47th Power Sources Conference 2016

Orlando, Florida, USA
13 – 16 June 2016

ISBN: 978-1-5108-5235-8

Printed from e-media with permission by:

Curran Associates, Inc.
57 Morehouse Lane
Red Hook, NY 12571

Some format issues inherent in the e-media version may also appear in this print version.

Printed by Curran Associates, Inc. (2018)

For permission requests, please contact Power Sources Conference at the address below.

Power Sources Conference
Palisades Convention Management
411 Lafayette Street, Suite 201
New York, NY 10003

Phone: (212) 460-8090 x 202
Fax: (212) 460-5460

mgoldfarb@pcm411.com

Additional copies of this publication are available from:

Curran Associates, Inc.
57 Morehouse Lane
Red Hook, NY 12571 USA
Phone: 845-758-0400
Fax: 845-758-2633
Email: curran@proceedings.com
Web: www.proceedings.com

PROCEEDINGS OF THE

47th POWER SOURCES CONFERENCE

13–16 JUNE 2016

Chairs' Welcome

Welcome to the Power Sources Conference 2016

Welcome to the 47th Power Sources Conference, taking place at the Wyndham Orlando Resort in Orlando, FL from June 13–16, 2016. This year's technical program reflects continued strong interest in high-energy batteries, fuel cells, and other portable and mobile power sources. We are sure that you will also enjoy the exhibition and social functions.

This is the best possible conference for obtaining information and meeting with key influencers in the military power sources arena. Get updates on new military and government needs and requirements, and learn about the latest power sources technology from both government and industry spokespeople.

Enjoy the Conference!

GENERAL CHAIRMAN
Dr. Robert P. Hamlen
Hamlen Enterprises LLC
Formerly Chief, Power Division US Army Communications-Electronics R&D Center

Table of Contents

Table of Contents

Table of Contents

Table of Contents

Table of Contents

Table of Contents

Table of Contents

Table of Contents

Table of Contents

Table of Contents

Table of Contents

Table of Contents

Author Index

Author Index

Author Index

Author Index

Author Index

Measurements of Lithium-Ion Battery Explosions

Thierry Carriere, Mitchell Hageman, Mike Tomlinson
ADA Technologies, Inc.
8100 Shaffer Parkway, Suite 130, Littleton, CO, 80127

Abstract: *Failing lithium ion batteries pose a significant threat to surrounding infrastructure and personnel. Effective battery containment must account for the potential pressure pulses created by failing batteries. In this study, commercially available cells were forced to failure in sealed pressure vessels. The resulting failure events were characterized in terms of the peak pressure change and peak pressure rise rate inside the vessels. It was found that battery failure events are highly stochastic, even for batteries undergoing the same abuse methods. The severity of failure events directly correlated with the amount of oxygen available in the sealed pressure vessels. The percentage of oxygen required to make a flammable fuel/air ratio was experimentally determined. It was concluded that oxygen deprivation through minimization of vessel free volume is a promising method of reducing the severity of battery explosions. This work has informed the design of a rugged, ultra-safe enclosure designed to protect against fire and over-pressurization threats from large format lithium ion batteries.*

Keywords: lithium ion batteries; abuse testing; fire; explosion protection; thermal protection; containment enclosure; laminated walls.

Introduction

The weight, volume and storage capacity benefits of current and future high-energy density storage systems make them attractive options to complete far-reaching and ambitious future US Navy missions. Both dormant and operational hazards associated with heat, fire, release of toxic materials and pressurized explosions are major concerns when these energy storage systems are installed in the same areas which are populated by personnel, sensitive equipment or vital structures. Safe packaging of these devices has lagged and as a result, a few significant events have taken place, highlighting the need for better tools to manage and control a possible uncontrolled release of stored energy. ADA Technologies is developing and testing a new, rugged, ultra-safe enclosure designed to withstand fire and explosion risks associated with large-format marine lithium-ion batteries of interest to the US Navy. The enclosure under development is designed to channel and contain released energy and protect nearby equipment and personnel.

A key safety feature of the enclosure is its pressure relief mechanism. Because lithium ion batteries can explode and ignite, it was necessary to characterize a notional worst case scenario, in particular in terms of overpressure and explosion strength. Battery fires have been extensively studied by several outfits including the FAA Technical Center, Sandia National Laboratories, Exponent, FM Global and others. However, little if any pressure data has been published. ADA Technologies has performed close to 90 battery failures to characterize the peak pressures that can be obtained from commercial lithium ion cells. From this work, ADA Technologies has designed and built a small-scale safety enclosure (700 x 600 x 600 mm) for shipboard high-energy density devices. The design was informed by flame exposure tests, battery explosion tests, and optimized for low weight and high internal volume. It is scalable, and full-scale shipboard enclosures (approximately 75 x 44 x 24 in) based on the same technology are being built this year. They will provide complete safety and allow the confident deployment of new, large-format lithium ion battery marine packs on board war ships.

Methods

Battery failures were performed in two sealed pressure vessels of volumes 10.9 gal and 1.9 gal. Each vessel was instrumented with thermocouples, a pressure transducer, and oxygen sensors. Batteries were forced to failure by several mechanisms, including overheating by conduction (hot plate), overcharging, and overheating by radiation (heating blanket). Three commercially available lithium ion cell types were used in these experiments: 18650s, 26650s, and 38120s. Each cell type was tested with a variety of failure mechanisms. A hot surface igniter was available and used in selected tests (via remote actuation) in each vessel to ignite vented gases from failing batteries. The experiments were characterized by the peak pressure obtained and the percent oxygen available in the vessel during ignition of flammable gases (whether ignition occurred with or without the assistance of the hot surface igniter). Selected experiments contained multiple pressure events (explosions) as fresh air, containing oxygen, was introduced into the vessel through an external valve if an explosion had completely depleted oxygen in the vessel.

At the conclusion of worst-case scenario testing, a small scale ultra-safe battery enclosure was designed and built. A proprietary laminate structure composed of a refractory material and an intumescent material was developed and used in combination with strong but lightweight stainless steel walls and frame. Pressure relief in the form of a large diameter burst disc was mounted onto the enclosure. The finished prototype can be seen in Figure 1.

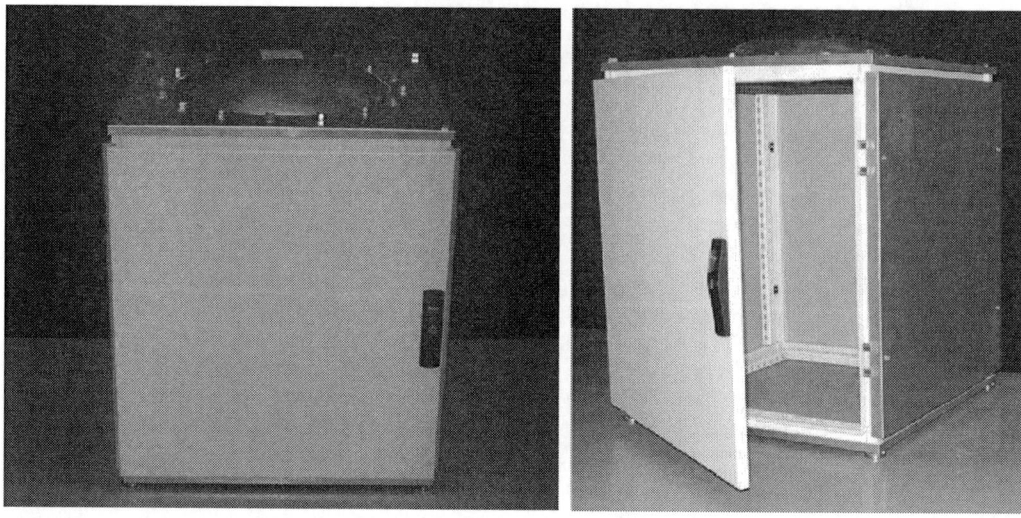

Figure 1. Small scale ultra-safe enclosure for fire and over-pressurization protection from lithium ion batteries.

Results and Discussion

Failing lithium ion cells of various types were found to produce highly stochastic peak pressures. In particular, the peak pressures did not correlate with the abuse method or the cell type. Figure 2 shows the range of peak pressures obtained from various cell types and abuse methods in the large pressure vessel (10.9 gal volume).

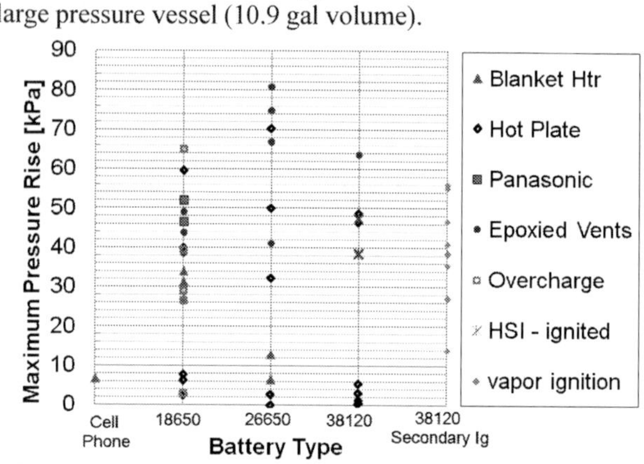

Figure 2. Summary of peak pressures from failures and ignitions achieved in the 10.9 gal pressure vessel.

Peak pressure is believed to be primarily driven by the combustion of flammable gases expelled from a battery during failure. The efficiency of combustion is driven by several factors, including the fuel composition (for example, vented electrolyte) and the fuel/oxygen ratio. During each failure event, both of these factors can vary from one battery to the next, depending on the initial conditions (how much air was in the vessel to start) and the specific compounds that are released from the battery during the failure event. This can explain the highly stochastic nature of the peak pressures that were obtained in these experiments. In order for the fuel/oxygen mixture to be flammable and allow for combustion, it must fall within a specific range of oxygen concentrations (upper and lower explosive limits, UEL and LEL). The flammability range (UEL-LEL) for the gases released by commercial lithium ion cells tested was experimentally approximated. Figure 3 shows the approximate upper and lower explosive limits, based on the data generated in this research.

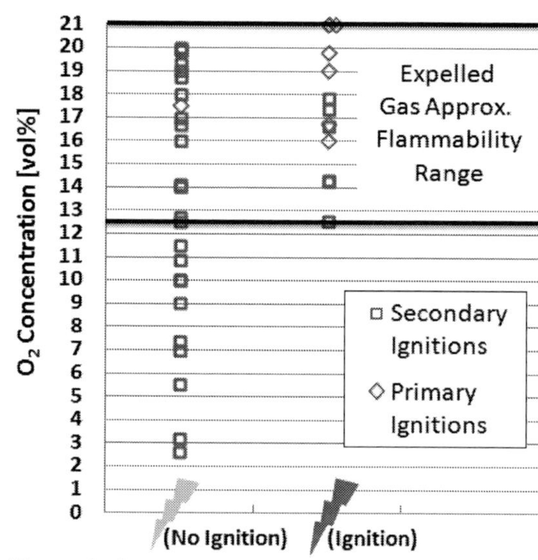

Figure 3. Oxygen concentrations for successful and unsuccessful ignition attempts after battery failures.

The experimental data suggests that vented gas ignitions can only occur in the approximate range of 12.5-21% oxygen (note that tests above 21% were not performed). Below the lower limit of ~12.5%, the fuel/oxygen ratio is too fuel-rich to support combustion. This scenario was frequently encountered in the small explosion vessel (1.9 gal volume) when an abundance of gases (fuel) were released from the failing cell. These presumably flammable gases lowered to oxygen concentration to the point where combustion was not possible. These results confirm that the possibility of an explosion via ignition of flammable gases is dependent on the oxygen availability. By limiting the oxygen availability, the severity of an explosion should be decreased. To test this, explosion strength was measured in vessels of two different internal volumes. The majority of the battery failures were performed in the larger, 10.9 gallon vessel. A vessel of 1.9 gallons was used to repeat several of the battery failure experiments. Figure 4 shows pressure traces for several 18650 cell failure tests in the large vessel.

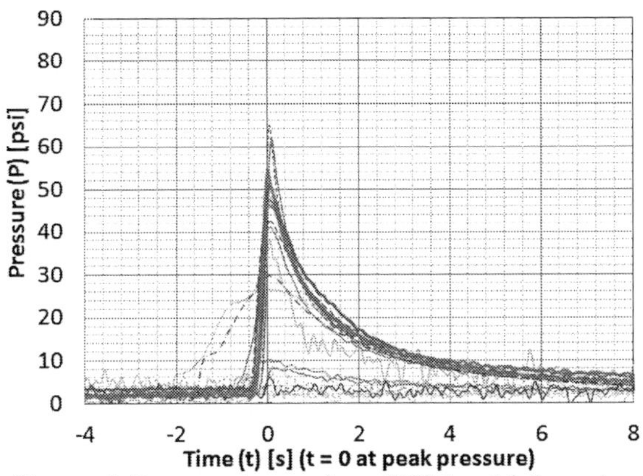

Figure 4. Pressure traces from 18650 cell failures in large pressure vessel.

The highest peak pressure obtained from 18650 cell failures in the large vessel was approximately 63 psi. For the small vessel, the highest peak pressure obtained was 12 psi (data not shown here). Similarly, the highest peak pressure obtained from 26650 cell failures in the large vessel was 86 psi while in the small vessel it was 12.5 psi. Failures with 38120 batteries were not performed in the small vessel. This difference in explosion strength between the small and large vessels supports the notion that oxygen availability is a primary driver of peak pressure. In this case, oxygen availability is directly correlated with vessel free volume. The larger the volume of the vessel, the more oxygen is initially available for combustion. This conclusion lends itself to a practical application: to decrease the severity of a potential battery explosion, the free volume in a battery containment enclosure could be minimized to limit oxygen availability. For enclosures housing lithium ion batteries, the packing configuration could utilize as much of the free space as possible. In such a case, vented gases from a failing battery could accumulate in an enclosure and mix with ambient air to form a fuel-rich, non-combustible mixture. While the resulting mixture might not be explosive as long as the compartment is closed or sealed, change in the fuel/oxygen ratio will likely happen through enclosure leakage or opening. The introduction of fresh oxygen could result in a rapid change of the equivalence ratio and the creation of a highly explosive mixture. Therefore the tactic of designing a system intentionally concentrating vented, flammable gases released by lithium ion batteries should be carefully considered before implementation.

The worst-case scenario testing described above helped inform the design of a rugged, ultra-safe battery enclosure for the housing of shipboard lithium ion batteries. The enclosure is composed of stainless steel walls and frame and a proprietary laminate structure built into the walls that affords thermal protection. Preliminary tests with various laminate configurations were performed to select the best combination of materials, including an intumescent material and a refractory material. Small scale flame tests were used to quantify the thermal performance of the laminates. Figure 5 shows an example of one of these tests. Once the laminate composition, structure and thickness were finalized, the small scale enclosure was constructed (see Figure 1). A large burst disc was integrated onto the enclosure to provide explosion protection. The weight of the enclosure came out to approximately 100 lb, placing the projected weight of the full scale enclosure far below the objective set forth by the US Navy.

Figure 5. Flame test performed on a laminate configuration during preliminary testing.

Currently, abuse testing is being performed on the enclosure to assess performance against various standard threats, specifically internal and external fire exposure, over-pressurization, and impact resistance. There are certain requirements for shipboard enclosures that must be met with regards to these threats before certification and deployment. Current testing is focusing on validating the enclosure design and modifying as necessary to meet these requirements. The fabrication of full-scale enclosures is planned for later this year.

Conclusions

Failing lithium ion batteries present a serious threat to personnel, equipment, and infrastructure in the surrounding area. Understanding the magnitude and physics of the threat are key to developing mitigation strategies such as safe containment to house these batteries. ADA Technologies performed over 90 battery failure experiments in sealed vessels to identify the worst case scenario for three commercially available lithium ion cells. This study revealed that a primary driver of explosion severity is the availability of oxygen for combustion. By limiting the free volume of storage containers for lithium ion batteries, the severity of an explosion can be minimized due to the rich nature of the fuel/oxygen ratio. However, the mixture could subsequently evolve into a highly combustible one with introduction of fresh oxygen. Based on these results, a small-scale rugged, ultra-safe enclosure for storage of lithium ion batteries was designed and manufactured. The enclosure incorporated a proprietary laminate structure to protect against thermal threats and a large burst disc to protect against over-pressurization. This technology is being developed for storage of shipboard lithium ion batteries for the US Navy, but its applications are far reaching for other industries that require safe storage of batteries.

Acknowledgements

The authors would like to thank Sarah Bernier and Norm Haberkorn of ADA Technologies for their help with this work. In addition, John Heinzel, Jason Ostanek, and Don Hoffman from the US Navy have provided invaluable feedback. Funding for this work has been provided by the Department of the Navy, Office of Naval Research under SBIR Phase II contract #N00014-14-C-0363.

Lithium Ion Battery Off-Gas Monitoring for Battery Health and Safety

Scott L. Swartz, Stephen R. Cummings, Nicholas B. Frank, and William J. Dawson

Nexceris, LLC
404 Enterprise Drive
Lewis Center, OH 43035

Abstract

Availability of robust and reliable gas detection for battery health monitoring is essential to the safe implementation and use of rechargeable batteries in military and commercial applications. Over-charged, degraded, and damaged batteries emit hazardous gases that can cause explosions if left unchecked. Leveraging its patented ceramic gas sensor technology platform, Nexceris has developed a monitoring system aimed at health and safety monitoring of lithium ion battery systems. Nexceris' off-gas monitor enables detection of electrolyte leaks from battery cells with sufficient early warning to prevent thermal runaway. Multiple inputs and outputs can be accommodated to meet the needs of each battery installation. For example, fault information supplied by a battery management system or auxiliary sensor can be used in combination with gas detection to diagnose battery health issues prior to an event. Multiple outputs including system shut-down, fire suppression and multiple alarms are possible. A complex algorithm has been incorporated in the control strategy to distinguish cell anomalies from potential catastrophic events. Because the monitoring system does not require physical integration with the cells, it offers the potential for redundant safety monitoring, even during transport or storage conditions.

Technology Overview

The starting point for this development effort was Nexceris' commercial hydrogen sensor, which was originally designed for hydrogen safety applications at concentrations approaching the lower flammability limit of hydrogen in air (which currently is sold into lead battery installations). This commercial platform was used and modified sensor formulations were evaluated to enable detection of flammable gases emitted from lithium ion battery electrolytes, such as diethyl carbonate and dimethyl carbonate. Nexceris has monitored the off-gassing characteristics to a range of operational and abuse conditions, including over-temperature, over-charging, and slow leak/pinhole tests in both pouch and cylindrical cells. Product development activities that have been completed to date include the design of prototype hardware and the vetting of fundamental sensing algorithms, and extensive testing to characterize the capability of the technology for detecting offgas from lithium battery cells under induced stressed conditions. The approach was demonstrated to provide an indicator of impending catastrophic failure in time for mitigations and well in advance of conventional battery failure detection approaches. An example of this capability is shown below in Figure 1, in which a battery cell was monitored for offgas using Nexceris' monitor while it was heated at a constant rate using a heater plate. A change in heating rate of the battery cell temperature was observed at 200 minutes when the cell began to self-heat (i.e., onset of thermal runaway). The sensor responded detected offgas from the cell well ahead of thermal runaway. The presence and quantity of offgas species were confirmed by third party analysis of gas samples collected during the test (the measured MEC content by shown by the green curve in Figure 1). The ability of the monitoring system to provide early fault warning for battery systems can increase the safety of these high energy density system by enabling mitigating actions before thermal runaway begins.

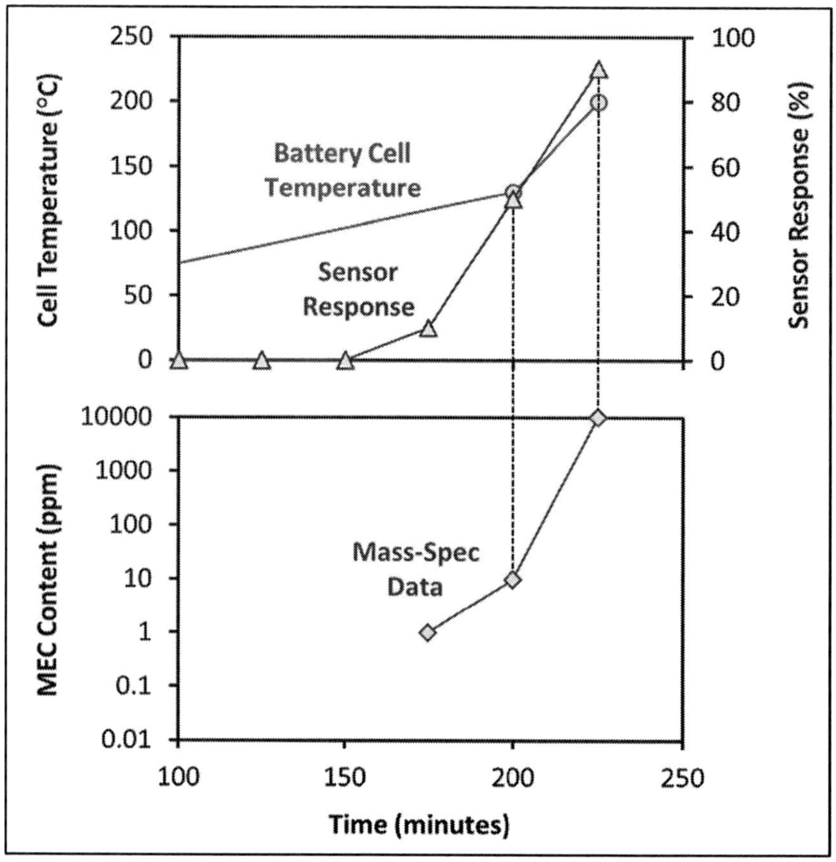

Figure 1. Results of lithium ion battery thermal runaway testing. Measurable responses to off-gassed methyl ethyl carbonate electrolyte were observed well in advance of thermal runaway

Production Description

The Nexceris battery monitoring system rapidly detects flammable gases emitted from damaged or degraded batteries. The monitoring system provides additional situation awareness of the condition of the batteries and can provide an alert so that action can be taken to avert a potential safety issue. Features, advantages and benefits of the battery monitor are summarized in Table 1.

Table 1. Features, advantages and benefits of Nexceris' lithium ion battery safety monitor

Features	Advantages	Benefits
Detects electrolyte prior to thermal runaway	Early warning	Can actuate shutdown or fire suppression
Can be combined with battery management system	Additional warning signal	Prevent false positives
Can be tailored for contained or uncontained configuration	Flexible design	Superior for many applications
Designed to take out environmental "noise"	Accurate in a range of configurations	Perfect for military, marine and commercial applications

Nexceris' lithium ion battery safety monitor is designed for flexible integration with a battery system to increase operational safety. Figure 2 shows a high level schematic of the operation of the monitoring system. Measurement of offgas from the batteries is provided by monitoring devices installed around the batteries. These devices provide return signals to the monitoring system controller which aggregates an array of signals using algorithms tuned to determine when electrolyte levels have become elevated. The monitoring system controller can then communicate with the battery system through the BMS or other systems to provide mitigating actions such as isolation of battery modules or fire suppression.

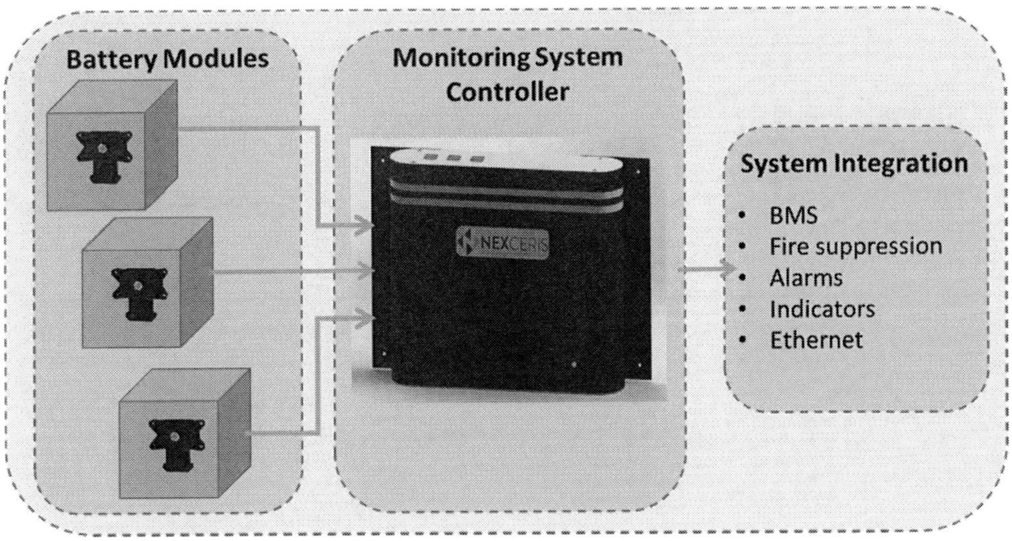

Figure 2. System function diagram for lithium ion battery safety monitor

An operational example of the monitoring system is shown below in Figure 3. This example shows how integration with the battery management system can provide additional system diagnostics when combined with convention monitoring of the BMS. Conventional monitoring provided by the BMS includes temperature and voltage measurements of from with the battery system. Anomalous behaviors from these signals will typically result in isolation or shutdown of battery modules within the system. The additional of offgas monitoring can provide additional situational awareness of the state of the battery system which can supplement existing logic and provide more rapid mitigating actions such as fire suppression.

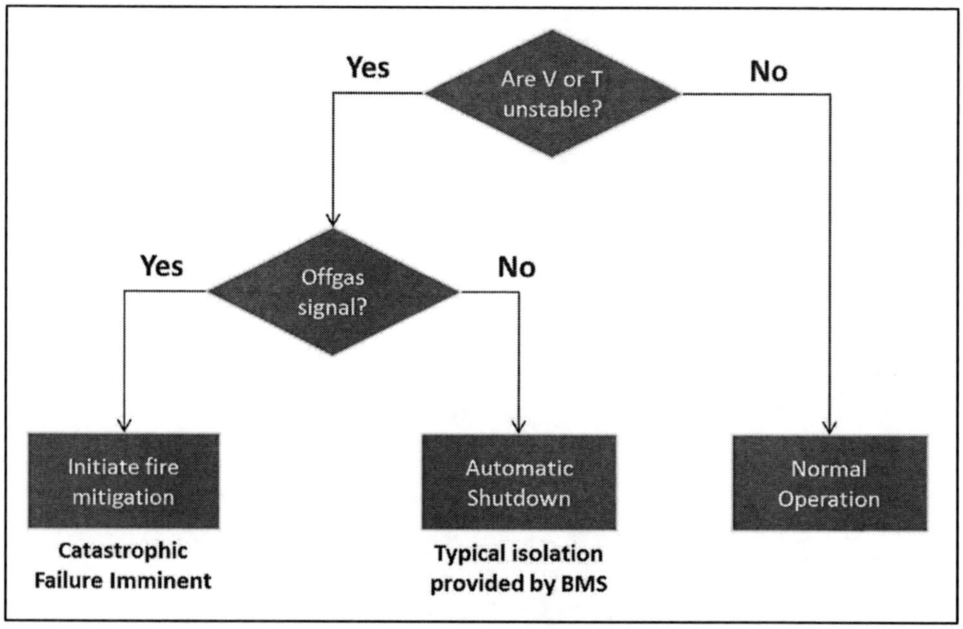

Figure 3. Offgas monitoring to supplement conventional BMS diagnostics with intelligent mitigating actions.

Acknowledgements

Funding for this work was provided under U.S. Department of Energy (DOE Contract No. DE-AR0000276) and by the U.S. Navy (NAVSEA Contract Numbers N65538-10-C-0035 and N00024-15-C-4002).

Diagnostic Technologies for Lithium-Ion Batteries: Internal Short Circuit Detection

Christopher H. McCoy[a], Thomas Kotwal[b], Chad Smutzer[b], Darrell King[b], Brian Barnett[a] and Suresh Sriramulu[a]
[a]CAMX Power, 35 Hartwell Avenue, Lexington, MA 02421
[b]TIAX LLC, 35 Hartwell Avenue, Lexington, MA 02421

Abstract: *We present technologies for detection of incipient internal short circuits in lithium-ion batteries for applications ranging from continuous, in-pack monitoring for improved safety and reliability to high-sensitivity diagnostics for manufacturing quality control, screening of cells for shorts prior to battery assembly or in other laboratory safety/forensic investigations. Challenges associated with detection of internal shorts are reviewed, and test data demonstrating the function and sensitivity of our technologies under a variety of realistic field conditions are presented and described.*

Keywords: lithium-ion; internal short circuit; battery safety; early detection.

Introduction

The superior energy and power on both a weight and volume basis of lithium-ion (Li-ion) battery technology has made this chemistry the clear choice for a number of DoD applications. However, this high energy content is a direct consequence of the use of active materials and electrolytes which are potentially extremely energetically reactive. Under certain triggers/abuses, Li-ion cells can experience thermal runaway, i.e., a rapid increase in cell temperature accompanied by venting, vent-with-flame, ejection of cell parts, fire and explosion. Internal short circuits (most typically attributable to metal contaminants in the cell) are the most commonly identified mechanism by which such events (i.e., safety failures) occur in the field. Internal short circuits causing failures in the field typically develop after some period of normal cell operation and occur in cells that passed all manufacturing safety and quality control screening. No adequate safety test to screen for future internal short development has been available, in part because these conditions develop slowly in the field and are not detectable at the point of manufacture.

We have developed multiple distinct, non-invasive and chemistry-agnostic technologies for sensitive early detection of internal shorts in Li-ion batteries before the shorts pose a thermal runaway threat. These technologies are based on extensive research into the underlying electrochemistry governing internal shorts, and on experience gained through safety audits of failures of Li-ion batteries in the field. They comprise hardware and software developed to utilize electrical markers only present when an internal short is present and deliver warning signals proportional to short severity. These technologies can be integrated with standard battery management electronics employed in Li-ion battery packs and provide early warning of incipient internal shorts that may lead to unsafe conditions. Furthermore, the internal short detection monitoring architectures are intrinsically suited to redundant implementations so that the system remains functional even if part of it is damaged or becomes non-operational.

We have advanced two of these technologies to the point that they are ready for implementation in battery systems. We present data showing rapid detection of both simulated and actual particle-induced internal short circuits including data demonstrating functionality in differing operational environments and battery designs. We discuss insights gained from audits of field-failures of Li-ion batteries as well as from an extensive research effort carried out to increase fundamental understanding of how internal shorts form and lead to safety incidents in the field. We will describe implementation options for internal short detection in Li-ion batteries and the benefits we foresee from adding this diagnostic technology.

Challenges of detection of internal shorts: Certain hurdles must be overcome for an internal short to be detected with sufficient sensitivity that early warning of a fault condition can be delivered. When a short first appears, is small in magnitude, high in resistance and drawing little current, its electrical signature is heavily masked by higher currents associated with normal cell operation, which are typically many orders of magnitude higher. Further, a minor short (e.g., 1000 ohms) has essentially negligible impact on cell impedance characteristics (e.g., 1ppm at 1kHz on a cell with 1 mΩ internal resistance) unless impedance data is acquired at very low frequencies with accompanying lengthy acquisition times. The default approach for detection of internal shorts is to monitor cell voltage over a sufficiently long period of time that voltage loss due to the internal short can be identified and sufficiently quantified (requiring, of course, that the cell is at rest and fully equilibrated). Table 1 shows detection times for voltage monitoring using the measurement capabilities in typical battery management ICs from leading manufacturers as well as the more sensitive detection technologies we have developed. Detection time for voltage measurement by battery management ICs was taken as the period required to acquire data to 10X minimum resolution (e.g., enough data to allow assessment /quantification of extent of voltage change) assuming ideal, noiseless performance. Real IC performance levels may, of course, yield slower detection. In this calculation, voltage resolution was taken as 0.376-0.61 mV, as specified for two recent offerings of major commercial products.

Table 1. Comparison of time-to-detect for different internal short detection methods/technologies.

Magnitude of the short resistance	Time needed to make an unambiguous determination of short presence in a 25 Ah cell		
	Typical BMS IC*	CAMX Power Short detection technologies	
		Technology 1	Technology 2
1000 Ω	26-42 hours	Real time	300 seconds
100 Ω	2.6-4.2 hours	Real time	30 seconds
10 Ω	0.26-0.42 hours	Real time	20 seconds

This engineering analysis, coupled with actual laboratory trials, led us to look for other means to achieve the sensitivity and rapidity of detection viewed as necessary for in-pack safety monitoring. In doing so, we identified reliable electrical signals that are present only when internal shorts are active in a cell. These markers therefore, serve as definitive indicators for the presence of internal shorts in cells. The detection of these electrical markers allows detection of internal shorts with a high degree of certainty, avoiding false-positive and false-negative responses. In essence, our technologies separate the target electrical signatures from signals impacted by normal cell current, changes in cell impedance with state-of-charge and cell aging, temperature effects, or other signals that might produce false positive or false negative detection outcomes.

Characteristics of internal shorts: We have been studying the nature and underlying electrochemistry of particle-induced internal shorts in lithium-ion cells for a number of years. We have created well over 500 particle-induced shorts in our laboratories under a variety of conditions. From this body of work we have found that internal shorts typically progress through several phases, initiating as very minor cell faults of high resistance (thousands of ohms or more), growing slowly for a period of time, followed by a period of more rapid growth, sometimes abruptly, to higher severity (or runaway). Aspects of this pattern of short development are seen in the data shown in Figure 1. For internal short detection to have utility and deliver enhanced safety profiles for in-pack monitoring applications, it needs to be of sufficient sensitivity to identify shorts before they grow large enough to present an imminent threat of runaway.

Applications for internal short detection: There are several different applications areas envisioned for internal short detection. They include:

- In-pack monitoring for safety and reliability;
- Quality control in the cell manufacturing process and reduction in aging periods needed to screen for internal short circuits;
- Cell screening prior to pack assembly, or in laboratory studies.

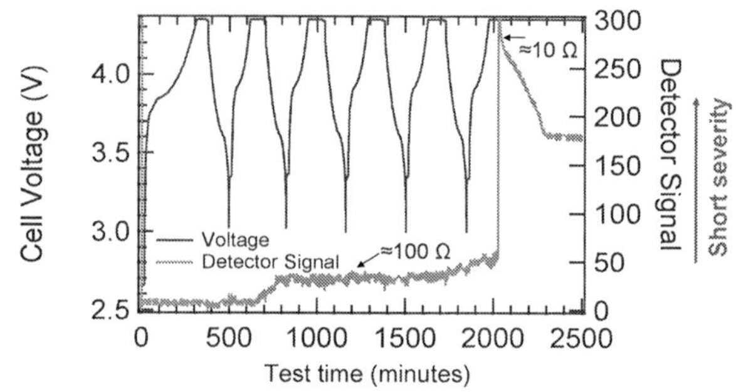

Figure 1. Cell voltage and output from our detection technologies monitoring a short created in a Li-ion cell by implantation of a metal particle. The detection signal (lower trace) shows the short initiate in the second cycle, grow to a moderate level (~ 100 Ω) for several cycles, and then abruptly spike to more dangerous levels (~ 10 Ω) in the sixth cycle.

In-pack monitoring for internal short circuits is an application where the internal short circuit diagnostic technology is integrated in battery management/monitoring electronics. The internal short circuit detection system reports status for the cells making up the battery and delivers warnings of any detected faults, including location and a gradation of severity. We have developed two distinct technologies for in-pack monitoring applications.

- The first (Technology I) offers real-time monitoring for the presence of internal short circuits and can operate continuously whether the battery is at rest, being charged, or delivering power.
- Our second technology (Technology II) was developed in response to tight cost constraints encountered in discussions with major automotive manufacturers considering implementing internal short circuit detection in plug-in hybrid electric and other battery electric vehicle platforms. Technology II offers the lowest cost and ease of implementation and can be directly integrated with existing battery management electronics designs, utilizing monitoring connections typically already in place in the form of cell/block voltage measurement connections.

In-pack monitoring for internal shorts must be able to detect the shorts while still small in magnitude but also track short growth in order to provide appropriate levels of warning. Thus, in-pack detection must deliver significant dynamic range with respect to the electrical resistance of internal short measured. In contrast, cell screening applications can be understood to place special importance on high sensitivity for good performance in screening out faulty cells. Cell screening applications are also generally likely to have a different cost sensitivity profile than in-pack detection applications given that the detection system implementation would be a bench-top instrument or piece of manufacturing line equipment. We have developed a third variant of our technology (Technology III) specifically aimed at high-sensitivity detection for the purpose of screening cells for the presence of internal shorts.

Results and Discussion

Detection technologies for in-pack safety monitoring and diagnostics: The first detection technology we present offers the highest level of in-pack monitoring. The hardware and software that make up the technology were specifically conceived to be able to identify the presence of internal shorts against a background of normal responses of cells to charge, discharge, aging, and temperature that can heavily cloak the signature of an internal short. Utilizing a monitoring architecture coupled with signal processing and analysis methodologies based on extensive laboratory investigations into internal shorts in lithium-ion cells, the technology is capable of detecting internal shorts with high sensitivity even while a battery is being charged or discharged.

We are currently implementing this technology for safety monitoring of Li-ion batteries used in a miner's cap lamp for underground mining applications. Figure 2 shows a photograph of the miner's cap lamp, and test data for this implementation are shown in Figure 3. These test results were produced by a prototype implementation of internal short circuit detection customized for use in mining cap lamps. The ultimate goal of such an implementation is to deliver an enhanced safety profile for lithium-ion batteries used in underground mines, where the consequences of a thermal runaway in an enclosed space are of serious concern in their own right, but are exacerbated by the potential for an explosive atmosphere.

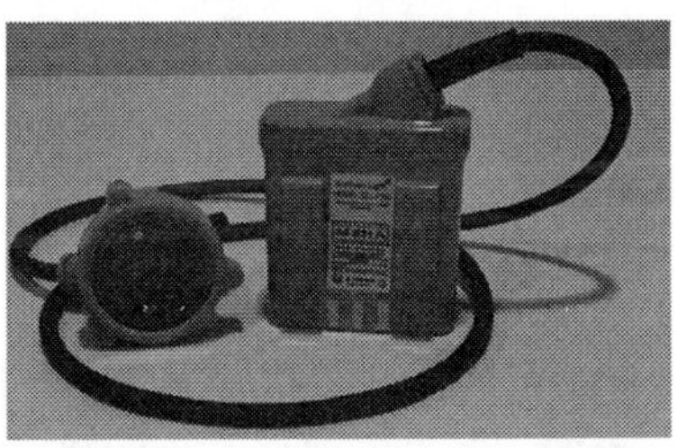

Figure 2: Lithium-ion miner's cap lamp system for which we are developing an implementation of our internal short detection technology.

Our second technology for in-pack detection of internal shorts is based on fundamentally different and distinct electrical interrogation and signal analysis methodologies. Test data and a photograph of one of our demonstration units are shown in Figure 4. Note that this demonstration unit is designed for convenience in bench-top use rather than demonstration of the much smaller footprint that would be achieved in an in-pack implementation. This particular demonstration unit has 12 monitoring channels that are user-configurable for modules or cell scanning tasks of fewer total units.

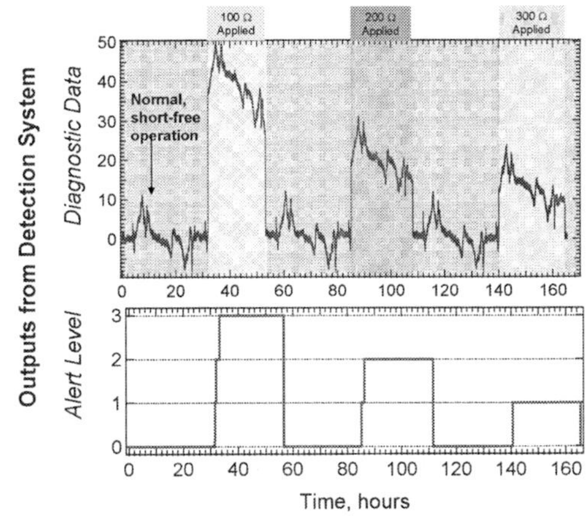

Figure 3. Test data from an implementation of our internal short circuit technology targeting improved safety of lithium-ion batteries utilized in underground mines. (top) The prototype was actively cycled using charge-discharge protocols simulating field conditions. Simulated shorts (load resistances) of the specified magnitudes were applied to one cell as indicated. (bottom) Detection system alert status output.

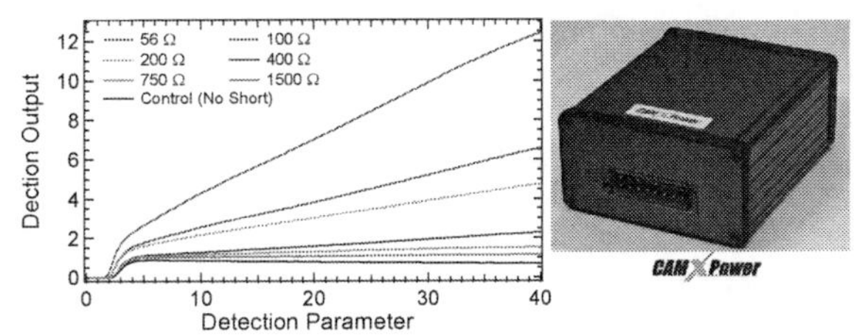

Figure 4. Technology II test data (left) and demonstration unit that generated the data (photo right). Data show the ability of the technology to resolve and grade the severity of differing short magnitudes for a 2.6 Ah 18650 cell. The control (no short) is the bottom trace, with progressively lower resistances moving upward from 1500 to 56 ohms.

One of the key challenges in detection of internal short circuits is that the larger the capacity of the cell, the more difficult it can be to identify the signs of an internal short. For example, if cell voltage is monitored over an extended period of time to look for a fall in voltage due to an internal short, the higher the capacity of the cell, the lower the impact of a given magnitude of internal short on cell voltage. An advantage of our detection technology is that sensitivity is not governed solely by cell capacity, and as a result sensitivity to internal shorts can be similar for cells of different capacities. For example, detection data are shown in Figure 4 for a series of simulated internal shorts in a 2.6Ah cell and Figure 5 shows the detection data for a 25Ah cell. It can be appreciated that detection of an internal short of a given magnitude becomes more challenging as total electrode area increases (proportionally larger dilution effect for certain electrical responses and thus a proportionally larger cloaking effect for internal shorts). However, the electrical interrogation method employed to produce the scan responses seen in the figure has sensitivity governed by factors that allow it to maintain sensitivity in larger vs. smaller cells. This attribute of our technology's performance is important because, while the electrical impact of an internal short on, for example, cell voltage decay, decreases with increasing cell capacity, the risk posed by an internal short of a given magnitude *does not*. Indeed, it can be appreciated that a thermal runaway event, because it is spawned in a relatively small area of cell electrode and is governed by factors that include the relevant chemical decomposition kinetics, local thermal environment and its impact on how rapidly local heating can be dissipated, and the power produced by the internal short, can be triggered by the same magnitude of internal short in cells large or small. Thus, it is critical to understand that while detectability of shorts is attenuated in larger cells, the risk profile is not.

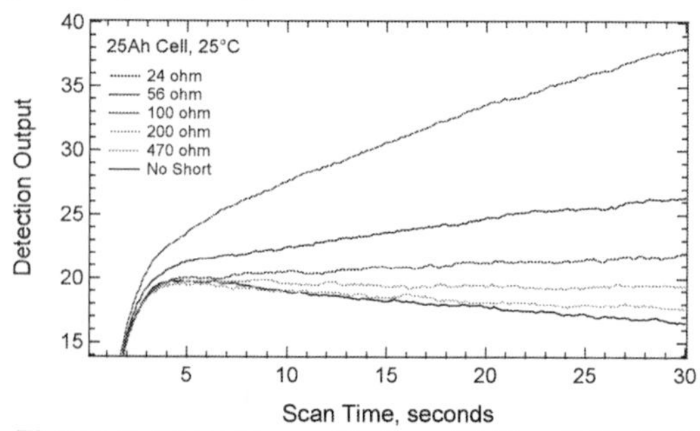

Figure 5. Detection profile for a 25Ah cell illustrating achievement of detection sensitivity comparable to that obtained (Figure 4) for a 2.6Ah cell. This contrasts with the factor of ten loss in sensitivity with simple long-term voltage monitoring for a 25 vs 2.6Ah cell.

Our in-pack detection technologies have been tested under a range of conditions including those requested as part of demonstration programs, with successful detection at the performance presented in this paper demonstrated from -30 to +55°C, from 0 to 100% state-of-charge, in cells from 1.5Ah to 75Ah, and for Li-ion cells representing the different common cathode chemistries.

Quality control in manufacturing and cell screening applications for internal short detection: Another set of applications we foresee for detection of internal shorts distinct from in-pack monitoring includes:

- quality control in the cell manufacturing process, e.g, reducing the aging time during cell formation;
- cell screening to look for internal shorts prior assembly of those cells into a battery system; or
- cell screening in the laboratory to screen for internal shorts as part of a safety or forensic evaluation.

The performance and cost priorities of these applications differ considerably from those of in-pack monitoring applications. In manufacturing or laboratory investigative applications it can be appreciated that a technology with the cost of an ordinary bench top piece of test and measurement equipment can be completely acceptable, whereas many in-pack applications might place more stringent restrictions on allowable cost. Further, screening of cells for internal shorts in any of the aforementioned applications likely demands the highest sensitivity levels in order to deliver the highest performance and effectiveness.

Building on our first-generation hardware implementation shown in Figure 4, we have developed a new implementation that is focused on cell screening applications. Test data for this implementation used to screen cells produced on our cell prototyping line is shown in Figure 6. The scan in the figure shows a cell with an actual, manufacturing defect-induced short that was identified using a ten-minute scan with our detection technology. The cell fails screening due to the rise in scan output versus the no-short reference (bottom trace) indicating a short. We routinely use the cell screening implementation of our detection technology to rapidly test cells produced in our prototyping facility for the presence of internal shorts. We are further advancing performance for cell screening to detect very minor (we are approaching successful detection of 1 MΩ) internal shorts.

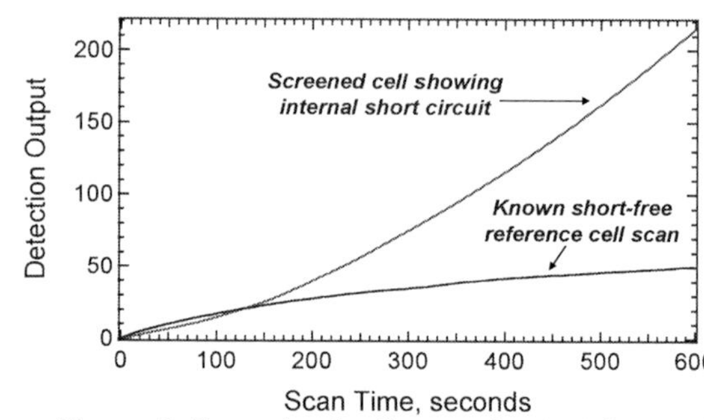

Figure 6. Example of cell screening test data and detection of a minor short showing identification of an actual manufacturing defect-induced internal short circuit found in a cell using a ten-minute scan (top trace). A known, short-free reference is shown for comparison (bottom trace). Our detection technology graded this short at ≈3000 ohms, confirmed by independent voltage and capacity loss measurements over a 32-day test period.

Acknowledgements

The authors gratefully acknowledge support of the Office of Mine Safety and Health Research (contract 200-2014-58751) to develop adaptations of our detection technologies for mining applications. With respect to this support, we note that *"The findings and conclusions in this presentation have not been formally disseminated by the National Institute for Occupational Safety and Health and should not be construed to represent any agency determination or policy. Mention of any commercial product does not imply endorsement."* The authors acknowledge support by Defense Logistics Agency of our work to further application of our detection technologies to reduce aging time required in cell manufacturing and provide sensitive screening of cells for internal shorts (SBIR contract HQ0147-15-C-8004).

Development of a Nonflammable Electrolyte for Li-Ion Batteries

Christopher Lang, Kenneth Rosina, Peter Moran

Physical Sciences Inc.
email: lang@psicorp.com

Abstract
Safer, higher performance cells are required to power next generation technologies. However, increasing battery's energy density tightens the required build tolerances and increases the potential for catastrophic system failure. This presentation will discuss Physical Sciences Inc.'s efforts to develop an electrolyte that increases battery safety. PSI will discuss its efforts to develop a nonflammable ionic liquid based electrolyte for use in high performance secondary lithium ion cells. Test data will demonstrate the nonflammability of the composite electrolyte system as well as the electrochemical and thermal properties over the desired temperature range. Test results from coin and pouch cells will not only highlight the performance, but also demonstrate the scalability of the developed electrolyte. Finally, the impact of the PSI electrolyte on cell safety under abuse conditions will be discussed.

Primary Conformal Wearable Battery

Eivind Listerud, Mario Destephen, and David Darch

EaglePicher Technologies, LLC
3220 Industrial Road
Joplin, Mo. 64801, USA

Abstract: *This paper covers a description of the primary conformal wearable battery developed by EaglePicher Technologies. It is designed to be robust, light-weight and flexible, with a nominal energy of 250Wh when discharged at 20W continuous power. The weight of the battery is 0.94kg. The battery has been subjected to extensive safety and abuse testing and this will be discussed in detail. The paper will also cover the battery management system, safety features, and give examples of electrical battery performance.*

Keywords: Portable power; Li/CF_x-MnO_2 hybrid battery; Conformal Battery; Bullet penetration testing; Impact testing.

Introduction

There is an ongoing effort by the Army focused on enhancing the load carriage distribution for the Soldier with a reduced weight burden and increased comfort. In that regard, the Army is specifically interested in the development of a conformal battery system designed to match the contour of a Soldier's SAPI body armor plate that will provide the soldier with a lightweight power pack for the increasing energy/power demands in the electronic battlefields of the 21st century. EaglePicher Technologies, LLC (EPT) has recently designed and developed a primary version of the Conformal Wearable Battery (CWB) that will deliver a significantly reduced weight burden in a conformal package, as well as much higher energy density than that of a Li/MnO_2-based battery. This paper will give a brief description of the battery before describing results from safety and battery performance testing under various conditions. Examples will cover impact testing and bullet penetration testing.

Battery Description

This primary CWB is a 24-cell 15V power pack based on a Li/CF_x-MnO_2 hybrid cell packaged in a flexible hermetic pouch. The pouch cell uses a CF_x-MnO_2 hybrid cathode, with paddle wound design in a flexible hermetic pouch. The conformal battery has dimensions of 19.5cm x 22.1 cm and is less than 2 cm thick. It weighs about 940 grams. The case design is shown in Figure 1 with a state-of-charge indicator (SOCI), a complete discharge device (CDD), and a connector. Note the grooves between the cell compartments. This is critical for achieving the right amount of conformability as required by the Army. While having these are inconvenient from a cell size and cell layout and wiring perspective, it is necessary to give the battery the right amount of flexibility. A careful tradeoff study was conducted to establish the optimum balance between the conformability and the energy in the battery, driven by the allowable cell size. Once this had been determined, extensive flexibility testing with subsequent electric testing was performed. An example of this can be seen in Figure 2. In addition to strength and flexibility considerations, the surface friction of the case material must also be evaluated. The battery should not be difficult to insert and remove from its designated location next to the SAPI armor plates, thus the coefficient of friction of the outer case surface must be below a certain threshold. Another consideration in the case design is chemical compatibility. The battery case material has been exposed to electrolyte solvent, as well as kerosene. The chemical testing has shown no significant effect on the case.

The battery will deliver over 250 Wh at a nominal voltage of about 15V under a 20W continuous load. It has a discharge capacity of about 17.6 Ah above 9V. The energy density at this rate is about 266 Wh/kg. The maximum continuous power draw is about 75W or 5A. It will operate in a temperature range from -20°C to 60°C. This is further detailed later in the paper.

Figure 1: Case design and layout, showing grooves between cell compartments, connector, CDD location,and SOCI.

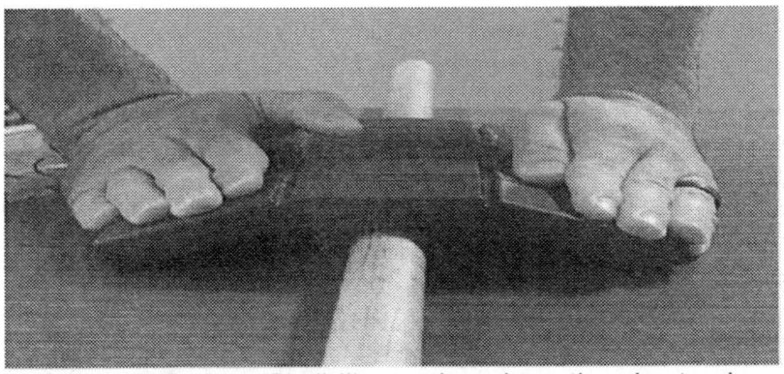

Figure 2: Battery flexibility testing along the short axis.

Battery SOCI and Protection System

EaglePicher Technologies has developed a battery protection and SOCI Printed Circuit Assembly (PCA) incorporating SBS/SMBus capability for the conformal battery pack. The PCA provides the following:

- Charge protection
- Over-current protection using fuses at both the cell and the battery level
- Temperature protection using multiple thermal fuses throughout the battery
- Complete Discharge Device (CDD)
- Temperature and Rate Compensated State-of-Charge Indicator (SOCI) with LED display. This can be seen in Figure 3. Testing of SOCI shows accuracy to within 10% of actual discharge data.
- Smart Battery Specification (SBS) 1.1 compliant communications interface (SMBus 1.1)

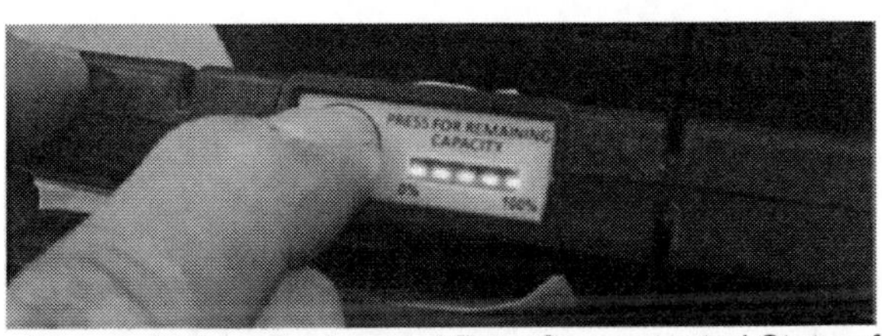

Figure 3: Temperature and Rate Compensated State-of-Charge Indicator (SOCI) with LED display.

Safety Evaluation

EaglePicher Technologies has conducted extensive safety and abuse testing of the primary CWB. Two of the more challenging tests that the Army requires the battery to pass are the bullet penetration and the impact tests.

Bullet Penetration Test

Three primary CWB batteries were exposed to the bullet penetration test as specified by the Army. These batteries were all at 100% SOC when subjected to the test and placed in front of a SAPI plate. Then each battery was shot three times using 7.62 mm ammunition. The last two were shot using 7.62 mm API tracer ammunition, one with the shots coming at an angle perpendicular to the battery surface, the other with the shots coming at a 45° angle to the surface. The back side of each of these two batteries can be seen in Figures 4 and 5, respectively. There were no sign of flames or fire in any of the three batteries. The maximum temperature observed in any of the batteries after the test was about 100°C.

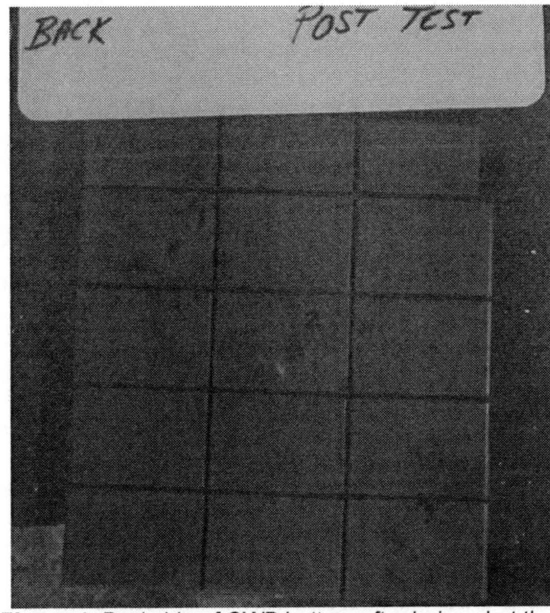

Figure 4: Backside of CWB battery after being shot three times with7.62 mm API tracer ammunition at an angle perpendicular to the battery surface.

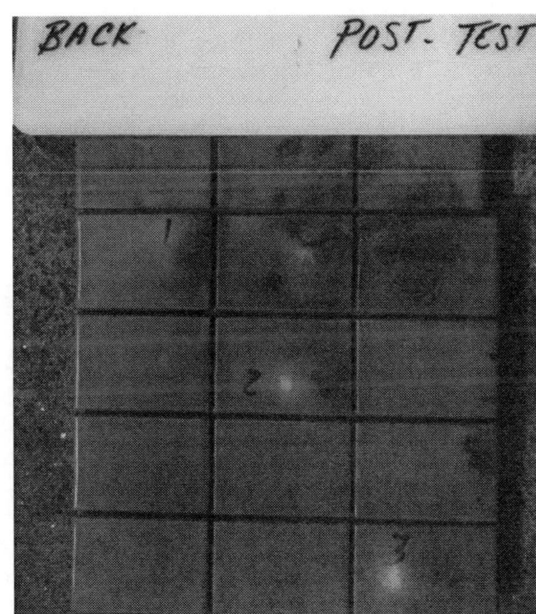

Figure 5: Backside of CWB battery after being shot three times with7.62 mm API tracer ammunition at a 45° angle to the battery surface.

Each battery was still at 100% SOC after the test. This was observed by using both the SOCI and by measuring OCV through the connector. The battery has been designed to still be functional after being exposed to gunfire.

Impact Test

Several primary CWB batteries have been exposed to the impact test. This test involves dropping a 16lb bowling ball on to the surface of the CWB battery from 3 feet up. This is to be done three times for each battery. After the impact test the battery must remain functional. Figure 6 shows an image of a ball hitting a battery during a test. This particular battery was impacted five times. After impact testing the same battery was subjected to a 20 W constant power discharge. The voltage profile of this test can be seen in Figure 7. It delivers about 240Wh. The battery was instrumented with internal thermocouples, showing the temperature did not exceed 45°C.

Prior to exposing this battery to an impact test, this same battery was also exposed to conformability testing, mechanical shock, random vibration testing, and transit drop testing. The transit drop test had a 26 drop requirement. Throughout this testing the battery was subjected to several 1 minute 20W loads to evaluate if any damage had been done to the battery. This will need to be considered when looking at the discharge profile in Figure 7 and the output of 240Wh.

Battery Performance

The CWB have been tested at a variety of rates and various environmental conditions. One of the baseline tests that EPT performs is a 20W continuous power discharge at room temperature. Figure 8 shows the outcome of two such tests. On the left in Figure 8 is a continuous 20W discharge showing that the conformal battery will deliver 250Wh in room temperature conditions. The plot on the right is the same test, except in this case the discharge was interrupted in order to perform other tests on the battery. The battery was discharged briefly at a 20W continuous load before it was exposed to 6 thermal cycles, similar to those specified for UN transportation testing. Subsequently it went through the UN sinusoidal vibration cycles 4 times in each axis. It was then discharged at 20W for another 3 hours. At this time the battery was subjected to a bend test of ninety deflection cycles, each cycle consisting of flexing the edges of the battery up and down a distance of 1in. from the centerline. This was then repeated along the other horizontal axes of the battery. After the bend test the battery was then fully discharged at 20W. It delivered 234Wh

Figure 9 shows how the battery performs in high and low temperature environments. The battery on the left in Figure 9 was discharged at about 55°C after a 4 hour soak at that temperature. This battery was subjected to 20W constant discharge and delivered 260Wh.The battery surface temperature reached about 72°C. On the right in Figure 9 is a battery that was discharged at about -20°C after a 4 hour soak at that temperature. This battery was also subjected to 20W constant discharge and it delivered 194Wh. The battery surface temperature in this case reached about 5°C.

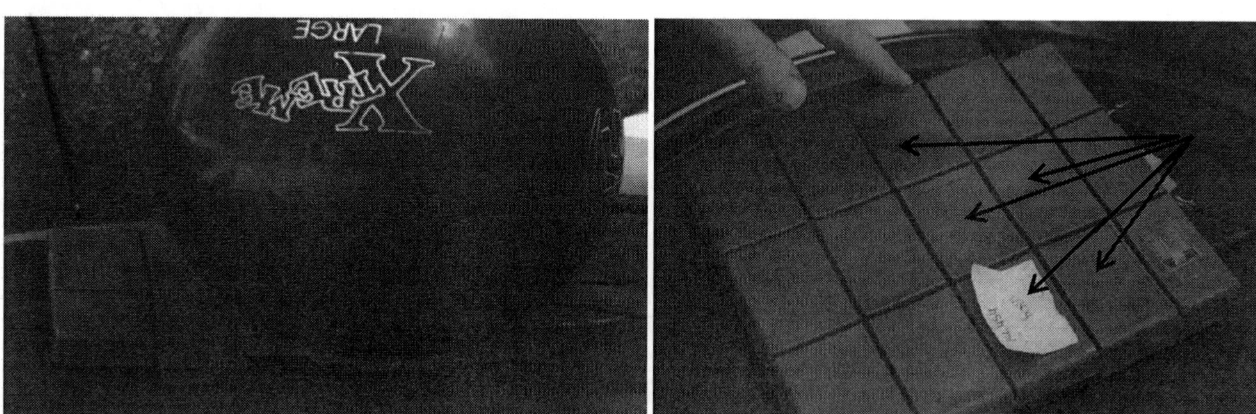

Figure 6: Instrumented battery subjected to the impact test. Photo is taken with a high speed camera. The bowling ball is dropped on several locations from 36 inches above the battery.

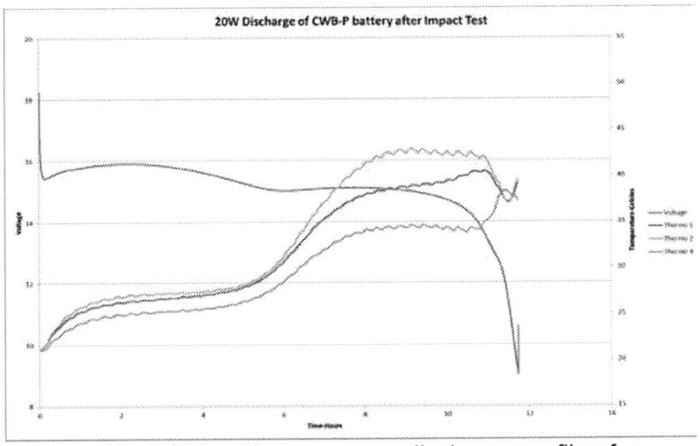

Figure 7: 20W continuous power discharge profile of battery after exposed to impact test.

Conclusion

EaglePicher has developed a primary conformal battery that is flexible, weighs less than 1.0kg, and will deliver 250Wh at room temperature. It will deliver over 190Wh at -20°C. It has a very robust design with numerous safety features that has been subjected to, and passed, bullet penetration and impact testing, in addition to numerous other safety tests.

Acknowledgement

Special thanks to CERDEC for supporting the primary conformal battery development. This material is released to the public domain in accordance with ITAR 22 CFR 120.11.

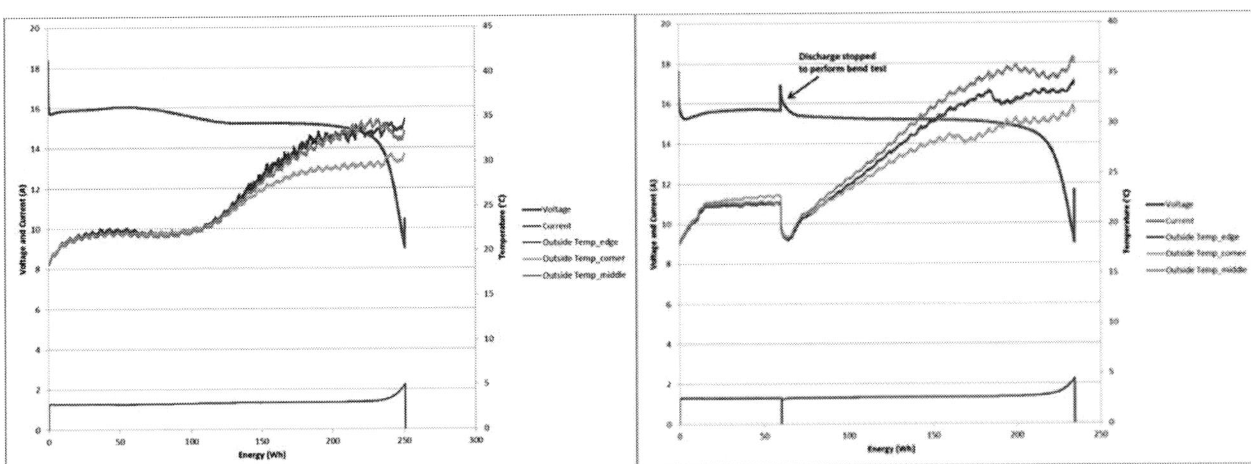

Figure 8: Discharge profile of CWB-P at 20W constant load in room temperature environment.

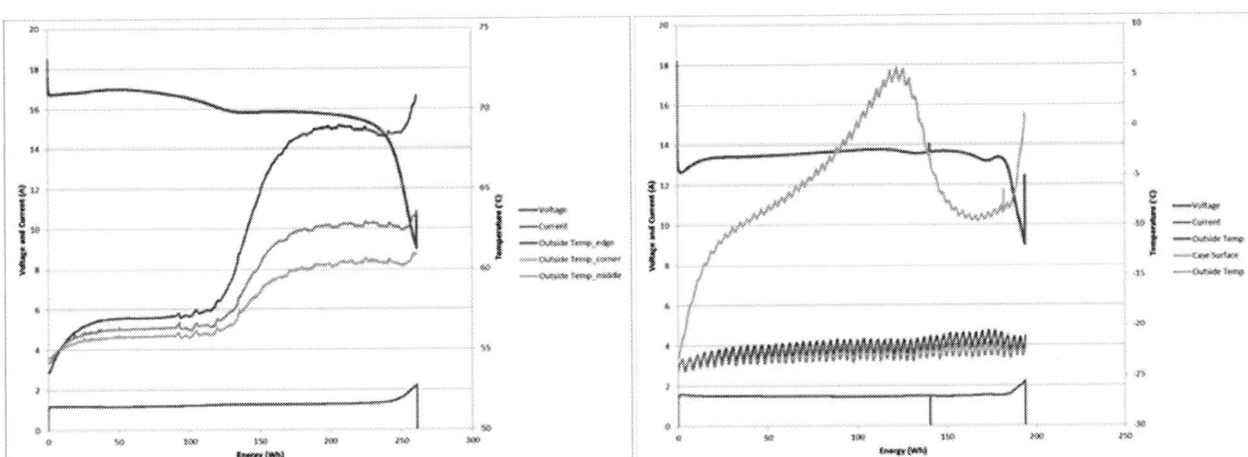

Figure 9: Discharge profile of CWB-P at 20W constant load at 55°C and -20°C.

Development of a High Temperature CFx Battery for Downhole Applications

Umamaheswari Janakiraman, Rebecca Cragun, Ernest Ndzebet, Mario Destephen, Dong Zhang and Greg Miller

Research and Development
EaglePicher Technologies, LLC
P.O. Box 47
Joplin, MO 64801
Contact Author: Mario Destephen

Abstract: *Downhole operation demands a battery which can operate efficiently at high temperature in severe shock and vibration environments. Lithium thionyl chloride battery has been the predominant technology for the downhole applications. Thionyl chloride is a corrosive liquid, which can cause environment and safety concerns during thermal runaway. EaglePicher Technologies (EPT) successfully developed a high energy density lithium carbon monofluoride (LiCFx) battery which can efficiently operate over a wide temperature range, (-20°C to 160°C). Moreover the high thermal stability of CFx enables enhanced safety advantages over the existing thionyl chloride battery. The performance and safety of EPT downhole battery was validated in D and sub DD configurations.*

Keywords: Downhole batteries; wide temperature operation range; electrolyte; thermal stability; carbon monofluoride (CFx).

Introduction

There is an increasing demand for the high-temperature batteries to power deep sea drilling devices. The oil and gas exploration is one of the most challenging industries in today's economy. The increasingly complex and sensitive technology utilized by oil and gas industries is specifically designed to meet the extremely challenging environments where they operate without compromising on safety. In some operations utilizing highly delicate instrumentation, batteries are the only option. So, the batteries must be absolutely reliable. Batteries used in the oil field industries are particularly important given the remote environment, and they must be able to withstand an enormous variety of operating temperatures, ranging anywhere from well below 0°C on Arctic oil rigs to very high temperatures of +150°C or higher during deep drilling. Moreover, the batteries also must last long enough to be of practical use in these industries. Drilling controls and measurement-while-drilling are the most demanding and critical of all battery applications. In these applications, tools are located just above the drill bit and are subjected to tremendous shock and vibration. The remote settings and difficulties presented when operating downhole in an oil well requires a high energy density and a safe battery with good endurance for the drilling operations.

Some batteries, such as the lithium/copper oxyphosphate, operate effectively at high temperatures but are less effective at low temperatures (≤ 25°C). [1] The lithium oxyphosphate batteries have to be heated up to > 50°C before discharge. The tool has to be lowered into the hole quickly before the battery cools down. This makes operations in cold weather problematic. On the other hand, it is a challenge for many lithium batteries with liquid electrolytes to operate at high temperatures (≥ 180°C).

So far, lithium thionyl chloride is the widely used chemistry for oilfield services due its high voltage, and thereby its high energy density. However, it has inherent limitations and safety issues. In the case of lithium thionyl chloride, the cathode active material is a corrosive and toxic liquid which becomes unstable at higher temperatures due to excessive pressure generation.[2] Both the high and low rate batteries are susceptible to explosion when shorted. Explosions can also result from battery over discharge and charging. The chemistry also exhibits a voltage delay upon load onset due to anode passivation, which is a function of storage temperature and time. As a result it has to be depassivated before use. Lithium anode passivation by thionyl chloride also leads to severe self-discharge during prolonged high temperature storage. Therefore, a high energy density and safe battery with consistent performance predictability over a wide temperature range is needed for downhole applications.

The development of a battery for oil and gas industry involves the selection of materials with good thermal stability, which includes anode, cathode, separator, case material, and electrolyte. The CFx cathode active material is inherently safe because it is stable and inert up to 400°C. Moreover, the lithium carbon monofluoride (Li/CFx) is an attractive 3V system and offers the highest theoretical energy density (~2180 Wh/kg) among the primary lithium chemistries. The theoretical energy density of lithium thionyl chloride is relatively lower (1470 Wh/kg) than the Li/CFx. Due to its high energy density, Li/CFx technology has the potential to replace the current lithium thionyl chloride technology. However lithium CFx batteries commonly use organic electrolytes which are flammable.

Considering the high temperature requirement for the downhole applications it is imperative to design the battery to ensure safety at high temperature operations. EPT has developed a Li/CFx battery for the downhole applications. This paper reports the discharge performance of EPT CFx D and sub DD batteries that can safely operate in a wide temperature range (-20°C to 160°C) with good rate capability. Further, the safety and shelf life characteristics of the EPT batteries are discussed.

Experimental

Carbon monofluoride (CFx) was first mixed well with specific amounts of commercial carbon. Binder was added to the above mix to make slurry which was then applied on a current collector to form the cathode. EPT proprietary electrolyte was prepared by mixing lithium salt and suitable additives in an organic matrix. Cylindrical D (or sub DD) size batteries were constructed with the CFx cathode, separator, electrolyte, and lithium or lithium alloy anode.

The developed D size CFx batteries were discharged from open circuit voltage (OCV) down to 1 V at a rate of $\geq$ 0.375 A (0.75A for sub DD) using an Arbin cycler. Batteries were tested in an environmental chamber between -20°C and 165°C. The thermal stability of the electrolytes was investigated through DSC using Netzsch DSC 200 F3 differential scanning calorimeter.

Results and discussion

The spirally wound D and sub DD Li/CFx batteries are shown in Figure 1.

Figure 1. EaglePicher Technologies high temperature Li/CFx batteries.

The CFx D sized batteries were initially tested at a rate of 0.375 A in environmental chambers to evaluate its capacity at different temperatures. Figure 2 illustrates the discharge curves of CFx D size batteries at different temperatures. These batteries used the EPT proprietary electrolyte. As can be seen in Figure 2, the developed electrolyte enabled the batteries to discharge over a wide temperature window (-20°C to 160°C). EPT batteries showed a high discharge capacity of 16 Ah at 150°C with an operating voltage of about 2.95V. Moreover, the batteries showed a high volumetric energy density of about 1000 Wh/L. A comparison with the existing thionyl chloride D size batteries in the market shows EPT batteries offer at least 20% higher capacity than the former over a temperature range from 21°C to 150°C when tested under similar conditions. In addition to the impressive performance at high temperatures, the batteries also showed good discharge efficiency at temperatures as low as -20°C. It is to be noted that the D sized batteries were able to be discharged at low temperatures without requiring a heater or a depassivation.

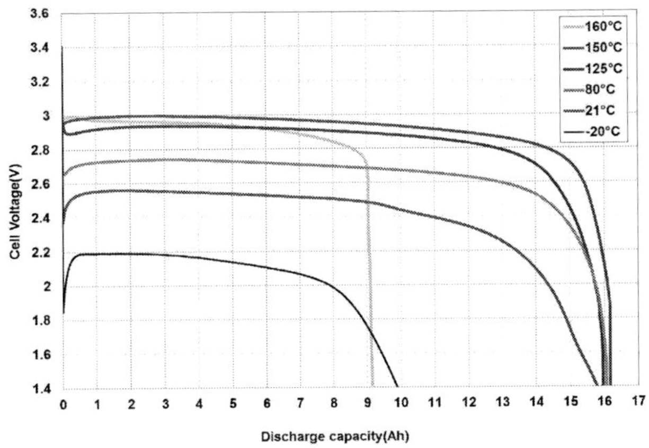

Figure 2. Discharge of EaglePicher Technologies D batteries at 0.375A between -20°C and 160°C.

The sub DD batteries showed similar discharge efficiency in the investigated temperature window (not shown). Besides the wide temperature window of operation, EPT CFx batteries also show high rate capability. Indeed, the batteries were able to discharge at 1.75A in pulse discharge at high temperatures. Due to the flat operating voltage the batteries were also able to discharge under power pulse protocol. The discharge profile of CFx D size batteries at 1.75A between 40°C and 125°C is shown in Figure 3. As can be seen, those batteries showed an average capacity of 15 Ah in the high rate pulse. Similar to the D sized batteries, the sub DD batteries also showed good rate capability. Figure 4 shows the discharge of sub DD batteries at 0.75mA continuous discharge and at 2A pulse discharge, respectively.

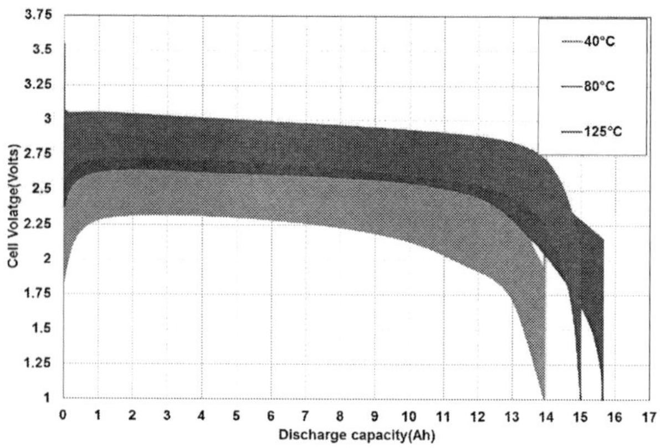

Figure 3. High rate pulse discharge of D batteries between 40°C and 125°C.

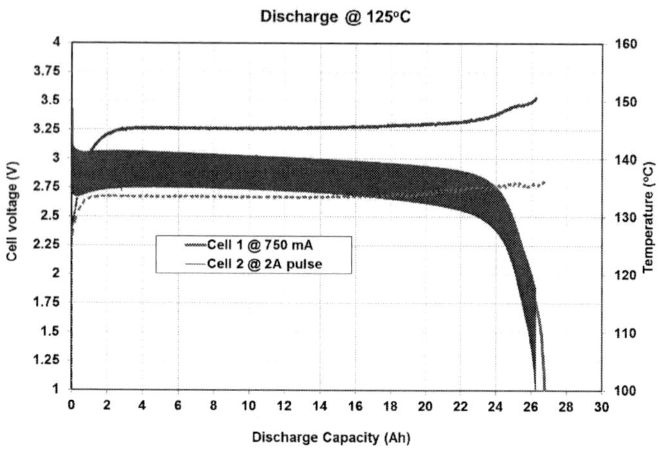

Figure 4. Moderate rate (0.75A) and high rate (2A) pulse discharge of sub DD batteries at 125°C.

The EPT high temperature CFx battery showed good shelf life upon storage up to 6 months at 60°C and RT (21°C). The stored batteries were discharged at 150°C. As illustrated in Figure 5, no loss in capacity was observed when the RT stored batteries were tested at 150°C after 6 months. Another battery stored at 60°C for 6 months showed a 3% capacity loss. Six months storage at 60°C is equivalent to about 10 years storage at RT. Therefore the expected self-discharge rate is <1%/year from this study, which is in good agreement with microcalorimetry data.

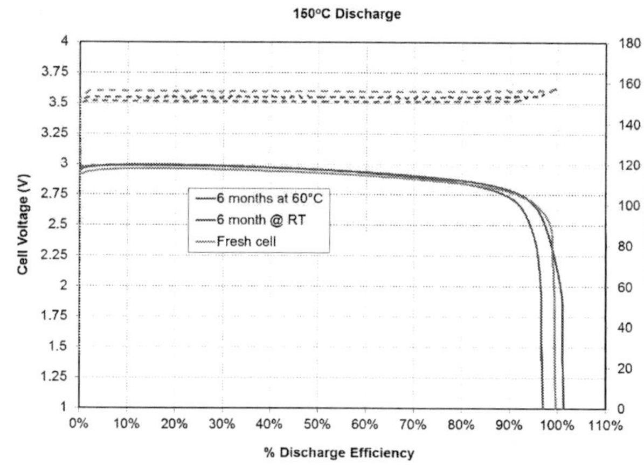

Figure 5. Discharge of downhole batteries at 150°C after storage at RT and at 60°C.

The observed good shelf life of EPT batteries is attributed to the electrochemical and thermal stability of the proprietary electrolyte up to 280°C as shown in Figures 6. The electrolyte was tested in the presence of lithium metal by differential scanning calorimetry (DSC). The endothermic peak appearing at 180°C is due to the melting of lithium metal.[3] However, the electrolyte showed good thermal stability in spite of the molten lithium and showed decomposition only about 300°C. The higher thermal stability of the proprietary electrolyte enables EPT CFx battery to safely operate at high temperatures. EPT also developed the next generation electrolyte with stability over 350°C to further extend the high temperature operation beyond 170°C.

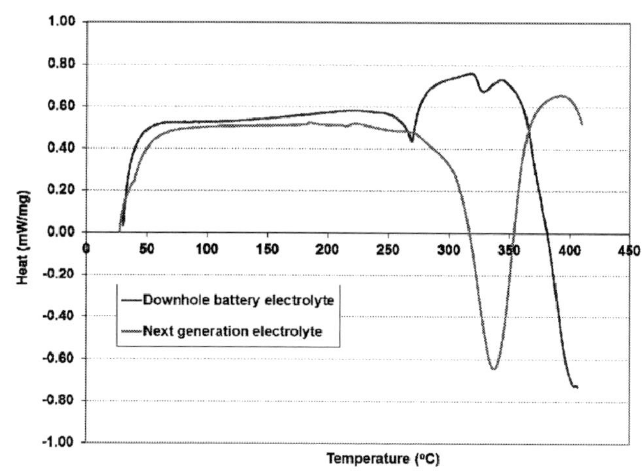

Figure 6. Differential scanning calorimetry (DSC) of electrolytes.

Aside from the exceptional discharge characteristics such as wide temperature operation range, high rate capability, and shelf life, the EPT batteries passed the safety tests required for transportation and downhole drilling operations. The tests include shock, vibration, short circuit, over discharge, and thermal cycling. To simulate the over discharge of the battery during drilling conditions, the test was performed at 125°C. The high temperature over discharge of sub DD battery for 40 hours is shown in Figure 7. As can be seen, the battery skin temperature stayed below 130°C during the entire duration of the over discharge test. The sub DD as well as D batteries also passed external short test at 55°C. The batteries also passed the shock and vibration tests. Nail penetration tests were done in addition to the above safety tests on the undischarged batteries. The batteries did not catch fire even after 48 hours following the nail penetration. The batteries passed all the safety tests, without a vent or fire. These safety test results further affirm the readiness of EPT CFx battery for downhole applications. It is generally considered that thermal runaway of lithium batteries occurs when the heat output exceeds thermal diffusion.[4] EPT CFx batteries were able to pass the recommended safety tests due to improvements in battery design.

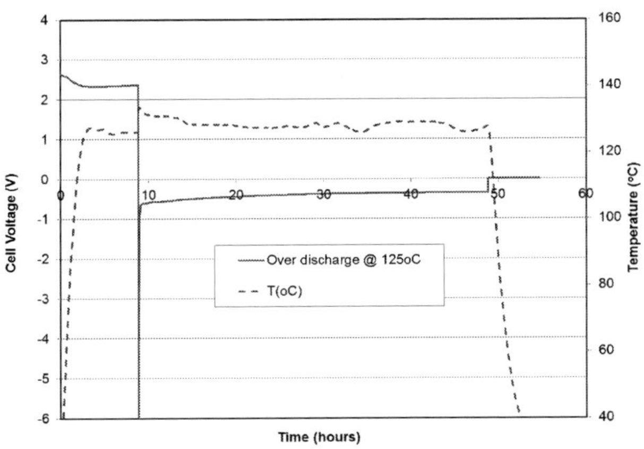

Figure 7. Over discharge test of sub DD at 125°C.

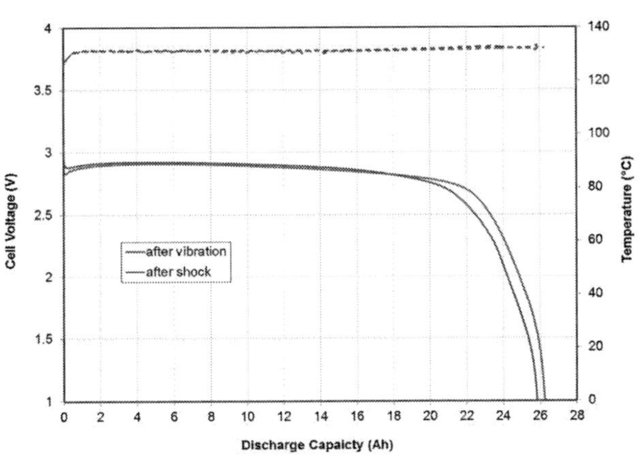

Figure 8. Discharge of sub DD battery at 750 mA post vibration and post shock tests.

The downhole batteries have to be tested for vigorous shock and vibration testing to ensure that they can withstand the drilling operation while supplying continuous power to operate the tool. To simulate this condition, the batteries were subjected to shock and vibration tests. The vibration test was a 20Grms random vibration between 30 and 500 Hz. The peak acceleration for shock test was 250G /2 ms. Following the shock and vibration tests, they were discharged at high temperature. EPT batteries delivered full capacity after the shock and vibration tests as shown in Figure 8.

Conclusion

Eagle Picher Technology has successfully developed Li/CFx batteries in D and sub DD configurations. The batteries show good discharge efficiency and rate capability over a wide temperature range from -20°C to 160°C. The cells show good shelf life, when discharged after 6 months of storage at 21°C and 60°C, respectively. Moreover, the D and sub DD size Li/CFx batteries passed all the recommended safety testing for transportation as well as operation in the oil field industry. The new EPT CFx battery is thus a promising technology for downhole applications.

Acknowledgements

This material is released to the public domain in accordance with ITAR 22 CFR 120.11

References

1. D. Hensley, M. Milewits, and W. Zhang, "Oilfield Review," *Autumn* (1998) 1- 57.
2. Y. Toyoguchi, T. Lijima, and M. Fukuda, "Active material for positive electrode of battery," *US patent,* no. 4271242, June 2, 1981.
3. N. Katayama et al, "Thermal stability of propylene carbonate and ethylene carbonate-propylene carbonate-based electrolytes for use in Li cells," J. Power Sources, 109 (2002) 321-326.
4. S. Tobishima and J. Yamaki, "A consideration of lithium cell safety," *J. Power Sources,* 81-82 (1999) 882.

Primary Lithium Batteries Using Hybrid Nanostructured CF_x/MnO_2 Cathodes

Stephen Lipka[1], Guandong Zhang[2], Christopher Swartz[1]
[1]Electrochemical Power Sources Group
University of Kentucky Center for Applied Energy Research
2582 Research Park Drive, Lexington, KY 40513
[2]Nanowise, LLC
3151 Custer Drive, Suite C, Lexington, KY 40517

Abstract: *Hybrid nanostructured cathodes were fabricated for use in primary lithium batteries. The cathodes were designed for pulse-power applications for naval sonobuoys. Results will be presented from a systematic study of the Li-MnO_2/CF_x/CNT batteries with different cathode compositions. The cells were tested at rates up to 5C. At higher C rates, the cells showed a capacity that is much higher than the sum value of the each individual component measured at the same discharge rate. Extremely high specific capacity combined with high power density was achieved; Li-MnO_2/CF_x/CNT batteries demonstrated a capacity of 270 mAh/g at a power density of 6242 W/Kg.*

Keywords: primary lithium battery; MnO_2; CF_x; sonobuoy; hybrid cathode

Introduction

Next generation, high pulse-power batteries are currently required for naval sonobuoys. The batteries must meet a plethora of requirements, including low cost, good battery safety, long shelf life, and the ability to discharge at required current densities under a variety of operational conditions, in addition to serving as a "drop-in" solution utilizing current sonobuoy battery form factors. Primary lithium batteries featuring hybrid cathode structures comprised of blends of MnO_2/CF_x have been previously demonstrated for various portable power-based military applications.[1] The use of a hybrid cathode structure allows for the advantageous utilization of excellent materials characteristics of both MnO_2 and CF_x. Heat-treated manganese dioxide is inexpensive, and is widely utilized in billions of primary Li/MnO_2 coin cells sold globally each year for consumer applications.[2] Li-CF_x primary batteries feature the highest theoretical capacity and energy density of any primary lithium battery, and offers many advantages, including long service life, low self-discharge, and the capability of operating over a wide range of temperatures.[3,4]

The overall objective of the project was to design, fabricate and test a primary lithium battery capable of meeting U. S. Navy sonobuoy pulse power performance metrics. The hybrid cathode architecture is based on an interpenetrating network of MnO_2 nanowires, CF_x nanospheres,[5] and carbon nanotube (CNT) based conductive additives in order to achieve both high power and specific capacities (Figure 1). The hybrid configuration of the cathode makes use of both the superior rate performance of MnO_2 and the higher specific capacity of CF_x active materials. The innovation is the three-component interpenetrating network configuration with the use of carbon nanotubes, which can enhance physical contact between cathode components, improve the rate of electron and lithium ion transport, and results in enhanced power capabilities. This novel Li-MnO_2/CF_x/CNT primary battery overcomes the shortcomings in the conventional Li-CF_x chemistry, such as low useful rate capacity of < C/50, self-heating at high discharge rates, and voltage delays. In addition, the synthesis techniques of active materials based on the hydrothermal process was developed to yield scalable cathode materials resulting in reduced cost of the battery.

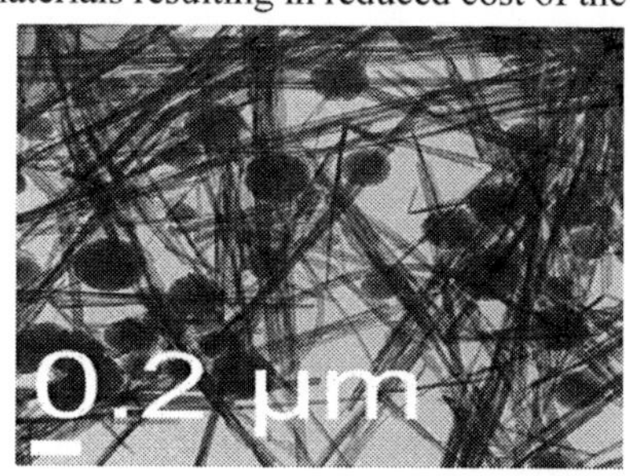

Figure 1. TEM of hybrid cathode architecture with nanostructured materials (63 wt.% MnO_2, 27 wt.% $CF_{1.244}$, 10 wt.% CNT).

Synthesis of α-MnO_2 nanowires

The α-MnO_2 nanowires were prepared by a hydrothermal method.[6] Additives were used in order to control the phase and morphology of the α-MnO_2 nanowires.[6] The hydrothermal reactions were performed in a 100 ml Teflon-lined stainless steel autoclave under autogenous pressure. The aspect ratio of the 1D α-MnO_2 nanowire can be controlled by the concentration of the reagents used in the hydrothermal reaction. As determined by SEM (Figure 2), the average diameter of the α-MnO_2 nanowires was ~ 30-40 nm, and the length was typically 5-30 µm, based on the reaction conditions.

Synthesis of spherical CF_x

Carbohydrate-derived, spherical carbon particles were also synthesized using a hydrothermal method.[5] The carbon particles were then carbonized, graphitized, and were fluorinated by Advance Research Chemicals, Inc. (Catoosa, OK). The degree of fluorination was determined by XPS, and was determined to be $CF_{1.244}$. The fluorinated carbon spheres had an average diameter of ~ 200-300 nm. Figure 3 is an SEM image of graphitized carbon spheres.

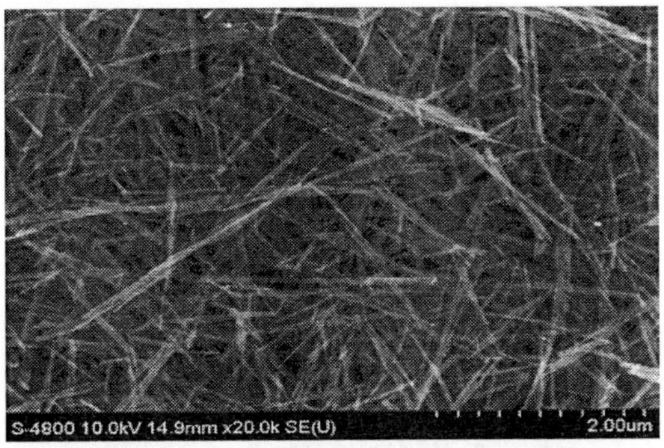

Figure 2. SEM of α-MnO_2 nanowires.

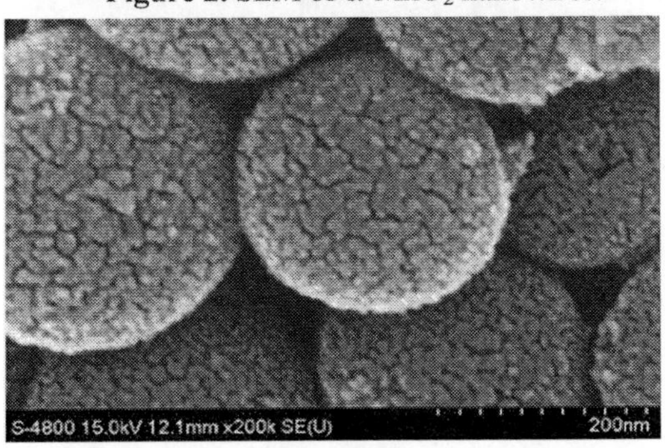

Figure 3. SEM of graphitized carbon spheres.

The multiwall carbon nanotubes utilized as the conductive additive in the three-component interpenetrating network were synthesized using a chemical vapor deposition method at the University of Kentucky Center for Applied Energy Research. The graphitized multiwall carbon nanotubes had a purity > 99%, an average outer diameter 24 ± 15 nm, an average inner diameter of 6 ± 2 nm, and a length: > 50 μm.

Electrode and cell fabrication

Cathode films were formed by mixing 90% α-MnO_2 nanowires or 90% $CF_{1.244}$ with 10% carbon nanotubes (CNT) in a methanol/water solution with sodium dodecyl sulfate (SDS). The mixture was then sonicated to produce a uniform suspension or slurry. The slurry was then cast onto a Celgard® 3501 polymer separator, and was washed and dried. The electrodes were then punched out from the dried sheet, and were pressed onto titanium mesh. The hybrid cathodes were created in a similar fashion, with varying weight percentages of α-MnO_2 nanowires and $CF_{1.244}$ added to the mixture, while 10 wt.% carbon nanotubes was kept constant in all electrode formulations. The cathodes were used in a two-electrode EL-Cell® with a lithium metal counter electrode (Acros), and a Celgard® 3501 separator. The electrolyte is 0.5M lithium tetrafluoroborate ($LiBF_4$) dissolved in 8:2 propylene carbonate (PC) and dimethoxyethane (DME). Cells were discharged at constant current on a MACCOR 4300 8-channel battery cycler from the open circuit voltage (VOC ~ 3.4 V) to 1.0 V, at various C rates based on the theoretical capacity.

Results

The electrochemical performance of the α-MnO_2 nanowires (theoretical capacity = 308 mAh/g) was evaluated first (Figure 4). The α-MnO_2 nanowires show excellent high rate discharge characteristics, with a capacity of 238 mAh/g at a C/10 rate, and a capacity of 163 mAh/g at a 5C rate. The composition of the cathodes is 90 wt.% α-MnO_2 and 10 wt.% CNT. No binder was added.

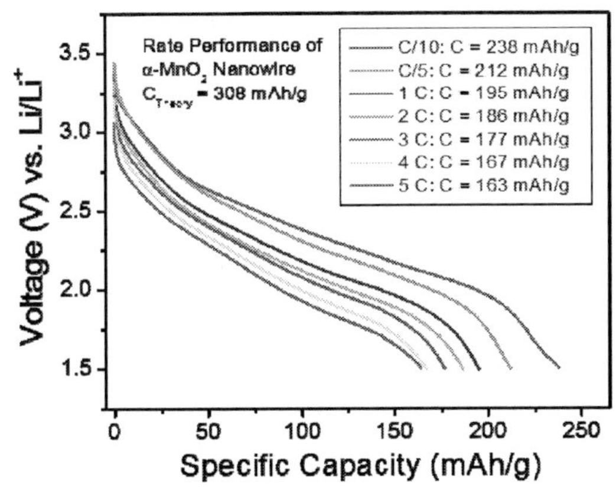

Figure 4. Capacity at varying C rates with α-MnO_2 cathodes.

The electrochemical performance of the fluorinated carbon spheres ($CF_{1.244}$; theoretical capacity = 936 mAh/g) was then evaluated at various C rates (Figure 5). The capacity was 751 mAh/g at C/10, and dropped to 199 mAh/g at C. The composition of the cathode was 90% $CF_{1.244}$, 10% CNT.

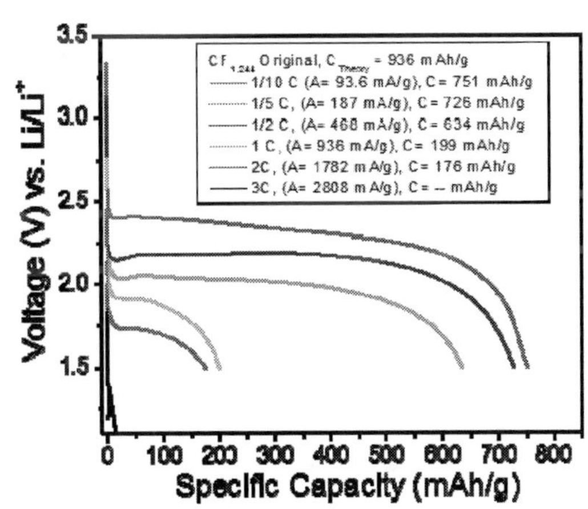

Figure 5. Capacity at varying C rates for $CF_{1.244}$ cathodes.

After the performance of the individual cathode components was quantified, a systematic investigation of the Li-MnO_2/CF_x/CNT batteries with different cathode compositions was performed. In these cathodes, the conductive filler CNT content was kept constant at 10 wt.% of the total mass. The total mass of the active materials combined (MnO_2 and CF_x) was kept constant at 90 wt.%. Three different mass ratios of α-MnO_2 nanowires to $CF_{1.244}$ were evaluated, including 70% to 30% (theoretical capacity = 496 mAh/g; 63 wt.% MnO_2, 27% $CF_{1.244}$), 50% to 50% (theoretical capacity = 622 mAh/g; 45 wt.% MnO_2, 45 wt.% $CF_{1.244}$), and 30% to 70% (theoretical capacity = 747 mAh/g; 27 wt.% MnO_2, 63 wt.% $CF_{1.244}$), respectively. The total theoretical capacity of the hybrid cathode is estimated as: $C_{total} = (C_{MnO2}\times W_{MnO2} + C_{CFx}\times W_{CFx})/(W_{MnO2} + W_{CFx})$; where W_{MnO2} and W_{CFx} are the mass of the α-MnO_2 nanowires and spherical $CF_{1.244}$, respectively (C_{MnO2} = 308 mAh/g, C_{CFx} = 936 mAh/g). The discharge data for the cathode composition of 63 wt.% MnO_2, 27% $CF_{1.244}$, and 10 wt.% CNT is shown in Figure 6.

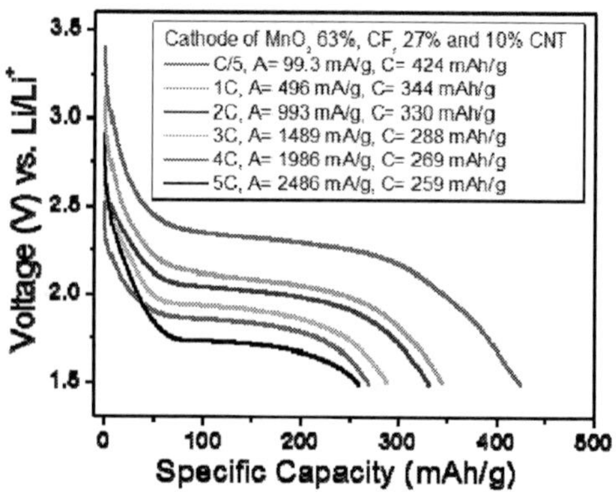

Figure 6. Discharge curves at varying C rates for cells with 63 wt.% MnO_2, 27% $CF_{1.244}$, and 10 wt.% CNT.

At a rate of C/5, the hybrid cathode (63 wt.% MnO_2, 27% $CF_{1.244}$) had an average discharge voltage of 2.34 V vs. Li/Li^+, and a capacity of 424 mAh/g (85% capacity utilization). At 5C the capacity dropped to 259 mAh/g (52% capacity utilization), and the average discharge voltage dropped to 1.74 V vs. Li/Li^+. The discharge data for the cathode composition of 45 wt.% MnO_2, 45% $CF_{1.244}$, and 10 wt.% CNT is shown in Figure 7.

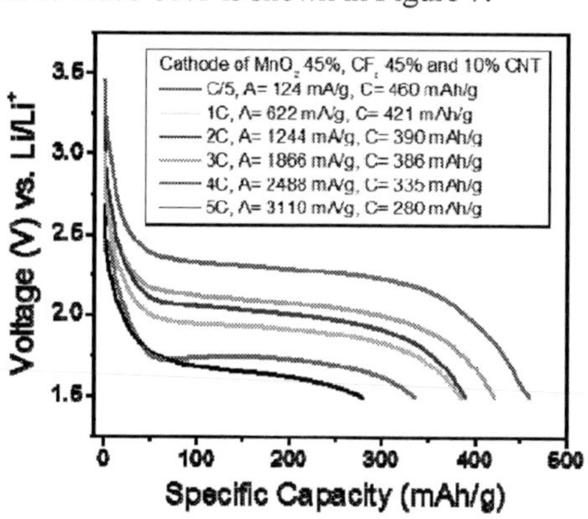

Figure 7. Discharge curves at varying C rates for cells with 50 wt.% MnO_2, 50% $CF_{1.244}$, and 10 wt.% CNT.

As seen in Figure 7, the hybrid cathode (45 wt.% MnO_2, 45 wt.% $CF_{1.244}$, 10% CNT) had an average discharge voltage of 2.31 V vs. Li/Li^+ at C/5, and a capacity of 593 mAh/g (95% capacity utilization). The higher theoretical capacity of this hybrid cathode is expected due to the higher $CF_{1.244}$ content in the electrode formulation. At 5C, the average discharge voltage drops to 1.63 V vs. Li/Li^+, and had a capacity of 280 mAh/g (45% capacity utilization), which is a lower discharge voltage and slightly higher capacity than the electrode formulation with 63% MnO_2 at 5C. The discharge data for the cathode composition of 27% MnO_2, 63% $CF_{1.244}$, and 10% CNT is shown in Figure 8.

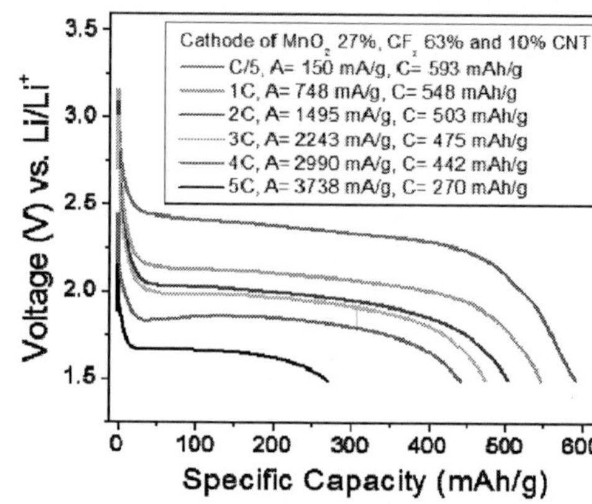

Figure 8. Discharge curves at varying C rates for cells with 27 wt.% MnO_2, 63% $CF_{1.244}$, and 10 wt.% CNT.

As seen in Figure 8, the hybrid cathode (27 wt.% MnO_2, 63% $CF_{1.244}$) had the highest capacity of the three hybrid cathode formulations at C/5 (593 mAh/g, 79% capacity utilization), along with the highest average discharge voltage (2.40 V vs. Li/Li^+). At 5C, the capacity was 270 mAh/g (36% capacity utilization), and the average discharge voltage was 1.67 V vs. Li/Li^+. A graphical summary of specific capacity vs. discharge rate is shown in Figure 9. The cathode formulation with the the highest $CF_{1.244}$ content (63%) had the highest specific capacity at all C rates tested, except at 5C.

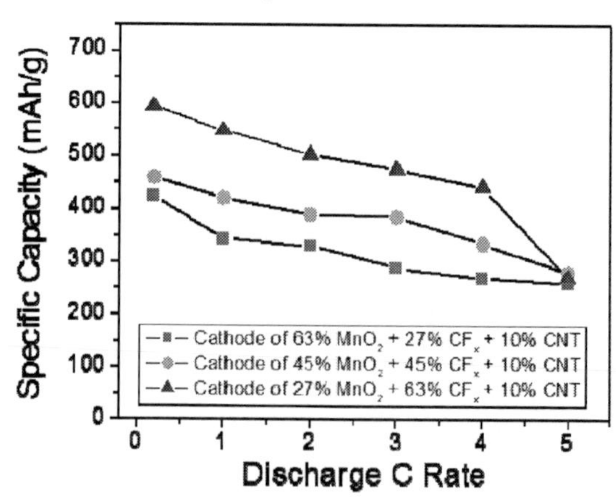

Figure 9. Specific capacity as a function of C rate for hybrid cathode formulations.

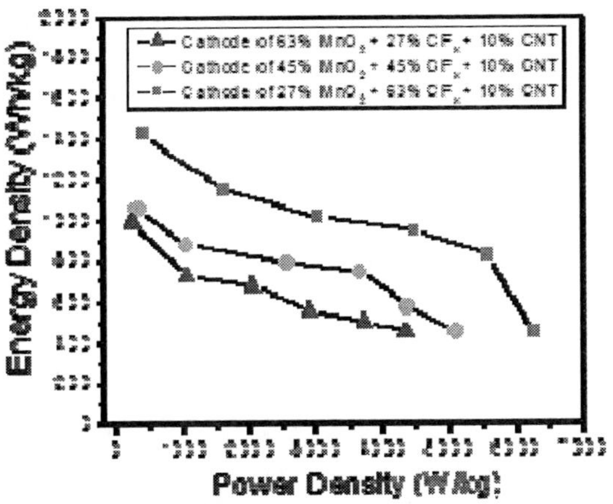

Figure 10. Ragone plot of Li-MnO_2/CF_x/CNT batteries with different compositions.

A Ragone plot summarizing energy density vs. power density is shown in Figure 10. The cathode formulation with 27% MnO_2, 63% $CF_{1.244}$, and 10% CNT achieved the highest energy and power densities, with a specific capacity of 270 mAh/g, an energy density of 451 Wh/kg, and a power density of 6242 W/kg (at 5C).

Summary

Table 1 is a summary of discharge data and various performance metrics for the hybrid cathode formulations used in this study. Nanostructured cathode materials were synthesized using hydrothermal methods, which are inexpensive and readily scalable. The individual components were successfully integrated into a cathode architecture with assistance of the surfactant SDS, resulting in the interpenetrating network of MnO_2 nanowires, CF_x nanospheres, and carbon nanotubes in the cathode. The cells with hybrid cathodes can work up to 5C. At higher C rates, the hybrid cathodes have a capacity that is much higher than the sum value of each component measured at the same rate. The hybrid configuration of the cathode makes use of both the superior rate performance of MnO_2 nanowires and the higher specific capacity of spherical CF_x active materials, and eliminates the shortcomings of the conventional Li-CF_x chemistry, such as low discharge rate capability, voltage delay, and most importantly, leads to significant improvement in the high rate discharge performance.

Acknowledgements

The authors wish to thank the Department of Defense and the Department of the Navy for SBIR funding (contract number N68335-15-C-0031).

References

1. Negrete, C. R.; Davenport, A. J. "Development in Hybrid Lithium CF_x/MnO_2 Technology for Military Applications." Proceedings of the 45th Power Sources Conference, 2012.
2. Tan, H.; Wang, S.; Lei, X. *Journal of the Electrochemical Society.* **2015**, *162*, A448.
3. Dai, Y.; Cai, S.; Wu, L.; Yang, W.; Xie, J.; Wen, W.; Zheng, J.-C.; Zhu, Y. *J. Mater. Chem. A.* **2014**, *2*, 20896.
4. Zhang, S. S.; Foster, D.; Wolfenstine, J.; Read, J. *J. Power Sources.* **2009**, *187*, 233.
5. Loth, M. A.; Kunadian, K.; Chen, R.; Graham, U.; Swartz, C.; Lipka, S. M. "Fluorinated Carbon Nanospheres for Primary Lithium/CF_x Batteries." Proceedings of the 45th Power Sources Conference, 2012.
6. Gui, Y.; Qian, L.; Qian, X. *Chinese Journal of Inorganic Chemistry.* **2009**, *25*, 668.

Table 1. Summary of performance metrics for hybrid cathodes.

Cathode Composition	Discharge Characteristics					
	C Rate	Current (mA)	Mean Point Voltage (V)	Capacity (mAh/g)	Energy Density (Wh/kg)	Power Density (W/kg)
MnO_2: 63%	C/5	99.3	2.34	424	992	232
CF_x: 27%	1C	496	2.11	344	726	1047
CNT: 10%	2C	993	2.04	330	673	2026
	3C	1489	1.94	288	559	2889
C_{Theory}:	4C	1986	1.87	269	503	3714
496.4 mAh/g	5C	2482	1.74	259	451	4319
MnO_2: 45%	C/5	124	2.31	460	1063	286
CF_x: 45%	1C	622	2.10	421	884	1036
CNT: 10%	2C	1244	2.03	390	792	2525
	3C	1866	1.94	386	749	3620
C_{Theory}:	4C	2488	1.74	335	583	4329
622 mAh/g	5C	3110	1.63	280	456	5069
MnO_2: 27%	C/5	150	2.40	593	1423	360
CF_x: 63%	1C	748	2.11	548	1156	1578
CNT: 10%	2C	1495	2.02	503	1016	3020
	3C	2243	1.99	475	945	4464
C_{Theory}:	4C	2990	1.86	442	822	5561
747.6 mAh/g	5C	3738	1.67	270	451	6242

High Energy Lithium Carbon Monofluoride (Li/CF$_x$) Pouch Cells

Thierry Le Gall, Girts Vitins, Philip Holland and Gary Mepsted

QinetiQ Ltd

Cody Technology Park, Ively Road, Farnborough, GU14 0LX, United Kingdom

Abstract: *QinetiQ has developed and optimized high-energy lithium carbon monofluoride primary cells (Li/CF$_x$) for space and defense applications and has tested their performance and safety in a number of different formats, as an alternative to lithium/thionyl chloride options. With a specific capacity of 864 mAh g^{-1} delivered at around 2.5 V, CF$_x$ offers a significant increase in specific capacity and energy compared to other cathodes. Therefore it is an attractive battery system for reducing weight and increasing mission duration. QinetiQ has recently optimized cathode composition and cell design to minimize expansion and maximize CF$_x$ utilization for higher specific energy. This paper reports on large format pouch cells, which deliver 36 Ah, high (95%) CFx capacity utilization and a specific energy of up to 770 Wh kg^{-1} and a volumetric energy of up 960 Wh dm^{-3} when discharged at C/75 rate at 20°C. Cell capacity has also been characterized at -15°C and 55°C. Thermal properties have been analyzed using accelerated rate calorimetry under adiabatic conditions showing that approximately 37% of the Li/CFx conversion reaction energy is produced as heat.*

Keywords: Primary lithium batteries; carbon monofluoride; pouch cells.

Introduction

Due to its light weight and a corresponding high specific capacity of 864 mAh g^{-1} delivered at around 2.5 V the Li/CF$_x$ (x = 1) electrode system is known to have the highest practical specific energy (ca. 2.20 kWh kg^{-1} active material) among well-known primary cell systems, e.g. 1.47 kWh kg^{-1} in Li/SO$_2$Cl$_2$ and 0.90 kWh kg^{-1} in Li/MnO$_2$. At the cell level, 240 Wh kg^{-1} have been achieved by Ultralife in cylindrical cells of Li/MnO$_2$ and 400 Wh kg^{-1} in pouch cells. So far, the highest specific energy reported for Li/CFx D-cells is 500 Wh kg^{-1} by Eagle Picher [1], where some variants include Li/CF$_x$-MnO$_2$. In the past, Li/CF$_x$ has been demonstrated in 18650 cylindrical cells with a capacity of 3.6 Ah at 2.5 V by Sandia National Laboratories [2]. Previously, QinetiQ has reported larger format Li/CF$_x$ pouch cells up to 600 – 650 Wh kg^{-1} [3]. Thin light-weight pouch cell packaging offers weight reductions and the prismatic (flat wound or stacked) cell shape provides better space utilization in rectangular battery packs compared with cylindrical cell assemblies. Therefore a higher energy density can be achieved with better packaging efficiency.

While Li/CF$_x$ is widely used in small coin cells and some cylindrical cell designs, large pouch cells appear unique in part because of some fabrication challenges.

Heat generation is well known in larger format Li/CF$_x$ cells due to the nature of conversion reaction:

$$Li + CF_x = x\,LiF + C \quad 864\ mAh\ g^{-1}$$

The Gibbs free energy predicts an open-circuit potential of around 4.57 V [4-8]. However the heat generation occurs as the practical cell discharge proceeds at 2.4 – 2.6 V at C/20 – C/100 rates [1,8,9], which is much lower than the thermodynamic value of 4.57 V. This inefficiency is related to several mechanisms. The high polarization with Tafel type behavior [5,7] has been associated with the activation energy required to break covalent C-F bonds [4], while other studies have related it to formation of an intermediate insertion compound, CLi$_x$F [6] or C(Li-Solvent-F)$_x$ [8,9] with subsequent crystallization of LiF and release of heat. Heat generation must be managed in larger cell and battery applications, particularly at higher discharge rates. While it can limit the upper discharge rates applied in higher temperature environments, it can be beneficial at low temperatures.

Attempts have been made to enhance CF$_x$ rate capability by reducing fluorination, with x in range 0.33 – 0.66, at the expense of specific capacity [10]. Zhang et al have explored cathode composites with added carbon nanotubes [11]. Such composites improve the conductive network around CF$_x$ particles without effecting CF$_x$ properties. The most effective method has been hydrothermal surface modification of CF$_x$ particles with reduced fluorination at the particle surface. In small laboratory cells the material has been demonstrated with an enhanced voltage of 2.6 V, capacity of 830 mAh g^{-1} at C/40 rate and a high rate capability, with a plateau voltage of over 2.1 V and a capacity of 700 mAh g^{-1} at 20C rate to a 1.5 V cut-off [12]. Such high discharge rates may not be applicable in larger batteries due to heat rejection issues.

In the present paper, large format Li/CF_x pouch cells with excellent performance characteristics, including high CF_x utilization, are demonstrated. The cells are suitable for military battery packs where lower battery weight and higher specific energy are required.

Experimental

Cell fabrication

Large format pouch cells were fabricated in dry-room (dew-point of -40°C) conditions at QinetiQ's pilot production facility. CF_x was processed into composite cathode ink dispersions in NMP to produce solid coatings comprising more than 90 wt.% CF_x (with x = 1). Cathode coatings in excess of 170 g m^{-2} were deposited onto Al-foil, calendared and subsequently cut to the required size cathode parts, which were vacuum-dried at 120°C. Electrodes were stacked with interleaved microporous separator (20 μm) and electrically connected using ultrasonic welding. Cold-formed laminate packaging material was thermally sealed around the electrode stacks. Standard 1 M $LiBF_4$ in PC/DME electrolyte was used, which offers a low density and good performance at low temperatures. The electrolyte volume was optimized to provide maximum specific energy over a wide temperature range.

Testing

Cells were discharged with constant current or constant power to 1.5 V using Maccor and Arbin multi-channel cyclers. Three cells were used in each test and typical or average data values are presented in this paper. Cell surface temperature was monitored by thermocouple mounted in the center of the cells.

Heat generation in cells was measured using an accelerated rate calorimeter under adiabatic conditions, which was calibrated using an alumina plate. Specific heat capacity of the cells was measured between 25° – 90°C and then cells were partially discharged and the generated heat was calculated based on the temperature rise and heat capacity. Discharges were stopped when temperature reached 90°C.

Results

Cell weight and dimensions

Cells (Figure 1) weighed 116.5 ± 0.5 g. Cell dimensions excluding tabs are 95.5 ± 0.5 mm in width and 137.5 ± 0.5 mm in length. Cell thickness is 7.3 ± 0.1 mm. Therefore the total volume is 96 cm^3, with a corresponding cell density of 1.21 g cm^{-3}. Post-mortem of a 95% discharged cell has confirmed complete cohesion and integrity of the cathode coat with no delamination evident.

Figure 1. 36 Ah Li/CF_x pouch cells

Discharge performance

Voltage profiles of two 36 Ah cells discharged at C/75 rate and room temperature are shown in Figure 2. Both constant current and constant power discharge plots are shown to exemplify that there is no significant difference between the two discharge regimes. Cells had an OCV of 3.5 V. The voltage rapidly dropped to around 2.3 V and recovered to a plateau of 2.6 V as the conductive carbon formed at CF_x particle surface. Cells delivered 36 Ah, which corresponds to 95% CF_x capacity utilization, confirming efficient cell operation. The average cell voltage was 2.52 V. Cell expansion was around 3%. The cells have delivered 90 – 92 Wh of electric energy corresponding to a specific energy of 767 Wh kg^{-1}.

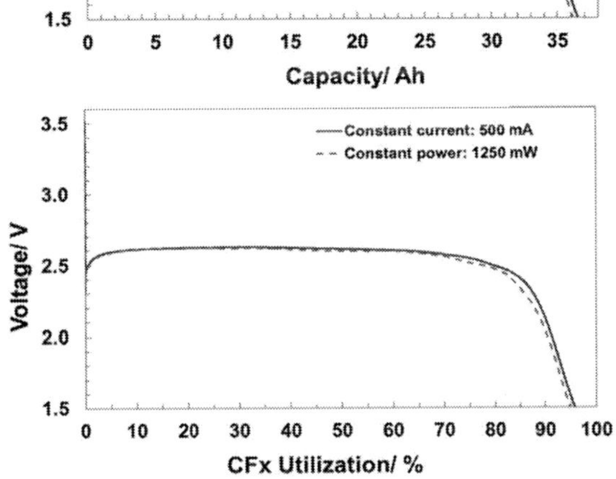

Figure 2. Voltage profile of 36 Ah Li/CF_x pouch cells at C/75 rate at 20°C

Cells were also discharged at -15°C and 55°C, and after two weeks storage at 55°C. The voltage profiles are shown in Figure 3.

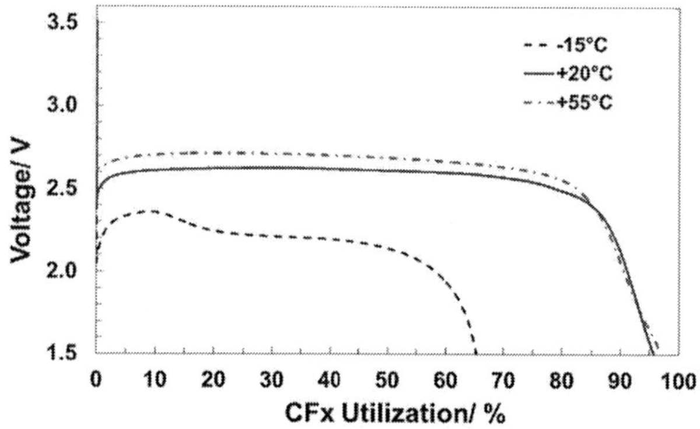

Figure 3. Voltage profile of 36 Ah Li/CF_x pouch cells at C/75 rate and different temperatures

The performance results are summarized in Table 1. Low temperature discharge is more challenging. The voltage profile is uneven and cells deliver a capacity of 24 Ah and lower utilization (64%). The low temperature performance improves if cells are discharged in a larger battery pack assembly where cells would be higher temperature. In contrast to the low temperature conditions cells deliver excellent performance at 55°C with 97% utilization and a specific energy reaching 810 Wh kg^{-1}. The cell thickness at this temperature decreases by 3%.

Table 1. Cell performance indicators at different environmental temperature and after storage at 55°C

Environment Temperature (°C)	Capacity (Ah)/ CFx Utilization (%)	Average Voltage (V)	Specific Energy (Wh kg^{-1})	Skin Temperature Peak (°C)
-15	25 / 65	2.16	444	-10
20	36 / 95	2.50	757	30
55	36 / 97	2.61	810	60
20 (after 2 weeks storage at 55°C)	35 / 95	2.50	744	30

Voltage profiles obtained at different discharge rates at 20°C are shown in Figure 4. As expected with increasing discharge rate both the cell voltage and CF_x capacity utilization slightly decrease to an average of 2.43 V and 93.7%, respectively at C/20 rate.

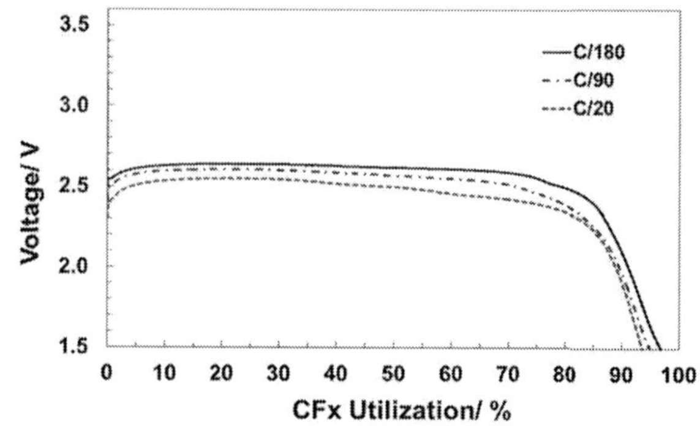

Figure 4. Voltage profile of 36 Ah Li/CF_x pouch cells at different discharge rates at room temperature

Thermal properties

The cell heat capacity (Cp) is 1.54 g J^{-1} $°C^{-1}$ at 20°C, as extrapolated from the plot in Figure 5. It agrees well with calculated figures based upon the inventory of cell components. It somewhat increases with temperature, which can be attributed to the properties of the liquid electrolyte comprising solvated ions and polar molecule interactions.

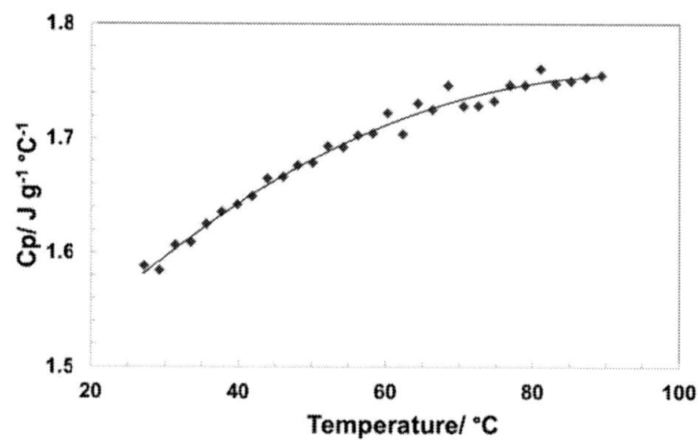

Figure 5. Heat capacity in 36 Ah Li/CF_x pouch cells

Calorimetric test results are summarized in Table 2. Three cells were discharged at 500 mA. The capacity was limited by the allowed maximum temperature (90°C). Tests at three temperatures, starting at -15°C, show good consistency in heat power and the corresponding heat energy. Based on the total energy released the electric energy efficiency is 63%, which broadly agrees with the discrepancy in the practical cell voltage 2.6 V and the thermodynamic value of 4.5 V. The heat generation effectively represents an overall IR polarization due to the mechanisms discussed above.

Table 2. Calorimetric test results for three cells at 500 mA

Discharged Current, Initial Temperature	500 mA, -15°C	500 mA, 20°C	500 mA, 55°C
Temperature Rise (°C)	106	69	33
Heat ΔH (kJ)	19.9	13.2	6.7
Electric Energy (kJ)	33.0	22.5	11.2
Energy Efficiency (%)	62.4	63.0	62.6
Discharge Capacity (Ah)	3.58	2.38	1.17
Average Heat Power per Cell (W)	0.77	0.77	0.80

Conclusions

QinetiQ has successfully fabricated and demonstrated large format Li/CF_x pouch cells with a practical capacity of 36 Ah, a specific energy of 760 ± 10 Wh kg^{-1} and a volumetric energy of 950 ± 10 Wh dm^{-3}. At lower temperature (-15°C) cells deliver reduced capacity and corresponding cathode utilization (65%) but at ambient and higher temperatures full capacity is delivered, even after prolonged storage at 55°C. Accelerated rate calorimetry studies have shown that the specific heat capacity of the cell is 1.54 g J^{-1} $°C^{-1}$ at 20°C and the electrical efficiency of the discharge process is 63%.

Acknowledgements

The authors wish to thank DSTL (UK) for funding.

References

1. Shmuel De Leon Energy Ltd., "Li/CFx Batteries - The Renaissance", *Report*, 14 January 2011.
2. G. Nagasubramanian, "Fabrication and Testing Capabilities for 18650 Li/$(CF_x)_n$ Cells", *Int. J. Electrochem. Sci.*, vol. 2, pp. 913-922, 2007.
3. E.I. Eweka, C.O. Giwa, G.O. Mepsted, K. Green, D. Scattergood, "Development of High Energy Density Small Flat Spiral Cells and Battery Pack on Lithium/Carbon Monfluoride (Li/CF_x)", *J. Power Sources*, vol. 162, pp. 841-846, 2006.
4. H.F. Hunger, G.J. Heymark, "Cathodic Discharge of Graphite Intercalation Compounds in organic Electrolytes", *J. Electrochem. Soc.*, vol. 120, pp. 1161-1168, 1973.
5. W. Tiedemann, "Electrochemical Behaviour of the Fluorographite Electrode in Nonaqueous Media", *J. Electrochem. Soc.*, vol. 121, pp. 1308-1311, 1974.
6. M.S. Whittingham, "Mechanism of Reduction of the Fluorographite", *J. Electrochem. Soc.*, vol. 122, pp. 1308-1311, 1975.
7. S. Davis, E.S. Takeuchi, W. Tiedemann, and J. Newman, "Simulation of the Li-CF_x System", *J. Electrochem. Soc.*, vol. 154, pp. A477-A480, 2007.
8. S.S. Zhang, D. Foster, J. Wolfenstine, and J. Read, "Electrochemical Characteristic and Discharge Mechanism of a Primary Li/CF_x Cell", *J. Power Sources*, vol. 187, pp. 233-237, 2009.
9. J. Read, E. Collins, B. Piekarski, and S. Zhang, "LiF Formation and Cathode Swelling in the Li/CF_x Battery", *J. Electrochem. Soc.*, vol. 158, pp. A504-A510, 2011.
10. P. Lam, R. Yazami, "Physical Characteristics and Rate Performance of $(CF_x)_n$ ($0.33 < x < 0.66$) in Lithium Batteries", *J. Power Sources*, vol. 153, pp. 354-359, 2006.
11. Q. Zhang, K.J. Takeuchi, E.S. Takeuchi, and A.C. Marschilok, "Progress Towards High-Power Li/CF_x Batteries: Electrode Architectures Using Carbon Nanotubes with CF_x", *Phys. Chem. Chem. Phys.*, vol. 17, pp. 22504-22518, 2015.
12. Y. Dai, S.Cai, L. Wu, W. Yang, J. Xie, W. Wen, J.-C. Zheng, and Y. Zhu, "Surface Modified CF_x Cathode Material for Ultrafast Discharge and High Energy Density", *J. Mater. Chem.*, vol. A2, pp. 20896-20901, 2014.

Synthesis and Electrochemical Performance of $Li_xMn_{2-y}Co_yO_{4-d}Cl_d$ Cathode Material

Terrill B. Atwater, Paula C. Latorre, and Ashley L. Ruth

U.S. Army, Aberdeen Proving Ground, MD

Abstract: *Lithium manganese oxide spinel is a potential candidate for Li-ion battery cathodes because of its low toxicity, comparable capacity, and low cost. However, this spinel suffers from capacity fading due to fracturing of the cell structure. Historically, cycle life enhancements of spinels have been achieved through transition metal doping on the "B" site of the lattice. In this effort, dopants of interest include compounds containing Group VIII Row 4 (Fe, Co, and Ni) elements, cobalt in particular. In addition to fabrication method variants of this material, the electrochemical performance and cycle life data of the Co "B" site and Cl "O" site manganese-based AB_2O_4 spinel is presented in this paper. Lithium electrochemical cells with Co "B" and Cl "O" site doping of a Mn-based AB_2O_4 spinel cathode have demonstrated the following: 1) full reversibility between 4.5 V and 2.0 V, 2) low charge/discharge overpotential between 4.5 V and 3.5 V, 3) high specific capacity of 240 mAh/g of active material, and 4) high rate charge and discharge.*

Keywords: Lithium and Li-ion battery, Lithium manganese oxide spinel, Spinel cathode, Co-doping, Cl-doping

Introduction

The benefits of lithium battery systems lie within their high energy density (Wh/L) and high specific energy (Wh/kg). Manganese dioxide (MnO_2) is an attractive active cathode material because of its high energy density and low material cost. Manganese dioxide is an intercalating compound for lithium that functions by solvating and desolvating lithium cations from the electrolyte in solid state. The lithium cations are deposited into the vacancies of the MnO_2 cathode crystal structure. The objective of this effort focuses on the limited cycle life of rechargeable lithium manganese-based electrochemical systems, namely capacity fading of the cathode. These two characteristics are considered the major technical hurdles in rechargeable lithium battery technologies.[1-4]

Background

Capacity fading is the loss of cycle capacity in a cell over the entire life of a battery system, limiting the practical number of cycles that may be used. In lithium battery systems, capacity loss is often attributed to the degradation of the active cathode material. This degradation is a result of changes in both composition and crystal structure of the active material that occur during charging and discharging of the cell. The crystal structure of the active material changes in coordination with the state of charge of the cell. This is linked to intercalation of lithium cations into the active material. Additionally, throughout the life of a cell, parasitic side reactions occur between the chemical species of the cell components. These include chemical dissolution and degradation of the active cathode material. Methods reducing this effect include changing the crystal structure and composition of the active material or eliminating these parasitic mechanisms through other means. Capacity fading is currently a major setback for rechargeable lithium cells and is therefore an active area of research.[2-9]

Manganese dioxide exists in different phase states or crystal structures. The common phases are referred to by the following prefixes: α, β, γ, and λ. α-MnO_2 is the most stable structure; it is a one-dimensional lattice containing both one-by-one, and two-by-two channels for lithium insertion/extraction. γ-MnO_2 is a one dimensional structure but has a one-by-two channel. λ-MnO_2 is created through the delithiation of Li-Mn-O type spinels ($Li_xMn_2O_4$). The crystal structure of the spinel is maintained through both delithiation and lithiation. The λ crystal structure is a three-dimensional cubic array. This structure promotes mechanical stability and adequate pathways for lithium insertion/extraction. λ-MnO_2 is perhaps the most preferred rechargeable phase on MnO_2. Degradation of the λ-MnO_2 crystal structure, forming α/γ-MnO_2 and other Mn_xO_y phases, reduces the capacity of the cathode material.[10-17]

A family of halogenated "B" site doped $AB_2O_{4-d}X_d$ lithium manganese spinel materials was synthesized and evaluated as a cathode for lithium and lithium-ion electrochemical systems. This spinel is formulated with the general stoichiometry $Li_xMn_2O_{4-d}X_d$, where $x \approx 1$ and d ranges from 0.005 to 0.3; this work was reported previously and also demonstrated in these current proceedings.[18-20] By introducing halogens into the starting material mixture and thereby into the final product, the synthesis process time of lithium manganese-based AB_2O_4 spinel materials is dramatically reduced. Additionally, when coupled with a lithium anode, the $Li_xMn_2O_{4-d}X_d$ material proved to be reversible to voltages as low as 2.0 V (where x is approaching 2). In order to stabilize the manganese to improve cycle life, Group VIII Period 4 elements (Fe, Co, Ni) were doped into the "B" site. This paper will present data relating to the Co-doped material while the Fe-doped material is presented in a complementary paper in these proceedings.

Experimental

A glycine nitrate combustion method was used to synthesize cobalt-doped chlorinated lithium manganese oxide spinel. Stoichiometric amounts of $Li(NO_3)$ and $Mn(NO_3)_2{\cdot}4H_2O$ and $Co(NO_3)_2{\cdot}4H_2O$ (Alfa Aesar) with $MnCl_3$ were mixed and then dissolved in distilled water. NH_2CH_2COOH (glycine, Alfa Aesar) was dissolved into the aqueous solution as a chelating agent in a 1:1 metal ion-to-glycine ratio. The solution was heated to 80 °C until the water fully evaporated and a gel was formed. The gel was heated further to 250 °C when auto ignition occured and formed metallic oxide ash. The ash was collected and ground in a mortar and pestle and fired at 600 °C for two to six hours to achieve the desired phase.

The $Li_xMn_{2-y}Co_yO_{4-d}Cl_d$ material was also fabricated using a solid state process where manganese and cobalt mixed metal oxides along is combined with Li_2CO_3 or LiOH as the principal starting material. Halogens were introduced into the starting material mixture and subsequent final product using lithium halide salts. The subsequent material mixture was ground using a random orbit mixer mill and was then heated at 600 °C in air.

Phase purity was determined using X-ray diffraction (XRD, Bruker D8 Advance, Cu-kα). Samples of $LiMn_2O_4$ (non-doped and non-chlorinated lithium manganese oxide) were synthesized via the above mentioned process without the halogen or Group VIII addition to determine structure changes that occurred. Both chlorine-to-manganese and Group VIII-to-manganese stoichiometry was determined from X-ray fluorescence spectroscopy (XRF, Bruker S2 Ranger). An Olympus metallograph was used to observe the morphology of the particles.

The experimental cells were composed of a lithium anode separated from the cathode by a nonwoven glass separator. The $Li_xMn_{2-y}Co_yO_{4-d}Cl_d$ cathode was fabricated by mixing together the active material, carbon, and polytetrafluoroethylene in an 85:10:5 by weight ratio, respectively. The cathode mixture was rolled to 0.04 cm and dried in a vacuum oven. A 0.075 cm thick lithium foil was cut using a 19.0 mm diameter hole punch. The cathode was cut into 2.85 cm^2 discs, resulting in a 0.13 g cathode. A 0.01 cm nonwoven glass separator was utilized for the separator and as a wick. The electrolyte used was 1 molar $LiPF_6$ in proportional mixtures of diethyl carbonate, dimethyl carbonate, and ethylene carbonate.

Cells were cycled with an ARBIN MSTAT4 battery cycler system controlled by MITS Pro software. The cells were charged and discharged from 4.5 V to 3.5 V, 4.5 V to 2.25 V, or 4.75 V to 3.5 V. The charge/discharge rates were maintained at 1.0 mA/cm^2 or 2.0 mA/cm^2. A rest period of 15 minutes between charge and discharge cycles was used to allow for cells to achieve equilibrium on all experiments.

Results

After formulation of the $Li_xMn_{2-y}Co_yO_{4-d}Cl_d$ material, the physical properties were evaluated using powder X-ray diffraction. The stoichiometry was verified with X-ray fluorescence. Figure 1 shows the X-ray diffraction pattern for a family of $Li_xMn_{2-y}Co_yO_{4-d}Cl_d$, where $x \approx 1$ and y ranges from 0.05 to 0.2 (bottom to top pattern). These patterns are representative for both the chlorinated and fluorinated $AB_2O_{4-d}X_d$ material. The undesirable Mn_2O_3 product was minimized by maintaining a slight $x > 1$ lithium stoichiometry.

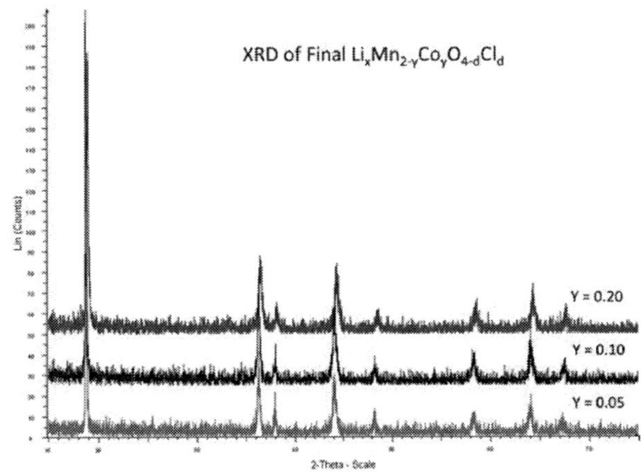

Figure 1. The X-ray diffraction pattern for a family of $Li_xMn_{2-y}Co_yO_{4-d}Cl_d$ where $x \approx 1$ and y ranges from 0.05 to 0.2.

In addition to identifying the resultant $Li_xMn_{2-y}Co_yO_{4-d}Cl_d$ spinel material, Figure 1 also shows a slight shift to higher 2-theta values (smaller d-spacing) with increasing cobalt concentrations as expected from the smaller ionic radius of cobalt versus manganese.

Figures 2-5 show the electrochemical characterization of the $Li//Li_xMn_{2-y}Co_yO_{4-d}Cl_d$ couple. Figures 2 and 3 show charge/discharge data displayed as a hysteresis plot and a differential capacity plot, respectively. These figures show the initial formation cycles for the $Li//Li_xMn_{2-y}Co_yO_{4-d}Cl_d$ electrochemical system. The reversible region for the $Li//Li_xMn_{2-y}Co_yO_{4-d}Cl_d$ electrochemical couple occurs where $0.25 < x < 1.80$ in a three-step thermodynamic charge/discharge profile. Figure 2 shows the high capacity capability approaching 240 mAh/g.

The figures reveal that a small portion of the low voltage (down to 2.25 V) discharge process is recharged at an elevated voltage rather than centered about the 2.9 V; Figures 2 and 3 show the corresponding charge peak at 3.65 V. The high voltage plateau is a pair of twin peaks centered on a 4.14 V and 3.99 V potential (4.11 V and 3.97 V for discharge) and the low voltage plateau is centered on a 2.95 V potential (2.81 V for discharge). The data displayed in the figures show the charge/discharge data at a slow, 100-hour rate, revealing the kinetic and thermodynamic properties of the system. The differential capacity curves show the low overpotential required for charge at the upper plateau, which is on the order of 0.05 V. The overpotential for charge at the low voltage thermodynamic region is on the order of 0.15 volts.

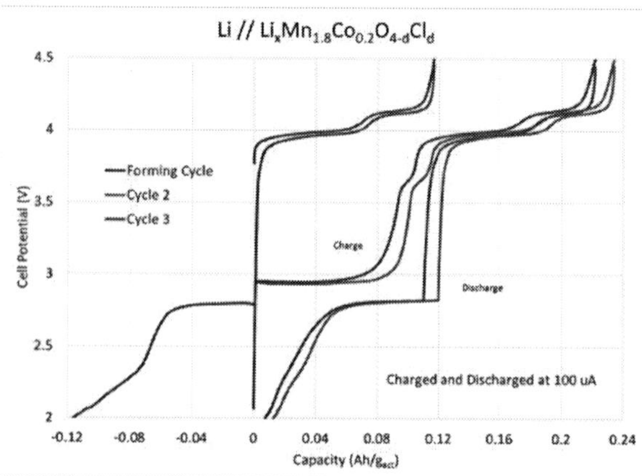

Figure 2. Galvanostatic data, displayed as a hysteresis graph (charge/discharge) of a representative Li//$Li_xMn_{2-y}Co_yO_{4-d}X_d$ electrochemical cell showing the formation cycle.

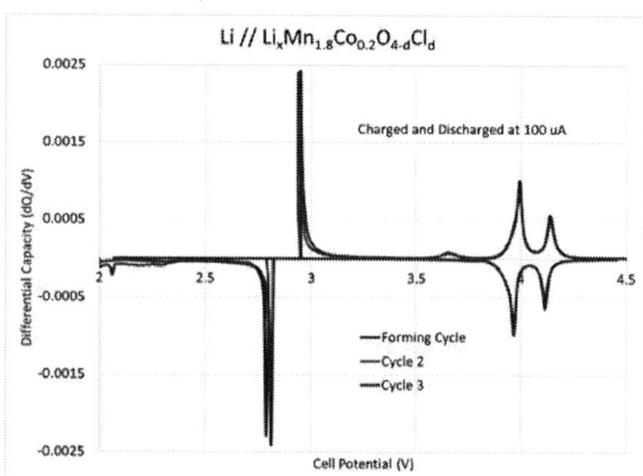

Figure 3. Galvanostatic data displayed as a differential capacity graph for a representative Li//$Li_xMn_{2-y}Co_yO_{4-d}X_d$ electrochemical cell showing the formation cycle.

Figures 4 and 5 display the charge/discharge data of a representative cell showing the thermodynamic stability of the Li//$Li_xMn_{2-y}Co_yO_{4-d}X_d$. Charge and discharge cycles were performed after cells were stored at various conditions and after repeated deep discharge cycling to 2.25 V. Storage included the following conditions: 1) 55 °C for 4 weeks on an unformed (as assembled) cell, 2) 55 °C for 4 weeks on a cell discharged to 3.5 V, 3) 20 °C for 12 weeks on a fully charged cell, and 4) 20 °C for 16 weeks on a cell discharged to 4.0 V. After the storage period, cells were cycled at 1 mA/cm^2 and their performance was comparable to "as assembled" cells tested under an equivalent load. This data is presented in Figure 4. After varied storage conditions, the performance of the cell is observed with periodic deep discharge to 2.25 V during one of ten normal upper voltage (4.5 V to 3.5 V) cycles up until cycle 100. The data shows minimal changes in the peak location and shape, indicating a robust chemistry under various conditions. The differential capacity traces displayed in Figure 4 show the stability of the $Li_xMn_{2-y}Co_yO_{4-d}X_d$ cathode material when coupled with lithium in an electrochemical cell.

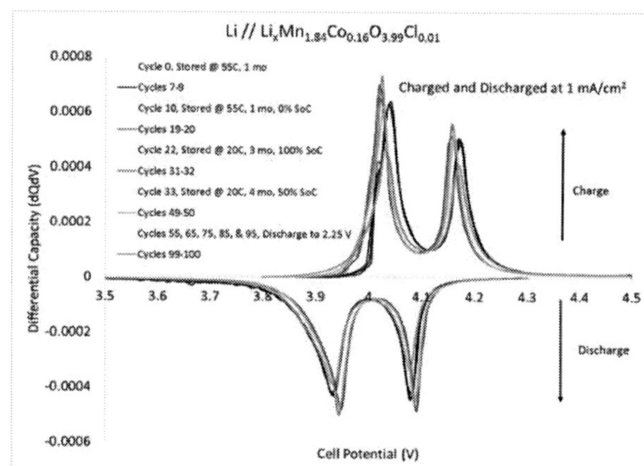

Figure 4. Galvanostatic data for a representative Li//$Li_xMn_{2-y}Co_yO_{4-d}X_d$ electrochemical cell subjected to repeated storage and subsequent deep discharge to 2.25 V.

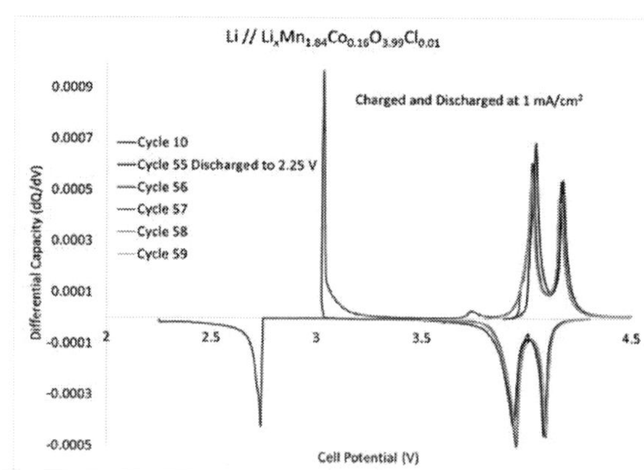

Figure 5. Galvanostatic data for a representative Li//$Li_xMn_{2-y}Co_yO_{4-d}X_d$ electrochemical cell showing thermodynamic stability.

Figure 5 displays the differential capacity traces for cycles 55-59 and compares them to cycle 10. This plot displays data for the same cell represented in Figure 4. No variations occurred between the deep discharge of cycle 55 and the consecutive cycles of 56 through 59. Cycles 56 through 59 also have very similar electrochemical behavior to cycle 10, even after the varied storage and cycling conditions. This data further demonstrates the stability of the $Li_xMn_{2-y}Co_yO_{4-d}X_d$ cathode material.

Conclusion

A cobalt-doped lithium manganese oxide spinel with chlorine addition was synthesized. X-ray diffraction confirmed the proper AB_2O_4 lithium spinel phase was achieved successfully. The $Li_xMn_{2-y}Co_yO_{4-d}X_d$ spinel cathode material was incorporated into an experimental button cell opposite a lithium metal anode, and charge/discharge cycling was performed to determine the electrochemical performance of the novel cathode. The $Li//Li_xMn_{2-y}Co_yO_{4-d}Cl_d$ system demonstrated a low overpotential of 0.05 V in the 4.5 V to 3.5 V regime. Additionally, this chemistry yielded a very high specific capacity, nearing 240 mAh/g. After long term storage under various temperature conditions, the cell continued to exhibit the same electrochemical performance upon further cycling as compared with early cycle life performance. The stability of the chemistry was further demonstrated through periodic cycling to low voltage (2.25 V); the cell remained reversible upon recharging and continued to cycle under the 4.5 V to 3.5 V regime with equivalent capacity at extended cycling as compared to early cycling. These results demonstrate desirable traits for incorporation into lithium-ion batteries for the military.

References

1. David Linden (Ed.); Handbook of Batteries 4th ed.; McGraw-Hill, 2011
2. Tarascom, JM, Guyomard D, *J. Electrochem Soc.*, Vol. 138, Oct. 1991, pg. 2864
3. Thackeray MM, etal, Mater Res. Bull., 1984, pg 179
4. Gabano, JP, Lithium Batteries; Academic Press; New York, NY; 1983
5. Liu, W-R, et.al., *J. Power Sources*, 146 (2005) pg. 233-239
6. Kang, Y-J, et.al., *J. Power Sources*, 146 (2005) pg. 237-240
7. Kang, S-H, Goodenough JB, *J. Electrochem Soc.*, Vol. 147, No. 10, October 2000, pg. 3621-3627
8. Kang, S-H, Goodenough JB, *Electrochemical and Solid State Letters*, Vol. 3, No. 12, (2000), pg. 536-539
9. Sun, Y-K, et.al., *Electrochemical and Solid State Letters*, Vol. 3, No. 1, (2000), pg. 7-9
10. Inoue, T and Sano, M, *J. Electrochem Soc.*, Vol. 145, No. 11, November 1998, pg. 3704-3707
11. Larcher, D et.al.; *J. Electrochem Soc.*, Vol. 145, No. 10, October 1997, pg. 3392-3400
12. Wen, SJ et.al., *J. Electrochem Soc.*, Vol. 143, No. 6, June 1996, pg. L136-L138
13. Shao-Horn, Y et.al.; *J. Electrochem Soc.*, Vol. 144, No. 9, September 1997, pg. 3147-3153
14. Armstrong AR, et.al.; *J. Solid State Chem.*, Vol. 145, 1999, pg. 549-556
15. Yang, XQ et.al., *Electrochemical and Solid State Letters*, Vol. 2, No. 4, (1999), pg. 157-160
16. Xia, Y and Yoshio, M, *J. Electrochem Soc.*, Vol. 143, No. 3, March 1996, pg. 825-833
17. Xia, Y et.al., *J. Electrochem Soc.*, Vol. 148, No. 7, July 2001, pg. A723-A72
18. Terrill B. Atwater and Paula C. Latorre, Proceedings 46th Power Sources Conference, June 2014
19. Terrill B. Atwater and Paula C. Tavares, Proceedings 45th Power Sources Conference, June 2012
20. Terrill B. Atwater and Paula C. Latorre, SAE Int. J. Materials and Manufacturing. 6(1):2013 doi:10.4271 ISSN: 1946-3979, Jan. 2013
21. US Patent No. 8,900,756, Terrill B. Atwater and Paula C. Tavares, December 2, 2014
22. US Patent No. 8,597,377, Terrill B. Atwater and Paula C. Tavares, December 3, 2013
23. Filed Patent and Trademark Office SN: 14/636,183, Terrill B Atwater, Ashley L Ruth and Paula C Latorre, March 2015
24. Filed Patent and Trademark Office SN: 14/497,620,Terrill B. Atwater, Ashley L Ruth and Paula C Latorre, September 2014

Low Cost, High Speed, Automated Laser Electrode Cutter

Stephen Cordova, Steven C. Arzberger and Weibing Xing

ADA Technologies, Inc.
8100 Shaffer Parkway, Suite 130
Littleton, CO 80127

Abstract: *Through the implementation of the latest in laser technology and scanning systems coupled with innovative design and automation, ADA has developed a cost effective laser cutting system projected to be 10x lower in cost than current, state-of-the-art (SOTA) laser cutting systems. Our system will ensure high quality cuts with excellent tolerances, reliability, repeatability and minimum maintenance. The elimination of sharp edges, burrs and debris will ensure safe operation, minimizing the chance of cell failure and thermal runaway from processed electrodes. We have developed a laser cutting system to replace "lifetime buy" systems such as dies to enable rapid, agile, flexible, cost-effective and high quality lithium ion (Li-ion) battery manufacturing for the rapidly evolving needs of the US military. The system is designed to be compact (bench top size), durable and robust, thus enabling easy integration into a battery assembly/manufacturing line. A low cost (< $250k), high speed (2-4 m/s cutting, 10's of electrodes/min.), high precision, flexible (easily variable cutting speeds/geometry), durable electrode cutter with unsurpassed cutting quality is envisioned as the end product. It is imperative to develop next-generation, cost-effective, flexible electrode cutting technologies, to enable a fast-paced US military through rapid innovation in Li-ion battery design, while enhancing quality and tolerances.*

Keywords: Laser; electrode cutter; automated; low cost; high speed; manufacturing; additive manufacturing; thin film; laser welding; laser processing

Introduction

ADA Technologies, Inc. (ADA) has designed, developed and planned for the prototype fabrication of a low-cost, automated, high-speed/high-throughput electrode cutting system capable of producing high quality electrodes in an additive manufacturing environment. Our design uses the latest in laser technology and scanhead systems coupled to innovative designs for automation, to realize a system with unparalleled performance in a compact and cost-effective (10x less than current laser cutter systems) format. The system will yield high quality cuts with excellent tolerances, reliability and repeatability, with minimum maintenance. The elimination of sharp edges, burrs and debris will ensure safe operation, minimizing the chances of cell failure and thermal runaway. The system has been designed as a fully automated system to deliver electrodes for planar and cylindrical cells of virtually any size and shape. ADA anticipates the system to be compact (bench top size), durable and robust. This will enable its easy integration into battery assembly/manufacturing lines. <u>A low cost ($150-$250k), high speed (4-5 m/s cutting, 10's of electrodes/min.), high precision, flexible (easily variable cutting speeds/geometry), durable electrode cutter with unsurpassed cutting quality is envisioned as the end product.</u>

Identification & Significance of the Problem or Opportunity

Growing Concerns over Safety of Li-ion Batteries: In the Boeing 787 first year of service, and after fewer than 100k total flight hours, at least four aircraft suffered fires from large-format Li-ion batteries (**Figure 1**).[1] While strict quality control processes were in-place during their battery manufacture efforts to prevent internal short circuits, the fires still occurred and their root cause remains unknown. The military has a keen interest in reducing the risk of catastrophic failure in Li-ion batteries.

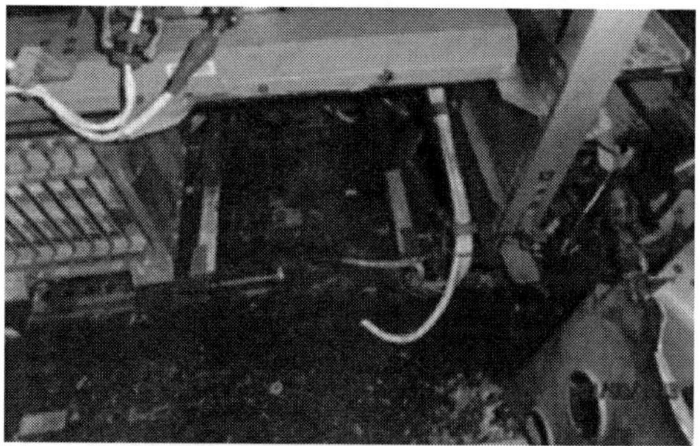

Figure 1. Damage in 787 electronics bay caused by a Li-ion battery fire.

Recent research has shown this kind of catastrophic failure involves a complex chain of events that could, perhaps, be interrupted through better design.[2] In general, failure is initiated by localized heating due to internal short circuit (*e.g.*, separator breach due to a manufacturing defect or a damaged separator due to external force), which can lead to "thermal runaway" within an isolated cell, the communication of excess heat to adjacent cells and subsequent deflagration of the entire battery system if left un-checked.[3] Further studies by the Department of Transportation, Research and Special Programs Administration showed that one of the leading causes of battery failure can be attributed to manufacturing defects[4], caused by undesirable metal impurities and electrodes with unacceptable edge tolerance and shards. Some of these impurities are incorporated by mechanical (metal) die cutters, which leave metal shards between the electrodes and separators. With repetitive cycling, the metal shard eventually punctures the separator, causing the positive and negative electrode to bridge, resulting in a short circuit. The short circuit produces high heat and ultimately leads to fire.

The Increasing Focus on Li-ion Battery Electrode Cutting Technologies: Compromising manufacturing technologies are often the reason for Li-ion battery failures. One of the biggest hindrances at present lies in the technology of electrode cutting. While traditional mechanical die-cutting technologies provide adequate quality and consistency in lower-energy battery systems, this manufacturing technology has become one of the main impediments toward the realization of the full potential of Li-ion chemistries. An enabling electrode cutting technique is essential in order to achieve exceptional tolerances with minimal edge debris and shards for minimizing catastrophic cell failure (hard short) or possible prolonged self-discharge (soft short). It is also imperative to replace "lifetime buy" systems such as dies to enable rapid, agile, flexible, cost-effective and high quality Li-ion battery manufacturing for the rapidly evolving needs of the US military. Hence, it is imperative to develop next-generation, cost-effective, flexible electrode cutting technologies, to enable a fast-paced US military through rapid innovation in Li-ion battery design, while enhancing quality and tolerances.

Laser Cutting of Electrodes

Laser cutting has emerged as the cutting technology of choice in many industries where speed and precision are emphasized The technology has proven to be a highly efficient and reliable manufacturing method that can potentially contribute to significant cost savings and quality improvements because it requires no consumables (*i.e.*, dies that wear out) and allows a greater degree of flexibility in manufacturing (*e.g.*, computer generated in "CAD style" software can generate special part designs and permit rapid development via iteration, with no new tooling costs). Recent advances in commercial lasers and laser power sources have enabled the technology to be applied to Li-ion battery electrode cutting.

Fundamentals of Laser-Assisted Cutting: High quality laser ablation cutting is dependent on many factors, such as: laser power, laser wavelength, laser type, beam quality, optics, power delivery method, expelling of melt, and material to be processed, etc. For Li-ion battery electrode cutting, the unit needs to provide sufficient intensity to ablate the electrode, but not excessive intensity as this may damage the product by adding excess heat. Intensity (laser power per unit area) can be expressed as:

$$\text{Intensity} = \frac{\textbf{\textit{Laser Power (W)}}}{\textbf{\textit{Irradiated Area (cm}}^2\textbf{\textit{)}}}$$

Hence, for effective laser cutting of electrodes, it is imperative to minimize the irradiated area by decreasing the spot size while providing a nominal amount of power for ablation for maximizing cutting speed while lowering cost and minimizing the heat affected zone (HAZ).

Conventional Laser Cutting (Gantry-Driven Lasers): With gantry-driven lasers (*e.g.*, **Figure 2**), the cutting head includes fixed beam delivery optics and a cutting gas delivery system that ejects the melt from the kerf. The cutting head is typically mounted on a robot or on the vertical axis of a Computer Numeric Control (CNC) machine tool system, which utilizes moving linear axes. This system has the advantage of an on-axis optical system with a very small spot size that can be generated and moved over very large fields since the beam is always orthogonal to the work piece. Optics are used to focus the collimated laser beam onto the work piece to achieve a small spot size.[5] Many difficulties arise with gantry-driven lasers, including achieving high speeds, precision and accuracy due to the movement of large masses over the cutting field, and cost. The moving linear axes are expensive and generate a large HAZ due to the relatively slow speeds. These systems are bulky and massive, requiring more workspace, and their accuracy is low and it gets worse with increasing unit size. Dynamics of the system constrain the maximum possible speed and acceleration. The programming of the cut-path also requires special attention, as the geometry of cutting path gets complex due to the momentum generated from the relatively large mass. Besides common process parameters such as laser power, speed, and spot size, etc., for conventional and remote laser cutting process, there are a number of other critical factors that affect the cut quality. For example, factors include nozzle size, distance of nozzle tip to the top of material surface, cutting gas type, gas pressure, and flow rate, etc. Compared to remote cutting the achievable cutting speed is significantly lower due to limitations in the available power and the maximum repetition rate.[6] Gantry-driven lasers are large, expensive and most deleteriously suffer from slow scan speeds that are not amenable to high speed Li-ion electrode cutting.

Remote Laser Cutting: Remote cutting technology is a relatively new laser cutting process that replaces the gantry for positioning of the laser light and focuses the laser beam with the help of quick moving mirrors. Remote laser cutting systems are capable of achieving spot speeds as fast as several meters/second. Due to low interaction time between the laser beam and component, the material is partially evaporated and desorbed, which leads to cleaner cuts and less edge burr effects than traditional gantry-driven laser cutting systems. The two essential components that have led to the success of remote cutting technology are advancements in: (1) optical beam scanning systems and (2) high brightness lasers that provide a highly efficient means of beam delivery.[7]

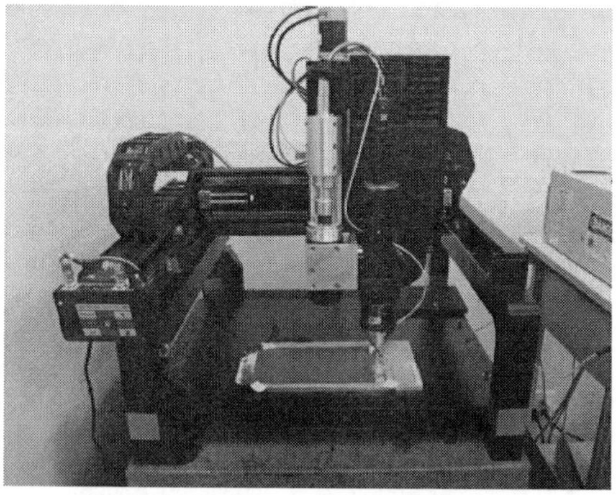

Figure 2. Typical gantry-driven laser.

Remote cutting utilizes well-established galvanometer scanner technology comprised of high-performance rotary motors that produce high dynamic beam deflection. The low mass and inertia of these systems enable high speeds (up to 15 m/s) and acceleration (up to 10 g). The material is cut by a combination of very high energy densities in a very small laser spot and very high speed beam movement; it does not require any cutting gas as the melt in the cut kerf is partially vaporized and partially ejected by very high vapor pressure under extreme conditions of temperature and melt pool dynamics. The image field size and the working distance are directly proportional to the focal length of the F-Theta focusing lens and are not adjustable. A larger field size requires a longer focal length, which in turn requires a better beam quality to generate small spot sizes. With the availability of high power and high brightness lasers such as fiber and disk lasers with excellent beam quality it is possible to achieve very small spot sizes < 20 μm with high power intensities ($>10^8$ W/cm^2).[7]

The downside of current remote laser cutting systems is that they utilize F-Theta lenses that can't adjust or achieve a large image field size to spot size ratio. A higher power continuous wave laser is also necessary, which substantially raises the cost of remote laser systems in comparison to gantry-driven laser systems. Further, these units are large, often requiring water-cooling systems that fill a large room. Finally, the increased power and larger spot size promote a much larger HAZ. This diminishes precision, accuracy and potentially compromises safety, once the electrodes are utilized in a Li-ion cell. *Hence, it is desirable to use advancements in laser cutting technologies that can address these current limitations and deliver high-quality, low-cost manufacturing capability for Li-ion battery electrodes.*

ADA Automated Laser Electrode Cutter (ALEC)

Approach: In contrast to the abovementioned laser cutting techniques, a 3-axis scanhead coupled to a relatively low power pulsed laser offers tremendous advantages. The ADA ALEC design significantly increases the image field size to spot ratio, which leads to desirable increases in cut quality and customization and flexibility. It is compact in size and significantly less expensive than existing systems. Because it is specifically tailored to_the problem of electrode cutting for Li-ion batteries, the ALEC will be able to process high quality electrodes for planar prismatic and cylindrical cells with high speed operation.

Preliminary Demonstrations with ADA Manual Electrode Laser Cutter (MELC): Using an ADA MELC as a precursor to the ALEC, we demonstrated electrode high speed (1.4 m/s) cutting of Li-ion electrodes while maintaining a very high cut quality (**Figure 3**). ADA has demonstrated the ability to cut high power electrodes (thin coatings) at a rate of 1.4 m/s and 1.0 m/s for the anode and cathode, respectively. Our MELC is equipped with a 30 W master oscillator power amplifier (MOPA) laser. We has also demonstrated the ability to cut high-energy anodes and cathodes (thick coatings) at a rate of 0.5 m/s and 0.4 m/s, respectively (**Table 1**). These high-energy electrodes represent the upper limit of SOTA manufactured electrode thicknesses, including anodes prepared from loading ~20 mg/cm^2 and cathodes of ~30 mg/cm^2. The goal of the fully developed ALEC is a fully automated laser cutter with a cutting capability of up to 5 m/s speeds. We anticipate the realization of this goal in the near future using a commercial laser and scanhead combination with a conventional thermal management system. A high power, efficient laser will translate to higher cut speeds while minimizing cost. Finally, the cutting speed far exceeds typical machine operations (*e.g.*, pick-and-place, unwind/wind, etc.) and will therefore not limit the overall electrode processing speed.

Figure 3. Still screenshot of Li-ion electrode being cut via remote laser ablation.

Figure 4 compares the cut quality and other attributes of electrodes prepared from stamping and laser cutting. Laser cut electrodes offer exceptional tolerance and precision, while stamped electrodes show a comparatively large deviation along a linear cut with the potential for shards or incomplete cuts. The cut quality varies with die use, progressively worsening with time. Our MELC and ALEC systems offer superior reliability with little to no required maintenance, whereas dies require substantial maintenance due to pronounced wear. The laser cutter is capable of cutting virtually any size electrode through a quick and simple software manipulation. Stamped electrodes, on the other hand, require a pair of dies for each cell footprint severely limiting flexibility to cell design. Finally, laser cut electrodes have substantially better cut-quality, a fact that is most prominently observed on thin power electrodes, without the formation of shards, burrs or furled edges; this essentially eliminates safety concerns and leads to higher performance products.

Table 1. Electrode cut speeds.

Electrode	*Current Collector Material*	*Current Collector Thickness, μm*	*Overall Electrode Thickness, μm*	*Maximum Cut Speed*, m/s*
High Power Anode	Copper	10	92	1.4
High Power Cathode	Aluminum	18	72	1.0
High Energy Anode	Copper	10	255	0.5
High Energy Cathode	Aluminum	18	188	0.4

*Maximum cutting speed determined by electrode fully cut; no perforations, scalloped edges or "hanging shards".

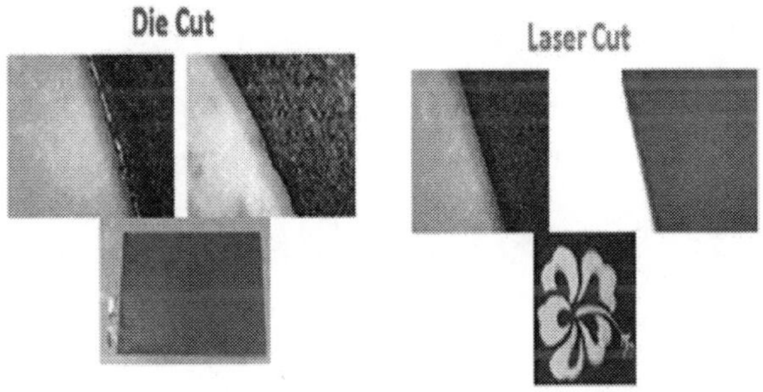

Figure 4. Comparison of die cut and laser cut electrodes.

Our MELC provides further flexibility due to the wide range of scanhead software capabilities. Using the simple and efficient CAD style software and laser output (laser power, scan speed and waveform), a user can rapidly machine electrodes/substrates in a variegated fashion. This represents a demonstration of some of the expansive capability of this machine. These advanced capabilities have the potential to open new areas of research in energy storage, among others.

Acknowledgements

The authors wish to thank Mather "Matt" Hutchens and Traci Myers of the Defense Logistics Agency (DLA) for their continued support and funding (contract HQ0147-15-C-800) in the development of this ALEC.

References

1. "Possible Solutions for the Battery Problem on the Boeing 787," © 2013 Isidor Buchmann
2. *Lithium-Ion Batteries Hazard and Use Assessment* by Celina Mikolajczak, et al. (Springer, 2012)
3. Vesely, B., "Fault Tree Analysis (FTA): Concepts and Applications," Presentation to NASA by Underwriters Laboratory. Web: 30 May 2013. http://www.hq.nasa.gov/office/codeq/risk/docs/ftacourse.pdf
4. http://www.ntsb.gov/investigations/fulltext/hzb0501.htm
5. Rahul Patwa1, Hans Herfurth1, Henrikki Pantsar1, (2012). High Speed Laser Cutting of Electrodes for Advanced Batteries, Fraunhofer Center for Laser Technology, University of Michigan, College of Engineering, Ann Arbor, MI
6. Herfurth H.J., Patwa R., Pantsar H. (2010), Laser cutting of electrodes for advanced batteries, in Proceedings of the LPM, Germany
7. Rahul Patwa1, Hans Herfurth1, Henrikki Pantsar1, (2012). High Speed Laser Cutting of Electrodes for Advanced Batteries, Fraunhofer Center for Laser Technology, University of Michigan, College of Engineering, Ann Arbor, MI

The G4 Synergetics Advanced NiMH Battery

William Gotts and John Weckesser
G4 Synergetics
bill.gotts@g4sinc.com

Abstract
G4 has developed a modular, low resistance, high power, large format rechargeable battery with integrated cooling based in part on an advanced Nickel Metal Hydride (NiMH) technology. G4's unique battery architecture incorporates a high electrode area therefore the module has a much lower resistance. The reduced resistance translates into less heat generated which then extends life and gives greater charge acceptance. It also translates into high current handling capability on both charge and discharge. In addition to the low resistance of the modules, G4's approach to alleviate excess temperature is to incorporate heat sinks between the cells to help dissipate the heat. In combination with the heat sinks, the module design can include fans or a centrifugal fan (depending on design/application) to draw the heat away. The combination provides rapid cool down so that the battery module can be safely and quickly recharged. The G4 battery system includes a Battery Management System (BMS) that allows further optimization of battery performance. The BMS controls specific parameters of the modules to keep the modules working within the desired depth of discharge range required for each specified project.

Advances in Low Cost Manufacturing with Reclaimed Electrode Materials

Steven Sloop
ssloop@onto-technology.com
OnTo Technology, LLC
Bend, Oregon, USA, 97703

Abstract: *This paper describes performance capabilities of recycled material in cells as a function of lithium-ion chemistry. The vertical integration of advanced battery recycling into battery manufacturing will significantly reduce material costs and address long term economic sustainability for the battery industry.*

Keywords: lithium-ion manufacture; recycle; critical materials; direct recycling.

Introduction

Lithium-ion constitutes a growing, multibillion-dollar market due to demand for batteries that can store energy and deliver power. Its applications range from small portable electronics to relatively large electric vehicles. Figure 1. graphically shows the demand for lithium-ion battery cathodes as a function of chemistry. In 2013, approximately 90,000 tons of cathode materials were manufactured, with an estimated value of \$2.4B. By 2025, the market is projected to grow to 330,000 tons and \$7.3B [1]. These market projections do not identify recycled material as a feedstock in cathode materials; but a modest use of 5% recycled cathode by 2025 has a potential value in excess of \$370M.

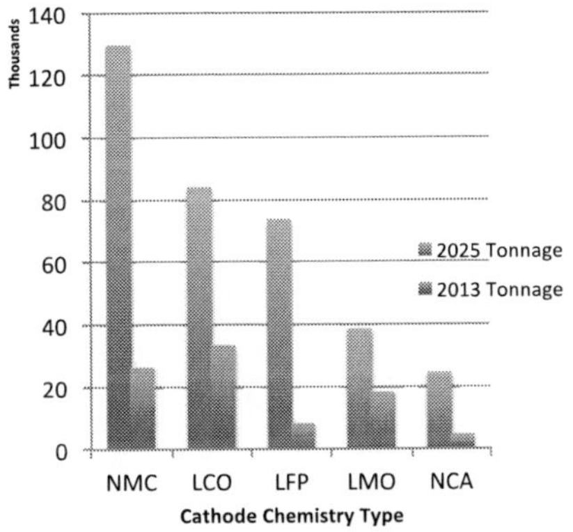

Figure 1: Li-ion electrode demand through 2025 (tons)
NMC: Li nickel manganese cobalt oxide
LCO: Li cobalt oxide
LFP: Li iron phosphate
LMO: Li manganese oxide "spinel"
NCA: Li nickel cobalt aluminum oxide

Cathode materials cost is an ongoing challenge, increased mining and recycling will help to maintain availability and margins in manufacturing; however, recycling in advanced batteries has not made inroads into manufacturing. In regards to battery manufacturing with recycling, the current pain points include:

(1) end-of-life recycling or disposal fees.

(2) unsustainable recycling yields.

(3) lack of manufacturing grade material from recycling.

(4) lack of reuse of critical materials such as lithium.

The energy investment in original manufacturing is essentially lost when batteries are recycled using hydrometallurgy or pyrometallurgy metals refining technologies. Metal refineries require sorted feedstock, as well as capital intensive infrastructure dedicated to advanced batteries primarily for cobalt and nickel recovery. Direct recycling offers a feasible pathway to way to conserve the energy invested into manufacturing highly engineered lithium metal oxides independently of cobalt/nickel content [2-3].

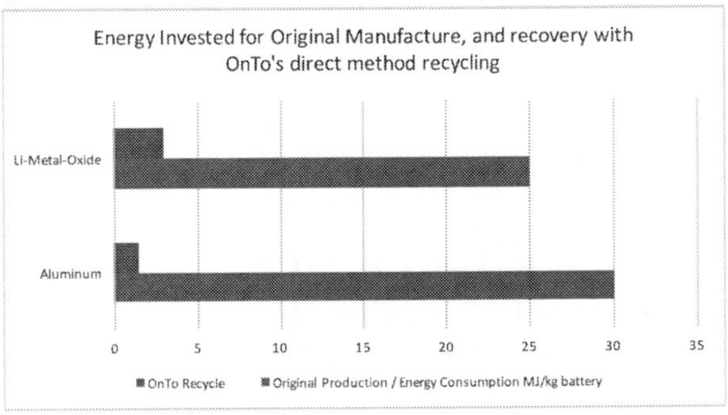

Figure 2: The energy consumed to produce lithium metal oxides and aluminum, and to recycle them with OnTo's direct methods.

Some direct recycling technologies use solid-state methods to reinstate lithium-metal-oxide stoichiometric ratios [4]. The processes employed here directly infuse lithium without using stoichiometric, classical solid-state methodology [5-6]. The direct processes reused the cathode materials, including lithium, saving the energy invested into original manufacture of the electrode material.

A successful electric vehicle (EV) commercialization will feature range (capacity), acceleration/fast charge (rate capability), safety (materials purity, engineering), and economic vertical integration of recycling. Chemistry is a basic factor in each aspect, and examples of EV chemistries and direct-recyclability are outlined below.

NMC's are an example of a chemistry with EV performance, and now direct-recyclability with this demonstration. Figure 3. shows long-term cycle life performance of recycled NMC, in which the capacity retention matches fresh material as a function of charge/discharge cycle. The material was harvested from electric vehicle grade batteries that were faded beyond 50% of their original capacity. The recycled material is compared with fresh material, both used simultaneously, side-by-side in building 2Ah cells.

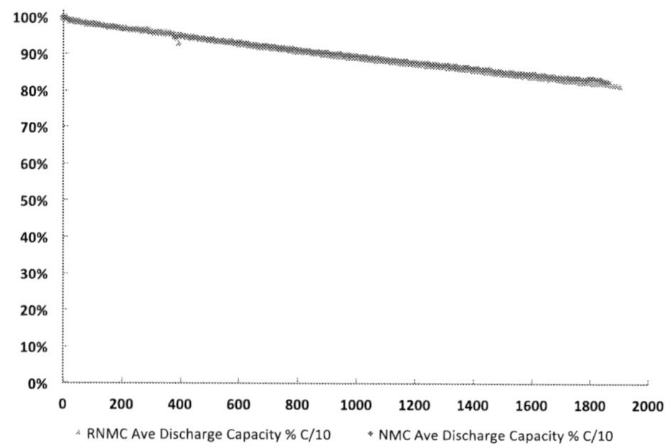

Figure 3. Recycled NMC Performance. Capacity retention vs. charge/discharge cycle for NMC and OnTo recycled NMC. New cells were prepared from 100% recycled electrode, and have outlasted the standard material in side-by-side cycle testing. The cell made from recycled material is shown along side the standard cell in the photo with a US quarter-dollar for size reference.

To improve EV performance and reduce costs, cathode mixtures may be used in manufacturing. Typically, these include lithium manganese oxide "spinel" with a layered metal oxide.

Figure 4 shows good cycle life performance in full test cells built from recycled material harvested from a commercial EV module.

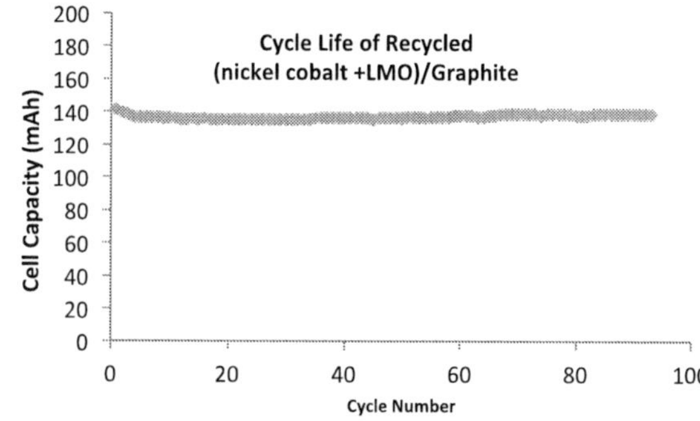

Figure 4. Mixed LMO Recycled Performance. Capacity retention vs. charge/discharge cycle for direct recycled nickel cobalt / spinel. New cells were prepared from 100% recycled electrode in a 140mAh cell.

Lithium iron phosphate (LFP), based upon the olivine structure, is another chemistry finding traction with EVs, buses and large scale energy storage systems (ESS) for grid, municipal power, and other applications. The chemistry is directly recyclable into new LFP cells. Figure 5 shows the proof of concept with recycled LFP evaluated alongside harvested LFP in small button cells with lithium metal electrodes. The voltage vs. discharge capacity of the recycled material is equal to theoretical capacity measurements expected for manufactured LFP formulations.

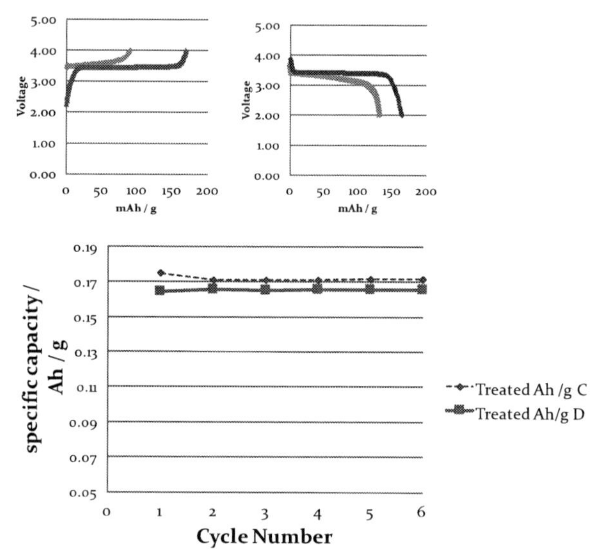

Figure 5. Direct Recycled LFP. The upper pair of graphs show the first charge and discharge cycle from harvested LFP (green) and processed LFP (blue). The lower graph is the specific capacity vs. cycle number for the recycled LFP sample. The theoretical capacity is expected to be 170mAh/g for the LFP sample.

Lithium cobalt oxide (LCO) is the prototypical Li-ion chemistry. It has received a lot of interest in recycling based upon cobalt recovery. Comparatively, direct recycling can produce low cost, high performance material at about 12% of the energy input required to produce new LCO from new lithium and recycled cobalt. Figure 6 shows the specific capacity vs. cycle number for recycled LCO.

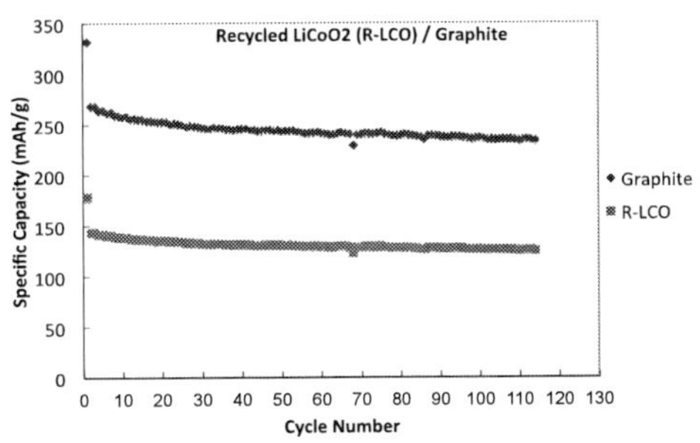

Figure 6. Direct Recycled LCO. The specific capacity vs. cycle number for the recycled LCO against (new) graphite. The theoretical capacity is expected to be 140-150mAh/g for the LCO sample.

Mixed layered oxides, such as NMC and LCO, are commercially produced. The flexibility of direct recycling was demonstrated on such a mixture. Figure 7 compares the discharge voltage vs. capacity for harvested and processed NMC/LCO and Figure 8 shows the cycle life for the recycled cell.

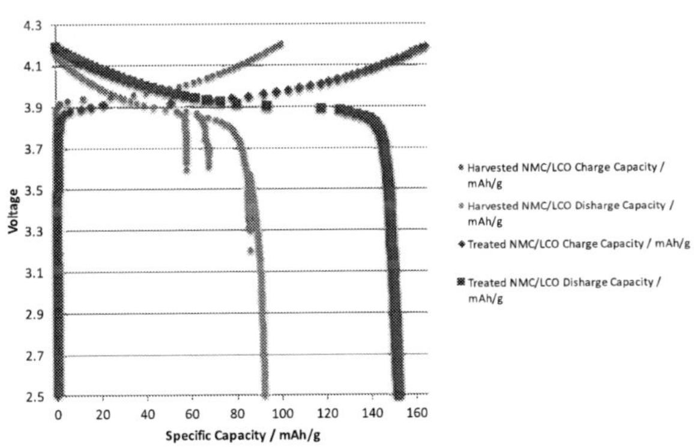

Figure 7. Voltage vs. Specific Capacity for Direct Recycled NMC/LCO mix. The direct treatment increased the specific capacity of the mixture of NMC/LCO from 92 mAh/g to 155 mAh/g.

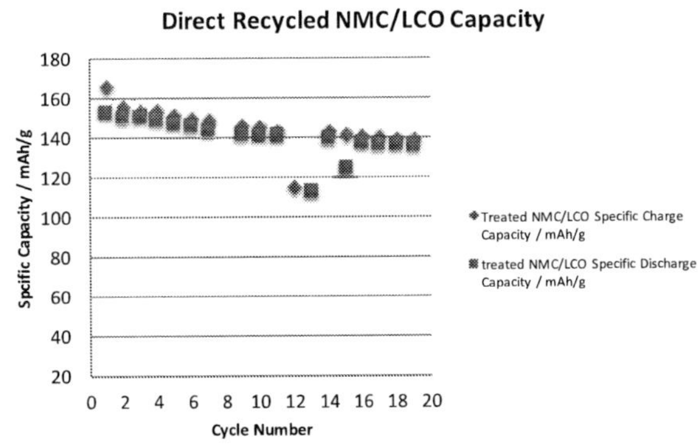

Figure 8. Specific Capacity vs. Cycle Number for Direct Recycled NMC/LCO mix. The Li metal/cathode cells maintain capacity over the preliminary examination.

A direct recycling feature includes improved purity of electrode materials. The process is able to remove trace metals from the electrodes. For example, a treated sample has 1/7th of the iron content that was measured in a commercial NMC sample. Figure 9 summarizes relative copper and iron trace metal content as a function of process.

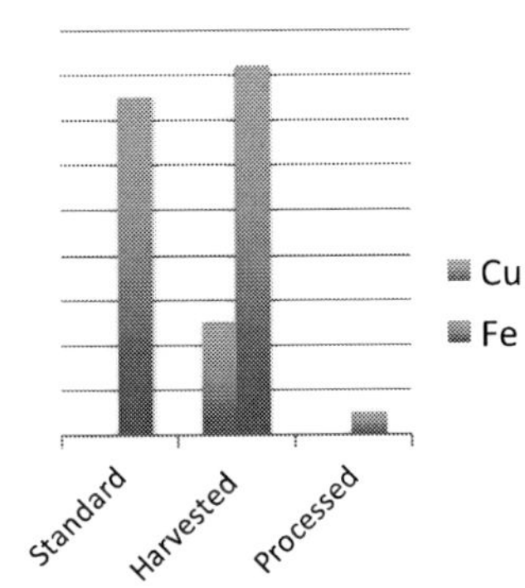

Figure 9. Relative trace metal content of NMC standard and recycled material. The direct recycle process significantly decreases, or eliminates the trace metal content in the electrodes.

Direct recycling produces high performance, low cost materials from the major electrode chemistries employed in the market from consumer electronics to electric vehicle applications. The suite of technologies is patented and developed by Dr. Sloop and OnTo Technology LLC.

Acknowledgements

Author S. Sloop acknowledges the funding received from NSF grants #1448061, #0750552; DOE grant #DE-SC0006336; and DLA contract SP4701-15-C-0098.

References

1. Pillot, C. *Proceedings of The International Battery Seminar and Exhibit* ***IBSE 2015*** Ft. Lauderdale, FL March 16, 2015.
2. Dunn, J.B.; Gaines, L. ; Sullivan, J.; Wang, M.Q. *Environ. Sci. Technol.* "Impact of recycling on cradle-to-gate energy consumption and greenhouse gas emissions of automotive lithium-ion batteries" 46 (22), 12704-12710, (2012)
3. Gaines, L. Sloop, S.; "EV Battery Recycling Technology: Challenges and Opportunities" ***IBSE 2016*** Ft. Lauderdale, FL, March 21, 2016.
4. Mathew, S.; Menon, K.; Scordilis-Kelly, C.; Saidi M.Y. "Method for Recovering Particulate Material from Electrical Components" U. S. Patent # 6,150,050.
5. Sloop, S. "Reintroduction of lithium into recycled battery materials" U. S. Patent # 8,846,225.
6. Sloop, S. "Reintroduction of lithium into recycled battery materials" U.S. Patent # 9,287,552.

Characterization of Safety Aspects of Li-ion Batteries for Maritime Applications

Sissel Forseth[1], Torleif Lian[1], Martin Gilljam[1], Preben J. S. Vie[2], Hanne Flåten Andersen[2] and Jan Petter Mæhlen[2]

[1]Norwegian Defence Research Establishment (FFI)
P.O. Box 25, N-2027 Kjeller, Norway

[2]Institute for Energy Technology (IFE)
P. O. Box 40, 2027 Kjeller, Norway

Contact Author Email: sissel.forseth@ffi.no

Abstract: *The Norwegian Defence Research Establishment (FFI) has long experience in battery safety. One of the major ongoing activities is related to safety and life of Li-ion batteries for maritime applications, in cooperation with Institute for Energy Technology (IFE). Several Li-ion cell chemistries are investigated by techniques such as Accelerating Rate Calorimetry (ARC) and Entropy Spectroscopy (ES). The observed shift in entropy spectrum after cycling at 5 °C can indicate a loss of active lithium. This result has implications for a marine vessel application in arctic waters, where the temperature in the battery room could be equivalently low. The next step will be to perform the ARC test on the cycled cells and relate the findings to the data obtained by ES.*

Keywords: Large Li-ion battery; enclosed space, safety characteristics; accelerated rate calorimetry; entropy spectroscopy;

Introduction

Li-ion batteries are widely used in electrical cars and consumer electronics and the Li-ion technology is considered mature for these applications. However, in maritime applications there are some issues to be solved, especially related to safety. The battery will in many cases be much larger and in the case of a submarine be in a confined space underwater.

It is well known that Li-ion batteries contain combustible materials and most of the chemistries do also release oxygen [1-3]. Flammable gases are also released upon heating [4]. Heating of the battery can be caused by internal flaws, *e.g.* particles from the cell production [5], poor battery management design or external incidents such as fire.

The degradation and ageing of Li-ion batteries could also contribute to instability and affect the safety performance. Hence, knowledge and the ability to predict capacity decay and the battery state of health will be vital information to enable safe and long-life operation. The changes in entropy spectra can be used as indicators of a battery`s state-of-health [6, 7]. Additionally Dubarry et al has shown that incremental capacity analysis during ageing gives (qualitative and quantitative) indications on the degradation mechanisms involved [8-10].

In order to ensure a proper design of the battery and the battery room in an electrical/hybrid electrical power vessel, all data from electrical and safety tests should be available. Physical dimensions of the room and systems for mitigating the consequences of a battery vent, battery fire and possible gas explosion must be included in the battery room design.

Since 2013 FFI and IFE are involved in a research project together with the Norwegian University of Science and Technology (NTNU), financed by the Norwegian Research Council and civilian maritime industry. One of the main topics is to investigate the effect of ageing and cycling on safety properties of different types of Li-ion cells. In this paper we will present results obtained from one of these cells and discuss them in a submarine context. With exception of ES, the other analyses have so far only been performed on new cells. The remaining work is due within the coming weeks.

Experimental

The investigated cell is a 6.0 Ah cylindrical cell from a well-known manufacturer. According to the manufacturer, it has a nominal voltage of 3.6 V and an energy density of 68.8 Wh/kg. It is a high power cell with a nickel oxide cathode and a carbon anode.

A large selection of the cells were cycled at 5, 25 and 45 °C at either 1C/1C or 3C/1.5C discharge /charge rates for long time. Every 100 to 200 cycles or every 14 days, all cells were characterized at 25 °C measuring remaining 1C and C/10 capacities.

A sample of the cell was opened in a glove box filled with argon, and the cell components were analyzed. Prior to opening, the cell was investigated by CT X-ray to identify a feasible region for cutting. The techniques used for materials characterization were Scanning Electron Microscopy (SEM) in combination with energy dispersive spectroscopy (EDS). Prior to the SEM investigation the cell parts were cleaned using dimethylcarbonate (DMC) in order to remove salts. Differential Scanning Calorimetry

(DSC) was used to identify the constituents of the separator.

The cell was investigated using an Accelerating Rate Calorimeter (ARC).The ARC uses a "heat, wait and seek" procedure. When an exothermic reaction in the cell is detected the ARC switches into adiabatic mode and this mode is maintained until 250 °C or until the heat generation of the cell is less than 0.02 °C/min. The cell state of charge was 100% and the atmosphere in the ARC was normal air.

The ageing mechanisms of the cells were studied by entropy spectroscopy (ES). ES reveals the entropy profile of the cell with respect to state of charge [6]. The entropy spectrum is specific to the anode and cathode chemistries of the Li-ion cell. The changes in entropy spectra can be used as indicators of a battery's state of health [6,7] and as a diagnostic tool for ageing mechanism. This method has been extended at IFE to record entropy spectra for cells up to 50 Ah size.

Results and discussion

Material characterization

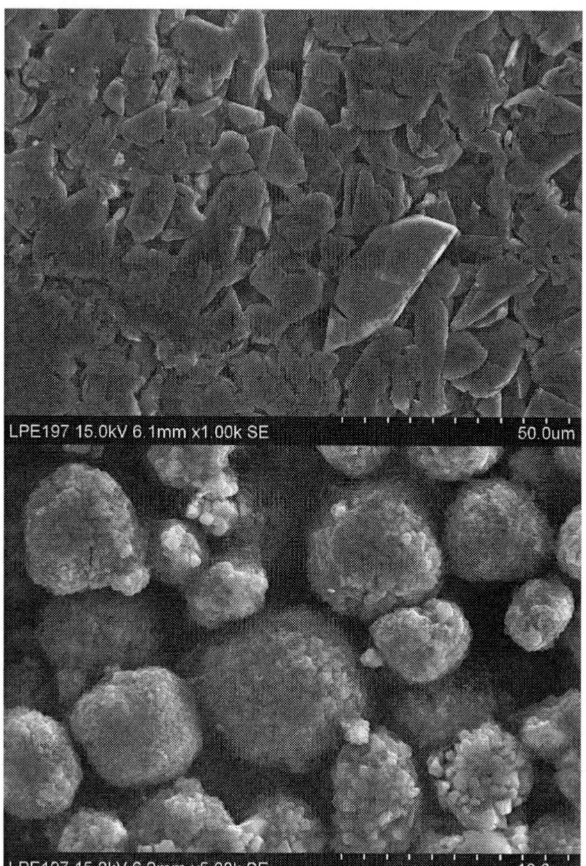

Figure 1. Secondary electron image of the anode (top) and cathode (bottom) of the investigated cell.

In Figure 1 the morphology of the anode and cathode of a new cell is shown. Combined with the results obtained from EDS, the flake shaped particles on the anode consist of carbon whereas the spherical agglomerates on the cathode side contain Ni, Co and Al. The approximate composition of the cathode was 79, 17 and 4 weight percent for Ni, Co and Al, respectively. This means that the cathode has a NCA-chemistry. The exact composition has to be determined by another technique e.g. X-ray diffraction.

The result from DSC on the separator is shown in Figure 2. Based on the endotherms occurring at 125 °C and 155 °C it is likely that the separator consists of polyethylene and polypropylene.

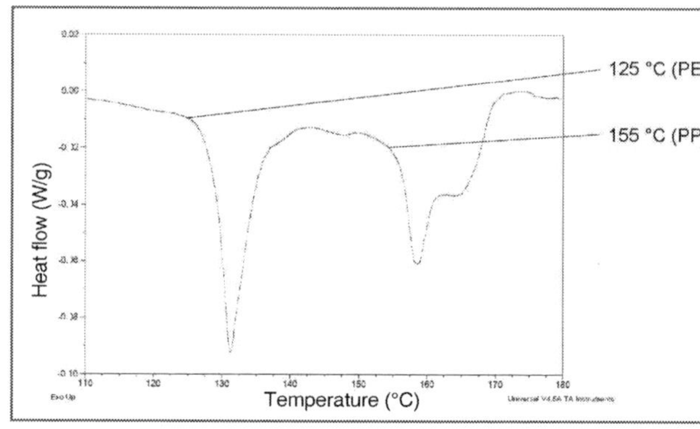

Figure 2. DSC on the separator.

Accelerating Rate Calorimeter (ARC)

There were performed 4 parallels of the ARC-test. The results are presented in Figure 3 and in Table 1.

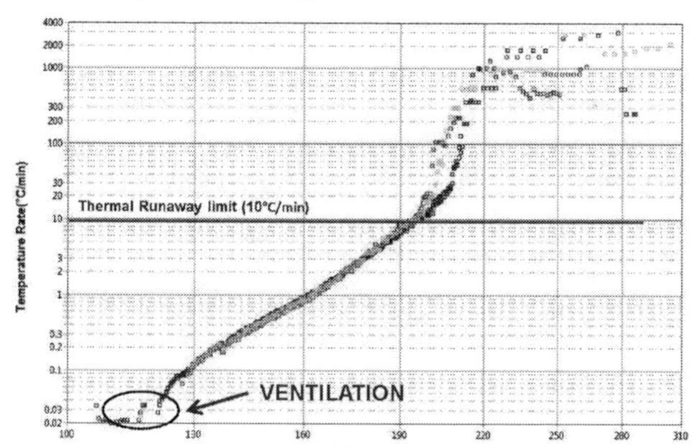

Figure 3. Temperature rate as a function of temperature obtained on new NCA cells.

Table 1. Results from ARC tests on the investigated cell (new cell).

Observed result	Temperature range (°C)
Weak exotherms (0.01 °C/min)	90-110
Onset temperature (0.02 °C/min)	106-116
Ventilation	113-120
Thermal runaway	190-195
Cells ignited the ventilated gas	250-300

As can be seen from Figure 3 and Table 1 onset of thermal runaway happens within a narrow temperature range, whereas the onset temperature for the other thermal incidents varies more. The variation in the results from the ARC-test is expected since the cells are heated far above their safe operational temperature range. From a submarine perspective it is important to note that the cells ignited the ventilated gases. A gas explosion in a submarine is not acceptable, but the probability of such an event could be reduced by using inert atmosphere in the battery room.

Figure 4. The investigated cell as received (top) and after (bottom) the ARC test.

All of the four investigated cells vented by opening the end cap opposite to the connector side (ref. Figure 4) as is specified from the battery manufacturer. This makes it easier to arrange the cells in a battery module in such a way that a thermal incident in one cell does not propagate to other cells.

Entropy spectroscopy

The change of entropy with ageing is illustrated in Figure 5. Here we observe a distinct shift of the full cell entropy spectrum after cycling a cell at 3C/1.5C discharge/charge rate at 5 °C for approx. 600 cycles. The remaining capacity of the cell was 75%. This shift can indicate a loss of active lithium, shifting the cycling window of the cell corresponding to a shift of the peak of about 25% SoC. Safety characterization of a cycled cell remains to be carried out. These results will be presented at the conference.

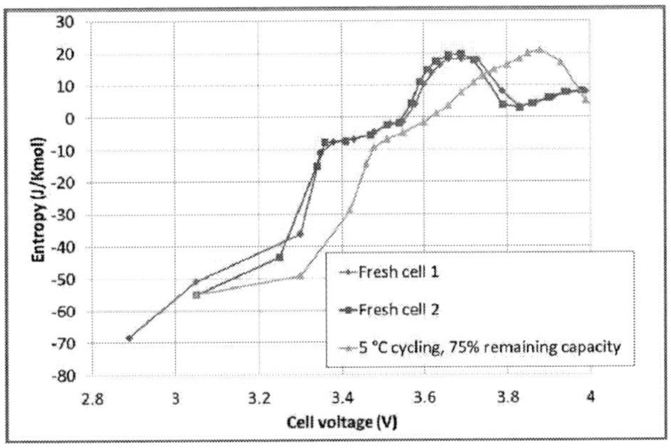

Figure 5. Entropy spectra for the 6 Ah cylindrical NCA-graphite cell. The 5 °C cell was cycled 600 cycles at 5 °C before obtaining the entropy spectrum.

Conclusion

Analyses of the examined cell concluded that the cathode is NCA (79:17:4) and the anode is carbon, while the separator consists of PP and PE. The un-cycled cells vented between 113-120 °C and thermal runaway onset temperature was approximately 192 °C. The cells ignited the ventilated gases, which is unacceptable in a submarine. The observed shift in entropy spectrum after cycling at 5 °C can indicate a loss of active lithium through lithium plating. This result has implications for a marine vessel application in arctic waters, where the temperature in the battery room could be equivalently low. Safety characterization of a cycled cell remains to be carried out. ARC results from a cycled cell compared to a new cell can reveal if the observed shift in the entropy spectrum relates to shifts in e.g. ventilation or onset temperatures. If high-rate charging at 5 °C has a negative influence on the safety properties of the battery, these conditions must be avoided.

Acknowledgements

The authors want to acknowledge the funding received from the Research Council of Norway. Helge Weydahl is acknowledged for his assistance in preparing this document.

References

1. MacNeil, D.D. and J.R. Dahn, "The Reaction of Charged Cathodes with Nonaqueous Solvents and Electrolytes: I. $Li_{0.5}CoO_2$." *Journal of the Electrochemical Society, 2001. 148(11): pp. A1205.*
2. Arai, H., et al., "Thermal Reactions Between Delithiated Lithium Nickelate and Electrolyte Solutions." *Journal of the Electrochemical Society, 2002. 149(4): pp. A401.*

3. Doughty, D.H., "A general discussion of lithium ion battery safety", *The Electrochemical Society Interface. 2012. pp. 37-44.*

4. Roth, E.P. 19, s-l.: ECS Transactions, 2008, Vol.11, issue 19, pp.19-41. 10.1149/1.2897969

5. Aircraft Incident Report, Auxiliary Power Unit Battery Fire Japan Airlines Boeing 787-8, JA829J, Boston, Massachusetts January, 2013, National Transportation Safety Board.

6. Viswanathan, V.V., et al., "Effect of entropy change of lithium intercalation in cathodes and anodes on Li-ion battery thermal management". *Journal of Power Sources, 2010. 195(11): pp. 3720-3729.*

7. Reynier, Y., R. Yazami, and B. Fultz, "The entropy and enthalpy of lithium intercalation into graphite". *Journal of Power Sources, 2003. 119: pp. 850-855.*

8. Dubarry, M., et al.,"Incremental capacity analysis and close-to-equilibrium OCV measurements to quantify capacity fade in commercial rechargeable lithium batteries". *Electrochemical and Solid State Letters, 2006. 9(10): pp. A454-A457.*

9. Dubarry, M. and B.Y. Liaw, "Identify capacity fading mechanism in a commercial LiFePO(4) cell". *Journal of Power Sources, 2009. 194(1): pp. 541-549.*

10. Dubarry, M., et al., *"Identifying battery aging mechanisms in large format Li ion cells"." Journal of Power Sources, 2011. 196(7): pp. 3420-3425.*

Safety of Lithium-Ion Batteries in Simulated Mining Environments

Stephen M. Lipka *, David T. Whitlow, Taylor Bramel, Christopher Swartz, Joanna E. Mroczkowska
Center for Applied Energy Research
University of Kentucky
2582 Research Park Drive, Lexington, KY, 40511, USA

Abstract: *Lithium-ion batteries are widely employed in portable power applications, including personal communications equipment in mining environments. Safety hazards of lithium-ion batteries are well documented, and many strategies have been developed to mitigate potential hazards associated with the use of various lithium-ion chemistries. The purpose of this study was to examine the safety of commercial lithium-ion batteries with variable cathode and anode chemistries at different states of charge in simulated underground mining environments, including air and air/CH_4 atmospheres.*

Keywords: lithium-ion batteries; mining safety; explosion; methane

Introduction

Lithium-ion batteries are increasingly ubiquitous in portable consumer electronic devices, including laptop computers, cellular phones, and tablet computers. Lithium-ion batteries are also finding widespread deployment in many additional applications and settings, including underground mining environments, where lithium-ion batteries are used as electrochemical power sources for cap lamps, and in tracking and communications equipment.[1,2] Battery safety is of paramount importance in any portable electronic device regardless of setting but it is particularly significant in enclosed and isolated areas such as passenger aircraft, or in underground mining environments, where potentially explosive methane/air mixtures can be ignited by a simple spark, which can be caused by shorting and thermal runaway of lithium-ion batteries.[4] This work focused on evaluating safety of commercially available batteries determined that batteries featuring lithium-titanate based anodes were to be the safest ones, regardless of state-of-charge, as minimal events or temperature changes were observed even after the most violent crushes. In general, lithium-ion battery safety for all cathode chemistries increased as the state-of-charge was diminished.

Experimental details

A custom-built battery crush test chamber utilized through the duration of the project is shown in Figure 1. Prismatic and cylindrical 18650 lithium-ion batteries were obtained from commercial vendors. The following cathode chemistries were used and evaluated: lithium cobalt oxide ($LiCoO_2$), lithium nickel manganese cobalt oxide (NMC), and lithium iron phosphate ($LiFePO_4$). In addition, the effect of anode chemistry on battery safety was determined using lithium titanate ($Li_4Ti_5O_{12}$) in place of the traditional graphite anode currently utilized in many commercial battery chemistries. All tested batteries were subjected to both wedge and flat plate crush tests, in order to determine the relative safety of each cathode chemistry under two crush speeds and various states-of-charge (SOC). Battery voltage, external cell temperature, and applied load were recorded for each crush test. Video recording of each crush test was also collected to document events.

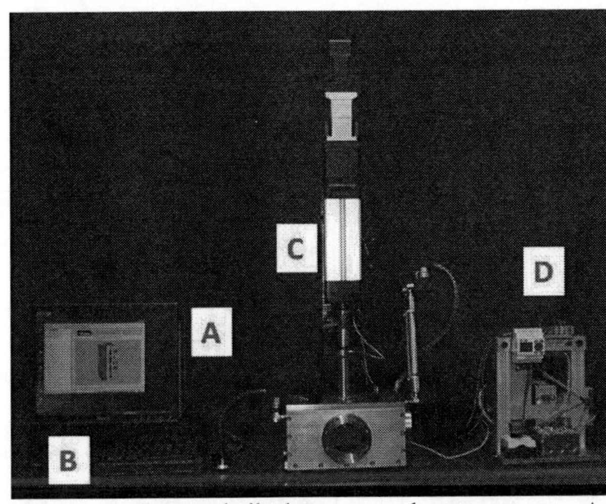

Figure 1. Custom-built battery crush test set up. A. personal computer, B. Measurement Computing data logger, C. electrical actuator and crush chamber, and D. command center houses buttons and switches that start and stop crushing sequences as well as adjust actuator height.

Results and Discussion

A 18650 lithium titanate battery (Model YJ18650) was obtained from a supplier in China, YJ Power Group LTD Capacity. According to the documentation, the manufacturer of the battery is TBK Electronics Co. LTD. The nominal capacity and cell voltage of the battery is 1300 mAh and 2.4 V, respectively. The battery has an energy density of 3.12 Wh. Using the lithium titanate anode lowers both the battery voltage and cell capacity. The battery had a non-traditional cell configuration with the positive and negative protruding from the battery header as pin connectors. The YJ18650 showing the positive and negative pin connectors extending from the header is presented in Figure 2.

Figure 2. TBK Electronics Co. LTD lithium titanate 18650 battery (Model YJ18650).

Because this was a unique configuration for a typical 18650 format, the battery was opened and the components were removed. Unravelling the contents immediately revealed the assembly and construction of the battery and how it differed from conventional 18650 battery construction. Figures 3 and 4 show photographs of the dissection of the TBK Electronics Co. LTD lithium titanate 18650 battery. Since the battery has the negative and positive exiting the header of the battery, the cylindrical case of the negative electrode is no longer electrically connected and is insulated from the metal cell canister. This is seen in the first image showing a green plastic insulating wrap around the jelly roll. Once the green plastic wrap is removed, the negative electrode is also wrapped with the battery separator. Unravelling the electrodes and separator revealed the method of attachment of the positive and negative pin connectors to the current collectors.

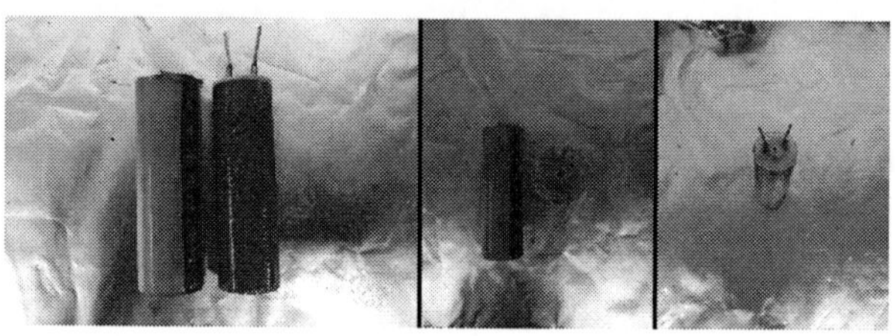

Figure 3. Disassembly of TBK Electronics Co. LTD lithium titanate 18650 battery (Model YJ18650) showing pin connectors and insulating jacket surrounding the jelly roll construction.

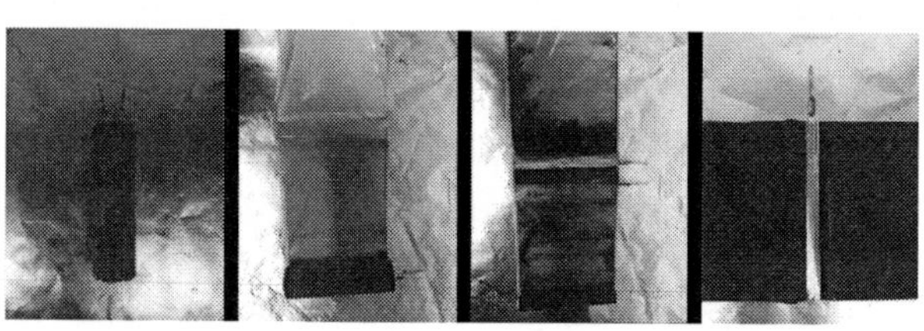

Figure 4. Disassembly of TBK Electronics Co. LTD lithium titanate 18650 battery (Model YJ18650) showing the separator and pin attachment to current collectors.

An enlarged image of the current collector/pin attachment is shown in Figure 5. It is interesting to note that both the positive and negative electrodes use an aluminum current collector as opposed to Al and Cu that are used as current collectors for the positive and negative, respectively in traditional Li-ion batteries.

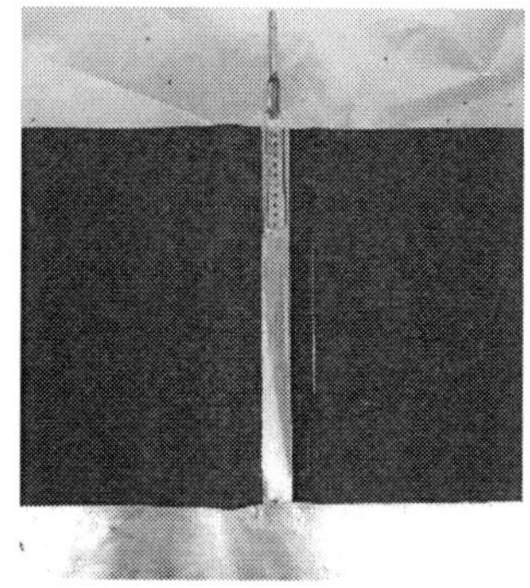

Figure 5. Photograph showing the attachment of the pin connector to the electrode current collector of TBK Electronics Co. LTD lithium titanate 18650 battery (Model YJ18650).

Battery crush tests for lithium titanate battery

Crush tests were performed on 18650 TBK Electronics Co. LTD lithium titanate battery (Model YJ18650) at 0.1 and 15 mm/s using a wedge penetrator at 40 °C in air at various states-of-charge (SOCs). All tests were performed in triplicate for each SOC. Representative data for selected crush tests are shown in Figures 6 - 7. As can be seen from these results, the battery did not short as evidenced by the fact that the cell voltage is maintained at about 2.4 V throughout the entire crush experiment. In addition, the battery cell temperature remained constant at approximately 40 °C and did not increase beyond the ambient temperature.

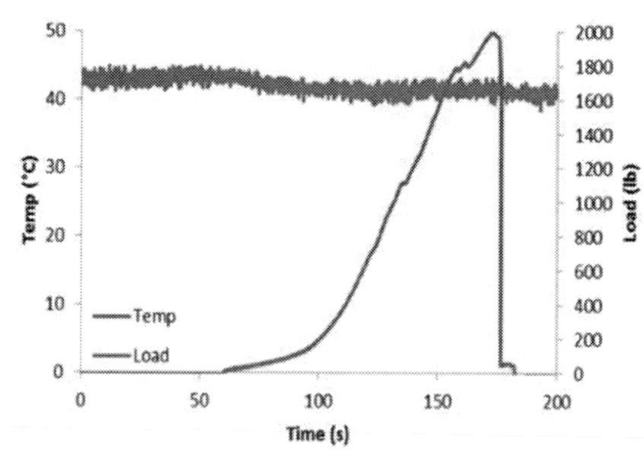

Figure 6. Cell temperature vs. applied load for 18650 TBK Electronics Co. LTD lithium titanate battery at 100% SOC (0.1 mm/s, 40 °C in air, wedge penetrator). Model YJ18650.

Triplicate runs were performed for each battery at both crush speeds and at all states of charge tested. Irrespective of crush speed or state of charge, no recorded event was observed for the lithium titanate batteries. Some of the batteries were nearly completely bisected by the wedge penetrator, as seen in the photographs in Figure 8.

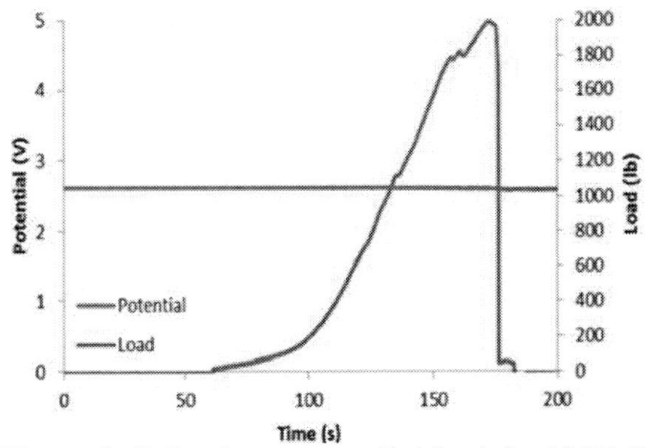

Figure 7. Cell voltage vs. applied load for 18650 TBK Electronics Co. LTD lithium titanate battery at 100% SOC (0.1 mm/s, 40 °C in air, wedge penetrator). Model YJ18650.

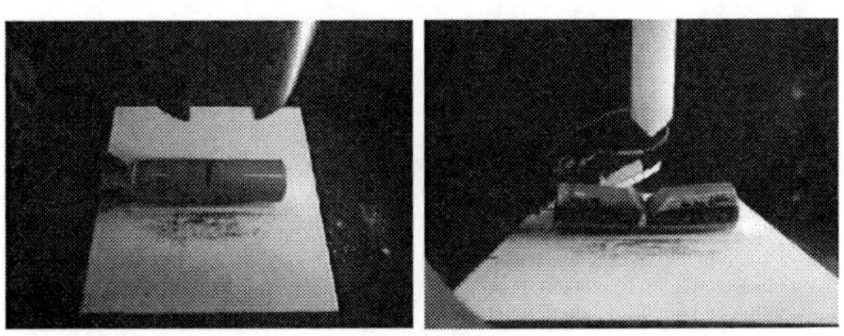

Figure 8. Images of 18650 TBK Electronics Co. LTD lithium titanate anode battery at 100% SOC (0.1 mm/s, 40 C in air) after wedge crush testing.

Battery crush tests for $LiCoO_2$/graphite battery

An additional 18650 lithium ion battery (Model YJ18650) was also obtained from YJ Power Group LTD, and was manufactured by TBK Electronics Co. LTD. The nominal capacity and cell voltage of the battery was rated at 2000 mAh and 3.7 V, respectively. The battery had an energy density of 7.4Wh. The reason for obtaining this battery was that it had the same cell assembly and configuration as the other battery manufactured by TBK Electronics Co. LTD having the LTO ($Li_4Ti_5O_{12}$) anode. We wanted to determine if the safety performance experienced by the LTO anode battery was due to the cell configuration or the LTO anode. Again, this battery had a non-traditional cell configuration with the positive and negative protruding from the battery header as pin connectors. The YJ18650 showing the positive and negative pin connectors extending from the header is shown in Figure 9. As shown, the battery has the positive and negative protruding from the header as pin connectors, a similar cell configuration to the battery with the LTO cathode. This battery contained a graphite anode and a Li-doped metal oxide cathode, which were confirmed by powder x-ray diffraction (XRD). A summary of the information on the two batteries is shown in Table 1.

Figure 9. TBK Electronics Co. LTD lithium ion 18650 battery (Model YJ18650).

Model No.	Capacity (mAh)	Cell voltage (V)	Cathode	Anode
YJ18650	2000	3.7	$LiCoO_2$	graphite
YJ18650	1300	2.5	$LiCoO_2$	$Li_4Ti_5O_{12}$ (LTO)

Table 1. Summary of 18650 cell specifications.

Crush testing of the 2000 mAh TBK Electronics 18650 battery (Model YJ18650) having the same cell construction and tab connections as the battery with the LTO anode was then performed under similar conditions. However, this battery contained a graphite anode instead of LTO. As noted previously, crush testing was performed in air using a wedge penetrator. Representative crush test data on this battery at 0.1 mm/s using a wedge penetrator at 40 °C in air at 100% SOC is shown in Figures 10 and 11, respectively.

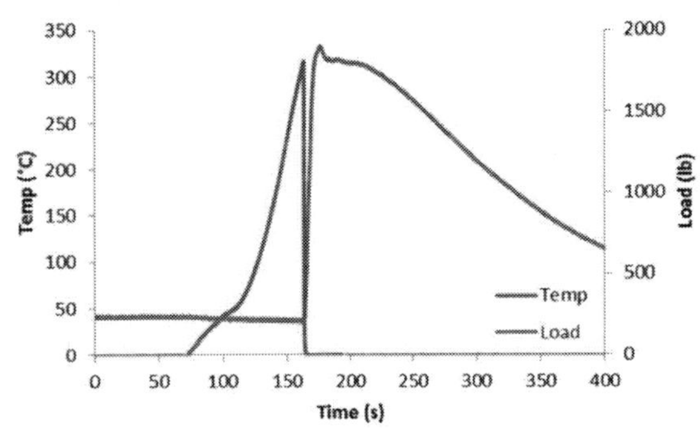

Figure 10. Cell temperature vs. applied load for 18650 TBK Electronics Co. LTD lithium ion battery (graphite anode) at 100% SOC (0.1 mm/s, 40 °C in air, wedge penetrator). Model YJ18650.

Unlike the battery having the LTO anode and exact cell configuration and construction, this particular cell resulted in a violent event when crushed in air using the wedge penetrator. As shown in Figures 10 and 11, the cell did short and for the most part experienced relatively high temperatures, one exceeding 330 °C. Based on these results, the conclusion would be that the LTO anode, along with the lower capacity (1300 mAh) and lower cell voltage (2.4 V) can be attributed to the improved safety of the cell and not the result of the cell construction. The evidence for the violence of the crush test for the $LiCoO_2$/graphite battery can be seen in Figure 12, and the partially melted Delrin® wedge penetrator is shown in Figure 13.

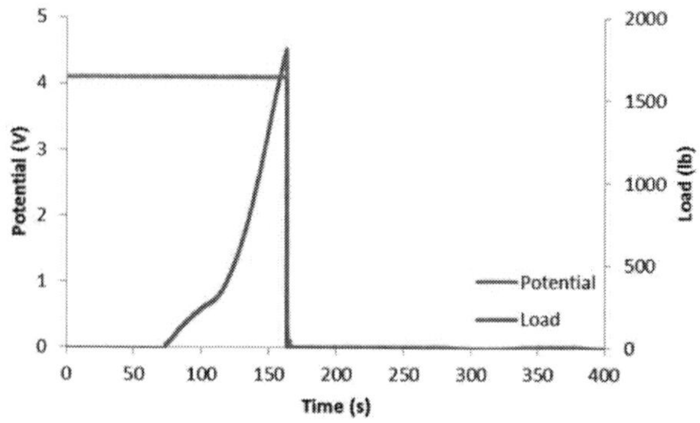

Figure 11. Cell voltage vs. applied load for 18650 TBK Electronics Co. LTD lithium ion battery (graphite anode) at 100% SOC (0.1 mm/s, 40 °C in air, wedge penetrator). Model YJ18650.

Figure 12. Images of 18650 TBK Electronics Co. LTD lithium-ion battery ($LiCoO_2$/graphite) battery at 100% SOC (0.1 mm/s, 40 °C in air) after wedge crush testing.

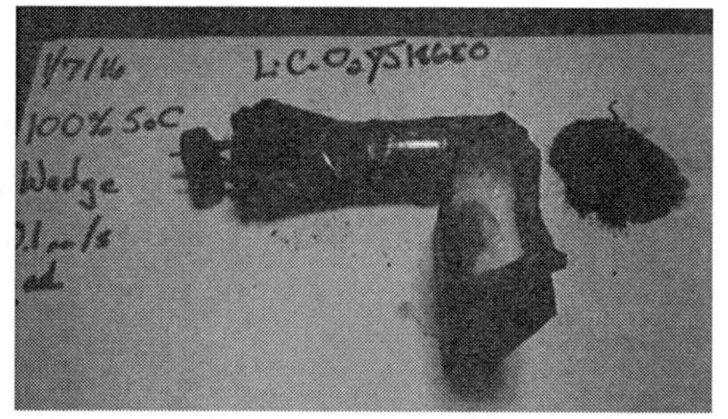

Figure 13. Remnants of the Delrin® wedge penetrator after wedge crush testing of the $LiCoO_2$/graphite battery at 100% SOC (0.1 mm/s, 40 °C in air).

Acknowledgements

The authors wish to thank the National Institute for Occupational Safety and Health for funding (contract no. 200-2013-56808).

References

1. Dubaniewicz, T. H. Jr.; DuCarme, J. P. *Journal of Loss Prevention in the Process Industries.* **2014**, *32*, 165.
2. Dubaniewicz, T. H. Jr.; DuCarme, J. P. *IEEE Transactions on Industry Applications.* **2013**, *6*, 2451-2460.
3. Abada, S.; Marlair, G.; Lecocq, A.; Petit, M.; Moynot-Sauvant, V.; Huet, F. *J. Power Sources.* **2016**, *306*, 178.
4. Lipka, S. M.; Rogers, F. III; Whitlow, D. T.; Bramel, T. "Probing Lithium-Ion Battery Safety in Mining Environments." Presented at the 228th Meeting of the Electrochemical Society, Phoenix, AZ, October 2015 (ECS abstract MA2015-02, 349).

Fundamental Aspects of Large-Scale Energy Storage System Safety

Summer Ferreira, Joshua Lamb, Christopher Orendorff, John Hewson, Babu Chalamala

Sandia National Laboratories
P. O. Box 5800, Albuquerque, NM 87185-0836

Abstract:
As the scale of energy storage systems increases, safety considerations grow commensurately with the amount of stored energy. The authors summarize a recent review of safety and reliability findings for battery storage and identify R&D gaps, particularly as batteries are scaled into system level hardware. While there have been a number of studies addressing failure of rechargeable batteries in portable computing and consumer electronics, with a small number of studies on electric vehicle battery systems, in the case of stationary batteries for grid energy storage, very little information exists on the fundamental aspects of safety. The aim of this review is to focus on the R&D needs that will allow the community to build on prior knowledge to address issues of abuse and safety for larger, grid scale energy storage systems. The primary focus of the review will be on the underlying materials science, electrochemical processes, and thermal kinetics that can lead to major safety events. Importantly, consideration will be given to identifying cell and system level interactions, how such interactions manifest into catastrophic failures, and the need to develop mitigation strategies.

To date, the safety of energy storage systems has been looked at almost exclusively through the narrow lens of cell level failures. While a greater understanding of cell level failures has been critical to the success of rechargeable batteries in consumer electronics, the complexity associated with the scale of energy in grid energy storage applications necessitates consideration of a wider range of system level issues related to power electronics, to power conditioning systems and to fire suppression of large energy storage systems and the surrounding physical infrastructure. Furthermore, the kinetic behavior of cell-level failure must take into account the probability of propagation and thermal runaway that is not indicated in smaller batteries of the same chemistry. In this paper, we will first provide a summary on the status of current research and outline the immediate and longer term R&D needs to advance the fundamental safety and reliability needs of the grid energy storage industry.

Keywords: Energy storage; thermal runaway; battery safety.

Introduction

Energy storage inherently has hazards associated with inadvertent release of stored energy. This is true whether the energy is stored as traditional hydrocarbon fuels, subject to fires, as pumped hydroelectric storage, subject to structural failures [1], or electrochemical energy storage subject to thermal runaway. In the case of hydrocarbon fuels, we are familiar with the hazards of fuel fires and developed safety systems to address critical issues. In the case of pumped hydro, we reduced the possibility of dam failures through engineering. In the latter case, thermal runaway of electrochemical energy storage devices has become a more significant issue with increasing system size and higher energy density. Of particular significance in terms of energy density is the prevalence of lithium-ion cells [2] with practical energy densities on the order of 0.5 MJ kg^{-1}. Examples of thermal runaway include lithium-ion cells reviewed in [3] several recent incidents with grid-scale storage facilities [4-6] and transportation systems [7]. One noteworthy aspect of these incidents is the uncertainty of best practices for fire fighting [4].

Factors that can lead to thermal runaway are reviewed in the next section. Recent research on failure in lithium-ion cells is briefly reviewed in the subsequent section. The extension of these results to larger systems is still incomplete, but recent research suggests important considerations as discussed in the section on Understanding failure in larger scale systems.

Factors leading to thermal runaway

The energy stored in electrochemical cells presents a potential source for energy release. Furthermore, electrochemical cells have additional complications relative to other chemical-energy storage systems. More specifically, in most batteries the oxidizing and reducing materials are held in close proximity such that failure of the separator can lead to the release of stored energy. While robust battery management systems can inhibit or reduce the propagation of cell level failures to the larger system, thermal dissipation of heat or the inclusion of reaction-inhibiting additives [8] appear to be the most promising approaches to mitigating thermal runaway when it does occur. Naturally, prevention of runaway is most preferable, and a range of studies have worked to understand possible causes. A range of mechanisms can lead to separator failure, including internal short circuits, mechanical damage and heating that might melt separator materials. Most of these failure mechanisms are reasonably well understood, and cell-level designs such as shutdown separators can reduce but not eliminate their possibility [9].

As will be discussed in the next section, elevated temperatures can lead to exothermic decomposition. Sources of elevated temperatures can include inappropriate installations with inadequate cooling or external thermal forcing from, for example, an external fire source.

While failure probabilities of individual cells are small, the large number of cells assembled into large-scale storage systems increases the probability of local failure, so an important question is the probability of propagation from a failing cell to adjacent cells [10]. In large-scale energy storage systems, the number of control and safety systems is significant, and the probability that point failures can lead to larger system failures can be addressed through probabilistic risk analysis or system-theoretic process analysis [11].

Cell-level lithium-ion studies.

The original prevalent chemistry for lithium-ion cells was based on a carbon anode and a lithium cobalt oxide ($LiCoO_2$) cathode. While this particular chemistry operated without incident under normal conditions, there is potential to go into highly energetic thermal runaway in abnormal scenarios. Significant research has occurred to understand these processes and the industry has moved to more robust cathode materials. Electrode materials based on spinel compounds and iron phosphates are e are significantly less hazardous, and are beginning to supplant $LiCoO_2$ as electrode materials.

Calorimetry measurements have been conducted on a range of cell chemistries, and these identify multiple reaction processes occurring over a range of temperatures [12-15]. Some of these processes are only mildly exothermic while others can lead to thermal runaway where the reaction accelerates through cell disassembly. These measurements provide insight into thermal processes inside cells, showing that measurable heat release can start to occur at temperatures as low as 90 to 120 C. These low temperature reactions have been identified and are primarily caused by the exothermic decomposition of quasi-stable organic lithium salts in the SEI layer [16]. The activation energy for this process has been measured to be in the range of 50 to 100 kJ/mol [17] so that rates increase rapidly with internal or external heating. As the unstable SEI layer decomposes into more stable components, additional lithium and electrolyte are able to react at increased rates as the temperature rises to form additional passivation layers on the anode particle surfaces [18, 19].

In addition to the reactions of the SEI layer, the electrolyte salt, $LiPF_6$, can decompose around 160 to 200 C into LiF and PF_5. PF_5 is a strong Lewis acid that can react with the alkyl carbonate electrolytes forming polymeric chains, or react with trace water to form HF and POF_3 that, in turn, can react to further decompose electrolytes [20].

Though these low temperature reactions are only mildly exothermic, they do result in significant gas generation leading to cell overpressure and potential rupturing of the seals. Measurements suggest that slightly more than 1 L/Ah (STP) of gas is generated during these low temperature processes [8]. Cells are designed so that gases are vented before the overpressure is too great. Vented gases will involve a gaseous jet that will also entrain liquid electrolytes; gases include products of partial oxidation of the alkyl carbonate electrolyte including CO_2 ($\approx$60%), CO, C_2H_4, CH_4 (together $\approx$20%) and H_2 ($\approx$10%) among others [21]. Because the gases and the electrolyte solution are flammable there is the potential for a dramatic burst of flame when venting occurs although this is not observed in all cells.

At somewhat higher temperatures, the cathode is observed to react with the electrolyte. For $LiCoO_2$ cathodes, these reactions start between 120 and 150 C [22] so that this overlaps the anode and electrolyte decomposition reactions. Other cathode materials are observed to react at higher temperatures including $LiMn_2O_4$ and $LiFePO_4$ [14, 15]. These reactions between the cathode and the electrolyte are strongly exothermic.

An important point to be made regarding the potential for heat release in thermal runaway for lithium-ion cells is that the electrolytes are flammable in air and can be oxidized by the cathode at sufficiently high temperatures as well. The energy density of typical alkyl-carbonate electrolytes is in the range of 10-20 MJ kg^{-1}, which is large enough that even the small quantities of electrolyte per cell represent the same energy release potential as the cell itself; that is the electrolyte oxidation potentially releases on the order of 0.5 MJ kg^{-1} [23].

Understanding failure in larger scale systems.

As the scale of the cells and packs increases, the surface to volume ratio decreases and this can reduce the opportunity to dissipate heat that is generated through normal operation or through local failure (i.e. localized internal short circuit). That is, a basic thermal balance between volumetric heat release and surface-area limited heat dissipation leads to a reduced ability to dissipate thermal energy that scales with the inverse of the shortest heat-transfer length scale (i.e. the diameter of a cell or thickness of a pouch). As cells are arranged into packs, modules and systems this shortest effective length scale will tend to increase. Recent work has shown that, while the net energy released in some larger format cells is similar when normalized by the stored energy, the normalized heat release rate increased though details of the construction of different size cells may play a role in this [24].

When multiple cells are arranged into packs, an important concern is the likelihood for single cell failure to propagate through the pack. The potential for propagation through a pack was modeled by Spotnitz et al. [25] and these results pointed out that cell-to-cell propagation is sensitive to the effective heat transfer between cells. This result is supported by testing: thermal runaway between cylindrical cells is less likely to propagate than that between pouch cells that are in more intimate thermal contact [10]. Tests have also shown that the electrical connectivity can affect the likelihood of thermal runaway propagation; specifically, when cells are connected in parallel and not electrically isolated during runaway of one cell, a resulting short circuit in the initially failing cell leads to the release of stored energy from the parallel cells [10]. This suggests the importance of electrical disconnects and fuses for system design.

If the hazard is associated with an external heat source like a fire, there is the potential to have heat flux from this source lead to thermal runaway in batteries. In recent testing the time to heat cells to temperatures where thermal runaway starts was shown to be significant relative to fire detection times, and it is possible to consider sprinkler suppression of fires in the time that it takes to heat the cells to thermal-runaway temperatures [26].

As in the case of the organic electrolytes, structural materials including polymer packaging and separators can provide significant sources of energy for heat release if flammable [23]. Structural materials also offer significant paths for heat dissipation or containment if thermally conducting or insulating.

To date, scientific analysis of hazards associated with large-scale storage systems is largely non-existent. Experimental results are absent from the literature in batteries larger than even a handful of cells. In such an environment, the response to incidents is typically to apply safety measures that are chemistry and design agnostic, and not rigorously evaluated through research. The result is safety that doesn't take into account the specific system needs. This can be counterproductive both in terms of the cost of ineffective fixes and in the failure to address actual risks. A similar situation can occur for first responders where nationally reported incidents may encourage ineffective response strategies for other systems. A significant need exists for a science-based approach for energy storage systems to identify:

- System-specific safety technologies and engineering design practices.
- Processes for response to incidences that might occur.
- Reflection of best practices in codes, standards and regulations.

These best practices must address specific differences among the range of technology options currently under consideration. In this paper only lithium-ion cell safety was discussed because the relevant cell or system level information for other relevant technologies (advanced lead-acid, sodium-sulfur and flow battery systems) are much less studied for off-normal event behavior, despite past accidental fires for both lead-acid and sodium-sulfur systems [4-6]. To achieve the needs listed above for stationary system scale technology the gap from cell and small string abuse testing must be supplemented by empirical studies up to larger pack designs, for a range of chemistries and for a range of scenarios. These results must be coupled with modeling efforts. Furthermore, ancillary systems including power electronics must be considered for evaluating risk and consequences in off-normal events. Finally, risk assessment must be incorporated along with mitigating factors such as location, adjacent material, ventilation, suppression and containment integrated into design, as well as first responder guidance. Such assessments must consider conflagration, thermal release, gas and spray release. Together this represents a significant research and development challenge.

Summary

In this paper a brief summary of existing safety issues existing for rechargeable batteries as energy storage systems is outlined. Hazards associated with individual lithium-ion cells and their component materials have been studied most extensively and this has led to material science improvements that are expected to contribute to safer energy storage in the future. However, studies for larger systems are extremely limited as are studies of alternate chemistries relevant for grid energy storage. The costs of larger systems suggest a comprehensive science and engineering approach to understand components and their assembly into systems that might minimize the most costly tests and accidents. This approach should involve coupled experimental and modeling aspects and should address the diversity of storage system chemistries and design approaches that exist and are being considered.

Acknowledgements

Sandia is a multiprogram laboratory operated by Sandia Corporation, a Lockheed Martin Company for the United States Department of Energy's National Nuclear Security Administration under contract DE-AC04-94AL85000. The authors gratefully acknowledge funding from the Department of Energy, Office of Electricity's Energy Storage Program. The authors would like to thank Dr. Imre Gyuk for his support and guidance of this effort.

References

[1] J. L. Ehasz and K. Paul, "Taum Sauk Upper Reservoir Failure: Report On Technical Reasons for the Breach," Bonneville Power Administration, 2006.

[2] B. Scrosati and J. Garche, "Lithium batteries: Status, prospects and future," *Journal of Power Sources,* vol. 195, pp. 2419-2430, May 1 2010.

[3] Q. Wang, P. Ping, X. Zhao, G. Chu, J. Sun, and C. Chen, "Thermal runaway caused fire and explosion of lithium ion battery," *Journal of Power Sources,* vol. 208, pp. 210-224, Jun 15 2012.

[4] U. Irfan, "Battery Fires Pose New Risks to Firefighters," in *ClimateWire,* http://www.scientificamerican.com/article/battery-

fires-pose-new-risks-to-firefighters/: Scientific American, 2015.

[5] J. Ferguson, "APS fire probed," http://azdailysun.com/news/local/aps-fire-probed/article_1de2e924-ab0a-5e71-9a3a-6942c2d1c9bb.html: Arizona Daily Sun, 2013.

[6] NGKinsulators, "Cause of NAS Battery Fire Incident, Safety Enhancement Measures and Resumption of Operations," http://www.ngk.co.jp/english/news/2012/0607.html, 2012.

[7] J. Lowy. (2013, 8-7-2014). *Overcharging batteries eyed in Boeing 787 mishaps.*

[8] G. Nagasubramanian and C. Orendorff, "Hydrofluoroether electrolytes for lithium-ion batteries: Reduced gas decomposition and nonflammable," *Journal of Power Sources,* vol. 196, pp. 8604-8609, Oct 15 2011.

[9] P. G. Balakrishnan, R. Ramesh, and T. P. Kumar, "Safety mechanisms in lithium-ion batteries," *Journal of Power Sources,* vol. 155, pp. 401-414, Apr 21 2006.

[10] J. Lamb, C. J. Orendorff, L. A. M. Steele, and S. W. Spangler, "Failure propagation in multi-cell lithium ion batteries," *Journal of Power Sources,* vol. 283, pp. 517-523, Jun 2015.

[11] D. Rosewater and A. Williams, "Analyzing system safety in lithium-ion grid energy storage," *Journal of Power Sources,* vol. 300, pp. 460-471, Dec 2015.

[12] D. D. MacNeil, T. D. Hatchard, and J. R. Dahn, "A comparison between the high temperature electrode/electrolyte reactions of LixCoO2 and LixMn2O4," *Journal of the Electrochemical Society,* vol. 148, pp. A663-A667, Jul 2001.

[13] D. D. MacNeil, D. Larcher, and J. R. Dahn, "Comparison of the reactivity of various carbon electrode materials with electrolyte at elevated temperature," *Journal of the Electrochemical Society,* vol. 146, pp. 3596-3602, Oct 1999.

[14] E. P. Roth, C. C. Crafts, D. H. Doughty, and J. McBreen, "Advanced Technology Development Program for Lithium-Ion Battereis: Thermal Abuse Performance of 18650 Li-Ion Cells, SAND2004-0584.," Sandia National Laboratories2004.

[15] D. D. MacNeil, Z. H. Lu, Z. H. Chen, and J. R. Dahn, "A comparison of the electrode/electrolyte reaction at elevated temperatures for various Li-ion battery cathodes," *Journal of Power Sources,* vol. 108, pp. 8-14, Jun 1 2002.

[16] D. Aurbach, B. Markovsky, I. Weissman, E. Levi, and Y. Ein-Eli, "On the correlation between surface chemistry and performance of graphite negative electrodes for Li ion batteries," *Electrochimica Acta,* vol. 45, pp. 67-86, 1999.

[17] Z. H. Chen, Y. Qin, Y. Ren, W. Q. Lu, C. Orendorff, E. P. Roth, *et al.*, "Multi-scale study of thermal stability of lithiated graphite," *Energy & Environmental Science,* vol. 4, pp. 4023-4030, Oct 2011.

[18] M. Broussely, S. Herreyre, P. Biensan, P. Kasztejna, K. Nechev, and R. J. Staniewicz, "Aging mechanism in Li ion cells and calendar life predictions," *Journal of Power Sources,* vol. 97-8, pp. 13-21, Jul 2001.

[19] B. Y. Liaw, E. P. Roth, R. G. Jungst, G. Nagasubramanian, H. L. Case, and D. H. Doughty, "Correlation of Arrhenius behaviors in power and capacity fades with cell impedance and heat generation in cylindrical lithium-ion cells," *Journal of Power Sources,* vol. 119, pp. 874-886, Jun 1 2003.

[20] S. E. Sloop, J. K. Pugh, S. Wang, J. B. Kerr, and K. Kinoshita, "Chemical reactivity of PF5 and LiPF6 in ethylene carbonate/dimethyl carbonate solutions," *Electrochemical and Solid State Letters,* vol. 4, pp. A42-A44, Apr 2001.

[21] E. P. Roth and C. J. Orendorff, "How Electrolytes Influence Battery Safety," *Electrochemical Society Interface,* vol. 21, pp. 37-41, Summer 2012.

[22] D. D. MacNeil and J. R. Dahn, "Test of reaction kinetics using both differential scanning and accelerating rate calorimetries as applied to the reaction of LixCoO2 in non-aqueous electrolyte," *Journal of Physical Chemistry A,* vol. 105, pp. 4430-4439, May 2001.

[23] P. Ribiere, S. Grugeon, M. Morcrette, S. Boyanov, S. Laruelle, and G. Marlair, "Investigation on the fire-induced hazards of Li-ion battery cells by fire calorimetry," *Energy & Environmental Science,* vol. 5, pp. 5271-5280, Jan 2012.

[24] C. J. Orendorff, J. Lamb, L. A. M. Steele, S. W. Spangler, and J. Langendorf, "Quantification of Lithium-ion Cell Thermal Runaway Energetics, SAND2016-0486," Sandia National Laboratories2016.

[25] R. M. Spotnitz, J. Weaver, G. Yeduvaka, D. H. Doughty, and E. P. Roth, "Simulation of abuse tolerance of lithium-ion battery packs," *Journal of Power Sources,* vol. 163, pp. 1080-1086, Jan 2007.

[26] B. Ditch, G. Yee, and M. Chaos, "Estimating the time-of-involvement of bulk packed lithium-ion batteries in a wharehouse storage fire," in *Fire Safety Science, Proceedings of the Eleventh International Symposium,* New Zealand, 2014.

Failure Mechanisms in Overdischarged Large-format Lithium-ion Cells

Christopher Hendricks, Daphne, Fuentevilla, and Azzam Mansour
Naval Surface Warfare Center Carderock Division
christopher.hendrick.ctr@navy.mil

Abstract
Lithium-ion battery safety has received extensive attention due to the proliferation of high capacity, high power cells and modules utilized in electric vehicle, grid, aerospace, and military applications. Overcharge, thermal abuse, and short circuit failure mechanisms have been well studied and documented in the literature; however, overdischarge has received less attention. While overdischarge itself is not considered a safety concern, recharging and cycling an overdischarged cell may lead to both safety and performance issues. Overdischarge can occur naturally through self-discharge of the cell or parasitic losses within a battery system. With battery-powered devices potentially left for long periods of time in storage, DoD interest in extending the shelf life of devices in the field, and proliferation of battery packs composed of large numbers of cells, there is an increased interest in determining limits of low voltage recharge and developing a methodology for determining safety limits. Furthermore, overdischarge is a class of safety risk that is inherent to the cell and cannot be prevented with passive protection devices. Overdischarge and subsequent recharge is associated with a number of undesirable side reactions within the battery. At low voltages, the anode's copper current collector becomes unstable in the organic electrolyte [1]. As a result, the copper can dissolve, migrate within the cell, and re-precipitate on the electrodes. Furthermore, the passivating solid electrolyte interphase (SEI) layer on the electrode surface can degrade as a result of overdischarge [2-3]. This can lead to side reactions between the electrolyte and the electrode with gas as a byproduct. Excessive gas generation can lead to performance loss, cell rupture, and/or thermal runaway. Copper dissolution has been investigated in lab-scale beaker cells [4-7] and small format lithium-ion cells [8]; however, the impact of copper dissolution in large-format (>30Ah) cells has not been investigated. This study evaluates the impact of overdischarge and subsequent recharge and reuse on cell performance and safety. We previously identified the presence of copper in large-format lithium-ion cells that had experienced overdischarge for an unknown length of time [9]. In this talk, we extend our investigation to identify the relationship between cell voltage and storage time on copper dissolution, SEI layer degradation, and gas generation. We also take a closer look at differences in the SEI layers of overdischarged cells and cells within their nominal voltage range through a study of the carbon and oxygen XPS spectra. 1.S.T. Myung et al. "Electrochemical behavior and passivation of current collectors in lithium-ion batteries," Journal of Materials Chemistry 21 (2011), pp. 9891-9911 2.H. Yoshida, et al., "Degradation mechanism of alkyl carbonate solvents used in lithium-ion cells during initial charging," J. Power Sources 68 (1997) 311-315 3.V. A. Agubra and J. W. Fergus, "The formation and stability of the solid electrolyte interface on the graphite anode," J. Power Sources 268 (2014) 153-162 4.M. Zhao et al., "Electrochemical stability of graphite-coated copper in lithium-ion battery electrolytes," Journal of the Electrochemical Society 147 (11) (2000) pp. 3983-3988. 5.M. Zhao et al., "Quantitation of the dissolution of the graphite-coated copper foil in lithium-ion battery electrolytes by flame absorption spectroscopy," Electrochimica Acta 49 (2004) pp. 677-681. 6.H. Maleki and J. N. Howard, "Effects of overdischarge on performance and thermal stability of a Li-ion cell," Journal of Power Sources 160 (2006) pp.1395-1402. 7.D. Fuentevilla, C. Hendricks, and A. Mansour, "Quantifying the Impact of Overdischarge on Large Format Lithium-Ion Cells," ECS Transactions 69 (20) (2015) pp. 1-4.

NSWC Crane 23 October 2012 Fire Event Engineering Root Cause Analysis Reportable Findings

Michael Chatelain, Samuel Stuart, Mark Tisher
NSWC Crane Division
Building 3235, Crane, IN
michael.chatelain@navy.mil
samuel.stuart@navy.mil
mark.tisher@navy.mil

Abstract: *A battery fire event occurred at NSWC Crane Division Building 3325 battery test facility on 23 October 2012 at approximately 23:00. This Navy Class A mishap resulted in a NAVSEA directed Safety Investigation Board (SIB) analysis with actionable recommendations included in their report. One recommendation from the SIB was to perform an Engineering Root Cause Analysis (ERCA) of the event and to distribute the findings to the broadest battery community possible.*

Keywords: Lithium; Lithium Battery; Fire; Root Cause Analysis; High Energy Density Battery; Automated Test System; Grounding; Common Mode; Power Supply; Power Pole Connectors; Common Ground Plane.

Introduction

The ERCA[1,2] of the 23 October Building 3235 Fire Event (which will be referred to as the Fire Event throughout the rest of this paper) developed Fire Event discovery and direction forward including defining attributing factors of the event that influenced outcome, impact, and implemented changes mitigating potentials of future events. The physical remains/condition of the post Fire Event area, the complexity of the testing involved in the Fire Event, and the number of possible causes significantly increased the difficulty of finding a true root cause of the Fire Event. The use of root cause analysis methodologies and the analysis of hypothesized conditions with supporting and refuting evidence led to the present understanding of probable root cause. The depth at which this root cause is defined stems from the use of design of experiments and theoretical computations.

Background Leading Up To Fire Event

NSWC Crane building 3235 battery test facility was designed in the early 1990's to test high energy and power lithium batteries. The building is comprised of three sections that function as separate buildings with regards to the operations and containment of tests. These three sections are considered zones and will be described as zones 1, 2, and 3. Zone 1 is general office configuration with standard single recirculating heating, ventilation, and cooling system (HVAC). Zone 2 has its own air emissions scrubbing capability with significant high power test capability and its own HVAC system that is a 100% makeup air system. Zone 2 has a fire suppression system and is separated from zone 1 with a 2 hour fire wall. A ramped entry floor at the zone 1-zone 2 transition prevents water from zone 2 entering into zone 1 if the fire suppression system were activated in zone 2. Zone 3 is the high abuse test area with re-enforced concrete exterior walls and 10 test vaults with TNT equivalency ratings per vault. The entire zone 3 air emissions are scrubbed and all water produced or used in this zone is contained for proper disposal. The HVAC units of zone 3 are zone specific with no sharing with other building zones.

Zone 3 had an Uninterruptible Power System (UPS) for the area, but it was non-functional the entire period of the test sequence involved in the Fire Event.

The test sequence configuration central to the Fire Event consisted of twelve high energy density (>500AHr) lithium thionyl chloride cells subjected to a temperature conditioned discharge test profile. The cells were located on a mezzanine above the test vaults in zone 3. The Test System used to control the test profile sequence was a commercial automated charge/discharge system with approximately 100 channels of control/load configured with 4 channels in parallel per cell to meet the potential current draw requirements throughout the entire cell life to voltage cut-off. The automated Test System was located on the ground level and was the only system recording and controlling this test sequence. The entire test configuration was calibrated, verified, and validated prior to beginning the test sequence on the actual cells. The load and monitoring cabling between the cells and the Test System were approximately forty feet in length for each cell and configured in a bundle using wire ties. The controller of the environmental enclosure was modified for this test sequence to maintain a higher temperature (76°F) environment than its original design allowed. The cells were inside this enclosure with a wooden rack used to maintain cell orientation and refrasil cloth was used to isolate the cells from the enclosure interior.

There were many co-located tests being performed in zone 3 while this testing sequence was running and storage of parts, materials, equipment, and other assets where located throughout zone 3 at the time of the Fire Event.

Fire Event State

The Fire Event resulted in significant acidic vapor and smoke damage to nearly all of zone 3 of the building. There was significant fire damage central to the fire focal point and to the materials, parts, and equipment near this area. Nearly all equipment and tools in zone 3 were no longer usable post fire. The post Fire Event condition of zone 3 required Industrial Hygiene (IH) monitoring to determine suitable conditions to allow the analysis team to enter the area. The earliest entry was over 24 hours after the fire was extinguished. During this time frame most of the exposed metal was significantly corroded due to the acidic atmosphere. The environmental temperature enclosure was no longer distinguishable as an environmental enclosure, equipment and materials near the fire location were severely burnt or completely ash, scrubber ductwork near this area was severely melted, and building structures received significant impacts from the venting cells. Power was disconnected to the entire building as part of the fire response and could not be restored until zone 3 was cleaned and compromised electrical conduit, transformers, breakers, and receptacles were repaired/replaced. The ERCA Team composed their evidence while working in these dark, compromised conditions throughout most of this investigation.

Root Cause Tools

The ERCA Team had significant obstacles to overcome to obtain factual evidence of this Fire Event. The physical remains of the key components associated with this Fire Event were destroyed to levels that made determination of initial triggering events difficult to state with confidence as would be desired for this type of investigation. The ERCA Team did use every piece of remains available to piece together evidence developing a timeline of events and potential root causes based on this evidence as well as ruling out potentials that could not have happened as a result of this evidence.

The ERCA Team utilized several RCA techniques to categorize, organize, and analyze the information obtained through the ERCA Team evidence search. Spreadsheets, mapping, photographs, drawings, and data plotting/ analyses allowed the ERCA Team to develop evidence. The ERCA team also interviewed key personnel resident to the building who were involved in the testing and others that were not involved to develop more robust evidence. Emergency Responders, Security guards, dispatch, and subject matter experts involved with the high energy density battery program were also interviewed to develop more evidence.

The ERCA Team utilized both a fishbone diagram, Figure 1, and Fault Tree Diagram, Figure 2, to capture all potential root cause contributing factors of this Fire Event.

The ERCA Team used Design of Experiments and hypothesis theory generation with supporting and refuting evidence to capture all conceivable root causes. Experiments using the actual Test System after it was cleaned and failing power supplies were replaced helped the ERCA Team direct the root cause down to a few critical parameters. The initial analyses provide the ERCA team with likely potentials for the root cause, but until the test system was evaluated, and data parameters recorded during the Fire Event were evaluated to duplicate these recorded parameters, the ERCA Team had only speculation. The Test System evaluation still had levels of uncertainty due to power supply change out and actual cell size and chemistry not available for the evaluation, but the ERCA Team matched loading and voltages as close as possible.

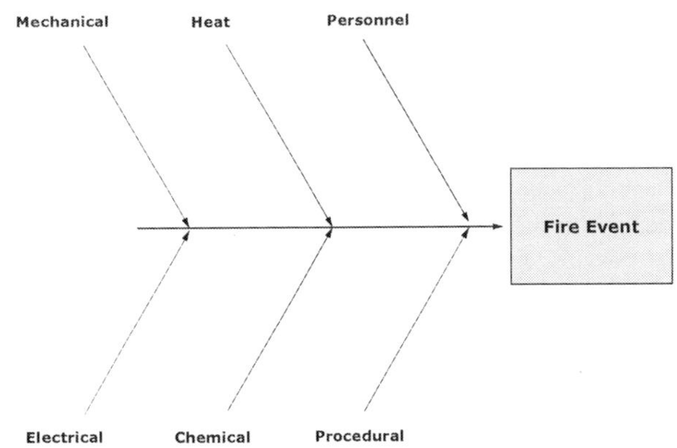

Figure 1. *ERCA Fishbone Diagram, Sub-Bones not shown, Major bone is electrical*

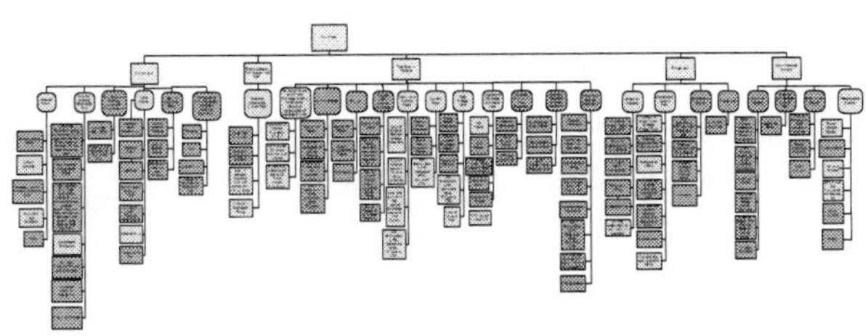

Figure 2. *Fault Tree Diagram, Showing complexity of Analysis*

SIB Contributing Factors to Fire Event Result

The ERCA Team had help from the SIB[3] and Judge Advocate General (JAG) investigations to develop personnel and procedural deficiencies associated with the Fire Event.

- There was no malfeasance determined from either of these investigation teams and the ERCA Team agreed with this determination based on their analysis. This does not mean there were no personnel errors associated with this Fire Event -- it means the errors had no purposeful intent for test disruption or facilities/equipment damage.

- The SIB determined several procedural issues that contributed to the Fire Event outcome, but were not the main root cause of the Fire Event.
- The SIB also determined improper risk analysis of this test scenario.
- The SIB determined lack of documented actions taken throughout the entire test sequence including decision process used to select test location.
- The SIB and JAG determined conflict of interest with individuals having dual positions which they identified as positions requiring separation.
- The SIB found significant housekeeping deficiencies including egress issues.
- The SIB determined a lack of battery training supplied to the Fire Department and Emergency Responders.

Root Cause

The root cause analysis indicated many varying potential root causes which could have contributed to this eventual Fire Event outcome. The personnel and procedural errors that were addressed above all had impacts in the Fire Event, but they were not the central root cause that drove the high energy density cells to failure.

There were other possible root causes, like a lightning strike or a rodent damaging the wiring or loads, but these potential root causes had no evidence that presented itself. Also, there is evidence based on Test System conditions that lead the ERCA Team to believe those types of occurrences could not have been the root cause of this Fire Event.

Some of the harder potential root causes to refute are the parts/materials falling on the cells while the discharge testing was ongoing that could have created inadvertent electrical paths. There is no evidence to prove or disprove materials or parts falling on the cells during the testing were the main cause of the Fire Event.

The evidence or conditions that the ERCA Team found most compelling throughout this investigation was the recorded data of the Test System. This data along with post fire evaluations of the Test System led the ERCA Team to conclude this data had significance to the root cause.

Voltage data showed that cell potentials shifted when the third discharge began on 6 of the cells. This condition was the key finding in the evidence that leads to the root cause of the Fire Event. This shift was repeated to a relatively close similarity during the post fire Test System investigation. The resulting stimuli this shift actually applied to the cells is still not fully understood, and this condition is unique enough that it has not been documented on this or other lithium thionyl chloride cells.

The ERCA Team analysis determined to some confidence that two triggers that were considered independent issues allowed the high energy density cells to be subjected to an abusive voltage stimulus. This stimulus was a combination of the failing/failed load power supply in series with the loaded and at rest cells and the improper seated power-pole connectors that are the Test System interface with the cells. The power supply shutdown or failing was proven to exhibit similar characteristics of voltage shifts. The improper seating of the power pole connectors was proven to provide a noisy voltage response which affected both recorded voltages and load response. These two factors working together approximately seven hours later sensitized the cells to a point that caused them to vent and start a fire within the environmental enclosure.

The ERCA Team did not have funding or cells available to repeat these stimuli to the actual high energy density cells. The verification that these triggers truly caused these cells to fail in the manner they did during this Fire Event will not be completed to that level.

The ERCA Team cannot absolutely state the root cause of the Fire Event was a combination of failing power supplies and improper seating of the power pole connectors.

The ERCA team can state it is the most likely root cause of this Fire Event.

Lessons Learned

The ERCA team developed many lessons learned and best practice guidance from this investigation into the Fire Event. Below are a few of the more critical lessons learned that the ERCA team gladly shares:

- A proper risk assessment is crucial when dealing with lithium battery tests, evaluations, and operations. All aspects of the tasking must be evaluated to determine the potential outcomes with respect to hazards and risks. Also, even if the tasking seems to have a low probability of worse case event, the worst case event should be evaluated with respect to the tasking. A proper risk assessment of this Fire Event would have not allowed the Test System used for the discharge test sequence without additional mitigations.
- Location of lithium battery operations must be evaluated for the process being performed and for any co-located and facilities impacts that may result. A proper evaluation of the discharge testing would not have allowed this operation to be performed on the mezzanine.
- Housekeeping is a very simple, but vitally important mitigation for any lithium battery operation or tasking.
- Proper training of operators, project personnel, and emergency responders is critical for safety of personnel, equipment, facilities, and environment.
- Separation of duties to avoid conflicts of interest is critical to properly assess appropriate risk and hazards[4].
- Utilizing equipment and tools for their intended use can significantly reduce operational risks.
- Proper documentation of actions and data recordings are necessary to meet the program and safety needs of the operations.
- Follow procedural documentation

Acknowledgements

The ERCA Team would like to acknowledge the NSWC Carderock led NAVSEA SIB team for their input and recommendations pertaining to this Fire Event and general best practice input. The ERCA Team also acknowledges the JAG Team for their fair, factual investigation into the personnel aspects of this Fire Event. Lastly, the ERCA Team would like to acknowledge the support and guidance from NAVSEA04, NAVSEA05Z, and NSWC Crane Division Command.

References

1. Managing to Lean, Version 1.0, October 2008, Lean Enterprise Institute
2. Risk Management Guide for DOD Acquisition 6th Edition, August 2006, Department of Defense Acquisition University, Fort Belvoir, VA
3. OPNAVINST5100.23G, Navy Safety and Occupational Health (SOH) Program Manual
4. NSWCCRANEINST5100.3, NSWC Crane Lithium Battery Safety Program, January 2015

High Rate Li/CF_x-MnO_2 Hybrid Technology Development

Mario Destephen, Ernest Ndzebet, Dong Zhang and Eivind Listerud
EaglePicher Technologies, LLC
3220 Industrial Road, Joplin, MO 64801

Abstract: *EaglePicher Technologies has developed a hybrid Li/MnO_2-CF_x technology capable of delivering high energy at high discharge rates at very low temperatures. Performance of the hybrid chemistry has been validated at up to 2C rate at a temperature between -40°C and 60°C. This technology offers a good opportunity for applications that require a combination of high power and high energy over a wide temperature range. This paper provides a general overview of recent progress in advanced hybrid technology at EaglePicher Technologies.*

Keywords: carbon fluoride; manganese dioxide; battery.

Introduction

Lithium/Carbon fluoride (Li/CF_x) is an attractive primary power source, because of its high specific energy, low self-discharge (less than 1% per year), excellent thermal stability, wide operating temperature range (-40 to 85°C), and improved abuse tolerance over other lithium systems. However, the roadblocks that prevent a wider market penetration of Li/CF_x chemistry are its initial voltage delay at low temperature, thermal management issue at high discharge rates, and its material cost. Several approaches have been used to address these issues including a partial substitution of CF_x by manganese dioxide to form hybrid cathode [1-2]. Using web-coating process similar to that in lithium-ion battery production, EPT has developed CF_x-MnO_2 hybrid cathode, which not only maintains all the favorable advantages of Li/CF_x but also provides the highest specific energy and excellent performance in wide temperature range as compared to other lithium primary chemistries.

This paper describes recent advances in the development of an CF_x hybrid chemistry that uses a mixture of CF_x and MnO_2 as cathode material. The cathode composition, cell design, and battery design were optimized for various applications including high rate batteries even at very low temperature.

Experimental

Materials and cathode process were described previously [3-5]. Carbon fluoride (CF_x) and electrolytic manganese dioxide (MnO_2) used in this work were commercially available materials. The hybrid cathodes were processed using EPT advanced web coating equipment similar to that used in lithium ion technology. The cathode composition and formulation were optimized to achieve high electrode density with enhanced rate capability.

Results and Discussion

Through extensive effort of several years, EPT has developed a high energy lithium primary cell technology that includes a CFx/MnO_2 hybrid cathode, a web coating process for the hybrid cathode, and proper electrolyte formulations. Among these features, MnO_2 helps reduce the heat generation, eliminate voltage delay and lower the material cost, while the web coating process provides a thin electrode that allows high rate capability. In addition, the carbon additive and its distribution in the cathode, as well as the cathode porosity was optimized to further enhance the rate capability. Further improvement was accomplished by optimized electrolyte formulation that contains low viscosity, low melting point solvents and optimal lithium salt concentration. In this section, we will discuss the performance of the hybrid chemistry for high rate applications.

High-Rate Hybrid Pouch Cell Development

Pouch cell with hybrid chemistry was developed to maximize cell discharge rate capability while maintaining the high energy density. The advantages for pouch cells are flexible in size design, high specific energy and inexpensive packaging material compared to hard case cells. Pouch cell format offers opportunities for better performance with reduced weight burden in portable power applications. The historic limitations for pouch cells include leakage, and swelling due to gassing and CF_x electrode expansion during discharge. Among these limitations, the major challenge for hybrid pouch cell is cell swelling due to the well-known swelling behavior of CF_x cathode during discharge. The higher the amount of CF_x in the hybrid cathode, the higher the extent of swelling was. The swelling will not only affect the battery integrity, but also will negatively impact the battery discharge performance in the pouch cell format. To address these limitations, optimized electrolyte formulation, CF_x type, pouch material selection and sealing conditions are key to mitigating the drawbacks. Figure 1 shows a picture of the high-rate hybrid pouch cell developed at EaglePicher.

The chemistry and design of the pouch cells were optimized by selecting proper cathode active material, cathode composition, carbon conductive additives, and binder. Also, for the active materials, the ratio of the amount of MnO_2 to CF_x was optimized in terms of its effect on swelling, heat generation, and energy density requirement for the high-rate battery. The cathode loading was optimized according to the process capability, energy density and power requirements for the battery. Cathode porosity was also optimized based on its effect on cathode swelling and energy density requirement for the battery.

Figure 1. Li/CFx-MnO2 Pouch Cell

Performance of the hybrid pouch cell was validated at up to 2C rate for a wide range of temperatures. Figure 2 illustrates the performance of pouch cells at different temperatures. As can be seen, the pouch cells were able to deliver high efficiency from -40°C to 60°C.

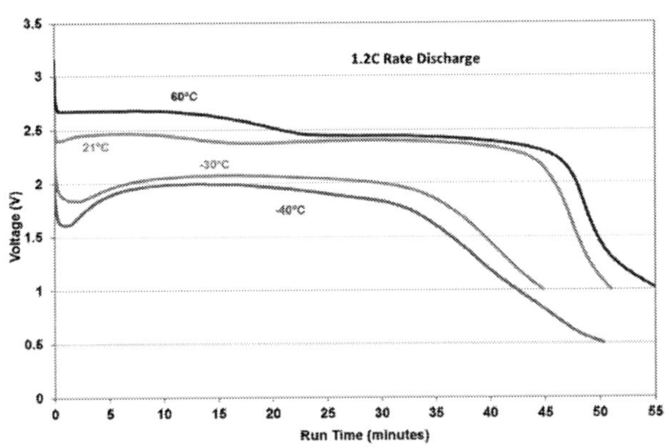

Figure 2. Discharge performance of pouch cells

Figure 3 show the discharge curves of pouch cells at 1, 1.5 and 2C rate at -40°C. In the figure it is seen that the cells exhibit good rate capability at -40°C, delivering 85 to 95% discharge efficiency. Another characteristic of the curves is that the higher the rate, the higher the cell discharge efficiency at -40°C. This can be explained by the heat effect of the battery. The higher discharge rate will generate higher amount of heat, making the battery discharge at a warmer temperature, thus working at a higher voltage, and delivering higher capacity.

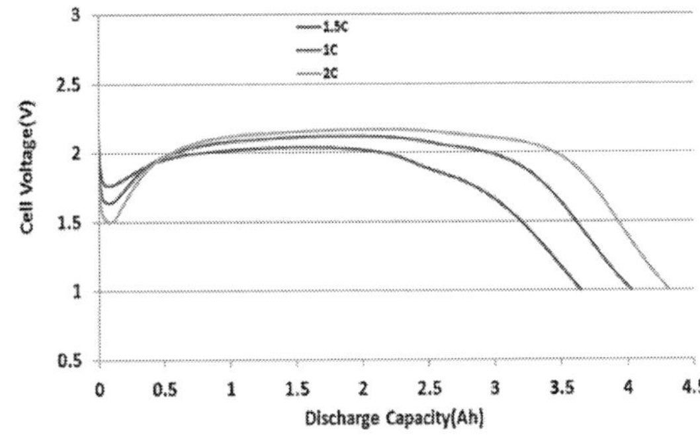

Figure 3. Pouch Cell Rate Capability at -40°C

Figure 4 shows a projection of the discharge power of a battery that contains 18 pouch cells. The battery would be about 13-cm long, with 18 pouch cells piled up inside. Each pouch cell was discharged at 2C rate. It is seen in Figure 4 that the battery is projected to deliver a maximum power of about 340W at a low surrounding temperature of -40°C. This indicates that the hybrid chemistry is a suitable power source for applications requiring high power capability in a wide operating temperature range.

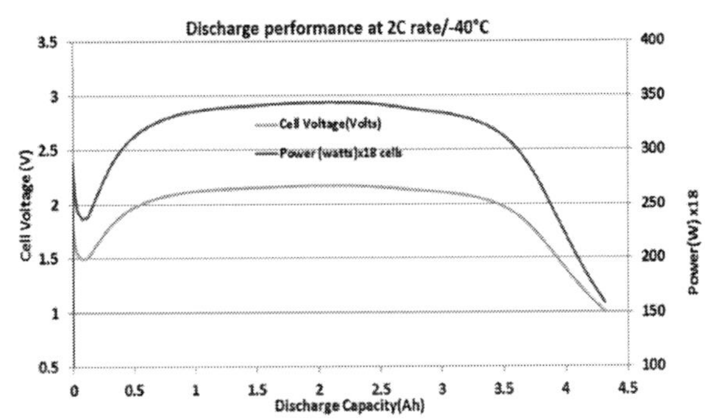

Figure 4. Projected Power Capability of a 18-Cell Battery

In summary, EaglePicher has made great progress in developing a high rate hybrid technology, with improved rate capability and extended operating temperature ranging from -40 to 60°C. The hybrid chemistry pouch cells provide an opportunity to develop lightweight, compact and versatile batteries for low and high temperature applications.

Further improvement opportunities include optimizing cell design and chemistry to extend operating temperature range (-50 to 70°C) without sacrificing rate capability and discharge efficiency; optimizing CF_x to MnO_2 weight ratio; incorporating carbon additive materials with improved conductivity and suitable physical structure;

optimizing cathode porosity; developing electrolyte with improved conductivity; evaluating aqueous binder; and incorporating electrolyte additives to improve cathode wettability.

Acknowledgement

This material is released to the public domain in accordance with ITAR 22 CFR 120.11.

References

1. Marple, J. W., "Performance characteristics of Li/MnO_2-CFx hybrid cathode jellyroll cells" *Journal of Powers Sources*, vol. 19, pp.325-335, 1987.
2. Leger, V. Z., "Non aqueous cell having a MnO_2/polycarbon fluoride cathode," US patent 4327166, April 1982.
3. Zhang, D., E. Ndzebet, and M. Yang, "Advanced Battery Chemistry for Portable Power," *Proceeding of the 44th Power Sources Conference*, Las Vegas, Nevada, 14-17 June 2010.
4. Destephen, M., D. Zhang, H. Bang, J. Wang, U. Viswanathan, and E. Ndzebet, "Advanced Hybrid Battery Chemistry for Portable Power," *Proceeding of the 45th Power Sources Conference*, Las Vegas, Nevada, 11-14 June 2012.
5. Destephen, M., D. Zhang, H. Bang, and E. Ndzebet, "Advanced Li/CFx-MnO2 Hybrid Technology Development," *The 46th Power Sources Conference*, Orlando, Florida, June 9-12, 2014.
6. Read, J., D. Foster, J. Wolfenstine, and S. Zhang, "Microcalorimetry of Li/CFx Cells and Discharge Mechanism", *www.arl.army.mil/arlreports/2009/ARL-TR-5043.pdf*, 2009.

Science & Technology Efforts Supporting Soldier Power at CERDEC

Michael Brundage
Chief, Tactical Power Branch,
US Army RDECOM CERDEC CP&ID
Michael.t.brundage2.civ@mail.mil

Abstract
Current and future warfighters rely heavily on electronics and electronic devices to maintain tactical superiority over their adversaries. These devices provide mission flexibility, agility, information dominance, and lethality, and they all require ever-increasing amounts of power and energy. Soldiers are called on to conduct constantly changing missions at the small unit operational levels (individual soldier, squad, and platoon), and each of these has their own unique power and energy requirements and Concepts of Operation (CONOPS). This presentation will describe in some detail the technologies and concepts that are currently under development and emerging at the US Army Research Development & Engineering Command (RDECOM), Communications-Electronics Research Development & Engineering Center (CERDEC), Command, Power & Integration Directorate (CP&ID), Power Division located at Aberdeen Proving Ground, Aberdeen, MD. CERDEC's current technology development programs addressing soldier and small unit power and energy (Tactical Power Generation (TPG) and Advanced Integrated Soldier Power (AISP)) will be highlighted. The presentation will also focus on requirements, priorities and 5-year and 10-year technology development program plans that will enable existing and potential academic and industry partners to better understand the Army's technical direction in terms of small unit power and energy.

Conductivity of Dense Li-ion Solid Conductors

Jeff Wolfenstine[1], Jan Allen[1], Travis Thompson[2] and Jeff Sakamoto[2]

[1]Army Research Laboratory
2800 Powder Mill Road
Adelphi, MD 20783
[2]University of Michigan
Department of Mechanical Engineering
Ann Arbor, MI 48109

Abstract: The Li-ion conductivity of three materials with different structures; $Li_{1.2}Sr_{0.1}Zr_{1.9}(PO_4)_3$, $Li_{0.33}La_{0.57}TiO_3$ and $Li_{6.5}Al_{0.25}La_3Zr_2O_{12}$ all consolidated to high relative density (>97%) was measured at room temperature. It was observed that $Li_{6.5}Al_{0.25}La_3Zr_2O_{12}$ exhibited the highest total conductivity of 5 x 10^{-4} S/cm. For $Li_{1.2}Sr_{0.1}Zr_{1.9}(PO_4)_3$ and $Li_{0.33}La_{0.57}TiO_3$ the total conductivity was 1.2 x 10^{-6} and 6 x 10^{-5} S/cm, respectively. Of the three, $Li_{6.5}Al_{0.25}La_3Zr_2O_{12}$ is the best choice for a solid Li-ion conducting electrolyte for use with a Li anode.

Keywords: structure; conductivity; grain boundary

Introduction

Solid Li-ion conductivity electrolytes are receiving attention because their use can lead to higher energy and safer batteries compared to current Li-ion batteries using organic electrolytes. One of the major requirements is high Li-ion conductivity. The Li-ion conductivity of a solid electrolyte is a function of crystal structure, chemistry and microstructure. It is the purpose of this paper to compare the ionic conductivity of three Li-ion conductors with different crystal structures; $Li_{1.2}Sr_{0.1}Zr_{1.9}(PO_4)_3$ (NaSICON structure), $Li_{0.33}La_{0.57}TiO_3$ (Perovskite structure) and $Li_{6.5}Al_{0.25}La_3Zr_2O_{12}$ (Garnet structure) all consolidated to high relative density (>97%).

Experimental

$Li_{1.2}Sr_{0.1}Zr_{1.9}(PO_4)_3$ [LSZP], $Li_{0.33}La_{0.57}TiO_3$ [LLTO] and $Li_{6.5}Al_{0.25}La_3Zr_2O_{12}$ [LLZO] powders were prepared using solid-state methods. LSZP and LLZO were consolidated to high relative density using hot-pressing. LLTO powders were consolidated to high relative density using a two-step procedure which consisted of sintering to about 94% relative density followed by hot-isostatic pressing. The phase purity after consolidation was determined by X-ray diffraction. The relative density was determined by comparing the measured density using the Archimedes' method (hexane as the immersion fluid) to the theoretical density determined by X-ray diffraction.

The microstructure (e.g., fracture mode/.grain size) of the specimens was characterized on fracture surfaces using scanning electron microscopy (SEM). Platinum or gold was sputter coated on the top and bottom sample surfaces. The impedance spectra of the samples at room temperature was characterized in the frequency range of 1 to 10^6 Hz using a 100 mV AC amplitude. From this information and the sample dimensions the bulk, grain boundary and total conductivity was determined by fitting the spectra using ZView software. The electronic conductivity was determined from DC polarization measurements on the same samples using a 1-3 V DC bias from the steady-state currents and sample dimensions.

Results and Discussion

X-ray diffraction confirmed after consolidation that LSZP, LLZO and LLTO were all single phase. The relative density of LSZP, LLZO and LLTO was 97, 98 and 99% respectively. The microstructure of the LSTP, LLZO and LLTO samples is shown in Figures 2-4 respectively. From Figures 2-4 the following can observed. Firstly, the fracture mode for LSZP was primarily intergranular. In contrast, LLTO and LLZO exhibited primarily transgranular fracture, which implies strong bonding across the grain boundaries.

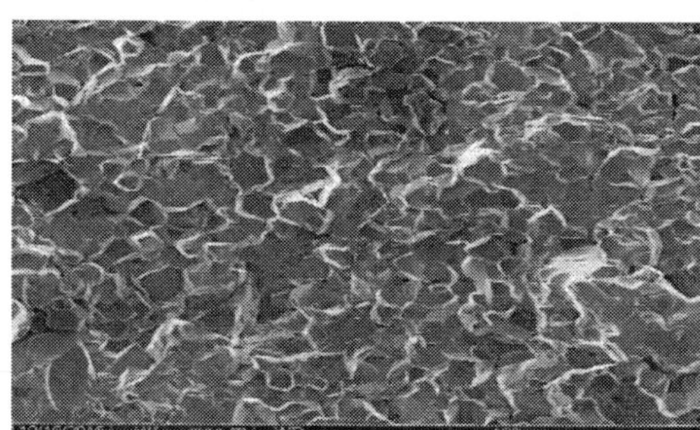

Fig. 1. $Li_{1.2}Sr_{0.1}Zr_{1.9}(PO_4)_3$ fracture surface.

Secondly the grain size of LSZP, LLZO and LLTO is about 15, 5 and 3 um, respectively.

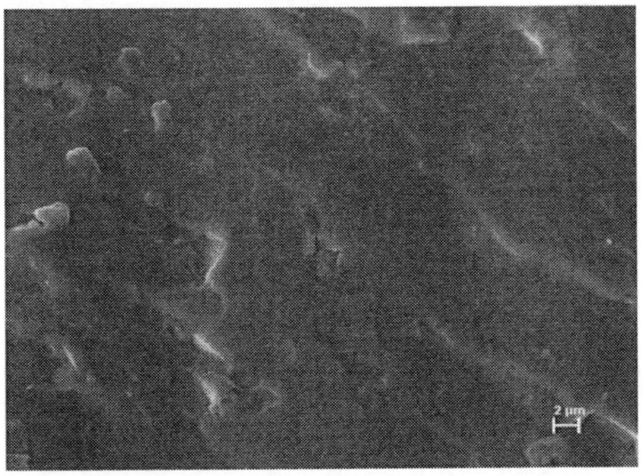

Fig. 2. $Li_{6.5}Al_{0.25}La_3Zr_2O_{12}$ fracture surface.

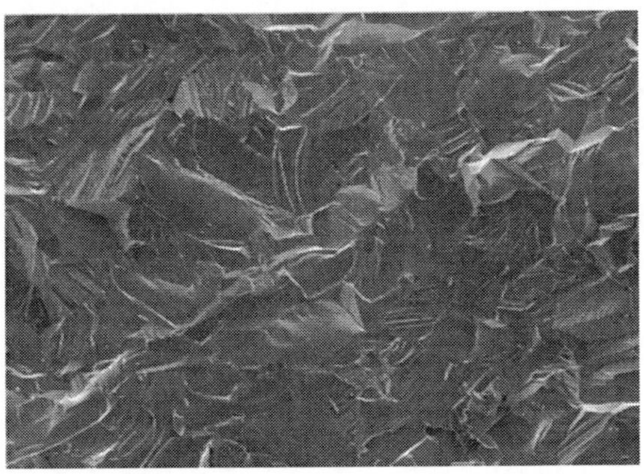

Fig. 3. $Li_{0.33}La_{0.57}TiO_3$ fracture surface.

A represenative impedance plot and polarization curve is shown in Figures 4 and 5, respectively. Analysis of the impedance data revealed that LLZO had the highest total conductivity (5 x 10^{-4} S/cm) followed by LLTO (6 x 10^{-5} S/cm) with LSZP the lowest (1 x 10^{-6} S/cm). LLTO had the highest lattice (1.5 x 10^{-3} S/cm) followed by LLZO (5.4 x 10^{-4} S/cm) with LSZP having the lowest (3.5 x 10^{-5} S/cm). The electronic conductivity values for the LLZO, LSZP and LLTO were 1 x 10^{-9}, 1 x 10^{-10} and 3 x 10^{-8} S/cm, respectively. The ionic transfer number for all three materials is approximately equal to unity. Thus, LLZO, LSZP and LLZO are potential solid Li-ion conducting electrolytes. It should be noted that LLZO is stable with Li at room temperature and that in first approximation LSZP should also be. However, LLTO is not stable with Li as a result of the reduction of some Ti^{+4} to Ti^{+3} leading to a mixed conductor. Consequently, LLZO is the best choice of the three to be used as a solid electrolyte when using Li as the anode.

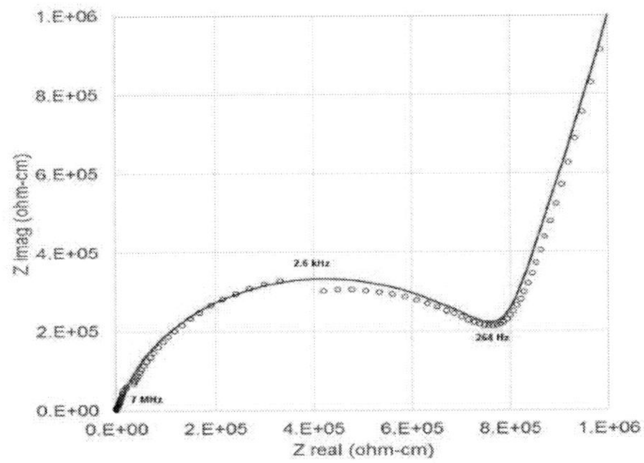

Fig 5. Impedance curve for $Li_{1.2}Sr_{0.1}Zr_{1.9}(PO_4)_3$.

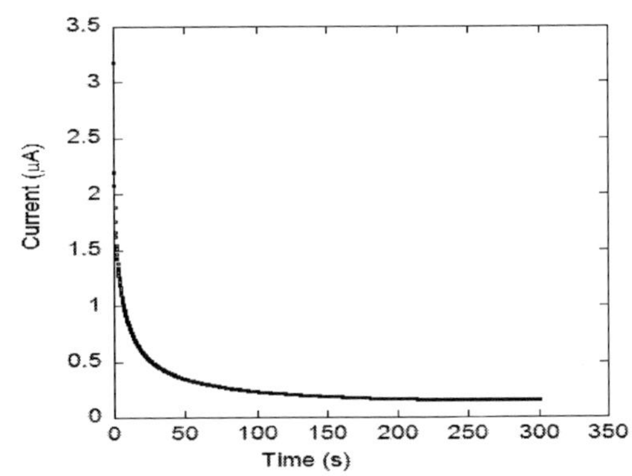

Fig. 5. Polarization curve for $Li_{0.33}La_{0.57}TiO_3$.

One interesting aspect of this study is that even though all three materials exhibited high relative density, the grain boundary resistance (R_{GB}) to the total resistance (R_T) of LSZP (about 70%) and LLTO (about 94%) is very high compared to LLZO (about 8 %). Analytical electron microscopy [1] for the case of LLTO has revealed the absence of Li at the grain boundaries, consequently, this can explain why this material exhibits a high R_{GB}/R_T. For the case of LSZP since, it has a NaSCION structure that cooling from high temperature to room temperature can result in microcracking at the grain boundaries if the grain size is too large [2]. The critical grain size to prevent microcracking for LSZP based on existing data suggests that it should be 3 um or less. Since the grain size of the LSZP material (about 15 um) is above the critical grain size, microcracking is expected and does occur as observed in SEM micrographs (Figure 6).

Fig 6. $Li_{1.2}Sr_{0.1}Zr_{1.9}(PO_4)_3$ fracture surface. The box shows microcracking at the grain boundary.

Summary

The Li-ion conductivity of three solid electrolyte materials with different structures; $Li_{1.2}Sr_{0.1}Zr_{1.9}(PO_4)_3$, $Li_{0.33}La_{0.57}TiO_3$ and $Li_{6.5}Al_{0.25}La_3Zr_2O_{12}$ all consolidated to high relative density (>97%) was measured at room temperature. $Li_{6.5}Al_{0.25}La_3Zr_2O_{12}$ exhibited the highest total conductivity (5 x 10^{-4} S/cm) of the three. The grain boundary resistance to total resistance for each material was determined. The high grain boundary resistance of $Li_{0.33}La_{0.57}TiO_3$ is a result of no Li at the grain boundaries. The high grain boundary resistance $Li_{1.2}Sr_{0.1}Zr_{1.9}(PO_4)_3$ is a result of microcracking at the grain boundaries. The low grain boundary resistance of $Li_{6.5}Al_{0.25}La_3Zr_2O_{12}$ is associated with its cubic structure. Of the three, $Li_{6.5}Al_{0.25}La_3Zr_2O_{12}$ is best choice for a solid Li-ion conducting electrolyte for use with a Li anode.

Acknowledgements

JW and JA would like to acknowledge support of the U. S. Army Research Laboratory. JS and TT would like to acknowledge support from the Battery Materials Research Program, Department of Energy (Award DE-EE-000682).

References

1. M. Cheng, K. Chen, C. Liang , C-W. Nan, R. Ishikawa, K. More, M. Chi (2014) Energy & Environmental Science 7:1638.
2. J. J.Cleveland, R. C. Bradt (1978) J. Am. Ceram. Soc. 61:478.

Anion Intercalation Compounds for Energy Storage

Jeffrey A. Read
U.S. Army Research Laboratory
RDRL-SED-C
2800 Powder Mill Road
Adelphi, MD 20783-1197

Abstract: *The challenge of building an electrochemical cell using graphite intercalation compounds at both electrodes is difficult due to the lack of suitable electrolytes. An electrolyte system based on monofluoroethylene carbonate (FEC) and ethylmethyl carbonate (EMC) has demonstrated improved stability on graphite cathodes when compared to other high voltage electrolytes, and forms a stable solid electrolyte interphase (SEI) on graphite anodes, which allows for full dual-graphite cells to be evaluated for energy storage*[1]. *There is a limited understanding as to the exact nature of the anion intercalate formed in these systems as well as the effect of solvent co-intercalation on cathode stability and structure, a critical factor in their cycling and storage performance. We recently characterized the* PF_6^- *intercalate from FEC:EMC using a number of in-situ techniques and determined that a stage I compound* $C_{20}PF_6$ *with anion in close contact with the graphite layers is formed at full charge. Significant volume change occurs in the graphite cathode due to expansion of the c-axis in graphite to allow for anion insertion. Solvent co-intercalation occurs at a rate of ~ 0.7 solvent molecules per anion with a strong preference for EMC over FEC to co-intercalate. This paper discusses the effects of anion intercalate structure on energy density, specific energy, and the cell design for an storage system based on anion intercalation.*

Keywords: in-situ studies; anion intercalation; dual graphite cells.

Introduction

Electrochemical cells that utilize a graphite intercalation compound (GIC) as cathode have been demonstrated by a number of researchers.[2,3,4,5,6,7,8,9] Anions that can be electrochemically intercalated into graphite include among others ClO_4^-, BF_4^-, PF_6^-, $AlCl_4^-$, $CF_3SO_3^-$, $(CF_3SO_2)_2N^-$, as well as the fluoride-anion acceptor complexes.[1-6,9] The dual-carbon cell with non-aqueous electrolyte was first proposed as a rechargeable battery in patents by McCullough et al.[10,11,12,13] In a dual-carbon cell, the lithium salt is electrolyzed on charge with the Li^+ being stored in the anode and the anion intercalating into the cathode. The salt is depleted from the electrolyte on charge and replenished upon discharge with the energy capable of being stored in practical cells depending on the concentration and molecular weight of the electrolyte salt.[14]

Anion intercalation into graphite occurs at potentials near 5V and therefore the oxidation of both electrolyte solvent and anion is of major concern. The electrolyte solvents that have been investigated previously include propylene carbonate, ethylene carbonate, dimethyl sulfoxide, dimethylformamide, ethyl methyl sulfone, and the ionic liquid $Pyr_{14}TFSI$. These solvents show varying degrees of stability at high potential, with EMS giving the best overall results in terms of capacity and efficiency. The stability of the electrolyte solvent has been cited as the reason for cycling efficiencies of less than 100% and the poor storage performance of the anion intercalated graphite.[9] These electrolyte solvents are poor choices for intercalation of lithium ions into graphite anodes as they co-intercalate causing exfoliation and destruction of the graphite anode lattice, although recent work suggest that SEI forming additives may be used to stabilize the graphite anode towards the ionic liquid electrolyte based on $Pyr_{14}TFSI$.[15] Electrolytes based on EC, a critical component in most lithium-ion electrolytes, shows poor stability at 5.2V with significant oxidation and gas generation and therefore cannot be used for dual-graphite cells. In order to make a dual-graphite energy storage system feasible, an electrolyte system capable of high efficiencies on both the anode and cathode needed to be found. Our recent work[1] suggests that the $LiPF_6$ FEC:EMC electrolyte system is a step in that direction, with sufficient stability on graphite cathodes and excellent stability on graphite anodes that allows for full dual graphite cells to be evaluated.

Studies on the exact nature of the PF_6^- intercalate of graphite have been undertaken in various solvent systems. These efforts have mainly used X-Ray diffraction, dilatometry, chemical analysis and NMR to try and determine the intercalate layer spacing (d_i), molecular orientation, and chemical composition of the intercalated anion. Billaud et.al. prepared PF_6^- intercalated HOPG by chemical oxidation using NO_2PF_6 dissolved in nitromethane.[16] In-situ XRD studies, chemical analysis, and thickness measurements all indicated that a stage II intercalate, $C_{48}PF_6(CH_3NO_2)_2$, where every other graphite layer is occupied with PF_6^- anion, had formed as the end product with an intercalate layer spacing (d_i) of 7.75Å. Touzain and Bonnetain studied the electrochemical intercalation of PF_6^- from propylene carbonate[17] and concluded that the final product of charge at 5.2V was the Stage I compound $C_{24}PF_6(PC)_4$ where every layer is intercalated with anion. This Stage I product could not be isolated for analysis, but the Stage II compound, $C_{48}PF_6(PC)_4$ was analyzed using ex-situ XRD and was determined to have a d_i of 14.0Å. Zhang and Lerner studied PF_6^- intercalation from $NaPF_6$ in PC and nitromethane using ex-situ XRD.[18] The stage I product $C_{24}PF_6$ was formed with the amount of solvent co-intercalation not determined. The stage I product intercalated from nitromethane was noted to be particularly stable with a d_i of 8.0 Å. Seel and Dahn studied the electrochemical intercalation of PF_6^- from ethyl methyl sulfone electrolyte.[5] In-situ XRD was performed and the stage II compound, $C_8(PF_6)_{0.5}$ was the predicted final composition with a d_i of 4.47Å. The degree of solvent co-intercalation was not determined.

Our recent work demonstrated that PF_6^- intercalated from FEC:EMC forms a series of compounds culminating in the Stage I composition $C_{20}PF_6$ at 5.2V[19]. We characterized the anion intercalate using in-situ XRD, in-situ dilatometry, gravimetry, and analysis of fully charged HOPG crystals. Determining the true structure of the anion intercalate is important as this will set limits on critical performance parameters for the dual-graphite cell. The structure determines the ultimate charge storage capacity, cathode swelling behavior, and charge transfer resistance, while co-intercalation of solvent will affect both rate capability and can determine electrolyte composition, concentration and volume. This paper discusses some of the effects our results have on the predicted energy density of an anion intercalation energy storage cell.

Discussion

The voltage versus specific capacity curve for the initial charge of an in-situ XRD cell is shown in Figure 1. Figure 2 shows the indexed phases plotted in log [relative intensity] format with assigned Miller indices in order to show the low angle, low intensity peaks. Assignment of the stage for each of the indexed phases is not possible using XRD alone as it is possible to have a stage I GIC with the same I_c unit cell dimension as a stage II GIC but with a different structure.

In order to determine the stage of each observed phase, in-situ dilatometry was performed on the same cell discussed above after the in-situ XRD and 10 full charge / discharge cycles had been completed. The large change in crystal thickness upon cycling (0.117 - 0.120 mm) was comparable to the initial thickness (0.117 mm) and represents a 100% change in thickness upon anion intercalation/de-intercalation. This magnitude of change is only consistent with the formation of a stage I intercalate at full charge with an intercalate layer spacing of 7.75 Å. The thickness of the crystal was measured post cycling and registered a final thickness of 0.272 mm, a 133% increase in thickness from the pristine crystal, in line with the 130-131% change expected for a stage I intercalate. Table 1 shows all of the indexed phases B-E′ with corresponding I_c axis unit cell dimension, the calculated values and the expected percent

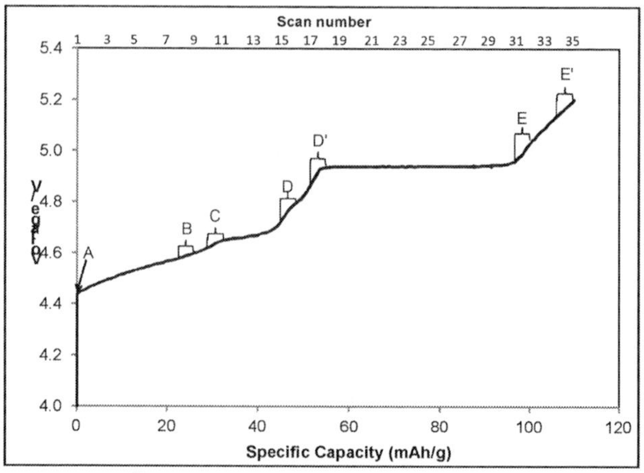

Figure 1. 1st charge curve of cell X4 during anion intercalation. Labels A-E' correspond to the XRD spectra shown in Figure 2.

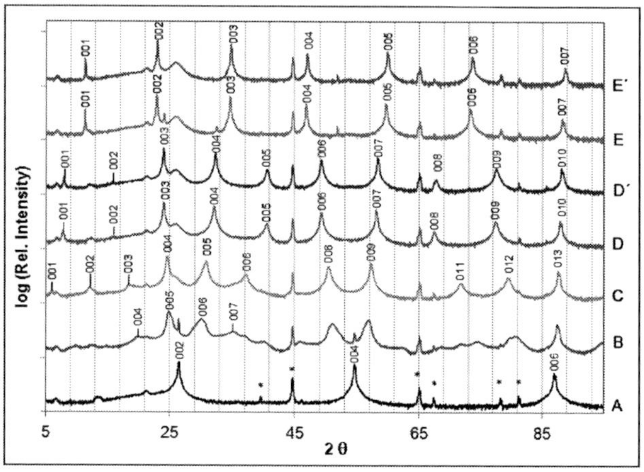

Figure 2. Indexed single phases A-E' from cell X4
* indicates peaks from aluminum pouch material.

Table 1. Observed phases with calculated I_c and percent expansion in c lattice over graphite (Δc).
Graphite layer spacing = 3.361 Å
$I_c = d_i + (n-1)3.361$Å.

Observed Phase	I_c	Calculated Stage	d_i = 7.755 / 7.725Å I_c	Δc
B	17.85	IV	17.84	33%
C	14.48	III	14.48	44%
D	11.11	II	11.12	65%
D'	11.09	II	11.09	65%
E	7.755	I	7.755	131%
E'	7.725	I	7.725	130%

expansion (Δc) in the I_c unit cell dimension with intercalation to the various stages I through IV. Two different values for d_i are used in these calculations with phases D' and E' calculated using the smaller d_i values as the lattice appears to contract upon the formation of these phases. Based on our results, we can calculate the size of the PF_6^- anion in the graphite layers from the stage I values in Table 1. Given the graphite layer spacing of 3.361Å and an intercalated layer spacing (d_i) of 7.755-7.725Å, the calculated diameter of the PF_6^- anion would be 4.394-4.364Å. This value is close to the diameter of the PF_6^- anion as calculated from the bond length of PF_6^- and the covalent radii of fluorine (4.36 Å) but smaller than the diameter based on ion volume (5.93 Å). The data would suggest that the PF_6^- anion is in close contact with the graphite sheets when intercalated.

Taking a closer look at both the in-situ XRD and dilatometry data, we can look for evidence of specific compositions, such as $C_{24}PF_6$, $C_{20}PF_6$, or $C_{18}PF_6$ being formed upon cycling. A comparison of the charge capacities for the formation of phases B-E' from a number of experiments along with the theoretical capacities of several anion intercalation compounds we can propose the following sequence of compositions:

$C_{24}PF_6$ (IV) → $C_{24}PF_6$ (III) → $C_{24}PF_6$ (II) → $C_{20}PF_6$ (II) → $C_{24}PF_6$ (I) → $C_{20}PF_6$ (I)

The transitions between $C_{24}PF_6$ stages are two phase in nature with the average number of graphite layers between anions changing over the course of the transformation, while the transitions between $C_{24}PF_6$ and $C_{20}PF_6$ stages can be thought of as solid solution transitions where more anion is simply packed between already intercalated graphite layers.

The XRD and dilatometry data give a good indication of the overall structure of the anion intercalation compound, but do not give the full composition. It has been found that the weight gain observed in a number of anion intercalation compounds is larger than can be accounted for by anion intercalation alone.[16,17,20] This extra weight gain has been determined to be due to the co-intercalation of solvent with the anion. We determined the weight gain of fully charged HOPG cathodes in 1.7m $LiPF_6$ FEC:EMC (1:1 w/w) electrolyte for a number of samples and the average increase in weight for a crystal is 92%, corresponding to ~0.7 solvent molecules for each PF_6^- anion. The fact that there is a range of weight uptake values might indicate that the solvent is poorly bound to the anion during the intercalation process and therefore a range of values is admitted, or that the crystals are not fully intercalated to the $C_{20}PF_6$ composition in all cases. In addition, it was determined using GC-MS, that there was a strong preference for co-intercalation of EMC with the PF_6^- anion, with the ratio of EMC:FEC at 10:1 in the fully intercalated crystal.

The basis for pursuing a dual-graphite energy storage cell is based on the idea that the cost will be lower than conventional Li-ion chemistries, mainly due to the fact that a transition metal cathode will not be used in the battery, and that the system will be safer than other grid storage batteries due to the fact that overcharge can be controlled by limiting the salt concentration in the electrolyte. The main drawback of the dual-graphite chemistry is that the specific energy and energy density is limited both by the anion intercalation capacity of the graphite, and by the amount of salt that can be dissolved in the electrolyte. Based on our results[1,19] that stage I $C_{20}PF_6$ is the maximum composition formed at 5.2V, and that upon discharge to 4.0V, stage IV $C_{24}PF_6$ is the lowest composition formed, the cycling capacity for the cathode under typical conditions is 89 mAh/g graphite. This is close to that observed for the best electrolyte systems studied. The maximum solubility of $LiPF_6$ salt in carbonate based solvents is typically in the range of 1.5 to 3M. For the electrolyte system we investigated, the maximum electrolyte concentration prepared was 2.0M.
To determine the energy density of an actual dual-graphite cell, the significant change in cathode volume has to be taken into account as the cell design will require allowances for expansion. If we allow for doubling the volume of the cathode active material, we estimate that the cathode porosity should be 60% in the uncharged state. Given this required porosity, we can calculate the energy density and specific energy for this dual-graphite cell if we use equations developed from the work of Dahn and Seel.[14] Assuming an anode thickness, we can calculate appropriately matched cathode and separator thickness and then the specific capacity and energy density from equations 1- 4 below:

$$t_c = \frac{t_a(1-\varphi_a)q_a}{(1-\varphi c)q_c} \qquad \text{Eq. 1}$$

$$t_e = \frac{t_a(1-\varphi_a)q_a\rho_a}{\varphi_s(M_d - M_c)R} - \frac{t_a\varphi_a}{\varphi_s} - \frac{t_a(1-\varphi_a)q_a\varphi_c}{(1-\varphi_c)q_c\varphi_s} \qquad \text{Eq. 2}$$

$$Wh/kg = \frac{V(M_d - M_c)R[t_a\varphi_a + t_c\varphi_c + t_e\varphi_s]}{(t_a + t_c + t_e)} \qquad \text{Eq. 3}$$

$$Wh/l = \frac{V(M_d - M_c)R[t_a\varphi_a + t_c\varphi_c + t_e\varphi_s]}{t_a(1-\varphi_a)\rho_a + t_c(1-\varphi_c)\rho_c + t_e\varphi_s\rho_e + t_e(1-\varphi_s)\rho_s} \qquad \text{Eq. 4}$$

Based on the parameters in Table 2, we calculate an energy density of 127 Wh/l and a specific energy of 107 Wh/kg for the dual-graphite cell. With a 20% de-rating for inert materials such as cell case, collectors, and

Table 2. Parameters for use in Eq. 1-4

Parameter	Value
Anode capacity, (q_a)	340 mAh/g
Cathode capacity, (q_c)	89 mAh/g
Molarity when charged, (M_c)	0.5M
Molarity when discharged, (M_d)	2.0M
Average cell voltage (V)	4.7V
Graphite density (ρ_a)	2.2 g/cm^3
Electrolyte density (ρ_e)	1.4 g/cm^3
Separator density (ρ_s)	1.0 g/cm^3
Anode Porosity (φ_a)	0.3
Cathode Porosity (φ_c)	0.6
Separator Porosity (φ_s)	0.75
Anode thickness (t_a)	100 µm
Cathode thickness (t_c)	670 µm
Separator thickness (t_s)	1160 µm
charge stored per liter of 1 M electrolyte solution (R)	26.8 Ah/liter M

tabs, these values become 102 Wh/l and 86 Wh/kg. These values are calculated in a way such that the capacities of the anode and cathode are matched, and sufficient anion is available in the electrolyte for the required charge storage capacity of both electrodes. The energy density and specific capacity are independent of the absolute electrode thicknesses. When compared to Li-ion cells, 600 Wh/l and 230 Wh/kg, these dual-graphite values are low and demonstrate that this system will not be competitive in conventional mobile applications due to the low energy density but could still provide significant specific energy for microgrid applications.

Conclusions

Anion intercalation compounds can be used as cathodes in dual-graphite cells utilizing FEC:EMC based electrolytes. With a demonstrated cycling capacity of 89 mAh/g between 4.0 and 5.2V, cells with specific energies approaching 90 Wh/kg could be built. The large volume expansion observed for the graphite cathode results in a significant reduction in energy density from previously calculated values[21] as sufficient cathode porosity has to be provided in the working actual electrode. The energy density and specific energy of dual-graphite cells is lower than conventional Li-ion, although for grid storage applications, cost, service life, and safety are the typically the most important factors. Cell safety needs to be explored for these dual-graphite systems to determine if it is significantly better than conventional Li-ion.

Acknowledgements

The author would like to acknowledge Dr. Janet Ho for help with dilatometry, Dr. Jan Allen for helpful discussion on XRD indexing, Dr. Kang Xu, and Dr. Arthur Cresce for electrolytes and the US Army Research Laboratory for financial support.

References

[1] J.A. Read, A.V. Cresce, M. H. Ervin and K. Xu, *Energy Environ. Sci.*, 7, 617 (2014).

[2] R.T. Carlin, H.C. De Long, J. Fuller, and P. Trulove, *J. Electrochem. Soc.*, **141** (7) L73 (1994)

[3] R. Santhanam, M. Noel, *Journal of Power Sources*, **66**, 47-54 (1997)

[4] R. Santhanam, M. Noel, *Journal of Power Sources*, **76**, 147-152 (1998)

[5] J.A. Seel and J.R. Dahn, *J. Electrochem. Soc.*, **147** (3) 892-898 (2000)

[6] W.C. West, J.F. Whitacre, N. Leifer, S. Greenbaum, M. Smart, R. Bugga, M. Blanco, and S.R. Narayanan, *J. Electrochem. Soc.*, **154** (10) A929 (2007)

[7] T. Ishihara, M. Koga, H Matsumoto, and M. Yoshio, *Electrochem. Solid State Lett.* , **10** (3), A74 (2007)

[8] N. Gunawardhana, G-J Park, N. Dimov, A. K. Thapa, H. Nakamura, H. Wang, T. Ishihara, M. Yoshio, *Journal of Power Sources*, **196**, 7886 (2011)

[9] T. Placke, O. Fromm, S.F. Lux, P. Bieker, S. Rothermel, H-W Meyer, S. Passerini, W. Winter, *J. Electrochem. Soc.*, **159** (11) A1755-A1765 (2012)

[10] F.P. McCullough, A. Levine, and R.V. Snelgrove, U.S. Patent 4,830,938 (1989).

[11] F.P. McCullough and A.F. Beale, U.S. Patent 4,865,931 (1989).

[12] F.P. McCullough, U.S. Patent 5,518,836 (1996).

[13] F.P. McCullough, U.S. Patent 5,532,083 (1996).

[14] J.R. Dahn and J.A. Seel, *J. Electrochem. Soc.*, **147** (3) 899 (2000)

[15] S. Rothermel, P. Meister, O. Fromm, J. Huesker, H.W. Meyer, M. Winter, T. Placke, *ECS Transactions*, **58** (14) 15-25 (2014).

[16] D. Billaud, A. Pron, F. Lincoln Vogel, and A. Herold, *Mat. Res. Bull.*, **15**, 1627-1634 (1980).

[17] A.J. Touzain and L. Bonnetain, *Carbon*, **19** 193-198 (1981).

[18] Z. Zhang and M. Lerner, *J. Electrochem. Soc.*, **140** (3) 742 (1993).

[19] J.A. Read, *J. Phys. Chem. C*, 119 (16) 8438 (2015)

[20] G.R. Miller, H.A. Resing, F.L. Vogel, A. Pron, T.C. Wu, and D. Billaud, *J. Phys. Chem.*, **84** (25) 3333 (1980).

[21] J.A. Read, A.v. Cresce, M. H. Ervin, and Kang Xu, *46th Power Sources Conf. Proc., Paper 20.1*

Multi-element Substituted Lithium Cobalt Phosphate Li-ion Cathode

Jan L. Allen, Joshua L. Allen, Samuel A. Delp
Jeff Wolfenstine and T. Richard Jow
Sensors & Electron Device Directorate
US Army Research Laboratory
Adelphi, Maryland, USA, 20783

Abstract: *There is an ever-growing need for higher energy batteries that are abuse tolerant. $LiCoPO_4$ is a promising cathode material to enable high energy, abuse tolerant Li-ion batteries owing to its relatively high discharge capacity of up to 167 mAh g^{-1} at a discharge potential of ~4.8V and the known abuse tolerance of phosphate based cathodes. However unmodified $LiCoPO_4$ shows a severe loss of discharge capacity upon multiple charge – discharge cycles owing to structure deterioration and electrolyte decomposition. The intense development of high voltage electrolytes and strategies that improve the cycle life, discharge capacity and rate capability have increased the interest in this material. Recent advances in chemical substitution of $LiCoPO_4$ and high voltage stabilizing electrolyte additives now show that capacity fade can be significantly reduced. This paper will review our most recent efforts on $LiCoPO_4$ electrode development for improving the energy and abuse tolerance of Li-ion batteries. We will discuss synthesis methods, transport measurements, substitutional chemistry of $LiCoPO_4$ and performance enhancements that result from reformulating the electrolyte.*

Keywords: Li-ion; battery; cathode; $LiCoPO_4$; phospho-olivine; phosphate; rechargeable; positive electrode

Introduction

Elemental substitution of solid state battery electrode materials through solid solution is a means to tune the electrode properties to achieve improved function. $LiFePO_4$ (LFP) with the phospho-olivine structure is a well-known 3.5 V, commercialized positive electrode for Li-ion batteries. Complete substitution of Fe by Mn, Co or Ni changes the voltage of discharge to 4.1, 4.8 and 5.1 V, respectively [1-3] thus increasing the maximum theoretical energy storage from 585 Wh kg^{-1} for Fe to 685, 802 and 852 Wh kg^{-1}, respectively. $LiMnPO_4$ therefore seems to be a next logical step from LFP to boost the energy density of resultant Li-ion batteries since it falls within the region where the electrolyte is stable. However, initial work on $LiMnPO_4$ phospho-olivines [1] made it clear that the rate capability was extremely poor. It was only through elemental substitution of part of the Mn by Fe, $LiFe_{1-x}Mn_xPO_4$, that Pahdi et al [1] was able to obtain a reasonable discharge capacity. The poor rate capability can be explained by the electronic structure of $LiMnPO_4$ relative to $LiFePO_4$. Since the electronic conduction in phospho-olivines is polaronic the conduction is through hopping of a polaron which is a positive charge localized on the transition metal [4], a local M^{3+}, from site to site through the crystal. In the case of Mn^{3+}, owing to the fact that Mn^{3+} is a Jahn-Teller ion a distortion of the Mn-O bonding occurs in octahedral coordination. During electronic conduction the entire distortion must jump from site to site and thus the electron transport is slow. The substitution of Fe for Mn creates the possibility for Fe^{3+} charge carriers that much more readily move throughout the structure. The 5.1 V $LiNiPO_4$ cathode might also be if interest to use owing to its very high theoretical energy density but it is unfavorable to use as a Li-ion cathode because its electronic structure's valence band maximum (VBM) is heavily hybridized with oxygen [4]. Thus, instead of oxidizing Ni^{2+} to Ni^{3+} during charging in a Li-ion cell, a peroxide is formed which is unstable and therefore likely to be evolved as molecular oxygen. This leave $LiCoPO_4$ which has mainly transition metal character at its VBM though less so than Fe and it therefore readily forms polarons. It is also not susceptible to the Jahn-Teller effect. The 4.8V discharge potential requires a charge to 5 V which is problematic for the electrolyte. However, $LiCoPO_4$ in Li-ion cells does not cycle well [5-7]. The charged species, $CoPO_4$ is thermally unstable with respect to $Co_2P_2O_7$ [8].

$2\,CoPO_4 \rightarrow Co_2P_2O_7 + \frac{1}{2}\,O_2$.

The elemental substitution of Fe^{2+}/Fe^{3+} for Co^{2+}, $Li_{1-\delta}Co_{1-x}Fe_xPO_4$ reduces this instability and greatly improves the cycle life [9]. This may be a result of the higher transition metal character at the VBM for $LiFePO_4$ relative to $LiCoPO_4$ [4] which reduces the likelihood of oxygen evolution to form $Co_2P_2O_7$. The use of an electrolyte additive [10] further improves the cycle life. Fe substituted $LiCoPO_4$ with an electrolyte additive is compared to $LiCoPO_4$ with standard electrolyte in Figure 1. Subsequent characterization of the transport properties of $LiCo_{1-x}Fe_xPO_4$ shows improved electronic and ionic conductivity [11]. The electronic conductivity increases because Fe^{3+} type polarons have higher mobility than Co^{3+} type polarons [4]. The ionic conductivity increases owing to the creation of Li^+ vacancies as charge compensation for the Fe^{3+} substitution for Co^{2+}. However, the capacity of $Li_{1-\delta}Co_{1-x}Fe_xPO_4$ is much less than the theoretical and elemental substitutions were further explored in order to try to increase the discharge capacity. The fact that Fe^{3+} was found to substitute for Co^{2+} in $Li_{1-\delta}Co_{1-x}Fe_xPO_4$ has led to an exploration of aliovalent cations which might substitute for Co^{2+} and improve the discharge capacity. Furthermore, elemental substitution can be used to reduce the reactivity of the $LiCoPO_4$ based with the electrolyte in order to improve the coulombic efficiency and thereby increase cycle life. The improved discharge capacity and cycle life of this multi-elemental substitution of $LiCoPO_4$ are reported here.

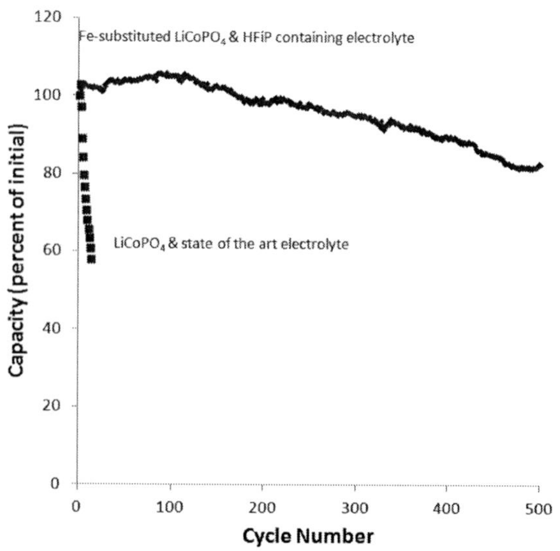

Figure 1. Comparison of cycle life of unsubstituted $LiCoPO_4$ with standard electrolyte versus Fe-substituted $LiCoPO_4$ with an electrolyte additive.

Experimental

Samples of $Li_{1+y/2}Co_{1-x-y}Fe_xM_y(PO4)_{1+y/2}$ with M = Cr, Ti, Al and / or Ga, $0 < y \leq 0.10$ and $0 \leq x \leq 0.2$ were prepared via a solid state route. Stoichiometric amounts of $Co(OH)_2$, LiH_2PO_4, Cr_2O_3, TiO_2, $Al(OH)_3$, Ga_2O_3, $FeC_2O_4.2H_2O$ and/or acetylene black (5 wt.% of final product) were ball-milled for 90 minutes then the mixture was heated at a heating rate of 10 °C min-1 to 700 °C under flowing N_2 and then the reactant mixture was held at this temperature for 12 h Samples of $Li_{1.025}Co_{0.99}Si_{0.01}Fe_{0.10}Cr_{0.05}(PO_4)_{1.025}$ (Fe, Cr- substituted $LiCoPO_4$) were prepared via the same method using $Si(OOCCH_3)_4$ as the Si source. The resulting crystalline phase(s) were identified using X-ray powder diffraction. X-ray data were collected using a Rigaku Ultima III diffractometer. For electrochemical testing, a composite electrode was fabricated by a slurry coating method. Using N-methylpyrrolidone (NMP) as solvent, a slurry was used to coat an Al foil substrate to produce a composite electrode of ca. 80 wt.% active, 10 wt.% polyvinylidene fluoride (PVDF) and 8 wt.% super-P carbon and 2 wt.% conductive carbon nanotube composite (CheapTubes.com). The electrode film was cut into small discs with an area of 0.97 cm^2, dried in drying oven at 80 °C in air before use. In a dry room (Dew point < -80 °C), Li/active coin cells (Hohsen Al-clad CR2032) were assembled using 3 layers of Celgard® 2400 as the separator and a 1.0 molal $LiPF_6$ solution in a 3:7 (wt.%) mixture of ethylene carbonate (EC) and ethyl methyl carbonate (EMC) electrolyte with 1 wt.% HFiPP (tris-hexafluoroisopropyl phosphate) or 2% TTSP (tris-trimethylsilyl phosphite). 100-150 µL of electrolyte was used per coin cell. Electrochemical testing was performed using a Maccor Series 4000 tester.

Results and Discussion

Singly substituted $LiCoPO_4$ in the absence of Fe did not show long cycle life therefore we focused on substituting elements in addition to Fe for Co including Cr, Ti, Al and Ga in order to find compositional modifications that can increase the discharge capacity of Fe-substituted $LiCoPO_4$ while maintaining long cycle life. We chose a nominal stoichiometry, $Li_{1+y/2}\,Co_{1-x-y}Fe_xM_y(PO_4)_{1+y/2}$, (M = Cr, Ti, Al and / or Ga) that favors substitution on the Co site and cation vacancies since substitution on the Li site would block Li-ion conduction. Figure 2 shows the capacity as a function of cycle for the compositions that were screened. Ti, Fe and Cr, Fe double modifications were found to be most favorable with respect to discharge capacity and cycle life. Furthermore, a composition level of 0.10 was found to be optimal for Fe and 0.05 for Ti or Cr based on longer cycling data not shown here. All samples show superior cycle life to $LiCoPO_4$ and increased discharge capacity relative to singly Fe-substituted $LiCoPO_4$, which in Figure 2 is labeled 20Fe and corresponds to nominal stoichiometry of $Li_{1-\delta}Co_{0.8}Fe_{0.2}PO_4$. The electrochemical performance and nature of this Fe-only substituted material as well as its electronic and ionic conductivity is described in detail by Allen et al. [9,11].

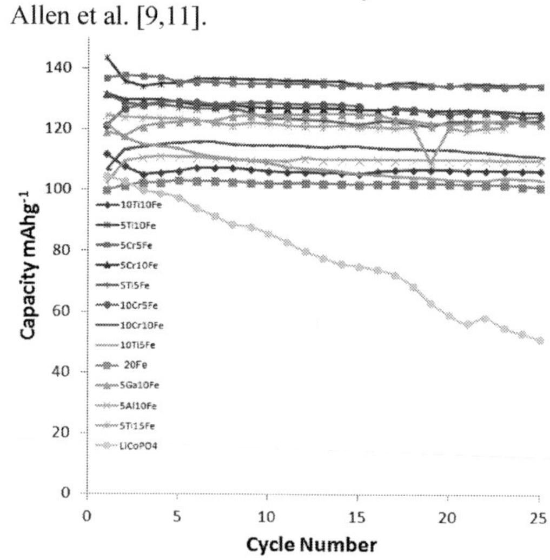

Figure 2: Discharge capacity and cycle life of doubly substituted LCP materials.

The most favorable properties in terms of high discharge capacity and long cycle life were observed for the composition $Li_{1.025}Co_{0.85}Fe_{0.10}Cr_{0.05}(PO_4)_{1.025}$. Its cycle life and discharge capacity compared to $Li_{1-\delta}Co_{0.8}Fe_{0.2}PO_4$ are shown in figure 3.

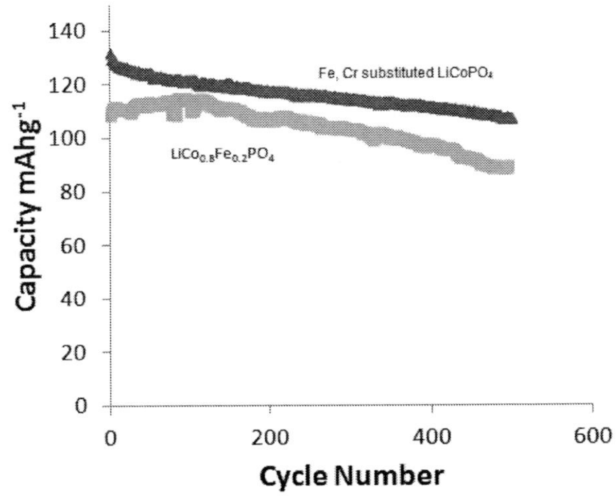

Figure 3. Comparison of cycle life and discharge capacity of Fe only substituted $LiCoPO_4$ to Fe, Cr - substituted $LiCoPO_4$.

It is clear from Figure 3 that the double substitution of Fe and Cr for Co leads to increased discharge capacity and better cycle life. However, even with the use of electrolyte additives the coulombic efficiency is too low at around 97.5% This inefficiency meaning that the charge capacity is greater than the discharge capacity is generally indicative of the electrolyte being decomposed on each cycle. Elemental substitution of Si for Co was then tried in order to reduce the reactivity of the electrode with the electrolyte and improve the coulombic efficiency owing to the increased bond strength of the Si-O bond relative to the Co-O bond which might therefore reduce its reactivity with the electrolyte. The improvement was substantial, increasing the coulombic efficiency to greater than 99% with this substitution of Si for 1% of Co. Using additional Si did not further improve the efficiency. The comparison of the discharge capacity, cycle life and coulombic efficiency of Fe, Cr substituted $LiCoPO_4$ versus Fe, Cr, Si substituted $LiCoPO_4$ is shown in Figure 4. Fe substitution improves cycle life. Cr substitution further improves cycle life and boosts the discharge capacity. Si substitution reduces the destructive reaction of the electrolyte with the high voltage cathode materials. In combination, the multi-element substituted $LiCoPO_4$ is able to achieve an energy density much greater than $LiFePO_4$ with good cycle life.

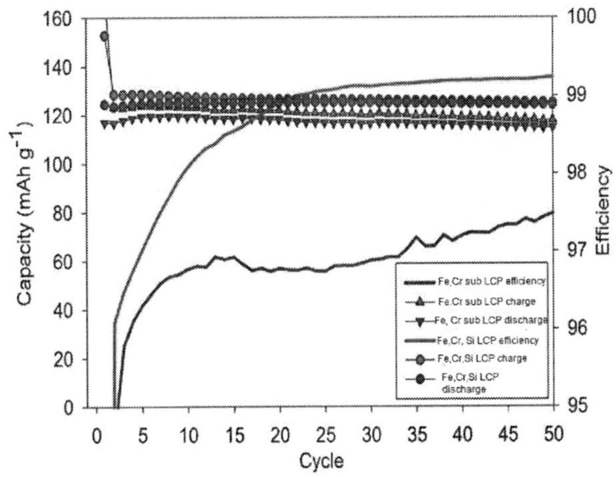

Figure 4. Comparison of cycle life, discharge capacity and coulombic efficiency of Fe, Cr- substituted $LiCoPO_4$ to Fe, Cr, Si - substituted $LiCoPO_4$.

Conclusions

It is clear that elemental substitution of solid state battery electrode materials through solid solution is a powerful means to improve the functional properties. Unsubstituted $LiCoPO_4$ has poor discharge capacity and cycle life and the 5 V operation is problematic for the electrolyte. Through multi-element substitution the cycle life, discharge capacity and the life of the electrolyte is substantially improved.

Acknowledgements

Authors acknowledge funding provided by the Army Research Laboratory.

References

1. Padhi, A.K., K.S. Nanjundaswamy, K.S., J.B. Goodenough, "Phospho-olivines as positive electrode materials for rechargeable lithium batteries," *J. Electrochem. Soc.*, vol. 144, pp. 1188-1194, 1997.
2. Amine, K., H. Yasuda, M. Yamachi, "Olivine $LiCoPO_4$ as 4.8 V electrode material for lithium batteries," *Electrochem. Solid State Lett.*, vol. 3, pp. 178-179, 2000.
3. Wolfenstine, J., J.L. Allen, "Ni^{3+}/Ni^{2+} redox potential in $LiNiPO_4$," *J. Power Sources*, vol. 142, pp.389-390, 2005.
4. Johannes, M.D., K. Hoang, J.L. Allen, K. Gaskell, "Hole polaron formation and migration in olivine phosphate materials," Phys. Rev. B, vol. 85, pp. 115106-11512, 2012.
5. Tadanaga, K., F. Mizuno, A. Hayashi, T. Minami, M. Tatsumisago, "Preparation of $LiCoPO_4$ for lithium battery cathodes through solution process," Electrochemistry, vol. 71, pp. 1192-1195, 2003.

6. Bramnik, N.N., K.G.Bramnik, T. Buhrmester, C. Baehtz, H. Ehrenberg and H. Fuess, "Electrochemical and structural study of $LiCoPO_4$-based electrodes," *J. Solid State Electrochem.* vol.8, pp. 558-564, 2004.

7. Wolfenstine, J., U. Lee,B. Poese, J.L. Allen, "Effect of oxygen partial pressure on the discharge capacity of $LiCoPO_4$," *J. Power Sources*, vol. 144, pp. 226-230, 2005.

8. Bramnik, N.N., K. Nikolowski, D.M. Trots, H. Ehrenberg, "Thermal stability of $LiCoPO_4$ cathodes, *Electrochem. Solid-State Lett.*, vol. 11, pp. A89-A93, 2008.

9. Allen, J.L., T.R. Jow, J. Wolfenstine, "Improved Cycle life of Fe-substituted $LiCoPO_4$," *J. Power Sources*, vol. 196, pp. 8656-8661, 2011.

10. Cresce, A.V., K. Xu, "Electrolytes in support of 5 V Li ion chemistry," *J. Electrochem. Soc.* vol. 158, pp. A337-A342, 2011

11. Allen, J.L., T. Thompson, J. Sakamoto, C.R. Becker, T.R. Jow, J. Wolfenstine, "Transport properties of $LiCoPO_4$ and Fe-substituted $LiCoPO_4$," *J. Power Sources*, vol. 254 pp. 204-208, 2014.

Sodium-ion Battery Materials: Advancement to Commercialization

Eungje Lee, Zonghai Chen, Guiliang Xu, Dehua Zhou, and Christopher S. Johnson*
Chemical Science and Engineering Division
Argonne National Laboratory
9700 S. Cass Avenue
Lemont, IL, USA, 60439

Jerry Barker*, Richard Heap, Noel Roche, Ruth Sayers, Chaou Tan, James Whitley, and Yang Liu
Faradion Limited
The Innovation Centre
217 Portobello
Sheffield, UK, S1 4DP

Abstract: *The rapid development of new advanced materials for non-aqueous sodium-ion batteries (SIBs) has enabled the fast turnaround of the cell chemistries into production level SIB battery modules with 140-150 Wh/kg stored energy. Notably this chemistry which uses hard carbon anodes and layered sodium transition metal oxide cathodes is durable, low cost and quite safe. This paper highlights these aspects, but also makes a case for the commercialization of SIBs which could serve as specialty batteries for military applications.*

Keywords: SIB; sodium ion; batteries; safety; carbon; performance; low cost

Introduction

Technical innovation and fast development of sodium-ion battery (SIB) electroactive materials and electrolytes led to the recent announcement of 140-150 $Wh.kg^{-1}$ energy density sodium-ion batteries (SIB) [1]. Engineering advancements and prototyping is rapid, actively borrowing from Li-ion battery technical know-how. While it may be argued that more widespread sourcing, low-cost, and availability of sodium precursors to synthesize active materials is advantageous to Li-ion, the recognition of the importance of enhanced safety and durability of SIB are also quite attractive qualities of the technology [2].

The discovery of new advanced higher-energy dense sodium materials continues to narrow the Li-ion battery energy gap [3]. Wide selection of sodium inorganic compounds (there are over 10000 more known sodium containing inorganic compounds compared to lithium containing compounds, for example), and engineered carbonaceous materials are capable to meet the different requirements of varied energy storage applications from commercial devices, large-scale grid systems, and potentially military batteries. Therefore, advances in sodium-ion batteries will rely on the development of novel materials as well as advanced characterization for complete understanding of materials and cell level behavior.

Impetus for SIBs

Certainly the availability of precursors or starting materials to make the active phases needed for sodium batteries is prevalent worldwide for sodium. Li sources for LIBs production are not scattered terrestrially like sodium, as for example, 50% of reserves are found solely in high dried lake beds in South America [2]. The sustainability of sodium is a mark of longevity of the technology over many years to come. In addition, the possibility of using Fe and Mn in cathodes as $Na[Fe_{1/2}Mn_{1/2}]O_2$ is equally appealing [3]. Moreover, since Al does not alloy with Na, Al current collectors (instead of copper) can be used on the negative (anode) side.

Existing Li-ion cell manufacturing lines for both pouch and cylindrical cells can be used for SIB production. Unlike other battery technologies, like Li-S or $Li-O_2$, no new approaches to re-define the builds are necessary. The existing infrastructure is in place.

In the near future we believe we can match best Li-ion in terms of cycle life, rate capability, energy density, and specific energy. Large-step improvements are possible for sodium-ion if more work is done in the field. Figure 1 shows the amount of publications over the last 2.5 decade time period. The lag in sodium-ion battery papers is quite apparent (blue bars) compared to lithium-ion (red bars) which has over thousands of papers published per year. However, this near-exponential trend for sodium-ion is following the track taken on lithium-ion over the course of the last 5 years. This bodes well and foretells that breakthrough in the technology is a matter of time and more effort through funding and future investment.

Performance Attributes

Cell design

One must first evaluate the rationale pursuit of sodium-ion from an energy density basis. For this reason, we have conducted BatPaC calculations that are processed for a 0.5 Ah pouch cell configuration with a power to energy ratio of

2 [4-5]. In Figure 2, we show the modeling results In this energy density model, which is graphed as cell (pouch) energy density as both a function of cathode capacity and anode capacity ($mAhg^{-1}$). We see a growth increase in energy density with cathode capacity increase, but only modest. However the energy density increase is more significant and correlated with anode capacity improvement. Thus, an intermetallic used in the system (usable capacity of 600 $mAhg^{-1}$) can provide a higher cell energy density. Note that metallic Na is the best conceivable anode, but would never be implemented in a full Na-ion battery due to safety concerns and high reactivity and instability.

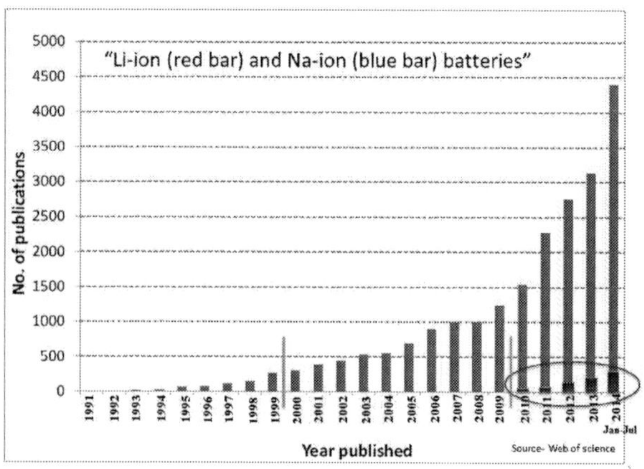

Figure 1. Number of publications per year for 'Li-ion' versus 'Na-ion' search terms. Na-ion papers are circled in blue, and number below 300 per year (2014) worldwide.

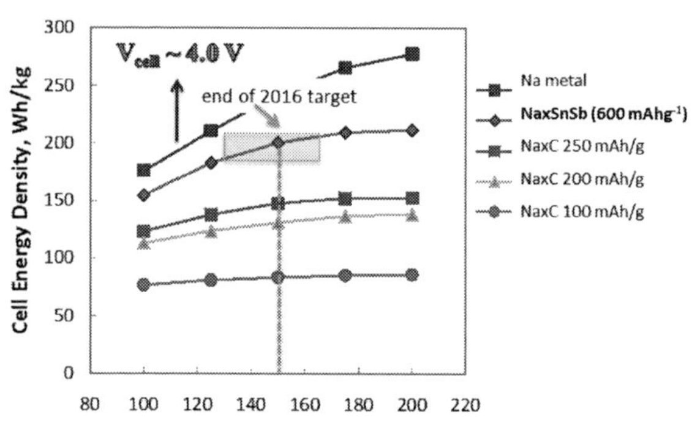

Figure 2. Pouch cell energy density as a function of both anode and cathode capacities. Anodes go from carbon to sodium metal, with an intermetallic anode shown and calculated based on 600 $mAhg^{-1}$ specific capacity. The nominal cell voltage used was 3.0 V.

In Figure 2, we hope to increase the energy density substantially by the end of 2016 to about 200 $Whkg^{-1}$. Note that these calculations use 3.0 V as the nominal cell output voltage at 50% SOC. However, if the voltage of the SIB can be increased to 4.0 V, then the cell energy density increases at least by 30% along the arrow marked in Figure 2.

New Materials – towards 600 $mAhg^{-1}$ Anode Capacity

Since the capacity of the anode drives the cell energy density, we are actively developing new anode materials. As discussed earlier, active material selections largely control the theoretical cell energy density. One such newly developed anode is SnO (divalent tin oxide) which is tested and characterized after high-energy ball-milling with carbon (i.e. SnO_C). The XRD diffraction pattern is shown in Figure 3, and the capacity with cycle number plot is given in Figure 4.

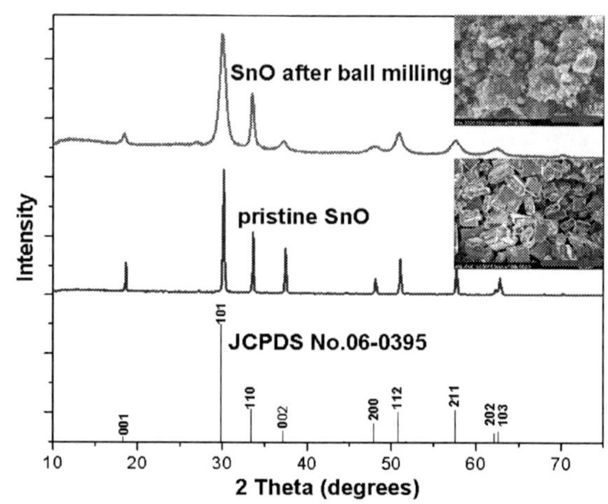

Figure 3. Top curve (red); SnO after ball milling with carbon (SnO_C), Middle curve (blue); as purchased SnO (Sigma – Aldrich), Bottom curve (black lines); JCPDS reference pattern for SnO.

It is clear in the top curve (red) that ball milling with carbon breaks down the particle size of SnO, causes some strain, but does not destroy the long-range crystal structure; the XRD pattern is still persistent for SnO. The SnO_C composite is about 65% SnO, and 35% carbon (SuperP).

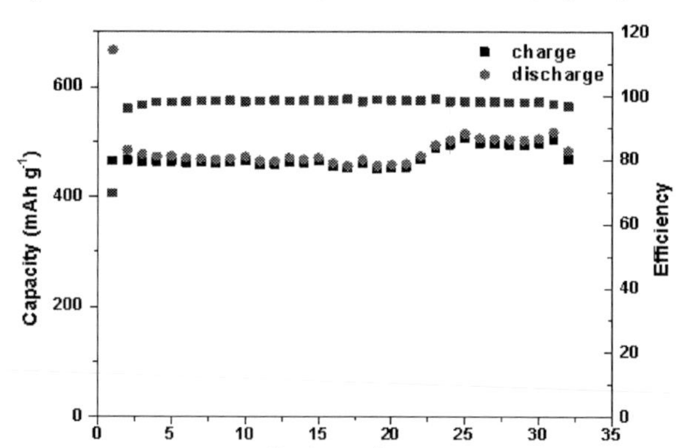

Figure 4. Specific capacity versus cycle number for a Na/SnO_C cell. The SnO_C demonstrates over 500 $mAhg^{-1}$ capacity.

The particle size of SnO in this case appears to be nanometer sized range which undoubtedly helps to buffer the large volume changes as sodium alloys with tin in a sea of volume-buffering amorphous sodium oxide (Na_2O). From the voltage profile (not shown), the behavior is not the same as pure Sn, or SnO_2 in sodium cells. No distinct Na-Sn alloy line phases are observed, and no crystalline Na_2O is observed *in operando* XRD diagnostic battery studies during pouch cell cycling. More work is underway to determine the mechanism of electrochemical reaction in this case.

At Argonne, we have done a majority of fundamental SIB materials research, particularly for cathode discovery. These include demonstrating fast cycling in Li-substituted sodium layered Ni-Mn oxides [6], demo of sodium Ni-Co-Fe containing layered oxides incorporated in full cells (with hard carbon anode) [7], and synthesis of high power P2-O3 stacked intergrowth layered oxide electrodes [8]. In addition, we are also interested in the behavior of iron in $NaFeO_2$ cathodes in sodium cells to determine the stability of Fe(IV) in electrochemical environments [9].

High Power Cathode for SIB

In fact sodium-ion batteries can incorporate high rate and high power cathode materials. Figure 5 highlights this feature whereby a P2-stabilized Li-substituted sodium nickel manganese layered oxide can yield single phase region, with less than 0.2% volume increase over movement of 0.5 Na atoms out of the structure [6]. The lithium stays in the structure and stabilizes the material at high states of charge. This observation is independently confirmed using electron microscopy and Li-solid state MAS NMR spectroscopy [10]. This cathode is thus capable of high rate and displays over 60 $mAhg^{-1}$ specific capacity even at a current density of 1.6 Ag^{-1} (25C). Thus, while sodium is larger in ionic radii than Li, and presumed to diffuse slower, it is not the case; P2-stacked layered structures offer tremendous phase stability and fast Na ion diffusion is possible.

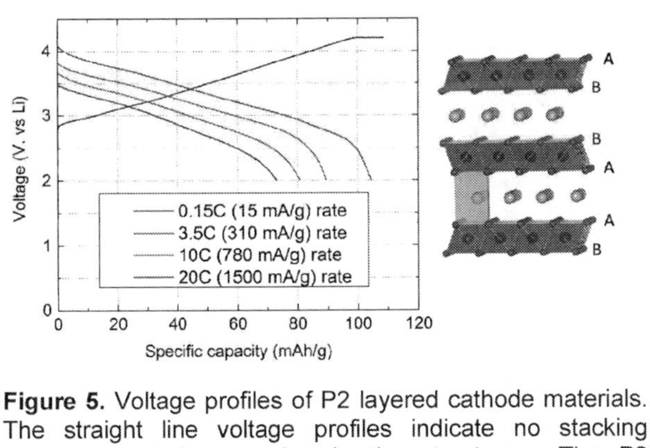

Figure 5. Voltage profiles of P2 layered cathode materials. The straight line voltage profiles indicate no stacking rearrangement is occurring in the structure. The P2 perspective schematic is shown to the right. The 'P' notation indicates a Na prismatic site, and the '2' designates a layer repeat unit of two; i.e. AABB stacking.

Faradion Ltd. Pouch cells and Modules

Working pouch cells and battery modules have been fabricated by Faradion Ltd. in the UK. As an example one is shown in Figure 6;, a 3.0 Ah prototype production pouch cell, situated next to an e-Bike energy-assist battery module consisting of 48 pouch cells (418 Wh). Note the form factor is essentially a stacked prismatic design analogous to LIBs, with cell in series and parallel strings with battery management circuitry.

Figure 6. 3.0 Ah pouch cell, and e-Bike working prototype battery module

The schematic of the cross-section of a Faradion Ltd. pouch cell is shown in Figure 7. Essentially the cathode is a layered sodium transition metal oxide, and the anode is a hard carbon. The cell is designed and optimized for energy; the electrode loading is ~ 3 mAh/cm^2. The voltage profile of the cell is given in Figure 8; cell was cycled between 1.0 to 4.3 V, with current rate of C/10. The voltage profile monotonically increases and decreases on charge-discharge indicative of Na (de)intercalation reactions. This type of cell has already demonstrated 150 cycles with negligible capacity fade with ~146 $mAhg^{-1}$. Modeling of the e-Bike module translates to only 14% energy loss over 600 cycles, certainly an acceptable value for specialized limited cycle life applications that may be implemented for military uses.

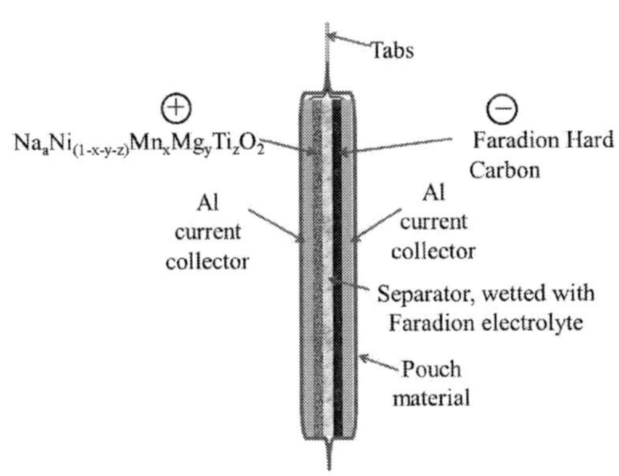

Figure 7. Cross-section of a typical single cell designed for pouch cell format. Note that the current collectors on both sides are aluminum.

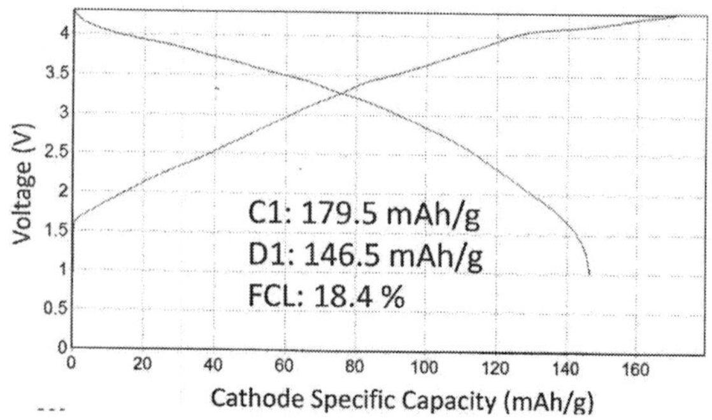

Figure 8. First charge-discharge voltage profile for a full cell, consisting of a layered TM oxide as cathode and hard carbon as anode.

Safety Attributes

0V Storage – Zero Energy Battery Transport

When one considers the ultimate safety aspects of large lithium batteries, it is critical to also think about transporting the batteries. While LIB batteries must be shipped in about a 30% SOC (energized cells) via a formation tap charge in order to avoid Cu current collector corrosion, the SIB can be shorted and sent into a zero energy state. Exactly this demonstration was done to show the behavior. For the experiment, the leads on the Al tabs on both sides of the battery were directly connected and the voltage brought to 0V. Subsequently, the cell was kept at 0V for 96 h, followed by a charge to 4.3 V, then it underwent normal cycling under nominal conditions. Result: absolutely no effect on safety or life of the cell was seen. Moreover the voltage profiles look extremely the same (Figure 8 vs. Figure 9a) when discharged under normal circumstances. The stable cycling shows the expected cathode capacity (Figure 9b). Even after 6 months storage in a zero energy state did not adversely affect the life and performance of the cell. The feature of using Al current collector on both electrodes contributes to the stability in addition to the choice of electrode chemistry. This is possible because Al does not alloy with Na. Certainly the durability of the cell is outstanding and can be leveraged, presenting an advantage, technologically over LIB.

Accelerating Rate Calorimetry (ARC) Studies

ARC studies give an indication of the thermal stability and durability of the cells. In Figure 10 is the result of ARC testing of pouch cells of $LiCoO_2$ (Li-ion), and $LiFePO_4$, LFP (Li-ion), along with the Faradion cell. All three cells are charged to the same state of stored energy. The results show lower heat evolution and increased onset temperature for self-heating with the Faradion cell and confirm a better safety threshold when compared to typical LIB. Table 1 lists the specific results (approximate numbers) from the testing.

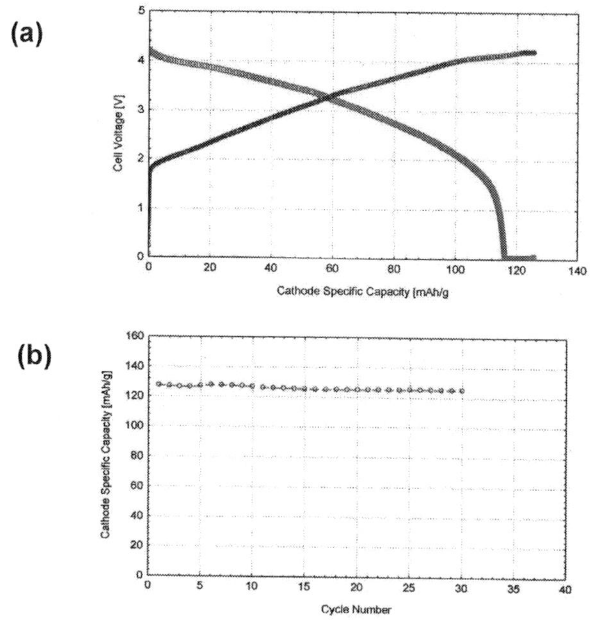

Figure 9. (a) Voltage profile of the shorted cell after 96 h, showing no performance decline; (b) capacity is stable post shorting shown to 30 cycles.

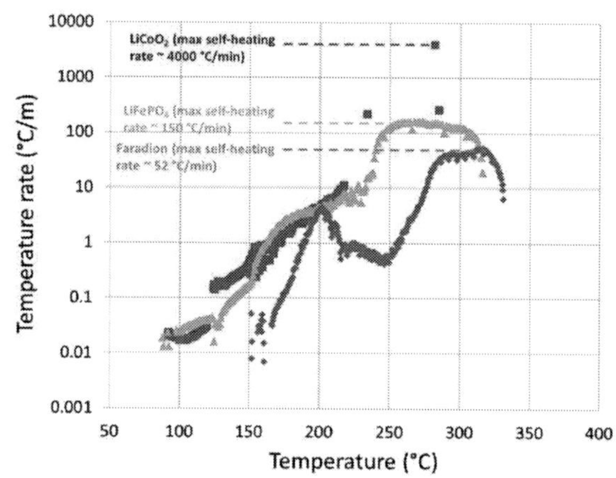

Figure 10. ARC studies comparing $LiCoO_2$, $LiFePO_4$ and SIB layered oxides cathodes chemistries.

Table 1. ARC Safety Summary

Cell	Onset T (°C)	Max self-heating rate (°C/min)
$LiCoO_2$	90	~4000
$LiFePO_4$	100	~150
Faradion	150	~52

An additional safety aspect comes in the form of the more thermally stable electrolyte used. SIBs can use propylene carbonate (PC) as the solvent of choice for the cell electrolyte chemistry. PC solven has a higher boiling point than the traditional straight chain di-esters used in LIB, for example EMC, or DMC. With a higher boiling point and a higher% fraction of low volatility behavior, then a greater safety margin is experienced during heating. In addition, PC is also a superior solvent for low temperature applications instead of EC:EMC type LIB blends and this factor will be important for batteries operated at below 0°C and lower temperatures.

Commercialization Prognosis

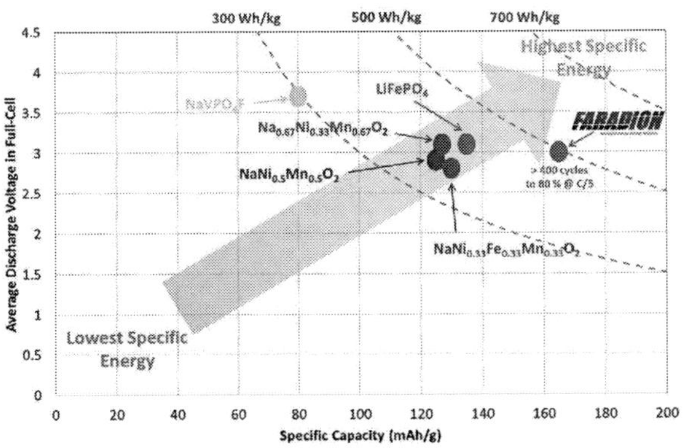

Figure 11. Projected energy densities as seen from cathode materials both for LILB and reported on for SIBs.

Commercially, early days are still happening for SIB, but we feel that the technology is very promising and timely as LIB is experiencing safety issues (e.g. exploding hoverboards, Boeing Dreamliner fire from faulty charged LIB in the hold, etc.). In addition there is always a concern with cost and supply issues of LIB as the EV market takes off. As seen in Figure 11, the energy density is very respectable at this point, and is seen to be higher than graphite/LFP technology. Note that with better active materials, optimized cell parameters, thicker electrodes then Faradion expects to push the specific energy to > 180 Wh/kg and beyond in the near future.

The demonstration of cell performance that are comparable to commercial LIB, but with better safety and lower material costs is the ultimate objective. Our current cost model suggests a total material cost of $128/kWh in the finished cell. If we assume material costs become around 50 % of the total battery pack cost, this equates to about $250/kWh for the pack. To note, as we move forward it is assumed that material costs will become a greater % of the overall cost, as this trend has been suggested by Tesla (Gigafactory) and others. As we go forward with optimized performance, and better active materials, the materials cost by 2017 are projected to be < $100/kg.

To summarize, at the very least, we see SIB as a durable, low cost battery technology capable of the following (1) drop-in replacement to LIB, and a (2) low-cost alternative; or a second product line.

In short, sodium-ion batteries are finding a niche in the market and we expect fast advances an implementation of new chemistry and materials into the batteries in a rapid succession of continued development and greater expansion of the technology.

Acknowledgements

Work supported by U. S. DOE, Office of Science under Contract No. DE-AC02-06CH11357.

References

1. Chemical & Engineering News (C&E News), July 20 2015, Vol. 93, Issue 29, pp 18-19
2. http://www.greentechmedia.com/articles/read/Is-There-Enough-Lithium-to-Maintain-the-Growth-of-the-Lithium-Ion-Battery-M
3. Yabuuchi, N., Kajiyama, M., Iwatate, J., Nishiwawa, H., Hitoni, S., Okuyama, R., Usui, R., Yamada, Y., Komaba, S., "P2-type Nax[Fe1/2Mn1/2]O2 made from earth-abundant elements for rechargeable Na batteries", *Nature Materials*, Vol. 11, Issue 6, pp. 512-517, 2012.
4. P. A. Nelson, K. G. Gallagher, I. Bloom, and D. W. Dees "Modeling the Performance and Cost of Lithium-Ion Batteries for Electric Vehicles" Chemical Sciences and Engineering Division, Argonne National Laboratory, ANL-11/32, Argonne, IL USA (2011).
5. http://www.cse.anl.gov/batpac/
6. D. Kim, S.-H. Kang, M. Slater, S. Rood, J. T. Vaughey, N. Karan, M. Balasubramanian, C. S. Johnson, "Enabling Sodium Batteries Using Lithium-Substituted Sodium Layered Transition Metal Oxide Cathodes", *Advanced Energy Materials*, Vol. 1., Issue 3, pp. 333-336, 2011.
7. D. Kim, E. Lee, M. Slater, W. Q. Lu, S. Rood, and C. S. Johnson, "Layered $Na[Ni_{1/3}Fe_{1/3}Mn_{1/3}]O_2$ cathodes for Na-ion battery application," *Electrochemistry Communications*, Vol. 18, pp. 66-69, 2012.
8. E. Lee, J. Lu, Y. Ren, X. Luo, X. Zhang, J. Wen, D. Miller, A. DeWahl, S. Hackney, B. Key, D. Kim, M. D. Slater, and C. S. Johnson, "Layered P2/O3 Intergrowth Cathode: Toward High Power Na-Ion Batteries", *Advanced Energy Materials*, Vol. 4, Issue 17, pp. 1400458, 2014.
9. E. Lee, D. E. Brown, E. E. Alp, Y. Ren, J. Lu, J.-J. Woo, and C. S. Johnson, "New insights into the performance degradation of Fe-based layered oxides in sodium-ion batteries: Instability of Fe^{3+}/Fe^{4+} redox in α-$NaFeO_2$", *Chemistry of Materials*, Vol. 27, pp. 6755-6764, 2015.
10. J. Xu, D. H. Lee, R. J. Clément, X. Yu, M. Leskes, A. J. Pell, G. Pintacuda, X.-Q. Yang, C. P. Grey, and Y. S. Meng, "Identifying the critical role of Li substitution in P2–$Na_x[Li_yNi_zMn_{1-y-z}]O_2$ ($0 < x, y, z < 1$) intercalation cathode materials for high energy Na-ion batteries", *Chemistry of Materials*, Vol. 26, pp. 1260-1269, 2014

Recent Progress with the Use of Garnet-type Superionic Conductors in Solid-State Batteries

Travis Thompson
University of Michigan, Department of Mechanical Engineering

Regina Garcia
University of Michigan, Department of Materials Science and Engineering

Donald Siegel
University of Michigan, Department of Mechanical Engineering

Logan Williams
University of Michigan, Department of Materials Science and Engineering

Jeff Wolfenstine and Jan Allen
Army Research Laboratory, RDRL-SED-C

Emmanouil Kioupakis
University of Michigan, Department of Materials Science and Engineering

Robert Schmidt
University of Michigan, Department of Mechanical Engineering

Seungho Yu
University of Michigan, Department of Mechanical Engineering

Jeff Sakamoto
University of Michigan, Department of Mechanical Engineering
jeffsaka@umich.edu

Abstract

In recent years, the push to move past conventional Li – ion battery technology has grown. Several advanced battery technologies and cell chemistries have been identified as promising candidates including i) solid-state batteries with Li metal anodes, ii) Li – S, and iii) flow batteries. Although an engineered solution using liquids may be possible for some of these options, a solid electrolyte is an enabling technology for each of the beyond Li – ion alternatives. Li7La3Zr2O12 (LLZO) with the cubic garnet structure is a promising solid electrolyte for advanced battery concepts such as solid-state Li-ion batteries. Cubic LLZO is a fast ion conductor, exhibiting 0.3 – 1 mS/cm depending on which particular dopant is selected. Besides affecting the conductivity, the dopant can impact the chemical and electrochemical stability against Li metal and at high voltages vs Li/Li+. This presentation will overview the requirements for solid electrolytes used in a solid-state battery configuration with an emphasis on LLZO. The electrochemical stability window, chemical stability with metallic Li, and film processing for full cells is discussed. A combination of DC and AC measurements are used to determine the electrochemical stability in the range 2 – 8 V vs Li/ Li+ for Al and Ta dopants. Additionally, measurements using diffuse reflectance UV/Vis spectroscopy and DFT computations were used to determine the band gap. Negligible electronic current is observed over the entire voltage range, although a change is observed near the band gap.

Metadielectric Materials for Energy Storage

Lev Mourokh[1,2,3] and Pavel Lazarev[3]

[1] Department of Physics, Queens College of CUNY, Flushing, NY 11367, USA
[2] The Graduate Center of CUNY, New York, NY 10016, USA
[3] Capacitor Sciences Inc., 1455 Adams Drive, Suite 2060, Menlo Park, CA 94025, USA

Abstract: *Energy storage units having both high energy density and high power density are crucial for further development of technology. As the limitations of the electrochemical batteries are impossible to overcome, the right answer should arrive from simpler devices and capacitor is the simplest. We show that high energy density can be achieved using layers of organic molecules with large second-order permittivity. Molecular polarizabilities and hyperpolarizabilities are calculated for various molecules using quantum chemistry software, and the expressions related them to macroscopic permittivities are derived. We believe that the proposed approach provides new opportunities for design of the energy storage devices.*

Keywords: energy storage; conjugated polymers; polarizability; hyperpolarizability; electron donors and acceptors.

Introduction: Energy Storage

Efficient energy storage is the key component in the development of various modern technologies. In the present time, the all-electric cars start to enter the vehicle market but they are still more expensive and less trustworthy than the usual ones. Electronic devices, which are omnipresent in modern society, are also heavily dependent on reliable energy storage modules. Moreover, renewable energy sources such as solar cells and wind turbines are sustainable and environmentally friendly, but their energy production is intermittent and the effective storage would make the energy available on demand. In the present time, the main storage devices are the batteries. The energy is stored electrochemically, i. e. carriers released in chemical reactions can enter electrical circuits. The energy density of batteries is very high and they are relatively cheap. During the charging process, the carriers (like lithium ions) are returned back to the source. This process is slow and, moreover, it degrades the battery material. Thus, the power density of the batteries is low and their lifetime is short due to the material damage. Furthermore, the batteries become less reliable at elevated temperatures. The alternative storage units are capacitors, where the energy is stored electrostatically [1]. The charging process is fast, leading to the high power density and the longtime reliability. The main shortcoming for capacitors is their low energy density. In order to overcome it, novel devices called supercapacitors have been developed [2]. They have the energy densities greater than those of conventional capacitors and power densities greater than those of batteries. However, there is still no structure having the power density comparable to standard capacitors and the energy density comparable to batteries [1]. Moreover, the cost of supercapacitors remains relatively high.

Introduction: Conjugated Supramolecules

In the present paper, we propose to use the conjugated supramolecules with large second-order permittivity to develop capacitors with high energy density and high power density. Conjugated supramolecules are molecular stacks with repeating units of fundamental monomers.

We propose to use aromatic molecules as our fundamental monomers. They are expected to have high polarizability and even exhibit metallic conductivity [3]. Accordingly, they are shown to have a high dielectric constant up to 2.0×10^5 (at 1 kHz) [4,5]. So large value is most probably due to the hyperelectronic polarization, which is the analog of the space-charge polarization in doped semiconductors. Certain electrons can be detached from the host atom and moved over to the other side of the molecule creating a large polarizability. The polarizability shows a non-linear dependence on the electric field and its magnitude is several orders larger than that of the electronic polarization, especially in the frequency range of kHz-MHz, which makes such systems most suitable for the energy storage purposes because its contribution is the largest at the static fields. Similar molecules were shown to exhibit strong non-linear optical properties [6] and, correspondingly, we can expect large hyperpolarazibilities in these structures.

The conduction can compromise the high dielectric strength of the dielectric. To avoid this, we propose to couple the aromatic molecules with high polarization to aliphatic alkyl tails having high resistance. The example of such molecules is shown in Fig.1. Growth of similar structures was discussed in Refs. [7,8]. Such combination naturally leads to the layered arrangement, with alternate layers having high permittivity and high breakdown voltage.

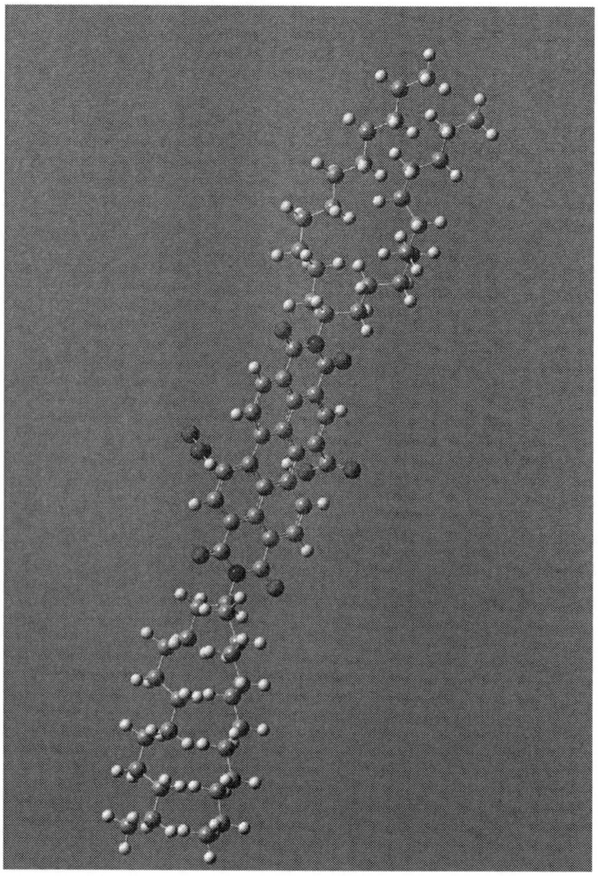

Figure 1. Molecular design for high energy density capacitors. Aromatic core with high polarizability is attached to alkyl tails with high resistance

Theory: Energy Density of Nonlinear Capacitors

The energy density of electric field is given by [9]

$$w = \int_0^D \vec{E} \cdot d\vec{D}' = \vec{E} \cdot \vec{D} - \int_0^E \vec{D} \cdot d\vec{E}'. \qquad (1)$$

For simplicity, we consider the isotropic and uniform situation with all the fields directed along the x-axis. In this case, for the nonlinear media the electric displacement can be written as

$$D = \varepsilon_0 \varepsilon^{(1)} E + \varepsilon_0 \varepsilon^{(2)} E^2 + \dots . \qquad (2)$$

Substituting Eq. (2) into Eq. (1), we obtain for the energy density

$$w = \varepsilon_0 \varepsilon^{(1)} \frac{E^2}{2} + \varepsilon_0 \varepsilon^{(2)} \frac{2E^3}{3} + \dots . \qquad (3)$$

For the flat-plate capacitor with the plate area A, plate separation d, applied voltage $V_{op}=E/d$, and linear capacitance without dielectric $C_0=\varepsilon_0 A/d$, the total stored energy is

$$W = \int w \, d\mathrm{Vol} = \varepsilon^{(1)} C_0 \frac{V_{op}^2}{2} + \varepsilon^{(2)} C_0 \frac{2V_{op}^3}{3d} + \dots , \qquad (4)$$
$$= \varepsilon_{eff} C_0 \frac{V_{op}^2}{2}$$

where

$$\varepsilon_{eff} = \varepsilon^{(1)} + \frac{4V_{op}}{3d} \varepsilon^{(2)} + \dots \qquad (5)$$

Thus, one can see that the dielectric with large second-order permittivity can be used for the heavy-duty capacitors especially if they are charged at large voltages.

Theory: Linear and Nonlinear Clausius-Mossotti Relations

Linear and nonlinear permittivities can be determined using the generalization of the Clausius–Mossotti relation in terms of polarizability and hyperpolarizability (second-order polarizability). Macroscopic polarization is given by

$$P = N p_{ind} , \qquad (6)$$

where p_{ind} is the induced dipole and N is the density of the dipoles. On the other hand,

$$P = D - \varepsilon_0 E = \varepsilon_0 \left(\varepsilon^{(1)} - 1\right) E + \varepsilon_0 \varepsilon^{(2)} E^2 + \dots . \qquad (7)$$

In the simplest Lorentz approximation, the induced dipole can be expressed in terms of the local field

$$E_{loc} = E + \frac{P}{3\varepsilon_0} , \qquad (8)$$

as

$$p_{ind} = \alpha E_{loc} + \beta E_{loc}^2 + \dots , \qquad (9)$$

where α and β are the polarizability and hyperpolarizability, respectively. In the capacitor structure, the external field will be applied along the main direction of the molecule, so $\alpha = \alpha_{xx}$ and $\beta = \beta_{xxx}$. Substituting Eqs. (8) and (9) into Eq. (6) and comparing to Eq. (7), we can equalize the coefficients with the same power of the electric field E. The linear term would give as the usual Clausis–Mossotti relation

$$\frac{\left(\varepsilon^{(1)} - 1\right)}{\left(\varepsilon^{(1)} + 2\right)} = \frac{N\alpha}{3\varepsilon_0} , \qquad (10)$$

whereas the quadratic term would provide the expression for the second-order permittivity, as

$$\varepsilon^{(2)} = \frac{N\beta}{3\varepsilon_0} \left(\varepsilon^{(1)} + 2\right) \left(1 + \frac{2}{3}\left(\varepsilon^{(1)} - 1\right) + \frac{1}{9}\left(\varepsilon^{(1)} - 1\right)^2\right). \qquad (11)$$

Here, N is the density of molecules. Thus, having the values for α and β it is possible to determine the first- and second-order permittivities and, correspondingly, the energy stored in the nonlinear capacitor.

Results

Proper molecular design is crucial for the achievement of high-polarizability structures. Using the Langhals perylene (LP) molecule, Fig. 2(a), as example of molecule with shorter conjugated system, we used extended conjugation of amidines with electron acceptor group NO_2 and electron donor group NH_2 to compare polarizabilities. In Fig. 2 (b), we show the structure with the single acceptor and donor groups at the apex positions (NAP_1), while in Fig 2 (c) the hypothetical structure with the double groups is presented (NAP_2).

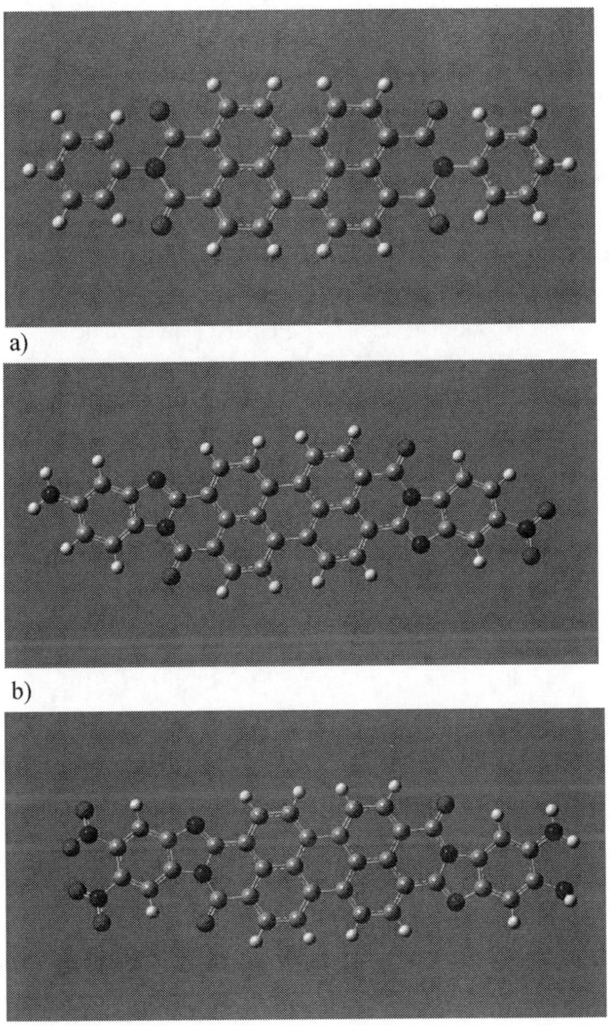

a)
b)
c)

Figure 2. (a) Langhals perylene; (b) Phenyl-perylene with the single NO_2 and NH_2 groups at the apex positions; (c) Phenyl-perylene with the double NO_2 and NH_2 groups. Carbon, hydrogen, nitrogen, and oxygen atoms are shown by grey, white, blue, and red colors, respectively.

Comparison of NAP_1 and NAP_2 allows us to get deeper insight on the dependence of the polarizabilities on the number of donors and acceptors.

These molecules are analyzed with Gaussian09 software [10], their polarizabilities and hyperpolarizabilities are determined using the B3LYP method with 6-31G basic sets and are given in Table 1. They are expressed in atomic units, 1 a.u $= e^2 a_0^2 / E_h$ for α and 1 a.u. $= e^3 a_0^3 / E_h^2$ for β, where e is the electron charge, a_0 is the Bohr radius, and E_h is the Hartree energy.

Table 1. Polarizabilities and hyperpolarizabilities for the molecules of Fig. 2

	LP	NAP_1	NAP_2
α	945	1252	1546
β	0.041	21106	119078

One can see that while the polarizabilities of these molecules are comparable, the hyperpolarizabilities are increased by several orders of the magnitude by the introduction of the donor/acceptor groups. It should be also noted that the doubling of these groups increases the hyperpolarizability by the factor of 5.

The values for the microscopic molecular polarizabilities can be recalculated to the macroscopic permittivities using Eqs. (10) and (11). However, linear Clausius-Mossotti expression, Eq. (10), would not provide accurate results at high molecular density of conjugated polymers because of so-called "polarization catastrophe", which happens when the right site of Eq. (10) becomes close to one [11]. To avoid these complications, we use the linear permittivity as a parameter to calculate the second-order permittivity, Eq. (11) and the effective permittivity, Eq. (5), involved in the expression for the energy density. From practical point of view, $\varepsilon^{(1)}$ can be understood as a dielectric constant at zero applied voltage and obtained values of ε_{eff} would provide the dielectric constant for the operation voltage of the capacitor. In Fig. 3 we show the dielectric constants for NAP_1 and NAP_2 as functions of the zero-field values at electric field V/d = 1 V/nm and the molecular density N = 3 10^{27} m^{-3}. It is clear that the low value of the hyperpolarizability for LP makes its dielectric constant independent on the applied voltage.

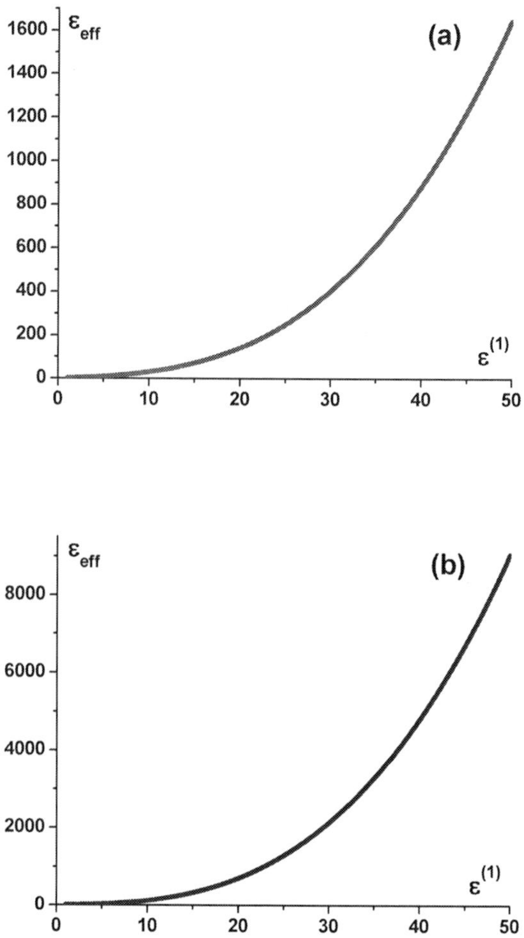

Figure 3. Dependence of the dielectric constant for the capacitor operation voltage on its zero-voltage value for (a) NAP_1 and (b) NAP_2.

One can see from this figure that even for the moderate values of the dielectric constant at zero applied voltage, the effective permittivity at operational voltages can reach very large values, which makes these structures very attractive for the energy storage applications. The reason for this phenomenology is the giant nonlinear response of these molecules to external electric field.

Conclusions

In conclusions, we propose to explore organic molecules with large second-order permittivity for the energy storage devices. Actual device would have a multilayer structure with alternate layers of the materials with high permittivity and high breakdown voltage. We derive the contributions of the second-order permittivity to the energy stored in the capacitor. The values of molecular polarizabilities and hyperpolarizabilities are calculated using the quantum chemistry software, Gaussian09. We show that introducing the electron acceptor group NO_2 and the electron donor group NH_2 to the molecule of perylene, it is possible to increase the hyperpolarizablity even if the polarizability remains essentially the same. The obtained values are used to determine the first- and second-order permittivities, as well as the effective dielectric constant involved in the expression for the energy density. We show that for our perylene-based molecules, the effective dielectric constant at the operational voltage is quite high, which allows us to use the proposed structures for the energy storage device applications.

References

1. X. Hao, A review on the dielectric materials for high energy-storage application, *J. Adv. Dielect.* **3**, 1330001 (2013).
2. B. E. Conway, Electrochemical Supercapacitors: Scientific Fundamentals and Technological Applications (New York, Kluwer-Plenum, 1999).
3. H. Shirakawa, E. J. Louis, A. G. MacDiarmid, C. K. Chiang, and A. J. Heeger, Synthesis of electrically conducting organic polymers: Halogen derivatives of polyacetylene, (CH)x, *J. Chem. Soc., Chem. Comm.* **16**, 578 (1977).
4. R. D. Hartman and H. A. Pohl, Hyperelectronic polarization in macromolecular solids, *J. Polymer Sci. Part A-1: Polymer Chem.* **6**, 1135 (1968).
5. C.-H. Ho, C.-D. Liu, C.-H. Hsieh, K.-H. Hsieh, S.-N. Lee, High dielectric constant polyaniline/poly(acrylic acid) composites prepared by in situ polymerization, *Synth. Met.* **158**, 630 (2008).
6. Ch. Bosshard, et al, Organic Nonlinear Optical Materials (Cordon and Breach Publishers, 1995).
7. H. Kim and J.-W. Park, Self-assembly of rod-coils consisting of tetraaniline and alkyl chains in different oxidation states, *J. Mater. Chem.* **20**, 1186 (2010).
8. Z. Shao, Z. Yu, J. Hu, S. Chandrasekaran, D. M. Lindsay, Z. Wei, and C. F. J. Faul, Block-like electroactive oligo(aniline)s: anisotropic structures with anisotropic function, *J. Mater. Chem.* **22**, 16230 (2012).
9. L.D. Landau, E.M. Lifshitz, and L.P. Pitaevskii, *Electrodynamics of Continuous Media*. Vol. 8, 2nd ed. (Butterworth-Heinemann, 1984).
10. Gaussian 09, Revision E.01, M. J. Frisch, et al, Gaussian, Inc., Wallingford CT, 2009.
11. Ch. Kittel, Introduction to Solid State Physics, 8th ed. (John Wiley & Sons, 2005).

Developments in the Material Fabrication and Performance of $LiMn_2O_{4-d}Cl_d$ Cathode Material

Paula C. Latorre, Ashley L. Ruth, and Terrill B. Atwater
U.S. Army RDECOM
Communications, Electronics, Research, Development and Engineering Center
Aberdeen Proving Ground, MD 21005

Abstract: *Lithium manganese oxide spinel materials exhibit promising electrochemical performance and good thermodynamic and kinetic stability when used as a cathode in lithium and lithium-ion electrochemical systems. An inherent disadvantage is their limited cyclability as a result of the energy barriers for removing lithium from the octahedral sites. This work incorporates chlorine into the lattice of the* AB_2O_4 *to help assist in lithium deinsertion from the octahedral sites. By introducing this chlorine into the starting material and the subsequent final product, the overall electrochemical performance is enhanced, which will be extremely useful in versatile applications.* $AB_2O_{4-d}Cl_d$ *materials were synthesized using both a solid state reaction method and a common ceramic glycine nitrate combustion process and were evaluated as a cathode for lithium and lithium-ion electrochemical systems. The data presented in this paper is the result of continuing fabrication efforts that allow for an even distribution of chlorine in the* $AB_2O_{4-d}Cl_d$ *material lattice. The material properties were verified using X-ray diffraction and X-ray fluorescence to determine the extent of chlorination into the lithium manganese spinel mixture. Electrochemical coin cells were fabricated and cycled between 4.75 V and 3.5 V at 1-2* mA/cm^2 *to determine cycle life capability and degradation processes.*

Keywords: Lithium manganese spinel; Lithium rechargeable batteries, Lithium-ion battery

Introduction

As portable electronic systems continue to advance in both complexity and capability, so does the need for an advanced portable power device that can meet the demands of current and future portable electronic systems. In the U.S. Army, many of these systems are utilized in a Command, Control, Communication, Computers, Intelligence, Surveillance, and Reconnaissance (C4ISR) environment, where the system must be capable of consistent operation for an allotted period of time. Therefore, the system's portable power device must also have equivalent operational reliability and safety requirements. Lithium and lithium-ion battery systems are highly sought after for rechargeable applications due to their high energy density (Wh/L) and high specific energy (Wh/kg), specifically to meet the rigorous requirements placed on them for operational field use. Lithium manganese oxide spinel ($LiMn_2O_4$) is a potential viable active cathode material for use in these versatile applications due to its low toxicity, good capacity, and low cost.

Background

Lithium oxide spinels are plagued by capacity fading, where a cell loses cycle capacity over the duration of its useable life. Capacity fading limits the cell's number of practical cycles, which in turn decreases the overall system availability once integrated into a product. In lithium battery systems, capacity loss is attributed to degradation in the active cathode material due to constant cycling. Degradation of the active material can be due to loss of crystallinity, alternative phase formations, or potential side reactions.[1-4] Methods to eliminate or mitigate this degradation effect include changing the crystal structure and composition of the active material.

Some studies have incorporated chlorine or fluorine into the starting material and have reported positive impacts on the active material's electrochemical performance.[5-7] However, the halide is not reported to be incorporated into the lattice structure. These studies used the standard processing method for lithium manganese oxide spinels and demonstrated an increase in capacity. However, capacity retention issues in regard to cycle life were observed between cycles 10 to 20.[6,7]

Our group has utilized two different processing methods to successfully introduce chlorine into the starting material and subsequently into the final product, enhancing the material's electrochemical performance. The first method involves a solid state process in which the anion, either fluorine or chlorine, is incorporated into the material.[8] This method has yielded active material which has previously reported cyclability to 20 cycles.[9-11] The second processing method incorporates chlorine into the bulk of the lithium spinel material via in-situ combustion synthesis. This paper will focus on the discussion and evaluation of both processing methods and their effect on cycle life performance.

Experimental

The active cathode material, $Li_xMn_2O_{4-d}Cl_d$, was fabricated using two different processing methods. The first processing method involved a reduced solid state process (SSP) where starting materials included MnO_2, Mn_2O_3, or Mn_3O_4, Li_2CO_3 or LiOH, and a halide salt, such as $LiClO_4$. The starting material mixture was grinded in a mortar and pestle until uniform. The subsequent mixture was then placed in an orbit mixer mill for one hour and then calcined in air at 600 °C for at least two hours. Multiple samples of the final material, $Li_xMn_2O_{4-d}Cl_d$, was produced with varying concentrations of the halide salt in order to determine the extent of halide retention in the crystal structure. The second material fabrication method used in this paper was a glycine nitrate combustion process (GNP) to synthesize $Li_xMn_2O_{4-d}Cl_d$. Lithium nitrate, along with hydrated manganese nitrate and halide salt (manganese chloride) were dissolved in deionized water. Glycine was then added to the aqueous solution as a chelating agent. The subsequent solution was then heated until the water fully evaporated. The resultant gel was then heated until auto ignition occurred, forming a black ash. Ash was then collected and grinded in a mortar and pestle until uniform. The material was then calcined in air at 600 °C for at least two hours. Both calcined final materials were then evaluated for their viability as cathode materials for rechargeable lithium batteries.

In order to determine if any structural changes occurred in each sample, a baseline material ($LiMn_2O_4$) was fabricated using a traditional sol-gel method. XRD and XRF were used to analyze and compare the structure of the resultant baseline material with $Li_xMn_2O_{4-d}Cl_d$ materials formed using both the SSP and GNP mentioned previously. Additionally, these three materials (prior to calcination) were also evaluated using thermogravimetric analysis (TGA) to observe the reaction thermodynamics.

Coin cells were fabricated using a lithium anode, an organic electrolyte, and a cathode using the $Li_xMn_2O_{4-d}Cl_d$ material to evaluate the thermodynamic and kinetic properties of the resultant $Li//Li_xMn_2O_{4-d}Cl_d$ electrochemical system. The lithium anode consisted of lithium foil that was approximately 0.075 cm thick and was cut using a 12.7 mm diameter hole punch. The cathode material consisted of $Li_xMn_2O_{4-d}Cl_d$, carbon black, and polytetrafluoroethylene (PTFE) in a ratio of 85:10:5. The cathode was cut into 1.0 cm^2 discs which were approximately 0.1 to 0.15 g. The anode and cathode were separated using a 0.01 cm nonwoven glass separator. The electrolyte medium used was a 1 molar solution of $LiPF_6$ with proportional mixtures of diethyl carbonate, dimethyl carbonate, and ethylene carbonate.

The electrochemical coin cells were cycled using an ARBIN MSTAT4 battery cycler system controlled by MITS pro software. The cells were discharged and charged from 4.75 V to 3.5 V at a rate of 1 mA/cm^2 to evaluate capacity retention. A 15-minute rest was introduced between charge and discharge cycles to allow for cells to reach equilibrium. Data was logged every 15 minutes or every 0.01 V during both charge and discharge.

Results

After the final active materials were fully calcined, their physical properties were evaluated using X-ray diffraction (XRD). Figure 1 shows the diffraction patterns of $Li_xMn_2O_{4-d}Cl_d$ formed using both SSP and GNP, shown as "b" and "c" respectively, where $x \approx 1$ and $d \sim 0.05$. The traditional $LiMn_2O_4$ spinel diffraction pattern is also shown for comparison. The peaks presented in each pattern correlate directly with the JCPDS file for $LiMn_2O_4$ spinel (00-018-0736). The lack of additional peaks indicate the achievement of a single phase spinel.

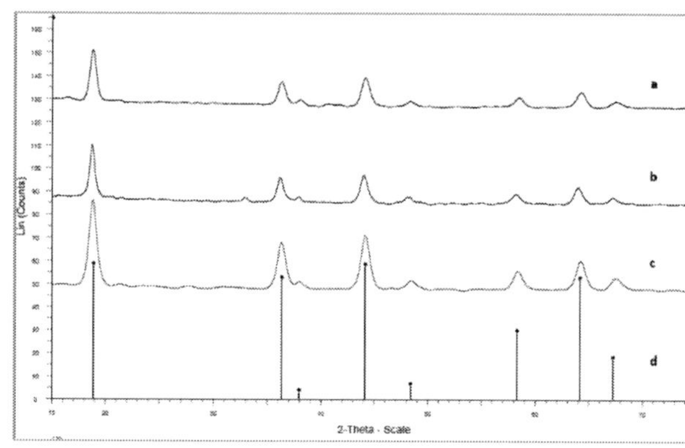

Figure 1. XRD patterns of $LiMn_2O_4$ (a), $Li_xMn_2O_{4-d}Cl_d$ made by SSP method (b), and $Li_xMn_2O_{4-d}Cl_d$ made by GNP method (c), along with JCPDS file for $LiMn_2O_4$ (d).

X-ray fluorescence (XRF) spectroscopy was also performed on all post-calcined materials to determine and characterize the elemental components of the material. Figure 2 shows the XRF results of $Li_xMn_2O_{4-d}Cl_d$ formed using both SSP and GNP. The figure shows similar material compositions with the exception of a peak intensity divergence at 2.63 keV. Peak intensities at this energy are 5206 and 2016 A.U. for $Li_xMn_2O_{4-d}Cl_d$ spinels made by SSP and GNP, respectively. These peaks correlate to the corresponding energy for chlorine, indicating a retention of Cl present in the sample after calcining. The Si, P, and S present in each sample are attributed to the sample holder, and Pd is from the X-ray source.

A series of $Li_xMn_2O_{4-d}Cl_d$ spinels were made via SSP, where $x \approx 1$ and $0.025 < d < 0.15$, to determine the extent of chlorine doping in the material through XRF. Figure 3 shows the weight percent of Cl in the sample prior to and after calcining the material. In each sample, the pre-calcination value of Cl is greater by approximately 50%.

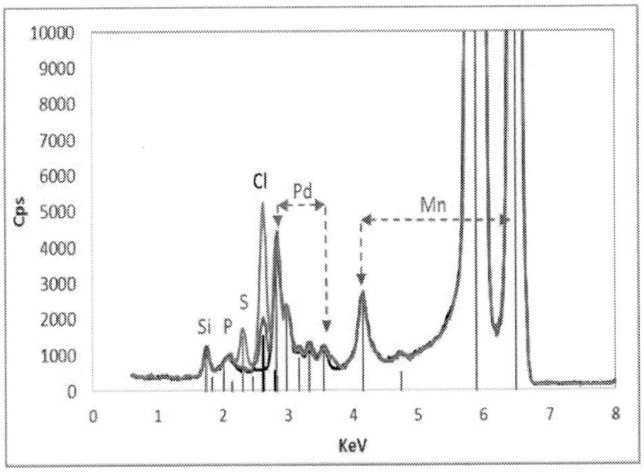

Figure 2. XRF of $LiMn_2O_4$ (black), $Li_xMn_2O_{4-d}Cl_d$ made by SSP method (blue), and $Li_xMn_2O_{4-d}Cl_d$ made by GNP (red).

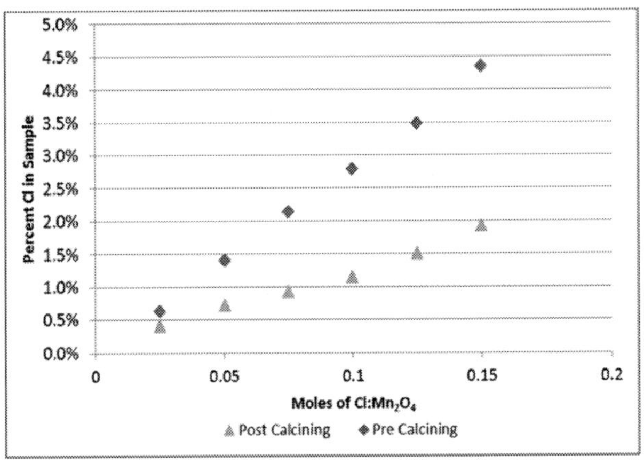

Figure 3. Weight percent of chlorine present in each sample before and after calcining using SSP method.

TGA was performed to determine the appropriate temperature of calcination for each process as well as the thermodynamics of the reaction. Figure 4 shows the resultant weight percent TGA curve for $Li_xMn_2O_{4-d}Cl_d$ spinel precursors using both processing methods. The TGA was performed in air from 30 °C to 750 °C at a rate of 10 °C/min. The dehydration of water molecules, which occurred between 30 and 100 °C, amounted to a 5% mass decrease, which was then normalized in the figure for the GNP process (shown in red). The calcining temperature of 600 °C could potentially be reduced, as the slow mass loss after 400 °C in the SSP material and 500 °C in the GNP material is probably attributed to Cl evolution. The figure demonstrates the comparative standard composition and formation of the spinel.

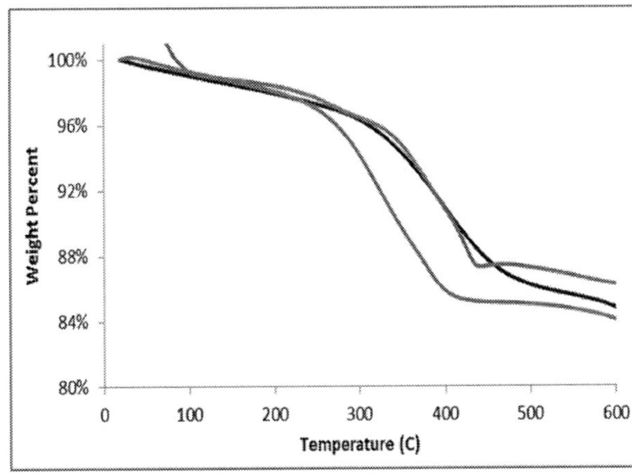

Figure 4. TGA of precursors of $LiMn_2O_4$ (black), $Li_xMn_2O_{4-d}Cl_d$ made by SSP method (blue), and $Li_xMn_2O_{4-d}Cl_d$ made by GNP (red) normalized to eliminate weight reduction due to water loss.

After material analysis was performed, the $Li_xMn_2O_{4-d}Cl_d$ spinel was utilized as the active cathode material in a $Li//Li_xMn_2O_{4-d}Cl_d$ electrochemical coin cell. Figure 5 shows the differential capacity of a representative cell, where the active material was made via GNP. Cells were cycled in their reversible region, between 4.75 V and 3.5 V[10-12]. The figure shows minimal IR shifts up until cycle 100, after which the features begin to slowly degrade, specifically the low voltage peak centered at 4.0 V. Degradation may be attributed to either conductivity or kinetic changes in the cell, leading to a lower coulombic efficiency.

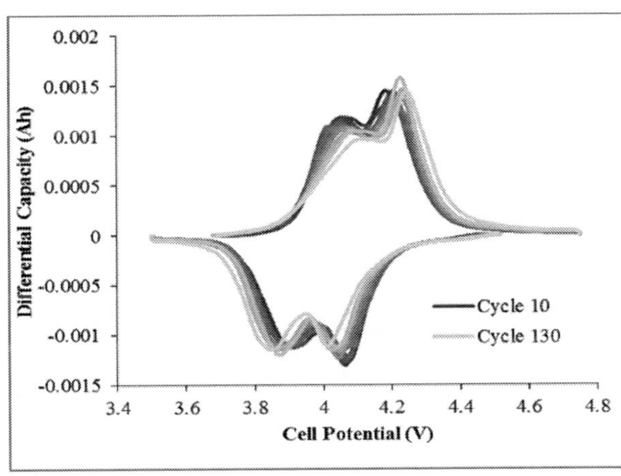

Figure 5. Differential capacity for a $Li//Li_xMn_2O_{4-d}Cl_d$ electrochemical cell made by GNP displaying 130 cycles.

Cycle life data of electrochemical cells were compared at varying degrees of Cl content present in the active material. The specific capacity for each cycle of three variant cells is shown in Figure 6. The first cell (depicted as "c") was made using the SSP process to produce $Li_xMn_2O_{4-d}Cl_d$ spinel, where $x \approx 1$and $d \approx 0.025$. The second cell (depicted as "b") was alternatively made using the GNP process to produce $Li_xMn_2O_{4-d}Cl_d$ spinel, where $x \approx 1$ and $d \approx 0.045$. Both of these cells demonstrate good cycle life with overcharge beginning to occur at cycle 100, which begins to impact the cell's performance. However, the cells are still able to retain 95% of their original capacity after 130 cycles. Comparatively, the third cell (depicted as "a") was made using the SSP process to make $Li_xMn_2O_{4-d}Cl_d$ spinel, where $x \approx 1$and $d \approx 0.05$. Cell "a" shows a decrease in capacity retention and cycle life, although it had the highest initial specific capacity at approximately 0.10 Ah/g. Cycles 39-48 were omitted due to shorting. Although the cell suffered significant shorting and capacity loss for 10 cycles, it was able to recover.

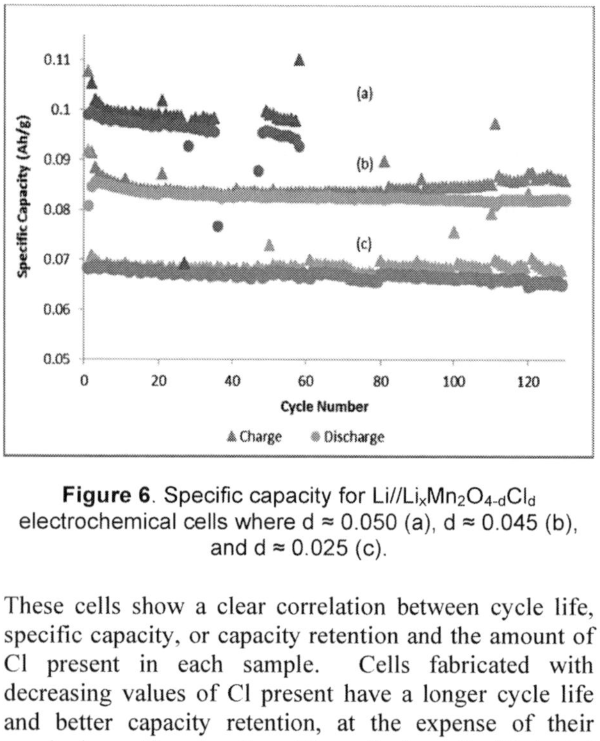

Figure 6. Specific capacity for $Li//Li_xMn_2O_{4-d}Cl_d$ electrochemical cells where $d \approx 0.050$ (a), $d \approx 0.045$ (b), and $d \approx 0.025$ (c).

These cells show a clear correlation between cycle life, specific capacity, or capacity retention and the amount of Cl present in each sample. Cells fabricated with decreasing values of Cl present have a longer cycle life and better capacity retention, at the expense of their nominal specific capacity. Alternatively, cells fabricated with higher Cl content present in the sample have a higher specific capacity with limited cycle life. However, these three cells were fabricated using different processing methods, two using SSP and the third using GNP. Further studies would have to be performed in order to conclude if the processing method had any additional impact on the cells' electrochemical performance. Additionally, these cells were cycled at high voltages and the electrolyte utilized may be insufficient at high voltage, causing the cell to fail prematurely.

Conclusions

Chlorine-doped lithium manganese oxide spinel was synthesized using two processing methods: a reduced solid state process and a glycine nitrate combustion process. Both of these processing methods drastically reduced the manufacturing cost and time to produce a single phase $LiMn_2O_4$ spinel material. Formation of a single phase material was confirmed via X-ray diffraction and Cl was verified to remain in the sample after calcination via X-ray fluorescence, although some Cl was lost during processing. Thermogravimetric analysis verified the proper thermodynamics during calcining to produce lithium manganese oxide spinel in all samples. $Li_xMn_2O_{4-d}Cl_d$ spinel was incorporated into the cathode of electrochemical coin cells paired with lithium metal. The coin cells demonstrate a correlation between cell performance and Cl present in the cathode material. Cells with lower Cl doping show good cycle life retention even when overcharging. Further testing and evaluation is recommended to evaluate high voltage electrolytes in order to mitigate capacity degradation. With further optimization, the robust LixMn2O4-dCld spinel materials will be promising active materials for future integration into lithium-ion batteries.

References

1. Reddy, Thomas B. *Linden's Handbook of Batteries*. Vol. 4. New York: McGraw-Hill, 2011.
2. Xia, H., Z. Luo, and J. Xie, *Progress in Natural Science*, vol. 22, pp. 572, 2012
3. Huang, H., C. A. Vincent, P. G. Bruce, *Journal of the Electrochemical Society*, vol. 146, pp. 3649, 1999
4. Xia, H. and M. Yoshio, *Journal of the Electrochemical Society*, vol. 143, pp. 825, 1996
5. Amatucci, G.G., N. Pereira, T. Zheng, I. Plitz, and J.M. Tarascon, *Journal of Power Sources*, vol. 81, pp. 39, 1999
6. Liu, W.R., S.H. Wu, and H.S. Sheu, *Journal of Power Sources*, vol. 146, pp. 232, 2005
7. Son, J.T., and H.G. Kim, *Journal of Power Sources*, vol. 147, pp. 220, 2005
8. Atwater, T. B., and P. C. Tavares, **US Patent No. 8,597,377**, December 3, 2013
9. Atwater, T. B., and P. C. Tavares, PC, **US Patent No. 8,900,756**, December 2, 2014
10. Atwater, T. B., and P. C. Tavares, *Proceedings of the 45th Power Sources Conference*, 2012
11. Atwater, T. B. and Latorre, P. C., *SAE Int. J. Materials and Manufacturing*, Vol. 6, no. 1,pp. 85-89, 2013
12. Atwater, T. B., and P. C. Latorre, *Proceedings of the 46th Power Sources Conference*, 2014
13. Amine et al, **US Patent No. 5,677,087**, October 14, 1997

Development of Soldier Wearable Fuel Cells

Tony Thampan, Shailesh Shah
US Army CERDEC

Abstract: *Communications-Electronics Research, Development, and Engineering Center (CERDEC) is developing wearable conformal fuel cell based power sources for dismounted Soldier applications in the US military. As part of this development, an AlH_3 based fuel cell system has been evaluated in ballistic tests and demonstrated in Soldier exercises. This work presents the results including promising performance during the 2016 Army Expeditionary Warrior Experiment (AEWE).*

Keywords: wearable; safety; fuel cell; Soldier demonstrations; AlH_3 ;

Introduction

Power and energy are critical to assure communications and situational awareness capabilities for Soldiers. To effectively deploy these capabilities on the Soldier and to avoid increased risks of musculoskeletal injuries higher energy power sources and energy sources are required. As a potential solution, the authors together with industry partners, are investigating Aluminum hydride based wearable fuel cells [1, 2, 3].

Aluminum hydride (AlH_3, Alane) is a covalently bonded, binary hydride which can release up to 10.1 wt. % H_2 resulting in a very high H_2 capacity at 0.149 kg H_2 L-1. While seven different polymorphs of AlH_3 (α, α', β, γ, δ, ε, and ζ) have been identified, this work utilized a metastable α-AlH_3 polymorph [4], which is the most thermally and hydrolytically stable form [5].

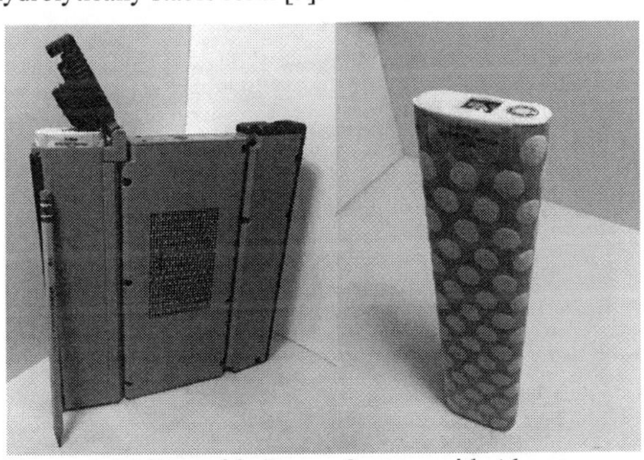

Figure 1 (a) Wearable Power System with Alane cartridge inserted. (b) Cartridge with thermal insulation wrap

Utilizing AlH_3, a PEM based fuel cell system have been able to provide a high energy density of 582 Wh kg^{-1} for a 1440 Wh load. This results in a significant weight savings vs. the conventional 150 Wh kg^{-1} Li-ion battery.

Table 1 Wearable Power System specifications

Parameter	Performance Overview
Power Rating	20W
Peak Power and Duration	35W for 10 min
Start-up Time	Instant with battery
Voltage	10-16.8 Volts
Energy Density for 72 hr (700 Wh) mission	354 Wh/kg
Dry Weight	1.12 kg (2.47 lbs)
System Volume	1.00 L
Dimensions	20.0 x 22.1 x 2.3 cm with flexibility to conform to SAPI plate
Battery Capacity	4x 9Wh = 36Wh total
Cartridge Capacity	85 Wh (0.12kg)
Cartridge Handling	Insulation on cartridge enables cartridge swapping without the use of gloves

This system has received positive soldier feedback [6] and was developed to a higher system maturity level as shown in Figure 1 and specifications provided in Table 1.

The system is based on a hinged design that allows it to conform (Figure 2) which is necessary for operation as a wearable device.

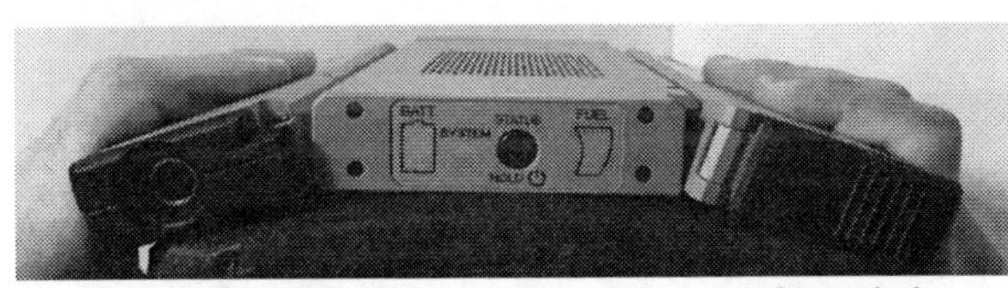

Figure 2: Wearable Power System in a conformal shape

Additionally the system has an internal battery that is charged by the fuel cell. This battery bus allows the system to meet transient high load demands, seamless load following and energy harvesting. The cartridge replacement is done by flipping open the cartridge chamber lid (Figure 1) and replacing the cartridge. During cartridge change out, power is supplied from the battery. The user interface is shown in Figure 3 and allows the operator to see the battery and cartridge state of charge.

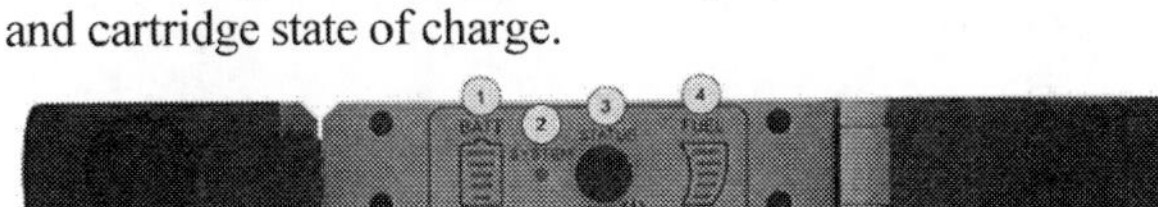

Figure 3: The system interface consists of 1) Battery State of Charge Gauge 2) System Status Indicator 3) Status / Fuel Cell Power Button and 4) Fuel Gauge

This work describes the developmental ballistic tests and soldier feedback on the operation of the systems at the 2016 Army Expeditionary Warrior Experiment (AEWE).

Experimental

The ballistic testing follows the performance specification sheet [7] protocol, in which the cartridge was mounted in a test fixture in different configurations with a vest and armor plate. As specified, the projectile was a 7.62 mm with a 2390 ft s^{-1} muzzle velocity. The cartridges SOC ranged from empty to fully charged.

The 2016 AEWE occurred at Ft. Benning GA and occurred over a 72 hours mission period including night missions. Data collection included power and energy data, using fuel cell's onboard memory storage capability, and a Soldier survey after the event.

Results and Discussion

Ballistic Tests The results of the cartridge tests are shown in Figures 4, 5 and 6. When the cartridge was mounted in the test fixture and ballistic tested, the impact resulted in a flash and flame. This is shown in Figure 4 (a) and the post impact results are shown in Figure 4 (b). However when the cartridge is mounted in the vest against an armor plate, no flame or flash was observed. The set up and post test results are shown in Figure 5 (a) and (b). It can be seen after impact, the AlH_3 powder is dispersed on vest.

Figure 4: (a) Cartridge ballistic test (b) Cartridge after test

Figure 5: (a) Cartridge ballistic test in vest again an armor plate. (b) Post test vest

Based on the pass criteria [7], the fuel cell cartridge should not injure the user when struck by bullets or shrapnel or present unsafe conditions. This includes avoidance of flame after impact. It appears from the testing with the cartridge in the vest, that when the cartridge powder is not allowed to disperse in the air, no flame is present upon ballistic impact. This design feature must be taken in account during the system design and safety qualification.

2016 Soldier Evaluation The Wearable Power System (WPS) was provided to Soldiers to integrate on their standard Modular Lightweight Load-carrying Equipment (MOLLE) vest as shown in Figures 6 (a), 6 (b), 7 (a) and 7 (b). Four soldiers were outfitted with the WPS, and mounted it on their vest according to their preference. Most soldiers chose to mount the system on their side or on the back.

Figure 6: WPS worn (a) in front (b) in the back

The WPS provided power to tactical radios, GPS and the NETT WARRIOR system. These systems allow enhanced communication and situational awareness for the Soldier.

Figure 7: (a) WPS worn on the side (b) Soldier operating Nett Warrior End User Device with power from WPS

During the missions the power and energy data was collected and is shown in Figure 8, 9 and 10. As shown in Figure 8, for a 72 h mission the average load was 8-10 W.

A total of 10 cartridges were changed. Not all had reached empty, but rather were changed at the user's discretion.

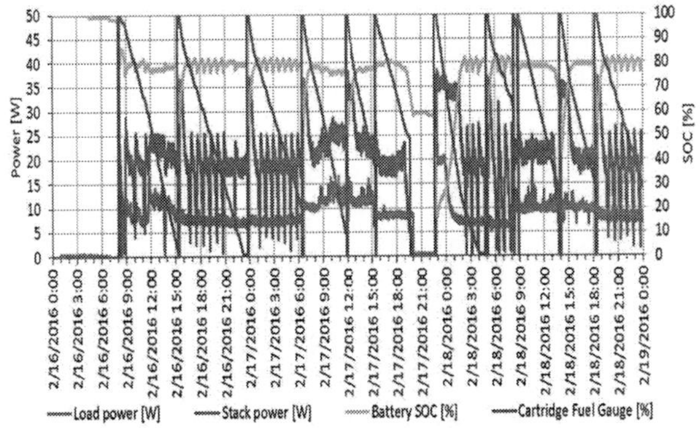

Figure 8: 72 h mission the average load was 8-10 W, with 10 cartridges changed.

Figure 9 show a subset of the data from a 72 hr mission profile. It can been seen there is consistent 10W load as the cartridge was being depleted. Upon start up the battery is used to initiate H_2 flow, and then the fuel cell stack provides power to recharge the battery. For the rest of operation, the stack power increases and decreases to maintain the battery SOC. The cartridge was removed with 19% remaining.

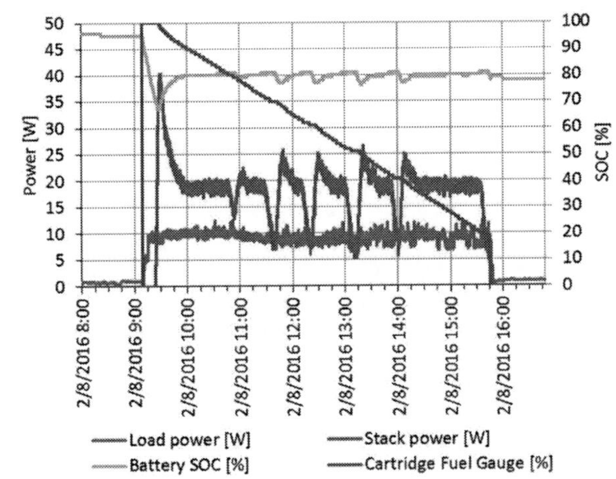

Figure 9: A subset of power /energy data from a 72 hr mission.

Figure 10 shows power /energy data at a high load period. This system has a high 20 -25 W load, with the fuel cell stack increasing output power to meet this demand, until 11:30. Starting at 13:00, the stack power is increased / decreased to match load, while keeping battery SOC at 80%.

<u>*Soldier Survey Response*</u> Four Soldiers utilized the WPS during the 2016 AEWE. Unfortunately two of the systems had technical failure with the control system resulting in poor reliability and negative feedback from the soldiers on their use. The two Soldiers whose systems worked properly were very favorable to the capability.

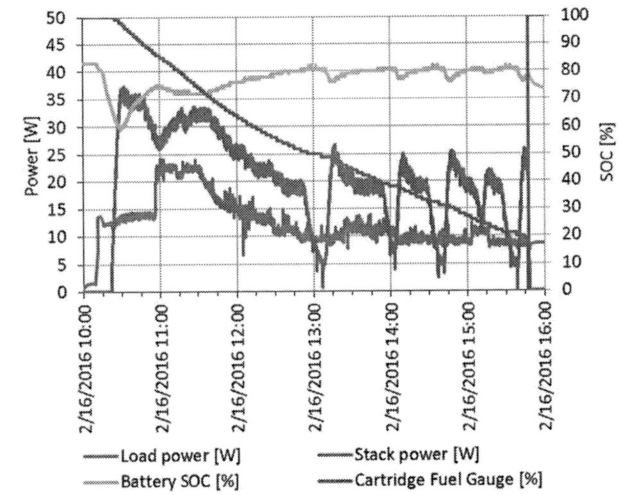

Figure 10: A subset of power /energy data with a high load period

Specifically the benefits included:

- A 55% weight reduction vs. CWB for 72 hr mission. This weight savings reduces the burden or allows for additional equipment or supplies to be taken
- Improved operational tempo for maneuvers. Utilizing the existing CWB, Soldiers must stop and recharge their batteries which impedes maneuvers. With the WPS, the cartridge replacement allows for a rapid operational temp without the need for battery recharging.

Conclusion

In conclusion the WPS has been evaluated at a the 2016 AEWE with a TRL 6. Although these prototype systems encountered reliability challenges, the systems provided significant weight savings and improved operational tempo. Future work will include increasing the TRL level to meet military performance requirements including verifying system safety in a battlefield environment.

References

1. T. Thampan, D. Shah, C. Cook, J. Novoa, S. Shah, J. Power Sources 259 (2014) 276-281
2. D. Shah, T. Thampan, Wearable Fuel Cell (WFC20) Technical Report, US ARMY, CERDEC/CPI/Army Power RDER-CPP-PS, June 13th, 2013
3. T. Thampan, T. Atwater, C. Cook, J. Novoa, A. C. Sutorik, Int. J. Hydrogen Energy (2016) *in press*

4. J. Graetz, J.J. Reilly, V.A. Yartys, J.P. Maehlen, B.M. Bulychev, V.E. Antonov, B.P. Tarasov, I.E. Gabis, J. Alloys Compd, 509S, (2011), S517-S528

5. A Paraskos, J. Hanks, and G. Lund, Insensitive Munitions and Energetic Materials Conference Proceedings, Miami, FL October 16, 2007

6. T. Thampan, E. Wooley, E. Durkin, After Action Report – CERDEC C4ISR Ground Activity E-15, FORT DIX, NJ. July 9, 20 – 23 2016

7. PERFORMANCE SPECIFICATION SHEET, MIL-PRF-32383/4 (CR) 6 March, 2013

Solid Acid Fuel Cell Portable and Remote Power System Developments

Calum Chisholm
SAFCell
calum.chisholm@safcell.com

Abstract

Solid Acid Fuel Cells (SAFC) operate at intermediate temperatures (~250°C), are inherently impermeable to gases, and transport "bare" protons through a solid electrolyte. These properties give SAFCs advantages over other fuel cell technologies in cost, durability, start/stop cycling, fuel flexibility, and simplified system design. SAFCell has developed SAFC stacks with very high tolerances to typical anode catalyst poisons such as carbon monoxide and hydrogen sulfide. SAFC stacks therefore run easily on commercially available fuels (e.g., propane and diesel), without complex reforming and fuel clean-up sub-systems required for lower temperature fuel cell technologies. In partnership with UltraCell, LLC., SAFCell has now demonstrated the advantages of SAFC stacks at the system level by developing pre-commercial remote area power systems (RAPS) and prototype portable power generators. Talk will give a high level overview of the SAFC technology and then describe ongoing efforts by SAFCell and UltraCell to develop and deploy power systems using SAFC stacks. Specifically, a 50W flex-fuel unit for man-portable power and a 50W methanol RAPS for the oil and natural gas sector. For both systems, the ability of the SAFC stack to reform CO and methanol greatly reduces system complexity, which simultaneously increases system robustness.

Hydrogen Separation Membranes for Power & Energy

Zachary William Dunbar
US Army Research Laboratory
Adelphi, Maryland 20783

Abstract: *Hydrogen separation palladium membrane technology enables selective removal of hydrogen from a stream of mixed gases. This enables a range of Army relevant technologies, such as the purification of hydrocarbon reformate into ultrapure hydrogen for fuel cell electric power, as well as novel membrane reactor configurations to generate fuels and chemicals in theater. ARL is developing novel, low cost, high flux membranes that eliminate many of the drawbacks of traditional palladium membrane technology.*

Keywords: palladium membrane; hydrogen separation; fuel processing; reforming; fuel cell

Introduction

The US Army has growing demands for portable electrical power. Battery technology is well suited for low power applications, and conventional internal combustion generators work well at high power ranges. However there is an intermediate range loosely defined here as approximately 50 W to 5000 W, where neither technology is ideal. Batteries suffer from poor energy density, while internal combustion engines have poor efficiency in this power range, in addition to being noisy, maintenance intensive and producing toxic emissions. This power range is an ideal range where fuel cell technology can contribute in the near future [1-2].

For military applications, a major limiting factor for fuel cell deployment is the source of fuel [2-4]. Compressed hydrogen is a non-starter on the battlefield, for both logistical and safety reasons. Energy dense liquid hydrocarbon fuels, on the other hand, hold promise to enable fuel cell technology by providing a convenient, dense, and safe alternative to compressed hydrogen. JP-8, a kerosene-like mix of long chain hydrocarbons, is the ideal liquid fuel for the Army since it is readily available on the battlefield and is well understood from a fuel handling and safety perspective. Unfortunately, to make JP-8 useable by a fuel cell it must undergo several fuel processing steps to transform it into hydrogen-rich reformate gas. The resulting gas is a high temperature mix of hydrogen and various reaction byproducts, some of which are detrimental to the fuel cell. Therefore, the reformate gas must be purified before being sent to the fuel cell.

In this work, the novel ultra-thin palladium-alloy membrane developed at ARL is characterized for hydrogen flux, stability, pressure tolerance, cost, and sulfur tolerance. The use of a palladium alloy improves tolerance to poisons frequently encountered to hydrocarbon reformate, enables lower temperature operation without hydrogen embrittlement and potentially reduces cost by replacing some of the palladium with less expensive base metals. In addition, a 'fuel to electric power' proof-of-concept demonstration is shown. Future directions such as higher temperature operation and membrane reactors are discussed.

Experimental Design

All microfabrication steps are conducted in the Adelphi Laboratory Center's Specialty Electronic Materials and Sensors Cleanroom (SEMASC).

Palladium and an alloying metal are deposited onto the polished side of a silicon wafer using co-sputtering, forming a dense metal film of approximately 1 micron in thickness. Photoresist is then spun over the metal surface, and patterned using standard commercial photolithographic techniques. The photoresist is exposed and developed, leaving a polymer mold. The wafer is placed in a nickel sulfamate plating solution, and a nickel layer is plated around the polymer mold. The plated nickel is in a grid-like pattern and will act as mechanical support for the palladium alloy. Afterwards, the polymer mold is chemically removed. Finally, the starting silicon wafer is removed, leaving behind the palladium alloy, supported by the patterned nickel metal support.

Figure 1. False-color SEM (scanning electron microscopy) cross-section of ARL's palladium membrane,

Results & Discussion

The palladium-copper alloy microstructure supported membranes are tested in a synthetic water-gas-shift type atmosphere (50% H2, 1-5%CO, 20% H_2O, balance CO_2). The membranes are able to separate hydrogen from this mixture with a selectivity of over 5000:1 (molecules hydrogen separated per molecule non-hydrogen). The flux shows little deactivate when the carbon monoxide concentration is increased from 1% to 5%, indicating good resistance against this known palladium membrane poison. Flux vs time is shown in Figure 2.

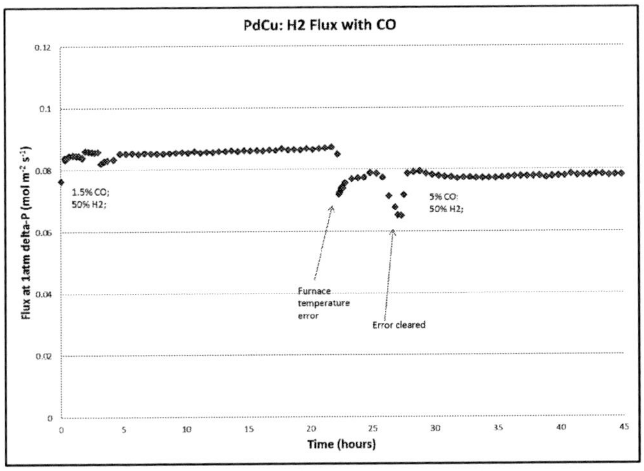

Figure 2. Hydrogen Flux vs time for a palladium-copper alloy exposed to a mixture of hydrogen and carbon monoxide on the feed side of the membrane

A proof-of-concept demonstration was also conducted, to verify the palladium-alloy membrane purifies reformate gas to a standard suitable for fuel cell electric power. The demonstration consisted of a scaled up palladium alloy membrane, approximately 11 cm^2 in area (3.8cm or 1.5 inches in diameter). Simulated reformate gas is feed to one side of the membrane, at atmospheric pressure. On the permeate side of the membrane, steam sweep gas is feed at atmospheric pressure. The permeate sweep gas is later condensed, leaving behind an atmosphere of pure hydrogen, which flows to a low temperature proton exchange membrane (PEM) fuel cell, running at constant power. Nominal fuel cell power is 300 mW. The PEM fuel cell will tolerate no more than 1 ppm carbon monoxide, per the manufacturer (Horizon). The output of the fuel cell is displayed in Figure 3.

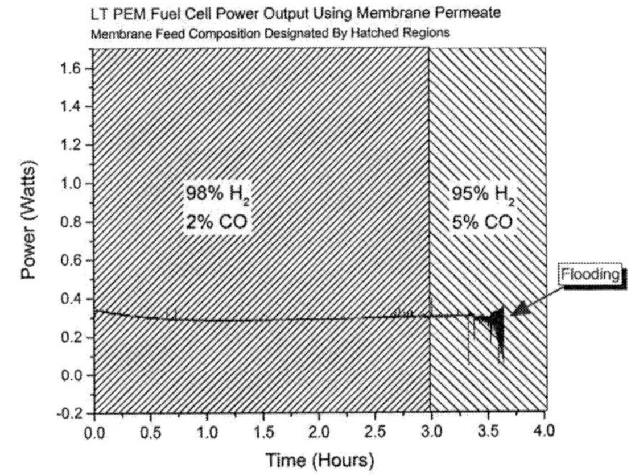

Figure 3. PEM fuel cell power outout over time, receiving hydrogen purified by palladium-copper alloy membrane. Feed hydrogen carbon monoxide concentrations indicated by hatched regions. Permating hydrogen to fuel cell is less than 1 ppm CO. Water flooding (unrelated to palladium-alloy membrane) forces halt to experiment before 4 hours.

Conclusions

Palladium membrane technology enables fuel cells (particularly low temperature PEM fuel cells) utilizing high energy density liquid hydrocarbons as fuel. Significant progress has been made in developing a palladium alloy membrane with a novel support architecture, which enables high hydrogen flux with great selectivity and favorable cost metrics. The membrane has been demonstrated to purify hydrogen streams of up to 5% (50,000ppm) carbon monoxide into 'PEM fuel cell quality' hydrogen. Future work will expand the membrane operating window to higher temperatures and improved resistance to hydrogen sulfide.

References

[1] S. Roychoudhury, M. Lyubovsky, D. Walsh, D. Chu, E. Kallio, Journal of Power Sources, 160 (2006) 510-513.

[2] A.S. Patil, T.G. Dubois, N. Sifer, E. Bostic, K. Gardner, M. Quah, C. Bolton, Journal of Power Sources, 136 (2004) 220-225.

[3] DOD 4140.25-M, DOD Directive 4140.25, (1993).

[4] V. Jayaraman, Y.S. Lin, J. Membr. Sci., 104 (1995) 251-262.

Developments in High Pressure Electrolysis to Enable Simplified and Efficient Hydrogen Fuel Production

Stephen Szymanski, Luke Dalton, Katherine Ayers
Proton Energy Systems, d/b/a Proton OnSite
10 Technology Drive
Wallingford, CT 06492

Abstract: *Proton Exchange Membrane (PEM) electrolysis combined with electrochemical compression in the same device is an attractive configuration to replace mechanical compressors. This solution combines the advantages of higher total efficiency, low noise output, and much higher reliability than mechanical compression due to the lack of moving parts. In addition, available mechanical compressors are large and heavy relative to an electrolyzer with the same hydrogen throughput. A study at Proton showed that footprint could be cut at least in half with high pressure electrolysis compared to low pressure electrolysis with mechanical compression, for a neighborhood-scale fueling station application. Efficiency losses in the electrochemical compression process are controlled by the Nernst equation, hydrogen permeation in the membrane, and resistance losses at the operating current density, which trade well vs. mechanical compression to relatively high pressures.*

Electrochemical compression can be accomplished directly in an electrolyzer stack, as is evidenced by Proton's 15 bar to 165 bar commercial electrolyzer capability. The compression at this output range is accomplished with very little voltage penalty. As the output pressure of the electrolyzer is increased beyond 165 bar, the proportion of energy consumption required to compress the hydrogen becomes a more significant contribution to the overall system energy consumption.. At higher generation pressures, back diffusion of the hydrogen across the MEA increases and represents an efficiency loss. The net result is a declining efficiency benefit as we approach typical vehicle fueling pressures (350 to 700 bar).

Recently, Proton has been focused on high pressure oxygen production (3,600 psi) for NASA's exploration missions, and 5,000 psi hydrogen production for a commercial energy storage application. Building off of Proton's 5,000 psi stack design, developed under the DOE funded "Home Fueler" program, Proton is able to provide an electrolyzer solution that eliminates the reliability and maintenance issues of mechanical compressors for both of these customers. In this paper, we will provide an update on the development of high pressure electrolysis technology for use in a variety of energy storage, fueling, and niche market applications.

Keywords: electrolysis; proton exchange membrane; hydrogen; energy storage; electrochemical compression.

Introduction

Proton OnSite has been serving a variety of hydrogen application needs for more than 20 years. Our customers have a wide range of hydrogen pressure requirements for their processes, ranging from just a few psi to 10,000 psi for vehicle fueling applications. As we evaluate system configurations to address these requirements, it is clear that higher pressure capability from the electrolyzer offers benefits in the areas of lower capital cost and energy usage in the downstream compression process. Increasing the "electrochemical" compression contribution is more economically and electrically efficient up to a certain point. Proton's work on high pressure electrolysis and compressor cells has provided an excellent data source for modeling of compression costs and energy consumption. It is apparent from this data that at high capacities, and very high pressures, there are crossing points where a combination of electrochemical and mechanical compression is the most efficient and viable solution.

Fundamentals of Electrochemical Compression

The PEM electrolyzer cell schematic is shown below:

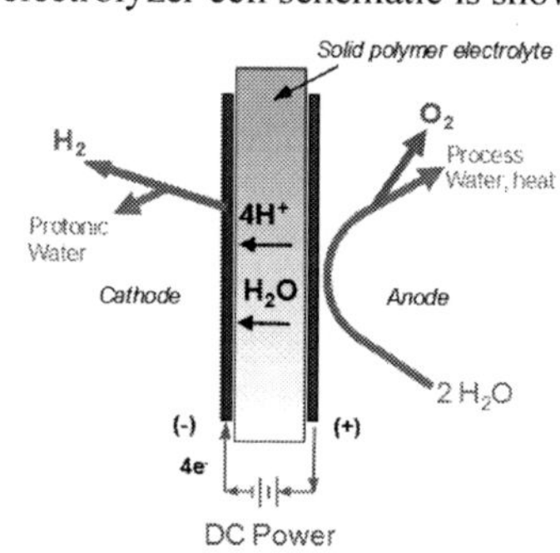

Figure 1. PEM electrolyzer cell schematic

The system operation of a PEM electrolyzer allows for the back pressuring of the hydrogen side of the cell stack, while maintaining a low (near ambient) pressure on the oxygen side. This differential pressure operation is a fundamental safety advantage for PEM electrolysis, in that it assures there is no opportunity for oxygen to cross over to the hydrogen side of the cell. Through several development programs, Proton has demonstrated differential pressure electrolysis up to 5,000 psi, and stack sealing at 7,500 psi.

At a modest range of operating pressures (200 to 2,400 psi), there is very little voltage penalty associated with the increased pressure, as shown in the figure below. The curves show cell voltage versus current density at three different operating points: 200 psi, 1100 psi, and 2400 psi.

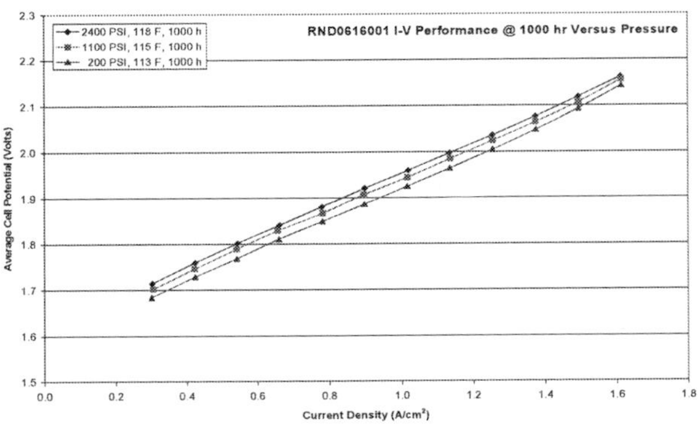

Figure 2: Voltage effect of increased pressure

When you look at the energy consumption of a PEM electrolyzer system over a larger range of hydrogen pressures, there are three primary processes involved: generation, drying, and compression. The energy for the electrolysis (generation) process itself is nearly independent of pressure. The energy use for drying is a relatively small contributor, and decreases proportionately at higher pressures (see Figure 3). This result is because the water content of the output gas is highly dependent on pressure. For example, increasing the hydrogen generation pressure from 200 to 2400 psi results in a 6X to 7X reduction in moisture, which significantly reduces the purge losses in the dryer system. It is really only the energy required for compression that increases as hydrogen generation pressure increases. Specifically, hydrogen permeation losses of the proton exchange membrane increase at high pressure. These efficiency effects need to be compared to mechanical compression losses over a similar pressure and flow range.

There is no inherent physical limitation to electrochemically compressing hydrogen to 875 bar, which is a common storage pressure for vehicle fueling. Previous reports[1,2] have demonstrated small scale electrochemical compression to these levels, for short periods of time. Proton has demonstrated sealing of electrochemical cells to 550 bar, and operated electrolysis cells at 350 bar differential pressure for over 2000 hours. However, many variables need to be considered in defining a solution capable of meeting the application requirements. First, the higher the compression pressure, the higher the mechanical stress on the membrane. If a thicker membrane is required to meet the pressure targets, either the operating efficiency decreases, or the current density has to be reduced, increasing capital cost. Second, higher differential pressure results in higher hydrogen crossover, a separate loss in efficiency that has to be accounted for. Therefore, each delivery pressure is likely to have a different optimum configuration. New advances in membranes may also help to reduce the crossover losses, especially for membranes specifically designed for compression applications, vs. materials optimized for fuel cell or electrolysis operation.

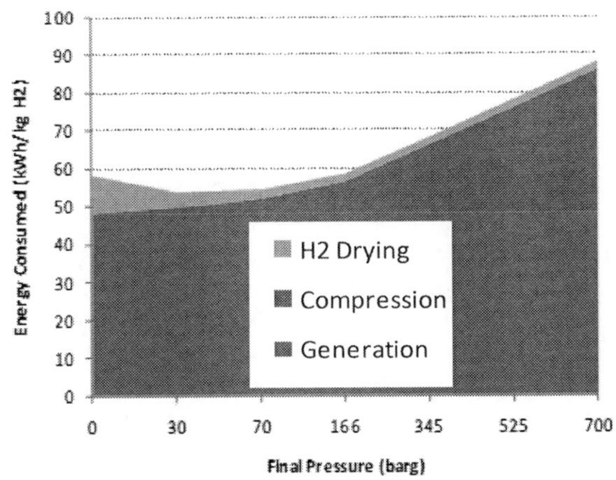

Figure 3: PEM electrolysis energy use versus pressure

Electrochemical vs. Mechanical Compression

Two common hydrogen fueling pressures have emerged for passenger vehicles, buses, material handling equipment, and other specialty vehicles: 350 bar (5,000 psi) and 700 bar (10,000 psi). When we evaluate the energy consumption required to compress hydrogen to these pressures, we can compare the total energy required based on different operating pressures from the electrolyzer. The following charts show total energy consumption per kg of hydrogen for a range of electrolyzer operating points. The first chart shows that for the 350 bar compression case, net energy is minimized when the electrolyzer is operating at 70 bar output pressure. For the 700 bar compression case, net energy is minimized when the electrolyzer is operating at 166 bar output pressure.

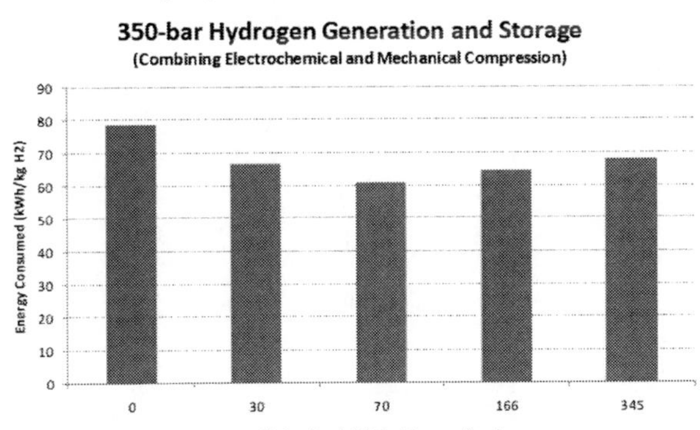

Figure 4: Net energy for 350 bar compression, as a function of electrolyzer output pressure

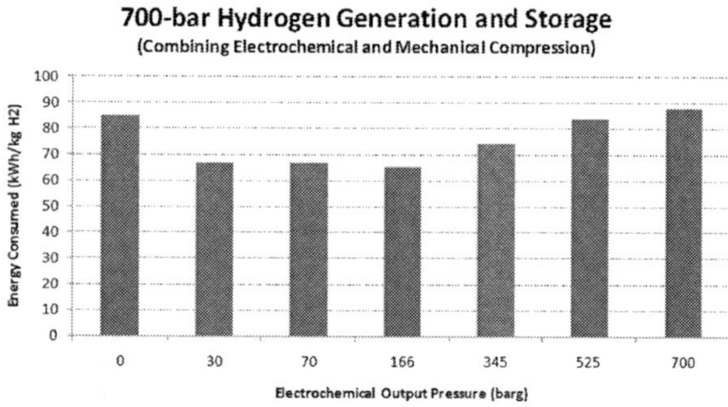

Figure 5: Net energy for 700 bar compression, as a function of electrolyzer output pressure

However, energy consumption is not the only factor in determining the optimal balance of electrochemical and mechanical compression for high pressure hydrogen applications. Pure mechanical compressors suffer from two major drawbacks. The first is contamination via lubricants that may be harmful to PEM fuel cells. By reducing the compression stages, the degree of contamination can be decreased. The second drawback is the maintenance cost and downtime of mechanical compressors. Compressors account for 23% of station events and 32% of station maintenance time[3], representing the number one cause of system downtime at current hydrogen stations. Typical compressor maintenance events take 4–6 hours and two technicians before getting the compressor online. In contrast, a PEM electrolyzer stack has no moving parts, and no inherent maintenance requirements. Also, Proton has demonstrated stack lifetimes of more than 60,000 hours, which represents a significant improvement over the operating life of compressors.

High Pressure Electrolysis Development

Proton is actively developing high pressure electrolysis capability in two configurations. The first is an anode feed stack that generates 5,000 psi hydrogen and ambient pressure oxygen, and is being designed for an energy storage application. The second is a cathode feed stack that generates 3,600 psi oxygen, and near ambient pressure hydrogen. This stack is being developed for NASA's future exploration missions, where they would like to eliminate the need for an oxygen compressor to fill the oxygen tanks on the astronaut's space suit. (It should also be mentioned that Proton has previously demonstrated 3,000 psi balanced pressure electrolysis on a DARPA program.) The two stack configurations utilize different materials and operate in different modes, but fundamentally share many design features.

350 Bar Hydrogen Generation

Initial work on the 350 bar stack design was conducted on a DOE program, and was focused on a small scale "home fueling" application. The system concept was to develop a low cost device that could be used to slow fill vehicles, particularly at night, in a residential setting. The design concept for the stack development was to adapt our commercial 86 cm^2 platform to a 350 bar capability. This stack geometry had already been modified to achieve a 165 bar hydrogen production pressure, and more than 20,000 hours of operation had been accumulated at this pressure. On the DOE program, Proton successfully designed and operated a one-cell stack at 350 bar pressure, and accomplished a stack sealing pressure of > 525 bar. Cell voltages were compared to a commercial 13 bar stack, as shown below.

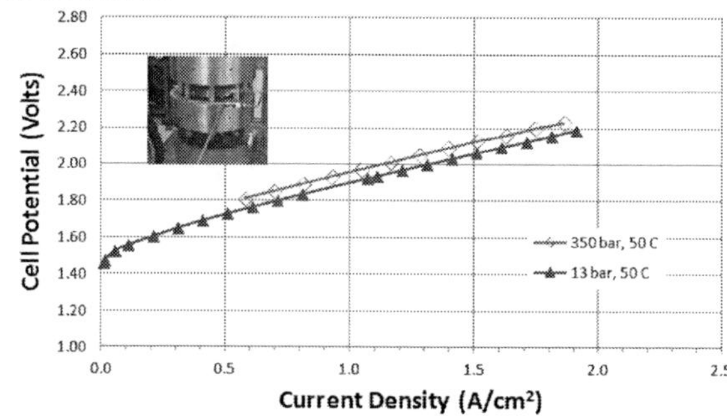

Figure 6: 350 bar voltage performance versus 13 bar

In addition, Proton was able to make some significant design improvements in advancing from the 165 bar stack to the 350 bar stack (see below). Ultimately, the goal was to develop a stack that was lower in cost and more readily manufacturable. In particular, the new stack design eliminated certain structural reinforcement components and allowed for the use of commercial tie rods and nuts.

Figure 7: 165 bar (L) vs. 350 bar stack design (R)

Subsequent to the conclusion of the DOE program, Proton engaged in a joint development activity with a commercial partner who will be integrating the 350 bar stack into their energy storage solution. The primary focus of this program is to scale the design to a 34 cell configuration that can produce 2 Nm^3/hr of hydrogen at 350 bar. Proton has built and is testing this design in our development lab as of this writing. Stable operation has been achieved for thousands of cell hours to date, see Figure 9.

Figure 8: 34-cell 350 bar test stack

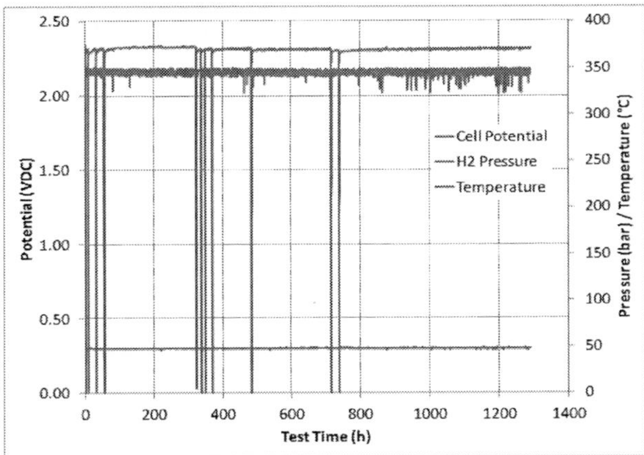

Figure 9: 350 bar stack showing stable performance

<u>245 Bar Oxygen Generation</u>

As previously mentioned, Proton is also developing a cathode feed stack for NASA's high pressure oxygen needs. NASA's system level analyses for multiple remote microgravity PEM electrolysis applications have consistently shown that a reactant water feed at the cathode results in the simplest and most robust electrolysis system for space applications. The reason for this system architecture selection is to accommodate the challenges associated with gas-liquid water phase separation in microgravity environments. Since reliable phase separation is such a challenge, employing cathode feed cells requires phase separation only in the hydrogen/water cathode circulation loop, as the PEM cell inherently yields a net flux of water toward the cathode and helps remove any liquid water from the anode. The disadvantage of this approach is that the anode requires water for the oxygen generation reaction. Therefore, other elements of the cell design need to be optimized to maximize performance.

In the Phase I project, Proton successfully demonstrated transition from an anode feed, high pressure hydrogen generation configuration to a cathode feed, high pressure oxygen generation configuration, based on Proton's 5000 psi stack platform. This effort involved opening up the flow field pathways through the cathode chamber and changing the pressure compensating elements from cathode to anode, with corresponding changes in the materials of construction. In the Phase II effort, this work is being extended to optimize the stack design for the application, and scale to a relevant stack height.

Figure 10 shows polarization curves at a range of operating pressures for the first test stack. As seen from the curves, the limiting current density decreases substantially from operation at ambient pressure to operation at 3600 psi. This result is likely due to the lack of available water at the anode, which decreases further as oxygen pressure is increased due to the hydraulic forces driving water to the cathode side of the cell and due to the decrease in relative humidity in the anode gas stream.

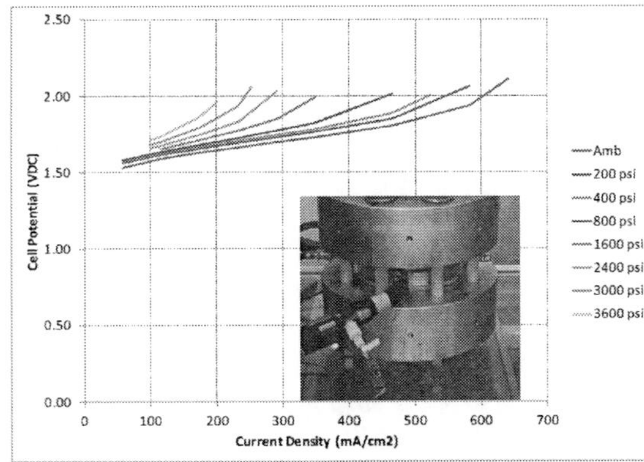

Figure 10: Polarization curves as function of pressure

Figure 11 below, shows stable operation achieved at 3,600 psi oxygen generation for the first 230 hours of operation.

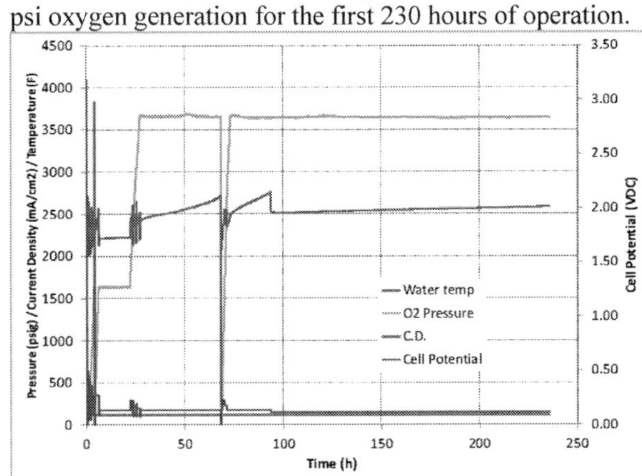

Figure 11: Stable operation in cathode feed mode

Summary

High pressure electrolysis is an enabling technology for eliminating unreliable and inefficient compressors for both hydrogen and oxygen service. For energy storage and small fueling applications, system simplification and cost reduction are also significant benefits to be derived from this technology. To address these emerging markets, Proton is developing both stack and system capability.

Acknowledgements

The authors would like to acknowledge the U.S. Department of Energy and NASA for their support in funding portions of this development effort.

References

1. http://www.hydrogen.energy.gov/pdfs/review14/pd048_lipp_2014_o.pdf
2. http://www.phaedrus-project.eu/userdata/file/Presentations/PHAEDRUS%20presentation%20at%20WES %20151012 %20by%20HyET%20Peter%20Bouwman.pdf
3. http://www.nrel.gov/hydrogen/images/cdp_infr_21.jp

Production of Synthetic Fuel from Anaerobic Digester Gas and Other Wastes

Lyman J Frost
Joseph J Hartvigsen
S. Elango Elangovan
Ceramatec, Inc
Salt Lake City, UT 84119 USA
lfrost@ceramatec.com

Abstract: *This paper discusses research conducted at Ceramatec related to production of synthetic fuels from various wastes using small scale Fischer Tropsch. The system designed and tested by Ceramatec indicates the ability to produce a modular, road-transportable system for the same capital as large plants. Ceramatec has demonstrated the production of FT liquids from various feedstock options, including: natural gas, synthesis gas from co-electrolysis, biogas, and solid fuels.*

Keywords: Fischer Tropsch; Synthetic Fuels; GTL; CTL; BTL; modular synthetic fuel plants

Introduction

Ceramatec has been involved in research associated with synthetic fuels for a significant period of time. It has demonstrated the ability to produce Fischer Tropsch (FT) fuels from a variety of feedstock sources (e.g. co-electrolysis of steam and carbon dioxide, gas output by an anaerobic digester, natural gas, and heavier hydrocarbons). Ceramatec started not with a technology but with an objective to design a system that could eventually be built on a small scale for the same operating and capital cost that large, world-class FT plants are built. Since there are limited sites that can provide the volumes of natural gas needed for these larger plants, a solution to smaller volumes of hydrocarbons to liquids was needed.

The energy industry has developed a model for economies of scale of building very large, very efficient, and permanently sited synthetic fuels plants. In order to process the diverse, dispersed, and small field resources that are available, a different model is required. The Ceramatec vision is a mass-produced modular unit that is sized to be road transportable, constructed of normally available materials in a factory, and designed for minimum capital and operating cost. What is lost in plant size is made up for in number of plants produced, and by mass manufacturing of innovative designs developed using modeling tools and developed around advanced catalysts and supports. The economics simply don't work for one-of-a-kind designs, built on-site for a small and transient feedstock.

Ceramatec's reactor design philosophy attempts to reduce the costs and risks associated with reactor design, fabrication and operation by the following means:

- Using fixed bed reactors
- Limiting reactor train module size to 12"x12"x48" for over the road mobility
- Employing removable catalyst bed elements for off-site catalyst service
- Designing pressure boundary components fabricated from standard industrial piping and fittings
- Design for thermal management based on high activity catalysts
- Simplify the process scheme to minimize capital
- Achieve low thermal variation in reactor radial and axial profiles

Technical

Ceramatec successfully demonstrated a XTL reactor element at 43mm diameter and expanded this to a 100mm diameter reactor. Reactors are interoperable with a variety of structured reactor inserts and can be charged with highly active conventional or hybrid catalysts.

A Comsol Multi-physics model was used to maximize the total reactor production rate by varying seven parameters defining the profile geometry. The total catalyst volume productivity was maximized subject to a constraint on the limiting temperature within the domain. A Monte-Carlo technique was used to find starting points for subsequent Nelder-Mead optimization to converge on local optima. This approach yielded some non-intuitive reverse taper fin solutions where heat gathering surface area was more critical than heat (Figure 1).

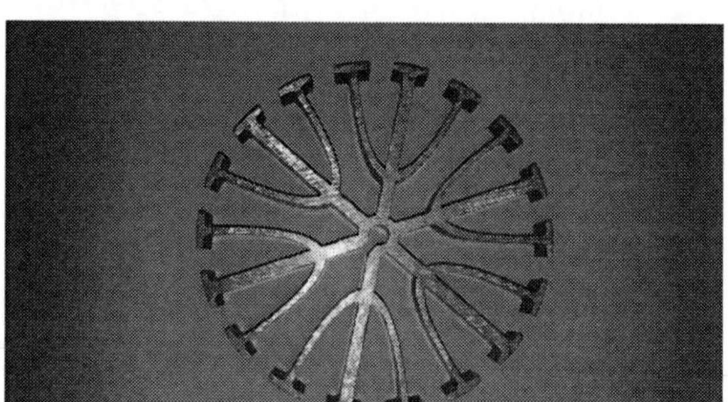

Figure 1: Reactor insert arrangement for thermal transfer

Ceramatec has an established synthetic fuels laboratory infrastructure with sufficient syngas generation and compression capacity to supply a 2 BPD reactor. The current laboratory implementation of this reactor is a ¼ length implementation of the 100mm reactor with a removable catalyst tube and a fixed cooling jacket. The cooling jacket features dual mode cooling with a forced convection pass on an annular zone in direct contact with the catalyst tube, surrounded by a boiling coolant outer shell. The forced convection pass coolant is held above the saturation pressure while the outer shell coolant is at saturation pressure. As the thermal stability of the 100mm diameter reactor is now proven, a 7-tube, ¼ length, 1 BPD reactor is in design to demonstrate a larger number of reactor tube elements.

The ¼ BPD GTL laboratory system is fed by a three (3) inch natural gas pipeline. After passing through a sulfur guard bed to remove any sulfur compounds, the synthesis gas is generated by a Ceramatec designed non-thermal plasma catalyzed reformer. This reformer is capable of processing up to 100 MSCF per day of high-BTU natural gas (i.e. enough for ~ 10 BPD of FT liquids). Figure 2 shows the reformer (~8' high; ~2' diameter).

Figure 2: 10 BPD Plasma Natural Gas Reformer

After production, the synthesis gas (CO and H_2) goes through several stages of compression. The first compression step uses a two-stage compressor with cooling to condense moisture after each stage (Figure 3). The synthesis gas exits the compressor at about 200 psig and is piped to an intermediate storage facility located external to the laboratory. When the intermediate storage in a 240 gallon 200 psig tank. When the tank is full, a second step of compression increases synthesis gas pressure to 800 psig and stores the material in two 500 gallon tanks (Figure 4). This serves as a buffer feedstock to the Fischer Tropsch reactor located within the laboratory.

Figure 3: Two-stage compression with cooling

Figure 4: Syngas storage (800 psig) and compressor

Each of the compression steps is sufficient to provide enough pressurized synthesis gas for ~ 2 BPD of FT liquids. The synthesis gas is then ready to be fed to the FT reactor. The reactor input is regulated to about 300 psig and is preheated prior to introduction into the FT reactor.

The FT reactor (Figure 5) operates at ~ 300 psig and ~225° C with internal heat transfer media to produce an even catalyst bed temperature in both axial and radial directions. The internal heat transfer structures have demonstrated the capability to maintain bed temperatures in a 4" reactor with a Co-Ru catalyst that varies by < 10° C.

Figure 5: FT reactor system (yellow skid)

The reactor has automated product collection for both light and heavy hydrocarbons (green skid in Figure 5). The system has a dual cooling system with integral cooling. A synthesis gas recycle system is also used to optimize utilization. The recycled synthesis gas is re-pressurized prior to mixing with the fresh feedstock. The cooling loop operates at atmospheric pressure by use of a synthetic coolant. At full production with a catalyst of appropriate activity the FT reactor (~5' high and 4" diameter) is capable of producing ~ ¼ BPD of FT liquids.

Ceramatec has done simulations on the production of FT liquids from anaerobic digester gas and other wastes. Anaerobic digesters produce a gas that is typically on the order of 60 - 75% CH_4 with the balance largely being CO_2. According to the USDA there were 88.5 million head of cattle in the United States in 2014. Based on typical manure yields and anaerobic digester conversions from Purdue University reports in 2014, this translates into ~1560 MMSCF (million standard cubic foot) per day of methane per day. Typical yields experienced by Ceramatec in its experiments demonstrate that 10 MSCF of methane yield about 1 barrel of mixed FT liquids. Thus, cattle waste by itself could generate on the order of 156 MBPD (thousand barrels per day) of hydrocarbons.

Ceramatec investigated the use of anaerobic digester gas using samples that were provided by Utah State University. The gas was cleaned of hydrogen sulfide prior to being run through the Ceramatec plasma reformer to generate synthesis gas. The synthesis gas was then run through the Ceramatec FT reactor to generate liquids. The resultant synthetic fuel was run through a bomb calorimeter at Utah State University to determine energy content and the analysis showed 46.5kilojoules per gram (note: diesel is ~46 KJ/g). A further laboratory analysis by Bureau Veritas Group indicated a Cetane rating for the fuel of ~60.2. The product distribution was as shown in Figure 6.

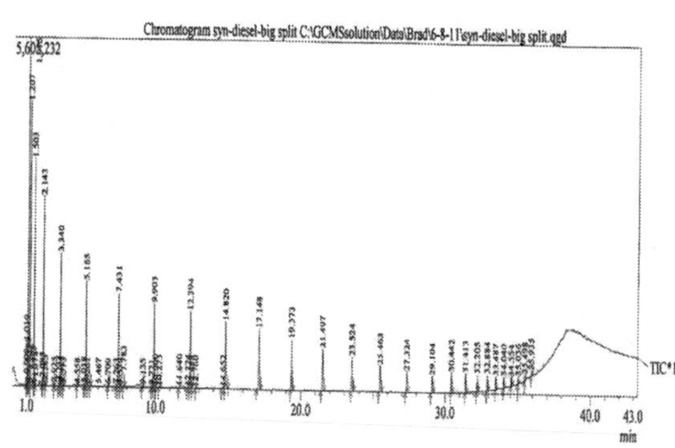

Figure 6: Chromatograph of FT liquids

The yield is typical of other yields that Ceramatec has seen in its laboratory work using the particular catalyst used for the referenced experiment. The distribution of product followed the ASF (Anderson – Schulz – Flory) distribution that is well known in FT work. The carbon number distribution depends on the particular catalyst and the operating conditions of the reactor. Figure 7 shows the carbon distribution with two different catalysts. The distribution in blue is with a standard Ceramatec Co-Ru catalyst and the distribution in red is with a hybrid catalyst that is designed to terminate carbon polymerization. The hybrid has a special support structure.

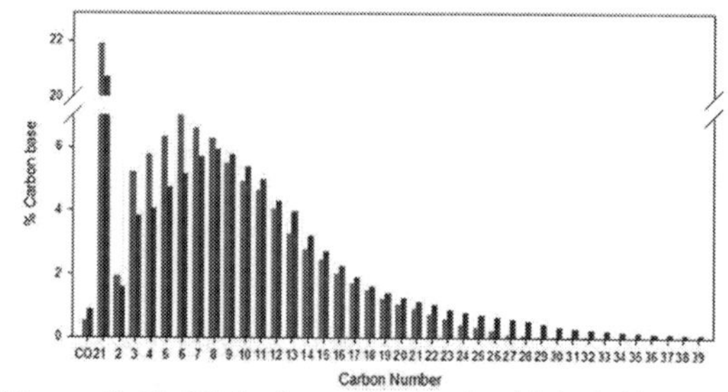

Figure 7: C distribution with standard & hybrid catalyst

The reactor has shown very stable operation and the catalyst used has demonstrated repeatable performance. The reactor was run for five hundred (500) hours and multiple product samples taken. The results tracked very well over time (Figure 8).

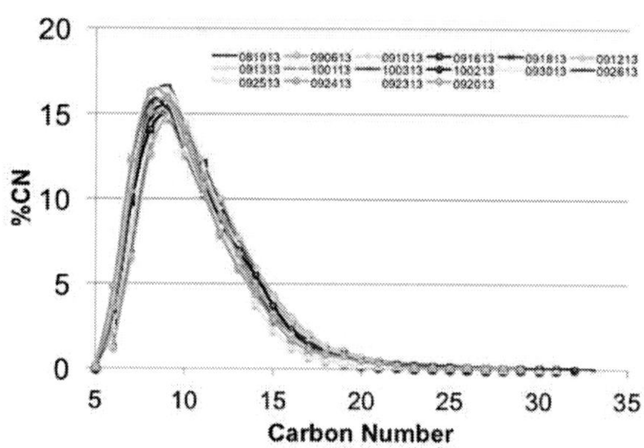

Figure 8: Plot of multiple samples from extended run

Ceramatec is currently building a 2 BPD system under a program funded by the United States Air Force and managed by DOE – NETL. The reactor will be initially tested using natural gas and then run on synthesis gas generated from a mixture of coal and biomass. The proportion of biomass has been selected to enable the production of Jet A fuel with less carbon emissions than would be generated if the fuel was produced from petroleum. The 2 BPD reactor will be combined with a new sulfur removal system that will remove the sulfur from the coal and generate a clean synthesis gas and a stream of elemental sulfur. The reactor will consist of seven (7) reactor tubes that are four (4) inches in diameter with the hybrid catalyst mentioned above. The reactor design is shown in Figure 9. The reactor tubes will be ~ fourteen (14) foot in length and will be water cooled pressure vessel. As can be seen in the figure, the tubes are arranged in a symmetrical arrangement.

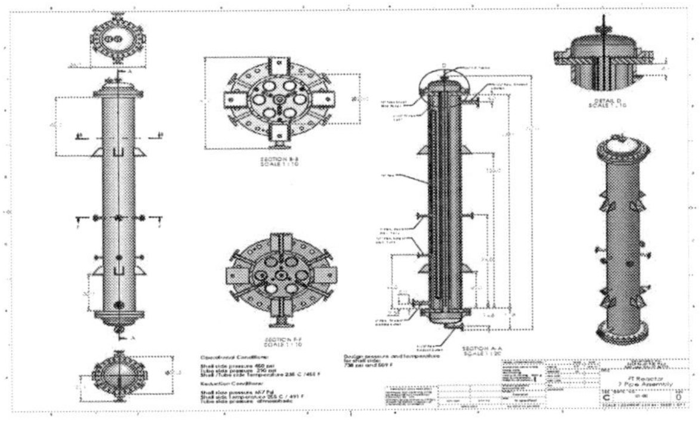

Figure 9: 2 BPD FT reactor for Jet A production

The stability of the reactor and catalyst in the laboratory has encouraged Ceramatec to design a 10 BPD pilot plant using the same components. The design was done in conjunction with an engineering and construction firm experienced in pilot plant construction. The 10 BPD pilot consists of three skids (skid 1 – 12'x12'x36'; skid 2 – 12'x12'x30'; skid 3 – 12'x12'x24') and a container for the synthesis gas compression. The plant is designed to operate on natural gas that has been largely cleaned of any sulfur compounds. The reformer operates in an autothermal mode using air and steam as oxidants. An artist's rendition of the facility is shown as Figure 8.

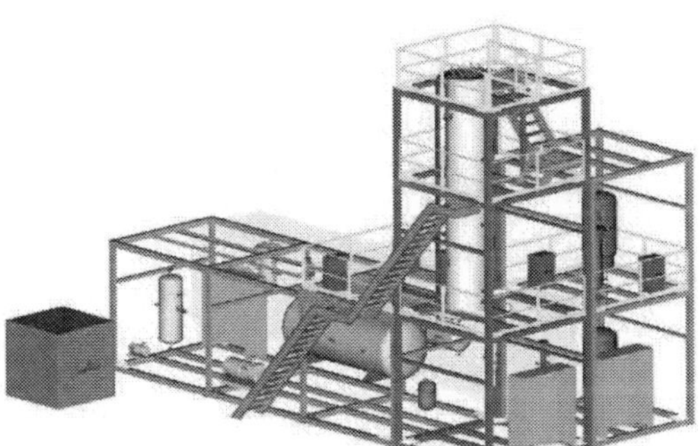

Figure 8: Proposed 10 BPD GTL facility

The compact size of the unit is made possible by the design of the FT reactor, operation of the reformer on air instead of oxygen, and the compact size of the reformer. It is contemplated that this GTL plant would be road transportable and could be deployed to remote sites to address flare gas or if a gasifier were added, to utilize waste at distributed locations.

Ceramatec has also designed reactors that are capable of producing ~ 100 BPD of FT liquids but meet the standards for being transported by road without special requirements.

Summary

Ceramatec has been conducting research in the design of systems for the production of FT liquids. Most of the research has been done using natural gas as a convenient feedstock. Other feedstock options have been tried, including anaerobic digester gas, synthesis gas from the co-electrolysis of steam and carbon dioxide, and various reformed heavy hydrocarbons. The results demonstrate the ability to construct a modular, transportable system that is cost effective. Current laboratory data indicates that it is possible to build FT systems in this size range that will match the efficiency, capital cost per BPD capacity, and operating cost of larger FT plants. This provides the capability to utilize hydrocarbon sources that are not presently cost effective.

Acknowledgements

Portions of the FT reactor testing and catalyst design have been supported by the State of Wyoming and by the Office of Naval Research. The US Department of Energy and the United States Air Force have also provided funding for portions of the technology. A majority of the funding has come from private sources.

Solar Fuel Production for a Sustainable Energy

Deryn Chu
US Army Research Laboratory

Robert, Mantz
US Army Reserach Office

Terry DuBois and Edward Plichta
US Army CERDEC

Nick Wu
West Virgina University

deryn.d.chu.civ@mail.mil

Abstract

The development of renewable and sustainable energy sources is one of the most significant scientific challenges facing the Department of Defense. Sun light is the most abundant renewable energy source and has great potential to meet future global energy demands. Solar fuels that convert solar energy to chemical energy stored as chemical fuels such as hydrogen and methanol. The direct photoelectrochemical water splitting to generate hydrogen has attracted attention world-wide due to their renewable fuel generation and benefit to the environment. Recently, numerous researchers have focused on artificial photosynthesis to convert sunlight, water and CO2 to organic fuels. The products derived from carbon dioxide reduction varies and includes methane, formic acid, methanol, etc., which depends on the reaction conditions. Using the photoelectrochemical technique, the photoelectrodes combine with catalysts enhancing reaction rates. The photo-electrochemical conversion of water to hydrogen and CO2 to small organic molecules as fuels has great potential to become a viable and economical technology. The development, characterization, and application of photocatalytic electrode catalysts to enhance photocatalytic reactions through extended light absorption will be discussed.

Applications of Inductive Power Transfer

Roger J Soar
Cynetic Designs Ltd
Kelowna, BC Canada V1Y 8J2 rsoar@shaw.ca

Keywords: inductive power; wireless power; wireless data; environmentally sealed; soldier systems; vehicle to soldier power

Introduction

Common to every piece of soldier portable electronic equipment is its requirement for electrical power which is provided in all cases via a battery source. The devices have different power needs and therefore the batteries for each device have different voltages, current and form factors. The merits of a wireless, inductively coupled charging or power transfer system alleviate significant power logistic issues that are created by the use of soldier mounted electronic devices. This type of system will continue to be ever more practical as advances in power management reduce peripheral device power requirement and allow an inductive charging system to be used to advantage.

There have been many discussions that have stated that the overall power requirement for the future soldier will increase. We also know that as the future warrior electronic ensemble is developed and component miniaturisation evolves, the number of small form factor batteries used in subsystem equipment will increase. These two scenarios when combined would predict that the future soldier will be managing a progressively larger number of small batteries. The daily power logistic plan for the future soldier must reduce system power issues down to the simplest maintenance task. To accomplish this design objective will take a number of progressively implemented stages. This paper will discuss the general principles of inductive charging then highlights three areas of application. The first application is between a vehicle seat and the central battery on a soldier; the second, where power from the central battery is distributed to load carriage pockets with integrated inductive charging capability to the devices carried within it; and third, a means to charge a weapon stowed on a vehicle. Future applications include inductive transfer of power to helmet sub-systems.

Inductive Power System Overview

Inductive Power Transmission and Receiving

A transmitting (TX) inductive power drive circuit uses an inductor-capacitor (LC) resonant tank circuit that inductively couples through alternating magnetic flux, the TX drive coil and a receiving (RX) coil that together form an air core transformer. The magnetic flux can transmit through any non-metallic material. The principle TX drive sub-circuits includes a microprocessor controlled oscillator circuit and a power MOSFET switch circuit that drives an alternating current through the inductive component of the LC tank circuit, the TX inductive power coil. For general power transmission, the resonant frequency of the power tank circuit would typically be selected within the range of 100-500 kHz, with an auto tune circuit that maintains resonance over a range of frequencies as external factors dictate. The resonant characteristics of the power TX tank circuit will change as the distance between the TX and RX coil distance changes, due to the mutual inductance between the TX and RX power coils varying. The mutual inductance between the TX and RX coils in turn changes the apparent inductance of the TX power coil and so affecting the resonant frequency of the tank circuit which can be monitored and modified by the micro-processor controller.

The remote RX circuit provides rectification of the received inductive alternating current (AC) power signal, regulates the voltage as required, and passes power to the battery charging and control circuit. The battery charging circuit monitors the charge required by the central battery and charges it accordingly when power is available from the TX inductive power coil via the RX inductive power coil.

Transmitter and Receiver Coil Construction

The TX inductive power coil maybe one of several geometries (cylindrical, planar, E-core) that allow it to be incorporated into its intended application. Coil windings of the TX and RX inductive

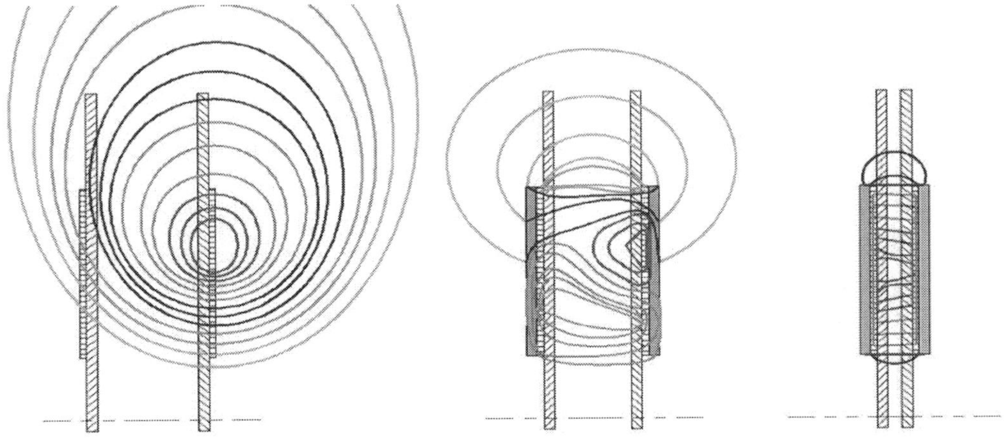

Figure 1. Representative illustration of the magnetic flux field lines for TX and RX inductive coils without ferrite backing, producing continuous free space radiation (left); with ferrite backing and 1cm air gap (middle); and with ferrite backing and 3mm air gap, demonstrating the effect of a tightly coupled radiation field and limited stray magnetic flux.

power coils may be wire wound using a variety wire types including conventional magnetic wire, multi-filament Litz wire, or multi-layer printed windings on flexible substrates.

The TX and RX inductive power coils may be air backed or, to aid in optimizing the efficiency of the inductive wireless power transfer between the TX and RX power coils, different shapes and thickness of ferrite backing can be employed to manipulate the shape of the coils magnet flux and form a tightly coupled, high efficiency air core transformer (Figure 1).

Typically direct current (DC) input to DC output conversion rates increase with inductive power output. Circuits employed by Cynetic Design can have efficiencies of 80% at 5 Watts output versus typical industry efficiencies of 75%, increasing to efficiencies of 88% or more at outputs of 20-40 Watts. Recent output capability of 60 Watts have been obtained at 86-88% efficiency (Figure 2).

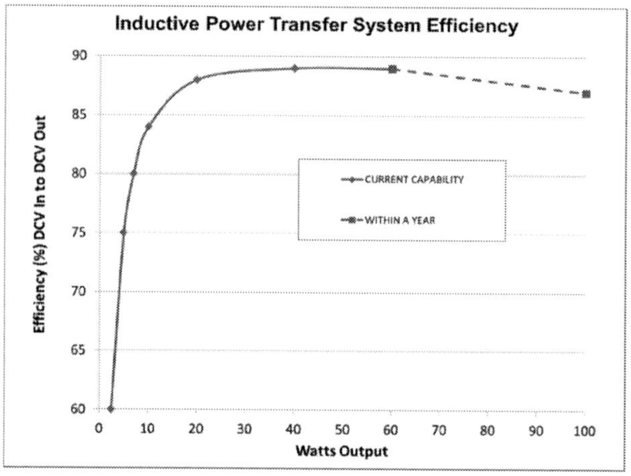

Figure 2. Conversion efficiency curve for increasing inductive power output

Inductive wireless power components have fundamental physical attributes that promote the design of an environmental proof system where no physical conductive electro-mechanical connection between TX and RX power components is required. The inductive system TX and RX coils can be sealed from the environment and may be fully submersed to any depth while operational. The system is unaffected by sand, dirt, snow, POL's (petroleum, oils and lubricants) and is easily cleaned of nuclear, biological and chemical (NBC) and other battlefield contaminants. Consequently inductive charging systems can be designed that meet required aspects of MIL-STD-810. In addition inductive TX and RX connectivity is not affected by the number of mating cycles, which for all intents and purposes is unlimited.

Example Inductive Applications

Vehicle Seat to Soldier Vest Power Transfer – Planar Coil Configuration

Both the US Army SWIPES (Soldier Worn Integrated Power Equipment System) and USAF BRITES (Battlefield Renewable Integrated Tactical Energy System) soldier power system employ a 150WHr conformal central power battery (CFB) that provides power to electronic devices distributed and carried on the soldier's tactical vest. Depending on the design and power management system protocols, inductive power received by a vest from a vehicle seat can be used to charge a central battery or can be ported directly to distributed devices on the vest. In an alternate system configuration it is possible that where there is no central battery carried by the user and even no power management system, the soldier's devices can be charged directly. Regardless of the CFB type and form factor, power management or distribution system, input power to the vest can be provided using an inductive power source. Two configuration options are available for seat to vest charging.

The planar coil system requires a 25cm elliptical transmitting planar coil placed within the seat back and a 20cm (dia.) planar coil located within an outer pocket on the back of the tactical vest. The TX power circuit on the seat continually polls or pings looking for an appropriate RX circuit to which it can provide wireless inductive power. Once an inductive connection is established between a TX power coil in the seat and a RX coil on the soldier, the rechargeable central or main power source battery would start to receive power. Currently power levels of 40-60 Watts can be provided through seat inductive planar coil charging.

The inductive RX coils (approx. 400g) with rectification sub-circuit and power conditioning electronics (30g), are placed in and around the back of the soldier's apparel such that the RX coil assembly is located close to the seat back and essentially on the same vertical axis as the TX power coil. The RX circuit of the inductive power transfer system, the AC rectification and voltage regulation circuit may be configured to provide a specific DC voltage to the battery charging circuit, with the voltage range typically in the range of 16-20volts DC (Figure 3).

It will usually be desirable to charge the soldier system central batteries as quickly as possible as the soldier may only be seated on the seat for a short time period. Cynetic Designs has demonstrated 50 Watt wireless charging implementations within Mine Resistant Ambush Protected (MRAP) vehicles in field trials conducted by CERDEC at Ft. Dix, and HMMWV trials with the USMC at Quantico.

Human Factor Considerations

As a population, the physical height of a user is comprised for the most part in the length of the legs and the length of the back, both of which vary independently of each other from one individual to another. The objective therefore, to be able to transfer inductive power from the seat to a seat occupant for the majority of the user population with equal efficiency, is not a straight forward task. Small lateral and vertical displacement can be accommodated using modified coil shapes such as elliptical or other geometries; however the RX coil height variance for a larger user group is too great to be efficiently accommodated with the application of a single TX coil. A method of accommodating the user population is facilitated by incorporating an array of multiplexed TX power coils that are embedded within the seat back. The seat occupant requires only a static RX coil assembly comprised of an individual coil that is located on the rear of his or her outer garment. The RX coil can then inductively couple with the one TX power coil within the TX power coil array that provides the best alignment and therefore the best power transfer efficiency.

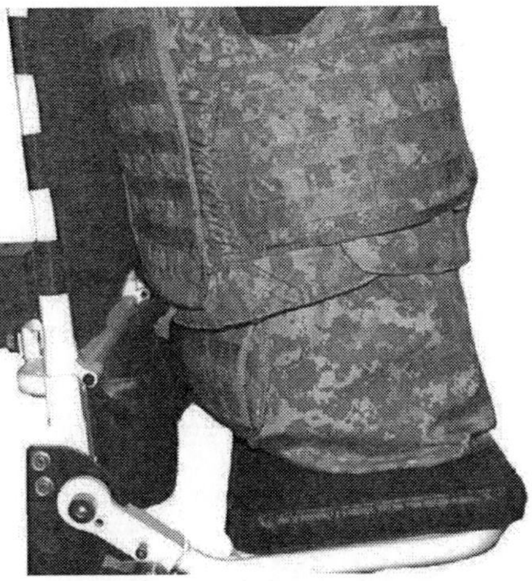

Figure 3. Installation of TX drive housing on back of seat, with primary inductive coil within seat back and secondary coil contained within vest plate pocket.

Vehicle Seat to Soldier Vest Power Transfer – Paddle Coil and Receptacle

An alternative to the application of a TX planar coil array in a seat back is inductive power transfer facilitated by placing a small (7 x 7cm) inductive TX paddle into a RX receptacle that is attached to a soldiers vest. The receptacle contains the RX voltage conditioning circuit which provides DCV charge power to the soldier system. The paddle can be placed into the receptacle once the soldier is seated, without any maintenance or pre-cleaning of either component. Regardless of the orientation of the soldier when seated he will continue to receive power until he stands up, separating the paddle from the receptacle without any action on the part of the soldier. Both the TX paddle and RX receptacle electronics are designed to be fully environmental proof and will transfer power in all adverse environments including if required, full submersion. The receptacle is designed with through holes so that no debris, ice or snow can collect within the receptacle.

Figure 3 Inductive paddle coil and vest receptacle for power transfer between seat and vest

The design of the TX paddle and RX inductive coils employ highly coupled ferrite backing which produces extremely low stray magnetic flux. The receptacle can be attached to the vest soldier system either directly or by a short cable with a user specified connector. Power out of 50 Watts (18VDC @ 2.8A) can be placed into a 6-8.0 ohm load, a typical charging load for large capacity central battery. Power transfer efficiency is typically in the order of 88%. In addition, the paddle and receptacle have been designed to allow the incorporation of low power Near Field Communication (NFC), Bluetooth, or Wi-Fi transceiver circuits to provide both wireless power and data transfer within a fully shielded enclosure. From a soldier weight saving perspective the 150Wh CFB weighs 1000g. The vest receptacle weighs 135g and can currently provide 95% charge to the conformal battery in 3 hours. For every one hour a soldier sits in a vehicle, the inductive power system represents a potential weight savings of 333g. With an anticipated future output of 100W, the system would realise a weight reduction of 660g per hour of soldier - vehicle time.

Wireless Charging on the Soldier Torso

Cynetic Designs has also developed technology that incorporates inductive charging technology into modular tactical load carriage pockets of the warfighter. Each pocket is fitted with a TX inductive power module that transfers power to the RX inductive module embedded either within an electronic device or its removable external battery.

All components on the system are charged on a demand basis, ensuring they are always at maximum readiness and fully optimizing the high energy density of the CFB. The internal rechargeable component batteries allow the component to have standalone operation for extended periods of time (similar to stock usage) however when they are returned to their charging location they are recharged back to 100% capacity or charged to levels according to a power manager setting. Fundamental to the future design is the ability to provide a power platform that provides active power management and graceful power degradation of peripheral devices. State of charge indicators can show main power depletion and a central power management device can preferentially dictate which devices continue to receive charge power. The multiple objectives attained by the technology are to reduce the overall number of types and weight of batteries carried by the soldier and to reduce the number of electro-mechanical power connections to handheld devices.

Tactical Radios

Concept demonstrators have been completed for the twist on Li ion batteries for tactical radios such as the PRC-148, 152 and 159 which can now be charged from an inductive modular pocket that eliminates the need for a charging cradle with electro-mechanical contacts in the base. The battery is attached to the desired radio then is slipped into a pouch containing the inductive TX insert. Two configurations are available. A custom battery with a three cell, 37Wh capacity, can be maintained at a greater than 80% charge using a RX inductive charging system integrated inside the original form factor of the battery. Alternately, an applique RX inductive battery charger (Figure 4) is available for attachment to stock batteries. The pocket insert is placed within a pouch and connects to a soldier system power port. Either configuration of inductively charged battery can be used in any environment including full submersion in saltwater. Power output of the charging system is 18 Watt for the 3 cell integrated inductive battery and 25 Watts for the applique system for a stock battery. Inductive efficiency for both formats is 80-88% (dependent on current draw in the charge cycle) with the Li ion battery charge circuit having an efficiency as high as 94%. A concept demonstrator has also been completed for an inductively charged battery for the Nett Warrior, PRC-154 Rifleman Radio.

Figure 4. 25Watt applique inductive charger and TX pocket insert for tactical radio battery

End User Device

Other small hand held devices that can be inductively charged include items such as smart phones, GPS, tactical flashlights etc. The inductively enabled pockets are connected to the vest power back plane and can be controlled and interrogated by a central power management system. Typical power output is 3-7 Watts. Figure 5 shows an inductive pouch for a Galaxy Note 2 cell phone, allowing it to be removed from the charging cradle without having to disconnect a power cable. With appropriate housings, any device including a tactical end user device (EUD) can be intelligently charged in all environments including full submersion. With the addition of wireless data communication using either NFC, Bluetooth or Wi-Fi to the cradle, a complete cable less and environmentally sealed EUD system is provided.

Figure 5. EUD is easily removable from the charging cradle without the need to disconnect cables.

Weapon System Charging

The inductive transfer of power to a weapon is facilitated by placing the stock of the weapon into a TX charging receptacle that receives electrical power from the vehicle and is attached to the floor of the vehicle beside each troop seat or multi-position gun rack. The stock of the weapon contains an integrated RX circuit and Li battery charger. Neither the TX or RX system components have any exposed electro-mechanical contacts or cables and are fully encased in plastic, making them completely insensitive to any environmental condition. In the case of maritime or riverine vessels, the stock can be engaged in the TX charging receptacle and charging initiated even when the receptacle and weapon stock are fully submersed. No maintenance or pre-cleaning of the stock is required prior to insertion into the charging receptacle. The receptacle is designed with a through hole for the stock so that no debris or fluids can collect within the receptacle.

Several design options for the RX coil and ferrite backing located within the weapon stock, allow the RX components to fit within the profile of the butt end of the stock of most weapons. The RX voltage conditioning unit and battery charger circuit are co-located with the coil and are intended for direct connection to a weapon system central battery. The current concept demonstrator modelled after an AR-15 type weapon, provides up to 40 Watts of charging power to a battery. All up weight for the weapon RX system components is 60g for a 40W RX coil, rectification and Li battery charging board. This compares to a 160gm, 36Wh Li battery.

Inductive Power and Wireless Data Communication

The miniature size of both NFC and Wi-Fi or Bluetooth transmit receive modules and the use of printed circuit or chip antennas allows these circuits to be embedded within many inductive power transfer systems. With the inductive power transfer operating at frequencies of under 500kHz, it is compatible with NFC's fundamental frequency of 13.56MHz, and Bluetooth or Wi-Fi systems operating in the range of 2.4 - 5.0GHz, allowing all three wireless technologies to co-exist and function within the same device.

The very close proximity of typically less than 0.5 centimeters for the RF transmit and receive antenna allow ultra-low power RF transmission to be utilized, which in conjunction with optimized shielding of the inductive housing and ferrites, provides a secure operational environment with little opportunity for device cross-talk.

Intellectual Property

All disclosures made within this paper are either patented or have patents pending.

Acknowledgments

Funding for development assistance of technologies described above has been received from US Army, CERDEC (BAA Funding); USMC, Gruntworks (BAA Funding); and the US Air Force, Wright-Patterson AFRL (SBIR Funding).

Autonomous Vehicles Achieving Long Endurance through Collaboration

Richard O. Stroman[1], William Adams[2], Keith Sullivan[2], John Palmisano[3], Randall Schur[2], Karen Swider-Lyons[1], and Alan C. Schultz[2]

[1]Chemistry and [2]Information Technology Divisions
US Naval Research Laboratory
4555 Overlook Ave SW
Washington, DC 20375

[3]Excet, Inc.
6225 Brandon Ave, Suite 360
Springfield, VA 22150

Abstract: *NRL is developing a group of autonomous vehicles which can collaborate to harvest and share energy. Built on the Packbot 510 platform, a "farmer" vehicle harvests solar energy with a rollable solar panel while "worker" vehicles carry out a mission. The farmer and workers rendezvous to share energy and information about the environment that will enable the group to operate more energy efficiently.*

Keywords: robot; collaborate; energy; optimization; mapping; autonomy, vehicle, UGV, solar.

Introduction

The capabilities of autonomous vehicles have improved dramatically over the past decade due in large part to advances in controls, navigation, autonomy, and payloads. Despite these improvements, most autonomous vehicles continue to rely on traditional energy sources which limit their range and endurance, and require resupply with the associated logistics burden. An ideal autonomous vehicle would operate indefinitely with minimal logistics burden by harvesting energy from the environment; efforts to develop solar-powered unmanned air vehicles (UAVs) [1] and soaring UAVs [2] have shown promise, while solar-powered unmanned ground vehicles (UGVs) have been used successfully for planetary exploration [3].

A major challenge for the development of energy-independent autonomous vehicles is the incompatibility of harvesting and mission design requirements. Often the best designs for energy harvesting have significant drawbacks for mission execution and vice versa. NRL is currently exploring a concept in which the individual members of a group of heterogeneous UGVs and UAVs are designed to harvest energy *or* carry out a mission, and then collaborate to share energy and energy-related information. Decoupling the energy harvesting and mission tasks may enable the group to be more effective because each member is then free to focus on one task and do it well. Collaboration among autonomous vehicles is not a new concept – there is a broad body of research on the subject [4] – but few efforts [5-8] have focused on energy. This work is unique in that it adapts the collaboration concept to harvesting, sharing, and efficiently managing energy in order to expand the energy limits of UGVs. Non-energy related mission constraints, such as time limits or denied access areas, are not included to ensure the results are energy-focused.

System Description

The experimental test group consists of one "farmer" vehicle which can harvest solar energy and two "worker" vehicles which can carry out search, sensing, and other missions. Fig. 1 shows a worker robot docked with the farmer for recharging. All three vehicles are based on the iRobot Packbot 510 platform. Autonomy is implemented by NRL on Intel NUC computers installed on each Packbot; they communicate with the Packbots through an iRobot API. All three robots carry a Carnegie Robotics Multisense SL, with trimodal sensors (3D stereo, laser, and video) and a high-resolution, high-accuracy 3D range sensor.

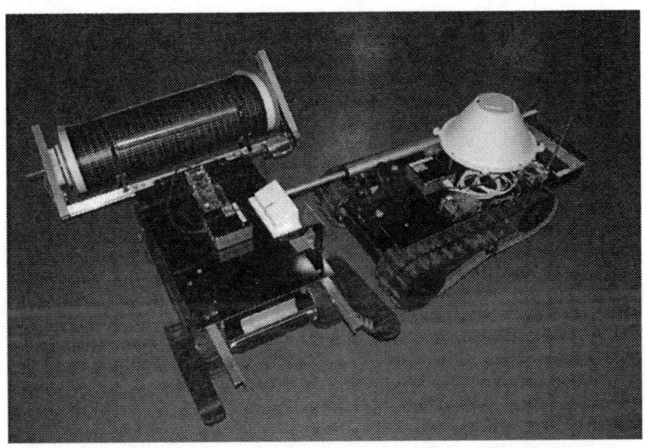

Figure 1. The farmer (left) with the solar array stowed and one worker (right) docked to recharge its batteries.

Farmer Vehicle: The farmer carries eight Ultralife UBBL02 (BB2590) batteries which are recharged by deploying the solar panel. The custom P3 Solar/Global Solar CIGS panel measures 25 x 371 inches and has a nominal power output of 600 W at AM1.5. Two Genasun maximum power point trackers (MPPTs) manage the solar panel and execute a constant current – constant voltage battery charging profile. State of charge, voltage, and current to each battery are monitored by a custom energy management board. Workers can access the farmer's battery pack via charging ports on each side of the farmer (second port not shown).

Worker Vehicles: Each worker carries four UBBL02 batteries which are recharged by plugging a probe into one of the farmer's charging ports. A Vicor DC/DC converter, modified to execute a constant current – constant voltage charging profile, draws current from the farmer battery pack to charge the worker battery pack. The worker can autonomously launch/recover/recharge a hexacopter for sensing and surveillance missions in areas inaccessible to a packbot. The hexcopter is recharged from the batteries on the worker (and from the farmer, when the farmer and worker are docked), so its energy is also derived from the solar panel.

Harvesting Energy

The farmer can deploy the solar panel, charge its batteries, and then stow the panel to transit to a rendezvous with the workers.

Solar panel deployment and rendezvous with the workers can be scheduled to avoid lost harvesting opportunities when the rates of harvesting and battery recharge can be predicted. For example, if the farmer batteries reach full charge at mid-day, then it will not be able to harvest additional energy despite the availability of sunlight. A rendezvous can be scheduled to occur when the batteries reach full charge so that the farmer can continue to harvest and distribute the additional energy directly to the workers.

The net solar power $\boldsymbol{P_s}$ supplied to the batteries is given by Eq. 1, where $\boldsymbol{\eta_s}$ is the solar panel efficiency, $\boldsymbol{\eta_m}$ is the MPPT efficiency, $\boldsymbol{S(t)}$ is the global horizontal solar irradiance at time $\boldsymbol{t}$, and $\boldsymbol{A_s}$ is the solar array area.

$$P_s(t) = \eta_m \eta_s S(t) A_s \qquad (1)$$

Battery state of charge is reported by the energy management board(s) and is used to estimate the remaining battery energy capacity, and then the net solar power is used to estimate the time until full charge. The solar irradiance at the farmer's location is estimated by the Bird et al. atmospheric model [9], which assumes clear skies. Variation in solar array efficiency with temperature is not considered.

A new feature is presently in development which will enable the farmer to determine when a shadow has impinged on the solar array, identify a better (no shadow) harvesting location, and then move there. Once the rate of harvesting falls below a threshold, the farmer retracts the solar panel and starts looking for a new charging location. The farmer analyzes images from the on-board camera looking for large bright regions, and then correlates these regions with satellite images of the operating area to estimate how long sunlight will cover the proposed region. The farmer then chooses the region with the longest potential sunlight coverage, proceeds to that location, and deploys the solar panel to resume charging.

Sharing Energy

There are two docking procedures: one between the farmer and worker ground robots, and another between the worker and hexacopter. Both procedures first use GPS (or a motion capture system indoors) to approximately position the two vehicles, and then control is switched to visual servoing based on AprilTags [10]. In both procedures, the target vehicle remains stationary during docking.

Docking between the worker and farmer proceeds in a similar fashion. Once the farmer is stopped, the worker uses GPS to align perpendicular to the farmer approximately 2 m away. Then, using its on-board camera, the worker tracks the AprilTag on the farmer (See Fig. 2 for the relationship between the AprilTag and docking port), and closes the distance between the two robots, keeping the AprilTag centered within the image. Depth from the stereo camera is used to determine when the worker is close enough to deploy the charging probe. An additional AprilTag on the charging probe is used to detect any misalignments that would prevent a successful docking, and if any misalignments are detected, the worker backs up approximately 2 m, and restarts the docking procedure.

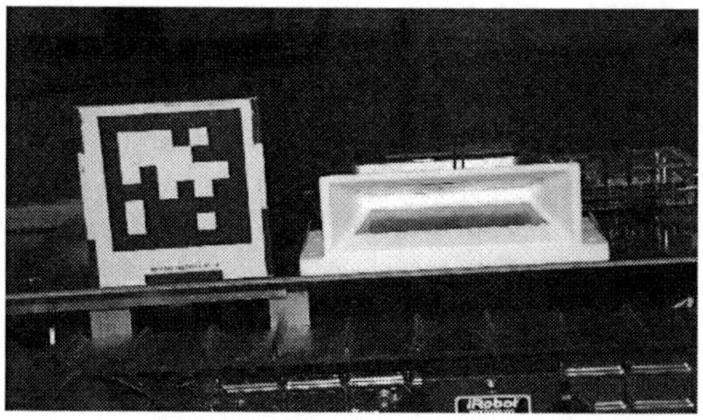

Figure 2. Charging port on the farmer with AprilTag for guiding the worker probe into the port.

The hexacopter starts its docking procedure by first flying over the worker robot's GPS location. Then, the hexacopter uses a bore-sighted camera to locate the AprilTag atop the landing code, and then uses a P-controller to keep the AprilTag centered within the image as the hexacopter descends. The landing cone design offers some leeway to account for drifting of the hexacopter.

Energy-Aware Route Planning

Tracked vehicles are robust and can operate in many different terrains, but they are also inefficient, making transit the most energy intensive activity for the farmer and workers. Furthermore, the energy consumed per unit distance traveled (J/m) and the energy consumed per angle turned (J/rad) can vary widely with terrain, speed, and inclination as shown in Fig. 3 and in [11]. The variation of energy cost suggests there should be one or more minimum energy cost paths between two locations in a varied terrain. Given the high energy cost of transit for these vehicles, finding the minimum energy cost path can yield gains in range, endurance, and mission flexibility. The key problems for minimizing transit energy cost are therefore (1) populating a terrain map with transit energy costs and (2) finding the minimum energy cost path through the map.

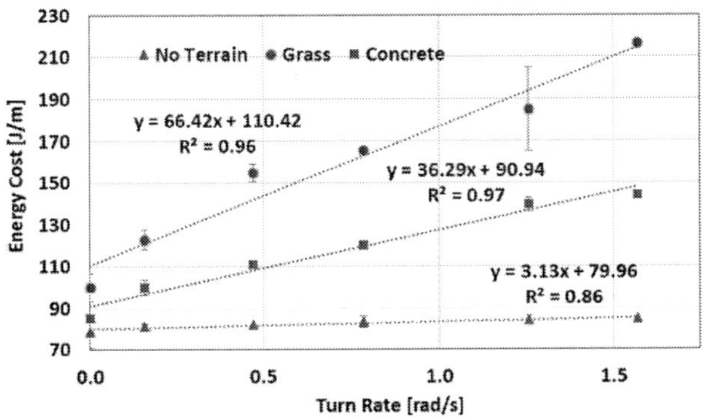

Figure 3. Transit energy cost measurements showing the influences of terrain type and turn rate for the Packbot 510. "No Terrain" is zero load, i.e. tracks raised off of ground.

Measuring Transit Energy Cost: The vehicle computers have access to real-time power consumption measurements from the energy management boards on each battery pack. Because the vehicles know where they are, they can store power consumption measurements in a geo-referenced map for later use. This information is useful for a group of vehicles that operate for long periods in one region and repeatedly cross the same areas. A few measurements can be applied more broadly if a satellite, aerial, or other image of the operating area containing terrain information is available. Such images can be segmented to define regions of similar terrain; then when a vehicle enters a segment and makes a measurement, the entire segment can be populated with transit energy cost data.

Transit energy cost varies with vehicle speed, but to make the energy cost discovery process practical for experiments, the farmer and workers travel at a fixed speed. Including speed in the energy cost discovery and path optimization processes would be a straightforward extension of the same approach with measurements made at a range of speeds in each new terrain.

Terrain classification is performed on-board the individual robots using only their cameras. The type of terrain – grass, concrete, gravel, bare dirt, asphalt, or sand – is determined through deep learning: individual images are fed through a deep neural network based on the widely applicable AlexNet architecture [12]. The output of the network has one neuron per terrain type. Once the robot knows what type of terrain it is currently traversing, it can populate map regions of similar terrain with energy consumption data or query the map to estimate how much energy is needed to drive across various terrains.

Sharing Transit Energy Information: The discovery of transit energy costs for a region will occur more quickly if the vehicles can share their measurements. The present system uses the Robot Operating System (ROS) to coordinate the activities of the vehicles and vehicle subsystems. Transit energy cost measurements are stored as shared geo-referenced maps in a ROS node. All three ground vehicles can write measurements to the map node and read the maps in order to compute energy efficient trajectories to their next destination.

Energy Cost Function: The ground vehicle paths between waypoints will approximate straight lines in regions with few obstacles, hence the path is a series of n straight segments of length $\boldsymbol{\ell}$ connected by n-1 in-place turns of angle $\boldsymbol{\theta}$ at the interior waypoint locations. With straight-line transit costs of $\boldsymbol{C_s}$ J/m for each segment and in-place turning costs of $\boldsymbol{C_r}$ J/rad for each turn, the total energy cost for a worker path is given by Eq. 2.

$$C_W = \sum_{1}^{n} \ell_k C_{s,k} + \sum_{1}^{n-1} \theta_k C_{r,k} \tag{2}$$

The farmer transit energy cost is complicated by the opportunity cost of stowing the solar array; the farmer loses an opportunity to harvest energy whenever it moves. The farmer transit energy cost is given by Eq. 3, which includes the energy expended in each solar array stow/deploy cycle $\boldsymbol{E_{sd}}$, the average rate $\boldsymbol{\overline{P}_s}$ at which the solar panel *could* produce power over the timescale of the move, and the farmer travel speed $\boldsymbol{v_F}$.

$$C_F = E_{sd} + \frac{\overline{P}_s}{v_F} \sum_{1}^{n} \ell_k + \sum_{1}^{n} \ell_k C_{s,k} + \sum_{1}^{n-1} \theta_k C_{r,k} \tag{3}$$

Plotting Trajectories to Rendezvous: The path planning goal is to find the rendezvous location which incurs the least total energy cost for all three robots, given their differing initial positions. The problem of finding a shortest (or otherwise optimal) path through a known environment has been extensively studied [13]. There are two separate methods used in this work to determine rendezvous location and optimal paths.

The first method treats finding the minimum energy-cost path between two points as a straightforward optimization problem in which the interior (non-endpoint) waypoint locations $\boldsymbol{w_2} \dots \boldsymbol{w_{n-1}}$ are the independent variables. Many techniques exist to find such minima; a Newton method and a genetic (evolutionary) algorithm to iteratively solve for the placement of n waypoints have both worked well. These approaches can identify minimum energy cost paths to a high resolution using interpolation to create a continuous environmental map. However, it is susceptible to local minima. The genetic algorithm tends to be more robust on a non-smooth transit energy cost map.

Finding the minimum energy cost rendezvous location is an extension of the single-path optimization problem, but with the following changes:

- The final waypoint location w_n becomes an independent variable and is constrained to be the same for all three vehicles.
- The interior waypoint locations for all three paths are independent variables which must be solved for simultaneously.

The second method uses a dynamic programming strategy to find the minimum energy cost paths through a discretized cost map. For each robot, the minimum energy cost path is calculated from the starting position to each other map region, using the energy cost functions given in Eqs. 2 and 3. Each map region then has a separate cost-to-go associated with it for each robot. These individual energy costs are summed, and the map region with the minimum total energy cost becomes the rendezvous location. The optimal path from each starting location to the rendezvous point is then already calculated. This approach is resolution complete, meaning that it gives the optimal solution given the grid resolution, and is globally optimal as grid resolution tends to infinity.

An example simulation is shown in Fig. 4, where paths from different starting locations to a minimum energy cost rendezvous location are shown for one farmer and two workers. The opportunity cost incurred by the farmer when solar energy is available will bias the rendezvous location toward the farmer's initial location, depending on the solar intensity. The (arbitrary, in this case) straight line transit energy cost is shown in the background. The vehicles make few turns, despite opportunities to take advantage of slightly lower straight line transit energy cost if they were to do so, due to the relatively high cost of turning.

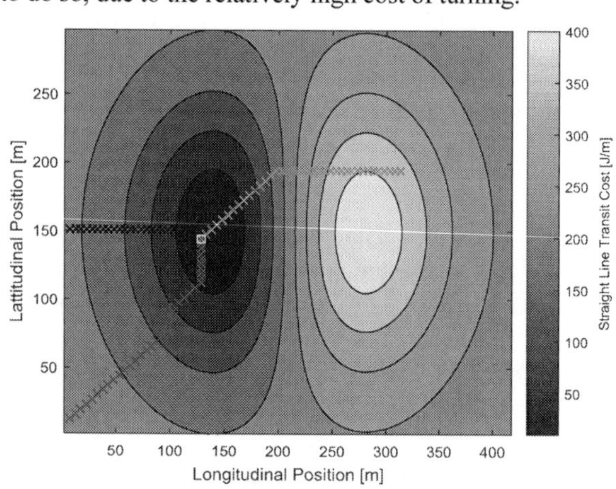

Figure 4. Minimum energy rendezvous location (yellow) and the paths to it for three vehicles starting in different locations. The straight-line transit cost mapped in the background of this example is arbitrary.

Status and Plans

At present the three vehicles have been fabricated, the farmer autonomously deploys and stows its solar panel, and all three vehicles dock autonomously to share energy. Codes to identify the minimum energy cost rendezvous location and paths to that location for all three vehicles have been completed. Mapping and terrain identification work and software integration are underway, with an anticipated demonstration of the complete energy harvesting/sharing/management system in summer 2016.

Acknowledgements

The authors acknowledge the Office of Naval Research, which is funding this work, and the Laboratory for Autonomous Systems Research at the Naval Research Laboratory, where much of the work has taken place.

References

1. P. Oettershagen, et al., *A Solar-Powered Hand-Launchable UAV for Low-Altitude Multi-Day Continuous Flight*. Proceedings of the IEEE Conf. on Rob. and Autom. (ICRA), 2015: p. 3986-3993.
2. J. Langelaan and D. Makovkin, *Optimal Persistent Surveillance using Coordinated Soaring*, AIAA Guidance, Navigation, and Control Conf.: 2014: pp 24.
3. J. L. Callas, *Mars Exploration Rover Spirit End of Mission Report*, NASA Report #JPL D-92756 (2016).
4. M. Brambilla, E. Ferrante, M. Birattari, and M. Dorigo, *Swarm robotics: a review from the swarm engineering perspective*, Swarm Intel. 7:1-41 (2013).
5. T. Dun-Ngo, H. Rapos, and H. Schioler, *Potentially distributable energy: Towards energy autonomy in large population of mobile robots.* Int. Symp. on Comp. Intel. in Robotics and Automation, (2007).
6. P. Zebrowski and R. T. Vaughan, *Recharging robot teams: A tanker approach.* 12th International Conference on Advanced Robotics, (2005).
7. J. Broderick, D. Tilbury, and E. Atkins, *Energy usage for UGVs executing coverage tasks.* Unmanned Systems Technology XIV, (2012).
8. P. Zebrowski, Y. Litus, and R. Vaughan, *Energy efficient robot rendezvous.* 4th Canadian Conf. on Computer and Robot Vision, Proceedings, (2007).
9. R. E. Bird, *A Simple, Solar Spectral Model for Direct-Normal and Diffuse Horizontal Irradiance*, Solar Energy, 1984, 32(4): p. 461-471.
10. E. Olson, AprilTag: *A robust and flexible visual fiducial system*, Proceedings of the IEEE Conference on Robotics and Automation (ICRA), 2011.
11. K. Boice, A. Leo, J. Lee, J. Paulson, M. Skalny, and T. Valascho, *Baseline Field Testing of BB2590 Lithium-Ion Batteries using an iRobot FasTac 510 Robot*, Army TARDEC report #21320, (2010).
12. A. Krizhevsky, I. Sutskever and G. E. Hinton, *ImageNet Classification with Deep Convolutional Neural Networks*, Proceedings of Advances in Neural Information Processing Systems, (2012).
13. S. M. LaValle, *Planning algorithms.* Cambridge University Press, (2006).

Evaluation of Spark Ignition Engines Converted for Operation on Heavy Distillate Fuels

Tony Thampan, Terry DuBois, Richard Scenna, and Michael Seibert
The Defence Science and Technology Laboratory, Salisbury, UK

Abstract:

To provide Soldier tactical power/energy utilizing existing logistics, while meeting size and weight requirements, portable Jp-8 gensets are required. As a potential solution, the Communications-Electronics Research, Development, and Engineering Center (CERDEC) together with industry have developed a variety of strategies for converting commercial-off-the-shelf (COTS) gasoline engines to burn heavy distillate fuels (e.g. JP-8) within an acceptable size and weight. The primary goal is to address a 1 kWe power need which is not support by existing compression ignition engines. There are a number of approaches being pursued for introducing JP-8 into spark ignition engines, including: atomization/vaporization of JP-8, modification of piston head to assist with low compression combustion of heavy fuels, and fuel reforming flowed by combustion. Performance of these technologies will be discussed, as well as insight into the combustion of heavy distillate fuel under spark ignition conditions, based on engine test stand data.

UK and NATO Standardisation Efforts for Dismounted Soldier Power

Darren Jonathan Browning
Platform Systems Division,
Defence Science and Technology Laboratory,
Salisbury, Wiltshire, UK, SP4 0JQ

Abstract: *This paper describes efforts within the UK and within NATO to standardise interfaces for soldier system power sources to aid interoperability within a nation's system and between international partners.*

The UK Ministry of Defence (MOD) is developing generic architectures for vehicles, bases and soldiers to improve integration and allow simpler upgrade and adoption of commercial off the shelf (COTS) technology. This paper discusses the UK Generic Soldier Architecture (GSA) and the requirements it may place on future batteries. The GSA is defining a common power and data interface to allow future equipment and power sources to be easily connected into an integrated soldier system.

NATO also has an aim to increase standardisation to enable greater interoperability between partner nations. The NATO Land Capability Group Dismounted Soldier Systems (LCG DSS) is tasked with improving standardisation and interoperability for the dismounted soldier. A number of STANAGS (Standard Agreements) are being written to allow the sharing of power sources and powered equipment between nations. Details of one such agreement (STANAG 4695 and the associated Allied Engineering Publication, AEP-95) which provides a dismounted soldier power connection will be discussed along with issues surrounding the standardisation of a combined NATO soldier power and data connector.

Keywords: standardisation; standardization; NATO; generic soldier architecture; GSA; STANAG 4695.

Introduction

Modern conflicts are generally undertaken by a coalition of forces consisting of elements from a number of partner nations. This trend is expected to continue and increase in the future. In addition, dismounted soldiers are now carrying ever increasing amounts of electronic capabilities and these need to be seamlessly integrated to each other and to host platforms. These trends lead to an increased drive for greater integration (within a system) and interoperability (between systems). Interoperability is important both between different platforms and elements of a single nation and between different nations. The UK MOD (Ministry of Defence) is addressing the problem of increasing integration and interoperability amongst and between its own forces by the development of generic architectures, the so called GXAs (Generic Architectures of different platforms). To date these comprise the Generic Base Architecture (GBA), Generic Vehicle Architecture (GVA) and Generic Soldier Architecture (GSA) [1]. These sit beneath the LOSA (Land Open Systems Architecture) which ensures the platforms can communicate with one another. Figure 1 summarises how these interact.

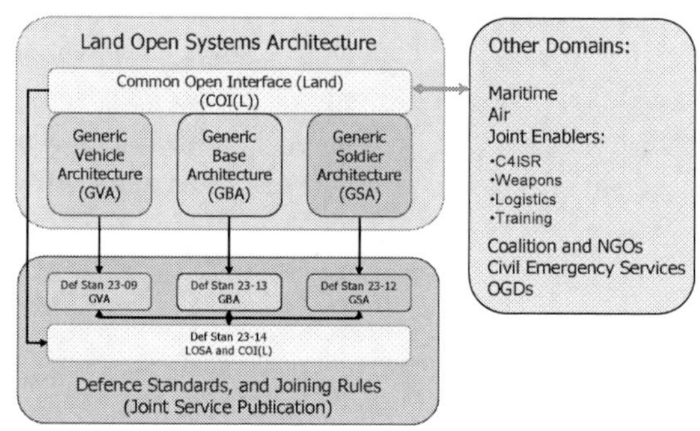

Figure 1. Relationship between UK LOSA and GXAs.

To address international soldier interoperability the UK is liaising with NATO and in particular NATO LGC DSS (Land Capability Group Dismounted Soldier Systems). LCG DSS is developing a range of STANAGS (Standards Agreements) to enable interoperability of NATO dismounted soldiers.

NATO LCG DSS STANAGS

NATO LCG DSS envisions that in coalition operations soldiers may need to exchange batteries or recharge each other's batteries. There may also be the need to exchange powered devices such as sights, electronic aids, radios etc. This will require a common connector and definition of expected power source parameters. The ultimate aim would be for NATO to use common soldier batteries. However, this is seen as unlikely in the near to medium term, although it remains an aspiration. NATO LGG DSS power team of experts (ToE) has therefore developed STANAG 4695; "ELECTRICAL INTERFACE SPECIFICATIONS FOR DISMOUNTED SOLDIER SYSTEMS (DSS) LEVEL 2 POWER CONNECTOR INTEROPERABILITY"[2]. STANAGs tend to be overarching documents and much of the technical detail is provided in the associated AEP (Allied Engineering

Publication) AEP 95. This STANAG and AEP has recently received sufficient votes from member nations and has been approved by the NAAG (NATO Army Armaments Group) for promulgation. It has now been sent to the NSO (NATO Standardisation Organisation) and will be released as a STANAG in due course. It should however be noted that until publication it is not a formally recognized STANAG.

It is hoped that NATO nations will start to adopt this connector on power sources and equipment requiring power. However, it is expected that legacy equipment will remain for a considerable period of time. Nevertheless, the existence of a standard NATO soldier power connector will mean that if all partner nations carry an adapter from their power source to the NATO power connector that this will enable interoperability without the need to carry adapters to every conceivable partner nation power source.

The NATO STANAG 4695 connector has been based around the US Nett Warrior power connector. It should however be noted that NATO does not specify a given manufacturer.

The key metrics for the connector are given below.

Table 1. Electrical characteristics of a STANAG 4695 compliant power source

	Level 2 Complaint Power Source
Voltage	8-32 V
Current	0-5 A
EMC	MIL-STD-461

Table 2. Pin assignments for a STANAG 4695 compliant connector

Contact location	Description	Terminal markings
1	V+ Battery Voltage	Batt +
2	V- Battery Voltage	Batt -
3	Charge +	Charge +
4	SMBus data	Data
5	SMBus clock	Clock
6	SMBus ID (10K Thermistor to Ground)	SB ID
7 (if present)	No connection or V+ Battery voltage	Blank/NC/Batt + (*2)

It should be noted that shielding to the connector casing is implied but not stated in this current version.

Further details are provided in STANAG 4695 and AEP 95. It should be noted that no document written by committee is perfect and almost as soon as STANAG 4695 was submitted the team identified ways in which it could be improved. It is therefore likely that an updated version will be written over the next few years. Therefore industry and users are encouraged to contact their national representative if they believe changes need to be made to facilitate implementation. One issue which is being debated is whether it is acceptable to have the 7th pin as optional. The concern is that if one nation arrives with a connector with 7 pins and another nation with a connector with 6 holes that these won't mate. It is therefore recommended that if a nation only wishes to use 6 connection points that the 7th central hole remains but is not electrically connected rather than being filled.

It is expected that in the first instance this STANAG will allow sharing of batteries but it is also intended to allow alternative power sources such as fuel cells and thermoelectric devices to be shared and ultimately energy harvesting devices such as solar panels and kinetic generators. This may require a device ID and the currently unused 7th pin could be used for this.

STANAG 4695 is for connectors passing power and power related data (i.e. SMBus) only. There is also a desire for some systems to be able to pass power and tactical data at the same time using a single connector. This is especially important on a dismounted soldier system where requiring two separate connectors to pass power and data on a small device will add additional mass and bulk. NATO LCG DSS is therefore starting work on a combined power and data connector. This is considerably more difficult given the fact that a wide range of soldier systems are already in operation or development and the data requirements of peripherals can be different. The current debate is over whether USB or Ethernet should be selected as the data protocol. It is likely that until a resolution can be found to this dilemma that two different NATO power and data connectors will be needed a "NATO power and USB" connector and a "NATO power and Ethernet connector".

This work is ongoing and will be progressed during the fall meeting in October in Prague.

NATO LCG DSS undertakes many other standardisation activities and another one of these is the development of a NATO Generic Soldier Architecture (NGSA). This is following the ethos of the UK GSA discussed below but may make different design decisions to reach an acceptable compromise between partner nations. This work is relatively immature and will progress over the next couple of years.

UK Generic Soldier Architecture (GSA)

The UK MOD has drafted a Generic Soldier Architecture for future dismounted soldiers. One of the aims of GSA is to control the interfaces on the soldier to develop an Integrated Soldier System (ISS) rather than what is often termed the "Christmas Tree" whereby items of new equipment are simply added to the dismounted soldier with limited consideration given to integration. It is also expected that the GSA will lead to cheaper through life upgradability, reduced weight and the easier adoption of COTS (Commercial off the shelf) technologies. The GSA is more wide ranging than just power and connectors but these are the only components which will be discussed here. The GSA was written by a working group consisting of military stakeholders and industry representatives. It is therefore hoped that it represents not only what is desired by the military but also what can be achieved and delivered by industry.

The GSA has taken the approach that all connector interfaces on the dismounted soldier will be the same. For example, the connection for a battery into the soldier system will be the same as for an item of equipment which will require both power and tactical data (radio, tablet etc). Therefore a soldier can place any item of equipment at any point on the system and it will work.

The current focus is on the torso system but it is ultimately intended that this will integrate to a power and data enabled weapon and helmet. Figure 2 shows how power and data flows around the system.

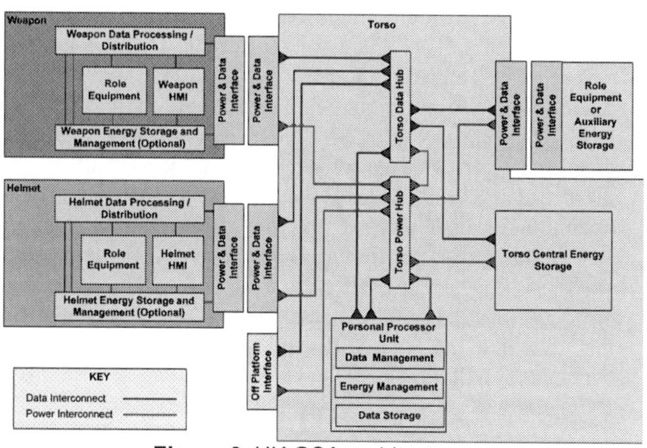

Figure 2. UK GSA architecture

After much debate and analysis the data format selected for the GSA was USB 2.0. This was selected over Ethernet due to the wide availability of commercial peripherals which use this protocol and the lower power consumption required to move data across the soldier architecture.

USB 2.0 requires two data wires. It also requires two power wires at 5 V to power USB equipment.

Some soldier equipment will have a higher power demand than that which can be supplied by USB 2.0. Therefore additional power lines are required. These have been defined as + 9-36 V, 5 A and ground. A third wire will also be needed to allow the battery to be charged *in situ*.

There was also a desire to minimise the number of pins used on any connector since pins and additional wires will add mass and cost to the system.

It is anticipated that future systems will be powered predominantly by a centralised power source (or possibly two for redundancy) rather than the discrete 10-14 different batteries carried by current UK dismounted soldiers. Most commercial and military rechargeable batteries communicate via the SMBus protocol. This requires a minimum of 2 wires and therefore pins on a connector. When these pins are considered along with the four USB pins and three additional power pins it was felt that this might lead to an excessively large and expensive connector. Therefore the decision was taken that there would only be one data format for the whole system, USB 2.0, and that any battery data would need to be communicated as USB 2.0 and not SMBus. The GSA pin assignments are shown in table 3.

Table 3. UK GSA connector pin assignments

Reference	Mnemonic	Description	Electrical
1	VBUS	USB 2.0 supply	+5V ±5%; 500mA Max
2	D-	USB 2.0 Data minus	90Ω ±15% characteristic impedance
3	D+	USB2.0 Data plus	90Ω ±15% characteristic impedance
4	USB 2.0 GND	USB2.0 Ground	0V; 500mA Max
5	VOUT	Power out	9V(Min) to 36V (Max); 5A Max
6	VIN	Power in	9V(Min) to 36V (Max); 5A Max
7	PWR-GND	Power Ground	0V; 5A Max

The GSA states that the case of the connector must provide shielding.

The GSA has defined its connectivity requirements but has yet to select a physical connector. Therefore although seven pins are required the numbers in the table above do not refer to specific pin allocations. The actual pin numbering will need to be defined once a connector has been selected since the proximity of one pin to another can affect performance. The vision for a future torso power and data system is that it will use flat textile based conductors and not traditional round cables. Therefore the future connector is expected to be low profile and to be able to mate directly to the torso system fabric. Traditional barrel connectors are not ideal for this. New connectors are therefore required. A number of companies are developing low profile connectors for applications such as these.

A range of demonstrators have been built to validate the GSA. Two different demonstration systems were built by different companies as part of the Man Worn Power and

Data (MWPD) 1 Technology Demonstration Programme (TDP) and this was further refined in a second phase (MWPD 2). MWPD 2 used a battery with a built in USB interface and this was shown to successfully communicate to the MWPD vest. However, it is recognized that the majority of soldier system batteries communicate via SMBus and to allow the MWPD vest to be powered by such batteries an adapter cable was built containing a small box which converts the battery SMBus data to USB data for compliance with the GSA system.

Conclusions

Future soldier systems are likely to be more integrated than they are today and if they are to remain flexible and upgradable an open architecture is required.

NATO LCG DSS is developing a range of STANAGS which will improve the interoperability of power sources and powered equipment between NATO nations. The first of these, STANAG 4695, defines a power and power related interface to allow batteries to be shared, either directly or via an adaptor.

Acknowledgements

The author would like to acknowledge all the hard working members of NATO LCG DSS and the UK GSA technical working group.

References

1. Defence Standard 23-12 Generic Soldier Architecture
2. NATO STANAG 4695

Energy Informed Operations: Mobile Military Microgrids

Marnie E. Bailey, Garrett C. Clarke, Michael Gonzalez, Nicholas Grossano, Jaclyn A. Lynch, Thomas F. Podlesak, Stefan G. Siegfried, Bradley J. Stanley, Darren Stephens, David O. Teicher and Tony M. Thampan

U.S. Army
Aberdeen Proving Ground, MD

Abstract: *Energy Informed Operations (EIO) seeks to improve the efficiency and reliability of mobile tactical microgrids. The U.S. military has approximately 100,000 small generators for use by military personnel in the field. Generators are the largest users of JP-8, the military version of Jet-A jet fuel, on the battlefield. The largest of these units is rated at 120 kW, with the vast majority being less than 25 kW. Existing generators of the Tactical Quiet Generator (TQG) type were fitted with a modification kit which enabled a microgrid controller to autonomously control each generator and read critical operational parameters remotely, via a standardized EIO MODBUS over Ethernet data interface. One or more such data enabled generators can be connected via Intelligent Power Distribution (IPD) ports to other generators or system loads. Of the latter, the largest and most significant are Environmental Control Units (ECUs), the most common of which are rated at 5 ton (60,000 Btu/hr) (17.6 kW thermal) cooling capability. Both the TQGs and the ECUs are controllable via corresponding EIO MODBUS over Ethernet standards. Over the past year, these microgrid systems have been tested at four field demonstrations held on U.S. Army bases in various parts of the U.S.A. The EIO microgrid, and encompassing components, were operated not only by EIO personnel but also by the end users, in this case actual soldiers. Reaction to the EIO microgrid, from soldiers with no specialized knowledge of electrical power systems to highly trained generator maintenance personnel, was very positive.*

Keywords: tactical microgrid; smart grid; generator; environmental control unit; MODBUS; Ethernet; fuel savings; EIO standard

Introduction

The U.S. Army supplies approximately 100,000 small mobile generators to all three of the U.S. Armed Services. These units range from 3 to 120 kW and are powered by JP-8 militarized Jet-A jet fuel. Electric power generation is the most fuel intensive use of energy on the battlefield, eclipsing vehicle propulsion. A deployed infantry division will consume approximately 300,000 U.S. gallons (1.13Ml) of JP-8 fuel per day. As a general rule of thumb, a U.S. Army division consumes its weight in fuel every 30 days. Fuel is usually delivered by 5000 U.S. gallon (18900 l) trucks. Fuel convoys are notoriously vulnerable to enemy attack. It has been shown [1] that on average 90 lives are lost per every 250 million gallons (945 Ml) of fuel delivered in recent conflicts in the Middle East. A case has been made that it may make more sense to transport fuel by air in the military theatre [2], taking advantage of both reduced vulnerability and speed of delivery. In either scenario, reduction in fuel consumption is highly desirable.

The current configuration of power generation is that a given set of loads are each driven by a dedicated generator. Often, the generator is not producing power at its peak efficiency (approximately 90% of rating). Operating a generator at less than peak efficiency not only wastes fuel but also can produce a phenomenon known as "wet stacking", in which unburned fuel collects in exhaust and causes the generator to foul.

A more desirable scenario is shown in Figure 1 Note how the individual generators are now networked both from a power and data standpoint, as are the loads. Power generation is not confined strictly to portable generators, but also to vehicle based systems and could also include renewables. Simulations have shown 37.5% fuel savings utilizing such a configuration versus the current configuration, resulting in reduced logistics.

Figure.1 Proposed fielded power generation structure and usage. Note the power and data networks, the integration of vehicles into the power system and the substantial quantity of fuel being delivered.

Energy Informed Operations (EIO)

The Energy Informed Operations (EIO) program focuses on developing an interface standard for an autonomous tactical microgrid architecture rated from 15 to 300kW that supports Army Contingency Basing. This architecture will support increased power availability and reliability, while reducing generator fuel usage and maintenance. Additionally, EIO supports the development of associated applications that allow optimization of power and energy resources based on mission objectives.

The EIO microgrid features open, standardized interfaces for communication and power interconnects with advanced control hardware and software that includes smart generation sources and Intelligent Power Distribution (IPD) units, as well as an EIO microgrid application providing enhanced grid awareness, analytics, and control of power resources. Moreover, the application hosts the EIO knowledge base providing a plethora of tools giving the right data, to the right user, at the right time (dependent on the task at hand, their intent, and their skill level).

In order to validate system functionality and effectiveness in a more dynamic environment, the authors have developed prototype hardware and software to demonstrate and test these standardized interfaces.

The Sustainability Logistics and Basing (SLB) Science and Technology Objective Demonstration (SLB-STO-D) executes field demonstrations to validate performance and collects data from emerging technologies for reductions in fuel, water and waste. EIO participates in these tests.

Field Tests

The authors brought various configurations of the EIO microgrid to several field tests-"experiments" in U.S. Army parlance-which are described below.

A. *Contingency Basing Integration Technology Evaluation Center (CBITEC)*

EIO participated in the SLB-STO-D 1000 man-camp exercise at the Contingency Basing Integration Technology Evaluation Center (CBITEC). It consisted of 14 type B-Hut shelters to be powered by the EIO grid. Each hut contained a 5 ton (60,000 Btu/hr) (17.6 kW thermal) environmental control unit (ECU) and lights, creating a load of approximately 8-9 kW maximum per hut. The huts were divided into 2 groups, which were referred to as the "A-block" and the "B-block". Due to issues with the data collection system, grid B data is not available. The EIO grid configuration for each block included two retrofitted EIO-standard compliant 60kW Tactical Quiet Generators (TQGs), and two EIO-standard compliant Intelligent Power Distribution units (IPDs), shown in Figure 2, with the necessary power and communication cables. The IPDs contain remotely controllable circuit breakers and contactors, which control the flow of power to the grid loads.

Figure 2. Intelligent Power Distribution (IPD) module, top view with cover removed. Circuit breakers are at center, data interface circuit boards (on edge) shown at top and bottom edge.

Each generator had been retrofitted with a modified digital control box. The modification involves replacing the baseline TQG control box with a new one containing the necessary EIO-standard compliant components, rendering the generator microgrid ready. Each modification kit contains a new digital controller, and the compatible supporting components such as a governor and voltage regulator that would enable synchronization and load sharing among the generators. The modification kit also includes a single board computer that functions as a translator between the vendor specific generator controller interface and the EIO-standard generator interface. This makes the generator data from the digital controller available to the grid, and allows the IPD to control the generator remotely. The new control box enables remote start/stop capabilities, synchronization, and makes data available to the user.

The IPDs distribute power and contain the intelligence that autonomously controls the grid. Each IPD has input and output ports that are monitored for power flow, and contactors that can be remotely actuated. When the grid is initialized, one of the IPDs becomes the "master", dictating commands to the connected IPDs and generators. Communication between grid sources/loads and IPDs utilizes Modbus over Ethernet. The grids are monitored through the EIO application, a visual computer interface that provides the user with power data in real-time, grid power analytics, and relevant mission critical alarms/reports.

The grid control algorithm is implemented so that turning on one generator would start the grid initialization process. This generator would become the isochronous (constant frequency/voltage) generator, and all discovered grid components (2 IPDs and 1 generator) would initialize in turn. The second generator would operate in droop mode, where the frequency is a function of the output power requested. The grid control actively changes the frequency set point of the droop generator to ensure that the grid frequency would be maintained at 60Hz regardless of load. Once the power required for the loads is established through measurement of total grid load, if the second generator is not required, it would shut off. Total grid load is actively monitored so that when the load approaches the maximum capacity of the isochronous generator (respective of user-defined spinning reserve), the second generator would turn on and provide power. Likewise, if the total grid load falls below the isochronous generator's minimum threshold (user-defined), the second generator would stop providing power. Matching the power generation capacity to the load allows for a reduction in generator run time and fuel usage.

Grid A power data from prescribed scripts and a soldier exercise can be seen in Figure 3. The scripts took place over four days. At these points, the graph shows incremental changes in load, and the second generator shuts off when it is not needed. The load profile displays the power usage from the soldiers who were in residence over the middle portion of the time period. For the majority of this time frame, power requirements remained relatively low so that the second generator did not need to turn on and provide power. Eliminating the need for a second generator to be running translates into significant fuel savings and reduction in runtime. Fuel consumption is shown in

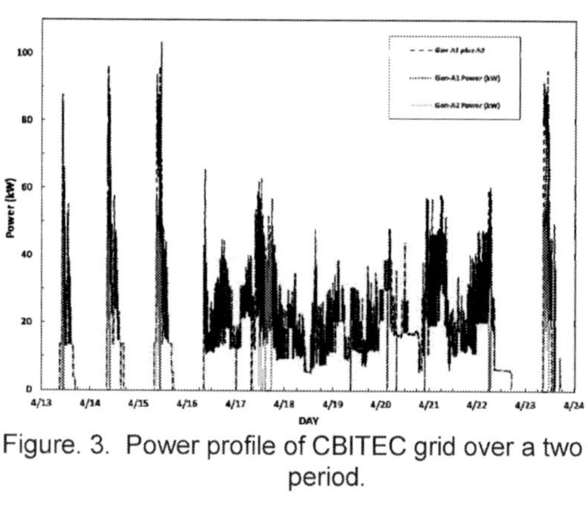

Figure. 3. Power profile of CBITEC grid over a two week period.

Figure 4, comparing the grid consumption to individually dedicated generators.

The baseline alternative to EIO would have been spot generation; two separate generators running constantly regardless of load because the maximum load, however infrequently it may be needed, is greater than the capacity of a single generator. Often when individual generation is used, both generators have small loads compared to total capacity, resulting in inefficient fuel usage. Figure 4 shows that having two generators run in a grid formation significantly reduces the amount of fuel needed to power the same load.

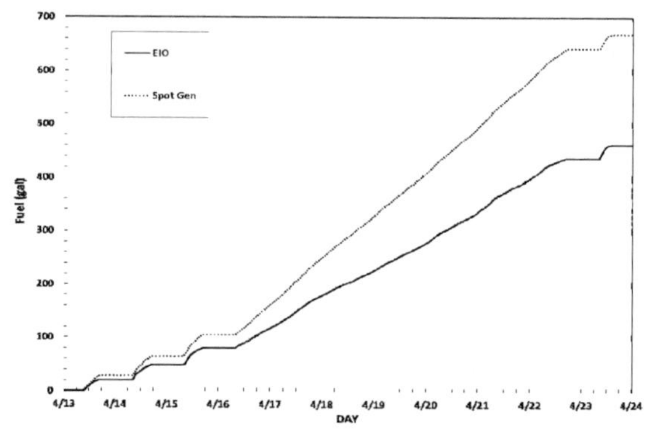

Figure 4. Fuel Consumption of EIO Grid A vs Dedicated Individual Generation

The fuel calculations were based on known values of fuel consumption per TQG as a function of the load it is powering. During the exercise portion, the amount of fuel consumed resulted in a fuel savings of 34% and a runtime savings of 50%. The exercise portion consisted of powering soldier-occupied tents as opposed to planned load profiles with incremented steps, and took place over a longer period of time than those scripts. The decreases in fuel usage and hours savings in this portion suggest that if the grid were to run for a longer period of time in a dynamic, real-world situation, the savings would continue to grow.

The reduction in generator runtime translates to less wear and tear on generator components and less frequent maintenance requirements. Oil changes on TQGs are recommended every 300 hours or 6 months. In the EIO configuration, the number of required oil changes could be cut in half, fewer spare parts and or swapping of systems would be needed, and the logistics burden would be reduced.

B. Base Camp Integration Laboratory (BCIL)

EIO participated in the 300 person camp exercise at the Base Camp Integration Laboratory (BCIL). This was a larger installation than the previous, involving 4 generators (2 60 kW, 2 30 kW) and 4 IPDs. The grid, in this configuration, powered 8 large barrack tents, a camp kitchen and camp shower, laundry, and latrine (lavatory) facilities.

The added layer of complexity created reduced reliability, largely in the data links. However, satisfactory data was obtained. Typical data is shown in Figure 5, which shows how a 60 kW generator was supplemented by two 30 kW generators, so as to automate the load following. The two 30 kW generators operated in droop mode and, when not producing power, were allowed to idle for 15 minutes before shutting down, thus being available for rapid transition back to power generation if needed.

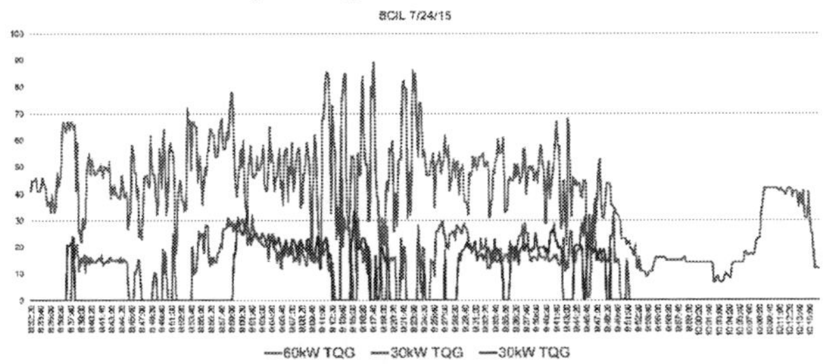

Figure 5. Typical data from the BCIL exercise, showing the power output of one 60 kW and two 30 kW generators and how they followed the load automatically.

The most difficult load to accommodate was that of the clothes dryer in the installation laundry, which cycled step loads of 35 kW every 30 seconds.

C. Integrated Capabilities Event (E15)

This experiment sought to integrate EIO with the U.S. Army's Condition Based Maintenance Plus (CBM+) program. The next step to accomplishing the EIO and CBM+ goals involved packaging the data transmitted from generators into a format CBM+ can understand. CBM+ uses a format called the Army Bulk CBM+ Data (ABCD) format. It is an extension to the Common Document Format (CDF) defined by the National Aeronautics and Space Administration (NASA). EIO developed the methods to package real-time data, culminating in an integration and experiment effort at the Integrated Capabilities Event (E15) [4].

The EIO configuration consisted of a 30kW retrofitted Tactical Quiet Generator (TQG) connected to an IPD and the EIO application. This single grid node provided power to an ECU, which was cooling E15's main tent. The ECU drew 6-7 kW of power when the ECU's compressor was engaged in cooling mode. Ideally the generator requires more load to operate efficiently, however the main focus of the demonstration was not efficiency of the microgrid configuration but the packaging of the real-time data provided by the generator and collected by the EIO application. The data was collected in ABCD format and provided to the CBM+ team.

The EIO single grid generated 12 days of ABCD files for both the TQG, and the IPD. EIO was successful in developing, testing and demonstrating that near real-time sensor data from microgrid components communicating using the EIO standards can be packaged into the CBM+ ABCD format and use the CBM+ architecture to provide the data to logistic systems for processing. This impacts the soldiers by stream-lining and semi-automating/automating solutions to power resources malfunctions. It also offers a path to accurate prognostics and diagnostics that predictively prevent, avoid or reduce malfunctions.

D. Network Integration Evaluation

The final demonstration was at the Network Integration Evaluation exercise. This is a large scale exercise designed to test data interoperability between U.S. Army systems. EIO sent 3 30 kW TQGs and 5 ECUs. EIO also powered a field refrigeration unit, which had an unexpectedly high inrush power of 60 kW-steady state being 7 kW-which caused a momentary system overload. The EIO grid responded quickly enough to prevent the overall system from being damaged, although it became readily apparent that communications delays can amplify transient behavior.

Of more significance than the overall system functioning was the reaction of the end users, which were ordinary soldiers with no particular expertise in electrical systems. They were able to make easy use of the system by means of the human-machine interface app. Interestingly, this interface was found to be more readily accepted by the junior, younger personnel, as opposed to the older, more senior personnel. This we attributed to the younger generation's greater familiarity with personal electronics and use of social media.

Future Work

EIO continues to refine its algorithms, apps and interfaces to produce a more reliable and versatile system. We will be returning to this year's the Base Camp Integration Laboratory exercise to demonstrate these improvements. Of particular interest is the integration of energy storage devices and inverters onto the grid. This would enable the addition of renewable energy devices, mainly solar photovoltaics and load leveling of the generators.

References

1. Valentina Prado et.al., "A Systematic Thermodynamic analysis of Fuel Consumption at Forward Operating Bases", in *Proc. of the 2011 IEEE International Symposium on Sustainable Systems and Technology*
2. Thomas F. Podlesak and Darren Z. Stephens, "Locational Marginal Pricing for Optimization of Energy Informed Operations", in Proc. of the 46th Power Sources Conference ,June 2014
3. Van T. Phu, Bradley J. Stanley, Jonathan F. Potter, Jeffrey P. Grossmann, Jon E. Hallander, Garrett C. Clarke, "Energy Informed Operations Software Application", CERDEC Technical Report, in preparation
4. Jon E. Hallander, Garrett C. Clarke and Bradley J. Stanley "Energy Informed Operations and Condition Based Maintenance Plus", CERDEC Technical Note, in preparation

Intelligent Energy for Asynchonous Tactical Energy Networks

Edward Shaffer, Bruce Geil, John Carroll
Army Research Laboratory

Darrell Massie
Intelligent Power & Energy Research Corporation

edward.c.shaffer.civ@mail.mil

Abstract

Recent military operations in the eastern Asia were characterized by instantiation of forward operating bases (FOBs) of various sizes and capabilities. The larger forward bases provided logistic, staging, and sustainment support to deployed units operating within geographic areas serviceable by these FOBs. These FOBs included various, non standard power and energy capabilities; in some cases tactical microgrids were implemented to realize "operational energy" goals to reduce logistics, improve energy efficiency, and enhance capabilities. The "lessons learned" in developing and deploying engineering solutions for improved power and energy capabilities and operational and tactical microgrids have provided a basis for further improving military generation, distribution, energy storage, power conversion, environmental control units, energy efficient structures, and renewables. In the near term, deploying an array of this improved energy and power hardware can be implemented as needed by a combination of standard military (eg TQGs, AMMPS, PDISE) and ruggedized commercial equipment; efforts are underway to standardize interfaces and connectors to enhance distribution and interoperability. Concepts for future military operations suggest a move away from large, enduring, fixed (in time and space) forward deployed bases. As such, the need for more agile, flexible, smaller footprint, rapidly reconfigurable energy and power capabilities will continue to grow. Current and planned military power and energy hardware provide limited solutions and assume a conventional fixed frequency AC generation and distribution architecture. This paper posits concepts and constructs for developing intelligent hardware and software based architectures toward realizing adaptable future energy systems. The Army has a unique opportunity to experiment in designing, developing, and implementing such tactical energy systems. These efforts are envisioned to leverage 1) "lessons learned" from recent deployments; 2) ongoing developments in SmartGrid technologies, which are also migrating from "top down, fixed grid" constructs to "bottom up, local /distributed energy resource" approaches; and 3) agile, self sensing, high speed/high density power electronics, power distribution, and energy storage components being developed at ARL.

Effect of Iron Disulphide, FeS_2, Decomposition on Modelling of Thermal Batteries

Andrew Grahame Ritchie
Farnborough, Hants GU14 0BE, UK
Email: andrew.ritchie20@btinternet.com

Abstract

The kinetics and thermodynamics of the thermal decomposition of iron disulphide, FeS_2, cathode material are discussed with relevance to the modelling of thermal battery performance.

Keywords

Thermal batteries; modelling; iron disulphide; pyrite

Introduction

Iron disulphide, pyrite, FeS_2, is the usual cathode material in thermal batteries. Its thermal decomposition has been discussed in connection with modelling of thermal battery performance [1]. The rate of thermal decomposition of iron disulphide in a flowing inert gas stream has been measured. However, modelling shows that the actual rate of iron disulphide decomposition in thermal batteries is much less. Two possible explanations have been proposed for this: (i) the iron disulphide is mixed with molten salts which inhibit the decomposition [1,2] and (ii) thermal batteries are sealed containers, so the sulphur vapour pressure from the decomposition of the iron disulphide reaches its equilibrium value and no further decomposition is possible [1]. The effect of molten salts was found to be minor, with only slight inhibition of the iron disulphide decomposition [1,2]. Thermal analysis studies using differential thermal analysis (DTA) in sealed containers showed strong inhibition of the decomposition [1]. However the thermodynamics were not considered in this work, though they have been briefly considered elsewhere [3]. This paper will consider the thermodynamics of iron disulphide decomposition and its effect on the rate of iron disulphide decomposition in thermal batteries and its inclusion in thermal battery modelling.

Iron - sulphur phase diagram

The phase diagram for the iron - sulphur system has been reported [4,5]. The essential points are that iron disulphide melts with decomposition at 743°C and cannot exist above this temperature, whatever the external pressure of sulphur vapour is applied. The sulphur vapour pressure over iron disulphide reaches 1 atmosphere at 697°C. The composition of pure crystalline iron disulphide is $FeS_{2.000}$ [6].

Thermal decomposition of iron disulphide

The equilibrium vapour pressure of sulphur over decomposing iron disulphide has been measured and compared with earlier works [7]. The recommended equation for the equilibrium sulphur vapour pressure over pyrite is (eqn. (6) of [7]):

$$\log_{10} p_{vap} = 16.2 - 15700/T$$

where p is in bar, T is in K.

Using this equation, the following vapour pressures for sulphur in equilibrium with iron disulphide are calculated:

T (°C)	T (°K)	Log10(P) (bar)	P (bar)	P (atm)	P (torr)
300	573.15	-11.192	6.42E-12	6.34E-12	0.000
350	623.15	-8.995	1.01E-09	9.99E-10	0.000
400	673.15	-7.123	7.53E-08	7.43E-08	0.000
450	723.15	-5.511	3.09E-06	3.05E-06	0.002
500	773.15	-4.107	7.82E-05	7.72E-05	0.059
550	823.15	-2.873	1.34E-03	1.32E-03	1.005
600	873.15	-1.781	1.66E-02	1.63E-02	12.423
650	923.15	-0.807	1.56E-01	1.54E-01	116.980
697	970.15	0.017	1.04E+00	1.03E+00	779.888
700	973.15	0.067	1.17E+00	1.15E+00	874.825
743	1016.15	0.750	5.62E+00	5.54E+00	4,213.298

Table 1: Decomposition pressure of iron disulphide.

The calculated decomposition pressure at 697°C using the above equation, 1.03 atm, is close to the measured pressure of 1 atm.

Discussion

The equilibrium sulphur pressure over iron disulphide reaches significant values in the temperature range 600 - 650°C, which is the temperature range over which most decomposition occurs (Figure 1 of [1]). Hence, in sealed containers in which the sulphur vapour is contained, this vapour pressure will be reached and further decomposition prevented.

Conclusion

Thermodynamic studies show that the vapour pressure of sulphur in a thermal battery, which is a sealed container, will inhibit iron disulphide decomposition, so modelling of thermal battery performance does need to take the thermodynamics of iron disulphide decomposition into account as the thermodynamic limiting vapour pressure will be reached in sealed containers, such as thermal batteries. Decomposition of iron disulphide will therefore be much less than at the same temperature in open containers. This is important for the modelling of the effect of iron disulphide decomposition on the performance of thermal batteries.

References

1. A. G. Ritchie and P. J Carter, Thermal Stability of Iron Disulphide, FeS_2, Cathode Material in Thermal Batteries, *Proceedings of the 38th Power Sources Conference*, pp 215 - 8, 1998.

2. P. J. Masset, Thermal Stability of FeS_2 Cathode Material in "Thermal" Batteries: Effect of Dissolved Oxides in Molten Salt Electrolytes, *Z. Naturforsch A,* vol 63, no 9, pp 596 - 602, 2008.

3. S. Schoeffert, Thermal batteries modeling, self-discharge and self-heating, *J. Power Sources*, vol 142, pp 361 - 9, 2005.

4. O. Kubaschewski, Iron - Binary Phase Diagrams, Springer Verlag, Berlin, pp 125 - 8, 1982.

5. M. Hansen and K. Anderko, Constitution of Binary Alloys, Genium Pub. Corp. New York, pp 704 - 8, 1991.

6. Unpublished analysis carried out by W. Westby, RAE, Farnborough.

7. Y. Hong and B. Fegley, The sulfur vapor pressure over pyrite on the surface of Venus, *Planet. Space Sci.*, vol 46, no 6/7, pp 683 - 90, 1998.

Salt Coated Zr/BaCrO$_4$ Heat Papers for Thermal Batteries

Chae-Nam Im, Byeong June Park, Seung-Ho Kang, and Hae-Won Cheong

Agency for Defense Development, Yuseong P.O Box 35, Dae-Jeon, 305-600 Korea
+ Corresponding author. Tel: +82-42-821-3688, Fax: +82-42-823-3400
E-mail address: imchw@add.re.kr

Abstract: *Excessive heat input to thermal batteries at the initial stage of activation can lead to a serious problem, such as thermal decomposition of FeS_2 cathode or melting of Li(Si) anode. This, in turn, not only reduces the battery capacity but also triggers thermal runaways. These transient thermal unstability can be significantly mitigated by the combustion temperature of heat papers. In this study, Zr/BaCrO$_4$ heat papers were prepared by paper-making process and molten salt, such as LiCl, KCl, and NaCl was spray-coated to suppress the peak burning temperature of heat papers. The peak burning temperature and the specific calorific output were decreased as the coated film thickness increased due to the latent heat of molten salt. Salt coating on the surface of Zr/BaCrO$_4$ heat papers remarkably alleviates the thermal decomposition of FeS_2 cathode and the melting of Li(Si) anode as well as Fe/KClO$_4$ heat pellet ignition by controlling the peak temperature, which results in the enhanced reliability of thermal batteries during the activation.*

Keywords: FeS_2 cathode, Zr/BaCrO$_4$ heat paper, Molten salt, Fe/KClO$_4$ heat pellet, Peak burning temperature

Introduction

Thermal batteries have excellent mechanical stability, reliability and long-term storage life. Because of these advantages, they have been used as the main or assistant power sources for guided weapons [1]. Li(Si)/FeS_2 thermal batteries, which are used mostly in these days, use inorganic salt as electrolyte which is inactive at room temperature [2]. The two principal heat sources are Zr/BaCrO$_4$ heat paper used only as fuse train and heat pellets, which are the primary heat sources. In this application, the fuse ignited by the initiator, in turn ignites the heat pellets, all the solid electrolytes are instantly melted into excellent ionic conductors [3]. At the initial stage of activation, excessive heat input to thermal batteries by the heat sources can lead thermal decomposition of FeS_2 above 550°C or the melting of Li(Si) above 700°C . It is reported that this not only reduces the battery capacity but also triggers thermal runaway (Figure 1). The danger of short circuit also increase in the decrease of electrolyte viscosity, which causes the leakage of molten salt by the high temperature of heat papers. These transient thermal unstability can be significantly mitigated by the width reduction of heat papers [4-6]. However, one of possible hazards caused by the high burning temperature of heat papers still exists in thermal batteries.

In this study, molten salt, such as LiCl, KCl, and NaCl was spray-coated to suppress the peak temperature of Zr/BaCrO$_4$ heat paper. Thermal properties of coated-heat paper such as peak temperature, burning rate, calorific output, and heat pellet ignition was measured. We have investigated the best condition to ignite the heat pellet and minimize thermal decomposition of FeS_2 cathode and melting of Li(Si) anode.

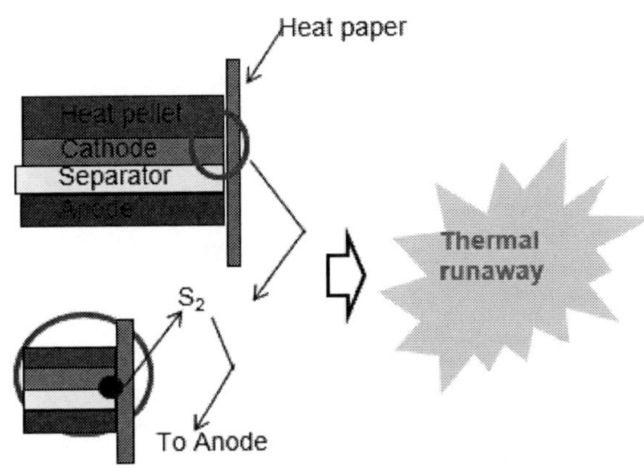

Figure 1. Schematic representation of thermal runaway scenario by Zr/BaCrO$_4$ heat paper.

Experiment

Fabrication of molten salt coated Zr/BaCrO$_4$ heat paper

While Zr itself is high sensitivity material and easily ignited in air, BaCrO$_4$ is low sensitivity material and not ignited in air. Zr (mean particle diameter: 2.0 μm), BaCrO$_4$ (mean particle size diameter: 1~2 μm), and two type of ceramic fibers (mean particle size diameter: 1 and 5 μm, respectively) is used. LiCl, KCl, NaCl molten salt for coating Zr/BaCrO$_4$ heat paper were used.

First, the slurry for heat papers was prepared to mix ceramic fibers with Zr/BaCrO$_4$ solution and organic binders that improve the adhesion between Zr/BaCrO$_4$ and fibers. The resulting slurry, which was about 98~99 % water by weight, was stirred for the effective dispersion and was deposited onto the wire mesh, followed by formation and dewatering of heat paper sheet (Figure 2). The heat paper sheet is rolled onto reels for handling and dried at 80°C for 24 hr. As shown in figure 3, molten salt (LiCl, KCl, and NaCl) was properly spray-coated on $Zr/BaCrO_4$ heat paper to suppress the peak temperature. After the coating, the heat papers was dried at 100°C for 24 hr.

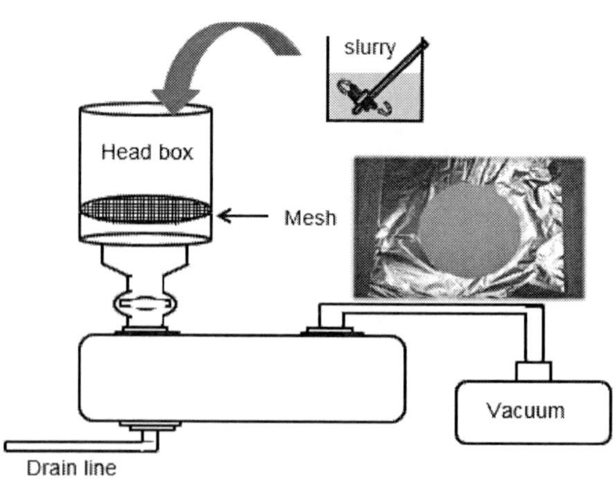

Figure 2. Schematic diagram of fabrication process for $Zr/BaCrO_4$ heat paper

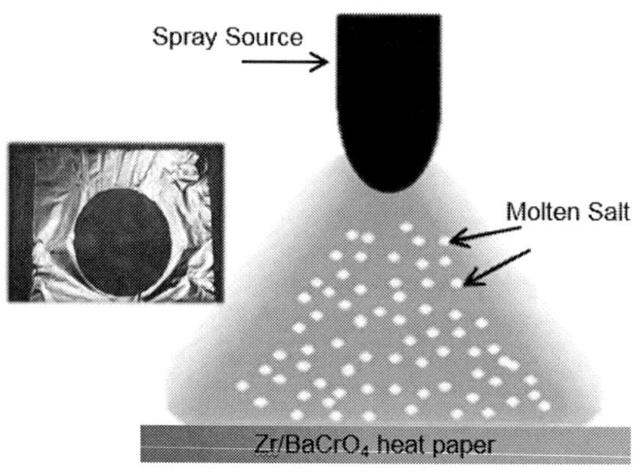

Figure 3. Spray coating of molten salt on $Zr/BaCrO_4$ heat paper

Thermal properties

The peak temperature and burning rate of slat-coated $Zr/BaCrO_4$ heat paper were measured by test apparatus as shown in figure 4. The peak temperature is measured via a thermocouple and the burning rate was calculated from the time difference of the electric potential when both wires are cut. Calorific output was measured using bomb calorimeter (Parr 6100, Parr Instrument Co.) in argon atmosphere. Igniting $Zr/BaCrO_4$ heat papers were investigated with the direct contact method by laser in order to determine the heat pellet ignition before and after salt coating.

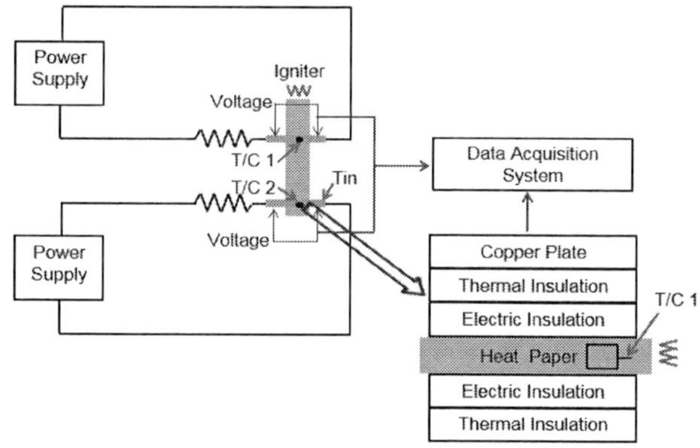

Figure 4. Peak temperature and burning rate test apparatus

Results and Discussion

Peak temperature

The peak temperature of LiCl-coated $Zr/BaCrO_4$ heat papers is shown in figure 5. The different coating thickness and peak temperature of $Zr/BaCrO_4$ heat papers is 0 µm, 20 µm, 50 µm, and 70 µm, and is 950.8°C, 690.9°C, 635.9°C, and 527.9°C, respectively. As coating thickness increases, peak temperature is decreased. However, cooling rate is flat at 50 µm coating around melting point of LiCl than other coatings because LiCl maintains the phage change until the end of latent heat storage.

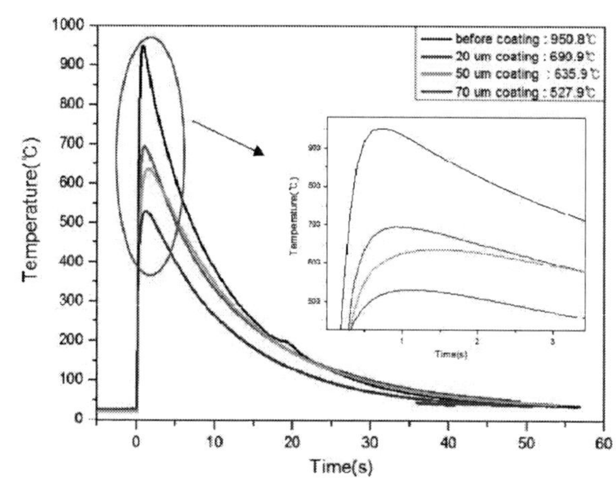

Figure 5. Peak temperature of $Zr/BaCrO_4$ heat paper before and after LiCl coating

Figure 6 and 7, similarly as figure 5, represents the peak temperature of KCl and NaCl-coated $Zr/BaCrO_4$ heat papers. Coating thickness of two heat papers is 20 µm, 50 µm, and 60 µm, respectively. Peak temperature of KCl-coated $Zr/BaCrO_4$ heat papers are 815.3°C, 775.1°C, and 665.9°C respectively. Peak temperature of NaCl-coated

$Zr/BaCrO_4$ heat papers are 813.5°C, 744.1°C, and 670.6°C, respectively. As shown in figure 6, phase change of KCl at 50 ㎛ that is around melting point at 770°C shows that slower cooling rate than other coatings. NaCl-coated $Zr/BaCrO_4$ heat papers not show such a phenomenon because thinner coating thickness than other molten salts means small time of maintaining the melting point.

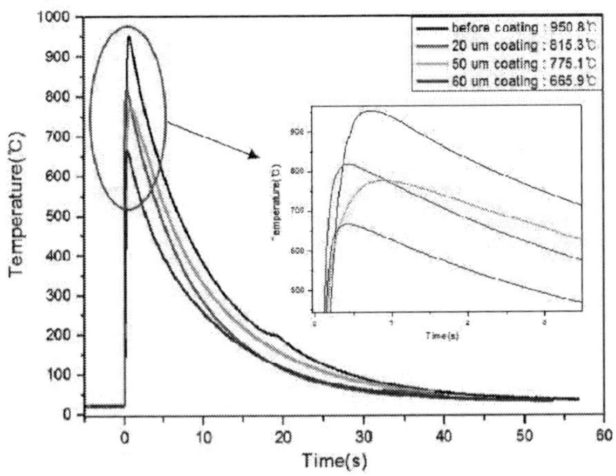

Figure 6. Peak temperature of $Zr/BaCrO_4$ heat paper before and after KCl coating

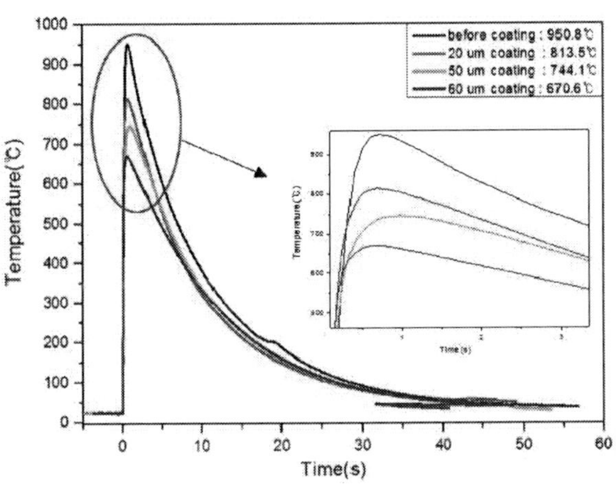

Figure 7. Peak temperature of $Zr/BaCrO_4$ heat paper before and after NaCl coating

Burning rate and calorific output

The particle size and specific surface area of reducing agent, Zr influence significantly the reaction rate of pyrotechnics [7, 8]. As shown in figure 8, burning rate of $Zr/BaCrO_4$ heat paper before salt coating is very fast at 74 ㎝/s because $Zr/BaCrO_4$ heat papers have the large specific surface. The increase of coating thickness of LiCl, KCl, and NaCl decline the burning rate of $Zr/BaCrO_4$ heat papers due to coating film rather than specific surface area. Existence of coating film thickness on $Zr/BaCrO_4$ heat papers interrupts the burn reaction and absorbs the heat which increase the reaction rate. It is also insensitive to the contact with oxygen. The calorific output of salt-coated $Zr/BaCrO_4$ heat papers is shown in figure 9. Calorific output are reduced because of the increased mass of non-exothermal parts

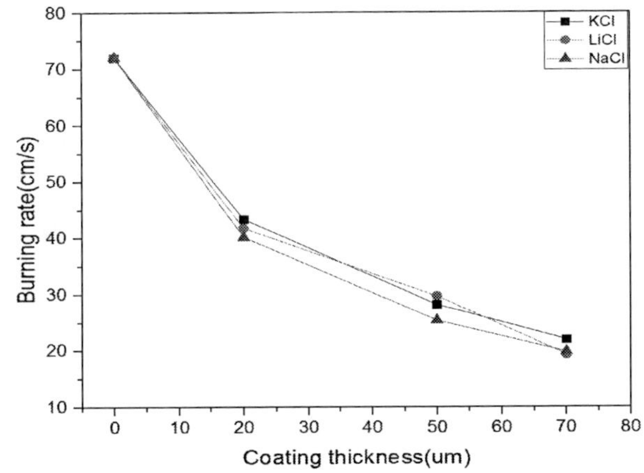

Figure 8. Burning rate of $Zr/BaCrO_4$ heat paper with different coating thickness

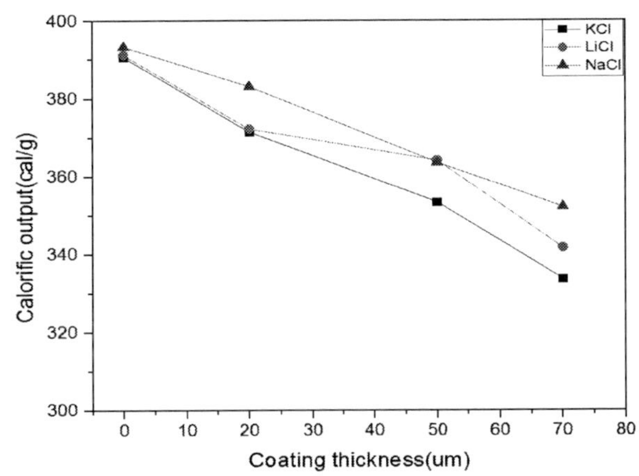

Figure 9. Calorific output of $Zr/BaCrO_4$ heat paper with different coating thickness

Heat pellet ignition test

In most modern pellet-type thermal batteries, heat papers are used only as fuse train to ignite the $Fe/KClO_4$ heat pellets. It is reported that the ignition temperature of heat pellets is about 440°C [9]. As shown in figure 10, It is tested with direct contact method to determine the heat pellet ignition when activated by salt-coated $Zr/BaCrO_4$ heat papers. All the salt coated $Zr/BaCrO_4$ heat papers ignited the heat pellets (Table 1).

Table 1. Heat pellet ignition test results

	LiCl-coated heat papers	KCl-coated heat papers	NaCl-coated heat papers
Heat pellet	Ignition	Ignition	Ignition

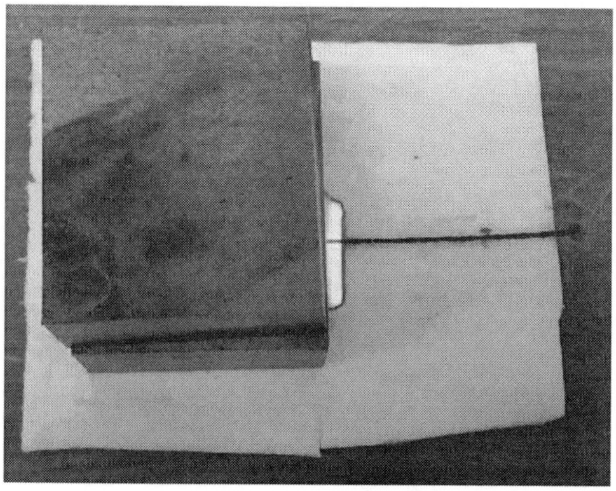

Figure 10. Heat pellet ignition test with salt coated $Zr/BaCrO_4$ heat paper

Conclusion

In this study, molten salt, such as LiCl, KCl, and NaCl was spray-coated to control the peak burning temperature of $Zr/BaCrO_4$ heat paper. As coating thickness increases, peak temperature was decreased. . However, cooling rate is flat at 50 μm coating around melting point of LiCl and KCl than other coatings because both molten salts maintain the phage change until the end of latent heat storage. LiCl 70 μm coated $Zr/BaCrO_4$ heat paper, which has the lowest peak temperature of 527.9 °C ignited the heat pellets. As a results, salt coating on the surface of $Zr/BaCrO_4$ heat papers remarkably alleviates the thermal decomposition of FeS_2 cathode and the melting of Li(Si) anode as well as heat pellet ignition by controlling the peak burning temperature, which results in the enhanced reliability of thermal batteries during the activation.

References

1. R. A. Guidotti, P. Masset, Journal of Power Sources, vol. 161, pp. 1443-49, 2006.
2. Y. S. Choi, S. H. Ha, H. W. Cheong, S. B. Cho, proceeding of 45th Power Sources Conference, pp. 539~541, 2012.
3. D. Linden, "Handbook of Batteries, Second Edition" (McGraw-Hill, Inc.,) pp. 22.1-22.20, 1994.
4. R. A. Guidotti, (SAND2006-1902, Sandia National Laboratories), 2006.
5. H. W. Cheong, S. H. Kang, J. M. Kim, S. B. Cho, Journal of Ceramic Processing Research, Vol. 13, Special. 2, pp. 198-201, 2012.
6. H. W. Cheong, S. H. Ha, Y. S. Choi, Journal of Ceramic Processing Research, Vol. 13, Special. 2, pp. 308-311, 2012.
7. B. Berger, Chimia, Vol. 58, pp. 363-368, 2004.
8. B. Berger, Propellants, Explosives, Pyrotechnics, Vol. 30, pp. 27-35, 2005.
9. B. Czajka, S. Styczynski, S. Tabat, D. Szal, and L. Wachowski, Central European Journal of Energetic Materials, Vol. 8, pp. 3-24, 2011.

Development of Porous MgO Preform through Tape Casting Technique to Fabricate a Thermal Battery Separator

Kyung-Ho Kim [a], Sung-Min Lee [a], Seung-Ho Kang [b], Chaenam Im [b], Hae-Won Cheong [b], Yoon Soo Han [a,]*

[a]Engineering Ceramic Team, Korea Institute of Ceramic Engineering and Technology, Icheon 17303, Korea
[b]Agency for Defense Development, Yuseong P. O. Box 35-41, Daejeon 34188, Korea

E-mail address: corundum69@kicet.re.kr

Abstract: *The development and test results of composite separator which consists of the porous ceramic preform and the infiltrated Lithium-based molten salt electrolyte is reported. The porous, thick film type of ceramic preform was fabricated using tape casting method with MgO and poly methyl meth acrylate (PMMA) materials, and then the molten salt was infiltrated into the sintered preform by dipping method. The porosity of MgO preform is a linear function of the amount of PMMA additions and the maximum porosity is 75%. The LiF-LiCl-LiBr system showed the best result on the high temperature test where cut-off voltage was over 100 seconds which was around 90% of performance compared to the pressed pallet type thermal battery.*

Keywords: Thermal battery; Porous MgO; PMMA; Separator; Tape casting

Introduction

Thermal battery which has very high power output and very long storage time without degradation has been mainly developed for the military purposes such as thermal-guidance weapons, guided bombs, and torpedoes [1]. The most commonly used electrochemical system in thermal batteries is Li-Al and Li-Si alloys/FeS_2 system, where a Li-based solid electrolyte is placed between them. The system consisting of electrodes and electrolyte are usually fabricated by uniaxial pressing the corresponding powders, which are very brittle under external loads. The electrolyte layer generally contains 30 percentage of MgO powder as a binder to hold the molten electrolyte [2-5]. To minimize the risk for fracturing as well as to enhance the electrochemical properties, however, the use of ceramic preform as a separator can be considered. In this study we report a method for fabricating thermal battery with highly porous MgO separator by tape casting and evaluate its torpedoes performance.

Experimental procedure

MgO powder (Scora, France) had an average particle size of about 50 nm. For additive as a pore former, PMMA (HLDP-040, DEAJUNG Chemical, Korea) with average particle size of about 10 μm was used. As a solvent, ethanol and toluene mixed by 50 vol% each was used, while PVB(BMSZ, >97%, SEKISUI Chemical Co., LTD, Japan) for the organic binder, DOP(Dioctyl phthalate, 99%, SAMCHUN Chemical, Korea) for the plasticizer, copolymer series(DISPERBYK-111, Altana Co., Germany) for the dispersant were employed. To obtain the optimum green sheet, slurries were prepared by changing the binder contents in comparison with the powder to the conditions of 5.5 to 9.5%, the representative formulation of which is shown in Table 1.

Table 1. Composition of the suspension for tape casting

MgO (wt%)	PMMA (wt%)	Dispersant (wt%)	PVB (wt%)	DOP (wt%)	Solvent (wt%)
6.36	18.86	0.30	52.12	3.05	19.32

To fabricate porous preform, MgO powder along with PMMA as the pore former were ball milled together with organic materials and solvent for 24 h, with the final slurry being obtained after undergoing aging for 24 h. Tape casting was conducted by pouring the slurry in a doctor blade set at the dam height of 300 μm, and moving the film at the velocity of 2.0 m/min, from which 100 μm-thick green sheets were finally produced. 300 μm-thick stacked sheets were prepared by application of 12 ton of load for 10 seconds after setting the table temperature of Stacking Machine at 40°C and overlapping several layers of the green sheet. To increase the forming density through tighter adherence of the stacked sheets, the sheets were pressed for 10 minutes at 70°C under 20MPa using a WIP(Warm Isostatic Press), and then the substrates were cut into the disc shape with the diameter of

50 mm. The sintering process under the oxidizing atmosphere was conducted in a box-type electric furnace at 1300 °C for 4 hours. Infiltration process was conducted in box type furnace by dipping the MgO preform into molten salt in graphite box at 500°C as shown in Figure 1. All processes were done in glove box where relative humidity was below 2% to avoid the hydration reaction of salts.

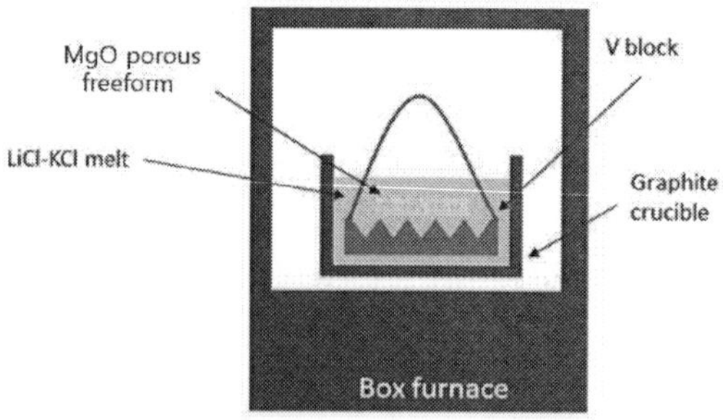

Figure 1. Schematics of molt salt infiltration process with MgO porous preform.

Results and discussion

Figure 2 shows the micrographs of the green sheet and the sintered MgO preform. In figure 2 (a), submicron size MgO particles are placed uniformly between tens of micron size of spherical PMMA particles which seems not to be deformed during uniaxial stacking process. In figure 2 (b), PMMA particles disappear and large pores are formed instead without the collapse of reticulated structure of MgO during sintering process.

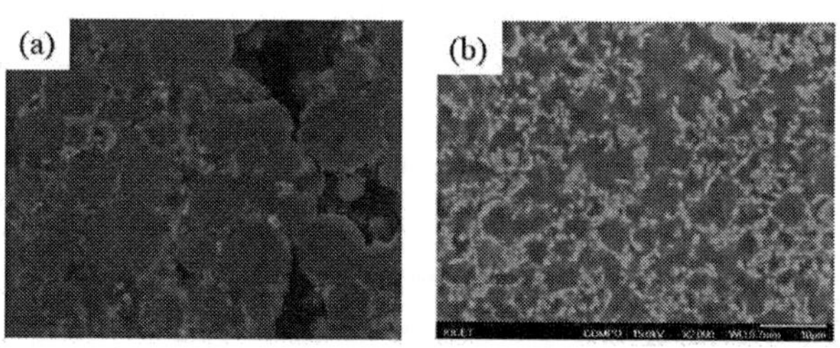

Figure 2. Cross sectional micrographs of (a) MgO green sheet with PMMA and (b) its sintered preform. Note that the pores in sintered preform are filled with polishing mount resin (dark grey) instead of molten salt electrolyte.

The cross sectional micrograph of MgO preform as a function of porosity is shown in Figure 3. The pore area (grey area in the images) increase as the content of PMMA increase. The MgO grains (white area in the images) look smaller in the specimen with larger porosity. The pores seems to be connected each other to make the three dimensional channels which means molten salt can flow in the preform and the infiltration process will occur.

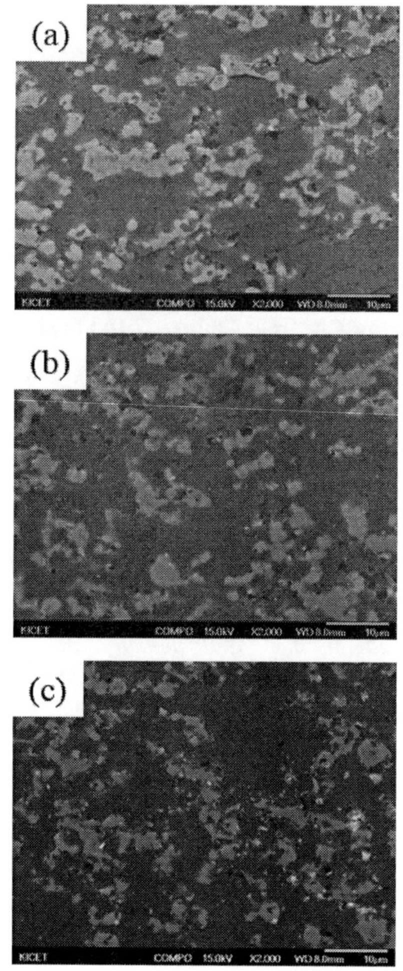

Figure 3. Cross sectional micrographs of MgO preform with (a) 65, (b) 70, and (c) 75 % of porosity.

To check out the uniformity of pore size distribution over MgO preform, the thin disc specimen was sliced into 8 sections and the cross sectional polished images are shown in Figure 4. No severe agglomeration of pores or MgO particles are observed and the tape casting process is acceptable as a fabrication process for high porous, 300 □m-thick preform.
Figure 5 shows the surface microstructure of MgO preform at different surfaced positions. It is important to investigate the surface microstructure which will be the interfaces with anode and cathode electrodes and has been believed to affect the performance of thermal battery in applications because if there is no surface open pores which is the end of the pore channels, the high performance of thermal battery would not be expected. As shown in figure 5, we can easily find out the open pore distribution is very uniform and this structure would leads to enable the molten salts or Li ions to flow in the pore channel and at the interface of separator and electrodes.

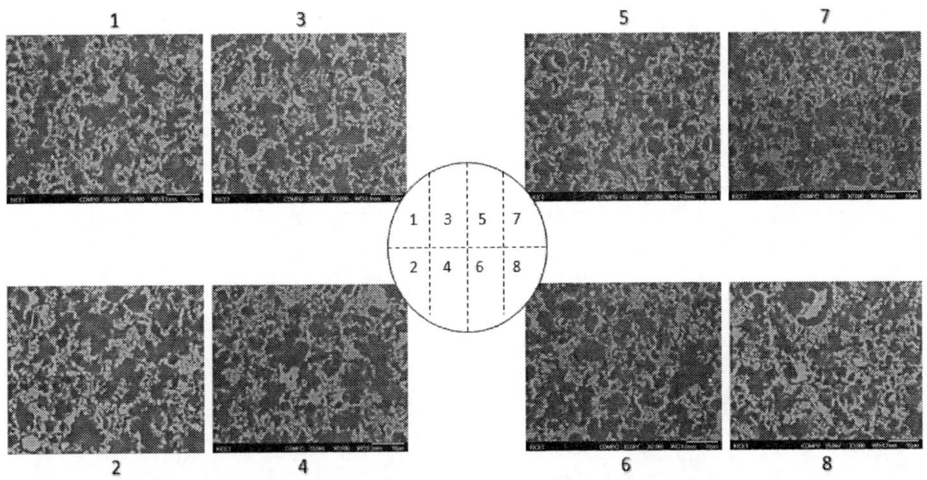

Figure 4. Cross sectional micrographs of the different 8 sections in the MgO preform.

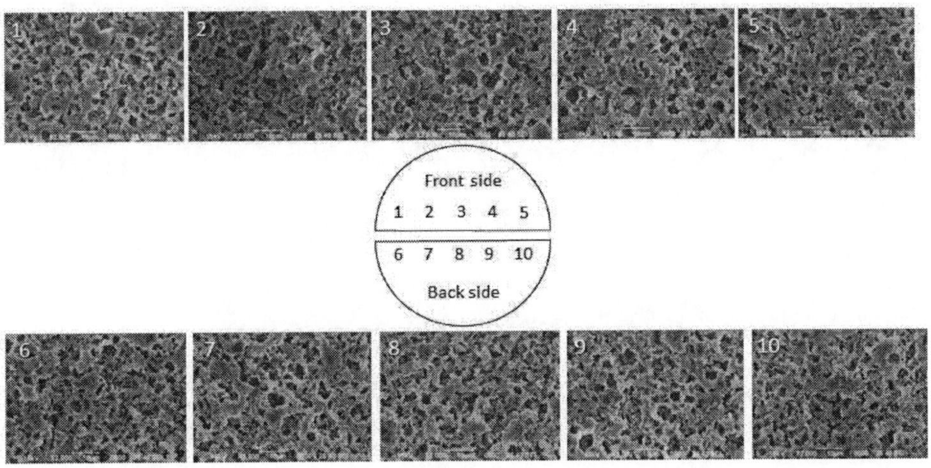

Figure 5. Surface microstructure of MgO preform. The position 1 to 5 correspond to the microstructures of upper side of the disc specimen and the position 6 to 10 correspond to the microstructures of bottom side of specimen.

The result of battery test is shown in figure 6. The MgO separator thermal battery with the composition of 22% LiF, 31% LiCl and 47% LiBr molten salt system shows the longest time, 107 seconds, to cut-off voltage in the output voltage versus ac current curve, which is around 90% of performance compared to the pressed pallet type thermal battery.

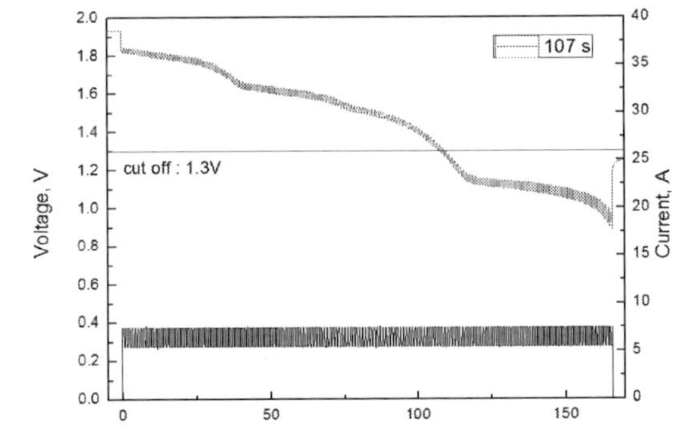

Figure 6. The output voltage versus ac current curve. The time to cut-off voltage at 500°C is over 100 seconds in LiF-LiCl-LiBr system.

The fracture surface analysis after high temperature battery test was carried out, and the microstructure of fracture surface of battery is shown in Figure 7. No molten salt was observed in the middle area of separator which had been filled with molten salts before high temperature battery test. However, if we look into the interface between separator and both electrodes, the dense layers which seems to be still filled with molten salts would be observed. This means that during the test the molten salts which can flow freely in the pore channels flow from the preform to both electrodes due to capillary force which occur from the difference of pore size. In other words, in this system the average pore size in the separator would be larger than that of both electrodes, so there is pressure difference which make molten salts flow. Moreover, we cannot find any evidence that the pore structure of separator is collapsed, which can squeezed the molten salts out to the both electrodes.

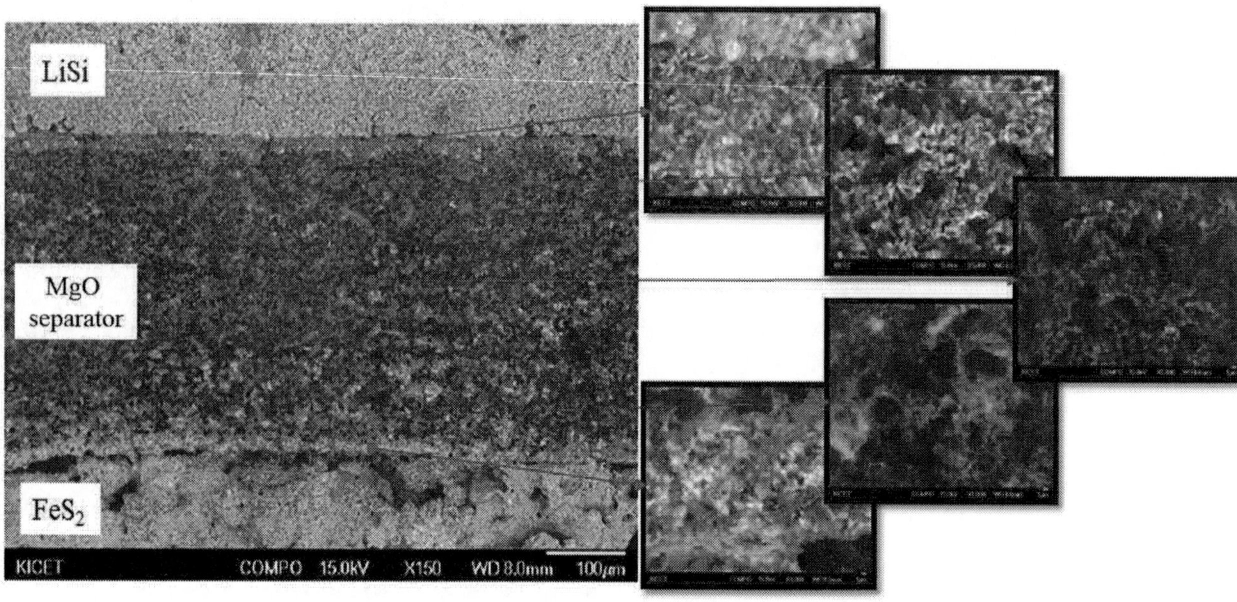

Figure 7. Cross sectional micrographs of fracture specimen after the high temperature battery test.

Conclusions

In the study, the high porous MgO preform was fabricated by tape casting and the thermal battery with LiF-LiCl-LiBr salt was tested after molten salt infiltration by dipping method. The porosity of MgO preform was controlled by changing the amount of PMMA spherical polymer addition and the highest porosity obtained with this method was 75 %. The high porous MgO preform has the uniform internal pore channels and the surface open pores which is believed to be important considerations for the thermal battery to show high performance during the application. The thermal battery shows good performance which the cut-off voltage in the output voltage versus ac current curve is 107 seconds. In the fracture surface analysis, we find that the molten salts flow to the both anode and cathode electrodes by capillary force due to the average size difference of pores in each separator and electrode which mean we can control life of thermal battery by controlling the pore sizes in the MgO preform.

Acknowledgments

This study was funded by the Agency for the Defense Development of Korea.

References

1. Klasons,V., in : Linden, D., (Ed.), *Handbook of Batteries*, 3rd ed., McGraw-Hill, New York, pp. 21.1–21.22, 2002.
2. Masset, P., and R.A. Guidotti, "Thermally Activated ("Thermal") Battery Technology Part II: Molten Salt Electrolytes," *Journal of Power Sources*, Vol. 164, pp. 397–414, 2007.
3. Masset, P., and R.A. Guidotti, "Thermally Activated ("Thermal") Battery Technology Part III a: FeS_2 Cathode Material," *Journal of Power Sources*, Vol. 177, pp. 595–609, 2008.
4. Masset, P., and R.A. Guidotti, "Thermally Activated ("Thermal") Battery Technology Part III b: Sulfur and Oxide-based Cathode Materials," *Journal of Power Sources*, Vol. 178, pp. 456–466, 2008.
5. Guidotti, R.A., and P.J. Masset, "Thermally Activated ("Thermal") Battery Technology Part IV: Anode Materials," *Journal of Power Sources*, Vol. 183, pp. 388–398, 2008.

Investigation of $CoNi_2S_4$ as Suitable Cathode Material for Use in Next Generation Thermal Batteries

[1]Kyriakos Giagloglou, [1]Julia L. Payne, [2]Christina Crouch, [2]Richard K.B. Gover, [1]Paul Connor, [1]John T.S Irvine

[1]University of St. Andrews, School of Chemistry, North Haugh, St Andrews Fife KY16 9ST, United Kingdom
[2]AWE, Aldermaston, Reading, RG7 4PR

Abstract: *In this work $CoNi_2S_4$ was synthesized by solid state reaction in sealed quartz tubes (10^{-3}Torr) and investigated as a candidate cathode material in thermal batteries. The structure of $CoNi_2S_4$ was determined by XRD and was an inverse spinel structure single phase material and cell parameters refined by WinXpoW program. The electrochemical properties of the batteries were investigated at 500°C by Galvanostatic Discharge. Li-Si alloy as anode, LiCl-KCl as electrolyte and MgO as separator were used. $CoNi_2S_4$ has a 2 step voltage plateau vs Li-Si, the first one at 1.75 Volts and the second one at 1.4 Volts at a constant current of 20 mA with capacity of 266 $mAhg^{-1}$.*

Keywords: solid state synthesis; cathode $CoNi_2S_4$; galvanostatic discharge at 500°C; high temperature lithium battery;

Introduction

Thermal batteries are electrochemical systems that convert chemical energy into electrical energy by means of an electrochemical oxidation-reduction reaction between the anode and the cathode electrode. These batteries operate in a similar manner to more common batteries and are able to provide higher power and long shelf life than common batteries. These batteries find usage in critical systems where high reliability is crucial. They are known for their ability to be stored for long periods of time (> 25 years), their ability to be started rapidly (< 1 s) and their ability to be discharged at extremely high rates compared to standard batteries [1]. Moreover, thermal batteries are used to supply power to ejector seats, guided munitions and emergency power systems on aircraft. Thermal batteries are composed of a number of individual electrochemical cells that have three key components: a cathode, an anode, and an electrolyte. In this case the thermal prefix is related to the electrolyte, a halide salt eutectic that is only ionically conductive when molten (>350°C). Contemporary cells often use a lithium alloy as the anode, a halide salt eutectic bound in an insulating porous material as the electrolyte and a transition metal sulfide as the cathode. These transition metal disulfides such as FeS_2, NiS_2 and CoS_2 are very common and all of these materials can supply voltages of ~ 1.7 V vs. $Li_{13}Si_4$ for their first electrochemical transition but also have further electrochemical transitions eventually terminating in complete reduction of the transition metal. Curiously, these proposed discharge pathways differ for all three disulfides [2]. In this work the preference is to use the $Li_{13}Si_4$ alloy as an anode which has the highest Li content and the minimum oxidation under dry-room conditions. It also has a potential of around 157 mV vs Li at 415°C [3]. The capacity of this alloy is 485 $mAhg^{-1}$ and it is preferred because the lithium diffusion in silicon is greater than in other alloys. We use the lithium chloride – potassium chloride eutectic electrolyte, which melts at 354°C and has become established for use in high temperature batteries and requires a minimum of 35 wt% MgO as binder. In this work $CoNi_2S_4$ is investigated as cathode material for use in thermal batteries. Normal spinel structures $A^{2+}B^{3+}{}_2S^{2-}{}_4$ are usually cubic close-packed structures with the S^- anions arranged in a cubic close-packed lattice and the cations A^{+2} and B^{+3} occupying some or all of the octahedral and tetrahedral sites in the lattice. The tetrahedral spaces are smaller than the octahedral spaces. B^{3+} ions occupy half the octahedral holes, while A^{2+} ions occupy one-eighth of the tetrahedral holes. $CoNi_2S_4$ is an inverse spinel structure as you can see in Figure 1 and has a different cation distribution in that all of the Co cations and half of the Ni cations occupy octahedral sites, while the other half of the Ni cations occupy tetrahedral sites [4]

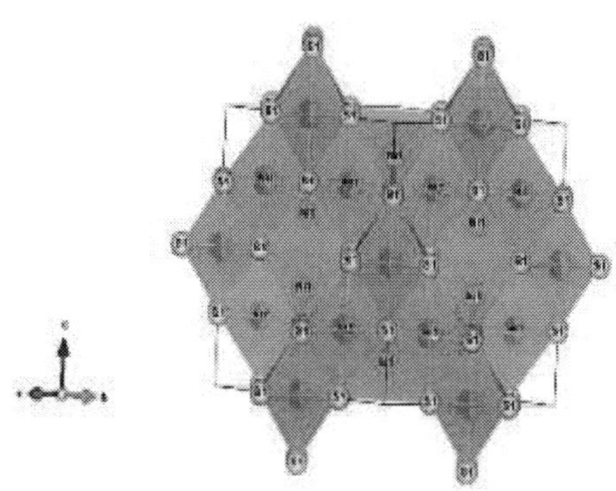

Figure 1. Crystal structure of $CoNi_2S_4$. Yellow atoms are Sulfur, Gray atoms are Nickel and Blue atoms are Cobalt. As you can see $CoNi_2S_4$ is an inverse spinel structure.

Experimental procedure

$CoNi_2S_4$ was synthesized by solid state reaction in sealed quartz tubes to ensure that was not oxidized. 0.77g of Nickel (Aldrich,-100mesh, 99%), 0.38g of Cobalt (Alfa Aesar,-325mesh, 99.5%) and 0.83g of Sulfur (Alfa Aesar,-100mesh, 99.5%) powders were used. All the powders were weighed out and mixed in a mortar and pestle in air and then sealed into evacuated (10^{-3}Torr) quartz tubes before the reactions were carried out inside a tube furnace. The tube furnace was heated and cooled down to room temperature at (1°C/min). The synthesis of $CoNi_2S_4$ has previously been reported by Knop and Huang [4]. Here the synthetic procedure (*via* a conventional solid state route) involved multiple firings at temperatures in the 500 °C-600 °C temperature range for 3 days, 2 days, 5 days, 6 days, 1 month and 20 days, *i.e.* a total of 66 days! We have recently had success in synthesizing the sample in just 8 days, in just two firing steps, by using ball milling as an intermediate step. The firings and the temperature of synthesis are presented in Table 1. Between firings there was ball milling in Argon for 4 hours to achieve homogeneity. X-Ray diffraction analysis was conducted in order to examine the cathode phase using a conventional X-ray powder diffractometer Panalytical Empyrean model having a Cu Ka1 1.540598 wavelength, operated at 40 mA and 45 kV. Scanning electron microscopy Jeol JSM-5600 model was used to study the morphology of the cathode powder. The cells were tested at high temperature and were investigated electrochemically by Maccor Model 5300 by Galvanostatic Discharge. High temperature discharge measurements were performed at a temperature of 500 °C using a furnace connecting to Maccor instrument. Fabrication of the composite cathode material for high temperature electrochemical investigation was made from $CoNi_2S_4$ by making a pellet by mixing 75 wt% active powder and 25 wt% Super P Carbon. Thermal cells were assembled in an argon-filled glove box by stacking a microporous separator containing 45 wt% MgO (Hallstar) and 55 wt% LiCl-KCl (Sigma Aldrich 99.99%) electrolyte between the cathode and the anode pellet. Anode pellet was made by mixed 75 wt% $Li_{13}Si_4$ (Lithium Rockwood) and 25 wt% LiCl-KCl. To prevent spillage, all 3 components comprising anode, separator and cathode were captured by a ceramic ring and were mechanically isolated (top and bottom) with foil graphite. The measurements were conducted under air atmosphere and thermal cells were introduced into a furnace set to the test temperature. While heating, the electrolyte melts and voltage starts to rise. For stabilization, the cell was maintained at relaxation mode for a short duration of 60 s and only then a constant current was applied.

Table 1. Firings and temperature of synthesis

1st firing	Ball milling	2nd firing
550°C for 1 day	300rpm 4hrs	550°C for 6 days

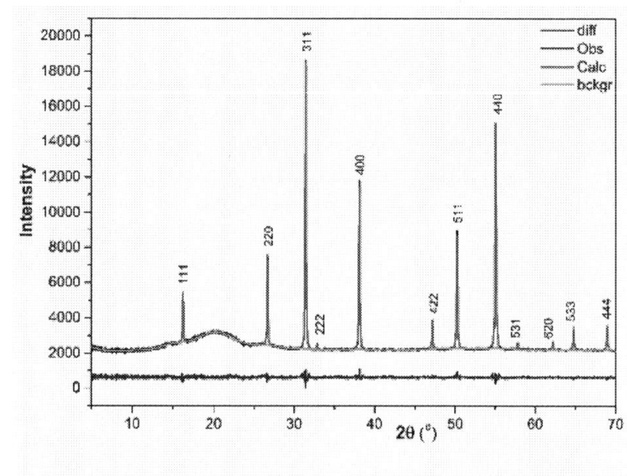

Figure 2. XRD pattern of $CoNi_2S_4$ refined by Rietveld Analysis. According to Rietveld Analysis $CoNi_2S_4$ is a pure phase. Numbers of wRp=0.0215, Rp=0.0164, Reduced Chi^2=1.174 can confirm a nice fitting. The peak at around 20° is from the silica substrate disc which is using for XRD.

Results and Discussion

Cathode material characterization

Synthesized $CoNi_2S_4$ material was studied by powder x-ray diffraction as presented in Figure 2 as collected from reflection geometry. $CoNi_2S_4$ was identified as single phase [4]. Using WinXpoW program the parameters of unit cell are a = 9.4239 Å and Space group Fd-3m. The morphology and the shape of the crystallites of $CoNi_2S_4$ was investigated by SEM and are presented in Figure 3.

Figure 3. SEM image of $CoNi_2S_4$ shows the shape of crystallites.

Electrochemical investigation at 500°C

$CoNi_2S_4$ was characterized electrochemically by Galvanostatic Discharge and Galvanostatic Intermittent Titration Technique GITT using the Maccor. Discharging was performed at a constant current of 20 mA. The experimental discharge capacity of $CoNi_2S_4$ approaches a value of 266 $mAhg^{-1}$. There is a flat voltage profile at 1.8-1.7 Volts and then a second step at 1.5 Volts as you can see in Figure 4. The electrochemical performance is still being investigated. The experimental capacity is calculated by

Maccor and then is multiplied by 3600s to convert in Coulombs. Then moles of electrons are divided by moles of active electrode to achieve x number which corresponds to the moles of lithium ions per moles of formula unit. Moreover the Maccor GITT procedure consists of galvanostatic discharge pulses, each 10 minutes long, followed by 5 minutes of relaxation time, with no current passing through the cell. In order to have sufficiently slow potential changes, a current of 10 mA has been chosen for discharge. GITT discharge pulses are applied each followed by a relaxation period. It can be noticed in Figure 5 the potential drops between the pulses and the relaxation times until potential of 0.5 Volts is reached. $CoNi_2S_4$ has an IR drop and the cell resistance is increasing during discharge from 10 Ω to 17.5 Ω as the electrode structure develops.

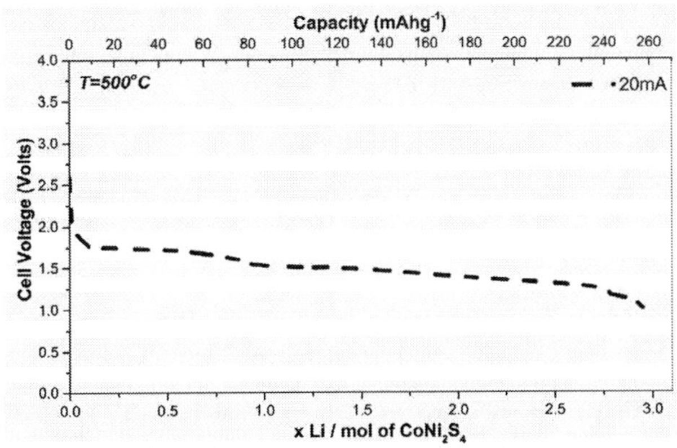

Figure 4. Galvanostatic discharge of $CoNi_2S_4$ at a constant current of 20 mA at 500°C. $CoNi_2S_4$ has a 2 step plateau as you can see in the graph.

Acknowledgments

Special thanks to AWE for their support and funding for this work.

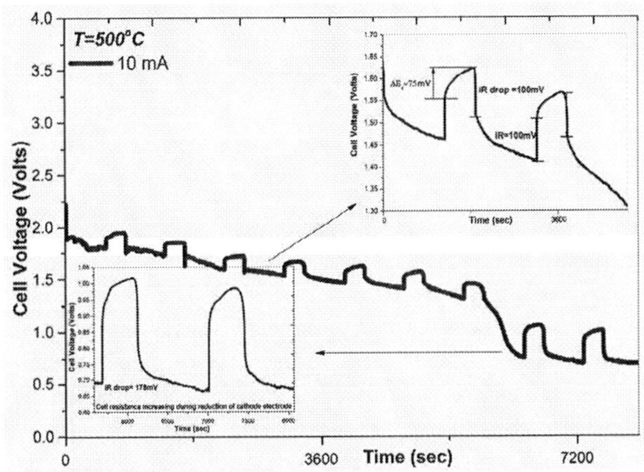

Figure 5. GITT of $CoNi_2S_4$ at a constant current of 10 mA at 500°C.Cell resistance is increasing during reduction of cathode electrode from 10Ω to 17.5Ω

Conclusions

High temperature discharge behaviour of pure phase $CoNi_2S_4$ synthesized by solid state reaction is presented in this work. At a temperature of 500°C the value of the working voltage plateau was recorded at a constant current of 20 mA and capacity of 266 $mAhg^{-1}$ was achieved. Potential value of 1.8-1.7 Volts [first plateau] and then of 1.5-1.4 Volts [second plateau] vs Li-Si for $CoNi_2S_4$ as seems to be stable at 500°C can define that material as promising candidate for thermal batteries applications. GITT shows that the cell resistance is increasing during the discharge reaction.

References

1. R.A Guidotti, P.Masset, *J. Power Sources* (2006) 161 p1443
2. S.K. Preto, Z. Tomczuk, S. von Winbush, M.F. Roche, *J.Electrochem. Soc.*, (1983) 130 p264
3. C.J. Wen, R.A. Huggins, *J. Solid State Chem.* (1981) 37 p271
4. Huang Chunghis, Knop O., *Canadian Journal of Chemistry*, (1971) 49 p598-602

Alumina Paper Separator Infiltrated with Molten Salts for Thermal Batteries

Hae-Won Cheong*, Seung-Ho Kang, Chae-Nam Im, Byung-June Park, and Jang-Hyeon Cho

The 4th R&D Institute – 4th Directorate, Agency for Defense Development
Yuseong P.O. Box 35-4, Daejeon, 305-600, Republic of Korea

Abstract: *Conventional electrolyte for thermal batteries is composed of eutectic salt, such as LiCl-KCl or LiF-LiCl-LiBr, blended with MgO binder to retain the molten salt. The powder mixture is compacted into pellets. The high content of MgO binder, however, incurs an increase in the internal resistance of the electrolyte. In this study, an alumina (Al_2O_3) paper separator infiltrated with molten salt was proposed as an alternative to the conventional pellet-type separator. The alumina paper with the bulk porosity of 96 % was used as a separator and the binary eutectic mixture (LiCl 45 wt.% - KCl 55 wt.%) was used as molten-salt electrolyte. Small amount of MgO binder was add to the electrolyte to reduce the leakage of molten salt. The wetting behavior, microstructure of alumina paper separators and discharge performances of single cells assembled with the separators were investigated. The discharge characteristics of the single cells with the alumina paper separators outperformed those with conventional pellet-type separators. The ceramic paper separator infiltrated with molten salt can be a promising electrolyte for thermal batteries.*

Keywords: electrolyte, molten salt, infiltration, ceramic separator, thermal battery

Introduction

Thermal batteries, which are heat-activated primary reserve power sources that adopt inorganic salt as electrolytes, are primarily used as power sources for military applications, such as in missiles, torpedoes, and munitions, due to their excellent power capability, robustness, and reliability [1, 2]. A Li(Si)/FeS_2 couple is one of popular electrochemical system and the electrolyte is composed of halide mixture, such as LiCl-KCl or LiF-LiCl-LiBr eutectic salt. These electrolytes are non-conductive solids at ambient temperature, which prevent self-discharge and corrosion of electrodes for decades. In order to retain the molten salt at high operating temperature around 500°C, MgO binder has been used to immobilize the molten salt usually. But the amount of MgO binder increases the internal resistance of thermal battery increase, which resulting in decrease of energy density [3]. Studies have been reported on glass filter separator and ceramic fiber separator [4-7] which has excellent mechanical strength and chemical stability at high operating temperature.

In this study, an alumina paper infiltrated with binary eutectic salt (LiCl-KCl) was proposed as an alternative for conventional MgO based separator. Microstructure of alumina paper separator, wetting behaviors of molten salt on alumina paper were analyzed. The discharge performance of Li(Si)/FeS_2 single cells assembled with the alumina paper separator was evaluated.

Experimental Details

Preparation of cathode and anode materials: Cathode powders consisted of 73.5 wt.% FeS_2 (45-100 μm, 98% pure, LinYi), 25 wt.% eutectic salt mixture (LiCl-KCl/MgO), and 1.5 wt.% Li_2O (<250 μm, 97% pure, Sigma-Aldrich). Li_2O was added as a lithiation agent to avoid voltage spikes, which frequently occur with FeS_2 cathode, at the early transient discharge state [1, 2, 8]. The anode comprised of 75 wt.% of Li(Si) alloys (Li 44.53 wt.% -Si 55.47 wt.%, Beijing General Research Institute), with 25 wt.% of the eutectic salt LiCl-KCl (LiCl 45 wt.% - KCl 55 wt.%). And the binary eutectic salt, LiCl-KCl (LiCl 45 wt.% -KCl 55 wt.%), was selected as the electrolyte material [8].

Preparation of cathode and anode pellets: Pellets with diameter of 30 mm for anode and cathode were prepared by conventional cold pressing. Anode powder mixture (Li(Si)/LiCl-KCl) and cathode powder mixture (FeS_2/LiCl-KCl/Li_2O) were pressed into a pellet under static compaction pressures of 2.94 ton·cm^{-2} and 5.89 ton·cm^{-2} respectively. The measured thickness and geometrically calculated density of the anode pellets were 0.48 mm and 1.04 g·cm^{-3} and those of cathode pellets were density were 0.33 mm and 3.21 g·cm^{-3}, respectively. In order to prevent the oxidation and contamination of each electrode material, all powder processing, pellet fabrication, and single-cell assembling process were prepared under dry air conditions of a relative humidity of less than 2%.

Preparation of ceramic separator infiltrated with molten salt: The binary eutectic salts with a ratio of 45 wt.% of LiCl and 55 wt.% of KCl were prepared as electrolyte and alumina paper which are known to be chemically stable at high operating temperature of thermal batteries was used as separator. Wetting and infiltration behaviors were measured using CCD camera (KSP-PRO320, Touptek.) with the resolution of 10 frames/second and the infiltration of molten salt was carried out in a glove box substituted with argon (Ar) atmosphere to prevent the contamination of eutectic salt during infiltration process. For the sufficient infiltration of molten salt into the alumina papers, the holding temperature of small-sized box furnace (C-14P, SENES) was set to 450°C and maintained for 30 min. The experimental equipment for wetting behaviors and infiltrations of molten salt has shown in Figure 1.

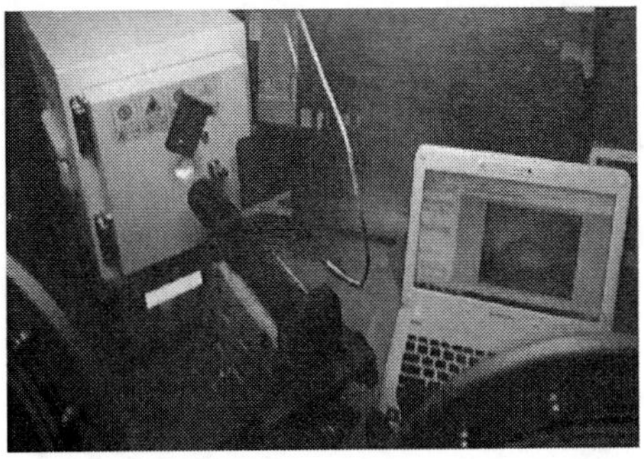

Fig. 1. Experimental equipment for wetting and infiltration of molten salt

Characterizations: Differential scanning calorimetry (DSC-131-EVO, SETARAM) was performed to verify the exact melting point of the fabricated eutectic salt. The temperature was ramped up with a heating rate of 10°C·min^{-1}. Scanning electron microscope (SEM, CX-1000S, Coxem) was used to verify the microstructure of alumina paper separator infiltrated with molten salt.

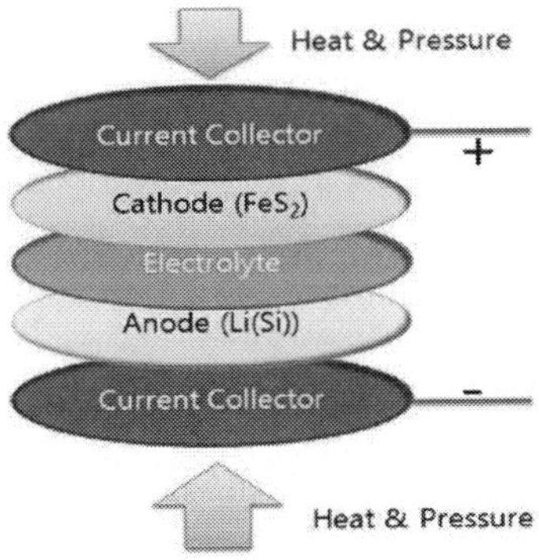

Fig. 2. Schematics of single cell discharge test [11]

Discharge performances: The cathode pellet, alumina paper separator infiltrated with molten salt, and anode pellet were stacked into single-cell, and the assemblies were inserted into a specially designed temperature-controlled heating press. For evaluating discharge performance, consecutive pulse currents with current densities of 810 mA·cm^{-2} (0.5 s) and 1,110 mA·cm^{-2} (0.5 s) were applied. Voltage data were directly measured using current collectors, and current data were measured using a shunt resister (221501, Yokogawa). All test data were collected at a sampling frequency of 100 Hz using a data acquisition system (DaqBook2005, IOTech).

Results and Discussions

Fabrication of eutectic salts: Figure 3 shows the DSC traces of molten salt fabricated with the composition of 44 wt.% of LiCl and 55 wt.% of KCl. The melting point of prepared eutectic salt was 358°C which is in accordance with the result (LiCl:KCl = 44.8:55.2) reported by P. Masset [9] and J. Sangster [10]. This means that the eutectic salt was properly prepared for intended composition.

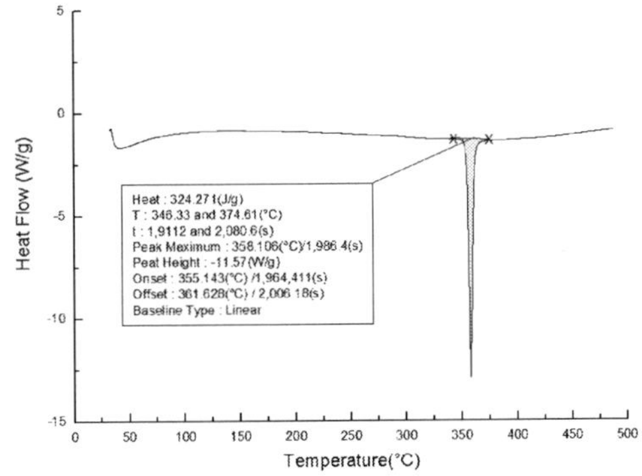

Fig. 3. DSC traces of eutectic salt (LiCl-KCl)

Microscopic analysis of ceramic felt separator: Figure 4 and Figure 5 show the microstructures and pore size distributions of alumina paper used as separator in this study. Fine fibers with the diameter of 10 um and coarse fibers are intertwined continuously and the fibers were fixed by chemically stable alumina-based binders. The measured porosity and median pore diameter of the felt were 78.7 % and 11.3 um respectively. The measured porosity was relatively low compared to that suggested by manufacturer (96 %). From the result of microstructure and porosity measurement, it could be concluded that the moving path of the lithium ions is ensured by the sufficient melting of eutectic salt after infiltration at 450°C.

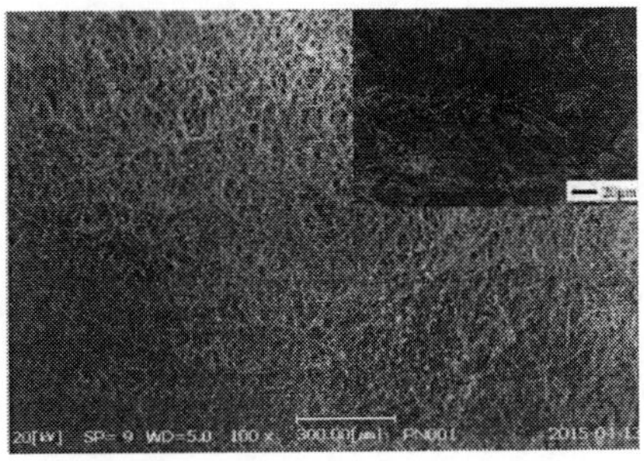

Fig. 4. Microstructure of alumina paper

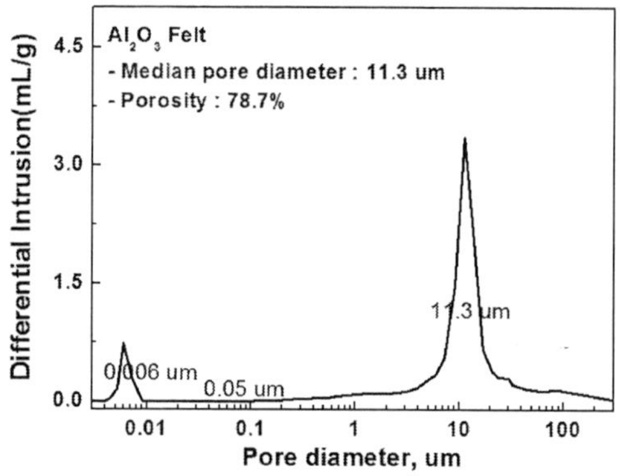

Fig. 5 Pore size distribution of alumina paper

Wetting behaviors and the infiltration of molten salt: Wetting behaviors of molten salt on alumina paper has shown in Figure 6. The eutectic slat began to melt around 375°C and the complete wetting occurred around 430°C. The molten salt was absorbed into alumina paper by the capillary force. The cross sectional image of alumina paper infiltrated with molten salt added with 1.0 wt.% of MgO binder to reduce the leakage of molten salt during operating has shown in Figure 7. The eutectic salt homogeneously mixed with MgO binder was densely infiltrated into alumina paper.

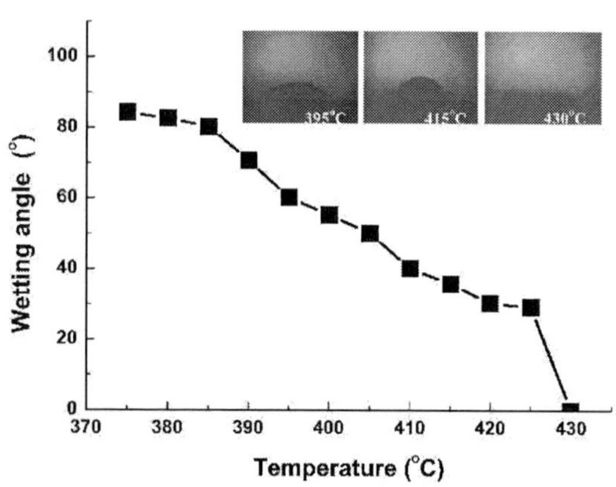

Fig. 6. Wetting behaviors of molten salt on alumina paper based on temperature

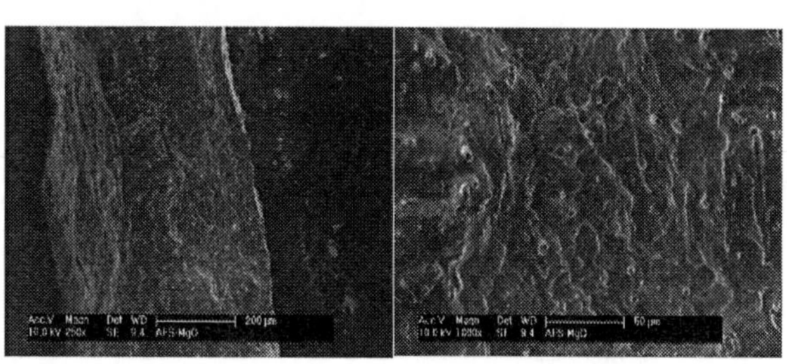

Fig. 7. Cross section of alumina paper infiltrated with molten salt at 450 °C

Discharge performances of single cells: Discharge performances of single cells assembled with alumina paper infiltrated with molten salt with the thickness of 0.3 mm and conventional MgO based separator have compared in Figure 8. The MgO based pellet type separator was fabricated with the thickness of 0.44 mm because it has easily broken when it compacted into pellet with the thickness of 0.3 mm. The discharge characteristics of single cells assembled with alumina paper separator infiltrated with only molten salt (APS) outperformed those of single cells assembled with alumina paper separator infiltrated with molten salt added with 1.0 wt.% of MgO binder (APS(MgO 1.0wt.%)) and conventional MgO based pellet type electrolyte. During the discharge at the temperature of 500°C, no noticeable leakage of electrolyte was observed in each case. The electrochemical capacity of single cell was decreased with the addition of MgO binder due to small infiltrated amount of electrolyte.

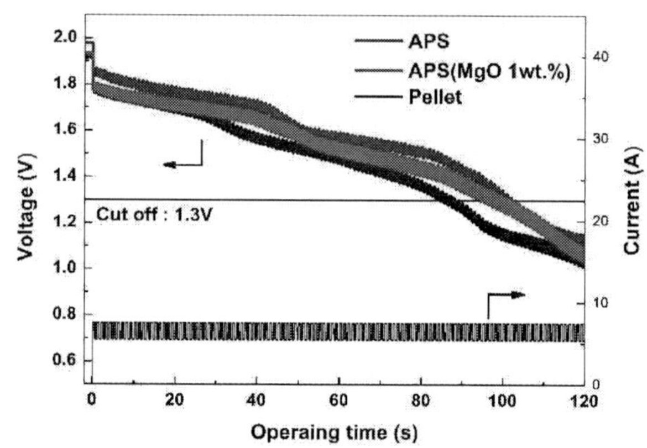

Fig. 8. Discharge performances of single cells

The obtained energy densities of single cells based on the size, weight and operation time with the cutoff voltage of 1.3 V were shown in Figure 9. The energy density of single cells with alumina paper separator infiltrated with molten salt improved by 14.3 % compared to that of single cells assembled with conventional MgO based separator. In case of alumina paper infiltrated with molten salt added with 1.0 wt.% of MgO binder, the operation time of single cell was slightly shortened from 98.8 second to 94.3 second. But the energy density was improved by 7.5 % because it was fabricated in thinner thickness (3.0 mm) compared to conventional pellet type separator (0.44 mm). This means the alumina paper infiltrated with molten salt can be one of promising candidates to substitute conventional MgO based separator with high energy density and improved mechanical and electrical properties.

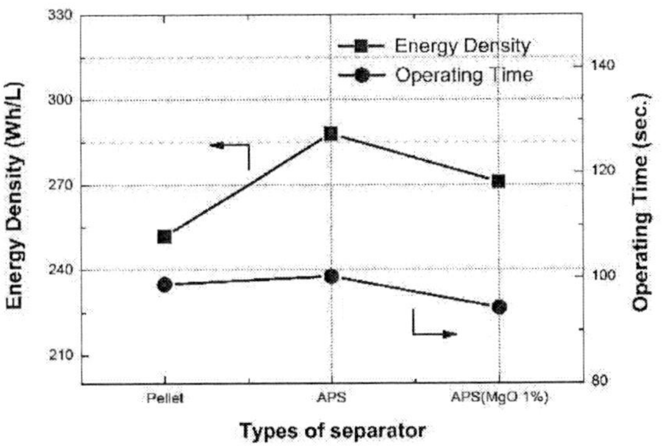

Fig. 9. Energy densities and operating time of single cells

Conclusions

The present study showed the feasibility of alumina paper separator as an alternative to the conventional MgO separator for thermal batteries. Alumina paper infiltrated with molten salt outperformed in discharge performance with thinner thickness and the energy density was improved by 14.3 % compared to that of conventional MgO based separator. Alumina paper separator infiltrated with molten salt can be one of promising separator for thermal batteries which should withstand severe operating conditions such as high operating temperature, high acceleration force and vibration environments with no conspicuous sign of a short circuit due to the excessive leakage of electrolyte.

Acknowledgements

The authors would like to thank professor Dang-Hyuk Yoon at Youngnam University for his contributions to this work.

References

1. R. A. Guidotti and P. Masset, J. Power Sources, 161 (2006) 1443
2. P. J. Masset and R. A. Guidotti, J. Power Sources, 177 (2008) 595
3. R. A. Guidotti and F. W. Reinhardt, SAND2006-2244
4. T. D. Kaun, Proc. of Power Sources Conference, P.12.1 (2004).
5. T. D. Kaun and M. C. Hash, Proc. of Power Sources Conference, 291 (2000).
6. T. D. Kaun and B. Lundeen, A. Hebden, and C. Bowen, Proc. of Power Sources Conference, 365 (2008).
7. H. W. Cheong, S. H. Ha and Y. S. Choi, J. Ceramic Processing Research. Vol.13, (2012) s308
8. H. W. Cheong, S. H. Kang, J. M. Kim and S. B. Cho, J. Ceramic Processing Research. Vol.13, (2012) s198
9. P. Masset. Ph. D. Thesis, National Polytechnic Institute of Grenoble, Grenoble, French (2002)
10. J. Sangster, A.D. Pelton, J. Chem. Ref. Data 12(2) 174 (1987)
11. Y. S. Choi, H. R. Ryu, H. W. Cheong, S. B. Cho and Y. S. Lee, Appl. Chem. Eng., 25, (2014) 161.

A Study of Thin Electrode Using Tape Casting Method without Organic Binder for Thermal Battery

*In Yea Kim[1], JaeHwan Ko[1], Hae-Won Cheong[2], and Young Soo Yoon[1]**

1 Department of Chemical and Biological Engineering, Gachon University Seongnamdaero 1342, 461-710 Gyeonggi-do, Republic of Korea
2 Agency for Defense Development, Daejeon 305-600, Republic of Korea

Abstract: The tape casting using organic binders have serious problem because they produce gases such as carbon dioxide and organic impurities gas at operation temperature of thermal battery. In this study, silicic acid is found suitable as an inorganic binder because it can enhance the mechanical and thermal stability of the electrodes. The thin electrodes were fabricated using different amount of silicic acid. The thin electrodes were analyzed to confirm the occurrence of gases at operating temperature by using thermogravimetric analyzer (TGA-DTA). In order to analyze the effects of silicic acid as an inorganic binder for thermal battery, the mechanical properties of thermal battery electrodes were investigated with different amount of silicic acid.

Keywords: Thermal battery, cathode, silicic acid, inorganic binder.

Introduction

Thermal batteries are primary reserve batteries that employ inorganic salt electrolytes that are non-conductive solids at ambient temperatures, where integral pyrotechnic materials scaled to supply sufficient thermal energy to melt the electrolyte. The standard technique for fabrication of electrodes for thermally activated thermal batteries involves cold pressing of anolyte, separator, catholyte, and tape casting. The pressures for pelletization increase the square of the diameter of the pressed pellets. This results in the need for expensive, high-capacity hydraulic presses for large-diameter pellets. Pressing large-diameter thin pellets is extremely difficult. This is compounded by the fact that pellets of this size tend to be quite fragile, which poses handling problems and reduces pelletization yields. Tape casting of electrode offers a solution to this problem. Tape casting technique can be very unique for thermal battery which can reduce the overall battery weight and volume. This, in turn, increases the energy density and specific energy of the battery, which is becoming increasingly important in many of today's military applications. Tape casting is a well-established technique used for large-scale fabrication of ceramic substrates and multilayered structures. A slurry consisting of the ceramic powder in a solvent, with addition of dispersants, binders and plasticizers, is cast onto a stationary or moving surface. However, organic binder have serious problem because they produce gases such as carbon dioxide and organic impurities gas at operation temperature of thermal battery (at 500 °C). In this study, in order to minimize former problems, silicic acid has been used as an inorganic binder instead of organic binder. Silicic acid is suitable as an inorganic binder because it can enhance the mechanical and thermal stability of the electrodes. The thin electrodes were fabricated using silicic acid (from 8 to 16 wt %). The structure of the thin electrodes was investigated by scanning electron microscopy (SEM) and energy-dispersive x-ray spectroscopy (EDS). The thin electrodes were analyzed to confirm the occurrence of gases at operating temperature by using thermogravimetric analyzer (TGA-DTA).

Experiment

Slurry formulation: In the present experimental condition, the tape casting slurry consisted of solvent, powder, dispersant, binder and plasticizer. To avoid competitive adsorption, the binder and plasticizer should be added after all of the others. The slurry was therefore prepared by two-stage ball milling procedure. Firstly, FeS_2 powders, LiCl-KCl electrolyte, solvent and dispersant mixed together by ball milling for 24 h with nylon jar and zirconia balls. Secondly, inorganic binder, plasticizer, solvent and zirconia ball were added. Different concentrations of binder and plasticizer system were tested. The processing program is shown in Fig. 1.

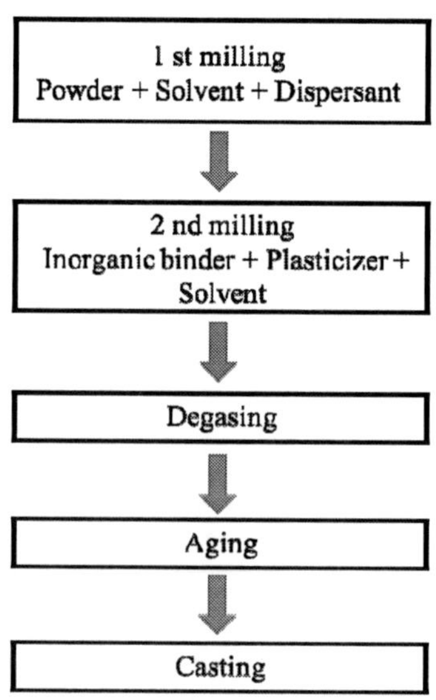

Figure 1. The processing program of tape casting

Data of the powders and main organic additives used in this experiment were summarized in Table 1.

Table 1. Data of the powder and the main organic additives used in this work.

Solvent	Acetone & Benzene
Inorganic binder	Silicic acid
Dispersant	BYK-111
Plasticizer	Dibutyl phthalate

Preparation sheet: Tape casting experiments were conducted by a self-made machine with a stationary container and a double-blade system. To ensure a uniform thickness of the sheet, the height of blade was adjusted by micrometer screws. Thin sheet used are SUS foil.

Thermal treatment: The tape was under two-stage thermal treatment . First stage was evaporation of the solvent in vacuum at 80 °C for 4hr. Second, samples were calcined at a heating rate of 3 °C min^{-1} to 500 °C for 2hr.

Result

The microstructures of green sheet surface are shown in Figure 2. At 6 wt% silicic acid distinct grain boundary was observed between FeS_2 powders. The electrode becomes denser with increasing content of silicic acid. The electrode becomes completely continuous at 8 wt% silicic acid. It confirmed the possibility of silicic acid as inorganic binder.

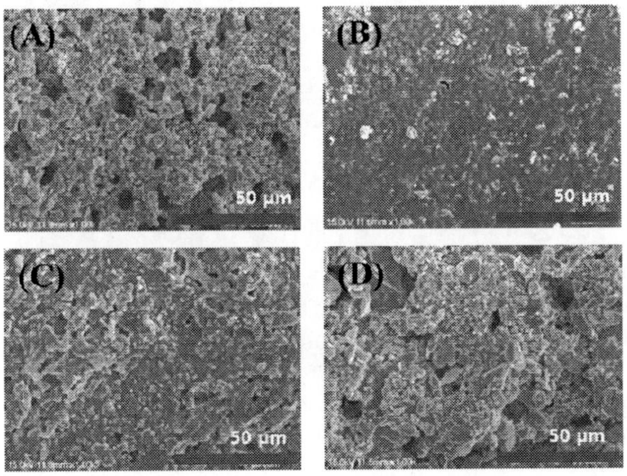

Figure 2. SEM micrographs of electrode surface with difference of inorganic binder (a) 6 wt% (b) 8 wt% (c) 10wt% (d) 12 wt %

The single cell discharge results of the reference, 8 wt % silicic acid samples are shown in Figure 3. At the beginning of discharge, the OCVs of the reference and 8 wt % silicic acid samples are approximately 1.9 V. The discharge test result of 8 wt % silicic acid sample is rapidly close to cut off voltage These results suggest that tape casting using silicic acid as inorganic binder performance of thermal batteries can be achieved.

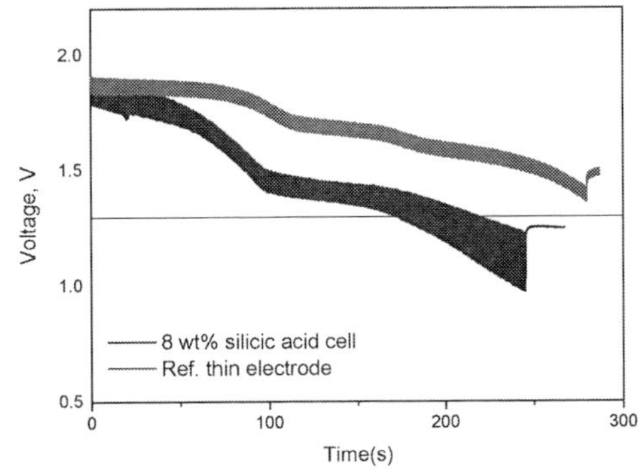

Figure 3. Single cell discharge results, discharged at 500 °C. (a) pristine (b) 8 wt% silicic acid cell

Acknowledgements

This research was supported by the Agency for the Defense Development of Korea.

References

1. Y.S Choi, S.B Cho, Y.S Lee, "Effect of the addition of carbon black and carbon nanotube to FeS_2," *Journal of Industrial and Engineering Chemistry, vol.20,* pp.3584-3589, 2014
2. P. Masset, R. A. Guidotti, "Long-life, multi-tap thermal battery development" *Journal of Power Sources* vol. 164, pp. 397-414, 2007.
3. P. Butler, C. Wagner, R. Guidotti, I. "Explosions Caused by Commonly Occurring Substances," *Journal of Power Sources*, Vol. 136, no. 2, pp. 240-245, October 2004.
4. Z. Yupinga, J. Donglianga, P. Greilb "Tape casting of aqueous Al2O3 slurries," *Journal of the European Ceramic Society,* Vol. 20, no. 11, pp. 1691-1679, October 2000.
5. A. Kristoffersson, E. Roncari, C. Galassi, "Comparison of different binders for water-based tape casting of alumina," *Journal of the European Ceramic Society,* Vol. 18, no.14 pp2123-2131, December 1998.

Current Sharing of Lithium-ion Cells in Parallel

David Wetz, Caroline Westenhover
Department of Electrical Engineering, Pulsed Power and Energy Lab
University of Texas at Arlington
Arlington, TX, United States, 76019

Abstract: *To supply sufficient power to a load electrochemical cells are connected in series and parallel to create a higher voltage, higher current battery. The varying ESRs of the parallel cells can create uneven current sharing, which is compounded by the different resistances among the tabs used to connect the cells. Data about current sharing of cells discharged in parallel was gathered. Maximum current difference between cells is calculated, then implications and future research areas are discussed.*

Keywords: lithium-ion battery; parallel cells; ageing; state of health.

Introduction

Recent developments in the US Navy have found ships moving to a more electrical architecture, meaning that the electrical load profiles on ship board have become more diverse. Ships of the future will employ more transient and higher power loads than previously deployed. While many high power transient loads are nearly ready for deployment into next generation ships, there is still a need to study the power systems involved in integrating these devices. Traditionally, shipboard electric loads have been powered by the ship's prime mover. These types of generators, while stiff sources, are not suited to high power surges or low power dips that occur very quickly with the new transient loads. One way to meet the demands of these new loads would be to increase the generator size so that it is large enough to provide for the peak loads, however this approach would be an inefficient use of weight and footprint. Research at the University of Texas at Arlington (UTA) and in Naval research laboratories show that energy storage devices, such as lithium-ion batteries, are capable of providing the transient power demands while allowing the prime mover to see a constant load power rather than a stochastic one.

To achieve the voltage, power, and energy required, many cells are assembled into battery packs in series/parallel. There are two possible ways to combine cells into a battery pack. In one configuration, all parallel cells are directly connected together, making balancing easier as they can directly pass current back and forth to maintain a constant voltage level. These parallel cells are placed in series with more parallel cells, creating a matrix of wiring connections. This can be complicated and costly as it can in be difficult to ensure that all parallel cells in a large pack are able to be in close proximity for direct connections, as seen in Figure 1 A. In a second configuration, battery modules are first created which contain a smaller percentage of the overall cells in parallel. These cells are stacked in series and the modules are then placed in parallel with other equivalent modules. This configuration offers flexibility in many ways such as module replacement and maintenance as well as more lax restrictions on footprint arrangement, this arrangement can be seen in Figure 1 B.

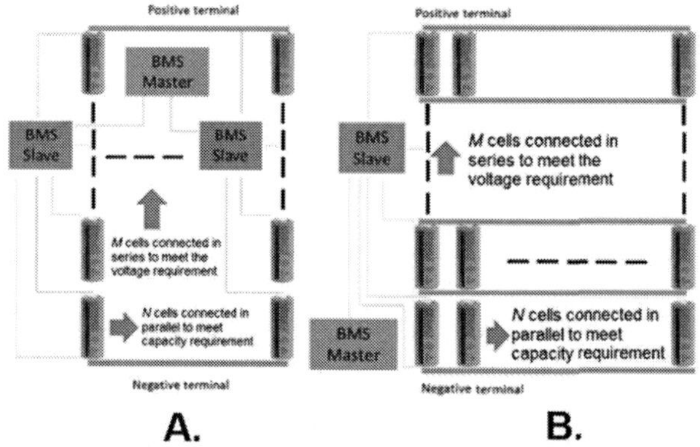

Figure 1. Alternate battery pack configurations

When placed in parallel, cells naturally maintain the same voltage but the current provided by each individual cell varies [1]. The cause for this unequal current sharing is not yet fully understood, but there are several suspected sources. The two discussed and investigated here are the variation in the equivalent series resistance (ESR) of each battery, and the resistance between cells due to the tabs used. This phenomena is important to identify because Gong et. Al [2] shows that once there is an imbalance in the State-of-Health (SOH), the whole pack begins to age at an accelerated rate. Fully understanding the source of this unequal current could help to identify the best balancing technique as presented by Ohio State University [3].

This paper will present a method for experimentally validating the cause of the difference in current sharing of a pack of parallel battery cells. The next section will discuss the experimental setup and test plan and the final section will present the results. Finally, conclusions will be drawn from the results, offering an explanation to the cause of this problem and future work will be recommended.

Procedure

Setup: A custom printed circuit board (PCB) was designed to measure the current and voltage from each individual cell. It was designed for five 26650 cells to be connected in parallel. A photo of the PCB is presented in Figure 2.

To measure the current in and out of each cell, a 300 $\mu\Omega$ current sense resistor (CSR) is placed in series with each cell's negative terminal and the PCB's common negative. Differential voltage monitors (DVMs) are connected across each cell's terminals to acquire isolated voltage measurements for each cell. The board was attached to a larger experimental set up which measured the cells temperature. This setup connected up to six boards for an up to 1S/30P battery.

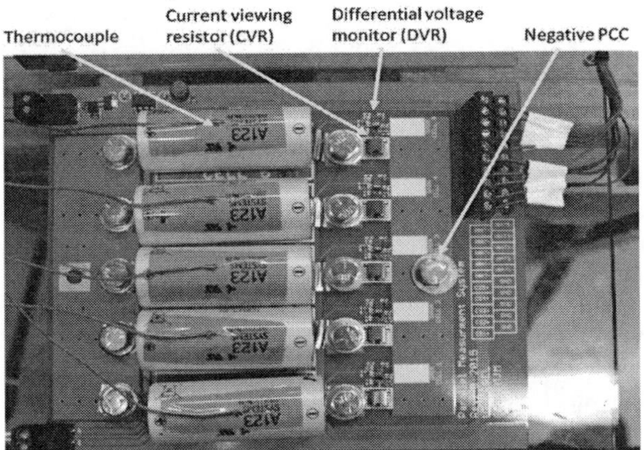

Figure 2. First Custom 1S/5P PCB for 26650 cells

The cells were each assigned to position 1-30 and those numbers are used throughout the results to identify the cells. The parallel connection of boards is made by bolting them into large copper bus bars, with electrical connections from each end of the positive and negative copper bars are made to connect to them to the programmable power supplies and loads. Voltage and current measurements are made using a dedicated National Instruments (NI) CompactDAQ (CDAQ) data acquisition and control system with each cells' thermal profile measured using NI 9213 CDAQ cards. The voltage, current, and temperature of each cell is sampled at 25 Hz during the experiment. The full experimental set up is pictured in Figure 3.

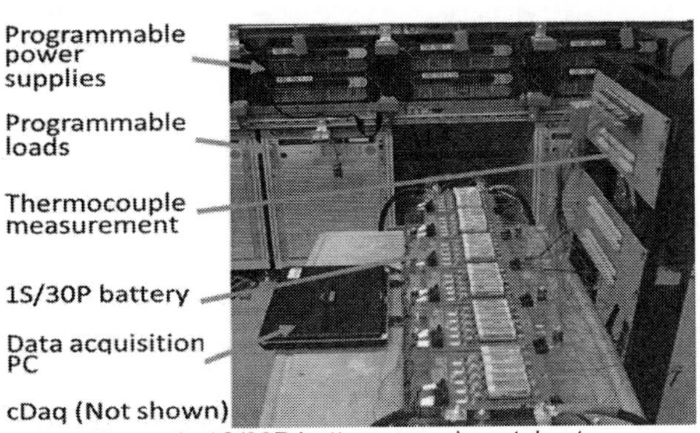

Figure 3. 1S/30P battery experimental setup

To ensure a high level of accuracy of the CSR, the gain of each cell's current monitoring circuit was carefully calibrated using a 0 A – 40 A ramp. The ramped current was measured simultaneously using a highly calibrated oscilloscope probe and the NI cRIO. The scale factor for each channel was calculated using the data from both measurements. This calibration method was performed on each cells CSR.

Pulsed Tests: The battery was put through a regimen of 1333W 30s on 5s off pulsed discharge. The first set of tests consisted of 50 pulses with a 20 minute constant current recharge in between each pulsed discharge. The second set of tests consisted of 100 pulses with a 20 minute constant current recharge in between each pulsed discharge. In both tests, the recharge point was determined to be whether the charged voltage setpoint was reached or whether 20 minutes had passed, whichever came first. In this paper, the data presented was extracted from the set of 50 pulses, the data from the 100 pulses yielded similar results in regards to the current sharing, which did not require exclusive presentation.

Results and Discussion

Below the total current, individual voltages, individual currents, individual temperatures, and a close up plot of the current for the last three pulses in a discharge are plotted in Figures 4 through Figure 8. The total current and individual voltages will give a clear picture into how the current demands change across the power profile. The individual currents along with the close up of three pulses will show how the cells split the demanded current between each cell. Additionally the individual temperature plots will show the temperature spread across the cells, during the charging and recharging phases.

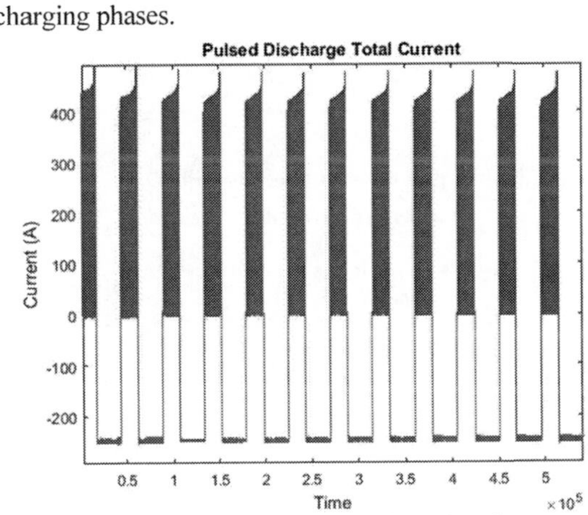

Figure 4. Total Current of all 30 cells

As can be seen in the graphs, especially in Figure 8, the current sharing is not balanced with the second iteration of the boards. The max current percentage difference between two different cells is 18.3%. This difference is significant when considering that temperature, a leading cause of cell aging, goes up as a function of   . This temperature difference can be seen in Figure 7. At each of the highest temperature points there is a temperature difference around 6.5°C, a 13.4% difference. A consistent 10% difference in temperature over the life time of the battery will make a large difference between the rates of aging for each individual cell. The current imbalance and the resulting temperature difference will lead to some cells having a more rapid increase in ESR than other cells.

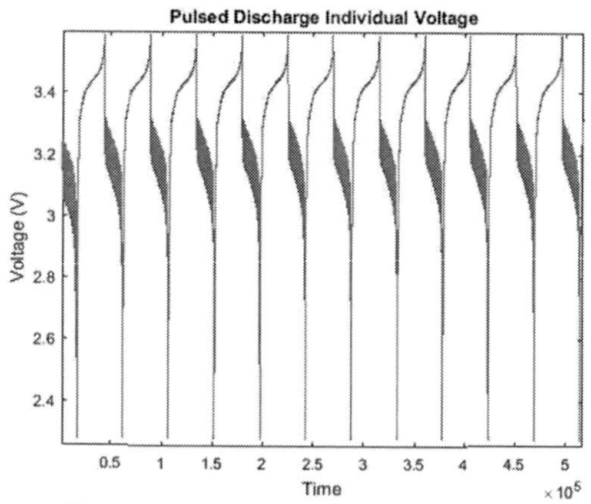

Figure 5. Voltage curves for all 30 cells

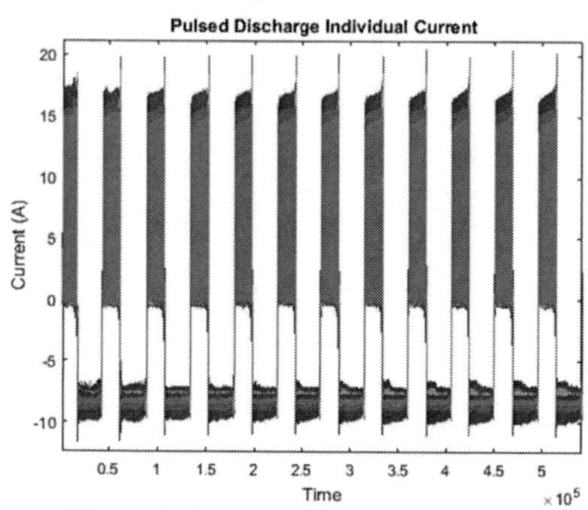

Figure 6. Current curves for all 30 cells

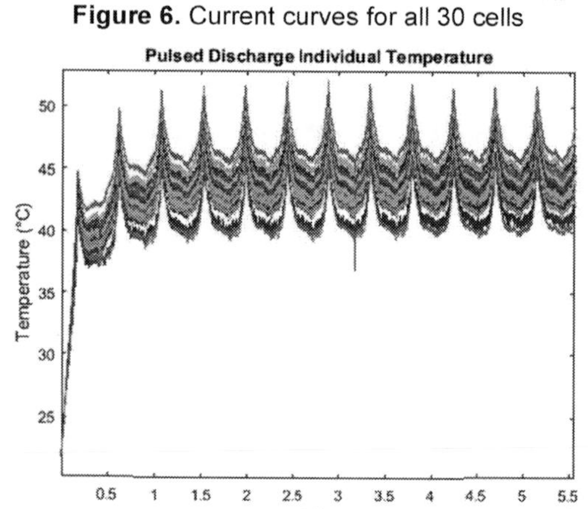

Figure 7. Temperature curves for all 30 cells

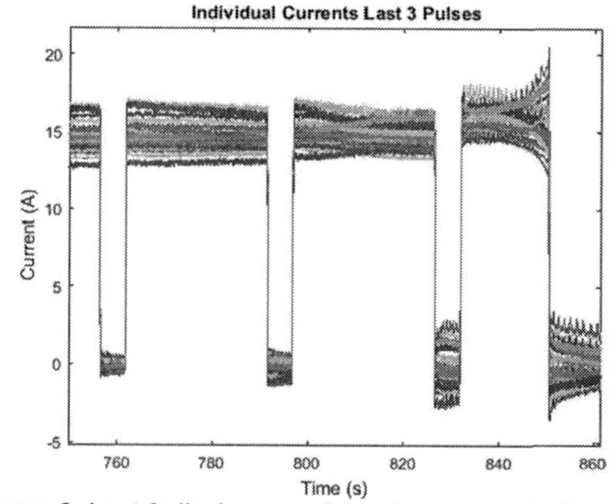

Figure 8. Last 3 discharge pulses show current mismatch

Conclusion

It is known that differences in ESR and individual tabs lead to significant current imbalances and that a sizable difference between the SOH in batteries in parallel can lead to acceleration in aging of the entire battery pack, however it is not known whether small initial resistance differences, in the form of ESR and tab resistance, will noticeably decrease the lifetime of a battery. Furthermore, if initial resistance differences do decrease the overall lifetime of the battery, what is the acceptable resistance span and what is the cost associated with going outside of that span? More data, taken across longer time spans, is needed to draw usable conclusions from these initial results so that accurate and precise conclusions can be drawn. A useful development would be models that accurately represent how cells act and degrade in parallel.

References

[1] Bruen, Thomas, James Marco, and Miguel Gama. "Current variation in parallelized energy storage systems." *Vehicle Power and Propulsion Conference (VPPC)*, pp. 1-6, Oct 27 2014.

[2] Gong, Xianzhi, Rui Xiong, and Chunting Chris Mi. "Study of the characteristics of battery packs in electric vehicles with parallel-connected lithium-ion battery cells." *Industry Applications, IEEE Transactions on* 51.2, pp. 1872-1879, Mar. 2015

[3] Welsh Jr, James D. "A comparison of active and passive cell balancing techniques for series/parallel battery packs." *M.S. Thesis University of Ohio,* (2009).

High Rate Characterization of a 76 V, 60 Ah Lithium-Iron-Phosphate Lithium Ion (LFP-LI) Battery for High Pulsed Rate Applications

Christopher Williams, Matthew Martin and David Wetz
University of Texas at Arlington

John Heinzel
Naval Surface Warfare Center, Philadelphia Division

wetz@uta.edu

Abstract

Electrochemical energy storage devices are steadily becoming more power and energy dense, bringing about the opportunity to more widely deploy them in high rate civilian and military applications. At The University of Texas at Arlington's (UTAs) Pulsed Power and Energy Laboratory (PPEL), a 76 V, 60 Ah lithium-iron-phosphate battery has been sized and evaluated under a constant power (42 kW), pulsed profile (5 second on/ 5 second off) similar to how they may be used to drive future pulsed power applications. Significant interest is placed in evaluating the cell/module balancing and cooling requirements with both forced air and liquid cooling technologies being evaluated. Metrics evaluated and presented here include power density, energy density, usable capacity, rate of capacity fade, impedance growth, and thermal profiles when operated at these high rates typically required of a directed energy system's prime power supply. Conclusions will be drawn to provide the audience with a better understanding of the role of each of these technologies in future pulsed power systems as well as design practices which can be followed based upon the lessons learned here.

A Pseudo-Plastic Flow Model for Slurry Deposition of Thin Film Cathodes

Martin R. Bachicha
Power Sources Technology Group
Sandia National Laboratories
Albuquerque, New Mexico, 87185-0614
mrbachi@sandia.gov

Abstract: *The standard industry method for producing cathodes used in thermal batteries is pellet pressing. Performed by manual operators, pellet pressing can be labor-intensive. The development of automated presses has helped reduce labor costs, but equipment and tooling costs for pellet pressing remain high. This paper explores an alternative method for producing cathodes from thin-filmed coatings produced by depositing catholyte slurry on a moving substrate. It is vital for the slurry to have a pseudo-plastic rheology. A MatLab program is presented that models pseudo-plastic flow behavior.*

Keywords: thin-film; tape caster, doctor blade, MatLab, pseudo-plastic flow model.

Introduction

This paper explores an alternative method developed at Sandia National Laboratories (SNL) for producing cathodes from thin-filmed coatings. The coatings are made by depositing slurry on a moving stainless steel or sacrificial substrate with a tape caster and doctor blade as shown in Figure 1.

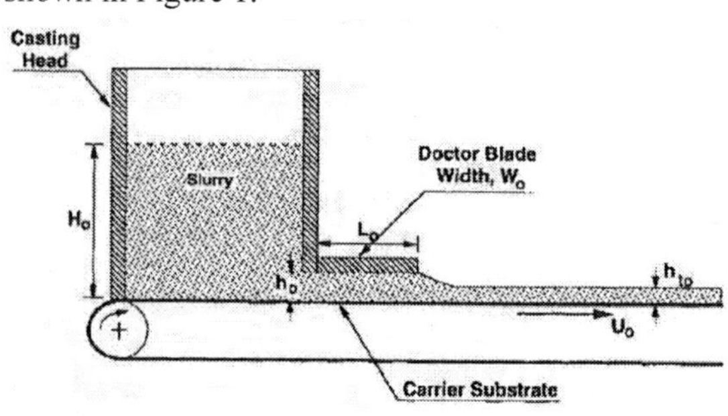

Figure 1. Schematic of a tape casting process[1]

Cathode slurry is generally formulated using a standard catholyte material (a mixture of FeS_2 powder and electrolyte binder) mixed with a solvent such as Xylene. Table 1 shows the composition of the cathode slurry used for this study.

Slurries that are used to coat thin-film thermal battery components must be formulated and blended so as to achieve a consistent pseudo-plastic rheology. A pseudo-plastic rheology is a key when depositing the slurry film in order to keep the film from running after depositing it on a moving substrate.

Table 1. Composition of Catholyte Slurry

Constituent*,^	Function	vol%
FeS_2	Active cathode	20.5
E1C+$MgCl_2$	Electrolyte	19.2
KX (50% resin in Xylene)	Binder	3.6
Sn (1:10, di-n-butyl dilauryl	Catalyst	0.1
Xylene	Solvent	56.6

*Mixed in Thinky ARE-310 Mixer for 5 min. at 1200 rpm;
^Sonicated for 6 intervals of 10 sec. at 50% power

It is also important for producing films with uniform thickness. A Thinky ARE-310 mixer was used to disperse the FeS_2 particles in the cathode slurry. A Branson Digital Sonifier was used to further break up agglomerates that may exist after mixing with the Thinky mixer. This also led to an improvement in the slurry's rheology. The rheology of the slurry can be

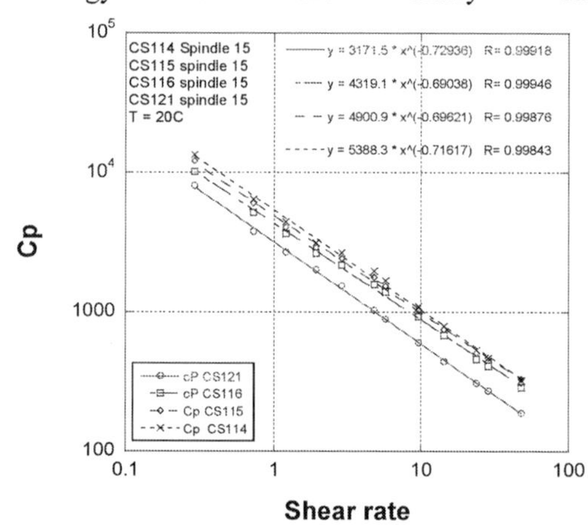

Figure 2. Rheology of Selected Cathode Slurries

shown to be pseudo-plastic by its rheology graph (Figure 2). The graph plots viscosity versus shear rate as measured by a lab rheometer. Slurry is pseudo-plastic if its viscosity decreases linearly when plotted on a log scale as shown in Figure 2. The rheology for these slurry samples showed a significant improvement after sonication and became pseudo-plastic in nature.

Model and Operational Parameters

It is important to understand and control the operational parameters of the tape casting system to help achieve a desired cathode film thickness from a pseudo-plastic slurry blend. A MatLab program was developed based on the solution of a model for generalized planar Couette flow in a doctor blade channel developed by Pitchumani and Karbhari[1]. Their model combines the Ostwald-de Waele rheological model (1) with the simplified Navier-Stokes flow equation (2).

$$\tau = m|\dot{\gamma}|^{n-1}\,\dot{\gamma} \tag{1}$$

$$-\frac{dp}{dx}+\frac{d\tau}{dy}=0 \tag{2}$$

The term $m|\dot{\gamma}|^{n-1}$ represents the effective viscosity as a function of shear rate, $\dot{\gamma}$. Note that the value of n determines the type of fluid as follows:

Table 2. Shear Rate Exponents of Fluid Types

N	Type of Fluid
< 1	Pseudo plastic
1	Newtonian fluid
> 1	Dilatant

Figure 3 shows the channel at the base of the doctor blade in Figure 1, illustrating the flow of the cathode slurry due to the pressure head caused by the height of the slurry in the doctor blade reservoir and the drag of the moving stainless steel substrate. There are two possible velocity profiles within the channel: (Case I) a monotonically decreasing velocity between the moving substrate and the doctor blade, and (Case II) a velocity profile with a maximum inside the channel.

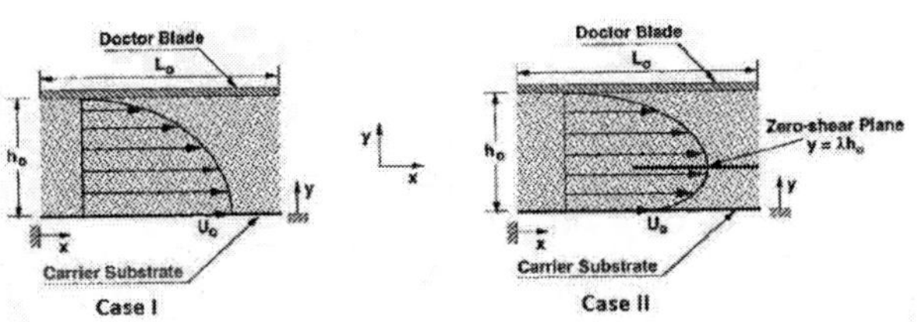

Figure 3. Generalized Fluid Flow Model for Tape Casting[1]

Note that:

$\dot{\gamma} = \frac{du}{dy}$ = shear rate or velocity gradient perpendicular to the plane of the shear

τ = shear stress in the x-y plane

u = fluid velocity in doctor blade channel

m = empirical constant sometimes called the flow consistency index

n = shear rate exponent (dimensionless).

The slurry parameters m and n can be determined from the fitted equations for the lines in the shear rate graph of Figure 2. The boundary conditions associated with equation (2) are as follows:

$$u(y=0) = U_O; \qquad u(y=h_O)=0 \tag{3a}$$

$$p(x=0)=p_\infty+\rho_{sl}gH_o; \; p(x=L_O)=p_\infty \tag{3b}$$

where:

U_O = speed of substrate

h_O = channel height or doctor blade gap

p_∞=ambient pressure

ρ_{sl} = slurry density

H_o= height of the slurry in the reservoir

g= gravitational constant

L_O= channel length (doctor blade width)

Assuming a constant pressure differential along the length of the channel, the pressure gradient term in Eq. (2) may be replaced by:

$$\frac{dp}{dx} = \rho_{sl}gH_o\,/L_O \tag{4}$$

The ultimate governing equation and boundary conditions are written in terms of dimensionless parameters ξ, φ, and α based on the Reynolds (5c) and Froude (5d) numbers of the slurry flow as shown.

$$\xi = \frac{y}{h_O} \tag{5a}$$

$$\varphi = \frac{u}{U_O} \tag{5b}$$

$$\text{Re}= \frac{\rho_{sl}\,U_O h_O}{m\left(\frac{U_O}{h_O}\right)^{n-1}} \tag{5c}$$

$$\text{Fr} = \frac{U_O{}^2}{gH_o} \tag{5d}$$

$$\alpha = \frac{\text{Re}h_O}{\text{Fr}L_O} \tag{5e}$$

The Reynolds number (Re) denotes the ratio of the inertial effects due to the motion of the carrier substrate to the viscous effects based on the shear rate of the drag flow. The Froude number (Fr) signifies the hydrostatic head effects due to the height of the slurry in the slurry reservoir, and α is a combined design flow parameter. Substituting the above terms into equations (1) and (2) results in the following governing equation and boundary conditions:

$$\frac{d}{d\xi}\left(-\left|\frac{d\varphi}{d\xi}\right|^{n-1}\frac{d\varphi}{d\xi}\right)= \alpha \tag{6}$$

$$\varphi(\xi=0)= 1; \qquad \varphi(\xi=1) = 0 \tag{7}$$

Integrating equation (6) once with respect to ξ we get

$$-\left|\frac{d\varphi}{d\xi}\right|^{n-1}\frac{d\varphi}{d\xi} = \alpha(\lambda\text{-}\ \xi) \tag{8}$$

where λ is a constant of integration. Pitchumani and Karbhari apply equation (8) to each of the two cases shown in Figure 3. They highlight the fact the fluid velocity is monotonically decreasing and the shear rate $d\varphi/d\xi$ is strictly negative in Case I and in Case II above the zero shear plane. Also, they show that the fluid velocity is monotonically increasing and the shear rate is strictly positive below the zero shear plane in Case II.

This results in the following equations for Case I and Case II.

Case I:

$$\left(-\frac{d\varphi}{d\xi}\right) = \alpha^N(\xi-\lambda)^N \qquad (9)$$

Case II:

Increasing velocity profile and positive shear rate:

$$\left(\frac{d\varphi^<}{d\xi}\right) = \alpha^N(\lambda-\xi)^N \qquad (10a)$$

Decreasing velocity profile and negative shear rate:

$$\left(-\frac{d\varphi^>}{d\xi}\right) = \alpha^N(\xi-\lambda)^N \qquad (10b)$$

where:

$$N = \frac{1}{n} \qquad (11)$$

Integrating equation (9) with respect to ξ and applying the boundary conditions of equation (7) results in the dimensionless velocity profile $\varphi(\xi)$ and a transcendental equation for determining the integration constant λ for Case I where there is a monotonic decrease in velocity between the moving substrate (ξ=0) and the doctor blade (ξ=1). Integrating equation (10a,b) with respect to ξ and applying the boundary conditions in equation (7), results in the dimensionless velocity profiles $\varphi^<(\xi)$ and $\varphi^>(\xi)$ for Case II where the velocity profile in the channel has a maximum. Also in Case II, where the velocity profile in the channel is at its maximum ($\xi = \lambda$), the two velocity profiles are equal. By equating the two profiles a transcendental equation is obtained for determining the integration constant λ for Case II. It should be noted in Case II that $\varphi_{max} > 1$, since $u_{max} > U_O$. For both cases, the transcendental equations for determining the integration constant λ, are solved for empirically using the MatLab ***fsolve*** function. They also provide equations for estimating film thickness, h_{film}, which are based on the continuity equation using the velocity profiles of each case and a film shrinkage parameter β.

Pitchumani and Karbhari, also provide a criterion for determining which of the two cases (I and II) is appropriate for a given set of parameters. They derive a critical value of α above which Case II will apply, and below which Case I will be applicable.

$$\alpha^* = \left(1+\frac{1}{n}\right)^n \qquad (12)$$

The criterion for deciding the appropriate case in terms of α and α^* can be written as:

$$\alpha \leq \alpha^* \quad \text{(Case I)}$$

$$\alpha \geq \alpha^* \quad \text{(Case II)}$$

The MatLab program solves for the critical value of α^* as a function of n, compares the actual value of α from equation (5e) to determine the case (I or II), and then solves the integration constant λ, dimensionless velocity $\varphi(\xi)$ and dimensionless film thickness h_{film}/h_0 for the appropriate case.

Production Runs

Using the slurry parameters as inputs, MatLab plots the velocity profile of the slurry in the doctor blade channel (Figure 4) and gives a prediction of the dried cathode film thickness. Overall the model was accurate and gave good results when compared with actual production runs. This was especially true for slurry lots with percent solids less than 78% and effective viscosities (μ_{eff}) of less than 235 centipoise. In these cases the model predicted dry film thickness close to the measured value. The values of casting and slurry parameters used in selected production runs along with calculated values of key model parameters are given in Table 3. A plot of theoretical film thickness versus casting speed for various reservoir slurry levels is shown in Figure 5.

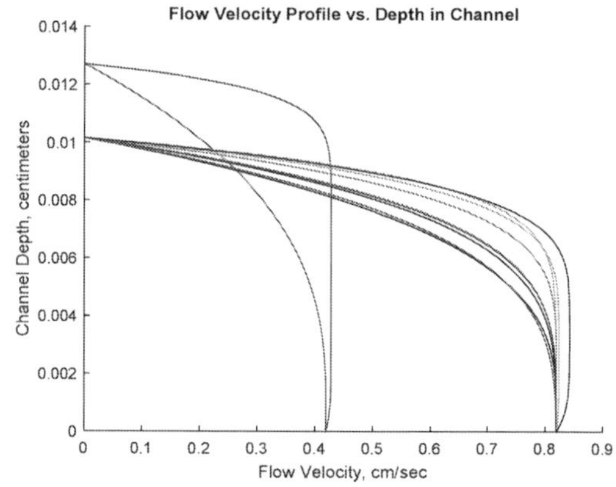

Figure 4. Velocity Profile of Flow in Channel

Additional Observations

The majority of lots have alpha (α) values that are near the critical value (α*). Hence all slurry lots are either Case II or in transition from Case I to Case II, a strong indicator that the cathode slurry is pseudo-plastic. The model can be used to examine what effect different settings of casting speed, doctor blade channel height, slurry reservoir depth, and slurry shear rate exponent have on cathode film thickness. Figure 5 shows the effect of reservoir slurry level on theoretical film thickness. Figure 6 demonstrates the effect the slurry shear rate exponent, n, has on film thickness. Plots in Figures 5 and 6 are based on a doctor blade gap h_0 of 0.01 cm, a shear rate index n of .28 and an m value of 4.0 unless otherwise noted.

Another key observation is that as the shear rate index n approaches 1 (i.e., as the fluid becomes Newtonian) the film thickness approaches $h_0/2$, or half the doctor blade channel height.

Table 3. Values of Casting and Slurry Parameters Used in Selected Production Runs

Lot No.	h_o, (cm)	U_o, (cm/sec)	m (Pa* sec^n)	n	ρ_{sl}, (g/cc)	% Solids	μ_{eff} (Cp)	(Re /Fr)	α	α*	B	h_{tp}, (cm)	h_{mod}, (cm)
1	0.013	0.42	8.3	0.12	1.89	72.3	385.7	46.4	2.32	1.31	1.033	0.013	0.012
6	0.010	0.82	4.0	0.27	1.97	73.3	162.7	46.9	1.88	1.52	1.157	0.010	0.009
9	0.010	0.82	4.9	0.30	2.17	76.8	230.8	36.4	1.45	1.56	0.999	0.008	0.008
10	0.010	0.82	4.3	0.31	2.12	74.8	208.7	39.3	1.57	1.56	0.988	0.008	0.008
12	0.010	0.82	3.9	0.26	2.19	78.5	153.6	55.0	2.20	1.51	1.003	0.009	0.009
13	0.010	0.82	3.2	0.27	2.08	78.1	129.1	62.3	2.49	1.52	1.042	0.010	0.009

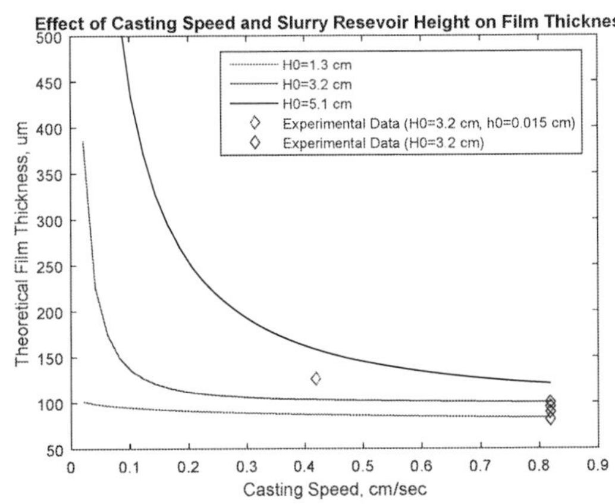

Figure 5. Effect of Casting Speed and Slurry Height

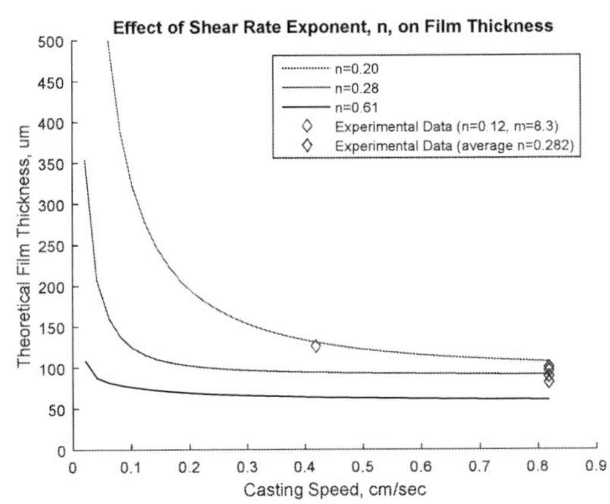

Figure 6. Effect of Shear Rate Exponent, *n*

Cost Impacts and other Benefits

A cost analysis was performed by Advanced Thermal Batteries (ATB)[2] for SNL in 2013 comparing the cost of making thermal batteries with traditional pellets versus the cost of making batteries with thin film cathodes. The analysis estimated a $10 savings per battery. This increased to $20 per battery if thin film anodes and separators are also made. The cost of installing a thin film coating line is on the order of $2 to $3 million, Thus, ATB concluded investing in thin film coating technology will be meaningful if "we look at technical benefit and/or large production on the order of 100K batteries per year." One technical benefit is that thin film coated components can be punched into alternate shapes, meaning batteries are no longer restricted to a cylindrical form factor.

Conclusion

Producing cathodes from thin film coatings made with catholyte slurry offers an effective alternative from the traditional pellet pressing manufacturing for high production volumes or for when battery manufacturers have a requirement for batteries with alternate shape factors. Pseudo-plasticity of the slurry is a key in order to make thin films of uniform thickness. A MatLab program was developed from a model for flow through a doctor blade developed by Pitchumani and Karbhari[1]. Their paper presented experimental data for the case of slurry with Newtonian flow characteristics. This paper validates their model with experimental data in the case of non-Newtonian, pseudo-plastic flow behavior.

Acknowledgements

Sandia National Laboratories is a multi-program laboratory managed and operated by Sandia Corporation, a wholly owned subsidiary of Lockheed Martin Corporation, for the U.S. Department of Energy's National Nuclear Security Administration under contract DE-AC04-94AL85000.

Sandia National Laboratories does not advocate any particular equipment, system, or vendor.

References

1. R. Pitchumani, V.M. Karbhari, Generalized fluid flow model for ceramic tape casting, J. American Ceramic Society, 78 (9) 2497-2503.
2. TFTB vs. Pellets Cost Analysis (2013 March)

Cathodes for High Rate, Long Cycle Life Lithium Sulfur Batteries

Qingliu Wu, Pu Zhang, Peter Aurora, and Michael Wixom
Navitas Advanced Solutions Group
4880 Venture Drive, Suite 100, Ann Arbor, MI 48108
mwixom@navitassys.com

Abstract: *Low cost and high capacity make lithium sulfur batteries (LSB) the next generation of lithium ion batteries. Practical application of LSB's remains limited by utilizing a limited fraction of the available sulfur and by fast capacity fading of sulfur cathodes. The root causes are poor electronic conductivity of the cathode combined with high solubility of intermediate polysulfide products during cycling. To overcome these limitations, Navitas is developing a conductive nanoporous ceramic host material for LSB cathodes. The nanoporous structure will better accommodate sulfur volume changes during cycling; its mechanical strength and conductivity will enable high utilization of sulfur; and its high affinity to both sulfur and polysulfides will minimize sulfur dissolution. The cathode material development and Li-S cell will be reported. Large format cell design and its potential application for aircraft F/A-18 battery will be discussed.*

Keywords: Lithium Sulfur Battery; Cathode; Conductive Ceramic; Nanoporous; Polysulfide; Cycle Life; UAV

Introduction

The LSB theoretically delivers specific energy of 2600 Wh/kg, which is 3-5 times higher than present state-of-the-art lithium-ion batteries. However, practical application of lithium sulfur batteries remains limited by low utilization of sulfur and by fast capacity fading of sulfur cathodes. The root causes of these limitations are poor electronic conductivity of the cathode combined with high solubility of intermediate lithium-polysulfide products that form during the charge/discharge processes. Poor electronic conductivity is due both to low intrinsic conductivity of sulfur, as well as to volumetric changes that degrade electronic connectivity in the cathode.

The keys to longer cycle life lie in improving the cathode conductivity and isolating sulfur and sulfides to the cathode [Manthiram 2013, 2014; Yang 2013]. The strategy of encapsulating sulfur within a conductive host matrix has emerged as an effective strategy to improve LSB performance. However, the sulfur-encapsulation approaches reported to date effectively trap non-polar sulfur, but not the polar polysulfide intermediates that form during discharge. This leaves polysulfide species free to dissolve and be transported to the anode where they undergo parasitic reaction resulting in the formation of dendrites and depletion of the anode.

To address these limitations Navitas has developed a novel nanoporous ceramic cathode that is low cost, highly conductive, stable, and with high affinity to both sulfur and polysulfides. This innovation enables lithium sulfur batteries to meet the high rate capability and longer cycle life required to meet military and civilian aircraft needs.

Advanced performance of the LSB cathode is achieved through the following features: (1) nanoporous structure accommodates sulfur volume change during cycling; (2) high mechanical strength and conductivity enables utilization of sulfur; and (3) strong affinity to both sulfur and polysulfides limits sulfur dissolution.

Experimental

Synthesis of Lithium Sulfur Cathode

Navitas ceramic cathode was fabricated through a two-step approach of preparing conductive nanoporous ceramic host and impregnating sulfur. The nanoporous ceramic host was fabricated through a high temperature reaction under controlled atmosphere in a tube furnace. Melt-diffusion was used to impregnate sulfur into the porous ceramic host.

Characterization

Physical properties: tap and true densities were measured with a tap density meter and a He pycnometer. BET surface area was measured with Micromeritics ASAP2020. Sulfur content was determined by TA Instruments TGA.

Morphology: The cathode composite phase and micro-structure was identified by using XRD, SEM, and EDAX.

Electrode Fabrication

LSB cathodes were fabricated by mixing a slurry containing active material, conductive additive, and binder in a Flacktec SpeedMixer. The prepared slurry was hand-cast on to Al foil. The coated cathode was then calendered to a desired thickness (porosity).

Cell Assembly

Li-S cathodes were evaluated in CR2025 coin cells. The cathode formulation was "80% active / 14% carbon black / 6% binder, and the cathode was calendered to 40% porosity. Li foil served as the anode.

Cell Test

Electrochemical performance was evaluated based on cell capacity, rate capability, and cycle life on Maccor cyclers. The cell was cycled over 2.6 to 1.8 V at +0.5C/-0.5C or +1C/-2C.

Safety Evaluation

Safety evaluation on the LSB cathode was performed by differential scanning calorimetry (DSC) using TA

Instruments DSC Q200. Three groups of Li-S cells were taken to full charge, 50% charge, and full discharge. Inside an argon-filled glovebox, the cells were disassembled and the cathodes were harvested and transferred into DSC pans and hermetically sealed. DSC measurement was carried out under N_2 at 30 - 350 °C with a heating rate of 5 °C/min.

Results and Discussion

Cathode Material Development

The ceramic host material was converted from a metal oxide precursor by thermal treatment at temperature < 1000 °C. After the conversion, the powder changed its color from white to black, indicating a completion of the reaction. The host material phases were identified and confirmed by XRD. The host material has a surface area of 100 m^2/g and porosity of 50%, as designed.

50 wt% sulfur was impregnated into the porous host. After the impregnation of sulfur, the S-ceramic composite exhibits the same black color as the initial host (Figure 1), indicating that sulfur was encapsulated inside the host, as desired, rather than on the surface. No yellow residue of free sulfur was observed on the surface. The sulfur content was confirmed by TGA as 50%.

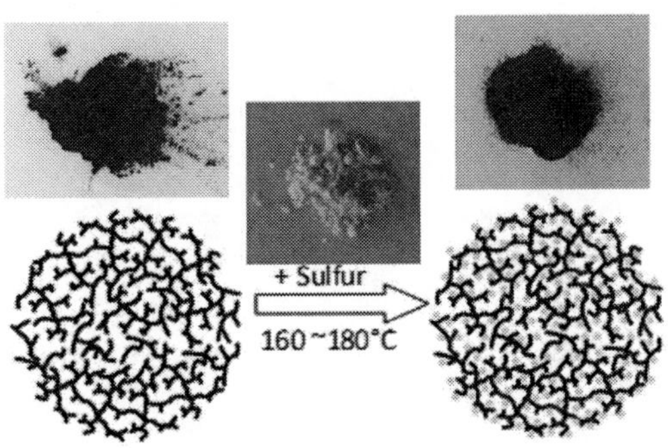

Figure 1. Illustration of the impregnation of sulfur into porous ceramic host. The black color of the sulfur composite indicated that sulfur was encapsulated inside the host, as desired, rather than on the surface.

LSB electrodes were fabricated using this sulfur-ceramic composite as active material. Baseline LSB cathodes were also prepared using microporous carbon as the sulfur host. The slurry mixing procedure and electrode coating process did not vary from conventional lithium ion electrode processes. Thus the new composite cathode fabrication can be readily adapted into industrial high volume production.

Electrochemical Evaluation

Capacity and Voltage

Formation cycles were performed on cells containing with both Navitas ceramic cathode and baseline porous carbon cathode. The charge/discharge profiles are shown in Figure 2. Both cells show two plateau-like features, one at 2.4 V and the other at 2.1 V. These two plateaus are characteristic of Li-S batteries corresponding to the reduction of sulfur to Li_2S_8, and Li_2S_6 to Li_2S_2 respectively. Within the voltage window of 1.8 - 2.6V, the initial discharge (or lithiation of the cathode) capacity of Navitas ceramic cathode is ~1000 mAh/g, which is much higher than that of baseline cathode (~600 mAh/g). The initial discharge step was followed by a charge step (or delithiation of the cathode). The Navitas ceramic cathode delivers a charge capacity of >900 mAh/g, much higher than the baseline at ~500 mAh/g. The higher capacity of the ceramic cathode most likely results from a lower sulfur dissolution, which is attributed to its higher affinity to sulfur / polysulfides than the baseline porous carbon host.

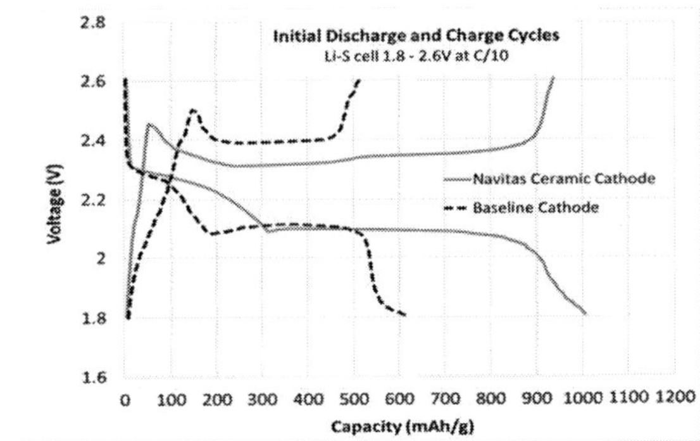

Figure 2. Voltage profiles of Li-S cells with Navitas ceramic cathode and baseline cathode respectively during the initial cycle.

Rate capability

The Navitas ceramic cathode shows promising rate capability due to its intrinsic conductivity. It retains 80% capacity at 1C and 73% capacity at 2C, which is 2X better than the porous carbon cathode baseline cell. LSB power density is primarily dictated by the balance between ionic and electronic transport in the cathode. As electrode loadings are increased to achieve high energy, capacity retention is reduced due to transport limitations as electrodes become thicker, less conductive, and lower in porosity. Therefore, one of the key benefits of the proposed conductive host material is to improve the electrode conductivity to enable capacity retention at high loading.

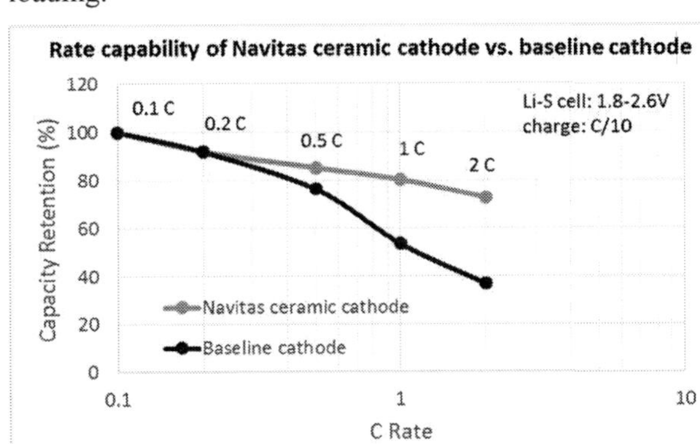

Figure 3. Rate Capability of Li-S cells with Navitas ceramic cathode and baseline porous carbon cathode. The cell with

ceramic cathode retains 80% capacity at 1C and 73% capacity at 2C, which is 2X better than the porous carbon baseline.

Cycle Life

Initial cycling results are promising and show clear advantage of Navitas ceramic cathode over the baseline cathode (Figure 4). During the first 30 cycles, the capacity of mesoporous carbon baseline dropped rapidly and only retained 45% of initial capacity after 100 cycles. However, 65% of initial capacity was preserved in Navitas ceramic cathode after 100 cycles. This advantage suggests that the intrinsic conductivity and high affinity to sulfur species of the ceramic cathode will enable longer LSB cycle life.

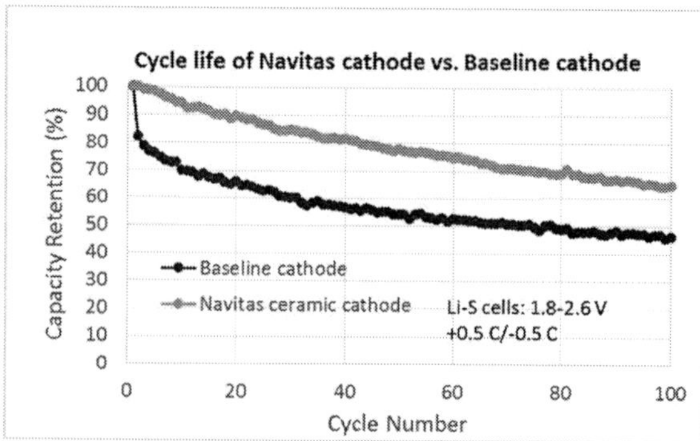

Figure 4. Cycling performances of Li-S cells with Navitas ceramic cathode (Gen I) and baseline cathode.

Performance Improvement

Although the new nanoporous ceramic cathode shows significant advantage in the initial test, practical applications will require further cycle life improvement.

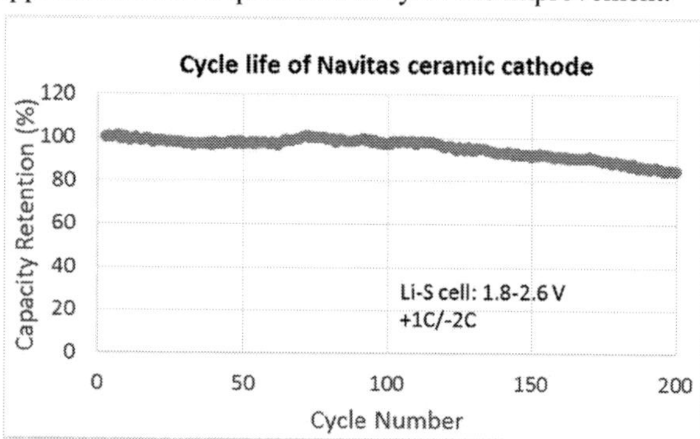

Figure 5. The cycling performance of Gen II Li-S cell. It retains >95% initial capacity after 100 cycles (vs. 65% of Gen I) and 85% even after 200 cycles.

Navitas is focusing on three areas to improve the performance:

The ceramic host structure has been modified to enhance its interaction to the sulfur species and to improve Li ion conductivity within the cathode structure.

A new binder alternative to PVdF was evaluated. The new binder provides stronger interaction with ceramic host to enhance the electrode integrity. The binder also helps to retain the sulfur inside the pores.

A new electrolyte system designed to reduce sulfur solubility has been developed and evaluated. This work is still on going.

Given the benefits of above component optimization, Gen II electrodes and cells were prepared and evaluated. Figure 5 clearly shows an improved cycle life of the Gen II Li-S cells which retained >95% initial capacity after 100 cycles (vs. 65% of Gen I) and 85% after 200 cycles.

Safety Test (DSC)

Differential scanning calorimetry (DSC) curves for Navitas ceramic cathode delithiated to different states (0%, 50%, 100%) are shown Figure 6. A NCM 523 (fully charged) baseline cathode is also included for comparison. It shows no significant exothermic decomposition up to 350 °C for the Li-S cathode, indicative of high safety advantages of the sulfur composite cathode over conventional lithium ion battery cathodes. This is consistent with results on the sulfur cathodes by other researchers [Song 2014].

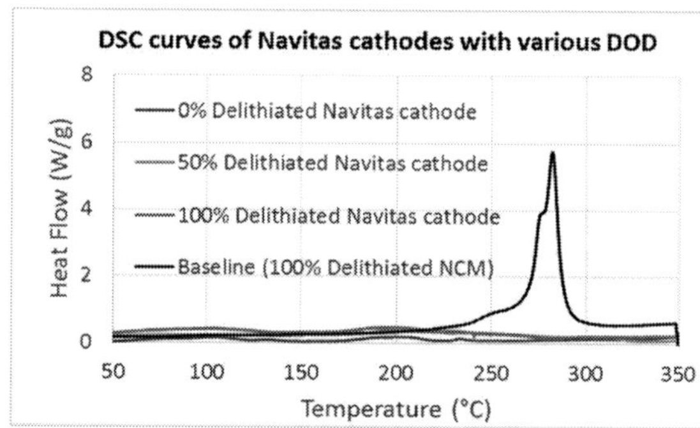

Figure 6. DSC curves of Navitas ceramic cathodes at deference states of delithiation (0%, 50%, and 100%) and 100% delithiated NCM 523 baseline cathode

Large Format Cell Design and Battery Application

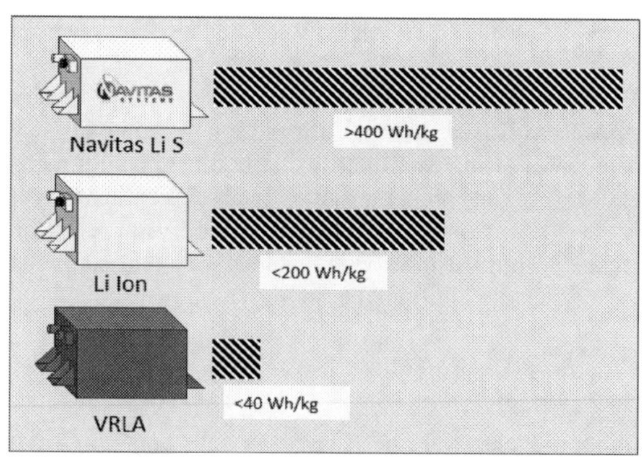

Figure 7. Illustration of batteries with different energy densities. Navitas LSB has 10 times and 2 times energy density of VRLA and conventional LIB respectively.

Future work will focus on scaling up the cathode material and maturing a cell design that meets form and function requirements for aviation batteries (e.g., a 26V, 30Ah battery in F/A-18 platform). When deployed in the aviation batteries, this technology will significantly reduce the weight, service life and maintenance requirements of legacy NiCad or lead acid batteries. The LSB technology will surpass state-of-the-art lithium ion batteries and offer superior safety and abuse tolerance. The potential benefit is summarized in Figure 7.

Conclusion

A Li-S cathode has been developed based on a conductive nanoporous ceramic host. The new cathode exhibits significantly higher capacity, better rate capability, and longer cycle life than the baseline mesoporous carbon LSB cathode.

The material hosts 50 wt% sulfur and has >800 mAh/g capacity. It retains 80% capacity at 1C rate and 73% at 2C rate, 2X higher than the baseline. It also retains 95% capacity after 100 cycles, and 80% after 250 cycles. The LSB safety is also demonstrated with DSC measurement. The novel host material is expected to enable LSB's to be deployed in both high energy and high power systems. Li-S batteries incorporating these cathodes will significantly reduce the weight, increase the service life and eliminate maintenance requirements of legacy NiCad or lead acid aviation batteries. The LSB technology will surpass state-of-the-art lithium ion batteries and offer superior safety and abuse tolerance. A 26V, 30Ah aviation battery in F/A-18 platform will be the initial target application.

Acknowledgement

This work was supported by US Navy SBIR program under the contract# N68335-16-C-0017. Navitas thanks Dr. Venkat Manivannan for support and technical guidance.

Reference

1. Manthiram, A., et al., "Challenges and Prospects of Lithium-Sulfur Batteries", *Accounts of Chemical Research*, 46, 1125-1134, 2013
2. Manthiram, A., et al., "Rechargeable Lithium-Sulfur Batteries", *Chem. Rev.*, 114, 11751-11787, 2014
3. Yang, Y., Zheng, G., Cui, Y., "Nanostructured Sulfur cathodes", *Chem. Soc. Rev.*, 42, 3018-3032, 2013
4. Song, J., et al., "Thermal Reaction of Lithiated and Delithiated Sulfur Electrodes in Lithium-Sulfur Batteries", ECS Electrochem. Lett., 3, A26-A29, 2014

Energy Storage Unit for 600V Micro Grid at Forward Operating Base

Neil Johnson, Richard Miller, Chad Hartzog
Navitas Advanced Solutions Group
Janie Hancock and Steven Kolhoff
US Army RDECOM-TARDEC
njohnson@navitassys.com

Abstract
Navitas Advanced Solutions Group has successfully designed and built an Energy Storage Unit (ESU) for use in military 600V micro-grids. The storage unit contains a 24 kW-hr battery pack for energy storage, a 180kW DC/DC converter to maintain a steady 600V output independent of battery pack SOC, and a self-contained cooling system for use up to 65 deg C. The ESU communicates with other components on the micro grid using government furnished equipment which then directs the ESU to either absorb or provide power/energy. The prototype ESU was tested to confirm safety, functionality and stability under significant load transients. The Army's goal is installation and startup of a 600V micro grid at a forward operating base in less than 20 minutes. The paper will discuss the architecture and address production readiness of the proposed solution.

Thermal Runaway Propagation Resistant Li-ion Battery Designs That Achieve > 180 Wh/kg

Eric Darcy
NASA-JSC
eric.c.darcy@nasa.gov

Abstract

In partnership with the National Renewable Energy Laboratory (NREL), we have invented (U.S. Patent #9,142,829) an on-demand internal short circuit (ISC) device that is activated by raising the cell temperature > 57 C, rather than > 130 C required without the device. We have achieved > 90% success rate in driving a 2.4Ah (~180 Wh/kg) cell design into thermal runaway with a device designed for an anode active material to cathode current collector short and using a non-shutdown separator. Building on this success, we are now implanting the device in a cell design exceeding 250 Wh/kg to learn its design vulnerabilities and effectiveness of safety features like shutdown separators, cathode coatings, current interrupt devices, positive thermal coefficient switches, center mandrels, cell vents, and crimped headers. We are providing our cells to researchers conducting in-operando tomography on cells during thermal runaway for first time video insight into the response of an 18650 cell to a thermal runaway that is internally induced by an internal short circuit instead of external driven by thermal, mechanical, or electrical abuse. This enables the study of conditions that replicate latent defect induced field failures with the most fidelity. As the specific energy of commercially available 18650 cell designs exceed 250 Wh/kg, we are presented with additional challenges for integrating them into safe, high performing (> 180 Wh/kg) battery designs for manned spacecraft applications. Specifically, these cell designs are susceptible to side wall rupturing and/or electrode jellyroll ejection during thermal runaway. Battery pack designs with such cell designs require cell interstitial materials that provide structural support to the cell cylindrical can walls. Thermal modeling and test verifications indicate that highly thermally conductive materials protect the adjacent cells much better than highly insulating materials. In addition, conductive heat sinks allow the cells to be much more tightly nested, saving volume. This leaves very little cell surface area for heating unmodified cells into thermal runaway for battery safety testing. In fact, the only way to achieve single cell thermal runaway in these battery designs is by triggering cells implanted with the ISC device (Figure 1). These tests give us insight into the impact of battery design features like cell-cell spacing, cell electrical isolating layers, and features that protect the adjacent cells from propagating into thermal runaway. Finally, battery flame arresting materials and vents are crucial to prevent flames and sparks for exiting battery enclosures. This Power Sources submission will be a first public forum disclosure of these results.

US Naval Lithium Battery Safety Program and Revision Three of the NAVSEA Technical Manual S9310-AQ-SAF-010

Dan Kieffner and Mark Tisher
Naval Surface Warfare Center – Crane Division
300 Hwy 361, Crane, IN 47522

Julie Simmons and Clint Winchester
Naval Surface Warfare Center – Carderock Division
9500 MacArthur Blvd, West Bethesda, MD 20817

Joseph Vignali, Elizabeth Donohue, and David Cherry
Naval Sea Systems Command
1333 Isaac Hull Ave SE, Washington Navy Yard, DC 20376

Abstract: *To assure that the safety risks associated with lithium and lithium-ion batteries fielded in all Naval applications have been characterized and accepted appropriately, the Navy employs a structured and tailored Lithium Battery Safety Program. One of the fundamental requirement documents used to implement this safety program is the Naval Sea Systems Command (NAVSEA) Technical Manual (TM) S9310-AQ-SAF-010. This TM was originally published in the 1970s as a supplemental document to educate and guide the program managers within the Navy who were running acquisition programs. It has been updated multiple times over the intervening years to address safety lessons learned as well as new technology insertion. The current revision, "Revision Two of the Naval Sea Systems Command (NAVSEA) Technical Manual for Navy Lithium Battery Safety Program Responsibilities and Procedures" of 15 July 2010 was issued as a replacement for Revision One, which was dated 19 August 2004. A new revision is planned for publication in late 2016. The new revision will harmonize the TM with the process changes enacted by the 12 August 2015 release of an updated Naval Instruction, 9310.1c, foremost of which is the delegation of Certification Authority for some lithium batteries and lithium-battery operated systems from NAVSEA to specific System Commands (SYSCOMS). It will also provide updates to guidance and requirements relating to lithium battery storage, transportation, firefighting and safety testing. This paper will highlight and discuss the major changes in between Revision Two and Revision Three of the NAVSEA TM S9310-AQ-SAF-010.*

Keywords: systems; safety; Navy; battery; lithium; lithium-ion.

Introduction

In response to failures associated with lithium batteries experienced by users, the U.S. Navy implemented a process guiding acquisition program personnel in selection and safety certification of lithium battery systems. Technical manual S9310-AQ-SAF-010 (TM), an unlimited distribution document, describes tests, usage, and logistics for lithium batteries; the latest version of the TM [1] was introduced in 2010. The TM guided safe introduction and operation of many systems containing lithium batteries; examples include the Joint Strike Fighter [2], radios [3], and unmanned systems [4]. In combination with other guidance documents, such as [5] and [6], potential effects on the larger system in which a lithium battery was used were analyzed and mitigated.

Multiple events have compelled a TM revision. Recent roles and responsibilities changes within the Naval acquisition structure forced a process change; the Naval Ordnance Safety and Security Activity is no longer the Lithium Battery Safety Program (LBSP) Authority. Technology maturity has allowed expansion of the exceptions list. Some logistics guidance has become obsolete.

In 2015, the team started development of TM Revision Three draft content. As recent feedback from users is incorporated, the subject document has continued through the review and revision stage. The following changes have interim approval but are subject to change; any major alteration or addition to these changes will be highlighted during the presentation.

Process Changes

The Department of the Navy designated Naval Sea Systems Command (NAVSEA) as the organization responsible for the Naval LBSP. NAVSEA has identified an official as the LBSP Authority, the person responsible for Naval lithium battery safety. The LBSP Authority has identified a Certification Authority (CA) at each of several Systems Commands (SYSCOMs) as the delegated certifiers of a new or existing lithium battery. Technical Agents, the Navy's lithium battery safety experts at the Carderock and Crane Naval Surface Warfare Centers, serve the CAs in an advisory role.

Although there are exceptions, Figure 1 summarizes the general process flow. A requesting manager or representative will consult with a Technical Agent. After review of initial data, the Technical Agent will confer with the CAs defined by the system. For aircraft systems, the Naval Air Systems Command (NAVAIR) CA is the contact; for Marine Corps systems, the Marine Corps Systems Command (MARCOR) CA is the contact; and the

NAVSEA CA is the contact for all other systems. The Technical Agent will check existing standardization and

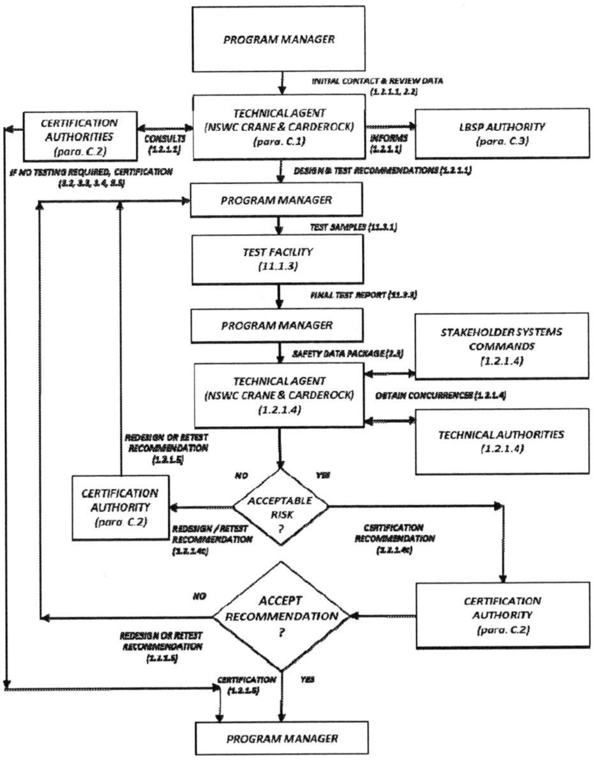

Figure 1. Process flow for lithium battery certification.

safety databases, consult with the CA, and use any other sources necessary to determine how to guide the requesting manager. If the proposed battery meets accelerated review criteria, or if existing data are sufficient, then the CA can review and certify the battery for the proposed use; otherwise, the Technical Agent will provide recommendations to the requesting manager. During execution of an overall program, the requesting manager will provide funding and test samples for testing at a SYSCOM approved test facility. After completion of testing, the requesting manager will provide test results and other relevant data to a Technical Agent for review. The Technical Agent will evaluate results, consult with impacted Technical Authorities and other agencies, and provide a recommendation to the CA. The CA will then provide either a certification or a recommendation for redesign or retest.

Accelerated Reviews and Test Exceptions

In [1], coin cells and certain commercial batteries did not require a safety data package; the sole requirement was for the requesting manager to provide a report describing the items to be purchased. In addition, [1] allowed the CAs to recommend members of a limited class of batteries for approval. In TM Revision Three, the unrestricted coin cell configuration will be expanded to allow two cells. Furthermore, commercial lithium ion battery packs with Underwriter's Laboratory approvals, used as recommended by the manufacturer, charged only using the manufacturer's recommended charger, and 100 watt-hours (Wh) maximum has been expanded from 18 volts maximum to 21 volts maximum and will be unrestricted. The size and chemistry content limits will be expanded for batteries that have only the reporting requirement as used for coin cells and COTS electronics using lithium ion batteries. The CA will have guidance that allows for accelerated review of batteries without additional testing; see Figure 2. For example, the NAVSEA CA may choose to certify a battery of 999 Wh for a surface ship application without conduct of additional testing. Regardless of the thresholds of Figure 2, the CA will retain authority to impose testing requirements if the battery is novel or otherwise not well-characterized by existing data models as required to mitigate an identified hazard.

PLATFORM TYPE	a. Maximum energy content	b. Maximum number of cells	c. Maximum cell capacity rating	d. Maximum battery voltage
Surface ship	Less than 1 kilowatt-hour (kWh)	50	30 Ampere-hours (Ah)	50.0 volts (V)
Submarine or submersible	30 Wh	3	3.5 Ah	12.6 V
Aircraft (outside of manned spaces)	300 Wh	8	15 Ah	32 V
Aircraft (manned spaces)**	300 Wh	8	15 Ah	32 V
Expeditionary, land-based	400 Wh	50	30 Ah	32 V

** - Limited to solid cathode primary or lithium-ion rechargeable technologies.

Figure 2. Potential threshold criteria for accelerated review and certification.

Design and Use

In addition to minor best practices changes associated with battery design, the usage paragraph will be greatly expanded to accommodate facility and test design best practices developed as the result of a recent significant battery test facility fire [7]. These best practices include test sample isolation, automatic fire suppression incorporation, and automated test circuit shutdown in the event of incident detection. Risk assessment and mitigations are beneficial.

Packaging, Handling, Storage, Transport, Disposal, and Emergency Response

There is some correlation between the volume of lithium batteries in a location and the magnitude of a worst credible mishap; however, the logistics of battery movement and storage can reduce the magnitude of an adverse unplanned event. The military agency and regulations responsible for guidance of disposal of military hazardous materials has changed. Emergency incident response personnel should be informed regarding the presence of lithium batteries and the nature of the hazards that can be encountered in response to a worst credible mishap incident.

Safety Testing

A new section of TM Revision Three includes an explicitly stated restriction on lithium battery test operations except at locations approved by the LBSP Authority and the facility Commanding Officer. Other new additions include designed isolation of test samples and risk assessment to ensure that the isolation cannot be breached during a worst credible mishap. Due to the low value of the test results when the test was executed as described, aging safety was eliminated as a required test for rechargeable batteries. In addition, the verbiage associated with lithium-ion battery cycling types of tests was adjusted to clarify intent.

The objective test passing criteria were expanded with additional clarifying information; see Figure 3. As indicated in TM Revision Three, an inability of a lithium battery or lithium battery-powered equipment to meet the objective test passing criteria does not automatically result in rejection of the equipment for service use. Batteries that fail to meet such criteria will be rejected only if a technical evaluation of the test results by the CA establishes that rejection is the appropriate course of action.

Platform	Criteria		
Submarines	Venting of gaseous/liquid/solid material and flames outside of the tes unit is prohibited. Local generation c heat resulting in temperatures greate than 100 degrees C is prohibited.	and	The peak pressure remains equal to or below 50 percent of the yield pressure or designed pressure release of the unit in any test that releases material into the platform.
Aircraft(1)	Venting of gaseous / liquid material is permitted. Venting of solid material and flames outside of the test unit is prohibited. Structural failure resultng in rupture of the test unit is prohibite	and	The peak pressure remains equal to or below 90 percent of the yield pressure of the unit in any test. Operation of a safety mechanism designed to release pressure is permitted.
Ships	Venting of gaseous/liquid/solid material is permitted. Venting of flames outside of the test unit is prohibited. Structural failure resulting in rupture of the test unit is prohibited.	and	The peak pressure remains equal to or below 50 percent of the yield pressure of the unit in any test. Operation of a safety mechanism designed to release pressure is permitted.
Land	Venting of gaseous/liquid/solid material and flames is permitted. Structural failure resulting in rupture of the test unit is prohibited.	and	The peak pressure remains equal to or below 90 percent of the yield pressure of the unit in any test. Operation of a safety mechanism designed to release pressure is permitted.
Naval R&D & Test Facilities	Venting or rupture of the test unit and release of toxic, flammable, or explosive gasses and materials, projectiles, and fire jets is permitted.	If	Non-expendable equipment and facility damage is maintained below the reportable threshold of MIL-STD-882 and supporting personnel are not injured.
(1) The preferred non-rechargeable chemistry for aircraft is solid cathode chemistry. Liquid cathode chemistries are highly corrosive and toxic. The location of the cell or battery in the aircraft will be closely scrutinized, especially regarding the possibility of toxic, corrosive gasses affecting crew members, passengers, or high priority equipment or systems.			

Figure 3. Passing criteria for test units by platform type.

Future Efforts

At the time that this paper was submitted for publication, Revision Three had progressed to intermediate review stages. It is expected that publication will occur in 2016. Because of the scope of changes, it is conceivable that users will request further modifications. Developer and user comments are welcome and encouraged.

Acknowledgements

The authors wish to thank Justin Govar, John Heinzel, Mark Hurley, and Nathan Kumbar for feedback on the content of the S9310-AQ-SAF-010 Revision Three drafts produced to date. The project was funded by the Naval Sea Systems Command Engineering Policy & Standards Division.

References

1. Naval Sea Systems Command. (2010). *Technical Manual for Navy Lithium Battery Safety Program Responsibilities and Procedures, S9310-AQ-SAF-010.* Retrieved from http://www.everyspec.com/USN/NAVSEA/NAVSEA_S9310-AQ-SAF-010_4137/
2. Hess, A., & Fila, L. (2002). The Joint Strike Fighter (JSF) PHM concept: Potential impact on aging aircraft problems. *IEEE Aerospace Conference Proceedings, 6*, 3021-3026. doi:10.1109/AERO.2002.1036144
3. Dominick, M., Thampan, T., Novoa, J., & Shah, S. (2012). U.S. Army CERDEC's Soldier-Wearable Fuel Cell Developments and Testing. *Proceedings of the 45th Power Sources Conference,* 219-222.
4. Ellsworth, N., Rottmayer, M., & Miller, R. (2012). Group I SUAS power system analysis. *Proceedings of the 45th Power Sources Conference*, 491-494.
5. Department of Defense (2012). *Department of Defense Standard Practice –System Safety, MIL-STD-882E.* Retrieved from http://www.system-safety.org/Documents/MIL-STD-882E.pdf
6. Naval Sea Systems Command. (2011). *High Energy Storage System Safety Manual, SG270-BV-SAF-010.* Retrieved from https://www.fbo.gov/index?s=opportunity&mode=form&id=4a4ef5f3e26e78711f743e2ec348d2ea&tab=core&_cview=0
7. Chatelain, M., Tisher, M., & Stuart, S. (2016). NSWC Crane 23 October 2012 Fire Event Engineering Root Cause Analysis Reportable Findings. *Proceedings of the 47th Power Sources Conference,* In publication.

Research Advances in Anion Exchange Membrane Electrolysis to Enable Low-Cost Hydrogen Energy Storage

Stephen Szymanski, Julie Renner, Nemanja Danilovic, Morgan George, Chris Capuano, Wayne Gellett, and Katherine Ayers

Proton Energy Systems, d/b/a Proton OnSite
10 Technology Drive
Wallingford, CT 06492

Abstract: *Hydrogen is a widely used industrial gas, and major contributor to CO_2 emissions when made from natural gas reforming. Hydrogen generation via water electrolysis is a zero carbon alternative when integrated with renewable energy storage applications. Key advantages of leveraging hydrogen as an energy storage medium are the flexibility and deployability it provides. Membrane-based electrolysis is an especially promising technology for hydrogen generation applications because of the lack of corrosive electrolytes, compact physical layout, and dynamic operating range due to the ability to generate hydrogen at differential pressures. Commercial membrane-based electrolyzers are based on proton exchange membranes (PEM). The key challenge with PEM electrolyzer systems is the high capital cost that results largely from precious metal catalysts and valve metal flow field materials in the cell stack. To date, the only pathway with promise to achieve platinum group metal (PGM)-free electrode formulations in membrane-based electrolysis cells is utilization of anion exchange membranes (AEMs). AEMs also enable the use of less expensive stainless steel flow field materials. The oxygen flow fields and separators combined with the membrane electrode assembly represent nearly 2/3 the cost in a PEM stack. Transitioning to these alternate materials can therefore save substantial cost.*

Proton has been developing AEM technology since 2010, and has made significant progress in understanding the limitations and potential of AEM chemistry. Progress has been made in membrane electrode assembly development, understanding stability, and system scale-up. While AEM technology is still far less mature than PEM, this progress points to the potential for AEM to enable a step-change in the cost of membrane-based electrolysis in the future.

Keywords: electrolysis; anion exchange membrane; non-precious metal catalysts; hydrogen; energy storage

Introduction

Hydrogen is a widely used industrial gas, with a large and expanding global market. The United States (U.S.) alone manufactures over 9 million tons of hydrogen annually. High-purity hydrogen is used in heat treating, generator cooling and as a laboratory carrier gas. Conventional power plants use hydrogen-cooled generators which require high-purity hydrogen to be effective. The most common way to produce hydrogen is by hydrocarbon steam reforming; however, the process is not carbon-neutral and represents a large environmental concern. As an example, hydrogen is needed to manufacture ammonia, and nearly all of the emissions (1.6 tons of CO_2 per ton of ammonia) are a result of using natural gas as the feedstock [1]. In addition, hydrocarbon steam reforming is difficult to scale-down. As a result, hydrogen is often produced at a central location and shipped, which increases the cost and carbon footprint. Water electrolysis offers a competitive production method because it is high-purity, on-site, uses water as the only feedstock, and can be easily integrated with renewable electricity sources, enabling green hydrogen production.

Hydrogen generation via water electrolysis is rapidly gaining international interest for renewable energy storage applications due to the flexibility and deployability it provides. Key advantages include 1) the ability to interconnect various infrastructures such as renewable electricity, transportation, and biogas upgrading, and 2) the ability to address very long timescales, such as seasonal variations in solar intensity. Renewable energy is becoming a significant part of the energy grid, triggering new challenges in managing supply and demand fluctuations. Denmark is striving for at least 50% wind power to serve their electricity demand by 2025 and Germany already has over 30 GW [2]. However, over 20% of Germany's available wind power is lost due to lack of transmission capacity, and this issue will become worse as the renewable penetration increases [3]. Thus, as intermittent renewable energy becomes more prevalent in Europe and in America, cost effective, flexible storage options become essential and hydrogen is the most versatile near term option.

To specifically address these opportunities, PEM-based electrolysis is an ideal near term technology because of the lack of corrosive electrolytes, compact physical layout, and dynamic operating range. The ability to generate hydrogen at differential pressures results in process intensification, with multiple processes occurring at once in a single device (generation, separation and compression). However, the PGM catalysts required for stability in the acidic membrane environment become a significant cost driver at megawatt scales, as other component costs have decreased with scale and manufacturing development. AEM technology represents a promising pathway to a step-change in the capital cost of membrane-based electrolysis.

PEM Status: What AEM is competing with

AEM-based electrolysis currently has many challenges to overcome to make it competitive with PEM technology. PEM-based systems are highly advanced, with over 60,000 hours of demonstrated durability. The performance of PEM-based systems is high compared to AEM-based systems and there are still opportunities for significant cost reduction in PEM systems. In addition, the manufacturing processes and supply chain are well-established for PEM systems, enabling steady scale-up progression and development. PEM cells have been scaled to over 700 cm^2 active areas, enabling the commercialization of MW-scale stacks and systems (Figure 1).

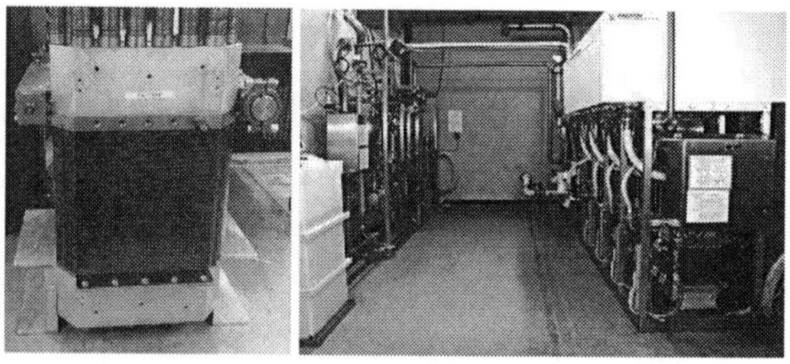

Figure 1. One 0.25 PEM MW stack (left) for the MW-scale electrolysis system (right).

The Importance of Capital Cost

While grid electricity cost is currently the major contributor to lifecycle cost for PEM electrolysis, in a renewable energy storage application, the economics are different. There are emerging scenarios pointing to a need to shift emphasis on reducing the capital cost of membrane-based electrolysis. In fact, work at the National Renewable Energy Laboratory (NREL) has shown that hydrogen production via electrolysis can be economical at \$0.02-0.03/kWh, as there are tradeoffs between capacity factor, capital cost and electricity [4]. Two areas where AEM-based electrolysis can make an impact are in catalyst, and bipolar assembly (plate and anode components) costs. Using the conservative assumptions below in Table 1, AEM would have the potential to save over \$40,000 per MW on catalyst alone. Additionally, moving from titanium-based components in the bipolar assembly to stainless steel would save over \$50,000 per MW.

Table 1. Cost savings in PGM catalyst loading per MW.

Total electrode area/MW	27 m^2
Total PGM loading	3 mg/cm^2
Catalyst cost assumption	~\$50/g
Catalyst cost/MW	>\$40,000

AEM Technology: Pros and Cons

The chemistry of alkaline electrolyte-based systems, such as potassium hydroxide (KOH) alkaline tank electrolyzers, allow for less expensive materials of construction and catalysts. However, the KOH liquid electrolyte systems utilize separator-based technology, which has a very low 'bubble point' mandating a balanced pressure design. Balanced pressure complicates system design and materials selection and requires significant hydrogen (H_2), oxygen (O_2), and caustic electrolyte volumes, necessitating ASME rated pressure vessels and hazardous classification. Controlled, active system shutdown is required to prevent hazardous cell pressure imbalance and H_2/O_2 recombination. In addition, maintaining the system electrolyte concentrations typically needs significant external processing and equipment, which requires the systems to have a much larger footprint than corresponding membrane-based systems. Alkaline KOH liquid electrolytes also suffer from high maintenance costs due to the extreme corrosivity of the carrier fluid, as well as the tendency to form sodium and potassium carbonates when exposed to air which precipitate and foul the porous separator and electrodes. Collectively, these drawbacks make KOH-based systems less ideal for integration with intermittent and dynamic renewable energy.

Proton is pursuing pathways for PEM technology which can reduce the current stack cost by over half (Figure 2, top). Changes include new flow field designs for the anode and cathode, which reduce raw material usage and labor, and reductions in catalyst loading based on novel electrode structures. Conversion to AEM-based analog (Figure 2, bottom) enables a step change to a new cost curve.

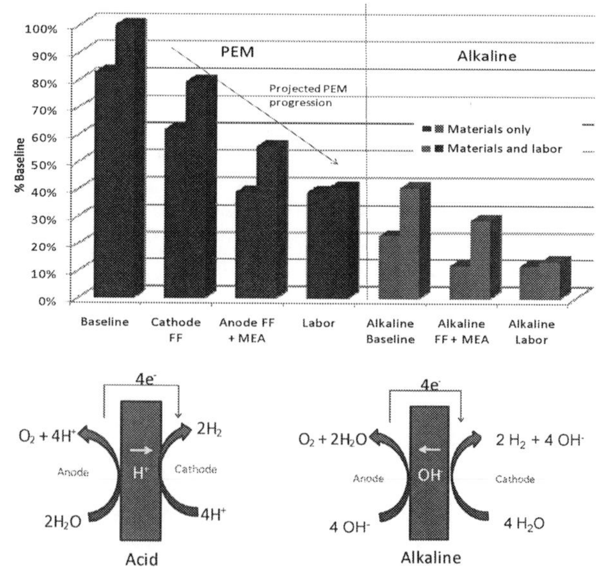

Figure 2. Top: Cost progression of design changes for PEM (left) and AEM (right) technologies. Bottom: AEM (right) versus PEM (left) electrolysis reactions.

AEM cells enable stainless steel flow fields, which are 80% lower in cost compared to titanium. AEM technology also enables the use of thinner membranes and cheaper catalysts, reducing the MEA cost by at least 50%. Finally, an AEM system would have the PEM advantages of differential pressure operation, pure water as the carrier fluid, and lower resistance than a liquid electrolyte system.

This step change in cost is achievable despite some of the technological challenges with AEM systems, including lower operating current densities, lower conductivity of alkaline membranes and lower stability of both membranes and ionomers compared to PEM materials. In addition, translation of catalyst activity from liquid electrolyte to ionomer has been problematic. Water transport and management is also a challenge in AEM cells versus PEM cells, because the hydrogen evolution reaction occurs in a fully flooded environment. To achieve differential pressure and a dry hydrogen stream in an AEM-based electrolysis cell, water is often fed on the anode side, and allowed to permeate through the membrane to the cathode. This represents a very different situation compared to the PEM analog.

AEM History at Proton OnSite

Proton was one of the first to pioneer an AEM electrolyzer concept through an ARPA-E GRIDS program. Over the course of the project, a test bed was established for AEM-based electrolysis capable of evaluating multiple materials. Proton and their collaborators made significant advances in membrane durability, electrode performance and cell development. The project culminated in an unprecedented 2000-hour electrolysis demonstration using AEM material developed at Los Alamos National Laboratory (LANL) while efficiencies for the AEM cell achieved values closer to the PEM cell than liquid KOH systems (Figure 3).

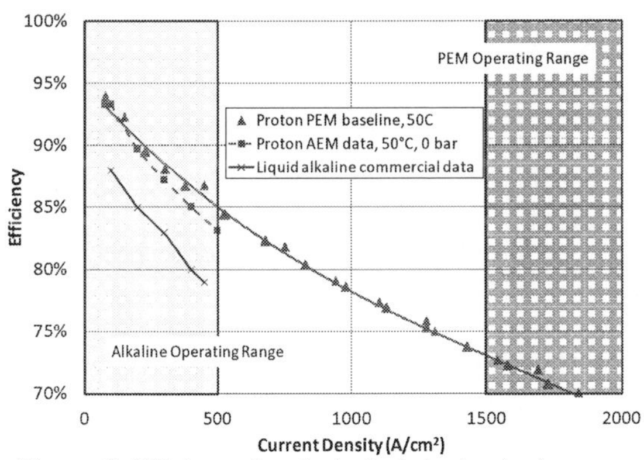

Figure 3. Efficiency for electrolysis technologies.

Critical Areas and Technology Road Map

Since the test bed developed under the GRIDS program was established, Proton OnSite has remained a leader in AEM-based electrolysis advancement, working across agencies (Department of Energy, ARPA-E, NYSERDA) and with many different collaborators. Proton OnSite has identified several key critical issues and has developed a technology roadmap to guide their AEM development efforts. Critical issues include the need for new stable membrane chemistries, process development to accommodate the new materials and AEM temperature sensitivity, as well as the understanding of catalyst-ionomer interactions. In the next section, Proton OnSite describes their recent progress collaborating with multiple partners to solve these issues.

Recent Progress

Electrode Processing Considerations

Alkaline-based ionomers are often used as binders and ion conductors in the electrodes made at Proton OnSite. Adhesion issues were manifesting during operation of the AEM electrolyzer on the anode side of the cell (Figure 5, left). It was hypothesized that the ionomer was the source of the adhesion problem, and some AEM materials have been shown to preferentially degrade in the presence of the oxygen evolution electrode.[5] Proton OnSite engineered their ink to incorporate binders with better adhesion and favorable electrode morphology (Figure 5, right). This result illustrates the challenge of developing materials to withstand the harsh conditions (high voltage and oxygen) at the anode in electrolysis. As discussed in the next section, stability of both the ionomer and membranes must be understood and considered in this environment.

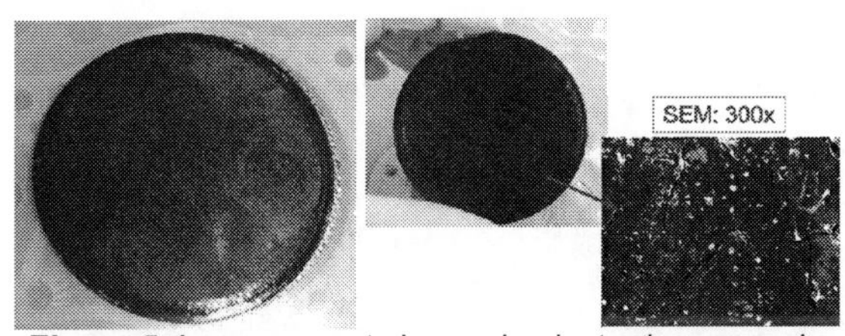

Figure 5. Improvements in anode electrode processing for better adhesion during operation.

Impact of Oxygen

In collaboration with researchers at the Illinois Institute of Technology (IIT), Proton OnSite investigated the development of PPO-C6-TMA-based membranes and ionomers.[6] As part of this work the effect of oxygen on the ionomer degradation in an alkaline environment was identified as a major problem (Figure 6).

Figure 6. Oxygen has an effect on ionomer stability in base. Solubilized samples were incubated in the presence and absence of oxygen in 0.5 M KOH at 60°C. The results indicate that oxygen plays a role in ionomer instability for this chemistry.

<u>Carbonate vs. DI Water</u>

Proton has conducted a variety of tests using both catalyst coated membranes (CCM) and gas diffusion electrodes (GDEs) showing that when potassium bicarbonate is added to the process water, the performance improves (Figure 7). Proton speculates a number of mechanisms for the improvement: 1) the electrolyte expands the anode active area, improving catalyst utilization 2) the electrolyte buffers CO_2 and improves ion transport, and 3) the electrolyte may stabilize the membrane and/or the ionomer.

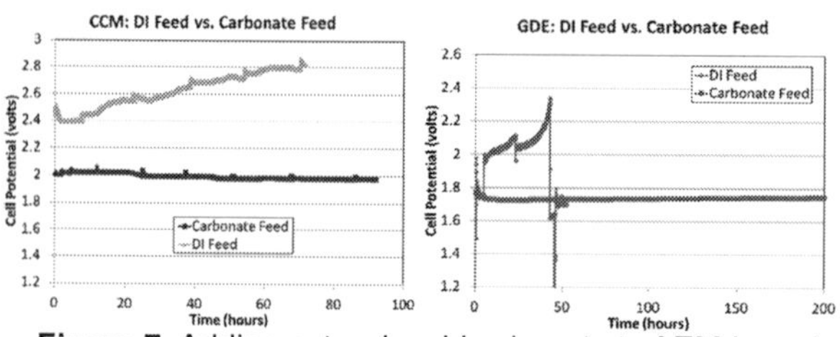

Figure 7. Adding potassium bicarbonate to AEM-based electrolysis process water shows increased durability and performance using both CCM and GDE configurations.

<u>Stack Scale Up</u>

Proton and their collaborators have also made great progress in scaling up AEM electrolysis systems (Figure 8).

Figure 8: Scaled lab prototype and stack (lower left corner) based on AEM technology.

Proton leveraged their existing commercial hardware and scaled up their standard 3-cell design to a 10-cell stack (Figure 8 inset) with a goal of producing 1 L/min of hydrogen at 500 mA/cm^2. The stack represented a high degree of cost reduction, utilizing lead ruthenate pyrochlore anode electrocatalysts for high activity,[7] reducing the precious metal loading, as well as an anode GDL fabricated with 316 stainless steel. The catalyst and flowfield material changes represent >80% and >90% cost reductions over the PEM baseline materials, respectively. The configuration was operated at 500 mA/cm^2 for over 500 hours utilizing potassium bicarbonate in the process water.

Summary

While there are still opportunities for cost and efficiency improvements in PEM electrolysis, AEM electrolysis has the future potential to make a step-change in the cost curve. While AEM electrolysis technology is still immature, Proton and their partners have shown rapid improvements in the capabilities of AEM stack materials including higher durability, higher performance, and the ability to scale up. Continuing advancements can be achieved through synergistic collaborations, leveraging future fundamental discoveries and utilizing Proton's robust AEM test bed. Major future challenges include understanding the impact of catalyst composition and structure as well as electrode structure and fabrication.

Acknowledgements

The authors would like to acknowledge the U.S. Department of Energy (contracts DE-SC0007574, DE-SC0013179, and DE-EE0006958), ARPA-E (DE-AR0000121), and NYSERDA (#38304) for their support in funding portions of this development effort. We also acknowledge collaborations with IIT, Northeastern University, Penn State University, Rutgers University, Los Alamos National Laboratory, Sandia National Laboratory, University of Delaware, University of New Mexico, Tetramer Technologies, and Cornell University on AEM projects.

References

1. IPCC Guidelines for National Greenhouse Gas Inventories. Chapter 3 – Chemical Industry Emissions. (2006).
2. Wind in power - European statistics. The European Wind Energy Association. (2011).
3. Bullis, K., Hydrogen Storage Could Be Key to Germany's Energy Plans. MIT Technology Review (2012).
4. Fall 2015 ECS meeting, Phoenix AZ, presentation by Bryan Pivovar
5. J. Parrondo and V. Ramani, J. Electrochem. Soc. 161 (10), F1015 (2014)
6. J. Parrondo, M. S. J. Jung, Z. Y. Wang, C. G. Arges and V. Ramani, J. Electrochem. Soc. 162 (10), F1236 (2015)
7. J. Parrondo, M. George, C. Capuano, K. E. Ayers and V. Ramani, Journal of Materials Chemistry A 3 (20), 10819 (2015)

Feasibility of the Al_2O_3 Felt as a Separator for Thermal Batteries

Sang Hyeok Chae [a], Seung-Ho Kang [b], Chaenam Im [b], Hae-Won Cheong [b], Kyung-Ho Kim [c], Yoon Soo Han [c], Sung-Min Lee [c], Dang-Hyok Yoon [a,]*

[a]School of Materials Science and Engineering, Yeungnam University, Gyeongsan 38541, Korea

[b]Agency for Defense Development, Yuseong P. O. Box 35-41, Daejeon 34188, Korea

[c]Engineering Ceramic Team, Korea Institute of Ceramic Engineering and Technology, Icheon 17303, Korea

E-mail address: dhyoon@ynu.ac.kr

Tel.: +82-538102561; fax: +82-538104628

Abstract: *Thermal battery is used as a power source for military weapons, which demands a high level of long-term stability without a significant decrease in capacity. Because the components for conventional thermal batteries are being manufactured by simple pellet pressing using a ceramic powder, however, a risk for electric short by the fracturing of the pellet always exists. Therefore, the use of Al_2O_3 felt separator was examined in this study to enhance the reliability of thermal batteries by minimizing the sudden failure of an electrolyte layer upon shock. To assess the feasibility of ceramic felt as a separator for thermal batteries, a commercial Al_2O_3 felt having 97% porosity was tested using binary LiCl-KCl and ternary LiF-LiCl-LiBr electrolytes. The wetting and loading behaviors of the molten electrolytes for the porous ceramic felt as well as the chemical stability of the felt were found to be adequate for practical applications.*

Keywords: Thermal battery; Ceramic felt; Separator; Electrolyte; Infiltration

Introduction

Thermal battery is a primary battery, which delivers a large amount of energy within a short time. Thermal battery is ideally suited to the field of strategic warfare applications, such as thermal-guidance weapons, bombs, and underwater mines [1]. Because of the nature of military weapons, the thermal battery should offer a high level of reliability, including long storage life of more than 10 years, without a significant decrease in capacity. After stacking the periodic layers of the unit cell to realize a desired output voltage along with a $Fe/KClO_4$ heat pellet at the end of the stack to activate the battery pyrotechnically, the thermal battery is hermetically sealed [2,3]. The most commonly used electrochemical system in thermal batteries is Li-Si (or Li-Al)/FeS_2 (or CoS_2), where a Li-based solid electrolyte is located between them. These components are fabricated by pellet pressing using the corresponding powder, which are very fragile upon a shock. The electrolyte layer generally contains 30 percentage of MgO powder as a binder to hold the molten electrolyte [2-7]. To minimize the risk for fracturing as well as to enhance the electrochemical properties, however, the use of ceramic felt as a separator can be considered. With these backgrounds, a porous Al_2O_3 felt having 97% porosity is tested to replace the conventional MgO-contained electrolyte layer. The wettability of molten LiCl-KCl and LiF-LiCl-LiBr electrolytes on the Al_2O_3 felt, and thermal stability of the felts at very corrosive molten electrolyte were evaluated along with the loading/leakage rates.

Experimental procedure

To evaluate the feasibility of porous Al_2O_3 felt (ALF-50, 97% porosity, > 99 wt. % pure, Zircar Ceramics, USA) as a separator, the wetting and loading behaviors of molten LiCl-KCl and LiF-LiCl-LiBr electrolytes on the separator were evaluated. A small-sized box furnace and a CCD camera connected to a lap-top computer were placed in the glove box, which can maintain a relative humidity of less than 2 %, to observe the in-situ wetting and infiltration behaviors of the electrolytes. After placing approximately 0.5 grams of the electrolyte powder on top of the felts, the samples were kept for 1 hour at 10°C lower than the melting point of each electrolyte for thermal equilibrium followed by continuous heating at a rate of 1°C/min, while recording the wetting and infiltration behaviors using a CCD camera.

To check the chemical stability and loading rate, the ceramic felt was infiltrated by soaking in the salt bath. The loading rate was calculated by considering the porosity after infiltration, the amount of electrolyte loaded in the felt was measured in the glove box using a scale accurate to 0.1 mg, while XRD was performed for the infiltrated samples. For the leakage rate measurement, the loaded felts were placed at 500°C for 30 minutes under the constant pressure of 130 Pa. Nine samples were used for the measurement of loading and leakage rates.

Results and discussion

According to the wetting test, 2 kinds of electrolytes showed full wetting at temperatures higher than their melting temperatures, as shown in Fig. 1.

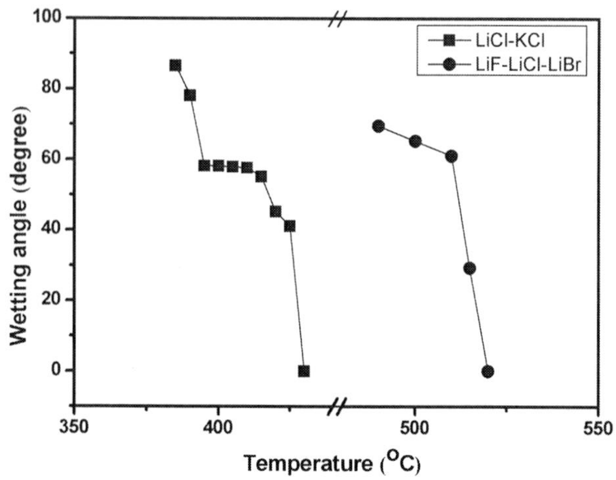

Figure 1. Behavior of the wetting angle for both electrolytes on Al_2O_3 as a function temperature.

The molten LiCl-KCl electrolyte formed a hemisphere upon melting at 415°C because of its high surface tension (123 dyne/cm, which is larger than that (72 dyne/cm) of water at 25°C) [8]. On the other hand, this molten electrolyte spread and wets the surface of the ceramic pellets as the temperature was increased to 430°C, even though a slight difference in wetting angle was observed among the samples. The full melting of the LiCl-KCl electrolyte occurs above 400°C under this continuously heating condition, although the melting temperature of this electrolyte was reported to be 354°C. The full melting of the LiCl-KCl electrolyte required approximately 1 hour when exposed at a constant temperature of 355°C, while the time decreased to less than 10 seconds at 430°C. Therefore, it appears that the melting of LiCl-KCl requires time to provide sufficient thermal energy corresponding to the latent heat for melting, when the electrolyte is exposed to the near melting temperature. This suggests that the operation of thermal batteries requires higher operating temperature than the melting point for the instant activation of thermal batteries with a LiCl-KCl electrolyte.

The LiF-LiCl-LiBr electrolyte fully wets the surface of the pellets at 530°C. However, the LiF-LiCl-LiBr electrolyte did not form a spherical shape upon melting, which might be due to its smaller surface tension (70 dyne/cm) than that (123 dyne/cm) of the LiCl-KCl electrolyte. Similar to the LiCl-KCl electrolyte, the LiF-LiCl-LiBr electrolyte fully wetted the pellets at 530°C which is much higher than the eutectic temperature of this composition (443°C).

Figs. 2 and 3 showed the infiltration behaviors of the LiCl-KCl and LiF-LiCl-LiBr electrolytes to the ceramic felt, respectively. The liquid LiCl-KCl and LiF-LiCl-LiBr electrolytes disappeared at 430 and 530°C, respectively, by infiltrating into the porous felts. The porous separator should hold a sufficient amount of molten electrolyte to achieve high ionic conductivity, while still separating the cathode and anode to prevent a short circuit. In addition, the separator should be sufficiently stable to resist the highly corrosive molten salt environment and maintain adequate mechanical strength for handling.

The chemical stability of the electrolyte in the very corrosive molten electrolyte environment is important for achieving a high ionic conductivity and reliability of the thermal batteries. Therefore, the formation of any Li-containing compounds by a reaction between the electrolyte and separator material was examined by XRD after dipping the felt into the molten electrolyte for 30 minutes. Fig. 4 shows the XRD patterns of the felt before/after infiltrated with the electrolyte. Based on the Rietveld analysis, the alumina felt is a pure nonstoichiometric η-alumina ($Al_{2.666}O_{3.999}$, reference code = 98-001-5806). Any intermediate compound formed from the reaction between the η-alumina and both electrolytes could be found, indicating the rigidness of the felt. When the alumina felt was exposed to the molten LiCl-KCl electrolyte, KCl and LiCl were the main phases along with the small presence of Li_2O_2 and metallic Li. Any intermediate compound formed from the reaction between the η-alumina and the LiCl-KCl electrolyte could be found, which might be due to the thermally rigid alumina felt. It can be estimated that a certain amount of LiCl is oxidized into Li_2O_2, while the remaining is existed as an amorphous phase based on the relative peak heights of the Li-containing phases.

The loading and leakage rate of the felt for the LiCl-KCl electrolyte were 93 and 10 wt. %, while those for the LiF-LiCl-LiBr were 92 and 21 wt. %, respectively. Overall, no significant barriers for the application of Al_2O_3 ceramic felt as a separator for thermal batteries were found, in terms of wetting, infiltration, chemical stability, and loading/leakage rate. The evaluation of electrochemical property of a thermal battery containing these felt materials is being evaluated.

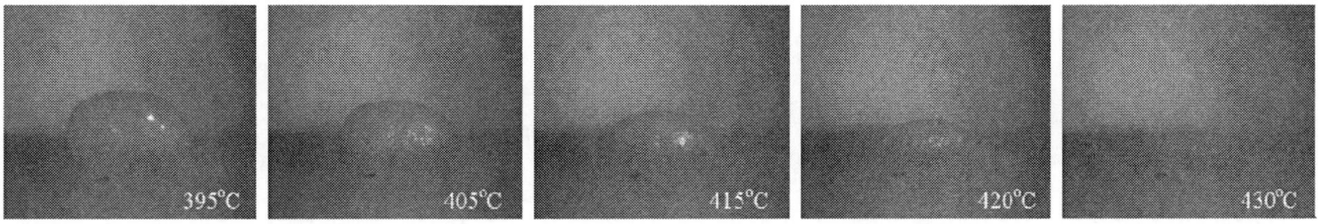

Figure 2. Infiltration behavior of the molten LiCl-KCl electrolyte on the porous alumina felt.

Figure 3. Infiltration behavior of the molten LiF-LiCl-LiBr electrolyte on the porous alumina felt.

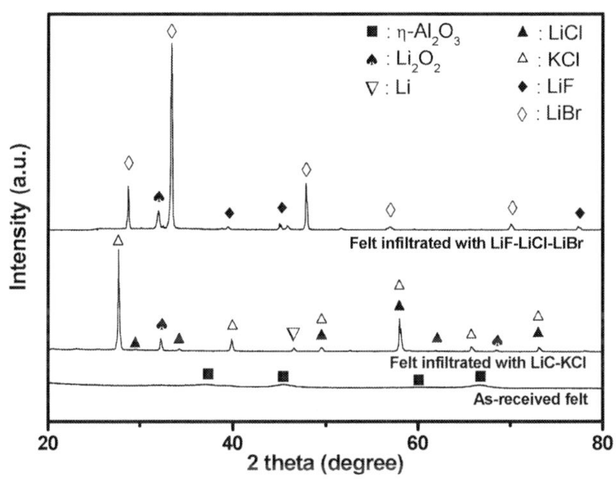

Figure 4. XRD patterns of the alumina felt before/after infiltration using both electrolytes.

Conclusions

To enhance the reliability of thermal batteries compared to the conventional pellet-pressed structure, Al_2O_3 ceramic felt was tested as a separator. The wetting, infiltration, loading, leakage, and chemical stability of the felt materials to the molten LiCl-KCl and LiF-LiCl-LiBr electrolytes were examined. The felt material showed good wetting and infiltration behavior for both molten electrolytes, while full wetting or infiltration could be achieved at temperatures higher than the melting point of both electrolytes. The loading rate of both electrolytes for the felt was greater than 90% along with leakage rates smaller than 21%, which are feasible for practical applications. The chemical stability of the felt in a molten electrolyte environment, which was confirmed by the examination of compounds formed upon exposure at high temperatures, showed that the ceramic felt is stable, exhibiting the presence of compounds having relatively low melting point, such as Li_2O_3 and metallic Li. Therefore, there was no possibility to decrease the ionic conductivity of the electrolytes by the immobilization of Li-ions. Overall, no significant barriers for the application of ceramic felts as a separator for thermal batteries were found.

Acknowledgments

This study was funded by the Agency for the Defense Development of Korea. The authors thank Vitzrocell Co., Ltd. for offering the electrolyte powder.

References

1. Klasons,V., in : Linden, D., (Ed.), *Handbook of Batteries*, 3rd ed., McGraw-Hill, New York, pp. 21.1–21.22, 2002.
2. Cheong, H.W., S. H. Ha, and Y.S. Choi, "Surface Modified Ceramic Fiber Separators for Thermal Batteries," *Journal of Ceramic Processing Research*, Vol. 13, no 2, pp. s308-s311, 2012.
3. Guidotti, R.A., F.W. Reinhardt, J. Dai, and D.E. Reisner, "Thermally Activated ("Thermal") Battery Technology Part I: An Overview," *Journal of Power Sources*, Vol. 161, pp. 1456–1464, 2006.

4. Masset, P., and R.A. Guidotti, "Thermally Activated ("Thermal") Battery Technology Part II: Molten Salt Electrolytes," *Journal of Power Sources*, Vol. 164, pp. 397–414, 2007.
5. Masset, P., and R.A. Guidotti, "Thermally Activated ("Thermal") Battery Technology Part III a: FeS_2 Cathode Material," *Journal of Power Sources*, Vol. 177, pp. 595–609, 2008.
6. Masset, P., and R.A. Guidotti, "Thermally Activated ("Thermal") Battery Technology Part III b: Sulfur and Oxide-based Cathode Materials," *Journal of Power Sources*, Vol. 178, pp. 456–466, 2008.
7. Guidotti, R.A., and P.J. Masset, "Thermally Activated ("Thermal") Battery Technology Part IV: Anode Materials," *Journal of Power Sources*, Vol. 183, pp. 388–398, 2008.
8. Cho, K.Y., D.H. Riu, D.G. Shin, K.H. Lim, E.J. Jin, H.E. Kim, S.H. Ha, and J.H. Choi, "Reaction Behavior of Ceramic Mat with Lithium Salt for the Electrolyte Separators of Thermal Batteries," *Journal of the Korean Ceramic Society*, Vol. 46, No. 6, pp. 587–591, 2009.

Transient Anion Formation in Electrospun Alkaline Exchange Membranes under Operating Conditions

*Jacob A. Wrubel, Aldo A. Peracchio, Brice N. Cassenti, Timothy D. Myles, Matthew B. DeGostin, Wilson K. S. Chiu**

Department of Mechanical Engineering
University of Connecticut
Storrs, CT, USA, 06269-3139

***Corresponding author: wchiu@engr.uconn.edu**

Abstract: *Carbon dioxide interactions in alkaline anion exchange membrane fuel cells can be a major limiting factor in their commercial use. The presence of carbon dioxide in the oxidant gas stream leads to the formation of carbonate and bicarbonate species in the electrolyte which lowers the membrane's conductivity. The formation of these species is studied here for isolated anion exchange membranes exposed to air. A model that describes transient hydroxide, carbonate, and bicarbonate evolution is developed to provide a quantitative understanding of the effects of this process. A Fiber Network model is also created to calculate transport properties that depend on the morphology of electrospun membranes. Predictions from these models are validated to analytical solutions, steady-state numerical results, and existing experimental measurements. The results described herein can used to better understand anion exchange membranes used in an operating fuel cell in the presence of carbon dioxide.*

Keywords: Anion exchange membranes; electrospun membranes; carbon dioxide; fuel cell

Introduction

Anion exchange membrane fuel cells (AEMFCs) offer several advantages over proton exchange membrane fuel cells (PEMFCs), including more facile oxygen reduction reaction (ORR) kinetics in alkaline environments which eases the requirement of expensive catalysts [1-4]. However a historical concern with AEMFCs is their susceptibility to carbon dioxide in the cathode gas stream which, once absorbed into the membrane, initiates carbonate- and bicarbonate-forming (CO_3^{2-} and HCO_3^- respectively) reaction schemes [1-5]. These ions, while still conductive, are less mobile and lead to a decrease in the membrane's conductivity [3]. Therefore it will be beneficial to quantitatively describe the transient and steady-state behavior of these membranes with respect to local concentrations of ionic species. An ion exchange model has been developed which describes the transient ion exchange process in an isolated AEM, which is used to predict the effects of carbon dioxide on membrane transport properties.

A new manufacturing technique for AEMs has recently been proposed which allows for a higher ion exchange capacity (IEC) of the membrane without sacrificing mechanical or chemical stability [2]. The process uses electrospinning to create "dual-fiber mats" of separated ionomer/uncharged polymer chains. The ionomer chains are then selectively cross-linked, while the uncharged polymer chains are selectively softened to flow and become the matrix for the cross-linked ionomer network, providing strength and stability.

To account for the complicated microstructure of electrospun membranes, a fiber network (FN) model has been developed to predict ionic conductivity by approximating the cross-linked ionomer chains as a random resistor network [5]. The simulated ionic conductivities are directly linked to the effective diffusivities of ions through the electrospun network. These physically relevant diffusivity values are used in calculating ion fluxes in the membrane.

The present work describes the results of the transient ion exchange model for an isolated AEM as well as the FN model.

Theory

a. Ion Exchange Model

In the ion exchange model [3], the hydrated pores of the fiber network are simulated as a one dimensional channel in which ionic transport and reactions take place. Ionic transport is governed by Fick's second law with an added reaction term that acts like a source:

$$\frac{\partial c_i}{\partial t} = \frac{\partial}{\partial x}\left(D_i^{eff}\frac{\partial c_i}{\partial x}\right) + \dot{R}_i \tag{1}$$

where i denotes the ionic species. In [3] the effective diffusivity D_i^{eff} is given by a Bruggeman model, but this can be substituted with values obtained by other models, e.g., the FN model (presented in the next section). The reaction source terms are given by the local equilibrium balance using the forward and backward rate constants for reactions $R1 - R6$ appearing below, which describe the hydroxide, carbonate, and bicarbonate formation scheme in the membrane alkaline environment.

$$CO_{2(aq)} + OH^- \leftrightarrow HCO_3^- \quad \text{(R1)}$$
$$HCO_3^- + OH^- \leftrightarrow CO_3^{2-} + H_2O \quad \text{(R2)}$$
$$H_2O \leftrightarrow H^+ + OH^- \quad \text{(R3)}$$
$$(TMA)OH \leftrightarrow (TMA)^+ + OH^- \quad \text{(R4)}$$
$$(TMA)HCO_3 \leftrightarrow (TMA)^+ + HCO_3^- \quad \text{(R5)}$$
$$(TMA)_2CO_3 \leftrightarrow 2(TMA)^+ + CO_3^{2-} \quad \text{(R6)}$$

Reactions $R4 - R6$ describe the association and dissociation processes involving the anionic species and the fixed cationic side groups (represented here as trimethylamine, TMA). The complete solution to eq. 1 provides concentration profiles $C_i = f(x,t)$ for the ten species that appear in $R1 - R6$. Initial and boundary conditions are described in more detail in [3], specifically for CO_2 for which $J_{CO_2}\big|_{x=0,L}$ is governed by Henry's law. All other species are assumed to have no fluxes in or out. In other words, carbonate and bicarbonate are only introduced via the source terms, and are allowed to accumulate in the membrane. In an operating membrane there would be boundary conditions for hydroxide, carbonate, and bicarbonate due to the electrode reactions, including the self-purging mechanism [6]. These are not considered here but will be in the extended model.

b. Fiber Network Model

The motivation in developing the FN model was to predict the ionic conductivity of a very complicated and non-uniform microstructure for which volume-averaged approaches may be insufficient. The FN model simulates the conducting fibers of an electrospun composite mat as a random resistor network for which the conductivity may be solved for using electrochemical fin theory [5]. Geometric considerations such as volume fraction of conducting factors, in plane vs. through-plane conductivity, and isotropic vs. anisotropic swelling are included.

The FN model uses input parameters describing a physical system to generate a simulated electrospun mat of straight, randomly oriented ionomers. Although the generated mat is two-dimensional, the model accounts for the difference between in-plane intersections and through-plane intersections due to the layering effect. To manage the size of the data set, the mat is reduced to a statistically representative element called a coupon. Contact points (in- and through-plane) within the coupon are then identified, as well as points where the fibers intersect the boundary of the coupon. After applying a potential at the boundaries, the current through each 'resistor' in the network can be solved for using Kirchhoff's circuit laws.

The conductivity of the individual fibers, σ_f, is assumed to be constant and known although the conductivity of individual fiber segments is difficult to determine in practice. Instead the effective conductivity of the entire mat, σ_{eff}, is usually reported. Therefore to compare the results of the FN model to experimental data, σ_f can be varied so that σ_{eff} fits one experimental data point, and then this value of σ_f is used for all other points. For a more detailed description and derivation the reader is referred to [5]. It should be noted that although conductivity in fibers is modeled after the electrical conductivity of e.g., a wire, the more physically relevant analogue is mass transport through a hydrated pore.

Results and Discussion

The FN model, when compared to experimental data, is shown to accurately describe the ionic conductivity in electrospun AEMs as parameters such as ionomer volume fraction and water content are varied. It was demonstrated that although volume-averaged approaches like porous media theory may sufficiently describe the system, they rely on accurate estimates of porosity and tortuosity. These estimates can be obtained from the FN model, but they may be overestimated because of the assumption of 1D transport along fibers. In general the FN model is well-suited to characterizing key design parameters in the manufacturing of electrospun membranes.

The results of the ion exchange model describe a rapid drop in the average hydroxide concentration in the membrane as carbonate accumulates. Once the membrane is essentially fully depleted of hydroxide, bicarbonate also begins to accumulate. The initial decrease in hydroxide results in a similarly sharp decrease in the membrane's conductivity since hydroxide ions have the highest mobility in the solution. There is also a gradual decrease in the conductivity after that as carbonate is converted to bicarbonate; the ions have similar diffusivities but carbonate's -2 charge gives it a higher conductivity. By the time the reactions reach equilibrium, the conductivity of the membrane will have dropped by 20-25%.

Conclusions

Thus far this Army Research Office sponsored project has seen the development of two models to predict the conductivity of electrospun AEMs; one with regard to processing parameters, and the other which demonstrates the effect of carbon dioxide on the membrane. The FN model is an important tool for this class of materials, as it predicts effective transport properties based on local morphology. Similarly, the ion exchange model is an important step in understanding the effects of carbon dioxide formation on the membrane's conductivity.

Future work will use the conductivity predictions from the FN model in an extension of the ion exchange model that will simulate a membrane in an operating fuel cell.

Acknowledgements

Financial support from the Army Research Office (award number W911NF-14-1-0298) is gratefully acknowledged. The authors would also like to acknowledge the support of and discussions with Dr. Cynthia Lundgren, Dr. Deryn Chu, and Dr. Kyle N. Grew of the U.S. Army Research Laboratory. The authors thank Prof. Peter N. Pintauro of Vanderbilt University for discussion on the electrospun membrane synthesis process.

References

[1] Varcoe J. R and R. C. T. Slade "Prospects for Alkaline Anion-Exchange Membranes in Low Temperature Fuel Cells," *Fuel Cells*, vol. 5, no. 2, pp. 187-200, 2005.

[2] Park A. M., Turley F. E., Wycisk R. J., and P. N. Pintauro, "Electrospun and Cross-Linked Nanofiber Composite Anion Exchange Membranes." *Macromolecules*, vol. 47, pp. 227-235, 2014.

[3] Myles T. D., Grew K. N., Peracchio A. A., and W. K. S. Chiu. "Transient Ion Exchange of Anion Exchange Membranes Exposed to Carbon Dioxide." *J. Power Sources,* vol. 296, pp. 225-236, 2015

[4] Grew K. N., Ren X., and D. Chu, "Effects of Temperature and Carbon Dioxide on Anion Exchange Membrane Conductivity," *Electrochem. Solid St.*, vol. 14, no. 12, pp. B127-B131, 2011.

[5] DeGostin M. B., Peracchio A. A., Myles T. D., Cassenti B. N., and W. K. S. Chiu, "Charge Transport in the Electrospun Nanofiber Composite Membrane's Three-Dimensional Fibrous Structure," *J. Power Sources*, vol. 307, no.1, pp. 538-551, 2016

[6] Matsui Y., Saito M., Tasaka A., and M. Inaba. "Influence of Carbon Dioxide on the Performance of Anion-Exchange Membrane Fuel Cells." *ECS Trans,* vol. 25, pp. 105-110, 2010.

Fuel Cell Powered Small Unmanned Aerial Systems

Deryn Chu, Rongzhong Jiang, Zachary Dunbar, Kyle Grew, and Joshua McClure
U. S. Army Research Laboratory,
2800 Powder Mill Rd., Adelphi, MD 20783-1107
Robert Mantz
U. S. Army Research Office
Research Triangle Park, N.C. 27709-2211
Kevin Chu
U. S. Army CERDEC. CP&I/Power Division
5100 Magazine Rd.
Aberdeen Proving Ground, MD 21005

Summary:
Small unmanned aerial systems (SUASs) have great potential for many different applications [1-4]. The SUASs are light-weight, man-portable, and capable of carrying payloads. SUASs can be broadly classified by their performance characteristics such as engine type, weight, speed, and endurance. Currently, small UASs are powered by lithium-ion or lithium polymer batteries; however, flight endurance is limited and requires frequent battery replacement. Frequent battery replacement is due to low capacity and energy density (less than 200Wh/Kg). Numerous research and development efforts have focused on alternative power sources. These alternative power sources technologies include such as solar cells and hydrogen based polymer electrolyte membrane fuel cells.

Long endurance small UAS flights have been demonstrated through the implementation of a propane fueled solid oxide fuel cell (SOFC) fuel cell system. A propane fueled SOFC stack has been shown to extend mission flight time. The research and development efforts presented here not only apply to small UASs, but also provide potential to the viability of extending mission operations for other unmanned systems applications.

Introduction:

The Army has identified the need for small, man-portable, autonomous and unmanned systems that can perform reconnaissance missions in confined spaces. SUASs have been used by many military forces throughout the world. Based on the National Defense Industrial Association (NDIA) reported, small unmanned systems have rapidly been adopted and adapted to meet requirements for operations in Afghanistan and Iraq during the last decade [5]. Currently, all of the SUASs used in these operations are powered by high power density lithium polymer or lithium-ion battery. The flight endurance is usually limited less than 2 hrs and requires frequent battery changes [less than 200Wh/Kg]. The weight and size of the small UASs are restricted the mounting of extra batteries. Since small UASs are mainly used for intelligence, surveillance, reconnaissance and target acquisition (ISRTA) missions.

Alternative methods to power small UASs that have been reported within the literature have included combinations of batteries with advanced high-efficiency photovoltaics cell (PVC) or high power/energy density fuel cell systems. Unmanned aerial systems have strict specific power and energy requirements. Traditional batteries can have a wide range of specific powers, but have limited specific energy. Therefore, power systems with improved specific energy are required to increase unmanned mission durations. Fuel cells have the promise to achieve all of these goals. Integrating fuel cell power sources offer improved flight endurances which can greatly benefit military units that use small UASs for ISRTA missions. Specifically, the extended on-site mission time can enable a small UAS to monitor targets-of-interest and their movement without losing contact. Further, a reduced number of UAS takeoffs and landings can help minimizing the risk of damages to the small UAS that are associated with hard landings. This translates to lower operational cost and shorter operational turn-around time.

Our research and development efforts are focused on the development of a high power and high energy density fuel cell systems to power unmanned systems. This technology uses a high power density solid oxide fuel cell (SOFC) with a high energy density hydrocarbon fuel (e.g., propane) to achieve a system with the required power density and energy density to extend mission flight duration. Under the Defense Advanced Research Project Agency (DARPA) Tactical Advanced Power Program with technical support from the Army Research Laboratory (ARL), an advanced high energy density and high power density propane fueled SOFC system has been successfully developed and integrated into the Stalker XE unmanned aerial system by Lockheed Martin, Inc. and the UltraElectronics AMI. Furthermore, this system also has been designed to handle environmental and operational stresses, such as a wide range of temperatures, weather, altitudes, vibration, and sudden impacts. However, this paper only reports the performance evaluation of the propane fueled SOFC power source used for UAS propulsion.

Results and Discussions:

Two 300W propane fueled portable solid oxide fuel cell systems have been evaluated at the ARL. The SOFCs are based on the yttria-stabilized zirconia (YSZ) electrolyte. Because SOFC electrolyte materials generally have low ionic conductivity at lower temperatures, SOFCs typically operate in the 800-1000°C range. With these elevated temperatures, SOFCs are offered the advantage of an ability to use carbonaceous fuels. On the other hand, it also introduces problems associated with carbon coking and the creation of a cell structure that involves bonding of the dissimilar ceramic materials. The individual cell's anode, cathode and electrolyte form a composite structure which must be able to survive heating and cooling cycles. This is a severe problem for a small power, portable application such as those being considered here. This problem is less severe for stationary applications where the SOFC system may be kept hot and running indefinitely once it is put into operation. For the two SOFC systems examined for this study, both were manufactured by the UltraElectronics AMI Inc. (Fig 1). One system was evaluated under thermal cycles (on/off) performance and the other system was evaluated under a long term operation performance without any thermal cycles (on/off). The system initial starts up via a BB2590 battery (warm up time ~30 minutes), after which the system provides power to recharge BB-2590 battery. The system power output for first two-to-three hours is lower than ~295W due to this recharging process.

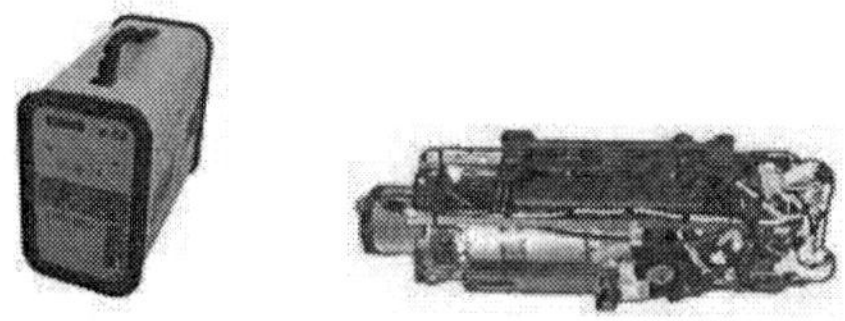

Figure 1. An UltraElectronics AMI 300W portable solid oxide fuel cell system and a 260W solid oxide fuel Cell stack for unmanned aerial system power.

Figure 2 shows the performance results from the thermal cycle study. The system enduring 36 thermal cycles is without any performance degradation. The 37th thermal cycle resulted in a reduced stack voltage, forcing approximately a 10% reduction in power. All tests were performed at constant current (i.e., at an initial load of 9.5A, and then 8.5A following the 37th thermal cycle), using commercial propane from standard 'bbq grill' 15 pound propane containers purchased from a local Home Depot. A sulfur trap (filter) was provided by Ultra Electronics to scrub the sulfur-containing odorant from the propane prior to it being feed to the fuel cell. Sulfur must be removed from the propane or it will poison the reformer and fuel cell catalysts.

The system performance decay from the initial 295 W to 260 W after the 36th thermal cycle may be due to the following possibilities: (1) degradation of the reforming system due to carbon deposition limiting the hydrogen supply, (2) each tubular SOFC cell may experience performance decay due to carbon deposition at the anode electrode, and/or (3) breakage one or several of the tubular cells. Further post-performance analysis will be necessary to uncover the underlying cause of the recognized performance decay.

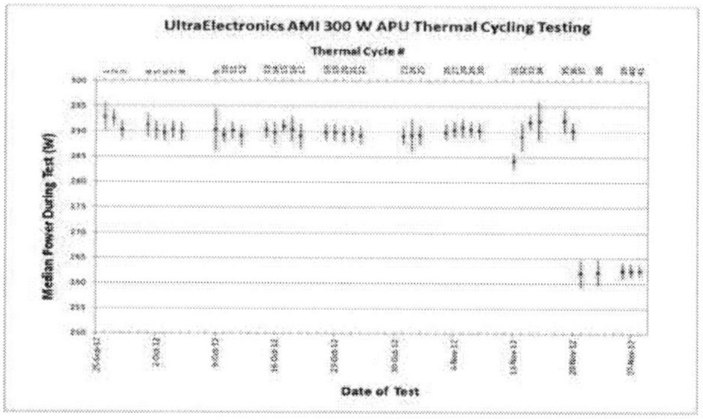

Figure 2. An Ultra Electronics AMI 300W portable solid oxide fuel cell system thermal cycling testing

The evaluation of a SOFC system performance under continuous operation is shown in the Fig. 3. For this test, the system's performance remains very consistent for more than 1,000 hrs. Because the continuous operation system performance met expectation, long term evaluation of performance was stopped. The main issue with maintaining performance during long term operations is the access and use of a quality fuel supply. Although the UltraElectronics systems runs well off of commercial propane, its sulfur trap (filter) has only a 250 hour lifetime (~ 10 day) before it must be replaced. However, it is hot swappable and able to be switched while the fuel cell is in a hot condition and without need to power down the fuel cell. In general, carbon deposition reactions occur more easily/frequently in the propane reforming reactor and in the fuel cell anode during the thermal cycling (from room temperature to solid oxide fuel cell operating temperatures ~800°C). For continuous operation, the carbon deposition reaction is less likely to occur. Both systems performed very well. Further development of this technology into a commercial product will be required and specific improvements in the areas of sulfur tolerant reforming catalysts and fuel cell catalysts (catalyst endurance) are needed. None-the-less, this design approach is an excellent option for meeting the demands of unmanned systems applications.

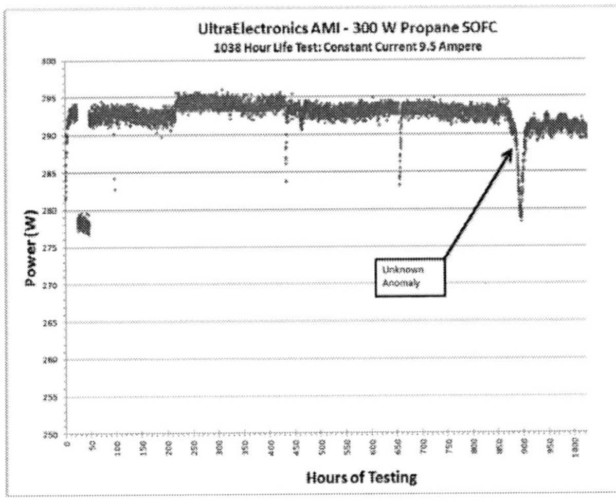

Figure 3. Performance of a 300W portable solid oxide fuel cell system under the continuous operation conditions.

Summary:

We have demonstrated a long endurance flight, small UAS through the implementation of a high energy density and high power density propane fueled SOFC stack. Based on our experience and studies, we recommend that a hybrid power source combining a high energy density device, such as a fuel cell, with a high power density device, such as a Li-ion battery, can provide an optimal power source for various small UASs, unmanned ground systems, and unmanned underwater systems applications. Propane fueled SOFC systems with high specific power and energy density would have direct application across the military in unmanned systems applications that currently rely on various battery technologies.

Acknowledgements: The authors want to thank Department of the Army, the Army Materiel Command and RDECOM for finical support. The program was initiated and funded by the DARPA. Small unmanned Aerials is development by Jennies and Lockheed Martin. Solid oxide fuel cell system is manufactured by UltraElectronics AMI Inc. Dr. Deryn Chu served subject matter expert (SME), contract technical represent (COTR) and Synchronized Pre-deployment & Operational Tracker (SPOT) for the program. Also want to thank Dr. Brian Holloway (the former DARPA Program Manager) for all of the supports.

References:

[1]http://www.youtube.com/watch?v=98BIu9dpwHU

[2]http://www.youtube.com/watch?v=98BIu9dpwHU&feature=player_detailpage

[3]https://www.youtube.com/watch?v=CYT4PFV_Hs

[4]http://www.suasnews.com/2015/03/34801/energyor-demonstrate-fuel-cell-powered - multirotor/

[5]http://www.ndia.org/meetings/5380/Pages/def

Lightweight System Design and Demonstration of a High Reliability, Air Independent, PEMFC Power System for Aerial and Space Applications

Robert Utz, Robert Wynne, Scott Ferguson, Mike Miller, Robert Sievers, & Ying Song

Teledyne Energy Systems
Hunt Valley, MD, USA 21031

Abstract: *Demand has increased in recent years for high reliability mobile power systems for space and aerial vehicles in both military and commercial applications. Batteries have traditionally supplied power in these applications, but the desire to extend mission duration and expand vehicle capabilities requires an increase in energy density that is difficult for batteries to achieve. Teledyne Energy Systems has designed a PEM fuel cell system using passive ejector driven reactant (EDR) circulation, integrated balance of plant, product water separation, and reactant humidification incorporated directly into the stack footprint to provide a solution that is both compact and light.*

This paper reviews subsystem testing of the lightweight PEM fuel cell system. The PEM fuel cell stack testing demonstrated optimum efficiency at 2 kWe of power during standard operation and up to 5 kWe of continuous power. Test status of the passive flow control and water management subsystems will be reviewed. Future work will include completion of subsystem testing, testing of the fully integrated system under expected operating conditions for potential applications of the lightweight PEMFC, and the pursuit of further mass reduction opportunities in the system design.

Keywords: PEM fuel cells; lightweight; unmanned aerial vehicles; hydrogen; launch vehicle; ejectors; passive controls; balance of plant

Introduction

Aerial and space vehicles require dependable and long lasting power sources to complete their intended objectives. Batteries are often chosen for these applications due to high reliability over other available power systems in challenging environments and stressful conditions. Battery designs are limited by the fact that power and energy are coupled. Using a battery for a low power, long duration application would require a significant increase in battery mass to satisfy the mission power profile. This is undesirable for both space and aerial applications due to critical system design constraints that would compromise the capabilities of the vehicles.

Launch Vehicles: Launch vehicle upper stages currently utilize batteries to provide power for controls during the mission. Potential regulations on deorbiting space debris and the desire for longer mission durations to extend capability per launch are driving the demand for more energy than the existing batteries can provide [1]. A PEMFC system could provide power for longer missions in place of existing batteries by drawing on the readily available excess hydrogen and oxygen from the propellant tanks. This minimizes the mass of the PEMFC system design by eliminating the need to include the reactants and storage tanks. Figure 1 depicts how the increase in system mass per unit of energy is much higher for the batteries currently used in the design than for a 1 kW PEM fuel cell system. Work has already begun on developing a PEMFC system for Atlas and Delta launch vehicles that pulls reactants from the preexisting LH2 and LOX tanks for upper stage propulsion and passively manages reactant conditioning, flow control, and system cooling [2].

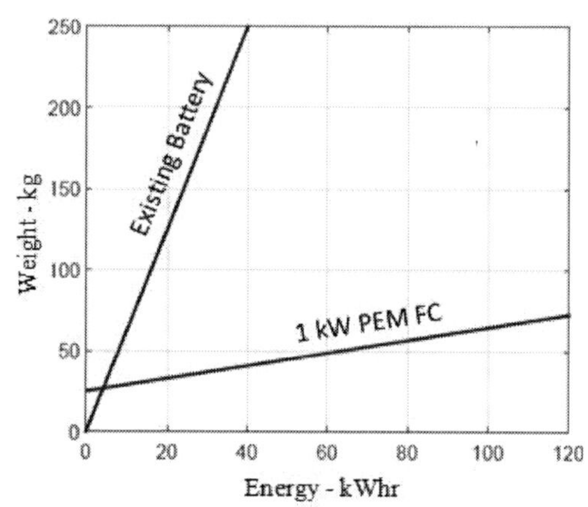

Figure 1: Launch Vehicle Energy Storage Comparison - Existing Battery vs 1 kW PEMFC System

Unmanned Aerial Vehicles: System mass is also a critical factor for unmanned aerial vehicle (UAV) system design. Batteries are frequently chosen as power sources for UAVs and work well for short mission durations. Existing battery technology prohibits the use of these vehicles for long duration (> 1 day) missions due to the mass necessary to meet the energy requirement. A potential approach to solving this problem is a regenerative fuel cell system (RFC), which contains a PEMFC stack, a PEM electrolyzer, and solar panels. During the day, the solar panels provide power to the UAV and to the electrolyzer, which converts water into hydrogen and oxygen for storage in tanks. At night, the hydrogen and oxygen is sent to the PEMFC to produce the power necessary to keep the UAV airborne. The water generated by the PEMFC is reused by the electrolyzer when sunlight is available again. This process could theoretically keep a UAV powered for months at a time without the need for refueling or maintenance. Having this capability would create a wide range of potential long flight time applications for UAVs that are not currently feasible.

Significant interest exists in the marketplace for a low mass energy system that can provide power for long mission durations. Meeting that demand requires deviating from most current PEMFC system designs in which cost and performance hold higher importance. This paper will outline the design approach to satisfy this need, demonstrate system capabilities through testing, and discuss future actions to validate and further improve the system.

Design Approach

A lightweight PEMFC system has been developed through the evolution of a passive integrated balance of plant design. Initial PEMFC system designs generated by Teledyne Energy Systems, Inc. (TESI), like the 117 cell, 12 kW system delivered to NASA Glenn in 2005 under a development program [3], incorporated active pumps for reactant flow control and mechanical means of water separation. Although operationally successful, the use of a large number of components relying on active control methods was seen as a design weakness for the intended application. A desire to increase system reliability and reduce parasitic power losses encouraged the pursuit of a passive balance of plant design. In the following years, TESI worked with NASA Johnson Space Center in making an ejector driven reactant (EDR) design with integrated regulator assembly to control gas flow rates and pressures [5]. The joint TESI-JSC developed integrated BOP and advanced regulator/ejector system lead to a full PEMFC system design and demonstration for an ONR program in 2012 [4] as well as a 22-cell fully integrated R&D demonstration system.

Figure 2: 22-cell Teledyne IRAD Test Asset and Close-up of Integrated Balance of Plant Endplate

Ejectors are desirable for PEMFC systems because they can provide a passive means of recirculating the reactants without excessive parasitic losses and lower reliability from moving parts in pumps. Ejectors can circulate the reactants at high stoichiometric flow rates, which promotes high efficiency and MEA durability, keeps reactant concentration uniform, and optimizes water concentration throughout the stack.

The initial development of the EDR system contained separate subsystems for reactant circulation, water removal, and humidification. Subsequent designs, like the 22-cell IRAD asset pictured in Figure 2, combined the separate subsystems into a single unit integrated within the stack assembly. The water management assembly removes product water and provides humidification to incoming gases in an electrically isolated but physically connected section of the fuel cell stack. This provides a compact system intended to minimize the overall volume of the fuel cell system while increasing reliability.

Figure 2 also shows a close up view of the integrated balance of plant endplate design mentioned above. The instrumentation, controls, and fluid ports are contained in a single structure, minimizing system volume and simplifying connections. The endplate contains multiple ejectors integrated together to expand the allowable power output of the system (in this instance, 700 W to 3 kW).

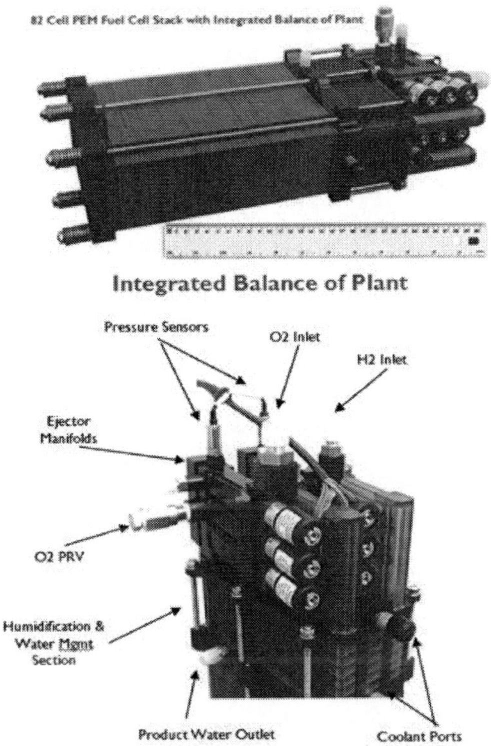

Figure 3: Demonstration model of the lightweight PEMFC system (a) and detailed view of integrated balance of plant (b)

The fully integrated system approach can be optimized for aerial and space applications by minimizing system weight through design modifications and component selection (see Figure 3). The cell active area was reduced and the bipolar plate and manifold designs were changed to decrease unit cell mass. The balance of plant endplate was split into multiple, smaller sections and composed of lighter weight materials where possible. Existing valves, pressure control devices, and pressure sensors were replaced with lower mass options. The end result is a design that maintains the high efficiency and dependable performance of previously demonstrated systems while greatly reducing overall mass.

Qualification & Demonstration Testing

Proving the capabilities of this design requires a full demonstration of a lightweight, fully integrated PEMFC system. Testing was completed or is in progress on individual components and subsystems to confirm expected performance of each segment of the design individually prior to full integration and allow for design adjustments, if needed. The separate subsystems are to be assembled together after independent performance verification of each component. The fully integrated system will be tested through expected demand profiles to demonstrate stable, continuous operation, load following, and high efficiency with minimal performance degradation.

Stack Design/Short Stack: Initial tests were performed on a small scale to characterize MEA behavior so that the full stack could be sized properly. A short stack (2-cell) was assembled using the updated 75cm^2 bipolar plate design and tested to confirm beginning of life performance using our existing MEA technology. The polarization curve shown in Figure 4 demonstrates high efficiency of the MEA in the 75 cm^2 format. Projected to a stack consisting of 112 cells, the performance pictured below would be capable of sustained, long term operation at 1.5 to 2 kW with the ability to produce greater than 5 kW of peak power.

Durability: A durability test at a constant current density of 350 mA/cm^2 was started on the short stack after completion of initial performance testing. After every 70 to 100 hours of operation at nominal conditions, the load was changed to a peak current density of 600 mA/cm^2 and then to a minimum current density of 123 mA/cm^2 for five minutes each. Performance curves and leak checks were performed every 1000 hours to track behavior and check for MEA failure. The test has reached 4500 hours of operation without failure and with minimal performance degradation at the time of publication. Cell voltage stability at constant current over the duration of the test can be seen in Figure 5. This level of durability would satisfy the mission profiles of many expected applications of the system and allow for use over multiple missions without the need to repair or replace the fuel cell stack. The durability test will continue until MEA degradation results in a failure, after which a failure investigation will take place and the degradation rate will be calculated.

Fuel Cell Stack: A stack consisting of 112 cells was built with the MEA and bipolar plate designs used in the short stack testing. The stack was tested independently of the integrated balance of plant and water management sections, shown in Figure 6, using actively controlled humidification, gas flow rate, and water separation. The test was done to verify MEA performance and efficiency

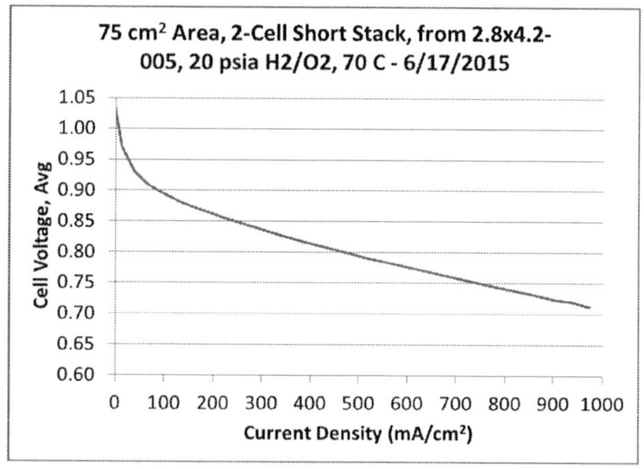

Figure 4: Short Stack Test - 75cm2, 2-cell, 20 psia, H2/O2, 70°C

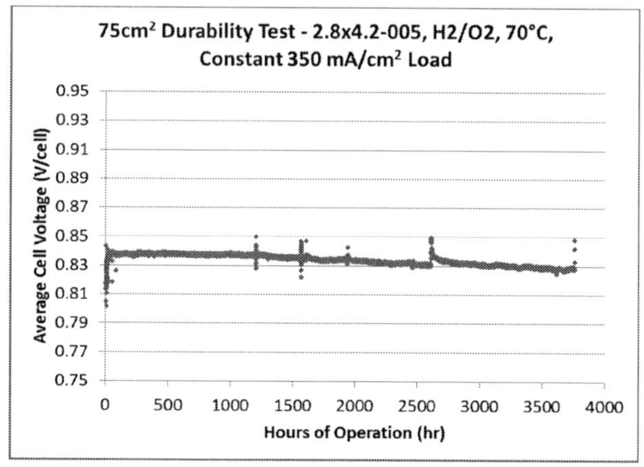

Figure 5: Durability Test - 75cm2, 2-cell, 20 psia, H2/O2, 70°C

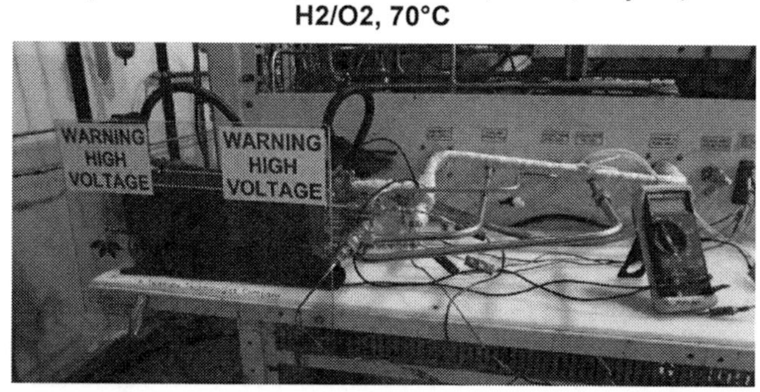

Figure 6: 112 Cell Lightweight Stack - Test Setup

prior to assembling the fully integrated system. A stack polarization curve is shown in Figure 7. The stack demonstrated the ability to produce 2 kW of power at lower current densities favorable for minimizing long term degradation and over 5 kW for short durations of peak power demand.

Ejectors: The ejector configuration was determined through CFD analysis and performance verification using actual expected H_2 and O_2 flow conditions (flow rate and pressure). The ejectors must be able to provide high

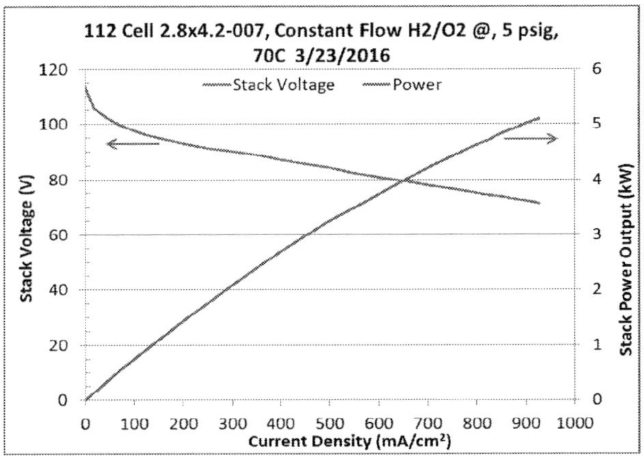

Figure 7: Fuel Cell Stack Testing - 112 cells, 20 psia, H2/O2, 70°C

stoichiometric flow rates over a wide range of operating conditions. The hydrogen and oxygen gas flow manifolds each have a set of 3 ejectors in parallel. The parallel ejectors are sized such that each provides a different flow rate at a common inlet pressure. Using valves to operate individual ejectors at a time or a combination of ejectors in parallel provides the wide range of gas flow rates necessary to maintain optimal stack performance over all power levels between 1 and 5 kW. Testing of the complete set of 3 ejectors each for O_2 flow is complete and has demonstrated the ability to provide stoichiometric flow rates of 2 or greater for all power levels between 1 and 5 kW. H_2 ejector testing has not been completed as of the submittal of this paper.

Figure 8: O2 Ejector Manifold with Passive Pressure Regulator - Test Setup

Water Management: The water management assembly must both remove water produced by the fuel cell and humidify the dry hydrogen and oxygen gas to maximize MEA efficiency. The water separation portion has been assembled and tested, verifying that 100% of the product water can be removed for up to 5 kW of power produced. The dry gas humidification section has not been assembled and tested as of the completion of this paper.

Future Work: Assembly of the integrated system will begin once testing of the H2 ejector manifold and water management sections is complete. Once integrated, the system will be put through a series of potential load profiles under expected operating conditions to test system capabilities. Operation of the previously built and tested 22-cell IRAD asset demonstrated rapid startup, load following, and continuous power for durations of over 300 hours. The lightweight system will be made to demonstrate each of the above scenarios, verifying that expected performance has been maintained in the new, lightweight design.

Conclusion

A lightweight PEMFC system with passive controls for use in space and aerial vehicle applications has been designed and manufactured. Testing at the subsystem level is currently in progress with integrated system testing to follow. Short stack tests demonstrated MEA performance with the new bipolar plate design and showed sufficient durability for expected mission profiles. The ejectors are being tested individually and integrated together to verify that sufficient stoichiometric flow rates can be provided to satisfy all PEMFC power levels. The water management section has demonstrated the ability to separate product water at up to 5 kW and will be tested to demonstrate successful reactant humidification. The fully integrated system will be assembled and subjected to a rapid startup and extended operation under changing load conditions. Future work will include longer duration testing of the integrated system, testing of additional power profiles of expected system applications, and further design refinements to minimize overall system mass.

Acknowledgements

The authors would like to acknowledge the United Launch Alliance for providing input into the system requirements of a lightweight PEMFC system for launch vehicles. The authors would also like to acknowledge the NASA Johnson Space Center for collaboration on the development and testing of the passive EDR design.

References

1. Gravlee, M., Reed, J., Bridges, C. 2014. "Orbital Disposal of Launch Vehicle Upper Stages" AIAA 2014-4343. AIAA SPACE Conference and Exposition 2014.
2. Ferguson, S., Miller, M., Sievers, B., Utz, R., Wynne, B., Reed, J., Kutter, B. 2016. "Fuel Cell Power System Development for LOX/LH$_2$ Upper Stage". IEEE Aerospace Conference 2016.
3. Loyselle, P., Prokopius, K. 2011. "Teledyne Energy Systems, Inc., Proton Exchange Member (PEM) Fuel Cell Engineering Model Powerplant. Test Report: Initial Benchmark Tests in the Original Orientation." NASA/TM-2011-216225. NASA Glenn Research Center, Cleveland, OH.
4. Wynne, B,. Diffenderfer, C., Ferguson, S., Keyser, J., Miller, M., Sievers, B., Ryan, A., Vasquez, A. 2012. "Development of a PEMFC Power System with Integrated Balance of Plant". 2012 Fuel Cell Seminar and Exposition.
5. Vasquez, A., Wynne, B., 2013. "Development of a High Reliability Compact Air Independent PEMFC Power System". 2013 Fuel Cell Seminar and Exposition

Hydrogenation of Carbon Dioxide to Useful Fuels

Terry G. DuBois[1], Michael L. Seibert[1], Richard M. Scenna[1], Deryn Chu[2]
[1]US Army Communications-Electronics Research, Development and Engineering Command (CERDEC)
Aberdeen Proving Ground, MD 21005
[2]US Army Research Laboratory, Adelphi, MD 20783-1138D

Abstract: *The United States Army desires to operate for extended periods of time in austere environments with limited logistics resupply. Fuel constitutes one of the largest logistics items on the battlefield and the Army is actively pursuing advanced, efficient power generating technologies, smart micro-grid power distribution approaches, as well as, load management techniques to reduce fuel consumption. Recent research on the catalytic synthesis of hydrocarbon fuels from carbon dioxide and hydrogen with renewable energy input, often termed "solar fuels", has raised the possibility of producing high value fuels within the military theatre of operation.*

Carbon Dioxide (CO_2) can separated into carbon monoxide (CO), which is a valuable precursor to numerous chemical products by reacting it with hydrogen. If hydrogen is manufactured by splitting water using low- or zero-carbon energy, then CO manufactured from captured CO_2 and water-derived hydrogen via the reverse water-gas-shift reaction (rWGS) would produce a "low carbon liquid fuel" and could eliminate, or reduce the logistic burden associated with JP-8 use in electric power generation on the battlefield. As a potential approach, the US Army Research, Development, and Engineering Command (RDECOM), together with academic partners, are investigating the combination of rWGS and fuel synthesis reactions to produce fuel.

This paper will highlight the development and evaluation of catalysts used to convert CO_2 into CO via the rWGS reaction. Iron and noble metal based catalysts were evaluated and their CO_2 conversion, CO selectivity, and stability will be presented. In addition, process evaluation of a system resulting in methanol/ dimethylether will be discussed.

Keywords: reverse water-gas-shift; hydrogenation; fuel synthesis; hydrocarbons fuels

Introduction

The Army has a critical need to provide the Small Unit the capability to continuously generate power for critical Platoon and Squad level C4ISR equipment for 72 hours or longer while operating as a dispersed and decentralized force in austere environments. Another Army need is to provide this continuous power generation capability without requiring a significant amount of fuel resupply. In order to address this problem, CERDEC is working to develop methods for using natural resources such as CO_2, water and alternative energies (i.e. solar) to produce synthetic hydrocarbon fuels of value to the Army. In this effort, the approach being explored is catalytic conversion of CO_2 to a hydrocarbon fuel using water and solar energy; often termed, solar fuel.

These self-produced fuels can be used as alternative sources for providing continuous power generation for Small Unit portable power systems enabling the Platoon as well as the Squad to operate dismounted in remote areas for multiple days under austere conditions. Moreover, the use of such self-produced fuels enables Net Zero operations not just for the individual Soldier, but for the Squad as well as the Platoon further reducing the Army's burden of relying on fuel resupply, thus saving fuel and potentially Soldiers lives.

The catalytic production of hydrocarbon fuels from CO_2 involves two process steps: (1) separation of CO_2 to CO through the reverse water-gas-shift (rWGS) reaction, and (2) fuel synthesis reaction. The catalytic conversion of carbon dioxide into carbon monoxide through the rWGS reaction (Eqn. 1) is considered one of the most promising routes for the conversion of CO_2 into fuels and chemicals.

$$CO_2 + H_2 \rightarrow CO + H_2O \quad \Delta H_{(298K)} = 41.2\ kJ/mol \quad [1]$$

The reaction is reversible and catalysts that are used for the forward water-gas shift (WGS) reaction are often found to catalyze this reaction as well. However, in contrast to the water gas shift reaction, the rWGS reaction is endothermic and consequently thermodynamics dictates that to achieve high conversions this reaction should be carried out at the highest practical temperature. Because the forward WGS catalysts usually operate at low temperatures, it is often found at high temperatures that the metallic particles of WGS catalysts aggregate and the catalyst rapidly loses activity.

In addition, because the reaction must be carried out at high temperatures, further reduction channels of the carbon monoxide into formaldehyde, methanol and methane can be active on many catalysts reducing the selectivity to the desired product, an issue that is absent when studying the water gas shift reaction. Useful novel catalysts must then be catalytically active, stable in the long term in the reactor and be highly selective to the production of carbon monoxide. Byproduct formation channels (such as methane or methanol) have to be minimized or eliminated.

A number of catalysts have been investigated for the rWGS reaction including Cu/ZnO [1] and Cu-Zn/γ-Al_2O_3 [2], PdZn [3], iron-containing catalysts, and Pt/CeO2 [4], Ni-CeO_2 [5], and others. However, no optimal catalyst has been identified and research is needed to find a material with the right stability and activity to be a practical catalyst.

Studies were conducted to examine the stability of bimetallics under operating conditions. At the same time, an experimental program that utilizes a medium-throughput reactor in combination with a fast micro-GC and mass spectrometry, was implemented to evaluate the proposed catalysts for this reaction. Iron and noble metal based catalysts were identified as promising candidates [6]. These catalysts were evaluated for stability and selectivity using a laboratory microreactor.

This paper presents modeling and experimental results of catalytic approaches to producing hydrocarbon fuels from carbon dioxide and hydrogen. The initial focus is on the first step in the process: reverse water gas shift reactions. Overall, hydrogenation of carbon dioxide can provide insight into challenges and opportunities into the possibility of fuel synthesis on the battlefield.

Experimental Apparatus

Experiments were performed on a two stage micro-reactor (a single reactor stage was used for the work here). A photograph of the micro-reactor is shown in Figure 1 and the process diagram is shown in Figure 2. The test bed consist of automatic high-pressure catalytic reactors which include valves and process layout inside a hot box (furnace). The hot box (SS304, max. temp. 200°C ± 1°C) preheats reactants and avoids the possibility of volatile reactant condensation. The reactor furnace (max. temp. 1100°C ± 1°C) uses radiant heaters for good thermal response and temperature distribution. The tubular reactor (SS316) is 9.1 mm ID by 300 mm length; the isothermal reaction zone (50 mm in length) is located in the middle of the reactor tube, supported on a 20-40 micron plate. Reactor temperature measurement uses a 1.5 mm, stainless steel sheaved, K-type thermocouple located in the reaction zone (without thermo well). Multi-port valves are Valco 6-port/2-position valves. Gas mass flow controllers (2 inlets gases, 1 outlet gas) are Bronkhorst (Hi-Tec, precision 1% FS, repeatability 0.1%). The liquid/gas separator includes a Peltier cooled condenser, separator and level sensor device (± 0.1 mm); with less than 0.5cc dead volume. All reactor data is computer controller and data is recorded at 1 second intervals.

Figure 1. Two stage microreactor

Analysis

Gases (carbon dioxide and hydrogen) were obtained from AirGas with a purity of ultra high purity (Grade 4.5).

The gaseous reformate stream was analyzed by an on-line gas chromatograph (Agilent Technologies, Micro GC 3000) with four columns using thermal conductivity detectors: (i) molecular sieve column (10 m x 0.32 mm), (ii) Plot U column (8 m x 0.32 mm), (iii) alumina column (10 m x 0.32 mm), and (iv) OV1 column (10 m x 0.15 mm x 2.0 μm). Multiple level calibration curves were used for all compounds with the calibration gases at 0.02% analytical tolerance.

For the data presented, fuel conversion is defined as:

$$CO_2 \text{ conversion } (\%) = \frac{(n_{CO_2})_{out}}{(n_{CO_2})_{in}} \cdot 100\%$$

where, n_x is the number of moles of x. The selectivity for carbon monoxide is defined as:

$$CO \text{ selectivity } (\%) = \frac{(n_{CO})_{out}}{\sum (n_C)_{out}} \cdot 100\%$$

Where, $\Sigma(n_c)$ is the sum of moles of all carbon species.

Under all test conditions the carbon balance was in the range of 100% ± 5%.

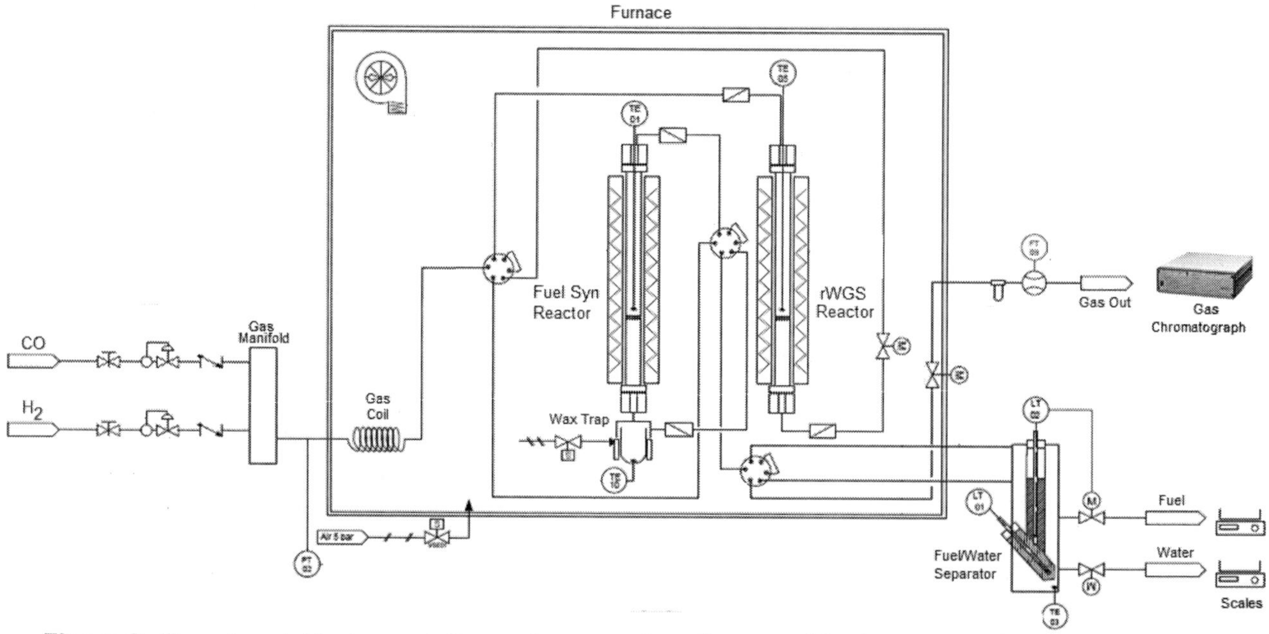

Figure 2. Experimental instrumentation and process flow diagram of the two stage micro-reactor test bed.

Discussion and Results

The rWGS reaction (Eqn.1) is an exothermic, equilibrium limited reaction that exhibits increasing conversion with increasing temperature. However, unwanted side reactions can occur; the Sabatier reaction (Eqn. 2), shown below, represents a common completing reaction.

$$CO_2 + 4H_2 \rightarrow CH_4 + 2H_2O \qquad \Delta H_{(298K)} = 165\, kJ/mol \quad [2]$$

Figure 3 show equilibrium modeling result of the rWGS and the Sabatier reactions. Although the Sabatier appears to be less likely to occur at elevated temperature, chemical kinetics, not shown, are much more favorable as temperatures increase.

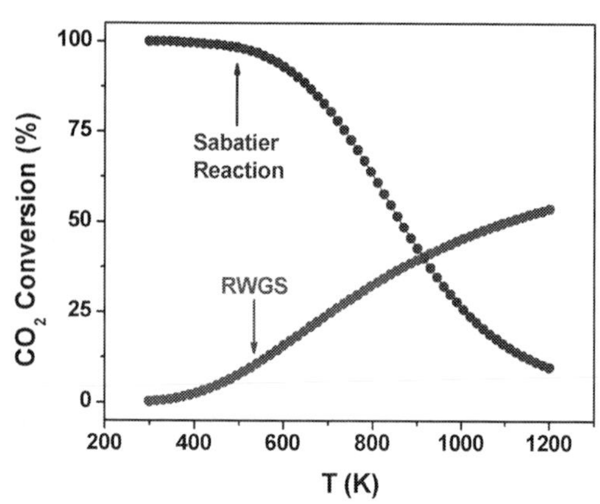

Figure 3. rWGS and Sabatier reactions under equilibrium conditions.

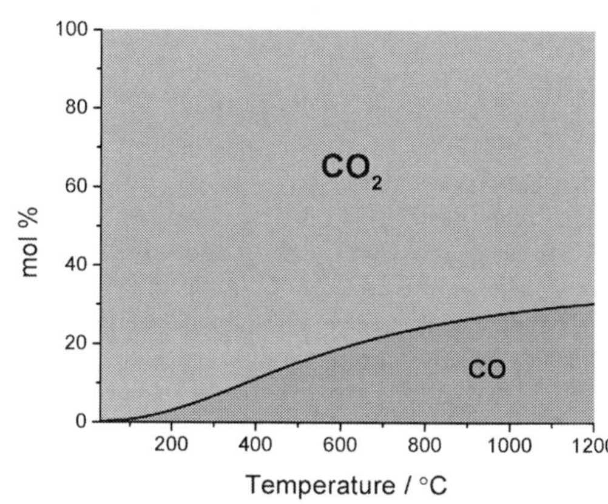

Figure 4. Concentrations of reverse water-gas-shift reaction under equilibrium conditions.

Equilibrium modeling of reverse Water-Gas-Shift: Figure 4 shows equilibrium predicted conversion of carbon dioxide to carbon monoxide as a function of temperature. From the figure, production of carbon monoxide increases with increasing temperature and begins to plateau at approximately 1200 °C; corresponding to a carbon monoxide concentration of approximately 35%. In order to produce carbon monoxide in high concentration, needed for fuel synthesis, a separation process with recirculation or membrane process will likely be needed. In addition, operation at high temperatures as equilibrium would indicate will present challenges with catalysts durability.

rWGS Experimental Evaluation: Figure 5 shows carbon dioxide conversion as a function of reaction temperature for a number of catalysts. The platinum based catalysts performed best achieving on the order of 80% of equilibrium predicted conversion. Noteworthy is that two non-noble metal catalysts (1% Ni/CeO_2 and 5% Fe-2.5% K/Al_2O_3) performed very well, and at temperature above 825 K, performed almost as well as the much more expensive platinum catalysts. Also, when you compare 5% Fe-2.5% K/Al_2O_3 and 5% Fe-1% K/Al_2O_3 the positive influence of potassium as a reaction promoter. Figure 6, shows that most catalysts resulted in high CO selectivity; exceptions were 1% Ni/CeO_2 and 1% $Pt-Ce/ZrO_2$.

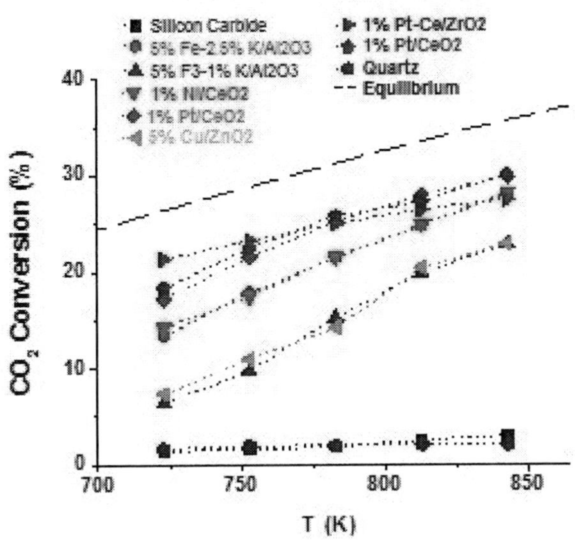

Figure 5. Carbon dioxide conversion under conditions of 180 cm^3/min CO_2 and 157 cm^3/min H_2 with 0.30 g catalyst.

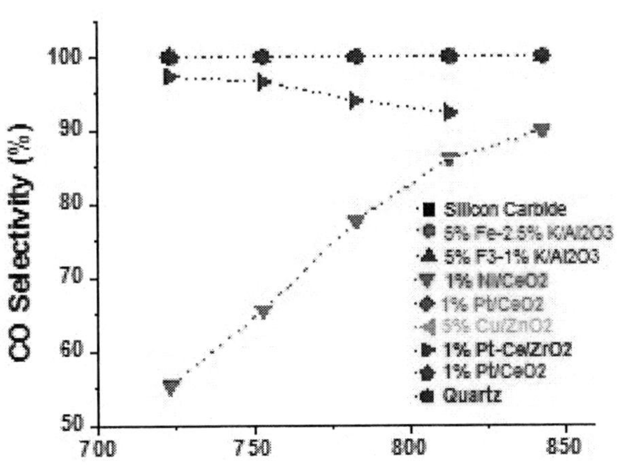

Figure 6. Carbon monoxide selectivity under conditions of 180 cm^3/min CO_2 and 157 cm^3/min H_2 with 0.30 g catalyst.

Summary

A number of catalysts were evaluated to determine their potential in supporting the rWGS reaction. Both noble metal (Pt) and non-noble metals (Fe, Ni) catalysts were evaluated. Although, noble metal catalysts supported the rWGS reaction better at temperatures below 800 K, above this temperature, 1% Ni/CeO_2 and 5% Fe-2.5% K/Al_2O_3 performed equally well and would make a more economical choice. In the future, additional experimental work is needed to investigate catalysts durability.

Acknowledgements

The authors gratefully acknowledge the *US Army Communications-Electronics RDE Center's* support in the form of an In-House Laboratory Independent Research project. Additionally, Prof. Lobo of the Center for Catalytic Science and Technology, University of Delaware and his group supported catalysis development and evaluation.

References

1 Yue L., Qi Fu, Flytzani-Stephanopoulos, M. Low-temperature water-gas-shift reaction over Cu- and Ni-loaded cerium oxide catalysts. *Applied Catalysis B: Environmental*, volume 27, issue 3, 7 August 2000, pp. 179-191.

2 Stone, F.S., Waller, D. Cu-Zn and Cu-ZnO/Al2O3 catalysts for the reverse water-gas-shift reaction. *Topics in Catalysis*, volume 22, issue 3, April 2003, pp. 305-318.

3 Dagle, R. A., Platon, A., Palo, D. R., Datye, A. K., Vohs, J. M., & Wang, Y. PdZnAl Catalysts for the Reactions of Water-Gas-Shift, Methanol Steam Reforming, and Reverse-Water-Gas-Shift. *Applied Catalysis A - General*, volume 342, issue 1-2, June 2008, pp. 63-68.

4 Goguet, A., Meunier, F., Breen, J.P., Burch, R., Petch, M.I., Faur Ghenciu, A. Study of the origin of the deactivation of a Pt/CeO_2 catalyst during reverse water gas shift (RWGS) reaction. *Journal of Catalysts*, volume 226, issue 2, September 2004, pp. 382-392.

5 Wang, L., Zhang, S., Liu, Y. Reverse water gas shift reaction over Co-precipitated Ni-CeO2 catalysts. Journ of Rare Earths, volume 26, issue 1, February 2008, pp. 66-70.

6 Wulfers, M.J., Loiland, J.A., Marinkovic, N.S., Lobo, R.F. Fe/γ-Al2O3 and Fe-K/γ-Al2O3 as reverse water-gas-shift catalysts. *Catalysis Science & Technology*, The Royal Society of Chemistry 2016.

Solid Oxide Fuel Cell Systems for Subkilowatt Power Generation in Expeditionary Manned or Unmanned Environments

Thomas Westrich
USSI

tom.westrich@ultra-ussi.com

Abstract
Individual warfighters require extremely lightweight, quiet, efficient, and reliable power sources for a variety of portable electronics and other applications in the modern battlefield without increasing the logistical burden. A solid oxide fuel cell (SOFC) fueled by JP-8 is considered a potential portable power system at the warfighter, squad, or platoon levels, especially if it meets the requirements of future soldier missions; primarily safety, low weight, high power, and high energy density. The JP-8 logistic fuel currently used in the battle field would be a logical choice as an energy source for SOFC fuel cell applications. However, the heavy hydrocarbons in the logistic fuels have to be converted to hydrogen-rich reformate in order to generate electricity by a SOFC. Additionally, the large sulfur content in logistics fuels places demands on the sulfur tolerance or filtration requirements of the system. Therefore, the SOFC power system should consist of an integrated system for logistic fuel processing and sulfur mitigation with a SOFC. The system integration of fuel processing and sulfur mitigation subsystems with the SOFC subsystem is an important development issue to be addressed, particularly to meet the weight requirements for many power platforms (~25lb for <1kW). No acceptable fuel cell solution has been provided that meets all of these requirements. However, several fuel cell systems have been developed which meet a partial list of requirements. For example, USSI has developed a 350W solid oxide fuel cell that is fueled by commercial propane. This system has a high specific power, and is capable of parallel operation to produce 1.2kW with less than 35lbs of packed weight. To reduce the development lifecycle, USSI is leveraging existing technologies to develop a functional JP-8 power system. This talk will focus on these integration challenges and achievements associated with the development of JP-8 fueled SOFC power system for military use at the squad and platoon level.

Fluoropolymer-Based Anion-Exchange Membranes and Ionomers with Strong Stability and High Performance for Alkaline Membrane Fuel Cells and Metal-Air Batteries

Shaoyi Xu, Shengdong Jiang, Weifan Sang, Yong Gao
Department of Chemistry and Biochemistry
Southern Illinois University
1245 Lincoln Drive, Carbondale, IL 62901
Ph: (618)453-4904; Email: ygao@chem.siu.edu

Rong Jiang
Midwest Energy Group Incorporated
150 E. Pleasant Hill Road
Carbondale, IL 62903

Abstract: Highly chemical stable anion-exchange fluoropolymers were synthesized as solid membranes and liquid ionomers. These materials demonstrated outstanding chemical and thermal stability under harsh alkaline conditions as well as desirable physical and mechanic properties—similar to those of Nafion™.

Keywords: anion-exchange; alkaline; electrolyte; membrane; ionomer; catalyst binder; alkaline membrane; fuel cell; zinc-air battery; fluoropolymer

Introduction

Anion-conductive polymeric electrolytes play significant roles in many electric devices. For example, anion-exchange membranes are utilized in alkaline membrane fuel cells (AMFCs) to separate the fuel of hydrogen or methanol from oxygen and transport hydroxide anions from the cathode side to anode. In AMFCs, ionomers are employed as catalyst binders for balancing the hydrophobicity/hydrophilicity, transporting hydroxide anions and diffusing oxygen in alkaline cathodes. A distinctive advantage of AMFCs over conventional alkaline fuel cells, which utilize a concentrated KOH aqueous solution as an electrolyte, is that AMFCs can have reduced effects from atmospheric CO_2—no K_2CO_3 or Na_2CO_3 precipitate is formed in AMFCs.[1] Anion-conductive polymers can also find applications in a new generation of zinc-air batteries. Solid-state and gel electrolyte membranes have been studied for constructing novel rechargeable zinc-air cells.[2]

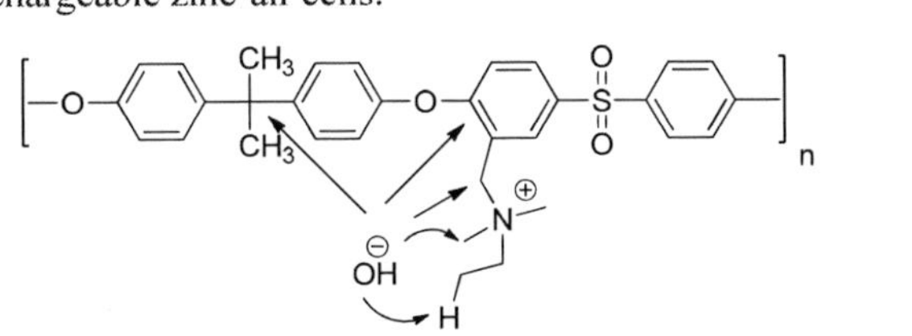

Scheme 1. An example of a polysulfone-based hydrocarbon membrane with a quaternary ammonium that have multiple OH^--labile functionalities—leading to the quick degradation of the membrane under alkaline conditions. Curved arrows show the attacks by the electron pair of OH^-.

Despite the importance of alkaline polymer electrolytes and the significant investments vested by federal funding agencies, limited progress has been made in discovering novel anion-conductive polymers that are suitable for AMFCs. The stability of anion-exchange polymers under harsh alkaline conditions (e.g., pH>14) and the cell operation temperature of ~ 80 °C still remains a bottleneck technology challenge.[1] For example, in scheme 1, a hydroxide anion, which is a potent base and nucleophile, can attack multiple functionalities of a polysulfone polymer via SN2 nucleophilic substitution or Hofmann elimination reactions[3]—leading to the degradation of this hydrocarbon polymer.

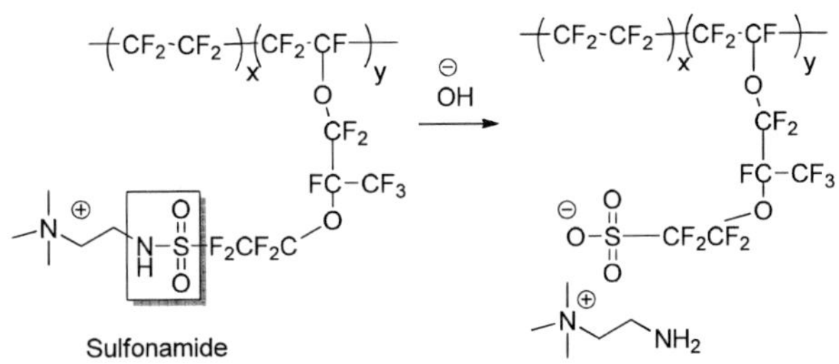

Scheme 2. An example of anion-exchange fluoropolymers that are analogues of Nafion™. Unfortunately, the sulfonamide bond that links a quaternary ammonium group is sensitive to hydrolytic reactions.

It is of interest to note that fluoropolymers such as PTFE and Nafion™ demonstrate superior chemical and thermal stability due to their highly fluorinated structure. Nafion™ has been widely employed as cation-exchange membranes and ionomers in proton-exchange membrane fuel cells (PEMFCs) and electrolyzers. In the past, attempts to synthesize anion-exchange fluoropolymers that are analogues of Nafion™ received limited success. For example, scheme 2 shows that the degradation of a sulfonamide-linked anion-exchange fluoropolymer by a base. The sulfonamide linker is labile to a hydroxide-promoted hydrolytic reaction while its quaternary amine group can also be cleaved by OH^- attacks (not shown in scheme 2). Thereby, the anion-exchange fluoropolymer counterparts of Nafion™, which are stable under harsh alkaline conditions, have not yet been achieved.

In this presentation, we will discuss our synthesis and preliminary evaluation of a group of fluoropolymer-based alkaline electrolytes. A novel free-radical desulfur coupling reaction that was recently discovered by our laboratory[4] has enabled us to graft the terminal of Nafion™ side chains with chemically stable anion-exchange group via a C-C bond. Such fluoropolymers were found to inherit the merits of Nafion™ polymers and many of our prototype electrolytes demonstrated impressive stability against alkaline and thermal degradations.[5,6]

Discussion

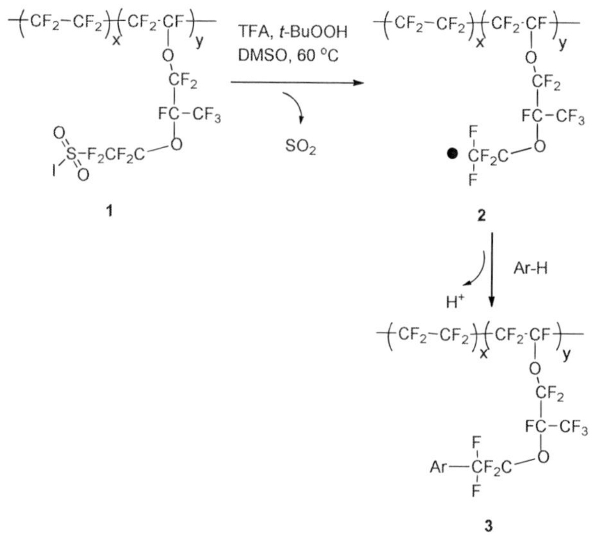

Scheme 3. A free-radical desulfur coupling reaction that was recently discovered by our group for the synthesis of anion-exchange fluoropolymers from the Nafion derivative of **1**. The aromatic or heteroaromatic -Ar group is attached to the polymer side chain via a C-C covalent bond.

Scheme 3 shows that the employment of a free-radical desulfur coupling reaction for grafting an aromatic or a heteroaromatic group of -Ar to the side chains of Nafion™. Fluoropolymer **1** is a sulfonyl iodide analogue of Nafion™, which can be achieved by two steps. The $-SO_2I$ group of **1** is very reactive. Upon the treatment of *t*-BuOOH as a radical initiator, $-SO_2I$ decomposes to yield a free-radical of **2**. SO_2 is the byproduct and the release of SO_2 gas makes this desulfur reaction thermodynamically favorable. This reaction is typically carried out in DMSO at 60-80 °C while trifluoroacetic acid (TFA) is used to facilitate the desulfur process. The free radical of **2** then attacks Ar-H to discharge H^+ and form a C-C covalent bond between the -Ar group and the side chain of **3**. It is noteworthy that unlike the sulfonamide in scheme 2, such a C-C covalent linker in **3** is resistant to hydroxide attacks—rendering the high chemical and thermal stability of fluoropolymer **3**.

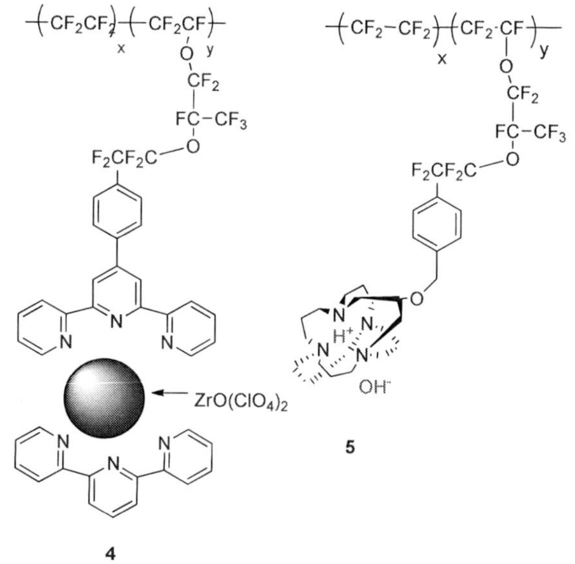

Figure 1. Fluoropolymer-based anion-exchange membranes: zirconium oxide (**4**) and proton cage (**5**) as anion-conductive groups.

Such a free-radical desulfur coupling reaction has been employed by our laboratory for the synthesis of a group of fluoropolymer-based anion-exchange electrolytes. Figure 1 shows a zirconium oxide nanocluster-doped composite membrane of **4**[5] and a fluoropolymer of **5** with proton cage as the anion-exchange group.[6] In **4**, the heteroaromatic ligand of phenyl-2,2':6',2"-terpyridine (PhTPY) is covalently linked to the side chain of the fluoropolymer via a C-C bond while in **5**, the proton cage is attached to the polymer side chain through a covalently bonded 1,4-phenylene group. Polymer **4** has in-plane ionic conductivity at 10.5 mS/cm at 25 °C and 29.9 mS/cm at 60 °C in de-ionized water. A Volhard titration test was carried out and membrane **4** was confirmed as an anion conductive material with an anion-exchange capacity (IEC) of 0.76 meq./g. At 25 °C, membrane **5** has an in-plane ionic conductivity of 9.1 mS/cm while at 60 °C, its ionic conductivity is increased to 20.2 mS/cm. The conductivity tests were carried out via a four-electrode method with a test sample immersed in de-ionized water.

It is well known that the ionic conductivities of alkaline membranes are generally lower than those of cation-conductive polymer membranes due to the mobility difference of a proton cation and a hydroxide anion. Commercial anion-conductive FAA HEM has an ambient-temperature conductivity of 17 mS/cm; A3 Ver2 was reported to be 2.6 mS/cm while AS-4 was found to be 13 mS/cm.[7] Some highly anion-conductive membranes were recently reported in literatures, but all these membranes are comprised of hydrocarbon polymers. In general, the long-term stability of hydrocarbon polymers under very strong alkaline conditions has not yet been demonstrated.[1]

Membrane **4** is comprised of poly(PhTPY), 2,2':6',2"-terpyridine, and $ZrO(ClO4)_2$. The heteroaromatic groups of PhTPY and terpyridine encapsulate and protect $ZrO(ClO_4)_2$ nanoclusters. Zirconium oxide is a known Lewis acid that has affinity towards a Lewis base. Hydroxide anions are transiently "bonded" to the acidic sites of $ZrO(ClO_4)_2$ nanoclusters and zirconium oxide serves as anion-exchange group for facilitating OH^- migration. The surface of a $ZrO(ClO_4)_2$ nanocluster can provide anchorage sites for transporting OH^- anions, which renders zirconium oxide as an anion-exchange group in membrane **4**. In polymer **5**, a proton cage[8] encompasses and protects a proton (H^+) cation. Hydroxide (OH^-) anions are loosely attracted by the cage but they can migrate from one cage site to another—leading to the hydroxide conductivity. H^+ forms weak hydrogen bonds with four surrounding nitrogen atoms of the cage—which reduces the positive charge density on each nitrogen atom—making the cage and H^+ less attractive for OH^- to attack. Such caged H^+ structures were known to withstand very harsh alkali conditions.[8] Membrane **5** has a thickness of 60 μm, which is compatible to commercial cation-exchange membrane Nafion™ NRE-212. The thickness of membranes can be easily varied by adjusting the amount of fluoropolymer casted in the dish. The ion-exchange capacity (IEC) of membrane **5** was found to be 0.88 mmol/g.

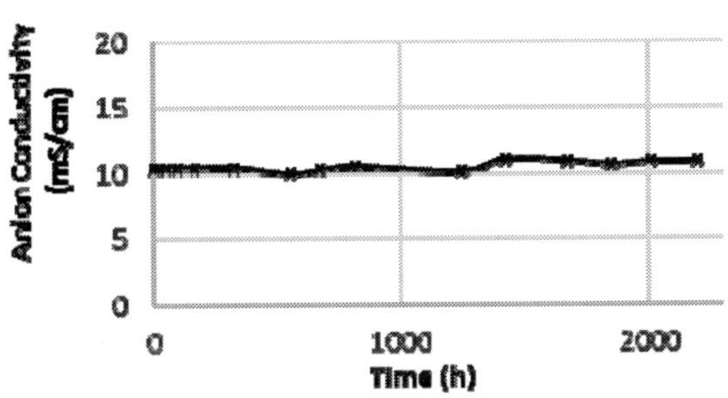

Figure 2. The ionic conductivity of membrane **4** at 25 °C in de-ionized water after the membrane was subjected to a 7 M KOH solution of 15% EtOH/85% H_2O at 120 °C for various time periods.

The chemical stability of membrane **4** was examined by a hydrolytic degradation test, in which the membrane was boiled in a 7 M KOH solution of 15% EtOH/85% H_2O at 120 °C in a reactor for 2,200 h. At a fixed time interval, the membrane was taken out, washed with de-ionized water and boiled in de-ionized water for 1 h prior to an ionic conductivity test (de-ionized water, 25 °C). Membrane **4** was found to show no loss of its conductivity after 2,200 h (> 3 months) (Figure 2). The mechanic properties of membrane 4 are also compared with those of N-115 (Table 1). The tensile strength and elongation at break properties of membrane **4** are compatible to those of N-115.

Table 1 Comparison of physical properties of membrane **4** and N-115.

	Membrane 4	N-115
Thickness (μm)	98	127
IEC (mmol/g)	0.76	0.90
Water Uptake (wt%)	20.5	38
Tensile Strength-MD, at Max Load (MPa)	4.1	4.9
Elongation at Break (%)	146	200

In summary, fluoropolymer-based alkaline membranes and ionomers were synthesized via a novel free-radical desulfur coupling reaction. The linker that tethers a polymer side chain and an anion-exchange group is comprised of a C-C covalent bond that is stable against hydroxide attacks and thermal degradation. Our fluoropolymers demonstrated high chemical stability—showing no sign of decomposition in a 7 M KOH solution at 120 °C for over 3 months—unprecedented in literatures. Continued work is currently carried out in the laboratory to further improve the anion conductivity of fluoropolymeric electrolytes and tailor their structures to meet the specific requirements for the applications of AMFCs, bipolar fuel cells, electrolyzers and zinc-air batteries.

Acknowledgements

This work in part was supported by the Department of Chemistry and Biochemistry at Southern Illinois University Carbondale.

References

1. J. R. Varcoe, P. Atanassov, D. R. Dekel, A. M. Herring, M. A. Hickner, P. A. Kohl, A. R. Kucernak, W. E. Mustain, K. Nijmeijer, K. Scott, T. Xu, and L. Zhuang, "Anion-Exchange Membranes in Electrochemical Energy Systems", *Energy Environ. Sci.*, 7, 3135-3191 (2014).
2. J. Fu, J. Zhang, X. Song, H. Zarrin, X. Tian, J. Qiao, L. Rasen, K. Li, Z. Chen, "A Flexible Solid-State Electrolyte for Wide-Scale Integration of Rechargeable Zinc-Air Batteries", *Energy Environ. Sci.*, 9, 663-670 (2016).
3. C. G. Arges, and V. Ramani, "Two-dimensional NMR spectroscopy reveals cation-triggered backbone degradation in polysulfone-based anion exchange membranes", *Proc. Natl. Acad. Sci USA*, 110, 2490-2495 (2013)
4. S. Xu, R. Jiang, and Y. Gao, "Synthesis and Performance Comparison of Perfluorobenzoic Acid and Perfluorobenzenesulfonic Acid Membranes", *J. Membr. Sci.*, 507, 63-71 (2016).

5. S. Xu, R. Jiang, S. Jiang, and Y. Gao, "Anion-Conductive Perfluoroheteroaromatic Composite Membranes: High Chemical Stability under Strong Alkaline Conditions", *J. Electrochem. Soc.*, 163, F688-F690 (2016).

6. S. Xu, R. Jiang, and Y. Gao, "Proton and Metal Cage-Based Anion-Conductive Fluoropolymers for AMFCs", Xu, S.; Jiang, R.; Gao, Y., *ECS Trans.*, 69, 391-402 (2015).

7. H. Yanagi, and K. Fukuta, "Anion Exchange Membrane and Ionomer for Alkaline Membrane Fuel Cells (AMFCs), *ECS Trans.*, 16 (2), 257-262 (2008).

8. M. Y. Redko, M. Vlassa, J. E. Jackson, A. W. Misolek, R. H. Huang, J. L. Dye, "'Inverse Sodium Hydride': A Crystalline Salt that Contains H^+ and Na^- ", *J. Am. Chem. Soc.*,124, 5928-5929 (2002).

The Usage of Alternative Energy in Naval Forces

Şenol Kirimli
kirimlisenol@gmail.com

Abstract
Operational Energy (OE) is the energy needed for exercising, acting, and sustaining armed forces and weapons platforms for military operations, and consists energy used by naval platforms, warplanes, combat systems, and tactical energy systems. Energy is a fundamental enabler of military operations for long. Energy, mostly petroleum is a prerequisite for military power. Today, The ability to deliver operational energy to where and when it's needed is at enhancing risk. For instance, the difficulty of moving energy across the last tactical mile of resupply, in the face of improvised explosive devices, irregular adversaries, and insurgent attacks will remain a part of the operational environment. Likewise, ability to project and sustain power in the operation area will be challenged by anti-access, area-denial (A2/AD) weapons able to target combat and logistics forces with long-range precision. The achievement of military operations depends on one fundamental resource: energy. The Navy objectives include increasing energy security and enhancing warfighter capabilities through the implementation of renewable energy. The Navy's energy goals should include: energy efficient acquisition, reduction of petroleum use, production of clean energy installations on shore. The navy should have more eco-warships and airplanes in addition to harness alternative energy. This study focused on navy's strategies how to install alternative energy resources.

Standard Architecture for Soldier Power System

Jasper Groenewegen[1], Norbert Haerle[2], Rianne 't Hoen[1], Mario Sonka[2], Fabrizio Parmeggiani[3], Matteo Sedehi[3], Carsten Cremers[4], Sophie Weixler[4]

[1] DNV GL, Utrechtseweg 310, 6812 AR Arnhem, the Netherlands
[2] Rheinmetall Defence Electronics GmbH, Brüggeweg 54, 28309 Bremen, Germany
[3] Larimart, V. di Torrevecchia 12, 00168 Rome, Italy
[4] Fraunhofer ICT, Joseph-von-Fraunhofer-Str. 7, 76327 Pfinztal, Germany

Abstract: *The European Defence Agency facilitates the development of a Standard Architecture for Soldier Systems (STASS). As a first step, a consortium consisting of Rheinmetall Defence Electronics, Larimart, Fraunhofer ICT and DNV GL is tasked to develop the soldier power system (SPS). The SPS will represent a comprehensive architecture for the power aspect of soldier systems. The purpose of this architecture is to promote interoperability and interchangeability for national dismounted soldier programs both at system and component level. The SPS will help to minimize physical, operational and cognitive burden of the soldier, stimulate continuous improvement of components and reduce costs.*

The SPS is a modular system starting with the core configuration for core devices and can be extended with connections to medium power group devices. A central rechargeable battery and the interface with power sources make it possible to organize the power consumption as flexible, lightweight and efficient as possible, without compromising on energy reliability.

The operational, system and technical architectural views on the soldier architecture will be presented. The type, task and length of a mission, as defined in the operational view, determine the energy need of a squad. The system view presents the modular STASS tailored for the three operational scenario's (low, medium and high activity intensity). The future technical view will describe the interfaces requirements to achieve an integrated squad power system and minimize the burden for the warfighter.

Keywords: Soldier Power System, modular soldier system, Standard Architecture for Soldier Systems.

Introduction

The European Defence Agency facilitates the development of a Standard Architecture for Soldier Systems (STASS). As a first step, a consortium consisting of Rheinmetall Defence Electronics, Larimart, Fraunhofer ICT and DNV GL is tasked to develop a standard architecture for the soldier power system (SPS). The SPS will represent a comprehensive architecture for the power aspect of soldier systems. The purpose of this architecture is to promote interoperability and interchangeability for national dismounted soldier programmes both at system and component level. The soldier power architecture will help to minimize physical, operational and cognitive burden of the soldier, stimulate continuous improvement of components and reduce costs.

The ambition of the soldier power architecture is to provide interfaces that comply with publically available open standards. The possibility for modular components to connect to the system via these interfaces promotes third party competition and makes it possible to connect COTS to the system. This will promote innovation, diversity and reduce the costs of an integrated soldier power system.

The soldier power architecture will provide guidelines on which devices are relevant to connect to the SPS and characteristics on the external power sources (EPS) that can provide energy to the SPS. By focusing on the interface between the SPS and these devices/ EPS, the soldier power architecture allows freedom for national choices within the core of the system, such as whether to connect the helmet with the vest using cable, wireless connection or no connection at all. Thus, the design of the core system of the SPS is a national concern, while the soldier power architecture focusses on the connection with devices and external power sources.

System architecture

The system architecture defines the power system on the squad level, since power sources within a squad are shared between soldiers. Also, depending on the weight that each soldier carries, spare batteries are distributed over the soldiers within a squad. The main aim for the system architecture is to minimize the number of types of batteries used in the squad and to make smart charging of these batteries possible. Minimization of the number of battery types is considered to be the primary solution for weight reduction as the risk of empty batteries is then addressed on a system level instead of an individual component level (3 spare batteries per system instead of for each piece of kit).

Squad Energy System: The squad energy system (Figure 1) consists of all power sources, energy storage and power consumers. These devices can be distributed in the following groups:

- External power sources (EPS); the EPS are the energy suppliers of the squad.
- Low power consumers (LPC); the LPC use less than 2.5 W per device and have stand-alone energy supply.

- High power consumers (HPC); the HPC use more than 15 W per devices and have stand-alone energy supply.
- Soldier power system (SPS); the SPS consists of the medium power consumers (MPC, 2.5 – 15 W) that are powered by a common energy source: the central rechargeable battery (CRB).
- Bulk charger (BC); the BC can connect to the EPS and charge the batteries in the squad energy system.

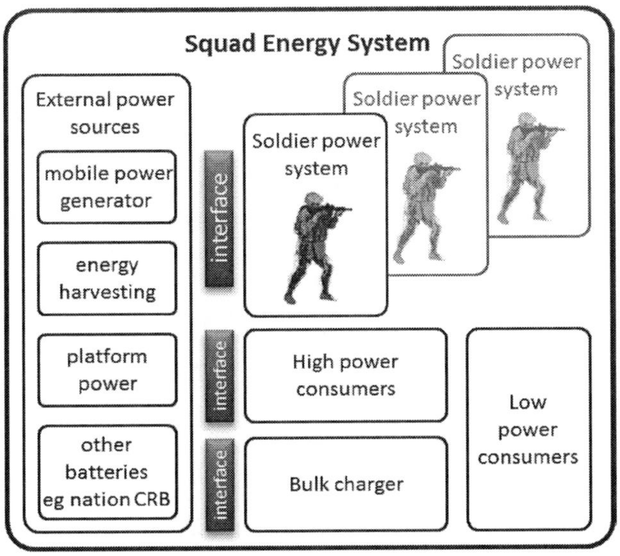

Figure 1. Squad Energy System

External power sources: The external power sources can be divided in four groups: mobile power generators (MPG), energy harvesting (EH), platform power (PP) and battery supply (BS). The MPG converts high energy density fuel into electrical energy, and therefore provides controllable power (for most efficient use). An EH converts renewable energy into electrical energy and provides erratic intermittent dirty power. PP is the use of power from a platform, such as a vehicle or helicopter. This can be either via direct link with constant conditioned power supply, or the resupply of batteries/ fuel. Central rechargeable batteries of another type or batteries that are bought locally form the fourth group. The BS can cope with a dynamic power load. Table 1 shows examples of power sources in each group and the categories that can be distinguished with corresponding characteristics.

Low power consumers: The low power devices will have a dedicated battery and will not be connected to the core system. Additional connection (cabling) adds more constrictions and weight than what would be saved by having a common energy source. Ideally, to minimize the logistic burden, only one type of low power battery is used. This limits the number of types and as such the total amount of spare batteries carried on a mission.

High power consumers: Connection of the high power devices to the central power system endangers the power security because of the possible large power draw. Also, since a HPC typically uses more than one battery during a mission, there is no advantage by using a common energy source. Therefore, the high power devices will be operated with a stand-alone power supply. Ideally, to minimize the logistic burden and increase flexibility, the same battery as the CRB in the soldier power system will be chosen. A direct link with an EPS (MPG or EH) for a hybrid power source could further minimize the weight burden of a HPC.

Table 1. External power sources

Type	Example	Category	Characteristics
MPG	Multi-fuel gen Fuel cell Diesel TEG	Small	Mobile Integrated hybrid power source SMbus protocol
		Medium	Mobile Autonomous charger SMbus protocol
		Large	Stationary AC/DC Connect to charger
EH	Solar Wind	Mobile	Connected to torso Intermittent power
	Knee generator EH backpack	Stationary	Connected to charger Intermittent power
PP	Vehicle Helicopter	Direct link	During transport
		Resupply batteries/fuel	Exchange batteries
BS	Local batteries CRB from other nations	Mobile	Exchange batteries Charging of batteries Provide dynamic load

Bulk Charger: The bulk charger interfaces with the external power sources and provides recharge capability for the CRBs. The SMBus protocol allows smart battery charging and prevents overcharging. The power conversion and conditioning functionalities are in the charger.

Soldier Power System

The SPS is a modular system starting with the core configuration for standard devices and can be extended with connections to medium power devices. A central rechargeable battery and the interface with power sources make it possible to organize the power consumption as flexible, lightweight and efficient as possible, without compromising on energy reliability.

Table 2. Characteristics of the energy consuming devices.

Type	Example	Characteristics
HPCiso	Counter-IED device	> 15 W Stand-alone power
HPCdata	Long range radio	> 15 W Data connection
MPCe	Intra-squad radio	2,5 – 15 W Ethernet connection
MPCu	Night Vision Goggle	2,5 – 15 W USB connection
LPCu	GPS	< 2,5 W USB connection
LPCiso	Flash light Aim point	< 2,5 W Stand-alone power

The SPS distinguishes standard devices and group devices. Standard devices are carried by every soldier in the squad and consist of an intra-squad radio for voice and position exchange, but also GPS and flash light. Group devices are only used by specific roles, such as commander display, long range radio and electronic counter measures.

An overview of the type of devices is given in Table 2. The devices are categorized by power consumption and data type. Medium power consumers can have a USB or ethernet data protocol. High power consumer might be connected to the SPS for data exchange, but have to be limited in power draw. Low power consumers that are connected to the core system for data sharing might as well use the central energy source to be powered.

The core configuration of the SPS consists of central power distribution, information and control (CP_{DIC}) that redistributes the energy available from the CRB and power sources, if connected, to the power consuming devices (Figure 2). The CP_{DIC} is a nation specific design: the power for the devices is provided by the CRB, which is charged by the power sources or the energy for the devices comes directly from the power source, while excess power is used to charge the CRB. SMBus protocol makes smart charging possible. Energy security can be provided by implementing a hold-up battery that can be charged via the CP_{DIC} in all power consumers or having a second CRB.

Sources that provide power can be 'clean', e.g. fuel cell or batteries, or 'dirty', e.g. solar energy or a vehicle. 'Clean' means that the power source shows a very limited level of spikes, ripple and noise within a defined voltage range (e.g. 8–18 V). Simple conditioning without particular filtering is sufficient to prevent damage to CRB or devices. 'Dirty' sources show a high level of spikes, ripple, noise and a wide voltage range (e.g. 8–36 V), which requires more complex filtering and power conditioning.

The external power adapter (EPA) converts 'dirty' power sources into 'clean' power. The EPA limits for example the current, to prevent damage. A data protocol sets the voltage to a standard level unless otherwise specified. The USB devices are set at 5 V, the ethernet between 8–18 V.

Within the soldier power system a number of subsystems can be distinguished as shown in Figure 3. The central subsystem is the vest with one or two CRBs. Depending on the national choice the helmet and weapon subsystems can be connected via a cable, wireless or can be stand-alone. The external power sources can be connected via direct link or used to charge the batteries. The backpack is a carrier system for devices and power sources. Using a power manager for distribution, information and control (DIC) batteries can be recharged or power can directly be used via a connection to the vest.

The weapon and helmet subsystems (Figure 4) can be a platform on their own with a dedicated central power source, typically smaller than the CRB. The advantage is that the separate devices can be powered centrally, which saves switching batteries of the devices one by one. Devices can be connected to the weapon subsystem using the physical interface as described in STANAG 4694 [1]. However, no technology standard describing the power and data transfer through this interface exists. This is a technology gap, we emphasize that this standard should be developed.

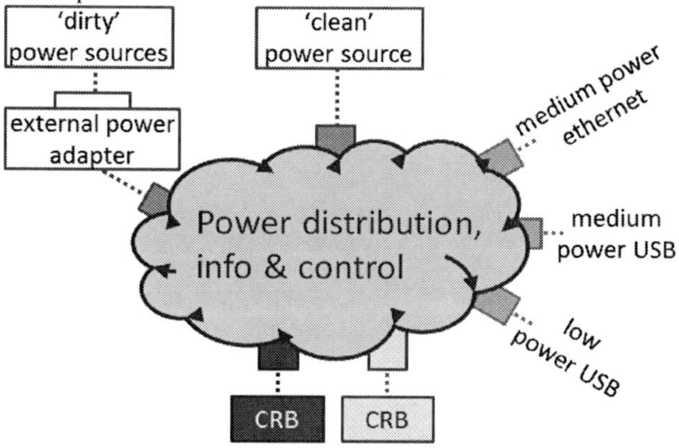

Figure 2. The power distribution, information and control within the soldier power system and with CRB are a national design choice. This $power_{DIC}$ cloud can be connected to external power sources (red) and devices (green).

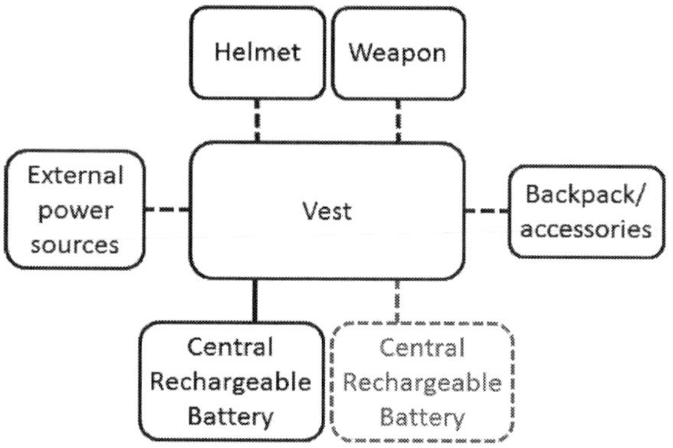

Figure 3. The subsystems within the soldier power system.

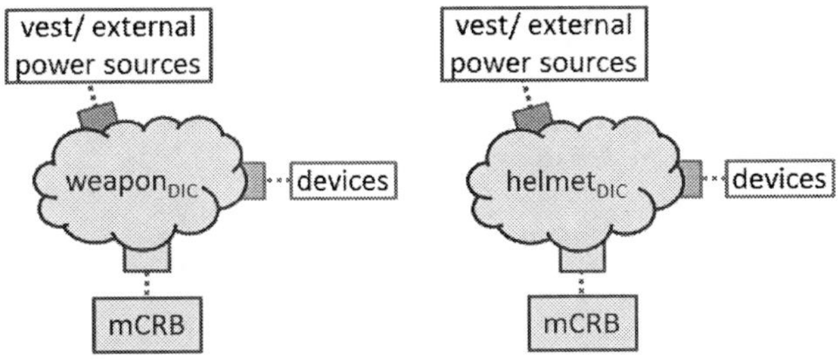

Figure 4. Schematic drawings of the weapon and helmet subsystems. The interface between the weapon devices and the weapon$_{DIC}$ is described in the STANAG 4694 (powered rail). No standard for the helmet interface exist.

Table 3. Summary of the characteristics of the low, medium and high intensity activities.

State of alertness	Low	Medium	High
Activity examples	Transporting Resting Safeguarding	Marching Patrolling	Assault Combat
Time duration	4 – 12 h	4 – 8 h	2 – 4 h
Movement	none/ low	medium	high
Cognitive burden	low	medium	high
Back pack	none/ light	medium/ heavy	light

Operational view

The type, task and length of a mission determine the total energy need of a squad. Three states of alertness's can be distinguished: low, medium and high. Their characteristics are described in Table 3. These states determine the power availability and recharge capability by means of mobile power generation, energy harvesting or direct link to platform power. For example, in the medium state, the soldier is in motion so may use kinetic energy harvesting or a fuel cell in his backpack. An example of the soldier power system configuration possible in the medium state is shown in Figure 5.

Conclusion

Minimization of the number of battery types is considered to be the primary solution for weight reduction as the risk of empty batteries is then addressed on a system level instead of an individual component level.

The STASS power architecture is a modular system defining types of external power sources and categories of power consumers. It acknowledges national core systems and identifies the interfaces to standardize on. Standard interfaces stimulate third party competition and makes it possible to connect COTS/MOTS devices to the system, which will promote innovation, diversity and reduce the costs of an integrated soldier system.

The EDA project will publish its full report by the end of 2016, providing a detailed description on the standard power interfaces for sources and consumers identified.

References

1. STANAG 4694, Accessory Rail, NATO, approved by LCG-DSS 8 May 2009.

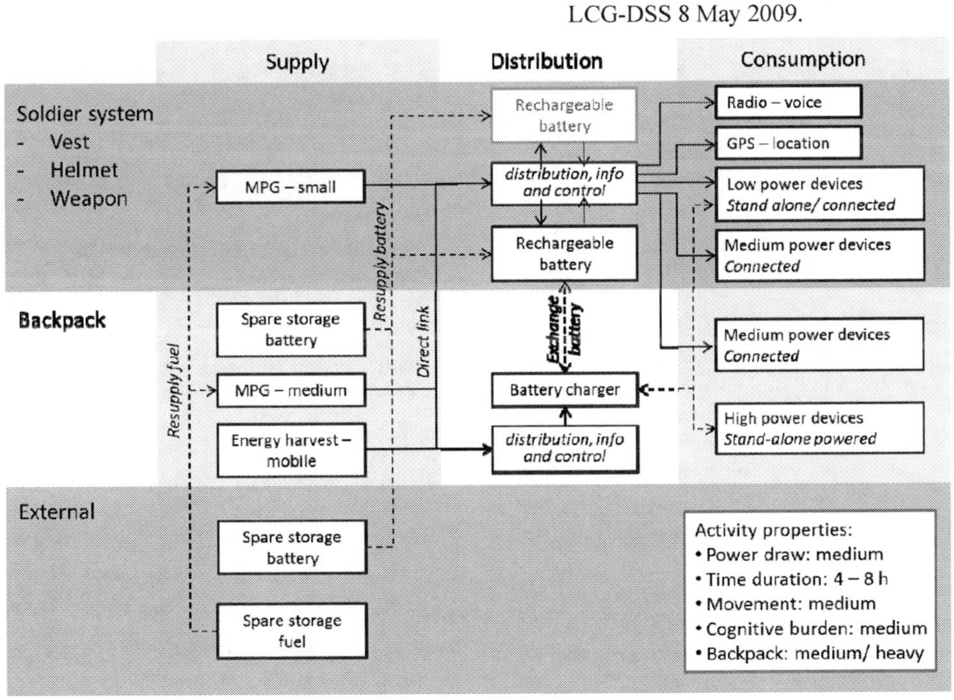

Figure 5. Soldier power architecture for activities with medium state of alertness

Power Sources for Dismounted Soldier Systems

Christopher John Ford[1], Robert James Luxton[2] and Jamie Francis Sheerin[3]
[1-3]QinetiQ Ltd. Batteries, Cables and Connectors, Fort Halstead, Building Q8, Sevenoaks, Kent UK TN14 7BP
[1]cford@QinetiQ.com, [2]rjluxton@QinetiQ.com, [3]jfsheerin@QinetiQ.com

Abstract: *This paper presents the assessment of candidate centralized power sources for Dismounted Soldier Systems (DSS). It tracks the project from definition of a mission profile based upon data for specific roles within a Squad to determine the performance and define the quantity, weight and volume for a range of mission durations based upon the characterization of each power source. We established the capability and performance of a hybrid system using an established fuel cell to recharge on manoeuvres. Using a sophisticated excel model we have been able to predict the consumption of power sources to determine swap outs for a specific mission and applied State of Health factors to illustrate the impact of using aged batteries. In our analysis we have been able to model the behavior of power source consumption under a variety of scenarios. We also concluded that there is work to be done to standardize the requirements for a DSS centralized power source.*

Keywords: Dismounted Soldier Systems; Power Sources;

Introduction

The demand for portable power for Dismounted Soldier Systems (DSS) is continually increasing. To provide the necessary capability for independent ISTAR (information-surveillance-target-acquisition-reconnaissance) operation, which utilises a growing portfolio of electronic tools the requirement for robust, uninterrupted power is ever increasing.

Recent assessments have shown that a soldier needs some 70 batteries of 7 different types weighing 7.2kg for a 72-hour mission.

The individual power for such devices ranges from 60μW for spotting sights to 120W for thermal imaging. With the advent of personal computers and the capability to stream video the power demands will increase further.

Under recent NATO Science and Technology (SET206) activities studies have been undertaken into manwearable power. The author has led a working group investigating the issues associated with these programmes and will provide a summary of the activity in this presentation.

Definition of the range of loads used for DSS established from 3 User communities

We established the specific power consumption from three reference papers [1, 2 and 3], which determined the load for the roles. This was applied to a range of rechargeable power sources (Figure 1) and using the individual characteristics we could then define the quantity, weight and volume for each mission. The characterisation loads were as follows:

- 2W continuous (UK Riflemen x 3 roles);
- 5W continuous (for information only);
- 10W continuous (US Team Leader / US Riflemen / UK Section Commander & 2IC also Norwegian Normal Soldier);
- 20W continuous (US Squad Leader / Norwegian High Power Soldier).
- Composite load 10W background with superimposed 30W pulses (40W total) applied for 1 minute in each 30-minute period during discharge (for information only).

Application of the load to a range of secondary batteries and fuel cells for a centralised power source

The range of candidate power sources comprised both primary and secondary systems; however the primary systems were discounted, for logistical reasons. The compliment of rechargeable power sources are shown in Figure 1.

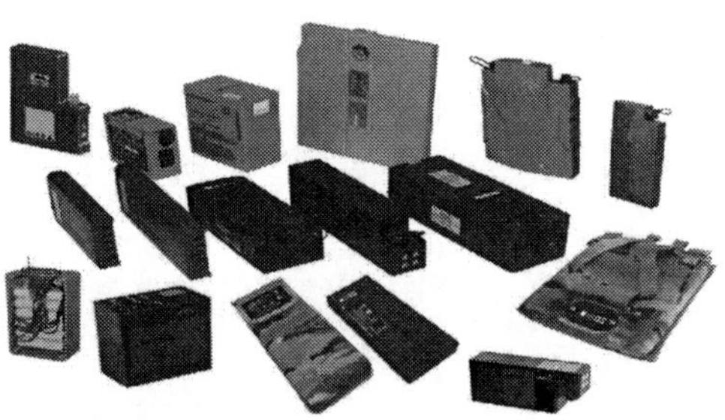

Figure 1: The range of candidate DSS power sources.

Characterising the range of power sources enabled us to determine the run time (h) and the specific energy (Wh/kg) under each load allowing us to predict the quantity, weight and volume of each power source for specific mission duration of 24, 48, 72, 96 and 120h.

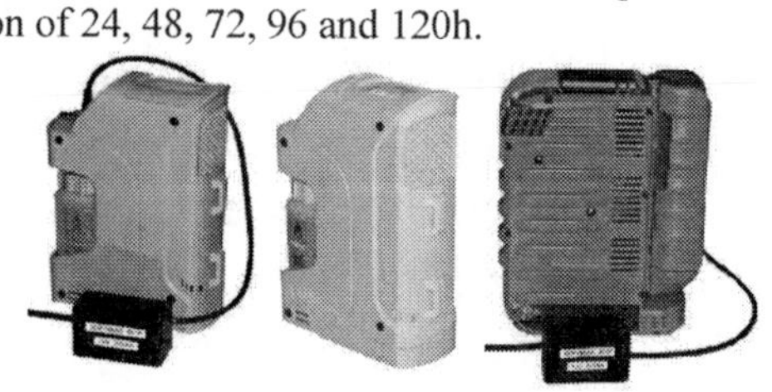

Figure 2: Example Fuel Cells.

Direct Methanol (SFC Jenny 600S) and Reformed Methanol (Ultracell XX55) fuel cells were also assessed (
Figure 2). To support the XX55 during start-up, and the pulse load which exceeds the Jenny output power, it was necessary to use an auxiliary battery.

Effects on the DSS in terms of weight, volume and quantity of power sources carried for the identified loads

Figure 3 shows the weight of a conformal battery compared to the Jenny 600S fuel cell. In this example the conformal is a factor of 4 times heavier than the fuel cell solution. The fuel cell results include "Start" and "End" weights the difference being representative of the fuel consumed during the mission.

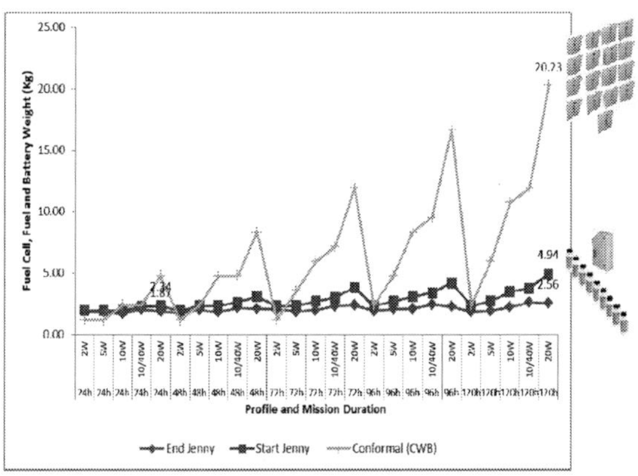

Figure 3: Comparison of a Jenny 600S Fuel Cell and the conformal battery

The overall analysis showed that a battery based upon a lithium ion type 18650 cells in a 4s3p configuration gave the best solution in terms of weight, quantity and volume. The closest commercially available test vehicle was to utilise one half of a high performance BB 2590/U product.

Effects of an example fuel cell used for opportunity charging during a typical DSS sortie

Of the two fuel cells the Jenny was considered our most favourable option due to its alignment with the DSS loads and portability.

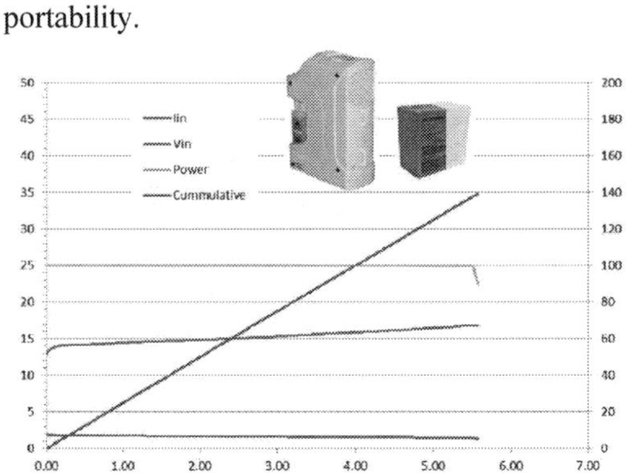

Figure 4: Charge characteristics of Jenny and the ½ BB2590/U

In order to use the fuel cell efficiently, we found it necessary to truncate the charge when the Jenny output reached 90%. The charge time was 5.6h and we recharged the battery to 88% of its full capability. Extending the charge duration to fully charge the battery would significantly reduce the efficiency of the fuel conversion.

Centralised Power and Distribution

The advent of intelligent textiles has enabled the distribution of centralised power to key outputs of the DSS equipment. In some instances the retention of smaller hold up batteries are still required.

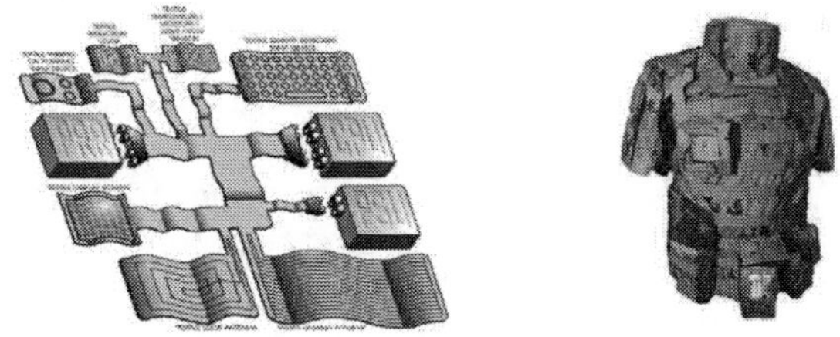

Figure 5: Examples of power distribution and DSS Vest.

The physical definition of equipment interface connectors with the intelligent network are proving an issue but work is in hand to define these requirements in STANAG 4695 and it's supporting AEP-95.

Modelling of typical DSS scenarios to show effects related to various phases of a typical DSS sortie.

Based upon work undertaken by NSRDEC [3] we produced a sophisticated excel model which could map the Squad power consumption profile for a 72 hour mission across the defined 10 phases.

We modelled the identified equipment and its power consumption in conjunction with the equipment usage by activity and the defined usage across the 10 phases of activity. This enabled the mapping of power consumption during the mission as shown in Figure 6 and Figure 7.

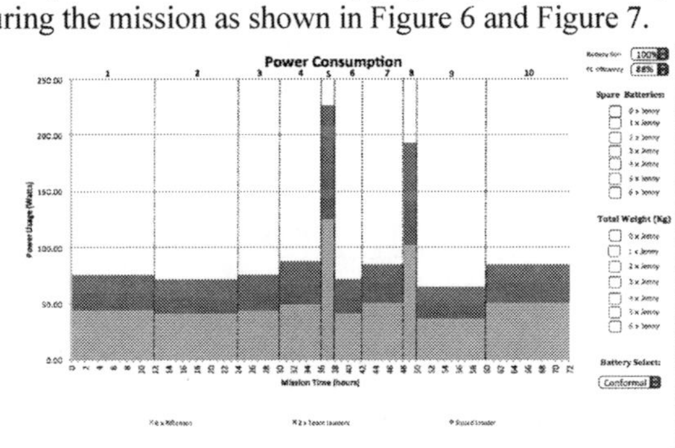

Figure 6: Power Consumption Profile

To the left of Figure 6 we enable the option to vary the State of Health (SOH), the charge efficiency, battery selection (conformal or ½ BB-2590/U) and whether we carried batteries only (0 x Jenny check box) or a number of Jenny fuel cells.

Upon selection the model creates the quantity of batteries, fuel cells and fuel cartridges required.

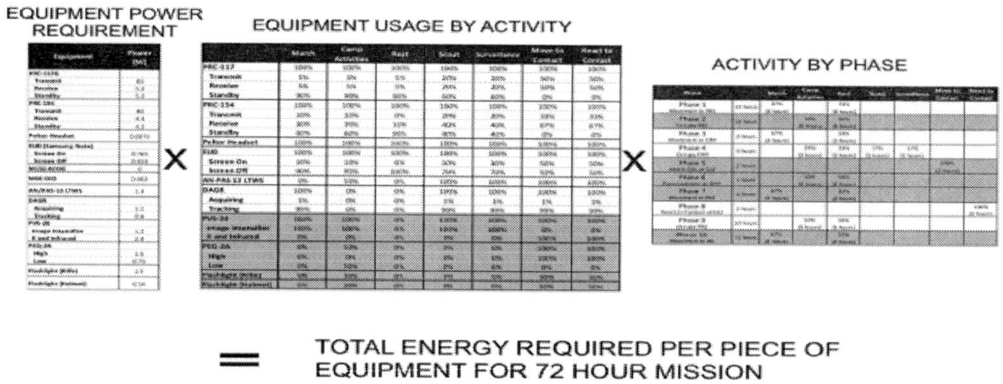

Figure 7: Power consumption analysis based upon the NSRDEC criteria

Demonstration of the impact on weight, volume and quantity of power sources related to the power source state of health

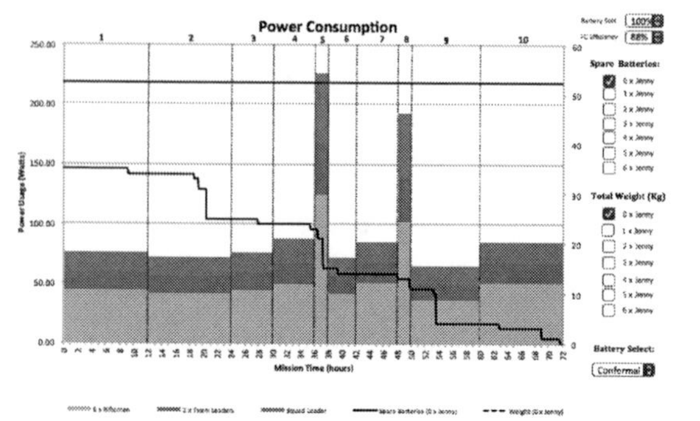

Figure 8: Power consumption for the Conformal battery at 100% SOH

Figure 8 shows the profile for the consumption of Conformal batteries within the 72h mission. The top horizontal line represents the weight of batteries carried which is a mass of 52.5kg representing 44 batteries. The stepped profile shows the consumption of charged batteries. It can be seen that a number of battery exchanges occurs during phase 5 (Attack to OBJ) which is not ideal.

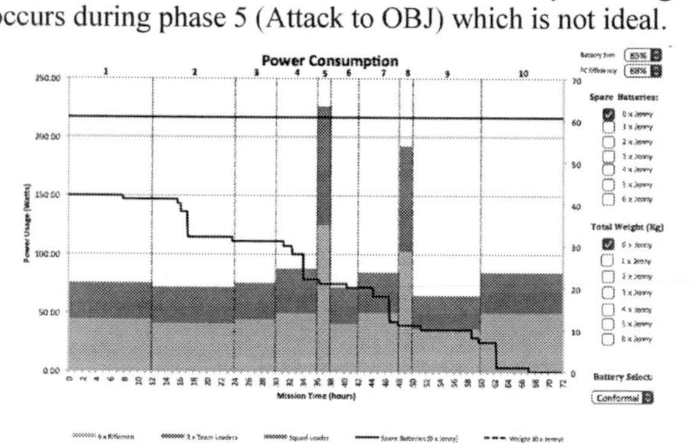

Figure 9: Power consumption for the Conformal battery at 85% SOH

Figure 9 shows the impact of utilising Conformal batteries at 85% SOH here we see the compliment has increased 51 batteries (Mass 60.7kg).

If we retain the 100% SOH population but now introduce 2 x Jenny 600S fuel cells into the mix we can reduce the compliment of Conformal batteries to 33 (Mass 45.44kg start weight and 43.18kg end weight). We would need 8 fuel cartridges and the squad would need to undertake 17 charge sequences. Note that the model is designed to prohibit charging during attack sequences (Figure 10).

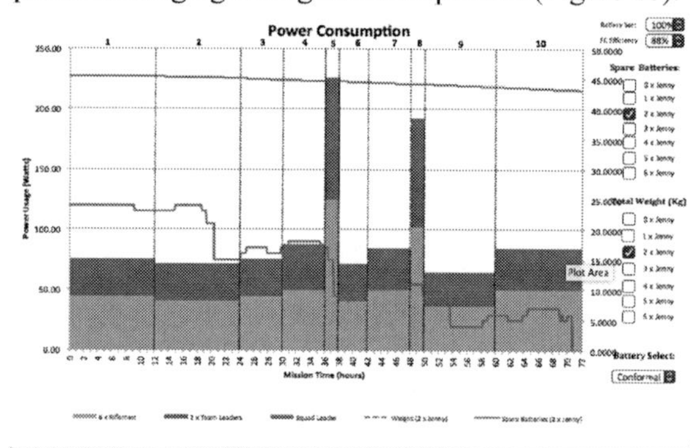

Figure 10: Power consumption for Conformal battery used in conjunction with 2 x Jenny 600S for charging

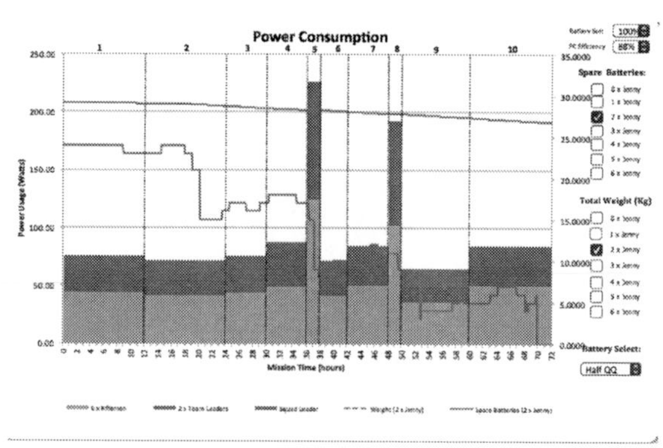

Figure 11: Power consumption for ½ BB-2590/U battery used in conjunction with 2 x Jenny 600S for charging

Figure 11 shows the consumption profile for the ½ BB-2590/U variant with 2 x Jenny 600S to charge during the mission. Here we see a distinct weight advantage in that we still require 33 batteries but the mass has reduced compared with the conformal to 29.13kg (start) and 26.82kg (end). 8 fuel cartridges were required and 17 re-charges were performed.

Limitation of current DSS power sources in terms of procurement and test specifications.

This study identifies a typical range of power sources and demonstrates their capabilities, which illustrates the choices to be made by the user. Its modelling techniques show that it is possible to predict power source performance and assist the DSS in planning for anticipated usage.

The range of product standards that support these power sources varies from comprehensive validation and test requirements to simple datasheets. Bearing in mind the austere requirements of the DSS there is an outstanding requirement to develop control standards for a format of battery suitable for this role.

Conclusion

The purpose of the model is to support mission planning. It enables the choice of power source and indeed regenerator to be assessed. The mapping of equipment can be modelled to suit the National DSS by defining the equipment portfolio. Having established the power consumption this can then be applied to the selected power source. However, we recognise that the model will only ever be as good as the data which supports it, and whilst it is relatively straight forward to measure power source performance and equipment loads, the usage pattern may be much more difficult to interpret.

Our model has also enabled the characterisation of SOH of the battery. Whilst it is recognised that a power sources energy density declines with age the ability to vary the SOH value enables the visualisation of the impact. Manufacturers are now beginning to include the SOH feature on their batteries and typically indicate when 80% of the rated capacity is reached.

In terms of the products characterised our scenario has shown that a battery construction utilising the lithium ion type 18650 cell has the greatest advantage in terms of the DSS role. When bearing in mind the logistical difficulties in the re-supply of the DSS reducing the weight burden must be one of the highest priorities. Furthermore the 4s3p configuration enables the construction of an ergonomic form factor.

SMBus technology enables the power source to be connected to an external energy source such that it can be regenerated from a range of harvesting offerings such as solar panels, dc to dc scavengers, wind and other auxiliary generators including fuel cell systems.

Acknowledgements

We wish to acknowledge the work of NSRDEC in defining the DSS Squad mission profile. We also wish to thank Bren-Tronics, Denchi-Power, Revision Military, SAFT and Ultralife, and for providing examples and test data. Defence Equipment and Support, Directorate of Technology (within the UK MoD) for providing the funding to undertake this project.

References

1. Electrical Power Supply for Military Ground Troops, Norwegian University of Science and Technology, Carl Gustaf Rye-Florentz, Oslo, Norway 16 May 2010
2. 130520.DCC RF BFM Power Consumption Database Issue 1.1 (UK)
3. NSRDEC 2021 Power and Data Architecture Study NSRDEC and Draper Collaboration. Section 2: 2013 Baseline Equipment and Usage Study 21 October 2013. Bruce Buckland (NSRDEC) et al. John Scudiere (Draper) et al.
4. RUSI Infantry: Capability, Burden and Technology, Intelligent Textiles: Reducing the Burden, Dr Stan Swallow and Asha Peta Thompson, February 2010.

Energy-Informed Soldier Mission Planning Through Simulation

Richard O. Stroman[1], Daniel J. Milliken[2], Eric A. Leadbetter[3], Karen Swider-Lyons[1], and Jonathan Novoa[4]

[1]Chemistry Division
US Naval Research Laboratory
4555 Overlook Ave SW, Washington, DC 20375

[2]EOIR Inc.
6165 Guardian Gateway, Suite J
Aberdeen Proving Ground, MD 21005

[3]Information Technology Division
US Naval Research Laboratory
4555 Overlook Ave SW, Washington, DC 20375

[4]Army Command, Power & Integration Directorate
5100 Magazine Road
Aberdeen Proving Ground, MD 21005

Abstract: *Soldiers presently lack quantitative methods to estimate the energy required or available (via harvesting) for a dismounted mission. Such estimates could enable Soldiers to reduce their battery weight burden and logistics tail. A smartphone app has been developed to simulate prospective missions and provide Soldiers with quantitative energy estimates for energy-informed mission planning. The app uses a device database, mission parameters, characteristics of the local environment, and planned energy resources to evaluate mission feasibility and final energy state (battery state of charge and fuel remaining).*

Keywords: simulation; soldier; energy; battery; solar; harvesting; mission planning.

Introduction

The growing burden carried by Soldiers to satisfy the energy needs of their equipment is a well-documented problem [1,2]. Reducing this burden is a goal of current DoD research and development, and to this end, the Naval Research Laboratory, EOIR, Inc. and CERDEC are collaborating to develop advanced Soldier power simulation tools. These new tools – the Soldier Power Simulation (SPS) and the Soldier Power Planner (SPP) – support the design and selection of Soldier power systems with the goal of helping Soldiers make energy-informed decisions in the field. The SPS is a Simulink model intended for engineering analysis, design, and optimization of Soldier power systems. It incorporates detailed component models, physical (current and voltage) links between components, and user-defined mission profiles and environments. The SPP is a mobile device app, supported by a MATLAB energy analysis code, intended for energy-informed mission planning in the field. It takes a less detailed approach to limit the setup burden on the Soldier and run quickly on a mobile device.

Soldier Power Simulation (SPS)

The SPS (see Fig. 1) is a collection of initialization scripts, data files, and Simulink blocks which represent a Soldier power system. Initialization scripts specify the initial system state, include or exclude components, input basic component data, and manage the storage and display of simulation results. Data files populate the look-up tables which underlie the empirical component models. Simulink blocks and the connections among them establish the system topology and the relationships between key state variables such as voltage and current.

Four major blocks comprise the SPS: *Battery*, *Sources*, *Loads*, *Power Manager*, and *Scenario*. The *Battery* block uses the battery current, battery state of charge (SOC), and ambient temperature to predict the battery voltage at each time step. The *Sources* block uses the Soldier activity, ambient temperature, and solar irradiation to predict the power provided by a solar array. The *Loads* block uses Soldier activity (mission element) and solar irradiation to predict the power consumption of common Soldier carried devices. The *Power Manager* block is an energy clearing-house which permits power to flow between the battery, sources, and loads while ensuring each system operates within its proscribed limits (e.g. battery minimum voltage) and the model conserves energy. Furthermore, the *Power Manager* block collects state data from the other blocks, collates it, and saves it to file(s) that are later post-processed to plot, report, and archive the simulation results. The *Scenario* block reads user-provided profiles describing Soldier activity and the environment as functions of time, and then provides these profiles to the other blocks as time dependent configuration parameters.

The *Battery* block presently includes options for a Palladium Energy CWB or an Ultralife BB-2590. Both battery models were developed empirically by fitting a simple equivalent circuit model to measurements at different temperatures. Model parameters are evaluated as functions of SOC and temperature at each time step by interpolating among the measured values.

The *Loads* block can estimate load power in two ways; either as a constant power, the value of which depends on Soldier activity, or as a user-defined power profile with respect to time. Average power values were obtained from measurements, device vendor specifications, and [3]. User defined power profiles can be in the form of a .csv file or MATLAB timeseries and can resolve variations down to the model time step size if desired.

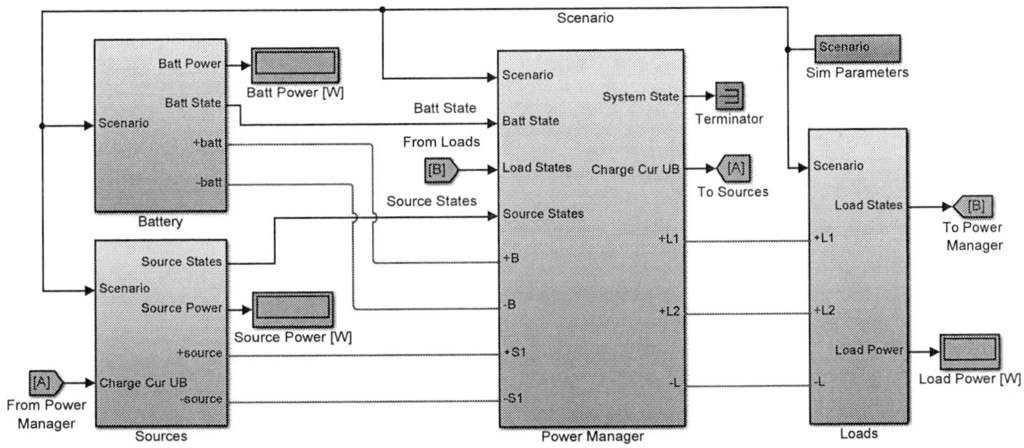

Figure 1. Top-level block diagram for the Soldier Power Simulation showing major sub-components and connections.

The present *Sources* block includes several solar arrays, but could be expanded to include kinetic and other energy harvesters, as well as external sources such as vehicle-mounted charging ports. Power harvested by the solar array is estimated by calculating the total global horizontal solar irradiance as a function of date, time, and location, and then applying the array's efficiency (with temperature correction). The energy harvested by devices which require setup or deployment (such as a rollable solar array) is forced to zero during incompatible activities. For example, the model understands that it is impractical to unroll a solar panel during an enemy engagement.

Once the simulation of a prospective power system is complete, the predicted component states are plotted vs. time to show how they perform together. This allows users to correlate performance with specific design features, control strategies, or aspects of the mission.

Soldier Power Planner (SPP) App

With the SPP app, Soldiers can use a simple graphical interface (Fig. 2) to input parameters for a prospective mission (duration, equipment, planned usage, etc.) and quickly receive an assessment of mission energy feasibility and the weight of energy-related equipment. If the mission is infeasible as planned (insufficient energy or too heavy), they can adjust the mission plan or equipment to identify a better combination. For example, they might find that shifting the start time of a patrol will enable them to make better use of a harvesting opportunity and carry fewer batteries.

Energy assessments are generated by a time-domain model that was developed in the MATLAB environment. The MATLAB code is compiled into C++ using MATLAB Coder, for execution by the app on a mobile device. The model uses mission parameters to estimate the load and harvesting power profiles with respect to time, and then calculates the net power required. The net power is used in conjunction with battery models to estimate battery state (i.e. SOC and voltage) vs. time.

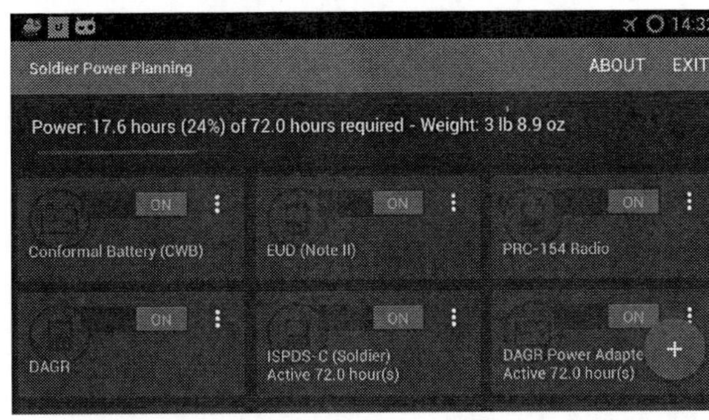

Figure 2. Screen capture of the SPP user interface.

The app has three main components: the GUI/front end code, the database, and the energy analysis code (EAC).

- The GUI/front end provides the interface presented to the solder, manages input parameters provided by the Soldier, and post-processes the mission energy analysis for display. The GUI shown in Fig. 2 has simple radio button inputs and sliders to configure the prospective mission.
- The SQLite database stores the energy-related characteristics of each device in the library, the input parameters from the Soldier, and the energy analysis results.
- The EAC reads input parameters and device characteristics from the library, simulates the mission, and then writes outputs such as mission duration and final Soldier energy state to the database.

The relationships between these components are shown schematically in Fig 3.

The mission is input as a total duration, list of devices carried, and the time "slices" during which those devices are active. Load power is based on average values from [3] and harvester power is based on either average values or

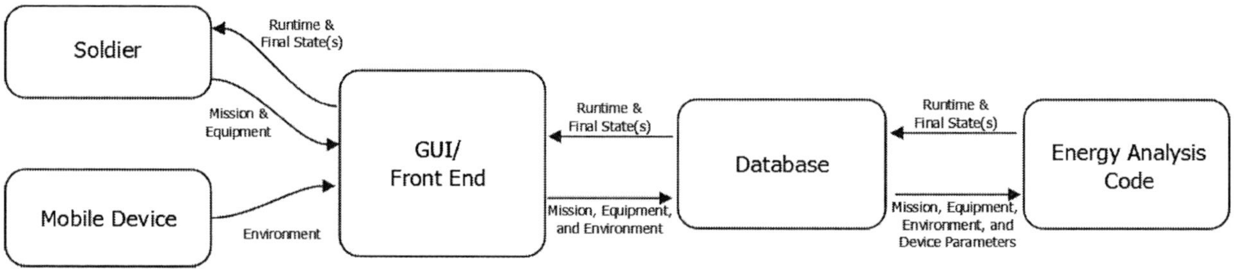

Figure 3. Schematic showing how the SPP estimates the evolution of Soldier power energy state.

device models which incorporate environmental influences, such as solar arrays.

In the SPP, devices are characterized as loads, batteries, harvesters, or generators. Batteries and generators differ in that batteries are bidirectional and generators have a fuel supply that must be tracked; otherwise they are treated the same way. Wearable fuel cells are an example generator for the purposes of SPP analysis. All systems in SPP must have at least one battery, but its capacity can be arbitrarily small to simulate harvester-only or generator-only systems.

The EAC (shown in Fig. 4) first evaluates the total load and harvester power at each timestep throughout the mission. Subtracting total load from total harvester power yields the power that must be supplied (or stored) by the battery(ies) and generator(s). Next, a loop evaluates battery and generator state (SOC and fuel consumption) at each time step in the simulation. When multiple batteries and/or a generator are present, a state machine swaps batteries and draws power from the generator in an effort to capture as much harvested energy as possible while minimizing the number of battery swaps and fuel consumed.

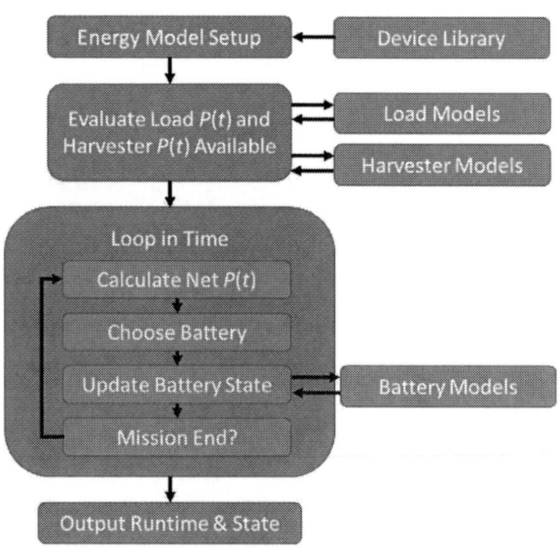

Figure 4. Schematic showing how the SPP estimates the evolution of Soldier power energy state.

Results are presented to the Soldier as a feasible runtime (which may be less than the desired mission duration) and the final battery states of charge and remaining generator fuel supply.

Status and Results

The utility of the SPP for mission planning is illustrated for one of many potential scenarios in Fig. 5. It compares the net power for a notional 72 h mission at Ft. Drum, NY in summer (21 June) and in winter (21 December). Connected devices include a radio (PRC-154), batteries (CWB and BB2590) and two solar panels (a rollable PowerFilm R28 and a continuously deployed Global Solar CIGS panel). The battery and solar panel models account for the influences of temperature and local clear-sky solar irradiance.

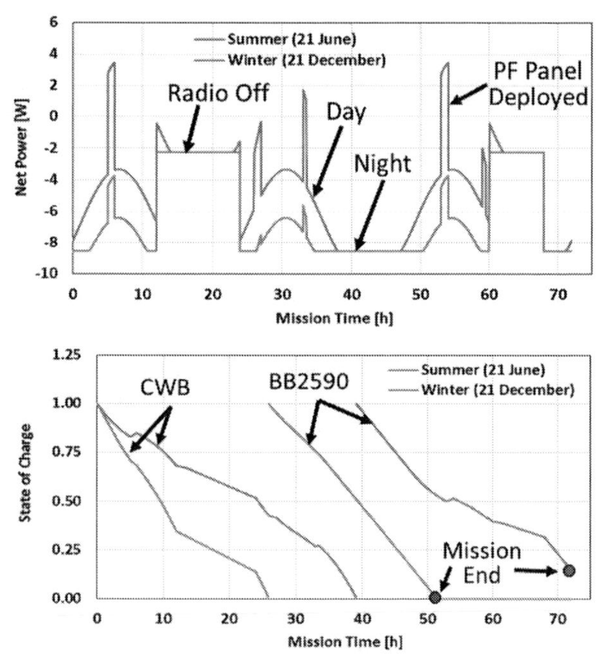

Figure 5. SPP results for a mission at Ft. Drum NY in summer and winter, illustrating the utility of simulation for estimating energy needs in different environments. Net power (net = harvested – load) at top and battery state of charge at bottom.

The simulation indicates the planned mission would be feasible in summer, but infeasible in winter – not a surprising result, but the simulation quantifies the energy deficit to make the difference actionable. The Soldier can choose an additional battery to satisfy the energy shortfall with confidence that it will be sufficient or plan additional harvesting to improve the likelihood of completing the mission in winter. Both adjustments to the mission plan are improvements over the present approach in which Soldiers often decide how many batteries to carry based on a subjective estimate of their needs.

Conclusions and Future Work

With respect to the SPS, we conclude that a detailed engineering model of a Soldier power system can provide useful insights into component interactions and the performance of different system architectures. Such models offer a valuable opportunity to analyze power systems in a well-defined and repeatable way that is difficult (or impossible) to achieve in field experiments. Properly validated models should play an important role in the development of future Soldier power systems.

With respect to the SPP, we conclude that it is feasible to run a detailed energy system simulation on a mobile device, and such simulations can provide Soldiers with useful insights during the mission planning process. The quantitative simulation results may be used to support energy informed operations by enabling Soldiers to select appropriate energy resources for a mission and take advantage of the best energy harvesting opportunities.

This work can proceed in several ways. In the near term, user evaluations and field validation of the model results are most important. Individual components and subsystems have been validated against measurements, but complete missions should be simulated and then executed to evaluate simulation accuracy. From a research perspective, the SPP app displays only the mission runtime and final state to the Soldier; the detailed output shown in Fig. 5 is generated but not displayed. There may be opportunities to use the detailed time indexed data to recommend actions, suggest alternative mission plans to leverage harvesting opportunities, or select equipment better suited to the mission. Additionally, tools such as SPP depend heavily on the quality of input parameters, and machine learning techniques could be used to update device parameters in the database so they reflect recent use patterns and improve the accuracy of future simulations of similar missions and environments.

Acknowledgements

The authors wish to thank the Army Communications-Electronics Research, Development, and Engineering Center for funding this work.

References

1. National Research Council, *Meeting the Energy Needs of Future Warriors*. 2004, Washington, DC: The National Academies Press. 136.
2. A. Wahlman, C. Clavin, R. Keller, D. Georgi, and J. Ayers, *An Assessment of the Challenges Associated with Individual Battlefield Power: Addressing the Power Budget Burdens of the Warfighter and Squad*, Institute for Defense Analysis, Paper P-5121 (2014).
3. S. Meredith and D. Bergmann, *Soldier Power: A Growing Operational Concern*, Infantry Professional Forum (2013).
4. B. Buckland, K. Shukla, A. R. Negron, D. Krasnecky, J. Scudiere, and V. Mittal, *NSRDEC 2021 Power and Data Architecture Study*, Natick Soldier Research Development and Engineering Center (2013).

Preliminary Analysis of Energy Harvesting Insole

[1]José Collazo, [1]Julianne S. Douglas, [1]Alexis Moy & [2]Christopher Mullen
[1]U.S. Army Communications-Electronics Research, Development and Engineering Center
Aberdeen Proving Ground, MD, USA
[2]Oak Ridge Institute for Science and Education, Belcamp, MD 21017

Abstract: *Modern advances in kinetic energy harvesting allow for a mobile and renewable source of power that decreases dependence on battery-stored energy. This alleviates part of the physical load that a soldier carries. Energy that is captured from the motion of the warfighter is used to charge a central battery. The electromechanical system resides in the boot insole, and mechanical power from the heel strike is converted into electrical power using a series of gears and an electromagnetic alternator.*

This study analyzes the risk, performance, and benefits of using energy harvesting insoles as additional power sources. The insoles are tested for maximum power achieved with variable electronic loads, walking speeds, and weights. Preliminary results suggest a direct relationship between the power output of the insoles and both the walking speed and pilot tester mass. It is shown that the performance of the unit tested approximates the manufacturer's specifications of average 0.04J/step.

Keywords: energy harvesting; kinetic; wearable; insole; testing; analysis; electrodynamics; generator; heel-strike; boot; alternator

Introduction

Today's dismounted Warfighter leverages C4ISR (Command, Control, Communications, Computers, Intelligence, Surveillance, and Reconnaissance) technology to maintain the tactical edge. Using these capabilities requires power that creates excess weight in the form of extra batteries and increased logistics due to additional resupply. Unfortunately, this solution is sub-optimal, as additional batteries will increase an already excessive load (approximately 100 lbs.) carried by the dismounted Soldier and occupy volume in the rucksack that could otherwise hold more essential mission supplies such as water, food, and ammunition. Recent advances in the fields of power and energy have produced energy harvesting systems which attempt to convert mechanical energy into electrical energy for the purpose of recharging batteries or powering electronic systems [1]. The U.S. Army has investigated several areas of kinetic energy harvesting, including heel-strike, knee-brace, and (both linear and rotary-based) suspended-mass induction technologies.

This study focuses primarily on an insole Energy Harvesting (EH) device that capitalizes on the Soldier's heel-strike along with the issues of analyzing its raw power output and comparing results across tests varying resistance, payload, and stride frequency.

Background

Energy harvesting is the production of off-grid electricity using ambient energy. The ambient energy could be the kinetic energy of a moving structure, the energy of sunlight, or the human thermal energy emitted as waste heat. An energy harvesting device collects the energy that would otherwise be wasted from the environment while minimally impacting the characteristics of its host structure or its surroundings [2]. Energy harvesting technology has been growing in relevance as small devices with lower power demand keep increasing in popularity [3]. Energy harvesters are being used in a variety of applications such as regenerative braking in electric vehicles, battery trickle charging, air pressure sensors in automobile tires, unmanned autonomous vehicles, implanted medical sensors, and structural health monitoring [4].

One solution is to implement a mechanical device actuated by the heel-strike that is able to be integrated into multiple types of footwear.

There are various energy harvesting methods that convert mechanical energy into electrical energy. Electromagnetic energy harvesters (also called induction energy harvesters) utilize a permanent magnet generator to provide electricity to an electrical load [2]. Normally, the generators are composed of a rotor, which houses magnets, and a stator, which holds stationary coils. Magnetic flux emitted from the magnets moves from pole to pole. This flux is arranged along the rotor such that the resulting magnetic field moves through the geometry of the coil, inducing a current. This voltage is used to energize an electrical circuit.

Generators work under the principles of the Maxwell equations that help describe the interplay between magnetic and electric fields [2]. The equation below, Faraday's law of induction, describes how a time (t) varying magnetic field (Φ_B) will induce an electric potential or voltage (V), which is proportional to the number of turns of the coil (N) that the magnetic field acts upon.

$$\mathrm{V} = -N\frac{d\Phi_{\mathrm{B}}}{dt}$$

where:

$$\Phi_{\mathrm{B}} = \iint B(r,t)\cdot dA$$

where N is number of turns of the coils, B is magnetic flux density, and dA is element of surface area. The magnetic field is a function of the size of the permanent magnet used and its material properties. The dot product of B and dA shows the directionality of the magnets to the coils.

Inductive energy harvesters can be categorized by how they achieve a relative velocity between the coil and the magnet. Rotational generator harvesters feature the flexibility to be used in applications that require a flat profile. This concept effectively integrates into a heel-strike application, as all of the surface area of the heel contributes to power generation.

The generator studied in this kinetic energy harvester (KEH) is a radial permanent magnet generator (PMG). Specifically, it is an external radial PMG, where the rotor spins on the outside circumference of the stator. A similar model to the one used is illustrated by Figure 1, the rotor in this case being permanent magnets (green) fixed on a rotating drum (red) and the stator being wound coils (blue) [5].

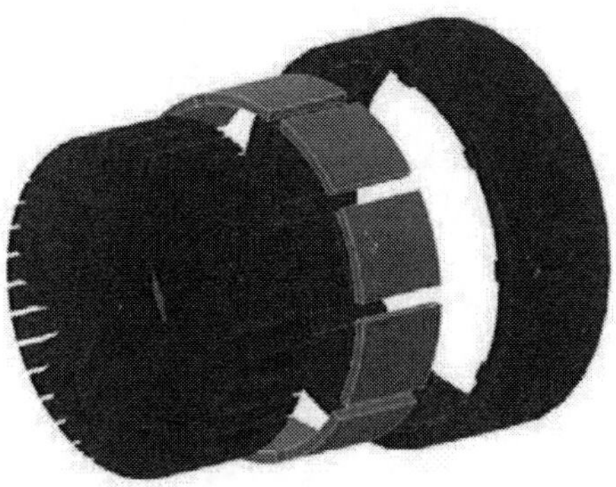

Figure 1: External Radial PMG Model [5]

Starner and Paradiso provide a good evaluation of the energy available for scavenging from human movement and identify walking as a prime source of energy. Their report on various human generated power techniques [6] showed that up to 67 W could be recovered during the human step (and around 20 W for footwear applications). However, it is estimated that less than half of the possible power output is accessible after mechanical and electrical inefficiencies.

This low efficiency and power output supports the importance of further optimization of device design and the experimentation process. Coil geometry also directly impacts the harvesting efficiency since the number of turns in the coil is proportional to the voltage. Magnet strength also directly affects the magnetic field necessary to induce a current in the coil. Greater insight into each parameter's effect on device performance and efficiency can be achieved by standardizing the experimental design and analysis protocol.

Experimental Design

The system tested in these experiments was a modified insole implanted with an electromechanical energy harvester, which consisted of a generator actuated by a downward translational heel-strike force. The vertical component of the heel-strike force was converted into rotational motion using a rack and pinion modified with a spring-return and gear train. The gear train is key in converting a vertical linear force to a horizontal force and subsequently to a rotational force to spin the rotor at optimal speed. It is important to note that this iteration of the design doesn't yet take advantage of the spring's recoil energy; it only harvests energy from the downward stroke. Improving this design is a focus of the next generation iteration.

Rather than developing a test bed to emulate heel-strike, two human pilot testers were utilized to more accurately represent the complex time-varying and multi-directional force profiles involved while walking. For ethics reasons, the only humans permitted to wear the insole harvester for this preliminary investigation were the authors [7].

A level treadmill was set to three pre-determined speeds for the pilot testers to walk at while the insole harvester was connected to the nearby National Instruments data acquisition hardware and LabVIEW software to measure the system's output voltage and current. Each pilot tester walked at 2.5, 3, and 4 mph while carrying weight on their backs to simulate two payloads each, giving a total of four unique payloads for comparison. The insole harvester was connected to the same resistive electronic load at every speed and payload condition. This equivalent resistance was selected to provide the maximum power output. It was found experimentally by calculating the average power output from the measured voltage and current of three 30-second trials for each resistance, ranging from 1 to 150 ohms, shown in the Results section.

Unfortunately, the subjects' walking gait characteristics were not accounted for beforehand and visual analysis of their gait characteristics showed marked differences.

Results

The equivalent circuit/resistance of the energy harvesting insole was experimentally determined by measuring the average maximum power output for each of three trials using various electronic loads ranging from 1 to 150 ohms. Figure 2 displays the average maximum power output for each of the resistances tested while hand actuating the unit. From the data, it is clear that the highest power output occurs at 9.8 ohms. The equivalent resistance of 9.8 ohms was then used for the remainder of the testing.

Preliminary data from the first subject indicates that indeed there is a direct relationship between the payload on the insole and the average power that was measured for the entire run at any given speed. As seen from Figure 3, pilot tester 1's (P1) overall payload acting on the device plays a critical role in the output average power. More power is produced at 200 lbs. of payload than at 170 lbs. This is likely because there is more kinetic energy available to be harvested by the device since more mass is participating in the actuation. As more weight translates to higher impact, the rotational acceleration from the gears increases, causing more induction in the generator. This behavior can be explained by is due to Faraday's Law of induction. Higher rotational acceleration will cause an increased change in the magnetic field ($d\Phi_B$) over time, therefore outputting a higher voltage.

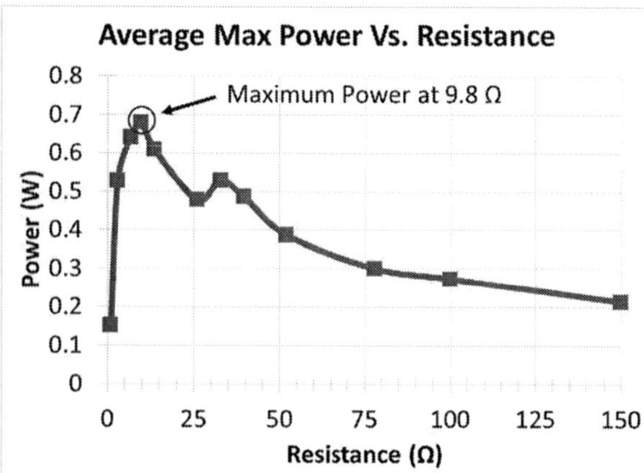

Figure 2: Average Max Power Vs Resistance

The slope of the graphs in Figure 3 and 4 indicates the force applied to the insole at the moment when the heel strikes, as seen below:

$$\frac{P}{v} = \frac{E/t}{v} = \left[\frac{kg \cdot m^2/s^3}{m/s}\right] = \left[kg \cdot m/s^2\right] = F$$

where P is power, v is velocity, E is energy, t is time, and F is force. Dimensional analysis was used to display the conversion of power and velocity to force.

As treadmill speed increases, vertical speed also increases because frequency is increasing while stroke remains constant, thereby proving the relationship between velocity and the force applied to each step. The regression in Figure 3 & 4 models the linear relationship between selected speed and power output in all our trials. Comparing Figure 4 with Figure 3, we see that pilot tester 2 (P2) has greater applied force per step than P1. This could be because P2 traveled a greater vertical distance per step at the same horizontal speed, making P2's vertical velocity and momentum larger. Again, it is important to point out that the subjects' walking gaits were not accounted for beforehand.

Inconsistent spread of data points in the various speeds is also illustrated in both Figure 2 and 3. When comparing the natural human walking speeds 2.5 and 3.0 mph with the faster 4.0 mph, the range of data at that speed is significantly larger. It is worth mentioning that on an average, the range of data at the higher speed (4.0 mph) is five times the range of the slower walking speed (2.5 mph).

This behavior illustrates that when the subject walks at a higher speed, the power output will be more inconsistent, as shown by the range of power outputs. The inconsistent steps at higher speeds also make it more difficult to properly actuate the generator.

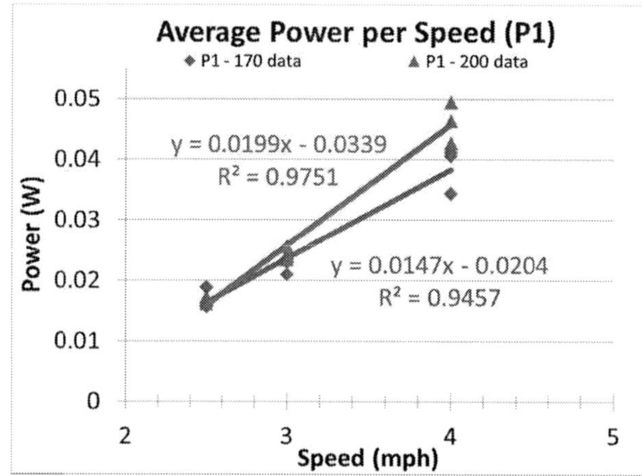

Figure 3: Average Power per Speed for Pilot Tester 1

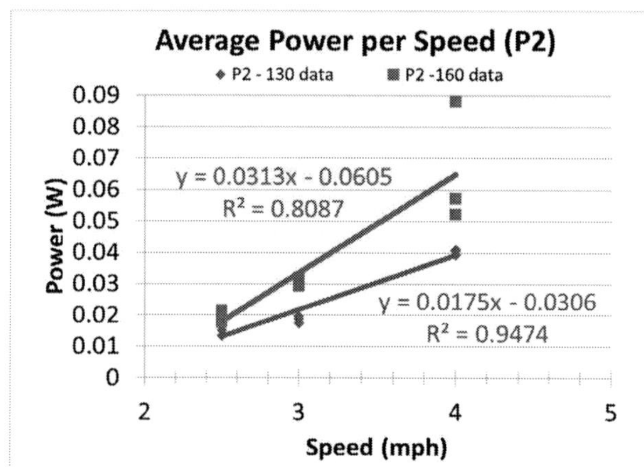

Figure 4: Average Power per Speed for Pilot Tester 2

Figure 5 illustrates the direct relationship between the selected walking speed and the average energy per step output of the harvester device. The average energy was calculated by summing all of the energy produced throughout the trial and dividing it by the total amount of steps the subject took.

The equation below explains the slope of each of the linear regressions in Figure 5, which is the average impulse *(I)* applied on the generator. Dimensional analysis was used to display the conversion of power and velocity to force.

$$\frac{E}{v} = \left[\frac{kg \cdot m^2/s^2}{m/s}\right] = [kg \cdot m/s] = [N \cdot s] = I$$

where v is velocity, E is energy, t is time, and I is impulse. It is important to note that once again the selected speed for the subject plays an important role in the energy production, as it also increases the size of vertical stroke that acts upon the insole naturally with increasing stride length. The impulse that P2 applied was consistently greater than P1 as seen from the slope on the linear equation. Even though P1 represents greater payload, P2 at 160 lbs was noted to have a more vertical inclined walking gait. From the data collected, the method of walking and the vertical distance the user achieves in the gait before the heel strike appears to be a determining factor in achieving maximum power output of the harvesting device.

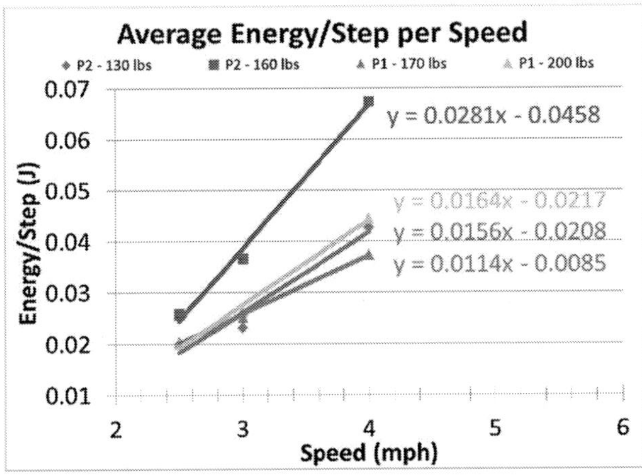

Figure 5: Average Energy/Step per Speed for Both Testers

As seen by the performance of both P1 and P2 in Figure 5 at the speed of 4 mph and the higher payloads, the EH does validate the vendor specification of 0.04 J/step.

Table 1 shows the similarities between the average force and the average impulse applied on the harvester. These values were calculated by using the previously stated equations for force and impulse, which are also the linear slopes of the regressions in Figures 3 through 5.

Subject	Subject Weight (lbs)	Avg. Force (N)	Avg. Impulse (N·s)
P2	130	0.017489	0.015634
	160	0.03137	0.028151
P1	170	0.01469	0.011447
	200	0.019906	0.016437

Table 1: Average Force and Impulse per Weight

Design improvements to the system for obtaining higher energy output are achievable. Some potential improvements include increasing stroke, frequency, and mass, optimizing coil geometry, and maximizing magnet strength. Since the kinetic energy ( ) input relies on mass and velocity (stroke times frequency), increasing the stroke length, frequency, and mass directly impacts the energy available to be harvested.

Conclusion/Further Work

A typical running shoe insole dissipates a relatively large amount of energy as heat. Shorten's analysis of the energetics of a shoe midsole worn by a 76 kg (167.5 lbs) runner suggests that a running shoe will dissipate between 2 and 10 J per step [8]. Future designs of energy harvesting insoles could instead turn this energy into electricity, without altering the comfort or energy expenditure of the person.

These results prove that test standards for radial inductive-based kinetic energy harvesting systems need to include frequency and load testing with metabolic input to get a reliable baseline performance characterization. Since walking gaits were not accounted for beforehand, future efforts will involve implementing motion capture technology to characterize different walking gaits in relation to power outputs. Further improved heel-strike EH prototypes will also be tested and compared with current performance data. Targeting human integration factors, such as coefficient of harvesting, and more comprehensive cost-benefit trade studies could also be beneficial in realizing the Army's search for energy independence.

Acknowledgments

This research was supported in part by an appointment to the Postgraduate Research Participation Program at the U.S. Army Communications-Electronics Research, Development and Engineering Center (CERDEC), administered by the Oak Ridge Institute for Science and Education

References

1. Rome, L.C., Flynn, L., Goldman, E.M., Yoo, T.D. "Generating Electricity While Walking With Loads." *Science* 309: 1725-1728, 2005.
2. Joyce, B.S., "Development of an Electromagnetic Energy Harvester for Monitoring Wind Turbine Blades," Virginia Polytechnic Institute and State University, (MSME Thesis). December 12, 2011.
3. Amirtharajah R., Chandrakasan A. P., "Self-powered signal processing using vibration-based power generation," *IEEE Journal of Solid-state Circuits*, no. 5(33), pp. 687-695, 1998.
4. Inman D. J., Priya. S. "Energy Harvesting Technologies", New York, NY: Springer, 2009.
5. Tarımer, İ. and Ocak, C. "Performance Comparision of Internal and External Rotor Structured Wind Generators Mounted from Same Permanent Magnets on Same Geometry" *Electronics And Electrical Engineering, No. 4(92), 2009*
6. Starner, T. Paradiso, J. "Human Generated Power for Mobile Electronics" *Piguet, C. (ed), Low Power Electronics Design, CRC Press*, 2004
7. CITI Program at the University of Miami "Human Subjects Research (HSR) Training"
8. Shorten, M. "Running Shoe Design: Protection And Performance" pp 159-169 in *Marathon Medicine* (Ed. D. Tunstall Pedoe) London, Royal Society of Medicine, 2000

Analysis Natural Gas SOFC-GT-ST-ORC Quadruple Cycle for Power Generation

Osagie Matthew, Hong Nyugen
and
Sen Nieh, Professor and Chair
Department of Mechanical Engineering
The Catholic University of America
620 Michigan Avenue, NE
Washington DC, USA, 20064
(202) 319-5170, nieh@cua.edu

Abstract: *Improvement of performances has been a major concern for the power industries. There has been many propositions over the past decade of single cycle ranging from the rankine/steam cycle (ST), brayton cycle/gas turbine (GT), organic rankine cycle (ORC), solid oxide fuel cell (SOFC), through combined cycle to triple cycle power generation, aimed at increasing energy efficiency, reducing cost and pollutants emission, such as PMs,* NO_x, SO_x, *CO, VOCs, etc. and lowering greenhouse gas* CO_2 *emission. Researchers and power plant owners at some point have integrated these cycles to achieve a higher efficiency. Of such category are the SOFC-GT, SOFC-ST, SOFC-ORC, GT-ST, GT-ORC, and ST-ORC hybrid, combined cycle power generation. Other research engineers have considered triple cycle power generation, such as SOFC-GT-ST, SOFC-GT-ORC, and SOFC-ST-ORC. This research examines a novel quadruple cycle power generation system that integrates SOFC, GT, ST and ORC using natural gas as the primary fuel. Mathematical modeling of the SOFC-GT-ST-ORC quadruple cycle are developed and investigated. Preliminary results show that up to 80% power plant energy efficiency is obtainable for this quadruple cycle; which is much higher than the single cycle (30% - 45%), combined cycle (50% - 60%), and triple cycle (60% - 70%) power generation.*

Keywords: Solid Oxide Fuel Cell; Gas Turbine; Steam Turbine; Organic Rankine Cycle.

Introduction

The outset of hydraulic fracturing has lead to the decline in the price of natural gas making it economically feasible for power generation. In addition to the other benefits such as lower carbon emission compared to coal. As a result, the use of natural gas as primary fuel in single, combined, triple cycles and other hybridized cycles such as SOFC-GT and SOFC-ORC is gradually increasing. For example, Kimura H et al replaced a coal-fired plant with a 1400°C f-type gas turbine combined cycle power plant to achieve 95% reduction in the oxides of nitrogen and 79% in the carbon emitted with no particulates and sulfur oxides [1]. Zhang X, et al wrote a review of integration strategies for solid oxide fuel cells with classical thermodynamic cycle in which the integration strategies is determined by higher efficiency, lower emission and better reliability [2]. Arsalis A, presented a thermoeconomic modeling and parametric study of hybrid SOFC-gas turbine-steam turbine power plants and concluded that a 10MWe SOFC-GT-ST hybrid triple pressure reheat exhibit a maximum efficiency of 73.8%, an average efficiency of 65.3% and a total efficiency of 68.4% [3].Similarly, Hung T C wrote on a conceptual series and parallel arrangement of a GT-ST-ORC toward optimal energy conversion [4]. Yan Z et al proposed a new power system by integrating SOFC-GT with ORC with liquefied natural gas as heat sink and found that the electrical efficiency reached 67.38% [5]. These sited research work aimed to utilize waste heat. The benefits of heat recovery include lowering CO_2 emissions and achieving more power output for the same amount of fuel [6].

This paper examines a novel hybrid of SOFC integrated with GT, ST and ORC, SOFC-GT-ST-ORC quadruple cycle. The energy analysis of the series and parallel configuration of the hybridized cycle is developed using CyclePad, CATT III programs and their power output and efficiency compared.

Configuration

The configuration of the SOFC-GT-ST-ORC is shown in figure 1. The system consists of compressors, heat exchangers, IRSOFC, combustor, turbines, pumps and a condenser. Compressed air and natural gas enters the SOFC. The exhaust gases from the SOFC undergo combustion. The combustion products are used to rotate the turbine. The exhaust products of the gas turbine goes through a heat exchanger to raise the temperature of the air and fuel entering the SOFC as well as the water entering the steam turbine and the organic agent, R134a, used as working fluid in the organic rankine cycle.

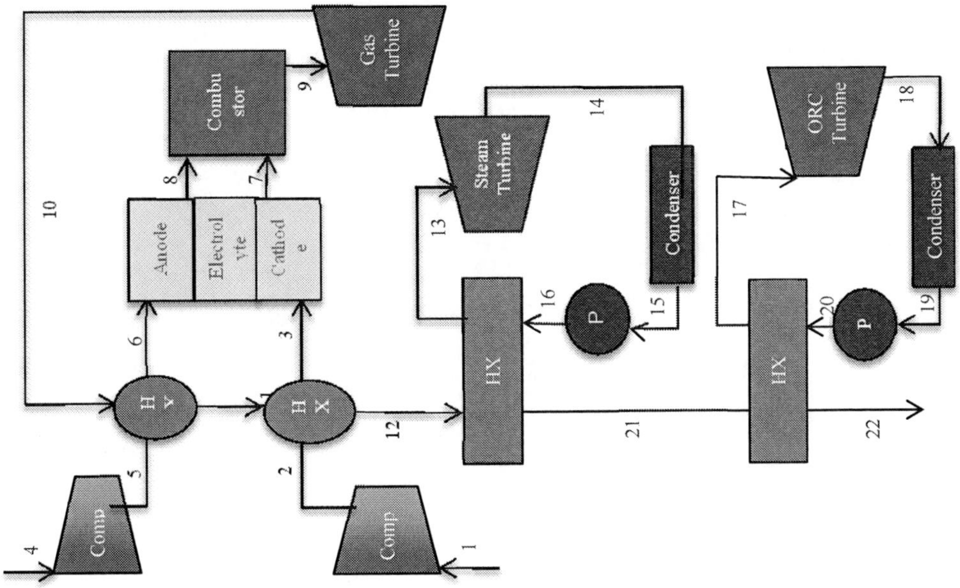

Figure 1. SOFC-GT-ST-ORC Quadruple Cycle

Modeling

SOFC:

Unlike classical power plants where the chemical energy in fuel is first converted to thermal energy, subsequently to mechanical energy and eventually to electricity, SOFC converts the chemical energy in fuel directly to electricity through an electrochemical process [7]. In SOFC, hydrogen in generated in the by steam reforming and was gas shift reaction.

$$CH_4 + H_2O \xleftrightarrow{steam\ reforming} CO_2 + 3H_2$$

$$CO + H_2O \xleftrightarrow{water\ gas\ shift} CO_2 + H_2$$

$$V_{sofc} = E_r - V_{act} - V_{ohm} - V_{conc}$$

$$E_r = -\frac{\Delta G^0}{2F} + \frac{RT_{sofc}}{2F} ln\left(\frac{P_{H_2}\sqrt{P_{O_2}}}{P_{H_2O}}\right)$$

$$V_{act} = \frac{RT}{2F} ln\left(\frac{J}{J_o}\right)$$

$$V_{conc} = -\frac{RT}{2F} ln\left(1 - \frac{J}{4000}\right)$$ [8]

$$V_{ohm} = J\sum_{k=1}^{4}\gamma_k$$

$$\gamma_k = \delta_k \alpha_k e^{(\beta_k/T)} \text{ Ohm-}m^2$$

$$\dot{\omega}_{sofc} = V_{sofc} * I$$

Gas Turbine:

$$\dot{\omega}_g = \dot{m}_{gt} C_p (T_9 - T_{10})$$

$$\dot{\omega}_{c,a} = \dot{m}_{air} C_p (T_2 - T_1)$$

$$\dot{\omega}_{c,f} = \dot{m}_f C_p (T_5 - T_4)$$

Steam Turbine:

$$\dot{\omega}_s = \dot{m}_{st} (h_{13} - h_{14})$$

$$\dot{\omega}_{ps} = \dot{m}_p (h_{16} - h_{15})$$

Organic Rankine Cycle:

$$\dot{\omega}_r = \dot{m}_{orc}(h_{17} - h_{18})$$

$$\dot{\omega}_{po} = \dot{m}_{orc}(h_{20} - h_{19})$$

$$\dot{\omega} = \dot{\omega}_g + \dot{\omega}_s + \dot{\omega}_r - \dot{\omega}_{c,a} - \dot{\omega}_{c,f} - \omega_{ps} - \omega_{po}$$

$$\eta = \frac{\dot{\omega}_{sofc} + \dot{\omega}}{\dot{m}_f * LHV}$$

Results and Discussion

Table 1. Ohmic Polarization Resistance Constants

Component	δ (m)	β (K)	α (Ω m)
Interconnection	0.000085	4690	0.0012
Electrolyte	0.00004	10350	0.0000294
Anode	0.0015	-1392	0.0000298
Cathode	0.0022	600	0.00008144

Table 2. Mixture States Composition in Percentage

States	O_2	N_2	CH_4	H_2O	CO_2	CO	H_2
1	21	79					
2	21	79					
3	21	79					
4			100				
5			100				
6			100				
7	9	91					
8				63	16	5	16
9	3	64		26	7		
10	3	64		26	7		
11	3	64		26	7		
12	3	64		26	7		

Table 1; list the constants for calculating the ohmic polarization voltage loss. Table 2, shows the composition of the states from 1 through 12.Table 3, list the thermodynamic properties of the states of the SOFC-GT-ST-ORC quadruple cycle.

Table 3. Thermodynamic States of SOFC-GT-ST-ORC

States	P (bar)	T (K)	$\dot{m}$ (kg/s)	h (kJ/kg)	s (kJ/kg k)	$\dot{\omega}$ (MW)
1	1	298	200	299	2.42	
2	4.3	452.1	200	453.6	2.42	30.92
3	4.3	840	200	842.9	3.04	
4	1	298	15	623.2	11.61	
5	4.3	393.3	15	861.5	11.61	3.575
6	4.3	400	15	863.2	11.62	
7	4.3	1040	160			
8	4.3	1040	40			
9	4.3	1873	200	1879	3.84	128
10	1	1235	200	1239	3.84	
11	1	846.7	200	849.6	3.46	
12	1	846.6	200	849.5	3.46	
13	13.33	823	28.14	3584	7.79	29.74
14	0.15	327.1	28.14	2527	7.79	
15	0.15	300	28.14	112.5	0.393	
16	13.33	300	28.14	113.8	0.393	0.037
17	21	355	57.13	446.3	1.75	2.239
18	6.63	298	57.13	407.1	1.7	
19	6.63	298	57.13	234.4	1.12	
20	21	300	57.13	235.5	1.12	0.063
21	1	360	200	361.2	2.61	
22	1	360	200	301	2.42	

Table 4 shows the system performance results. A cell voltage of 0.767 V was attained.at a current density of 500mA/cm^2. The SOFC generates a power of 125.5MW. Figure 2, shows the T-S diagram of the SOFC-GT-ST-ORC quadruple cycle. The exit temperature of the SOFC contributes to raising the final inlet temperature of the gas turbine.

Table 4. Performance Result of SOFC-GT-ST-ORC

ΔH (kJ/mol)	-241.8
ΔS (kJ/mol K)	-44.37
ΔG (kJ/mol)	-158.7
E_r(V)	0.937
V_{sofc} (V)	0.767
LHV (kJ/mol)	802.3
U_f	0.82
I (A)	5.934*10^8
J (mA/cm^2)	500
V_{act}(V)	0.171
V_{ohm}(V)	0.009
V_{conc}(V)	0.011
$\dot{\omega}$ (MW)	125.5
P_{sofc} (MW)	455.4
η(%)	77

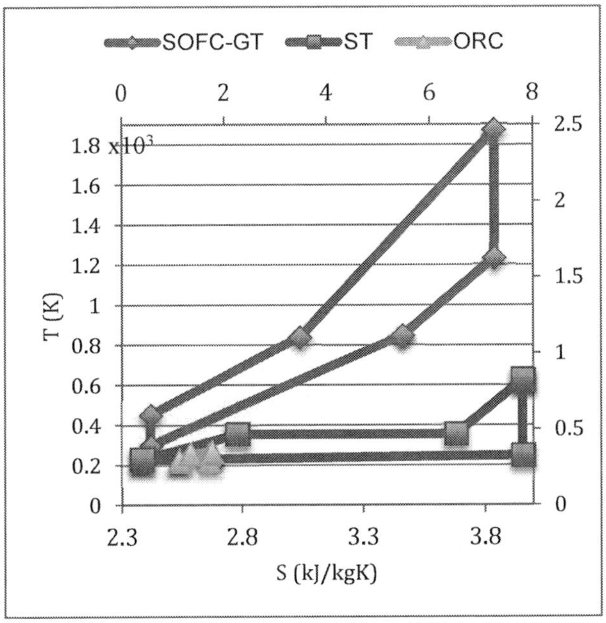

Figure 2. T-S diagram of the SOFC-GT-ST-ORC Quadruple Cycle

Summary

A natural gas SOFC-GT-ST-ORC quadruple cycle is developed. The study shows that 77% efficiency is obtained higher than single (30-45%), combined (50-60%) and triple cycle (60-70%) and other hybrid of SOFC, GT, ST and ORC. This is possible because the waste heat from the gas turbine was utilized both in the steam cycle and organic rankine cycle. The SOFC generates about 72% of the power while GT, ST and ORC put together generates about 28%. Although the work of the gas and steam turbine might be encroached upon, it creates room for the work in the ORC. Future work would include optimizing the cycle, the effect of change in pressure, temperature, mass flow rate and fuel utilization factor in the efficiency in plug flow.

References

1. Kimura H, Inoue N, Fujimoto K, Nishimura H, Honda M, " Replacement of Coal-fired Thermal Power Plant with Highly Efficient GTCC Power Plant with Latest Green F-type Gas Turbine, Mitsubishi Heavy Industries Technical Review Vol. 48 No. 1, March 2011
2. Zhang X, Chan S.H., Li G, Ho H, Li J, Feng Z, "A Review of Integration Strategies for Solid Oxide Fuel Cells", Journal of Power Sources, 2009
3. Arsalis A, "Thermoeconomic Modeling and Parametric Study of Hybrid SOFC-Gas Turbine-Steam Turbine Power Plants Ranging from 1.5 to 10MWe", Journal of Power Sources, 2008
4. Hung T. C., "Triple Cycle: A Conceptual Arrangement of Multiple Cycle Toward Optimal Energy Conversion", Journal of Engineering for Gas Turbines and Power, 2002
5. Yan Z, Zhao P, Wang J, Dai Y, "Thermodynamic Analysis of an SOFC-GT-ORC Integrated Power System with liquefied natural gas as heat sink", International Journal of Hydrogen Energy, 2013
6. Siemens AG, "Waste Heat Recovery with Organic Rankine Cycle", Siemens Energy Sector, 2014
7. Milewski J, Swirski K, Santarelli M, Leone P, "Advanced Methods of Solid Oxide Fuel Cell Modeling", Springer 2011, pp 8-9.
8. Bove R, Ubertini S, "Modeling Solid Oxide Fuel Cells: Methods, Procedures and Techniques", Springer 2008, pp 246-248
9. Akkaya A V, "Electrochemical model for performance analysis of a tubular SOFC", Int'l Journal of Energy Research, 2007

Reducing Fuel Consumption through Hybrid Power Systems and Advanced Electronics

Norman Bessette and Gary Simon
Acumentrics SOFC Corporation
19 Walpole Park South, Walpole, Ma 02081

Abstract: Future battlefield power requirements necessitate energy flexibility. At one time generators were the only option but now with advancements in energy storage and renewables more options exist. This paper will detail some of the advancements being made to include these technologies to reduce the required fuel needed in the operating theater.

Keywords: power; TQG; fuel cell; solar; energy storage; Wankel; rotary engine.

Introduction

Future battlefield power requirements necessitate energy flexibility. While generators were once the only option, new renewable technologies such as solar and fuel cells, and new battery technologies such as Li-ion and ultimately flow batteries, are finding their way to that battlefield. This results in large fuel savings, reducing logistical requirements and supply chains, freeing the warfighter for the mission at hand. The right-sizing and reliability of such systems, however, becomes significantly more complex. Solar power availability depends on weather and location, and thus has a relatively low reliability for that reason. At the other end of the spectrum AMMPS generators boast a meant time between failure of at least 750 hours, but require fuel and operate at 70-72dB.

Reducing or eliminating the fuel requirement for a mission necessitates the combination of available technologies; generators for reliability, and renewable and efficient resources for significant fuel reduction as well as advanced storage technology. As such, Acumentrics is working on all fronts from renewable technology integration of solar and fuel cells to advanced power density Wankel cycle generators to smart electronics to modulate and prioritize the most efficient power sources.

For renewable platform integration Acumentrics is working in partnership with SolAero Tech on an ONR sponsored program entitled Renewable Sustainable Expeditionary Power (RSEP) which is focused on integration of solar panels and a 3kWe fuel cell operational on JP-8 to cut fuel consumption by over 40% relative to a base load TQG.

For advanced power management, Acumentrics is working with ONR on a program entitled High Energy Storage Module (HESM) for use with tactical generators and advanced energy storage. The HESM system provides intelligent power management by controlling power draw from a TQG and four discrete DC sources, prioritizing power drawn from each source to maximize fuel reduction as the HESM also provides the capability to double the power output of the TQG for periods of time by providing withdrawal from storage.

For advancing generator technology Acumentrics is working in partnership with Freedom Motors on an advanced engine utilizing improvements to the Wankel system to increase both power density as well as fuel efficiency. This system also has the ability to improve the MTBF of existing TQG's.

This paper will examine each of these evolving advanced technologies and explain the integration of each to provide a highly efficient power module for military use.

Renewable Sustainable Expeditionary Power (RSEP)

To provide ultimate flexibility to our forward operating personnel, reliance on fuel supply and the associated logistics needs to be reduced. The present 3kW TQG generator has an efficiency of at most 25% making it a liability to the mobility of these troops. To meet the military's goal of a 40% reduction in fuel usage the military has contracted SolAero Tech and Acumentrics to develop a system integrating a JP-8 fueled 3kWe SOFC unit with a deployable solar array. This unit, depicted below in Figure 1, contains a JP-8 fueled 3kWe SOFC unit as well as a deployable solar array capable of 2kW. The unit contains electrical energy storage and 80 gallons of fuel as well as a power distribution box for providing AC or DC power. The unit is trailer mounted on the military's standard LTT-MCC trailer and comes in at slightly below 4000 lbs.

This program is in its final year of development and will culminate in a TRL6 level unit provided for initial testing at Carderock in the fall.

High Energy Storage Module (HESM)

The High Energy Storage Module (HESM) program is intended to allow for better balancing of power among available power sources as well as "right sizing" of generators for a mission avoiding the need for redundancy or over sizing which results in excessive weight and expense, lower efficiency and thus higher fuel usage for the military. The program builds off of Acumentrics' long history in power electronics and power management to provide this hybrid solution. The product under development has the ability to:

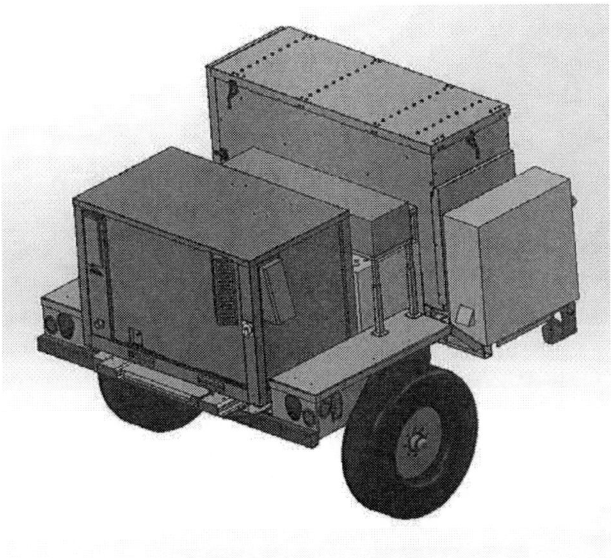

- **Load Sharing**: The HESM will source load power to the maximum capability of its DC inputs, such as solar or a fuel cell, reducing the load the generator must source. If the available renewable sources have sufficient capability the generator can be turned off.
- **Peak Shave:** provide transient load power when the load exceeds the rating of the single TQG.
- **Ride Through:** provide power from storage devices or other DC sources when the TQG is being brought on-line.
- **Energy Storage Charge:** Charge back a multitude of energy storage devices when there is excessive DC or AC power available.
- **Stand Alone:** Operate power solely from a DC renewable source when the supply exceeds the load.

Figure 2 below shows the overall schematic as well as the unit itself in the lower left hand corner. The unit will have the capability to convert any of the DC sources to the AC output at 90% efficiency. The volume of the unit will be 17" wide x 21" deep and not exceed 14" height. Weight shall be less than 200lbs supporting a four-man carry.

As the military's forward power needs are constantly changing, as are the devices from which that power is derived, adapting to these needs and the elimination of fuel will require the integration of multiple DC devices for the production of AC power. The HESM system will provide that interface. It will come with the capability and flexibility to adapt to new energy storage and power generation technologies as they become available. It will

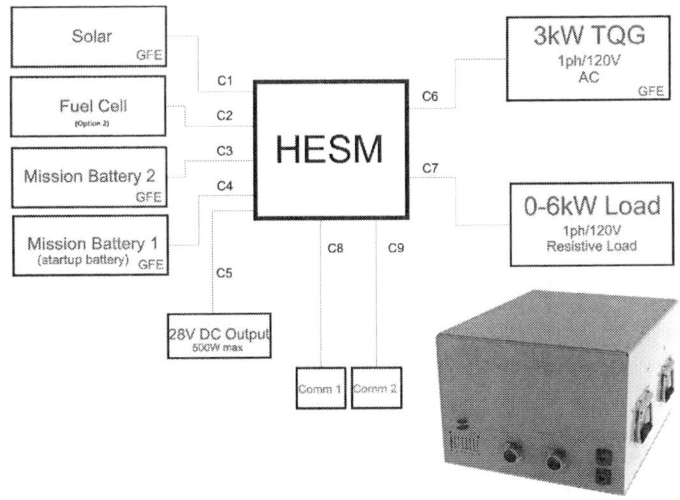

maintain the very high reliability factor that can be achieved with the new AMPS generators through interface with those systems. It will minimize fuel consumption by load sharing with renewable sources and shutting off the generator as possible based on the load profiles. Finally, it allows right-sizing of the generator systems to the average load with the potential for extended peak operation over the capability of a generator alone.

Advanced Generators Leveraging the Wankel Cycle

Existing TQG's suffer from high weights and low power density values resulting in logistical burdens in forward operating theaters. These generators also suffer from low mean time between repairs and mean time between overhauls. Freedom Motors (FM) has developed and demonstrated a family of rotary engines, the rotopower engine, with two models reaching the beta production stage (150cc and 530cc) with a third model (27cc) demonstrated. Figure 3 below compares the piston engine to its rotary equivalent. The rotary engine realizes a factor of 7 reduction in weight and factor of 3 in volume. A 40% noise reduction has also been achieved. Work remains on improving the overall efficiency of the generator through combustor design to exceed that of a standard piston engine and operate on JP-8 fuel as well as ruggedization of a unit capable of meeting military specifications. Once complete, integration with the HESM design above will provide a lightweight highly efficient unit for forward operating personnel.

Acknowledgements

The authors would like to thank ONR for its funding for the HESM program under contract N00014-12-C-0652 and its funding of the RSEP program under contract N00014-12-D-0251/0002. We would like to specifically acknowledge the support of Scott Coombe, Don Hoffman, and Ed House of ONR. We would also like to thank the support of Solearotech as our partner on the RSEP program.

		Displacement	HP	Weight	Volume	Emissions	Critical Parts
Piston Engine		100cc	2.8	28 lbs.	1.5ft^3	Meets emissions standards for California without catalytic converter	12
Rotapower Engine		27cc	2.8	4 lbs	.5 FT^3	Emissions far below California emissions standards without catalytic converter	3

Experimental Testing and Analysis of an Asymmetrical Supercapacitor Module Device for Sustainable Power Delivery

Wenhua H. Zhu and Bruce J. Tatarchuk*

Center for Microfibrous Materials
Department of Chemical Engineering, Auburn University
212 Ross Hall, Auburn, AL 36849-5127
*tatarbj@auburn.edu, zhuwenh@auburn.edu
http://wp.auburn.edu/cm3/

Abstract: *An asymmetrical supercapacitor module device with 300 F at an operating window between 4.0 volts and 14.5 volts was tested and evaluated via DC techniques using modern equipment. Charge and discharge characteristics were obtained on the capacitor module at an initial 25 A current load. Energy and power density were assessed on the supercapacitor module. Four lithium iron phosphate (LFP) cells were separately adjusted to a bottom-balance of 2.1 V level and then connected in serious to form a high-energy powerful battery pack. DC pulse methods were employed to characterize and evaluate two types of advanced power devices. The hybrid power system consisting of the supercapacitor module in parallel with a 12.8 V Li-ion 4-cell pack in series has been successfully tested as a functioning hybrid device for power delivery and energy storage need. The preliminary results and analysis on hybrid power capability are reported in details with experimental pulse load data.*

Keywords: supercapacitor; hybrid power device; high power delivery; renewable energy; energy storage and conversion.

Introduction

The weakness of the Lead-acid, Ni-MH, and Li-ion battery packs as well as PEM fuel cell systems can generally be supplemented by the irreplaceable power features of supercapacitor power modules[1]. A supercapacitor stores energy through the electrical charge in the double layer at the electrode-electrolyte interface, mostly in porous carbon or activated charcoal with high surface area[2]. This unique structure design via two carbon electrodes insulated by a thin porous separator provides this type of capacitor power module with unusual higher energy density at contrast with traditional capacitors[3]. Double layer capacitors do not have any dielectrics in general, but in contrast, the effective thickness of the similar "dielectric" is particularly thin in the double layer and many functional arrays in the porous particle structures contribute to the double layer charges at the interface due to the driving forces of the electric field. The porous nature and double layer charges translate it to a highly reliable capacitance. It can recapture up to 90%, braking energy during frequent start-stops, accelerate the engine at high power demands, and can also assist the fuel cell powered vehicle very quietly but powerfully. The supercapacitor module is suitable for a short distance range or many heavy duty start-stops[4]. It is still necessary for some applications to store more energy in the power system for a short period of use or recapture more energy for longer distance requirements. Although the Prius batteries can only recapture *ca.* 50% of the braking energy, the Lead-acid batteries, Ni-MH, and Li-ion battery packs are all find their suitable applications for various on-board energy storage tasks. The Li-ion LFP cells and battery packs are quickly applied to many energy storage areas such as mobile laptops, electric bicycles, and hybrid vehicles. Some applications need storage for a certain amount of energy but for a short period of high power need, and this gives the concept of a hybrid power device, also called a hybrid power system. The hybrid power combines high power feature of the supercapacitor and high energy storage of the advanced rechargeable battery. In the present work, an asymmetric capacitor module was characterized using an updated high-power equipment. The hybrid system with two types of power devices, *i.e.* a supercapacitor module and a four-cell LFP battery pack was operated together as a hybrid power source for performance assessments.

Experimental

The supercapacitor module consists of 10 asymmetric capacitors connected in series as a package, and four Li-ion LFP batteries are also linked in series as single battery pack. The capacitor module and battery pack can be characterized separately, and two above energy storage devices can also work together as a hybrid power device. It was set up with proper connections (up to 600 A) for further testing and evaluation. The accurate factory data and parameters were corrected and updated as the following description. This supercapacitor module is the 10EC104 type by KBi, with a mass weight of 4.79 kg and a dimension of 26.5 cm in length, 6.3 cm in width, and 16.3 cm in height. The capacitor module can be operated in the range from 4.0 V to 14.5 V. It is a type of the advanced capacitor with asymmetrical structures, also named as a NiOOH/C hybrid capacitor. The positive electrode of the capacitor uses nickel hydroxide electrodes, the electrolyte is utilized *ca.* 30% potassium hydroxide solution, and the negative electrode is employed the activated carbon electrodes.

Four lithium iron phosphate (LFP) cells were adjusted to a bottom-balance of 2.1 V level and then connected in serious to form as a high-energy powerful battery pack. The nominal voltage of the battery pack is summed as 12.8 V based on

3.2 V nominal voltage of single Li-ion LFP cell. The battery pack was normally charged to 60% of the rated capacity, approximately at a level of *ca.* 60% SoC (state-of-charge). The cell has DC equivalent series resistance no more than 1 mOhm with a specific power of *ca.* 1600 W kg^{-1}. Its energy density at cell level is *ca.* 80 Wh kg^{-1}. The voltage limit is recommended as 2.0 V during a pulse discharge process. The cell operating temperature is within the range from −15°C to 60°C but is recommended to be charge between 0°C and 40°C. The battery pack was well maintained within this operating temperature range requirement. The asymmetric supercapacitor power module is positioned in the ambient room-temperature environment. During the hybrid power assessments, the capacitor module was firstly charged up to an identical voltage with the battery pack at 60% SoC. It was then installed in parallel with the Li-ion LFP battery pack to form as a hybrid power system. The Arbin BT-MP battery tester, directly connected to the supercapacitor module terminals, was applied to the hybrid system characterization. The hybrid power system was subsequently conducted various tests and evaluation according to proper characterization profiles.

Results and discussion

Supercapacitor Energy Storage Mechanism and Battery Chemistry in the Hybrid Power Devices: Electrochemical supercapacitors offer visible advantages in power capability, high cycle life, long working and calendar life, no or low maintenance requirements. The initial electrochemical capacitor uses aqueous solution such as potassium hydroxide, and the operating voltage is limited to *ca.* 1.2 V per unit cell (nominal at *ca.* 0.9 V). For energy storage enhancement, the organic electrolyte is applied to replace KOH electrolyte and the capacitor unit cell voltage can be greatly increased. Typically, an ammonium salt dissolved in an organic solvent such as propylene carbonate can be used as the organic electrolyte[4]. And the symmetric capacitors can obtain 2.3~2.7 V rated voltages per unit cell but in addition with disadvantages of low temperature performance and long-term stability concerns.

For further durable energy-storage needs, an asymmetric capacitor can be established with two different capacitor electrodes in series. One electrode with high surface area is the same as that in the symmetric capacitor using electrostatic energy stored in the double layer; another capacitor electrode is taken from the battery electrode. This single battery electrode uses the faradaic energy storage, *i.e.* through electron charge/discharge transfer reactions at the electrode-electrolyte interface to realize the conversion between chemical and electric energy. The depth-of-discharge (DoD) of the battery electrode is very low and it convinces longer cycle life. The asymmetric capacitor design contributes a unique feature for electrode self-balancing with using of aqueous electrolyte and insignificant overcharge, because of gas recombination mechanisms available for quite a few battery electrode such as nickel hydroxide electrodes.

The battery pack in this work consists of 4 Li-ion LFP cells in series for a nominal voltage of 12.8 V. This is also called lithium iron phosphate battery using graphite as anode insertion material and $LiFePO_4$ as cathode active material [5]. Its low electrical conductivity of the LFP cathode was providentially solved by particle size reduction and conductive coating technology [6]. Another obstacle using the olivine LFP as cathodes for the industrial development is that the ionic conductivity is particularly sensitive to any impurity that is able to block a channel, thus preventing Li^+-ion diffusion to all sites in the channel[7]. This problem is fortunately resolved because it is now probable to produce the electrode material free of impurities. As a whole, the dimension reduction of the LFP particles to nanosize delivers short Li^+-ion diffusion paths within the positive electrode. In addition, the synthesis of carbon-coated LFP enhances the electrical conduction between particles ensuring high rate capability and preventing particles agglomeration. Furthermore, the use of high quality of the enhanced LiFePO4, impurity-free materials as positive electrodes makes it possible for the nano-structured cathode in a Li-ion LFP cell to remarkably deliver a reversible capacity of *ca.* 160 mAh g^{-1}. These efforts make this type of Li-ion cells with low-cost, long cycle life, better calendar life than layered $LiCoO_2$ chemistry, exceptional thermal stability, slower capacity deterioration, non-toxicity, and high rate capability for proper power delivery and rapid energy capture needs. The olivine $LiFePO_4$ material derived from the triphylite mineral family exhibits reputable chemical and thermal stability at contrast with layered $LiCoO_2$ and spinel $LiMn_2O_4$ cathode structures. This is mainly resulted from the strong P-O bonds in the olivine LFP framework instead of the weak Co-O or Mn-O bonds when runaway overheating, circuit shorting, or out gassing. As an outcome, the LFP cells in series as a pack were chosen to work together with the asymmetric electrochemical capacitor module as a hybrid power device for pulse power tests and evaluation for various task duties.

Energy and Power Density Assessment on Asymmetric Capacitor Module: Charge and discharge cycle features of the supercapacitor module is shown in Figure 1. It is charged at 25 A to a constant voltage of 13.0 V and then discharged at 25 A to 6.5 V, rest for 30 s. Six low-power cycles reveals the capacitors in series in good working condition. Updated Ragone plots of the asymmetric capacitor module is shown in Figure 2. Theoretically, it has a maximum stored energy from 4.0 V to 16.0 V. But for a preferred operating window, the volatge is range from 4.0 V to 14.5 V and the optimal voltage window is ranged from 6.5 V to 13.0 V. The actual available energy stored in the capacitor is based on the system allowable operating range in considering of the life cycle needs. In general, less energy is stored if the system is operated at a lower voltage window such as discharge from 13.0 V to 6.5 V cutoff range. The Ragone plots of the asymmetric capacitor module shows that the power module has super power capabilty in spite of lower specific energy of no more than 2.0 Wh kg^{-1} at unit weight level.

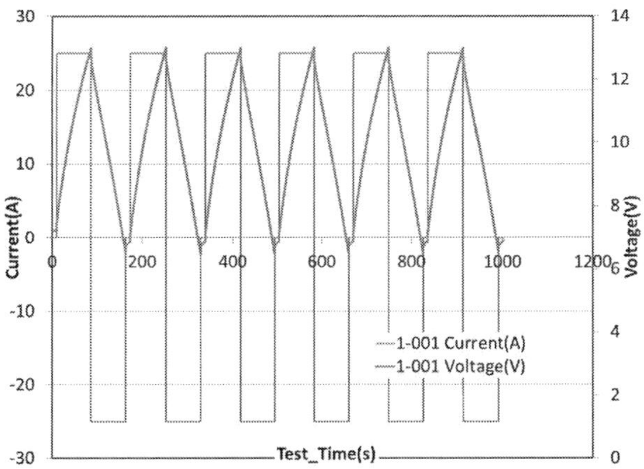

Figure 1. Charge and discharge cycle features of the supercapacitor at 25 A charge to a constant voltage of 13.0 V and 25 A discharge to 6.5 V, rest for 30 s for 6 cycles.

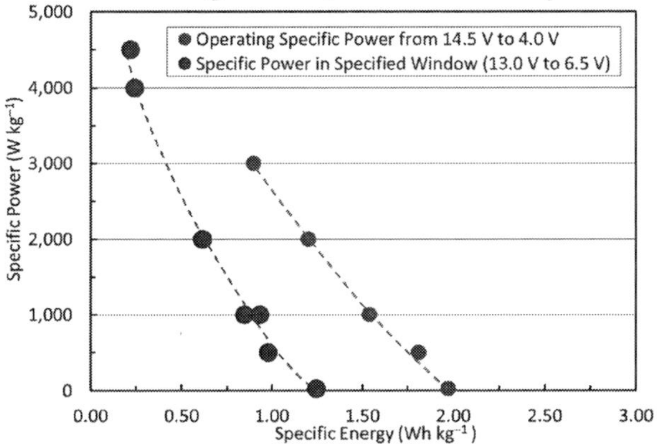

Figure 2. Measured specific power versus specific energy at two specified voltage windows for the supercapacitor module. The values of specific power and specific energy are both based on the factory unit weight of 10.57 lbs[1].

Charge and Discharge Characteristics of the Li-ion Battery Pack: The Li-ion LFP cells were received normally with *ca.* 10-20% SoC. The Li-ion battery pack consists of four single cells linked in series with suitable cooling capability (no more than 60°C at the battery surfaces). The energy stored device was charged up to 14.0 V at 75 A and then discharged at 150 A down to 9.2 V end-of-discharge voltage (EoDV) for system performance assurance before pulse load tests. The battery pack was initially cycled at a level of 83% SoC. The testing results reveal that the battery power system and electrical connections are reliable and the power pack are ready to work together with the asymmetric capacitor module for cranking and hybrid pulse tests.

Pulse Cranking on the Supercapacitor Module Device: The capacitor power module was charged at 25 A until the voltage cutoff at 13.0 V end-of-charge voltage (EoCV). For the actual engine cranking, the applied current may increase to 580 A or 880 A. Here the modified cranking profile was chosen for examination of current pulses during the cranking periods. The applied currents during testing are changed from 120 A to 580 A as shown in Figure 3. Using the modified cold cranking profile, the supercapacitor was operated under a duty cycle of 16.67% and a frequency of 0.0833 Hz at different load levels. The result shows that it successfully runs more than 6 cranks and maintains more than 7.5 V voltage at 120 A load. If the cranking current increases to 300 A, it still lasts for 3 complete cranking cycles. It reaches the 4.0 V lower voltage operating limitation and stops in the middle of the 4th cranking cycle. At a high current of 580 A, the single capacitor module can only operate for one complete cycles due to limited energy storage in the power device. From the above cranking tests, it reveals that the capacitor module can run up to 300 A load for assisting a battery engine startup due to concerns of cold weather or the expensive battery system duration.

Hybrid Power Assessment of the Supercapacitor Module in Parallel with a Li-ion 4-Cell LFP Battery Pack: In some particular field applications, the hybrid power technology can combine the battery and capacitor's advantages. The hybrid pulse power characterization (HPPC) profile is originally applied to observe its discharge pulse and regenerative pulse power capabilities at a closely full charge state (*ca.* 100% SoC for battery) for both the minimum and maximum power-assist goals (10-s discharge, 40-s rest, and 10-s regeneration). The regular test procedure uses constant current at levels derived from the manufacturer's maximum rated discharge current. Considering the available equipment power capability, a modified HPPC profile is initially applied to evaluate the supercapacitor in parallel with a Li-ion LFP battery pack as a hybrid power device for evaluating potential pulse power applications.

The Li-ion cells of the battery pack in the hybrid power system were separately charged to *ca.* 60% SoC level in the beginning (60% charge input associated with the factory rated capacity). It was then connected in parallel with the asymmetric supercapacitor module device at the similar OCV voltage level. For further understanding of the hybrid power performance, the hybrid power module is conducted performance assessments under a certain hybrid pulse load profile. The Arbin battery tester was connected to the hybrid device with the same positive and negative terminals before the pulse loading tests. The hybrid power system was performed investigations through the same modified hybrid pulse power characterization profile. The duty cycle is 16.67% as shown in Figure 4 at a frequency of 0.0167 Hz with a load current of 120 A for 10 sec, rest for 40 sec and then charge under a charge current of 90 A for 10 sec for 10 cycles.

The hybrid test results reveal that the hybrid power device is capable of performing the pulse power function with proper

[1]Specific energy (Wh kg^{-1}) and specific power (W kg^{-1}) are better terms for description of energy and power levels per unit weight. Here the measured and calculated value of specific energy (Wh kg^{-1}) is revised and corrected in considering of the actual energy output per factory unit weight. In the excel sheet, it was inappropriately assessed without accurate factory weight in the preliminary work [8,9] for specific energy values (Wh kg^{-1}) in the Ragone plots.

energy capture ability and also maintain the stable pulse loading output voltages. As shown in Figure 4, the response voltage decreases with 10-s energy consumption at 120 A load. The voltage recovers quickly during the initial 40-s rest period and increases sharply during 10-s replenishing charge (similar to the energy-regenerative process). During each HPPC cycle, the hybrid power device has a loss of 300 A·s capacity, but the pulse curves including the response voltage are actually stable at the peak and bottom locations. Due to the better rate capability of the Li-ion battery chemistry than the Lead-acid battery chemistry, the acceptance of the 1st charge regeneration is improved with the assistance of Li-ion battery pack[8]. The noises for the pulse charge current is also removed due to the use of a newer Arbin battery tester.

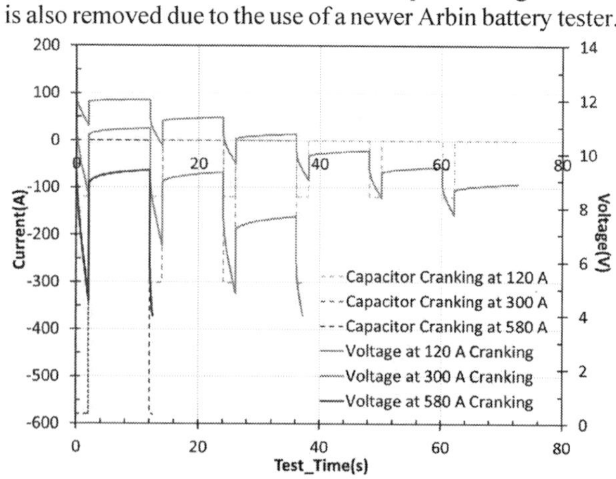

Figure 3. Supercapacitor cranking profiles in the energy-stored power module under pulse power testing using a modified cold cranking profile, operating under a duty cycle of 16.67% and a frequency of 0.0833 Hz at different loads.

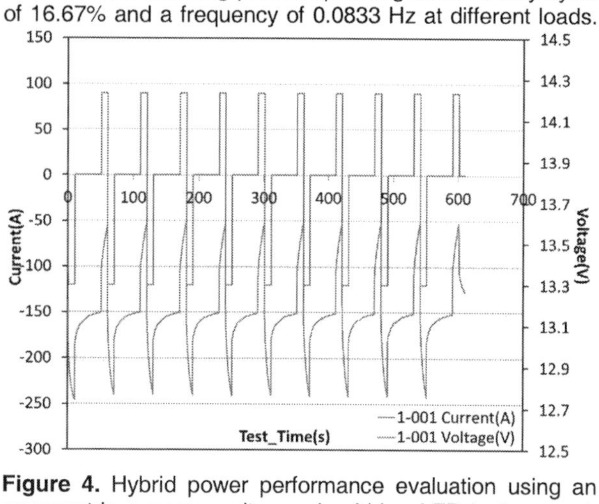

Figure 4. Hybrid power performance evaluation using an asymmetric supercapacitor and a Li-ion LFP battery pack under a modified hybrid pulse power characterization (HPPC) profile. The system was operated via a duty cycle of 16.67% and a frequency of 0.0167 Hz with a load current of 120 A for 10 sec, rest for 40 sec, and then under a charge current of 90 A for 10 sec. The following cycle is repeated after the 1st 60-s cycle period.

In the future work, the further results using this HPPC profile for testing and evaluation of the hybrid power source is to be included with more detailed current response during charge and discharge cycles for the Li-ion batteries in the hybrid module device.

Summary

In this study, an asymmetric supercapacitor power module was characterized using a modern high power equipment up to 580 A load. It was connected together in parallel with a high rate Li-ion LFP four-cell pack as a hybrid power device. This hybrid power system was performed the tests and assessment using a modified cranking profile under a duty cycle of 16.67% and a frequency of 0.0833 Hz at different loads. Tests were also conducted on the hybrid power system using a modified HPPC profile under a duty cycle of 16.67% and frequency of 0.0167 Hz with a load current of 120 A for 10 sec, rest for 40 sec, and then under a charge current of 90 A for 10 sec. The supercapacitor module can be positively operated using the modified cranking profile for 6 cycles at 120 A load current. This capacitor module in parallel with the 12.8 V Li-ion LFP pack as a hybrid power device has been successfully assessed using the modified HPPC profile. The hybrid power system is expected to have an enhanced power delivery and energy storage capability for specific applications such as cold weather, heavy duty trucks, or rapid energy capture for regenerative braking requirements.

References

[1] T.S. Balasubramanian and S.K. Chopra, "Evaluation of supercapacitor- battery hybrid pack for pulse power application," in *Advances in Sensors for Aerospace Applications* 2007, pp.1-7.

[2] B.J. Tatarchuk, "Method of optimizing composite preparation for electrical properties: maximum capacitance electrodes," WO9118698A1, 1991, pp.1-47.

[3] Tecate Group. Ultracapacitor & Supercapacitor, *https://www.tecategroup.com/ultracapacitors-supercapacitors/ultracapacitor-FAQ.php*, 2014.

[4] J.R. Miller and S.M.Butler,"Capacitor energy storage for stationary-power applications," in *Proceedings of the Battcon 2004 Conference*, 2004, pp.4.1-8.

[5] A.K.Padhi, K.S.Nanjundaswamy, and J.B. Goodenough, "Phospho-olivines as positive-electrode materials for rechargeable lithium batteries," *Journal of the Electrochemical Society,* vol. 144, pp.1188-1194, 1997.

[6] S.Y. Chung, J.T. Bloking, Y.M. Chiang, "Electronically conductive phospho-olivines as lithium storage electrodes," *Nature Materials,* vol.1, pp.123-128, 2002.

[7] K. Zaghib, A. Guerfi, P. Hovington, A. Vijh, M. Trudeau, A. Mauger, *et al.*, "Review and analysis of nanostructured olivine-based lithium recheargeable batteries: Status and trends," *J. Power Sources,* vol. 232, pp.357-369, 2013.

[8] W. H. Zhu and B. J. Tatarchuk, in *Proceedings of the 46th Power Sources Conf.*, 2014, pp.391-394.

[9] W. H. Zhu and B. J. Tatarchuk, *Applied Energy,* vol. 169, pp.460–468, 2016.

Hybrid Electrical Energy Storage System Implementing High Energy Supercapacitors

Stephen Cordova, Steven C. Arzberger and Weibing Xing
stephenc@adatech.com, stevena@adatech.com, weibingx@adatech.com
ADA Technologies, Inc.
8100 Shaffer Parkway, Suite 130
Littleton, CO 80127

Abstract: *ADA Technologies, Inc. (ADA) has demonstrated the feasibility of an unprecedented lithium ion (Li-ion)/supercapacitor Hybrid Electrical Energy Storage System (HEESS). Our technology is positioned to afford significant pulse power (projected ~ 10 kW/kg) in a high-specific energy system (100-150 Wh/kg). The system is enabled via a constant-current regulator that isolates the battery from the supercapacitor to improve the end-to-end efficiency from the battery to the load, while accounting for the relative diminutive rate capability of the high-energy Li-ion battery. The pulse power capability is provided by an ADA supercapacitor technology that possesses ~ 10x the energy (15-20 Wh/kg at cell level) of commercial supercapacitor products. This leads to a significantly improved duty cycle – duration, magnitude and frequency of the pulse.*

Keywords: Supercapacitor, ultracapacitor, hybrid, energy, Li-ion, battery, high energy, pulse power

Introduction

A HEESS comprised of a supercapacitor to buffer/filter high rate pulse currents, coupled to a high-energy battery, would allow for an efficient storage device that maximizes energy density and can deliver pulse power characteristics (duty cycle, pulse amplitude, frequency, etc.). Such an HEESS would enable the combination of many disparate energy devices providing valuable mass and size savings.

In essence, supercapacitors serve as a compliment to a primary energy source (battery), which cannot repeatedly provide quick bursts of power. Supercapacitors are capable of repetitive cycling (several hundreds of thousands of cycles) across a wide range of rate and temperature. This holds tremendous potential to extend the life of current systems and provide additional mass savings through the elimination of the heating/cooling architectures required by battery systems.

A hybrid device will permit high charge/discharge currents to be accepted via an isolated supercapacitor. Indeed this is important because a Li-ion battery can be compromised when rapidly charged at a high state-of-charge, which is known to lead to deteriorated performance and significant safety concerns.

ADA has demonstrated the technical feasibility of an unprecedented performance HEESS. We have: (1) used analytical simulations to predict the performance of an HEESS based on the combination of a commercial Li-ion battery bank and an ADA supercapacitor cell bank, with autonomous electronic controls, (2) illustrated HEESS capabilities through empirical demonstrations, (3) demonstrated unprecedented specific energy in our high energy supercapacitors and (4) demonstrated ADA large format supercapacitor performance. These efforts are prologue to a HEESS hardware demonstration. We anticipate a demonstration device with a specific energy of > 150 Wh/kg and significant pulse power.

Identification & Significance of the Problem or Opportunity

Burden of Today's Soldier: Today's soldier carries a significant number of electronic devices to maintain an advantage on the battlefield. Each device has its own unique power profile necessitating multiple electrical energy storage (EES) devices to be carried. This burdens the soldier's mobility and effectiveness, and may compromise mission success.

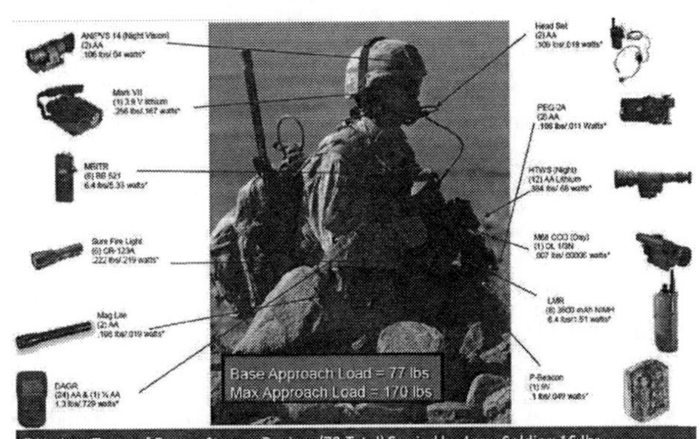

Figure 1. Various items carried by a soldier on a typical mission. Soldier may carry seven various types of energy storage devices (70 total) for a total of 16 lbs. on a typical mission.[1]

An example of a soldier's equipment burden during a typical mission is shown in **Figure 1**. With increasing frequency, electronic devices require high power, often pulse power, and high-energy; a dichotomous pair that, until recently, required multiple energy storage devices. Since pulse power characteristics tend to be deleterious to the life of traditional high-energy batteries, this necessitates inefficient oversizing of the battery and DC-bus architecture. Alternatively, supercapacitors are capable of providing very high repetitive pulse power profiles but suffer from a low energy density prohibiting their sole use.

Constant Current Architecture

A constant current architecture was designed and developed by Pedram. A software simulator SIMES[2] (**Figure 2**, left) was used to predict hybrid performance with this different electronics architectures, leading to a fundamental understanding of HEESS performance potential, and promising designs. Pedram designed a hybrid prototype (**Figure 2**, right) from a 115 Wh Li-ion battery bank, a 163 Wh lead-acid battery bank and a 8.13 Wh supercapacitor bank. This was used to validate the hybrid design benefits and the validate the use of the constant current electronics architecture.

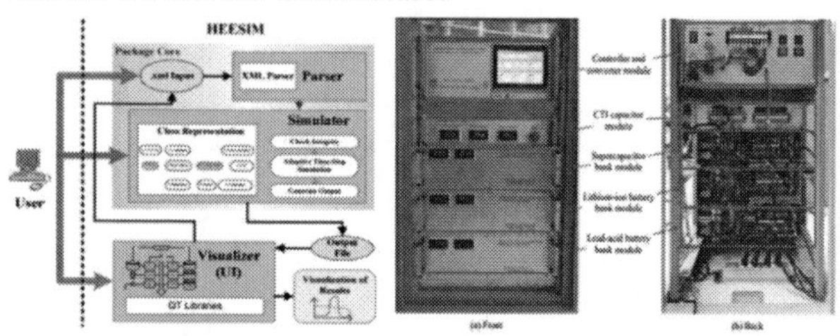

Figure 2. SIMES: a HEESS performance simulator (left) and prototype HEESS (right).

An ADA HEESS was conceptualized based on commercial high energy Li-ion battery cells, ADA high specific energy supercapacitor cells and a constant current regulator architecture. Analytical tools were used with empircal data inputs, leading to the predicted performance of a range of possible designs that represent an unprecedented combination of power (pulse power) and energy (see **Figure 3**).This results from the discreet isolation of each energy storage bank,[3] and the load. This also established desirable performance tailorability characterics for the ADA HEESS, which represent the ability to address a range of applications. This is possible through design adjustments in the relative Li-ion/supercapacitor percentages to meet the specific pulse power requirement(s).

Pedram defined three fundamental charge management policies: (1) a charge allocation from a power source to a set of EES banks,[4,5] (2) a charge replacement from EES banks to load devices,[6] and (3) a charge migration between EES banks to improve the HEESS availability and responsiveness.[7] Optimal control policies based on convex optimization and heuristic search algorithms were derived. Pedram established effective logarithmic-time algorithms for HEESS fault detection and tolerance.[8] This led to the development of a state-of-health (SoH) joint charge management algorithm and HEESS models, leading to significant safety improvements.[9] This SoH model also provides meaningful extensions over prior SoH degradation models, which are limited to predictions for battery cycle life charge/discharge for arbitrary charge/discharge patterns. The models employ effective cycle decoupling techniques. SoH modeling will provide a dynamic means to adjust charge allocation throughout life increasing the HEESS efficiency and safety characteristics.

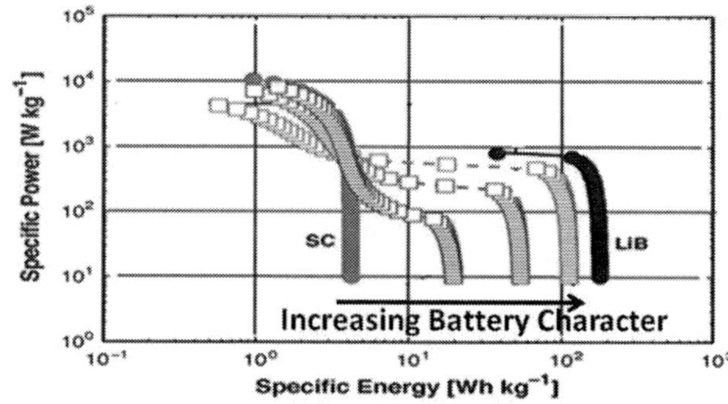

Figure 3. Analytical model results displayed as specific energy vs. specific power, which demonstrate ADA HEESS performance potential. The solid red profile depicts a supercapacitor (SC) and the solid black depicts a Li-ion battery (LiB). The intermediate profiles correspond to hybrid configurations with increasing battery character (from left to right).[10]

The coupling of a high energy supercapacitor with a high energy Li-ion battery via a constant current regulator will: (1) maximize pulse power capability, (2) extend operational life, (3) maximize operational temperature range and (4) maximize safety characteristics. The device pulse power capability is enhanced with a higher energy supercapacitor. For example, ADA high specific energy supercapacitors that provide 10x the energy (15-20 Wh/kg, at cell level) of a commercial supercapacitor significantly improve the duty cycle—duration, magnitude and frequency of pulse characteristics. We can also tailor the energy storage banks and electronics architecture to a specific charge/discharge protocol to maximize capability.

HEESS Empirical Demonstration: Pedram developed a novel and enabling battery/supercapacitor hybrid system based on a constant-current regulator (**Figure 4**). This design isolates the battery from the supercapacitor, leading to significant improvements in energy efficiency. A battery/supercapacitor HEESS is suitable for applications of relatively small scale such as embedded platforms, desktop and server applications. In comparison, a hybrid architecture comprising a parallel connection does not perform well when the supercapacitor capacity is small. This is due to the low energy density or relatively high current demands. The constant current regulator serves to maximize the pulse power capability of the high energy supercapacitors while accounting for the relatively low rate capability of the high energy Li-ion batteries.

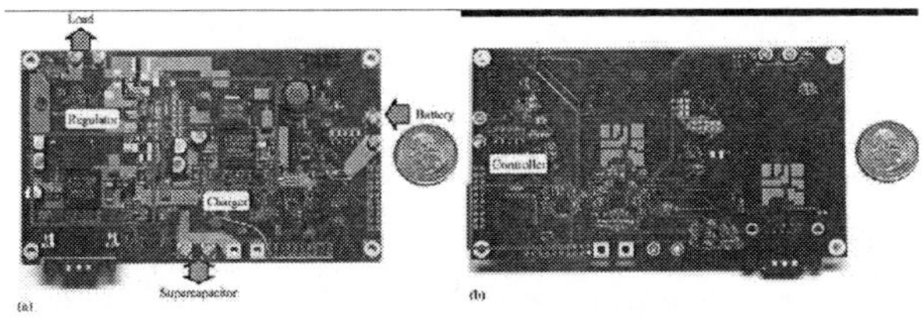

Figure 4. Hybrid power controller board; (a) top and (b) bottom views.

ADA HEESS Architecture: The ADA HEESS design includes energy storage banks with converters, a charge transfer interconnect (CTI) and a main micro-controller block. It is based on the demonstrated general HEESS architecture that was established by Pedram. This architecture controls the HEESS operation by sensing and providing feedback to the electrical energy storage bank charge and discharge currents, and the CTI voltage. The HEESS architecture has been generalized to support multiple CTIs and mesh network-based interconnects. Each HEESS component was modeled including the batteries, supercapacitors and power converters. All modeling efforts were based on empirical date inputs obtained from hardware demonstrations.[11]

The Pedram constant current regulator electronics package was designed to minimize the energy loss and capital cost of the system, and satisfy load requirements. Hardware demonstrations *revealed a 7.7% energy efficiency improvement was achieved (in deliverable energy density), when compared to an identical system based on a parallel connection*, for a HEESS demonstration article comprised from a battery and a supercapacitor.

ADA's High Energy Supercapacitors

ADA developed and offers high energy supercapacitor electrodes and cells for large format applications. We have demonstrated high specific energy (15-20 Wh/kg) supercapacitors with excellent rate and life cycle stability performance. Supercapacitor performance includes discharge capacity specific values of 88 to 92% at 1000 C rate and near complete capacity retention without fade for > 30,000 cycles.

ADA fabricated 20 F supercapacitor prototype cells (**Figure 5**) within the volume allotment of a commercial 10 F supercapacitor product. Our cells displayed more than double the capacitance, and more than triple the specific energy. We project an additional specific energy improvement of 2-4x will be achieved with cell material optimization and/or the selection of a high voltage electrolyte. This prototype development effort demonstrates the inherent potential in ADA's supercapacitor technology.

Figure 5. An ADA 20 F supercapacitor prototype cell.

A rate evaluation of the ADA 20 F supercapacitor prototype was performed in comparison to the 10 F commercial product (**Figure 6**). The ADA supercapacitor showed nearly double the capacitance at a lower mass than the commercial product. This led to a specific energy of 2-4x, which was rate dependent (as anticipated). The relatively high energy of the ADA supercapacitor technology was predicted to afford a substantial increase in pulse power capability.

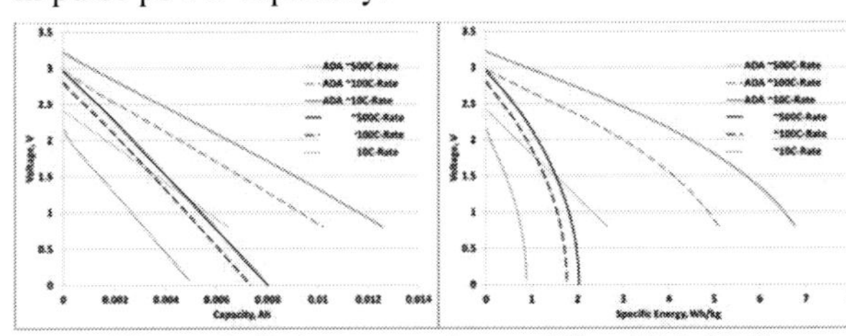

Figure 6. Rate comparison of the ADA 20 F supercapacitor (green) and commercial 10 F supercapacitor (blue); capacity (left) and specific energy (right) based data sets.

ADA also designed and fabricated a large format, 280 mAh (325 F) supercapacitor cell (**Figure 7**, left). This cell was designed to fit efficiently within a BB-x590 enclosure. **Figure 7** (right) displays the cell discharge performance at various rates. This supercapacitor cell was observed to possess a specific energy of 11.5 Wh/kg at 10C rate, with little to no specific energy decrease with continuous rates up to 50C. Cell performance values were used to predict the performance of an ADA BB-x590 HEESS. The high capacitance and high power, including pulse and continuous, was predicted to yield significant HEESS pulse power. The design also included a large cell footprint with appreciable lead volume to efficiently dissipate joule heating generated from high currents.

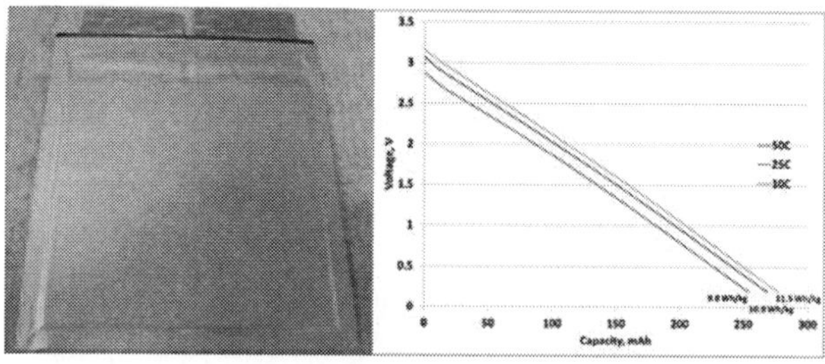

Figure 7. Supercapacitor designed specifically for the BB-x590 HEESS (left) and discharge curves for an ADA high energy supercapacitor designed for an ADA BB-x590 HEESS.

Acknowledgements

The authors acknowledge the contributions and support of Dr. Ken K. Ho, Naval Facilities (NAVFAC; contract number N39430-14-C-1505) and Mr. David Chapman, Air Force Research Laboratories (AFRL; contract number FA9453-15-M-0493) in the development of the ADA high specific energy supercapacitor technology. We also acknowledge the contributions and support of Dr. Robert Mantz, Army Research Laboratories (ARL; contract number W911NF-15-P-0013) in the development of the ADA HEESS technology.

References

1. Patrick J. Taylor, Army Research Laboratory, DOE Thermoelectrics Applications Workshop, 3-6 Jan. 2011.
2. S. Yue, D. Zhu, Y. Wang, N. Chang, and M. Pedram, "SIMES: a simulator for hybrid electrical energy storage systems," Proc. of the Int'l Symposium on Low Power Electronics and Design, Sep. 2013.
3. Y. Kim, J. Koh, Q. Xie, Y. Wang, N. Chang, and M. Pedram, "A scalable and flexible hybrid energy storage system design and implementation," Journal of Power Sources, vol. 255, no. 1, Jun. 2014, pp. 410-422.
4. Siyu Yue, Di Zhu, Yanzhi Wang, Younghyun Kim, Naehyuck Chang and Massoud Pedram, "SIMES: A Simulator for Hybrid Electrical Energy Storage Systems," in Proceedings of IEEE/ACM International Symposium on Low Power Electronics and Design (ISLPED), pp. 33-38, 2013.
5. Q. Xie, Y. Wang, Y. Kim, N. Chang, and M. Pedram, "Charge allocation for hybrid electrical energy storage systems," Proc. of the International Conference on Hardware/Software Codesign and System Synthesis, Oct. 2011.
6. Q. Xie, Y. Wang, M. Pedram, Y. Kim, D. Shin, and N. Chang, "Charge replacement in hybrid electrical energy storage systems," Proc. of Asia and South Pacific Design Automation Conference, Jan. 2012.
7. Y. Wang, X. Lin, Y. Kim, Q. Xie, M. Pedram, and N. Chang, "Sing-source, single-destination charge migration in hybrid electrical energy storage systems," IEEE Trans. on VLSI Systems, vol. 22, no. 12, Dec. 2014, pp. 2752- 2765.
8. Y. Wang, X. Lin, M. Pedram, and N. Chang, "Online fault detection and fault tolerance in electrical energy storage systems," Proc. of PES General Meeting, Jul. 2014, pp. 1-5.
9. Y. Wang, X. Lin, Q. Xie, N. Chang, and M. Pedram, "Minimizing state-of-health degradation in hybrid electrical energy storage systems with arbitrary source and load profiles," Proc. of Design Automation & Test in Europe Conference & Exhibition, Mar. 2014, pp. 1-4.
10. Picture adapted from: D. Cericola, P.W. Ruch, R. Kötz, P. Novák, A. Wokau,n J. Power Sources, 195-9 (2010) 2731–2736, Simulation of a supercapacitor/Li-ion battery hybrid for pulsed applications.
11. Y. Kim, S. Park, N. Chang, Q. Xie, Y. Wang, and M. Pedram, "Networked architecture for hybrid electrical energy storage systems," Proc. of the 49th Design Automation Conference, Jun. 2012.

1 kW, Single-Soldier Portable, JP-8 Generator

Subir Roychoudhury, David Spence, Curtis Morgan, Francesco Macri Richard Mastanduno and Anthony Anderson

Precision Combustion, Inc.
aanderson@precision-combustion.com

Abstract

Requirements for Platoon Power Generation (PPG) as identified by the Army include lightweight, JP-8 fueled, single soldier portable 1 kW generators. Precision Combustion, Inc. (PCI) has developed a simple and compact conversion kit that modifies lightweight, spark ignited (i.e. gasoline) engines to operate on JP-8. The approach is different from other developers attempting to modify gasoline engines to operate on JP-8. A novel approach consisting of "octane matching" seamlessly operates lightweight commercial off the shelf generators on JP fuels. A 1 kWe (nominal), single soldier portable generator, operating on JP-8 and diesel has been advanced to TRL 7 with support from CERDEC via testing at the Base Camp Integration Laboratory (BCIL) at Ft. Devens, MA. Operation with JP-8 as well as diesel, gasoline, and biofuels has been examined. Military applications of interest include power generation for battery charging and as tactical gensets supporting small unit power requirements. Precision Combustion, Inc. (PCI) utilizes its patented Microlith® catalyst technology for achieving this breakthrough. Performance data from this generator will be presented. This includes weight, durability, service intervals, engine specific data (oil analysis, engine temperatures, etc.). Key system characteristics, including efficiency, life, system performance, and hybridization, will be presented. The generator includes custom power and control electronics to enable both AC and DC output. It was hybridized with an internal rechargeable battery. Data from endurance and MIL-SPEC testing will be reported. These show the suitability of the generator for meeting the Army's weight and efficiency targets while demonstrating durable and reliable operation.

Cost Benefit Analysis of the Wearable Fuel Cell vs. the Conformal Wearable Battery as the centralized power source for the Dismounted Soldier

Shailesh Shah[a], Steven Aviles[b], Angela Travers[c], Tony Thampan[a]
[a] U.S. Army RDECOM, CERDEC, Aberdeen Proving Ground, MD 21005
[b] U.S. Army MCOE, Fort Benning, Georgia 31905
[c] U.S. Army PM SWAR, Fort Belvoir, Virginia 22060

Abstract: *Today's Warfighter is equipped with a range of technologies nearly all of which derive their critical performance from energy. Power demands unfulfilled at each echelon creates an energy gap at the next higher echelon. The Small Unit Power (SUP) Capability Development Document (CDD) [1] released by the Maneuver Center of Excellence (MCoE) in 2013 has recommended the use of a an Integrated Soldier Power and Data System – Core (ISPDS-C) that distributes power from a core central power source to up to four connected peripherals to maintain an 80% or higher level of charge of peripheral batteries. The thin and ergonomically designed Conformal Wearable Battery (CWB) is the current choice for a ruggedized central power source. This approach reduces the need for spare batteries for each peripheral during extended missions. The ISPDS-C provides the ability to interface peripheral systems seamlessly with a variety of energy sources. It can also monitor the energy status of SUP systems, to plan and manage energy resources to best accomplish mission objectives. In a prior paper[2], we looked at the impact of substituting a Wearable Fuel Cell (WFC) for the CWB as the central power source. In this paper, we expand the Cost Benefit Analysis (C-BA) to determine the "should cost" of the WFC and its fuel cartridge. We examine the costs where it is competitive with the CWB for a set of fielding options of the recommended equipment to support 72-hour mission durations in austere environments. We have compared the use of the WFC and its benefit on "cost," "soldier load," "convenience," and "logistics."*

Keywords: Soldier load, cost, logistics, convenience, rechargeable batteries, primary batteries.

Background: Soldiers carry a significant amount of equipment (e.g., communication and location devices) that is powered by multiple batteries and types, and they are therefore burdened by having to use/carry replacement batteries. The U.S. Army - MCoE in Fort Benning, Georgia released a CDD [1] for SUP that has addressed the power gaps from all angles. Each echelon has power distribution battery charging and power generation capability as described below.

Platoon:

- *Modular Universal Battery Charger (MUBC)* Provides lightweight, scalable, and robust capability to charge multiple battery types.
- *Platoon power generation capability* Provides sufficient power to recharge and power all platoon equipment and fulfill residual power gaps at the squad and Soldier level.

Squad:

- *Squad Power Manager* Provides useable power from multiple energy sources.
- *Squad power generation capability* Provides source of power in austere environments where no power source exists.

Soldier:

- *Integrated Soldier Power and Data System Core* (ISPDS-C).
- *Soldier power generation capability* Provides supplemental power to the conformal battery thus extending time between battery exchanges.

The preferred approach for providing power to small units in the field is one that decreases Soldier load and logistical footprint and allows them to self-sustain for up to 72 hours in an austere environment. It should also minimize the number of battery types and quantities, reduce the frequency of battery exchanges mid-mission and reduce the overall cost. A complete list of the qualitative and quantitative factors that must be considered in the analysis is shown in Table 6.

The CWB is the current choice for a ruggedized central power source in the SUP suite of equipment. The Army is also developing a Wearable Fuel Cell in the same form factor as the CWB as a potential replacement for the CWB [2]. In this case, the energy need for the 72 hours is met by carrying additional cartridges of fuel. Since fuel cells are a "primary solution," this would eliminate the need to carry a platoon generator, universal battery chargers, and fuel that would be required for charging conformal and BB-2590 batteries needed for the 72- hour mission. This is a significant advantage, since it avoids the additional burden of carrying a bulky 30-lb. generator and associated fuel and saves the Infantry Brigade Combat Team (IBCT) the trouble of charging the conformal batteries during the mission. Figure 1 shows an example of a fuel cartridge and WFC being developed by the Army and its associated metrics.

Fuel Cartridge 80 Wh / 100 g	Wearable Alane Fuel Cell - 2 lb.

Figure 1

The impact of substituting the CWB with the WFC for a set of possible SUP fielding options has been examined in a prior paper [3]. It should be noted that though the analysis presented refers to the Alane-based WFC being developed by the Army, it is independent of the fuel cell/fuel technology used in the WFC. The prior analysis[2], failed to include a cost comparison of the CWB versus WFC for the courses of action (COAs) considered. This paper includes a cost comparison for the fielding options considered and presents preliminary data on bullet penetration tests performed on the Alane fuel cartridge.

SUP Benefit Assessment:

This paper has considered the following four courses of action (COAs):

COA 1 – MAINTAIN STATUS QUO/BASELINE

- Small Units carry rechargeable batteries with no recharge capability forward.
- Planned resupply every 24 hours.

COA 2 – FULL FIELDING OF SUP EQUIPMENT

- Soldier Power Manager, Platoon Generator, Squad Generator, Soldier Generator, and ISPDS-C with 2 x Conformal Wearable Batteries (CWBs).

COA 3 – PARTIAL SUP FIELDING WITH WFC

- Soldier Power Manager, Squad Generator, Soldier Generator, and ISPDS-C with 1 x Wearable Fuel Cell (WFC) and fuel cartridges.

COA 4 – FULL SUP FIELDING WITH WFC

- Soldier Power Manager, Platoon Generator, Squad Generator, Soldier Generator, and ISPDS-C with 1 x Wearable Fuel Cell (WFC) and fuel cartridges.

The projected BOI of SUP equipment for a dismounted infantry platoon is shown in Table 1 below.

Table 1: Power Generation/Supplying Systems per COA

Generation Capability Assumptions	COA 1	COA 2	COA 3	COA 4
Platoon Power Generation (PPG)	0	1	0	1
Squad Power Generation (SqPG)	0	5	5	5
Soldier Power Generation (SoPG)	0	40	40	40
ISPDS-C w/ 2 Conformal Batteries	0	40	0	0
ISPDS-C w/ 1 Wearable Fuel Cell	0	0	40	40

The power output and weight of each SUP component considered in Table 1 is given in Table 2:

Table 2: SUP Equipment Metrics

Generation Capability Assumptions	Power Output W)	Maximum Weight (lbs.)
Platoon Power Generator (PPG)	> 900	< 30
Squad Power Generation (SqPG)	> 100	< 3
Soldier Power Generation (SoPG)	10	1
ISPDS-C w/ 2 Conformal Batteries	> 10	5.85

The various power consuming equipment and their associated battery particulars are given in Table 3.

Table 3: Infantry Platoon IBCT BOI – Systems Using Rch - Batteries

DEVICE	Battery Type	Batteries per System	Equip Run Time (hrs.)	BCT System BOI
AN/PRC-154 (Rifleman Radio)	Rifleman Radio Battery	1	8	40
AN/PRC-148	MBITR Battery	1	12	6
AN/PRC-119F	BB-2590	1	33	2
AN/PSC-5 SATCOM	BB-2590	2	17	1

In order for the units to be self-sustained for 72 hours they must be equipped with the sum-total of the energy needed for the period. While COA 1 assumes this energy need is met by the resupply of batteries every 24 hours, for COAs 2 - 4 this energy need is met by carrying extra batteries/fuel cartridges and recharging batteries using the SUP equipment. The specific energy contribution assumed from each SUP equipment over the 72- hour period is shown in Table 4. Also shown in Table 4 is the carry weight imposed by the SUP equipment. It should be noted that the carry weight of the PPG is assumed zero, since it is assumed that the PPG is not an item that will be carried by the Soldier, but rather transported to a location and stored for use during stops in a mission. The power generation equipment at all levels that provide the energy to charge batteries is assumed to operate at ~ 66% efficiency. Based on the specified hours of operation, the net energy available from each piece of equipment over 72 hours is given in the last column of Table 4.

Table 4: Power Generation/Supplying Systems

Generation Capability Assumptions	Carry Wt. lbs.	Power (W)	Hrs/ Day	Wh/ day	Wh/ 72 hr
Platoon Power Generation (PPG)	0	600	2	1200	3600
Squad Power Generation (SqPG)	6.5	66	3	198	594
Soldier Power Generation (SoPG)	1	6.6	3	19.8	59.4
ISPDS-C w/ 2 Conformal Batteries	5.85	various	24	150	450
ISPDS-C w/ 1 WFC + 4 x 115 Wh cartridges	4.71	various	24	150	450

The inventory of power equipment that is carried by a 40 - person Infantry Platoon for each COA is given in Table 5.

Table 5: Power Equipment Inventory for Each COA

ITEM	COA 1	COA 2	COA 3	COA 4
Rifleman Radio Battery	360	60	40	40
MBITR Battery	36	12	12	12
BB-2590	6	4	6	4
BB-2590	10	4	10	4
Conformal Wearable Battery (CWB)	0	80	0	0
Platoon Power Generator	0	1	0	1
Squad Power Generator	0	5	5	5
Soldier Power Generator	0	40	40	40
ISPDS-C	0	40	40	40
JP-8	0	1	0	1
Universal Battery Charger (MUBC)	0	3	0	3
Alane Fuel Cell	0	0	40	40
Alane Fuel Cartridges*	0	0	160	160

* Assumes each cartridge has 115 Wh of energy.

The C-BA for each COA is based on the quantitative and qualitative factors shown in Table 6 below. Each factor was assigned a "weight" based on the relative importance of the factor.

Table 6: Evaluation Factors Considered and Weighting

Evaluation Factor	Nominal Power Output	Maximum Weight
	PERFORMANCE	
Load – Weight/Bulk (Batteries Saved)	Soldier load with relation to battery weight.	14
Energy Management	How effectively power can be managed.	17
Recharge Time	The amount of time required to recharge equipment.	11
Mission Interruptions/ Frequency	The amount of time between having to stop to replace batteries in systems.	20
Autonomy	Ability to charge independently at the lowest level.	10
Ergonomics/Ease of Use	Complexity of operating the system.	8
Environmental Flexibility	Impact of environmental conditions on capability.	6
	LOGISTICS	
Training	The amount of training needed.	5
Logistics Footprint/Supply Chain	ILS requirements (i.e., temperature, space, humidity, disposal).	5
	PROGRAMMATICS	
Producibility	Ability to manufacture the power system in required quantities.	4

The benefits assessment was based on Multi-Criteria Decision Making (MCDM). In MCDM, the COAs are scored relative to the benefit (non-cost) evaluation factors defined above. Decision analysis software (Logical Decisions Portfolio © (LDP)) was used to implement and document the assessment. Each COA was reviewed and scored against each benefit evaluation factor, using the performance scales. For the most part, the COAs were assessed on a relative basis, where the best COA for a particular factor received a 100 score and the worst scoring 0, based on how the COAs compared to each other [4]. The assessment was based on available data and the knowledge and expertise of the SMEs. The total weight of equipment carried by the soldier for each COA and the final total weighted benefit score is given in Table 7.

Table 7: Total Weight and Weighted Benefit Score for Each COA

COA	Total Weight Carried in lbs.	Weighted Benefit Score
1	359	39
2	455	73
3	359	79
4	386	78

Note that the total weight is just one of the factors that affects the weighted benefit score.

As can be seen from Table 7, the weighted benefit score of COAs 2-4 is nearly the same; however, there is a significant weight penalty associated with COA 2 that uses the CWB. While COA 2 is a reasonable approach, the SUP equipment adds to soldier burden and mission responsibility in terms of charging batteries. Each platoon is required to carry and maintain a 900 W generator, fuel (JP8), and three Universal Battery Chargers (UBCs) to recharge the CWBs and other batteries in their inventory. On cloudy days, the use of fueled generators may need to be increased beyond the proposed 2 hours/day (see Table 4) to make up for the energy that could not be tapped from the sun.

Table 8 gives the benefit scores assigned to the different options for each category. It is worth noting from Table 8 that the WFC options (COA 3 and COA 4) had lower scores for "Mission Interruptions" since the current cartridge capacity is lower than the capacity of the CWB, requiring more frequent cartridge changes than CWB recharges. This disadvantage can be overcome by designing cartridges with increased capacity over what is available today.

Table 8: Evaluation Factors Considered and Scores

Category	Weight	COA 1	COA 2	COA 3	COA 4
Load	14%	82	0	100	73
Energy Management	17%	0	90	70	90
Recharge Time	11%	100	40	100	80
Mission Interruptions	20%	0	100	75	75
Autonomy	10%	0	100	70	85
Environmental Flexibility	8%	100	90	75	75
Ease of Use/Ergonomics	6%	0	100	100	100
Training	5%	100	70	60	50
Logistics/Supply Chain	5%	0	100	60	70
Producibility	4%	100	50	60	50
Weighted Benefit Score	100%	39	73	79	78

SUP Cost Assessment:

Cost comparison for each COA was performed with the help of the Business Management Director at Project Manager Soldier Warrior (PM SWAR). Cost models were used to estimate the total Life Cycle Cost Estimate (LCCE) associated with each COA based on the fielding plan provided by MCoE. In this case, the plan included fielding and sustainment of the SUP suite of equipment to 40 IBCT's over a period of 20 years. The LCCE is the sum of the Research, Development, Test, and Evaluation (RDTE) cost for new SUP equipment, procurement cost for initial fielding over the several years over which the fielding would be accomplished (OPA), and Sustainment Costs (OMA) that include maintenance and replacement costs over the life cycle, calculated in base year dollars. The fuel cell cost that was assumed for the cost estimates is $500 per unit and the fuel cartridge cost was varied from $20 to $5 per 115 Wh cartridge.

Figure 2 is a plot of the total cost (given in base year 2013 dollars) that is associated with each COA plotted versus the cost of the fuel cartridge.

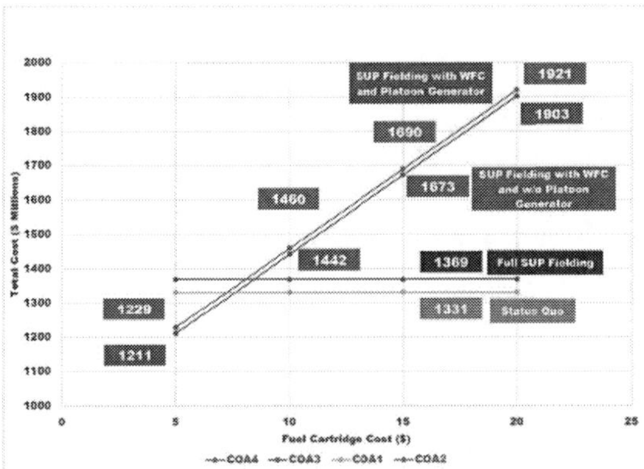

Figure 2: Impact of Fuel Cartridge Cost on Total Cost for COAs 1-4 at Fuel Cell System Cost of $500

It can be seen from Figure 2 that the total life cycle costs in COAs 3 and 4 are below the baseline costs for COA 1 and the full SUP fielding option of COA 2, only when the cartridge costs below ~ $7.

Figure 3 shows the impact of fuel cartridge cost on the OMA costs associated with the SUP equipment included in COAs 1-4. Since COA 1 is the baseline status quo option, the OMA costs associated with SUP equipment is zero. It can be seen that the OMA cost for COAs 3 and 4 is comparable to the OMA cost for COA 2 only when the cartridge cost is ~ $5.

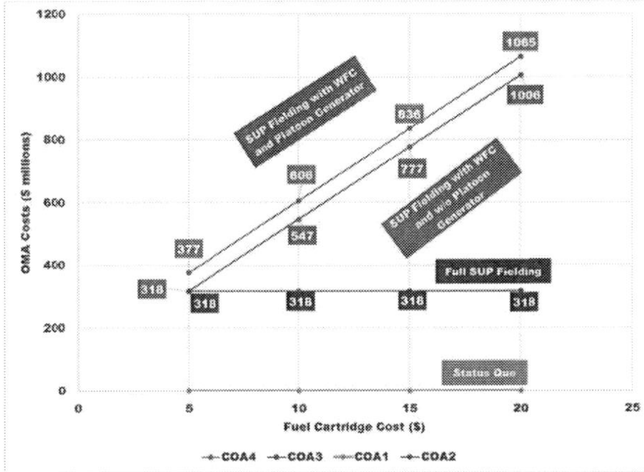

Figure 3: Impact of Fuel Cartridge Cost on OMA costs for COAs 1-4 at Fuel Cell System Cost $500

Ballistic Tests: Preliminary ballistic tests on the Alane fuel cartridge have been conducted with mixed results. It was noted that if the bullet penetration results in dispersion of the Alane fuel from the cartridge compartment, it can cause the fuel to ignite. However, if the fuel remains contained in the cartridge after bullet penetration, ignition is prevented as a result of the limited oxygen availability. A complete evaluation of cartridge safety is planned, including testing of the fuel cartridge while operating the fuel cell. CERDEC is working closely with contractors to answer the above questions and mature the technology for Wearable Fuel Cells.

Conclusions: The WFC has a significant weight advantage over the CWB option for a centralized power source in the SUP suite of equipment. The current cost of Alane fuel makes the cost of the fuel cartridge prohibitively expensive. Implementation of large-scale Alane production and development of electrochemical routes to manufacture Alane are likely means of making the cartridges affordable for the Army.

References

1. Mr. Graham K, and Major Allen J., "Capability Development Document for Small Unit Power (SUP) Increment:1", Department of the Army, MCoE, Operational Energy Branch, Soldiers Division, Fort Benning, GA 31905-5000, 26 Sep, 2013.
2. T. Thampan, D. Shah, C. Cook, J. Novoa, S. Shah, "Development and Evaluation of Portable and Wearable Fuel Cells for Military Use," *Journal of Power Sources,* vol. 259, pp. 276-281, August 2014.
3. Shailesh Shah, T. Thampan, S. Aviles, D. Shah and C. Cook; "The Impact of Rechargeable Batteries on Soldier Missions", Proceedings of the 46th Power Sources Conference, 2014.
4. Mr. Graham K, and Major Allen J., "Other Appendices for Capability Development Document for Small Unit Power (SUP) Increment:1", Department of the Army, MCoE, Operational Energy Branch, Soldiers Division, Fort Benning, GA 31905-5000, 26 Sep, 2013.

Advanced PEM Fuel Cell MEAs for High Performance and Durability for Undersea and Space Power

Ying Song, Bob Wynne, Scott Ferguson, Rob Utz, and Bob Sievers
Teledyne Energy Systems, Inc.
10707 Gilroy Road, Hunt Valley, MD USA 21031

Abstract: *Over the past 30 years, Teledyne Energy Systems, Inc. (TESI) has developed PEM fuel cells stack designs and system operational algorithms to meet various space and undersea needs. A wide range of mission profile power levels can be provided by TESI's developed hydrogen/oxygen PEM fuel cell systems. One key aspect to achieving high performance and durability of PEM fuel cell systems is the advanced PEM fuel cell MEAs designed with features that are tailored to the specific applications. This paper provides an overview of TESI's MEA design, development, and evaluation progresses as well as the different aspects of stack performance, efficiency and durability that have been achieved.*

Keywords: PEM Fuel cell, stacks, MEAs, performance, durability

Introduction

Fuel cells are recognized as efficient, silent, clean energy conversion systems with the power density necessary for the weight and volume requirements for space flight and underwater vehicles. Proton Exchange Membrane (PEM) fuel cell technology has been receiving more attention as a possible alternative to the internal combustion engine for aerospace and underwater applications. It operates at relatively low temperatures, offers quick start-up times, and requires only hydrogen and oxygen for operation. The core of a fuel cell system is the fuel cell stack. PEM H_2/O_2 stack is superior for aerospace and underwater applications compared to other fuel cell technologies because it has higher efficiencies (~70%) when operated on H_2/O_2 and water is the only reactant product that is easy to store onboard with no product gases to trap or dump overboard, enabling a fully closed, air-independent, neutrally buoyant system. The membrane electrode assembly (MEA) as one the primary components in the fuel cell stack is critical for higher stack performance to meet energy requirements and durability to fulfil multi-missions. In this paper, we focus on air-independent H_2/O_2 PEM fuel cells as a means of meeting performance and durability targets at TESI for both aerospace and underwater applications. Achievements in stack/MEA development are presented.

Fuel Cell Development at TESI

TESI, a division of Teledyne Technologies (NYSE: TDY), located in Hunt Valley, Maryland, is a technology leader in the fields of electrolytic, thermoelectric and fuel cell systems, manufacturing and supporting customer around the globe [1]. Our mission is to provide unique energy solutions through superior products capable of operation in the harshest environments. Typical markets for these technologies are space, undersea, and terrestrial remote power. TESI is always an active designer and manufacturer of hydrogen and fuel cell systems. For over 12 years, TESI has been developing PEM fuel cell technology for space applications under contracts directly funded by NASA. The efforts were initiated to develop a PEM fuel cell system for the next generation reusable launch system. The high efficiency and high power density fuel cell stacks and systems were designed, built, and tested up to TRL 5/6 using pure hydrogen and oxygen as reactants. All this experience has given TESI the technical expertise to develop and deliver aerospace quality fuel cell systems [2]. TESI also addressed on design and environment constraints of the underwater vehicles and focused on fuel cell stack design and system integration for undersea applications under a subcontract primarily funded by ONR [3]. The experiment working with both NASA and Navy programs has given TESI the technical expertise to develop and deliver high quality PEM fuel cell systems appropriate for space launch and UUV vehicles.

TESI has designed and manufactured PEM fuel cell systems to provide significant technical and cost advantages compared to other competing solutions. TESI's integrated balance of plant (BOP) results in a significant reduction in system volume, parts count, leak points, and piping runs. A typical compact and passive integrated BOP is shown in the Figure 1. TESI has developed a purge system with intelligent control algorithms to effectively remove the impurities while minimizing the loss of reactants. The capabilities to incorporate gravity independent water management system enable the fuel cell membranes to maintain at optimal hydration levels while simultaneously removing excess byproduct water. This results in a compact fuel cell package with no pumps or moving parts, no bulky external water separators and no humidifiers. It greatly reduces piping requirements. In addition, the ejector driven reactant system (EDRS) has been successfully developed and demonstrated at TESI that replaces the pumps for recirculation reactants through the fuel cell flow fields. It has no moving parts to fail and no power consumption with a low cost and high reliability.

TESI specifically designed H_2/O_2 PEM fuel cell stacks allow the system to operate optimally in a non-air environment with a fast rate of rise from ambient to operating temperature for quick start up from a hibernation or shut-down state and faster response to changes in power demand. TESI's fuel cell stacks utilize high efficiency MEAs that has been proven robust under a wide range of duty cycles to meet specific needs for under water and space applications. As the core of a fuel cell stack, MEAs have been properly designed and manufactured that provide much greater repeatability and robustness in assembly and performance than traditional approaches.

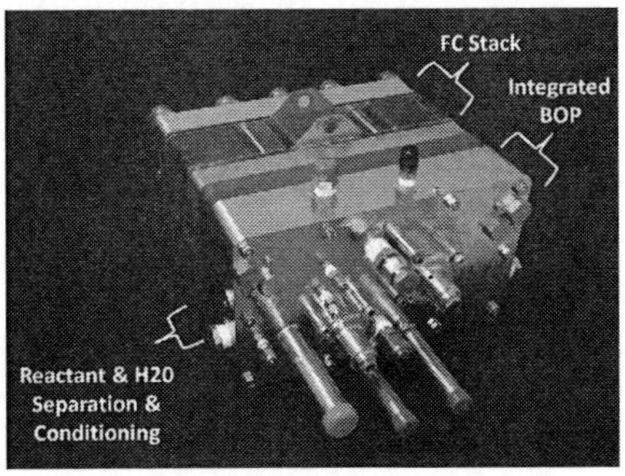

Figure 1. Compact and Passive Integrated Balance of Plant (BOP).

MEA Design and Performance Evaluation

Membrane Design Point and Configuration: Two major factors decide MEA applications, high power density and extended lifetime. In order to achieve them, MEAs have been carefully designed and examined. Thin reinforced membranes are selected for MEAs to ensure ionic conductivity and long durability. The membranes are coated with different types of catalyst by various coating techniques for high surface area to enhance catalytic activity. Catalyst loading is optimized and a higher loading is preferred to maximize the reactant utilization. Meanwhile the ionomer in the catalyst layer is carefully investigated since it contributes to electrochemical reaction and water management. MEAs have been designed to tolerate different hydration/dehydration conditions. A perimeter seal is also developed for flexibility to handle MEAs with or without a non-ionomer border around the membrane, better control of compression especially on the GDL/catalyst interface, and elimination of gas permeation from the active area to the edge of the membrane and outside of the stack.

MEA Performance Evaluation: MEA performance generally can be evaluated from room temperature to 90°C at an operational pressure from zero to 50 psig. It's noted that no substantial increase in cell voltage is observed with a minimal gain in efficiency as temperature increases above 70°C. There is a significant increase in MEA performance as the reactant pressure increases. Our typical operation conditions are 70°C at 30 psig. Figure 2 shows a typical polarization curve of the fuel cell stack built with two cells at the test conditions. The effect of reactant stoic on the MEA performance is studied usually from the minimum 1.0 stoic which is a non-flow through mode to a relatively higher stoic which depends on the reactant flow rates provided by BOP to satisfy all power levels. The effect of stack/MEA orientation has been investigated to ensure the voltage and efficiency can be orientation independent. The obtained results, as shown in the Figure 3, indicate that the cell orientation, vertical and horizontal, has no significant impact on cell voltages over current densities.

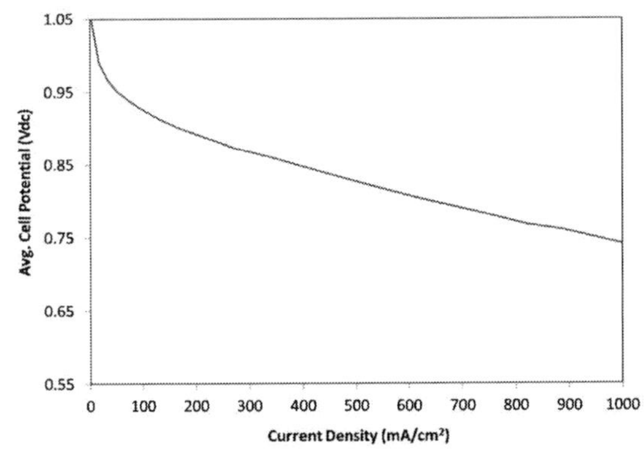

Figure 2. Typical Polarization Curve of Fuel Cell Stack at 70oC and 30 psig

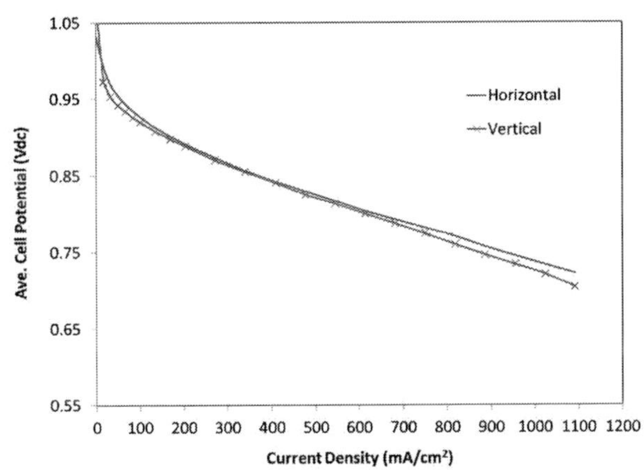

Figure 3. Fuel Cell Stack Built with Specific MEAs Show Performance Orientation Independent

The ability of MEA to handle inert is investigated. It's known that the inert built up in the stack may cause MEA performance loss. The experimental study was carried out to investigate the effect of the helium concentration in both hydrogen and oxygen. Compared to the high purity reactants, a 5 to 30 mV loss of MEA performance is observed from low to high current density. After the reactants were switched to the pure gases, 100% performance recovery is easily obtained. It illustrates that high performance and efficiency of MEAs in the fuel cell system can be maintained with the reactants refreshed through a TESI's proprietary gas purging design while maintaining a closed cycle operation. Figure 4 shows a proprietary purge process can maintain efficiency over long duration of operation while maintaining a closed cycle operation [4].

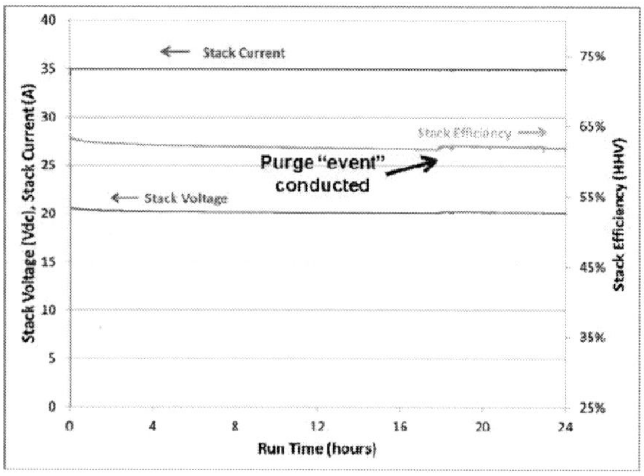

Figure 4. High Performance and Efficiency of MEAs in the Fuel Cell System to Be Maintained through a TESI's Proprietorial Gas Purge Process

The water management in the MEA and fuel cell is also very important. A lot of optimization work has been done to further improve the ability of MEA to handle different situation from completely dry to over flooded. The product water produced in the fuel cells during operation can be effectively managed. The water back diffusion from cathode to anode can be minimized. This is optional depending on the system requirements. MEAs are designed and manufactured to meet different requirements. In addition, product water management and in-cell water removal have been simplified to keep the fuel cell system more compact.

MEA Long Term/Life Durability

Another barrier for acceptance of fuel cell as the practical power source is durability under a wide range of operational conditions. For different applications such as space flight and undersea vehicle, the requirements for MEA lifetime vary and the test conditions might be significantly different. TESI has successfully demonstrated MEA/fuel cell durability in the past years [5]. The stacks built for NASA in 2005-2006 are in use up to date. Figure 5 shows the durability test results from one of our 4 cell stack with over 13,000 hours life. One of the MEAs degraded in 12,000 hours developing a high gas crossover rate, detected by cell voltage loss.

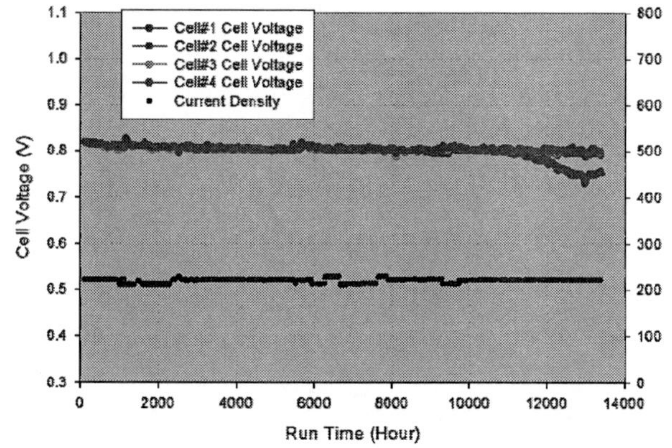

Figure 5. Over 13,000 hour MEA Life Durability Demonstrated

A two-cell short stack was tested under equivalent mission load to determine the durability of MEAs that were designed in an advanced configuration. It was tested through mission cycles from low to high current densities to meet the customer's requirement. It completed about seven load profiles and demonstrated over 7,500 hours of operation before a cross-leak was detected, as shown in Figure 6.

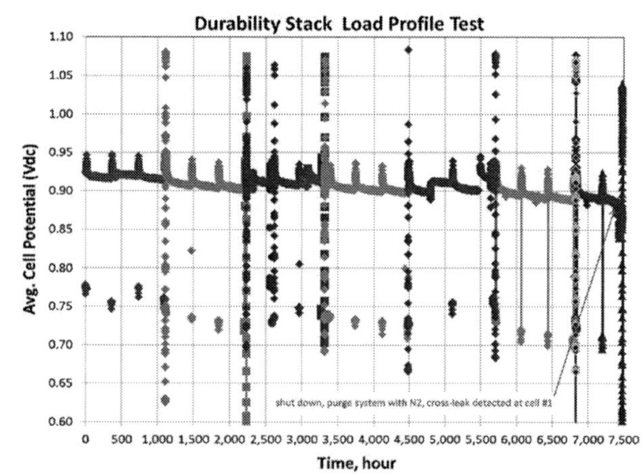

Figure 6. Two-Cell Stack Demonstrated over 7,500 Hours of Operation under Equivalent Mission Load

Summary

TESI's unique design and manufacturing processes for PEM fuel cell systems provide significant technical and cost advantages. TESI's fuel cell stacks/MEAs after complete optimization and integration approaches have exhibited much greater repeatability and robustness in assembly and performance than the traditional approaches. High performance and durability of PEM fuel cell stack/MEA are successfully demonstrated for undersea and space power.

Acknowledgements
Authors want to acknowledge the funding received from NASA and ONR and the support by Teledyne Energy Systems, Inc. the Internal Research & Development Projects

References
1. Teledyne Energy Systems, Inc. website http://www.teledynees.com
2. Bob Wynne, Scott Ferguson, John Keyser, Ying Song, Bob Sievers, Arturo Vasquez, "*Development of a High Reliability Compact Air Independent PEMFC Power System*," Fuel Cell Seminar & Energy Exposition October 2013
3. Ying Song, Bob Wynne, Scott Ferguson, Johnny Alston, Rob Utz, Bob Sievers, "*High Performance and Durability PEM Fuel Cell MEA for Undersea and Space Power*," Fuel Cell Seminar & Energy Exposition, November 2014
4. Bob Sievers, Scott Ferguson, Mike Miller, Ying Song, Rob Utz, Bob Wynne, "*Development and Demonstration of a High Reliability Compact Air-independent PEMFC Power Systems for Autonomous Vehicles*," IAPG Chemical Working Group Meeting, September 2015
5. Ying Song, Bob Wynne, Mark Hoberecht, "*Hydrogen/Oxygen PEM Fuel Cell Stack Durability Testing for Aerospace Applications*," Fuel Cell Seminar & Exposition, October 2008

Desulfurization of JP-8 Fuel with Mixed Metal Oxides for Fuel Cell Applications

Terry G. DuBois and Richard Scenna
US Army
Communications-Electronics Research, Development, and Engineering Center
Email: terry.g.dubois.civ@mail.mil

Abstract: *In 1988, the US military identified JP-8 as the preferred battlefield fuel for all ground and land-based forces. Military grade jet fuel (JP-8) is a kerosene based fuel that is very similar to commercial grade Jet-A1 fuel, but contains some additional trace additives. The maximum allowable sulfur content of JP-8 is 3000 ppmw; fairly high when compared to commercial grade diesel at 15 ppmw sulfur. Fuel cell power units exhibit militarily attractive operating characteristics, such as: low aural and visible signatures and high efficiency. However, fuel cell systems employ heterogeneous reforming catalysts and electro-catalysts that are susceptible to deactivation when exposed to sulfur compounds, even at relatively low sulfur concentrations. Therefore, sulfur removal from JP-8 is critical for the introduction of military fuel cell power systems.*

An attractive approach for liquid phase desulfurization of JP-8 is selective adsorption, coupled with air regeneration. The adsorbent materials being used consist of a proprietary combination of metal oxide compounds, some of which support fuel pyrolysis. The adsorption beds are configured in a dual bed arrangement allowing continuous operation (one bed adsorbs, while the second bed is regenerating). Sulfur adsorption takes place under conditions of 150 psig, 400 °C, and a liquid hourly space velocity (LHSV) of 0.5 to 1.5 hr^{-1}. Experimental results show that high yields (>90% for single pass, >95% with recycle) can be achieved. The absorbents demonstrated long life and excellent performance while undergoing over 1000 hours of testing and 120 thermal cycles. The paper will provide background on the need for JP-8 desulfurization and detailed data on the performance of the desulfurizer, quantifying sulfur reduction as a function of time, impact to the characteristics of the desulfurized fuel, and projections on the potential of this approach to fuel cell power unit needs.

Keywords: jet fuel, regenerable desulfurization, sulfur adsorption, fuel processing, catalysts deactivation.

Introduction

Fuel cells hold promise as a more efficient, convenient, and low emission power generation systems for portable devices and stationary power plants [1,2]. Due to the high energy density and the existing infrastructure for liquid hydrocarbon fuels (eg. gasoline, diesel, and jet fuel) these fuels are attractive for mobile fuel cell applications [3,4]. The selection of JP-8 as the preferred military fuel was based on: flight and ground force safety, good low temperature operations, worldwide availability, and interoperability with NATO forces [5]. Military grade jet fuel (JP-8) is a kerosene based fuel that is very similar to commercial grade Jet-A1 fuel, but contains trace additives, such as: static dissipating additive, corrosion inhibitor/lubricity improver, fuel system icing inhibitor and may contain antioxidant and metal deactivator [6]. Jet fuels are middle distillate fuels consisting of hundreds of hydrocarbons that are broadly defined in terms of boiling point range, aromatic content, heating value, sulfur content and other physical characteristics. JP-8 contains organic sulfur compounds with total sulfur content ranging up to 3000 parts per million by weight (ppmw), and for most catalytic processes the sulfur level needs to be reduced before it can be catalytically reformed, as sulfur is a poison to most reforming and fuel cell electrode catalysts. Regenerative fuel desulfurization can be utilized to enable military use of fuel cell power units.

Recent decisions to lower emission from vehicles through reducing the sulfur and aromatic content in transportation fuels resulted in a number of approaches for sulfur removal. Hydrodesulfurization (HDS) is a conventional method that is being employed by the refineries to produce low sulfur gasoline and diesel in order to meet environmental regulations [7]. However, this method is not well suited for mobile fuel cell applications, as the process requires severe conditions such as high temperature (300-400 °C) and high hydrogen pressure (30-130 atms). Alternative methods such as adsorptive desulfurization, oxidative and extractive desulfurization, biodesulfurization, etc., are being explored to produce ultra-low-sulfur liquid transportation fuels [7,8]. Among various alternative methods, adsorptive desulfurization is considered to be more promising. ConocoPhillips Petroleum Company has commercialized a process known as S Zorb for producing low-sulfur gasoline [9]. The process is based on reactive adsorption occurring over a solid adsorbent at elevated temperatures up to 400 °C and pressures up to 400 psig by use of a relatively small H2 stream. Similarly, the Research Triangle Institute reported a TReND (transport reactor naphtha desulfurization) process for the deep desulfurization of naphtha over a metal oxide-based adsorbent around 400 °C with minimal hydrogen consumption [10].

In this paper, we describe the experimental evaluation of a mixed metal oxide sulfur absorbent in an air regenerable approach for organic sulfur removal from JP-8 fuel, using adsorptive desulfurization.

Experimental Apparatus

Figure 1 shows a picture of the regenerative desulfurization test apparatus and Figure 2 presents a schematic of the experimental instrumentation and process flow diagram of the unit. The desulfurization module is designed to produce a low-sulfur, condensed fuel stream from military JP-8 logistic fuel. It employs a proprietary mixed metal oxide desulfurization absorbents that operates at elevated temperature (450 °C) and pressure (~1136 kPa). Desulfurization of JP-8 to less than 10 ppmw sulfur is the design target. Desulfurization is accomplished by passing the fuel through a heated sulfur absorbent that selectively abstracts sulfur from the fuel. The desulfurization beds are 0.8 L in volume and contain 0.68 kg of absorbent per bed. Thermocouples (K-Type, 1/16" OD) were placed at approximately 25.4 mm from the entrance and exit of each bed. The sulfur absorbent is periodically regenerated with air (flow rate of 2.5 slpm to 4.0 slpm), releasing the absorbed sulfur as a mixture of hydrogen sulfide and sulfur oxides. The cycle time for one absorption period is 271 minutes. Continuous desulfurization of fuel is accomplished by utilizing two absorption beds in parallel, with one absorbing sulfur while the other simultaneously regenerates. Start-up time from ambient temperature was approximately 18 minutes. For all data presented in this manuscript, the input fuel flow was 6 ml/min. (approximately equivalent to flow needed for 1 kWe net output when incorporated into a fuel cell power source).

Figure 1. Air regenerative desulfurization test bed.

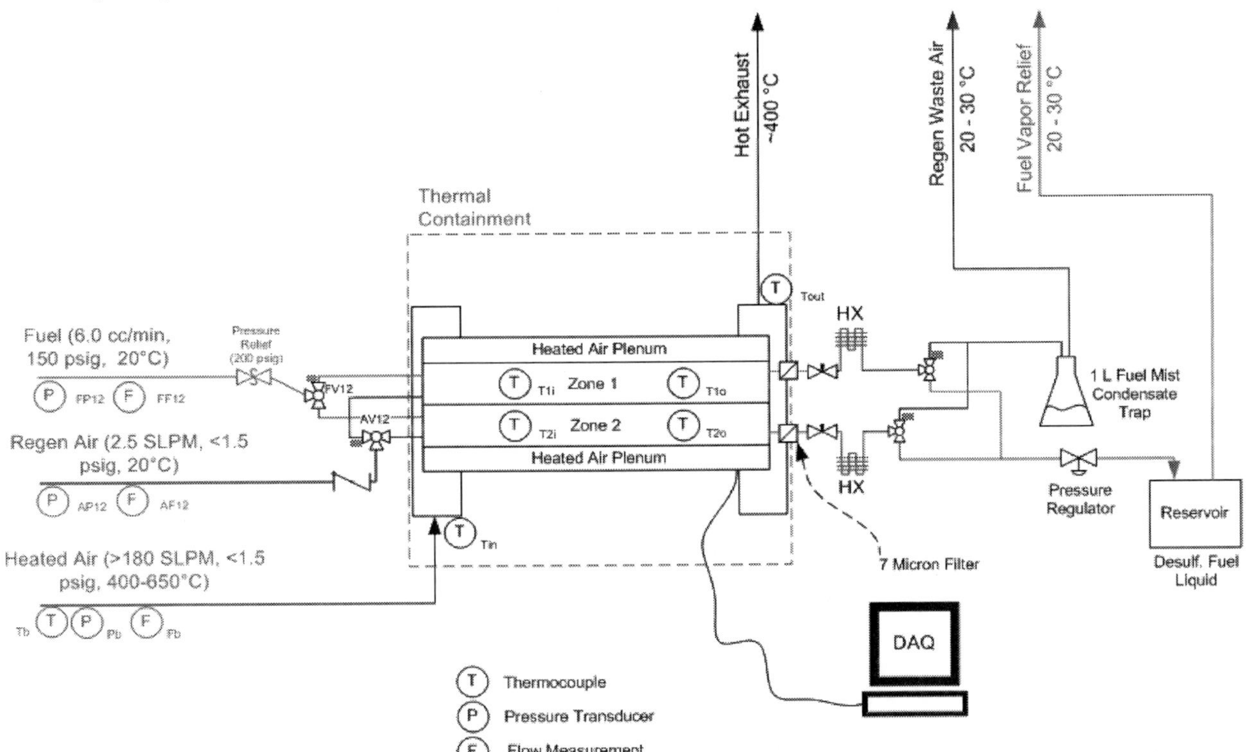

Figure 2. Experimental instrumentation and process flow diagram of the desulfurization test bed.

Analysis

Fuels (JP-8) were obtained from a commercial supplier and from the Air Force Research Lab all meeting MIL-DTL-83133 requirements. Fuels with different total sulfur content were blended when needed. For data presented in this manuscript, unless otherwise stated, all JP-8 fuel used as a source contained 400 ppmw total sulfur, with input flow rate of 6 ml/min., 450 °C average bed temperature, and 1136 kPa (150 psig) operating pressure.

Total sulfur analysis was performed using an Analytik Jena Elemental Analyzer (Ea3100) with sulfur detection via ultraviolet (UV) fluorescence. The instrument calibration range is from 0.1 ppmw to 1000 ppmw.

The gaseous components were analyzed by an on-line gas chromatograph (Agilent Technologies, Micro GC 3000) with two columns with thermal conductivity detectors: (i) molecular sieve column (10 m x 0.32 mm), and (ii) Plot U column (8 m x 0.32 mm. Multiple level calibration curves were used for all compounds with the calibration gases at 0.02% analytical tolerance.

Gaseous flow was measured by an Alicat Scientific MW series mass flow meter, accuracy of ± (0.4% reading + 0.2% FS). Fuel mass measurements: Scientech Balances, model SL2000, ±0.01g (fuel input), and a PGL Precision Balances, model PGL 20001, ±0.1g (fuel output).

For the data presented, fuel yield is defined as:

$$\text{Fuel yield (wt\%)} = \frac{(\text{hydrocarbon fuel})_{out}}{(\text{hydrocarbon fuel})_{in}} \cdot 100\%$$

where, the hydrocarbon fuels are in mass quantities. Alternatives the yield based on fuel energy content is defined as:

$$\text{Fuel yield (energy \%)} = \frac{(\text{hydrocarbon fuel})_{out} \cdot LHV_{fuel_{out}}}{(\text{hydrocarbon fuel})_{in} \cdot LHV_{fuel_{in}}} \cdot 100\%$$

where, LHV_x is the lower heating value of fuel x.

Discussion and Results

An experimental desulfurization test bed was constructed for the evaluation of a proprietary sulfur absorbent consisting of mixed metal oxides and some catalytic materials. The resultant output from the absorbent bed is a gaseous stream of vaporized, desulfurized fuel and lighter reformed gases (primarily hydrogen).

Desulfurizer test bed operation and performance: Figure 3 shows a typical temperature and pressure operating profile for a single absorption cycle. Upon startup both the absorption and desorption beds are externally heated by air using an inline heater (Farnam Heat Torch HT150) operating at 1500W. Once the bed inlet temperature reached 400 °C, fuel begins to flow into the absorption bed where the pressure is maintained at 1136 kPa (150 psig) by a back pressure regulator. Adsorption of sulfur can be seen in the temperature profile as mildly exothermic with an elevated temperature "wave" traveling from the front of the bed to the rear as the "time-on-stream" increases. As desulfurization begins in one bed, air begins to flow into the regeneration bed, where strongly exothermic oxidation reactions occur.

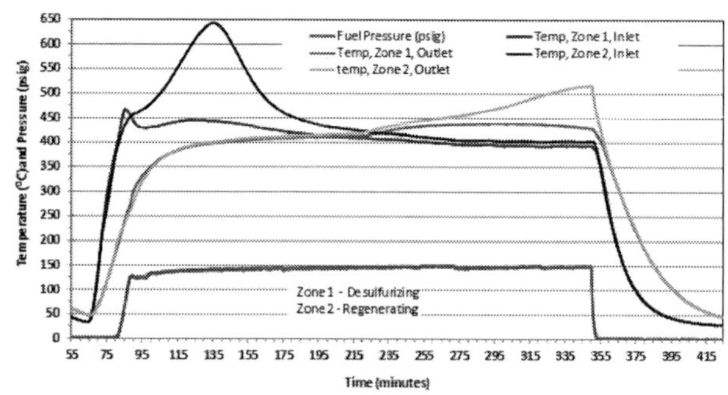

Figure 3. Operating characteristics.

Performance throughout a sorption cycle: Figure 4 shows fuel input and output flow rates along with cumulative yield during a sorption cycle. The flow of desulfurized fuel begins approximately 9 minutes into the desulfurization cycle. The mass fuel flow in, is 4.4 g/min. and the output is at a steady (i.e. linear) 4.1 g/min. The desulfurized fuel yield increases with length of cycle time, and when looked at on a liquid mass basis, achieves a yield of 90-92.5%.

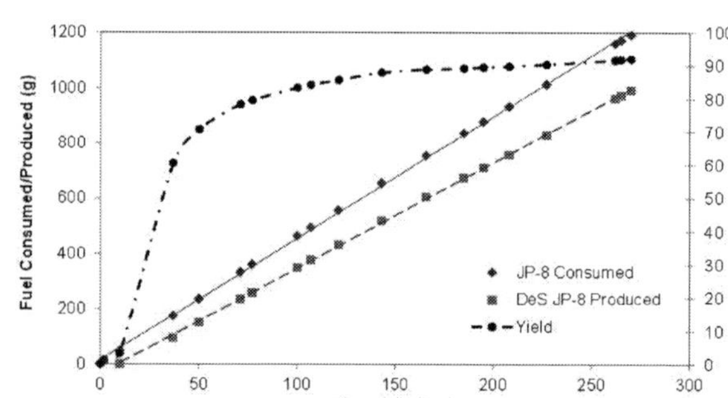

Figure 4. Desulfurized fuel production and yield.

Figures 5 and 6 show the analysis of the composition of the gaseous components of fuel desulfurization and the total flow rate as a function on time. The largest gaseous components are hydrogen (70-80 mol%) followed by methane (5-10 mol%). The flow varies over the sorption cycle, peaking at 820 cc/min. (at 110 minutes into the cycle); with an average flow over the cycle of approximately 450-500 cc/min. On an energy basis, the yield of desulfurized product (both fuel and gas) is 94.9 - 95.2%.

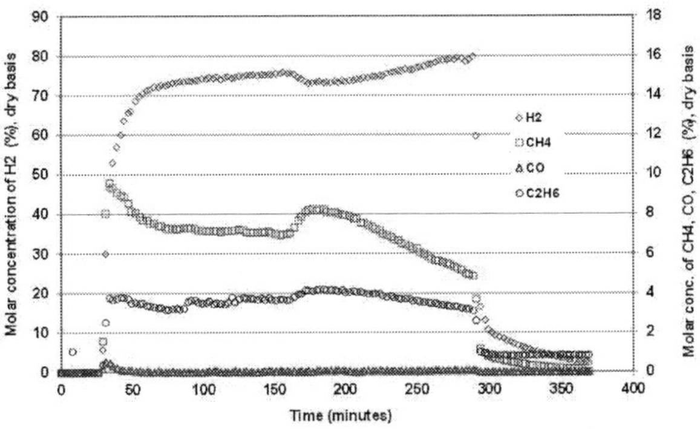

Figure 5. GC analysis of non-condensing components of desulfurization.

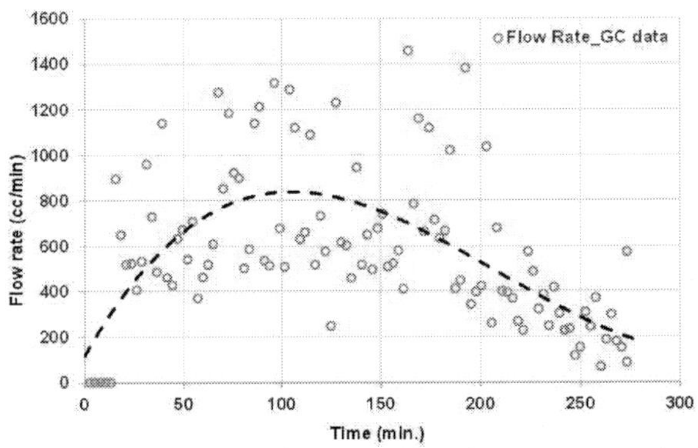

Figure 6. Flow rate of non-condensing component of desulfurization.

Long-term Performance: An experimental objective in evaluating the absorbents was to determine the rate of absorbent degradation over a prolonged period of operation. Figure 7 shows the change in desulfurized fuel over 500 hours time-on-stream and 100 absorption/regeneration cycles. The initial absorption capacity with a 10 ppmw sulfur breakthrough is 1.52 mg $S_{absorbed}/g_{absorbent}$. A 0.32% degradation in absorption capacity over 500 hours of on-stream operation and 100 absorption/regeneration cycles was noted.

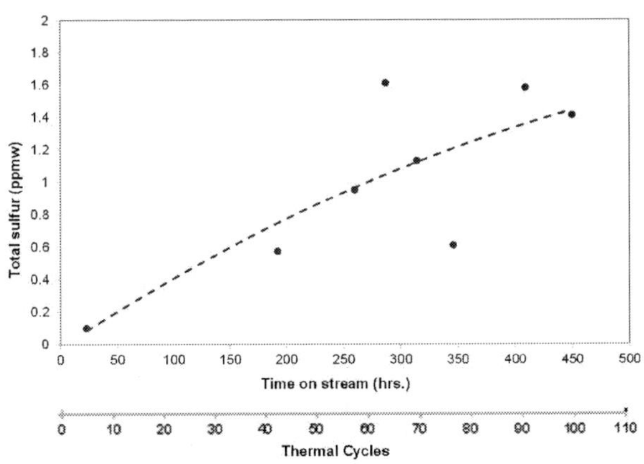

Figure 7. Effects of operating time and thermal cycling on absorption performance.

Summary

Successful operation of an air regenerative JP-8 fuel desulfurizer was demonstrated. Very good absorbent durability was achieved the greater than 500 on-stream operating hours and more than 105 absorption/regeneration cycles with 0.32% degradation. Product yields of greater that 90% (weight basis) and greater than 94% (energy basis) were demonstrated.

Acknowledgements

The authors gratefully acknowledge the *US Army Communications-Electronics RDE Center's* support of this effort. In addition, we gratefully acknowledge the contributions of Dr. Mark Fokema (Aspen Products, Inc.), Mr. Will Wihlborg (Thermo Fischer Scientific), and Dr. Tim Edwards (AFRL).

References

1 Song C. Fuel processing for low-temperature and high temperature fuel cells; challenges, and opportunities for sustainable development in the 21st Century. *Catal. Today* 2002, vol. 77, pp. 17-49.

2 Ashok P., DuBois T., Sifer N., Bostic E., Gardner K., Quah M., Bolton C. Portable fuel cell systems for America's Army: technology transition to the field," *J. of Power Sources* 2004, Vol. 136, pp 220-225.

3 Krause T., Kopasz J., Rossignol C., Carter J., Krumpelt M. Catalytic Autothermal Reforming of Hydrocarbon fuels for Fuel Cell systems. *Prepr. Pap. – Am. Chem. Soc., Div. Fuel Chem.* 2002, vol. 47, p. 542.

4 Fukunaga T., Katsuno H., Matsumoto H., Takahashi O., Akai Y. Development of kerosene fuel processing system for PEFC. *Catal. Today* 2003, vol. 84, p. 197.

5 Stucker JP, Schank JF, Dombey-Moore B. Assessment of DoD fuel standardization policies, National Defense Research Institute; February 23, 1995. ISBN: 0-8330-1546-X.

6 Military specification MIL-T-83133D – turbine fuels, aviation, kerosene types, NATO F-34 (JP-8), NATO F-35; January 29, 1992.

7 Song C. An overview of new approaches to deep desulfurization for ultra-clean gasoline, diesel, and jet fuel. *Catal. Today* 2003, vol. 86, p. 211.

8 Velu, S.; Ma, X.; Song, C. Selective adsorption for removing sulfur from jet fuel over zeolite-based adsorbents. *Ind. Eng. Chem. Res.* 2003, vol. *42*, p. 5293.

9 Babich, I. V.; Moulijn, J. A. Science and technology of novel process for deep desulfurization of oil refinery streams: a review. *Fuel* 2003, vol. *82*, p. 607.

10 Turk, B. S.; Gupta, R. P. RTI's TReND process for deep desulfurization of naphtha. *Prepr. Pap.sAm. Chem. Soc., Div. Fuel Chem.* 2001, *46*, 392.

Comparing Hydrogen and Hydrogen-Rich Reformate Enrichment of JP-8 in an Open Flame

Michael L. Seibert
US Army Communications, Electronics, Research, Development and Engineering Center (CERDEC)
Aberdeen Proving Ground, MD 21005

Sen Nieh
Professor and Chair
Department of Mechanical Engineering
The Catholic University of America
620 Michigan Ave, N.E.
Washington, DC 20064

Abstract: *Hydrogen enhanced combustion of JP-8 provides an additional control parameter for external combustion based power sources. Previous work showed benefit of hydrogen enhanced combustion for external combustion based power sources. Since hydrogen enriched combustion is made possible by fuel reforming of logistics fuels, reformate is a more realistic source in a fielded system. It is a mixture of hydrogen, carbon monoxide, carbon dioxide, and nitrogen (with trace amounts of lower hydrocarbons).*

Tests evaluated the temperature profiles of dual fueled flames using JP-8 and either hydrogen or a bottled mixture representing fuel reformate. Figure 1 shows increased temperature at 3 cm above the fuel nozzle with either form of hydrogen addition. Both supplemental fuels move combustion earlier, allowing more stable combustion and potential for reduced size. JP-8 flow rate was reduced to maintain fuel energy input at a constant 5.5 kWth. In comparing two cases, the important factor was the flow rate of hydrogen. The energy from carbon monoxide in the reformate does not contribute to improving combustion.

This research also compared methods of hydrogen addition. It was added with either the atomizing air or the secondary air. These tests showed that availability of oxygen is important as well. For example, hydrogen through the nozzle produces additional changes to the flame structure due to the combustible mixture of hydrogen and air in the nozzle. The equivalent hydrogen flow rate of reformate in the nozzle does not produce the same effect because the air in the nozzle is replaced by the other gases in the reformate (CO, CO_2, and N_2).

Hydrogen enrichment tests establish the benefit of dual firing hydrogen and JP-8. These reformate tests show the variables that must be considered in implementing this technique in a practical system.

Keywords: hydrogen; fuel reforming; external combustion; jet fuel

Introduction

Hydrogen enhanced combustion of JP-8 provides an additional control parameter for external combustion based power sources. This research compares the use of pure hydrogen with a representative mixture of hydrogen-rich reformate containing hydrogen, carbon monoxide, carbon dioxide and nitrogen.

This work builds on previous research efforts to provide JP-8 fueled power below 2-kW. It combines the concepts of oxygen enriched combustion [1] with the availability of hydrogen produced by logistics fuel reformation[2].

Other researchers have demonstrated the use of hydrogen enriched combustion in diesel engines [3], gas turbines [4,5], and lower hydrocarbons [6,7]. In previous research, hydrogen is shown to shift JP-8 combustion earlier, and to increase flame stability [8].

Experimental Set-up

Measurements are made of a 5.5 kWth open flame. An air siphon nozzle sprays JP-8 droplets upward, as shown in Figure 1. Approximately 10% of the air required for combustion is supplied through the nozzle. This air is used both to atomize the fuel and pull it from the fuel tank. The nozzle is mounted within a 1.5" tube supplying additional combustion air. Hydrogen and hydrogen-rich reformate can be introduced to either the atomizing air or the secondary air supply. Temperature is measured through the flame by three thermocouples sweeping horizontally through the flame. The temperature at each location is averaged over 15 seconds. A string potentiometer measures and records the thermocouple locations. The combined location and temperature data provide a detailed thermal profile of the flame.

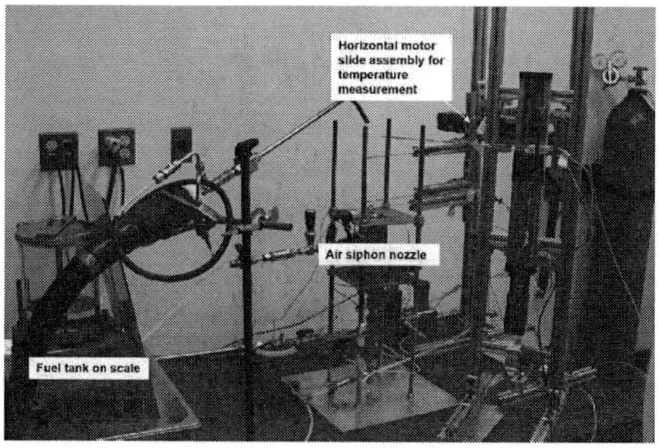

Figure 1. Experimental set-up shown air siphon nozzle and thermocouple stands.

Results

Temperature profiles of a JP-8 flame and two hydrogen enriched JP-8 flames are shown in Figure 2. Hydrogen in the secondary air is shown to move combustion earlier as shown by the higher temperatures at 1.4 and 3.1 cm. With hydrogen in the nozzle air, the earlier temperature increase is accompanied by a change in the structure of the flame caused by the premixed hydrogen and air in the nozzle. The premixed hydrogen and air create a center temperature peak, and increase the temperature more rapidly in the early flame.

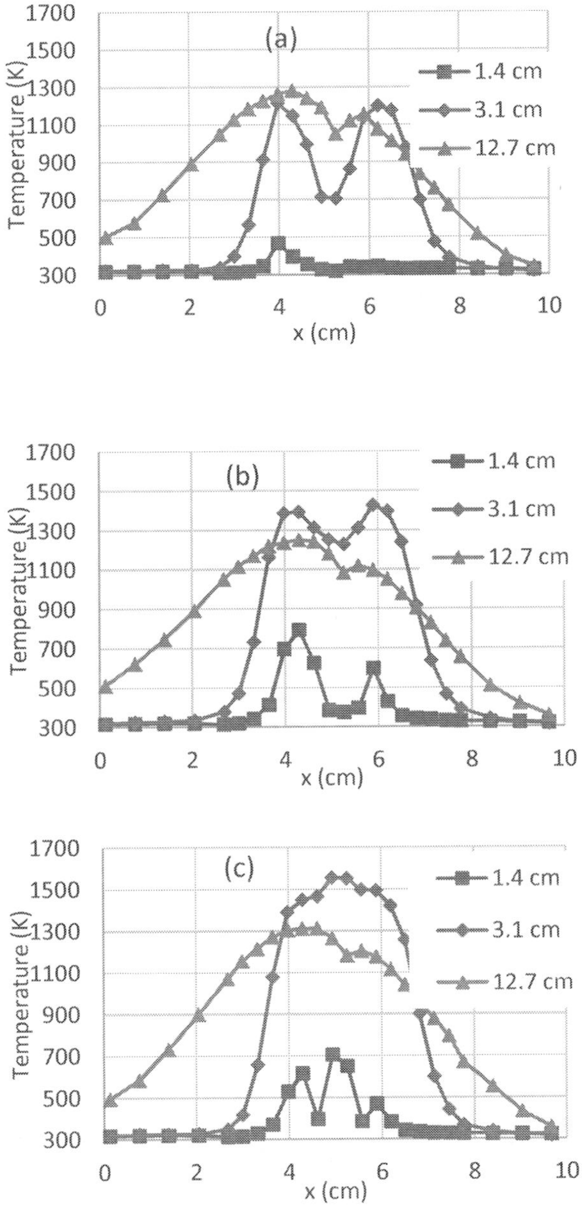

Figure 2. Lateral temperature profiles of a) JP-8 flame, b) JP-8 with H2 in secondary air, and c) JP-8 with H2 in the nozzle air.

Tests were done using mixtures of simulated reformate to move hydrogen enriched combustion closer to practical applications. These consist of a gas mixture containing the major components of the products of fuel reformation, i.e. hydrogen, carbon monoxide, carbon dioxide, and nitrogen as shown in Table 1.

Table 1. Simulated reformate composition [2].

CO_2	CO	H_2	N_2
7.3%	18.1%	34.5%	Balance (~40.1%)

Lateral temperature sweeps at 1.4 and 3.1 cm show the early flame structure with the simulated reformate in Figures 3 and 4. At 1.4 cm, temperatures at the edge of the flame are raised by approximately 100 K relative to a JP-8 only flame. As expected, increasing the energy fraction from reformate increases the temperature. At 3.1 cm, the temperature increase at the edge of the flame is less pronounced, but the center temperature increases by 200 K with 20% energy contribution.

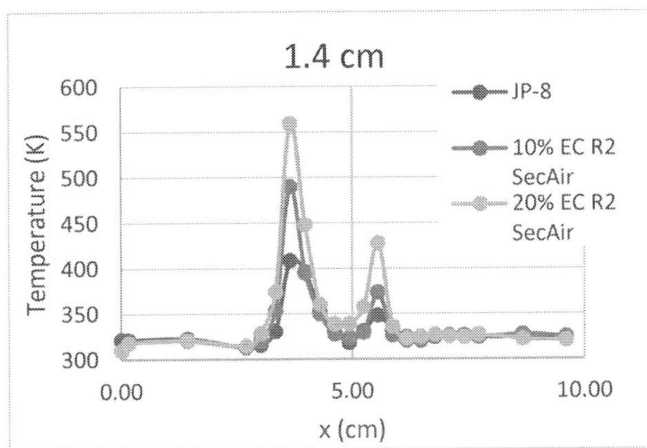

Figure 3. Lateral temperature profile at 1.4 cm comparing JP-8 and JP-8 with 10 and 20% of the energy supplied by simulated reformate in the secondary air.

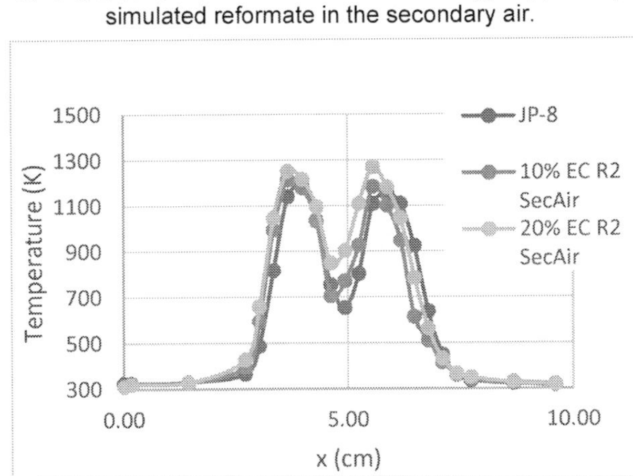

Figure 4. Lateral temperature profile at 3.1 cm comparing JP-8 and JP-8 with 10 and 20% of the energy supplied by simulated reformate in the secondary air.

With hydrogen rich reformate added to the nozzle, there is less temperature increase on the edges of the flame, as shown in Figure 5. The temperature increase in the center is less pronounced as well. On the sides, there is no added gaseous fuel to enhance combustion at the mixing interface. In the center, unlike pure hydrogen, the nozzle mixture in this configuration does not form a strong pilot flame. This is because the other components of reformate displace the oxygen needed for premixed combustion.

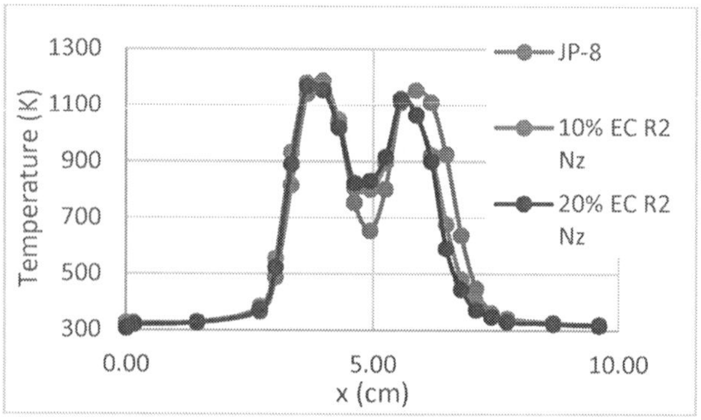

Figure 5. Temperature profiles at 3.1 cm showing reformate addition to the nozzle.

The advantage of hydrogen enriched combustion is more significant using pure hydrogen, than when using hydrogen-rich reformate. Figure 6 show the temperature profiles at 3.1 cm for both hydrogen and reformate in the secondary. For comparison, hydrogen and reformate each contribute 20% of the energy in the respective flames. In the secondary air, hydrogen raises the temperature at the side peaks 150 K hotter than reformate, and 350 K hotter in the center dip. In application, there would be benefit to using pure hydrogen if it was available. Recent research in palladium membranes shows they can be used as filters to produce a nearly pure hydrogen stream [9].

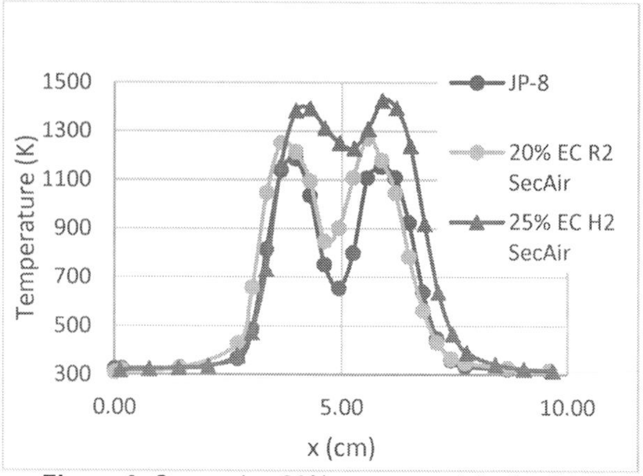

Figure 6. Comparing 20% energy contribution from reformate and 25% from pure hydrogen in the secondary air at 3.1 cm.

Much better agreement is seen between reformate and hydrogen when comparing solely on the basis of hydrogen. At 20% energy contribution, the reformate is at 11 slpm which amounts to 4 slpm hydrogen. The temperature profile of this flame is shown in Figure 7 at 3.1 cm. The JP-8 flames enriched with pure hydrogen show higher temperature than the reformate flame. The reformate temperature profile matches the hydrogen temperature profile better when compared on a hydrogen flow rate basis than when compared on an energy contribution basis. This indicates that while carbon monoxide in the reformate technically provides chemical energy to the flame, it does not contribute to shifting the flame earlier and reducing standoff distance.

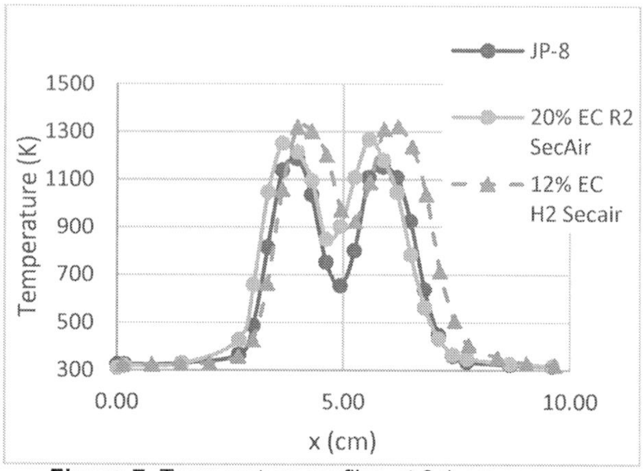

Figure 7. Temperature profiles at 3.1 cm compare hydrogen-rich reformate and pure hydrogen in the secondary air.

The reformate through the nozzle does not provide good agreement with hydrogen through the nozzle, even when compared on the basis of hydrogen flow rate. Figure 8 compares the temperature profiles of a JP-8 flame with 11 slpm reformate (4 slpm hydrogen) with 4 slpm pure hydrogen at 3.1 cm. The temperature profile of the reformate enriched flame follows the JP-8 only flame at 1.4 cm. At 3.1 cm, the temperature dip in the fuel rich center is not as deep with reformate as with JP-8 only.

The dominant feature when hydrogen enrichment is done through the nozzle is the center temperature peak or pilot flame. This is clearly present in both figures for the flames enriched with pure hydrogen but not with reformate. As noted above, this configuration has 4 slpm hydrogen and 7 slpm air in the nozzle which is very close to the stoichiometric ratio for hydrogen combustion (Φ=1.36). 20% energy contribution from reformate requires 11 slpm which displaces all the air through the nozzle. Since there is no oxygen in the nozzle, no center flame is formed. The 10% energy contribution from reformate case has 6 slpm reformate and 4 slpm air in the nozzle. While this provides a combustible proportion of hydrogen and oxygen, the flow rate is not enough to create the center flame effect. This is true with pure hydrogen as well. Using 2 slpm pure hydrogen in the nozzle does not produce enough heat to generate a separate pilot flame even with sufficient oxygen for full combustion.

In the secondary air configuration, the amount of hydrogen is the important factor in comparing enriched flames. The energy content of carbon monoxide does not provide a measureable benefit over JP-8. In the nozzle configuration, the ratio of hydrogen and oxygen in the nozzle is also important. With carbon monoxide, carbon dioxide, and nitrogen displacing air, the conditions for a "pilot flame" are more difficult to achieve with reformate. A combustible hydrogen-air mixture can substantially speed droplet heating and vaporization, and move combustion earlier. This can allow a smaller, more stable combustor.

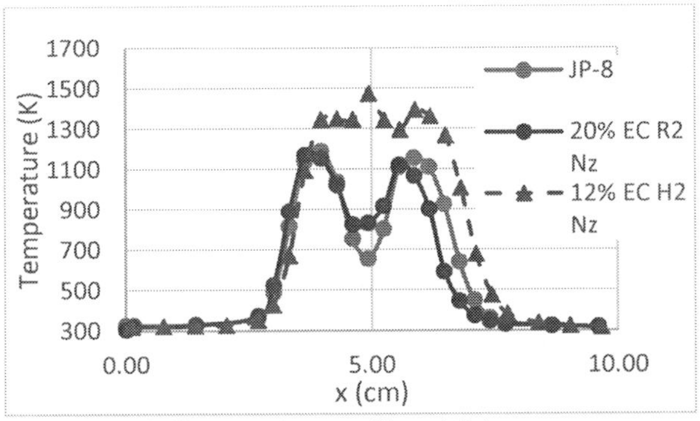

Figure 8. Temperature profiles at 3.1 cm compare hydrogen-rich reformate and pure hydrogen in the nozzle.

Summary

Hydrogen enriched combustion has been demonstrated as a control parameter for external combustion based power sources. The present research uses hydrogen-rich reformate as the source of hydrogen. It is shown that for the same amount of hydrogen in the secondary air, the effect on combustion is similar with pure hydrogen or with hydrogen-rich reformate. Added hydrogen shifts combustion earlier, raising temperature, and increasing flame stability. Carbon monoxide in the reformate adds energy, but does not change the combustion performance due to its lower flame speed. Hydrogen-rich reformate has substantially less impact in the nozzle than pure hydrogen. This is due to other gases (N_2, CO, and CO_2) displacing oxygen, preventing the formation of the pilot flame.

References

1. Coombe HS, Nieh S, Polymer membrane air separation performance for portable oxygen enriched combustion applications, *Energy Conversion and Management* (2007)Volume 48, Issue 5, Pages 1499-1505
2. DuBois TG, Nieh S, Selection and performance comparison of jet fuel surrogates for autothermal reforming, *Fuel* (2011) vol 90 1439-1448
3. Abu-Jrai, A., Tsolakis, A., Megaritis, A. "The influence of H_2 and CO on diesel engine combustion characteristics, exhaust gas emissions, and after treatment selective catalytic NO_x reduction." *International Journal of Hydrogen Energy* 32 (2007) 3565-3571
4. Burguburu, J., Cabot, G., Renou, B., Boukhalfa, A.M., Cazalens, M., "Effects of H2 enrichment on flame stability and pollutant emissions for a kerosene/air swirled flame with an aeronautical injector" *Proceedings of the Combustion Institute* 33 (2011) 2927-2935
5. Burguburu, J., Cabot, G., Renou, B., Boukhalfa, A.M., Cazalens, M., "Comparisons of the impact of reformer gas and hydrogen enrichment on flame stability and pollutant emissions for a kerosene/air swirled flame with an aeronautical fuel injector" *International Journal of Hydrogen Energy* 36 (2011) 6925-6936
6. Schefer, R. W. "Combustion of Hydrogen-Enriched Methane in a Lean Premixed Swirl Burner." *Proceedings of the 2001 Department of Energy Hydrogen Program Review*
7. Kumar, P. and Mishra, D.P. "Experimental investigation of laminar LPG-H_2 jet diffusion flame." *International Journal of Hydrogen Energy* 33 (2008) 225-231.
8. Seibert, M.L., and Nieh, S., "Measurements of Hydrogen Enriched combustion of jet fuel in open flame." Proceedings of the ASME Power and Energy Conference, June 2016, Charlotte, NC
9. Z. Dunbar, "Hydrogen purification of synthetic water gas shift gases using microstructured palladium membranes," *Journal of Power Sources,* vol. 297, pp. 525-533, 2015

Development of Nickel Zinc Technology for Military and Civilian Energy Storage Applications

Rhodri W. Evans, Stephen L. Vechy*, Andrew C. Loyns, Christian Oettel**, Alfonso S. Pensado**, Borislav S. Leshtanski** and Scott Lichte ***

Engineering and Technology, EnerSys Limited, Newport, United Kingdom
***Reading, PA, USA**
*****Warrensburg, MO, USA**
****EnerSys - GAZ Geräte- und Akkumulatorenwerk Zwickau GmbH, Zwickau, Germany**

Abstract: *Nickel Zinc technology was originally developed and patented in 1901 by Thomas Edison. The historical performance limitation has been the cyclic capability and stability of the rechargeable system. Recently, technological advancement and development activities have addressed this issue. The aqueous Nickel Zinc electrochemical system offers very attractive levels of both energy density and power density combined with good cyclic capability across a broad and flat electrical discharge spectrum. The energy and power performance metrics of today's advanced Nickel Zinc technology offer significant improvement compared to lead-acid battery configurations and approach the metrics of lithium-ion battery systems.*

EnerSys has invested and focused on the development of Nickel Zinc cells and batteries to evaluate the performance for a range of applications. At this stage of our activity, it has become increasingly apparent that Nickel Zinc electrochemical systems can offer several very attractive performance attributes that align well to the demands for both military (such as combat vehicles) and civilian markets (such as Uninterruptible Power Systems).

Our paper will focus on results of electrical characterization (including constant current and constant power performance), float life testing to date, open circuit (stand loss) testing, cycle life evaluation, high power discharge, charging options, charge acceptance/efficiency, and abuse testing.

Keywords: Nickel Zinc chemistry; maintenance free cells; technology characterization.

Introduction

The introduction of the Nickel Zinc (NiZn) electrochemical couple into a rechargeable battery was described by Edison in the year 1901 [1]. Since that time, many approaches were undertaken to develop and establish NiZn batteries in the commercial market [2]. However, the technology was only successful in a few niche applications.

The NiZn technology is based on a $Ni(OH)_2$ cathode and a ZnO / Zn based anode which are electrically separated by a separator material. The OH- conductivity between the two electrodes is provided by an aqueous KOH solution. The proceeding electrode reactions, taking place at the anode (negative electrode) during charge and discharge, are shown in equation 1-3 [2, 3]. Note the generation of gaseous oxygen and hydrogen during over-discharge and over-charge, respectively (equation 4 and 5).

Anode

$$Zn + 2OH^- \underset{\text{charge}}{\overset{\text{discharge}}{\rightleftarrows}} Zn(OH)_2 + 2e^- \quad (1)$$

$$Zn(OH)_2 + 2OH^- \leftrightarrow ZnO_2^{2-} + 2H_2O \quad (2)$$

$$ZnO_2^{2-} + H_2O \leftrightarrow ZnO + 2OH^- \quad (3)$$

$$2OH^- \rightarrow \tfrac{1}{2}O_2 + H_2O + 2e- \quad (4)$$

$$2H_2O + 2e^- \rightarrow H_2 + 2OH^- \quad (5)$$

The proceeding electrode reactions, taking place at the cathode (positive electrode) during charge and discharge, are shown in equation 6 [2,3]. Note the generation of gaseous hydrogen and oxygen during over discharge and over charge, respectively (equation 7 and 8).

Cathode

$$2NiOOH + 2H_2O + 2e^- \underset{\text{charge}}{\overset{\text{discharge}}{\rightleftarrows}} 2Ni(OH)_2 + 2OH^- \quad (6)$$

$$2H_2O + 2e^- \rightarrow H_2 + 2OH^- \quad (7)$$

$$2OH- \rightarrow \tfrac{1}{2}O_2 + H_2O + 2e^- \quad (8)$$

Equations 2 and 3 represent side reactions which take place at the anode subsequently to the actual discharge reaction (Eq. 1). However, they do not proceed with a similar reaction rate and do not contribute to the generated/consumed electrical current. The species $Zn(OH)_2$, generated during discharge, is soluble in water. Hence, the deposition of solid ZnO (Eq. 3) does not take place at the exact position where the Zn particle was located before the discharge. This results in a relocation of the active material on the anode with increasing cycle life and is often referred to as the so called "shape change effect". Consequently, the reaction chain from $Zn(OH)_2$ to ZnO is of high importance for the cell chemistry and cell life, as this "shape change effect" leads to a reduction of the electrochemical active surface area of the electrode (passivation, agglomeration, etc.) [4,5].

Experimental

Unless otherwise indicated, the results presented in this paper were acquired using single cell and battery arrangements, made within the NiZn facilities of EnerSys. The basic test unit is a prismatic single cell, with a rated capacity of 100Ah. The cell is designed to be maintenance free; no electrolyte top-up or refill is required during the life of the cell. The specific energy of the single cell, as shown in Figure 1, is in the range of 66Wh/kg. The energy density is 135Wh/l as the cell has a volume of about 1.25 liters.

Figure 1. EnerSys prismatic NiZn prototype cell

Test Results & Discussion

Power Capability Characterization: The capacity behavior of the NiZn technology at different constant power discharge loads is shown in Figure 2. The graph shows for 10 different discharge loads, ranging from 50W up to 1000W, and the available Ah discharge capacity of the tested cell. The displayed data was recorded with a fresh 100Ah NiZn prototype cell, described above. The discharge was terminated during the test at the pre-defined cutoff voltage of 1.25V. The cell delivered throughout the complete discharge power range a capacity larger than 100Ah, underlining the strong high-power/high-energy capability of the NiZn technology.

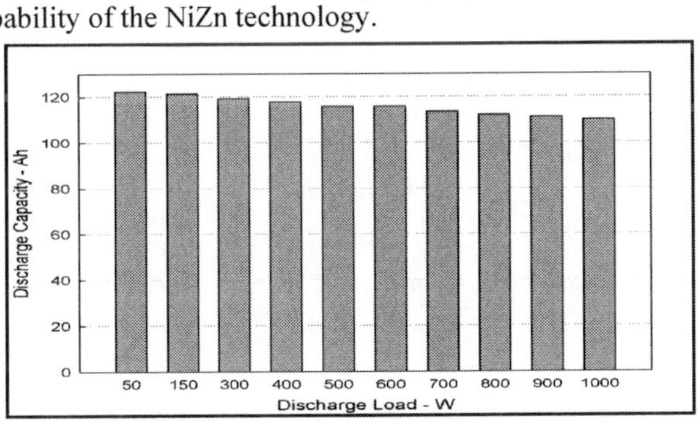

Figure 2. Discharge Ah capacity of a 100Ah NiZn prototype cell at different constant power discharge loads between C/3 and 6C rates

High Power Pulse Discharge (HPPD) testing is shown in Figures 3 and 4 below. After the initial 50%DOD at 100A rate, the cell completed five roundtrips of variable 30s pulse discharges while maintaining temperature <+30°C.

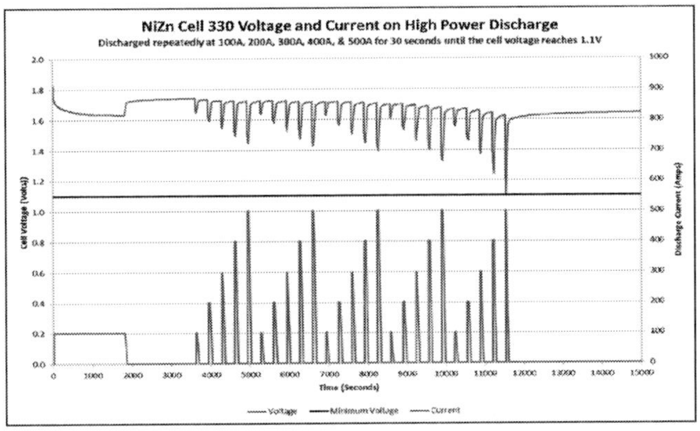

Figure 3. HPPD showing variable discharge current pulses and voltage response at variable states of discharge

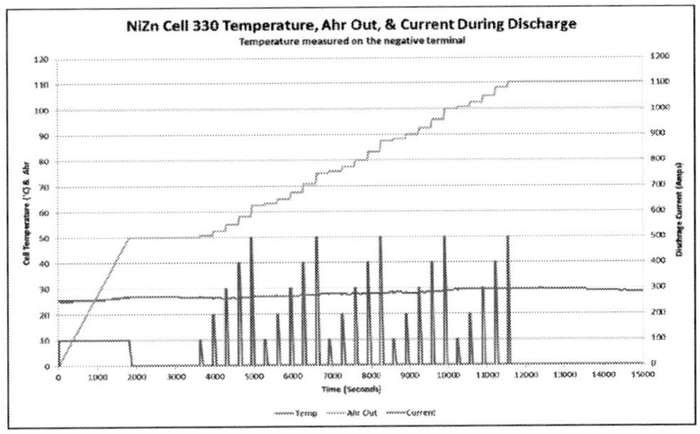

Figure 4. HPPD showing variable discharge current pulses and cumulative Ah discharge output along with demonstrating isotherm conditions.

The DC resistance of the cell remained at 0.5 mΩ until 88Ah removed, and increased to 0.7mΩ at 100Ah removed, finally achieving 1.0 mΩ at EOD delivering 110.3Ah total, providing 14 seconds at 500A during the last step before hitting the 1.10V cutoff. Given the pre-HPPD C/10 capacity of this cell was 120Ah, this shows the NiZn cell can deliver up to 500A (5C rate) while between +25°C and +29°C temperature while at 92%DOD of available capacity – which equates to 5C rate high-power engine-starting capability down to approximately 8-10% state of charge.

Open Circuit (Stand Loss) Characterization: The ability for the NiZn technology to undergo successful storage is another crucial performance factor to characterize. One dozen new, fresh prototype 100Ah NiZn cells were fully charged at 1.90V to 100%SOC, and then stored at +25°C for 13 months. The cell open circuit voltages (OCV) for this group started at 1.88V average and fell to about 1.80V within the first 30 days. The cell voltages fell very slowly over the next 12 months to final OCV's between 1.73V and 1.75V after the full 13-month storage period. The residual capacities (when tested at the 100A C1 discharge rate to 1.10V) ranged between 31Ah-42Ah, signifying about 30%-40%SOC which equates to between 5%-6% capacity loss/month. The first recharge used 100A to a 5A end of charge current cutoff input and ranged between 116-118Ah; the subsequent discharge at 100A to 1.10V cutoff yielded between 117Ah-119Ah output. This confirms the ability for fresh, new cells to provide 100% capacity recovery on the very first recharge with >98% coulometric charge efficiency.

Abuse & Safety Characterization: The safety of installed battery technology is of crucial importance. Therefore, the characterization of the NiZn technology for safe operation has been established.

The over-charge of a battery, caused for example by a malfunction in the utilized charger technology, is a realistic scenario in the field of battery applications. Figure 5 shows the results of controlled over-charge tests carried out with a NiZn 100Ah prototype cell. During the test, the charge current was set to 20A (i.e. C/5) and the cell voltage was limited to 2.1V, being at least 150mV above the nominal value. During the test, the temperature was recorded, and is plotted along with the course of the current, cell voltage, and charge capacity.

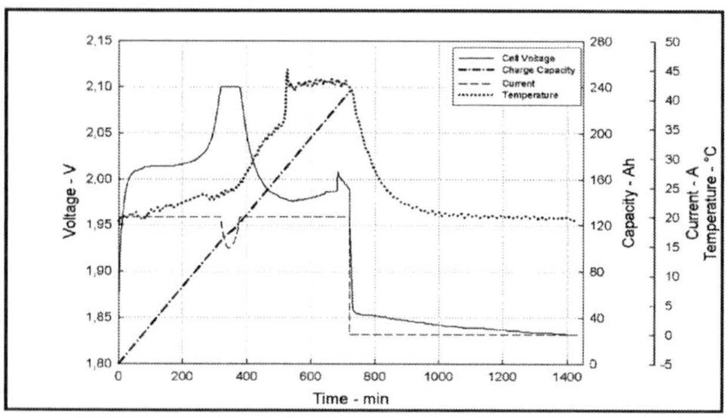

Figure 5. Controlled overcharge of a NiZn prototype cell with 20A at 2.1V for 12h

The graph shows that the cell voltage increased at the start of the test quickly to a value of about 2.01V, followed by a voltage plateau for about 300 minutes (~100Ah input). Subsequently, the cell voltage increased exponentially up to the set limit of 2.1V. As this limit was reached the charge current was consequently reduced by the electrical circuit. It dropped below 15A, and increased afterwards back to its set value of 20A. At the moment when the current value again reached 20A, the cell voltage started to decrease to a minimal value of 1.97V, followed by a secondary maximum slightly above 2V. After 720 minutes, the current was set to 0A, and the voltage and temperature were recorded until the total test duration of 1440 minutes was reached. In total, a capacity of 236Ah was applied to the cell during this test. During the test, the cell did not show any visual signs of structural instability and after the test no external damage was visible.

The recorded temperature data, which peaked at +45°C, gave no indication of an uncontrollable reaction (i.e. thermal runaway).

The behavior of the NiZn technology during over discharge is shown in Figure 6. Here, the cell was discharged with 100A to a cell voltage of 1V, followed by a discharge with 10A to a cell voltage of 0.3V. The discharge cut-off voltage of NiZn under standard conditions is in the range of 1.3V. Hence, the cell was discharged by about 1V below its standard cut off voltage. Figure 6 shows the course of the voltage, the current, the cell wall temperature, and the charge capacity as a function of time.

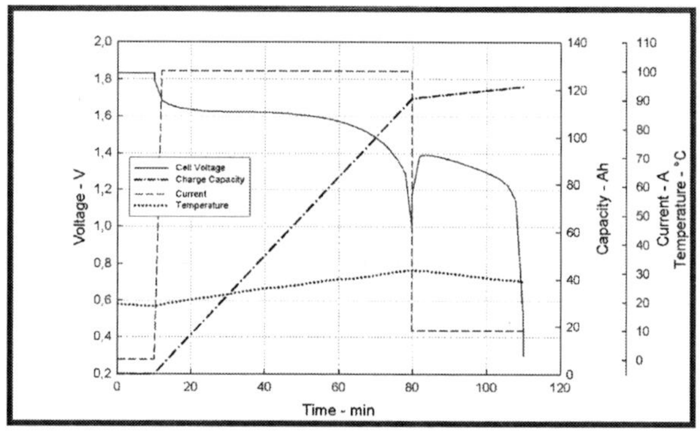

Figure 6. Controlled overdischarge of a NiZn prototype cell down to 0.3V

The discharge with a current of 100A started after 10 minutes. The voltage shows the standard course of a cell voltage during discharge, which is explained in detail within industry literature [7]. During this first discharge step, the temperature at the cell wall increased to maximum of 31°C. The switch of the discharge current from 100A to 10A is visible at 80 minutes. Here, the cell voltage recovered from 1V to about 1.4V, and decreased subsequently to 0.3V at the 110 minute mark. During this second discharge step, only 5Ah were discharged, whereas the cell delivered approximately 116Ah during the 100A discharge step. The cell wall temperature decreased in this period from 31°C to 27°C. Similar to the over-charge operation, no signs of an uncontrolled reaction proceeding within the cell could be observed. The structure of the cell was not harmed and no deformations could be observed.

The reliability and robustness of a battery system is improved, if the battery exhibits the property to allow a safe recharge starting at 0% state of charge. In order to determine the recovery of the NiZn technology after an extended period at 0% state of charge (SoC), a NiZn 12V 100Ah prototype battery was stored under standard conditions in discharged state for 21 days with a 2-Ohm resistor connecting both battery terminals. Subsequently to these 21 days, the battery was recharged with a current of 10A (C/10) in order to determine the remaining recoverable battery capacity. Figure 7 illustrates this experiment by plotting the course of the current, the voltage, and the capacity as a function of time during the charge and discharge steps which occurred after the 21 days of storage at 0%SOC. The battery was charged continuously with 10A up to a charge capacity of 125Ah. During this process, the battery voltage increased, first rapidly, then more slowly up to a voltage of 15.04V, or 1.88VPC. This behavior is to be expected and resembles the general charge behavior of a battery [7]. After a short rest period of 30 minutes, the discharge of the battery was started. As shown in Figure 7, the discharge current was 10A and the battery delivered a capacity of 100 Ah. This test demonstrated the ability of the NiZn technology to recover from an abusive, extended storage period while in a 0% SOC (and 0V terminal voltage) over-discharged condition without exhibiting a decrease of the available capacity.

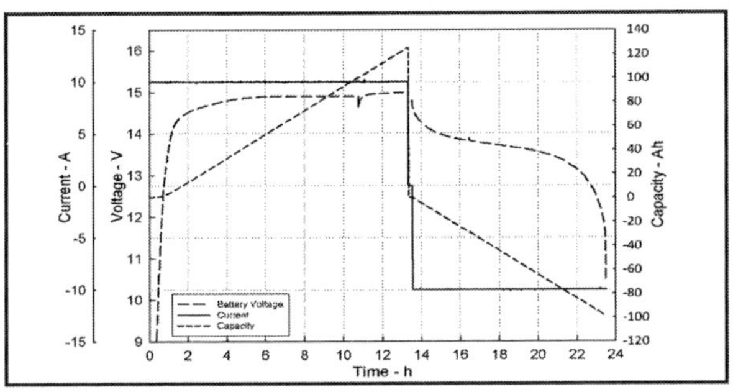

Figure 7. Recovery of an 8 cell 12V 100Ah NiZn prototype battery after 21 days at a 2 Ohm short circuit.

Application Standard Characterization: The Telcordia GR—4228: Clause 5.14 test procedure represents an industry standard test regime designed for lead- acid batteries. The test is characterized by the 100%DOD complete deep discharge of the 100Ah test cells, at 3 different discharge current rates. The recharge in between the different rate discharges is realized by charging for 24h at a voltage of 1.9V with a current limit of 10A. For the benefit of a clean illustration, the graph shows only the data of one cell of the test group (as the other cells performed equally). The achieved discharge capacity over the test cycle life for 3 different discharge rates is displayed in Figure 8. At the beginning of the test, each cell exhibited an available discharge capacity of more than 100% of its rated capacity.

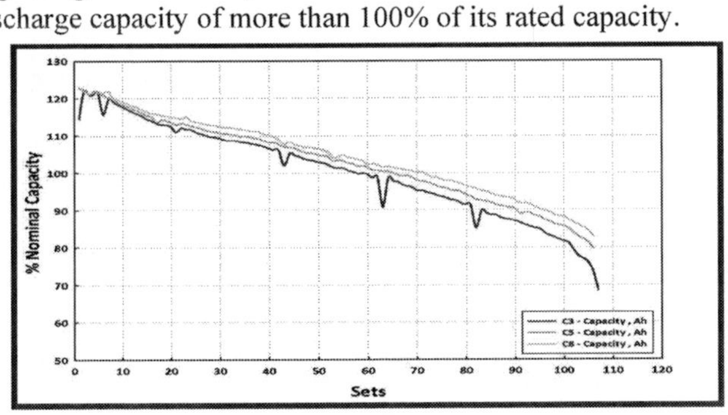

Figure 8. Telcordia GR-4228:Clause 5.14 results of NiZn prototype single cells.

The graph illustrates the cells passed, under the defined test conditions [6], the 53 cycle sets mark. The end of the cell life is defined in this test at the 80% nominal capacity mark. After 53 cycle sets, the cell capacity dropped from 120%–125% down to 100%–105% of the nominal capacity.

Conclusion & Outlook

The test results demonstrate the potential of the NiZn technology in both high and low discharge rates, deep cyclic performance and response to long-term storage. It was shown that the available capacity of a NiZn cell does not drop significantly with increasing load demands in the tested constant power load window, and the technology can deliver 5C power when as low as 10% state of charge. The self-discharge appears reliable at between 5-6%/month when at +25°C; however, the OCV correlation to %SOC needs further study. The NiZn technology exhibited very stable behavior during the over-charge, over discharge, and recovery tests, and no signs of a thermal runaway or hazardous cell conditions were observed. Additionally, it was demonstrated that the NiZn technology has the capability to be reactivated after deep discharge to 0V and a consecutive storage time of 21 days. Industry lead-acid standard tests, adapted to the NiZn technology, are ongoing. The 100%DOD Telcordia test showed an exceptional achievement of ~100 cycle sets and >300 total individual cycles.

In summary, it can be stated that the NiZn technology is a safe aqueous chemistry with many benefits for a wide range of applications including the military and civilian energy storage markets. The optimization and industrialization of the technology is ongoing.

Acknowledgment

The work described in this paper is based on NiZn technology developed by PowerGenix, and thanks go to Jeffrey Phillips and LinJun Wang of that company for their support.

References

[1] T.A.Edison, Brit. Patent GB190120072-A (1901)

[2] Thomas B.Reddy, Linden's Handbook of Batteries, 4th ed, 2011, chapter 23: J..Phillips and S.Mohanta.

[3] J.Jindra, "Sealed nickel-zinc cells",JPowerSources,vol 37, pp. 279-313,1992

[4] F.R. McLarnon, and E.J.Cairns, " The Secondary Alkaline Zinc Electrode", J.Electrochem.Soc.,vol 138, pp. 645-664,1991

[5] J.Jindra, "Progress in sealed Ni-Zn cells, 1991-1995",JPowerSources,vol 66, pp. 15-25,1997

[6] International Standard GR-4228 - CORE, Issue 02, 2013, " Valve-Regulated Lead-Acid(CRLA) Battery String Certification Levels Base on Requirements for Safety and Performance"

[7] Thomas B.Reddy, Linden's Handbook of Batteries, 4th ed, 2011, chapter 3: D. Linden

Betavoltaic Performance Under Extreme Temperatures and Hybrid Configurations

Tom Adams[1], Shripad Revankar[2], Peter Cabauy[3], Bret Elkind[3], and Darrell Cheu[2]

[1] Naval Surface Warfare Center, Crane Division, Crane, IN 47522 USA

[2] School of Nuclear Engineering, Purdue University West Lafayette, IN 47907 USA

[3] City Labs, Inc. Homestead, FL 33030 USA

Abstract: *Longevity of sensors and portable devices are severely limited by temperature, chemical instability, and electrolyte leakage issues associated with conventional electrochemical batteries. Betavoltaics, which operate similar to photovoltaics, can operate in a wide temperature range safely without permanent degradation. Though not a new concept, which began in 1950's and peaked in mid 1970's, research has been minimal and sporadic until recent advancements in ultra-low power electronics and materialization of low power applications. The technology is rapidly maturing, generating research, and development in increasing beta emitting source and semiconductor efficiencies. This study presents an update on betavoltaic technology, results from temperature evaluation on commercially available General Licensed betavoltaic cells, development of hybrid system for latent and burst power, modeling and simulation techniques and results, and current and proposed research and development. Betavoltaic performance was successfully demonstrated for wide temperature range (-30°C to 70°C). Short circuit current and open circuit voltage were used to compare electrical performance. Results indicate that the open-circuit voltage and maximum power decreased as temperature increased due to increases in the minority carrier concentration.*

Keywords: Betavoltaic; radioisotope power source; energy harvesting; hybrid battery; solid-state battery; beta emitter; p-n junction; latent power; low power; modelling.

Introduction

Radiation interaction with materials can have beneficial uses, such as in betavoltaic cells, a type of radioisotope power source where the kinetic energy associated with beta (β-) decay is converted into electricity. Though not a new concept, research and development has been minimal for many years due to limited low-power applications, rapid semi-conductor degradation, limited availability and high cost of suitable radioisotopes, and public perception. Novel and compelling need-based applications are emerging in the military, intelligence, commercial, and medical markets that can utilize the diminutive energy produced from such cells. Present-day micro-electromechanical systems and electronic devices make betavoltaics an attractive alternative to electrochemical batteries enabling applications to perform for much longer periods in extreme temperatures. Unlike conventional electrochemical batteries, commercially available betavoltaics can operate in excess of 10 years over temperatures ranging from -55°C to 150°C [1]. Because the technology is far from mature, many challenges and issues remain to be solved to improve efficiency and energy density, and reduce cost, which will be discussed in the background section of this paper.

Little performance data exists on current betavoltaic technology. Furthermore, temperature behavior and aging phenomena are not known. Betavoltaics made by City Labs are being evaluated under temperature and other external forces such at electric fields, magnetic fields and high energy radiation in the form of neutrons and gamma rays. The results will provide a benchmark for inserting betavoltaics into applications. A model is being developed to assess the temperature effects on performance to assist designers in using the technology and identify critical areas that can be improved. Eventually, previously developed surface beta flux models using MC-SET (Monte Carlo Simulation of Electron Trajectories in solids) [2] will be coupled to the model.

Radioisotopes are encountered by everyone daily and are used safely in many locations, such as households, hospitals, retail stores, and aircraft. For example, smoke detectors rely on americium-241 for sensing smoke. Hospitals use radiographic imaging devices and tracers in many of their treatment protocols. Tritium is used in many products, such as exit signs, gun sights, and watches to provide illumination. Promethium-147 (^{147}Pm), a byproduct of nuclear fission, has been used to illuminate gauges for aircraft. Before these devices become available, a General License in the form of a Sealed Source & Device Registration (SSDR) is required from the U.S. Nuclear Regulatory Commission (NRC). Naturally occurring radioisotopes, such as potassium-40, tritium (T), and carbon-14 are routinely found in the human body from ingestion of food and water. Cosmic radiation is constantly present where exposure increases with altitude.

Background

The first betavoltaic battery was developed in 1953 at RCA by Rappaport. The device yielded an efficiency of only 0.2% and degraded rapidly due to radiation damage from the beta source, strontium-90 [3]. Several others continued research using ^{147}Pm but were only able to achieve <1%

efficiency [4, 5]. The most promising effort in the early history of betavoltaic developments occurred ca. 1974 through research led by Olsen at the Donald W. Douglas Laboratories [6, 7]. Olsen's Betacel battery exhibited a 4% efficiency using ^{147}Pm and silicon p-n junctions. Over 285 patients received pacemakers powered by the Betacel batteries, 60 patients inside the United States. German and U.S. medical institutions were seriously considering the Betacel for wider use. The United States Atomic Energy Commission (USAEC) had authorized the licensing in the United States of a Clinical Investigation Program that allowed the implantation of 50 Betacel pacemakers per month [8]. However, strides in lithium battery development entered onto the scene and were subsequently selected for pacemakers instead [9].

Most research and development in the last 10 years has concentrated on designs using tritium; since the radiation damage is low and thus easily shielded, and relatively available. City Labs successfully produced tritium betavoltaic prototypes in 2008 (Figure 1), that are still operating. The NanoTritium™ betavoltaic was granted a NRC General License which is approved for manufacture and sales within the United States.

Figure 1. City Labs' NanoTritium^{TM} betavoltaics.

Theory of Operation

A betavoltaic cell creates electricity similar to a photovoltaic or solar cell. In a betavoltaic cell, electrons are produced indirectly via the kinetic energy of the beta particles interacting within the semiconductor. The basic concept of operation is shown in Figure 2. The beta particle enters the p-n junction and collides with atoms creating electron-hole pairs (EHP) as it slows down. A portion of the kinetic energy is lost to the lattice. A 5 keV particle creates 1000 or more EHPs, and those created near the intrinsic or depletion region contribute to the generated current collected at the contacts. The number of EHP is proportional to the band gap energy of the material, the minimum energy for an electron to move to the conduction band, and the number of defects or traps where recombination occurs. The holes are accelerated to the p-side collector and the electrons are accelerated to the n-side collector. EHPs created outside the depletion layer quickly recombine and provide a net current of zero. With a load connected, the electrons travel from the n-side, through the load and back to the p-side. The electrical characteristic for a single diode is shown in Figure 3. The peak power occurs about 0.8V and can be used in a constant current mode or constant voltage mode, depending on the application. The cells can be stacked in parallel and series.

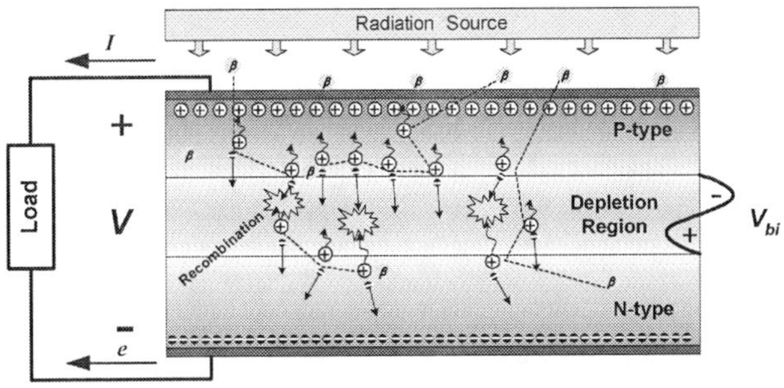

Figure 2. Overview of a betavoltaic cell.

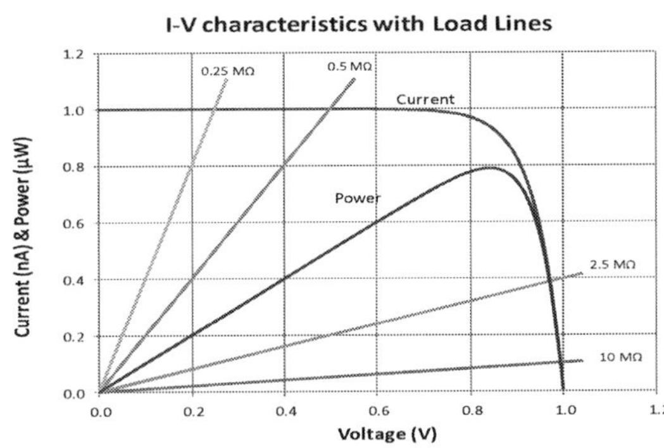

Figure 3. Typical I-V characteristics of a Betavoltaic cell

Hybrid Designs

Combining the betavoltaic in parallel with a solid-state lithium rechargeable (secondary) battery can provide latent and burst power for many applications. In a design using a Cymbet 50 µAh lithium solid-state rechargeable battery, the operating temperature is limited to 85°C, the maximum operating temperature of the battery. The power of the betavoltaic will be based on burst power required and duty cycle of the sensor. Various methods of controlling the betavoltaic current to prevent overcharging the solid-state battery is being investigated. A hybrid design, shown schematically in Figure 4 will alleviate self-discharge losses at high temperatures.

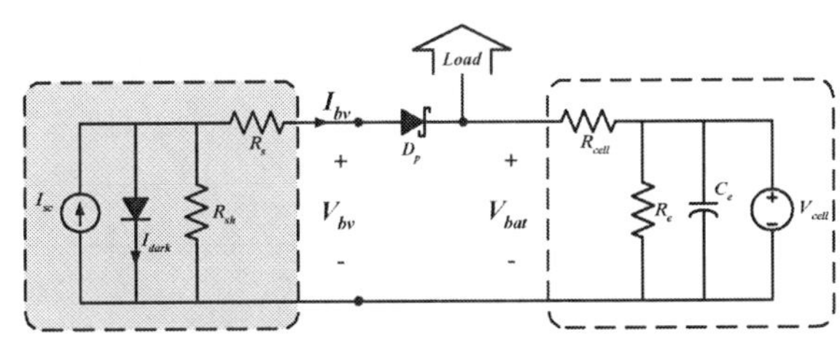

Figure 4. Hybrid betavoltaic and Lithium battery

Temperature Performance Results

Betavoltaics were evaluated under temperature from -30°C to 70°C by applying a voltage and sinking the current using a Keithley 2602B source measurement unit. For individual cells, Current-voltage (I-V) curves were acquired by stepping the voltage from 1.00 V to -0.10 V in steps of 1 mV and measuring the current. Figure 5 shows I-V curves measured on Sample BV07. From cold to hot, the open-circuit voltage, V_{oc}, decreased from 0.95V to 0.65V while the short-circuit current (I_{sc}) increased from 82 to 86 nA. Because of the strong temperature dependence on voltage, the maximum power increases with decreasing temperature.

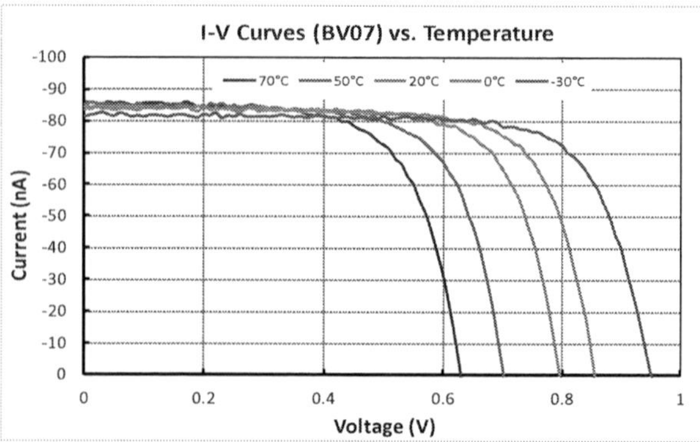

Figure 5. I-V curves of Sample BV07 at temperatures from -30°C to 70°C

Six betavoltaic cells connected in series were evaluated from -30°C to 70°C. I-V curves were acquired by stepping the voltage from 5.00 V to -0.10 V in steps of 5 mV and measuring the current. Figure 6 shows that betavoltaics can operate in series where V_{oc} and I_{sc} operate similar to individual cells. To fully charge the battery to 4.1V in a hybrid design, seven betavoltaic cells in series are needed at 70°C while five cells are needed at -30°C. The lithium solid-state rechargeable battery performance evaluated under temperatures from -30°C to 70°C show the charge/discharge times increase by 20% from the coldest temperature. A hybrid design that operates at both extremes requires control circuitry that is being developed to prevent overcharging the battery.

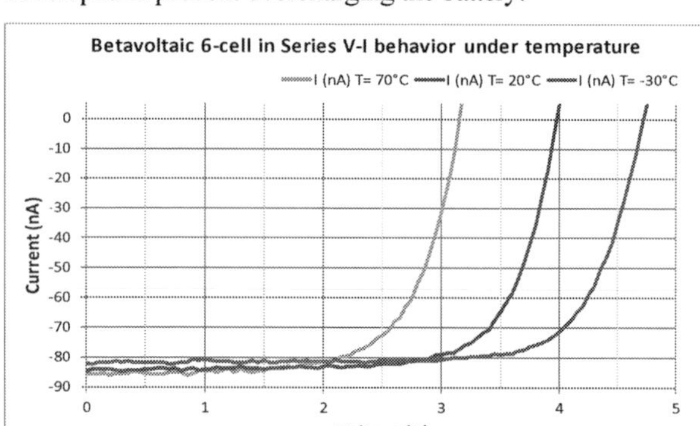

Figure 6. I-V curves of six samples (BV07-BV11) connected in series at temperatures from -30°C to 70°C

A plot of V_{oc} versus temperature for samples BV06 and BV07 in Figure 7 indicates it decreases at rate of 4.0 and 3.2 mV/K, respectively. The difference in the V_{oc} versus temperature rate is a function of the p-n junction properties, which indicated the variability between lots when they were made.

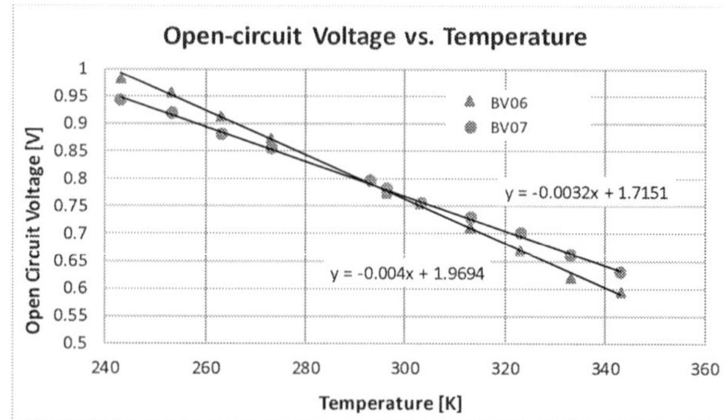

Figure 7. V_{oc} versus temperature for Samples BV06 and BV07

The sensitivity of current and temperature was evaluated by plotting I_{sc} versus temperature. Figure 8 shows that current decreases with temperature at a rate of 0.025 and 0.044 nA/K for Samples BV06 and BV07, respectively. The large difference between the current is due to the passivation quality of the p-n junction surface when the beta source activity is the same. is positive showing an increase of current with temperature current existing at each temperature.

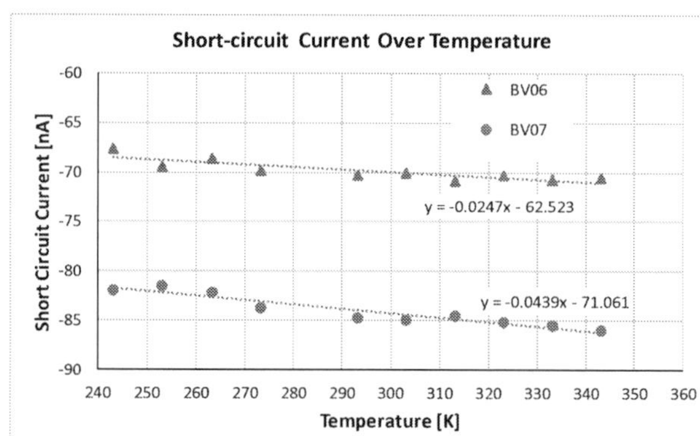

Figure 8. I_{sc} versus temperature for Samples BV06 and BV07.

Modelling Temperature Effects

From the evaluation results, the voltage varies with temperature much greater than current. A model is needed to quantify and estimate this fluctuation while providing insight into the parameter that cause it. Betavoltaics can be modeled using the Shockley equation shown in Eq. 1, where I is the net output current from ionization, I_o is the saturation or dark current, q is the electron charge (1.602×10^{-19} C), V is junction or bias voltage, n is the ideality factor, k is Boltzmann's constant (8.617×10^{-5} eV/K), T is the temperature in Kelvin, and I_L is the ionization current. Since $I_L >> I_o$, the output current is negative which indicates current production [10].

$$I(V) = I_0\left(\exp\left(\frac{nkT}{q}\right) - 1\right) - I_L \quad (1)$$

Under open circuit conditions when $I = 0$, the Shockley equation reduces to Eq. 2 where I_o can be found based on V_{oc} and n, which is based on semiconductor properties and can be set to 1 for the initial model. According to the equation, voltage should increase with temperature. However, experimental results indicate that this is not the case, where the voltage actually decreases with temperature.

$$V_{oc} = \frac{kT}{q}\ln\left(\frac{I_L}{I_0} + 1\right) \quad (2)$$

Since the activity of the beta emitting source does not change vary with temperature, I_o must cause the voltage to reduce as temperature increases. I_o is proportional to the square of the intrinsic carrier density or concentration, n_i, (free electrons) and is given by Eq. 3, where D_n and D_p are the diffusion coefficients of electrons and holes respectively, L_n and L_p are the diffusion lengths of electrons and holes respectively, and N_a and N_d are the doping concentrations of electrons and holes respectively [11].

$$I_o = qn_i^2\left(\frac{D_n}{L_nN_a} + \frac{D_p}{L_pN_d}\right) \quad (3)$$

The effects of temperature are significant with the intrinsic carrier concentration as shown in Eq. 4 where the band gap energy E_G, which is a function of material and temperature, N_C and N_V, the density of states in the conduction and valence band respectively, are considered independent of temperature [10, 11].

$$n_i = \left(N_CN_V\right)^{\frac{1}{2}}\exp\left(\frac{E_G}{2kT}\right) \quad (4)$$

The dark current I_o was found from the experimental results by Eq. 2 using V_{oc} and I_L equal to I_{sc}. The calculated I_o versus temperature is shown in Figure 9 indicates that dark current does increase greatly with temperature. The constant C is the lumped parameter of the variables in Eqs. 3 and 4 that do not depend on temperature.

Conclusion

Betavoltaic power sources are a safe enabling technology for military and commercial applications that require very long operating life under harsh environmental conditions. Hybrid designs where betavoltaics trickle charge a solid-state battery or capacitor offer potential uses in sensors and surveillance devices. The fact that betavoltaics deliver more power as temperature decreases makes them a suitable replacement for cold temperature applications where batteries fail. Though performance degrades at higher temperature, it is not permanent and returns to its same performance as temperature lowers. The technology is far from maturity with much room for improvement. Understanding effects of temperature and other external forces on performance will assist designers in using the technology and research in identify critical areas that can be improved.

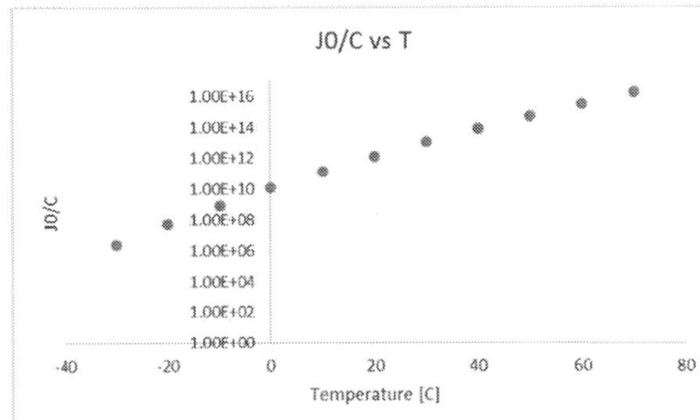

Figure 9. Calculated Dark Current I_o vs. Temperature

Acknowledgements

I would like to thank Naval Surface Warfare Center, Crane Division for the Naval Innovative Science and Engineering Section 219 program (NISE 219) funding to conduct this research. This work was done in a laboratory at Purdue University under the direction of Dr. Robert Bean and consultation of Radiological and Environmental Management.

References

1. Olsen, L.C., P. Cabauy, and B.J. Elkind, *Betavoltaic power sources.* Physics Today, 2012. **65**(12): p. 35-38.
2. Napchan, E., *MC-SET - Monte Carlo Simulation of Electron Trajectories*, 2008, [Computer Software].
3. Rappaport, P., *The electron-voltaic effect in pn junctions induced by beta-particle bombardment.* Physical Review, 1954. **93**(1): p. 246.
4. Flicker, H., J.J. Loferski, and T.S. Elleman, *Construction of a promethium-147 atomic battery.* IEEE Transactions on Electron Devices, 1964. **11**(1): p. 2-8.
5. Manasse, F.K., J.J. Pinajian, and A.N. Tse, *Schottky barrier betavoltaic battery.* IEEE Trans. Nucl. Sci, 1976. **23**(1).
6. Olsen, L., *Betavoltaic energy conversion.* Energy Convers., v. 13, no. 4, pp. 117-127, 1973. **13**(4).
7. Olsen, L. *Advanced betavoltaic power sources*. 1974.
8. R. Franco, M.L.S. *Benefits and Risks of Promethium Battery-Powered Pacemakers*. in *Advances in Pacemaker Technology*. 1974. Erlagen Springer-Verlag.
9. Olsen, L.C. *Review of betavoltaic energy conversion.* 1993.
10. Neamen, D.A., *Semiconductor physics and devices: basic principles*2003: Irwin, Inc.
11. Zemen, M., *Solar Cells*, 2010, Delft University of Technology: Delft, Netherlands.

A Theoretical Approach for using an Integrated Vision System to do Quality Checks during the Production of Thermal Batteries

Martin R. Bachicha[1] *and Graham E. Bartlett*[2]

[1]Power Sources Technology Group
Sandia National Laboratories
Albuquerque, New Mexico, 87185-0614
mrbachi@sandia.gov

[2]Integrated Quality Group LLC
Albuquerque, New Mexico, 87107
iqgroup@msn.com

Abstract: *Inspections to guarantee battery stack integrity have traditionally been performed by quality assurance personnel. To this end, this paper describes a theoretical approach for using a commercial visual inspection system to perform the quality inspection of thermal battery stacks during a battery production build. The vision system can take pictures of the battery stack prior to the wrapping operation. Image quality and registration can be further optimized using the MatLab Image Processing Toolbox. In theory, the Visual Inspection System can compare a battery stack to a battery that meets requirements. By comparing a stacked battery to the baseline, the vision system should be able to identify stacking defects if they exist.*

Keywords: Keyence Vision System; MatLab; Image Processing; Image registration; Inspection

Introduction

A thermal battery is a single use device that uses a chemical thermal source to produce electricity. It has multiple cells that are linked to provide the required power needed for a specific application. Cells are composed of an array of very thin pellets, including anodes, cathodes, heat pellets, separators and collectors, stacked one on top of another in a specific order. The stacked cells are enclosed in a metal container.

Building thermal batteries requires high attention to detail to ensure the various types of pellets and components that make up the battery are correctly placed in the stack. Inspections to guarantee battery stack integrity have traditionally been performed by quality assurance personnel. This paper describes an approach for using a commercially bought Keyence Visual Inspection System to perform the quality inspection of thermal battery stacks during a battery production build. The Keyence system can take pictures of the battery after it has been stacked and prior to the wrapping and closure welding operations. In theory, it can perform a real time quality assurance check of a battery stack to a known good battery stack. The vision system can also be used to inspect X-rays of recently assembled batteries by comparing them to the "baseline" X-ray of a known good battery. All in all, the Keyence Vision System is an efficient tool for verifying that the battery has been correctly assembled and for identifying stacking defects if they exist.

Methodology

The battery image file is represented by a two dimensional matrix where the pixel location (x,y) of the image signifies the column and row numbers of the matrix with an intensity value at each pixel location. Because all of the components are some shade of gray in our application we use the gray scale, where intensity values range from zero (black) to 255 (white). In order to detect an edge, there has to be a difference in gray scales. The table below shows the average gray scale values and their spread of gray scale values inside the inspection region within a stack. In the Keyence system, we identify a small section of the pellet to analyze. Within that region there will be small variations in density (brightness).

Table 1. Gray Scale Values

Pellet	Ave. Gray Scale Value	Ave. Density
Separator	160	NA
Anode	33	4
Heat	59	8
Cathode	55	5

The grayscale value of the separator pellet is so different from the other pellets that it is not a problem to identify. In addition, the difference between the anode and the separator is quite distinct and an edge between the two is identifiable. On the other hand, the heat – cathode edge is a definite challenge and at times, the software analysis cannot locate the edge. A key challenge in using the Keyence Visual Inspection System is to improve the contrast and sharpness of the image by improving the lighting or performing image processing on the pictures, allowing each heat and cathode pellet to be detected.

Variation in Pellet Thickness

For an average thermal battery, the pellets range in thickness from 0.7 mm for the heat pellet to 0.13 mm for the collector with the other pellets having about a 0.3mm thickness. All but the collector are made from compressed powder, making them very fragile. It is easy for an operator, wearing gloves, to pick up more than one pellet by mistake.

For our process at Sandia National Laboratories (SNL), fabrication of the pellets is consistent, yielding a thickness standard deviation of approximately 0.0017 mm for the anode, cathode, and separator pellets. SNL's commercial partner, which automates the process, has a higher standard deviation, but is still well within engineering tolerances. Because of this, the probability of a tolerance stack-up causing a false negative by emulating a double or missing pellet in the stack is negligible.

Battery Assembly

In SNL's process, one technician stacks the pellets, one pellet at a time. An inspector watches the process to ensure the pellets are in the right sequence and the technician has picked up one pellet at a time.

In a study submitted to the National Nuclear Security Administration (NNSA) by SNL [1], the study found that inspectors correctly rejected 85% of defective items and incorrectly rejected 35% of acceptable parts. Use of a phased inspection approach based on inspector confidence ratings was not an effective or efficient technique to improve the overall accuracy of the process. Results did verify that inspection is a workload-intensive task, dominated by mental demand and effort. Nuclear Security Enterprise inspection results were not vastly superior to the industry average of 80%. Because of the criticality of a power source for nuclear weapons, 80% is not good enough. A more reliable inspection method is needed.

After the stack is assembled, the stack is compressed with several hundred pounds of force before being wrapped and sealed. While the compression reduces the variation between pellets, it also makes repair of a faulty stack very difficult, resulting in broken pellets and increasing the probability of battery malfunction.

Solution: Keyence Vision Inspection System

SNL examined a number of commercially available vision inspection systems and settled on a Keyence system because of its flexibility and built in analysis tools. As soon as the stack assembly process is complete, the stack is placed in front of the camera and a picture taken. In less than a second the software identifies any errors based on the inspection criteria.

The issues with using any vision inspection system are primarily lighting and battery placement with respect to the camera. A reference image is used as a standard and the inspection process and criteria are programmed into the system with respect to the standard. All subsequent images are compared to the reference, including the inspection criteria. If the batteries to be inspected are not in exactly the same position, magnification and focus as the standard, the criteria will not be met.

All of the pellets are various shades of gray. Correct lighting, meaning bright enough to bring out the subtle differences in the shades of gray while not producing glare, is critical.

The Keyence system analyzes pixels to provide the required results. It starts with a known good standard and either performs a one to one comparison of the standard with the image of the object to be inspected or carries out a series of geometrical instructions to compare. For example, if one wants to inspect a fabricated part for integrity, the system will compare the object with the standard and if they are not identical, the system will register an error.

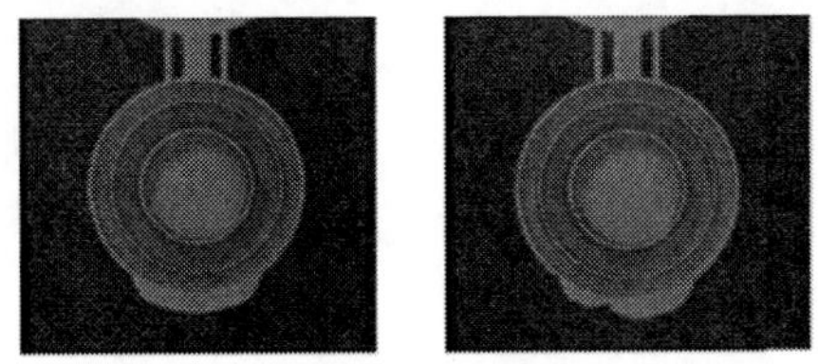

Quality Image　　Defective Image

Figure 1. Images of Good and Defective Parts

Using the Keyence system's geometric recognition capability, if the user is looking for an edge, the system will first identify the location of the edge on the standard and then will look for the same edge on the inspected object. For a given object, there can be as many types of features as one needs to look at. The software comes with an extensive library of tools.

Figure 2 shows an image of an uncompressed stack in its fixture. Figure 3 shows a close-up image of a cell, illustrating the different shades of gray of each pellet and the need for image enhancement. The two white cells are separator pellets. If we want to know if a pellet is missing or if there are two of the same pellets, we can compare the thickness of the cell with the standard. We first go to the standard and identify the top and bottom edges of the cell. We then identify a range to allow for variation. The system compares the object with the reference standard and provides go/no-go result.

Figure 2 (left). Uncompressed Stack

Figure 3 (above). Zoom into stack to show individual cells

Early Attempts in using the Keyence System

The earliest attempts at programming the Keyence system identified errors 100% of the time, but also gave several false negatives. The problem was not with the Keyence system, but the variation in an uncompressed stack. In many cases, as can be seen in Figure 4, the edge is shifted over to one of the internal edges of the cell instead of the outside edges; consequently the width of the cell fails the test.

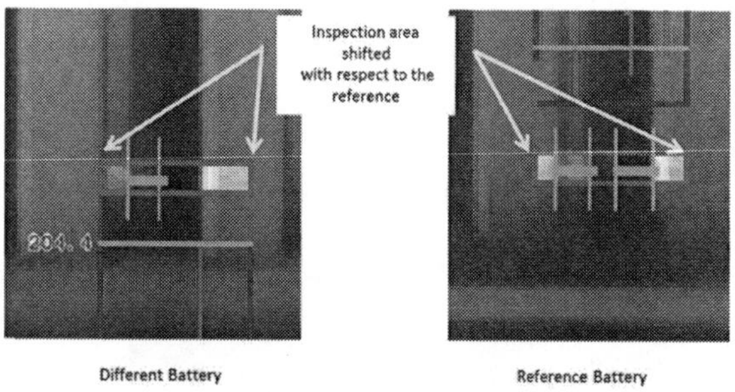

Figure 4. Inspection Area Shift from Pellet Variation.

Figure 5 shows a comparison of the close-up images from two different batteries zoomed to the same magnification, one of which is the reference standard. Since the pellets in each stack vary in thickness, these small variations in pellet thickness can cause the distance of an edge to the reference point to be slightly off, causing a false negative when comparing the image to the reference standard. There is a need to "pre-register" each stack image to the same magnification and scale as the standard in order to make a valid comparison of a battery to the baseline.

Image Sharpening and Registration

The MatLab Image Processing Toolbox can be used to sharpen and register battery images. Connectivity can be established between the Keyence system and a laptop using an Ethernet cable. Images are then imported into MatLab using the ***imread*** function.

Figure 5. Comparison of images of two different batteries (one of which is the reference standard)

MatLab can then be used to sharpen the images. If images are not already grayscale, they are first converted to a grayscale image using the ***rgb2gray*** function. The MatLab ***imsharpen*** function then further sharpens the image.

After sharpening the images, the next step is to choose control points on each battery to register the production image to the reference standard. Control points are pixel locations from features in the battery image that are common to all batteries of the same battery type. They are used to scale or register two images of different batteries to each other. MatLab has a ***Control Point Selection Tool*** that can be used to select control points from an image. Since it is a manual tool, however, it does not lend itself well to an automated production process. Thus, ***custom MatLab code*** was written to find the appropriate control points.

First MatLab finds the edges of the key components in the battery stack—edges of cathodes, anodes, electrodes, etc. MatLab finds the edges using the ***edge*** function. Once edges have been identified, the pixel locations of the edges can be stored using the ***bwboundaries*** function. "Control points" can then be chosen from key edges in each image. For our analysis, the edges representing the positive and negative electrodes were chosen as they are effectively the start and end of the battery stack. The custom MatLab code locates the first pixel from each of these edges on both the reference and production batteries and uses them as control points.

Using these control points as inputs, the Image Processing Toolbox then computes the geometric transformation matrix using the ***fitgeotrans*** function. The production image, when multiplied with the transformation matrix, registers it to the standard image. This is done using the MatLab ***imwarp*** function. The production and reference images are now both to the identical scale and magnification. After performing the image sharpening and registration, the pre-processed images are then exported back into the Keyence Vision Inspection System using the ***imwrite*** function so a valid comparison of the production battery image to the reference standard can be performed. A flowchart of the MatLab Image Processing program is shown in Figure 6.

Photos of battery X-rays taken before and after image enhancement and registration are shown in Figure 7. They exhibit a subtle improvement in image sharpness and quality and are now registered to the standard reference image. They are ready to be tested for quality assurance by the Keyence Vision System.

Future Production Builds

Plans to use a Keyence Vision System integrated with the MatLab Image Processing Toolbox in a thermal battery build are scheduled for May 2016. The Keyence Visual Inspection System will perform the quality assurance analysis on batteries to ensure pellets and other parts have been properly installed in the correct quantities and order.

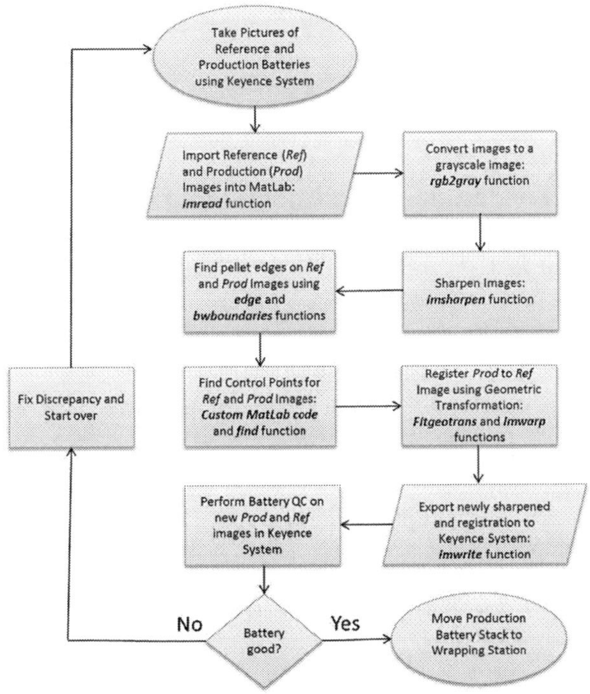

Figure 6. Flowchart for MatLab Image Sharpening and Registration Program.

Estimated Return on Investment

The following are some of the benefits of using an image inspection system. A Keyence system costs roughly \$15,000, while a MatLab license with the Image Processing Toolbox costs roughly \$3,000. The total system cost is around \$18,000. Financial estimates range from \$12.50 to \$40.00 per battery for in-process inspection. Assuming an inspection cost of \$25 per battery, a battery manufacturer would only need to build 720 thermal batteries over 2 years to achieve a 2-year payback on labor cost.

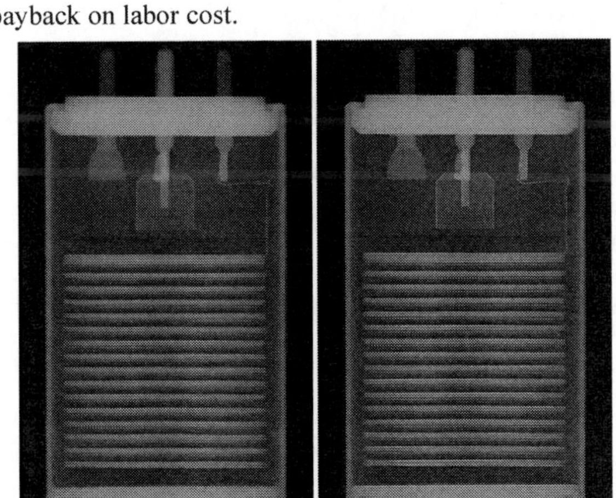

Figure 7. Comparison of Battery Image before and after Image Enhancement and Registration

Human inspectors are only 80%-85% accurate, while a vision system is 98% accurate. This means using an image system vastly improves quality with a potential for improved yields and reduced scrap costs. As people retire, training qualified inspection personnel is a recurring cost. Knowledge and experience will be captured in the vision system. Automating the inspection will also improve productivity by eliminating a second person for the stacking effort.

Risk Reduction is also a factor. Our suppliers are at risk of tornados and hurricanes affecting their production. Since SNL is primarily a research and development organization, it faces the challenge of meeting production requirements in case a vendor is put out of business by inclement weather. The vision system will be one step in improving our throughput.

Conclusion

If your inspection requirements involve human eyes and the object has either fine detail or difficult shading discrimination, the Keyence Vision Inspection System and the MatLab Image Processing Toolbox are powerful tools for battery producers.

Acknowledgements

Sandia National Laboratories is a multi-program laboratory managed and operated by Sandia Corporation, a wholly owned subsidiary of Lockheed Martin Corporation, for the U.S. Department of Energy's National Nuclear Security Administration under contract DE-AC04-94AL85000.

Sandia National Laboratories does not advocate any particular equipment, system, or vendor.

References

[1] Visual Inspection Reliability for Precision Manufactured Parts (2015 Dec)

Using Human Factors to Develop Automated Energy Harvester Test Systems

Julianne S. Douglas[1], Alexis Moy[1], José Collazo[1], Courtney A. Haynes[2], and Maria K. Talarico[2]

[1]U.S. Army Communications-Electronics Research, Development and Engineering Center, Aberdeen Proving Ground, MD, USA

[2]U.S. Army Research Laboratory, Human Research and Engineering Directorate, Aberdeen Proving Ground, MD, USA

Abstract

Highly trained Warfighters equipped with the most advanced technologies are key to the United States military's tactical advantage. A large portion of these advanced technological capabilities, especially those used by dismounted Warfighters, require DC power sources. Typically, these sources are batteries that must be recharged or disposed of after each use. Unfortunately, the energy in each battery comes at a price. Today's dismounted Soldier carries more weight than ever before in US history and a significant portion of that weight is batteries.

Energy harvesting may help to minimize the weight burden by producing electricity from excess motion to reduce the number of spare batteries carried. Kinetic energy harvesting is the conversion of excess motion energy (in this case from Soldiers' movement) into useable electrical energy. This energy can be used to recharge Soldier electronics. Unfortunately, no military test standards and protocols are pre-existing for this novel, cross-discipline technology. Therefore, creating an accurate, representative test mechanism to emulate torso motion and a corresponding Standard Operating Procedure have become the focus of this effort.

This paper endeavors to verify the Warrior Torso Test Stand (WATTS) performance against human factors and requirements documentation. Specific metrics for validation include step frequency and stroke (which combine into vertical speed), payload, and center of mass (COM) position versus time mapping. Experimental validation of this state-of-the-art motion emulator is compared to previously acquired human motion capture and COM data collected by Army Research Laboratory (ARL) in collaboration with the authors from the Communications-Electronics, Research Development, and Engineering Center (CERDEC). A correlation factor will be determined later for various sets of conditions (i.e. walking at 3 mph with 40 lbs. strapped to the back of the torso). This factor will be used in future tests to correct for known baseline differences between the motion of the unit being tested in the WATTS and the human motion data.

Keywords: Energy Harvesting; Test Apparatus; Verification; Validation; Soldier; Warrior; Torso; Emulator

Introduction & Background

The Army is exploring many different avenues to provide Soldiers with energy on-the-move to sustain the battery life of systems during extended duration missions via kinetic energy harvesting. Industry is also looking at ways to harvest energy to power the next generation of wearable health monitoring sensors and portable electronics. One of these devices is an energy harvesting backpack (EHB) that converts mechanical energy from the user's gait into electrical energy to recharge batteries or power electronic systems. The EHB is an assault pack with a spring suspension mounted to a rigid backpack frame. The pack oscillates in response to the vertical displacement of the user's center of mass and converts the potential energy of the spring into electrical energy.

With all of the advancements in energy harvesting devices, there is a need for a standardized test protocol to ensure comparable results. However, a reliable and repeatable test apparatus has not been previously developed to evaluate devices like the EHB that produce power from human movement.

Some of the requirements to build a test apparatus to satisfy the rigorous evaluation needs for torso-wearable energy harvesting devices stemmed from a collaborative study between CERDEC and ARL. In this study, researchers gathered human kinematics and metabolic effects. The main goals were to: 1) quantify the amount of energy generated from an EHB while the user is walking at various speeds, 2) compare the kinematics, kinetics, and available kinetic energy of the EHB versus the assault pack, and 3) determine the biomechanical effects of the EHB system on the user versus assault pack. Human subjects walked on an instrumented treadmill at incline and decline grades at 3 mph and a second self-selected pace while wearing an EHB or the standard Army assault pack.

The WATTS is a test apparatus that emulates the forward lean angle and vertical COM motion of the average Warfighter's torso. It approximates the vertical component of walking and running motion of an average human Soldier torso by oscillating up and down with an adjustable angle. CERDEC has begun validation testing on the WATTS to see how accurately this new system moves like a human torso. The WATTS provides CERDEC the capability to perform reliable and repeatable laboratory-grade, developmental testing over extended mission sets. This capability will be used for many future dismounted soldier devices and enables more successful collaboration and partnering with other Army and Joint organizations, industry, and academia.

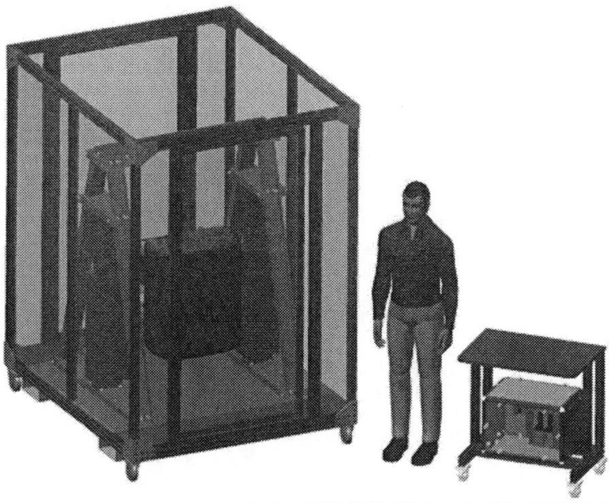

Figure 1: Warrior Torso Test Stand (WATTS)

Figure 1 illustrates the WATTS system tested in this validation. This system employs two variable speed actuators with a controller that allows for easily adjustable stroke length and torso angle to emulate the movement of the human torso. A software graphical user interface (GUI) is used to control the electromechanical actuators, which are used to manipulate the stroke length and frequency. The WATTS also employs a manually adjustable torso angle to simulate the forward torso lean angle of Soldiers as a result of carrying weight on their backs. The torso angle can be adjusted from 0 to 30 degrees in increments of 5 degrees. The red line in Figure 2 illustrates the torso angle.

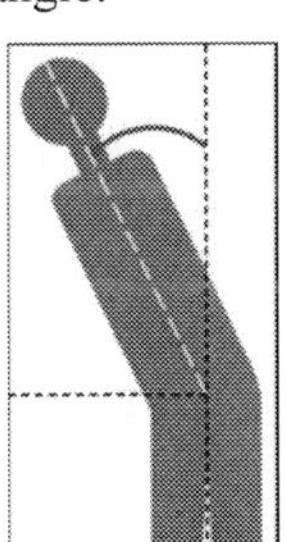

Figure 2: Calculated trunk angle and WATTS torso angle

Experimental Design

There are several aspects of experimental design and analysis that differ between human subject testing and torso emulation on an automated mechanical test apparatus. Selection and manipulation of input and control variables for each of these evaluation environments is where the majority of differences originate. The ARL-CERDEC human subject study controlled treadmill speed (and therefore human gait speed), grade, and backpack payload weight. Each subject's unique walking, or gait, characteristics were natural to the conditions with no cadence, or frequency, control. Vertical COM displacement, or stroke, may have been influenced by stride length which is a function of multiple factors including treadmill length, gait speed, and leg length. Dependent measures from this human platform included voltage and power output of the EHB, ground reaction forces and loading rates, body lean and knee flexion angles, motion of the body center of mass, vertical motion of the EHB, spatiotemporal gait characteristics, and metabolic cost. In contrast, the WATTS controls backpack payload weight, torso angle, and vertical COM displacement (via stroke and frequency inputs).

The data was collected, for both the ARL-CERDEC study and the validation of the WATTS, at three different 20 second intervals per trial condition once steady state was attained.

For the ARL-CERDEC study, vertical displacement of the human moving at a specific horizontal speed as a function of time was collected. The output of the WATTS was current data from a laser that was pointed at one of the actuators that was converted to distance. This distance was used to validate the stroke that was set on the GUI.

The displacement data is given as a current. The position is calculated by normalizing the range then calculating the range proportion represented by the measured current and adding the start of the measuring range distance. The change in displacement and change in time is used to calculate the velocity.

Results

The most challenging aspect of designing and testing wearable energy harvesters is the direct interaction between the subject and wearable device. Integrating with humans and emulating human movement is a complex issue. There are many situations in which machines cannot replicate human movement, simply because of the unpredictable and fluid nature of human motion. The preliminary results discussed in this paper are an illustration of this point.

Figure 3 shows one cycle each from a human and the WATTS set to emulate that specific human's average stroke and frequency. The vertical COM motion of a human wearing 40 lbs. in an Army Assault Pack while walking at 3.0 mph on a level treadmill, and the WATTS vertical torso motion wearing the same Assault Pack and while set to a 5 degree torso angle, 1.76 in. stroke and 1.77 Hz frequency. The two cycles shown were selected specifically as an example of the similarities seen between the human and the WATTS. For these cycles illustrated above, the human COM vertical motion has a calculated stroke, frequency, and torso angle of 1.63 in, 1.76 Hz, and 6.51 degrees, respectively, and the WATTS torso stroke, frequency, and torso angle measures 1.65 in, 1.76 Hz, and 5 degrees, respectively.

In each of the figures 3-8, the blue (D_h[in]) curve represents the vertical displacement of the human torso. The gray (V_h[in/s]) represents the vertical velocity of the human torso at a specific frequency. The red (D_w[in]) curve shows the displacement, or stroke, of the WATTS. The yellow (V_w[in/s]) curve shows the vertical velocity of the WATTS at a specified frequency.

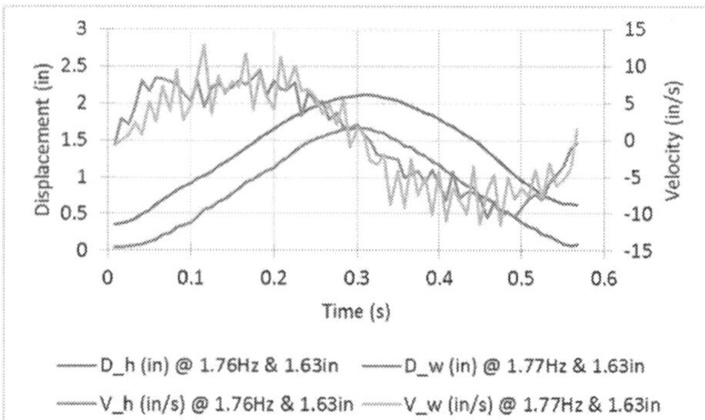

Figure 3: Comparison of similar frequencies and strokes for human (h) at 1.76Hz and 1.63in and WATTS (w) at 1.77Hz and 1.63in displacements (D) and velocities (V)

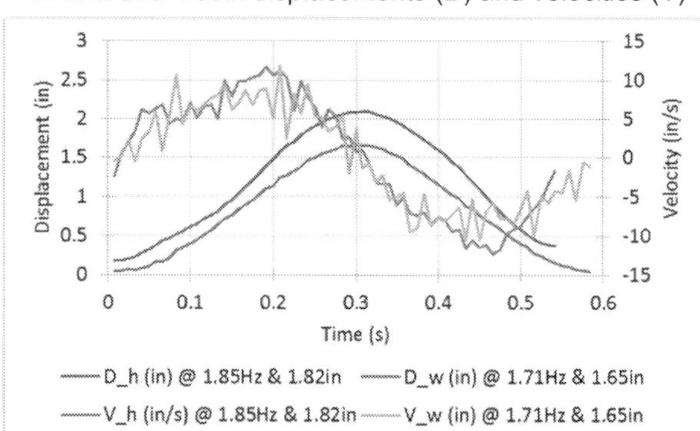

Figure 4: Comparison of frequencies and strokes for human (h) at 1.85Hz and 1.82in and WATTS (w) at 1.71Hz and 1.65in displacements (D) and velocities (V)

However, there can be deviations as well. An example is shown in Figure 4 of one cycle where the WATTS and human motions are close to the tolerance limits in the same conditions as in Figure 3 with the same person.

Figures 3 and 4 illustrate the derivative relationship between displacement and velocity. Each of the displacement curves can be approximated by and since the derivative: – is clearly recognizable through the noise, it is clear these are velocity curves. The WATTS generally has more noisy derivative curves than any human test subject likely due to its actuators resistances or EMI output interfering with the measurement system.

Figure 5 and Figure 6 compare the motion of the WATTS to the motion of a human. In Figure 5, the blue line's peaks and valleys change height and, in conjunction with Figure 6, it becomes clear that there are some frequency variations in play causing the accelerated phase shift seen in Figure 6. This makes it clear that humans can exhibit far more changes in their gait than the WATTS can with constant frequencies and strokes. The significance of that lies in the velocity and therefore all the quantities that are calculated from velocity, perhaps the most important being kinetic energy. Given the relationship between velocity and kinetic energy, velocity is important in determining the quantity of energy harvested by each unit the WATTS will test.

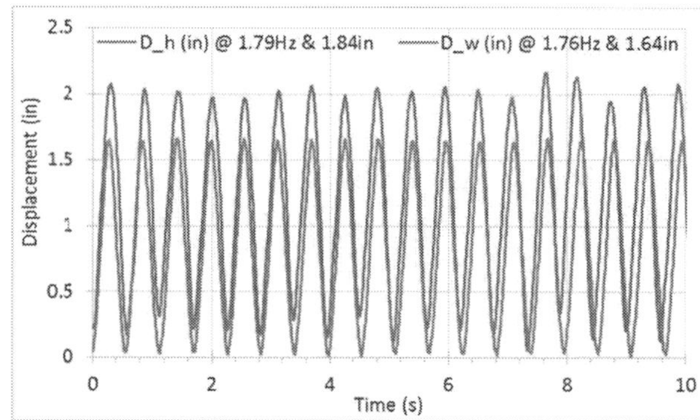

Figure 5: Comparison of position versus time curve variances between human (blue) and WATTS (orange) motion over a 10 second time period

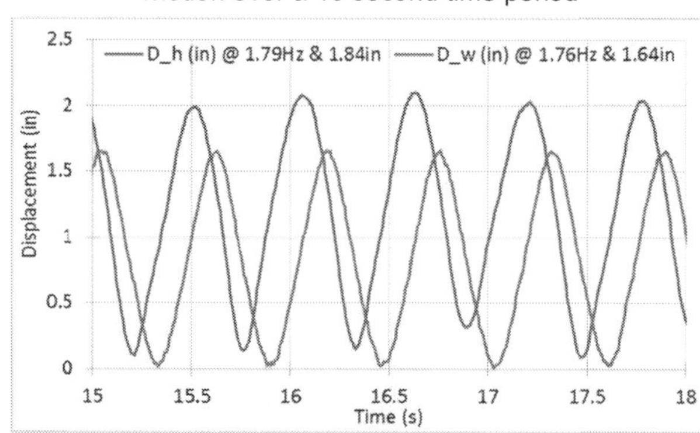

Figure 6: Motion discrepancies build over time

Figures 7 and 8 show the rate of change in torso position over time for the human subject (gray) and the WATTS (yellow). It is more evident from velocity than position data shown in earlier figures that the WATTS and human subject are fairly in sync. However, because the velocity data is more normalized, it also shows the phase shift more clearly than the position data. Figure 8 below is a perfect example of the human-WATTS phase shift. Further analysis is required to determine if the velocity phase shift could be the correlation factor correcting for the known baseline differences between the motion of the unit being tested in the WATTS and the human motion data.

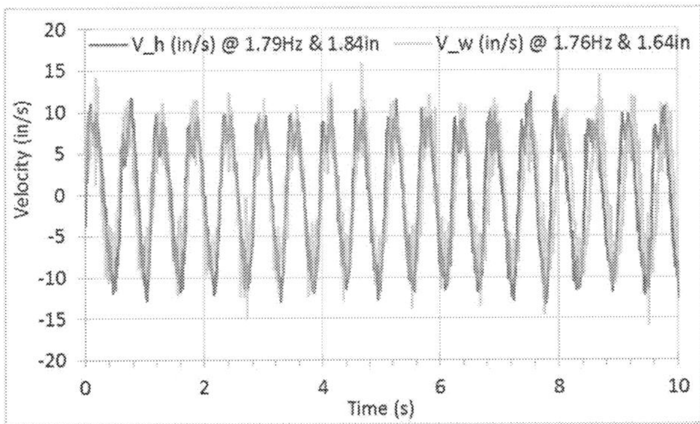

Figure 7: Comparison of Velocity versus time curve variances between human (gray) and WATTS (yellow) over a 10 second time period

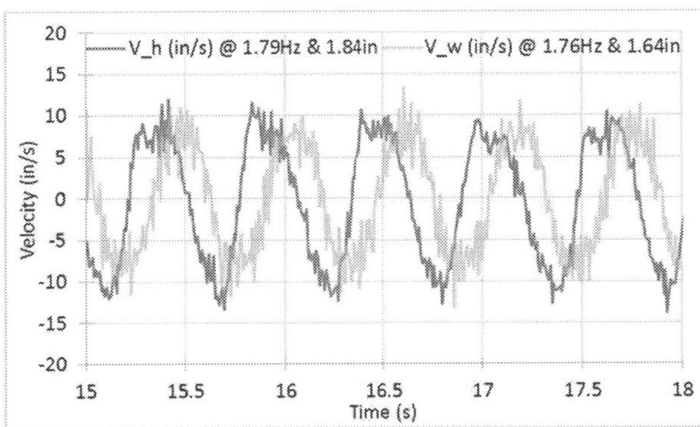

Figure 8: WATTS's velocity (yellow) is lagging human subject's velocity (gray) due to human frequency and stroke variances

Validation of this kinetic energy harvester test apparatus would be incomplete without analysis of the kinetic energy the WATTS imparts to the unit under test. Continuing the case from earlier, 35 lbs. in a 5 lb. assault pack was harnessed to the torso and tested at the following inputs: 5 degree torso angle, 1.76 in. stroke, and 1.77 Hz frequency. The total kinetic energy of the moving assault pack after 20 seconds on the human was approximately 200 mWhrs as shown in Figure 10. This equates to approximately 36 W of potential power from the motion of the pack that could potentially be harnessed by a device. Conversely, it appears to be approximately 160 mWhrs after 20 seconds on the WATTS in Figure 9. This equates to approximately 28.8 W of potential power, which is less than on this particular human test subject.

One interesting aspect to note in Figure 10 is that the human torso displacement (light blue line), which represents the human gait cycle, correlates directly to a spike in instantaneous kinetic energy (green line) when the slope of the displacement curve is negative. Looking closely at Figure 10, another relationship also becomes discernable. It appears that the majority of the kinetic energy is produced during the braking or negative work cycle of the gait where the person is slowing down.

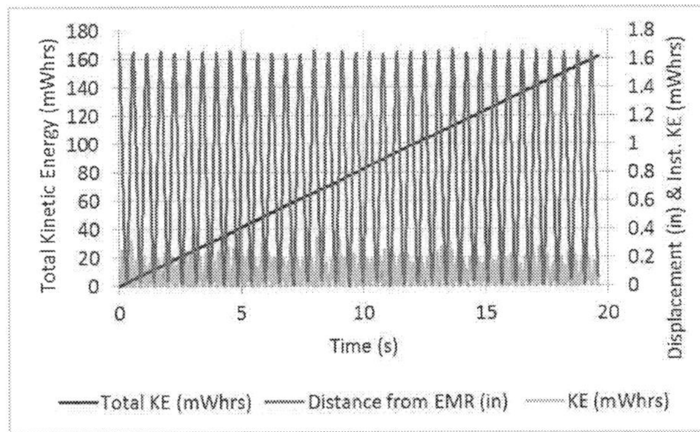

Figure 9: WATTS Total and Transient Kinetic Energy

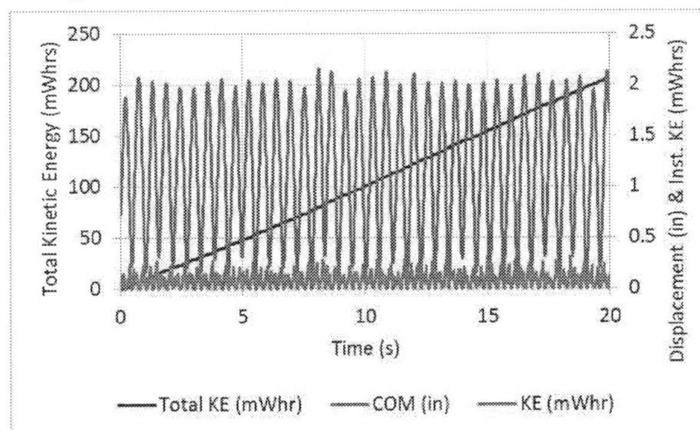

Figure 10: Human Total and Transient Kinetic Energy

Conclusions & Future Work

The traditional means of testing kinetic energy harvesting devices has always been through the use of human subjects. The WATTS does not replace human subject testing, but rather adds valuable information that can be used to better evaluate the effect and efficiency of energy harvesting systems and their interaction with humans. These preliminary results suggest that the WATTS is an accurate, representative test apparatus that has the ability to emulate the human torso. The WATTS provides a new capability to the US Army and opens a new door for future efforts with other agencies and private industry to be able to validate computer models and simulate long-term missions. This enables more accurate predictions of what a Warfighter will need during a mission. Future technology will include improvements to harvester efficiency and tuning such as linear actuators, advanced mechanical gearing, and ergonomic decoupling.

Acknowledgments

This research was supported in part by the US ARL Human Research and Engineering Directorate in collaboration with the CERDEC, through an inter-organization collaboration effort/agreement between the ARL and CERDEC. This study was entitled "Quantifying Energy Generation Capacity of an Energy Harvesting Backpack and Biomechanical and Metabolic Effects on the User."

High Power Li-ion Cells for Hybrid, More Electric Aircraft (MEA) and Directed Energy Weapon (DEW) Applications

Frank J. Puglia, Stuart Santee, Svetlana Trebukhova, Boris Ravdel, Christine Cook
Yardney Division
EaglePicher Technologies, LLC
East Greenwich, Rhode Island, USA, 02892

Abstract: *High performing More Electric Aircraft (MEA) and Directed Energy Weapons (DEW) require electrical power and energy far beyond their predecessors. For MEA, this includes providing discharge power and the ability to absorb energy from regeneration events across a wide range of temperatures. Current Li-ion batteries are not capable of supporting 100C-200C re-charge rates without the risk of lithium plating and accelerated degradation. A hybrid approach can be used to meet the energy and power requirements. For DEW, the primary need is for high discharge rates with a reasonable recharge rate. The temperature requirements for DEW applications are generally narrower. This is a result of the existing need for thermal control in other parts of the weapons system and the fact that cell energy efficiency is enhanced with a temperate environment. The requirements for DEW can be further divided into terrestrial and airborne applications. Airborne applications typically have stricter mass and volume requirements that greatly influence the choice of chemistry. A rechargeable Li-ion cell with high power capabilities and a thermally efficient design greatly enhances the capabilities of new high power systems. A second use of hybridization discussed in the paper is to couple high power batteries or capacitors with lower power technologies, such as metal air batteries, to provide improved life, power and environmental tolerance. This presentation focuses primarily on the Yardney Division of EaglePicher Technologies' development of high power, Li-ion and hybrid systems for the most demanding MEA and DEW applications.*

Keywords: Directed Energy, Hybrid, More Electric Aircraft, Aluminum Air, High Power, Safety, Thermal, Pulse, Continuous, Yardney

Introduction

The demand for electrical power, especially highly variable electrical power demand, has outstripped the development of any one chemistry to support the needs. Man portable applications are looking for specific energy values that exceed 350Wh/kg. This can be met by several technologies such as Aluminum-Air batteries and Li-CFx batteries. However, neither of these high energy density technologies can support C-Rate or higher discharges. The solution for the power needs is sometimes for the soldier to carry multiple batteries and operate them in parallel. A good compromise solution is to place either a capacitor bank or high power Li-ion battery in parallel with the high energy system. A second application where hybrid systems are showing great promise is Directed Energy Weapons. This paper shows that Li-ion batteries are very well suited to meet the discharge power demands for DEW. The rate capability of the Li-ion technology allows for the batteries to store as few as five "shots" or discharges worth of energy. In this case, the ability to store fewer discharges implies improved rate capability and additional discharges can come from placing units in parallel. Ideally the number of shots would be equal to the time that the target is accessible and the recharge time should be less than the time for new targets to be presented. This can be seconds to minutes or hours. Charge-to-discharge ratios ranging from 2:1 to 30:1 have been discussed. For the shorter durations it may not be practical for the load to extract power from the vehicle electrical bus. In this instance, a primary battery or fuel cell may result in the lowest overall mass to meet the mission profile. A third place where hybrid systems are the best approach to meeting performance requirements is in stabilizing the electrical bus of More Electric Aircraft (MEA). This applies to both military and commercial aircraft. The previous application, DEW, where the platform may be required to recharge the DEW energy storage capacitors or batteries is an extreme example of varied bus loading. The more typical bus loading noise is due to the electrically controlled flight surfaces, radars, etc. In such an application, the best performance is likely the combination of a very high power Li-ion battery and a very high power capacitor bank. The performance of individual components for these types of systems is discussed within this paper. Emphasis is given to the design and performance of high power Li-ion batteries to meet the power side of the requirements.

Man Portable Systems

The mass of the energy load carried by the soldier has been well documented. Rechargeable batteries are lower cost but invariably lower energy density. Primary batteries are higher energy density but are often limited in power and partially used batteries are usually discarded at the end of a mission. Yardney has developed a high energy density, Aluminum-air battery. This, roughly 100Ah, Aluminum air battery can be used alone or in hybrid mode. Hybrid systems used/modeled include using other primary batteries in parallel, such as SO_2, Thionyl Chloride batteries, Rechargeable Li-ion batteries; and more recently capacitors with next generation DC/DC converters. Each of these options, in order, represents an additional increase in power and operating temperature range.

Figure 1 shows the 24V, 100Ah Aluminum-air battery previously developed. This box has two chambers, one for the Al-Air portion and a separate area into which any number of hybrid systems can be installed.

Figure 1: 100Ah, 24V Aluminum-Air Battery Pack With Isolated Section for Hybrid Integration

The Aluminum-air battery pack, containing about 2.9kWh of energy, has a specific energy of about 676Wh/kg. The peak power from the system is about 5Amps or 90Watts. The power from a hybrid system, with just a lead acid battery for power, can easily increase to 350 Watts with a decrease in the specific energy from ~450Wh/kg. More advanced systems, such as those being developed by ElectroStandards Laboratories, can increase peak power and time at power, with a much smaller mass and volume penalty. Figure 2 shows some test data for a single Aluminum-air cell. This cell was tested at various long pulse rates with a two Watt background load. The pulse power tested ranged from 2.7Watts to 4.3Watts. It was known from previous testing that the 5.0Watts was the approximate limit for the systems. This is approximately a C/30 discharge rate. There are two known rate limiting processes for the higher rate pulses. The first is a passivation type of impedance. This explains why, at the highest pulse, the voltage increases (improves) throughout the one minute duration of pulse. The second rate limiting factor is related to the diffusion of oxygen. Figure 3 demonstrates that the system can support the pulse loads for extended periods. In this particular example approximately 70Ah of capacity was discharged. All testing was performed at 20°C. Additional capacity is available at both lower rates and lower voltage cutoffs. The increase in polarization at this depth of discharge is the focus of continued development.

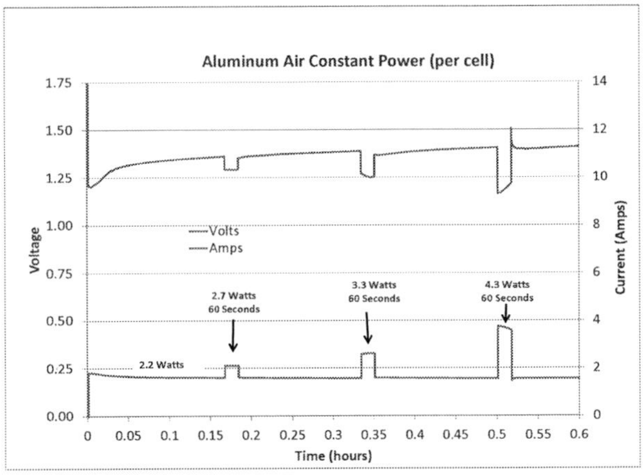

Figure 2: Single Cell Test Data at Various Pulse Rates with a background load.

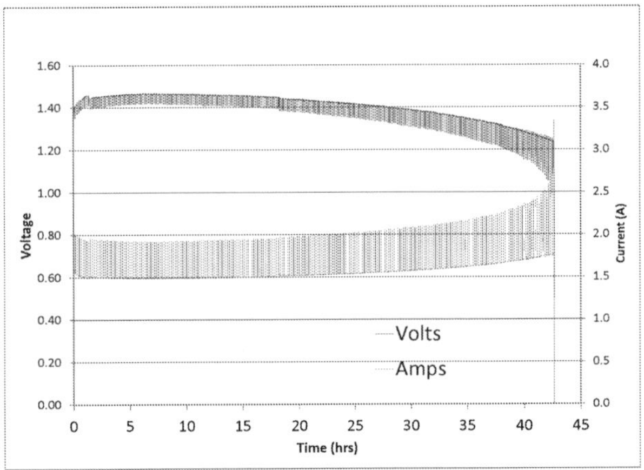

Figure 3: Single Cell Test Data with 2W/3W Pulse Profile.

There are many systems that are viable for the "energy" portion of a hybrid battery. Aluminum air systems have the advantage of requiring no maintenance before use and having a shelf life that can exceed ten years before activation. Furthermore, the battery can be recharged by replacing the stack and electrolyte. The stack and electrolyte salt, carried dry, offer an excellent method for doubling the available energy at only an additional 50% of mass.

Vehicle Level Hybrid Systems

More Electric Aircraft, both commercial and military, are finding that the constant and bi-directional loads placed on the battery are resulting in reduced battery life. The reduced battery life is primarily due to the higher operating temperatures of the battery. If the battery is removed from the electrical bus, the voltage on the electrical bus experiences very wide and rapid voltage changes. In general, such noise on the electrical bus is known to be a contributing factor to premature failure of electronics. Given the cost of electronics on aircraft, this is highly undesirable. The noise is bi-directional since motors for the flight control surfaces operate in generator mode when in reverse. This puts large amounts of excess energy onto the bus. The noise on the electrical systems will only get worse when Directed Energy Weapons, (DEW) are ultimately integrated into aircraft. Such systems will likely employ a combination of the aircraft generator, batteries, capacitors, and fuel cells to stabilize the electrical bus.

The team of the Yardney Division of EaglePicher, PC Krause and Associates, Northrop Grumman and John Miller Enterprises has been studying this problem under the Hybrid Energy Storage Module (HESM) Area #1 program. The modelling and test results within that program have found that the optimum solution is highly dependent on the mission profile and source of the noise. For all applications, the team has found that very high power Li-ion batteries are able to respond within the timeframes necessary to support even the most aggressive noise loads. Figure 4 shows a generic example of 70C charge and discharge pulses on a high power Li-ion cell at 25°C. Both charts have the same range on both axes. When the cells are held near a middle state of charge the polarization is bi-directionally equal. This is not necessarily the case at different states of charge. There is also no indication of a lag in response to the voltage. Longer duration pulses have been evaluated with similar results. This illustrates the viability of using Li-ion cells directly to absorb voltage spikes on vehicle platforms that originate from the cycling of electrical equipment. An obvious consequence of holding the battery at 50% state of charge is the loss in specific energy if the battery energy is needed for other loads such as emergency power.

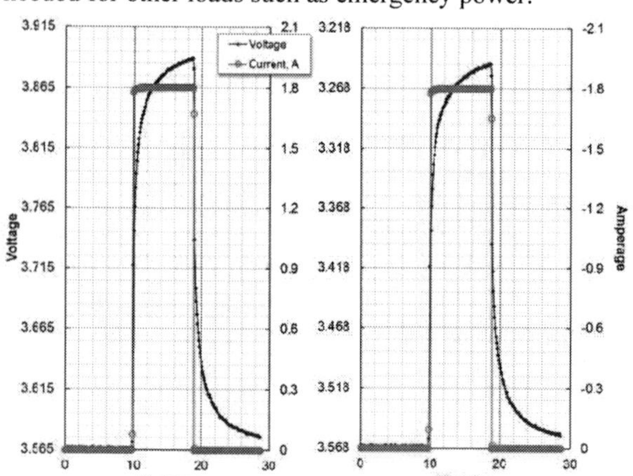

Figure 4: 70C Charge and Discharge Pulses on a Li-ion Cell.

Directed Energy Weapons (DEW)

The power capability available from the highest performing Li-ion batteries can meet the requirements of most Directed Energy Weapons. The performance of the batteries can be highly dependent on rate and temperature. As most DEW systems will have thermal management available it is reasonable to design around an ideal operating temperature. The Yardney team has identified approximately 35°C as the ideal balance between performance, self-discharge rate and cycle life for most applications. Shorter life applications could realize a modest improvement in power density by operating at higher temperatures. Figure 5 illustrates the relationship between the cathode discharge capacity and energy and the discharge rate. Testing was performed at 25°C and thus the results, especially at higher rates, are somewhat below optimum. At discharge rates up to 60C there is very little difference in the energy that can be delivered by two second pulses or through continuous discharge. At the 100C discharge rate an advantage of up to 20% is observed when the system is allowed to have rests of 5 seconds or more between the pulses. By the 180C discharge rate, approximately 50% of the energy can still be extracted above the normal 2.5V cutoff if rests between pulses are equal to or greater than ten seconds. If no rests, or just a 1 second rests are used, the available energy is just ~15% of theoretical energy.

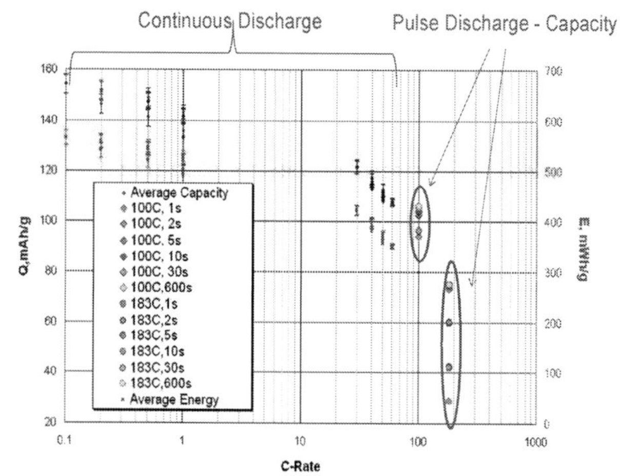

Figure 5: 25°C Cell Chemistry Performance for Various Rates and Pulse Durations

This chemistry has been integrated in prismatic cells with capacities of 5Ah, 14Ah and 18Ah. Figure 6 shows the performance of the 18Ah cell at a 41P (~800Amp) continuous discharge rate. The discharge curves for 20°C and 35°C are both shown. The combination of the higher operating voltage and increased capacity for the cells at 35°C allows those cells to deliver 10% more energy. As the cells are viable for MEA as well as DEW, Figure 7 shows the performance of the 18Ah cell at 2000Amps and after a cold soak at 0°C. The 900gram cell delivers over 5.2kW for more than three seconds. When integrated into a 24V battery with a 18V cutoff, the power for three seconds for a 7S battery at 0°C is 37kW (50HP) from a battery with a project mass just over twenty pounds.

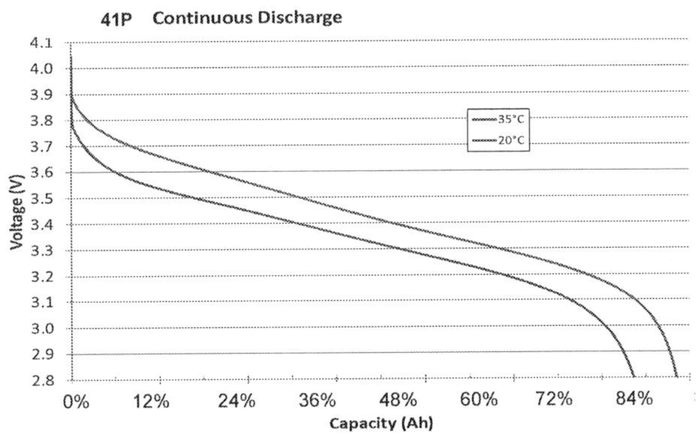

Figure 6: Constant Power Discharge (41P) of the 18Ah Cell at 20°C and 35°C.

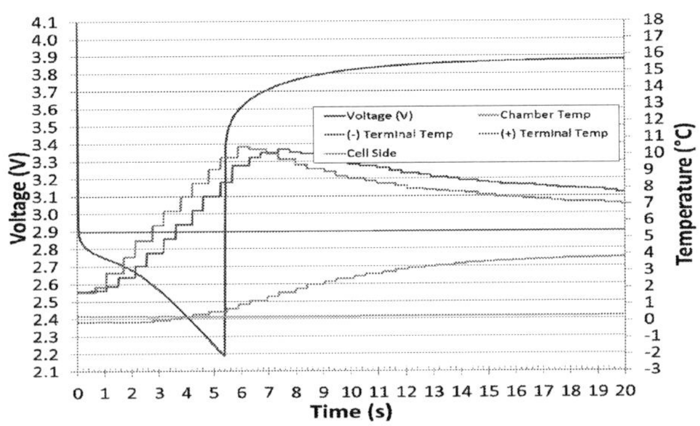

Figure 7: 2000Amp Discharge of the Cells Cold Soaked at 0°C, with Voltage and Temperature Plots.

Each of the 5Ah, 14Ah and 18Ah batteries has been incorporated in modules with integrated cooling. Using the 18Ah cell, the team worked with General Atomics Aeronautical Systems, Mission Systems Division to develop the high power module shown in Figure 8. This battery operates at over 75kW/2000Amps. This is more than 9 kW/l continuous at the final module level.

Figure 8: 50Volt Battery Module Capable of Power up to 70kW.

Summary

The Yardney Division of EaglePicher has developed cells and modules with integrated cooling that are capable of delivering over 9kW/liter at the battery level. As a result of the highly efficient cooling afforded by the high aspect ratio prismatic cell design, the system is able to operate with a very high duty cycle without overheating. This product line is optimized for standalone and hybrid systems supporting the MEA and DEW markets.

Acknowledgements

The authors of this paper would like to acknowledge the support the these efforts that came from NAVAIR Pax-River (Michael Allen, Mark Hurley and Venkat Manivannan); ElectroStandards Laboratories (Dr. Ray Sepe), Wright Patterson Air Force Base (Seana McNeal, John Narius) and General Atomics (Robb Mansfield, Chuck Hayman, Justin Schwartz, Mike Perry).

Design and Implementation of a Centralized Power Supply for a Precision Guided 120mm Mortar Projectile

Edward Bukowski, Peter Muller, Benjamin Topper and Douglas Petrick

Guidance Technologies Branch / Lethality Division
Weapons and Materials Research Directorate
U.S. Army Research Laboratory
Aberdeen Proving Ground, Maryland, USA, 21005
edward.f.bukowski4.civ@mail.mil

Abstract: *The Precision Universal Mortar Attack (PUMA) effort is an Office of Naval Research (ONR) Future Naval Capabilities (FNC) Program which is developing the technologies needed for low cost, high precision mortar fires. The primary deliverable product of PUMA is a guidance kit designed to enhance the performance of existing mortar ammunition. The U.S. Army Research Laboratory (ARL), working in collaboration with the Naval Surface Warfare Center – Dahlgren Division (NSWCDD), has developed several custom technologies for enabling the precision guidance, trajectory shaping, and range extension of 120mm mortars. These technologies include a GPS-based Guidance Electronics Unit (GEU), a Control Actuation System (CAS), and a Centralized Power Supply (CPS). The CPS consists of Lithium-Ion Polymer (LiPo) cells and battery protection circuitry that provides cell balancing and protects against over-charge and over-discharge conditions. The CPS was custom-designed to efficiently use the space available, and is a rechargeable and removable unit that integrates into the CAS module. It has been experimentally validated to survive up to 10,000G's in setback acceleration. It has also been successfully utilized during several PUMA flight demonstration experiments. This paper will provide additional details on the development and execution of the CPS design including a presentation of recorded flight experimentation data.*

Keywords: lithium-ion polymer; PUMA; 120mm Mortar

Introduction

The U.S. Army Research Laboratory (ARL) is the fundamental research laboratory of the U.S. Army Research and Development Command (RDECOM) and employs a science and technology campaign essential in assuring the continued land power dominance of the U.S. Army. The Guidance Technologies Branch (GTB) has developed a variety of advanced concepts and innovations that are aimed at enhancing the capabilities of gun-launched, precision-guided munitions as part of this ARL campaign. These innovations have led to the design and implementation of a variety of low cost, high reliability diagnostic and Guidance, Navigation and Control systems for a wide range of ballistic projectiles [1] [2].

For the past several years the Office of Naval Research (ONR) has been sponsoring ARL research in precision guided munitions technologies. In particular, ARL has been working in collaboration with the Naval Surface Warfare Center – Dahlgren Division (NSWCDD) on the Precision Universal Mortar Attack (PUMA), an ONR Future Naval Capabilities program. The main deliverable product of PUMA is a guidance kit designed as an upgrade to existing mortar ammunition. It is an integrated system solution for enhanced mortar engagements by enabling precision guidance, trajectory shaping and range extension. NSWCDD is the principle investigator for this effort, with ARL serving as the lead developer and integrator [3].

The PUMA guidance kit employs a modular design which allows for alternate configurations and provides flexibility for deployment across several platforms. It was initially demonstrated on an 81mm mortar airframe and its performance was characterized over a series of successful flight experiments which included a controlled divert demonstration and several guide-to-hit demonstrations [4].

The guidance kit was then transitioned to a 120mm mortar airframe (Figure 1). During this transition, upgrades were made to several of the system modules which included the addition of a centralized power supply (CPS) for powering the kit. Instead of multiple power supplies located throughout the various modules, the CPS provided a central power location in a module that was easily accessible and could be removed and replaced if required. The upgraded PUMA guidance kit was successfully integrated onto a 120mm mortar airframe and characterized over a series of successful flight experiments.

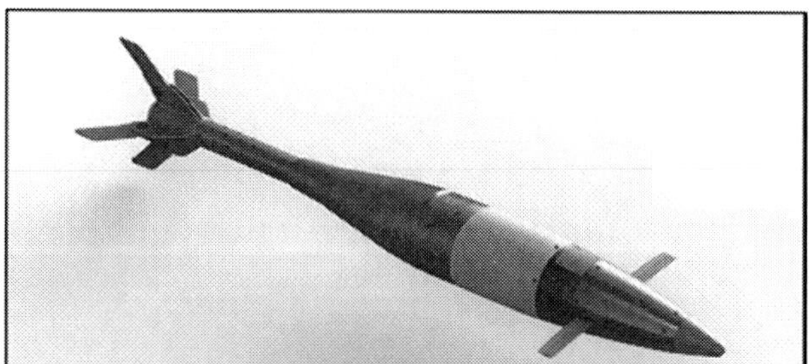

Figure 1. PUMA Guidance Kit on 120mm Mortar Airframe

PUMA Power Budget

The CPS is responsible for providing power to two of the PUMA modular sub-systems, the Control Actuation System (CAS) and the Guidance Electronics Unit (GEU).

The CAS (Figure 2) is a single axis control unit with a pair of command-deployable super-caliber canards driven by a commercial-off-the-shelf (COTS) voice coil system. It also provides canard position and velocity feedback information to the GEU as part of the closed loop guidance. The CAS requires an operating voltage between 15 and 21 volts (V), 18V nominal, and can draw an average of 1 amp (A) with spikes up to 6A. This results in an average power requirement of 18 watts (W) with spikes up to 108W. However, the CAS is only utilized during a guided flight and only operates after canard deployment which typically occurs once the projectile reaches apogee. Once activated, the CAS requires power for the remainder of the projectile flight which is approximately 60 to 80 seconds.

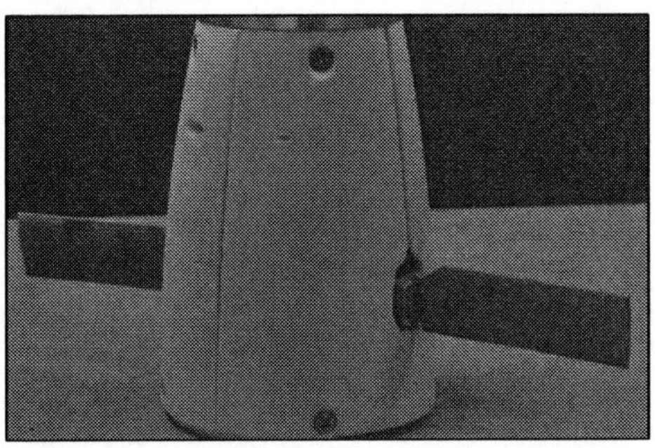

Figure 2. PUMA Control Actuation System

The GEU (Figure 3) contains an on-board Digital Signal Processor (DSP) that manages the on-projectile guided flight operations such as guidance law, navigation filter, launch detection and vehicle state estimation. The unit also contains a GPS receiver, inertial navigation sensors, and a CAS command and control board. The GEU requires a nominal operating voltage of 4V with a nominal current draw of 1A over the entire flight of the projectile. However, for the demonstration phase of the program, there was a requirement for the GEU battery to run for a minimum of 30 minutes. This was in order to support laboratory bench-testing, pre-flight module functionality checks and pre-flight configuration of the GPS receiver.

Figure 3. PUMA Guidance Electronics Unit

CPS Development

During the PUMA 81mm mortar demonstration, both the GEU and CAS contained their own individual power supplies. As the design was transitioned to the 120mm mortar airframe, these power supplies were consolidated into a central CPS module that was located within the upgraded CAS module. Improvements to the CAS structural aero-shell allowed for additional volume within the CAS to be dedicated to the CPS (Figure 4).

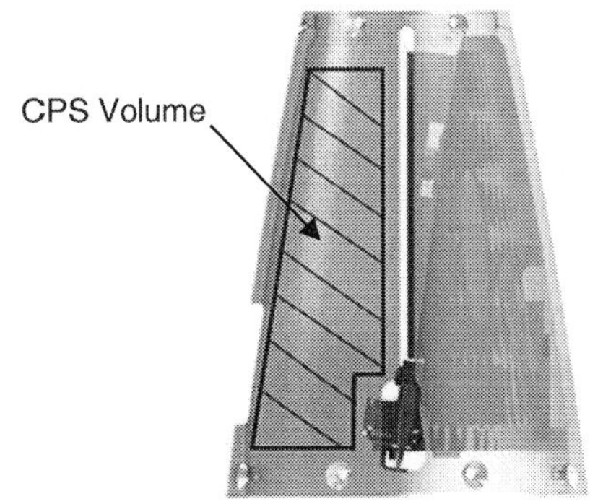

Figure 4. Volume dedicated for the CPS within the CAS

In addition to meeting the requirements outlined in the PUMA power budget, the CPS also needed to be rechargeable, removable, and operational during and after gun launch. The module was also required to include circuitry for cell balancing and over-charge/discharge protection, as well as an easily accessible user interface for on/off control, external power and battery charging.

The final CPS design used Lithium-Ion Polymer (LiPo) batteries consisting of 250 milliamp-hour (mAh) capacity cells. These cells were chosen primarily because they were rechargeable, had a high discharge rate capability (up to 25 times their rated capacity, or 25C) and were small enough (34mm x 16mm x 6mm) to fit within the CPS battery cavity. The cells were also of low cost (less than $20 each) and commercially available. LiPo cells have also performed very well in high-G ballistic environments in the past [5] [6]. Within the CPS, the CAS battery consisted of five cells wired in series for a nominal battery voltage of 20V and capacity of 250mAh. The GEU battery consisted of four cells wired in parallel for a nominal 4V, 1Ah battery. A preliminary performance evaluation of these batteries verified that they would meet the PUMA power specifications. Multiple CAS batteries were evaluated under a constant 2A load (i.e. discharge current) and produced an average runtime of 8 minutes prior to a 15V cutoff (Figure 5) which exceeded the PUMA required runtime of 80 seconds. The GEU batteries were discharged under a constant 1A load and produced an average runtime of 60 minutes prior to a 3V cutoff (Figure 6) which also exceeded the PUMA required runtime of 30 minutes.

Additional experiments were conducted on the CAS battery to verify high-G survivability. Two CAS batteries were evaluated on a high-G drop table at acceleration levels of approximately 10,000G's. Since the CAS is not powered during gun launch, the batteries were evaluated with no load applied. The open circuit voltage of each battery was monitored during the high-G event and no significant changes were observed (Figure 7). At the conclusion of the experiments, the batteries retained full functionality. Since both the CAS and GEU batteries are comprised of the same model cells, and the GEU is in a low power state with a minimal load on its battery (around 8mA) during gun launch, it was concluded that these results also verified the high-G survivability of the GEU battery without conducting additional experiments.

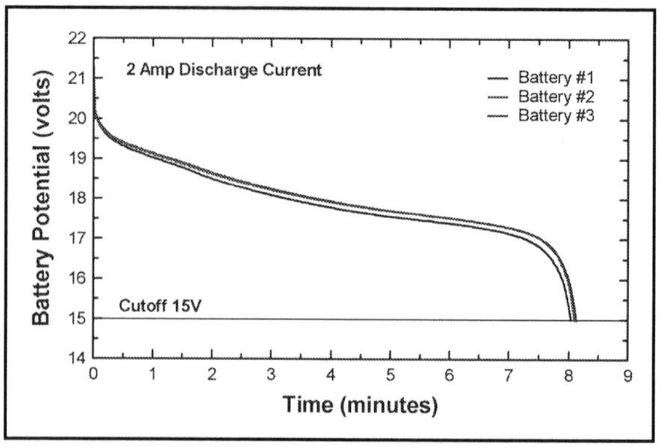

Figure 5. CAS Battery Discharge Curves

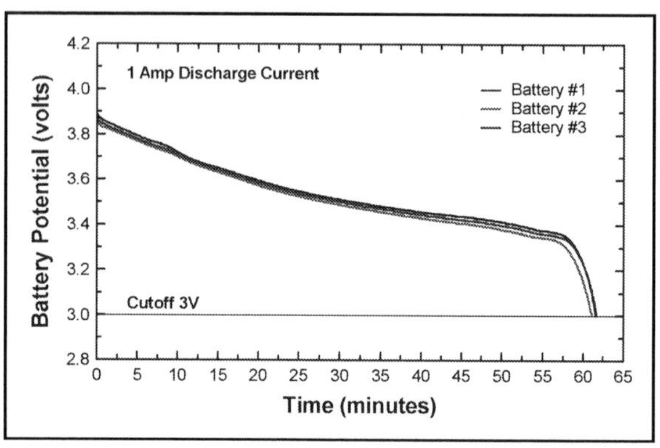

Figure 6. GEU Battery Discharge Curves

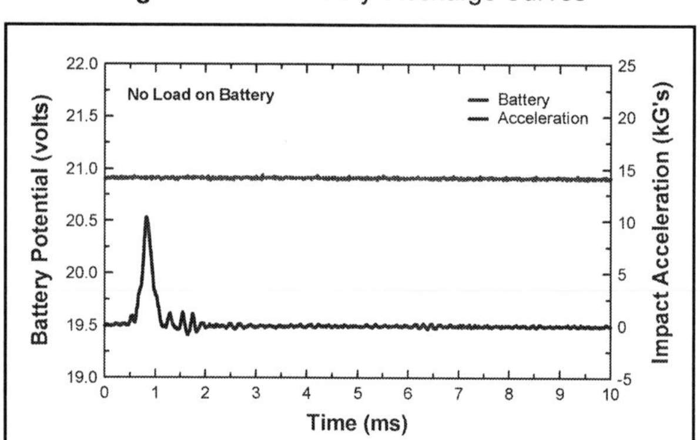

Figure 7. High-G Acceleration Performance of CAS Battery

CPS Final Design

In addition to the CAS and GEU batteries, the CPS contains a unique set of printed circuit boards custom designed to fit within the CPS housing (Figure 8).

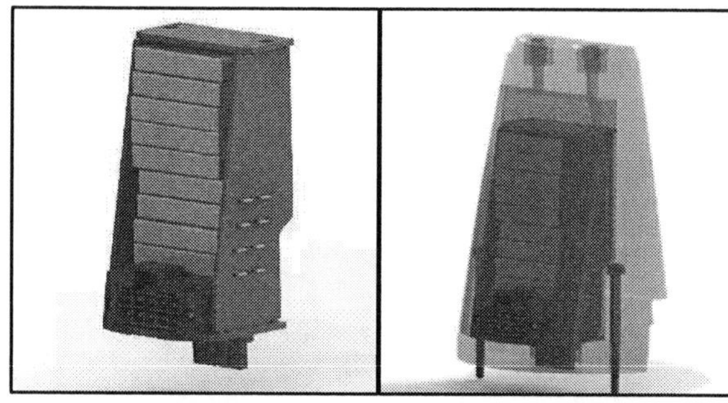

Figure 8. CPS Circuit Boards and Batteries

The boards form an interconnected "cage" around the cells which are soldered together without any board-to-board connectors. The tabs on the LiPo cells are also soldered directly to the circuit boards eliminating excess wiring. The circuitry on these boards provides three main functions: LiPo cell protection, battery on/off control, and a battery bypass for operating on external power. The LiPo cell protection circuit monitors the individual cell voltages during charging and discharging of the batteries. When charging the batteries, the circuit protects against cell over-voltage and over-current conditions and provides automatic cell balancing and open-cell detection. During discharge, the circuit protects against cell under-voltage and pack over-current and short-circuit conditions. Threshold values for all of these conditions are user-programmable enabling a great deal of system design flexibility. A ruggedized external connector on the side of the fully-assembled module provides a secure interface for charging the batteries, providing external power, and controlling the on/off circuitry within the module. Once assembled the CPS is protected by an outer housing made of glass filled polyamide, a rapid prototyping material (Figure 9). The housing is fabricated using a selective laser sintering 3-dimensional printing process. The material itself was chosen because it had the best strength properties of any of the additive manufacturing materials available.

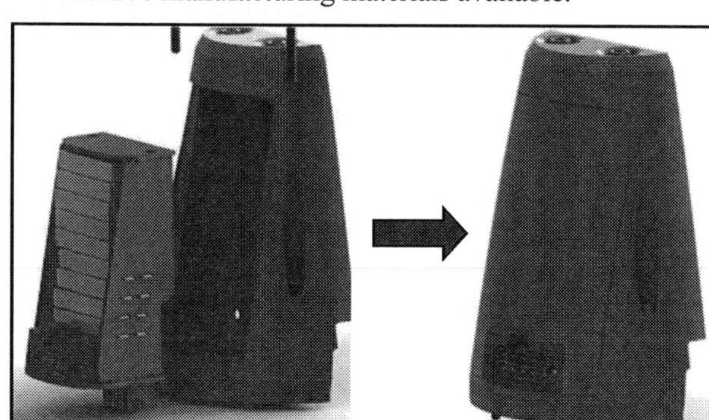

Figure 9. Complete CPS Module

Experimental Flight Demonstration

In 2014 the PUMA 120mm mortar guidance kit was evaluated over a series of flight demonstration experiments with varying degrees of success. A CPS module was included within each guidance kit and successfully powered the GEU and CAS modules during each flight experiment. An on-board diagnostic telemetry system, also known as a Recoverable Instrumented Test Article (RITA), was also utilized during each flight experiment to verify proper GEU and CAS operation. Inertial sensor data, GEU command data, and CAS power information were all transmitted by the RITA module to a ground station where it was recorded for later interrogation.

The desired operation of the CAS throughout a typical flight experiment is as follows: in a resting state during the initial portion of flight; activate upon canard deployment; then remain operational for remainder of the flight. While active, the CAS will draw varying amounts of current depending on the amount of force necessary to either maintain or alter the projectile trajectory. The CAS operates based on commands provided by the GEU.

Analysis of in-flight CAS voltage and current data (Figures 10-13) verified proper operation of the CPS. For the first 20 to 25 seconds of flight, the CPS maintained a nominal 20.8V with no load applied. Upon CAS activation, the CPS still maintained an average of 20 to 20.5V for the remaining 25 to 30 seconds of the flight. The CAS voltage also dropped no lower than approximately 18V even under loads just under 6A. At no time did the CAS voltage drop below operational limits and the CPS met all of the specified power requirements.

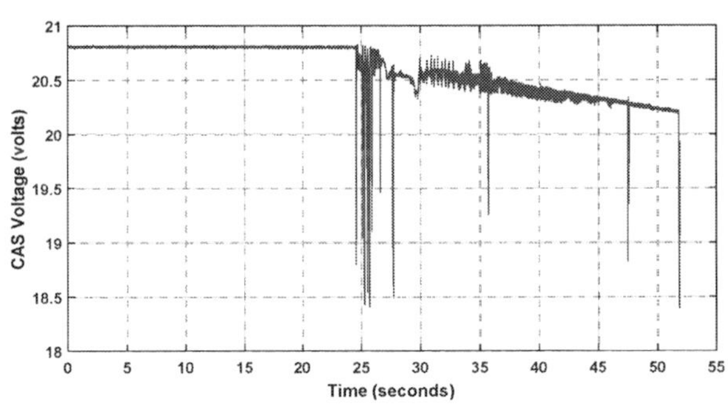

Figure 10. CAS Voltage during Flight Demonstration T3

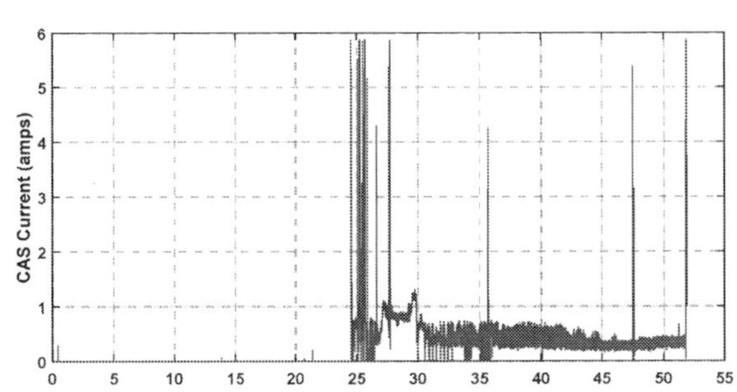

Figure 11. CAS Current during Flight Demonstration T3

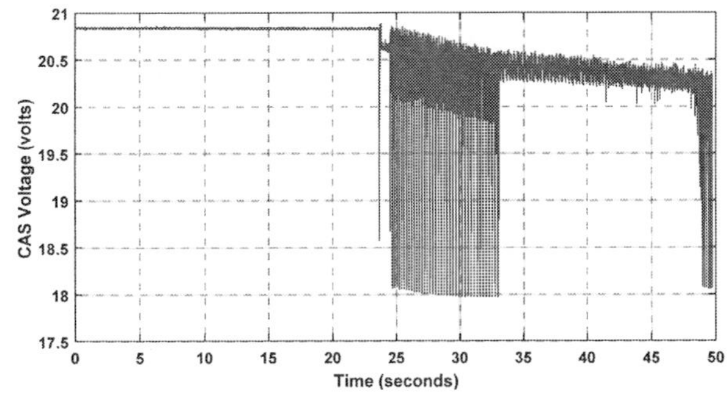

Figure 12. CAS Voltage during Flight Demonstration T7

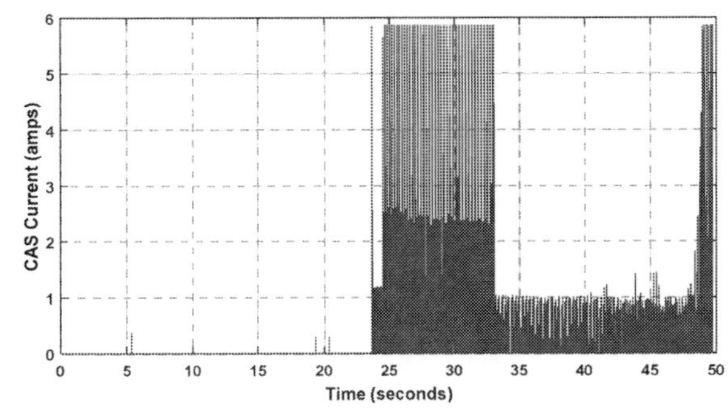

Figure 13. CAS Current during Flight Demonstration T7

Conclusions

This effort resulted in the successful design and development of a Centralized Power Supply module which utilized COTS LiPo cells and custom printed circuit boards for powering the GEU and CAS modules of the PUMA 120mm Mortar Guidance Kit. The CPS included precision battery protection circuitry which provided cell balancing, open cell detection, and user programmable limits for preventing cell over-voltage, cell under-voltage, pack over-current, and pack short-circuit conditions. The CPS module enabled a successful set of flight demonstration experiments for the PUMA 120mm mortar guidance kit program.

References

1. Fresconi, F., Celmins, I., Ilg, M., Maley, J., "Projectile Roll Dynamics and Control with a Low-Cost Skid-to-Turn Maneuver System," *U.S. ARL*, ARL-TR-6363, March 2013.
2. Grzybowski, D., Peregino, P., Davis, B., "Development of a Telemetry-Enabled High-G Projectile Carrier," *U.S. Army Research Laboratory*, ARL-TR-6099, September 2012.
3. Steelman, S., "Precision Universal Mortar Attack (PUMA)," *NDIA 2012 Joint Armaments Conference*, May 2012.
4. Steelman, S., "Precision Universal Mortar Attack (PUMA)," *NDIA 46th Annual Gun & Missile Systems Conference*, August 2011.
5. Bukowski, E., "Evaluation of Commercial-off-the-Shelf Lithium Batteries for use in Ballistic Telemetry Systems," *U.S. Army Research Laboratory*, ARL-TR-4840, June 2009.
6. Bukowski, E., "High Impact Shock Survivability Study of Lithium Ion Polymer Cells for use in Ballistic Applications," *44th Power Sources Conference*, June 2010.

Design, Construction, and Evaluation of 1000 V Valve Regulated Lead Acid (VRLA) and Lithium-Ion Batteries

Matthew Martin, Christopher Williams, Kendal Mckinzie, David Wetz, Clint Gnegy-Davidson and Isaac Cohen

University of Texas at Arlington

John Heinzel

Naval Surface Warfare Center - Philadelphia Division

wetz@uta.edu

Abstract

The US Navy has notionally defined the requirement for a 1000 V battery to operate as both a transient buffer as well as the prime power supply for a host of electrical systems on board the next generation of electrical ships. Since the number of applications demanding a 1000 V battery are limited, little is published in the literature concerning the design and operation challenges facing the development of these high voltage batteries. To help fill this knowledge gap, the University of Texas at Arlington's (UTA's) Pulsed Power and Energy Laboratory (PPEL) has designed and assembled two 1000 V batteries to serve as design cases and experimental test beds. One battery is constructed in a 75S/2P format using 13.5 V valve regulated lead acid (VRLA) modules while the other is constructed in a 288S/1P format using 30 Ah cylindrical lithium-iron-phosphate (LFP) lithium-ion cells. A novel data acquisition and controls system has been installed to evaluate each batteries electrical and thermal performance as well as transient voltages associated with the erection of 1000 V batteries. In this presentation, the design of the two batteries will be presented along with the experimental research performed thus far.

Li-Ion Conformal Wearable Battery

Eivind Listerud, Mario Destephen, and David Darch

EaglePicher Technologies, LLC
3220 Industrial Road
Joplin, Mo. 64801, USA

Abstract: *This paper describes the Li-Ion conformal wearable battery developed by EaglePicher Technologies. It is designed to be robust, light-weight and flexible, with a nominal energy of 150Wh and a weight of 1.18kg. The considerations in terms of balancing conformability, energy, and cell size will be discussed. The paper will also cover the battery management system, safety features and specific safety tests, and give examples of electrical battery performance.*

Keywords: Portable power; Li-ion battery; Conformal Battery; Battery management system.

Introduction

EaglePicher Technologies, LLC (EPT) has long been a leader in the development and production of batteries for portable power applications. It is currently developing the next generation of light-weight batteries for the soldier using both a primary chemistry (covered in another presentation for this conference) and a secondary Li-Ion chemistry. In this regard EaglePicher has developed a Li-Ion battery to decrease the wearable energy footprint and increase energy independence for the Soldier. The battery needs to be flexible to match a Soldier's SAPI body armor plate and offer increased comfort and enhanced load carriage distribution. In addition, the battery must reduce the weight burden and offer increased energy density.

EaglePicher's Li-Ion Conformal Wearable Battery (CWB) will deliver a significantly reduced weight burden in a conformal package while supplying improved energy density. This paper will give a brief description of the battery before describing some of the efforts involved in the analysis, design, and the development of this battery. Trade-off considerations will be discussed; showing how conformability, cell size, and pack energy have to be balanced in order to achieve optimum performance based on the Army's targeted goals. Results from safety and battery performance testing under various conditions are included.

Battery Description

The secondary CWB is a thin lightweight battery with a *flexible* form factor that is designed to match the contour of the Soldier's body for improved mobility and agility. The case design and the layout of the battery can be seen in Figure 1. Grooves between the cell compartments can be seen, as well as the vent and the state-of-charge indicator. The main connector is on the lower right side while the charge pins are located on the back. The battery can be charged through either contact port. The battery provides a 14.4 Volt nominal voltage and delivers 150 Wh. It will operate from -20°C to 60°C. The battery will deliver 10.5 Ampere hours and operates in a voltage range from 10 to 17.2 Volts with a life greater than 224 cycles. The battery assembly consists of Lithium-Ion pouch cells. A significant driver behind using pouch cells was the stringent weight criteria set forth by the Army. Nominal weight for the battery is 1.18 kg and the energy density is 128Wh/kg. The maximum continuous current is 5 Amps.

Figure 1: Case design and layout, showing grooves between cell compartments, vent, and SOCI.

Conformability

Several challenging technical hurdles have been overcome in enabling this design to fulfill the Army's needs of significant weight reduction while still supplying the required energy and power in a conformal package. Among the most challenging requirements was the flexibility criterion. The battery must be able to flex its edges a certain distance from its horizontal center axis repeatedly while still operating throughout the entire temperature range. The required movement of the edges is shown in Figure 2. In order to accomplish this multiple design factors had to be considered. Case material candidates were extensively evaluated based on factors from chemical compatibility, surface friction, and strength of materials. An example of a finite element analysis performed on a model of a potential design is shown in Figure 3. The material must possess the right combination of flexibility, strength, and durability.

Perhaps one of the more critical design decisions during the development of the battery was the size of the cells to use. Optimization of cell size had to be considered not just in light of the energy requirements but also in terms of the flexibility of the battery. Make the cell size large enough to optimize the entire interior volume of the case and the battery will not be conformal enough. Make the cell size small enough to enhance flexibility and the battery will not have enough energy. Once the optimum balance between cell size and flexibility was determined, the final design underwent extensive flexibility testing. An example of this is pictured in Figure 4. The top picture shows a battery deflected along the longer side of the battery. The bottom image shows the test performed along the short side. This was performed at both room temperature and at -20°C and always followed by electronic testing to make sure no damage was done to any interior battery components.

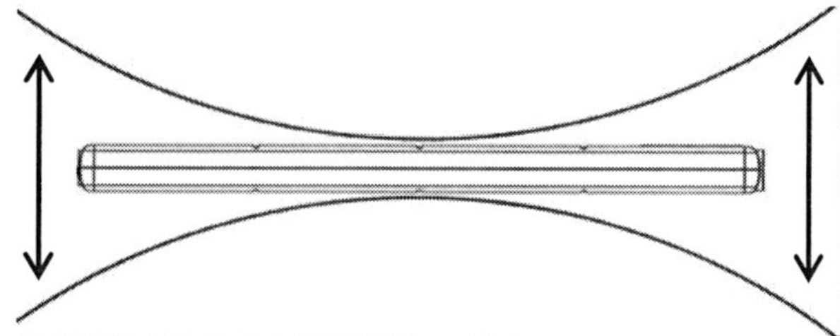

Figure 2: Required movement of edges of a conformal battery.

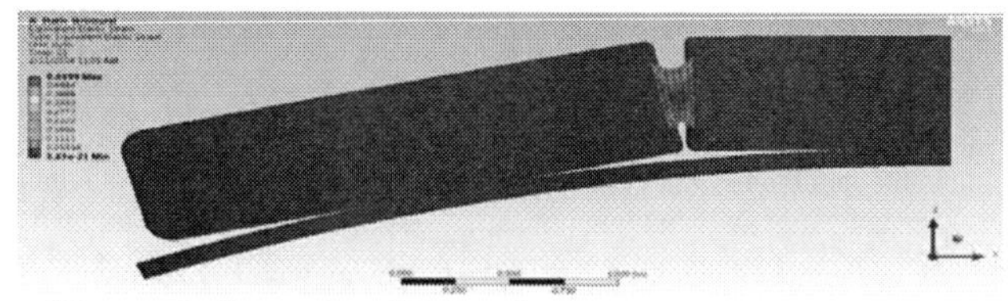

Figure 3: Example of finite element analysis for battery flexing subjected to bending requirements.

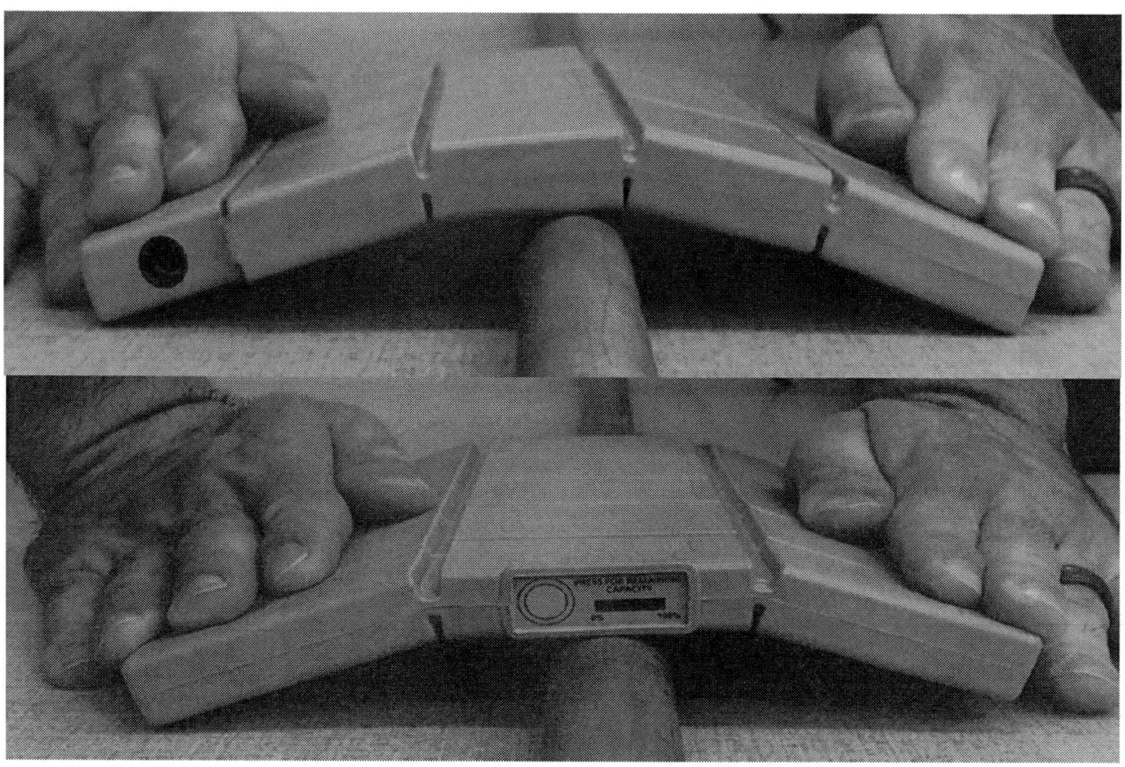

Figure 4: Battery subjected to conformability test. The typical test consisted of flexing the battery 100+ times in both vertical directions, along both horizontal center axes. The test was always followed by a discharge/charge cycle.

Battery Management System

The Li-Ion CWB contains a Battery Management System (BMS) to protect the cells and control battery operations. The BMS is responsible for operating the internal cell balancing, the charge/discharge FETs, and the SOC indicator. The SOCI can be seen in Figure 5. There are two ports for charging, giving it the ability to charge from either a connector or charging contacts. It has SMBus communications compliant with Version 1.1. It will also monitor for the following fault conditions:

- Over Temperature
- Under Temperature
- Over Current
- Over Voltage
- Under Voltage

The battery contains numerous safety features, including both non-resettable and resettable thermal devices. Numerous current fuses are also located throughout the battery and a vent is located in the external battery case.

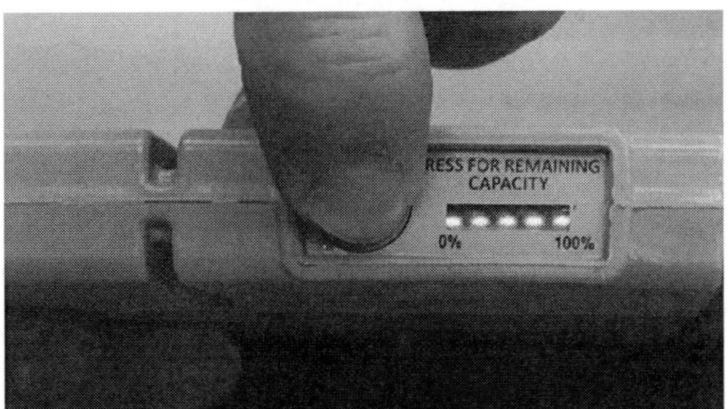

Figure 5: Temperature and Rate Compensated State-of-Charge Indicator (SOCI) with LED display.

Safety Testing

As previously mentioned, the choice of going with a pouch cell was partly driven by the weight target. In addition the pouch approach has shown to provide enhanced safety. A critical safety test that has been performed on the pouch cell is the nail penetration test. Cells at 100% SOC were instrumented with thermocouples and then subjected to the nail penetration test. As seen in Figure 6, the maximum temperature observed was about 94°C. Otherwise the test was uneventful. This test has special significance in light of the Army's bullet penetration requirement at the battery level.

Overcharge of Li-Ion batteries is always a concern. The CWB battery contains a BMS that will monitor virtual cell voltages and interrupt the battery charge when any virtual cell voltage exceeds the pre-set value of 4.32V. Figure 7 shows battery test data recorded during an overcharge test. The battery was to be charged at a constant current of 2.1A until the battery voltage reached 17.8V. This is significantly higher than the recommended maximum charge voltage of 17.2V. The recorded voltage and current profile can be seen in the graphics on the left in Figure 7. As the battery voltage reaches 17.19V the current is cut off and the charge stops. In the plot on the right of Figure 7, the voltage profiles of each of the virtual cells corresponding to the battery voltage are shown. The maximum voltage of any of the virtual cells is 4.32V. For additional safety, there are two more overvoltage thresholds as part of the battery design.

Overcharge testing has also been performed at the cell level. A pouch cell have been charged to 5.5V (22V at battery level) at a charge rate of 1.15A. After 6 hours the charge rate was less than 1mA. The maximum temperature was about 60°C before the temperature went back to room temperature.

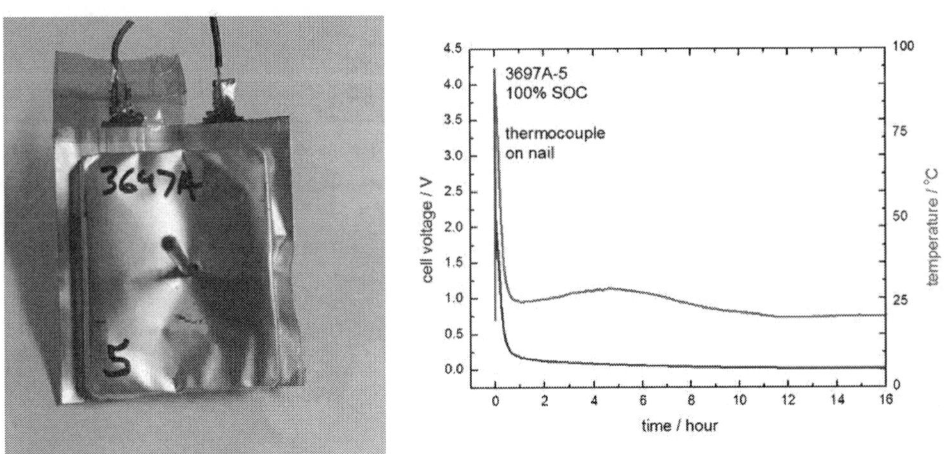

Figure 6: Image of pouch cell after nail penetration test and the temperature profile during testing.

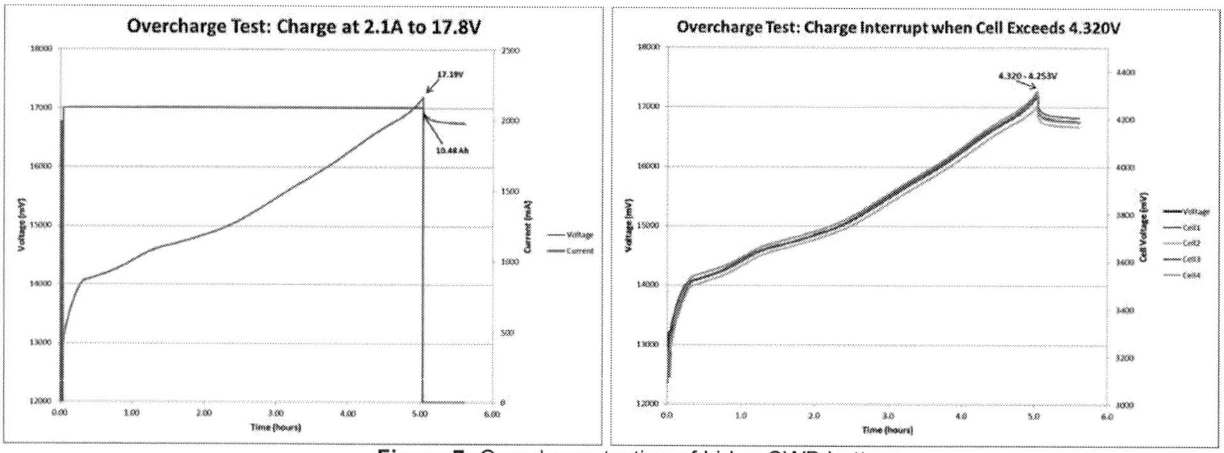

Figure 7: Overcharge testing of Li-Ion CWB battery.

Battery Performance

Discharge testing at the battery level shows that the battery will deliver over 150Wh when discharged at a C/5 rate. This can be seen in Figure 8. At the maximum discharge rate of 5A (C/2), the decrease in energy output is small and the battery still delivers over 140Wh. These cycles have been performed with a charge rate of 3.5A (C/3).

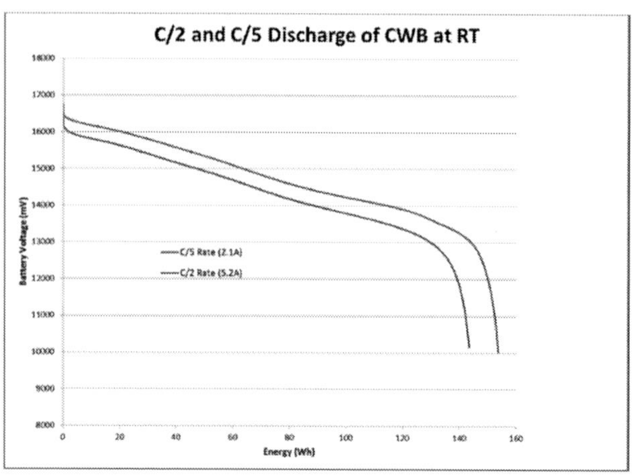

Figure 8: C/2 and C/5 discharge profiles during RT testing.

The battery has also been subjected to cold temperature discharge testing. Figure 9 shows the discharge profile at -20°C after a cold soak of 4 hours at that temperature. At a rate of C/5 the battery delivers over 110Wh.

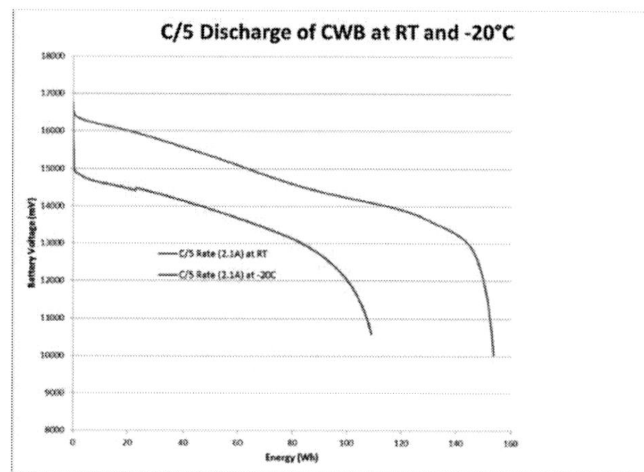

Figure 9: C/2 and discharge profiles during RT and -20°C testing.

Conclusion

EaglePicher has developed a Li-Ion conformal battery that is flexible, weighs less than 1.2kg, and will deliver 150Wh. It has a robust design with numerous safety features that has been subjected to numerous tests. It meets the Army's conformability requirement using the right balance between cell size and case flexibility.

Acknowledgement

Special thanks to CERDEC for supporting the rechargeable conformal battery development. This material is released to the public domain in accordance with ITAR 22 CFR 120.11.

First Generation Lithium-Ion 6T Battery Development

Neil Johnson, Chad Hartzog, Boris Mikhaylenko, Laurence Toomey
US Army RDECOM-TARDEC
njohnson@navitassys.com

Abstract

Navitas Advanced Solutions Group has demonstrated a 24V first generation lithium-ion 6T ground vehicle starter battery based on automotive grade, high volume domestic production lithium iron phosphate cells. Pre-production prototype batteries are currently undergoing electrical testing at US Army TARDEC and Navitas ASG. The first generation battery has demonstrated 60Ah, 800 Cold Cranking Amperes at -18°C while maintaining voltage >14.4V, and over 2,000 deep cycles. The battery's mass is 22 kg, almost half the mass of a 40 kg state of the art 12V lead-acid 6T battery. Fifteen first generation batteries are undergoing S9310 US Navy lithium battery safety testing at NSWC Carderock. It is expected that Navitas' 6T battery will be approved for land and shipboard transportation and use.

Second Generation Lithium-Ion 6T Battery Development

Chris Silkowski[1], Mike Wixom[1], Neil M. Johnson[1], Chad Hartzog[1], Laurence Toomey[2], and James Mainero[2]

[1]Navitas Advanced Solutions Group
4880 Venture Drive
Ann Arbor, MI 48108

[2]US Army RDECOM-TARDEC
6501 E. 11 Mile Road
Warren, MI 48397

Corresponding Author Contact: csilkowski@navitassys.com

Abstract: *Navitas Systems Advanced Solutions Group has successfully assembled custom-design large format lithium-ion cells and an exploratory prototype 24V second generation lithium-ion 6T battery. The prototype cells were tested and prototype battery performance was projected: 90 Ah and 1,100 Cold Cranking Amperes could be delivered, a marked improvement compared with the first generation 24V lithium-ion battery's 60 Ah and 600 CCA. The ultimate goal is to provide the capability of two 12V, 120 Ah, 1,100 CCA lead-acid 6T batteries using the space of a single 24V lithium ion battery. This exploratory prototype battery serves as the technical foundation of the next phase of second generation battery development, in which the ultimate second generation device will be improved to 120 Ah, 1,400 CCA goals and validated to the point of production readiness.*

Keywords: Navitas, 6T battery, starter battery, lithium-ion, cold crank, silent watch.

Introduction

The 12V lead acid 6T battery has provided starting power and energy for military ground vehicle systems for decades. As the needs and missions of the modern Army evolve, it is evident that a battery possessing substantially greater capabilities must be adopted. Incumbent 12V lead acid 6T batteries are heavy (two-man lift), require regular maintenance recharging, and deliver only 300-400 deep discharge cycles (needed for Silent Watch operations). Two 12V batteries are required to service 24V vehicle electrical systems. Improved 24V batteries containing much greater energy and power content are desired, as well as a greater service life under modern usage profiles and the ability to communicate status and state of health to the user. The ultimate goal is to provide the capability of two 12V lead acid batteries using the space of a single 24V lithium ion battery.

Navitas Systems Advanced Solutions Group (ASG) has developed a first generation (Gen 1) 24V li-ion 6T product[1] based on COTS 20Ah pouch cells to TRL 7. Figure 1 shows the Gen 1 battery. An exploratory second generation (Gen 2) product based on a Navitas customized cell, featuring optimized chemistry and cell design, was developed to TRL 5. Built upon this foundation work, the increasingly evolved, production-intent Gen 2 6T is now under development. An overview of Navitas' Gen 2 cell and battery, cell performance data, and performance projections of Gen 2 batteries are presented herein.

Figure 1. Navitas Gen 1 6T Lithium-Ion Battery

Navitas Gen 2 Lithium-Ion 6T Battery Overview

The goal of the Gen 2 lithium-ion 6T battery program is to produce an ideally 24V, 120Ah, appropriately safe, affordable, and high power device capable of both starting combustion engines under extreme cold weather conditions and supporting silent watch needs.

Table 1 shows Gen 2 6T battery performance goals and a comparison of lead acid, Navitas Gen 1 and projected Gen2 24V batteries. Due to the high power design needed to deliver 400 cold crank amperes (CCA) at -40°C, the projected battery may not meet objective Gen 2 capacity and energy targets, but does boost capacity and energy density by at least 65% over Gen 1, boosts cold crank at -18°C to 1,300 CCA, delivers 1000+ deep cycles, and weighs 40% less than a single lead acid 6T battery—or 70% less than the pair of lead acid batteries normally needed to service a 24V vehicle.

Technical Approach

Gen 2 6T battery performance levels present a challenging goal—perhaps beyond the capabilities of current practical state of the art lithium-ion battery technology. To approach Gen 2 battery goals, all aspects of the battery must be considered and optimized, in particular the component cell chemistry and cell mechanical design.

Table 1. Gen 2 24V lithium-ion 6T battery goals and Navitas battery performance.

Parameter	Lead Acid 6T	Navitas Gen 1 6T	Navitas Gen 2 6T (proj.)	Gen 2 6T Target
Capacity of Single Battery (Ah)	120 at 12V	60 at 24V	Min. 100 at 24V	120 at 24V
Energy Density (Wh/L)	102	110	185	220
Cold Crank, 30s (CCA at -18°C)	1,225	700	1,300	1,400
Cold Crank, 30s (CCA at -40°C)	400	150	400	400
Operating Temperature	-46 to +71°C	-46 to +71°C	-46 to +71°C	-46 to +71°C
Cycle Life (cycles at 80% DOD)	360	1,000++	1,000+	1,000+
Mass needed for 24V vehicle (kg)	80	22	25	20 – 30

Gen 2 6T Cell Chemistry: The Navitas Gen 1 6T battery is based on 20Ah lithium iron phosphate (LFP) pouch cells produced domestically in high volume by A123 Systems. LFP is a remarkably safe cell chemistry, capable of very long cycle life in excess of 2,000 deep cycles; however, LFP is limited to energy densities ~170 Wh/L at battery pack level. As such, a move to a more energetic metal oxide chemistry is necessary to achieve Gen 2 6T performance levels. Navitas has developed and qualified a high power graphite/NMC chemistry capable of supporting >200 Wh/L at battery level. This performance of this chemistry in 9Ah test cells was reported previously in detail[2]. Briefly, cold crank performance equivalent to 1,500 CCA was demonstrated, along with discharge functionality to -46°C and cycle life of 1000+ deep discharge cycles.

Gen 2 6T Cell Design, Exploratory Metal Can Cell: the 20Ah pouch cells used in Navitas' Gen 1 battery are assembled together in a module that also incorporates aluminum heat sink fins between every pair of cells (to conduct heat efficiently in/out of the module) as well as one compliant pad per every two cells, which allows the module to be compressed to a set length. This is a necessity when using pouch cells, as cell thickness can vary by ±0.2mm per cell. With a 20+ cells per module, these tolerances can result in poor module length control and modules which no longer fit into the battery case or mate accurately with set internal anchor points. The heat sink fins and compliant pads occupy 10-20% of the module volume, impacting volume usable for energy storage. As such, Navitas' cell design strategy was to eliminate or minimize these inactive materials by evolving the cell's design from pouch to a 45Ah high power metal can prismatic cell. Figure 2 shows the metal can cell.

Using a can cell, heat sinks are eliminated as the cell packaging serves this purpose. An optimized width, length, and thickness were adopted to efficiently fill the battery housing. Cell thickness is increased, leading to greater packaging efficiency and elimination of compliant pads. Cell thickness tolerances are reigned in, allowing further elimination of compliant pads or the use of thinner pad stock. Cell performance is shown in the Cell Testing Data section below.

Figure 2. Navitas Gen 2 6T 45Ah Lithium-Ion Metal Can Prismatic Cell

Exploratory Prototype Gen 2 Battery: a prototype 90Ah Gen 2 6T battery was constructed using fourteen 45Ah metal can prismatic cells (7S2P configuration). The battery module, featuring heavy duty plastic end plates which also act as anchor points to the battery case, is shown in Figure 3. The prototype battery was assembled into a cast aluminum Gen 1 6T battery case. Basic BMS functionality (CANBus communication, cell voltage and temperature measurements) was verified, but no substantial electrical testing was conducted. Projected battery performance is shown in the Battery Performance Projections section.

Figure 3. Navitas Exploratory Prototype Gen 2 6T Battery Module, Composed Of Metal Can Prismatic Cells

Gen 2 6T Cell Design, Development Pouch Cell: To achieve a viable price point for the Gen 2 6T battery, high volume cell manufacturing must be leveraged. Unfortunately for the 45Ah metal can cell, very few established volume manufacturers of large format metal can prismatic cells exist in North America, and those that do are currently dedicated to serving their primary markets (e.g., consumer automotive). As such, a course correction has been made to re-orient cell development back toward large format pouch cells, which can be produced by several North American manufacturers. The current design direction is to leverage large format pouch cells, oriented horizontally within the battery housing to optimally fill the allowable volume. This configuration will by necessity have to re-adopt some of the inefficiencies of the original module; however, a battery capacity of min. 100+Ah is projected using this cell and module design. Figure 4 shows the current design concept. Large form factor cells minimize packaging inefficiencies.

Figure 4. Navitas Development Gen 2 6T Battery Concept Featuring Large Form Factor Pouch Cells

Cell Testing Data

Exploratory 45Ah Metal Can Cell: the electrical performance of the prototype 45Ah cell was measured. Cold crank testing at -18°C verified that this cell is capable of delivering 12C+ rate (1,100+ CCA at battery level) while maintaining voltage above 2.29V (16V / 7 cells in series). Figure 5 shows the cold crank pulse response.

Cold crank testing at -40°C verified that this cell is capable of delivering 4C rate (400 CCA at battery level) while maintaining voltage above 2.29V. Figure 6 shows the cold crank pulse response.

Continuous discharge capability of the prototype 45Ah cell was measured over the -46°C to +23°C temperature range. As the cell chemistry was designed for low temperature operation, little reduction in available energy is observed in the -20°C to +23°C range. At -46°C, the battery is capable of delivering 41% of the energy available at 23°C at a 3.0V cut off, and 52% of the energy available at 23°C at a 2.5V cut off. Figure 7 shows the discharge performance.

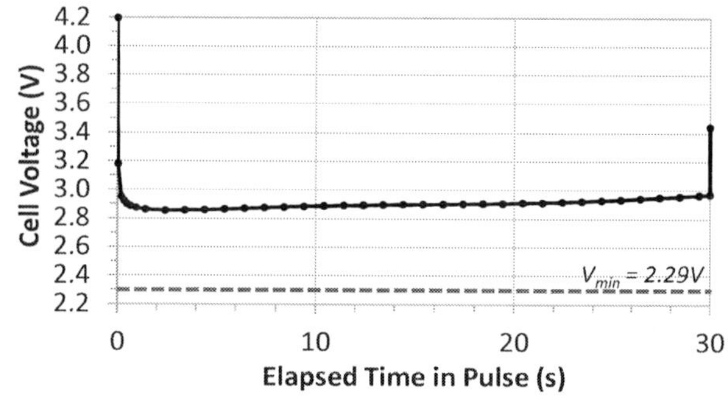

Figure 5. Cold Crank Pulse Response of Navitas 45Ah Gen 2 6T Cell, -18°C, 12C Rate Pulse

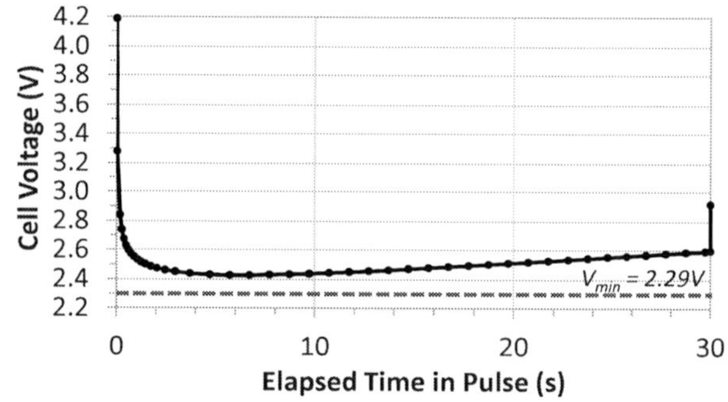

Figure 6. Cold Crank Pulse Response of Navitas 45Ah Gen 2 6T Cell, -40°C, 4C Rate Pulse

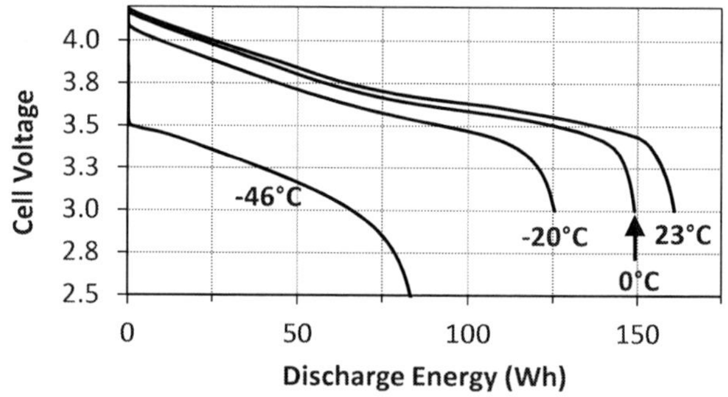

Figure 7. Discharge Performance of Navitas 45Ah Gen 2 6T Cell in the -46 to +23°C Temperature Range, 0.1C Rate

Cycle life testing of the 45Ah cell is currently underway. It is expected that deep discharge cycle life of the 45Ah cells will be consistent with that of the previously-tested 10Ah cells, 1,000+ cycles.

Battery Performance Projections

Exploratory Prototype Gen 2 Battery: based on single cell testing data, the performance of the exploratory Gen 2 6T battery was projected at 90Ah, 1,100CCA, 1,000+ deep discharge cycles.

Development Gen 2 Battery: based on 45Ah cell data and models of the large format pouch cell in development, the Gen 2 6T battery in development is expected to deliver 100+Ah, approximately 1,300 CCA at -18°C, 400 CCA at -40°C, and 1,000+ deep discharge cycles, based on an affordable cell produced in North America.

Conclusions

Navitas Advanced Solutions Group's Gen 2 6T lithium-ion ground vehicle battery is projected to offer a significant boost to 24V lithium-ion 6T battery performance, and a substantial increase in performance and capabilities above commercial state of the art lead acid 6T batteries. Capacity, energy, cold crank, low temperature operation, and power will all be enhanced. 100+Ah, 1,300 CCA at -18°C, 400 CCA at -40°C, and 1,000+ deep discharge cycles are possible with the Gen 2 lithium-ion cell chemistry in an optimized cell form factor. Battery cost and supply chain security will be controlled by producing cells on a high volume manufacturing line in North America. With this performance level, battery logistics and maintenance burdens will be reduced, while enabling vehicles to carry significantly greater energy to service silent watch needs.

Acknowledgements

Navitas wishes to thank Alion Science and Technology, the National Advanced Mobility Consortium (NAMC), and the U.S. Army RDECOM Tank Automotive Research, Development and Engineering Center (TARDEC) Energy Storage Team for their partnership and financial support of this work.

References

1. N. Johnson, et. al., "First Generation Lithium-Ion 6T Battery Development," *Proc. 47th Power Sources Conference*, 2016.
2. C. Silkowski, et. al., "24V Lithium-Ion 6T Battery Cell Chemistry Development," *Proc. 46th Power Sources Conference*, 2014

Effect of Oxygen Content at Various Steam to Carbon Ratios in a Distributed Reactor

Richard Scenna[a], Terry DuBois[a], Ashwani K. Gupta[b]
[a] US Army Research, Development and Engineering Command, CERDEC, CPI
[b] University of Maryland, Department of Mechanical Engineering, College Park, MD 20742

Abstract: *This work investigates the non-catalytic chemical decomposition of a JP8 fuel under wet distributed reforming conditions. Small amounts of steam added to the reactor resulted in high (up to 81%) reforming efficiency, which is much greater than that reported previously using conventional non-catalytic reforming. Reformate consisted of high concentrations of both hydrogen (21-24%) and carbon monoxide (20-23%). Syngas composition was governed by the availability of oxygen, steam, and heat to activate partial oxidation, steam reforming, and water gas shift reactions. The results demonstrate sound viability of a non-catalytic reformer.*

Keywords: Fuel Reforming, Fuel Processing, Wet Partial Oxidation, JP8

Introduction

The addition of small amounts of steam (S/C<1.0) to partial oxidation, called wet partial oxidation, has been shown to enhance reformate quality over conventional dry partial oxidation. Typically, reformers are employed to generate hydrogen for large-scale industrial applications (such as refineries and ammonia plants), but they can also be used to operate fuel cells using logistically available fuels such as JP8, diesel, or gasoline. Fuel cells are not directly compatible with most logistical fuels, since they require a hydrogen fuel stream. A reformer can act as an intermediary device converting the incompatible logistic fuel into a more usable form (syngas) for the fuel cells. Each fuel cell type has unique requirements and tolerance for syngas composition. A solid oxide fuel cell can accept a wide range of reformate quality, as it is capable of utilizing both hydrogen and carbon monoxide. Proton exchange membrane or phosphoric acid fuel cells require high purity hydrogen and are easily poisoned by carbon monoxide. The U. S. Army CERDEC is increasingly interested in developing more efficient power sources, but is constrained by the need to operate with the available logistical fuels (JP8).

Conventional reforming of JP8 typically employs noble metal catalysts to enhance reformate yield, achieving efficiencies of 75-90%. However, high sulfur concentrations found in JP8 (3000ppm_w) will deactivate common reforming catalysts [1]. To prevent this, fuel desulfurization or sulfur tolerant catalysts are required [2]. Kerosene and diesel fuels are known to have issues with coke formation on the catalyst surface [2]. Although this can be mitigated by operating with excess oxidizer, it reduces the overall reforming efficiency.

A non-catalytic approach avoids these issues, while also reducing the reformer cost. Non-catalytic reformers operate under super-adiabatic conditions to enhance conversion (porous media or with heat exchangers). However, the higher reactor temperatures promote the cracking of hydrocarbons leading to soot formation (up to 40%) and thermal damage [3]. Non-catalytic reformers typically operate at lower efficiencies (60-70%) than catalytic reformers (75-90%)[2–5].

Previous studies have shown that the distributed reaction regime suppresses soot formation and enhances reformate quality[6]. Entrainment reduces peak temperatures, while elevating averaged reactor temperature. This results in faster kinetics without the potential of reactor damage. The entrainment of reactive species into the exhaust stream promotes additional kinetic pathways at earlier locations in the reactor.

Steam is commonly employed in the catalytic reforming process as either a primary or secondary oxidizer[4]. Catalytic reactors use steam to enhance syngas yields, which also reduce soot formation and protects the catalysts. Limited information is available in the literature on non-catalytic reactors employing steam[7].

Steam promotes both steam reforming and water gas shift reactions, which enhance hydrogen concentrations in the syngas. The addition of steam delays ignition, thus elongating mixing time of reactants before ignition occurs. Steam increases turbulent velocity while reducing laminar flame speed of the reaction, to promote a more distributed reaction condition.

However, only a limited amount of steam should be added to avoid detrimental effects to the reforming process. The endothermic nature of the steam reforming reactions reduces the reactor temperature, which limits the chemical kinetics. In addition, the enhanced volumetric flow rate reduces the average residence time of reactants in the reactor.

This works examines the distributed reaction regime using steam to enhance both conversion and reformate quality under wet partial oxidation conditions. Oxygen and steam content were varied to enhance the understanding of the relationship between exothermic partial oxidation reactions and endothermic steam reforming reactions.

Experimental Design

The experimental test stand was similar to the design used in our previous works, except for the addition of a steam vaporizer[6]. Fuel, air, and steam were independently heated and mixed prior to injection. The mixer was selected to minimize residence time (3ms) while providing 99.99% mixing efficiency. The air flow rate was fixed at 30 SLPM, while fuel and steam flow rates were varied to adjust oxygen to carbon and steam to carbon ratios. Prior data reveals that optimum results should be between steam to carbon ratios of 0.0 to 0.50[7]. Steam to carbon ratios were increased further until reformate quality degraded. The fuel/air/steam charge, held at 375°C, was injected into the reactor.

The reactants were injected through a single injector located at a central location in the cylindrical reactor[6]. Injecting from a single central location allowed uniform entrainment all around the injected jet. The reactor was initiated through an igniter located opposite of the injector location. The product gases were exhausted through two outlets adjacent to the injector on the same side. This configuration is referred to as reverse flow configuration since the reactants and products are required to reverse direction before exiting the reactor. In contrast, a plug flow reactor allows reactants and products to flow through the reactor with no change in direction.

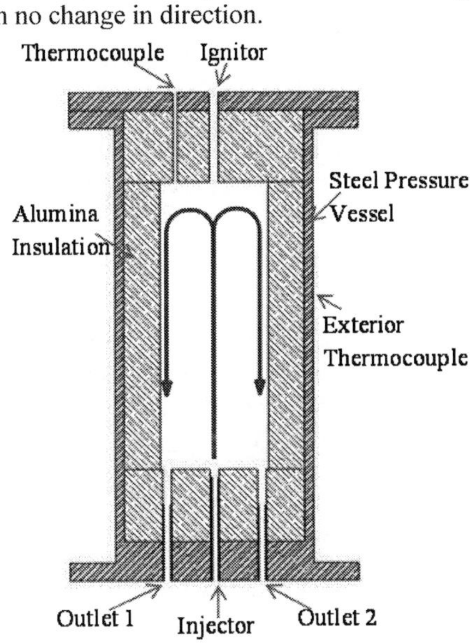

Figure 1. A schematic diagram of well insulated reactor.

The reactor consisted of two layers. The outermost layer consisted of a steel pressure vessel, which maintained the reactor pressure and allowed sealed connections to the reactor. The outer pressure vessel was maintained at 800°C by an external tube furnace (not shown in Fig 1). This promoted near adiabatic conditions by reducing the temperature gradient in the reactor. If the reformer was incorporated into a fuel cell hot box, this would be considered as a realistic working condition. The inner layer was composed of a high purity alumina insulation ($97\%_{mass}$), which served to protect the outer steel pressure vessel and retain heat. A high purity alumina insulation was chosen to prevent reductions by syngas.

Reformate quality was monitored using a four channel gas chromatograph (GC) calibrated to three primary standards each composed of 10-14 hydrocarbons. Each standard has an analytical tolerance of 0.17%. The gas chromatograph was able to detect hydrocarbons up to C6. Prior to the gas chromatograph, a filter, and condenser were included to mitigate the transport of soot, particulates or water into the GC. A carbon balance of 95-100% was achieved. To avoid flow disruption, temperature was not directly measured.

Results and Discussion

The addition of steam improved the reformate quality as compared to the dry partial oxidation case. Only trace amounts of steam and oxygen were needed to produce a noticeable change in reformate quality. Steam to carbon (S/C) and oxygen to carbon (O/C) ratios were varied over the range: S/C=0.0 - 0.25 and O/C=1.04 -1.15. Oxygen to carbon ratios below 1.04 was restricted due to low conversion.

The addition of steam, even in trace amounts (S/C~0.01), drastically increased both hydrogen and carbon monoxide concentrations in the syngas. The syngas composition consisted of high concentrations of both hydrogen (21-24%) and carbon monoxide (20-23%). Concentrations of other gases did not vary much over the range of oxygen to carbon ratios examined here, with the exception of hydrogen, see Figs. 2-5. Previous work showed that small changes in oxygen to carbon ratio had a limited effect on syngas composition [8].

Reformate chemical composition is the result of the balance between the faster, highly exothermic partial oxidation reactions (R_1), the slower endothermic steam reaction (R_2), and water gas shift reaction (R_3). Steam reforming is more desirable as it generates higher yields of hydrogen, but it is limited by its endothermic nature and potential quenching. Partial oxidation is an exothermic reaction, but it produces lower yields of hydrogen. If excess steam is available after the oxidative and steam reforming reactions, the water gas shift reaction can shift the composition of reformate to produce additional hydrogen. The faster oxidative reactions are considered to occur before the slower steam reforming and water gas shift reactions.

$$C_xH_y + \left(\frac{x}{2}\right) O_2 \rightarrow \left(\frac{y}{2}\right) H_2 + xCO \qquad (R_1)$$

$$C_xH_y + xH_2O \rightarrow \left(x + \frac{y}{2}\right) H_2 + xCO \qquad (R_2)$$

$$CO + H_2O \rightarrow H_2 + CO_2 \qquad (R_3)$$

Under ideal conditions, only a limited amount of fuel will be oxidized to generate the heat necessary for endothermic steam reforming reactions. However, the reactor temperature must be maintained so as not to reduce the overall reaction rate. Excess oxygen will increasingly oxidize fuel (partial oxidation) and reduce the amount of fuel available in undergoing steam reforming reactions. Excess oxygen also has the potential to oxidize reformate. However, insufficient oxygen reduces both reactor temperature and activity of steam reforming reactions, resulting in reduced conversion. It was noted that fuel conversion increased with increase in oxygen to carbon ratio, see Fig 6. This was most notable at steam to carbon ratios of 0 to 0.05, wherein the conversion was low.

At an O/C ratio of 1.04, there was insufficient oxygen for full conversion, see Fig. 6. Under these conditions, the addition of steam to partial oxidation was only beneficial between S/C ratios of 0.01 to 0.10. At S/C ratios in excess of 0.10, the excess steam promoted the formation of lower molecular weight hydrocarbons (such as, methane and acetylene), while reducing hydrogen concentrations, see Figs. 4-5. This was attributed to reduced reactor temperatures caused by the excess steam.

The availability of excess steam activated the water gas shift reaction. As expected at the onset of water gas shift reaction an increase in steam to carbon ratio showed a small increase in both hydrogen and carbon dioxide concentration, along with small corresponding decrease in carbon monoxide, see Figs. 2-3.

Increasing oxygen to carbon ratio to 1.08 increased reformate quality. The reformer demonstrated high reforming efficiency of 81% with hydrogen concentrations of 24%, see Fig. 2 and Fig. 7. These concentrations and performance are very similar to those of catalytic reformers and demonstrate the feasibility of employing non catalytic reforming approach as a replacement for catalytic reformers in a solid oxide fuel cell systems.

The additional oxygen content caused an increase in both steam reforming and partial oxidation reactions to cause near full conversion (99%). At O/C ratio of 1.08, there was sufficient steam, air, and heat to convert fuel through steam reforming and partial oxidation reactions, but the amount of steam was insufficient to activate the water gas shift reaction. This was shown by the reactor achieving full conversion and higher efficiency at O/C ratio of 1.08 than that at 1.04. Increase in S/C ratio increased carbon monoxide formation and a decrease in carbon dioxide formation, which indicates the water gas shift reaction was not active. At O/C ratios of 1.08 and higher, there was sufficient heat available so that the increased steam content did not promote formation of additional hydrocarbons, as seen at O/C = 1.04.

This phenomenon is not typically seen in either catalytic wet partial oxidation or autothermal reforming. Generally, catalytic reactors use greater amounts of steam (S/C=1.0-2.0) than what used in the present study (S/C=0.0-0.25), which is sufficient to activate both steam reforming and water gas shift reactions[4]. However, previous non-catalytic literature has recommended lower S/C ratios[7].

However, at higher oxygen to carbon ratios (O/C>1.08), the activity of oxidative reactions increased, reducing the amounts of fuel available to undergo steam reforming. This resulted in increased conversion at lower O/C ratios, but reduced hydrogen concentrations. As steam reforming reactions became less active, excess steam became available to support water gas shift reaction. After full conversion, increase in steam content caused a drop in carbon monoxide and an increase in both hydrogen and carbon dioxide concentration, see Figs. 2-3. This supports the assertion that water gas shift was active.

Excess oxygen appears to impact the formation of hydrogen more than the formation of carbon monoxide. An increase in the amounts of oxygen caused a reduction in hydrogen, see Fig. 2. Since the distributed reactor entrains hot reactive gases prior to ignition, hydrogen is more readily oxidized than other gases (such as, CO, CH_4, C_2H_2), which causes a more pronounced effect on the amounts of hydrogen concentration.

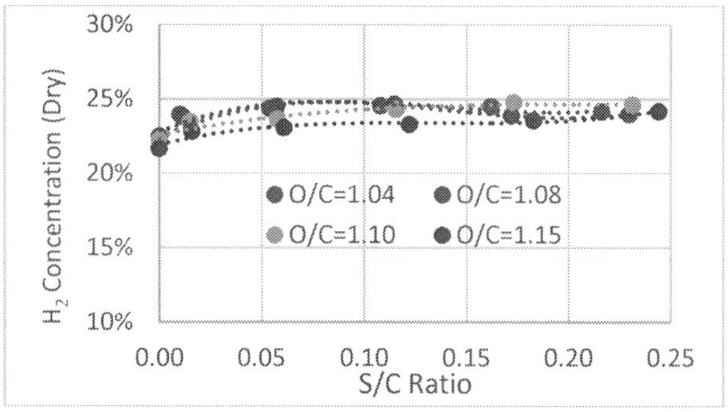

Figure 2. Hydrogen concentration at S/C=0.0 to 0.25 and O/C=1.04 to 1.15

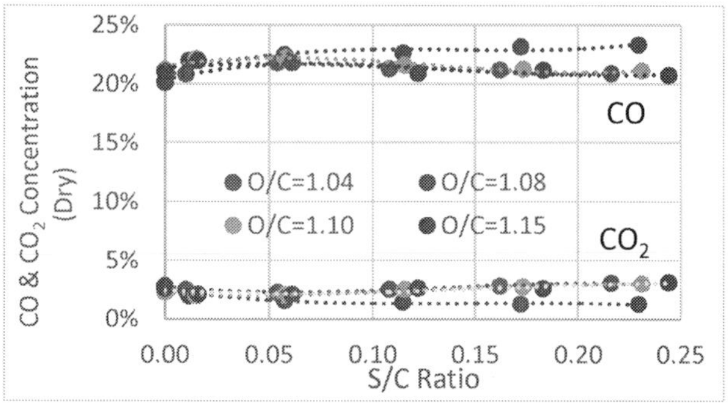

Figure 3. Carbon monoxide and carbon dioxide concentration at S/C=0.0 to 0.25 and O/C=1.04 to 1.15

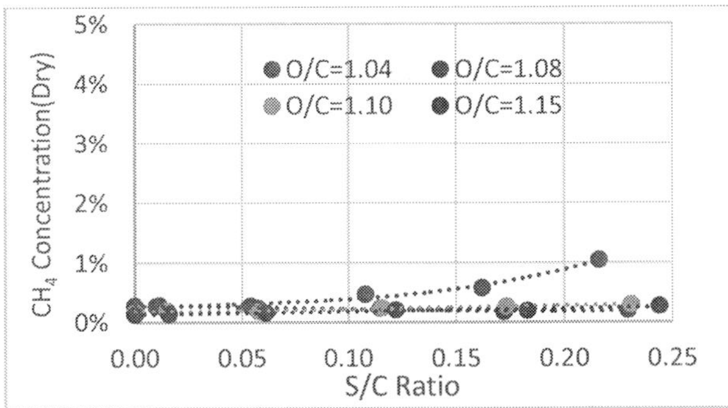

Figure 4. Methane concentration at S/C=0.0 to 0.25 and O/C=1.04 to 1.15

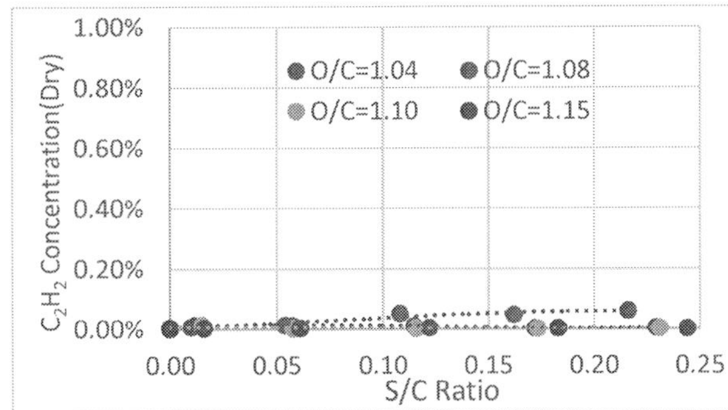

Figure 5. Acetylene concentration at S/C=0.0 to 0.25 and O/C=1.04 to 1.15

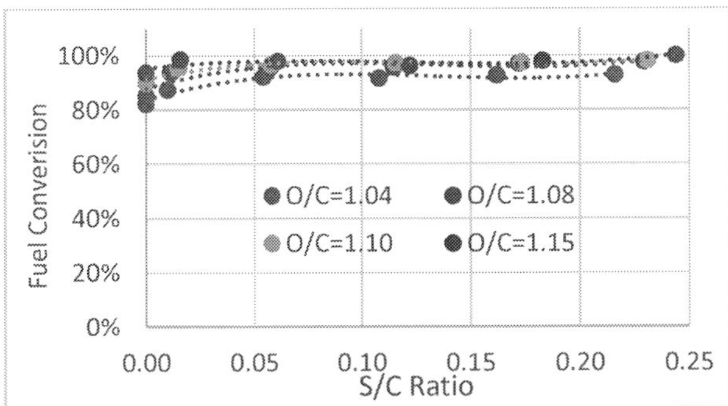

Figure 6. Fuel conversion at S/C=0.0 to 0.25 and O/C=1.04 to 1.15

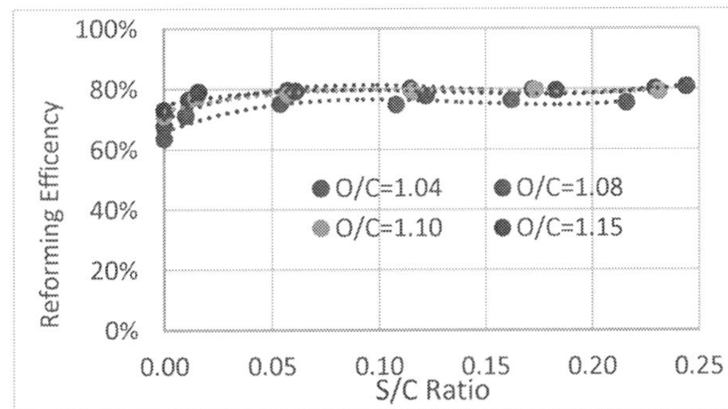

Figure 7. Reforming efficiency at S/C=0.0 to 0.25 and O/C=1.04 to 1.15

Conclusions

JP8 fuel reforming under wet partial oxidation conditions demonstrated a substantial increase in the reformate quality. With small concentrations of steam, the reactor achieved high reforming efficiency of 75-81%, and is comparable to catalytic reforming. Syngas was composed of high concentration of hydrogen (21-24%) and carbon monoxide (20-23%). Methane (0.13-1.04%) and trace amounts of acetylene (0.0-0.03%) were the only hydrocarbons detected. These results demonstrate the viability of non-catalytic reforming of JP8 fuel.

Syngas composition was governed by the availability of oxygen, steam, and heat to active partial oxidation, steam reforming, and water gas shift reaction. Insufficient oxygen (O/C=1.04) resulted in slower kinetics and inability to fully activate the steam reforming reactions. At peak performance (O/C=1.08) there was sufficient steam, air, and heat to convert all the fuel through steam reforming and partial oxidation reactions, but insufficient steam to activate the water gas shift reaction. Excess oxygen (O/C>1.10) enhances oxidative reactions, reduce fuel available to undergo steam reforming reactions to subsequently limit the performance.

Acknowledgment

The authors acknowledge the support of the US Army ILIR program. Distribution A

Reference

[1] Department of Defense, U. S. of A., 2013, MIl-DTL-83133J. http://quicksearch.dla.mil

[2] Lee, I. C., and Chu, D., 2003, Literature review of fuel processing. www.dtic.mil

[3] Smith, C. H., Pineda, D. I., Zak, C. D., and Ellzey, J. L., 2012, "Conversion of jet fuel and butanol to syngas by filtration combustion," Int. J. Hydrogen Energy, **38**(2), pp. 879–889. aladinrc.wrlc.org

[4] DuBois, T., 2011, "Oxygen-Enriched Fuel Reforming of Heavy Liquid Hydrocarbon Fuels for Fuel Cells," Catholic University of America. http://aladinrc.wrlc.org/

[5] Pastore, A., and Mastorakos, E., 2011, "Syngas production from liquid fuels in a non-catalytic porous burner," Fuel, **90**(1), pp. 64–76.

[6] Scenna, R., and Gupta, A. K., 2016, "Partial oxidation of JP8 in a well-insulated distributed reactor," J. Fuel Process. Technol., **142**, pp. 174–181.

[7] Roth, K., and Wirtz, S., 2007, "Investigation of soot formation during partial oxidation of diesel fuel," Chem. Eng. Technol, **30**(6), pp. 782–789.

[8] Scenna, R., and Gupta, A. K., 2015, "Partial oxidation of jp8 in a distributed reactor," J. Fuel Process. Technol., **134**, pp. 205–213.

Production of Hydrogen from Various Feedstock Options Using Non-Thermal Plasma Catalyzed Reforming

Lyman J. Frost
Joseph J. Hartvisgsen
S. Elango Elangovan

Ceramatec, Inc
Salt Lake City, Utah 84119

Abstract: Ceramatec has developed a method for reformation of various hydrocarbons using a non-thermal plasma system to catalyze the reformation process. The plasma provides the same type of catalytic activity as a solid catalyst but since the plasma is constantly renewed it is not sensitive to sulfur or various other contaminants that adversely affect traditional solid catalysts. The reformer can operate in a partial oxidation or steam reforming mode but these modes are usually combined in an autothermal process. Any hydrocarbon that can be vaporized can be reformed with the system. The reformer can operate with air, oxygen enriched air, or pure oxygen as an oxidant. The reformer uses the non-thermal plasma to form radicals to promote reforming much as would occur with a solid reforming catalyst. The reformer has been deployed in the field in sizes as large as 1 MMSCF per day of natural gas. The plasma unit has the advantages of being insensitive to sulfur (i.e. it is essentially a continually renewing catalyst), creating a highly active reforming zone, being fuel flexible, and being capable of operating in a number of orientations for packaging.

Keywords: Reforming JP-8; plasma reforming; logistic fuel reforming; non-thermal plasma

Introduction

Operation on liquid hydrocarbon logistic fuels drawn from any available infrastructure, or from onboard the vehicle, is an absolute requirement for a truly useful and practical fuel cell power system for military applications. Unfortunately, catalytic steam reforming of these fuels has proven difficult due to adverse effects from the high aromatics content and deeply-bound sulfur on catalyst activity. In partial oxidation, catalytic partial oxidation (CPOX), and autothermal reforming (ATR) processes, a sub-stoichiometric amount of air is combined with the fuel, and the mixture is burned (either with or without a catalyst) to generate synthesis gas used to fuel the fuel cell. Conventional partial oxidation processes have been plagued with soot and carbon deposition issues, and in some cases, the soot management system may be larger and more complex than the reformer. The thermal mass of the catalyst in the case of CPOX or ATR operation, the hydrogen required in a hydro-desulfurization system, and the operational difficulties associated with the partial oxidation process make each of these processes difficult to use for compact synthesis gas production.

Non-thermal plasma reforming is an approach that solves many of the above problems. This approach uses a low-amperage, high-voltage plasma arc to catalyze the reforming of the heavy hydrocarbons. The energy needed to complete the reformation process can be introduced by burning a portion of the fuel or by heat integration with the rest of the system. Much as would be accomplished by a solid catalyst, the non-thermal plasma creates radicals that promote the reforming process. Unlike the solid catalyst, the non-thermal plasma approach is not sensitive to sulfur since it is constantly renewed with each plasma arc generated and since there are no catalyst sites for sulfur to deactivate. The plasma does not eliminate the sulfur from the synthesis gas but as stated the reforming process is not sensitive to this sulfur. Sulfur still needs to be eliminated if downstream processes are sensitive to sulfur.

Likewise, without the solid catalyst bed there is no thermal mass that must be heated to temperature and thus start-up time is substantially reduced. The unit may be started in a partial oxidation mode and then switched to steam reforming as temperatures sufficient to produce steam are reached. This provides substantial flexibility in operations by going from exothermic to endothermic operations dependent only on control algorithms and the mode that makes the most sense at a point in time. The system is flexible, sulfur tolerant, and consumes a minimum of the energy value of the synthesis gas produced. The system does need some electrical energy to produce the plasma (i.e. ~ 1-3% of the energy in the input fuel).

Non-thermal Plasma Reformer:

Introduction

Ceramatec has developed an innovative, integrated process that retains the thermodynamic advantages of steam reforming and combines it with the robust, highly energetic reaction zone characteristic of partial oxidation. The reformer operates as a non-thermal plasma-catalyzed, autothermal reformer. The process is easily scalable for use in compact power systems, ranging from a few kilowatts to hundreds of kilowatts, can be used to reform various hydrocarbons to produce synthesis gas, or used to produce hydrogen. A laboratory-scale reformer (Figure 1) is compact, with an internal volume of 0.6 L and a reformation capacity of 5 kWt fuel rate. The plasma reformer generates a highly active, non-thermal plasma source of non-equilibrium electric discharges that act as an activation source for plasma chemical reactions.

The device has at least two diverging knife-shaped electrodes along which multiple electric discharges glide. The vaporized hydrocarbon to be reformed is expanded between the electrodes and drives the electric arc along the electrodes. Progress of the electric discharge is shown in Figure 1 (right). A high-voltage, single- or poly-phase, relatively low-current discharge is generated across a gas flow between the electrodes. The discharge forms at the closest point, spreads along the electrodes, and disappears and another discharge immediately forms at the initial spot. The geometry of the electrodes, flow conditions, and characteristics of the power supply determine the path of the arc. The electrodes do not need to be cooled, so the electrical energy is directly and totally transferred to the processed gas. The voltage can be as high as 20,000 volts. Multiple discharge systems can be installed for large gas flow rates. Any gas or vapor can be directly processed.

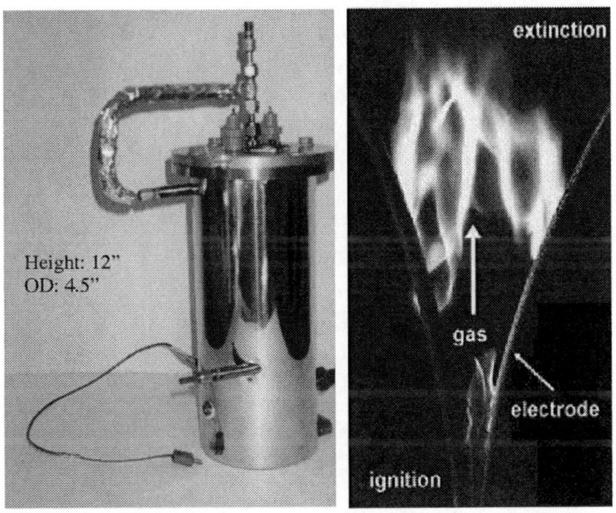

Figure 1. Plasma reformer: 5-kWt JP-8 reformer (left); view of the electrodes (right).

Plasma Reformer Sizing

The reformer has been built in a number of other sizes besides the small unit shown in Figure 1. Figure 2 shows a larger unit operated in conjunction with a Fischer Tropsch gas-to-liquids system capable of about two (~2) barrels per day of FT liquids (~8' tall x 20" diameter; 1 kWe input). Figure 3 shows five (5) larger reformers on a common manifold used in an ammonia plant in Peru. Each of these reformers is capable of reforming 1 MMSCFD of "wet" natural gas (~1250 BTU/SCF). The reformer does not need a pre-reformer to process the wet gas. Each reformer is ~15' tall, 5' in diameter, and uses about 4 kWe of electric input. The reformer uses enriched air (41% O_2) to yield the ratio of H_2:N_2 required for the ammonia reactors after removal of the CO_2. The reformer shown in Figure 2 has been used to reform natural gas, anaerobic digester gas, high sulfur diesel, mixtures of heavy hydrocarbon solvents, and other volatile liquids like glycerol.

Figure 2: Reformer for 2 BPD FT reactor

Figure 3: 5 x 1 MMSCFD plasma reformers

Input Feedstock

The reformer has been used with a variety of feedstock options. As mentioned, any hydrocarbon that can be volatilized can be reformed. A sample of military grade jet fuel (JP-8) with a total sulfur of 430 ppmw and an aromatic content of 15.3 vol% was reformed. A reformate gas analyses for operations in both a partial oxidation and a steam reforming mode is shown in Figure 4. Even with the 15% aromatic content of the JP-8, there was only about 1.5 volume % of methane in the reformate and negligible higher hydrocarbons.

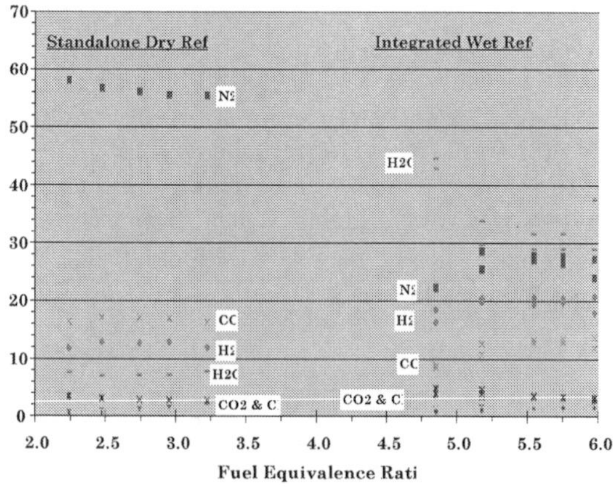

Figure 4: Analysis POX and Steam Reforming of JP-8

The reformer was also used to reform on an in-situ basis the residual tars and oils exiting a biomass gasifier operating at ten (10) TPD. A multi-stage version of the reformer was installed immediately after a cyclone separator used to remove particulate matter. Pictures of the reformer being readied for installation and installed are shown in Figure 5. The design of the unit was based on laboratory data developed using mixtures of Benzene – Toluene – Xylene (BTX) with some heavier compounds added. Data for a typical laboratory run is shown in Table 1. The output gas stream was run through a water gas shift to adjust the H_2:CO ratio prior to being fed to a mixed alcohols synthesis step. The experiments used steam and air as oxidants for the autothermal reforming.

Figure 5: Reformer for residual tars and oils

Table 1: Input and Output for Reforming BTX

	Dry Gas	Air In	O_2 In	H_2O In	BTX In
Run	L/min	L/min	L/min	g/min	g/min
4	50	52	0	1.7	5.9

			Mole %	Output			
Run	H_2	N_2	CO	CO_2	BTX	CH_4	H_20
4	12	54	21	7	0	3	6

A plasma reformer was also used to reform anaerobic digester gas (~75% methane, 25% CO_2). The sulfur compounds and siloxanes had been removed from the input gas stream prior to being entered into the reformer. The reformer used a combination of steam and air as oxidant for the autothermal reforming to generate a synthesis gas at an approximate 2:1 ratio of H_2:CO. The synthesis gas mixture was fed to a Fischer Tropsch reactor operating at 225° C and 300 psig to produce liquid hydrocarbons. The output was analyzed to by ASTM methods and showed a energy density of 46.5 KJ/gram (diesel is ~46 KJ/gram) and a very good 60.2 cetane rating.

Recently, a test program was conducted that reformed a mixture of solvents condensed from a paint booth with the objective of producing hydrogen for fuel cell powered fork lifts. The gas stream from the reformer would be run through a activated carbon filter to remove any residual hydrocarbons, sent to a water gas shift reactor to maximize hydrogen content, fed to a pressure swing absorption system to remove CO_2, and then stored for use by the fork lifts. The tests used pure oxygen and steam as the oxidants and operated in an autothermal mode. The input hydrocarbons were vaporized prior to entry to the reformer and mixed with steam to prevent carbon formation as the mixture was preheated. The input solvents were a mixture of long chain hydrocarbons and cyclic hydrocarbons provided by the customer from actual operations. The output gas stream was analyzed using an on-line gas chromatograph. A small slip stream was fed to an open burner to monitor flame color. The data showed good conversion. The data for residual hydrocarbons on a typical run is shown in Figure 6 and a picture of the flame for the same run is shown in Figure 7.

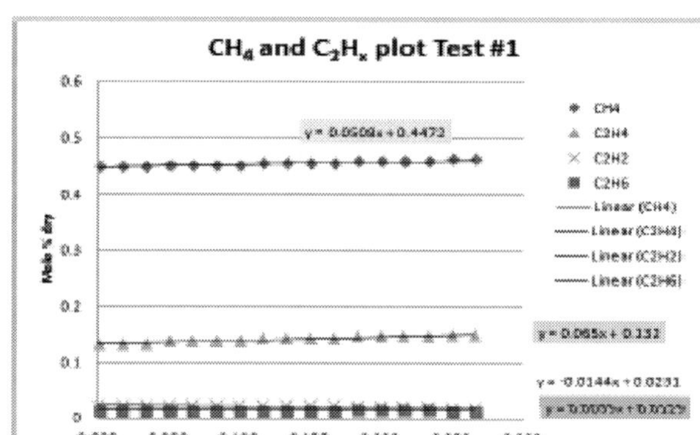

Figure 6: Residual Hydrocarbons – Reformed Solvents

The clear blue color of the flame from the synthesis gas shown in Figure 7 indicates very little in the way of residual hydrocarbons. This fact was confirmed by the GC analysis shown in Figure 6 and a subsequent analysis of samples that were extracted from the output stream and sent to an external laboratory for analysis.

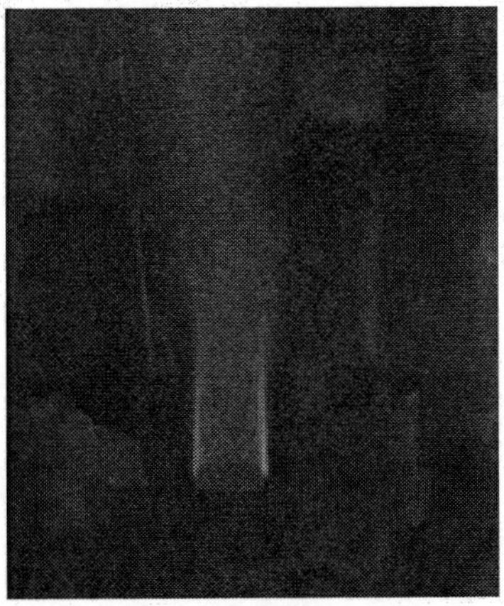

Figure 8: Flame from Reformed Solvents

One of the problems with reforming of heavy hydrocarbons such as the solvents in the testing is the formation of carbon. Some of the more refractory hydrocarbons undergo cracking when exposed to high temperatures and various forms of carbon can be created. The change in pressure was monitored during the solvent reformation and it actually showed a slight decrease. A plot of the ΔP at the start of the tests is shown in Figure 9.

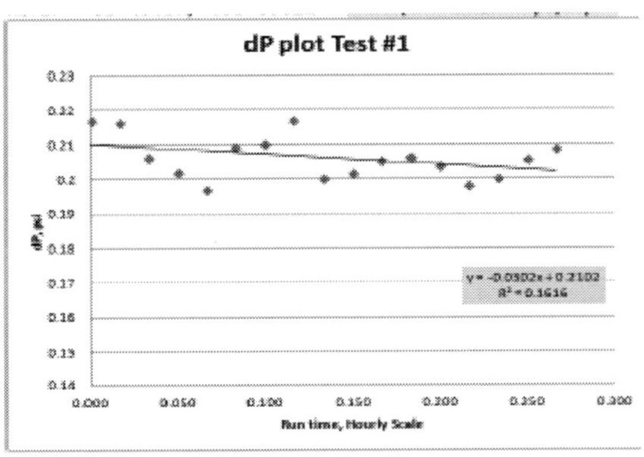

Figure 9: Pressure Drop - Initial Testing

The trend continued over time with later tests showing the same slight downward trend in pressure drop. A composite of pressure drop data from tests 8 - 11 is shown in Figure 10. The unit was not cleaned between tests.

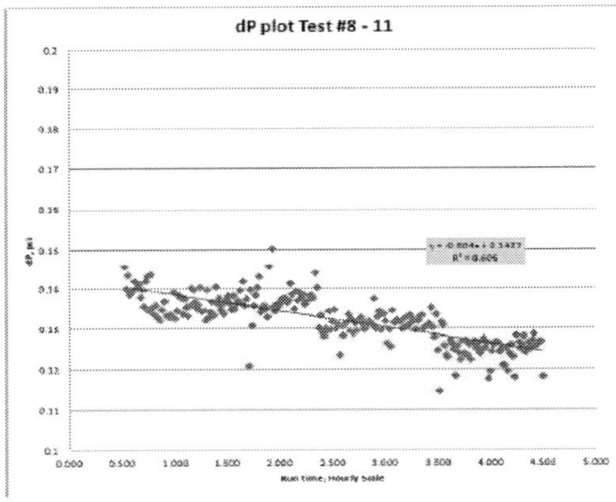

Figure 10: Pressure Drop – Latter Tests

Summary:

Ceramatec has developed a reforming technology that can successfully reform a variety of hydrocarbons. Anything from natural gas to mixtures of cyclic hydrocarbons has been shown to reform successfully. The plasma-catalyzed reformer has been demonstrated to be sulfur-tolerant in reforming feedstock containing over 1000 ppmw total sulfur and in excess of 15 volume % aromatics. Non-methane hydrocarbon slip is negligible. The reformer operation is soot free as evidenced by low pressure drop change and the power consumption for the plasma is on the order of 1 – 3% of fuel LHV. When combined with a water gas shift reactor and an appropriate gas cleaning system, the reformer can provide a stream of hydrogen similar to that generated by a steam methane reformer.

Acknowledgements:

Some of this work has been supported by various agencies of the United States Department of Defense, the United States Department of Energy, and the State of Wyoming. Much of the work has been funded by private corporate entities. Basic technology development on the plasma reformer was done in conjunction with ECP in France.

Revealing Chemical Mechanisms of Solid Oxide Fuel Cells with Operando Optical Studies

Syed N. Qadri[1,2], John D. Kirtley[1,2], Daniel A. Steinhurst[3], Bryan Eichhorn[4], Robert Walker[5] and Jeffrey C. Owrutsky[2]

[1] Naval Research Laboratory/National Research Council Postdoctoral Fellow
[2]Chemistry Division, Code 6111, U. S. Naval Research Laboratory, Washington, DC 20375, USA
[3]Nova Research, Inc., Alexandria, VA 22308. USA
[4] Department of Chemistry and Biochemistry, University of Maryland, College Park, MD 20742, USA
[5] Department of Chemistry and Biochemistry, Montana State University, Bozeman, MT 59717, USA

Abstract: *Solid oxide fuels cells (SOFCs) are promising devices for fuel-flexible and efficient power generation. The high temperatures (>700 °C) required for operation enable the use of a variety of fuels. However, avoiding degradation by carbon deposition remains a challenge. Innovative operando optical methods, including Raman and infrared emission spectroscopy (FTIRES) as well as near infrared thermal imaging (NIRTI) have been used to demonstrate that operating SOFCs with dry or steam reforming of methane shows more cooling on anode surfaces but less carbon formation than for methane alone. In previous studies of hydrocarbons other than methane, cooling due to fuel cracking on the anode correlated with more carbon formation. The cooling trends observed with methane fuels depend on operating temperature (700-800 °C) and reforming conditions. Anode cooling with steam reforming is intermediate between dry reforming and plain methane while carbon accumulation correlate with less cooling. The amount of carbon formed was demonstrated using electrochemical oxidation while monitoring the evolution of species over the anode. Electrochemical oxidation measurements indicated that more carbon was formed with cells operating on methane fuel and dry reformed methane produced the least. FTIRES corroborates these results by showing there is more carbon dioxide and carbon monoxide produced by electrochemical oxidation of carbon after the fuel stream is terminated. The results of these optical studies indicate that both steam and dry reforming of methane are viable for SOFCs in terms of decreased carbon accumulation during operation.*

Keywords: solid oxide fuel cells; operando spectroscopy; thermal imaging; in situ studies; methane reforming

Introduction

Carbon deposition from the use of hydrocarbon fuels leads to anode degradation and has been the focus for solid oxide fuel cell (SOFC) material research. When using simple hydrocarbons such as methane and methanol, the anode is susceptible to carbon formation. Reforming with steam and carbon dioxide can be effective in alleviating carbon formation during operation, but these methods would benefit from systematic approaches to improve SOFC durability. Direct *operando* methods are needed to better understand the conditions that influence fuel chemistry and stability of electrodes. Recently, *operando* optical techniques that directly probe the SOFC anode have been developed, including Raman spectroscopy to track molecularly specific surface features,[1-2] near infrared thermal imaging (NIRTI) to temporally and spatially resolve surface temperature changes,[3-4] and Fourier transform infrared emission spectroscopy (FTIRES)[5] to measure mid-infrared emissive signatures of gas species over the anode. These studies among others have provided direct observation of the chemical and structural evolution of the electrode as well as reaction products under various conditions. However, many mechanistic details at the anode remain elusive.

Despite extensive reports on the use of Ni-YSZ (yttrium stabilized zirconia) and ceria based anodes for electrode materials in solid oxide fuel cells, previous work has primarily utilized post-facto testing and electrochemical analysis. The current work describes experiments that probe 1) infrared emission spectra from reforming/electrochemical products and 2) surface temperature changes from Ni/YSZ anodes of working cells. Most work reported previously shows data collected separately using each technique, but recently we have begun measuring emission spectra and surface temperature changes simultaneously using a novel duplex technique that combines FTIRES with NIRTI. All *operando* measurements have been performed on fully operational SOFCs at 700 - 800 °C. This report details first how dry reforming of methane can influence surface cooling of an operating SOFC anode. CO is shown to be an important intermediate that is modulated by different reforming conditions. Carbon deposition on Ni-based anodes is quantified with FTIRES and electrochemical methods. This manuscript then describes a targeted approach that assesses carbon removal using steam. Measurements from FTIRES and NIR thermal imaging indicate that carbon was oxidized to CO and CO_2 early, and to CO_2 only as more carbon was removed from the anode. Ultimately, this study is part of a larger effort to understand chemical mechanisms under a variety of hydrocarbon fuels and conditions, including fuel cell and electrolysis modes with particular regard to how these are influenced by electrochemical load.

Experimental

SOFC Apparatus. The optically-accessible assembly used has been discussed previously.[5] Ni-YSZ anode-supported cells (MSRI) were used in addition to Ni-YSZ electrolyte-supported (Nextech Materials). The assembled SOFC manifold was placed inside a tube furnace and heated to 700-800 °C. A CaF_2 window is used to seal the front of the furnace and an additional 50.8 mm OD alumina tube bridges the space between the furnace and the duplex FTIR spectrometer and camera. The entire optical path is purged with nitrogen or argon. The duplex set-up (Figure 1) relies on using a beamsplitter to transmit (~95%) emission for FTIRES and reflect a small portion (~5%) for NIRTI. A 2 mm thick CaF_2 window is used as the beamsplitter and it is antireflection coated to avoid a double image. Images were collected using a program written with LabView v8.5 and calibrated with a thermocouple.

Flows into the SOFC were regulated with mass flow controllers (Brooks Instrument). Constant flows of 150 sccm and 65 sccm Ar were delivered to the cathode and anode, respectively. Fuel measurements were taken under an additional 25 sccm CH_4 and 4 sccm H_2O for steam reforming. Dry reforming of methane was carried out with 25 sccm CH_4 along with 25 sccm CO_2. Cell polarization was maintained and electrochemical measurements were conducted with a potentiostat (Gamry Reference 3000 Potentiostat/Galvanostat/ZRA). Voltammetry and electrochemical impedance measurements were made before, during, and after each trial to monitor cell function (data not shown). The maximum current (I_{max}) recorded for each cell before trials was used as a benchmark for cell performance, and then used to standardize under-load conditions between different cells and trials, which are defined at 3/4 I_{max}. Open circuit voltages (OCV) were recorded to electrochemically monitor leaks and degradation.

FTIRES Measurements. All spectra were taken with a Mattson Instruments, Inc. spectrometer (Model #: RS-10000). The source was removed from the optical path and an external mirror was used to redirect emission from the SOFC anode into the detector. Data were collected as 16 averaged scans with a resolution of 0.5 cm^{-1} over a range of 500-4000 cm^{-1}. Two successive sets of data were collected. The first set of spectra was taken during fuel exposure while the cell current was increased in increments. Each trial was ~ 600 s long and FTIRES scans were started at every 100 s after the beginning of each trial. Background scans were taken immediately prior to fuel exposure. All data were corrected versus the most recent background and baselines are leveled with a linear correction.

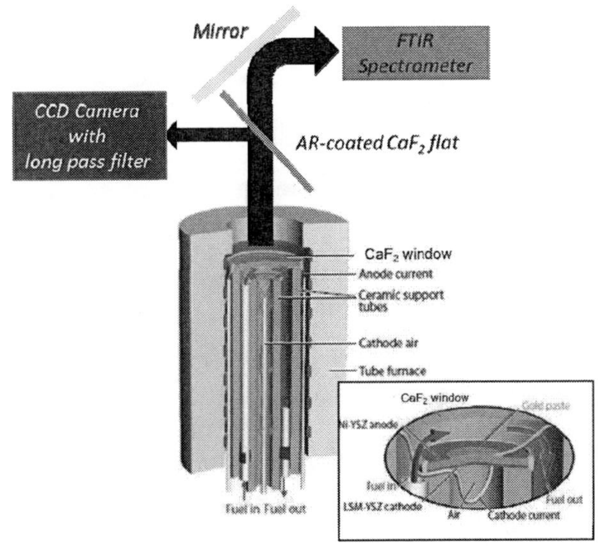

Figure 1. Diagram of SOFC duplex setup. Red arrows indicate direction of fuel flow to anode, while blue arrows indicate direction of oxygen flows to cathode. Adapted from R.J. Kee.

Results and Discussion

Methane Reforming

An intriguing result from our simulated biogas (BG) SOFC studies is that the dry reforming of methane, using carbon dioxide, is a heterogeneous process that results in more anode cooling than occurs with methane alone. This is evident in the thermal images and temperature time series (Figure 2) when the fuel is introduced.[6,7] In previous studies of larger hydrocarbons and alcohols, cooling due to fuel cracking on the anode correlated well with increased carbon formation. The cooling from dry reforming is strongest at 800 °C and weakest at 700 °C.

Carbon was also monitored on the surface of anode-supported cells using Raman spectroscopy and throughout the bulk anode using FTIRES with chronopotentiometry. Raman spectra collected during SOFC operation show that more surface carbon is formed with methane relative to to dry reformed methane. The amount of carbon formed was also measured with FTIRES after the fuel stream was terminated.[6,7] FTIRES corroborated the Raman results by showing there was more CO_2 and CO produced by electrochemical oxidation of anodic carbon after trials when only methane had been the fuel. More CO and CO_2 were observed for biogas than methane during operation, which is expected since CO_2 is a component of the fuel stream.

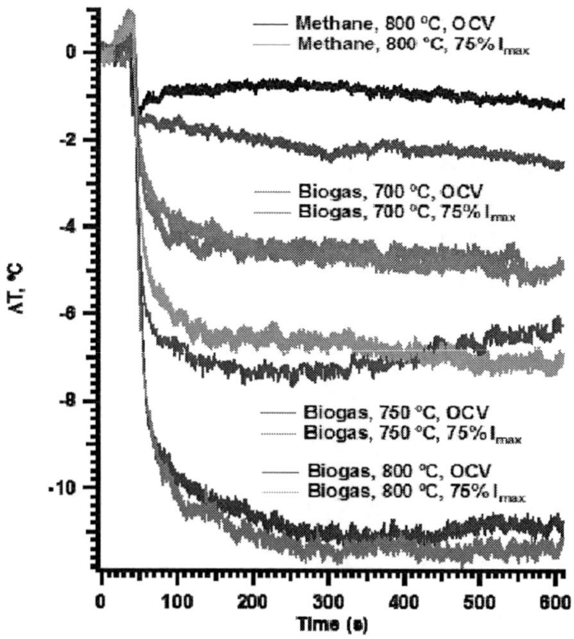

Figure 2. Time-series plots of temperature changes observed on anode-supported SOFCs for CH_4 and BG at various temperatures and load conditions.[7]

In our current work, we explore how SOFC operation with steam reforming compares to with plain methane and dry reforming. The amount of carbon formed on the anode surface was also characterized by spectrochronopotentiometry (SCP) under various conditions, including a range of temperatures. Steam reforming of methane results in an intermediate amount of cooling between plain and dry reforming of methane, and also an intermediate amount of carbon at the temperatures tested (Figure 3). FTIR emission spectra were collected for each reforming series (Figure 4). The intensity of the $CO_{(g)}$ band was greater with steam or dry reforming. These data suggest that CO is a reforming product.

Carbon gasification by steam in operational SOFCs.

An additional study relevant to the steam reforming mechanism used H_2O to remove carbon preformed by exposing an anode-supported cell to CH_4. The SOFC was first exposed for ~10 min to CH_4, followed by a ~10 min purge to remove CH_4, followed by introduction of H_2O. Figure 5 shows that H_2O oxidized carbon to CO and CO_2 initially, and this was accompanied by the strongest surface cooling. Later, only CO_2 formed and was associated with less surface cooling. A steep rise in cell potential coincident with decreasing CO_x products at the end of the trial indicates that carbon was completely oxidized. The sharp drop in "temperature" after 1500 s is likely instead an emissivity change as Ni is oxidized.

These studies when compared with theoretical studies predict that carbon oxidation by steam may favor the endothermic formation of CO gas when more surface CO is present (at early times, when surface carbon is also abundant), while the less endothermic formation of CO_2 gas is favored when less surface CO is present.

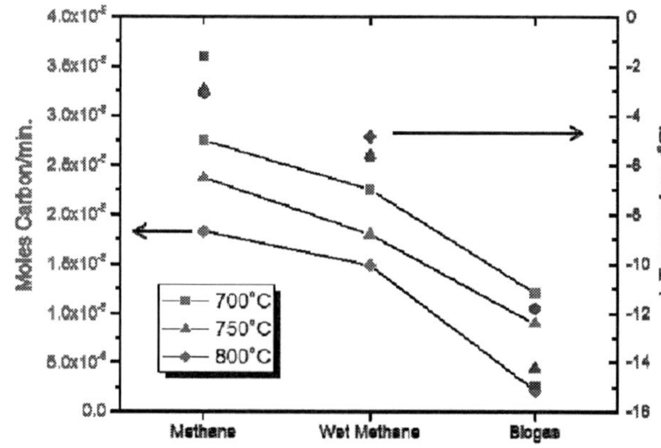

Figure 3. Comparison of carbon deposition rates and surface temperature changes during fuel exposure for reforming conditions identified on the x-axis. Data shown were taken under 75% I_{max} load on anode-supported cells.

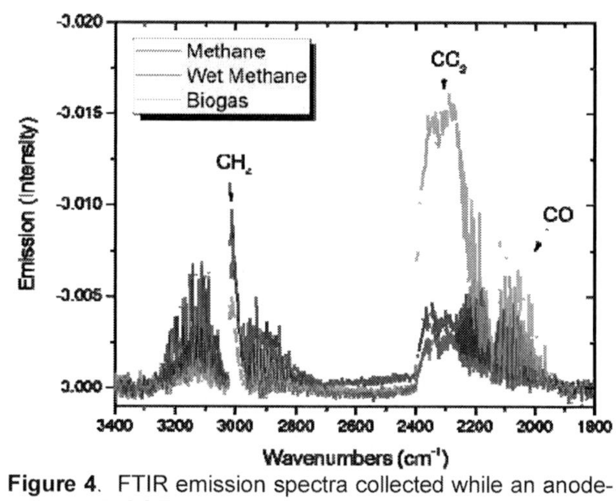

Figure 4. FTIR emission spectra collected while an anode-supported SOFC operated (800 °C) with plain methane (red), steam-reformed methane (blue) and dry reformed methane (green).

Conclusions

A duplex system that combines NIRTI and FTIRES has been demonstrated to more reliably correlate temperature changes in working SOFCs and for identification of fuel intermediates and products. IR

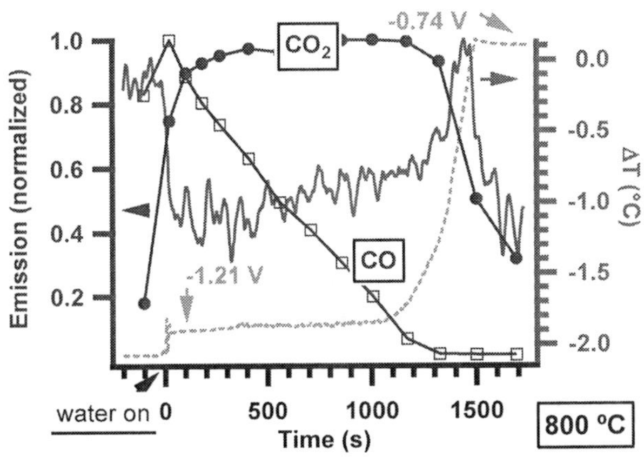

Figure 5. Normalized emission intensities (left axis) of CO_2 (2292 cm^{-1}, blue closed circles) and CO (2094 cm^{-1}, blue open squares) are plotted against time while steam oxidizes carbon on an anode-supported SOFC at 800 °C. Surface temperature changes were measured simultaneously (solid, red line, right axis). These ΔT values have been smoothed with a 100-point boxcar average and are relative to conditions (H_2/Ar) prior to the preceding methane exposure. Open circuit voltage (dashed light blue) is also shown (no axis).

signatures of CO product are stronger under reforming conditions. This is the first report highlighting a duplex technique of thermal imaging and IR spectroscopy of gas-phase and surface species on a working electrode. These *operando* studies provide clear evidence that polarization and temperature affect chemical and physical processes at the anode. Furthermore, these techniques provide data that can be used to evaluate the success of models that accurately describe SOFC chemistry.

Acknowledgements

We thank the Office of Naval Research for funding. We also acknowledge helpful discussions with Dr. Harold D. Ladouceur and Dr. Andrew B. Baronavski (NRL). SNQ and JDK thank the National Research Council for their postdoctoral fellowships.

References

1. Park, S. E.; Chang, J.-S.; Lee, K.-W. *Carbon Dioxide Utilization for Global Sustainability: Proceedings of the 7th International Conference on Carbon Dioxide Utilization* **2004**, 153.
2. Graves, C.; Ebbesen, S. D.; Mogensen, M.; Lackner, K. S. *Renewable and Sustainable Energy Reviews* **2011,** *15* (1), 1-23.
3. (a) Benson, E. E.; Kubiak, C. P.; Sathrum, A. J.; Smieja, J. M. *Chemical Society Reviews* **2009,** *38* (1), 89-99; (b) Savéant, J.-M. *Chemical reviews* **2008,** *108* (7), 2111-2112.
4. Ebbesen, S. D.; Mogensen, M. *Journal of Power Sources* **2009,** *193* (1), 349-358.
5. Pomfret, M. B.; Owrutsky, J. C.; Walker, R. A. *Analytical chemistry* **2007,** *79* (6), 2367-2372.
6. Kirtley, J. D.; Pomfret, M.B.; Steinhurst, D.A.; Owrutsky, J. C.; Walker, R. A. *Phys. Chem. Chem. Phys.* **2014,** *16*, 227.
7. Kirtley, J. D.; Pomfret, M.B.; Steinhurst, D.A.; Owrutsky, J. C.; Walker, R. A. *J. Phys. Chem.* **2015,** *C 119*, 12781
8. Kirtley, J. D.; Halat, D.M.; McIntyre, M.D.; Eigenbrodt, B.C.; Walker, R. A. *Anal. Chem.* **2012,** *84*, 9745-9753.

High Temperature Polymer Electrolyte Fuel Cell Developments for the Mobile Power Generation from Logistic (Liquid) Fuels

Carsten Cremers, Maria S. Rau, André Niedergesäß, Florina Jung, Karsten Pinkwart, Jens Tübke
Department for Applied Electrochemistry
Fraunhofer Institute for Chemical Technology (ICT)
Joseph-von-Fraunhofer-Str. 7, 76327 Pfinztal, Germany

Abstract: The tolerance of HT-PEMFC against fuel impurities expected in reformed logistic fuels was investigated on catalyst and single cell level. It could be shown, that standard platinum catalyst at the typical operation temperature of a HT-PEMFC show already a high level of tolerance against main impurities such as ethene or toluene. The tolerance for toluene includes a tolerance for small amounts of thiophene which was present as impurity in the toluene sample. Hydrogen sulphide as usual model substance for sulphurous compounds is tolerate up to about 20 ppm. Here it could be shown that a modification of the catalyst with an additional base metal component can increase the tolerance and even provide hydrogen sulphide oxidation capabilities.

On a fuel cell module level the integration of a typical reformed methanol HT-PEMFC module with a battery electric passenger car was investigated. Because of the very similar operation temperatures of HT-PEMFC stack and methanol steam reformer the realisation of a rather compact system was possible. Analysing the properties of the fuel it will be shown that methanol operated system might be an alternative in particular for cold environments.

Keywords: fuel cell; HT-PEMFC; fuel processing; logistic fuels; methanol

Introduction

The generation of electrical power in the range of a few kW to few tenth of kW is becoming more and more important for modern military operation; e.g. for the recharging of larger numbers of secondary batteries for dismounted soldiers in forward operating bases or as auxiliary power unit on board of a military vehicle during silent watch operations. In many of these situations power generation with low noise and IR signature and/or low emissions is required. Thus the use of fuel cells as power generators is in principle beneficial. One of the draw backs of today's fuel cells is, however, the selection of fuels which can be used with them. In order to be logistically viable it would be best if a standard logistic fuel such as NATO F-34 Jet fuel or NATO F-56 diesel fuel could be used. The fuel should however be at least liquid, easy to handle and readily available.

The use of logistic fuels will require the use of a reformer in order to convert the long chain hydrocarbon fuel into a hydrogen rich gas stream which can be further used in the fuel cell. As the logistic fuels allow for high level of organic and sulphur organic impurities the fuel stream will also contain higher level of impurities. One class or impurities are aromatic compounds. For LT-PEMFC as has been reported that toluene as model aromatic compound can significantly reduce the performance of a LT-PEMFC (1). Another substance class which might be present are alkenes. For the model substance ethene no significant effects on LT-PEMFC were reported if the fuel was highly humidified (2). The level of humidification in HT-PEMFC is, however, often lower. Finally, CO and hydrogen sulphide are known impurities in reformed gas streams. Former studies by Schmidt and Baurmeister have shown that HT-PEMFC have a high tolerance to CO in absence of H_2S which is however reduced if H_2S is presence simultaneously (3).

In this study the effect of these model substances on Pt/C catalyst under HT-PEMFC conditions was investigated using a set-up which allowed for the parallel investigation of the products formed by online mass spectrometery. Test results were partly verified also in single cell test.

Because of the operation temperature of 160 °C which is rather close to the steam reforming temperature of methanol of about 250 °C and the high tolerance of CO HT.PEMFC systems using reformed methanol have become commercial for stationary applications. In this study the integration of such a module into battery electric passenger car as range extender was investigated.

Experimental set-up

The main part of the work was done using a set-up for differential electrochemical mass spectrometry under HT-PEMFC conditions which was recently developed in our group (4). The set-up used here was slightly modified compared to the version described in (4) by changing the ethanol pump and evaporator against mass flow controllers to dose hydrogen and the gaseous test substances to the working electrode compartment. For tests with toluene the gas stream was bubbled through a flask with toluene at ambient temperature so that the gas flow was saturated with toluene at ambient temperature. For the catalyst tests small circular gas diffusion electrode were prepared from commercial 20% Pt/C catalyst (Johnson & Matthey) as described earlier (5).

Single cell tests were conducted in a commercial test rig "Evaluator C050" by FuelCon AG Germany. The MEA specimens were fixed in the contained cell fixture qFC 25/100 by balticFuelCells Germany. MEAS tested in this study were purchased either from Danish Power Systems Type Daprozol® 101 or from Advent. Break-in of the MEAs was always conducted in accordance with the manufacturer's recommendations.

For the vehicle integration a reformed methanol fuel cell module with integrated methanol steam reformer and liquid could HT-EMFC stack Type H3 5000 from Serenergy was considered. The system was configured with an integrated DC/DC converter to give an output voltage of 450 VDC to match the vehicles intermediate circuit voltage.

Results impurity tolerances

Despite of the low humidity level under which the catalyst tests were performed the presence of 20 ppm of ethene in H_2 had a slightly positive effect on the potentiostatic measured currents at higher potentials. In this potential region also a slight increase of the CO_2 release is observed. Thereby the main part of CO_2 is most likely being released from the carbon support (cf. fig 1).

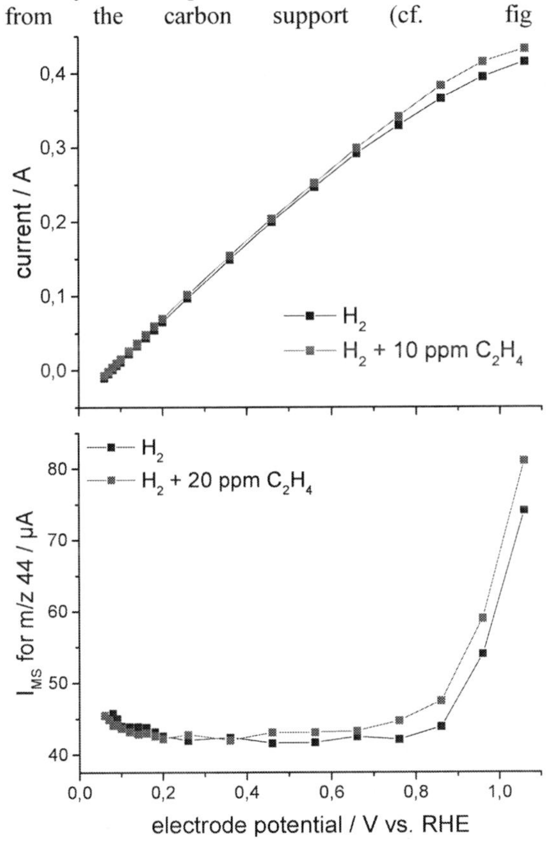

Figure 1. Faradaic current and MS data for the hydrogen oxidation reaction at a Pt/C electrode in presence and absence of 20 ppm ethene

This result is confirmed by single cell tests. Here upon a repeated start-stop cycling accelerated stress test protocol executed with hydrogen with 10 ppm of ethene as impurity showed no degradation for intermittently recorded iV-curves (cf. fig.2).

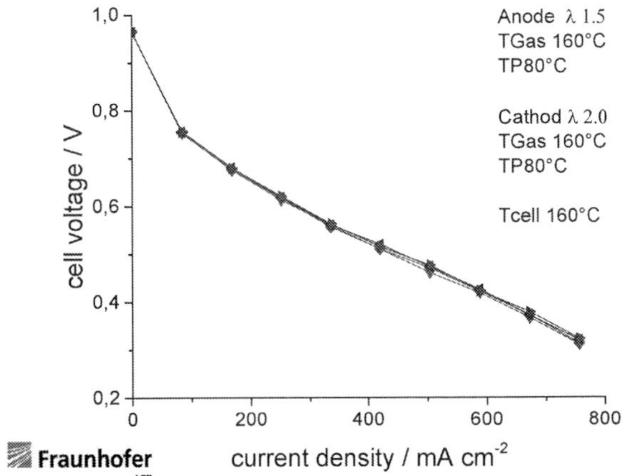

Figure 2. iV curves of an Advent MEA recorded intermittent to a start-stop AST protocol under operation with H_2 + 10 ppm C_2H_4 fuel and air

For toluene as impurity no effect is apparent at low potentials. At very high potentials a slight reduction of the catalyst is observed (cf. fig. 3).

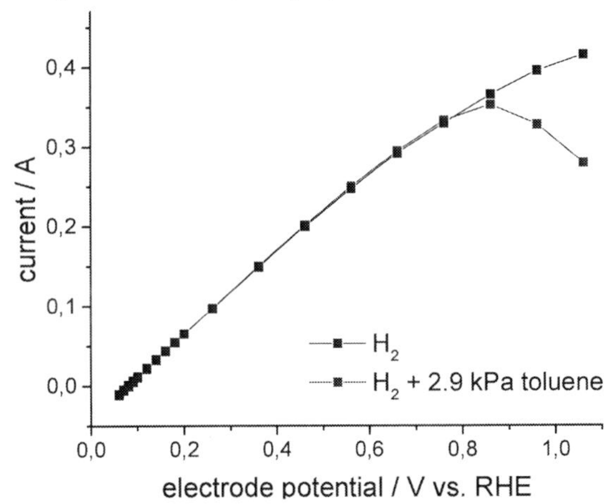

Figure 3. Faradaic current of the hydrogen oxidation in at Pt/C for pure hydrogen and hydrogen saturated with toluene at ambient temperature

In the mass spectrometer it can be observed that the thiophene peak at m/z 83 gets reduced at these high potentials (cf. fig 4)

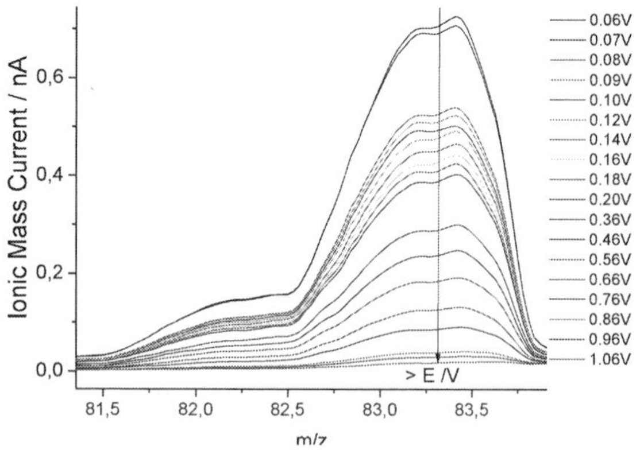

Figure 4. Potential dependence of the thiophene mass spectrum signal observed via MS during the oxidation of toluene saturated hydrogen

The presence of hydrogen sulphide itself will cause a lost of activity of platinum especially in the relevant low potential region. However, by adding another base metal M this effect can be over compensated (cf. fig. 5)

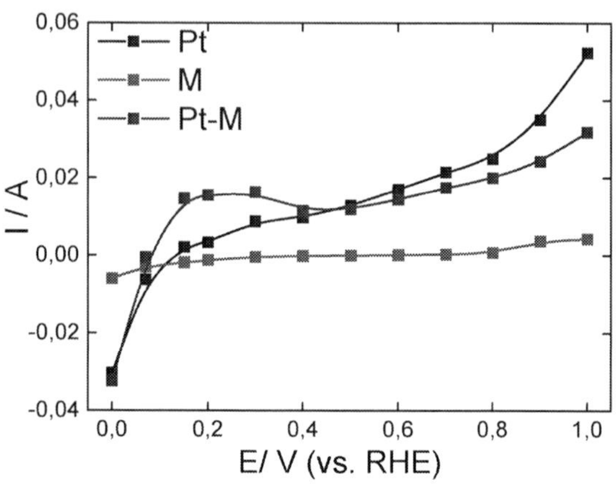

Figure 5. Potential dependence current response of different electrodes in a 40 vol% H2S balance H2 atmosphere at 145 °C

On MEA level high level it was shown by Danish Power Systems that a modification of the electrode to increase its durability under operation with highly humidified fuel gases (cf. fig. 6 upper). For the same type of MEA we could show that the modification also enhances the MEAs performance for operation with hydrogen sulphide containing gases as well as its stability under these operating conditions (cf. fig 6 lower).

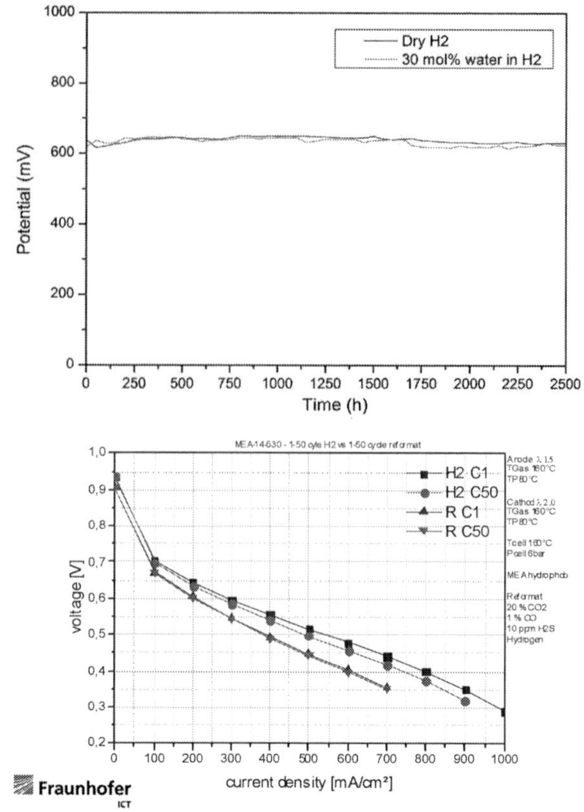

Figure 5. Stability of new Dapozol® 101 MEA operated with highly humid fuel gas (d.p. 80 °C), upper continues load at 200 mA cm^{-2}, lower using start-stop cycling as accelerated stress test with hydrogen and synth. reformate as fuel.

Results fuel cell vehicle integration

An important factor for the safe integration of the fuel cell into the vehicle in a confined space is the safe removal of the produced heat. Basically heat can be transported to and from the stack via the anode supply and exhaust, the cathode supply and exhaust and the coolant. Using technical data provided by Serenergy the thermal load on the three pathways was estimated. It was found that at high electrical loads the main part of the thermal energy will be removed via the cooling cycle. Albeit the heat rejected via the cathode exhaust can still achieve close to 2 kW and thus should not be neglected. As the anode input is always slightly warmer than the stack the system exhibits a small net heat uptake on the anode side (cf. fig. 6). This needed to be considered in the system integration where isolation of the cathode exhaust line in the mounting box and of parts close to the chassis is required.

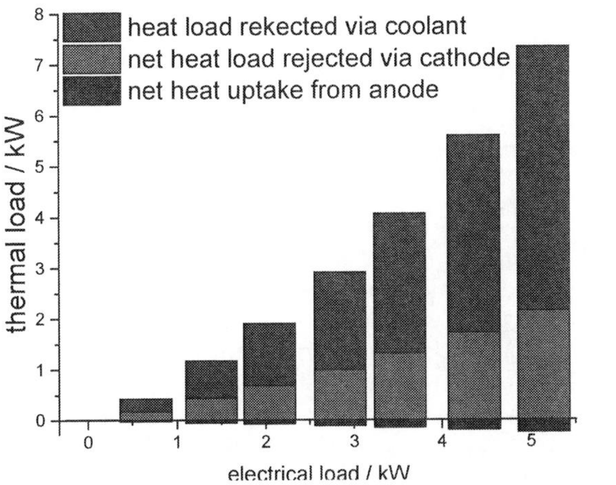

Figure 6. Estimated load dependent heat dissipation from a 5 kW rated H3 5000 RMFC module

This was taken into account for the system integration design shown in fig. 7.

With respect to possible military usage of such systems the use of methanol water mixture might be of interest as they offer a lower freeing point than most conventional fuels (cf. fig. 8)

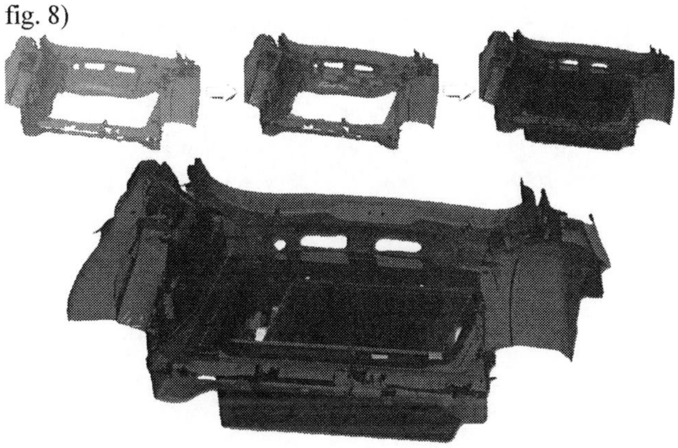

Figure 7. Vehicle integration of a 5 kW reformed methanol HT-PEMFC module in to a compact class battery electrical passenger car

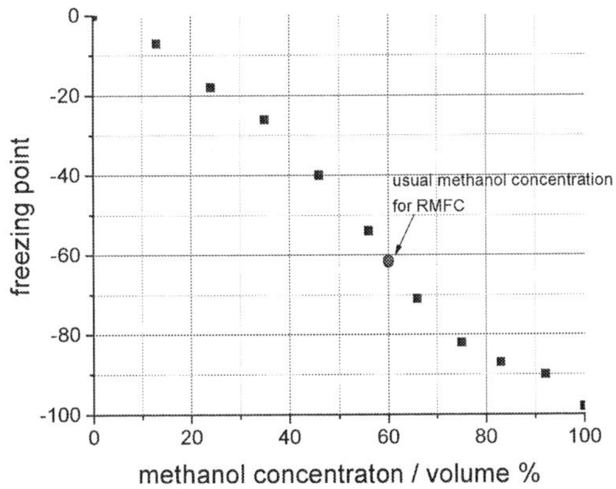

Figure 8. Estimated load dependent heat dissipation from a 5 kW rated H3 5000 RMFC module.

Acknowledgements

Financial support of this work by the following organisations is gratefully acknowledged.

German Federal Ministry for Economics and Energy and European Commission in the Frame Work of the Electromobility+ project FCCF-APU (www.fccf-apu.eu)

State of Baden-Württemberg in the framework of the project REM030 (www.rem2030.de).

German Federal Ministry for Defence, Bundeswehr Research Institute for Materials, Fuels and Lubricants (WIWeB) under contract E/E210/AF020/CF062

References

1. R. W. Lindström, T. Åkermark and G. Lindbergh, *Electrochimica Acta*, **55**, 7643 (2010).
2. K. Kortsdottir, R. W. Lindström and G. Lindbergh, *International Journal of Hydrogen Energy*, **38**, 497 (2013).
3. T. J. Schmidt and J. Baurmeister, *ECS Transactions*, **3**, 861 (2006).
4. C. Niether, M. S. Rau, C. Cremers, D. J. Jones, K. Pinkwart and J. Tübke, *Journal of Electroanalytical Chemistry*, **747**, 97 (2015).
5. M. Rau, C. Cremers and J. Tübke, *International Journal of Hydrogen Energy*, **40**, 5439 (2015).

Sulfur Tolerant, Compact, Portable Fuel Reformer System

Subir Roychoudhury, Christian Junaedi, Saurabh Vilekar
Precision Combustion, Inc.
sroychoudhury@precision-combustion.com

Abstract

Successful development of efficient fuel cell systems fueled with practical fuels is highly dependent on the effectiveness and durability of reforming systems for supplying H2 or stack-quality syngas and permitting stable, coke-free system operation. Some of the present challenges affecting widespread deployment of fuel cell power generation solutions are sulfur poisoning, coke formation, and water recovery for water neutral operation. Practical liquid fuels include distillate fuels such as military jet fuels (consisting of up to 3000 ppmw sulfur), diesels or kerosene, as well as renewable fuels such as bio-diesels. Making these fuels suitable for use in the fuel cell stacks requires: i) reformation of the fuels to minimize higher hydrocarbon content in the reformate to an acceptable level (depending on the fuel cell type); ii) achieving sulfur cleanup to <1 ppmv in the reformate stream in a practical and compact package; iii) process intensification (by closely integrating steam generation, sulfur cleanup, and reforming catalyst in an ultra-compact package); and iv) incurring low parasitic losses and minimized costs by implementing off-the-shelf balance-of-plant (BOP) components. In addition to sulfur-tolerant and coke-free reformer operation, water neutrality is an essential component to the power generation systems. This requires efficient water recovery and separation from the exhaust stream of the fuel cell stack. The ability to achieve all of these objectives demands practical fuel processing systems and fuel cells as well as robust flow management/fluid interface, thermal management, and control algorithms. Precision Combustion, Inc. (PCI) has designed, developed, and demonstrated a small-scale fuel reformer system for adaptation to a single-person portable (1 kWe) fuel cell generator application. The fuel reformer includes the reactants mixing section, reforming catalyst, steam generation heat exchanger, and sulfur trap. It was then integrated with the required BOP components, including fuel/water/air pumps, fuel and water tanks, filters, valves, and controls in a compact package for a stand-alone reformer demonstration system prototype (see Figure). The fuel flexibility (diesels, biofuels, and JP-8) and sulfur tolerance (up to 3000 ppmw sulfur) of this fuel reformer system have been demonstrated, with minimal degradation over long-term operation. Test results showed that the fuel reformer was able to reform JP-8 containing up to 3000 ppmw sulfur, without any upstream sulfur cleanup, in an extremely compact and lightweight package. Fuel cell-quality reformate was produced with <1 ppmv sulfur where the sulfur was removed from the reformate stream as H2S via a readily replaceable filter downstream of the reformer. 70 – 85% reforming efficiency (depending on the fuels tested) was achieved. A 2:1 turndown was also shown. The reformer system was integrated with a 1 kWe SOFC stack and tested for 500 hours to demonstrate fuel cell operation with sulfur laden JP-8 fuel. The test was successful and validated that the reformer system was suitable for meeting the Army's size, weight, and efficiency targets while demonstrating durability (multi 1000-hr operation projected), readiness for integration with 0.3 – 1 kWe fuel cells, and fuel flexibility..

High Current Pulse Discharge of Lithium Air Primary Battery

***Clifford Cook,*[†] *Terrill Atwater,*[†] *Paula Latorre,*[†] *Eugene Nimon,*[‡] *& Steve Visco*[‡]**
[†]US Army, RDECOM, CERDEC
Aberdeen Proving Grounds, MD
[‡] PolyPlus Battery Company
Berkeley, CA

Abstract: *The U.S. Army Communication-Electronics Research, Development, and Engineering Center (CERDEC) and PolyPlus Battery Company have recently achieved a high current pulse discharge of a state of the art lithium air battery, a 4-cell, 2-parallel, 2-series (2p2s) configuration, primary battery. Each cell contains a protected lithium anode, an aqueous electrolyte, and porous carbon cathode. Average battery weight began at 163 g; at the end of discharge average weight was 174 g. Battery OCV was 6.9 V and was discharged at a constant current (CC) of 63 mA with a pulse discharge every hour. The pulse cycle was allowed to continue until CC discharge reached a cutoff voltage of 3.0 V. The cycle repeated 96 times with a maximum current of 943 mA (current density of 11.2 mA/cm^2) was achieved, the highest reported to date for lithium air batteries.*

Keywords: Lithium Air; Pulse Discharge; Current Density; Solid Electrolyte; Aqueous Electrolyte; Air Cathode; .

Introduction

The lithium air battery consists of a lithium metal anode electrochemically coupled through an air cathode to readily available oxygen in the atmosphere. The theoretical specific energy is 13.6 kWh/kg.[1] However, a more practical specific energy of 3,582 Wh/kg should be utilized since the oxygen produces a solid discharge product.[2] At 3,582 Wh/kg, this still gives the lithium air battery a significant advantage over lithium ion (theoretical specific energy = 448 Wh/kg) and is the primary driving force for research and development efforts. Two lithium air systems have been developed, non-aqueous and aqueous.[3] This system uses the aqueous approach, which is governed by the following electrochemical reactions:

Anode: $Li^0 \rightleftharpoons Li^+ + e^-$ -3.045 V
Cathode: $O_2 + 2H_2O + 4e^- \rightleftharpoons 4OH^-$ +0.401 V
Overall: $4Li^0 + O_2 + 2H_2O \rightleftharpoons 4LiOH$ 3.45 V

The historic drawback for this system is on open-circuit and low-drain discharge, the self-discharge of the lithium metal can be rapid due to parasitic corrosion reactions. Control of this parasitic reaction and storage of the generated LiOH product is key to realizing the full potential of the lithium air battery.

In this study, we have discharged several lithium air cells and batteries in 2p2s configuration. The testing including a constant current discharge of a cell resulting in 798 Wh/kg and the pulse discharge of a battery with remarkably high current density, 11.2 mA/cm^2, the highest reported to date for lithium air batteries. In addition, these batteries are capable of extremely high energy density, ~500 Wh/kg.

Experimental

Description of cell. This particular system can operate at high columbic efficiencies because of the addition of a protective film, a sealed solid electrolyte anode system known as a protected lithium electrode (PLE). [4-6] The PolyPlus PLE is a hermetically sealed anode system containing two solid electrolyte sheets sandwiching an interfacial electrolyte and lithium foil. The exposed solid electrolyte provides intimate contact with the aqueous electrolyte and cathode, while preventing water and other reducible species from reaching the lithium metal within. The interface electrolyte is needed to maintain ionic contact as the lithium metal is depleted during discharge. In addition, it will prevent lithium from chemical reaction with the solid electrolyte. The solid electrolyte, $Li_{1.3}Al_{0.3}Ti_{1.7}(PO_4)_3$ (LATP) is a water stable, high Li^+ conducting (~10^{-3} S/cm) glass ceramic. The storage of the discharge products is done with the cathode system shown in Figure 1. The double sided cell design is needed to accommodate the lithium volume change during discharge. From top to bottom: The cell casing is perforated to allow air flow. The gas diffusion electrode (GDE)/cathode contains a gas diffusion membrane, carbon Teflon coating, and thin film Ti current collector. The gas diffusion membrane is needed to regulate air flow. The carbon/Teflon coating is needed to facilitate a triple phase

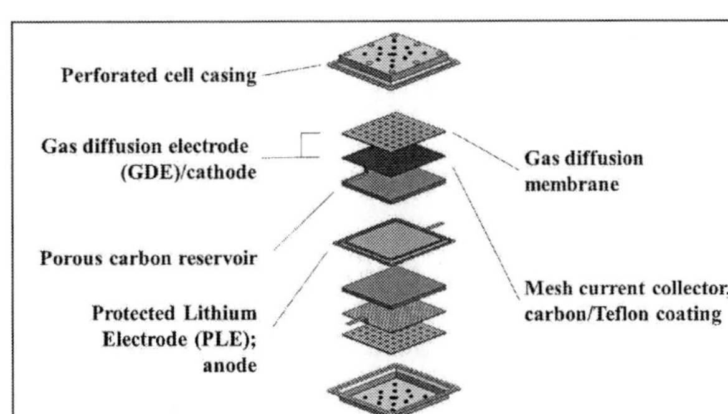

Figure 1: Exploded view of primary lithium air cell.

boundary. Carbon acts as a charge transfer medium for the electrochemical reaction, while Teflon prevents the cathode from flooding either with aqueous electrolyte (located in the porous carbon reservoir) or external humidity. Finally, the porous carbon reservoir holds the aqueous electrolyte and by-products of the electrochemical reaction.

Experimental set up. All batteries and cells were discharged with an Arbin battery cycler with MITS Pro Software. Ten PolyPlus Li-Air cells, 10 Ah, were discharged in ambient conditions at room temperature. All cells were weighed and averaged 36.1 g +/- 0.5%. Cells #1 and #2 were stored for 49 days in ambient conditions before discharging. The schedule was as follows: Rest for 1 hour monitoring open circuit voltage. Continuous discharge at various discharge currents (see Table 1) until reaching cutoff voltage of 1.5 V. All cells were discharged under ambient conditions with no humidity control (RH ranging from ~45% to 74%) and in the horizontal position with the exception of cell #2, which was placed in the vertical position. All battery cells were configured 2p2s and discharged in a Russells model GD-32-3 humidity/environmental chamber, which was held constant at 25 °C in 50 % relative humidity. The test fixture is shown in Figure 2 and prototype battery is shown in Figure 3. Batteries were discharged using either a constant current (CC) or pulse discharge. Constant current profile: rest at OCV for 2 hours, constant current (CC) discharge at 63 mA (0.75 mA/cm^2) until reaching cut-off of 3.0 V. Pulse discharge profile: rest at OCV for 2 hours, CC discharge at 63 mA (0.75 mA/cm^2) with a pulse discharge every hour. Pulses were done by ramping current at 5 mA/sec until voltage drop reached 2.0 V. The system was then returned to CC discharge at 63 mA (0.75 mA/cm^2).

Table 1: Summary of results including operating voltage, discharge current, capacity, and energy density to 1.5V.

† indicates cells that were stored 49 days in ambient conditions prior to discharge
‡ indicates vertical position

Cell	Discharg e Current	Current Density	Total Capacity	Specific Energy
	(mA)	(mA/cm^2)	(Ah)	(Wh/kg)
1†	12.7	0.6	10.6	798.5
2‡†	12.7	0.6	9.8	747.2
3	21.1	1.0	6.4	487.5
4	21.1	1.0	6.6	515.3
5	12.7	0.6	6.9	501.0
6	12.7	0.6	8.1	575.9
7	21.1	1.0	4.0	327.7
8	21.1	1.0	5.8	454.1
9	42.3	2.0	4.9	383.9
10	42.3	2.0	4.7	361.1

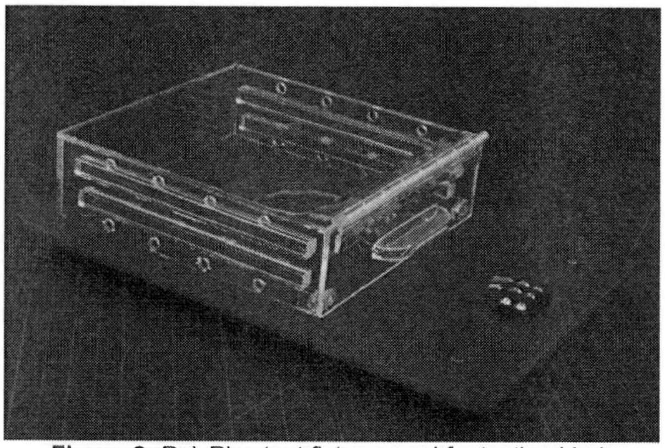

Figure 2: PolyPlus test fixture used for testing Li-air batteries. Allowed for proper air flow above and below the battery.

Results and Discussion

Cell data has been summarized in Table 1 and Figure 4. Cell testing has demonstrated a 10 Ah cell capable of 798 Wh/kg at a discharge rate of 12.7 mA with ambient humidity of ~ 45% as shown in Table 1 and Figure 4. This cell was stored 49 days at room temperature and pressure with air ports taped off in order to display long term storage potential. As shown here, storage did not adversely affect delivered capacity or cause voltage delay on start up. In addition cell #2, which achieved 747 Wh/kg at 12.7 mA, was suspended in a vertical position to show orientation independence. Cells #5 and #6, also discharged at 12.7 mA without storage, show an interesting voltage drop demonstrated in blue and green lines in Figure 4, respectively. This is likely to due to flooding of the positive electrodes at high relative humidity (~ 74%). Unfortunately, because of the drastic change in ambient relative humidity, a direct comparison between storage and immediate discharge cannot be made here. Cells #3, #4, #7, and #8 were discharged at 1.0 mA/cm^2 and averaged 5.7 Ah where cell #7 is an outlier at only 4.0 Ah capacity. In addition cell #3 and #8 show some signs of the same failure

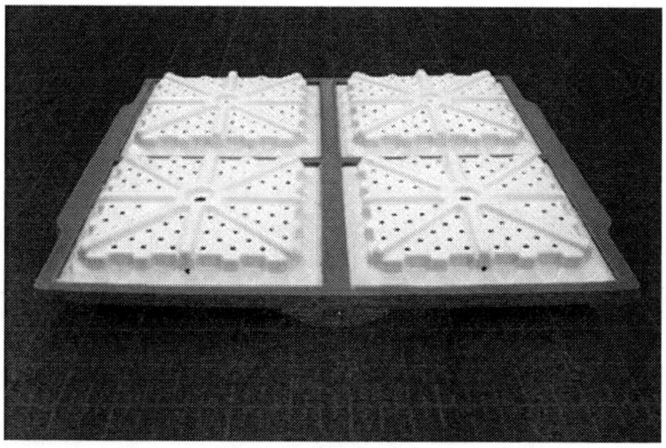

Figure 3: Image of the PolyPlus Li-Air battery used in this study.

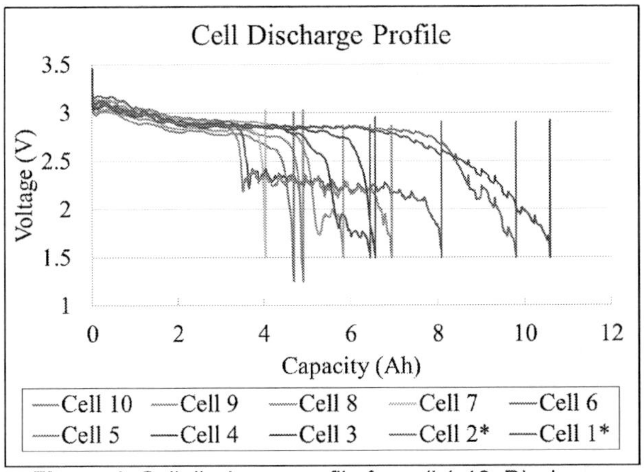

Figure 4: Cell discharge profile for cell 1-10. Discharge current: cells 1, 2, 5, and 6 at 12.7 mA; cells 3, 4, 7, and 8 at 21.1 mA; cells 9 and 10 at 42.2 mA. * annotates cells were stored for 49 days prior to discharge.

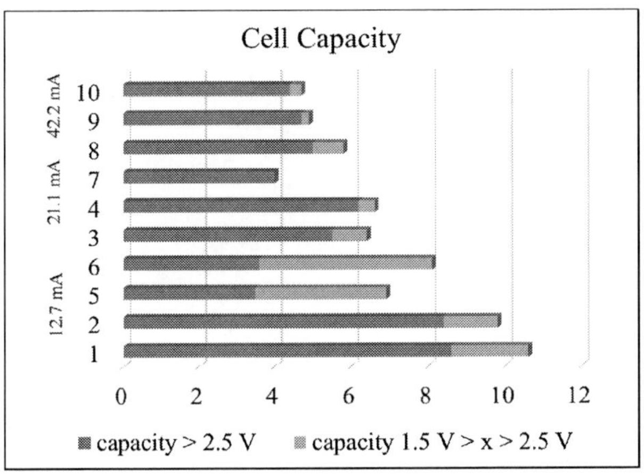

Figure 5: Bar graph summarizing of cell data showing capacity (Ah) at < 2.5 V (darker color) and capacity between 1.5 and 2.5 V (lighter colored). Current is displayed on the left axis: cells 1, 2, 5, and 6 at 12.7 mA; cells 3, 4, 7, and 8 at 21.1 mA; cells 9 and 10 at 42.2 mA.

experienced in cell #5 and #6. Figure 5 is a summary of the cells with capacities at voltages > 2.5 V and voltages between 1.5 and 2.5 V to better visualize the capacity obtained after the partial failure. Finally, cell #9 and #10 were discharged at 2.0 mA/cm^2 and provided approximately ½ of the rated capacity and 372 Wh/kg energy density, which is still a significant improvement over current Li-ion technology. Additional work is needed to improve the performance over a broad range of relative humidity.

Battery testing has demonstrated 502 Wh/kg at a discharge rate of 62 mA (0.75 mA/cm^2) with 25 °C, humidity of 50%. The 2p2s configuration is rated at 20 Ah. All battery weights averaged 163.3 g (+/- 0.3 g) prior to testing and 174.3 (+/- 0.3 g) post testing. The increase in weight is expected as the byproducts of the electrochemical reaction, LiOH, build over the discharge. OCV displayed in Figures 6 and 7 is between 6.9 V. The discharge profile shown in

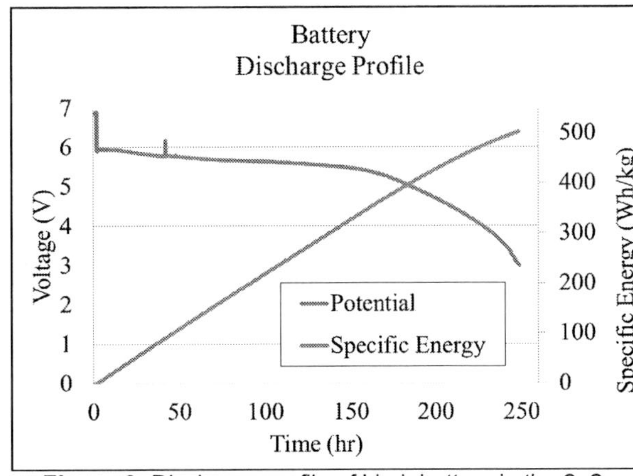

Figure 6: Discharge profile of Li-air battery in the 2p2s configuration discharged at 63 mA (0.75 mA/cm^2) displaying ~500 Wh/kg.

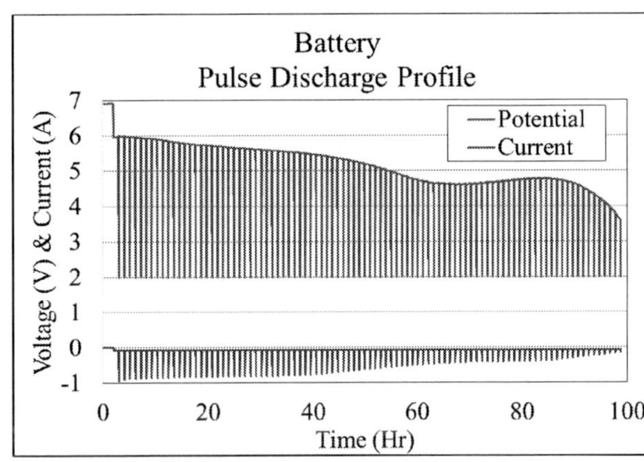

Figure 7: Pluse discharge profile of Li-air battery in the 2p2s configureation.

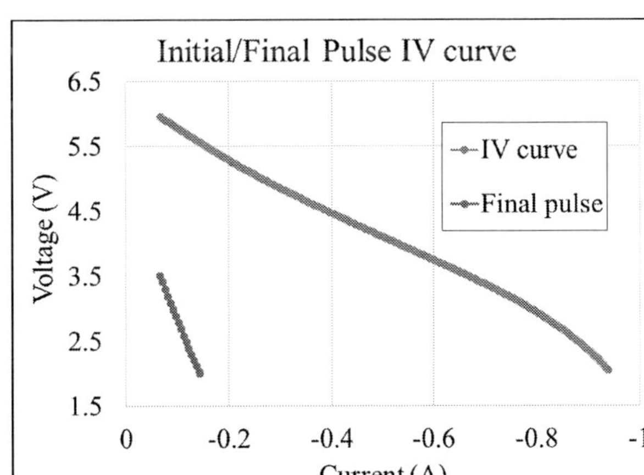

Figure 8: IV curve of initial/final pulse.

profile shown in Figure 6 is consistent with primary battery discharge and shows an operational voltage of 5.54 V, capacity of 12.6 Ah, and energy density of 502 Wh/kg. The decrease in energy density is expected with the additional weight of the housing and leads needed for battery assembly. The pulse discharge profile was chosen to simulate the duty cycle of a ground sensor with occasional power spikes during data transmission. Figure 7 shows the Li-air battery was capable of 96 pulses over 100 hours, with a capacity of 6.96 Ah, energy density of 208 Wh/kg, and an initial discharge of 943 mA (11.2 mA/cm^2). This is the highest reported current density achieved with the Li-air battery system. Closer inspection of the initial/final pulse is shown in Figure 8. The voltage current relationship can be expressed using the following equation[1]:

$$V=V_0-[(\eta_{ct})_a+(\eta_c)_a]-[(\eta_{ct})_c+(\eta_c)_c]-iR_i=iR$$

Where V_0 is the open-circuit voltage; $(\eta_{ct})_a$, $(\eta_{ct})_c$ are activation polarization or charge transfer overvoltage of the anode or cathode; $(\eta_c)_a$, $(\eta_c)_c$ are concentration polarization at the anode or cathode; i is the operation current; and R_i is the internal resistance of the cell. Upon inspection of the curve the majority appears linear until reaching ~0.8 A where concentration polarization is believed to increase with the increased current requirement. This is due in large part to limited mass transfer of O_2 in the cathode. As the discharge continues a build-up of by-products, LiOH begins to clog the pores increasing resistance and further limiting O_2 transport. This is evident in the final discharge curve with a much steeper slope.

Conclusion

The Li-air cells shown here have demonstrated near 800 Wh/kg, which is a significant achievement. These cells however require additional work to improve the performance over a broad range of relative humidity. The Li-air batteries made from these same cells has shown 500 Wh/kg and a current density as high as 11.2 mA/cm^2, also a significant achievement in the Li-air system. In addition, these batteries have shown the ability to be pulse discharged up to 96 times before depletion.

References

1. Linden, D., Reddy, T.B. (eds.) *Linden's Handbook of Batteries* 4th ed. New York: McGraw Hill. 2011.
2. Bruce, P.G.; Freunberger, S.A.; Hardwick, L.J.; Tarascon, J.-M. *Nature Materials*. 11, pp 19-29, January 2012.
3. Imanishi, N., Luntz, A., & Bruce, P. (Eds.). (2014). *The Lithium Air Battery: Fundamentals* (pp. 1-22). New York: Springer.
4. US Patent 7,645,543
5. US Patent 7,282,295
6. US Patent 7,824,806

Catalysis of the Oxygen Electrode Reactions in Lithium-air Batteries

K. M. Abraham*, Iromie Gunasekara, Sanjeev Mukerjee
Department of Chemistry, Northeastern University, Boston, MA 02115
Edward J. Plichta and Mary A. Hendrickson
US Army RDECOM CERDEC C2D
Army Power Division, RDER-CCA Aberdeen Proving Grounds, MD 21005

Abstract: *There is world-wide interest in the development of a rechargeable Li-air battery based on the Li/O_2 chemical couple because of its high theoretical specific energy of 5200 Wh/kg and low materials cost. The four-electron oxygen reduction reaction (ORR) in non-aqueous electrolytes used in these batteries proceeds through the intermediates LiO_2 and Li_2O_2 before being converted to Li_2O at appropriate potentials. Our studies have revealed that the kinetics and mechanism of the various reactions in the overall reduction of O_2 to Li_2O are influenced by the electron donor-acceptor properties of the solid catalyst employed in the porous carbon electrode and the non-aqueous electrolyte used in the battery.*

Key Words: Li-air battery, non-aqueous electrolytes, OR catalysis.

Introduction:

The phthalocyanine macrocycle is a strong electron accepter which facilitates the axial coordination of the metal center in metal phthalocyanines (MPC) (I) with ligands such as O_2 and its reduction products having a range of electron donor characteristics.

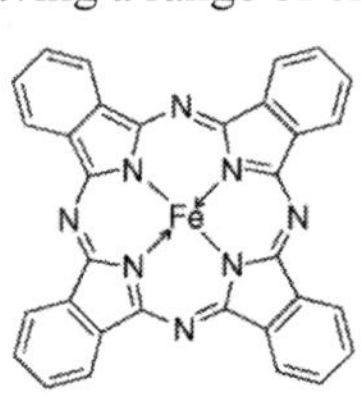

(I) Iron(II) Phthalocyanine

A few prior studies have reported ORR/OER catalysis of the O_2 electrode by these metal-N_4 complexes in non-aqueous electrolyte-based Li-O_2 batteries (1-5). In this paper we provide evidence of the tunability of the redox potential of the iron(II) phthalocyanine by changing the electron donor property of the ligating solvent molecule. Our results demonstrate that ORR catalysis on the metal-N_4 center can be tuned with respect to the electron donor property of the organic electrolyte via the solvates, $Li^+(solvent)_n$, formed between the organic solvent and Li^+. We also show that iron(II) phthalocyanine can be transformed into insoluble solid catalysts by appropriate high temperature processing of carbon black/FePC mixtures making them potentially useful for practical Li-air batteries. These results extend our previous observations of ORR on uncatalyzed electrodes in non-aqueous electrolytes that O_2 reduction is strongly coupled to the Lewis acid-base properties of the electrolyte used. A typical electrolyte for Li-air battery is composed of a solution of a Li salt in an organic solvent. Based on the electron donor property the solvents can be classified either as low donor number or high donor number solvents. Generally a solvent is said to be high donor number when its Guttmann Donor Number (DN) is greater than about 20 and a low donor number solvent when its DN is lower than 20. In this paper we show that ORR catalysis in non-aqueous electrolytes is coupled both to the Donor Number of the electrolyte solvent and the electronic configuration of the transition metal ion in the metal phthalocyanine catalyst, MPC, where M = Co or Fe, embedded in the porous carbon cathode. These results are reported in this paper.

Results and Discussion

We have found that ORR catalysis can proceed via either a homogeneous (Outer Helmholtz Plane, OHP) or a heterogeneous (Inner Helmholtz Plane, IHP) reduction pathway depending on the Donor Number of the organic solvent and the d electron configuration of the MPC catalyst present in the porous carbon electrode. In high number solvents such as dimethyl sulfoxide, DMSO (DN = 29.8) the initial one-electron reduction of O_2 to O_2^- occurs in a homogeneous Outer Helmholtz Plane reaction because of the relatively high stability of the $Li^+(DMSO)_n^-$-O_2^- ion pair specie in solution. A heterogeneous Inner Helmholtz Plane reaction catalyzed by the metal in the MPC is favored in electrolytes in low Donor Number solvents such as acetonitrile, MeCN (DN=14.1) and tetraethyleneglycoldimethyl ether, (TEGDME (DN=10.5).

Cyclic voltammograms recorded on a glassy carbon (GC) electrode in Ar saturated 1mM FePC solutions in 0.1 M $LiCF_3SO_3$ / DMSO and 0.1 M $LiPF_6$/ DMSO electrolytes are shown in Figure 1. Three pairs of redox reactions are observed. The Fe(II)/Fe(I) reversible reaction with a reduction peak at 2.62 V is consistent with the changes observed in the in-situ Raman spectrum at this potential (Figure 2). While all the peaks in the Raman spectrum obtained at open circuit potential (3.02 V) are due to the DMSO solvent, new Raman peaks appear at 260, 584, 745, 1000 cm^{-1}, and between 1100-1500 cm^{-1} when the electrode potential is scanned to slightly below the 2.62 V peak. It is important to review the electronic configuration of Fe presented in Scheme 1 as a function of its oxidation state to understand the Raman spectra since the Fe oxidation state changes during the potential scan.

Scheme 1: Iron (Fe) *d* electron configurations of FePC dissolved in DMSO as a function of the oxidation state of iron.

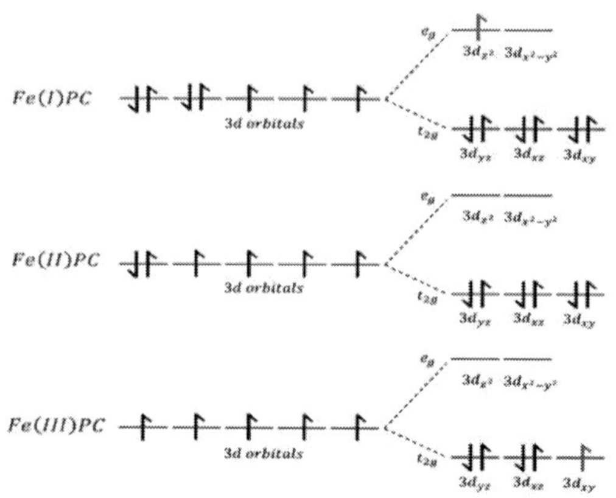

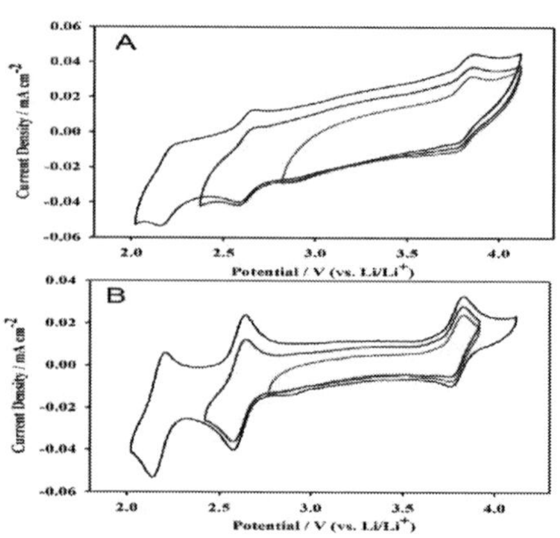

Figure 1: Cyclic voltammograms recorded on a glassy carbon electrode in argon purged 1 mM solution of FePC in A) 0.1 M $LiPF_6$/ DMSO and B) 0.1 M $LiCF_3SO_3$/ DMSO. Scan rate is 10 mV s^{-1}. The potentials are indicated versus a Li/ Li^+ reference electrode. CVs depicted in different colors represent current-voltage scans recorded at different potential windows.

In solvents such as DMSO which can form coordination bonds with electron acceptor centers, Iron(II) Phthalocyanine is six coordinated(6,7) in the structure, $(DMSO)_2Fe(II)PC$, containing two DMSO molecules as shown in in the equation in Scheme 2. At the open circuit potential the metal center in this structure is in the Fe(II) state.

Scheme 2: Equations [1] and [2] representing Fe(II)/Fe(I) Redox Reactions in DMSO

$$(\mathrm{DMSO})_2\mathrm{Fe(II)PC} + e^- \leftrightarrow [(\mathrm{DMSO})_2\mathrm{Fe(I)PC}]^- \quad [1]$$

$$[(\mathrm{DMSO})_2\mathrm{Fe(I)PC}]^- \leftrightarrow [(\mathrm{DMSO})\mathrm{Fe(I)PC}]^- + \mathrm{DMSO} \quad [2]$$

Scheme 3: Equation 3 representing Fe(I)PC Reduction in DMSO

$$[(\mathrm{DMSO})\mathrm{Fe(I)PC}]^- + e^- \leftrightarrow [(\mathrm{DMSO})\mathrm{Fe(I)PC}]^{2-} \quad [3]$$

When the electrode is polarized to lower potentials, the Fe(II) is reduced to Fe(I) which has the $(xz,yz,xy)^6(z^2)^1$ electronic configuration. If the DN of the coordinating molecule is high as in DMSO, a six coordinated complex having the Fe(I) electronic configuration is unstable and the redox potential of Fe(II)/Fe(I) is shifted downwards (equation 1) compared with that in a low DN solvent-based electrolyte, eg. $LiPF_6$/TEGDME that does not readily complex with Fe(II)PC. This shift of the Fe(II)/Fe(I) redox potential related to the nature of the electrolyte is profound and affects the mechanism of O_2 electrochemistry

As shown in equation [2] in Scheme 2, the $(DMSO)_2Fe(I)PC$ formed by reduction releases one of the two DMSO molecules to form an asymmetric five coordinated complex. The planarity of the $(DMSO)_2Fe(II)PC$ molecule is lost during this transition and the changes that appear in the Raman spectra below 2.6 V are consistent with these symmetry changes.

When Fe(I)PC is further reduced as displayed in Figure 1, the electron is acquired by the PC macrocycle (Scheme 3) reducing the phthalocyanine macrocycle moiety. This is reflected by the new Raman peaks that appear at 1425 and 1490 cm^{-1} in Figure 2 when the electrode is polarized down to 2.20 V. These Raman peaks can be attributed to the pyrrole C-C and C-N stretching vibrations arising from the reduction of the macrocycle ring as depicted in the equation of Scheme 3.

The oxidation of Fe(II) to Fe(III) that appears at 3.8 V in the reverse scan (in $LiCF_3SO_3$/ DMSO and in $LiPF_6$/ DMSO) is a two-step reaction where the electron transfer is followed by substitution of a coordinated DMSO molecule by an anion as depicted in Scheme 4. The strength of the coordination bond between the anion (X^-) in solution and the Fe(III) center determines the redox potential of the Fe(II)/ Fe(III) couple. That is, the oxidation of the Fe(II) to Fe(III) occurs at a lower potential if the anion forms a stronger bond with the Fe(III)PC formed from the oxidation (6, 8). This in turn is determined by the electron donor property (DN) of the anion. As we have shown (9) before, $CF_3SO_3^-$ has a DN of 16.9 as opposed to PF_6^- with a low DN of 2.5.

Scheme 4: Equations 4 and 5 representing Fe(II)/ Fe(III) oxidation reaction in DMSO

$$(DMSO)_2Fe(II)PC \leftrightarrow [(DMSO)_2Fe(III)PC]^+ + e^- \quad [4]$$

$$[(DMSO)_2Fe(III)PC]^+ + X^- \leftrightarrow (DMSO)Fe(III)PCX + DMSO \quad [5]$$

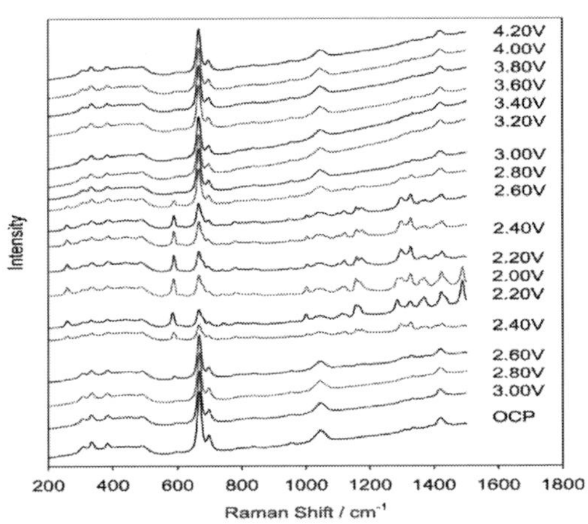

Figure 2: In-situ Raman spectra obtained at the carbon electrode at different potentials versus Li/ Li^+ in argon purged 1 mM FePC dissolved in 0.1 M $LiCF_3SO_3$/ DMSO

We have also studied the redox behavior of FePC/Vulcan-based catalysts in argon saturated electrolytes in DMSO and the data obtained, consistent with the preceding results, are discussed later in the section dealing with catalyzed ORR. Overall FePC showed similar redox behavior in acetonitrile-based electrolytes except that the various redox peaks are observed at higher potentials. The solubility of FePC in acetonitrile (MeCN) is much less than in DMSO and, as a result, we used a saturated solution of FePC in MeCN-based electrolytes to study FePC electrochemistry

In heterogeneous Inner Helmholtz plane (IHP) catalysis in low DN solvent-based electrolytes, the electronic configuration of the metal ion in the MPC must be appropriate for the formation of a co-ordination bond between the MPC and the superoxide O_2^- . This is achieved with transition metal ion electronic configuration of $[Ar]4s^03d^7$ (or $t_{2g}{}^6e_g{}^1$ configuration in the 3d electronic level) found in Co(II)PC and Fe(I)PC. Thus, FePC catalyzes O_2 reduction in the reduced Fe(I)PC state, as opposed to CoPC which catalyzes ORR in its normally stable Co(II)PC state (4,5), both possessing the $[Ar]4s^03d^7$ electronic configuration.

We have tested the performance of Li-air cells with FePC catalysts embedded in ketjenblack (KB) carbon obtained by heat-treating FePC/KB carbon mixtures at 300 and 600 °C in argon atmosphere. Both the FePC/KB(300) and the FePC/KB(600) catalysts doubled the cycle life of Li-O_2 battery cells compared to those tested without these cathode catalysts in the porous electrodes. . The data are summarized in Figure 3. These Li/O_2 cells were cycled with a capacity limit of 400 mAh g^{-1} (Figure 3). The two catalyzed cells with FePC/KB(300) and FePC/KB(600) survived through their 40th cycle with 100% capacity utilization. This is a two-fold increase in cycle life compared to the un-catalyzed Li-O_2 cell (Figure 3C). The other notable feature is the overall lower charge voltage of the catalyzed cells in early cycles which suggest that the catalysts also exert activity for the oxidation (OER) reactions. WE note that the oxygen evolution overpotential increased after each discharge cycle. This behavior is most probably associated with the degradation of the FePC catalytic sites by the oxygen reduction intermediates and the insulating lithium peroxide accumulating at the carbon cathode with repeated charge/discharge cycling.

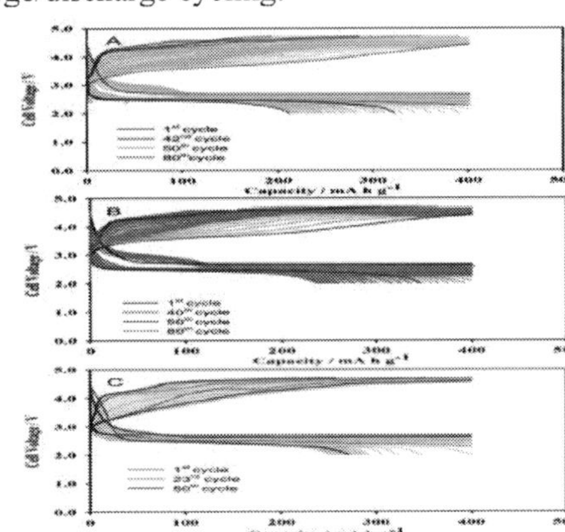

Figure 3: Cycling performance obtained for A) FePC/KB(300) B) FePC/KB(600) C) uncatalyzed(Ketjenblack) cells in 1 M $LiCF_3SO_3$/ TEGDME. The cell discharge capacity is limited to 400 mAh/g. The charge limit is 4.65V.

By limiting the capacity utilization of the Li-O_2 cell

to 400 mAh g^{-1} in the battery cell, the electrodes remain active to catalyze the charge reaction. Interestingly, our XRD and Raman spectral analyses of the products from discharged $Li-O_2$ cells indicated the presence of both lithium superoxide (LiO_2) and Li_2O_2, providing further support for the discharge reaction mechanisms in these cells utilizing the catalyzed electrodes.

Acknowledgment: Financial support from the US Army Cerdec contract No: GTS-S-15-015 is gratefully acknowledged.

References

1. Abraham, K. M.; Jiang, Z., Journal of the Electrochemical Society 1996, 143 (1), 1-5.

2. Fierro, C.; Anderson, A. B.; Scherson, D. A., Journal of Physical Chemistry 1988, 92 (24), 6902-6907.

3. Shui, J.-L.; Karan, N. K.; Balasubramanian, M.; Li, S.-Y.; Liu, D.-J., Journal of the American Chemical Society 2012, 134 (40), 16654-16661.

4. Trahan, M. J.; Gunasekara, I.; Mukerjee, S.; Plichta, E. J.; Hendrickson, M. A.; Abraham, K. M., Journal of The Electrochemical Society 2014, 161 (10), A1706-A1715.

5. Trahan, M. J.; Jia, Q.; Mukerjee, S.; Plichta, E. J.; Hendrickson, M. A.; Abraham, K. M., Journal of The Electrochemical Society 2013, 160 (9), A1577-A1586

6. Kadish, K.; Guilard, R.; Smith, K. M., *The Porphyrin Handbook: Phthalocyanines: spectroscopic and electrochemical characterization.* Academic press: 2003; Vol.16

7. Jones, J. G.; Twigg, M. V., *Inorganic Chemistry* **1969,** *8* (10), 2120-2123.

8. Milaeva, E.; Speier, G.; Lever, A. The redox chemistry of metallophthalocyanines in solution; DTIC Document: 1992.

9. Gunasekara, I.; Mukerjee, S.; Abraham, K. M. In Microelectrode Investigations of Oxygen Reduction Reactions in Lithium-Air Batteries, ECS Meeting Abstracts, ECS Meeting Abstracts, October 27, 2013; ECS Meeting Abstracts, 2013; p 449.

Lithium-Oxygen Cell based on Exfoliated Nitrogen-doped Graphene Nanosheets Cathodes and Ionic Liquid Electrolytes

Padmakar Kichambare and Stanley Rodrigues

Air Force Research Laboratory, Aerospace Systems Directorate

Wright-Patterson Air Force Base, Ohio 45433-7252.

Abstract: *Exfoliated nitrogen-doped graphene nanosheets (Ex-N-GNSs) as well as blend of Ex-N-GNSs with nitrogen-doped commercial carbon (Hybrid 1) cathodes have been evaluated in 1-butyl-1-methylpyrrolidinium bis-(trifluoromethylsulfonyl)imide, $PYR_{14}TFSI$, ionic liquid for application in lithium-oxygen batteries. In these cells $PYR_{14}TFSI$-lithium bis-(trifluoromethylsulfonyl)imide (LiTFSI) was employed as electrolyte. Compared to Hybrid 1 cathode, Ex-N-GNSs cathode exhibits higher cell capacity. However, glavanostatic cycling for Hybrid 1 cathode showed good performance with a discharge capacity of 1350mAh/g. The discharge capacity of Ex-N-GNSs cathode fades with cycling. These results demonstrate that Ex-N-GNSs based cathodes with ionic liquid electrolyte are potential components for design of lithium-oxygen batteries.*

Keywords: exfoliated nitrogen-doped graphene nanosheets; scanning electron microscopy; ionic liquid electrolyte; ionic conductivity; lithium-oxygen battery

Introduction

Lithium-oxygen batteries are attractive, high energy density electrochemical power sources anticipated to impact future technologies [1]. Although these cells operate on a simple chemical reaction between lithium ion and oxygen radical species, there are significant technical challenges that need to be overcome for successful development of these cells. Oxygen cathode structure, electrolyte decomposition, poor reversibility of electrochemical process, sensitivity to humidity, and cell design are some of the challenges [2]. In particular, the material architecture of oxygen cathodes and electrolytes play a key role in governing the electrochemical performance of lithium-oxygen battery.

Recently, Ionic liquids (IL) have been investigated as electrolytes [3,4] for lithium-oxygen cells. IL are promising electrolytes due to their negligible vapor pressure, non-flammability, wide electrochemical stability window, high thermal and chemical stability. The use of 1-butyl-1-methylpyrrolidinium bis-(trifluoromethylsulfonyl) imide ($PYR_{14}TFSI$)-lithium bis-(trifluoromethylsulfonyl) imide (LiTFSI) as ionic liquid electrolyte has been reported in lithium-oxygen cells [3]. These studies demonstrated that these cells exhibit a high capacity of 4500 $mAhg_{carbon}^{-1}$, 98.5% coulombic efficiency and a very good reversibility of electrochemical process. In addition, ternary mixed IL electrolytes consisting of PYR14TFSI, 1-butyl-3-methylimidazolium bis-(trifluoromethylsulfonyl) imide (BMIMTFSI) and LiTFSI were utilized to enhance cyclic performance of these cells [5]. Stability of $PYR_{14}TFSI$ ionic liquid in lithium-oxygen cells has been reported by Piana *et al* [6]. The specific energy and cyclability of these cells is governed by oxygen reduction and evolution reactions rates at cathode and their corresponding potential. Effect of binder-free inverse opal carbon as cathodes for lithium-oxygen cell in $PYR_{14}TFSI$ was investigated [4]. Various materials, such as carbon based nanostructured materials, noble metals and metal oxides have been investigated as electro-catalysts for energy storage applications [7]. Among these materials, graphene nanosheets (GNSs) is an efficient electro-catalyst for oxygen reduction reaction (ORR) and oxygen evolution reaction (OER). In addition, GNSs has excellent electrical conductivity, distinct morphology, and large surface area. GNSs have been employed as oxygen cathode in fuel cells and show a higher discharge voltage under acidic condition [8]. GNSs, nitrogen-doped graphene nanosheets (N-GNSs) were also employed in non-aqueous lithium-oxygen cells as cathode material that demonstrated an exceptionally high discharge cell capacity [9].

In continuation of our work on lithium-oxygen cells [10], we report here the use of exfoliated nitrogen-doped graphene nanosheets (Ex-N-GNSs) and blend of Ex-N-GNSs with nitrogen-doped carbon (Hybrid 1) cathodes with $PYR_{14}TFSI$-LiTFSI ionic liquid electrolyte in lithium-oxygen cell. Furthermore, temperature dependence of the ionic conductivity of $PYR_{14}TFSI$-LiTFSI electrolyte has been determined.

Experimental Details

Commercially available GNSs (Angstron Materials, Inc.) were heated in a vacuum oven at 250 °C to remove any residual surfactant. These GNSs were used for further work. Ex-N-GNSs were prepared using procedure described in our previous work [10]. $PYR_{14}TFSI$ (98%, Sigma-Aldrich) and LiTFSI (Sigma-Aldrich) were dried overnight under a vacuum at 120 °C.

A scanning electron microscope (SEM), (JEOL JSM-6060) was used to observe the morphologies of the specimens. The surface areas of the specimens were determined by nitrogen adsorption / desorption measurements at 77 K (Micromeritics ASAP 2020). The porosity of cathode material was characterized by a gas pycnometer (Micromeritis, Accu Pyc II 1340). Galvanostatic charge-discharge measurements of the specimens were conducted using a computer controlled VersaSTAT 4 (Princeton Applied Research) electrochemical workstation. Ionic conductivity measurements were performed using impedance spectroscopy. The ac impedance measurements were carried out in the frequency range from 1 Hz to 10^6 Hz using a VersaStat 4 (Ametek, USA) Frequency Response Analyzer (FRA) in a potentiostatic mode, with RMS ac voltage of 10 mV at temperatures between -60 °C to 75 °C. All measurements were carried out at atmospheric pressure. The cell assembly was thermally equilibrated for at least 30 minutes for each temperature measurement.

Powders of Ex-N-GNSs and Hybrid 1 were used to fabricate the oxygen cathode. Hybrid 1 was prepared by mixing nitrogen-doped carbon (mixture of nitrogen-doped Calgon activated carbon and Ketjenblack carbon in 40:60 wt % ratio) and Ex-N-GNSs in 50:50 wt% ratio. These powders were mixed and dispersed in N-methyl-2-pyrrolidone (NMP) using sonication for 90 min. This process was carried to load cathode materials in the open voids of nickel foam used as current collector. Subsequently, the cathode specimen was dried overnight at 120 °C under vacuum. A lithium-oxygen cell with a 1 cm^2 area was fabricated using a Swagelok type cell in a dry room with controlled moisture content. Nickel foam with Ex-N-GNSs/Hybrid 1 was used as working cathodes along with lithium metal as anode and a glass fiber (Whatman, GF-A) separator soaked with ionic-liquid electrolyte. LiTFSI was dissolved in $PYR_{14}TFSI$ in a 1:9 molar ratio to obtain the ionic-liquid electrolyte. The lithium-oxygen cells were discharged with constant current of 50 μA. Electrochemical impedance spectroscopy (EIS) measurements on the lithium-oxygen cells were conducted before and after discharge/charge measurements. All electrochemical tests on these cells were carried under oxygen atmosphere.

Results and Discussion

The morphology of the working cathode was examined under SEM. Figure 1a shows the SEM micrograph of Ex-N-GNSs that reveal the wrinkled, porous, 3D architectures with interconnected pore channels of Ex-N-GNSs. Figure 1b is the morphology of Hybrid 1 that

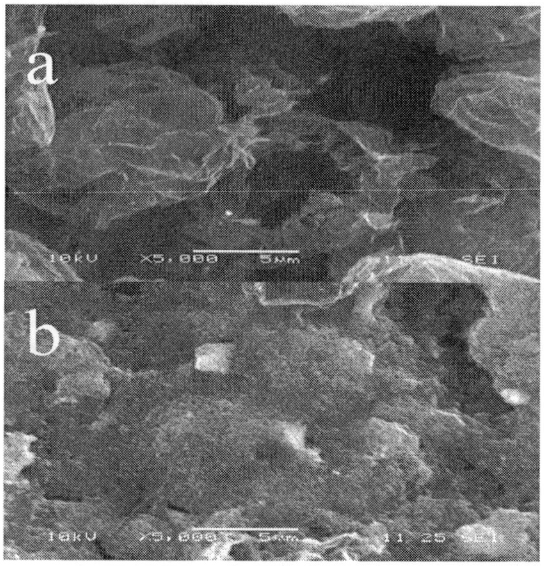

Figure 1. SEM image of (a) Ex-N-GNSs and (b) Hybrid 1

exhibits a fibrous and flake or plate like structure. This favorable morphology facilitates oxygen transport and

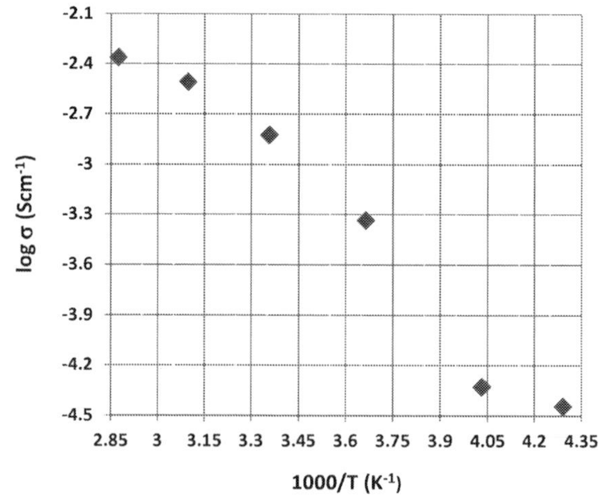

Figure 2. Temperature dependence of ionic conductivity of $PYR_{14}TFSI$-LiTFSI

provides enough voids to accommodate discharge products. Nitrogen adsorption–desorption isotherm measurements were carried at 77 K. The Brunauer-Emmett-Teller (BET) area of Ex-N-GNSs and Hybrid 1 were found to be 685 and 900 m^2/g, respectively (Table 1). The remarkable nitrogen uptake above the relative pressure ratio of 0.40 has been observed in BET isotherm and is due to the condensation of nitrogen in mesoporous Ex-N-GNSs. The pore size distribution of Ex-N-GNS and Hybrid 1 indicates a wide variation in pore size. Such high porosity helps to improve cell capacity.

The ionic conductivity of the $PYR_{14}TFSI$-LiTFSI was measured as a function of inverse temperature as shown in Figure 2. It is observed from Figure 2 that the ionic conductivity increases with temperature and the ionic conductivity does not follow the typical Arrhenius behavior. There is an abrupt change in the conductivity for IL in the temperature range from 0 °C to -40 °C. At 25 °C, the conductivity value is 1.49 $mS.cm^{-1}$.

Based on the high surface area with porous structure of Ex-N-GNSs and Hybid 1 as well as high ionic conductivity of $PYR_{14}TFSI$-LiTFSI electrolyte, lithium-oxygen cells with 1 cm^2 active area were fabricated. The electrochemical performance of Ex-N-GNSs and Hybrid 1 was evaluated. Figure 3 shows the discharge profiles of the lithium-oxygen cells with Ex-N-GNSs, and Hybrid 1 cathode. The cells were reversibly charged and discharged using current of 50 μA at 25 °C. The open circuit voltages (OCV) of lithium-oxygen cells fabricated with Ex-NGNSs and Hybrid 1 were 3.12 and 2.9 V, respectively. The difference in OCV is likely because of

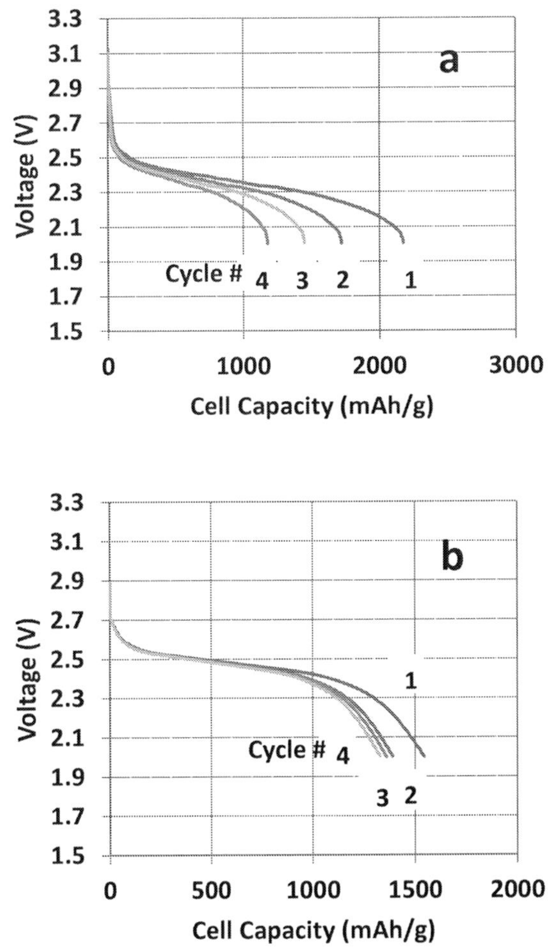

Figure 3. Discharge profiles for a lithium-oxygen cell at 25 °C using (a) Ex-N-GNSs) and (b) Hybrid 1

internal series resistances between various cell components as well as activation polarization of the cathode. Initial discharge cell capacity, normalized with the weight of carbon materials in the cathode, for Ex-N-GNSs and Hybrid 1 cathodes were found to be 2175 and 1544 mAh/g, respectively. Cell capacity for Ex-N-GNSs cathode decreased continuously with cycling and delivered capacity of 1178 mAh/g at the end of 4th cycle. On the other hand, cell with Hybrid 1 cathode showed a gradual decrease in cell capacity and delivered capacity of 1328 mAh/g at the end of 4th cycle. Figure 3 also shows that Ex-N-GNSs cathode has higher voltage plateau than Hybrid 1. Lower discharge cell capacity of Hybrid 1 cathode is most probably due to the poor O_2 diffusion in Hybrid 1 matrix caused by clogging of porous Hybrid 1 cathode with the discharge products. Better capacity retention with cycling for Hybrid 1 is due to meso/micro porous structure of carbon with embedded Ex-N-GNSs.

Table 1. Physical and electrochemical properties of Ex-N-GNSs and Hybrid 1

Cathode Materials	Ex-N-GNSs	Hybrid 1
Surface Area (m^2/g)	686.6	900
Pore Volume (cm^3/g)	1.86	1.9
Average Pore size (nm)	11.36	11.86
Porosity (%)	24.5	30
Open Circuit Voltage (V)	3.12	2.9
Specific Capacity (mAh/g)	2175	1544

Electrochemical impedance spectroscopy (EIS) was used to investigate the electrochemical performance of cathode in the lithium-oxygen cell. Typical Nyquist plots before and after discharge for Ex-N-GNSs and Hybrid 1 are shown in Fig. 4. Nyquist plots before initial discharge

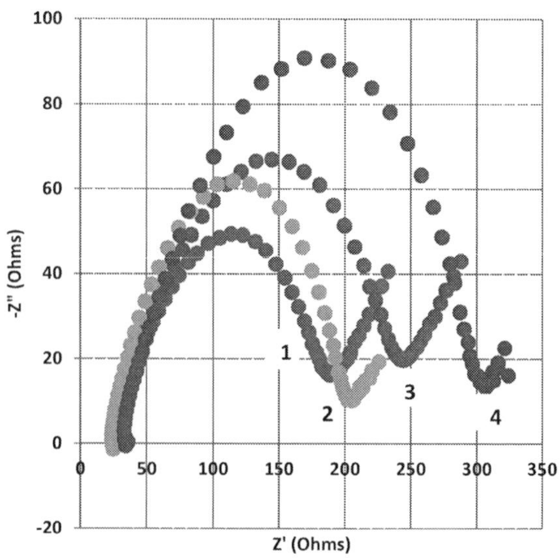

Figure 4. Nyquist plots for a lithium-oxygen cell at 25 °C for Ex-N-GNSs) and Hybrid 1 cathode before (1 and 2) and after (3 and 4) discharge, respectively, in oxygen atmosphere

exhibit low charge-transfer resistance for Ex-N-GNSs and Hybrid 1 indicating faster charge-transfer kinetics. Compared to Ex-N-GNSs cathode, Hybrid 1 cathode shows large increase in charge-transfer resistance after discharge and this increase is ascribed to the clogging of pores with deposition of discharge products. EIS results combined with discharge characteristics lead to conclusion that the Ex-N-GNSs has higher catalytic activity towards ORR in the oxygen cathode, thereby exhibiting higher cell capacity. However, Hybrid 1 cathode shows better capacity retention with cycling due to highly meso/micro porous structures of Hybrid 1.

Conclusion

In conclusion, this work demonstrates electrochemical performance of lithium-oxygen cell with ionic liquid as electrolyte with cathode formulation based on GNSs. The first discharge cell capacity of the cell with cathode of Ex-N-GNSs and Hybrid 1 were found to be 2175 and 1544mAh/g of active cathode material, respectively. This work highlights the importance of novel cathode architecture and opens up a promising approach to develop highly efficient oxygen electrodes for lithium-oxygen cells.

Acknowledgements

This research was supported by the Air Force Research Laboratory, Wright-Patterson Air Force Base, Ohio.

References:

1. Abraham, K.M. and Z. Jiang, "A Polymer Electrolyte-Based Rechargeable Lithium/Oxygen Battery", *J. Electrochem. Soc.*, vol. 143, pp. 1-5, 1996.
2. Girishkumar, G., B. McCloskey, A.C. Luntz, S.D. Swanson, and W.J. Wilcke, "Lithium-Air Battery: Promise and Challenges", *J. Phys. Chem. Lett.*, vol. **1**, pp. 2193-2203, 2010.
3. Elica, G.A., J. Hassoun, W.-J. Kwak, Y.-K. Sun, B. Scrosati, F. Mueller, D. Bresser, S. Passerini, P. Oberhumer, N. Tsiouvaras and J. Reiter, "An advanced Lithium-Air Battery Exploiting an Ionic Liquid-Based Electrolyte", *Nano Lett.*, vol. **14**, pp. 6572-6577, 2014.
4. Olivares-Marin, M., P. Palomino, J.M. Amarilla, E. Enciso, and D. Tonti, "Effect of Architecture on the Electrochemistry of Binder-free Inverse Opal Carbons as Li-Air Cathodes in an Ionic Liquid-Based Electrolyte", *J. Mater.Chem. A*, vol. **1** pp. 14270-14279, 2013.
5. Ara, M., T. Meng, G.-A. Nazri, S.O. Salley, and K.Y. Simon, "Ternary Imidazolium-Pyrrolidinium-Based Ionic Liquid Electrolytes for Rechargeable Li-O_2 Batteries", *J. Electrochem. Soc.*, vol. **161**, pp. A1969-A1975, 2014.
6. Piana, M., J. Wandt, S. Meini, I. Buchberger, N. Tsiouvaras, and H.A. Gasteiger, "Stability of a Pyrrolidinium-Based Ionic Liquid in Li-O_2 Cells", *J. Electrochem. Soc.*, vol. **161**, pp. A1992-A2001, 2014.
7. Ren, X., S.S. Zhang, D.T. Tran, and J. Read, "Oxygen Reduction Reaction Catalyst on Lithium/Air Battery Discharge performance", *J. Mater. Chem.*, vol. **21**, pp. 10118-10125, 2011.
8. Yoo, E., J. Nakamura, and H. Zhou, "N-Doped Graphene Nanosheets for Li-Air Fuel Cells under Acidic Conditions", *Energy Environ. Sci.*, vol. **5**, pp. 6928-6932, 2012.
9. Xiao, J., D. Mei, X. Li, W. Xu, D. Wang, G.L. Graff, W.D. Bennett, Z. Nie, L.V. Saraf, I.A. Aksay, J. Liu, and J.-G. Zhang, "Hierarchically Porous Graphene as a Lithium-Air Battery Electrode", *Nano Lett.*, vol. **11**, pp. 5071-5078, 2011.
10. Kichambare, P. and S. Rodrigues, Graphene Nanosheets Based Cathodes for Lithium-Oxygen Batteries", *C- J Carbon Research*, vol. **1**, pp. 27-42, 2015.

Correlation of Pore Size and Discharge Capacity in Li-air Battery with Carbon Nanotube Foams as Cathodes

Chao Shen[(a)(c)], Teng Liu[(d)], Mei Zhang[(b)(d)], Jim Zheng[(a)(c)(e)*], Mary Hendrickson[(f)], and Edward Plichta[(f)]

[(a)]Department of Electrical and Computer Engineering and [(b)]Department of Industrial and Manufacturing Engineering, Florida A&M University and Florida State University, Tallahassee, FL 32310; [(c)]Aero-Propulsion, Mechatronics and Energy Center, [(d)]High Performance Materials Institute, and [(e)]Center for Advanced Power Systems, Florida State University, Tallahassee, FL 32310; [(f)]Army Power Division, RDER-CCA, 5100 Magazine Road, Aberdeen Proving Ground, MD 21005

Abstract: It is generally accepted that the porosity, pore size, pore volume and surface area of the cathode material can affect the discharge capacity of Li-air battery. In this study, the reported tunable three-dimensional CNT foam affords the opportunity to estimate the influence of cathode pore structure on the discharge capacity of Li-air battery. A series of CNT foams were synthesized with high porosity and desired macropore size and used as Li-air battery cathodes. A direct inverse correlation between the carbon pore size and cell discharge capacity was proposed. Based on combined study of galvanostatic discharge, microscopy, porosimetry and modeling, we found that partial utilization of total pore volume caused by electrical passivation was the main factor limiting the discharge capacity.

Keywords: Li-air battery; carbon material; pore size; galvanostatic discharge; discharge capacity

Introduction

In recent years Li-air battery has attracted considerable attention due to its extreme high specific energy [1, 2]. The cathode plays a significant role of electron transfer and Li_2O_2 storage in rechargeable Li-air battery. Good electronic and ionic conductivity, fast oxygen diffusion, stable mechanical integrity and sufficient surface area and porosity are required for Li-air battery cathode [3]. It is generally accepted that the porosity, pore size, pore volume and surface area of the cathode material can affect the discharge capacity of Li-air battery. In order to correlate the battery performance with characteristics of cathode structure, it is useful to test materials with well-defined pore architectures. This can be realized through template based methods of preparation. In this work, a simple and scalable template based method for manufacturing three-dimensional carbon nanotube (CNT) foam as Li-air battery cathode was being reported. CNT foams were synthesized using poly(methyl methacrylate) (PMMA) microspheres as a template and Polyacrylonitrile (PAN) as a precursor to create crosslinking connections between CNTs [4, 5]. The porosity and the pore size of the CNT foam can be tuned easily by adjusting the concentration and particle size of the PMMA microspheres. The assembled CNT foam has a hierarchically porous structure and the pore size ranges from several nanometers to tens of micrometers.

The CNT foam owns various physical characteristics for the potential use as advanced Li-air battery cathode material. Excellent electrical behavior of CNT itself and the effective crosslinking connections between CNTs result in high conductivity. The macropore forming the three-dimensional carbon network promotes oxygen transport as well as electrolyte wetting. The large void volume provides storage space for the solid discharge product Li_2O_2. The high surface area extends the tri-phase (solid-liquid-gas) regions to favor discharge reaction. The freestanding architecture eliminates the potential issue of binder decomposition during cell operation.

We began by fabricating a series of CNT foams with high porosity and desired macropore size. Li-air cells were built and tested with the punched CNT foams as cathodes for single galvanostatic discharge performance. The test result was combined with microscopy, porosimetry and modeling to determine the main factor limiting the discharge capacity.

Experimental

Figure 1 described the synthesis pathway of CNT foam. The fabrication process of CNT foam started from making PAN/DMF solution. 1 weight percent of PAN was dissolved in Dimethylformamide (DMF). The PAN/DMF solution was then added to multi-walled carbon nanotube (MWCNT) with the weight ratio of PAN to MWCNT as 0.5, and proper amount of isopropyl alcohol (IPA) was added. The mixture was well dispersed by high power sonication (Misonix Sonicator 3000) for 30 min. Then PMMA spheres with desired size and weight were added to the CNT/PAN/IPA suspension. The followed 10-min bath sonication helped the mixture to reach a uniform dispersion of PMMA spheres in the suspension. After this, the mixture was put into vacuum filtration system to make the CNT/PAN/PMMA solid gel, which was further dried to remove IPA and DMF. The CNT foam was obtained through two thermal treatments, i.e. at 300 °C for 3 h in air and then at 1200 °C for 1 h in nitrogen with 80 ml min^{-1} flow rate. During the 1st thermal treatment, the PMMA microspheres were depolymerized and expelled while the PAN precursor was stabilized. In the 2nd high temperature treatment, the stabilized PAN precursor was carbonized to form graphitic structures among the CNTs. In this experiment, the weight ratio of PMMA to MWCNT was

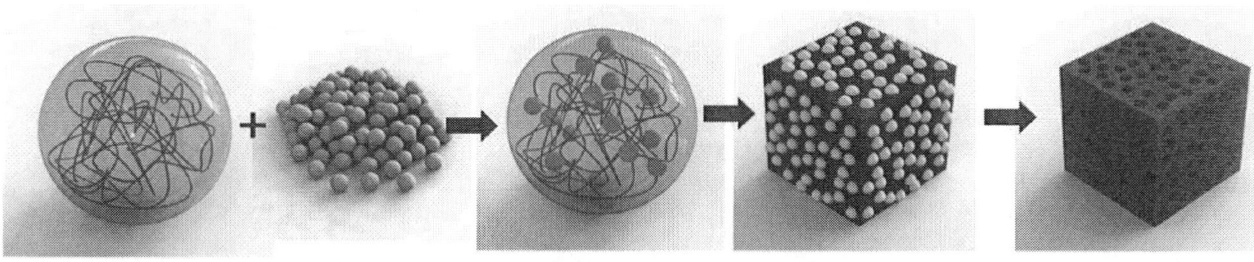

Figure 1. A schematic illustrating the synthesis pathway of CNT foam.

17 and the diameters of the PMMA spheres were 6±2, 9±2, 19±2, 23±2, and 27±2 μm. The samples obtained were denoted by CNT6, CNT9, CNT19, CNT23, CNT27, respectively, where the numbers represent the average size of macropore in CNT foams. The sample porosity was ~98% and the thickness was ~150 μm as pristine.

Scanning electron microscopy (SEM, JEOL-JSM7401F, 10 KV) was used to characterize the morphology of the CNT foam. The porosimetry of the samples were measured using a surface analyzer (Autosorb iQ Micropore Instrument) from nitrogen gas adsorption-desorption isotherms at 77K. All samples were outgassed at 200 °C for 2 h prior to the test. The Brunauer–Emmett–Teller (BET) specific surface areas were determined from the linear portion of the adsorption isotherm. The pore size distributions were calculated using the Barrett–Joyner–Halenda (BJH) method applied to the adsorption branch of the isotherm. The phase identification of the discharge product was conducted by X-ray diffraction (XRD) using a Siemens D500 diffractometer with CuK_α radiation source. Previous to the analysis the discharged cathode was washed with TEGDME solvent and dried in the glovebox. The sample was then transferred into the XRD chamber using a hermetically sealed aluminum sample holder with a thin transparent polymer film window.

The CNT foams were directly punched to disks with diameter of 0.625 inch (15.875 mm) and used as Li-air battery cathodes. Li-air cells were built in an argon atmosphere glovebox by stacking a lithium metal anode, a piece of glass fiber separator and a punched cathode in sequence into an electrochemical testing cell (ECC-AIR, EL-CELL GmbH, Co, Germany). The thickness of the cathode was controlled as 100 μm with a stainless steel ring spacer during cell operation. The electrolyte was made with 1 M $LiCF_3SO_3$ in TEGDME, which is a low-vapor-pressure ether that proved to be stable against superoxide attack [6]. Discharge measurements of the cells were carried out in 1 atm. oxygen gas at room temperature using an Arbin Instruments (Arbin-010 MITS pro 4.0-BT2000) controlled by a computer. The fresh Li-air cells were discharged to 2 V at a constant discharge current density of 0.013 mA cm^{-2}. The specific discharge capacities were calculated based on the weight of cathode materials without electrolyte.

Result and discussion

Figure 2 (a) and (b) presented the cross-sectional SEM images of pristine CNT6 and CNT27 sample, respectively. The cellular structure exhibited the geometry of a major spherical void with pore size in the order of micrometer. These cells were close-packed and interconnected with each other through the junctions of carbonaceous walls. The dimension of the spherical voids clearly depended on the size of the PMMA spheres template. Figure 2 (c) provided the zoom-in image of CNT6 sample, which revealed that the cell walls consisted of numerous minor cellular pores with sizes of 200-500 nm. Figure 2 (d) showed the SEM image of CNT27 sample after discharge. The carbon surface was deposited with a thin layer of solid discharge product Li_2O_2. The major voids of the samples remained open, suggesting a low pore utilization rate when the discharge reaction was terminated.

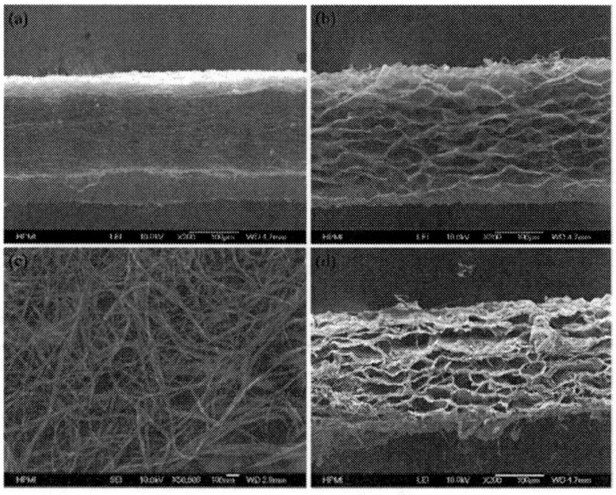

Figure 2. SEM images of CNT foams as pristine (a-c) and after discharge (d).

Figure 3 presented the first discharge voltage profile of Li-air batteries with different cathodes. It can be seen that CNT27 gave the lowest specific capacity of 3,330 mAh g^{-1}, while CNT6 delivered the highest specific capacity of 10,313 mAh g^{-1}. The first discharge profile demonstrated a clear inverse correlation between the cathode macropore size and the cell specific discharge capacity.

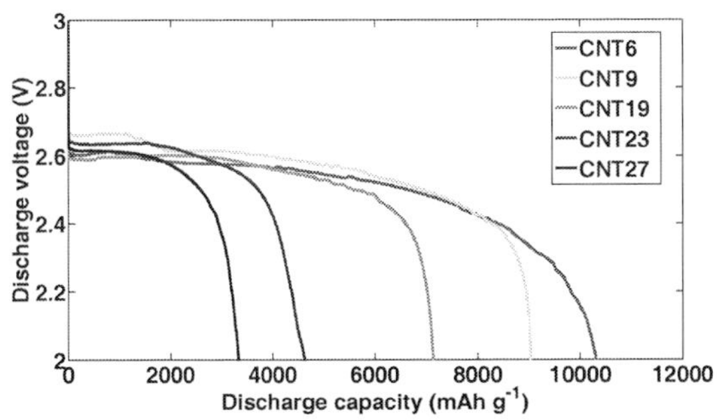

Figure 3. The first discharge voltage profile of Li-air battery with different CNT foam cathodes at a current of 0.013 mA cm^{-2}.

Figure 4 showed the isotherm of CNT6 sample and it exhibited type IV characteristics according to the IUPAC classification of six sorption isotherms [7]. The isotherm figures suggested that the CNT foam sample contained both micropores and meso- or macropores consistent with the hierarchical structure observed under SEM imaging. The BJH pore size distributions of different samples were shown in Figure 5. It is clear that the pore size distributions share a

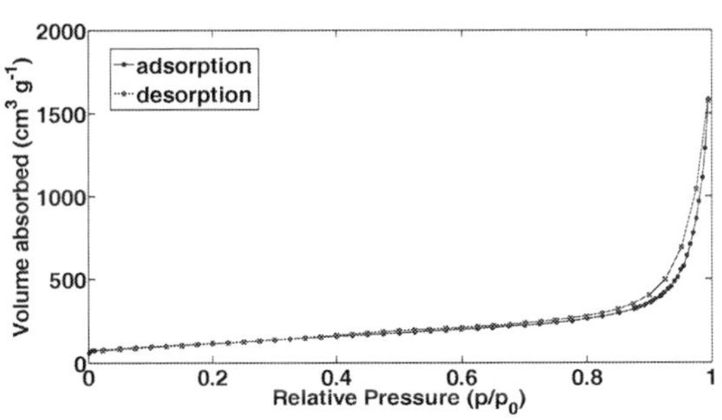

Figure 4. Nitrogen adsorption-desorption isotherm of CNT6 sample.

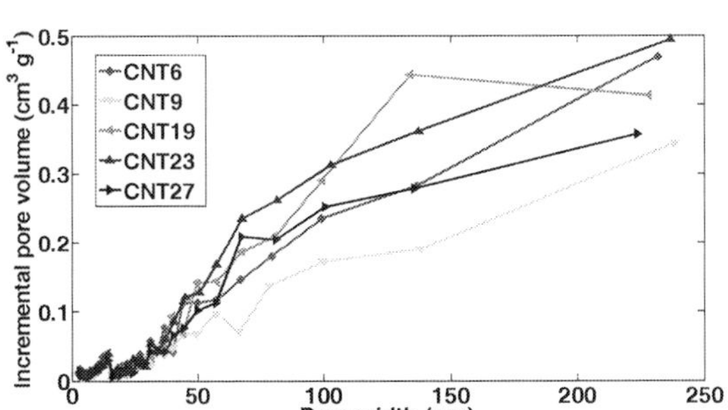

Figure 5. BJH pore size distributions of CNT foam samples.

similar hierarchical structure and the macropore occupies a significant fraction of the pore volume. In Table 1, we summarized the measured results of the surface area, pore volume and average pore size of different CNT foam samples. Among them CNT27 exhibited the highest value of 451 m^2 g^{-1} for BET surface area. For pore volume, CNT19 had the highest value of 2.66 cm^3 g^{-1}. On the other hand, CNT9 showed the lowest value of surface area and pore volume. One can see that the simple proportionality of the cell specific discharge capacity to either surface area or pore volume was not observed in this case. The correlation of the capacity with the average pore size in the measured range did not comply either. It indicated that the microstructure rather than the nanostructure of the cathode may be the main factor causing the capacity difference.

Table 1. Surface area and pore characteristics of CNT foam samples.

Cathode material	Surface area (m^2 g^{-1})	Pore volume (cm^3 g^{-1})	Average pore size (nm)	Specific capacity (mAh g^{-1})
CNT6	425	2.45	38.8	10313
CNT9	358	1.79	30.8	9032
CNT19	445	2.66	32.9	7149
CNT23	431	2.29	32.4	4635
CNT27	451	2.06	24.7	3330

To achieve maximum discharge capacity for a given cathode structure, the oxygen reduction reaction (ORR) must be maintained until the solid discharge product Li_2O_2 fill the total void volume of the cathode. However, Li_2O_2 is known to hinder the oxygen transport and charge transfer pathways due to its electrical passivation nature, thereby limiting the utilization of total pore volume. In order to understand the pore filling mechanism in the cathode, especially in the case with sufficiently large pores, we assumed that a thin layer of Li_2O_2 with thickness of t formed as the discharge product inside the carbon pores. As shown in Figure 6, for pores with radius smaller than t, the pore volume can be fully filled. For pores with radius larger than t, the pore volume was partially utilized. Assume the average radius of these pores is R_{av}, then the pore utilization rate of the partially filled pore can be calculated as the ratio of Li_2O_2 deposition volume to the total volume of the pore. When the discharge reaction is terminated, the total pore volume for Li_2O_2 deposition can be determined as:

$$V_d = \left[1 - \left(1 - \frac{t}{R_{av}}\right)^3\right](V_{tot} - V_f) + V_f \qquad (1)$$

where V_{tot} is the total pore volume of the cathode and V_f is the pore volume that can be fully filled by Li_2O_2.

If R_{av} is significantly larger than t, the pore utilization rate for partially filled pore will be relatively small, limiting the total pore volume for Li_2O_2 deposition.

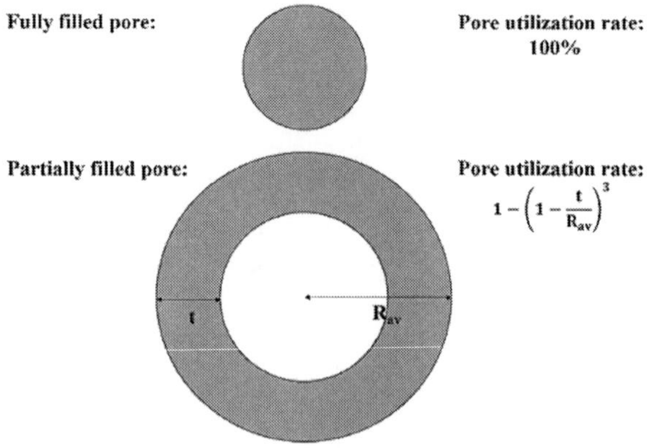

Figure 6. A schematic illustration of the pore filling model.

The calculated pore volume can be correlated with the discharge capacity using (1), assuming only the 2-electron discharge reaction with Li_2O_2 as the only product occurred:

$$V_d = \frac{Qm_cM_d}{2\rho_dF} \quad (2)$$

where Q is the discharge capacity, m_c is the weight of cathode, M_d is the molar weight of Li_2O_2 (45.88 g mol^{-1}), ρ_d is the buck density of Li_2O_2 (2.31 g cm^{-3}), F is the Faraday constant.

Due to the similarity of V_{tot} and V_f between different samples, with this model one would deduce the correlation as a reduced capacity with the increase of average pore size of partially filled pore. If we assume that a thin layer of Li_2O_2 with thickness of 10 nm formed inside the carbon pores as derived from the XRD pattern using the Scherrer equation, then the average partially filled pore sizes and pore utilization rates of the samples can be calculated as listed in Table 2. The calculated R_{av} tracked the average macropore size well and the value reduction resulted from the compression of the sample during assembly and the inclusion of mesopores in the calculation. The CNT6 sample yielded a much higher pore utilization rate of 27.4% than that of CNT27 sample, which can account for the 3-fold increase in the specific discharge capacities.

Table 2. Pore size calculation result of CNT foam samples.

Cathode material	R_{av} (nm)	Pore utilization rate (%)
CNT6	110	27.4%
CNT9	123	24.3%
CNT19	232	13.0%
CNT23	268	11.2%
CNT27	364	8.2%

Conclusion

In this work, a simple and scalable template based method for manufacturing three-dimensional CNT foams was reported. CNT foams were synthesized with high porosity and desired macropore size and used as Li-air battery cathodes. The well-characterized macropore size regime spanned a range unpresented in the literature for Li-air battery cathodes. A direct inverse correlation between the carbon macropore size and cell specific discharge capacity was proposed. Microscopy, porosimetry and modeling were conducted to study the influence of pore structure on the discharge capacity. It revealed that partial utilization of total pore volume caused by electrical passivation was the main factor limiting the discharge capacity.

Acknowledgements

This work was supported by US Army Power Division under contract No. GTS-S-15-014.

References

1. Akhtar, N. and W. Akhtar, "Prospects, challenges, and latest developments in lithium–air batteries," *Int. J. Energy Res*, vol. 39, no. 3, pp. 303–316, 2015.
2. Imanishi, N. and O. Yamamoto, "Rechargeable lithium–air batteries: characteristics and prospects," *Mater. Today*, vol. 17, no. 1, pp. 24–30, 2014.
3. Lu, J., L. Li, J. B. Park, Y. K. Sun, F. Wu and K. Amine, "Aprotic and aqueous Li–O_2 batteries," *Chem. Rev*, vol. 114, no. 11, pp. 5611-5640, 2014.
4. Cui, Y. and M. Zhang, "Cross-links in Carbon Nanotube Assembly Introduced by Using Polyacrylonitrile as Precursor," *ACS Appl. Mater. Interfaces*, vol. 5, no. 16, pp. 8173–8178, 2013.
5. Cui, Y. and M. Zhang, "Fabrication of cross-linked carbon nanotube foam using polymethylmethacrylate microspheres as templates," *J. Mater. Chem. A*, vol. 1, no. 44, pp. 13984-13988, 2013.
6. Black, R., S. H. Oh, J. H. Lee, T. Yim, B. Adams and L. F. Nazar, "Screening for superoxide reactivity in Li-O_2 batteries: effect on Li_2O_2/LiOH crystallization," *J. Am. Chem. Soc.*, vol. 134, no. 6, pp. 2902-2905, 2012.
7. Sing, K. S. W, "Reporting physisorption data for gas/solid systems with special reference to the determination of surface area and porosity (Recommendations 1984)," *Pure Appl. Chem.*, vol. 57, no. 4, pp. 603–619, 1985.

Ceramic Polymer Composite Electrolytes (CPCE) for a Wearable Li-Metal Battery

Brian Henslee
Cornerstone Research Group
Jitendra Kumar
University of Dayton Research Institute
Guru Subramanyam
University of Dayton

hensleeb@crgrp.com

Abstract

A battery used in a wearable or conformal electronic has significant weight and volume constraints. The volumetric packaging cost is significant and most of the packaging structure is dedicated to encapsulating sensitive electrolytes, aqueous or aprotic. Solid electrolytes are a path forward that provides battery performance durability, and safety while facilitating the use of flexible battery packaging materials that translate to low cost, high-density, conformal, wearable batteries. The full potential of solid electrolytes can only be realized if improvements in processing cost and stability with ultra high energy systems is improved resulting in a disruptive energy density beyond the Li-ion technology. In particular, research and development of solid-state flexible electrolytes capable of coping with massive structural reconfigurations required in next-generation electrodes such as Si, SnO_2, sulfur is needed. We will present novel methods to create flexible Ceramic Polymer Composite Electrolytes (CPCE) films for conformal and wearable lithium metal batteries such as extrusion, solution processing, spray drying, and polymer compounding with LISICON ceramics. Structural, thermal, electrical, and electrochemical characterization of the CPCE films will be presented. Battery performance of wearable battery cells (Li-Sulfur, Li-O_2) based on free-standing and flexible electrolyte (CPCE), anode and cathode will be discussed.

High Voltage Aqueous Redox Flow Batteries Based on Low Cost Electrolytes

Christopher Swartz and Stephen Lipka
Electrochemical Power Sources Group
University of Kentucky Center for Applied Energy Research
2582 Research Park Drive, Lexington, KY 40513

Abstract: *Redox flow batteries are an emerging technology suitable for grid energy storage applications. One distinct advantage of redox flow battery systems is the ability to decouple the energy density and capacity of the system from power performance. Higher capacities are achievable through the use of larger electrolyte storage tanks and higher concentrations of electroactive species, while higher power densities are achievable through the use of larger stacks. Many of the currently deployed systems are based on vanadium electrochemistry, and the search for electrolyte chemistries based on inexpensive redox couples is of great interest. One major goal for this research program was to develop higher voltage anolytes (relative to vanadium) based on aqueous manganese electrochemistry.*

Keywords: grid storage; redox flow batteries; aqueous electrolytes; manganese electrochemistry

Introduction

The capability to store electricity is set to become an integral component of the future electrical grid. Emerging technologies found in the grid storage portfolio include pumped hydro energy storage, compressed air energy storage, thermal and flywheel energy storage, and various electrochemical energy storage options, including redox flow batteries. Redox flow batteries (RFBs) are secondary battery systems suitable for large-scale, stationary energy storage applications, and are capable of storing large quantities of energy (MWh) and power (MW).[1] Redox flow batteries share many similarities with fuel cells, and are rechargeable, modular battery systems where energy storage and power performance can be decoupled from one another due to the battery architecture, and both can be scaled independently. The all-vanadium redox flow battery represents the current state-of-the-art in flow battery technology, and numerous demonstration units have been installed worldwide, ranging from kW, kWh units to MW, MWh capabilities. The relatively high cost of these systems has prevented widespread adoption of flow battery technology, and new flow battery systems featuring lower cost chemistries and ion exchange membranes (when compared to vanadium and Nafion®, respectively) remain highly attractive candidates to move flow batteries along on a forward trajectory to the commercial marketplace.[1,2] A flow battery schematic illustrating the battery architecture is shown in Figure 1.

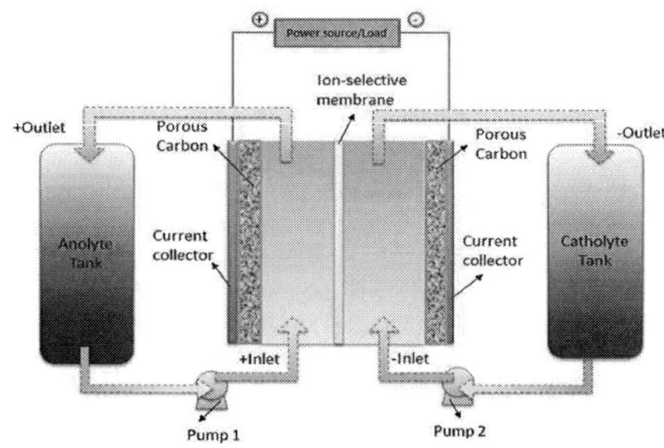

Figure 1. Schematic of a redox flow battery.

The specific purpose of this work was to develop and demonstrate the efficacy of manganese-based anolytes as a suitable alternative to vanadium anolytes for redox flow batteries. Manganese electrochemistry is attractive for three principle reasons, including a higher reversible potential for Mn^{2+}/Mn^{3+} than VO^{2+}/VO_2^{+}, higher natural abundance, and lower cost than vanadium. Flow battery anolytes based on the Mn^{2+}/Mn^{3+} redox couple have been reported in the literature, and the high standard electrode potential of Mn^{2+}/Mn^{3+} (1.51 V) has been utilized in manganese anolyte (Mn^{2+}/Mn^{3+})/vanadium catholyte (V^{2+}/V^{3+}) redox flow batteries, featuring a theoretical open circuit voltage of 1.77 V.[2,3] The usage of manganese anolytes can lead to a higher cell voltage, yet the disproportionation reaction of Mn^{3+} is a technical hurdle that needs to be resolved in order for manganese-based anolytes to find widespread utility in redox flow batteries.[2,4,5,6] The disproportionation reaction of Mn^{3+} is shown in Equation 1.

$$2Mn^{3+} + 2H_2O \longrightarrow Mn^{2+} + MnO_2 + 4H^{+} \text{ (Eq. 1)}$$

We have successfully demonstrated the ability to cycle manganese-based anolytes in a flow cell configuration for hundreds of cycles, with minimal degradation in cell performance, with the use of novel electrolyte additives to inhibit MnO_2 precipitation. Manganese-based anolytes are also capable of cycling at higher voltages than vanadium anolytes with high cell performance metrics, including coulombic, voltage, and energy efficiencies typically ranging from 75-100%, and achievable volumetric energy densities > 20 Wh/L, which are comparable to currently deployed vanadium redox flow batteries.

Experimental

Three electrode half-cell measurements, including cyclic voltammetry experiments were performed at room temperature using quiescent conditions with various electrolyte formulations. Graphite working electrodes were employed in the cells, along with a graphite or DSA counter electrode, and a Ag/AgCl reference electrode. Redox flow batteries were assembled using SGL carbon felt or SGL 10AA carbon paper as the electrode materials in the anolyte and catholyte compartment, respectively. Interdigitated graphite flow fields were utilized both compartments of the cell. A reference electrode (Ag/AgCl) was embedded in the graphite flow field used in the manganese electrolyte compartment, in order to monitor and control the potential of the positive electrode. Ion exchange membranes, including proton exchange membranes (Nafion® 212) and anion exchange membranes (Fumasep FAP-PP-375) were used to separate the anolyte and catholyte compartments during cycling. Electrolytes were pumped through both compartments using a ColeParmer Masterflex L/S economy drive peristaltic pump, at flow rates ranging from 10-30 mL/min. For V/Mn full cell testing, the vanadium catholyte compartment was sparged with nitrogen during cycling to remove oxygen, and to prevent oxidation of V^{2+}. Constant current charge/discharge experiments were performed at apparent current densities ranging from 10-125 mA/cm^2, based on the apparent surface area of the graphite flow field.

Results

A representative cyclic voltammogram for the standard manganese anolyte formulation used in the full cell cycling studies is shown in Figure 2. The electrolyte formulation is 1.2M $MnSO_4$, xM additive in 3M H_2SO_4. The purpose of the electrolyte additive was to stabilize Mn^{3+} in solution, and to prevent the disproportionation reaction of Mn^{3+} to form MnO_2. The potential for the Mn^{2+}/Mn^{3+} redox couple is +1.28 V vs. Ag/AgCl, with a peak separation of 0.467 V, and a peak current ratio (anodic peak current/cathodic peak current; I_a/I_c) of 1.19.

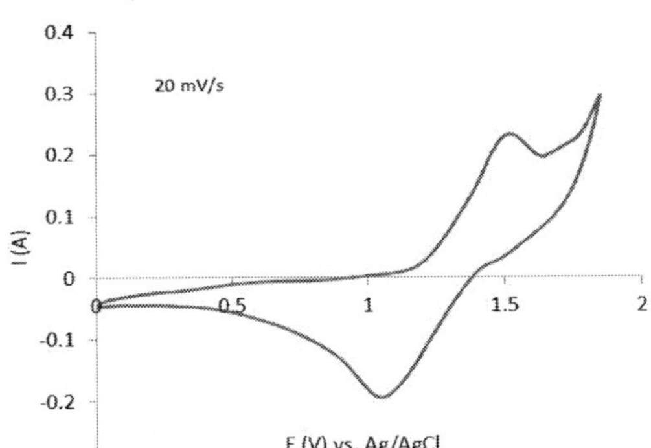

Figure 2. Cyclic voltammogram for standard manganese anolyte formulation. Sweep rate = 20 mV/s.

The manganese anolyte was then cycled in a full cell configuration at various applied current densities. A current density of 125 mA/cm^2 was achieved at a maximum charge voltage of 1.275 V vs. Ag/AgCl, before cell performance metrics began to fall off significantly, as seen in Figure 3a. The manganese-based half cell had a coulombic efficiency (CE) of 99.3%, a voltage efficiency (VE) of 91%, and an energy efficiency (EE) of 90.4%. The capacity utilization of the manganese anolyte was 63% (Figure 3b), with a calculated energy density of 18 Wh/L.

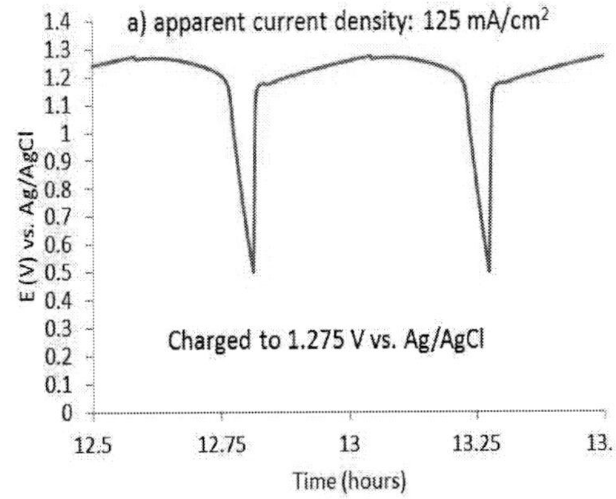

Figure 3a. Constant current charge/discharge data for manganese anolyte (125 mA/cm^2).

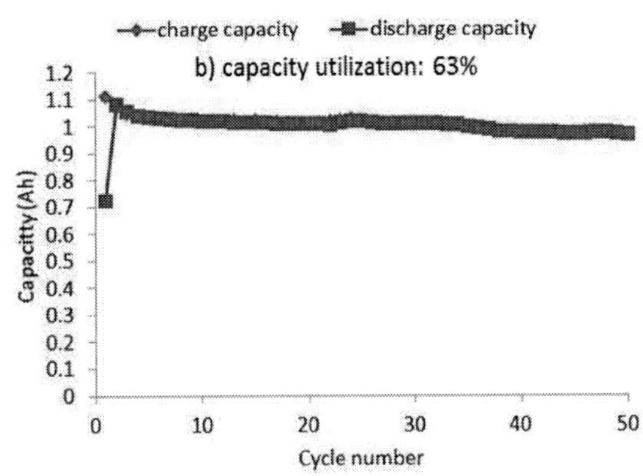

Figure 3b. Charge and discharge capacity data for 50 cycles at 125 mA/cm^2.

Control of the charge voltage is of critical importance for redox flow batteries that utilize manganese anolytes, due to the high anodic potential of Mn^{2+}/Mn^{3+}. Overcharge typically led to significant gas evolution and oxidation of the carbon electrodes and graphite flow field, respectively. Overcharge also led to significant precipitation of MnO_2, and significantly reduced cycle life for the cell.

Control of the charge voltage was also imperative for maximization of the charge and discharge capacity of the manganese electrolyte. For example, the maximum charge voltage that can be achieved for the manganese anolyte is 1.30 V vs. Ag/AgCl at an apparent current density of 46 mA/cm^2, leading to a maximum capacity utilization of 77.5% (Figure 4a and 4b). Table 1 is a summary of cell performance metrics for the manganese anolyte at 46 mA/cm^2, with three different charge voltages. Increasing the charge voltage by 50 mV (from 1.25 V to 1.30 V vs. Ag/AgCl) leads to a dramatic increase in both the capacity utilization and energy density for the manganese anolyte, achieving > 21 Wh/L, as seen in Table 1.

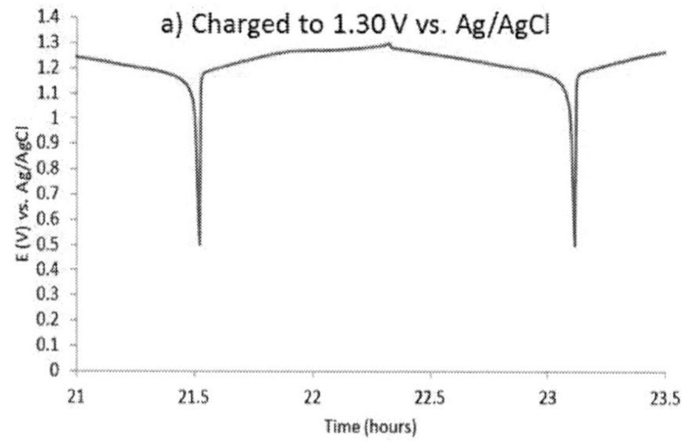

Figure 4a. Charge and discharge data at 46 mA/cm^2; charged to 1.30 V vs. Ag/AgCl.

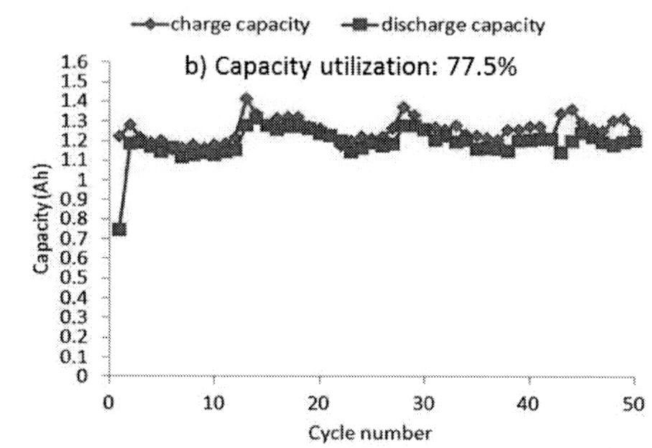

Figure 4b. Charge and discharge capacity data for 50 cycles at 46 mA/cm^2; charged to 1.30 V vs. Ag/AgCl.

Charge voltage (vs. Ag/AgCl)	CE (%)	VE (%)	EE (%)	Capacity utilization (%)	Energy density (Wh/L)
1.25	97.1	87.1	84.6	29.5	8.55
1.275	98.6	87.6	86.4	50.9	14.96
1.30	96.3	81.7	78.7	77.5	21.47

Table 1. Summary of cell performance metrics for anolyte at 46 mA/cm^2, at different charge voltages.

Cycle life studies for the manganese anolyte were also performed by cycling at different apparent current densities and charge voltages, as seen in Figure 5, and are summarized in Table 2. SGL carbon felt was used as the conductive carbon electrode for the cycling experiments. As seen previously, the capacity utilization for the electrolyte increased with charge voltage. The coulombic efficiencies for the cell were > 95% over 800 cycles, irrespective of apparent current density. Comparison of regions E, G, and H (charge voltage = 1.275 V vs. Ag/AgCl) show that increasing the apparent current density has no effect on coulombic efficiency, and only leads to minor decreases in the voltage and energy efficiencies at the higher apparent current densities.

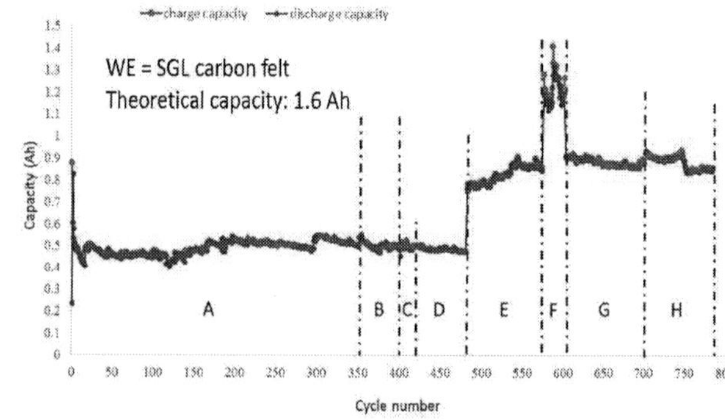

Figure 5. Cycle life data for manganese anolyte to 800 cycles.

region	C rate	Apparent current density (mA/cm^2)	Charge voltage on positive electrode (V vs. Ag/AgCl)	Capacity Utilization (%)	CE (%)	VE (%)	EE (%)	Energy density (Wh/L)
A	C/2	23	1.25	28.2	97.8	89.3	87.3	8.25
B	C/4	11.5	1.25	29.1	94	91.6	86.1	8.22
C	C/8	5.75	1.25	31.5	100	96.1	96.1	9
D	C	46	1.25	29.5	97.1	87.1	84.6	8.55
E	C	46	1.275	50.9	98.6	87.6	86.4	14.96
F	C	46	1.30	77.5	96.3	81.7	78.7	21.47
G	1.5C	69	1.275	53.9	98.7	77.4	76.4	13.82
H	2.25C	103	1.275	53.2	99	77.9	77.1	14.2

Table 2. Summary of cell performance metrics for manganese anolyte.

V/Mn Full Cell Testing

The successful demonstration of a functional V/Mn redox flow battery was then achieved using equal volumes of the fully optimized manganese anolyte (1.2M $MnSO_4$, xM additive in 3M H_2SO_4), in conjunction with a vanadium catholyte (1.2M V^{2+}/V^{3+} in 3M H_2SO_4). Replacement of the vanadium anolyte with manganese resulted in a redox flow battery with a higher cell voltage (E_{cell} = 1.77 V). The cell charge and discharge reactions are shown below in Figure 6.

$$Mn^{2+} \underset{\text{discharge}}{\overset{\text{charge}}{\rightleftharpoons}} Mn^{3+} + e^- \qquad E = +1.29 \text{ V vs. Ag/AgCl}$$

$$V^{3+} + e^- \underset{\text{discharge}}{\overset{\text{charge}}{\rightleftharpoons}} V^{2+} \qquad E = -0.483 \text{ V vs. Ag/AgCl}$$

$$E_{cell} = 1.77 \text{ V}$$

Figure 6. Half-cell reactions for V/Mn redox flow battery.

Cyclic voltammetry data illustrating the V/Mn electrochemistry is shown in Figure 7. The data was generated in a half-cell configuration using a graphite working electrode, a DSA or graphite counter electrode, and a Ag/AgCl reference electrode.

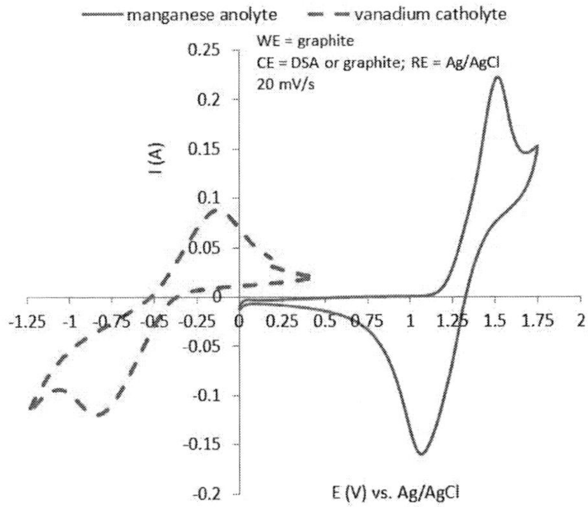

Figure 7. Cyclic voltammetry data demonstrating V/Mn redox reactions (sweep rate = 20 mV/s).

The cell utilized SGL carbon felt for the manganese anolyte, and surface-functionalized SGL 10AA carbon paper was used as the electrocatalytic electrode for the vanadium catholyte. In order to minimize crossover of electroactive metal cations, an anion exchange membrane (Fumasep FAP-450; 50 microns thick) was employed in the cell. The cell was cycled at an apparent current density of 23 mA/cm^2, with a maximum charge voltage of 1.185 V vs. Ag/AgCl used for the manganese anolyte. The full cell voltage profile was obtained using a digital data recorder, and is shown in Figure 8. The full cell charge voltage was 2 V, with a coulombic efficiency of 93.9%, a voltage efficiency of 70%, and an energy efficiency of 65.7%. The V/Mn redox flow battery had 35% capacity utilization and an energy density of 14.77 Wh/L.

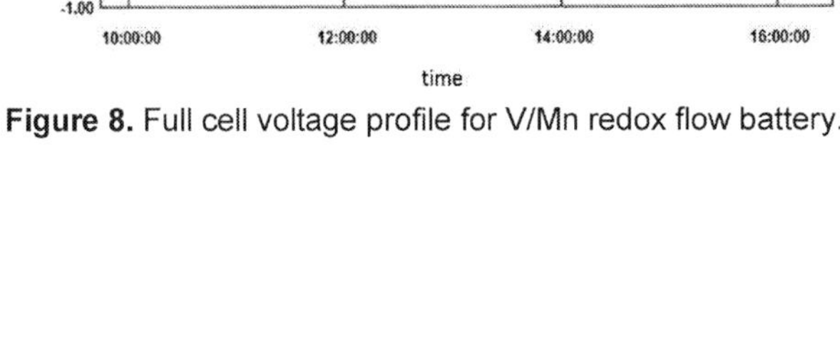

Figure 8. Full cell voltage profile for V/Mn redox flow battery.

Conclusions

Manganese anolytes were successfully optimized and demonstrated in a full cell configuration. In order to prevent disproportionation of Mn^{3+} to form MnO_2, two major strategies were adopted, including the use of electrolyte additives to stabilize Mn^{3+}, and inclusion of a reference electrode to monitor and control the potential of the manganese electrode, in order to prevent overcharge. The manganese anolyte was cycled for over 800 cycles, with over 300 cycles at > 50% depth of discharge. A high voltage (2V) aqueous redox flow battery utilizing an anion exchange membrane was then demonstrated using the V/Mn cell chemistry.

Acknowledgements

The authors wish to thank ARPA-E for funding (contract number DE-AR000260), and Thomas Kodenkandath and ITN Energy Systems, Inc. for helpful discussions.

References

1. Wang, W. et al. *J. Power Sources.* **2012**, *216*, 99.
2. Xue, F.-Q. et al. *Electrochimica Acta.* **2008**, *53*, 6636.
3. Hong, T.; Xue, F. "Investigation on manganese (Mn^{2+}/Mn^{3+})-vanadium (V^{2+}/V^{3+}) redox flow battery." 2009 Asia-Pacific Power and Energy Engineering Conference (APPEEC).
4. Swartz, C. R.; Lipka, S. M.; Rogers, F. III; Chen, R.; Kodenkandath, T. "Aqueous Manganese-Based Electrolytes for Redox Flow Batteries." Presented at the 226th Meeting of the Electrochemical Society, Cancun, Mexico, October 2014 (ECS abstract MA2014-02, 616).
5. Swartz, C. R., Lipka, S. M., Long, K. F.; Kodenkandath, T. "Manganese-Based Redox Flow Batteries for Grid Energy Storage," Presented at the 228th Meeting of the Electrochemical Society, Phoenix, AZ, October 2015 (ECS abstract MA2015-02, 115).
6. Soloveichik, G. L. *Chem. Rev.* **2015**, *115*, 11533.

Next-Generation Rechargeable Zinc Batteries based on Advanced 3D Electrode Designs

Joseph F. Parker, Christopher N. Chervin, Debra R. Rolison, and Jeffrey W. Long

Surface Chemistry Branch – Code 6170
U.S. Naval Research Laboratory
Washington, DC 20375, USA
Contact Author Email: jeffrey.long@nrl.navy.mil

Abstract: *Zinc-based alkaline batteries offer compelling alternatives to Li-ion batteries in terms of improved safety and lower cost. Although well-established for commercial and military applications in primary (single-use) forms such as Zn–air and MnO_2–Zn, poor cyclability has hindered the broader use of Zn batteries. Conventional Zn electrodes, typically powder-composite forms, suffer from non-ideal current flux, leading to low Zn utilization and dendrite formation upon extended cycling. We have redesigned the Zn anode in a "sponge" form factor that mitigates many of the historic limitations of Zn batteries. In this study, we demonstrate that Zn sponge anodes achieve Zn utilization up to ~90% (740 mA h g_{Zn}^{-1}) when discharged in either primary Zn–air or Ni–Zn cells. During discharge we periodically sample the corresponding cells to determine open-circuit voltage and impedance as a function of state-of-charge (SoC). The 3D-interconnected "wiring" of metallic Zn within the core of the sponge architecture maintains low cell impedance, even to high depths-of-discharge.*

Keywords: zinc–air; nickel–zinc, battery; three-dimensional; state-of-charge

Introduction

Ongoing safety concerns with Li-ion batteries are driving the search for alternative batteries that provide competitive energy density but which are less prone to catastrophic failure. The family of Zn-based batteries (*e.g.*, Zn–air and Ni–Zn) offers compelling options because they can deliver high specific energy in safe, low-cost forms. Zinc batteries have a long history for primary (single-use) applications but have been much less successful in rechargeable configurations, principally because the conventional electrode constructions used for Zn anodes (*e.g.*, packed-powder bed) lead to particle passivation/isolation and dendritic growth during long-term cycling.

In order to overcome the Zn dendrite problem as well as increase the upper-limit discharge capacity of Zn-based batteries, we have architecturally redesigned the Zn anode in a three-dimensional (3D) sponge morphology [1,2]. The Zn sponge design provides: (*i*) an inner core of Zn that is retained throughout battery charge/discharge to facilitate long-range electronic conductivity within the volume of the electrode; (*ii*) amplification of electrified interfaces to distribute current uniformly throughout the electrode structure, eliminating dendrite-forming high current densities; and (*iii*) confined void volume elements within the interior of the porous anode that promote saturation/dehydration of zincate to ZnO at lower zincate concentrations, thus preventing shape change.

We have demonstrated that such Zn sponges achieve 90% Zn utilization (728 mA h g_{Zn}^{-1}) in a primary Zn–air cell and dendrite-free cycling under charge/discharge conditions in a Ni–Zn cell [3]. In this paper, we evaluate Zn sponges as they are exhaustively discharged in prototype cells, paired with either carbon–cryptomelane–Teflon® air cathodes or NiOOH cathodes. We periodically sample the open-circuit voltage and cell impedance as a function of state-of-charge (SoC) and compare the resulting trends for these two related cell chemistries.

Experimental

Zinc Sponge Fabrication: Zinc sponge anodes were prepared as previously described.[1] Briefly, Zn, sodium dodecylsulfate, and carboxymethylcellulose are emulsified in a water:decane mixture for 20 min and poured into cylindrical polypropylene molds. After air-drying for 24 h, the released Zn objects (dried, but fragile) are heated in a two-step thermal treatment, first to 410 °C in argon to initiate Zn particle fusion, followed by heating in static air to 665 °C to thermally oxidize the surfaces of the Zn backbone while the 3D structure continues to form. The surface ZnO of the sponges is reduced *ante experimentum* in 6 M KOH.[1]

Preparation of Zinc–Air Cells: The reduced Zn sponge electrodes are infiltrated with 6 M KOH and dipped in a 6 M KOH/poly(acrylic acid) gel electrolyte, as reported previously [1]. The electrolyte-infiltrated Zn sponges are then placed atop a Sn current collector [4]. A single Freudenberg nonwoven separator is placed between the anode and the carbon–cryptomelane–Teflon® air cathode. A Ni wire is used as the positive external terminal contact. The single-discharge experiments are performed at constant current current density of 5 mA cm^{-2}, with a capacity cut-off for each cell representing 20, 40, 60, and 80% DOD_{Zn}.

Preparation of Nickel–Zinc Cells: The reduced Zn sponge electrodes are infiltrated with an electrolyte mixture of 6 M KOH + 1 M LiOH, with 8 wt % solid $Ca(OH)_2$ at the Zn sponge surface and within the pores [3]. The electrolyte-infiltrated Zn sponges are then placed atop a Sn current collector. A two-layer separator system is applied between the Zn and the NiOOH cathode—first a Celgard 3501 and then a 700/28K Freudenberg nonwoven. A second 700/28K Freudenberg separator is placed on top of the NiOOH cathode to ensure electrolyte availability for the cathode, which is often starved of hydroxide during charging [4]. The NiOOH cathode is harvested from a charged BPI AA battery (Amazon.com), wrapped in a Ni mesh current collector, and pressed to 1,500 psi for 1 min. A Ni wire is used as the positive external terminal contact. The single-discharge experiments were performed at a constant current density of 10 mA cm^{-2}, intermittently paused at 5 % DOD_{Zn} increments to sample OCV and cell resistance.

Results and Discussion

The inner metallic wiring of Zn sponges confers several desirable characteristics: (*i*) high Zn utilization when discharged in primary mode [1,2]; (*ii*) containment of discharge products that are then available for the recharge reaction; and (*iii*) enhanced uniformity of current distribution to suppress the emergence of electrochemical hotspots where dendrites would otherwise grow [5]. We have demonstrated that the sponge form factor leads to high Zn utilization in Zn–air cells (up to 91% DOD_{Zn}; 745 mA h g_{Zn}^{-1}) (Figure 1). A drawback of the Zn–air system, with its flat discharge profile, is that the state-of-charge (SoC) is not immediately ascertainable from passive observational studies, such as open-circuit voltage and electrochemical impedance spectroscopy [6].

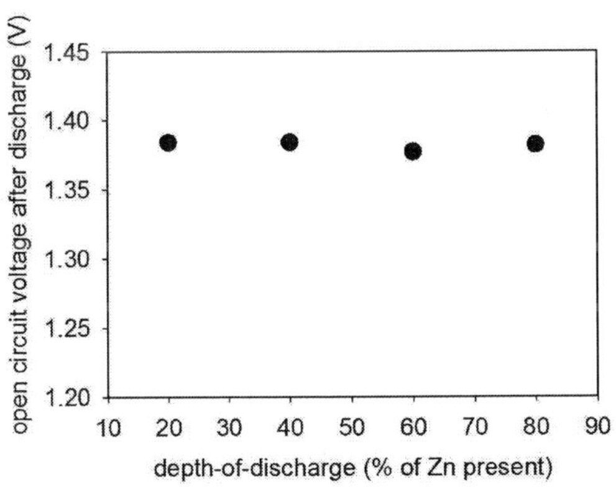

Figure 1. Open-circuit voltage of Zn–air cells at various depths-of-discharge.

The uncertainty in the Zn–air SoC stems from the nature of the two electrodic reactions: the cathodic reaction involves the reduction of oxygen, but the catalyzed air cathode does not undergo a redox reaction itself, so it is not expected to contribute to any changes in conductivity or resistivity of the cell as a function of depth-of-discharge. Similarly, the anodic Zn reaction is very fast and the Zn electrode is not very polarizable [7], so long-range conductivity, especially as wired into our Zn sponge electrodes, will force the Zn–O_2 redox couple to thermodynamically dominate the open-circuit voltage so the accumulating and poorly conductive ZnO will play a negligible role. We have previously demonstrated that the long-range connectivity and retention of inner-wiring, even to high DOD_{Zn} (Figure 2), leads to minimal changes in the cell resistance [2].

Figure 2. Scanning electron micrographs of Zn sponge electrodes before (left) and after (right) discharge to 80 % DOD_{Zn} in Zn–air cells.

Figure 3 shows a sample discharge of a Ni–Zn cell, intermittently sampling the OCV and impedance at 5% DOD_{Zn} increments (~ 41 mA h g_{Zn}^{-1}). Cells discharged with this sequence reached an average total depth-of-discharge of ~ 89 % (~ 730 mA h g_{Zn}^{-1}). The OCV reading at the end of each 1-h pause step is plotted versus the depth-of-discharge (Figure 4). The OCV decreases as the state-of-charge decreases, an observation that differs from the analogous Zn–air experiment highlighted in Figure 1; the Zn–air example serves as a control for the Zn/ZnO electrode because the potential of the air cathode is unchanged throughout the course of discharge. In the case of Ni–Zn cells, the NiOOH electrode is reduced to the less conductive $Ni(OH)_2$ upon discharge [8]. The differing OCV trends in the Ni–Zn case are therefore attributed to the formation of $Ni(OH)_2$, which dominates the observed OCV changes in the two-electrode cell.

The resistances of the Ni–Zn cells are averaged and plotted as a function of depth-of-discharge (Figure 4). In congruence with the OCV measurement, the cell resistance increases as more NiOOH is converted to the more insulating $Ni(OH)_2$. Again, this trend differs from that observed in Zn–air cells [2], where the cell resistance is largely unaffected by the depth-of-discharge.

In conclusion, changes in the OCV and cell resistance during discharge in Ni–Zn batteries are sufficiently distinguishable to design systems that monitor SoC. Alternatively, the relatively unchanged OCV and cell resistance during discharge in Zn–air batteries are ideal from an operational perspective, but complicate the assessment of SoC and will require more sophisticated diagnostics.

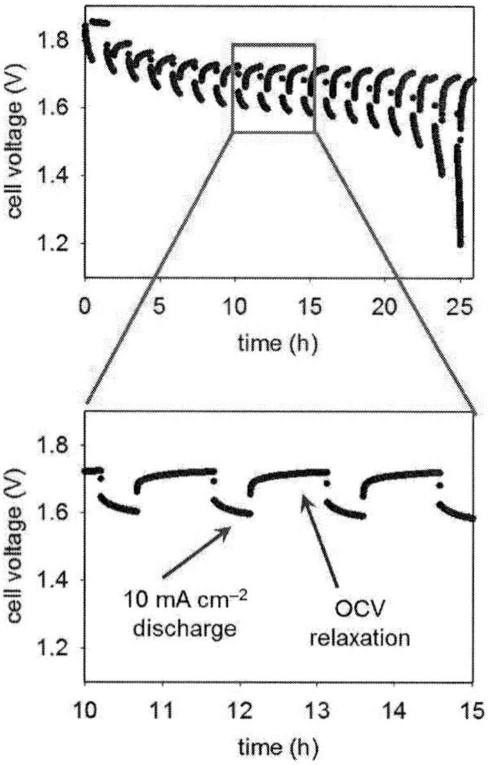

Figure 3. Discharge profile for a sample Ni–Zn cell with intermittent pausing at 5% DOD_{Zn} intervals to assess OCV as a function of state-of-charge.

Acknowledgements

The information, data, or work presented herein was funded by the U. S. Office of Naval Research.

References

1. Parker, J. F., Chervin, C. N., Nelson, E. S., Rolison, D. R., and J. W. Long, "Wiring Zinc in Three dimensions Re-writes Battery Performance–Dendrite-Free Cycling," *Energy & Environmental Science*, vol. 7, pp. 1117–1124, 2014.
2. Parker, J. F., Nelson, E. S., Wattendorf, M. D., Chervin, C. N., Long, J. W., and Rolison, D. R., "Retaining the 3D Framework of Zinc Sponge Anodes upon Deep Discharge in Zn–Air Cells." *ACS Applied Materials & Interfaces*, vol. 6, pp. 19471–19476, 2014.
3. Parker, J. F., Pala, I. R., Chervin, C. N., Long, J. W., Rolison, D. R., "Minimizing Shape Change at Zn Sponge Anodes in Rechargeable Ni–Zn cells: Impact of Electrolyte Formulation." *Journal of the Electrochemical Society*, vol. 163, pp. A351–A355.

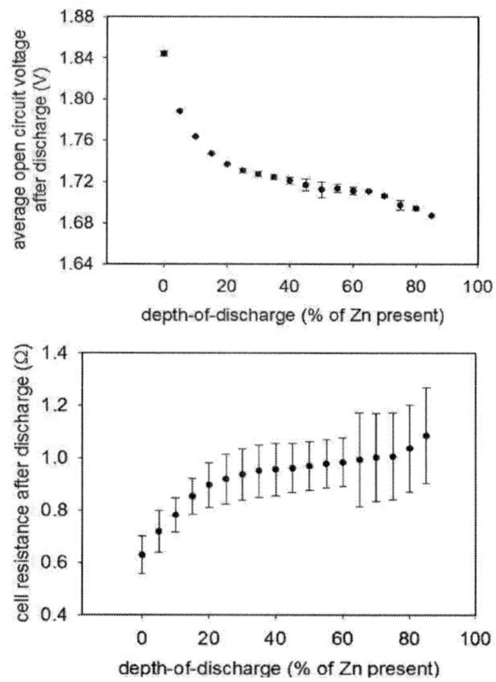

Figure 4. (top) plot of the average open-circuit voltage of Ni–Zn cells as a function of state of charge and (bottom) the corresponding average resistance of the same cells.

4. Bonnick, D. and Dahn, J. R., "A Simple Coin Cell Design for Testing Rechargeable Zinc–Air or Alkaline Battery Systems." *Journal of the Electrochemical Society*, vol. 159, pp. A981–A989, 2012.
5. McBreen, J., "Rechargeable Zinc Batteries," *Journal of Electroanalytical Chemistry*, vol. 168, pp. 415–432, 1984.
6. Şanal, E., Dost, P, and Sourkounis, C. "Electrotechnical Investigation of Zinc-Air Cells for Determination of Cell-Parameters for a Battery Management System." 4th *International Conference on Renewable Energy Research and Applications*, pp. 1157–1161, 2015.
7. Cai, M. and Park, S.-M. "Oxidation of Zinc in Alkaline Solutions Studied by Electrochemical Impedance Spectroscopy." *J. Electrochem. Soc.*, vol. 143, pp. 3895–3902, 1996.
8. Koshel, N. D. and Malyshev, V. V., "Measurement of the resistivity of the electrode NiOOH/$Ni(OH)_2$ solid phase active substance during the discharge process." *Surface Engineering and Applied Electrochemistry*, vol. 46, pp. 348–351, 2010.

Smart Sealed Rechargeable Silver-Zinc Cells for Plug-and-Play, User-Friendly Batteries in Manned and Unmanned Undersea Vehicles

Bryan D. Hirschorn, Michael A. Solis, and Thomas T. Terjesen

BST Systems, Inc.
78 Plainfield Pike Rd. Plainfield, CT, USA, 06374

Abstract: *BST Systems, Inc. is the first company to have developed a large-format (> 100 Ah) sealed and completely maintenance-free, rechargeable silver-zinc (Ag-Zn) cell. The Smart Sealed Ag-Zn (SS-Ag-Zn) features two innovations – an automatic gas balancer (AGB) and microprocessor-based algorithm-driven smart system manager (SSM) – that together with a commercial catalyst automatically manage gases to maintain low, sub-atmospheric internal pressure (negative gauge) for the life of the cell. BST has successfully configured the technology to meet the weight and dimension specifications of the military designation MK89 cell and is scheduled to power a SEAL Delivery Vehicle (SDV) with this technology in a 2016 sea-trial.*

For batteries powering large manned undersea and unmanned undersea vehicles ((UV and UUV) such as the Dry Combat Submersible (DCS), SS-Ag-Zn provides an unmatched combination of energy density (185 Wh/kg, 400 Wh/l), continuous power density (100 W/kg, 200 W/l), pulse power density (500 W/kg, 1000 W/l), increased cycle life, and safety, with lower cost of ownership and operation. SS-Ag-Zn significantly outperforms similar batteries constructed of lithium-ion cells, which in order to provide adequate safety, require a large number of small format cells (18650s) with significant spacing and interstitial materials to prevent thermal run-away, which results in practical battery-level specific energies and energy densities that are less than that provided by SS-Ag-Zn.

Keywords: silver; zinc; safe; sealed; hydrogen; aqueous; rechargeable; maintenance; aerospace; underwater vehicles.

Introduction

The US Navy is embarking on UUVs to substantially increase its intelligence and surveillance capabilities in the offshore and coastal battle space and USSOCOM is initiating the Dry Combat Submersible (DCS) program for SEAL delivery to replace the Advanced SEAL Delivery System (ASDS). Both UVs require a large energy storage system that is safe, user-friendly, has high energy density to meet the mission requirements and can be recharged in the vehicle with little or no maintenance and attention.

Smart Sealed Ag-Zn (SS-Ag-Zn) overcomes many of the perceived limitations of conventional Ag-Zn batteries. Smart Sealed Ag-Zn cells are factory activated and sealed, completely eliminating end-user activities and eliminating the continuous maintenance (purge and N_2 backfill) that was required of conventional Ag-Zn to mitigate hydrogen gas released in confined spaces. The unique sub-atmospheric pressure operation of SS-Ag-Zn enhances charge efficiency, providing a 20% improvement in cyclic capacity retention, resulting in delivered capacity that is greater than the rated minimum for 50-100 cycles. BST's robust separator system has demonstrated 2 years of wet-life in the field and now coupled with the unique feature of water returned to the electrolyte during SS-Ag-Zn operation, up to 3 years of wet-life is expected. Further enhancement of BST's separator system is being evaluated for cycling of a cell on its side eliminating the historical limitation of charging upright only. Orientation-independent charging is essential to many UUV special applications, which are both vertically and horizontally docked.

The development of sealed silver-zinc cells, and other aqueous batteries, have been attempted in the past through the use of stoichiometric hydrogen/oxygen recombination catalysts within cells [1-4]. Such recombination catalysts are not in use in silver-zinc cells because they are not effective with the non-stoichiometric gas generation, which leads to hydrogen gas accumulation within the cell and unacceptable pressures. Prior to BST's Smart Sealed technology, a completely maintenance-free (for the lifetime of the battery), sealed silver-zinc battery had been unattainable due to the inability of the catalyst to recombine the gas mixtures produced by the cells for the entire duration of the cell's practical life.

In 2014, in the proceedings of the 46th Power Sources Conference, BST reported on the SS-Ag-Zn technology, which at that time was in the development and demonstration phase (TRL 4-5) [5]. In this proceeding, BST reports on the performance of SS-Ag-Zn prototype cells (TRL 6-7), which were fabricated and tested in the last two years, and will discuss the qualification and sea-trial demonstration programs (TRL 8-9) scheduled for completion in the next 12 months.

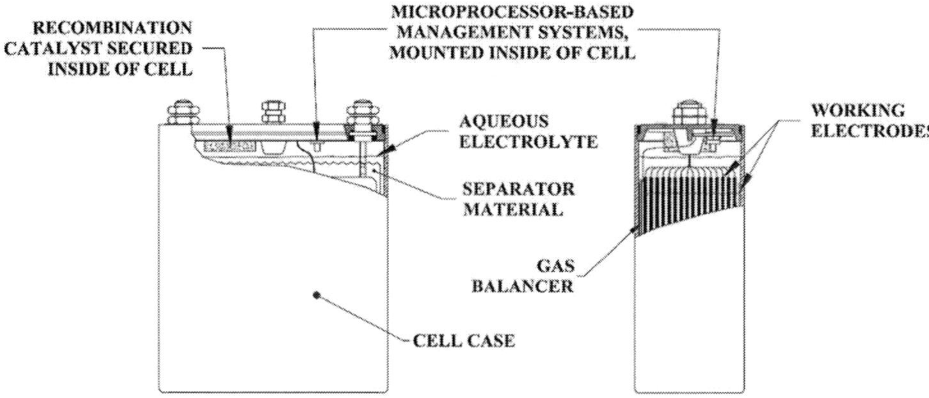

Figure 1: Schematic of the SS-MK89 cell.

Method

Hydrogen gas is generated non-synchronously and non-stoichiometrically (in excess) compared to oxygen gas during normal operations (discharge, charge, open-circuit stand) of a silver-zinc battery. Recombination catalysts are ineffective for the purposes of sealing silver-zinc batteries and other aqueous battery systems. BST Systems, Inc. has developed a Smart Sealed Ag-Zn (SS-Ag-Zn) cell which overcomes the difficulty associated with non-stoichiometric gas. The SS-Ag-Zn comprises a hydrogen/oxygen gas recombination catalyst, an automatic gas balancer (AGB), and a Smart System Manager (SSM) based on microprocessor control through a proprietary algorithm driven by a sensor. The SSM includes a power supply that draws needed energy from the cell. The components of the SS-Ag-Zn are located within the cell envelope. The AGB supplies oxygen automatically when there is insufficient oxygen, on a stoichiometric basis, inside the cell. The stoichiometric hydrogen/oxygen mixture recombines at a catalyst surface in the headspace, forming water or water vapor, which results in a low and sustainable pressure maintained within the sealed cell.

The Smart Sealed technology can be configured at the cell level (described above) or the battery/module level. When the Smart Sealed technology is configured at the battery/module level, the AGB component resides in each cell of the battery, and the other components (SSM and gas recombination catalysts) are located in a collection chamber within the battery housing. Advantages of the cell level versus battery/module level configuration are discussed in greater detail in reference 5.

Experimental

The development of SS-Ag-Zn was internally funded (IR&D) first and then through SBIR programs (Contract N00024-12-C-4119) iteratively, with the overall objective of developing a Sealed, maintenance-free, upgraded version of the current MK89 cell. The military designation MK89 cell is the power source for the SEAL Delivery Vehicles (SDV) and Shallow Water Combat Submersibles (SWCS) and may potentially be used as the power source for other vehicles when launched. Therefore, the challenge was to develop a Smart Sealed MK89 cell (SS-MK89) at equal or better electrical performance with the Smart Sealed components configured within the dimensional and weight specifications of the MK89, such that the SS-MK89 cell could act as a drop-in replacement for the conventional MK89 cell for current and future applications.

The SS-MK89 prototype cells, shown in Figure 2, were cycled individually following a protocol similar to the Acceptance Test method used on conventional MK89 cells. The cells were sealed under a vacuum pressure following a vented formation cycle. Full (100%) discharges at 60 A to a 1.20 V cut-off were performed on cycles 5, 15, 25, 35, 45, and 50, and all other discharges were timed (5 h) to 300 Ah. All charges were 10 A to 2.02 V cut-off.

Figure 2: Image of SS-MK89 prototype cell that meets the dimensional and weight requirement of a conventional MK89. The Smart System Manager and Gas Recombination Catalyst are located on the underside of the cover and the Automatic Gas Balancer is located in the cell electrode pack.

Statement A: Approved for Release. Distribution is unlimited

Results and Discussion

Smart Sealed Cells: During SS-MK89 prototype cell cycling internal cell pressure and output capacity was measured and evaluated. The internal cell pressure of a SS-MK89 cell as a function of cycle number is shown in Figure 3. It is seen that low, sub-atmospheric pressure was maintained for a full 50 cycles. The cell operated continuously without gas release well below the safety relief valve threshold of 20 psig. Power required to operate the SSM is supplied by the cell, thus the cell is self-contained.

The average discharge capacity of the SS-MK89 prototype cells as a function of cycle number compared to the average discharge capacity of conventional MK89 cells is shown in Figure 4. It is seen that the cyclic capacity retention of SS-MK89 cells is approximately 20% better than conventional MK89 cells. The improvement is attributed to the unique sub-atmospheric pressure operation of the SS-MK89 cells which enhances charge efficiency and electrode balancing, which is a natural consequence of the overall Smart System operation. The initial and end-of-rated-cycle-life (50) energy densities of the SS-MK89 prototype cells were 185 Wh/kg (400 Wh/l) and 133 Wh/kg (285 Wh/l), respectively.

Orientation Independent Charging: Orientation-independent charging may be required in some special UUV applications which are both vertically and horizontally stowed in the host vehicle. BST advised potential customers that Ag-Zn batteries can be discharged on their side (edge or face), but must be charged upright to prevent the development of slow-shorts. The customers asked BST for data to validate the advice. Recently, BST has cycled conventional MK89 cells that were discharged on their edge (electrodes racked) and face (electrodes stacked), but were charged upright. As shown in Figure 5, the cells that discharged on their edge demonstrated typical cyclic capacity retention (305 Ah on cycle 50), while cells that discharged on their face showed improved cyclic capacity retention (350 Ah on cycle 50).

For UVs and UUVs that are vertically stowed in the host vehicle, Ag-Zn batteries can be designed such that cells are upright during stowage and on their side (edge or face) during mission (horizontal). For UVs and UUVs that are both horizontally and vertically docked, orientation independent charging will be necessary as charging of cells in their non-upright positon will occur. BST has demonstrated that MK89 cells that charge on their side are limited to approximately 20 cycles. Currently, BST is testing a separator system design that it believes will enable orientation independent charging that will meet the rated cycle life (50 cycles) of the MK89.

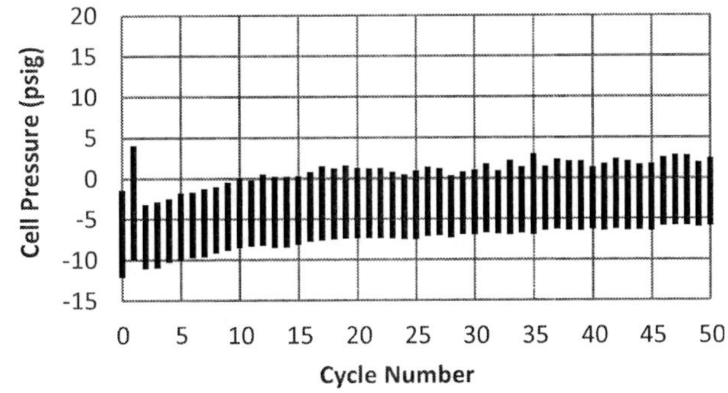

Figure 3: Internal cell pressure as a function of cycle number for a SS-MK89 prototype cell. The bars represent the pressure range over the complete cycle (charge/discharge/open-circuit).

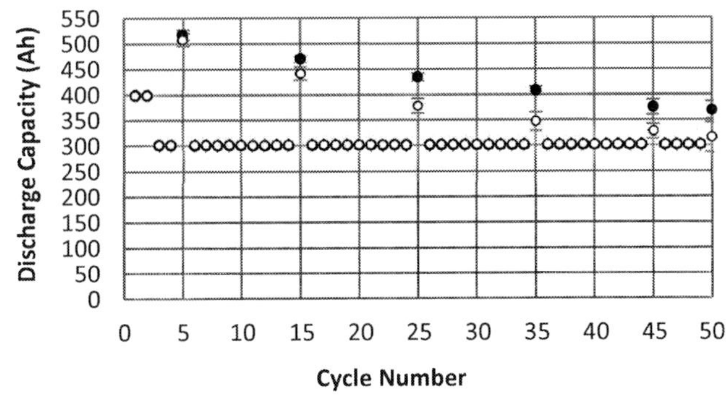

Figure 4: Average discharge capacity as a function of cycle number for SS-MK89 (closed circles) prototype cells compared to average discharge capacity for conventional MK89 cells (open circles).

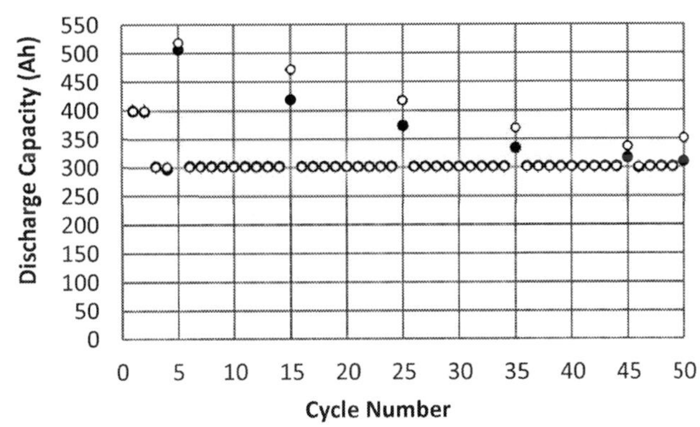

Figure 5: Average discharge capacity as a function of cycle number for conventional MK89 cells charged upright and discharged on their edge (closed circles) and charged upright and discharged on their face (open-circles).

Statement A: Approved for Release. Distribution is unlimited.

Conclusions and Future Work

BST Systems, Inc. has demonstrated lifetime sealed, safe operation of Ag-Zn prototype cells within the weight and dimensional constraints of the military designated MK89 cell type utilizing its patent-pending Smart Sealed (SS) technology. The SS-Ag-Zn technology overcomes many of the perceived limitations of conventional Ag-Zn battery, and enables safe, user-friendly, high-energy dense batteries for demanding applications in confined spaces, such as UVs. SS-Ag-Zn provides an unmatched combination of energy density, power density, safety, and cost-effectiveness and is the ideal power source for military applications with few missions per year.

SS-Ag-Zn cells are production-ready and will power a SEAL Delivery Vehicle in 2016. Under the SBIR Phase II.5 program, an SDV will be fitted with SS MK89 cells in the last quarter of 2016 for a complete field evaluation and validation of the cited benefits.

BST Systems, Inc is currently working on a separator system design that it believes will enable orientation-independent charging, which is essential for new UVs that are both horizontally and vertically stowed. Furthermore, operating cells on their face (plates stacked) enables better capacity retention and hence longer cycle life and more energy throughput over life. When BST demonstrates this successfully, it will enhance the attractiveness of Ag-Zn batteries and will allow more flexibility in UV design and operation.

Acknowledgements

The authors wish to thank and acknowledge the support of NAVSEA PMS 399, NSWC – Crane Division and Portsmouth Naval Shipyard (PNSY) for their support of this effort through the SBIR program.

The authors also thank the BST team for their support on this program.

References

1. Gaines, L., "Secondary Silver-Zinc Battery Technology," *Journal of the Electrochemical Society*, vol. 13, no. 2, pp. 61C-67C, 1969.
2. Misra S.S., T.M. Noveske, S.L. Mraz, and A.J. Williamson, "The Role of Recombination Catalyst in VRLA Cells," *Journal of Power Sources*, Vol. 95, pp. 162-173, 2001.
3. Levy I., A. Charkey, "Gas Recombination Assembly for Electrochemical Cells," *Energy Research Corporation,* US Patent 4810598, 1989.
4. Charkey A., "Sealed Zinc Secondary Battery and Zinc Electrode Therefor," *Energy Research Corporation,* US Patent A 5460899A, 1995.
5. Hirschorn B., Solis M.A., Terjesen T.T., "Development of Sealed, Large-Format Silver-Zinc Batteries and Cells for Department of Defense Applications," *Proceedings of the 46th Power Sources Conference,* pp. 513-516, 2014.

A Safe, High Energy Density Aluminum Subsea Energy Source

Thomas Milnes

Open Water Power, Inc.
Tom@OpenWaterPower.com

Abstract

Currently, the US Navy is pushing for breakthrough new energy technologies to support the fielding of a large manned and unmanned undersea vehicles as well as subsea sensors and equipment. The Navy has expressed a significant goal of trying to achieve 10X greater energy density than lithium ion batteries, but have typically opposing requirements for much greater safety than what exists today. This presentation will describe breakthrough new capabilities of an aluminum-seawater battery technology that was developed under a joint MIT/Lincoln Laboratory effort and spun out into a new venture, Open Water Power. This developmental technology has demonstrated 7-10X the energy density of lithium-ion while demonstrating significantly higher safety than any previously tested batteries. Results of recent Carderock Testing will also be discussed.

Low Cost Catalysts Synthesized from Non-Noble Metal Oxides and FeNx-Doped Graphene for Alkaline Fuel Cells

Rongzhong Jiang, Dat T. Tran, and Joshua P. McClure
Sensors and Electron Devices Directorate, U.S. Army Research Laboratory
2800 Powder Mill Road, Adelphi, MD 20783-1197

Abstract: *A nanocomposite material composed of* $Mn_{1.5}Co_{1.5}O_4$ *and* FeN_x*-functioned graphene* ($Mn_{1.5}Co_{1.5}O_4$-FeN_x/C) *was synthesized. The crystal structure and elemental composition of the bimetal oxide were determined by X-ray diffraction. The surface morphology of the nanocomposite was characterized with transmission electron microscopy and scanning electron microscopy. The catalytic activity for oxygen reduction reaction (ORR) was analyzed by electrochemical method. The enhancement of activity for ORR at the nanocomposite material is attributed to a synergistic effect from the bimetal particles and a synergistic effect from the* FeN_x/C *nano sheets. The nanocomposite material is able to catalyze 4-electron oxygen reduction to generate water in alkaline media with high kinetic rate. Finally, the activity and stability of the nanocomposite material were compared with that of 40% Pt supported on active carbon.*

Keywords: Nanocomposite; ORR; Synergistic effect; Non-noble metal oxides.

Introduction

Fuel cells are high efficient energy conversion devices, in which catalysts are one of the most important materials. The state of the art catalysts for fuel cell are expensive noble metals, including platinum black and platinum-based metal alloys. For a proton exchange membrane fuel cell, the catalyst covers about 60% of the cost of a fuel cell stack in automobile applications [1]. Further commercialization of fuel cells needs to solve the problems of high cost, low performance, and fast degradation of materials in the fuel cell components. Development of alkaline electrolyte membrane fuel cell (AEMFC) could use non-noble metal catalysts, and lower the overall cost [2-4]. Recent years, much attention has been paid to non-noble metal oxides for possible cathode catalysts in AEMFC [5-8]. Major challenges of using metal oxides for fuel cell catalysts are poor electrical conductivity and unsatisfactory activity. Furthermore, the catalytic reaction is incomplete, having 20% to 50% of oxygen reduced through 2-electron reaction to hydrogen peroxide, instead of 4-electron reaction to water in alkaline media. Our goal of this research is to minimize the product of hydrogen peroxide in the process of oxygen reduction reaction (ORR), and improve the activity and stability of non-noble metal oxides. We have investigated a series of metal oxides, Mn_2O_3, Co_3O_4 and $Mn_{1.5}Co_{1.5}O_4$. The catalytic activity was evaluated by supporting the metal oxides on 70% graphene nano platelets (GNP). We have achieved in enhancing the catalytic activity from mono-metal oxide to bimetal oxide, then to a nanocomposite composed of $Mn_{1.5}Co_{1.5}O_4$-FeN_x/C. However, the metal oxides do not catalyze oxygen 4-electron reduction, having some of the oxygen reduced only to hydrogen peroxide through the 2-electron reaction. Therefore, we have synthesized a nanocomposite material, $Mn_{1.5}Co_{1.5}O_4$-FeN_x/C, which contains the metal oxides and a functional carbon FeN_x/C. Here we report the synthesis and characterization of this non-precious nanocomposite material for catalytic oxygen reduction in alkaline media.

Experimental

The $Mn_{1.5}Co_{1.5}O_4$ was synthesized by the following procedure. 1g $CoC_2O_4{\bullet}2H_2O$ and 1g $MnC_2O_4{\bullet}2H_2O$ were mixed with 3 ml aqueous NH_4OH, ground to a paste, and dried at 70°C. The dry mixture was put in a ceramic boat and heat-treated at 400°C in the presence of air for two hours. A bimetal oxide with black color was obtained, and determined to be $Mn_{1.5}Co_{1.5}O_4$by XRD and EDS. The Mn_2O_3 and Co_3O_4 were synthesized by weighing 2g $MnC_2O_4{\bullet}2H_2O$ and 2g $CoC_2O_4{\bullet}2H_2O$, respectively, and following the same procedure as that of making $Mn_{1.5}Co_{1.5}O_4$, except processing and heat-treating them separately. The FeN_x/C was synthesized according to our previous reports [9] and briefly described here. 1g hemin and 1g GNP were uniformly dispersed in 50 mL N, N-Dimethylformamide (DMF). After drying on a hot-plate, the mixture was placed in a ceramic boat and placed in a tubular furnace for heat-treatment for 2 hours under a nitrogen atmosphere at 600 °C. The $Mn_{1.5}Co_{1.5}O_4$-FeN_x/C nanocomposite was synthesized by ultrasonic processing of $Mn_{1.5}Co_{1.5}O_4$ and FeN_x/C to decrease the large particle size and form nano-sized boundaries. A Branson Sonifier 450 was used for providing the ultrasound source. Here, 32 mg $Mn_{1.5}Co_{1.5}O_4$ and 75 mg FeN_x/C were mixed in a small beaker containing 4 ml 1-propanol and 4 ml water. The beaker containing samples were cooled with an ice bath, and processed at duty cycle 40 and output control 8 for 20 minutes. After ultrasonic treatment an ink-like solution was obtained, containing 4 mg/ml $Mn_{1.5}Co_{1.5}O_4$ dry sample and 9.4 mg/ml FeN_x/C. The dried material from the ink is called $Mn_{1.5}Co_{1.5}O_4$-FeN_x/C nanocomposite, and sent for XRD, SEM, TEM, and EDS analyses. The ink was directly used for electrochemical analysis by adding 5% Nafion solution as binder. The samples of Mn_2O_3/C, Co_3O_4/C, and $Mn_{1.5}Co_{1.5}O_4/C$ were also prepared by ultrasonically mixing with 70% GNP in ice-cooled water.

X-Ray Diffraction (**XRD**) were obtained from a Rigaku Ultima III instrument with Cu Kα radiation (λ = 1.5418 Å) using a Bragg-Brentano Configuration. The measurements were conducted with a scan rate of 1.0 degree (2θ) per minute; and each diffraction data point was collected at intervals of 0.02 degree (2θ) for the total spectrum range of 10 to 80 degree (2θ). A FEI QUANTA 200F instrument was used for scanning electron microscopy (**SEM**). The samples for SEM image were prepared by directly loading a small amount of catalyst powder on a sample holder. Transmission electron microscopy (**TEM**) were obtained with a high-resolution JEOL 2100 FE instrument equipped with an EDAX X-ray detector and a high angle annular dark field (HAADF) detector. Energy-dispersive X-ray spectroscopy (**EDS**) were obtained during the measurements. Before imaging, a solution was prepared by adding 5 mg of the catalyst into 5 mL of 1-propanol followed by a short ultrasonic bath (Branson 3510) treatment. An aliquot of ink was loaded onto a QUANTIFOIL ®–Holey Carbon Films (0.6 μm hole, 1.6 μm space 300 mesh copper grid, Electron Microscopy Science) with a micro-pipette, and the samples were dried overnight at room temperature.

A Pine Bipotentiostat RDE4 was used for electrochemical characterization. A glassy carbon (**GC**) disk electrode (0.196 cm^2) and a ring-disk electrode were used. The ring-disk electrode had a GC disk electrode (0.247 cm^2) and a Pt-ring electrode (collection coefficient 0.37). A catalyst sample was first suspended in 1:1 water/1-propanol solution with a small bottle and cooled with ice. The catalyst ink was prepared by ultrasonic treatment with a Branson Sonifier 450 at a duty cycle 40 and output control 8 for 10 minutes. The final content of catalyst was 4 mg/ml metal oxides ($Mn_{1.5}Co_{1.5}O_4$, or Mn_2O_3 or Co_3O_4). Then, 10 μl of catalyst ink was coated on a GC disk working electrode (0.196 cm^2), and dried at 40°C for over 60 minutes. The final coating on the GC disk electrode contained 95% total catalyst and 5% dry Nafion with total metal oxides loading of 0.2 mg/cm^2. An ink of 40% Pt/C was prepared with the same procedures as that of metal oxide samples. The final loading of 40% Pt/C on the GC electrode was 0.2 mg/cm^2. For the rotating ring-disk electrode (**RRDE**) experiment, the final metal oxides loading was 0.16 mg/cm^2. The catalyst coated electrode was mounted onto a Pine ASR rotator and used as the working electrode. All voltammetrical experiments were performed in argon (Ar) or O_2 saturated 0.1M potassium hydroxide (KOH) solution at room temperature (20 ± 1°C). A three electrode glass cell was used for electrochemical study containing three compartments separated by porous ceramic layers. A platinum wire counter electrode and a saturated calomel reference electrode (**SCE**) were used in the cell. The experimental results were reported based on reversible hydrogen electrode (**RHE**). The difference between SCE and RHE was experimentally determined with an SCE and a fresh-prepared RHE in 0.1M KOH solution in the same electrochemical cell. The current density reported in this article is based on the geometrical area of the GC disk electrode (mA·cm^{-2}), which can be changed to (mA·mg^{-1}) by simply multiplying a factor of 5 according to the mass of the catalyst loading.

Results and Discussion

The composition and morphology of several metal oxides were characterized with XRD, including mono metal oxides Mn_2O_3, Co_3O_4, and bimetal oxide $Mn_{1.5}Co_{1.5}O_4$. The XRD result shows that the metal oxides are highly crystalized. Their structures and compositions were determined as Mn_2O_3, Co_3O_4, and $Mn_{1.5}Co_{1.5}O_4$, respectively. The crystallite size of $Mn_{1.5}Co_{1.5}O_4$ (11.8 nm) is significantly smaller than that of Mn_2O_3 (21.3 nm) or Co_3O_4 (24.5 nm) by Scherrer Equation. The surface morphologies of Co_3O_4, Mn_2O_3, $Mn_{1.5}Co_{1.5}O_4$ and $Mn_{1.5}Co_{1.5}O_4$-FeN_x/C are initially screened with SEM, as shown in Figure 1. Many small particles of Co_3O_4 are seen, which are aggregated together to form cylindrical shapes with diameter ~250 nm, and length ~500-2000 nm. The SEM of Mn_2O_3 shows irregular polyhedrons containing many small ditches with ~10-30 nm width. Many micro particles of $Mn_{1.5}Co_{1.5}O_4$ are aggregated together to form granule shapes with irregular sizes. The SEM of $Mn_{1.5}Co_{1.5}O_4$-FeN_x/C shows irregular shapes with many large and small pores.

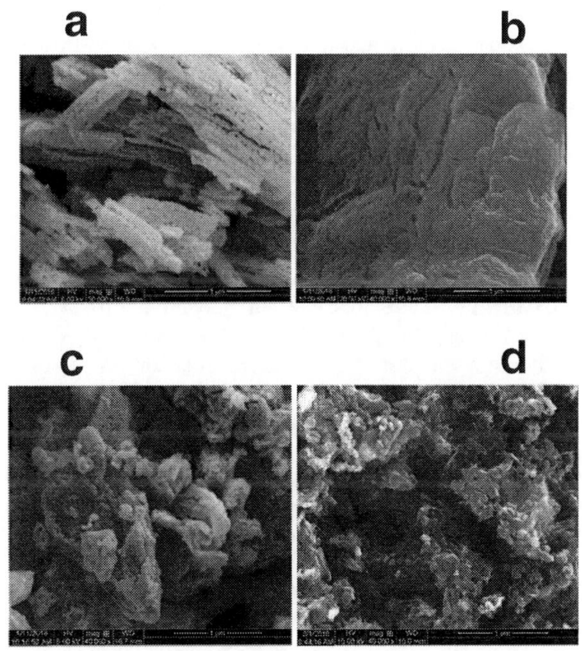

Fig. 1. SEM Images of Co_3O_4 (a), Mn_2O_3 (b), $Mn_{1.5}Co_{1.5}O_4$ (c), and $Mn_{1.5}Co_{1.5}O_4$-FeN_x/C (d).

The fine structures of these materials are examined with TEM, as shown in Figure 2. The TEM image of $Mn_{1.5}Co_{1.5}O_4$-FeN_x/C shows some small darker and round regions, which are identified as $Mn_{1.5}Co_{1.5}O_4$ particles. The positions of GNP can also be recognized from the larger and lighter regions. However, the boundaries between $Mn_{1.5}Co_{1.5}O_4$ particles and GNP are unclear, which implies that the nano boundaries are well formed between the two materials without gaps. From the TEM image of unsupported $Mn_{1.5}Co_{1.5}O_4$, the particle size of it was estimated as around 10–20 nm.

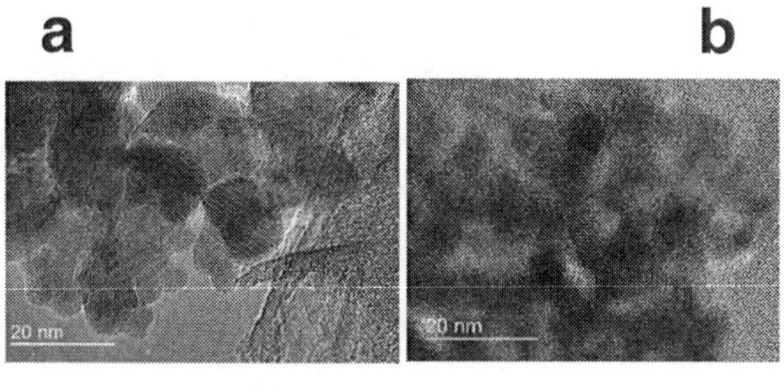

Fig.2. TEM images of $Mn_{1.5}Co_{1.5}O_4$-FeNx/C (a) and $Mn_{1.5}Co_{1.5}O_4$-FeNx/C (b).

The catalytic activity is analyzed by a method of rotating disk electrode (**RDE**). Figure 3A shows polarization curves of mono-metal oxides, bimetal oxide, and $Mn_{1.5}Co_{1.5}O_4$-FeN_x/C nanocomposite coated RDEs in O_2 saturated 0.1M KOH. The limiting current of ORR increases apparently in the order of $Mn_{1.5}Co_{1.5}O_4$/C > Mn_2O_3/C > Co_3O_4/C. The half wave potential shifts to more positive potentials. The enhancement of activity at the bimetal oxide over mono-metal oxides is attributed to a synergistic effect of different metal atoms in the bimetal crystal. It is interesting that when we functioned the catalyst support from blank carbon to FeN_x doped carbon, further catalytic activity enhancement was seen. The highest limiting current and the most positive half wave potential (0.82V) are achieved at $Mn_{1.5}Co_{1.5}O_4$-FeN_x/C nanocomposite coated RDE. The enhancement of catalytic activity at $Mn_{1.5}Co_{1.5}O_4$-FeN_x/C nanocomposite can be attributed to a secondary synergistic effect of ORR, where the oxygen molecules are catalyzed by two types of catalytic sites, or the bimetal atoms, Mn-Co, at the $Mn_{1.5}Co_{1.5}O_4$ site; and the Fe atoms at FeN_x/C site. The polarization curves of these catalysts coated RDEs are further analyzed by Tafel plots as shown in Figure 3B. The $Mn_{1.5}Co_{1.5}O_4$-FeN_x/C nanocomposite has the smallest Tafel slope, which indicates an advantage of fast electron transfer between the oxygen molecules and the catalyst coated electrode. The number of electron transfer and the yield of intermediate product, H_2O_2, for ORR are obtained by RRDE experiment. Figure 4 shows plots of the number of electron transfer and the yield of H_2O_2% versus disk potential. The yield of H_2O_2 is potential dependent, and a peak yield appears at ~0.6V. The peak yield of H_2O_2% at the $Mn_{1.5}Co_{1.5}O_4$-FeN_x/C nanocomposite is less than 5%. The very small percentage of H_2O_2 production is probably because a small part of electrode area is incomplete coverage by the catalyst. Apparently, the $Mn_{1.5}Co_{1.5}O_4$-FeN_x/C nanocomposite mainly catalyzes 4-electron oxygen reduction. The mechanism of ORR at the $Mn_{1.5}Co_{1.5}O_4$-FeN_x/C nanocomposite is explored. When oxygen molecules are diffused into the nano boundaries between the bimetals and the FeN_x/C, they are catalyzed simultaneously by the bimetal site, Mn-Co, and the FeN_x site. If any intermediate product, H_2O_2, is generated at the Mn-Co surface, it will be continuously reduced at the FeN_x site. The FeN_x/C is not only able to catalyze 4-electron O_2 reduction to water, but also it is able to catalyze 2-electron H_2O_2 reduction to water with excellent activity [9-10].

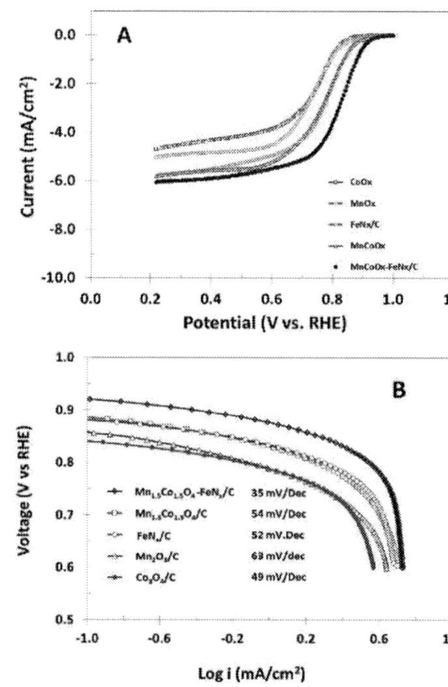

Figure 3. (A) Polarization curves of various catalyst coated electrodes in O_2 saturated 0.1M KOH, 10 mV/s, rotation rate 1600 rpm. (B) Tafel plots obtained from the results in (A).

The catalytic kinetics for ORR at the nanocomposite catalyst $Mn_{1.5}Co_{1.5}O_4$-FeN_x/C is investigated by analyzing the polarizations curves at different rotation rates, and making Koutecky-Levich plots. The result of Koutecky-Levich plots also demonstrated that oxygen is reduced by 4-electron reaction at the $Mn_{1.5}Co_{1.5}O_4$-FeN_x/C coated electrode. The kinetic rate constants for ORR at $Mn_{1.5}Co_{1.5}O_4$-FeN_x/C nanocomposite coated electrode are obtained from the Koutecky-Levich plots (See Table 1). At 0.7V the kinetic rate constant is 7.6×10^{-2} $cm \cdot s^{-1}$.

The activity and stability of $Mn_{1.5}Co_{1.5}O_4$-FeN_x/C nanocomposite are compared with commercially available Pt catalyst containing 40% Pt and 60% active carbon (40% Pt/C). The catalyst loadings on the electrode were 0.2 mg/cm^2 for the metal oxide and 40% Pt/C samples, respectively. 5% Nafion was added as a binder in all catalyst coatings. There is 60 mV half wave potential difference between $Mn_{1.5}Co_{1.5}O_4$-FeN_x/C (0.82V) and 40% Pt/C (0.88V). At 0.7V the activity of $Mn_{1.5}Co_{1.5}O_4$-FeN_x/C reaches 95% of 40% Pt/C. The catalytic stability is also compared by chronoamperometric test at 0.7V and 900 rpm rotation rate. The approximately paralleled curves were obtained, which indicates that the catalytic stability of the $Mn_{1.5}Co_{1.5}O_4$-FeN_x/C is comparable to that of 40% Pt/C for the duration of the experiment.

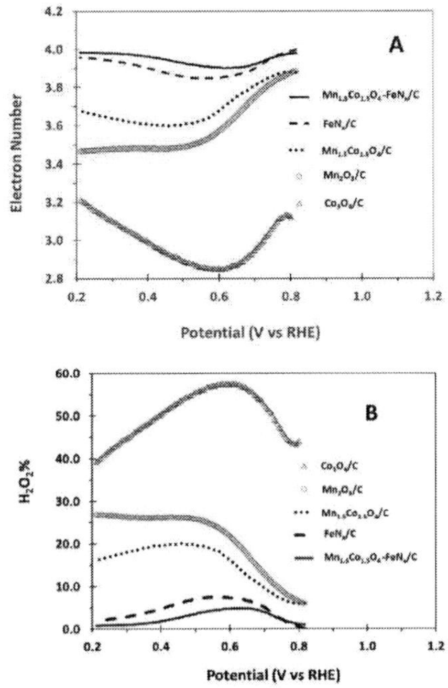

Figure 4. Plots of electron transfer number versus disk potential (A) and plots of H_2O_2% generation versus disk potential (B).

Table 1. Kinetic rates at nanocomposite catalyst $Mn_{1.5}Co_{1.5}O_x$-FeN_x/C coated electrode in O_2 saturated 0.1M KOH.

Kinetic Rate ($cm \cdot s^{-1}$)			
0.8V	0.7V	0.6V	0.5V
1.4×10^{-2}	7.6×10^{-2}	11.7×10^{-2}	24.9×10^{-2}

Conclusion

In this study we demonstrated a method of making non-precious nanocomposite material for ORR catalyst and achieved synergistic effects for bimetallic catalysts for the oxygen reduction reaction. A non-noble mono-metal oxide's catalytic activity can be enhanced by incorporating a second non-noble metal element into its crystal structure to generate a nano crystal material with uniform elemental spatial distribution. The addition of the second metal in the crystal structure into a mono-metal oxide results in smaller crystallite size, particle size, and higher active surface area for the bimetal oxide, leading to higher catalytic activity. The catalytic activity of the bimetal oxide can be further enhanced by supporting it on a functional carbon material containing FeN_x functional groups. The bimetal oxide, the functional carbon and the electrolyte form nano boundaries, which are the actives sites for catalytic oxygen reduction. The FeN_x group functions as a mediator to remove H_2O_2 intermediate generated in the catalytic process of oxygen reduction, and promoting oxygen to be catalyzed through a complete 4-electron reduction. Our work provides a new pathway in design and synthesis of novel non-precious nanocomposite catalysts.

Acknowledgements

The authors would like to thank Dr. Wen-An Chiou and Dr. Sz-Chian Liou at University of Maryland for assisting TEM and STEM analyses. Thanks to Dr. Cynthia Lundgren for helpful discussions. Finally thanks to the U.S. Department of the Army and U.S. Army Materiel Command for supporting this work.

References

1. Marcinkoski, J.; James, B. D.; Kalinoski, J. A.; Podolski, W.; Benjamin, T.; Kopasz, J. J. Power Sources 2011, 196, 5282–5292. "Manufacturing process assumptions used in fuel cell system cost analyses"
2. Luo, Y. T.; Guo, J. H.; Liu, Y. H.; Shao, Q.; Wang, C. S.; Chu, D. J. Membrane Science 2012, 423–424, 209–214. "Copolymerization of methyl methacrylate and vinyl-benzyl chloride towards alkaline anion exchange membrane for fuel cell applications"
3. Li, Y. S.; Zhao, T. S.; Liang, X. X. J. Power Sources 2009, 187, 387. "Performance of alkaline electrolyte-membrane-based direct ethanol fuel cells"
4. Switzer, E. E.; Olson, T. S.; Datye, A. K.; Atanassov, P.; Hibbs, M. R.; Fujimoto, C.; Cornelius, C. J. Electrochimica Acta 2010, 55, 3404. "Novel KOH-free anion-exchange membrane fuel cell: Performance comparison of alternative anion-exchange ionomers in catalyst ink.
5. Ma, Y. Y.; Wang, R. F..; Wang, H.; Key, J. L.; Ji, S. J. Power Sources 2015, 280, 526-532. "Control of MnO_2 nanocrystal shape from tremella to nanobelt for enhancement of the oxygen reduction reaction activity"
6. Wang, Y. G.; Cheng, L.; Li, F.; Xiong, H. M.; Xia, Y. Y. Chem. Mater. 2007, 19, 2095-2101. "High Electrocatalytic Performance of Mn_3O_4/Mesoporous Carbon Composite for Oxygen Reduction in Alkaline Solutions"
7. Xu, J. B.; Gao, P.; Zhao, T. S. Energy Environ. Sci., 2012, 5, 5333–5339. "Non-precious Co_3O_4 nano-rod electrocatalyst for oxygen reduction reaction in anion-exchange membrane fuel cells"
8. Dong, H. Q.; Chen, Y. Y.; Han, M.; Li, S. L. Zhang, J.; Li, J.S.; Ya-Qian Lan, Y.Q.; Z Dai Z. H.; Bao, J. C. J. Mater. Chem. A, 2014, 2, 1272–1276. "Synergistic effect of mesoporous Mn_2O_3-supported Pd nanoparticle catalysts for electrocatalytic oxygen reduction reaction with enhanced performance in alkaline medium"
9. Jiang, R. Z.; Chu, D. J. Power Sources 2014, 245, 352–361. "Comparative study of $CoFeN_x$/C catalyst obtained by pyrolysis of hemin and cobalt porphyrin for catalytic oxygen reduction in alkaline and acidic electrolytes"
10. Jiang R. Z. Chu, D. J. Electrochem. Soc. 2000, 147 (12), 4605. "Remarkably Active Catalysts for the Electroreduction of O_2 to H_2O for Use in an Acidic Electrolyte Containing Concentrated Methanol"

Development of Anion-Exchange Membrane Direct Methanol Fuel Cells: Stack Tests for a Portable Power Source

Tilman Jurzinsky, Florina Jung, Carsten Cremers, Karsten Pinkwart, Jens Tübke
Applied Electrochemistry
Fraunhofer Institute for Chemical Technology ICT
Joseph-von-Fraunhofer-Str. 7, 76327 Pfinztal, Germany

Abstract: *A 5-cell anion-exchange membrane direct methanol fuel cell (AEM-DMFC) short stack has been build up with in-house fabricated membrane electrode assemblies (MEAs) and end plates. While commercially available Hypermec™ 4020 by Acta S.p.A. was used as cathode catalyst, the anode consisted of an in-house made $Pd_3Ni_{0.5}Ru_{0.5}/C$ catalyst making the stack free from platinum and therefore less costly than proton-exchange membrane based direct methanol fuel cells (DMFCs). The $Pd_3Ni_{0.5}Ru_{0.5}/C$ catalysts exhibits high catalytic activity and is able to utilize the fuel more efficiently than compared Pt/C or Pd/C catalysts as differential electrochemical mass spectrometry measurements show that the methanol oxidation on $Pd_3Ni_{0.5}Ru_{0.5}/C$ catalyst results in higher CO_2 current efficiencies. Each cell of the stack has an area of 30 cm^2 giving the stack an overall area of 150 cm^2. Taking the stack volume of 0.242 L and weight of 0.468 kg into account the stack exhibits maximum power densities of 64 W L^{-1} and 33 W kg^{-1}, respectively. The overall maximum power of 15.4 W was recorded at a stack potential of 1.2 V at 60 °C and with 4M CH_3OH + 5M KOH solution and oxygen as anodic and cathodic fuels, respectively.*

Keywords: Alkaline; Electrochemical; Catalysis; Palladium; Differential Electrochemical Mass Spectrometry (DEMS).

Introduction

The increasing need of energy for modern electronic devices used by dismounted soldiers creates a necessity for a power supply, which is easy to refill/recharge, lowers logistic complexity, makes the soldier independent from the availability of a power grid and decreases weight burdens for the individual soldier. Proton-exchange membrane based Direct Methanol Fuel Cells (DMFCs), which were already tested as portable power source by the German and United States Army, offer higher energy densities than most primary batteries and thus are able to reduce the weight burden for dismounted soldiers. Besides this, DMFCs are easy to refill and only alcohol needs to be resupplied resulting in a reduction of logistic burdens. A wider introduction of DMFCs is mainly hindered by the high costs of the systems. [1] The major driving force of DMFC costs are the platinum based catalysts for the anode and cathode of the fuel cell.

Recent studies revealed that the electrocatalytic activity of Pt/C catalyst with respect to alcohol oxidation reaction is higher in alkaline media manifested by higher current densities and smaller overpotentials. [2] As other metals like Pd are also showing enhanced electrocatalytic activity in alkaline media, this leads to the possible employment of other catalysts than Pt. Especially bimetallic PdM/C [3–5], metal oxide promoted Pd/C [6,7] and trimetallic catalysts [8,9] were successfully identified as potential substitutes for Pt/C as methanol oxidation reaction catalyst in alkaline media.

In the past decade anion-exchange membrane (AEM) research took big steps towards higher ionic conductivities and longer lifetime making anion-exchange membrane direct methanol fuel cells (AEM-DMFCs) more feasible. A disadvantage of AEM-DMFC is the carbonation of the AEM by CO_2 from the air feed or even from the alcohol oxidation reaction itself. Resulting pH reduction causes loss of reactivity for alcohol oxidation [10]. Because of this carbonation issue, most research groups proposed the addition of 2 – 5 M KOH to the fuel solution in order to maintain a high performance [11,12].

In a former study we investigated Pd_XNi/C catalysts for methanol electro-oxidation and tested these catalysts in fuel cell set-up [3]. In this work, these catalysts are further modified resulting in trimetallic $Pd_3Ni_{0.5}Ru_{0.5}/C$ catalysts, which were electrochemically characterized in half cell and full cell measurements. Finally, $Pd_3Ni_{0.5}Ru_{0.5}/C$ catalysts were employed in an overall platinum-free AEM-DMFC short stack of 5 cells. The stack was assembled by a mixture of in-house fabricated and commercially available components. The stack assembly and operation at various conditions will be described.

Experimental

Anode catalysts were prepared as described in former studies. [3]

Electrocatalyst evaluation: Chronoamperometry (CA) and cyclic voltammetry (CV) experiments were conducted to study the electrocatalytic activity towards methanol oxidation reaction.

In a standard 3-electrode set-up, Pt foil of large area was used as counter electrode and mercury/mercury oxide electrode (MMO) as reference electrode. The working electrode was a glassy carbon disc (5 mm in diameter with a geometric area of 0.196 cm^2) covered with a thin layer of catalyst. In a first step, 2 μl of catalyst ink (solvent: ethanol;

binder: PTFE) was pipetted on top of the glassy carbon disc. Secondly, the pipetted solution was dried in order to form the desired catalyst layer. The electrolyte used was 0.5M KOH + 0.5M CH_3OH solution deoxygenated by Ar.

CA tests were carried out at an oxidation potential of -0.2 V (vs. MMO) for 1000 s. CV evaluations were carried out at 25 mV s^{-1} covering a potential window from -0.8 to 0.3 V (vs. MMO). For all electrochemical experiments a SP-300 potentiostat (Bio-Logic SAS) was used at room temperature. All differential electrochemical mass spectrometry (DEMS) measurements were done as described in former studies. [4,5]

Thermogravimetric analysis (TGA, TGA 2950, TA instruments, temperature range: 30-700°C, heating rate: 10°C min^{-1}, in air atmosphere) allowed for the examination of the metal loading on carbon. Catalyst composition was evaluated by inductively coupled plasma optical emission spectroscopy (ICP-OES) on an iCAP 6300 ICP Spectrometer (Thermo Fisher Scientific). For that reason, residue material from the TGA measurement was dissolved in aqua regia and analyzed via ICP-OES. Transmission electron microscopy (TEM) images were done using a Libra (Zeiss) transmission electron microscope with 120 kV acceleration energy and LaB_6 cathode. TEM image analysis was realized via ImageJ (1.48v, NIH) software. Particle size distribution histograms from the TEM images were made by metering the size of 1000 particles.

Membrane electrode assembly: The membrane electrode assembly (MEA) for stack tests consisted of an AEM (A201, Tokuyama), anode and cathode. Both electrodes were fabricated by spray-coating electrocatalyst ink consisting of catalyst, PTFE and H_2O onto SGL Sigracet 10AA and Freudenberg H2315 as anode and cathode liquid/gas diffusion layers, respectively. PTFE contents in the resulting catalyst layers were 5 wt% and 12.5 wt% for anode and cathode, respectively. The anode catalyst loading was 10 mg cm^{-2} corresponding to a metal loading of 2 mg cm^{-2}, while the cathode catalyst (Hypermec™ 4020 by Acta S.p.A.) loading was 4 mg cm^{-2}. To form a MEA the electrodes were hot-pressed with the AEM at 60 °C and 70 N cm-2.

Stack assembly: MEAs with an active area of 30 cm² containing $Pd_3Ni_{0.5}Ru_{0.5}/C$ as anode catalyst were fabricated as described before. Five of these were connected in series by using graphite bipolar plates with incorporated 3-serpentine flow fields. To prevent leakage one silicone sealing was used on each side, anode and cathode. Current collector and bipolar plates were used from the commercial available DMFC short stack of Baltic Fuels Cells GmbH. In-house made end plates, which are significantly lighter than commercial ones, were used to fix the stack and supply it with fuels. The stack was tightened slightly with 6 screws and a torque of 1 Nm. Table I summarizes the components used and the stack specifications. As shown in Figure 1 the stack temperature was measured in middle of the short stack. Therefore, a Type K thermocouple was fastened between the bipolar plates.

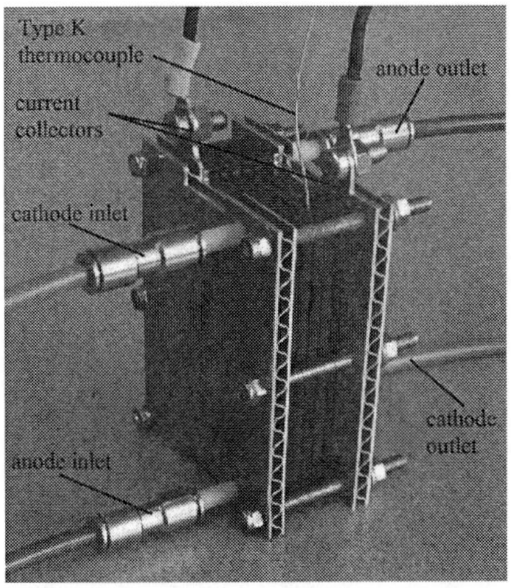

Figure 1. Image of the 5-cell AEM-DMFC stack with in-house made end plates

Stack testing: The short stack was run under various operation conditions. Anodic and cathodic fuel flow rates were constant throughout all experiments with 10 ml min^{-1} and 200 ml min^{-1}, respectively. Operation parameters like temperature, anodic electrolyte composition and back-pressure on cathode side were varied to further investigate the behavior of the stack. Stack temperature was mainly controlled by pre-heating the anodic fuel via a continuous-flow heater and was stable to a variance of ±1.0 °C.

To obtain experimental results that reflect the performance of the stack, a sequence of potentiostatic measurements were performed holding each potential for 3 min (time proven to be enough to measure steady state currents), while the current delivered through the cell/stack was recorded. In resulting U-I curves, the current considered in the plots is the one measured after 3 min. Additional to U-I curves, the stack was also tested under a constant load. Therefore a current of 6 A (= 200 mA cm^{-2}) was applied over a period of 120 min and the corresponding potential was monitored. Autolab PGSTAT potentiostat with 20 A booster (Eco Chemie B.V.) was used for stack tests.

Table I. Technical Specifications of the AEM-DMFC stack.

Area	
Cell	30 cm²
Stack	150 cm²
Stack	
Number of Cells	5
Cell pitch	< 3 mm
L x W x H	95 mm x 75 mm x 34 mm
Volume	0.242 L
Weight	0.468 kg

Results & Discussion

Physical characterization of the electrocatalysts: Table II summarizes the catalysts tested for their potential use in AEM-DMFCs and the data obtained from thermogravimetric, elemental and TEM characterization.

Table II. Summary of synthesized electrocatalysts and parameters obtained from TGA, ICP-OES and TEM.

Catalyst	Loading	Catalyst composition Pd:Ni(:Ru)	d [nm]
Pd/C	21.0	1.00:0.00	2.4 ± 0.7
Pd_3Ni/C	19.6	1.00:0.98	3.0 ± 0.7
$Pd_3Ni_{0.5}Ru_{0.5}/C$	19.7	3.00:0.47:0.51	3.2 ± 0.9

Thermogravimetric analysis reveals that the catalysts exhibit a loading of around 20 wt% of overall metal on carbon which was the desired value. Following ICP-OES measurements identified the elemental composition. As shown in Table II the found Ni and Ru contents are slightly different to the calculated values but in acceptable margin.

TEM imaging was done to investigate the morphology of the catalysts. All catalysts contain nano-sized metal particles of round shape which are disposed evenly on the carbon support. With the addition of Ni to the catalyst, the average particle size becomes slightly larger compared to the mean particle size of 2.4 nm for plain Pd/C. For $Pd_3Ni_{0.5}Ru_{0.5}/C$ the particles are bigger with a mean size of 3.2 nm. Pt-Nanoparticles in the range of 3 - 6 nm were found to be more catalytically active than bigger particles (4 - 32 nm). [13] Hence, it is suggested that the found small particle sizes for the catalysts are favorable.

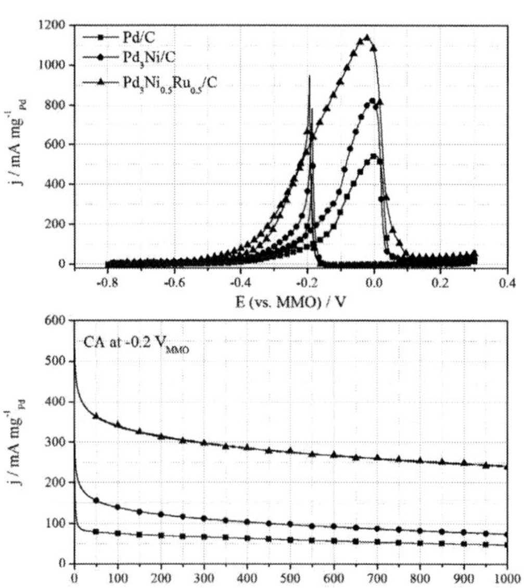

Figure 2. CV (up) and CA (down) obtained in 0.5M CH_3OH + 0.5M KOH solution for Pd/C, Pd_3Ni/C and $Pd_3Ni_{0.5}Ru_{0.5}/C$.

Electrochemical characterization: CV and CA tests could reveal that electrocatalyst with Ni mixed to Pd exhibits higher mass current densities and lower methanol oxidation onset potential. As shown in Figure 2 the catalytic activity of Pd-based catalyst is further improved by adding Ru to the catalyst.

$Pd_3Ni_{0.5}Ru_{0.5}/C$ exhibits a more than 2 times higher peak mass activity of 1137.3 mA mg^{-1}_{Pd} compared to Pd/C. Also, $Pd_3Ni_{0.5}Ru_{0.5}/C$ shows the lowest onset potential for methanol oxidation in this study with -0.484 V (vs. MMO) Compared to Pd_3Ni/C the electrocatalytic activity of $Pd_3Ni_{0.5}Ru_{0.5}/C$ is strongly enhanced by the addition of Ru. Potentiostatic measurements at an oxidation potential of 0.2 V (vs. MMO) reveal that the mass current density after 1000 s holding the potential is more than 6 times higher for $Pd_3Ni_{0.5}Ru_{0.5}/C$ than for Pd/C.

Besides standard electrochemical measurements, the CO_2 current efficiency (CCE) from methanol oxidation at various oxidation potentials was determined by DEMS for all of the catalysts. Figure 3 summarizes the obtained data for the catalysts. While the addition of Ni alone to Pd has a negative effect on the ability to completely oxidize methanol to CO_2 on Pd_3Ni/C, the further addition of Ru enhances the formation of CO_2 from methanol oxidation reaction. Pd/C and Pd_3Ni/C show CCE values below 50% regardless of applied potential. Hence, it is concluded that the incomplete oxidation of methanol to side products like formaldehyde and formate is mainly happening on Pd/C and Pd_3Ni/C. For $Pd_3Ni_{0.5}Ru_{0.5}/C$ the CCE values are higher than 50% at potentials ≥ 0.6 V (vs. RHE), which means that CO_2 is the main product of methanol oxidation on this catalyst at these oxidation potentials.

Compared to CCE values of Pt/C from a former study in the same DEMS setup, $Pd_3Ni_{0.5}Ru_{0.5}/C$ is able to outperform Pt/C regarding the efficient use of the anodic fuel as $Pd_3Ni_{0.5}Ru_{0.5}/C$ reaches significantly higher CCE values than Pt/C. [5] Hence, $Pd_3Ni_{0.5}Ru_{0.5}/C$ was chosen as anode catalyst for further stack tests.

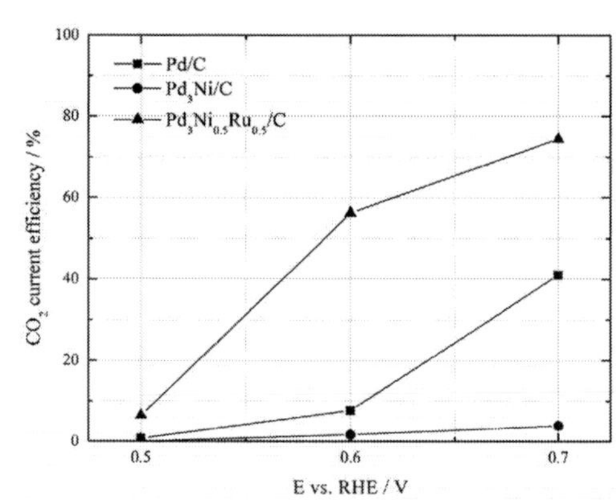

Figure 3. CO_2 current efficiencies of the electrocatalysts in dependency of the applied oxidation potential.

Stack tests: The MEAs for the stack tests were prepared without anion-exchange ionomer binder in catalyst layers. Thus, it is unlikely that the stack will work properly without any electrolytic supplements like KOH. To evaluate the changes in stack power caused by different electrolytic compounds, several tests with different anodic fuel compositions were done. As shown in Figure 4, various fuel compositions were tested while O_2 was used as cathodic fuel. Addition of 5M KOH to the fuel was found to be the fuel composition with the highest power densities possible in former single cell investigation. [12] As expected, the stack exhibits a low current with a maximum of only 1.1 A at 1.0 V stack potential when fuelled with 4M CH_3OH (without any electrolytic support). Related to the overall electrochemical active are of the stack, this corresponds to a power density of 7.3 mW cm^{-2}. Varcoe et al. demonstrated a power density of 8.5 mW cm^{-2} in AEM-DMFC single cell tests under similar conditions. [14] By adding $KHCO_3$ to the fuel the maximum stack power raises to 1.9 W or 1.8 W for the addition of 2M $KHCO_3$ or saturated $KHCO_3$, respectively. Still, obtained stack power is too low for a cost-effective usage of the stack. Stack performance is significantly increased by the addition of KOH. Best performance were reached by adding 5M KOH to 4M CH_3OH with 15.4 W at 1.2 V and a maximum current 15.3 A. It is desirable to operate a stack at average cell potentials of 0.4-0.6 V in order to yield higher conversion efficiencies and thus energy densities. At 2.5 V stack potential the power obtained with 4M CH_3OH, 4M CH_3OH + 2M $KHCO_3$ and 4M CH_3OH saturated with $KHCO_3$ is below 1 W whereas the power output with addition of KOH is up to 23 times higher. This underlines the mandatory usage of KOH as fuel supplement when working without an anion-exchange ionomer binder in catalyst layers.

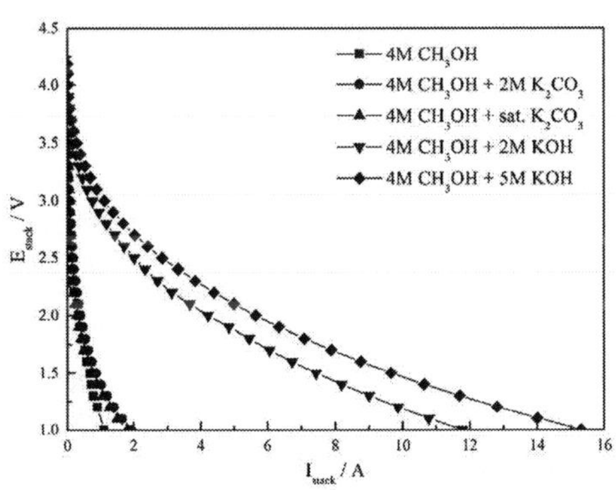

Figure 4. The influence of different electrolytic supplements in the anodic feed on the stack performance.

Conclusion

It was successfully shown that $Pd_3Ni_{0.5}Ru_{0.5}/C$ exhibits superior catalytic activity towards methanol oxidation reaction and ability to completely oxidize methanol to CO_2 over Pd/C or Pd3Ni/C. Therefore, a stack with $Pd_3Ni_{0.5}Ru_{0.5}/C$ as anodic catalyst was assembled and tested under various conditions.

The AEM-DMFC short stack was built completely free from Platinum and exhibited a maximum power of 15.4 W when fuelled with 4M CH_3OH + 5M KOH solution and dry O_2 at the anode and cathode, respectively. Taking the stack volume and weight into account the stack exhibits maximum power densities of 64 W L^{-1} and 33 W kg^{-1}, respectively. While addition of KOH increased the stack performance substantially, $KHCO_3$ as an electrolytic supplement was not able to enhance the stack as significant. Consequently, an AEM-DMFC stack is only cost-effective when fuelled with a solution of methanol and high amounts of KOH. As KOH in the fuel is likely to react with CO_2 from the air to $KHCO_3$, it is mandatory to prevent the carbonation of the fuel when it is stored for a long time at air.

Further experiments on the stack regarding the influence of back-pressure on the cathode and how the presence of CO_2 in the cathodic feed influences the performance will be presented at the conference.

References

[1] G. Apanel, E. Johnson, *Fuel Cells Bulletin* **2004**, *2004*, 12.

[2] A. Tripković, K. Popović, B. Grgur, B. Blizanac, P. Ross, N. Marković, *Electrochimica Acta* **2002**, *47*, 3707.

[3] T. Jurzinsky, C. Cremers, F. Jung, K. Pinkwart, J. Tübke, *International Journal of Hydrogen Energy* **2015**, *40*, 11569.

[4] T. Jurzinsky, P. Kammerer, C. Cremers, K. Pinkwart, J. Tübke, *Journal of Power Sources* **2016**, *303*, 182.

[5] T. Jurzinsky, R. Bär, C. Cremers, J. Tübke, P. Elsner, *Electrochimica Acta* **2015**, *176*, 1191.

[6] C. Xu, Z. Tian, P. Shen, S. P. Jiang, *Electrochimica Acta* **2008**, *53*, 2610.

[7] K.-H. Ye, S.-A. Zhou, X.-C. Zhu, C.-W. Xu, P. K. Shen, *Electrochimica Acta* **2013**, *90*, 108.

[8] R. M. Modibedi, T. Masombuka, M. K. Mathe, *International Journal of Hydrogen Energy* **2011**, *36*, 4664.

[9] R. Awasthi, R. N. Singh, *Catal. Sci. Technol.* **2012**, *2*, 2428.

[10] R. Parsons, T. VanderNoot, *Journal of Electroanalytical Chemistry and Interfacial Electrochemistry* **1988**, *257*, 9.

[11] L. Ma, H. He, A. Hsu, R. Chen, *Journal of Power Sources* **2013**, *241*, 696.

[12] A. Katzfuß, V. Gogel, L. Jörissen, J. Kerres, *Journal of Membrane Science* **2013**, *425-426*, 131.

[13] A. V. Tripković, K. Popović, J. D. Lović, V. M. Jovanović, A. Kowal, *Journal of Electroanalytical Chemistry* **2004**, *572*, 119.

[14] J. R. Varcoe, Slade, R. C. T., *Electrochemistry Communications* **2006**, *8*, 839.

XPS Characterization of TiO_2 for Photo-assisted Adsorptive Desulfurization Applications

Mingyang Chi, Xueni Sun, Achintya Sujan, and Bruce J. Tatarchuk*
Center for Microfibrous Materials
Department of Chemical Engineering, Auburn University
212 Ross Hall, Auburn, AL 36849-5127
***brucet@eng.auburn.edu, mzc0054@auburn.edu**

Abstract: *Sulfur compounds in hydrocarbon fuels can result in permanent poisoning of fuel cell electrodes and catalysts. Adsorptive desulfurization for stationary and mobile fuel cell power systems has gained importance in recent years due to environmental concerns and the requirement of clean energy. Recently, a novel photo-assisted adsorptive desulfurization technique was developed in our lab. An improvement in desulfurization performance is observed when anatase TiO_2 is treated by UV irradiation prior to and during breakthrough experiments. In order to understand the mechanism and the effect of UV irradiation of active sites on TiO_2 surface, X-ray Photo-electron Spectroscopic (XPS) studies of UV treated and un-treated TiO_2 samples were conducted. XPS results illustrate a difference in surface composition of samples. From O 1s narrow scan spectra, a shift in peak position and peak intensity can be observed. Based on XPS results, it is evident that UV treatment produces more isolated hydroxyl groups on TiO_2 surface. These isolated hydroxyl groups exist for a prolonged period and improve the desulfurization capacity of TiO_2. It is envisioned that with the application of photo-assisted adsorptive technique reported in this study, ultra-deep removal of sulfur compounds in model fuels can be achieved.*

Keywords: Desulfurization, Adsorption, Titanium dioxide, Photo-catalysis, UV, XPS

Introduction

Desulfurization of liquid fuel cells is an important step since the toxicity and corrosivity of sulfur compounds causes serious damage to fuel cell electrodes and catalysts. Stringent regulations have been applied to limit the maximum sulfur emissions in many countries around the world [1,2]. Ultra-deep removal of various sulfur compounds in fuel cells has gained more importance recently. Among variety of desulfurization methods [3], such as hydro desulfurization (HDS), catalytic oxidation, biological removal, and membrane separation, etc., adsorptive desulfurization is efficient and promising due to its low energy requirement and scalability [4]. Photo-oxidative desulfurization has already been reported to be efficient [5]. TiO_2 has been widely applied in photo-catalysis, semiconductors, and adsorbents for various purposes such as energy production, water splitting, environmental purification, and fuel cell pretreatment [6]. Recently, our lab has developed a novel and efficient photo-assisted adsorptive desulfurization (ADS) based on TiO_2 materials. A significant improvement in desulfurization performance is obtained when commercial anatase TiO_2 is irradiated by UV before and during breakthrough experiments. Besides, TiO_2 adsorbent regeneration was also carried out by thermal treatment in flowing air.

X-ray photoelectron spectroscopy (XPS), is an analytical technique capable of analyzing the surface composition as well as chemical states of each element on the sample surface. XPS has been applied in researches on all kinds of materials [7]. Both ex-situ and in-situ methods have been developed to discover the chemical properties of functional materials [7]. Taking advantage of this advanced analytical technique, the mechanisms for the UV induced enhancement in desulfurization of commercial anatase TiO_2 materials can be studied.

In this work, a comprehensive investigation of the mechanisms for the enhanced desulfurization performance of UV treated TiO_2 was carried out by in-situ XPS measurements. UV induced isolated hydroxyl groups on surface improve the desulfurization capacity of TiO_2. Thermal treatment at 450 °C under moisture free conditions can effectively regenerate the TiO_2 adsorbent.

Experimental

Anatase TiO_2 (ST61120, Saint Gobain Norpro, BET surface =162.89 m^2g^{-1}, pore volume= 0.46 cm^3g^{-1}) support was studied for photo-assisted adsorptive desulfurization activity. 3.2 mm pellet were crushed to 850-1400 um for breakthrough experiments. These particles were then calcined at 450 °C in flowing air for 2 h. To obtain an optical XPS spectra, TiO_2 particles were further crushed to 75-150 um for XPS analysis. Breakthrough experiments were carried out in a fixed bed reactor, using model fuels containing 3500 ppmw total sulfur benziothiophene in n-octane.

Figure 1 shows the schematic diagram of the photo-assisted desulfurization and thermal regeneration system. 10.0 g of adsorbent was vertically packed in a quartz tube reactor. 16 mm (inner diameter) and 62 mm (length) quartz tube reactor was used for breakthrough experiments. Quartz wool was used to pack and support both end of the reactor. The adsorbent bed was purged with UHP N_2 to remove any moisture and oxygen. A peristaltic pump was used to pump model fuel into the bed after N_2 treatment. The flow rate was 0.5 $mLmin^{-1}$ (LHSV~ 2 h^{-1}). In order to ensure complete wetting of the adsorbents particles in the reactor as well as minimize bed channeling, challenge fuel was admitted from the bottom of the bed.

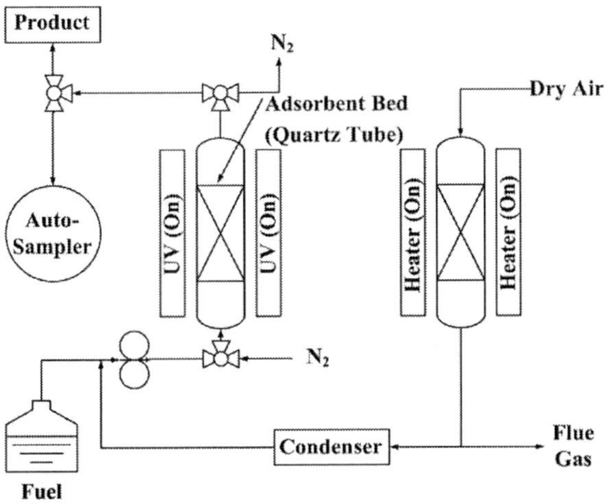

Figure 1. Experimental setup for photocatalytic adsorptive desulfurization and thermal regeneration units.

Figure 1 also illustrates that two UV lamps were placed symmetrically on both sides of the quartz tube reactor. UV lamps were turned ON as soon as the model fuel was admitted through the reactor. The time delay was estimate to be less than 3 seconds. As a control, another breakthrough experiment was conducted under dark conditions (no UV treatment) in the same setup. To eliminate the potential interference from other light sources, the reactor was covered with alumina foil that also helps focus all the UV-radiation in the reactor. Liquid samples at outlet were collected every 5 minutes for the first 1h of experiment and then every 10 minutes for the remaining period of the experiment. Samples were then analyzed by Antek Sulfur Analyzer. To further examine the effect of UV, TiO_2 was pretreated with UV irradiation for 2 h prior to the breakthrough experiment. After UV treatment, challenge fuel was pumped into the packed bed reactor.

In situ XPS experiment was carried out by AXIS Ultra DLD (Kratos Analytical LTd) X-ray photoelectron spectrometer. The end station consists of a fast entry load lock, sample treatment chamber (STC), and a sample analysis chamber (SAC). The sample was treated by a UV source mounted on the UHV flange of the load lock section, which is under ultrahigh vacuum condition (~ 10^{-9} torr) as shown in Figure 2. After 2 h UV treatment, sample was directly transferred into the analysis chamber. To investigate the effect of UV irradiation on the TiO_2 surface, XPS measurements were conducted for calcined TiO_2 adsorbent. Lastly, a TiO_2 sample was UV irradiated outside the chamber to examine the impact of H_2O and O_2 in air on this UV induced photo-adsorptive phenomenon. After this step, the sample was loaded into XPS analytical chamber. In other words, TiO_2 sample that was treated by UV in load lock was called UV treated TiO_2. TiO_2 sample that was UV treated in air was called UV pretreated TiO_2 in this article.

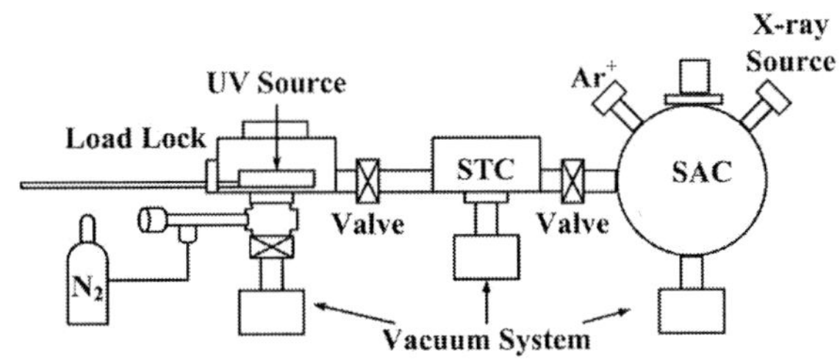

Figure 2. Configuration of XPS apparatus equipped with UV light.

A radiation with pass energy of 20 eV was used to measure high resolution spectra for the following elements: C 1s, O 1s, and Ti 2p.To offset the binding energy shifts caused by charging effect, C 1s spectrum obtained on a clean surface was constrained at 284.6 eV. All the spectrums were corrected by the same amount for the binding energy calibration. In order to obtain peak positions and peak intensities for surface species, Shirley background and Gaussian-Lorenzian line shapes were utilized for peak fitting with XPSPEAKS (version 4.1). Core level peaks were deconvoluted by fitting with Gaussian-Lorenzian (30%-70%) peaks.

Results and Discussion

A significant improvement in desulfurization capacity can be observed from breakthrough experiments shown in Table 1. As shown in Table 1, desulfurization capacity of TiO_2 increased from 2.45 mgS g^{-1} without UV treatment to 4.05 mgS g^{-1} for UV treated sample. From Table 1, it is apparent that UV irradiation before or during breakthrough experiments can enhance the desulfurization capacity of TiO_2 by approximately the same magnitude under the same test condition.

The enhancement in desulfurization capacity of TiO_2 adsorbent can be explained from an XPS perspective shown in Figure 3 and Figure 4. There is no significant difference in the C 1s and Ti 2p narrow scan spectra in UV treated and un-treated TiO_2. This implies that during 30 minutes time scale measurement, UV irradiation did not cause any change of Ti element.

From O 1s narrow scan spectra shown in Figure 4, a significant difference can be observed from the UV treated and non-treated TiO_2 particles. The peak at 529.7 eV can be assigned to TiO_2 oxide and the shoulder at 531.5 eV

Table 1. Sulfur removal capacities of calcined TiO_2 under different conditions

Operation Condition	No UV	UV-assisted ADS	UV pre-treated TiO_2
BT Cap @ $C/C_0 = 0.01$ (mg S/g adsorbent)	2.45	4.05	4.29
SAT Cap (mg S/g adsorbent)	3.90	5.63	5.95

belongs to hydroxyl groups (-OH). Figure 4 apparently illustrates the UV treated TiO_2 sample has more surface hydroxyl groups than the un-treated sample. The peak area ratio of OH^- to lattice O^{2-} is 0.31 for un-treated TiO_2 and 0.41 for UV treated TiO_2 and 0.46 for UV pretreated TiO_2 as shown in Table 2. In addition, the intensity of TiO_2 oxide peak for UV treated sample is by a limited extent smaller than that of un-treated sample as shown in Table 1. Thus, UV irradiation can cause a conversion of lattice TiO_2 oxide atoms to surface hydroxyl groups.

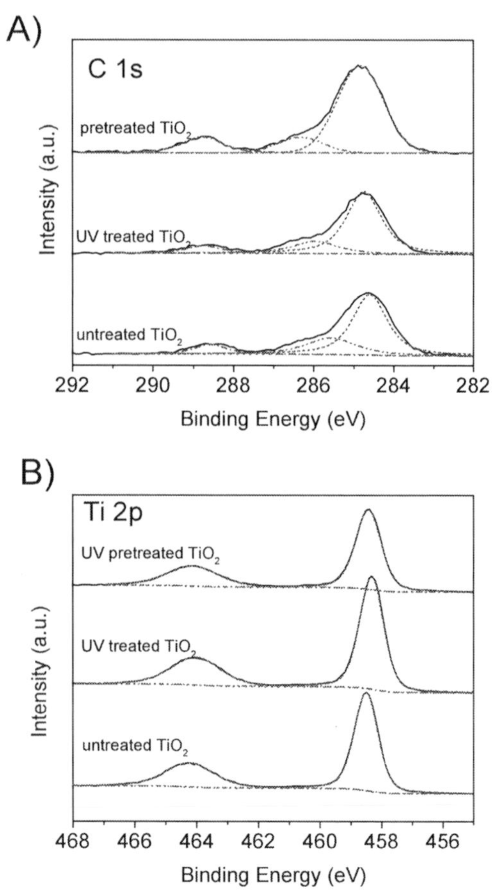

Figure 3. High resolution XPS spectra of A) C 1s and B) Ti 2p for TiO_2 samples under different treatment conditions.

A significant increase in surface hydroxyl groups was obtained for UV pretreated TiO_2 in air and UV treated TiO_2 under UHV conditions. Since there was no difference in Ti elemental species, O_2 in air can hardly be the reason for such an increase. On the other hand, UV irradiation can trigger the photo-catalytic reactions between TiO_2 and H_2O in air or reactions between TiO_2 and chemisorbed H_2O and produce more surface hydroxyl groups.

Table 2. Peak areas of O^{2-} and –OH species in TiO_2 under dark, UV treatment, and UV pretreatment

	Area of Bulk O^{2-}	Area of -OH	Ratio of $-OH/O^{2-}$
Un-treated TiO_2	20266.47	6267.482	0.31
UV Treated TiO_2	17523.02	7246.014	0.41
UV pretreated TiO_2	15881.07	7363.397	0.46

The mechanisms of the UV induced photo-assisted adsorptive desulfurization enhancement can be explained as the following formula:

$$Ti\text{-}O\text{-}Ti + H_2O_{\text{(chemisorbed)}} \rightarrow 2Ti\text{-}OH$$

It is established that surface hydroxyl groups can improve sulfur removal capacity of TiO_2 [8].These surface hydroxyl groups exist for a long period (up to 8 weeks) both under vacuum and atmosphere conditions. It was shown earlier that, the desulfurization capacity of UV irradiated TiO_2 was enhanced and this positive effect was maintained for up to 8 weeks.

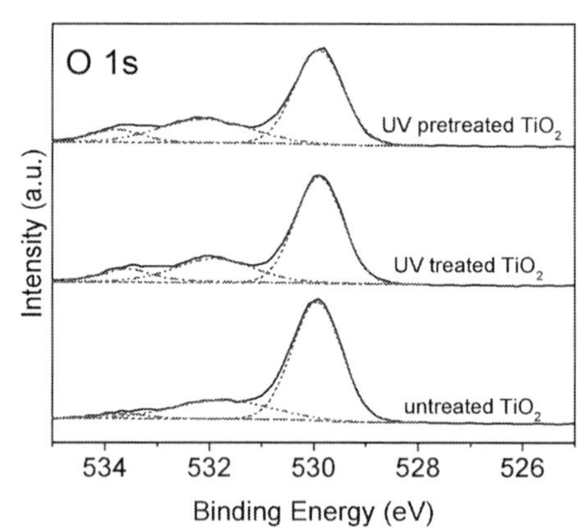

Figure 4. High resolution XPS spectra of O 1s for TiO_2 samples UV pretreatment in air, UV treatment at UHV, and no UV treatment conditions.

Conclusion

UV induced photocatalytic adsorptive desulfurization for commercial TiO_2 adsorbent improved the sulfur removal capacity by 65%.This enhancement resulted from UV photo-assisted reaction between TiO_2 lattice oxides with chemisorbed water. Both in-situ and ex-situ XPS measurements showed the peak at 531.5 eV corresponding to surface hydroxyl groups enlarged due to UV irradiation. In other words, UV treatment can produce additional surface hydroxyl groups. Moreover, UV induced surface hydroxyl groups are active for prolonged periods without significant decrease in breakthrough capacity based on prolonged stability of the O 1s peak. This study shows that UV induced photo-assisted adsorptive desulfurization method is simple and efficient. Future work will be focused on modification of TiO_2 adsorbent, in terms of doping, increase in surface area, etc. followed by study of fundamental mechanisms using multiple characterization techniques.

Acknowledgements

This work was supported by the United States Army TARDEC under Contract W56HZV-07-C-0577. The authors would also like to thank Dwight Cahela, Dr. Wenhua Zhu of the Center for Microfibrous Materials at Auburn University and Dr. Rui Xu from Chemical Engineering Department of Auburn University for their inputs on various aspects of this work.

References

1. Campos-Martin, J. M., M. C. Capel-Sanchez, and J. L. G. Fierro. "Highly efficient deep desulfurization of fuels by chemical oxidation." Green Chemistry 6.11 (2004): 557-562.
2. Jiang, Xue, Huaming Li, Wenshuai Zhu, Lining He, Huoming Shu, and Jidong Lu. "Deep desulfurization of fuels catalyzed by surfactant-type decatungstates using H 2 O 2 as oxidant." Fuel 88, no. 3 (2009): 431-436.
3. Kim, Hyung-Tae, Ki-Won Jun, Hari Shankar Potdar, Young-Seek Yoon, and Myung-Jun Kim. "Desulfurization of odorant-containing gases by sorption on Cu/ZnO/Al2O3: Effects of sulfur compounds." Energy & fuels 21, no. 1 (2007): 327-332.
4. Vecchi, Paul A., Arkady Ellern, and Robert J. Angelici. "Synthetic, Structural and Binding Studies of the 4, 6-Dimethyldibenzothiophene Complex [(η5-C5Me5) Ru (CO) 2 (η 1 (S)-4, 6-Me2DBT)] BF4: Toward an Understanding of Deep Hydrodesulfurization." Journal of the American Chemical Society 125, no. 8 (2003): 2064-2065.
5. Zhu, Wenshuai, Chao Wang, Hongping Li, Peiwen Wu, Suhang Xun, Wei Jiang, Zhigang Chen, Zhen Zhao, and Huaming Li. "One-pot extraction combined with metal-free photochemical aerobic oxidative desulfurization in deep eutectic solvent." Green Chemistry 17, no. 4 (2015): 2464-2472.
6. Ni, Meng, Michael KH Leung, Dennis YC Leung, and K. Sumathy. "A review and recent developments in photocatalytic water-splitting using TiO2 for hydrogen production." Renewable and Sustainable Energy Reviews 11, no. 3 (2007): 401-425.
7. Fujii, T., F. M. F. De Groot, G. A. Sawatzky, F. C. Voogt, T. Hibma, and K. Okada. "In situ XPS analysis of various iron oxide films grown by NO 2-assisted molecular-beam epitaxy." Physical review B 59, no. 4 (1999): 3195.
8. Lin, Daohui, and Baoshan Xing. "Adsorption of phenolic compounds by carbon nanotubes: role of aromaticity and substitution of hydroxyl groups."Environmental science & technology 42, no. 19 (2008): 7254-7259.

Smart Catalytic Performance of Pd Based Multi-metallic Nano Structures on MnO2 Support for DEFC: A Non-Pt and Non Carbon Approach

Jayati Datta

Department of Chemistry, Indian Institute of Engineering Science and Technology, Shibpur

Abhishek De

Department of Chemistry, Indian Institute of Engineering Science and Technology, Shibpur
jayati_datta@rediffmail.com

Abstract

Among the new technologies, fuel cell has emerged as one of the best green energy alternatives to the current fossil fuel based power sources, with tremendous prospect that the 21st century can expect. Since the last decade, besides the hydrogen fed proton exchange membrane fuel cells (PEMFCs), concerted efforts are made on using small alcohols, featuring higher volumetric and gravimetric energy densities, better energy efficiency and comparatively easy transportation, as liquid feed, in direct alcohol fuel cells (DAFC). Among the low molecular weight alcohols, ethanol in fact is a renewable energy source as it can be easily produced in large quantities by the fermentation of sugar containing agricultural raw materials and even from organic fraction of municipal wastes. Furthermore, use of bio-ethanol in fuel cell has significant advantage of being nearly CO2 neutral since the carbon dioxide produced in the process is consumed for biomass growth, offering a nearly closed carbon loop. In this respect, search for cheap and efficient CO-tolerant catalysts remains one of the most challenging tasks for the successful development of commercial direct ethanol fuel cell (DEFC) systems. The present trend is the use of non-Pt materials preferably Pd-based anode catalysts designed with a combinatorial approach by addition of multiple metals or metal oxide promoters to increase the ethanol oxidation kinetics in ambient environment. These catalysts are designated with improved functional properties at the reaction centers and electronic effects resulting from the electron transfer between the co-metals. A number of factors that are responsible for such enhanced catalytic activity are changes in M−M interatomic distance, number of nearest neighboring metal atoms, d band vacancies, metal content on the surface and so on [1-5]. In the present investigation we demonstrate that incorporation of Co and Ni into Pd matrix drastically reduces the charge transfer resistance and arrest the rapid current decay during ethanol oxidation in alkaline environment, indicating excellent tolerance towards ethanolic residues. Moreover, the usage of non carbon MnO2 support for low level Pt or completely Pt free multimetallic nano-particles is found to exhibit outstanding oxidation current density, reduced overvoltage and appreciable power density output in an in-house fabricated anion-exchange membrane DEFC. In summary, the co-metal partnership within the multi-metallic framework supported by MnO2 not only shows capability of extracting the best possible number of electrons from the alcohol fuels, harnessing more energy, at the same time, ensure affordability by bringing down the cost of the catalyst material and also eliminates the typical involvement of carbon in the fuel cell catalyst matrix. Some of the typical features for the above study are shown in Figures 1-4. References 1. Yanchun Zhao, Lu Zhan, Jianniao Tian, Sulian Nie, Zhen Ning, Int. J. Hydrogen Energy, 2010, 35, 0522-10526. 2. Yan-Jie Wang, David P. Wilkinson and Jiujun Zhang, Chem. Rev. 2011, 111, 7625–7651. 3. Wei Sun, Andrew Hsu, Rongrong Chen, J. Power Sources 2011, 196, 4491–4498. 4. Abhijit Dutta, Achintya Mondal, Jayati Datta, J. Power Sources, 2015, 283, 104-114. 5. Abhijit Dutta and Jayati Datta, J. Mater. Chem. A, 2014, 2, 3237–3250.

High Capacity, High Power, Multifunctional Lithium-Ion Polymer Cells for Military, Electric Vehicles, and Storage Applications

Denguo Wu[(1)], J. Fan[(1)], Anh V. Le[(2)] and Yu Qiao [(2)]
[(1)]American Lithium Energy Corporation (ALE), 1485 Poinsettia Avenue Suite 118, Vista, CA 92081
jfan@americanlithiumenergy.com
[(2)]University of California, San Diego, 9500 Gilman Dr. MC 0085, La Jolla, CA 92093-0085

Abstract:
ALE, an advanced lithium ion battery company located in San Diego County, is developing a multi-functional battery for EV applications. For this project, ALE is extending battery functionality beyond the role of being a power source of the electric vehicle. Specifically, ALE is designing this multifunctional battery to replace designated non-critical parts of the electric vehicle's framework to serve the dual role of providing a power source and providing physical protection against crush or impact as a mitigating capability. Our design approach enhances the battery's specific energy density, while decreasing EV cost by reducing the overall weight and cost of the electric vehicle itself.

ALE's multi-functional battery, when embedded as part of the EV architecture, can enable the EV to achieve a 300 miles range at a very competitive cost. To achieve our multi-functional battery performance and cost-savings objectives, ALE is integrating the mechanical and electrochemical additives into the multi-functional cell so that the battery configuration not only delivers a power source, but also serves as a safety mechanism. The safety capability derives from the overcharge protector and kinetic energy absorber that perform physical protection when the EV, and its batteries, are involved in a crush or impact due to car crashes or accidents. ALE has performed testing on cell performance and abuse tolerance, and our test results demonstrate the feasibility of this novel approach. Our design for a multi-functional EV battery also provides similar performance, safety, and cost benefits to military vehicles.

Keywords:
High Energy; High Power; Safe Multi-functional Li-Ion Cell; EV Batteries

Introduction
Energy density, cost, and safety are three highly correlated factors for EV batteries. A battery with a high energy density cell does necessarily lead to a battery having high energy density and low cost. This is because a highly efficient battery thermal system and a strong battery container may be required to mitigate safety risks. These factors diminish the battery's specific energy density, while increasing its cost. It is therefore advantageous to develop an EV battery optimized at a higher architectural level, e.g., the vehicle level. ALE's novel approach is very relevant for many military applications having both high energy and high safety requirements, as discussed below.

Results and Discussion
Cell Behavior in Impact or Mechanical Shock In Figure 1, ALE presents the coin cell temperature profiles of reference for conventional baseline coin cell, and our multi-functional coin cell with a unique mechanical shock additive as exhibited during an impact or mechanical shock test.

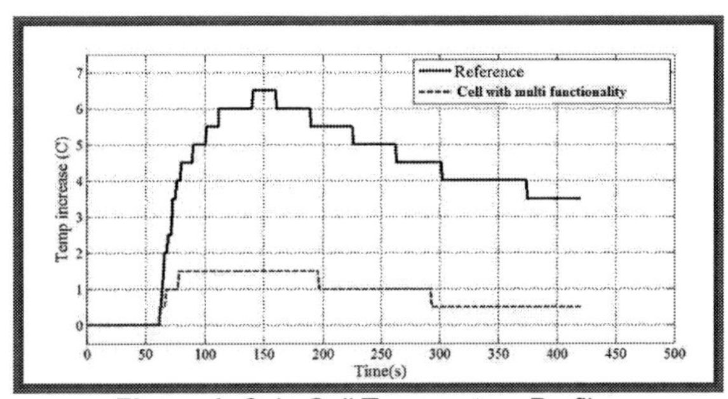

Figure 1. Coin Cell Temperature Profiles During Impact Tests

In the above test, the fully charged coin cell was placed in a fixture and impacted by a metal rod at a controlled speed per UL standards [1]. The multi-functional cell has a lower temperature than the conventional cell. This is because our cell with its mechanical shock additive becomes powerless and inert when a mechanical shock or impact exceeds its design limit. Our cell chemistry is designed to protect the cell from thermal run-away in cases when an internal short results from a significant EV impact.

In Figure 2, ALE presents our 10Ah multi-functional cell voltage and temperature profiles during our impact test. The multi-functional cell passed the test with a maximum temperature of 65°C as shown in Figure 3. During the impact test we performed, the conventional 10Ah cell exploded. (Not shown due to limited space).

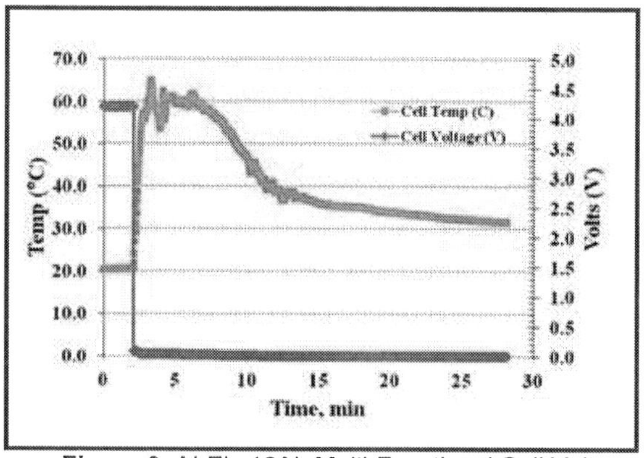

Figure 2. ALE's 10Ah Multi-Functional Cell Voltage and Temperature Profiles During Impact Test

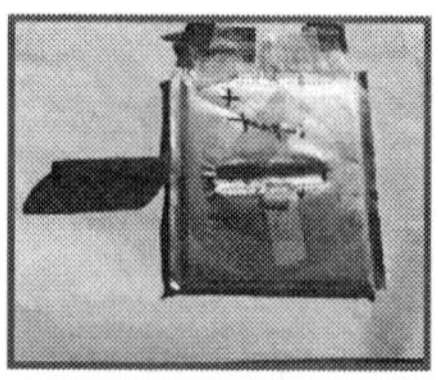

Figure 3. Photo of Cells after Impact Test

Cell Tolerence in Overcharge Test:

In Figure 4, ALE presents cell temperature and voltage profiles during the 12V-10A or 1C over charge test for our 10Ah multi-functional cell. The cell passed this test without fire or explosion. The maximun cell temperature is about 85°C. The conventional 10Ah cell caught fire during the impact test (not shown due to the limited space).

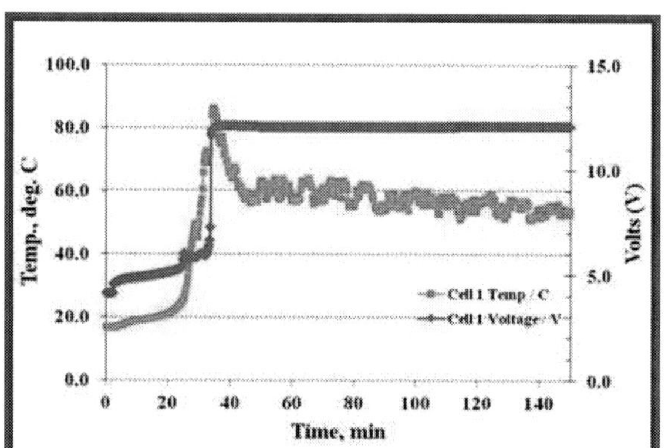

Figure 4. Cell Voltage and Temperature Profiles During 12V-1C (or 10A) Test

Cell Rate Capability and Cycle Life:

In Figure 5, ALE presents the a) cell discharge capacity at different currents and b) the cell capacity vs. the cycle number during 0.3C discharging and 0.5C charging cycle life test at room temperature. Our cell delivers about 90% of its capacity at 45A or 4.5C, which is effective for most applications. The cell lost only about 3% capacity after over 90 cycles, which is very high performance. No significant effect is seen from the additives, including the mechanical additive and the electrochemical additive.

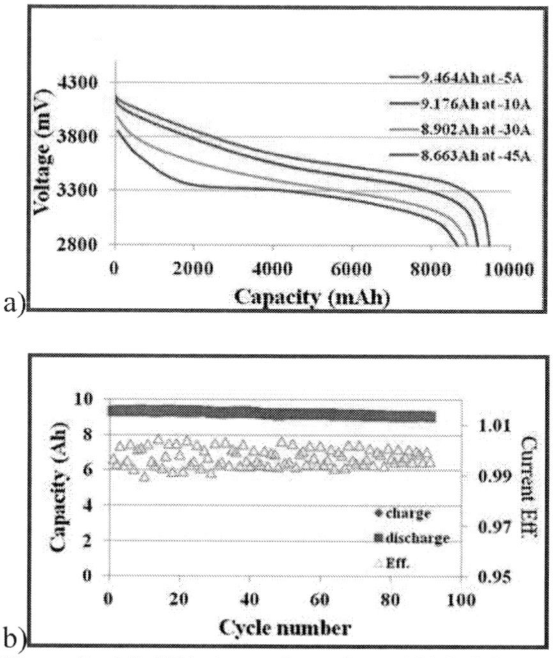

Figure 5. a) Cell Discharge Capacity and b) Cell Capacity and Efficiency vs. Cycle # at 100% DOD, 0.8C Charging, 0.8C Discharging

Multi-functional Cell for Military Application:

ALE's advanced multi-functional cell's high energy density makes it extremely useful in many military applications where space and weight are highly constrained. For instance, ALE's multi-functional cell can be made to be an integral part of bullet-proof vests. This enables the vests to not only protect the dismounted soldier from enemy fire, but also provide critical power needed for completing ground missions. ALE's multi-functional cell can continue to safely operate after suffering a certain kinds of bullet shots. Our multi-functional, bullet-resistant vest can extend combat mission time by an additional 72 hours without any increase in the dismounted soldier's weight load.

Conclusions

ALE's multi-functional lithium-ion polymer cell provides not only high-energy and high-power but also safety protection in unwanted situations where an electronic circuit fails, or the electronic circuit has little effect (such as an internal short) when embedded and becomes an integrated part of the EV architecture. ALE's multi-functional cell exhibits outstanding mechanical and electrochemical abuse tolerance, in contrast to cells available on the commercial market. ALE's multi-functional cell passes overcharge and impact tests. We can design and physically configure our lithium-ion polymer cell to comply with any military conformal requirements as well as additional custom specification for other military batteries and devices with unique specifications.

Reference

[1] UL 1642-2012

Acknowledgements

This ALE research is supported by the Advanced Research Projects Agency – Energy (ARPA-E) under Grant No. DE-AR0000396. Program Directors Dr. Chris Atkinson and Dr. John Lemmon and Dr. Dawson Cagle from ARPA-E are greatly appreciated for their support and guidance.

Development of Higher Energy Density Li-Ion Batteries

Christopher Lang, Kenneth Rosina and Peter Moran
Physical Sciences Inc.
lang@psicorp.com

Abstract
Higher energy density batteries are required to power next generation technologies. A significant amount of research has been devoted to developing new materials with increased capacity and performance. In order to minimize the cell weight, new cell design techniques are also required that minimize the mass fraction of the inactive components. This presentation will discuss Physical Sciences Inc.'s efforts to construct cells offering a ~25% increase in cell energy density as compared to cells built with current components and techniques. Test results from coin and pouch cells will highlight the cycling performance and impact on final cell energy density upon integrating the new technologies.

Development of High Energy and High Power Lithium-ion Polymer Cells for LMAMS Munition and Small UAVs *

Zhiqiang Xu and Chul Chai**
SKC Powertech, Inc.
Mt. Olive, New Jersey

William J. McMahan and Steven E. Horn
U.S. Army, Aviation and Missile Research, Development, and Engineering Center (AMRDEC)
Redstone Arsenal, AL

Abstract: *This work was performed under a contract supported by U.S. Army, Aviation and Missile Research, Development, and Engineering Center (AMRDEC) to develop low-temperature high rate and high energy lithium-ion polymer batteries for Lethal Miniature Aerial Munitions System (LMAMS) munitions (small UAS). Existing cells and batteries lack high power capabilities under cold soaking which negatively impacts their use in training and/or combat missions. Specifically, the lithium-ion polymer cells of existing batteries deliver 1.85Ah and are only functional above 5℃. At completion of Phase 1 SKCP developed comparably sized prototype cells that deliver 2.15Ah and demonstrated a much higher power at both low (down to -20℃) and high temperature. Under Phase 2, SKCP increased the cell capacity from 2.15Ah up to 2.7Ah (605060V42 for 4.2V operation), 3.1Ah (605060V44 for 4.4V operation), and 3.37Ah (605060V45 for 4.5V operation). All Phase 2 cells demonstrated a much improved power performance, an increase of ~46% over existing COTS cells, at both low and high temperature.*

Keywords: High power; high energy; Li-ion cell; low-temperature operation; LMAMS munitions; UAS.

Introduction

The LMAMS system needs a battery to ensure that duration and peak power capabilities are met over a wide operating temperature range. Existing batteries have limited capacity to meet the mission duration and lack of power capabilities after low temperature soaking, which limits their use in training and/or combat missions.

Under Phase 1, SKC identified the polymer Li-ion cells limiting factors for high rate (or fast discharge) performance over a wide temperature range. In response, SKC modified the cell design and developed electrodes, electrolytes, and processes that maximized power performance at low temperatures.

One of the objectives for Phase 2 was to develop new cell formulation that would substantially increase the UAS flying time without any physical changes in cell weight or dimensions and without sacrificing power and temperature performance. The battery cells will maintain a high-rate discharge from cold soak of 0°C (threshold) or -20°C (objective) and continue discharging at lower rates, without dropping below the minimum voltage cutoff. To meet the objective, the new cells should have a gravimetric energy density of over 300Wh/Kg and a volumetric energy density of over 690Wh/L. This paper describes SKCP's efforts for developing a high power / high energy cell with superb low temperature power capability.

Experimental

$LiCoO_2$ and/or $LiMn_2O_4$ were used as cathode materials. Modified graphite and/or graphene nano-platelets served as anode materials. Electrode fabrication utilized slurry-coating technology with either Polyvinylidene Fluoride (PVDF) or Styrene Butadiene Rubber (SBR) as a binder. Electrolyte solutions are generally consisted of one or two lithium salts dissolved in two to four solvents. These additive Lithium salts were made in-house. Solutions were prepared in a dry room (<1% humidity) and transferred to a glove box, inside of which the salt and polymer gelling agents were added before use. All separators in this project were either polyethylene (PE) or polypropylene (PP) with a thickness of 7um~16um and porosity 40~50%, which were obtained from a variety of vendors. The 6~8 um thin separators were specially made by SKC Co. Ltd.

The cell dimensions of 6.0mm x 50mm x 60mm is based on SKCP's pouch design. The design employed a stacking process, in which electrodes were sandwiched in a Z-folded one-piece separator. The electrodes were vacuum-dried for at least 5 hours at 65°C-85°C prior to and after the assembly. Inside the glove box, electrolyte was injected into the pouch to activate the cells. After allowing sufficient time to allow the electrodes and separator to be fully saturated, the cells were gelled at

* DISTRIBUTION A - Approved for public release; distribution unlimited. Review completed by the AMRDEC Public Affairs Office (9APR2014, Control No. PR0904)

elevated temperatures, pre-charged, degassed, formed, and aged. All cells were formed and tested on either the Maccor 4000 or Arbin BT-2000 automated test system.

Results and Discussion

Table 1 lists the UAS cell specifications. Another objective for the cells in Phase 2 was that each cell for the UAS system meet or exceed the following Discharging Protocol: pulse current 17 amps for 10 seconds then maintain 25W, ideally for 30 minutes at ambient room-temperature (RT) and at cold soak of -20°C without dropping below the minimum 3V/cell voltage cutoff limit. The cells are required to be 40g (+/- 5%) in weight and 6.0mm x 50mm x 60mm in dimension, the SKCP 605060 cell format, corresponding to a Gravimetric Energy of over 300Wh/Kg and a Volumetric Energy Density of over 690 Wh/L.

Table 1. Requirement of UAS Cell Specifications

Item	Specification	
Cell Dimensions	Thickness: 6.0 +/- 0.3 mm max after initial full charge	
	Width: 50.0 +/- 0.3 mm	
	Height: 60.0 +1.5/-0.0 mm	
Nominal Capacity and energy (Wh)	Existing competitor cells	Objective cells
	1.9 Ah (0.2C) 7.0Wh	>3Ah (12.5Wh)
Charging Voltage	4.2V	4.2 or higher
Nominal Voltage	3.7V	N/A
Discharge Cut-off Voltage	3.0V	3.0V
Cell Weight	40 g max	40g (+/- 5%)

The Phase 1 cell design optimization and cell component development resulted in the 605060 (2014 version) cell with 2.15Ah (0.2C) and over a 93% capacity at 10C (RT). These cells met the dimensional and weight requirements (39.7g and 5.9mm x 50mm x 60mm) and demonstrated a much improved low-temp power performance compared to existing cells, and that could be discharged following the Discharging Protocol at temperatures approaching -20°C. However, the objective goal for each cell in Phase 2 is to deliver a much higher capacity with a better power capability at low temperature. Based on chemistries identified under Phase 1 along with further cell design optimization and through the use of the latest advanced cell components, SKCP has successfully developed a new 4.2V cell (605060V42) along with other high-volt cells, 4.4V and 4.5V (605060V44 and 605060V45) with comparable cell form factors. The comparative operation parameters are shown in **Table 2**.

Table 2. UAS cell basic parameters and performance comparison

Cell Type (605060)	Competitor cell	SKCP Cells			
		605060 (2014)	605060V42	605060V44	605060V45
Weight(g)	>37.0	39.7	41.0	39.0	37.5
Capacity (Ah) at C/4	1.840	2.156	2.73	3.1	3.37
Energy (Whr)	7.021	8.283	10.56	12.2	13.4
Gravimetric Energy Density (Wh/Kg)	189.8	208.6	257.5	312.8	357.2
Volumetric Energy Density (Wh/L)	381.2	472.0	586.7	677.8	744.4

A discharge capacity comparison of the newly developed cells is shown in **Figure 1.** This includes cell versions: 605060V42, 605060V444, 605060V45, and 605060V46. These cells deliver a much higher capacity and higher voltage plateau than the existing competitor cells and the old SKCP 605060 (2014 version). The 605060V46 cell delivered over 4Ah but showed an over-limit thickness. [Note: Two SKCP cells have successfully undergone UN/DOT 38.3 testing, the 605060V42 (4.2V version, 2.7Ah) and 605060V44 (4.4V version, 3.1Ah).]

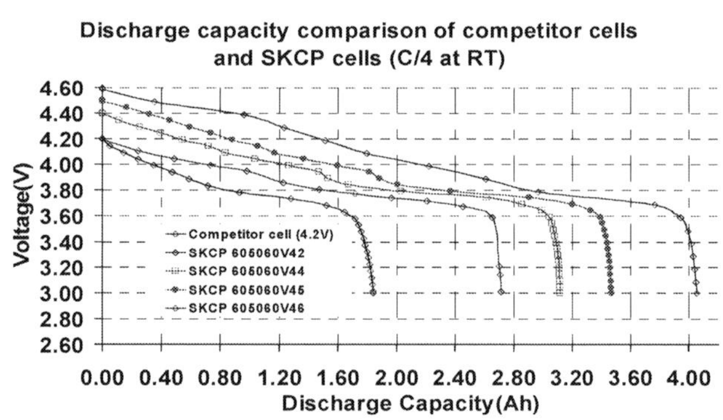

Figure 1. Comparison of Discharge Profile of UAS cells (0.2C and RT)

The power performance is detailed in the following figures: **Figures 2 – 5.** The cell performance tests were conducted under the proscribed Discharge Protocol and were evaluated specifically at low temperatures. These figures show that both the 605060V42 and 605060V44 are capable of high-rate discharge from cold soak of 0°C (threshold) and the -20°C (objective); and continue to discharge at lower rates, without dropping below the minimum voltage cutoff.

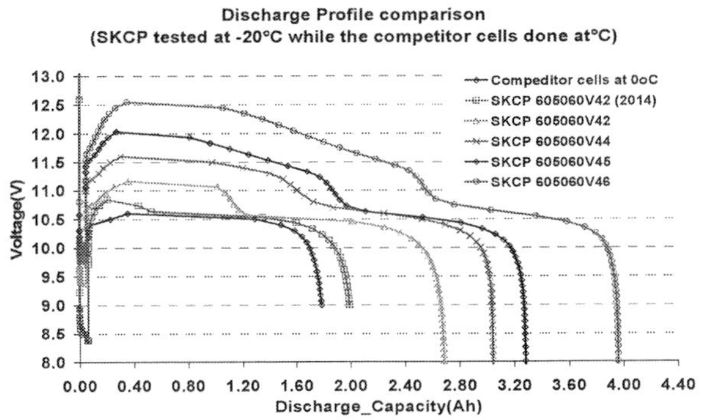

Figure 2. Comparison of discharging profile of three cells in series at objective temperature of -20°C, discharge protocol: 17A pulse discharge for 10 seconds then constant power (25W/cell) discharge to 7.5V (9V is the required cut-off limit)

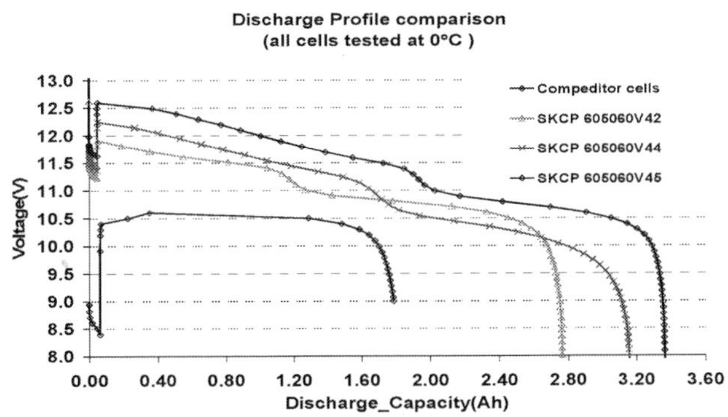

Figure 3. Comparison of discharging profile of three cells in series at threshold temperature Of 0°C, following the discharge protocol.

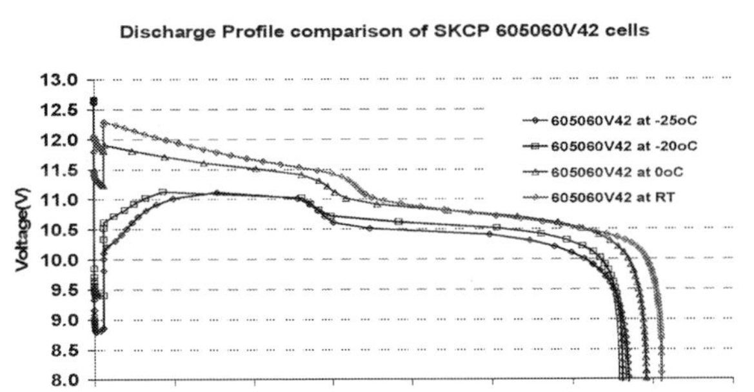

Figure 4. Comparison of discharging profiles of three 605060V42 cells in series at various temperatures, following the discharge protocol.

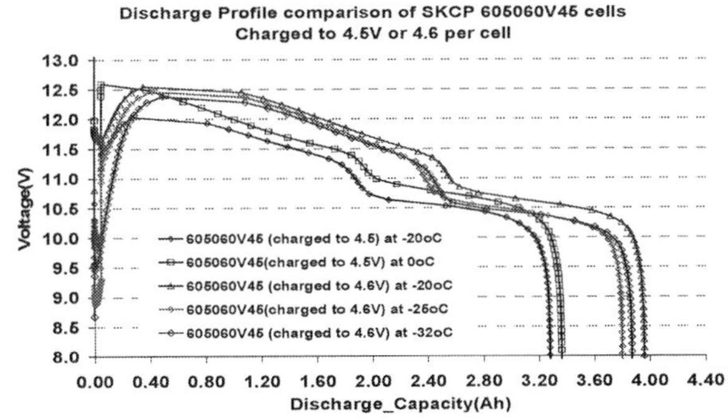

Figure 5. Comparison of discharging profile of three high-volt operation cells in series tested from threshold temperature (0°C), to objective temperature (-20°C), and ideal temperature (-32°C), following the discharge protocol.

Along with tests demonstrating cell performance under the discharging protocol, SKCP also conducted cell testing with respect to overcharging, storage life, and charging rate.

The overcharging tests were conducted on the 605060V42 and the 605060V44 cells. For this test, a 5.1V was applied to the 2.7Ah 605060V42 cells and 5.3V was applied to the 3.1Ah 605060V44 cells. Both passed the overcharging tests without displaying smoke or fire and maintained a max temp below 40°C. On the 605060V42 cells, no gassing was observed after the overcharging tests; this indicates that there is a possibility of developing a 5V cell, which would be applicable for LMAMS munitions and other small UASs. Figure 6 plots the overcharging results for the 605060V42 cell.

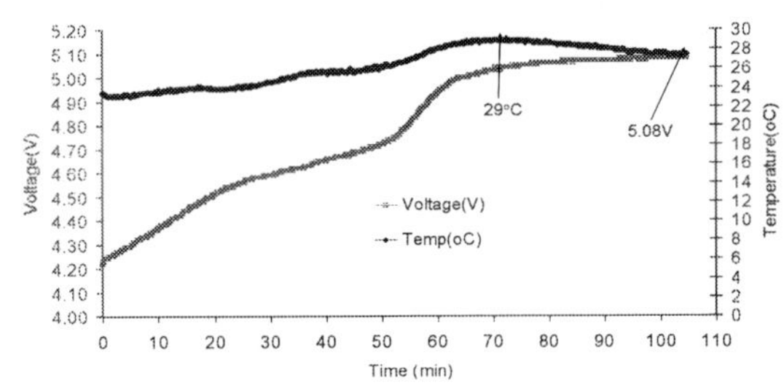

Figure 6. Over charging tests on 2.7Ah 605060V42 cell. 2.7A constant current to 5.1V tapping to 0.1A

Storage monitoring tests were used to determine the most appropriate charging state for cell/battery storage. These tests were conducted on the 605060V42 and the 605060V44 cells over a 72/19 day period, respectively. These cells were stored at two different charge levels, 3.8V and 4.2V, and three different temperatures, 45°C, Room Temperature (RT), and 0°C. The results are shown in **Table 3**. For both cell types, storage at 4.2V resulted in significant permanent loss in capacity, especially at higher temperatures. As an example, the 4.2V charge 605060V42 cell lost 19%, 6-7%, and 2-3% (Ah) capacity for 45°C, RT, and 0°C, respectively. Whereas, the cells that were stored with a 3.8V charge showed an almost negligible permanent (Ah) capacity loss, especially at RT and lower temperatures. Both cell types showed similar trends with respect to storage charge and temperature. Therefore, storage for these cells are shown to be optimized when stored with a 3.8V charge and at ambient room temperature and below.

Table 3. Capacity retention after storage at variable charged voltages and temperatures

2.7Ah 605060V42 (aging condition)	4.2V charged cells			3.8V charged cells		
	45°C	RT	0°C	45°C	RT	0°C
Capacity (Ah) after 72 days (Recharged to 4.2V)	2.18 (80.7%)	2.53 (93.7%)	2.633 (97.5%)	2.64 (97.8%)	2.68 (99.3%)	2.7 (100%)
3.1Ah 605060V44 (aging condition)	4.4V charged cells			3.8V charged cells		
	45°C	RT	0°C	45°C	RT	0°C
Capacity (Ah) after 19 days (Recharged to 4.4V)	2.66 (85.8%)	2.90 (93.5%)	3.05 (98.4%)	3.046 (98.3%)	3.074 (99.2%)	3.09 (99.7%)

One of the rechargeable cell requirements for the LMAMS system is to have a charging time of no more than 1 hour given a 1C rate. For the 605060V42 cell, the 1C rate is 2.7A. The charging rates for these cells were tested at ambient room temperature for rates from 0.25C to a 3C rate. Prior to testing, all the cells were charged to an initial capacity of 800mAh (~30% nominal capacity). This capacity was chosen to limit the charging time within 1 hour without sacrificing charge capacity. As shown in the **Figure** 7, at a 1C-rate, the cell reached 4.2V after 40 minutes. The cell can be considered to have a total capacity (including pre-charged capacity) of a least 93%. If a tapping (trickle) charge of C/20 (0.135A) is applied for 15 – 16 minutes, the cell will be fully charged within 55-56 minutes. Therefore, the 605060V42 cell meets the charging requirement of less than 1 hour given a 1C rate. These cells are also capable of using the fast charging rates, 2C (5.4A) or 3C (6.1A), for charging under 30 minutes without sacrificing the cell capacity. At temperatures of 0°C, these cells can be charged to 85% capacity. The 605060V44 cells have been observed with similar charging rate characteristics.

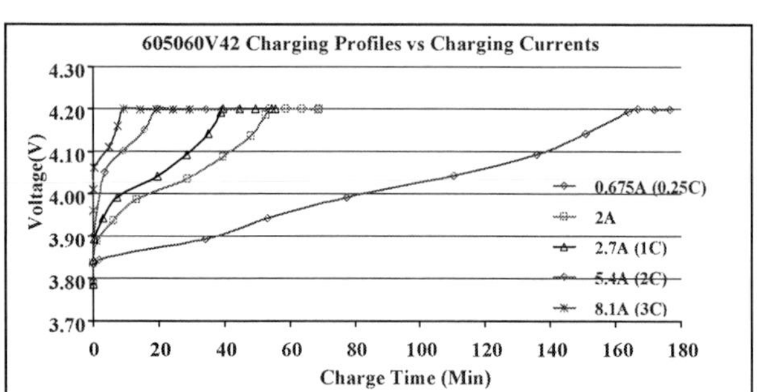

Figure 7. Charge profiles with Variable C-rates at RT

Conclusions

Under this program, SKCP met or exceeded the requirements. The cell design optimization produced high energy density / high power Li-ion cells with excellent low-temperature performance. The two Li-ion cells developed under Phase 2, the 605060V42 at 2.7Ah and the 605060V44 @ 3.1Ah, have energy densities of 257.5 Wh/kg and 312.8Wh/Kg, respectively. Both cells have undergone and passed UNDOT testing. These high energy cells exhibited excellent power performance at ambient room-temperature and at cold soak temperature of -20°C without dropping below the minimum 3V/cell voltage cutoff limit.

Future works may include cycle life improvement for the 4.2V cells and the other high-volt operational cells.

References

1. Zhiqiang Xu, Zhiwei Zhang, Chul Chai, and William J. McMahan, "Development of Low-temperature and High-rate Lithium-ion Cells for LMAMS Munition", *46th Power Source Conference*.
2. Zhiqiang Xu, Chi Kyun Park, Zhiwei Zhang, Chul Chai, "Organic Lithium Salt Electrolytes Having Enhanced Safety for Rechargeable Batteries and Methods of Making the Same", *US Patent 20060068295.*
3. "High-Rate Rechargeable Lithium-Ion Battery", *SKC Powertech/US Army Communications-Electronics Command Contract W15P7T-04-C-P016*
4. "High Energy and High-Rate Rechargeable Lithium-Ion Battery", *SKC Powertech/US Army Communications-Electronics Command Contract W15P7T-05-C-R009*
5. "The Development of Novel Electrolytes for Polymer Li-ion cells with wider operating temperature ranges"*SKC Powertech/US Army Communications-Electronics Command Contract W15P7T-06-D-A402*
6. Chi Kyun Park, Zhiwei Zhang, Luying Sun, Chul Chai, "High ionic conductivity gel polymer electrolyte for rechargeable polymer batteries", *US Patent 6,841,303*

Acknowledgement

The authors gratefully acknowledge U.S. Army AMRDEC for funding this work under the contract W911NF-11-D-0001 DO# 0247 and SKC Co. Ltd for help in providing separator material.

High Energy Li-ion Cells Based on CAM-7™ Cathode Material

Jane Rempel, David Ofer, Adrian Pullen, Daniel Kaplan, Brian Barnett, and Suresh Sriramulu

CAMX Power

35 Hartwell Avenue, Lexington, MA 02421

Abstract

CAMX Power has developed CAM-7, a versatile high-performance cathode material platform for Li-ion batteries that enables both high energy and high power batteries. CAM-7 is being considered for a wide range of civilian and DoD applications. In this paper we highlight three CAM-7-based cell designs that extend the performance of Li-ion technology beyond what has been historically demonstrated: (a) 250 Wh/kg 18650 cells that can operate at -40°C; (b) small pouch cells that can deliver 270 Wh/kg at 5C rate; and (c) 18650 cells with an available energy of 180 Wh/kg at a pulse power of 700 W/kg.

Keywords

Lithium-ion; Li-ion; 18650 cells; pouch cells;

Introduction

Li-ion batteries are attractive for many DoD applications owing to their excellent combination of energy and life. However, COTS Li-ion cells still do not offer high enough energy density (both volumetric – Wh/L and gravimetric – Wh/kg) to enable the mission profiles and durations desired for many current and anticipated DoD applications. To a large extent, the cathode material in a Li-ion cell limits the achievable energy density. $LiCoO_2$ (LCO) cathode material is predominantly used in COTS high energy density Li-ion cells. The past two decades have seen a steady increase in the energy density of Li-ion cells with LCO cathode material primarily through improvements in cell engineering and more recently, improvements in the LCO cathode material that allow for higher voltage operation. However, cell manufacturers have exhausted the cell energy increases possible with LCO; further increases can come only from implementation of new cathode materials. Although COTS cells with emerging $LiNi_{(1-x-y)}Co_yMn_xO_2$ (NCM) or $LiNi_{0.80}Co_{0.15}Al_{0.05}O_2$ (NCA) cathode materials are available, these cells typically have lower energy density than cells with LCO-based cathodes. Furthermore, commercial high-energy Li-ion cells are not suitable for many DoD applications where capability for low-temperature operation or high rate continuous discharge or pulse power operation is desired.

Recognizing this need for cathode materials that can enable higher energy density cells, CAMX Power has developed a stabilized $LiNiO_2$-based cathode material platform, CAM-7, that combines high capacity and high average discharge voltage with excellent rate capability and long life. The CAM-7 platform enables higher energy Li-ion cells than commercial cathode materials as shown in the comparison plot in Figure 1. CAM-7 materials are able to support high discharge capacity, while also enabling long cycle life as shown by the data in Figure 2.

In a materials development effort spanning more than 10 years, we have resolved challenges historically associated with high-nickel $LiNiO_2$ class cathode materials; challenges such as synthesis reproducibility, electrode slurry stability, high-temperature cycle life, and thermal stability. CAM-7 is now being commercialized for several civilian applications worldwide. Production of CAM-7 is being scaled up to 50 metric tons per year in our pilot plant (Figure 3) located in Rowley, MA, and we recently announced the first licensee for larger-scale production [1].

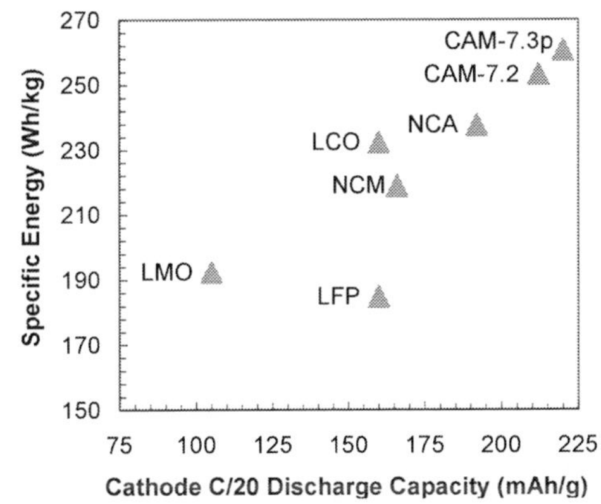

Figure 1: Comparison of the estimated cell-level specific energy of CAM-7 cathode materials with commercial off-the-shelf cathode materials in identically designed cells with graphite anode. LFP is $LiFePO_4$, and LMO is $LiMn_2O_4$. 4.2V charge, except for LFP - charged to 3.6V.

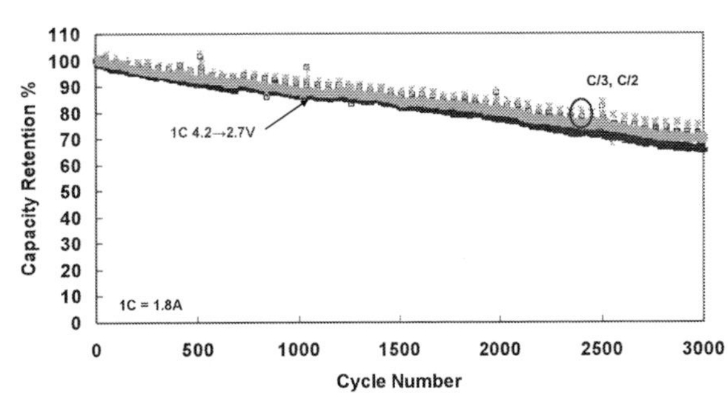

Figure 2: CAM-7/graphite cells have excellent cycle life. Data shown are for 18650 cells fabricated at CAMX Power with CAM-7 cathode and graphite anode. Cycling conditions: 4.2V - 2.7V, C/2 charge/1C discharge.

Figure 3: Photograph of CAMX Power's CAM-7 cathode production pilot plant with a nominal capacity of 50 mT/y located in Rowley, Massachusetts. A new furnace is being purchased to enhance synthesis throughput and plant flexibility.

Versatility of CAM-7 Cathode Material

Because of its unique combination of high capacity and high rate capability, CAM-7 is attractive for a wide range of applications and cell designs. By combining CAM-7 with different anode materials, electrode designs, and electrolytes, we have developed cell designs for a wide range of applications. Figure 4 summarizes the key attributes of these cells, showing tradeoffs in typical performance metrics. In this paper, we present data for the high-energy cells. In an accompanying paper being presented at this conference, we highlight the performance of high-power cells wherein CAM-7 is combined with lithium titanate anode for extremely long-life cells capable of operation at -50°C or supporting very high bi-directional (charge and discharge) power capability (10 kW/L).

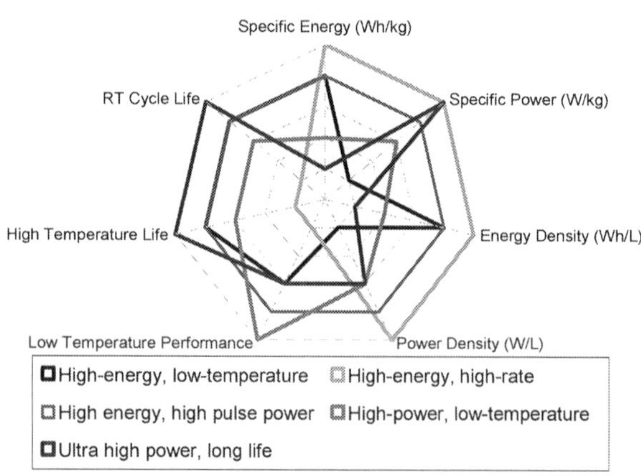

Figure 4: Spider chart summarizing the combination of attributes of specific cell designs developed and demonstrated with CAM-7 cathode material.

The following sections present performance data for three CAM-7/graphite or CAM-7/Si-based anode cell chemistries with high specific energy:

A. 18650 cells with specific energy of ~ 250 Wh/kg at RT, ~ 140 Wh/kg at -30°C, and ~ 50 Wh/kg at –40°C;

B. Small (7cc) pouch cells with specific energy of 300 Wh/kg at low rates and up to 275 Wh/kg at 5C rate; and

C. 18650 cells with an available energy of 180 Wh/kg at a pulse power of 700 W/kg (10s).

A) High-energy cells with excellent low temperature performance

We developed a CAM-7/graphite cell for DoD applications that combines high specific energy with long life and excellent discharge performance even at -40°C. Figure 5 shows the discharge voltage curves of CAM-7/graphite 18650 cells fabricated at CAMX Power. The inset table shows that the measured specific energy was 247 Wh/kg for these cells. Note that the specific energy at the jelly roll level is 290 Wh/kg. Our cells also have excellent low-temperature performance as shown in Figure 6 when compared to commercial high specific energy cells. Further improvement in specific energy can be obtained by using state-of-the-art 18650 cans. Essentially, the inside diameter of our 18650 cans is 17.3mm,whereas it is ~ 18 mm for newer, state-of-the-art 18650 cans, allowing more material to be packed in the newer cans. Hence, further improvements in specific energy can be achieved by using these state-of-the-art cans.

These CAM-7/graphite 18650 cells, using an earlier version of CAM-7 that has since been upgraded, were also independently evaluated at the Army Research Laboratory (ARL) as part of a Phase II SBIR program. The results of the evaluation were summarized in a report [2], and a key chart from this report is reproduced as Figure 7. This ARL report concluded (for DoD use) *that these cells were ideal for applications where cycle life is imperative, even in extreme conditions.*

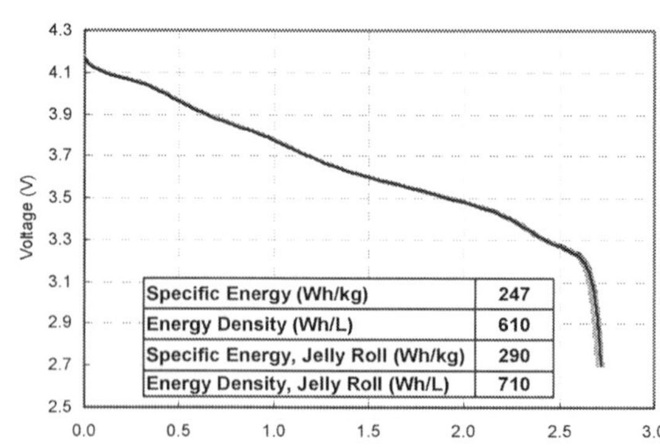

Figure 5: Discharge curves for CAM-7/graphite 18650 cells designed for very high specific energy. The cells were charged to 4.2 V and discharged to 2.7 V.

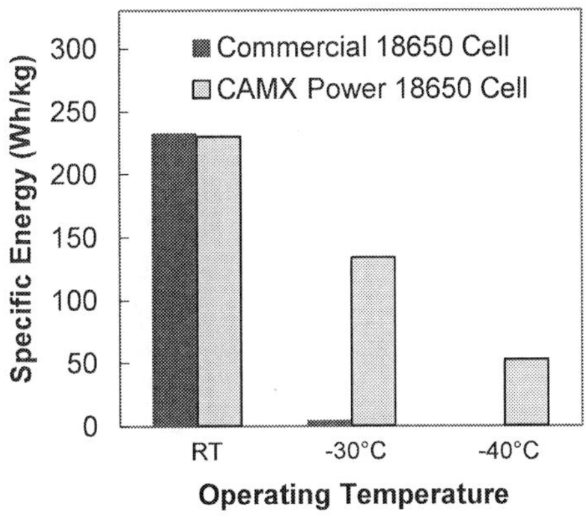

Figure 6: Comparison of delivered specific energy at different temperatures of COTS 18650 cells with CAM-7/graphite high-energy 18650 cells. 4.2 V – 2.7 V.

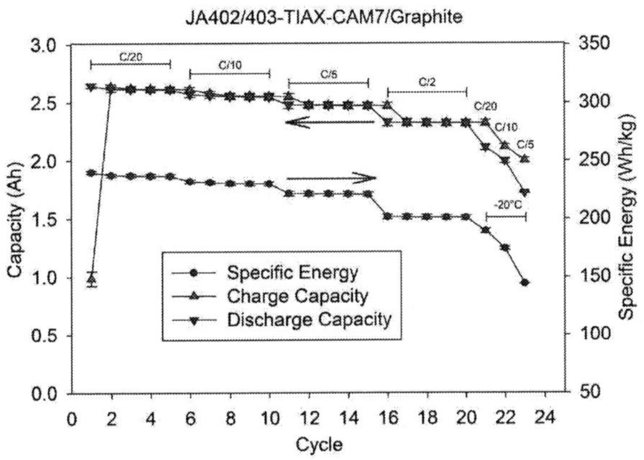

Figure 7: Measurements by ARL on CAM-7/graphite high-energy 18650 cells delivered to ARL as part of a Phase II SBIR project. Data are from [2]. Room temperature (25 °C, cycles 1–20) and low-temperature (–20 °C, cycles 21–23) rate cycling of high energy 18650 cells.

B) High-energy cells with excellent rate capability

A typical Li-ion cell designed to provide high specific energy cannot simultaneously support high rate discharge. This tradeoff occurs because high-loading, thick electrodes have to be employed to minimize the amount of inactive materials (e.g., current collectors and separator) employed in the cell. The ion transport limitations in such thick electrodes increase electrode polarization during high rate discharge and hence reduce the energy delivered during discharge. In contrast, when high capacity active materials are employed, high cell specific energy can be achieved even with thinner electrodes, and the rate capability of the cell can be preserved. A key requirement, of course, is that the active materials themselves be capable of supporting very high discharge rates.

We combined CAM-7 with silicon-based anodes to break through the energy/rate limitations of conventional Li-ion chemistries. We combined silicon-based materials sourced from a leading domestic supplier with CAM-7, high-performance commercial separators, and a specially formulated electrolyte in custom-designed 48 x 30 x 5 mm pouch cells. Figure 8 shows a photograph of the pouch cell, which has a measured capacity of 1.1 Ah at C/5 rate. The rate capability performance of this cell is shown in Figure 9. This cell has a specific energy of ~ 300 Wh/kg at low rates, and ~ 270 Wh/kg at a discharge rate of 5C.

Figure 8: Photograph of 1.1 Ah CAM-7/Si pouch cell. Performance of this pouch cell is shown in Figure 9.

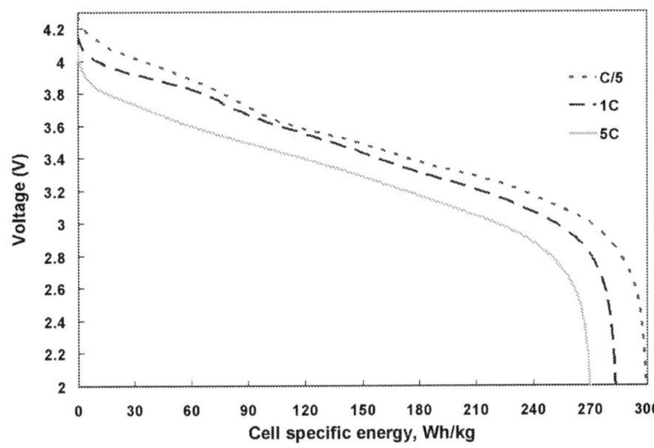

Figure 9: Discharge specific energy of the CAM-7/Si pouch cell shown in Figure 8 as a function of C-rate. The CAM-7/Si pouch cell delivers ~ 270 Wh/kg at 5C rate.

C) High-energy cells with excellent pulse power capability

Typically, Li-ion cells that are designed for high energy content cannot also simultaneously support high pulse power capability over a wide state-of-charge (SOC) range. Consequently, the 'available energy' for pulse power applications is significantly lower than the rated energy for the cell.

DOE's HPPC test is typically used to measure the available energy for pulse power applications. To maximize the available energy for pulse power operation, we combined high-capacity CAM-7 cathode material with a SiO_x/graphite blended electrode. These cells can deliver ~ 180 Wh/kg of available energy for a 10 s discharge pulse power of 700 W/kg (Figure 10). Moreover, by implementing cell hardware with reduced resistance, further improvement in power in comparison to baseline CAM-7/graphite cells can be achieved (Figure 11).

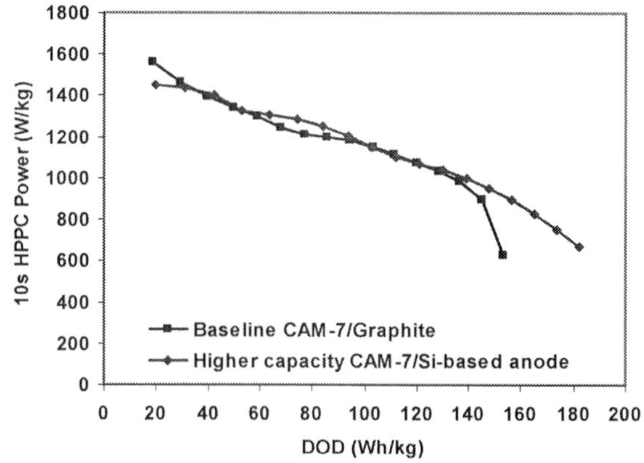

Figure 10: Measured discharge pulse power capability of CAM-7-based 18650 cells designed for pulse power applications. The CAM-7/silicon anode-based cells can achieve 700 W/kg with an available energy of 180 Wh/kg.

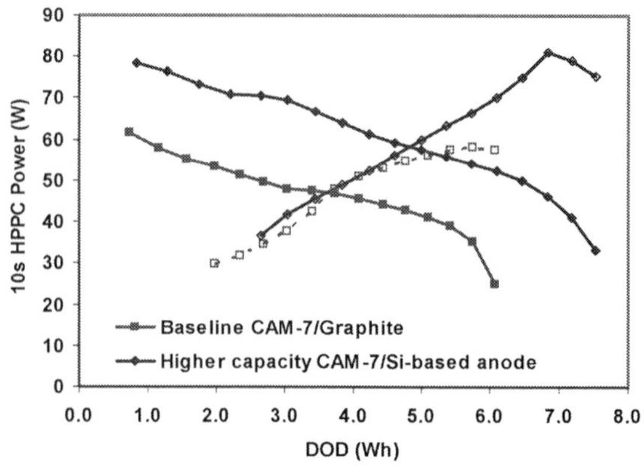

Figure 11: Performance of CAM-7-based 18650 cells designed for pulse power applications. The power capability was measured according to DOE's HPPC test procedures with 5A discharge and 3.75A charge 10s pulse.

The cells with the blended silicon/graphite anode and high capacity CAM-7 cathode also cycle well. Figure 12 shows the room temperature cycle life for these cells when cycled over a 90% SOC range, or from 4.1 V to 2.7 V.

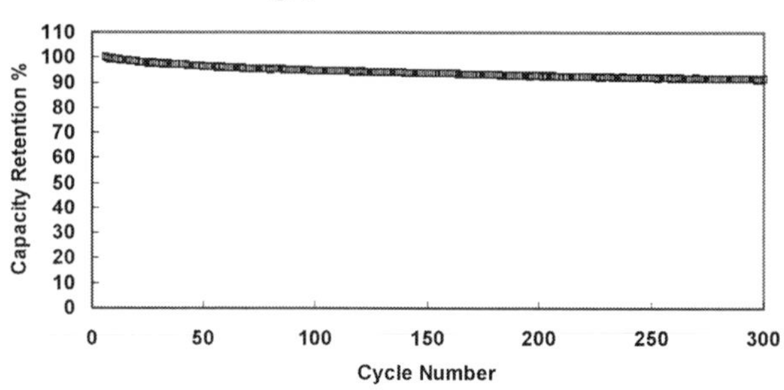

Figure 12: Cycle life of the cells from Figure 10 cycled between 4.1 V and 2.7 V, C/2 charge and 1C discharge.

Conclusions

CAM-7 cathode material enables very high specific energy cells for a wide range of applications and allows cell developers to pursue improved combinations of high power and high energy. The examples shown in this document highlight the versatility of the CAM-7 platform. CAM-7 can be combined with graphite, silicon-based anodes, or LTO-based anodes to achieve high specific energy densities for a wide range of duty cycles. We have demonstrated CAM-7 based cells that extend the performance envelope of Li-ion technology:

A. 18650 cells with specific energy of ~ 250 Wh/kg at RT, ~ 140 Wh/kg at -30ºC, and ~ 50 Wh/kg at –40ºC;

B. Small pouch cells with specific energy of 300 Wh/kg at low rates and 270 Wh/kg at 5C rate; and

C. 18650 cells with an available energy of 180 Wh/kg at a pulse power of 700 W/kg (10s).

These cell designs were primarily developed for specific applications of interest to the DoD and the DOE. We are interested in customizing these cells for other specific DoD applications. We are further interested in working with DoD agencies and their preferred cell suppliers to transition these cell designs to larger-scale production, so that they can be fielded for DoD applications. We will also be able to supply CAM-7 powder from our Massachusetts-based cathode production for DoD use.

Acknowledgements

We gratefully acknowledge financial support for some of the work presented in this document from the US Government, and specifically through grants W911QX-12-C-0001 and DE-EE0006452.

References

[1] Please see press release at: http://www.camxpower.com/2016/04/joint-news-release-camx-power-llc-and-basf/

[2] Allen JL, Allen JL, Delp SA, Jow TR. (2014). Evaluation of TIAX High Energy CAM-7/Graphite Lithium-Ion Batteries at High & Low Temperatures, U.S. Army Research Laboratory.

CAM-7/LTO Lithium-Ion Cells for Robust, High Power Batteries

David Ofer, Daniel Kaplan, Celine Yang, Sharon Dalton-Castor, Brian Barnett, and Suresh Sriramulu

CAMX Power
35 Hartwell Avenue
Lexington, MA 02421

Abstract: *CAMX Power is developing Li-ion pouch cells based on its CAM-7 cathode material and commercially available LTO anode material to provide high power, high charging rate capability, long life and safety in defense applications, start-stop vehicle batteries, and stationary power applications.*

Keywords: pouch cell; lithium-ion; high power, CAM-7; lithium titanate.

Introduction

Lithium-ion cells employing lithium titanate (LTO) anodes offer unique advantages that could prove to be critically enabling for a number of vehicular and storage applications. Although they have lower energy than conventional Li-ion cells, they can be charged extremely rapidly and at very low temperatures (even at -50°C), they have very high stability and safety, and they can have very long life. CAMX Power (spun off from TIAX LLC) is developing Li-ion technologies that match LTO anodes with our high energy, high power CAM-7 cathode material for military 6T vehicle batteries, start-stop vehicle batteries, and large-scale stationary storage batteries. The CAM-7 cathode material has the highest combined capacity and rate capability of any market-ready Li-ion cathode material (Figure 1), and is especially well-suited for implementing in long-lived, robust, safe LTO-anode pouch cells and batteries.

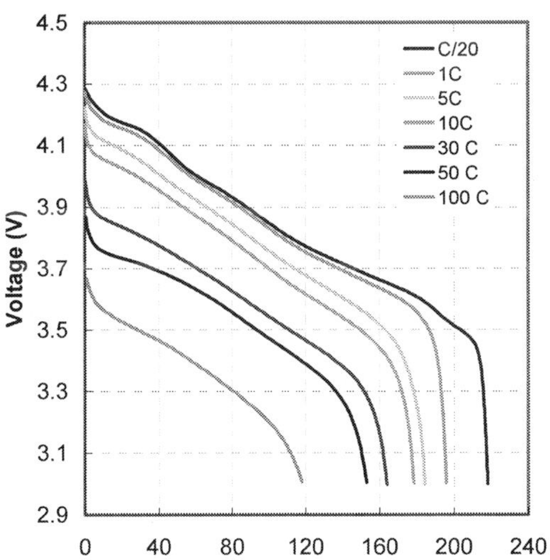

Figure 1. Discharge low loading (~2 mg/cm^2) CAM-7 electrode in a coin cell vs. a Li metal counter electrode. The cell was charged in CCCV mode to 4.3 V, and discharged at rates shown on basis of 200 mAh/g 1C rate.

CAM-7 is a dopant-stabilized $LiNiO_2$-class cathode material with a unique combination of high energy content and power capability as shown in Figure 1, making it ideally suited for both high energy density cells and high power cells. CAM-7 is made by a readily scalable solid-state synthetic process, and its chemical composition, morphology, and synthesis procedures can be tuned to optimize it for specific applications and electrode processing conditions. A 50 t/y pilot plant for producing CAM-7 is operating in Rowley, Massachusetts. CAM-7 cathode material was recently licensed for the purpose of scaling up production and bringing it to the global marketplace in high volume.[1]

LTO-anode Li-ion cells are known to have excellent cycle life and safety; however elevated-temperature gassing is reputed to be an issue for LTO-anode pouch cells.[2] CAMX Power has found that by using adequately purified active materials and electrolyte in suitable cell designs, CAM-7/LTO pouch cells can be made to have excellent elevated-temperature durability as well as low-temperature and high power performance. In addition to these characteristics, CAM-7/LTO cells can be discharged to the 0V condition and stored for extended periods without impacting performance. Different aspects of CAM-7/LTO pouch cell design and performance have been developed and characterized in SBIR programs sponsored by the Army, the Navy, the Defense Logistics Agency and the Department of Energy. A summary of key results obtained in those various programs follows.

CAM-7/LTO Cell Performance

6T battery application: Much of CAMX Power's (previously as TIAX) CAM-7/LTO pouch cell development work has been directed towards the 28 V, 6T battery application, where battery improvements are desired for enhanced Silent Watch capability. This effort has targeted low-temperature power delivery and charge acceptance capability as well as stability and life, and the technology has been implemented and demonstrated in pouch cells of capacity ranging from 100 mAh to 3 Ah. To meet the 6T battery operating voltage range requirements,[3] the CAM-7/LTO chemistry is best implemented in a 11-series cell, 4-6 parallel cell configuration. Cell designs with electrode loadings in the range of 1.3 to 1.7 mAh/cm^2 have been evaluated for their balance of energy/power characteristics, and are projected to provide pouch cells and 6T batteries with attributes in the range shown by Table 1.

Electrode mAh/cm^2	Cell Wh/kg*	Cell Wh/l	6T Ah	6T Wh
1.7	90	190	80	1925
1.3	83	177	74	1725

Table 1. Attributes of pouch cell and 6T battery designs.
*measured in 3 Ah pouch cells

The per-cell operating voltage limits in the 11-series 6T design are 2.59V sustained charging voltage and 1.31V cold-cranking voltage limit. The excellent low-temperature performance of the CAM-7/LTO cell technology under 6T-relevent conditions is illustrated by Figure 2, which shows the 30 sec.-duration pulse power capability of a 130 mAh unfixtured (no clamping pressure) pouch cell at -18 °C.

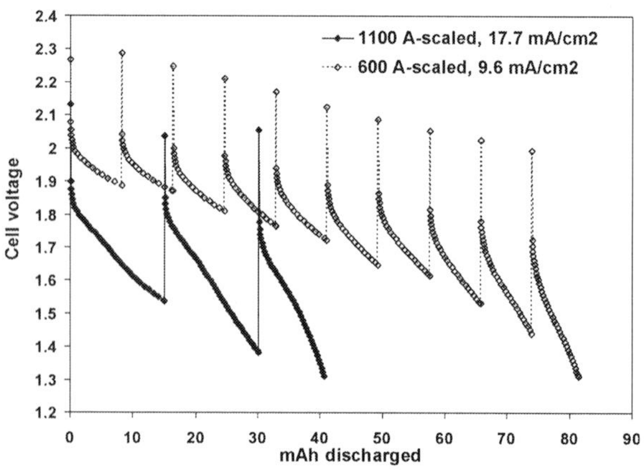

Figure 2. Capacity delivered during sequential scaled 30 second duration pulse discharges of a 130 mAh CAM-7/LTO pouch cell at -18 °C, pulsed at current densities corresponding to those expected for 600A and 1100A discharge of a 6T battery made with identical electrodes at loading of 1.3 mAh/cm^2. Cell charged to 2.59V and discharged to 1.31V, corresponding to operation of an 11-series-cell 6T battery, with 30 minute rests between pulses to minimize effects of self-heating.

The CAM-7/LTO cell technology also readily meets the 6T cold cranking requirement for delivery of a 30 sec.-duration 400A pulse at -40 °C. Excellent low-temperature performance of the CAM-7/LTO cell technology has been measured even at temperatures as low as -50 °C.

Figure 3 shows constant current continuous charge and discharge curves for a 3 Ah CAM-7/LTO pouch cell at -50 °C. Over half of the cell's capacity is delivered at the C/5 rate, and the cell can be charged to half its capacity at the 1C rate if the voltage limits are expanded to allow charging termination at 3.0V. We expect negligible self-heating at these rates, indicating that the measured performance is an inherent feature of the materials employed.

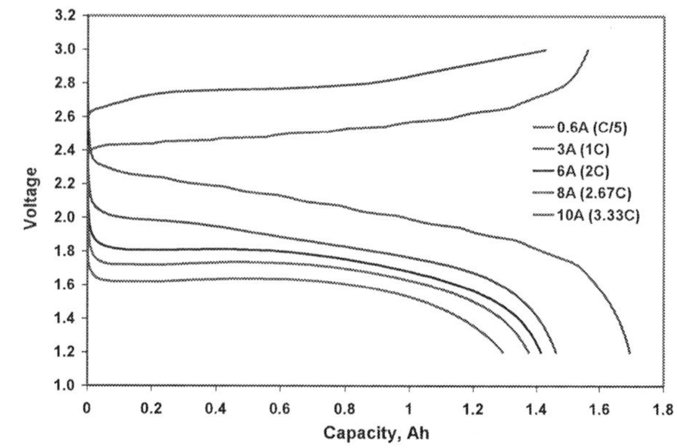

Figure 3. Continuous constant current charge and discharge characteristics of a 3 Ah, 1.7 mAh/cm^2 loading CAM-7/LTO pouch cell at -50 °C.

Figure 3 data suggest that for discharge at -50 °C at rates of 2C and higher, self-heating of this larger (3 Ah) cell helps to improve its rate capability, as indicated by increasing evidence of voltage delay with increasing rate.

This same low-temperature-optimized CAM-7/LTO pouch cell technology also has excellent tolerance for elevated temperature exposure, as illustrated by Figure 4, which shows discharge capacity vs. cycle number for 2C/2C cycling to 2.65V (60 mV above 6T charge voltage requirement) of a 2.7 Ah CAM-7/LTO pouch cell at 70 °C, as well as a photograph of the cell after 200 full cycles.

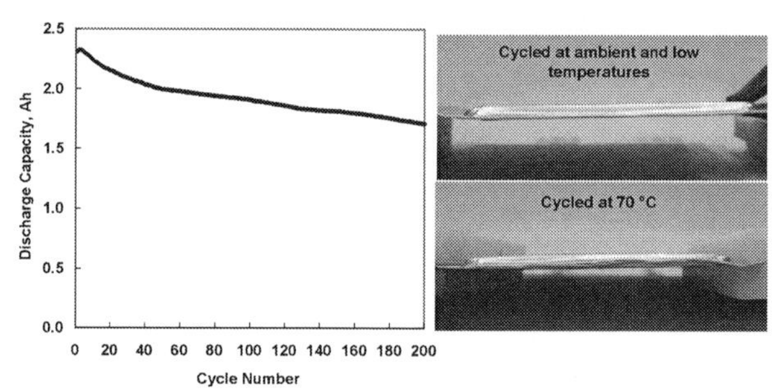

Figure 4. Left: Discharge capacity of an unfixtured 2.7 Ah CAM-7/LTO pouch cell cycled 200 times between 1.4V and 2.65V at 2C/2C rate at 70 °C. Right: Side-on photograph of pouch cell after 70 °C cycling compared to cell cycled only at ambient and low temperatures.

Although Figure 4 clearly shows that the cell undergoes significant capacity loss and impedance increase, it also shows no discernible change in the cell's profile, suggesting that relatively little gassing occurs even under conditions of excessively high charge voltage and extremely high temperature.

Although the low-temperature CAM-7/LTO cell chemistry can degrade at high state of charge and 70 °C, it cycles very stably at the 6T-specific charge voltage and less extremely elevated temperatures. Figure 5 shows discharge capacity vs. cycle number for 10C/10C cycling to 2.59V of 120 mAh CAM-7/LTO pouch cells at 45 °C and a photograph of a cell after 1000 full charge-discharge cycles.

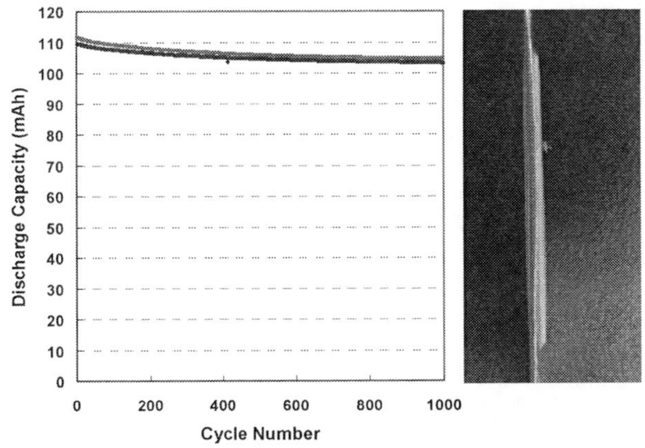

Figure 5. Left: Discharge capacity of 2 unfixtured 120 mAh CAM-7/LTO pouch cells cycled 1000 times between 1.31V and 2.59V at 10C/10C rate at 45 °C. Right: Side-on photograph of one cell after 45 °C cycling.

The pouch cells shown in Figure 5 did not gas or swell at all. The Figure 5 data also highlight this cell technology's rapid charge acceptance capability (10C charging).

Another exciting attribute of the CAM-7/LTO pouch cells is the ability to be stored at 0V without performance degradation. In fact, these cells can be stored even at 60 °C after being completely de-energized by discharge to 0V without any degradation. Figure 6 shows ambient-temperature discharge curves of a 1 Ah CAM-7/LTO pouch cell before and after being stored for 1 week at 60 °C in the 0V condition, demonstrating no deterioration of the cell's performance.

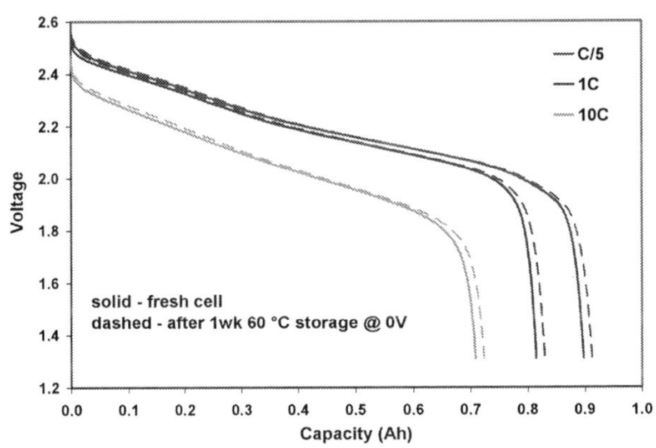

Figure 6. Ambient-temperature discharge curves of an unfixtured 1 Ah.

A battery's ability to tolerate discharge to 0V and storage at significantly elevated temperatures without damage to performance can greatly reduce the logistics burdens presented by Li-ion batteries because it eliminates the need for maintaining the batteries' charge status and controlling the environment in which they are stored, and also eliminates the safety concerns associated with storing and transporting large volumes of densely packed batteries.

The safety of the CAM-7/LTO pouch cell technology has been demonstrated in nail penetration tests. Figure 7 shows voltage and temperature results for nail penetration testing of a charged 2.85 Ah cell.

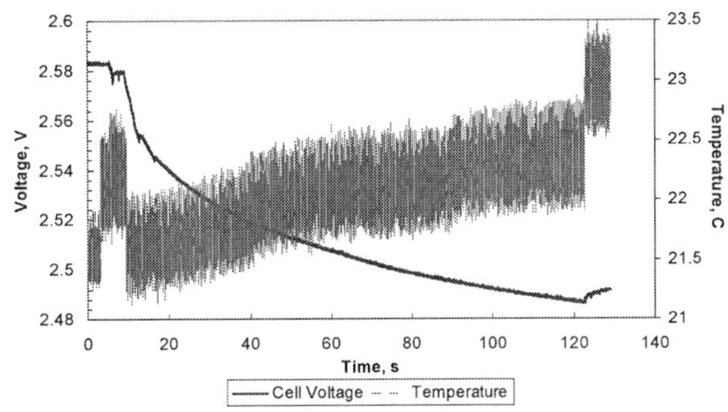

Figure 7. Voltage and surface temperature of 2.85 Ah CAM-7/LTO pouch cell during nail penetration test. Cell was fully charged to 2.65V. Nail speed set at 1 cm/sec.

The data in Figure 7 indicate that a short of relatively high resistance (estimated to be in the 1.5-3 ohm range) is formed by the nail penetration, and cell discharge through this short results in only a very small temperature increase (about 1 °C in a 2 minute period). This level of safety and abuse tolerance make the technology very attractive for large batteries and commercial vehicles.

Commercial vehicle application: The CAM-7/LTO cell technology has ideal characteristics for use in start-stop micro-hybrid vehicle batteries, for which its excellent low-temperature performance, long life, and high rate charging capability are essential. Figure 8 shows the excellent performance of a 120 mAh CAM-7/LTO pouch cell when tested to the scaled cold cranking requirements at -30 °C of the DOE Battery Test manual for 12V Start/Stop Vehicle Batteries,[4] calling for 3 consecutive pulse trains of 0.5 sec. at 6 kW and 4 sec. at 4 kW, with 10 sec. intervening rests.

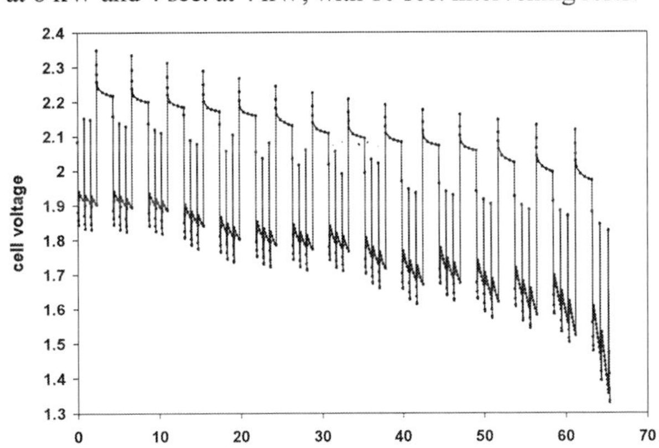

Figure 8. Pulse discharges of a 120 mAh CAM-7/LTO pouch cell at -30 °C at 16.5 mW/cm^2 and 11.0 mW/cm^2, with 2 mAh step-down at 0.5C rate between pulse trains.

The data in Figure 8 were collected between a charge voltage of 2.43V and discharge voltage cutoff of 1.33V, corresponding to operation of a 6-series-cell start/stop battery, and show that a battery based on this 1.2 mAh/cm^2 loading cell design can meet the cold cranking requirement across over 55% of its state of charge range. CAM-7's voltage/capacity characteristic (Figure 1) makes it well-suited for implementation opposite LTO in a 6-series-cell design, which in turn limits the maximum charge potential of the cathode material and greatly enhances life for a 7 liter start-stop battery design that is nevertheless projected to provide 750 Wh energy content.

Sationary power application: The CAM-7/LTO technology's high charge acceptance capability, high stability and long life make it very attractive for large-scale stationary power applications. As one metric for their potential utility in applications such as load leveling, CAM-7/LTO cells have been benchmarked against commercial ultracapacitors to evaluate their ability to provide similar power and life with higher energy density. Figure 9 compares the cycling at power density projected to correspond to 5 kW/l in an equivalent-electrode 18650 cell for a CAM-7/LTO coin cell and a commercial 3F ultracapacitor.

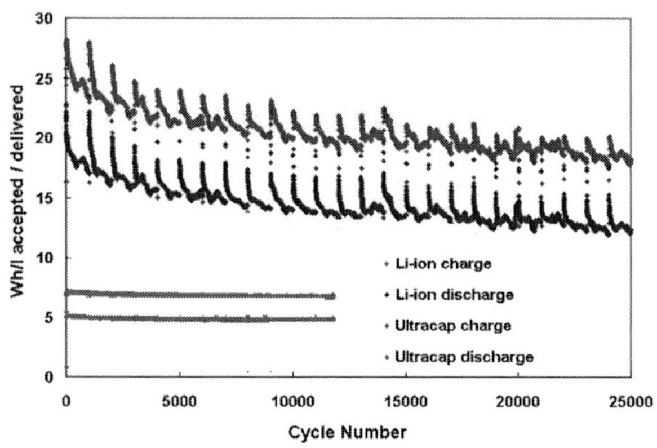

Figure 9. Charge and discharge energies for continuous 5 kW/l constant power cycling of a CAM-7/LTO Li-ion coin cell between 1.0 V and 2.65 V and a 3F ultracapacitor between 1.0 V and 2.85 V scaled to 18650 cell-level energy density. Li-ion cell cycling was interrupted at 1000 cycle intervals for rate capability measurements.

During the Figure 9 continuous 5 kW/l cycling, the 1.7 mAh/cm^2 Li-ion cell is cycled across only ~10% of its SOC range, but still with about 3 times the energy density of the ultracapacitor. Importantly, it cycles with approximately the same 70% energy efficiency as the ultracapacitor. The narrow SOC cycling range also results in low cycling-induced degradation of the Li-ion cell; it maintains capability for high energy density acceptance and delivery of high power (~20% decline as compared to ~5% decline for the ultracapacitor).

Lower loading CAM-7/LTO pouch cells achieve still higher power densities and higher energy density for high power charge acceptance and delivery. Figure 10 summarizes results for 8.5 kW/l (normalized to actual cell volume) pulse charge and discharge capability testing of a 130 mAh CAM-7/LTO pouch cell before and after 1,000 10C/10C cycles at 45 °C (with results like those in Figure 5). The triangular region formed under the intersection of the charge and discharge energy vs. SOC curves defines the SOC range over which the cell can both be charged and discharged by a given energy amount at constant power, important for load leveling batteries, and the figure shows that high power capability is retained well after elevated-temperature cycling.

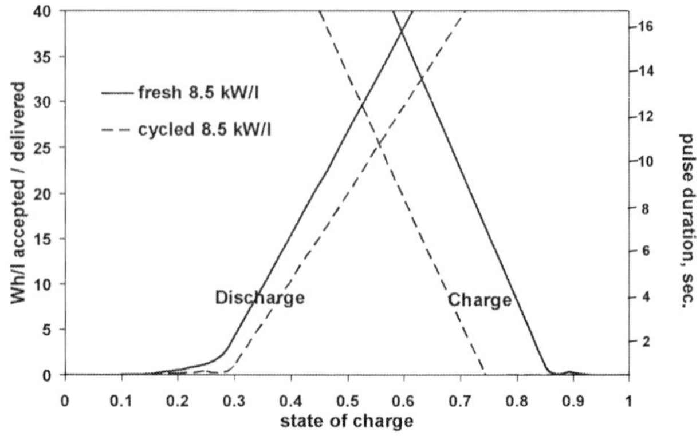

Figure 10. 8.5 kW/l pulse capability as a function of SOC between 2.59V charge and 1.31V discharge limits for an unfixtured 130 mAh, 0.5 mAh/cm^2 CAM-7/LTO pouch cell before and after 1,000 10C/10C cycles at 45 °C.

Conclusions

Li-ion pouch cells based on CAM-7 cathodes and LTO anodes offer an excellent combination of high power, high energy density, long life and safety for many applications.

Acknowledgements: This material is based upon work supported by the U.S. Army under Contract No. W56HZV-11-C-0065, by the Navy under Contract No. N39430-14-C-1506, by the Defense Logistics Agency under Contract No. HQ0147-15-C-8003, and by the Department of Energy under Contract No. DE-FOA-0001227.

References

1. https://www.basf.com/us/en/company/news-and-media/news-releases/2016/04/P-US-16-036.html
2. a) M. He, E. Castel, A. Laumann, G. Nuspl, P. Novak, E. J. Berg, *J. Electrochem. Soc.* **162**, A870 (2015). b) C. R. Fell, L. Sun, P. B. Hallac, B. Metz, B. Siska, *J. Electrochem. Soc.* **162**, A1916 (2015).
3. MIL-PRF-32143, Appendix A.
4. U.S. Department of Energy Vehicle Technologies Program, Battery Test Manual for 12 Volt Start/Stop Vehicles, INL/EXT-12-26503, 2013.

Frequency-based Probes and Charging Methods for Li-ion Battery Safety

Corey T Love[1], Tatyana Reshetenko[2] and Don Mase[1,3]
[1]Chemistry Division, US Naval Research Laboratory, Washington, DC, USA 20375
[2]Hawaii Natural Energy Institute, University of Hawaii-Manoa, Honolulu, HI, USA 96822
[3]EXCET, Inc., Springfield, VA, USA 22150

Abstract: This work aims to provide new insights into the design of optimal charging regimes for increased performance and safety of commercial lithium-ion cells at low temperatures. The mass transport and charge transfer limitations that exist within a lithium-ion cells during low temperature recharging lead to lithium plating and a corresponding loss in capacity retention. We leverage the state-of-health frequency determined by impedance spectroscopy for a commercial cell, 316 Hz, to generate pulse charging waveforms with similar time constants. From there, we vary the magnitude of the current amplitude as well as the current on and off times to determine the best pulse charging regimes for capacity retention at low temperatures.

Keywords: lithium-ion battery; battery safety, impedance spectroscopy; diagnostic; state-of-health; pulse charging; low temperature; lithium dendrite; lithium plating

Introduction

In previous reports we have shown the effect of low temperature charging on lithium dendrite formation and the propensity for internal short circuits [1] as well as the ability to probe lithium-ion battery state-of-health [2,3] and internal temperature [4] through an informed single-point impedance technique. We build upon these works to present new insights into optimal charging regimes for increased performance and safety of commercial lithium-ion cells, specifically for low temperatures. Figure 1(a) below is the frequency-based impedance response of an 18650 cell showing a minima at 316 Hz, corresponding to the ideal frequency for optimal ion and electron charge transfer within the cell. Figure 1(b) is the temperature-based impedance response of an 18650 cell at 316 Hz showing a minima around 40°C, corresponding to the ideal temperature to facilitate efficient mass transport within the cell's electrodes and electrolyte. We combine these two phenomena to produce unique charging regimes for (1) pulse charging at low temperatures to avoid degradation and dendrite formation and (2) constant current charging at idealized temperatures for maximum efficiency and rechargeability. This presentation will provide new insights and strategies to directly address low temperature performance and safety and also comment on novel heating strategies to maintain optimal temperatures for safe and efficient recharging.

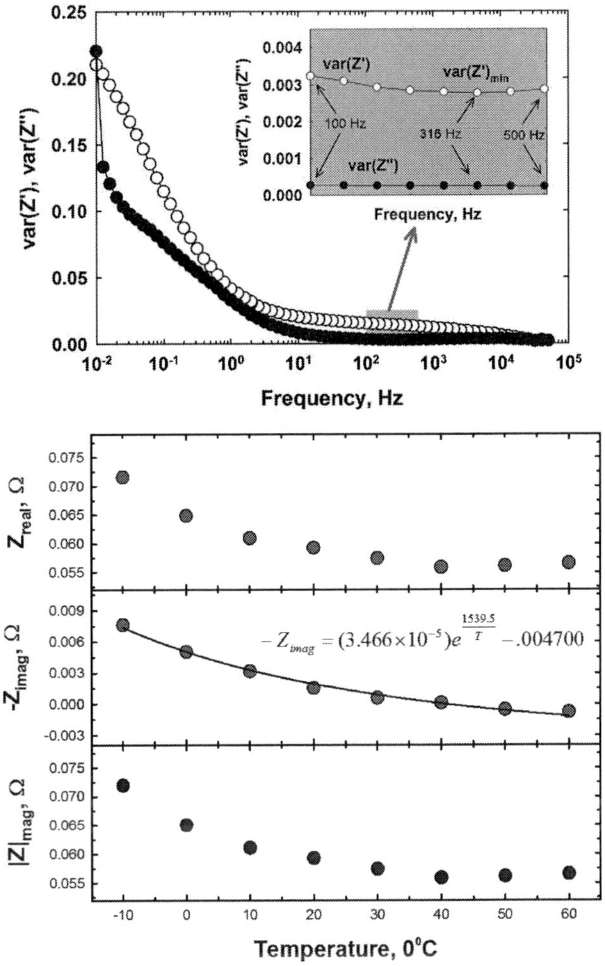

Figure 1. (top figure) Variance in real and imaginary impedance responses between 0 and 100% SOC taken at 10% SOC increments as a function of perturbation frequency showing a minimum near 316 Hz; and (bottom figure) real, imaginary and magnitude of impedance response at 316 Hz perturbation frequency over wide temperature range between -10°C and 60°C showing a minimum resistance to electronic and ionic mobility near 40°C.

Experimental

Figure 2 shows a schematic representation of the sinusoidal impedance perturbation at the state-of-health frequency (f_{SOH} = 316 Hz) where the current amplitude is 0.52 A corresponding to a C/5 current rate.

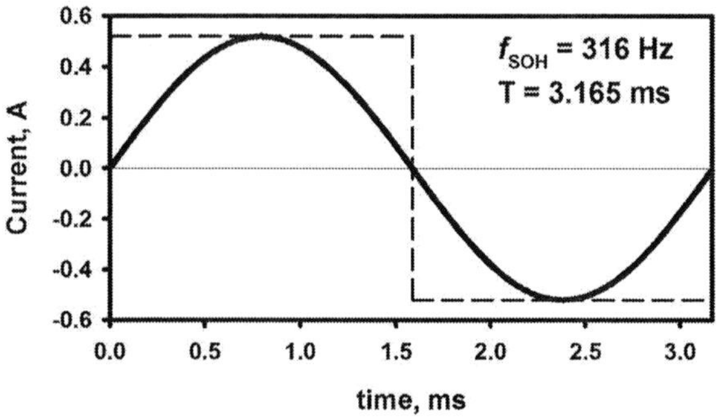

Figure 2. Schematic representation of sinusoidal impedance perturbation at 316 Hz with a current amplitude of 0.52 A (C/5). The wave period for the positive and negative current peaks is 3.165 ms.

The sinusoidal perturbation in Figure 2 is used to generate similar square-wave forms for pulse charging. Figure 3 shows three pulse charging waveforms of varying current amplitudes, current on times & zero current off times and on/off ratios (γ). Commercial 2.6 Ah 18650 lithium-ion cells were cycled using the constant current (CC) and pulsed-current (PC) profiles indicated in Table 1.

Table 1. Constant current and pulsed-current charging regimes for 2.6 Ah 18650 lithium-ion cells cycled between 2.75 – 4.2 V at 20°C and 0°C for 50 charge/discharge cycles.

Charging Regime	current	t_{on}	t_{off}	γ
CC	1.3 A (C/2)	-	-	-
PC1	1.3 A (C/2)	1.58 ms	1.58 ms	1
PC2	1.3 A (C/2)	0.79 ms	2.37 ms	3
PC3	0.65 (C/4)	3.17 ms	3.17 ms	1

A Keithley 2602B SourceMeter was used to charge and discharge the commercial 18650 cells. A laptop running LabVIEW provided remote control of the SourceMeter, including automated testing, data display, and data recording. The SourceMeter has the capability of pulse charging the battery with precise timing; this timing was confirmed by observing the pulses using an oscilloscope (Tektronix TDS 2004B). The basic experimental setup is illustrated in Figure 4. During steady charging (constant current or constant voltage) and steady discharging conditions, the LabVIEW program directly commands the SourceMeter (for example, by setting a voltage limit and then requesting a constant current). However, during pulse charging a different method of SourceMeter control is needed due to the precise timing desired for the pulses and the measured data. In this case, a script file (.tsp) that resides in the SourceMeter's NVM (non-volatile memory) is called by LabVIEW. The SourceMeter then executes that pulse charging script until LabVIEW aborts the script when the recommended upper voltage cutoff is reached, 4.2 V. All discharge cycles were performed at CC = 1.3 A. Temperature studies were performed in an environmental chamber where each cell was equilibrated at 0°C or 25°C for at least 2 hours prior to galvanostatic cycling.

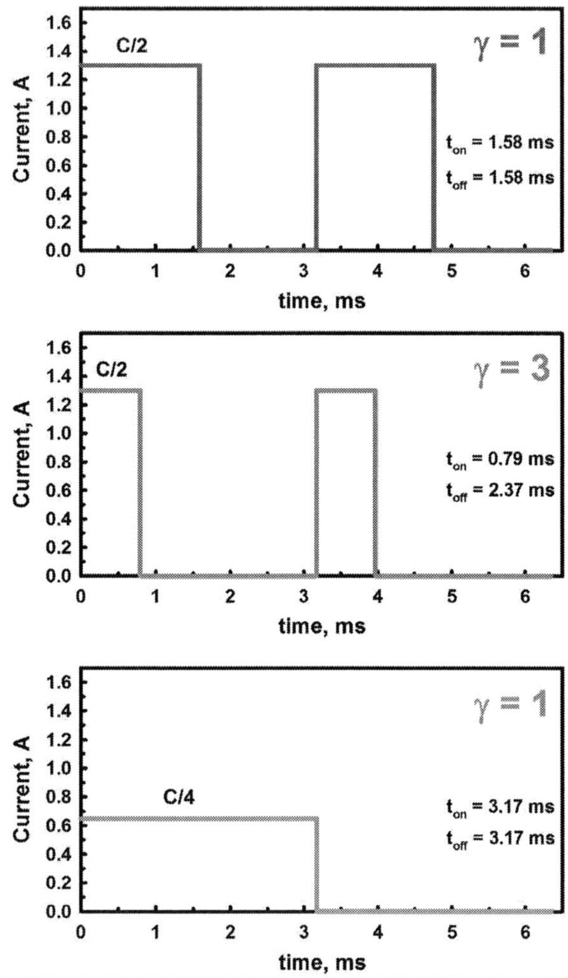

Figure 3. Square wave pulse charging profiles and scaled charge currents developed from f_{SOH} in Figure 2: top panel (PC1); middle panel (PC2); and bottom panel (PC3). The term γ, is the ratio of t_{on}/t_{off}.

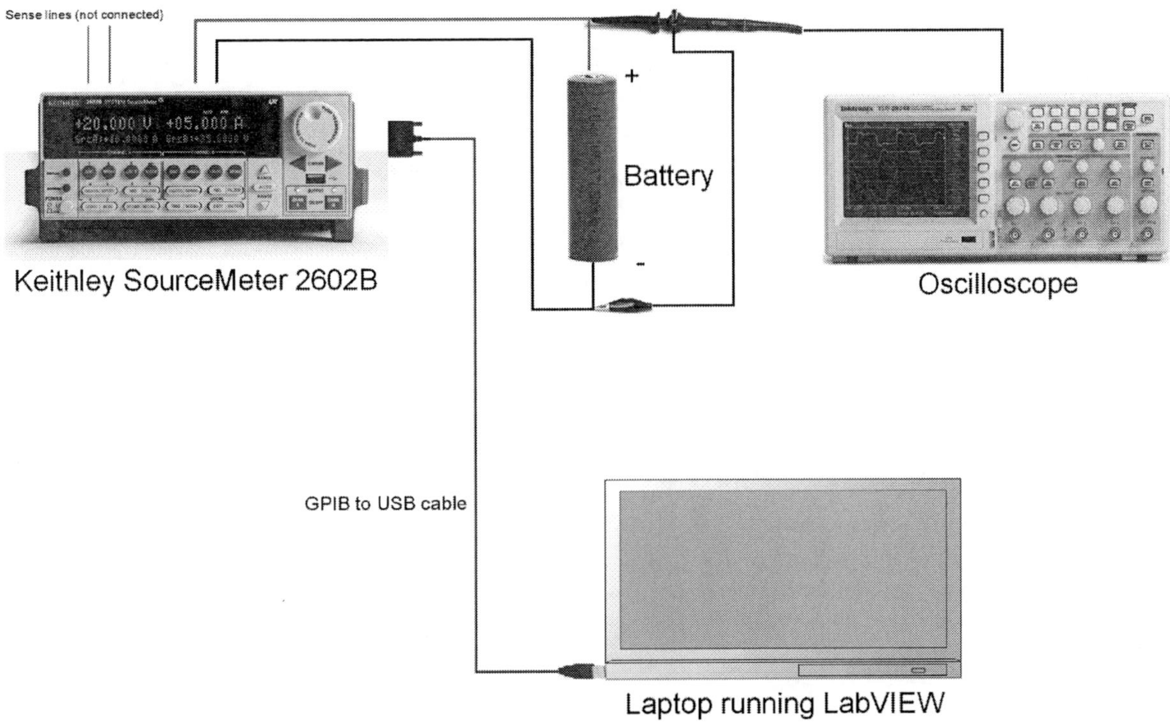

Figure 4. Illustration of experimental setup used to generate and control high precision pulse current waveforms for charging lithium-ion batteries.

Results

The effect of low temperature charge/discharge cycling during constant current (CC) charging is given in Figure 5. The initial decrease in capacity at low temperature is attributed to increased cell impedance as a result of hindered mass transport and charge transfer. The steep decrease in capacity retention with 0°C cycling is due to plating of lithium metal on the anode surface which reduces the amount of lithium ions available for intercalation and energy storage processes. There is little capacity fade in the cells cycled at 25°C over the first 50 galvanostatic cycles.

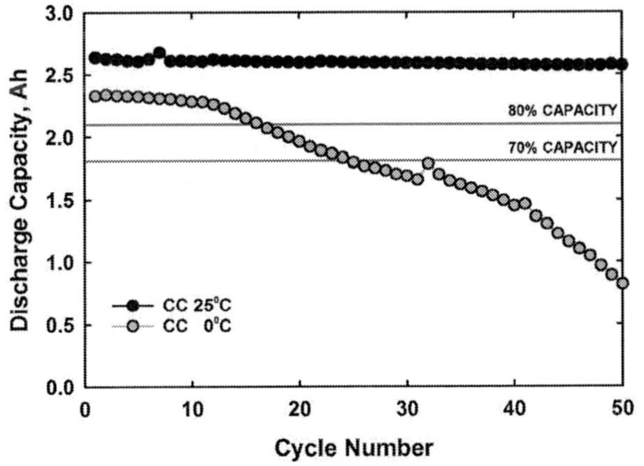

Figure 5. Discharge capacity during the first 50 cycles of constant current (CC) charge/discharge at 25°C and 0°C.

Acknowledgements

The authors thank the Office of Naval Research for financial support of this collaborative effort between the US Naval Research Laboratory and the Hawaii Natural Energy Institute at the University of Hawaii-Manoa.

References

1. Love, C.T., Baturina, O.A. and Swider-Lyons, K.E., "Observation of Lithium Dendrites at Ambient Temperature and Below," *ECS Electrochemistry Letters*, Vol. 4, no. 2, pp. A24-A27, 2015.
2. Love, C.T. and Swider-Lyons, K.E., "Impedance Diagnostic for Overcharged Lithium-Ion Batteries," *Electrochemical and Solid-State Letters*, Vol. 14, no. 4, pp. A53-A56, 2012.
3. Love, C.T., Virji, M.B.V., Rocheleau, R.E. and Swider-Lyons, K.E., "State-of-Health Monitoring of 18650 4S Packs with a Single-Point Impedance Diagnostic," *Journal of Power Sources*, Vol. 266, pp. 512-519, 2014.
4. Spinner, N.S., Love, C.T., Rose-Perhsson, S.L and Tuttle, S.G., "Expanding the Operational Limits of the Single-Point Impedance Diagnostic for Internal Temperature Monitoring of Lithium-ion Batteries," *Electrochimica Acta*, Vol. 174, pp. 488–493, June 2015.

Neural Network Models Using Multiple Indicators for State of Charge and State of Health

John Olson
TDA Research, Inc.
Wheat Ridge, CO 80033
jolson@tda.com

Abstract: *Accurate diagnostics and prognostics are important features desired in battery management systems (BMS). TDA Research is developing battery models based on neural networks (NN) that are ideal for use in a BMS. We introduce the concept of using multiple indicators for both state of charge and state of health models to increase the accuracy of the models.*

Keywords: neural network model; battery management system; BMS; state of charge; state of health; diagnostic; prognostic; conditional awareness; lithium-ion; lithium iron phosphate

Introduction

The Navy is developing advanced electric power and propulsion technologies for their fleet to increase the electrical power for sensors and weapons and decrease the use of fossil fuels [1, 2]. Advanced systems maybe composed of a variety of energy storage packs of differing chemistries. Further, battery packs may be changed out across the platform's lifecycle, causing costly certification and control systems changes. The Navy has indicated an interest in standard, sophisticated battery management systems [3].

TDA Research is developing models based on neural networks (NN). NNs were one of the first artificial intelligence (AI) algorithms, and have become one of the most utilized AI algorithms for a wide variety of applications [4].

For use in a BMS, battery models must have several characteristics. They must have fast computations, since calculations typically occur at the cell level and large packs can have hundreds of cells. They must rely exclusively on data collected by the BMS or derived from that data. They must have good accuracy over the entire life of the battery. They must converge to solutions if iterative solving is used. Most first principles models or even semi-empirical models in the literature cannot meet these criteria. While 1st principles models can accurately predict SOC and SOH they are complex, computationally difficult and solved iteratively (convergence issues). Semi-empirical models (e.g., equivalent circuit models) while simpler are almost completely dependent on resistance and capacity parameters, which although accurate do not necessarily correspond to real, measurable battery properties.

Many believe that SOC determinations using current integration are accurate for BMSs. However, although current integration itself can be extremely accurate, the total charge capacity (Ah_T) must also be determined over the life of the battery for accurate SOC calculation since SOC = Ah / Ah_T. Accurate determination of Ah_T over life can be challenging, especially for applications never reaching full discharge. This is not the only shortcoming of current integration and issues exist for extended rest (self-discharge and parasitic drains) and extended hybrid cycling (drift). NN models can meet these challenges.

NNs are a form of algorithms which are adept at evaluating non-linear and noisy data having complex relationships, like battery data. The NN models are a learning algorithm, where training data (typically large data sets) are used to create the model. NN models are particularly well suited for use with BMSs. Their compiled output consists of one multi-input equation capable of fast calculations.

TDA is developing NN models for calculation of state of charge (SOC) and state of health (SOH). Our models have been improved by increasing accuracy for transient data, by incorporating multiple indicators and adding input factors of pre-SOC and pre-SOH.

Improved Transient Response

We presented our initial NN models at the last Power Sources Conference. Although they were excellent with steady state response they did not respond well to transient data [5]. Although we recognized these limitations at the time, we didn't fully understand their origin. After further study, we determined the issues were due to the dAh/dV differential input parameter, where dAh is the change in Ah and dV is the change in cell voltage. This is a powerful input data because it has its maximum response at mid-SOC where the voltage curve of the lithium iron phosphate (LFP) cell is at its flattest [5]. The cell voltage has a variable transient response due to the time dependence of the cell resistance (R). We have now improved our models by substituting the differential input parameter dAh/dOCV, where dOCV is the change in open circuit voltage. We obtain OCV by calculation using real time measurements of R, V and I

$$OCV = V + I * R \quad (1)$$

where I is the rate of current, V is cell voltage and R is the cell resistance. We obtain R using the slope of the current – voltage data and time smooth this value. Although this method of determination of R is not the most accurate method, since it does not discriminate for time dependence of R, it has proven to be accurate enough for the NN model calculations. These improvements allow our newer models to successfully handle transient data.

Training Data

The development of the training data is the first step in creating NN models. Our training data is based on cycle life testing of K2 Energy high power 26650 LFP cells of nominal 2.6 Ah capacities. Although we have developed models for both charge and discharge, for the purposes of this paper we will discuss discharge models only, but most results and conclusions are applicable for charging as well.

We show the capacity fade of the LFP cells versus temperature in Figure 1. The small amount of 'noise' in

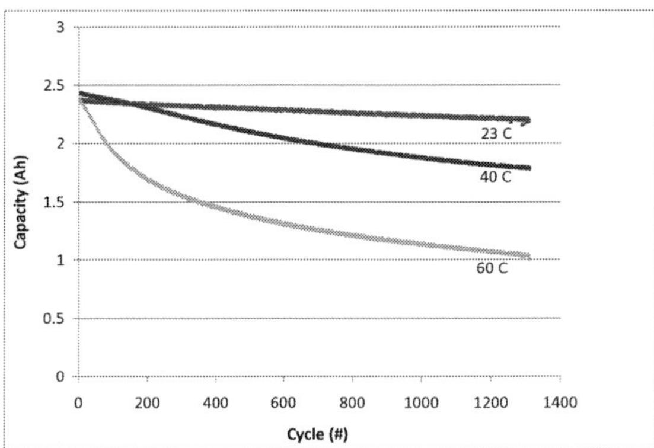

Figure 1. Capacity fade summary data for three LFP cells used in the NN models.

the plots is indicative of the slight changes of capacity with discharge rate (Peukert effect). The 23° C and 40° C cells are still cycling, while the 60° C cell has reached end of life.

The raw data consists of current (I), voltage (V), temperature (T), capacity (Ah), total capacity (Ah_T) and time (t). From these data we derived values for cell resistance (R), differential time (dt), differential capacity (dAh), Ah throughput (AhT), open circuit voltage (OCV), differential capacity with respect to open circuit voltage (dAh/dOCV), pre-state of charge (pre-SOC), pre-state of health (pre-SOH), state of charge (SOC) and state of health (SOH). SOC is calculated by

$$SOC = Ah / Ah_T * 100 \quad (2)$$

where parameters are as previously defined.

SOH is calculated by

$$SOH = Ah_T / Ah_N * 100 \quad (3)$$

where Ah_N is the initial charge capacity. Both pre-SOC and pre-SOH use the SOC and SOH results from the prior calculation.

Multiple Indicators

While our earlier models used input data representative of a discharge curve, we recognized that both SOC and SOH could be characterized by multiple indicators. In some cases the indicator might be represented by a single input data to the model, while for others (e.g., curve analysis) several input data are required.

For SOC, we have identified four relatively independent indicators, namely: Ah, OCV, curve analysis and pre-SOC. Ah refers to current integration which we have already discussed. Open-circuit voltage (OCV) is directly correlated to SOC, although this relationship is non-linear. OCV is only slightly dependent upon temperature (as defined by the thermodynamic entropy) but can change due to changes in the active material on the battery plates. We also use curve analysis as represented by the multiple inputs: current, voltage, temperature and dAh/dOCV. These input parameters are analogous to our original NN models [5]. The other independent input parameter is pre-SOC. Here we use the SOC calculated in the last iteration, as an input in the current calculation. This is analogous to a recursive formula where the current value is obtained using modifications to the previous value. It has the effect of reducing the data space for the calculation and increasing accuracy.

One of the challenges of using multiple indicators in a NN model is the possibility that one indicator will dominate the response of the others. This is not desired, because effectively the use of multiple indicators is reduced to only one. For example, the pre-SOC/pre-SOH input is a very strong indicator. Generally, the NN model will use this input almost exclusively. The influence of the different inputs can be accessed by most NN software and amounts to a sensitivity analysis. One technique we have used to modify the response of the input data is to constrain the weights of the input data.

We will now describe the results of both our SOC and SOH models.

SOC NN Model

As described, our multiple indicator SOC model uses four indicators. We used a simple NN architecture consisting of three layers: the input layer, the hidden layer and the output layer. The hidden layer used 5 nodes, tanh activation functions and back propagation using Levenberg-Marquardt solving. We used

NueroDimensions' NeuroSolutions Pro software to create our models. We recognize there are an intimidating number of variables you can use to create NN models, and it is beyond the scope of this paper to delve into these. However, we have found that the key issues are the input data and the amount of information in your data set. We have trained the same data sets with different NN architectures and gotten close to the same results.

We used the same cycle life data to extract subsets for training data, cross-validation data and test data. Although we ensured we did not use the identical discharges in the three sub-sets, a more ideal method would be to have completely independent data sets. This will occur in our further development. The bounds of our model are defined by the data shown in Figure 1.

Figure 2 shows the results of the SOC NN model

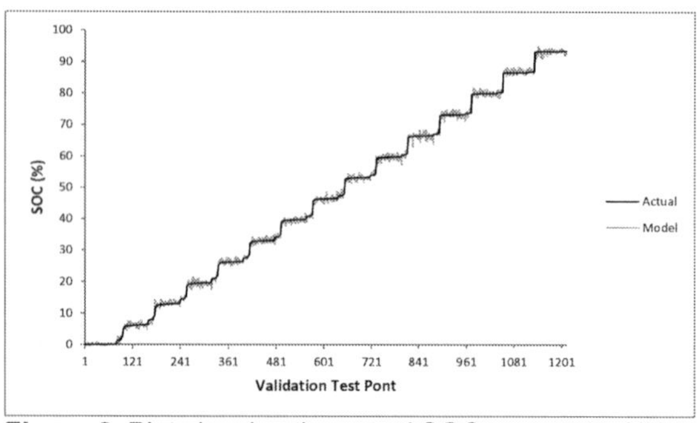

Figure 2. Plot showing the actual SOC versus the NN model results.

compared to the actual results. The test data set was comprised of a total of 16 discharges; 5 each from the 23° C and 60° C data sets and 6 from the 40° C data set. Within each temperature data set, the discharges spanned the cycle lives shown in Figure 1. Thus, the predictions take into account the declining capacities shown in Figure 1. The plot has 15 plateaus (including at 0% SOC or the end of discharge). It is a simple line plot, so there are 16 data points on each plateau corresponding to the 16 different discharge curves. It is clear from the plot that the errors appear to be random and evenly distributed. The absolute average error (actual result – model result) was 0.6% with the maximum error being 4.6%. In Figure 3 we look at the errors sorted from low to high. The number of test points less than 1% error is 81% and those greater than 2.5% only represent less than 0.5% of the test points.

Figure 4 shows the same data as in Figure 3 where we now compare the errors to a SOC calculation using current integration where the total capacity is not adjusted for capacity fade. These errors range as high as 55% and become larger with increasing life (as the accuracy of the

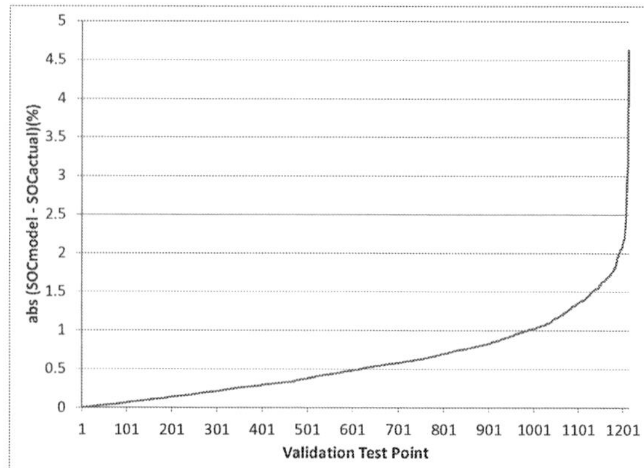

Figure 3. Plot of sorted errors showing that 81% of test points have errors < 1%.

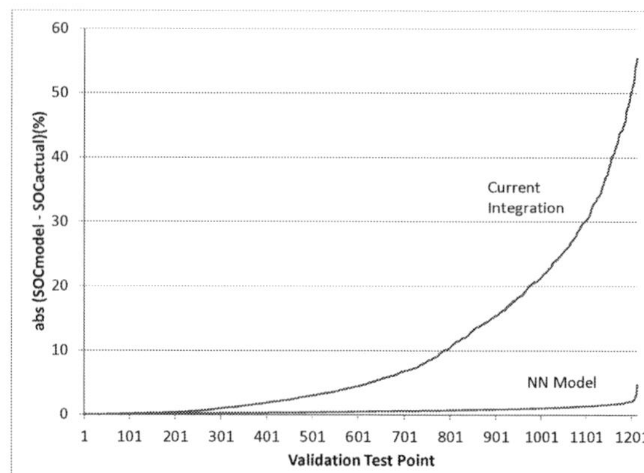

Figure 4. Same data from Figure 3 compared to a SOC calculation where the total capacity is not adjusted for capacity fade.

constant total capacity declines). This would be the magnitude of the current integration error over the life of the battery if the total capacity is kept constant.

SOH NN Model

In a similar manner to that described for SOC we constructed NN models for SOH. Here we define SOH as 100% when the cell is new (1st cycle) and 0% for a capacity of 0 Ah. It would be trivial to change this definition to make a SOH of 0 equal to 20% loss of capacity, 50% loss or whatever value is chosen.

For the SOH model we have determined four indicators, namely: total capacity (Ah_T), cell resistance (R), Ah throughput (AhT) and pre-SOH. Again these are data that a BMS assumed to be operating from the time a battery is new can collect over the life of the battery. We used the same NN model architecture used for the SOC model and the same data sets.

Figure 5 shows the results of our model compared to actual results. For this plot you can again observe plateaus. Here each plateau corresponds to a single discharge. They are ordered in three groups starting at 23° C and proceeding to 60° C. The start of each temperature

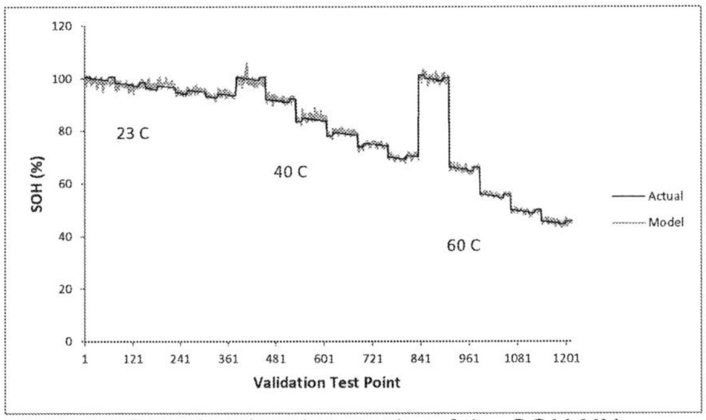

Figure 5. Plot showing the results of the SOH NN model compared to the actual values.

segment is evident by the profile close to 100%. As with the SOC model, the errors appear to be randomly distributed. The average error was equal to 0.9% and the maximum error was 5.9% which is evident in the 100% plateau of the 40° C data. The sorted errors are shown in Figure 6. Although the errors are slightly higher than the SOC model, their distribution is similar. For the SOH model, over 82% of the test points have errors < 1.5%. The percentage of test points with errors > 4% are only less than 0.7%.

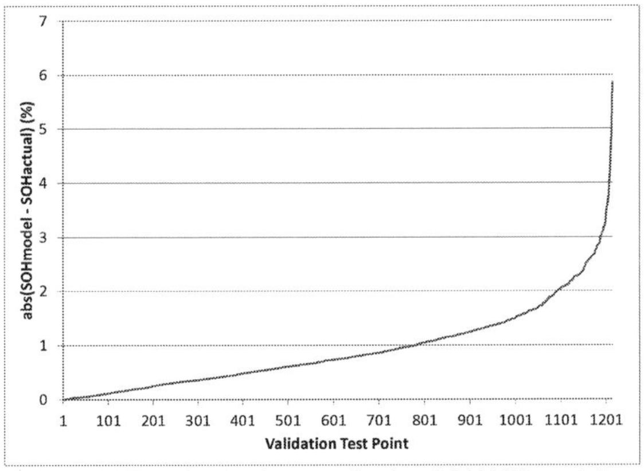

Figure 6. Plot of sorted errors for the SOH NN model.

Conclusions

NN models have been shown to be useful for the calculation of SOC and SOH, particularly for BMS applications. The final compiled model consists of one equation with multiple inputs and thus there are no concerns with the model converging in real time and they are capable of fast calculations.

We also highlight the shortcomings of current integration which depends on knowledge of the total capacity for an accurate SOC determination. If total capacity is not adjusted for capacity fade then errors as large as 55% may occur later in the battery life.

Although multiple input data is normal for NN models, we show our efforts to develop models based on multiple indicators. This provides a means to increase model accuracy by using several independent indicators for either SOC or SOH. In particular, we define four indicators for SOC consisting of current integration, open circuit voltage, curve analysis and pre-SOC. We also define four indicators for SOH consisting of charge capacity, Ah throughput, resistance and pre-SOH.

We have demonstrated models for a LFP cell that accurately predicts SOC and SOH over the life of the battery. For the SOC model we obtained an average error of 0.6%, where 81% of the test points had errors less than 1%. The SOH model had an average error of 0.9% and 82% of the test points had errors less than 1.5%. Further improvement of the models is expected with continued refinement.

Acknowledgments

This paper is based upon work supported by the Naval Sea Systems Command under Contract No. N00024-14-C-4011. Any opinions, findings and conclusions or recommendations expressed in this material are those of the authors and do not necessarily reflect the views of the Naval Sea Systems Command.

References

1. http://greenfleet.dodlive.mil/files/2010/04/Adv-Energy-Storage.pdf
2. http://energy.gov/videos/arpa-e-2011-keynote-ray-mabus-secretary-navy
3. http://www.navsea.navy.mil/Media/Naval Power Systems Technology Development Roadmap - Distribution A – 14 May 2013 - Final.pdf
4. http://uhaweb.hartford.edu/compsci/neural-networks-history.html
5. Olson, J., Heinzel, J., *Proceedings of the 46th Power Sources Conference,* Paper #33.4, Orlando, FL, June 9-12, 2014.

Algorithms for Advanced Battery Management System Design

Balakumar Balasingam, Niranjan Raghunathan, Krishna Pattipati and Yaakov Bar-Shalom
University of Connecticut
bala@engr.uconn.edu

***Abstract*—At the current rate of growth in battery operated devices (such as electric vehicles, portable electronic equipment, wearable electronic devices, household appliances, aerospace equipment and so on), a significant portion of the global energy consumption is about to happen through batteries. It is important that these batteries, or any other form of electrical energy storage system, be efficient in order to avoid contributing additional carbon emissions because of their usage. A battery management system (BMS) helps to achieve efficient power management through the accurate estimation of state of charge (SOC), state of health, time to shut down and remaining useful life of a battery (or a battery-pack). By exploiting these estimated quantities, the BMS generates optimal charging waveforms that aim to improve the charging time/energy efficiency, while ensuring the safety of its operation. Developing a BMS is a challenging adaptive estimation and control problem that requires modeling and on-line parameter identification of electrochemical device characteristics across temperature changes, SOC variations, and age. The BMS algorithms should be developed in such a way that they are robust and easily implementable in practical systems. This paper summarizes the new features, capabilities and functionalities of a robust BMS being developed by the authors.**

Keywords: Li-ion batteries, Battery management systems, battery fuel gauge, state of charge, state of health, power fade, capacity fade, time to shut down, remaining useful life.

I. Introduction

Rechargeable batteries, such as Lithium-ion (Li-ion) batteries, have become increasingly commonplace in our day-to-day lives and critical for a sustainable future. A wide range of devices, such as electric/hybrid vehicles, portable electronic equipment, wearable electronic devices, household appliances, aerospace equipment and renewable energy storage systems use different types of rechargeable batteries. Most of these batteries are made out of electrochemical components and their complete behavior is not fully understood yet. Such an understanding is important for reliable, safe and widespread use of those devices powered by batteries. The objective of a battery management system (BMS) is to develop ways for the accurate estimation of state of charge (SOC), state of health (SOH), time to shut down (TTS) and remaining useful life (RUL) of the battery (or battery-pack) and to exploit those estimated quantities in order to develop optimal charging algorithms while ensuring the safety of the device and efficiency of its operation (see Figure 4). Developing a BMS is a challenging adaptive estimation and control problem that requires modeling and on-line parameter identification of electrochemical device characteristics across temperature changes, SOC variations, and age. The BMS algorithms should be developed in such a way that they are easily adoptable in practical systems; they should be able to work for different kinds of storage devices that are independently manufactured; and they should be efficient in terms of computational complexity and parameter storage so that they can be implemented in miniature devices, such as smart watches. Under all these circumstances, the BMS algorithm should fulfill its general requirements: providing accurate information of the battery state and facilitating efficient, safe and fast charging.

A BMS consists of two important blocks: a battery fuel gauge (BFG) and optimal charging algorithm (OCA). Based on the measured voltage across battery terminals, load current and temperature of the battery, the BFG (see Figure 2) computes the SOC, SOH, TTS and RUL of the battery. The optimal charging algorithm (see Figure 3) exploits the BFG outputs to generate optimal charging waveforms that minimize power/heat dissipation and charging time while maximizing battery life. Next, we discuss the relevance of BMS in different domains and briefly discuss the functionalities of a robust BMS algorithm developed by the authors.

II. Application of the Proposed Battery Management System in Different Domains

The BMS is designed to address varying challenges depending on the application. In electric vehicles (EVs), the charging time has to be reduced without compromising the safety and longevity of the battery pack (rapid charging causes excessive heating which compromises safety). With the state of the art charging technology, it takes up to an hour to charge an electric vehicle from empty to full and this is a major bottleneck of electric vehicles in replacing hydrocarbon based automobiles on the road. This requires the development of rapid charging algorithms that are able to quickly charge batteries without compromising their safety and longevity. In portable and wearable electronic devices, such as smart phones, tablets and smart watches, the BMS algorithm is expected to consume minimal computational resources while providing highly accurate storage management functionalities. Due to the computational bottlenecks, existing fuel gauging algorithms in portable electronic devices are highly inaccurate as they are mostly implemented with low resolution approaches, such as table look-up method. Highly accurate BMS algorithms will

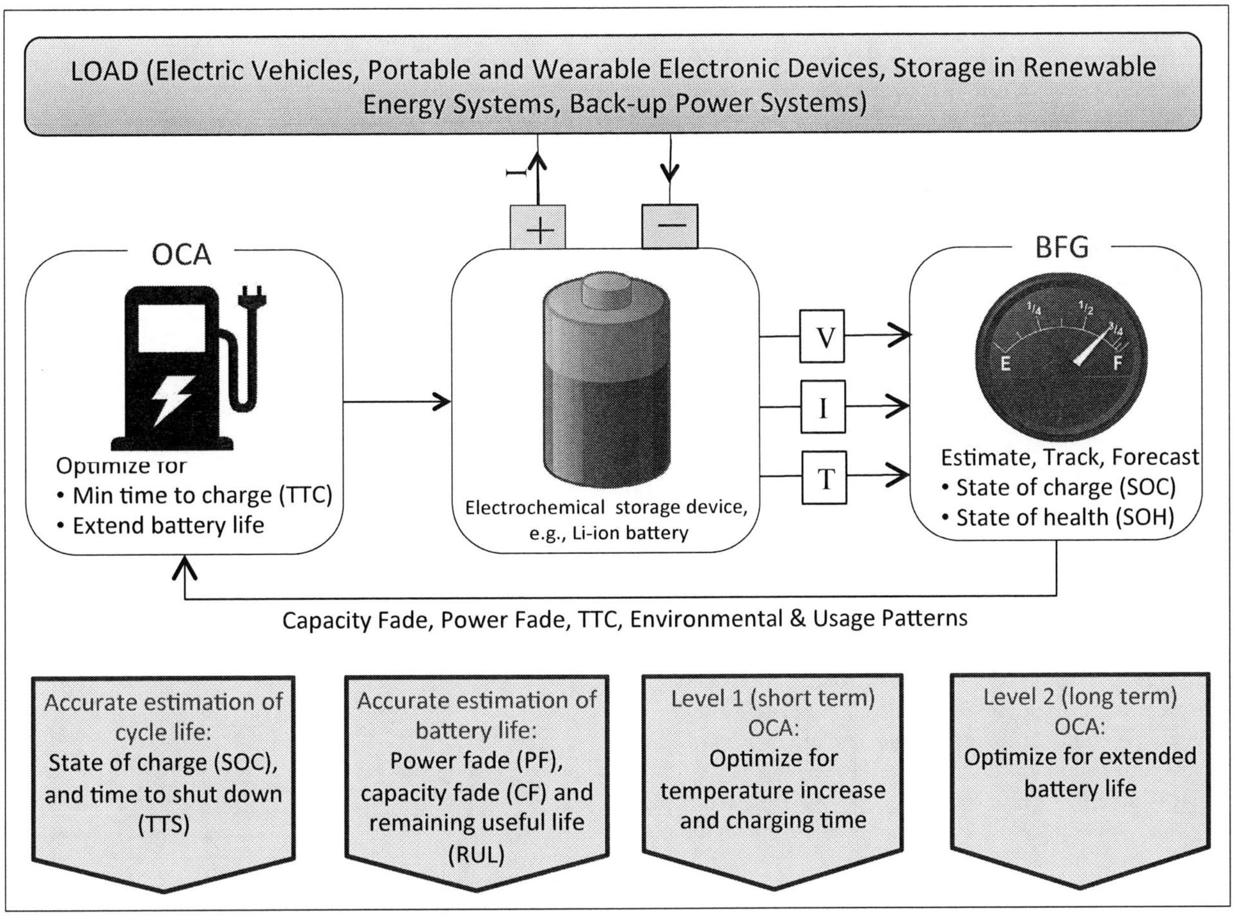

Fig. 1: **Battery management system (BMS).** Functional block diagram.

increase the cycle life and longevity — in practical applications this means that, the devices can be quickly charged and can be used for longer periods without recharging, all without affecting the longevity of the battery. In renewable energy storage applications the BMS algorithm should be able to handle unexpected and rapid flow of power in both directions. Renewable energy sources, such as solar panels and wind farms, produce power at unexpected rates; the battery arrays used to store excess energy should be managed in such a way that the safety and longevity of the storage system is not compromised.

In all of the above applications, there are several other challenges being faced by today's BMS community. State of the art BMS algorithms are based on offline computed OCV-SOC parameters using sample batteries [15]. The electrochemical properties of the batteries are such that the OCV-SOC curves differ for different battery models (due to differences in chemical compositions, shape etc.). The state of the art faces two important challenges *OCV parameter storage and identification* and the fact that *the battery behavior changes based on usage pattern.* These two challenges motivate the need for practical BMS algorithms that are not dependent on OCV-SOC parameters that were computed using sample batteries. Lack of accurate mathematical models is another area in which the state of the art of BMS suffers. The existing BMS validation methods [16], [17], [18], [12], have several limitations [8], [4] that can be improved through the development of accurate models. At present, there is no standardized way to evaluate an SOC tracking algorithm and it is nearly impossible to compare and evaluate the efficacy of two different BMS algorithms. Testing these algorithms on a model generated data helps to objectively evaluate different modules of the algorithms (such as parameter estimation, capacity estimation and SOC tracking).

The overall objective of a BMS include *accuracy, computationally efficiency* and *robustness*. The BMS solution developed by the authors contribute to the above objective by offering the following important features.

1) *Normalized OCV modeling approach.* A normalized OCV model [15] avoids excessive OCV-SOC parameterization.
2) *Voltage drop model.* The details of a novel voltage drop model that allows online, linear estimation of equivalent circuit model (ECM) parameters is presented in [5].
3) *Robust capacity estimation method.* A robust battery capacity estimation approach is detailed in [6].
4) *Robust parameter estimation method.* Online parameter estimation approaches for different ECM and how to address the possibility of multiple ECM representations

depending on battery state (charge, discharge, rest, etc.) is addressed [5].

5) *Robust SOC tracking approach.* The SOC tracking algorithm that is based on robust, online ECM parameter estimation [5] and robust, online capacity estimation [6] is presented in [7].
6) *Characterization-free (online) FG development.* Many of the existing BMS algorithms depend on offline characterization based on sample batteries. Considering the number of vendors making rechargeable batteries, the BMS algorithm is expected to store data corresponding to a large number of battery chemistries. The objective of an online FG algorithm is to adaptively estimate the characterization parameters along with other desired fuel gauging variables [3], [11].
7) *Battery aging models.* A level-1 optimization algorithm aiming to prevent battery aging through optimal charging needs to understand the various aspects of aging as a result of environment variables, such as temperature, and usage patterns (e.g. patterns of depth of discharge (DoD)). Accurate empirical models that can be used for this purpose are discussed in [2], [1].
8) *Universal BMS algorithm development.* Battery systems largely differ based on their application: batteries used in notebooks, tablets, smart phones and smart watches all have different characteristics. Developing a BMS system that is able to service many types of devices will result in many benefits: in the consumer electronics arena, it will reduce the amount of electronic clutter and will result in inexpensive devices to the consumer; in the automobile industry, it will result in cost reduction and more accurate BMS functionalities. A universal BMS solution is currently being developed by the authors.
9) *Computationally efficient algorithm development for BMS.* Computationally simpler, yet highly accurate, BMS algorithms are desired in portable and wearable electronic devices. Existing BMS algorithms in consumer electronic devices achieve computational reduction at a significant cost of accuracy. Several methods being developed by the authors in order to fully understand the computational implications of a BMS algorithm, such as *duty-cycle analysis*, *Sensitivity analysis of parameter and capacity estimation analysis*, and *computational simplification methods*.
10) *Battery model development.* The objective is to present models that are closer to a real battery behavior in terms of critical prognostic measures, such as SOH and RUL in response to environment variables (such as temperature) and usage metrics (such as the pattern of depth of discharge). Such a model will help in testing and rigorous evaluation of BMS algorithms prior to implementation. There is significant interest in accurate battery model development [13], [19], [20].
11) *Level 1 optimal charging algorithm.* details how to optimize against battery aging [1].
12) *Level 2 optimal charging algorithm.* details how to optimize against temperature rise and charging delay [2].
13) *Integrated BMS solutions* [14] details integration of BFG and OCA.
14) *Rigorous BMS validation techniques.* BMS validation is one of the least discussed topics in the literature. Details of rigorous BFG validation is discussed [4], [8].

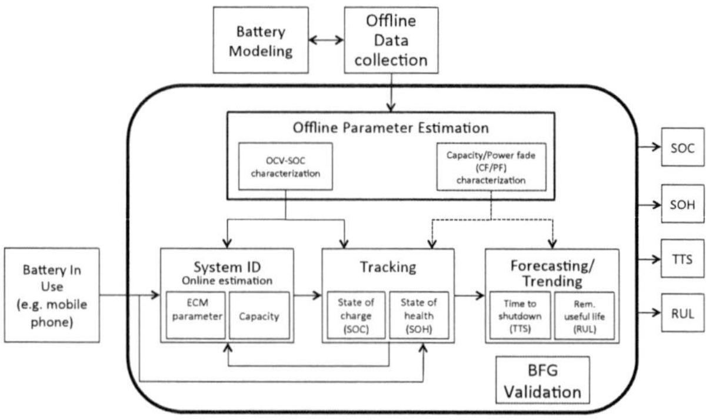

Fig. 2: **Battery fuel gauge (BFG).** In depth details of the robust BFG algorithm can be found in [15], [5], [6], [7], [3], [8], [4], [11], [9], [10].

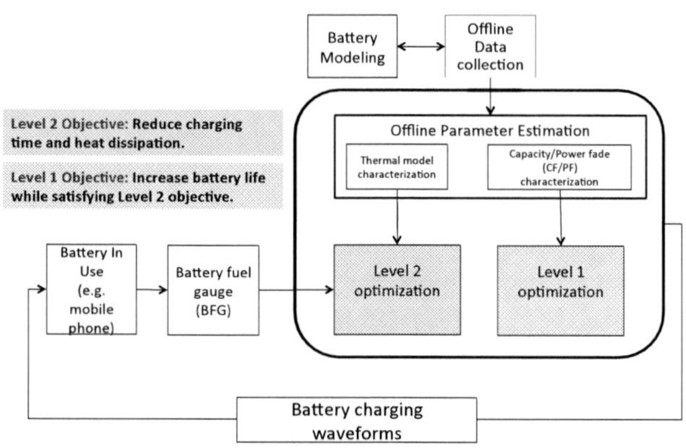

Fig. 3: **Optimal charging algorithm (OCA).** In depth details of the robust BFG algorithm can be found in [2], [1].

III. Conclusions

In this paper, we described the components of a robust battery management system (BMS) developed by the authors. The robust BMS includes features such as online battery capacity estimation, online parameter (battery impedance) estimation and optimal charging waveform generation. The accuracy and robustness of the proposed BMS are achieved through several key contributions, such as the *normalized open circuit voltage modeling*, *voltage-drop electrical equivalent circuit model*, *total least square (TLS) estimation of battery capacity*, *robust battery capacity estimation through fusion*, *recursive least square (RLS) tracking of parameters*, and *state-space model correlation modeling & mitigation*.

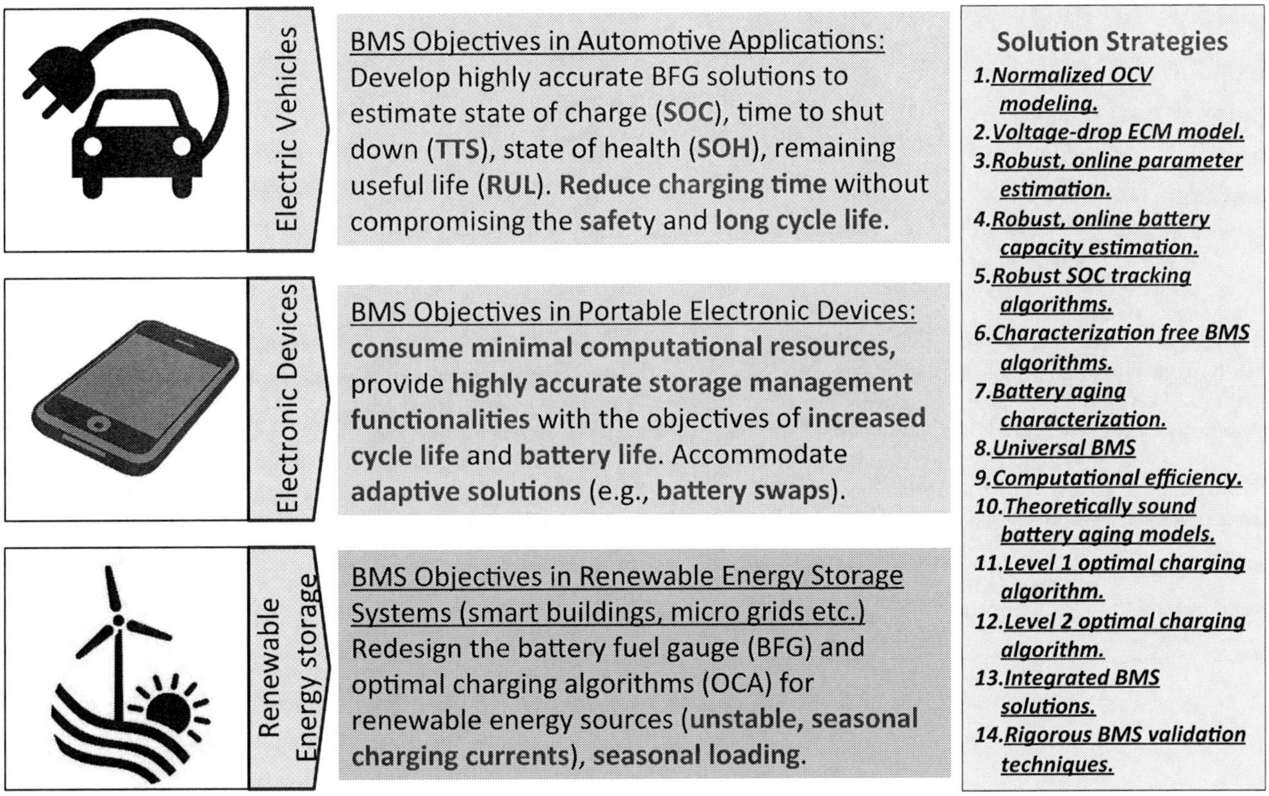

Fig. 4: **The relevance of BMS in different domains.** Challenges and the summary of solution strategies.

REFERENCES

[1] A. Abdollahi, X. Han, N. Raghunathan, B. Balasingam, K. Pattipati, and Y. Bar-Shalom, "Optimal battery charging, part II: Minimizing time-to-charge, energy loss, and temperature rise for general equivalent electrical battery model, capacity modeling and battery life management," *Journal of Power Sources*, 2014, (under review, 2016).

[2] A. Abdollahi, X. Han, G. V. Avvari, N. Raghunathan, B. Balasingam, K. Pattipati, and Y. Bar-Shalom, "Optimal battery charging, part I: Minimizing time-to-charge, energy loss, and temperature rise for OCV-resistance battery model," *Journal of Power Sources*, 2015.

[3] G. V. Avvari, B. Balasingam, K. Pattipati, and Y. Bar-Shalom, "A battery chemistry-adaptive fuel gauge using probabilistic data association," *Journal of Power Sources*, vol. 273, pp. 185–195, Jan 2015.

[4] G. V. Avvari, B. Pattipati, B. Balasingam, K. Pattipati, and Y. Bar-Shalom, "Battery fuel gauge validation on portable li-ion battery cells," *Applied Energy*, Sep. 2015.

[5] B. Balasingam, G. V. Avvari, B. Pattipati, K. Pattipati, and Y. Bar-Shalom, "A robust approach to battery fuel gauging, part I: Real time parameter estimation," *Journal of Power Sources*, vol. 272, pp. 1142–1153, Dec. 2014.

[6] B. Balasingam, G. V. Avvari, B. Pattipati, K. Pattipati, and Y. Bar-Shalom, "A robust approach to battery fuel gauging, part II: Real time capacity estimation," *Journal of Power Sources*, vol. 269, pp. 949–961, Dec 2014.

[7] B. Balasingam, B. Pattipati, G. V. Avvari, K. Pattipati, and Y. Bar-Shalom, "Robust battery fuel gauge algorithm development, Part 3: State of charge tracking", *International Conference on Renewable Energy Research and Applications*, 2014.

[8] B. Balasingam, G. V. Avvari, K. Pattipati, and Y. Bar-Shalom, "Performance analysis results of a battery fuel gauge algorithm at multiple temperatures," *Journal of Power Sources*, vol. 273, pp. 742–753, Jan 2015.

[9] B. Balasingam, B. French, Y. Bar-shalom, B. Pattipati, K. Pattipati, J. Meacham, T. Williams, G. V. Avvari, and T. S. Hwang, "Battery state of charge tracking, equivalent circuit selection and benchmarking," U.S. Patent Application 20 140 244 193, 2014.

[10] B. Balasingam, B. French, Y. Bar-shalom, B. Pattipati, K. Pattipati, J. Meacham, T. Williams, G. V. Avvari, and T. S. Hwang, "Battery state of charge tracking, equivalent circuit selection and benchmarking," U.S. Patent Application 20 140 244 225, 2014.

[11] B. Balasingam, B. Pattipati, C. Sankavaram, K. Pattipati, and Y. Bar-Shalom, "An EM approach for dynamic battery management systems," *International Conference on Information Fusion* pp. 2110–2117, July 2012.

[12] X. Chen, W. Shen, Z. Cao and A. Kapoor, "A novel approach for state of charge estimation based on adaptive switching gain sliding mode observer in electric vehicles," *Journal of Power Sources*, 246, 667-678, 2014.

[13] P. Notten, H. Bergveld, and W. Kruijt, "Battery Management Systems: Design by Modeling," *Kluwer Academic Publisher*, 2002.

[14] B. Pattipati, B. Balasingam, A. Abdollahi, G. V. Avvari, K. Pattipati, and Y. Bar-Shalom, "Integrated battery fuel gauge and optimal charger," *IEEE Autotest Conference*, 2014.

[15] B. Pattipati, B. Balasingam, G. V. Avvari, K. Pattipati, and Y. Bar-Shalom, "Open circuit voltage characterization of lithium-ion batteries," *Journal of Power Sources*, vol. 269, pp. 317–333, Dec. 2014.

[16] G. L. Plett, "Extended Kalman filtering for battery management systems of LiPB-based HEV battery packs: Part 1. Background," *Journal of Power sources*, 134(2), 252-261, 2004.

[17] G. L. Plett, "Extended Kalman filtering for battery management systems of LiPB-based HEV battery packs: Part 2. Modeling and identification," *Journal of Power sources*, 134(2), 262-276, 2004.

[18] G. L. Plett, "Extended Kalman filtering for battery management systems of LiPB-based HEV battery packs: Part 3. State and parameter estimation," *Journal of Power sources*, 134(2), 277-292, 2004.

[19] G. L. Plett, "Battery Management Systems, Volume I: Battery Modeling," *Artech House Publishers*, 2015.

[20] G. L. Plett, "Battery Management Systems, Volume II: Equivalent-Circuit Methods," *Artech House Publishers*, 2015.

Faster Charging with Virtual Voltage Termination Technology

Chris Turner
Inventus Power
cturner@inventuspower.com

Abstract

Faster Charging with Virtual Voltage Termination Technology Virtual Voltage Technology (VVT) from Inventus Power™ improves upon the standard CCCV (Constant Current Constant Voltage) charging method for Li-ion batteries. Typical CCCV charge control does not account for impedances through the full charging circuit and the resulting voltage drop between the actual charger output and the cells. Our VVT technology can improve efficiency resulting in up to 30% faster charge times or 30% less power required for the same charge time. Because of the improved efficiency, VVT has also been used in systems with built in charging to help reduce thermal issues created by AC to DC conversion inside of batteries employing built in chargers. Thermal issues associated with ultra-fast charging can also be mitigated with VVT technology. We will give examples of how VVT could be implemented to potentially improve other current fast charge methods in the market. The Inventus Power™ VVT technology is market validated with millions of batteries and chargers in the market using VVT since the introduction several years ago. The presentation, given by Chris Turner, Vice President, Technology at Inventus Power™, will provide case studies and data to further explain VVT's benefits as well as other related charging technology.

A Novel Li-ion Capacitor and Li-ion Battery Internally Hybrid Energy Storage Cell

***Jim P. Zheng*[(a)(b)(c)], *J.S. Zheng*[(b)(d)], *S. Yturriaga*[(b)], and *M. Hagen*[(a)(b)]**

[(a)]Department of Electrical and Computer Engineering, Florida A&M University and Florida State University, Tallahassee, FL 32310; [(b)]Aero-Propulsion, Mechatronics and Energy Center and [(c)]Center for Advanced Power Systems, Florida State University, Tallahassee, FL 32310; [(d)]School of Automobile Studies, Tongji University, Shanghai, China, 201804

zheng@eng.fsu.edu

Abstract: *We have demonstrated a new hybrid electrochemical device, which combines the Li-ion battery (LIB) and the electrochemical (EC) capacitor advantages. The voltage profiles for cells shows that at low current, the new device has a higher energy density than EC capacitor. In a hybrid cell, the cathode electrode is an inner combination of LIB material (e.g. $LiCoO_2$) and EC capacitor material (activated carbon), and anode electrode is Li intercalating carbon such graphite, hard carbon, soft carbon, and their mixture. The advantage of this hybrid cell is that, at a low output, it will reflect the characteristic of LIB and provide a high energy density; while at a high output, the hybrid cell may exhibit the feature of EC capacitor and provide a high power density; consequently, a high power density and a high energy density can be achieved.*

Keywords: Li-ion capacitor; Li-ion battery; hybrid energy storage; specific energy; specific power

Introduction

Li ion battery (LIB) and electrochemical (EC) capacitor are considered as the most widely used energy storage systems because they can produce a high energy density and a high power density, respectively. But they stand at two ends of the spectrum and presently it is impossible for a LIB or EC capacitor to achieve the twin demands of high energy density as well as high power density on their own [1], owing to the intrinsic chemistry restrictions and the kinetics involved. In a LIB, the Li ions move from the negative electrode to the positive electrode during discharge, and this process can provide a large chemical energy. However, the power density is quite low due to the slow movement and intercalation of Li ions. But in an EC capacitor, the main source of energy results from the electrolyte adsorption/desorption on the electrode to form electric double-layer capacitance (EDLC), which is a much faster process and therefore, EC capacitors have a high power density. But at the same time, they exhibit a very low energy density.

The Li-ion capacitor (LIC) is a new energy storage device which consists of an EDLC cathode and a Li-ion battery (LIB) anode, between which the ions shuttle during charge and discharge processes. The LIC not only retained all the advantages of EDLC such as specific power >5 kW/kg and cycle life > 100,000 cycles; but also had higher specific energy of 15-30 Wh/kg and higher maximum cell voltage of 4.1 V than that of EDLC [2,3]. Because the potentials of anode and cathode as well as the maximum cell voltage of LIC is comparable to that of LIB, it allows the LIC and LIB to be assembled in one package as a monolithic LIB and LIC hybrid cell. The energy density and power density of the hybrid cell will be designed to meet the requirements by a reasonable distribution of the ratio between LIB and LIC electrodes in a hybrid cell as shown in Fig. 1.

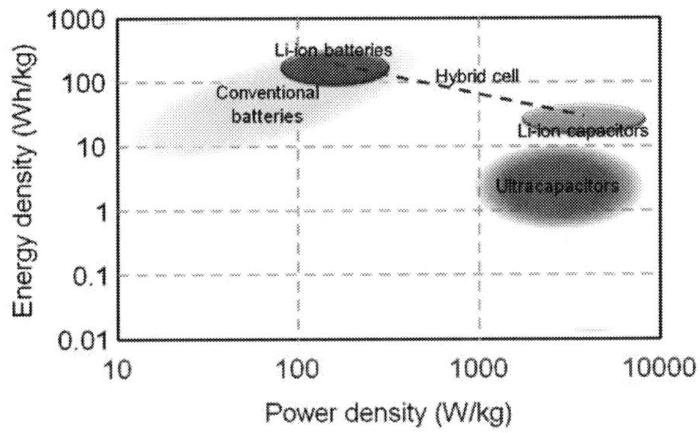

Fig. 1 Rogane plot showing energy density vs. power density for batteries, supercapacitors, Li-ion capacitors, and hybrid cells

Experimental

Commercial active materials were used for both the positive and negative electrodes as received. The slurry mixture of the negative electrode was made of hard carbon (HC) and 5% polytetrafluoroethylene (PTFE) in N-methyl-2-pyrrolidone (NMP) as a binder by the mass ratio of 92:8. After the slurry was prepared, the doctor blade method was employed to spread the prepared slurry onto a 10 μm thick Cu foil substrate.

The positive electrode based on AC was prepared by coating a slurry mixture of activated carbon (AC) and PTFE binder in NMP solvent by the mass ratio of 9:1. The positive electrode based on $LiCoO_2$ was prepared by mixing 85% active material, 10% carbon black, and 5% PTFE in NMP. After the slurry was prepared, it was coated onto an Al foil substrate by the mentioned doctor blade method. Finally, all electrodes were dried at 120 °C for 12 h to remove the solvent and water. After all the electrodes were dried, a hot-roll pressing process was employed to prepare electrodes sheets of desired thickness. All the electrode sheets were kept in the dry room and punched out into circular electrodes with a diameter of 1.27 cm.

The stabilized lithium metal powder (SLMP), used as obtained from FMC Lithium, was applied onto the surface of the prefabricated HC anode electrodes in an argon atmosphere in a glove box. Two-electrode Swagelok-type cells were assembled to characterize the performances of cells. Cells were charged and discharged under a constant current density of potentials from 2.0 to 4.1 V. The electrolyte was 1 M $LiPF_6$ in ethylene carbonate (EC): dimethyl carbonate (DMC) at a ratio of 1:1 by weight.

The electrochemical performance of the cells based on different cathode was measured by an electrochemistry instrument and the electrochemical impedance spectrum (EIS) for the cells was measured in the frequency ranging from 1MHz to 0.1Hz. The resulted spectrum was fitted by Gamry Echem Analyst program. The morphology of the electrodes was observed by scanning electron microscope (SEM). The difference electrochemistry devices with a cathode of $LiCoO_2$, $LiCoO_2$/AC and AC are referred to as LiB, HyLiC and LiC, respectively.

Result and discussion

Fig. 2 shows the voltage profiles for LIB, LIB/LIC hybrid, and LIC cells in the voltage range of 4.1-2.0 V under a constant current of 0.4 mA/cm^2. All cells were cycles in a potential range of 2.0-4.1V. The specific energy of LIB, LIB/LIC hybrid, and LiC cells were observed to be 344 Wh/kg, 149 Wh/kg, and 59 Wh/kg based on electrodes, respectively. Fig. 3 shows the voltage profiles of the first three cycles for LIB, LIB/LIC hybrid, and LIC cells under a constant current of 4 mA/cm^2. At this higher rate, the energy densities of LiB, LIB/LIC hybrid, and LIC cells were observed to be 6 Wh/kg, 31 Wh/kg, and 46 Wh/kg, respectively. LIB/LIC hybrid cell clearly outperforms the LIB at high rates. These results clearly demonstrate that LIB/LIC hybrid cell combines the high specific energy characteristics of LIB at lower rates and high power specific power characteristics of LIC at higher rates.

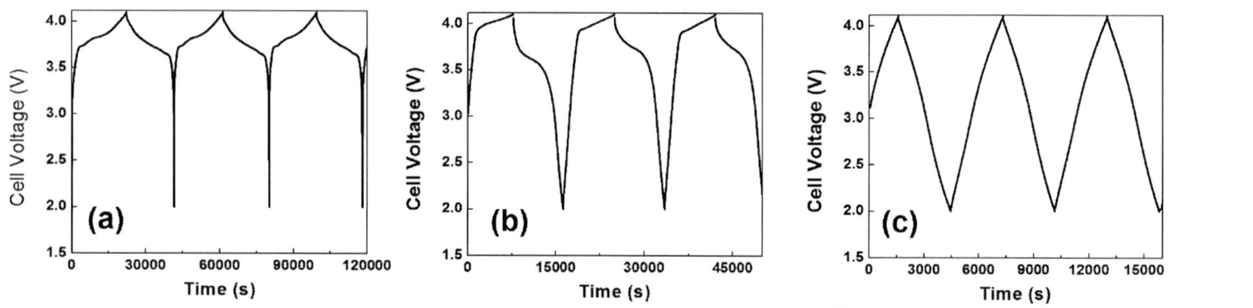

Fig. 2 Voltage profiles of cells with a charge and discharge current of 0.4 mA/cm^2: (a) LIB, (b) LIB/LIC hybrid, (c) LIC cells.

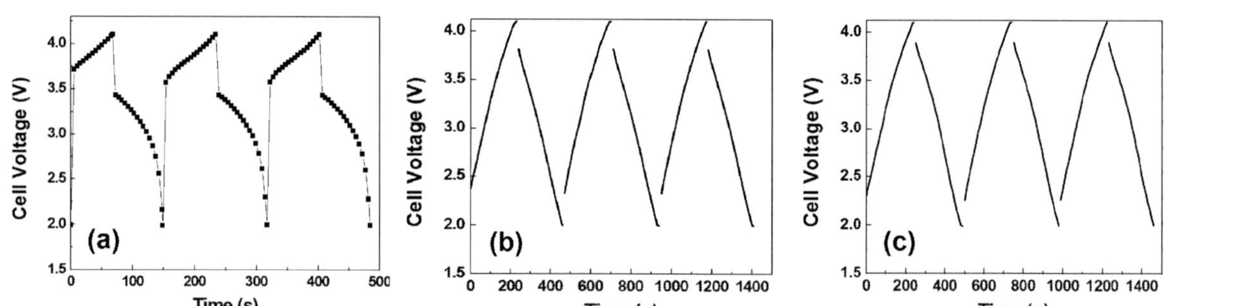

Fig. 3 Voltage profiles of cells with various positive electrodes with a current of 4mA/cm^2: (a) LIB, (b) LIB/LIC hybrid, (c) LIC cells.

Furthermore, the specific energy and the specific power of the LIB/LIC hybrid cell was investigated and compared with that of LIB and LIC cells. Three cells were discharged under constant power mode and Fig. 4 shows the Ragone plot based on the weight of activate materials.

The specific energy decreases with the increase in specific power for all cells, which means it is a greater challenge to realize an energy storage device which can satisfy the dual demands of a high specific energy as well as a high specific power. When the specific power is less than 250 kW/kg, LIB demonstrates a higher specific energy than others. While with a specific power higher than 250 kW/kg, LIC performs better than others with the highest specific energy.

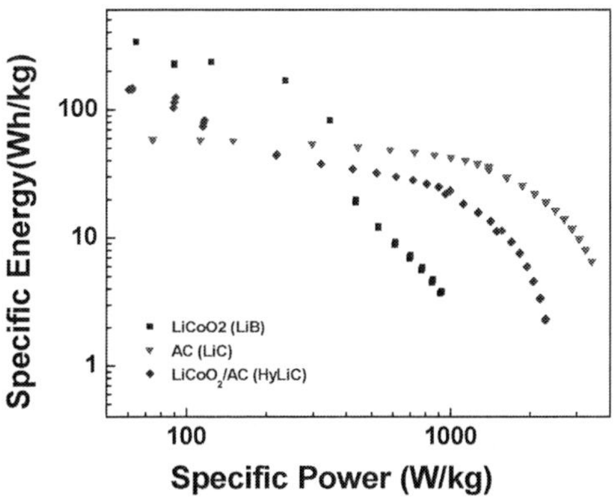

Fig. 4 The Ragone plots of cells based on different cathodes.

Conclusion

To combine the advantages of LIB and LIC, a novel electrochemical energy storage device of internally hybrid of LIB/LIC cell was developed. This cell balanced the voltage between LIC and LIB and provides high energy and power densities. The voltage profiles for cells show that at low currents, the new cell has a higher energy density than LIC. At a high currents, this device has a higher energy density than LIB. The Ragone plot proves that this novel device has the advantages of LIB and LIC, and can make a balance between the energy density and power density, therefore, can satisfy the demand of high energy density and high power density of energy storage system.

Acknowledgements

This work was supported by PNNL/DOE under contract No. 249389 and US Army Research Lab under contract No. W911NF-15-2-0103.

References

1. Y.-G. Cho, Y.-S. Kim, D.-G. Sung, M.-S. Seo, H.-K. Song, *Energy & Environmental Science*, 7, 1737-1743 (2014).
2. W.J. Cao and J.P. Zheng, "Li-ion Capacitors with Carbon Cathode and Hard Carbon/SLMP Anode Electrodes", *J. Power Sources*, **213**, 180 (2012).
3. W.J. Cao, J. Shih, J.P. Zheng, and T. Doung, "Development and characterization of Li-ion capacitor pouch cells", *J. Power Sources*, **257**, 388 (2014).

Nanoscale Polymers as Solid-State Electrolytes and Dielectrics in Next-Generation Batteries and Capacitors

Jeffrey W. Long, [1] ***Jean M. Wallace,*** [2] ***Megan B. Sassin,*** [1] ***and Debra R. Rolison*** [1]

[1]Code 6170, Surface Chemistry Branch
U. S. Naval Research Laboratory
4555 Overlook Avenue SW
Washington, DC USA 20375

[2]Nova Research, Inc.
1900 Elkin Street, Suite 230
Alexandria, VA USA 22306
Contact Author Email: jeffrey.long@nrl.navy.mil

Abstract: *We are developing a class of energy-storage devices in which all cell components (cathode, electrolyte/dielectric, anode) interpenetrate in three dimensions (3D) and where separation distances between opposing electrodes are reduced to the tens-of-nanometers length scale. The most challenging component of a fully integrated 3D battery or capacitor architecture is the electrolyte/dielectric phase, which must serve as a physical and electronic barrier between the positive and negative electrodes, among other functions. Initiated chemical vapor deposition (iCVD) methods offer a promising approach for generating conformal, nanoscale polymers in the non–line-of-sight conditions inherent to complex 3D architectures. We are adapting iCVD protocols to generate nanoscale siloxane-type polymer coatings that function as a dielectric in native form or solid-state electrolyte when infused with Li^+ salts. The basic structure and composition of iCVD-derived polymer coatings are assessed at planar substrates (e.g., carbon films) using such techniques as profilometry and infrared spectroscopy, while solid-state electrical properties are evaluated using AC and DC methods.*

Keywords: battery; capacitor; dielectric; polymer; electrolyte; solid-state; lithium.

Introduction

Energy-storage devices that are redesigned with all cell components interpenetrating in three dimensions (3D) and with minimized separation distances between opposing electrodes offer the potential for superior energy and power density [1–3]. The most critical constituent of these 3D designs is the dielectric/electrolyte phase that serves as a physical and electronic barrier between the positive and negative electrodes while also providing other key functions such as ionic conduction or dielectric charge storage. The non–line-of-sight conditions within complex 3D architectures limit the available fabrication protocols with which to generate conformal, nanoscale dielectric coatings. We previously explored electropolymerization as a route to synthesize ultrathin polymers at conductive substrates ranging from simple planar electrodes [4,5] to various porous architectures, including aerogel-like metal oxides [6,7] and carbons [8] as well as carbon-coated silica fiber paper [9]. Such polymer coatings can be transformed into solid-state electrolytes by incorporating salts [4] or by electropolymerizing a charged monomer [5].

Initiated chemical vapor deposition (*i*CVD), developed by Gleason and co-workers, is another promising method with which to generate conformal, nanoscale polymers in a controlled fashion [10,11]. This technique offers the advantages of liquid-free processing but can be performed under more benign conditions (*e.g.*, lower temperature) compared to typical CVD routes to polymers. Although initially demonstrated at simple planar substrates, *i*CVD protocols have been extended to coat more complex porous substrates such as trench arrays patterned into silicon [12] and carbon-coated silica fiber paper [8].

Gleason and Dunn recently reported that ultrathin *i*CVD-generated polysiloxane films can be converted from dielectrics into solid-state electrolytes by incorporating lithium salts, with the resulting ionic conductivities ranging from 10^{-11} to 10^{-8} S cm^{-1} [13–15]. In the present report, we adapt established *i*CVD protocols for the polymerization of 1,3,5-trimethyl-1,3,5-trivinyltricyclosiloxane ("V3D3") to apply ~ 40 nm–thick polymer coatings at planar pyrolytic carbon substrates. We investigate the AC and DC electrical characteristics of the resulting poly-V3D3 films, both in their native form and after salt-impregnation with $LiClO_4$ and discuss the implications of those findings for the design of next-generation 3D batteries and capacitors.

Trivinyltrimethylcyclotrisiloxane
"V3D3"

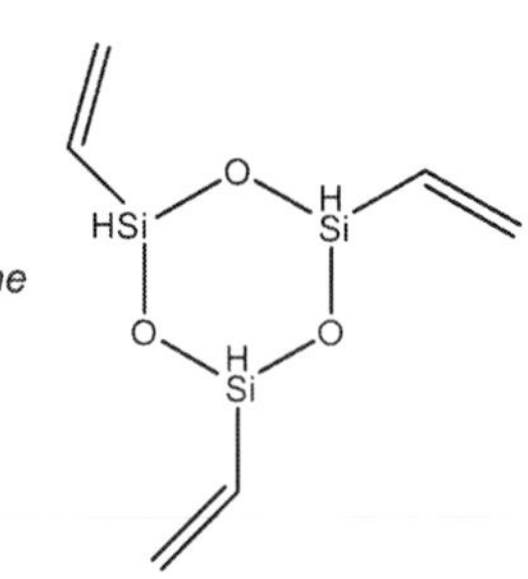

Experimental

Fabrication of substrates. Carbon substrates were prepared by modifying previously reported CVD procedures [16]. Briefly, sections of fused silica plates (G.M. Associates), were cut to 1 cm × 3 cm using a Dremel tool, calcined in a muffle furnace at 500 °C for 4 h in air, and then inserted into an alumina tube mounted in a tube furnace (MTI OTF-1200X). The temperature of the tube furnace was ramped to 1000°C at 10°C min^{-1} under an argon atmosphere, and after stabilization at 1000°C, the gas flow was alternated between benzene-saturated argon (100 cm^3 min^{-1}) for 7 min and pure argon for 10 min, cycling three times. Samples were removed after the furnace cooled to room temperature; the resulting substrates are hereafter denoted as "CVD-carbon". Gold-coated glass slide substrates were prepared using Denton Vacuum Desk IV Sputter Etch Unit.

Initiated chemical vapor deposition of poly-V3D3. Various planar substrates (CVD-carbon, Au-coated glass, and silicon wafers) were coated with poly-V3D3 using a commercial deposition chamber (GVD Corporation, Cambridge, MA). The monomer (1,3,5-trivinyl-1,3,5-trimethylcyclotrisiloxane: V3D3, >95%, Gelest) and the initiator (di-tert-butyl peroxide, TBPO 98%, Aldrich), were heated to 25 °C and 50 °C, respectively; lines from the source jars to the reaction chamber were held at 70 °C to avoid vapor condensation. The flow of initiator was maintained at 2 sccm with a computer-controlled mass-flow controller. The V3D3 monomer was then introduced to the chamber using a manual regulator valve with the target chamber pressure set to 370 mTorr. Thermal excitation was achieved by resistively heating Nichrome wire at 35 V (~2 A). Deposition time was 15 min under these conditions. For the CVD-carbon substrates, one end was masked with Fluorglas tape (as a point for future electrical contact).

Materials Characterization: Thickness measurements for both the CVD-carbon and *i*CVD-polymer films (on silicon wafer substrates) were collected using a Tencor Alpha-Step D-120 stylus profilometer. Fourier-Transform infrared spectra were collected on poly-V3D3-coated Au-glass slides using a Nicolet 6700 and grazing-incidence stage.

Solid-State Electrical Measurements. Selected poly-V3D3-coated CVD-carbon substrates were soaked in 0.5 M $LiClO_4$/propylene carbonate solution for 18 h at room temperature, and then quickly rinsed with propylene carbonate prior to drying in vacuum oven (60 °C, 24 h). All electrical measurements were performed in a N_2-purged glovebox (Plas-Labs, 830-ABC). Top electrical contact was made through a drop of Hg suspended from a 1-mL syringe and contacting a Cu wire for external connection [4]. Bottom electrical contact was made via alligator clip to the uncoated section of the CVD-carbon. Both electrical leads were connected to a Gamry Ref 600 potentiostat, with the CVD-carbon attached to the working electrode lead and the Hg-drop contact attached to shorted reference/counter leads. Impedance spectroscopy was performed at open-circuit voltage (OCV) with a ±100 mV AC perturbation over a frequency range of 100 kHz to 0.1 Hz. Current–voltage (*i*–V) scans were collected in cyclic voltammetry mode at 10 mV s^{-1}, initially scanning to/from 0.5 V, followed by obtaining another impedance spectrum, and repeating the cycle with increasing positive voltage limits (1.0, 1.5, 2.0, and 2.5 V).

Results and Discussion

The thickness of poly-V3D3 coatings deposited with 15-min monomer exposure was assessed on polymer-coated silicon wafers by first scraping sections of the polymer from the substrate using a razor blade and then tracing across the resulting interface with a stylus profilometer. A typical profile is shown in Figure 1, which shows a polymer thickness of ~40 nm.

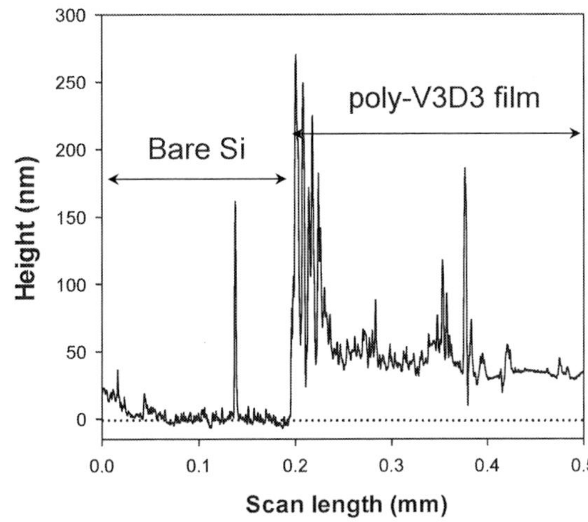

Figure 1. Profilometer trace of poly-V3D3 film on Si wafer.

Chemical structure was assessed using reflectance IR methods on poly-V3D3-coated Au-glass slides. The resulting spectra, shown in Figure 2, are consistent with those previously reported by Gleason and co-workers [11]. We observed no obvious changes in the spectra after

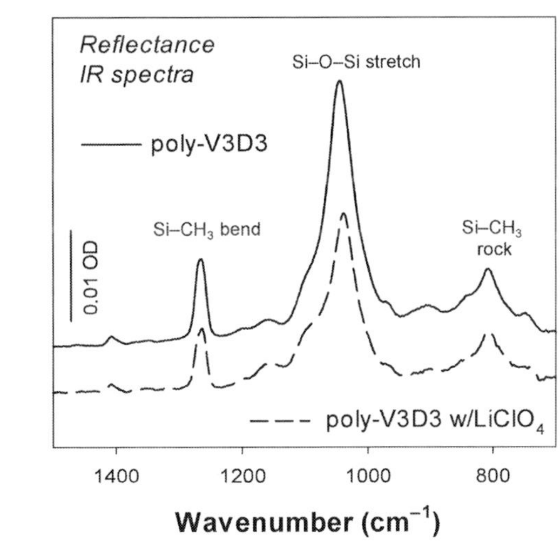

Figure 2. Infrared spectra of poly-V3D3 films on Au-glass.

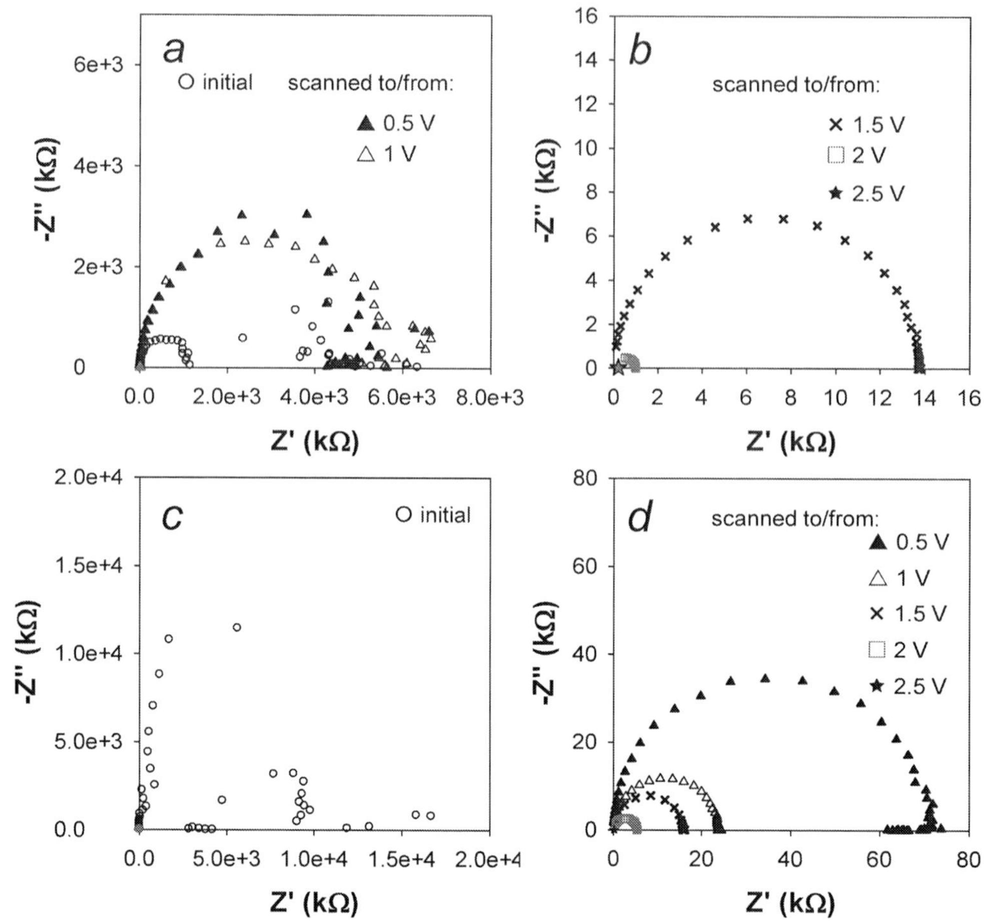

Figure 3. Impedance spectra for poly-V3D3 on CVD-carbon in: (*a*,*b*) as-deposited form; and (*c*,*d*) after soaking in $LiClO_4$/PC. All spectra are recorded under open-circuit conditions, but where indicated, after scanned-voltage tests to/from the indicated positive voltage limit.

soaking the poly-V3D3 film in $LiClO_4$/propylene carbonate solution (as described in the Experimental section).
The electrical characteristics of both as-deposited and $LiClO_4$-infused poly-V3D3 films on CVD-carbon substrates were assessed using AC and DC measurements. Initial impedance spectra for both samples (Figure 3a,c) show very high (MΩ-level) impedance, with little distinction between the two. Although impedance arcs are present, these do not necessarily indicate ionic conduction, but may arise from stray capacitance in the experimental setup. The seeming absence of ionic conductivity in the initial $LiClO_4$-containing polymer film was unexpected, considering the prior reports of solid-state ionic conductivity in similar poly-V3D3 materials [13].

After analyzing these initial impedance results, we proceeded by applying a sequence of DC and AC measurements in which the poly-V3D3 film was subjected to voltage-sweep tests (Figure 4) to progressively more positive voltage limits, interspersed with additional impedance measurements. For voltage sweeps to/from 0.5 V the current trace is similar between as-deposited and $LiClO_4$-containing poly-V3D3 films, but currents are an order of magnitude greater for the $LiClO_4$/poly-V3D3 film when the positive limit is 1.0 V; the resulting ohmic response is indicative of a small leakage current, as previously described by Rhodes et al. [4]. Further extending the voltage limits to > 1.5 V leads to dielectric breakdown, which is expected for polymer films that are in this nanoscale thickness range [4].

Biasing the poly-V3D3 films during these voltage-sweep measurements has a significant impact on their impedance behavior, as shown in Figure 3. Within the voltage window prior to dielectric breakdown, the as-deposited poly-V3D3 is not markedly changed but the $LiClO_4$/poly-V3D3 becomes significantly more conductive, with well-defined impedance arcs that intersect the real axis at 72 and 24 kΩ after the 0.5

and 1.0 V scans, respectively. We posit that the electric fields imposed across the polymer film (2.5×10^5 V cm^{-1} field strength for 1-V bias at 40-nm thickness) induce ordering of the polymer–salt domains to generate more efficient pathways for electrical conduction. The impedance behavior of as-deposited and $LiClO_4$/poly-V3D3 films converges again, but at very low impedance (<1 kΩ) that would indicate electrical shorting between the contacting electrodes,

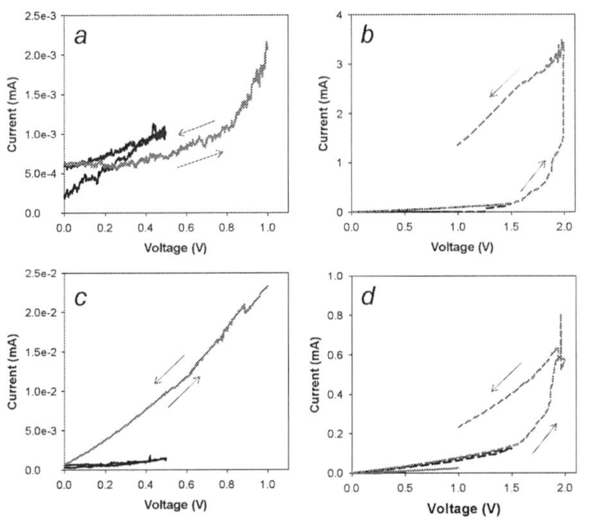

Figure 4. Voltage-sweep measurements for poly-V3D3 on CVD-carbon in: (*a*,*b*) as-deposited form; and (*c*,*d*) after soaking in $LiClO_4$/PC.

a consequence of the dielectric breakdown that both samples undergo at >1.5 V conditioning.

Acknowledgements

Support for this research was provided by the U.S. Office of Naval Research. This publication has been approved for Public Release.

References

1. Long, J. W., Dunn, B., Rolison, D. R., and White, H. S., "Three-Dimensional Battery Architectures," *Chemical Reviews*, Vol. 104, pp.4463–4492, 2004.
2. Rolison, D. R., Long, J. W., Lytle, J. C., Fischer, A. E., Rhodes, C. P., McEvoy, T. M., Bourg, M. E., and Lubers, A. M., "Multifunctional 3D Nanoarchitectures for Energy Storage and Conversion," *Chemical Society Reviews*, Vol. 38, pp. 226–252, 2009.
3. Oudenhoven, J. F., M., Baggetto, L., and Notten, P. H. L., "All-Solid-State Lithium-Ion Microbatteries: A Review of Various Three-Dimensional Concepts," *Advanced Energy Materials*, Vol. 1, pp. 10–33, 2011.
4. Rhodes, C. P., Long, J. W., Doescher, M. S., Fontanella, J. J., and Rolison, D. R., "Nanoscale Polymer Electrolytes: Ultrathin Electrodeposited Poly(Phenylene Oxide) with Solid-State Ionic Conductivity," *Journal of Physical Chemistry B*, Vol. 108, pp. 13079–13087, 2004.
5. Rhodes, C. P., Long, J. W., and Rolison, D. R., "Direct Electrodeposition of Nanoscale Solid Polymer Electrolytes via Electropolymerization of Sulfonated Phenols," *Electrochemical and Solid State Letters*, Vol. 8, pp. A579–A584, 2005.
6. Long, J. W., Rhodes, C. P., Young, A. L., and Rolison, D. R., "Ultrathin, Protective Coatings of Poly(*o*-phenylenediamine) as Electrochemical Proton Gates: Making Mesoporous MnO_2 Nanoarchitectures Stable in Acid Electrolytes," *Nano Letters*, Vol. 3, pp. 155–1161, 2003.
7. Rhodes, C. P., Long, J. W., Doescher, M. S., Dening, B. M., and Rolison, D. R., *Journal of Non-Crystalline Solids*, Vol. 350, pp. 73–79, 2004.
8. Long, J. W., Dening, B. M., McEvoy, T. M., and Rolison, D. R., *Journal of Non-Crystalline Solids*, Vol. 350, pp. 97–106, 2004.
9. Sassin, M. B., Long, J. W., Wallace, J. M., and Rolison, D. R., "Routes to 3D Conformal Solid-State Dielectric Polymers: Electrodeposition versus Initiated Chemical Vapor Deposition," *Materials Horizons*, Vol. 2, pp. 502–508, 2015.
10. Murthy, S. K., Olsen, B. D., and Gleason, K. K., *Langmuir*, Vol. 18, pp. 6424–6428, 2002.
11. O'Shaughnessy, W. S., Gao, M., and Gleason, K. K., "Initiated Chemical Vapor Deposition of Trivinyl-trimethylcyclotrisiloxane for Biomaterial Coatings," *Langmuir*, Vol. 22, pp. 7021–7026, 2006.
12. Baxamusa, S. H. and Gleason, K. K., "Initiated Chemical Vapor Deposition of Polymer Films on Nonplanar Substrates," *Thin Solid Films*, Vol. 517, pp. 3536–3538, 2009.
13. Chen, N., Reeja-Jayan, B., Lau, J., Moni, P., Liu, A., Dunn, B., and Gleason, K. K.,"Nanoscale, Conformal Polysiloxane Thin Film Electrolytes for Three-Dimensional Battery Architectures," *Materials Horizons*, Vol. 2, pp. 309–314, 2015.
14. Reeja-Jayn, B., Chen, N., Lau, J., Kattirtzi, J. A., Moni, P., Liu, A., Miller, I. G., Kayser, R., Willard, A. P., Dunn, B., and Gleason, K. K., "A Group of Cyclic Siloxane and Silazane Polymer Films as Nanoscale Electrolytes for Microbattery Architectures," *Macromolecules*, Vol., 48, pp. 5222–5229, 2015.
15. Chen, N., Reeja-Jayan, B., Liu, A. D., Lau, J., Dunn, B., and Gleason, K. K., "iCVD Cyclic Polysiloxane nad Polysilazane as Nanoscale Thin-Film Electrolyte: Synthesis and Properties," *Macromolecular Rapid Communications*, Vol. 37, pp. 446–452, 2016.
16. Lytle, J. C., Zimmerman, T. N., Pettigrew, K. A., and Rolison, D. R., "Carbon Ductwork with Nanometric Walls and Micron-to-Submicron Inner Diameters," *ECS Journal of Solid State Science and Technology*, Vol. 2, pp. M3078–M3083, 2013.

Hemp-derived Activated Carbons for Electrochemical Capacitors

Wei Sun [a], Stephen M. Lipka [b], Christopher Swartz [b], David Williams [c], Fuqian Yang [a]*

[a]Materials Program, Department of Chemical and Materials Engineering
University of Kentucky, Lexington, KY 40506, United States
[b] Center for Applied Energy Research,
University of Kentucky, Lexington, KY 40511, United States
[c] Department of Plant and Soil Sciences
University of Kentucky, Lexington, KY 40546, United States
*Corresponding authors

Abstract: *Activated carbons are prepared from raw hemp stem via hydrothermal processing and chemical activation. The obtained biochar is converted into activated carbons of low-dimensional structures and used to construct the electrodes of supercapacitor cells. The electrochemical performance of the activated carbons used in the supercapacitor cells is dependent on hydrothermal processing conditions and the mass ratio of KOH/biochar in the chemical activation. Excellent electrochemical performance metrics are achieved, including a specific capacitance of 160 F/g, and a high energy density of 19.8 Wh/kg at a power density of 21 kW/kg. Both the specific capacitance and capacitance retention increase with surface area and mesoporous fraction. A simple relationship between the specific area capacitance and the fraction of micropores is proposed, via the rule of mixtures, and is supported by the experimental results. This relationship reveals the effect of the distribution of pore sizes on the specific area capacitance of electrochemical double layer capacitors.*

Keywords: hemp; hydrothermal synthesis; activated carbons; supercapacitors

Introduction

Electrochemical double layer capacitors (EDLCs) are attractive energy storage devices, which store energy in an electrical double layer (EDL) of electrolyte ions at the electrode/electrolyte interface[1,2]. Various materials have been used in the electrodes of electrochemical double layer capacitors, including carbon-based materials[3], metal oxides [4,5] and conductive polymeric materials[6], among which activated carbonaceous materials have attracted great interest due to large surface area[7], porous structures, good conductivity and good physical and chemical stability[8,9].

Hydrothermal synthesis is a simple and economical method to produce micro/nano-scale carbon spheres with controllable sizes, using small molecules (i.e. xylose, glucose)[10-12] or macromolecules (i.e. starch, cellulose)[13,14] as precursors. These carbonaceous materials have been utilized as active materials in electrochemical energy storage after thermal processing, and exhibit good electrochemical performance. Due to its many attractive qualities industrial hemp recently became a promising material for numerous applications. As reported by Wang et al.[15] it can successfully be used to prepare activated graphene via hydrothermal processing and chemical activation. The resulting material had high surface area and a large amount of mesopores, and the supercapacitor electrode made from the hemp-derived graphene exhibits good electrochemical performance at different temperatures when tested in an organic electrolyte. However, only the hemp-bast fiber was utilized in the study, which is 20-25% of the biomass of hemp[16], leaving 75-80% biomass which likely can be carbonized and activated for energy storage applications. Given the potential applications of hemp-derived carbonaceous materials in energy storage, hemp hurd was utilized as a precursor in this work to prepare activated carbons for EDLCs via hydrothermal synthesis. The activated carbons were used to prepare the electrodes of EDLCs, and the electrochemical characteristics of the EDLCs with an organic electrolyte were investigated.

Experimental details

The activated carbons of low-dimensional structures were prepared by hydrothermal synthesis (HTS), which was followed by chemical activation. Raw hemp hurd was added to deionized (DI) water or 1 wt.% sulfuric acid and hydrothermally treated for 24 h at 200 °C. The product (biochar) was collected by filtration, washed in DI water and dried. The biochar was mixed with potassium hydroxide in different mass ratios (biochar/KOH) of 1:1 (a-1), 1:3 (a-3) and 1:5 (a-5). The mixture was thoroughly ground in a mortar and then heated to 800 °C in a nitrogen atmosphere and chemically activated for 1 hr. The activated carbon was washed with DI water until the pH 7 and dried at 90 °C for 12 hr. Activated carbons were characterized by a scanning electron microscope. To determine the surface area and pore structure of the activated carbons, the nitrogen adsorption – desorption isotherms were measured by an automated gas adsorption analyzer (Micromeritics). To prepare electrodes the activated carbon was mixed with graphite and PTFE (polytetrafluoroethylene) in a mass ratio of 92:5:3. The mixture was heat-treated at 110 °C for 30 min, then milled in a mortar until a sheet was produced. The sheet was then rolled to obtain thickness of 65-80 μm. Circular discs with a 12 mm diameter were punched out and used as the electrodes of electrochemical double layer capacitors. The prepared electrodes were placed on two carbon current collectors, separately, which were assembled together with a polymeric separator (CELGARD 3581) between them. The organic electrolyte was 1.8M $TEMABF_4$/PC.

Cyclic voltammetry (CV) and constant current charge/discharge experiments were performed at room temperature with a Gamry G750 Potentiostat. Electrochemical impedance spectroscopy was carried out with a Schlumberger SI 1260 impedance/gain-phase analyzer. ECC-STD test cell (EL-CELL, Germany) was used for electrochemical characterization.

Results and Discussion

Figures 1a-1b show the morphologies of the biochars derived from hemp hurd via the hydrothermal synthesis at 200 °C in two different solutions of DI water and 1 wt.% H_2SO_4. As depicted on the micrographs the morphologies of the hurd-biochars are relatively the same, independent of the liquid solutions. The similar structure of the carbons activated with different concentrations of KOH indicates the same role of the reaction between KOH and biochar in the formation of morphologies during activation as shown on Figures 1c-1f.

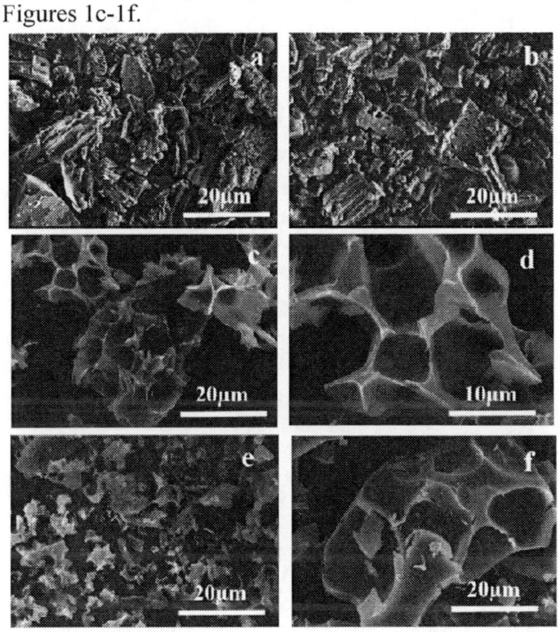

Figure 1. SEM images of the biochars derived from the hemp hurd in different liquid solutions: (a) DI water, (b) 1 wt.% H_2SO_4; SEM images of the chemically activated carbons with different mass ratios of KOH to biochar: (c-d) 3:1, (e) 1:1, and (f) 5:1.

It is known that chemical activation of carbon materials can lead to the formation of porous structures and an increase in surface area. Figure 2a shows the nitrogen adsorption-desorption isotherms for the activated carbons of Hurd-a-x. The isotherms for the activated carbons of Hurd-a-1 and Hurd-a-3 show a Type I profile, which is a typical microporous profile, while the isotherm of Hurd-a-3 shows a broad knee indicating a wide distribution of pore sizes. The isotherm of Hurd-a-5 is similar to a Type IV profile, suggesting the presence of a mesoporous structure. From the distribution of the pore sizes of the activated carbons (Fig. 2b), one can note that the average size of pores and fraction of mesopores increase with the increase of the mass ratio of KOH to biochar, in accord with the results shown in the isotherms (Fig. 2a).

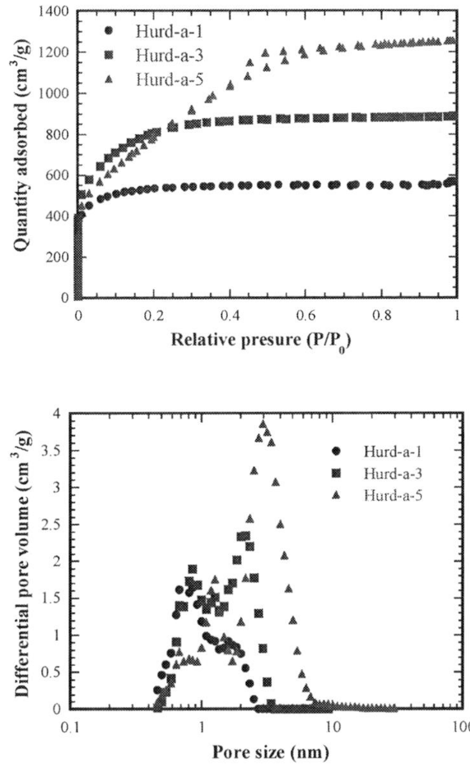

Figure 2. Surface properties of the activated carbons obtained from Hurd-a-x: (a) nitrogen adsorption-desorption isotherms, and (b) distribution of pore sizes calculated from the adsorption isotherms via the DFT.

In general, the surface properties of the biochar vary significantly with the hydrothermal conditions, and it is not necessary for a biochar with a larger surface area to produce activated carbon with a larger surface area after chemical activation than the activated carbon produced from a biochar with a smaller surface area under the same activation conditions. There are various factors, such as the surface and chemical properties of biochar, which determine the surface properties of the corresponding activated carbons.

Figure 3 shows the cyclic voltammogram (CV) for the supercapacitor cells made from the activated carbons of Hurd-a-x. The quasi-rectangular shape of the CV curves is observed for the supercapacitor cells made from Hurd-a-5 and Hurd-a-3, indicative of capacitive charge storage. This result implies rapid current response to the change of voltage from 0 to 2 V and fast ion transport during charging and discharging. The supercapacitor cell made from Hurd-a-1 exhibits less favorable electrochemical performance with relatively more distortion in the CV curve. The specific capacitance displays an increasing tendency from Hurd-a-1 to Hurd-a-5.

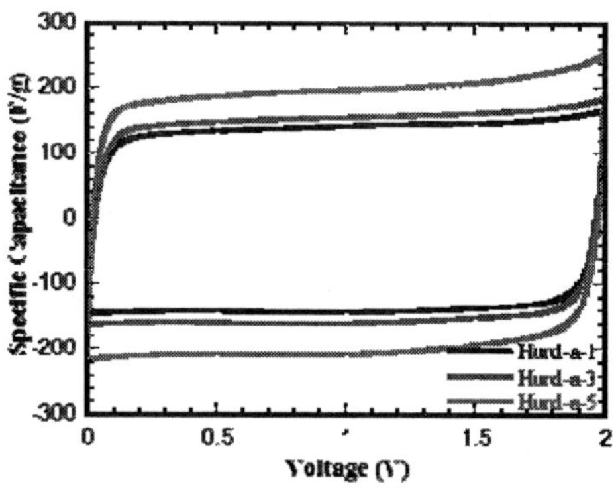

Figure 3. CV curves (scan rate: 0.05 V/s) of the supercapacitor cells made from the activated carbons of different biochar.

Figure 4 shows the charge/discharge curves of the supercapacitor cells made from the activated carbons of Hurd-a-x. The current density was 10 A/g. The charge/discharge behavior is highly reversible, and the discharge curves display linear behavior, and are approximately symmetrical to the corresponding charge curves. The linear behavior of the charge/discharge curves demonstrates excellent capacitive characteristics of the supercapacitor cells.

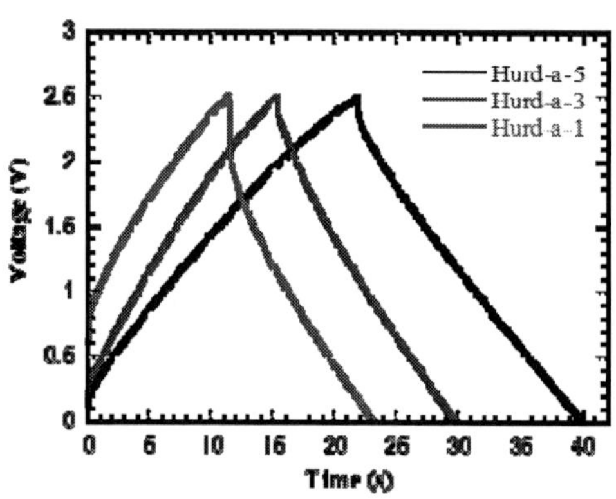

Figure 4. Galvanostatic charge/discharge curves (current density: 10 A/g).

Figure 5 shows the variation of specific capacitance with current density for the supercapacitor cells made from the activated carbons of Hurd-a-x. The specific capacitance increases with the increase of the mass ratio of KOH/biochar. The increase of the mass ratio of KOH/biochar improves the capacitance retention.

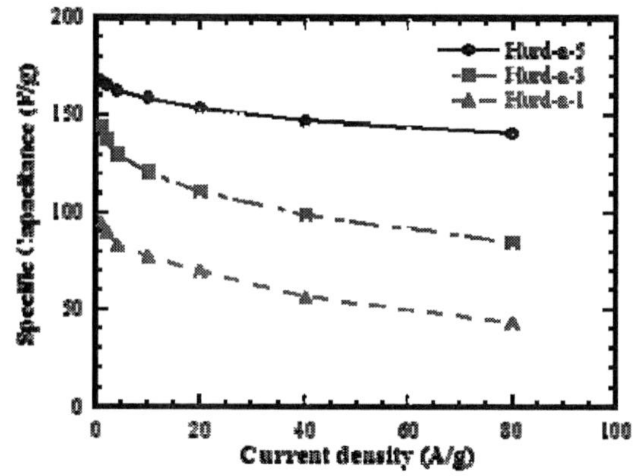

Figure 5. Variation of specific capacitance with current density.

Summary

In summary, activated carbons were prepared from raw hemp stem (hurd) as a precursor via hydrothermal processing and chemical activation. Controlling the experimental conditions, activated carbons of low-dimensional structures with high surface area and large fraction of mesopores were formed. The activated carbons were used to construct the electrodes of supercapacitor cells. The electrochemical performance of the cells was characterized. Excellent electrochemical performance of a specific capacitance of 160 F/g and a high energy density of 19.8 Wh/kg at a power density of 21 kW/kg was achieved. The specific capacitance and capacitance retention both increase as both surface area and mesopore fraction increase. For the same mass ratio of 5:1 for KOH/biochar, the supercapacitor cells made from the biochar hydrothermally synthesized in sulfuric acid possess higher capacitance than those made from the biochar obtained in DI water. The specific capacitance gradually decreases with increasing current density, and the supercapacitor cells made from the activated carbons prepared by using sulfuric acid in the hydrothermal process feature high capacitance retention.

A simple relationship between the specific area capacitance and the fraction of micropores was proposed, via the rule of mixtures. The experimental results support the relationship for the supercapacitor cells made from the activated carbons with R_{micro} larger than 57%. There exists the effect of current density on the specific area capacitance. For supercapacitor cells with the same fraction of micropores, a larger specific area capacitance can be achieved via a smaller electric current.

The process reported in this study provides an economic and effective method to prepare electrochemically active materials of high-performance from biomass and biowastes. The usage of low cost biomass can further reduce the cost of the material syntheses and provide the possibility to economically produce activated carbon materials in a large quantity.

Acknowledgements

The authors would like to acknowledge the financial support of the NSF EPSCoR grant 1355438 (Powering the Kentucky Bioeconomy for a Sustainable Future). FY is grateful for the financial support from the KSEF (KSEF-148-502-15-341).

References

1. A. Burke, *Journal of Power Sources*, 2000, **91**, 37-50.
2. A. S. Arico, P. Bruce, B. Scrosati, J.-M. Tarascon and W. Van Schalkwijk, *Nature Materials*, 2005, **4**, 366-377.
3. A. Chu and P. Braatz, *Journal of Power Sources*, 2002, **112**, 236-246.
4. G. Yu, L. Hu, M. Vosgueritchian, H. Wang, X. Xie, J. R. McDonough, X. Cui, Y. Cui and Z. Bao, *Nano Letters*, 2011, **11**, 2905-2911.
5. B. J. Lee, S. Sivakkumar, J. M. Ko, J. H. Kim, S. M. Jo and D. Y. Kim, *Journal of Power Sources*, 2007, **168**, 546-552.
6. Y.-Y. Horng, Y.-C. Lu, Y.-K. Hsu, C.-C. Chen, L.-C. Chen and K.-H. Chen, *Journal of Power Sources*, 2010, **195**, 4418-4422.
7. Y. Zhu, S. Murali, M. D. Stoller, K. Ganesh, W. Cai, P. J. Ferreira, A. Pirkle, R. M. Wallace, K. A. Cychosz and M. Thommes, *Science*, 2011, **332**, 1537-1541.
8. A. Pandolfo and A. Hollenkamp, *Journal of Power Sources*, 2006, **157**, 11-27.
9. Y. Wang, Z. Shi, Y. Huang, Y. Ma, C. Wang, M. Chen and Y. Chen, *The Journal of Physical Chemistry C*, 2009, **113**, 13103-13107.
10. R. Demir-Cakan, P. Makowski, M. Antonietti, F. Goettmann and M.-M. Titirici, *Catalysis Today*, 2010, **150**, 115-118.
11. R. Cakan, *Chemical Communications*, 2008, 3759-3761.
12. S.-A. Wohlgemuth, F. Vilela, M.-M. Titirici and M. Antonietti, *Green Chemistry*, 2012, **14**, 741-749.
13. M.-M. Titirici, M. Antonietti and N. Baccile, *Green Chemistry*, 2008, **10**, 1204-1212.
14. C. Falco, N. Baccile and M.-M. Titirici, *Green Chemistry*, 2011, **13**, 3273-3281.
15. H. Wang, Z. Xu, A. Kohandehghan, Z. Li, K. Cui, X. Tan, T. J. Stephenson, C. K. King'ondu, C. M. Holt and B. C. Olsen, *ACS Nano*, 2013, **7**, 5131-5141.
16. N. Stevulova, J. Cigasova, A. Estokova, E. Terpakova, A. Geffert, F. Kacik, E. Singovszka and M. Holub, *Materials*, 2014, **7**, 8131-8150.

Flexible, Printed Ultracapacitors for Use in Extreme Environments

Erik S. Handy[1], Kathleen A. Maleski[2], Tyler S. Mathis[2], Katherine L. Van Aken[2], Yury Gogotsi[2], Giuseppe L. Di Benedetto[3], James L. Zunino III[3]

[1]SI2 Technologies, Inc., North Billerica, MA 01862, USA, ehandy@si2technologies.com

[2]Department of Materials Science and Engineering, and A. J. Drexel Nanomaterials Institute, Drexel University, 3141 Chestnut Street, Philadelphia, Pennsylvania 19104, USA, gogotsi@drexel.edu

[3]Advanced Materials Technology Branch, U.S. Army Armament Research, Development and Engineering Center, Picatinny Arsenal, NJ 07806, USA, giuseppe.l.dibenedetto.civ@mail.mil

Abstract: *SI2 Technologies, Inc., Drexel University, and the U.S. Army Armament Research, Development and Engineering Center are developing a flexible, printed ultracapacitor for use in extreme environments. This novel device can be rolled up or folded into arbitrary shapes, and then inserted unobtrusively into an open cavity within a weapon system. The device may also physically-conform to curved surfaces, such as the inner cylindrical wall of an artillery round. The ultracapacitor can then power the round's onboard electronics or initiate a bridgewire detonator, for example. This offers significantly more physical integration options than are available using rigid, commercial off-the-shelf (COTS) batteries and capacitors. Due to its minimal volume and weight, the ultracapacitor will allow for larger munitions payloads and/or greater launch distances. A distinctive feature of the ultracapacitor is its suitability for use in extreme heat and extreme cold environments. Drexel's novel carbon nanomaterials and room temperature ionic liquids (RTILs) are key to achieving this goal.*

The use of additive manufacturing for building the ultracapacitor largely eliminates costly conventional manufacturing processes. Materials printing requires no product-specific tooling that must be stored and maintained (e.g., shadow masks for vacuum deposition). SI2 has considerable experience with the printing of electronic materials (e.g., roll-to-roll inkjet printing of electrically-conductive inks). SI2's materials are printed directly from a computer file in an ambient environment, greatly simplifying product design changes. As such, different printed ultracapacitors can be manufactured on the same production line without equipment modification. This supports the manufacturing of both low-volume Department of Defense (DoD) ultracapacitors (e.g., for munitions and soldier radios) and high-volume commercial ultracapacitors (e.g., for wearable electronics). An overview of flexible, printed ultracapacitor development and results to date will be presented.

Keywords: ultracapacitor; additive manufacturing; materials printing; flexible; nanomaterials; carbon; extreme environments.

Introduction

A broad range of current and emerging Army platforms require low-cost, rugged, flexible energy storage devices, but this need remains unmet by COTS products. Like many batteries, COTS ultracapacitors are rigid, and the end user is warned not to bend an ultracapacitor's leads lest the device's glass seal be broken. Armament systems require flexible, ruggedized energy storage devices that can be bent and inserted into spherical/cylindrical cavities within small rounds. Here, these power sources would take up little space and add negligible weight. A flexible power source could also be integrated into munitions to support single- or multi-point initiation. Bridgewire detonators, in particular, require rapid power dissipation to support bridgewire heating and, in some cases, explosion. Ultracapacitors are ideal for this kind of power delivery.[2] Flexible ultracapacitors could also be integrated with soldiers' uniforms for wearable power (e.g., for soldier-worn friend-or-foe identification systems).[1]

Further, a low-cost, precision manufacturing method is essential for integrating power sources with flexible substrates. Manufacturing approaches described herein will save both space and weight when ultracapacitors are incorporated into munitions, radios, or unmanned systems, for example. To maximize in-service reliability (lifetime) of these power sources, precision patterning of ultracapacitor components is critical to prevent microvoid formation. Microvoids (e.g., in electrodes) can cause electric field concentration, leading to generation of high current impulses and device failure during fast charge/discharge.

The Army's need for power sources to operate across a broad temperature range is also critical. Neither COTS ultracapacitors nor COTS flexible batteries can function at extreme temperatures. These temperatures range from arctic climates to high desert heat, months of hot tarmac storage, or in-flight aero-heating conditions. Current power sources often fail to operate at low temperatures (e.g., due to loss of ion mobility), and may leak and/or discharge their energy prematurely at high temperatures. Hence, there is a need for novel approaches to manufacturing rugged, flexible ultracapacitors that exhibit enhanced, reliable performance.

Flexible Ultracapacitors

To address this need, our team is developing a flexible, all-weather ultracapacitor that operates across a wide temperature range (**Figure 1**). Our innovative ultracapacitor technology uses a flexible polymer package and room temperature ionic liquid electrolytes (RTILs). RTILs are liquid salts that exhibit larger voltage windows and greater electrochemical stability when exposed to extreme temperatures.[1] By extension, ultracapacitors fabricated with specially formulated RTILs are much less temperature-sensitive than currently-available energy storage devices.[1] Further, our roll-to-roll manufacturing approach enables inexpensive ultracapacitor production (i.e., printing of functional inks directly onto flexible packaging). The resulting flexible devices can be bent, folded, and/or rolled into the required shapes. This unique combination of technologies is key to providing low-cost power for a range of current and emerging electronics applications.

During initial studies, it was demonstrated that ultracapacitors with our novel carbon electrodes could operate within a 3V voltage window **(Figures 1-2)**, meeting or exceeding many Army requirements. Replacement of conventional ultracapacitor components with additively-manufactured analogues (e.g., printed ink current collectors) made ultracapacitor fabrication more scalable. Notably, stable 3V operation was achieved even when the printed current collectors were made using silver ink. (Silver normally corrodes in both aqueous electrolytes and ionic liquid electrolytes at $\leq$3V). Ultracapacitors made using these components show performance parity with conventionally-made devices.

These early ultracapacitors were composed of flexible components, but the components were initially sandwiched between rigid PTFE backing plates. Hence, these were effectively still rigid devices. Guided by previous Army research, the next step was to demonstrate fully-flexible ultracapacitors. Here, the rigid PTFE backing plates were replaced with flexible, heat-sealable polymer substrates (**Figure 3**). When our novel carbon electrodes and RTIL electrolytes were combined in a flexible package, a fully-flexible device capacitance of 60-70 mF was achieved. As shown in **Figure 3**, when

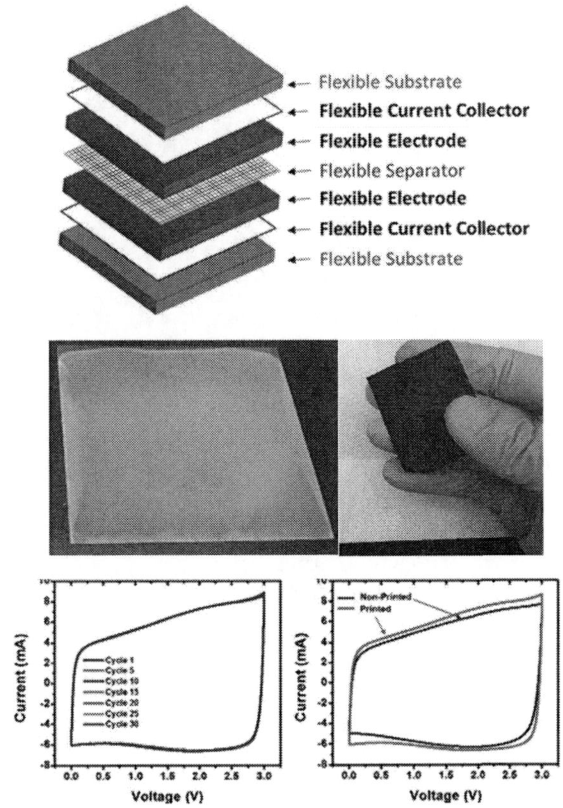

Figure 1. Ultracapacitors using printed components, ionic liquid electrolytes, and novel electrodes exhibit stable operation and performance parity with conventionally-manufactured ultracapacitors.

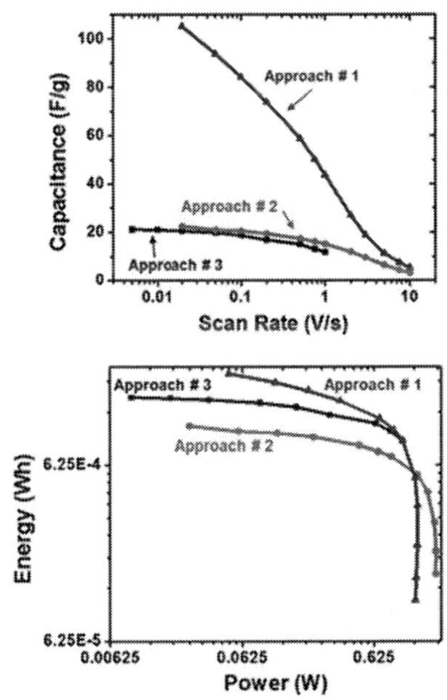

Figure 2. Power and stored energy can be varied based on the ultracapacitor fabrication approach used.

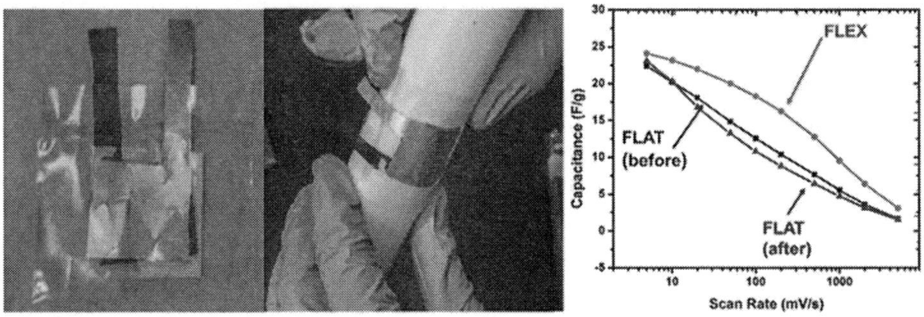

Figure 3. Flexible ultracapacitors exhibit comparable rate behavior whether flat or flexed (bent).

tested in bent ("flexed") configuration, the flexible device performed just as well as (if not better than) when it was tested in flat configuration. With redesign and optimization, our team further demonstrated that devices like this could be rolled up into cylinders less than 0.2" in diameter without compromising device performance (20-25 F/g at 5 mV/s; see **Figure 4**).

Ultracapacitors for Use at Extreme Temperatures

Temperature extremes will have the greatest effect on the behavior of the ultracapacitor electrolytes. Aqueous and organic electrolytes are most susceptible to side reactions occurring within the cell; these reactions lead to electrolyte degradation. With increased temperature, the rate of charge/discharge will increase due to higher ionic mobility. However, at extremely high temperatures, the operating voltage is reduced and electrolyte degradation is more pronounced. Alternatively, at extremely low temperatures, ionic mobility is reduced, and electrolytes can even freeze.

Thanks to RTILs, our ruggedized devices will provide power over a wide temperature range, from extreme cold to extreme heat. The electrolyte ions needed for ultracapacitor operation remain mobile in many climates. (RTIL electrolytes will also support a wide voltage range, i.e., 0-3V). Whereas conventional electrochemical double-layer capacitor electrolytes (e.g., propylene carbonate) are useful over the -25°C to +80°C range, ionic liquid electrolytes support ultracapacitor operation over the -50°C to 100°C range.[3]

Additionally, the relationship between electrode pore size and ionic liquid ion size is extremely important for optimizing capacitive performance.[2] We have previously found that maximum capacitances are obtained when the pore and ion sizes are the same.[4-5] Pore size selection is especially important when choosing a porous carbon electrode material. If the pores are too small, the ions will not go into the pores and capacitance will be very low. On the other hand, if the pores are too big, the entire surface area of the pores will not be utilized since the ion is much smaller than the available space.

To date, we have demonstrated flexible ultracapacitor operation at 0°C. We have also shown that low-temperature storage (followed by room temperature operation) of our flexible ultracapacitors is straightforward. In the latter case, we used a simple Styrofoam box, a thermometer, and dry ice to cool the environment and enclose the device. After a device was cooled to roughly -78°C and then warmed back to room temperature, it could recover and cycle electrochemically.

Low-Cost Additive Manufacturing of Ultracapacitors

As noted earlier, SI2 is using its patterned printing technique to build ultracapacitor components. SI2 has developed Direct Write (also known as Digital Printing) techniques to form electronic circuitry directly from a computer file (e.g. ink jet printing – see **Figure 5**) without any tooling, masks, etc. SI2's Direct Write technologies enable the manufacture of conformal and flexible electronic systems with geometric features ranging from 200-1000+ microns. These Direct Write processes operate in an ambient environment, eliminating the need for costly and slow-to-operate vacuum equipment and conventional plating and etching techniques. SI2 uses two Direct Write processes in-house: micropen dispensing for printing high-viscosity pastes onto flat and curved

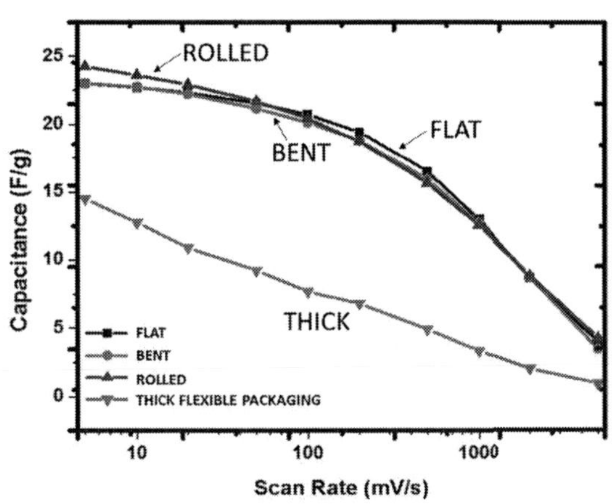

Figure 4. Rolled-up, flexible ultracapacitors perform as well as flat, flexible ultracapacitors, and perform better when the flexible packaging used is thin.

surfaces, and inkjet deposition for printing dilute liquids onto large area flat substrates. These techniques are well-suited to printing current collectors and electrodes onto flexible ultracapacitor packaging.

SI2's commercial grade (vs. consumer) inkjet hardware is capable of printing on up to 44" wide substrates (see **Figure 5**) with roll to roll substrate pay-out/take-up and in-line ink drying. The inkjet software allows for long uninterrupted printed lengths with either a continuous design or a repeating pattern.

Roll-to-roll printing affords high product volumes at low cost. Per-ultracapacitor costs will be kept low by automating the manufacturing process in this way, reducing human labor and the associated likelihood of error. Further, automated printing ensures that only as much device material as is needed is deposited, minimizing waste and keeping costs down.

Looking Ahead

In the next phase of this research, printing will be used more extensively to pattern the carbon-based electrodes for the ultracapacitors. At a minimum, the ultracapacitor current collector may continue to be manufactured using inkjet printing of metallic ink. As mentioned earlier, silver ink is quite common, and was used successfully in flexible ultracapacitor fabrication.

Beyond DoD applications, the flexible ultracapacitors described here can support new commercial harsh-environment electronics, as well. For example, the ultracapacitors can provide power to wireless sensors that monitor the structural health of bridges, buildings, and aerospace vehicles. These ultracapacitors can also help flexible batteries to provide high-power pulses (e.g., for wireless data transmission), prolonging battery life. The novel manufacturing techniques and materials incorporated into our all-weather devices may enable a range of next-generation Army and commercial electronics.

Figure 5. SI2 has roll-to-roll inkjet capabilities for flexible ultracapacitor printing.

Acknowledgements

U.S. Army STTR funding (Contract # W15QKN-15-C-0007) is gratefully acknowledged.

References

1. Jost, K.; Dion, G.; Gogotsi, Y., "Textile energy storage in perspective," *Journal of Materials Chemistry A* **2014,** *2* (28), 10776-10787.

2. Beidaghi, M.; Gogotsi, Y., "Capacitive energy storage in micro-scale devices: recent advances in design and fabrication of micro-supercapacitors," *Energy & Environmental Science* **2014,** *7* (3), 867-884.

3. Tsai, W. Y.; Lin, R. Y.; Murali, S.; Zhang, L. L.; McDonough, J. K.; Ruoff, R. S.; Taberna, P. L.; Gogotsi, Y.; Simon, P., "Outstanding performance of activated graphene based supercapacitors in ionic liquid electrolyte from -50 to 80 degrees C," *Nano Energy* **2013,** *2* (3), 403-411.

4. Simon, P.; Gogotsi, Y., "Materials for electrochemical capacitors," *Nature Materials* **2008,** *7* (11), 845-854.

5. Gogotsi, Y., "Not just graphene: The wonderful world of carbon and related nanomaterials," *MRS Bulletin* **2015,** *40* (12), 1110-1121.

Synergistic Effects of $CsPF_6$ Additive and Propylene Carbonate Content on Enhanced Performances of Graphite Electrode in Lithium-Ion Batteries

Wu Xu,[a] Hongfa Xiang,[a] Jianming Zheng,[a] Donghai Mei,[b] Pengfei Yan,[c] Ruiguo Cao,[a] Sarah D. Burton,[c] Mark H. Engelhard,[c] Mark E. Bowden,[c] Chongmin Wang,[c] Ji-Guang Zhang[a]

[a] Energy and Environment Directorate, [b] Physical and Computational Sciences Directorate, [c] Environmental Molecular Sciences Laboratory, Pacific Northwest National Laboratory (PNNL) Richland, WA 99354, USA

Abstract: *Propylene carbonate (PC) has a wide liquid range and low cost but it is seldom used in lithium-ion batteries because of its continuous co-intercalation into the graphene structure and the eventual graphite exfoliation. Here we report that cesium cation (Cs^+) can direct the formation of a good quality solid electrolyte interphase (SEI) on graphitic anode in PC-rich electrolytes through its passively "preferential" solvation by ethylene carbonate (EC) and the subsequent higher reduction potential off the complex cation. PC-decomposition and graphite-exfoliation are effectively suppressed by adjusting the EC/PC ratio in electrolytes to allow a reductive decomposition of Cs^+-$(EC)_m$ (m=1 or 2) solvates preceding that of Li^+-$(EC)_a(PC)_b$ ($0 \leq a,b \leq 4$ and a+b=3 or 4). PC content in the $CsPF_6$-containing electrolytes has significant effect on the performance of graphite electrode and an optimal PC content of 20% by weight is identified in the EC-PC-EMC (ethyl methyl carbonate) solvent mixtures with 30% EC content. The synergistic effects of Cs^+ additive and appropriate amount of PC enables the formation of a robust, ultrathin and compact SEI layer on the surface of graphite electrode, which is only permeable for de-solvated Li^+ ions and enhances the electrochemical performances of graphite electrode. The fundamental finds also shed light on the importance of manipulating and maintaining the electrode/electrolyte interphasial stability in various energy storage devices.*

Keywords: Cesium cation; Propylene carbonate; Solid electrolyte interphase; Graphite exfoliation; Lithium-ion battery

Introduction

Lithium (Li)-ion batteries (LIBs) have achieved great successes in portable electronic devices since 1991 and have now begun to penetrate applications in hybrid and pure electric vehicles and smart grid. The majority of state-of-the-art LIB systems contain a graphite anode, a nonaqueous $LiPF_6$/organic carbonate electrolyte, and a lithium transition metal oxide or lithium transition metal phosphate cathode. The solvent systems are normally the mixtures of cyclic carbonates such as EC and/or PC and linear carbonates such as dimethyl carbonate (DMC), EMC and diethyl carbonate (DEC). EC has been proven to be an indispensable ingredient that is responsible for forming SEI on graphite electrode surface during the initial charging process. The SEI prevents further intercalation of solvent molecules into graphite structure and the continuous decompositions of electrolyte components, so its quality dictates the performance of graphite as anode in LIBs.

It is well known that a large amount of EC in the electrolytes leads to inferior performance of LIBs at low temperatures because of the high melting point of EC (36.4°C). The replacement of EC with PC in all or part could enhance the low temperature performance or widen the operation temperature window of LIBs since PC has a much lower melting point of −48.8°C. Unfortunately, PC cannot form a stabilized SEI on graphite surface and it also continuously co-intercalates into the graphite with solvated Li^+ ion, leading to exfoliation of graphite and consequent capacity loss. Although some additives can form an SEI on graphite anode in PC-containing electrolytes, thicker SEI layers are resulted that negatively compromise important characteristics such as rate capability, low-temperature performance, and cycling stability at elevated temperatures.

In this work, we first systematically investigated the role of cesium cation (Cs^+) in the SEI formation mechanism effects in conventional $LiPF_6$/carbonate electrolytes with PC, then investigated the effect of PC content in this electrolyte system on the performances of graphite electrode in both Li||graphite half cells and graphite||$LiNi_{0.80}Co_{0.15}Al_{0.05}O_2$ (i.e., NCA) full cells. Details of the investigations are reported and discussed below.

Experimental

Materials: $LiPF_6$, LiTFSI, EC, PC and EMC of battery grade were purchased from BASF and used as received. Fluoroethylene carbonate (FEC) was bought from Solvay Chemicals. $CsPF_6$ (≥99.0%) was ordered from SynQuest Laboratories and dried at 65°C for 4 days under vacuum before use. Coated graphite (MAG-10, 1.53 mAh cm^{-2}) and NCA (1.50 mAh cm^{-2}) electrodes were provided by the CAMP Facility at ANL, and dried prior to use. High-purity Li chips (15.6 mm in diameter and 0.45 mm in thickness) were procured from MTI Corporation. The electrolyte solutions were prepared in an argon-filled glovebox in which both moisture and oxygen contents were controlled below 5 ppm.

Electrochemical tests and cell cycling performance. Electrochemical performances of Li||graphite half cells and graphite||NCA full cells with different electrolytes were evaluated in coin cells in 0.005 ~ 1.2 V and 2.5 ~ 4.3 V vs. Li/Li^+, respectively. Galvanostatic charge-discharge tests were performed on Arbin BT-2000 battery testers. A 1C rate corresponds to a current density of 1.5 mA cm^{-2} in the present work. Unless specified otherwise, the cells were subjected to two formation cycles at a C/20 rate at room temperature (RT), followed by cycling at different current densities under different temperatures.

Characterization. Surface morphologies of cycled graphite electrodes were measured by scanning electron microscopy (SEM), high resolution transmission electron microscopy (HRTEM), X-ray photoelectron spectroscopy (XPS) and optical microscope. The solvation properties were analyzed by ^{17}O nuclear magnetic resonance (NMR) and electrospray ionization mass spectrometry (ESI-MS).

Computational calculations. Density functional theory calculations were performed to calculate the Gibbs free energies of solvates to determine the Li^+ and Cs^+.

Results and Discussion

Effect of Cs^+ on electrochemical behavior of Li||graphite half cells: To evaluate how Cs^+ affects the electrochemical behavior of graphite in PC-rich electrolytes, electrolytes of 1.0 M $LiPF_6$ in EC-PC-EMC (5:2:3 by wt.) with and without 0.05 M $CsPF_6$ (denoted as E1Cs and E1, respectively) were tested in Li||graphite half cells, along with the electrolyte of FEC additive in E1 at 2 wt.% (or 0.25 M) (E1FEC) and the state-of-the-art electrolyte in absence of PC (1.0 M $LiPF_6$ in EC-EMC 3:7 by vol., E2). It is seen from Figure 1A that E1 shows a long plateau between 0.7 V and 0.5 V indicating extensive PC reduction and subsequent graphite exfoliation. This plateau is greatly suppressed when 2% FEC is added, but it does not disappear completely. However, the addition of 0.05 M $CsPF_6$ completely inhibits this parasitic process. The Cs^+-additive also significantly increases the first cycle Coulombic efficiency (84% for E1Cs, 67% for E1FEC, and 30% for E1), which is comparable to the 88% for E2. The above results demonstrate that 0.05 M $CsPF_6$ functions much more effectively in suppressing PC interfacial reactions than 2% FEC.

The irreversible reductions of the electrolytes on graphite surface can be distinguished from the differential capacity plots shown in Figure 1B and 1C. The conspicuous cathodic peak at ~0.5 V in E1 or E1FEC is attributed to the PC-reduction process at the graphite. It disappears when Cs^+ is present. When carefully examining the cathodic curves between 1.1 and 0.7 V, a small reductive peak at 0.75 V for all three electrolytes can be ascribed to the electrochemical reduction of EC molecules in Li^+-$(EC)_m$ solvates, which contributes part of the formed SEI. A third cathodic peak at a higher potential (~0.95 V) in E1FEC should correspond to the reduction of FEC, which greatly suppresses the reductive decomposition of EC at 0.75 V. It is also indicated from Figure 1B and 1C that the Cs^+-additive slightly increases the peak area or the irreversible capacity corresponding to the peak at 0.75 V for E1 decomposition in the reduction process.

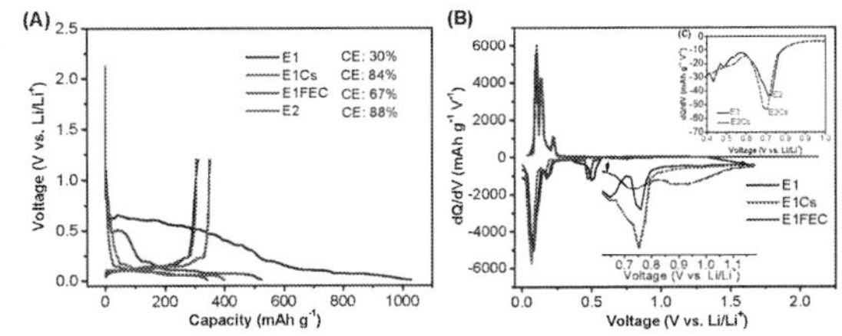

Figure 1. Electrochemical behavior of various $LiPF_6$-based electrolytes in Li||graphite half cells. (A) Lithiation/de-lithiation profiles of E1, E1Cs, E1FEC and conventional E2. (B) Comparisons of differential capacity (dQ/dV) plots of E1, E1Cs and E1FEC as well as E2 and E2Cs for the 0.75 V peak (insert). (Copied from ref. [1])

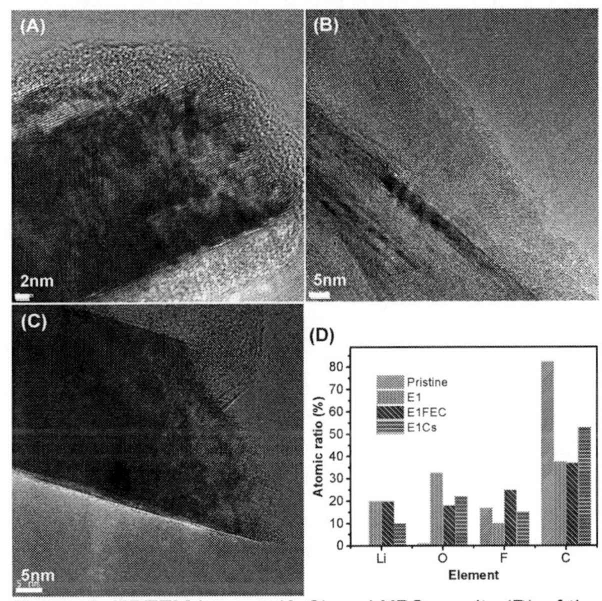

Figure 2. HRTEM images (A-C) and XPS results (D) of the graphite electrodes from Li||graphite half cells after discharged to 0.3 V in the first discharge process from (A) E1, (B) E1FEC and (C) E1Cs. (Copied from ref. [1])

Characterization of SEI layers on graphite anodes: Graphite electrodes recovered from Li||graphite cells initially discharged to 0.3 V vs. Li/Li^+ were analyzed by using various ex-situ techniques. At the chosen voltage, the SEI should have been generated but without Li^+ intercalation into the graphite. The HETEM image in Figure 2A shows that the graphite particle in E1 is covered by a thick (>6 nm) SEI only after the initial discharging process without lithiation, which should be resulted from the extensive reductive decompositions of electrolyte components and specifically PC solvent. When FEC is present, a thinner (2~4 nm) but uneven SEI film is formed on the graphite surface (Figure 2B). An ultrathin (<2 nm) and uniform SEI layer is found on the graphite surface from E1Cs (Figure 2C), indicating that Cs^+ additive significantly suppresses the SEI formation and growth.

The XPS results (Figure 2D) show that the SEI from E1Cs has higher C content and lower Li content than those formed in E1 and E1FEC, suggesting that the SEI layer formed in E1Cs consists of more organic species than inorganic species.

Solvation in Cs^+-containing electrolytes and Cs^+-induced SEI mechanism: ^{17}O NMR and ESI-MS are widely used to determine the solvation conditions in electrolytes. As shown in the ^{17}O NMR plots (Figure 3A), Cs^+ causes much less displacement in the C=O chemical shift ($\Delta\delta$ = 1.1 ppm) than Li^+ does ($\Delta\delta$ = 11.6 ppm), indicating that Cs^+ is a much weaker Lewis acid than Li^+; therefore, Cs^+ should have less coordination with cyclic carbonate solvent molecules and its solvation number should be less than Li^+. This is accordance with literature reports that the coordination number for Li^+ in nonaqueous solvents is normally ~4 [2] and for Cs^+ is <2 [3].

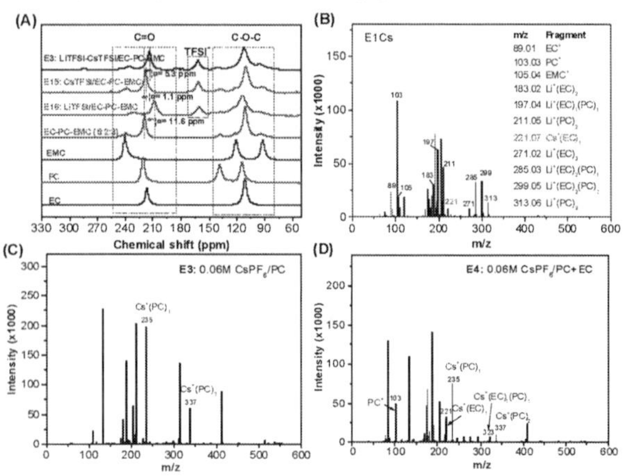

Figure 3. (A) ^{17}O NMR spectra of various solvents and electrolytes. (B) ESI-MS results of electrolyte E1Cs. (Copied from ref. [1])

ESI-MS analysis on E1Cs (Figure 3B) shows a strong peak at *m/z* of 221 for Cs^+-$(EC)_1$, but it does not show the signals for Cs^+-$(PC)_1$ (m/z 235) and Cs^+-$(PC)_2$ (*m/z* 337). The latter two solvates have been detected in E3 (0.06 M $CsPF_6$ in PC) without EC in the electrolyte (Figure 3C). To clarify whether Cs^+ prefers EC over PC, the electrolyte of 0.06 M $CsPF_6$ in EC-PC (E4) was made to be Li^+-free with sufficient populations of both PC and EC. The result demonstrates that Cs^+ prefers PC over EC (Figure 3D) just like Li^+ reported by Xu and coworkers [4]. In E1Cs, the Li^+:Cs^+:EC:PC:EMC molar ratio is 1:0.05:6.49:2.24:3.30 and the PC population is not sufficient to solvate Li^+, thus the absence of Cs^+-$(PC)_n$ (n=1,2) in E1Cs is clearly the result of Li^+ competition. In other words, in such PC-rich electrolytes, Li^+ acts like a PC-scavenger, while Cs^+, losing the competition for PC molecules, would be passively solvated by EC molecules.

The energies of the lowest unoccupied molecular orbitals (E_{LUMO}) for solvates Cs^+-$(EC)_m$ (m=1,2) and Li^+-$(EC)_a(PC)_b$, where 0≤a,b≤4 and a+b=3 or 4 were calculated. The two Cs^+-$(EC)_m$ solvates have E_{LUMO} in the values of −4.3 ~ −3.5 eV, much lower than any PC-containing Li^+-solvates (−2.6 ~ −2.0 eV). The lower LUMO energy of a molecule suggests a higher reductive potential. Thus the results indicate that the two Cs^+-$(EC)_m$ solvates would serve as the preferential interphasial precursor and experience the electrochemical reduction at the graphite surface prior to any Li^+-$(EC)_a(PC)_b$ solvates do, leading to an SEI that bears heavy chemical signature from EC solvent in Cs^+-$(EC)_m$ solvates, which is schematically depicted in Figure 4.

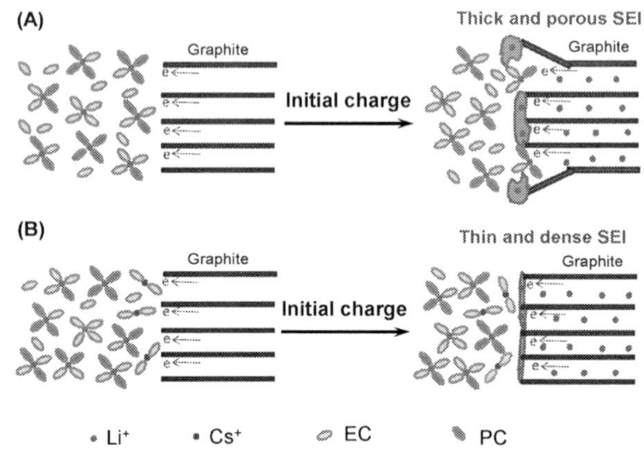

Figure 4. Schematic mechanism of SEI film formation promoted by Cs^+. (A) In a conventional electrolyte, Li^+ favors PC to form solvates. (B) In a Cs^+-containing electrolyte, due to the preferential formation of Li^+-$(PC)_n$ solvates, Cs^+ coordinates with EC molecules and its solvates have priority to be electrochemically reduced. (Copied from ref. [1])

As shown in Figure 5, the graphite||NCA full cells with E1 only deliver a low capacity <50 mAh g^{-1} after the formation cycles (Figure 5A), owing to the extensive PC reduction and graphite exfoliation. The addition of $CsPF_6$ or FEC successfully suppressed PC reduction (Figure 1). The $CsPF_6$ additive leads to better performances than FEC because of its thinner, uniform and more conductive SEI film on graphite anode (Figure 2C). Even after 100 cycles at 60°C, the SEI on graphite anode from E1Cs is still uniform with a thickness of ~1.5 nm (not shown here), indicating almost a constant interphasial morphology for E1Cs electrolyte. The Cs^+-effect on interphase could be extended to other electrolyte formulations. Figure 5D shows that another electrolyte E5Cs with 0.04 M $CsPF_6$ in 1 M $LiPF_6$/EC-PC-EMC (2:1:7 by wt.) can significantly improve the low-temperature discharge at −30°C and −40°C when compared with the state-of-the-art electrolyte E2. The high capacity retention at such low temperatures apparently benefited from the ultrathin SEI layer and its low impedance (not shown here).

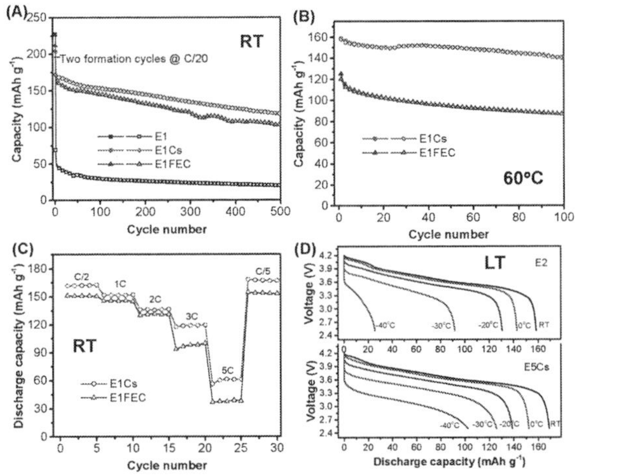

Figure 5. Cell performances of graphite||NCA full cells between 2.5 and 4.3 V after 2 formation cycles. (A, B) Cycling at RT (A) and 60°C (B) at C/3 charge and 1C discharge. (C) Rate capability at C/5 charge and then discharge at various C-rates. (D) Low temperature discharge performance at C/5 rate. (Copied from ref. [1])

Effect of PC contents: The effect of PC content in the 1.0 M $LiPF_6$/EC-PC-EMC electrolytes with 0.05 M $CsPF_6$ on the performances of graphite electrode was evaluated in half cells and full cells (Figure 6). The EC content in the EC-PC-EMC mixtures was fixed as 30% by weight. Apparently, the Cs^+ additive cannot completely suppress the PC intercalation during the initial formation cycle when 30% PC is in the solvent mixture (E30PC-Cs). When PC is in 10 and 20% (E10PC-Cs and E20PC-Cs), Cs^+ additive totally suppress the PC intercalation and the graphite electrode shows voltage profiles resembling to those in the control electrolytes (E0PC-Cs and E-control). However, E20PC-Cs shows the best long-term cycling stability in graphite||NCA full cells, indicating the optimal PC content is 20% by weight in the solvent mixtures.

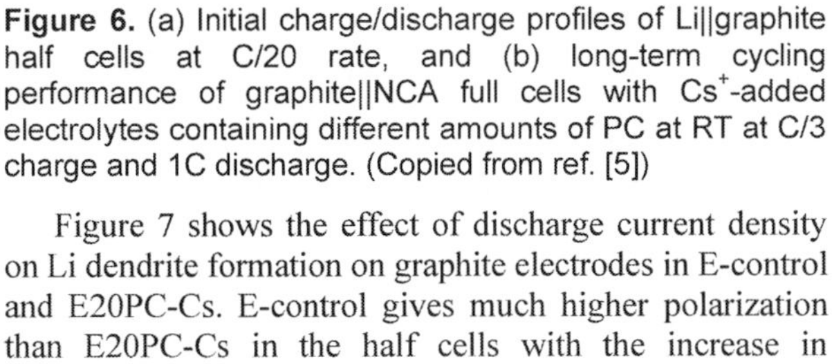

Figure 6. (a) Initial charge/discharge profiles of Li||graphite half cells at C/20 rate, and (b) long-term cycling performance of graphite||NCA full cells with Cs^+-added electrolytes containing different amounts of PC at RT at C/3 charge and 1C discharge. (Copied from ref. [5])

Figure 7 shows the effect of discharge current density on Li dendrite formation on graphite electrodes in E-control and E20PC-Cs. E-control gives much higher polarization than E20PC-Cs in the half cells with the increase in discharge current density. E-control leads to form some Li dendrites on graphite electrode at a current density of 0.5 mA cm^{-2} (Figure 7d) and more Li dendrites at higher current densities of 1.0 and 2.0 mA cm^{-2} (Figure 7e, f). In comparison, E20PC-Cs results in much less Li dendrite formation on the graphite electrode surface (Figure 7g-j).

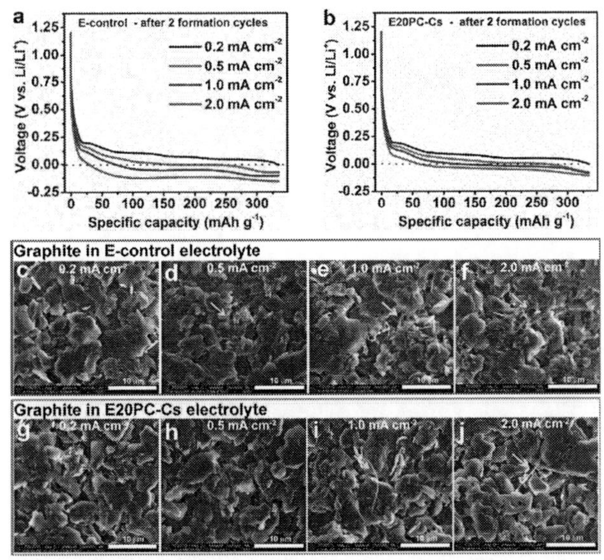

Figure 7. Lithiation voltage profiles of graphite electrodes in Li||graphite half cells with (a) E-control and (b) E20PC-Cs at different discharge current densities ranging from 0.2 to 2 mA cm^{-2}. (c-j) SEM images of graphite electrodes in E-control (c-f) and E20PC-Cs (g-j) at (c, g) 0.2 mA cm^{-2}; (d, h) 0.5 mA cm^{-2}; (e, i) 1.0 mA cm^{-2}; and (f, j) 2.0 mA cm^{-2}. (Copied from ref. [5])

Acknowledgements

This work was supported by the Assistant Secretary for Energy Efficiency and Renewable Energy, Office of Vehicle Technology, Advanced Battery Materials Research Programs of U.S. Department of Energy (DOE). The microscopy and spectroscopy measurements were performed in the Environmental Molecular Sciences Laboratory, a national scientific user facility sponsored by DOE's Office of Biological and Environmental Research and located at PNNL. The authors thank Drs. K. Xu and A. Cresce of U.S. ARL for conducting ESI-MS tests and Mr. Bryant Polzin of ANL for supplying coated NCA and graphite electrodes.

References

1. H. Xiang, et al., *ACS Appl. Mater. Interfaces*, 2015, **7**, 20687.
2. E. Cazzanelli, et al., *J. Chem. Phys.*, 1997, **107**, 5740.
3. H. Ohtaki, *Pure Appl. Chem.*, 1987, **59**, 1143.
4. A. von Wald Cresce, O. Borodin, K. Xu, *J. Phys. Chem. C*, 2012, **116**, 26111.
5. J. Zheng, et al., *ACS Appl. Mater. Interfaces*, 2016, **8**, 5715.

Paper 24.2

Pages 376-379

WITHDRAWN

Functional Ionic Liquid based Electrolytes

Surya Moganty
surya@nohms.com

Abstract

NOHMs Technologies is developing functional ionic liquid based hybrid electrolytes for high energy density, high voltage, and high power batteries for EV and military applications. The composition of electrolytes greatly affects the cell performance from rate capability, lithium cycling efficiency, and capacity retention at various temperatures to tolerance against electrical, mechanical and thermal abuses. Ionic liquids offer a host of attractive properties, including ultralow vapor pressure, high thermal stability, high ionic conductivity and wide electrochemical stability, which make them attractive as electrolytes. However, there are some physical property limitations that to-date has made them unattractive for lithium battery applications. High viscosity and the fraction of the ionic conductivity of the electrolyte arising from mobile lithium ions (i.e. the so-called lithium transference numbers) are typically low for these materials, which make cells assembled using ionic liquid electrolytes prone to large polarization during operation of the cell. These limitations can be easily overcome by blending ionic liquids with appropriate co-solvents. These hybrid electrolytes simultaneously overcome the poor thermal & electrochemical stability and safety problems that have plagued lithium battery electrolytes for years while still maintaining high conductivity. They provide a platform for engineering electrolytes with both chemical and interfacial tunability that beyond improving safety, expand the range of available battery form factors. During the presentation, we will show how the ionic liquid functionality affects the SEI formation on the graphite anode and high voltage stability. We intend to answer the following questions: 1) functional ionic liquid and co-solvent formulations to achieve a >4.5V electrolyte, 2) is the capacity fade dependent on the upper voltage cut-off, and 3) how the electrolyte formulations improve the capacity retention of at high voltages and elevated temperatures using 200 mAh pouch cells.

Solvation of the Sodium Ion in Carbonate Electrolytes

Arthur Cresce, Joshua Allen, Selena Russell
US Army Research Laboratory

Mallory Gobet, Jing Peng, Steven Greenbaum
Hunter College, City University of New York

Reginald Rogers
Rochester Institute of Technology

Kang Xu
US Army Research Laboratory

arthur.v.cresce.civ@mail.mil

Abstract

In lithium ion batteries, there is good evidence for a link between the competitive solvation condition of the lithium ion and the ability of solvents to form an effective solid electrolyte interphase on electrode surfaces, especially the surface of the graphite anode. In the typical lithium ion electrolyte, ethylene carbonate is paired with another solvent of lower donicity and lower melting point. Near the electrode, it can be demonstrated that the preference of Li+ for ethylene carbonate results in an interphase layer composed significantly of ethylene carbonate reduction products. In sodium ion batteries, similar solvents can be used to shuttle Na+ between electrodes; ethylene carbonate is still a common component of electrolytes used to examine sodium ion electrodes and cell performance. So far, however, the solvation preferences of Na+ have not been characterized and exploited in sodium ion battery research. This work will describe the solvent preferences of Na+ in ethylene carbonate-based electrolytes, and how this preference affects the performance of sodium ion batteries using a hard carbon anode. Various types of solvation characterization will be discussed, and a more complete picture of Na+ as a battery chemistry will be developed.

Thermal Characterization of Molten Salt Battery Materials

Stephen L. Hodson[1,2], Edward S. Piekos[1], Robert A. Sayer[1], Scott A. Roberts[1], Christine C. Roberts[1]

[1]Engineering Sciences Department
Sandia National Laboratory
PO Box 5800, Albuquerque, New Mexico, 87185

[2]Purdue University
School of Mechanical Engineering
610 Purdue Mall, West Lafayette, IN 47907

Abstract: *Molten salt batteries are particularly useful power sources for radar and guidance systems in military applications such as guided missiles, ordinance, and other weapons. Molten salt batteries are activated by raising the temperature of the electrolyte above its melting temperature using pyrotechnic heat pellets. The battery will remain active as long as the electrolyte is molten. As a result, the thermal processes within the components and interactions between them are critical to the overall performance of molten salt batteries. A molten salt battery is typically thermally insulated using wrappable and board-like insulation materials such as Fiberfrax wrap, Fiberfrax board, and Min-K insulation. The Fiberfrax board and Min-K insulation are composites of alumino-silicate and fumed silica-titania, respectively. In this work, the thermal conductivities of the Fiberfrax board and Min-K insulation are measured under different uniaxial compressive states and ambient environments. The thermal conductivity of the mixed separator pellets (LiCl/MgO/KCl) was also measured along with its contact resistances with interfacing members. To measure the thermal quantities, a steady-state reference bar with thermocouples was employed. The resulting values serve as inputs to a thermal model that aims to predict lifetimes of the batteries. Improvements to a thermal model for an example battery due to the revised thermal property values are discussed.*

Keywords: Thermal batteries; thermal conductivity; separator; Min-K; Fiberfrax; insulation; 1D reference-bar

Introduction

The overall performance of molten salt batteries is dictated by complex multiphysics consisting of electrochemical processes, mechanical responses, and thermal transport mechanisms. The molten electrolyte and separator [LiCl/KCl, MgO] serve as the battery's hub by providing an ionically conductive path between the anode [Li(Si)] and cathode [$CaCrO_4$ or FeS_2]. Depending on the application, the desired lifetimes can vary between a few seconds and one hour [1], which is partially dictated by the cooling rate of the molten electrolyte. To mitigate cooling, molten salt batteries are packaged with insulation materials such as Fiberfrax board and Min-K thermal insulation. The latter is often employed in molten salt batteries that require long lifetimes [2]. These insulations are included at the top and bottom of the battery stack and are compressed under force before the battery can is sealed. Other Fiberfrax insulation is wrapped around the stack under tension.

Predictive models for molten salt battery activation can be improved with high fidelity measurements of thermal properties such as heat capacity and thermal conductivity. Specifically, non-molten separator thermal conductivity is necessary for predicting rise time whereas insulation thermal conductivity has been found to be a great source of uncertainty in predicting the lifetime of the battery [2]. Currently, the insulation thermal conductivity is not implemented as a function of strain in the Sandia multiphysics model for battery activation (TABS v 3.0).

Various techniques, either steady state or transient, can be employed to measure thermal conductivities of materials and each has advantages and disadvantages. Transient techniques such as laser flash, thermoreflectance, and photoacoustic provide quick determination of thermal conductivities relative to steady state techniques, but generally require prior knowledge of the density and heat capacity of the material. Steady state techniques such as reference bar and infrared thermography do not require knowledge of the density and heat capacity, but are not suitable for rapid characterization of large quantities of samples. In this work, a steady state technique [4] was used to measure the thermal conductivities of the separator pellets as well as annealed Fiberfrax board and Min-K insulation materials in different ambient environments and compressive stresses which are congruent with common molten salt battery packaging protocols.

Experimental Setup

The separator material was formed by mixing, melting, and grinding LiCl/KCl electrolyte salt with MgO to form a powder. The mixture was then hydraulically pressed to form LiCl/MgO/KCl pellets of varying thicknesses. Pellets were all 1.75 g/cm^3 in density.

The Fiberfrax board and Min-K insulation materials were purchased in a variety of thicknesses from Unifrax and Morgan Thermal Ceramics, respectively. The insulation materials were then annealed in dry air at 600°C for 4 hours to remove moisture and stored in a dry environment until tested. SEM images showing the cross-section of the insulation materials are shown below in Figures 1(a) and (b).

The steady state reference bar technique is based on the ASTM D470-06 standard for measuring thermal conductivity and contact resistance and is used to measure the thermal conductivity of the different materials as well as the contact resistance with stainless steel 304 (SS304)

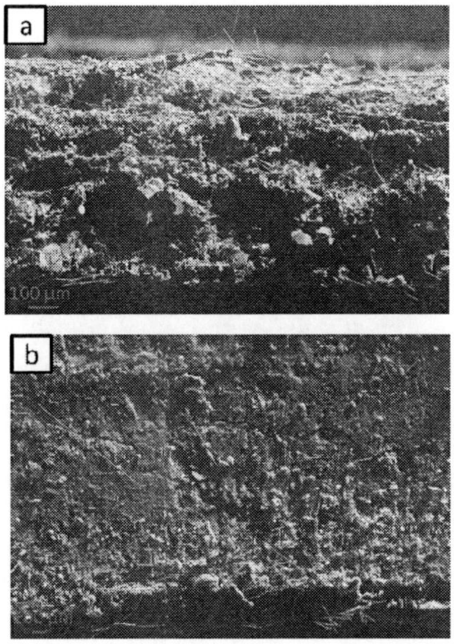

Figure 1. Cross-sectional SEM images of (a) annealed Fiberfrax board and (b) annealed Min-K.

and Macor heat flux meters. The system, shown in Figure 2 uses thermocouples to measure the temperature gradient in the heat flux meters while a mechanical translator compresses the interface to a load which is measured by a load cell. The mechanical translators are terminated with flat plates which are also cooled and heated to constant temperatures. The system has the capability to measure thermal properties in Ar, He, N_2, air, and vacuum, which can simulate the hermitically sealed environment of the battery and gases released during chemical reactions. Note that thermal conductivity values measured by this technique are solely in the cross-plane direction.

When compressed to a constant strain, Fiberfrax and Min-K insulations are known to undergo stress relaxation for extended periods of time. Therefore, both load and strain were measured simultaneously during measurements. Strain was recorded using a camera image of the sample.

The thermal model that accompanies the measurement technique is based on the one dimensional heat conduction equation and depending on the ambient environment (vacuum or gas), includes radiative and convective losses to the surroundings. The temperature throughout the stack is determined by solving Eq. 1 below:

$$\frac{d}{dx}\left(k_{HFM}\frac{dT}{dx}\right)-\varepsilon\sigma\left(T^4-T_{surr}^4\right)-h\left(T-T_\infty\right)=0 \qquad \text{Eq. 1}$$

where T is the temperature in the stack along the direction x, k_{HFM} is the thermal conductivity of the heat flux meter, ε is the emissivity of the heat flux meter, σ is the Stefan-Boltzmann constant, T_{surr} is the temperature of the surroundings that exchange thermal radiation with the heat flux meters, h is the convective heat transfer coefficient and T_∞ is the average temperature of the ambient gas. The total thermal resistance between the top and bottom heat flux meters is determined by fitting Eq. 1 to the temperature profiles in the heat flux meters using COMSOL. For the separator pellets, SS304 heat flux meters were chosen while Macor heat flux meters were chosen for the insulation materials. Note that the thermal conductivity of the Macor heat flux meters was determined by testing the material against SS304 bars of known thermal conductivity. The temperature profile and the thermal conductivity of the heat flux meters are used to determine the heat flux, temperature drop, and ultimately the thermal resistance across the interface. In Eq. 2 below, the total thermal resistance between the heat flux meters (R_{total}) comprises of two contact resistances (R_{TCR}) that are in series with the bulk (intrinsic) resistance (R_{bulk}) of the material of interest:

$$R_{total}=R_{bulk}+R_{TCR}=\frac{t}{k}+R_{TCR} \qquad \text{Eq. 2}$$

where t and k are the thickness and thermal conductivity of the material of interest, respectively. The thermal conductivity can be determined by measuring the total thermal resistance between the heat flux meters for different thicknesses of the material of interest. This produces a linear relationship between thermal resistance and material thickness in which the inverse slope of the linear relationship is the thermal conductivity and the y-intercept is the contact resistance. The uncertainties associated with this measurement technique include thermocouple error, uncertainty in estimating the thickness, regression uncertainty, and sample to sample uncertainty.

Results and Discussion

Thermal conductivity measurements on the separator pellets (LiCl/MgO/KCl) were conducted within the pressure range of 400 and 2250 kPa and an average interface temperature (material temperature) of approximately 45°C. Due to the fact that the molten salt battery materials are moisture sensitive, the system was purged with dry air (5-10% humidity) during thermal testing. Tests were conducted on mixtures of three distinct thicknesses of 0.5, 1, and 2 mm. The thermal conductivity of the mixture and contact resistance with the heat flux meters were estimated by a linear fit to the measured thermal resistance and mixture thicknesses for interface pressures of 400, 1700, and 2250 kPa.

The variation in the measured thermal resistance for samples of the same thickness is greatest at lower interface pressures and smallest at the highest interface pressure. This indicates that the sample to sample uncertainty decreases with increasing pressure and that the misalignment between the separator pellet and heat flux meters is mitigated as the pressure increases. The thermal conductivity and contact resistance as functions of interface pressure are shown below in Figure 3(a) and (b), respectively. The error bars include the sample to sample, linear fit, and thermocouple uncertainty.

The thermal conductivity of the separator pellets remains constant with interface pressure with a mean value of 2.30 W/mK with a lower and upper bound of 2.08 and 2.49 W/mK, respectively, at an interface pressure of 2250 kPa. As expected, the contact resistance of the separator pellets with the heat flux meters monotonically decreases with interface. Therefore, the separator pellets are not being affected by the compressive stress that is applied during the measurement, except that the contact with the instrument bars improves.

Thermal conductivity measurements on the Min-K and Fiberfrax board insulation materials were conducted at compressive stresses of 350 and 500 psi with an average material temperature of approximately 55°C. To assess the thermal transport mechanisms across the insulation materials, the samples were tested in both air and vacuum ambient environments. The test sequence was as follows: (i) air at 350 psi, (ii) vacuum at 350 psi, (iii) vacuum at 500 psi, and (iv) air at 500 psi. Figures 4(a)-(d) below shows the linear fits to the measured thermal resistances in air and insulation thicknesses for the aforementioned test sequence. Vacuum data was also obtained but is not shown. The error bars include errors due to thermocouple readings and estimation in material thickness. With coefficients of determination ranging between 0.86 and 0.99 for the experimental data presented in Figure 4, a linear fit properly describes the change in thermal resistance with material thickness. As such, the thermal conductivity of each material can be determined by the inverse slope of the linear fit. The thermal conductivity values for both insulation materials are summarized in Table 1 below and are in good agreement with the work of Guidotti et al. [2]. Note that the contact resistances between the insulation and Macor heat flux meters are not shown because the intrinsic (bulk) resistance of the insulations dominates thermal transport.

The changes in thermal conductivity with respect to the ambient environment and compression are consistent between the Min-K and Fiberfrax board insulations. When the test chamber is evacuated, the thermal conductivities decrease by 25% and 43%, respectively. Upon compression to 500 psi in vacuum, the thermal conductivities increase by 19% and 16%, respectively. When air is subsequently introduced into the test chamber to atmospheric pressure, the thermal conductivities increase by 50% and 78%. Comparing the thermal conductivities in air at 350 and 500 psi shows that compression of the insulations in air results in an increase in thermal conductivity of 25% and 19%, respectively.

The changes in thermal conductivity of the insulation materials suggest that the ambient environment and compressive stress serve significant roles in thermal transport throughout the insulation materials. Depending

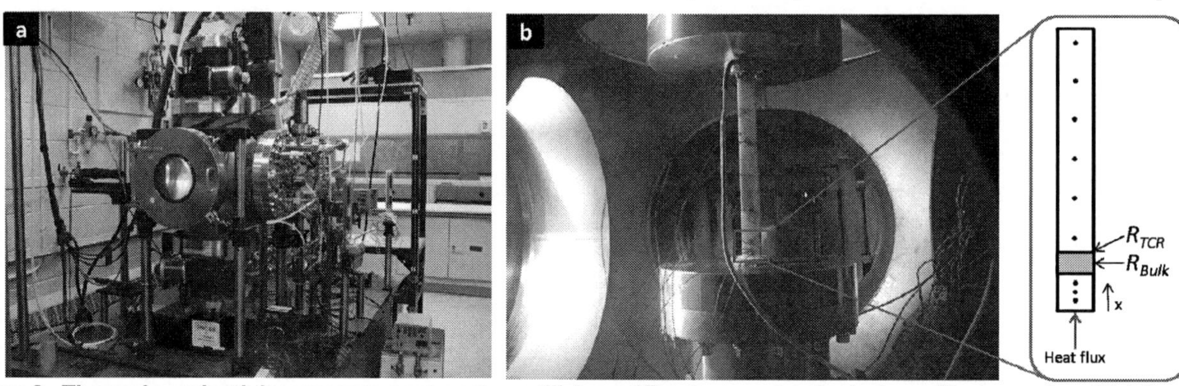

Figure 2. Thermal conductivity measurement system utilizing a 1D reference bar technique. Photographs of (a) the vacuum chamber and (b) the heat flux meters (HFMs) instrumented with thermocouples.

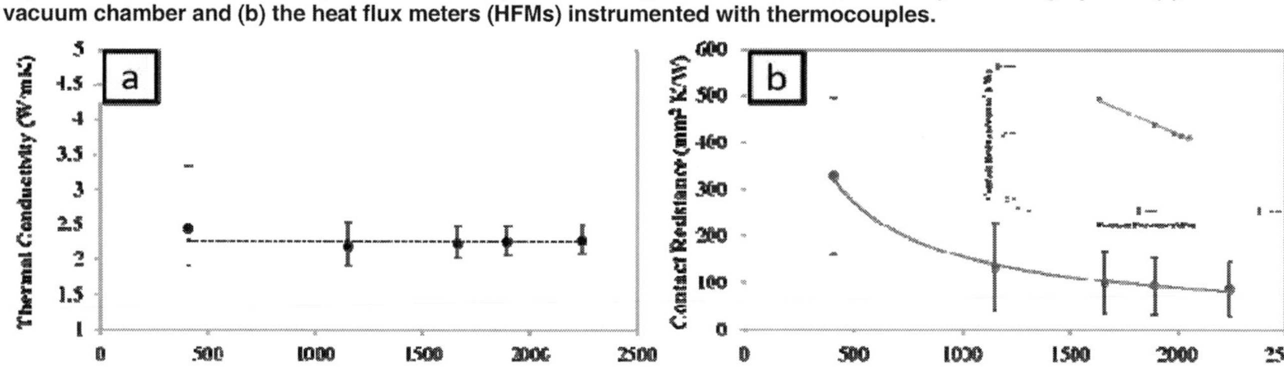

Figure 3. (a) Separator thermal conductivity and (b) Separator-heat flux meter contact resistance as a function of contact pressure. Inset: Contact resistance vs. pressure on a log-log scale

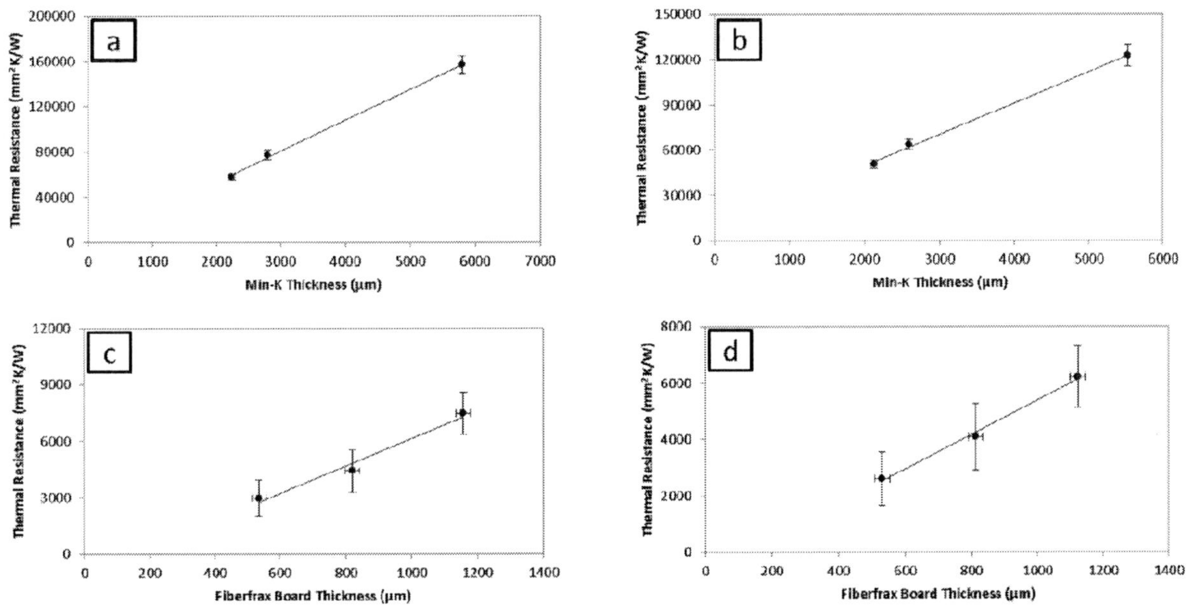

Figure 4. Thermal resistance in air as a function of insulation thickness for (a) Min-K at 350 psi, (b) Min-K at 500 psi (c) Fiberfrax board at 350 psi and (d) Fiberfrax board at 500 psi.

on the porosity of the insulation materials, thermal transport through the air medium can serve as a parallel pathway for heat transfer. In this sense, the thermal conductivity of the insulation materials is an effective thermal conductivity that comprises of thermal transport through the alumino-silicate (Fiberfrax board) or fumed silica-titania (Min-K) as well as the air medium. In the absence of the latter, thermal transport is relegated only through the solid medium. The granular and fibrous microstructure as observed in the cross-sectional SEM images in Figures 1 suggest that upon compression, the insulation materials densify and larger microscopic contact regions between the constituent particles of the insulation materials are formed, which ultimately increases the thermal conductivity.

Table 1. Thermal conductivity (W/mK) of Fiberfrax board and Min-K insulations under different conditions

k (W/mK)	**Min-K**		**Fiberfrax**	
Compressive stress (psi)	Air	Vacuum	Air	Vacuum
350	0.036	0.027	0.138	0.079
500	0.048	0.032	0.164	0.092

Conclusions

A steady state reference bar technique was employed to measure the thermal conductivities of the separator pellets (LiCl/MgO/KCl) and thermally insulating materials (Fiberfrax board and Min-K). The separator thermal conductivity was measured to be approximately 2.30 W/mK and constant within the pressure range of 400 and 2250 kPa. The effective thermal conductivity of the Fiberfrax board and Min-K insulation materials were measured to be on the order of O(0.1) W/mK and O(0.01) W/mK, respectively, at 350 and 500 psi. The thermal conductivities exhibited dependence on both the ambient environment and compressive stress.

Acknowledgements

Sandia National Laboratories is a multi-program laboratory managed and operated by Sandia Corporation, a wholly owned subsidiary of Lockheed Martin Corporation, for the U.S. Department of Energy's National Nuclear Security Administration under contract DE-AC04-94AL85000.

References

1. R. A. Guidotti, F. W. Reinhardt, and T. Kaun. “Characterization of Small Vac. Multifoil Containers for a One-Hour Thermal Batt.,” *Proceedings of the 40th Power Sources Conference*, pp. 299, 2002.
2. Trembacki, B. L. et al. “Uncertainty Quantification, Verification, and Validation of a Thermal Simulation Tool for Molten Salt Batteries”, *Proceedings of the 47th Power Sources Conference*, 2016.
3. R. A. Guidotti and M. Moss. “Thermal Conductivity of Thermal-Batt. Insulations,” Technical Report SAND 95-1649, Sandia National Laboratories, August 1995.
4. “Standard Test Meth. for Thermal Trans. Prop. of Thermally Conductive Elect. Insulation Mat.,” Annu. B. ASTM Stand., pp. D5470–06, 2011.

Evaluation of Aerogel Insulation for Thermal Batteries

Joe Edington and Alex Cotton
EaglePicher Technologies, LLC
1215 West C Street
Joplin, MO 64801

Abstract
EaglePicher Technologies has modeled and built test batteries to evaluate the advantages of aerogel insulation in thermal battery applications. Thermal property information was used to predict the performance of flexible aerogel blanket insulation for two different battery designs using AllBatt modeling software. The model predictions indicated that aerogel blanket insulation would produce a substantial improvement over traditional thermal battery wrap insulation. Based on these findings, test batteries were built to verify the predicted performance improvement. Batteries were also tested through operating and non-operating environments to verify that the aerogel insulation would survive real world battery applications. This paper presents the findings of this study.

Keywords: Thermal batteries; aerogel insulation.

Introduction
Thermal battery performance is largely dependent on heat management. The battery must maintain a sufficient temperature to keep the molten salt electrolyte hot enough to provide low impedance to ionic movement throughout the performance life of the battery. Practically speaking, all of the heat in a thermal battery is released within the first few seconds following activation of the pyrotechnic heat sources. Afterward, thermal insulation in the battery provides the only means of managing the internal temperature of the battery.

Thermal insulation in thermal batteries typically consists of semi-rigid insulating discs located at either end of the battery stack and flexible insulation blankets that wrap around the diameter of the cell stack. The needed characteristics of the flexible wrap limit the materials that can be used. These characteristics include:

- Sufficient strength for wrapping operation
- Low thermal conductivity
- Non-reactive with cell stack component at operating temperature (including lithium intermetallics)
- Structural integrity under non-operating and operating environmental conditions
- Flexible and conformal to cell stack

Typical thermal battery wrap materials are alumina-silica fiber blanket materials, such as, Fiberfrax. These materials show good chemical resistance, strength, and flexibility; however, thermal conductivity for this material is somewhat higher than is exhibited by high performance insulation materials, such as, Microtherm and Min-K. Typically, the high performance insulations lack the flexibility or non-reactivity to be used against the cell stack. This leads to the use of multiple-material wrapping schemes in many applications that require better thermal insulation than Fiberfrax can provide.

One recent breakthrough in flexible thermal insulation is the incorporation of silica-based aerogels in a flexible ceramic blanket material. This material offers the flexibility, strength, and conformal characteristics of Fiberfrax with low thermal conductivity associated with higher performance materials. This paper presents the evaluation results of one such material (Aspen Pyrogel) by EaglePicher Technologies.

Thermal Modeling of Aerogel Insulation
Thermal property values were provided by Aspen Aerogel and incorporated into AllBatt, a thermal battery modeling software, to evaluate the potential advantages of Pyrogel insulation in multiple thermal battery designs. Models were run using Pyrogel as partial and complete replacements for the existing insulation scheme in these batteries. The model results indicated marked improvement in heat retention for all designs; however, the largest improvement was seen by replacing the Fiberfrax wrap directly adjacent to the cell stack.

Figures 1 and 2 show the predicted temperature profiles of two different battery designs using Pyrogel in place of the current insulation schemes. In both cases, predicted heat retention was improved markedly by the Pyrogel insulation. Battery #1 is a current production battery with a running life of less than 5 minutes. Battery #2 is a development battery with a very low current draw and a longer operating life. Predictive models were run at high and low temperature extremes for battery #1 in Figure 1. The predictive model was run at ambient temperature only for battery #2 in Figure 2.

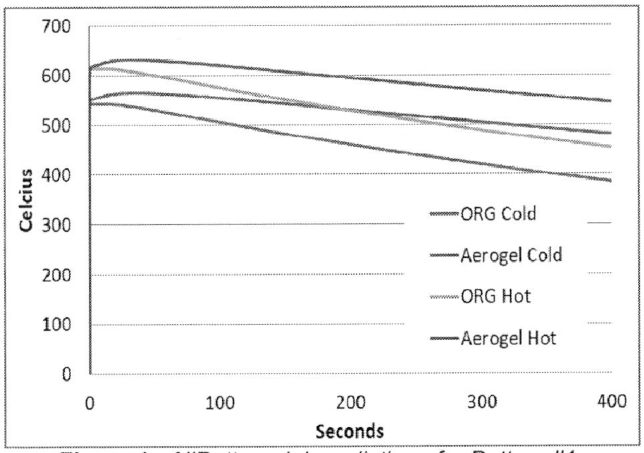

Figure 1: AllBatt model predictions for Battery #1.

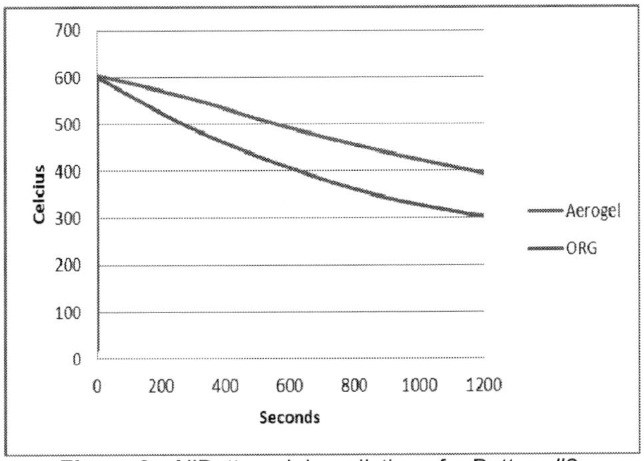

Figure 2: AllBatt model predictions for Battery #2.

Battery Performance with Aerogel Insulation

Test batteries of each type were built using the modeled insulation schemes to see if the modeled predictions would be reflected in real batteries. These tests also provided hands-on production experience with the Aerogel insulation to evaluate properties such as, handling, conformability, strength, and flexibility. An experienced operator was selected to wrap both the control batteries and the Aerogel batteries and provide comment. The Aerogel insulation was found to be somewhat stronger than Fiberfrax of a comparable thickness. The Aerogel was not quite as flexible as Fiberfrax and required more care while taping in place; however, the Aerogel conformed well to the cell stack and the overall properties of the Aerogel insulation were suitable for the intended use. From a wrapping perspective, the Aerogel insulation was superior to the other higher performance insulating blankets typically used by EaglePicher in terms of handling during the wrapping operation.

Both test battery types were fired using their typical load profiles. Following testing, selected batteries were dissected to examine the condition of the battery stacks and insulation and to look for signs of side reactions with the cell stack. The Aerogel insulation directly adjacent to the cell stacks did not show any signs of scorching beyond that which is typical next to the pyrotechnic heat source pellets. It appeared that the chemical stability between the lithium-based anode pellets and the Aerogel insulation was acceptable.

Figure 3: Outer Aerogel Wrap

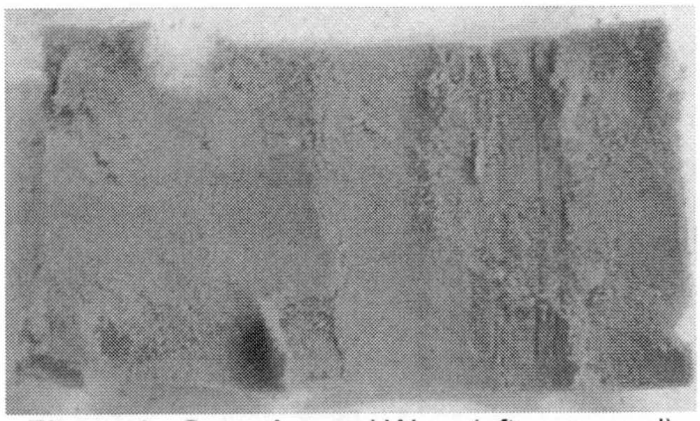
Figure 4: Outer Aerogel Wrap (after removal)

Figure 5: Inner Aerogel Wrap

The operating life of Battery #2 was improved by approximately 250 seconds using an equivalent thickness of Aerogel insulation versus the original wrapping scheme. This constitutes an improvement of approximately 40%. The agreement between the predicted and measured behavior is within reason.

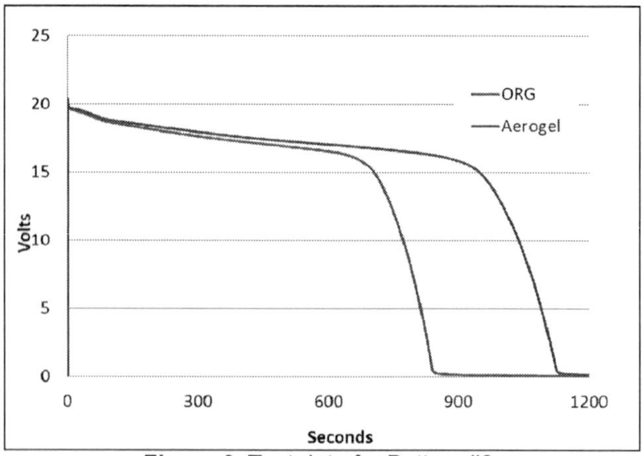

Figure 6 Test data for Battery #2.

Environmental Testing of Aerogel Insulation

Based on the improved electrical performance observed for battery #1, an expanded test set was built to evaluate the performance of the Aerogel insulation in non-operating and operating environmental conditions. Test environments included temperature extremes, random vibration, and shock. The test batteries were examined using Computed Tomography (CT) in the original condition, following non-operational environments, and following performance testing to look for signs of damage (Figure 7). Additionally, following performance testing, selected batteries were dissected to inspect the insulating wraps and cell stacks for sign of damage.

Non-operating vibration testing was performed along both the longitudinal and transverse axes with a vibration ranging from 0.75 to 3.5 Grms for a duration of 195 minutes, Figures 8 and 9. Non-operating shock was half-sine 1000 G with a duration of 10 msec along the longitudinal axis, Figure 10. Following non-operational testing, real time X-ray inspection showed no damage to the insulating wraps or the edges of the cell stack. These batteries were activated at hot and cold temperature extremes. The battery performance indicated that the non-operating environments had no deleterious impact on battery performance.

Figure 7: Post-Environment CT Images

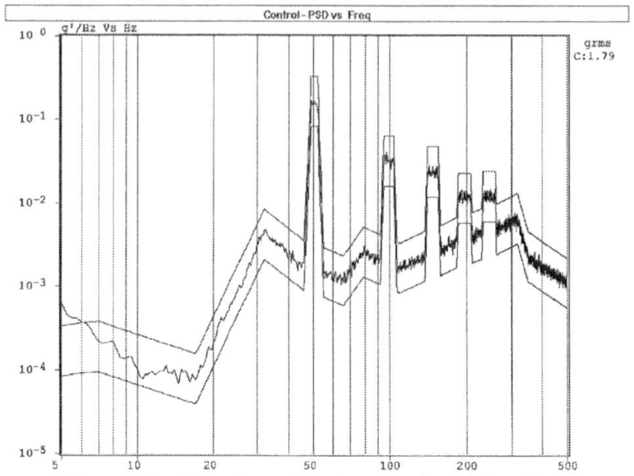

Figure 8: Non-Operating Longitudinal Vibration.

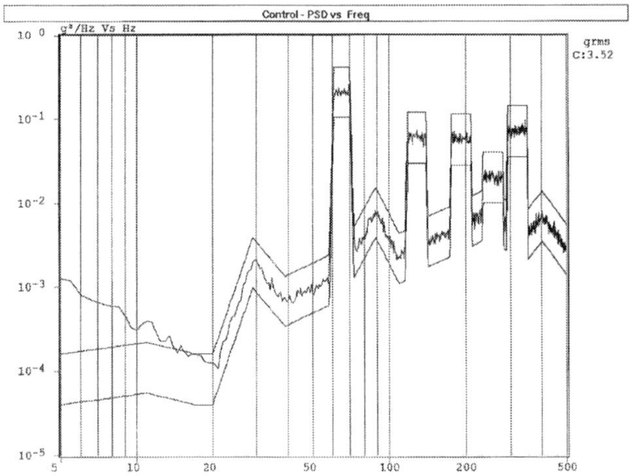

Figure 9: Non-Operating Transverse Vibration.

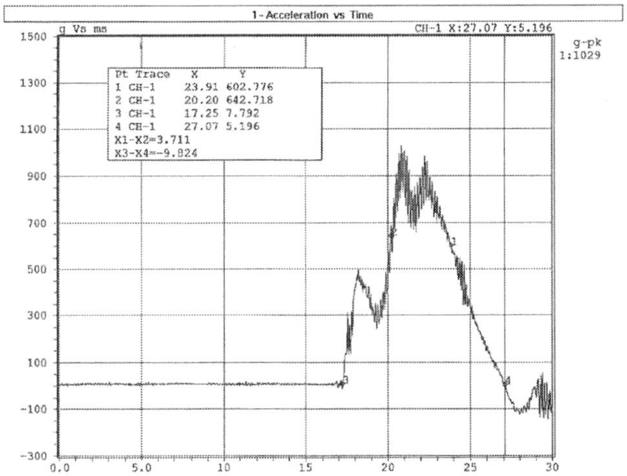

Figure 10: Non-Operating Shock.

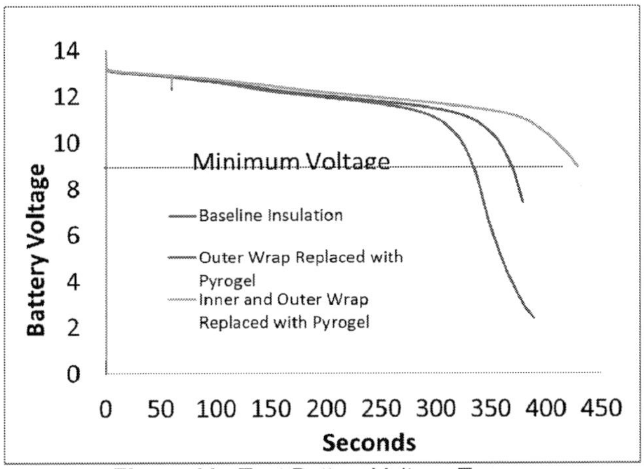

Figure 11: Test Battery Voltage Traces

Following performance testing, selected batteries were dissected to examine the condition of the Aerogel wraps for signs of damage and interaction with the cell stack during operation. No signs of damage or side-reactions were noted in the analysis.

Summary

Aerogel insulation was incorporated into an existing thermal battery design. Model predictions indicated that the aerogel insulation would improve heat retention within the battery. Test batteries were built and tested that verified the improved performance. Additional batteries were exposed to environmental conditions (vibration and shock) to determine the suitability of the aerogel insulation in real battery environments. All test batteries indicated that the aerogel insulation was acceptable for usage in thermal batteries and can provide a significant design advantage.

Figure 12: Outer Aerogel Wrap Exposed to Dynamic Environments

Figure 13: Outer Aerogel Wrap Exposed to Dynamic Environments (after removal)

Figure 14: Inner Aerogel Wrap Exposed to Dynamic Environments

Acknowledgements

EaglePicher would like to acknowledge Aspen Aerogels for supplying the aerogel material and thermal property information used in this study.

Recent Advances in Thin Film Based Thermal Batteries

Arsen G. Gevorkyan, Ronen Cohen and Ofer Raz*

Power Sources Department
Rafael LTD.
POB 2250, Haifa, Israel, 3102102
Contact information: oferra@rafael.co.il, +972-73-3355814

Abstract:

Molten salt thermal batteries are traditional power sources for various military applications. The combination of wide operational temperature range, high power density, shelf life of more than 20 years and maintenance free storage are unsurpassed by any other battery technology. Recent weaponry developments emphasized on "smarter", small volume, integral solutions drive for development of batteries with higher power density, smaller thermal footprint and ability to suit different volume geometries. Traditionally, powder pressing is used in preparation of thermal battery components. This technology is limited to circular geometry and minimum thickness. In the last few years significant efforts were put into development of various thin film technologies to overcome these limitations. Those technologies are supposed to allow production of thermal batteries with reduced volume and increase efficiency of system volume usage.

In this paper, we report on our recent progress in development of thermal batteries based thin film components. These advances allowed production of reproducible and robust cells with performance similar to conventional pressed pellets. Moreover, batteries assembled with those thin film components made possible the reduction of at least 35% in stack height which have resulted in significant battery volume and mass decrease of more than 20%.

Keywords: Thin film; Thermal batteries; Tape casting

Introduction

Tape casting was chosen by most thermal batteries manufacturers as most promising technology for production of new generation products. Most noticeable advantages of tape casting among other thin film technologies are low cost, wide range of suitable materials, process flexibility, simplicity and scalability. In addition, it allows production of electrodes with various shapes and significantly thinner than pressed ones. As a result, components manufactured using tape casting enable battery design to be more efficient in regards to material and volume utilization. Such thermal batteries will also have smaller thermal footprint allowing even more compact designs in customers' applications.

Tape casting process usually begins with preparation or purchasing of ceramic powder. Powder quality is defined by interplay of its specific surface area, density and average particle diameter (D_{50}) [1]. The slip preparation starts from mixing the powder with solvents and surfactants or deflocculants. The former is holding media for all other slip components while the latter is used to improve powder particles dispersion. The next step is homogenization of obtained slurry with binder and plastisizers or softeners. Softeners are usually divided into type I plastisizers intended to facilitate "green" tape flexibility and type II plastisizers intended to increase its plasticity. Polymeric binder is one of the most important components in tape casting process. It plays crucial role in all processing steps: in slurry it controls slip viscosity, in "green" tape it serves as a matrix to hold particles together and during decomposition it should leave minimum residues while below sintering temperature. The properties of the slurry such as viscosity, homogeneity and dispersion stability have a direct influence on the quality of the cast slip. Thickness of the slip is generally defined by the doctor blade gap but is also influenced by the carrier speed and the slurry level in doctor blade reservoir. Afterwards the casted slip should be dried to obtain the "green" tape. In general, drying is accelerated by heating to increase production capacity. However, excessive heating might cause various tape defects such as skin formation and cracks. In order to obtain "white" ceramic parts, the "green" tape is cut to desired shape and sintered.

Most thermal batteries R&D laboratories have put significant efforts in producing thermal batteries based on thin film components. J. Edington et. al [2] reported on first experiments with thin film thermal battery components in 2008. In following publication additional performance improvements and development of heat pellets by tape casting were demonstrated [3]. In 2012 thin film battery with satisfactory performance was developed [4]. The battery had 15% volume reduced compared to a one produced using conventional technology. In the same year D-shaped thermal battery was demonstrated but showed somewhat deteriorated performance compared to circular design. Another group [5] demonstrated thermal battery prepared using tape cast components as thin as 100 micron and functional battery with those components in 2008. D. Harney developed all thin film design with total cell thickness of about half millimeter excluding heat pellet resulting in more than 30% stack volume and weight reduction compared to pressed pellets. The battery was designed with emphasis on rise time which was slightly slower compared to conventional pressed pellets design [6]. The issue was solved later by J. Reining [7]. At different development steps most groups had issues with thin film battery performance which will be discussed below.

Results and discussion

In previous report by our lab [8] preparation of thin film thermal battery components using tape casting was demonstrated on single cell. It was shown that pellets with thicknesses as low as 100μm might be produced using tape casting and their electrical properties are comparable to some degree to those of pressed pellets. The material was flexible in its "green" state and could be easily formed using punch or other cutting methods.

It was shown that thin film cathode capacity and open circuit voltage (OCV) were somewhat lower compared to pressed pellets. Recently, performance of the thin film components was significantly improved regarding capacity, open circuit voltage and resistance on a single cell level. As shown on Figure 1 the specific capacity and average potential of electrodes are similar to standard pressed cell performance, while the conductivity is ~20% higher in the cathode and ~20% lower in the anode.

Though reduction of pellets thickness is generally favored it is not always benefits battery performance. Guidotti [9] reported that the thinner battery components are more prone to internal shortcuts resulting in thermal runaway especially when pellets thickness is less than 250μm. Therefore, despite the ability to produce very thin components there are great challenges associated with implementation of those components in thermal batteries. Our thin film materials and battery design developments allowed successful production of thin film battery with components as thin as 150μm. New design was proposed to currently manufactured battery with significant capacity excess of over 300% which is solely attributed to limitations of pressing technology. The discharge performance of production and thin film battery are shown at Figure 2. It might be noted that both batteries have very similar performance. The potential of thin film battery descend somewhat faster which is related to lower pellets capacity. Battery composed of pressed pellets on the other hand has significantly faster increasing resistance than that of the thin film battery. It is assumed that the better resistance consistency in thin film battery resulted from higher surface area resulted from smaller powder particles. Both batteries satisfy specification requirements while thin film battery has significantly reduced components weight as demonstrated at Table 1. Over-all thinner components allowed significant reduction of more than 20% in total battery weight and volume (Figure 3). Despite numerous material improvements separator weight could not be reduced below the weight of regular battery which we relate to issues previously described by Guidotti [9].

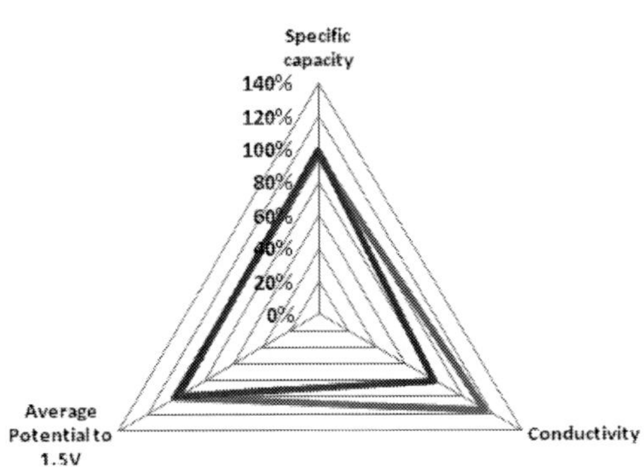

Figure 1. Performance comparison of thin film cathode (red) and anode (blue) to pressed pellets in single cell tests

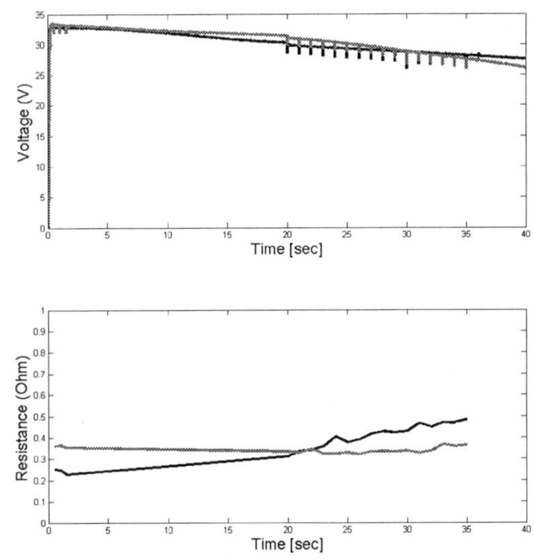

Figure 2. Comparison of pressed (black) and thin film (red) batteries performance.

Table 1. Comparison between pressed and thin film components on a mass basis

	Production	Thin film
Anode	100%	46%
Separator	100%	100%
Cathode	100%	33%
Heat Pellet	100%	70%
Cell weight	100%	64%

Figure 3. Picture of production (right) and thin film battery (left)

Also, an investigation of performance of the thin film thermal batteries under various environmental conditions is currently conducted. Preliminary studies have shown that these batteries have good tolerance to high acceleration shocks and vibrations. According to our recent results no limitations are caused by use of thin film battery components. Following this progress, activities of a production line assembly have started and are expected to be completed in a couple of years.

Summary and Conclusions

A short review of tape casting process and recent developments in thin film thermal batteries was made. Current state of thin film thermal battery technology in Power Sources department of Rafael was reported. It was demonstrated that currently produced tape casting materials were improved compared to previously reported results. Battery assembled from newly developed components performed on the level of pressed pellets. Yet, mass of the stack was reduced by 35% the mass and volume of the battery were reduced by more than 20%. The tape casting process undergoes continuous optimization to allow stable high capacity production of components for new and currently produced products.

References

[1] R. E. Mistler and E. R. Twiname, Tape Casting Theory and Practice, Westerville: The American Ceramic Society, 2000.

[2] J. Edington, G. Swift and C. Lamb, "Development of Thin Components for Thermal Batteries," in Power Sources, 2008.

[3] J. Edington and J. Baumann, "Thin Cell Components for Thermal Batteries," in Power Sources, 2010.

[4] J. Edington and J. Baumann, "Thin Component Thermal Battery Development and Process Scale-Up," in Power Sources, 2014.

[5] J. K. Pugh, A. Lang, E. Dayalan and D. Harney, "Tape Cast Technology as Applied to Thermal Batteries," in Power Sources, 2008.

[6] D. Harney, "Thin Film Thermal Batteries," in Power Sources, 2010.

[7] J. Reining, "Thin-Film Technology for Thermal Battery Applications," in Power Sources, 2012.

[8] T. Leviatan, S. Cohen, I. Eliel, G. E. Shter, A. Cohen, V. Beilin and G. S. Grader, "Thin Layer Electrochemical Components for High Power Thermal Batteries," in Power Sources 45, 2012.

[9] R. A. Guidotti, "Thermally-Related Safety Issues Assiciated with Thermal Batteries," Sandia National Laboratories, Albuquerque, 2006.

Development and Application of New Heat Source Materials for Thermal Batteries

Michael Ding and Frank Krieger

U.S. Army Research Laboratory
2800 Powder Mill Road
Adelphi, MD 20783, USA
michael.s.ding.civ@mail.mil

Nicholas Leventis

Department of Chemistry
Missouri University of Science and Technology
Rolla, Missouri 65409, USA

Abstract: *Described here are two new approaches to developing suitable heat source materials for thin-film thermal batteries. The first approach is the adaptation and use of a nano-layered bi-metallic foil with the two metal components reacting to each other rapidly and exothermically once the reaction is initiated. The second and most recent approach is an aerogel-based preparation route for making monolithic, nano-/micro-porous iron matrix with particles of a perchlorate salt deposited in the pores as the oxidant. These materials are inherently more suitable than the traditional pressed-pellets of particulate mixtures of iron and potassium perchlorate for use as heat source materials in thin-film thermal batteries.*

Keywords: thermal battery; thin-film thermal battery; heat source; pyrotechnic; nano-layered; aerogel; porous; perchlorate salt.

Introduction

The heating component in a thermal battery is critically important for the activation and operation of the battery. Traditionally, the material for this component is mostly in the form of compressed pellets of Fe and $KClO_4$ particulate mixtures, with Fe always in excess to endow the pellets with desired mechanical and electrical properties both before and after the exothermic redox reaction [1, 2]. As such, these pellets suffer from poor mechanical cohesion and integrity, low materials utilization, and inflexibility in form factor, and are therefore inherently unsuitable for application to thin-film thermal batteries.

With the recent rise of interest in thin-film thermal battery technologies, various forms of new heating materials have been under study and development that are particularly suited for this type of thermal batteries. An early group of materials to have received such attention is a nano-layered bi-metallic foil material, with the two metal components reacting to each other rapidly and exothermically once the reaction is initiated. One particular type of materials from this group, NanoFoil, was studied and characterized extensively for its potential to replace the traditional heat pellets in thermal batteries, and was tested for such use in both pressed pellet and thin-film thermal batteries [3-7]. This series of work culminated in a 12-cell NanoFoil-heated thin-film thermal battery prototype, with significantly reduced volume (stack), much shortened rise time (<100 ms), reasonable performance, and negligible internal gas generation during operation [8, 9].

Our most recent focus has been on producing a novel type of pyrotechnic materials, based on an aerogel preparation route, as the new heating material for thermal batteries and particularly for thin-film thermal batteries [10]. Instead of starting out with Fe and $KClO_4$ particles and pressing them into green pellets to use in thermal batteries as is traditionally done, we first made a monolithic, nano-/micro-porous Fe matrix in the shape of a pellet through a modified aerogel chemical route. This porous Fe matrix was then infiltrated with a perchlorate salt solution (mostly $LiClO_4$ but also $NaClO_4$ and $KClO_4$). Upon thorough drying, particles of the perchlorate salt deposited in the pores of the Fe matrix, thus forming a monolithic Fe-$LiClO_4$ pyrotechnic material. On testing and characterization, the best of these samples have shown good promise in their initiation and burning and in their mechanical and electrical properties as regards their applications as heating materials for thermal batteries. Furthermore, the new materials preparation route is significantly less expensive than the traditional method of NanoFoil production, and offers many new and effective ways of controlling and tailoring the materials structure and properties.

NanoFoil as Heat Source Materials

Developing a complete, fully functional thin-film thermal battery requires a compatible new heat source material with a set of properties drastically different from that of the traditional pressed pellets. One of the first answers to this requirement is the adaption and use of NanoFoil, a trademarked metal foil made of alternating layers of aluminum and nickel, each only about 100 nm thick. This foil material has been shown to possess many inherent advantages as a new heat source material for thin-film thermal batteries, such as rapid propagation of reaction front and heat delivery with no gas generation, flexible form factor, mechanical integrity, and safety against accidental initiation. But it also posed many new challenges, such as reliable initiation, control of peak skin temperature, and high cost [3-7]. For these reasons, we carried out a series of experiments and measurements on this material to adapt it for use in thin-film thermal batteries, culminating in the prototyping of a 12-cell NanoFoil-heated thin-film thermal battery.

In the following we summarize the experiments and test results on the 12-cell NanoFoil-heated thin-film thermal battery prototype [8, 9]. NanoFoil discs of 0.75-inch diameter as the heating component were made from sputtered bimetallic foil of aluminum (Al)-nickel (Ni) of 150 μm thickness. Thin-film components of anode/electrolyte and cathode were prepared with a coating method at Sandia National Laboratories. In a dry room of 74% relative humidity, these components were assembled into a 12-cell battery stack with nichrome wires and heat paper strips at appropriate places for initiation and with 3-mil-thick stainless steel discs appropriately inserted as thermal buffers to suppress the temperature surge experienced by the components on either side of the NanoFoil discs. This stack was then wrapped tightly with glass tapes for thermal insulation and mechanical stability, its electrode and match leads were properly connected to a battery header, the assembly was lowered into a battery can, and the case was finally hermetically sealed with a laser welder.

As plotted in figure 1, the prototype battery performed well under the current load of 142 mA (equivalent to 50 mA/cm^2). The runtime of 50 s was satisfactory considering the limited heat contents of the NanoFoil discs and the short-time nature of the targeted applications, as well as the stack resistance, voltage plateau, and power capability. The voltage-time curves of figure 1 give a rise time of about 100 ms, a significant improvement over the earlier similar battery stacks and other technologies. This can be more clearly seen in figure 2, which plots together the rise time curves of the prototype battery with two other batteries, one with the pressed-pellets for the anode and cathode-electrolyte and a pyrotechnic heat source, and one with anode and cathode-electrolyte pellets and NanoFoil discs as the heat source.

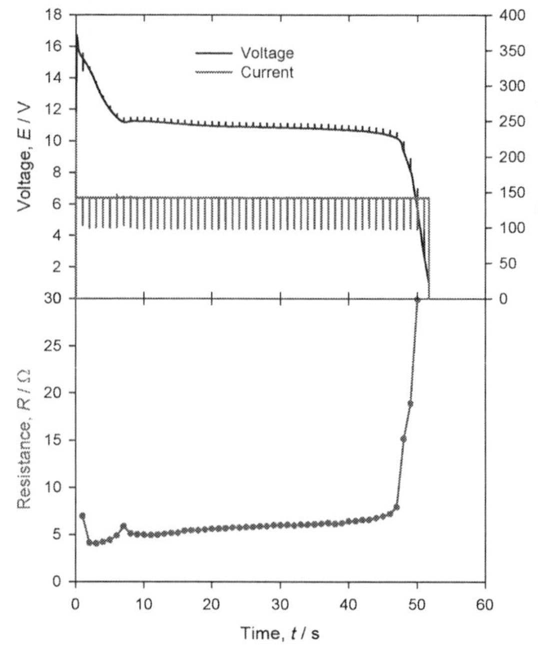

Figure 1. Discharge performance (top plot) of the 12-cell prototype NanoFoil-heated thin-film thermal battery device and its stack resistance-time curve (bottom plot).

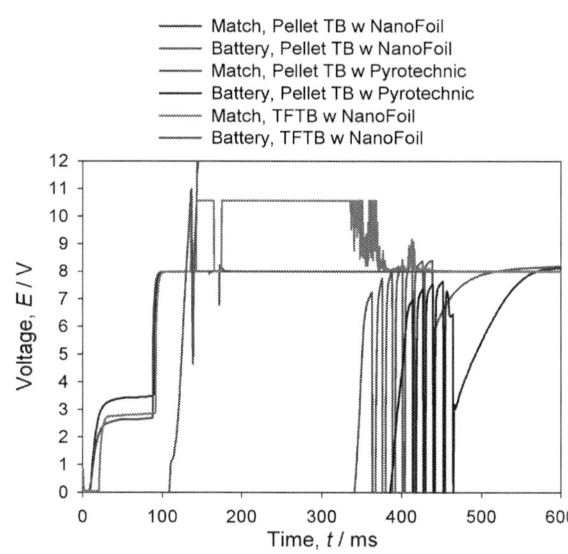

Figure 2. Improvements in rise time of the prototype NanoFoil-heated thin-film thermal battery device over a traditional pressed-pellet thermal battery and a NanoFoil-heated pressed-pellet thermal battery.

Fe-Aerogel-Based Materials as Heat Source

The second approach to developing a suitable heat source material for thin-film thermal battery is our recent efforts on producing a monolithic, nano-/micro-porous iron matrix with a perchlorate salt (mostly $LiClO_4$ but also $NaClO_4$ and

$KClO_4$) particles deposited in the pores, based on an aerogel preparation route, as described below [10].

A typical procedure for preparing such a piece of heat source material started out with carbothermal reduction of interpenetrating networks of polybenzoxazine (PBO) and iron oxide nanoparticles, as depicted in figure 3. Excess carbon was burned off at 600 °C in air, and oxides produced from partial oxidation of the Fe(0) network were reduced back to Fe(0) with H_2 at different temperatures (temp) ranging from 300 to 1300 °C. For temp > 400 °C, these nano-/micro-porous iron samples were free of carbon and oxide, as identified here on with H_2-reduction temperature as Fe-temp.

These different Fe-temp samples were subjected to a variety of measurements and characterization steps for their structural, mechanical, and electrical properties. Figure 4 shows some examples of such structural characterization by scanning electron microscopy. As can be seen, with increasing H_2-reduction temperature, the Fe particles grow larger and the inter-particle connections become thicker and stronger due to the action of sintering, with a concurrent reduction in sample porosity and increase in bulk density as observed in separate measurements. Concurrent improvements in mechanical strength and electrical conductivity were also observed.

To produce the final monolithic, pyrotechnic heat source material for thermal batteries, the Fe-temp samples were infiltrated with a perchlorate salt solution, mostly $LiClO_4$ but also $NaClO_4$ and $KClO_4$, and then dried thoroughly, thus forming a nano-/micro-porous iron matrix with its pores coated with a perchlorate salt deposit as the oxidant. Testing of these pyrotechnic samples for their ignition and burning behaviors was carried out in air with an open flame for initiation and a fast camera for recording. In general, samples reduced at temp ≤400 °C fizzled out upon initiation, those between 500 and 900 °C exploded, and those reduced at temp ≥950 °C reacted rapidly with a glow without much change in the physical dimensions of the sample. The last reaction behavior is demonstrated in figure 5 with the photographs of two samples (Fe-1200 and Fe-1300), and is desirable in a heat source material for thermal battery applications.

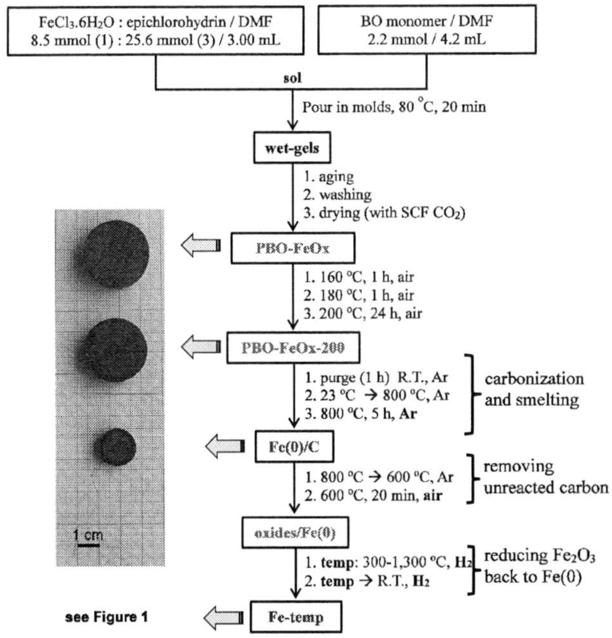

Figure 3. Steps in the preparation of Fe(0) aerogel samples with corresponding changes in the appearance of a typical sample.

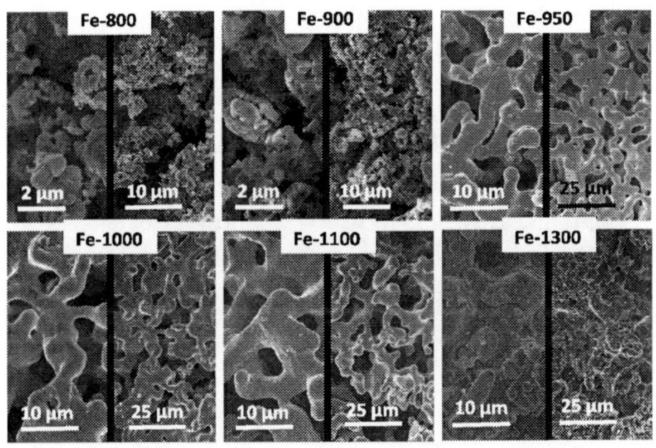

Figure 4. SEM micrographs of samples with different H_2-reduction temperatures (indicated as Fe-temp) and at two different magnifications (as indicated).

Figure 5. Initiation and burning behavior in air of samples of Fe-1200 and Fe-1300 loaded with $LiClO_4$ particles.

Conclusions

To develop a suitable heat source material for thin-film thermal batteries, two approaches were taken as described here. Adaption of NanoFoil for this use is the earlier approach and has reached a more mature stage, with the material studied systematically and modified for improvement, culminating in the prototyping of a 12-cell NanoFoil-heated thin-film thermal battery with a short rise time, reduced volume, decent performance, and negligible gas generation. To reduce the cost of production and further improve the properties of the material, a second approach was recently taken to develop an aerogel-based chemical route to produce a monolithic, nano-/micro-porous iron matrix with particles of a perchlorate salt deposited in its pores as the oxidant. The best of these materials have demonstrated desired behaviors of ignition and burning and promising electrical and mechanical properties for applications as heat source for thermal batteries.

Acknowledgements

We thank the Office of the Secretary of Defense and the Joint Department of Defense (DoD)/Department of Energy (DOE) Munitions Technology Development Program and the Army Research Office (Cooperative Agreement No. W911NF-12-2-0029) for their financial support, and the Advanced Power Sources Group of Sandia National Laboratories for their technical collaboration.

References

1. Lamb, C. M. in: Linden's Handbook of Batteries, 4th ed.; Reddy, T. B.; Linden, D., eds.; McGraw-Hill Companies, Inc., New York, 2011, p. 36.1.
2. Guidotti, R. A., and Masset, P. J., Power Sources, 2006, 161, 1443.
3. Ding, M. S., Krieger, F. C., Swank, J. A., Poret, J. C., McMullan, C. W., and Chen, G., "Use of NanoFoil as a New Form of Heat Source in Thermal Batteries," ARL-TR-6141; U.S. Army Research Laboratory: Adelphi, MD, 2012.
4. Ding, M. S., Krieger, F. C., Swank, J. A., Janow, C. W., Delnick, F. M., and Branson, E. D., Proc. 45th Power Sources Conference, Las Vegas, NV, June 11–14, 2012, p. 623.
5. Ding, M. S., Krieger, F. C., Swank, J. A., Poret, J. C., Chen, G., and McMullan, C. W., Proc. 43rd Power Sources Conference, Philadelphia, PA, July 7–10, 2008, p. 635.
6. Ding, M. S., Krieger, F. C., Swank, J. A., Poret, J. C., McMullan, C. W., and Chen, G., Proc. 43rd Power Sources Conference, Philadelphia, PA, July 7–10, 2008, p. 615.
7. Ding, M. S., Krieger, F. C., Swank, J. A.; McMullan, C. W., Chen, G., and Poret, J., Proc. 43rd Power Sources Conference, Philadelphia, PA, July 7–10, 2008, p. 377.
8. Ding, M., Krieger, F., Swank, J., Proc. 46th Power Sources Conference, Orlando, FL, June 9–12, 2014, p. 530.
9. Ding, M. S., Krieger, F. C., Swank, J. A., "Developing NanoFoil-Heated Thin-Film Thermal Battery," ARL-TR-6664; U.S. Army Research Laboratory: Adelphi, MD, 2013.
10. Leventis, N., Donthula, S., Mandal, C., Ding, M. S., Sotiriou-Leventis, C., Chemistry of Materials, 2015, 27, 8126.

Electrolyte-Binder Powder Processing to Improve Manufacturability of Thermal Battery Separator Pellets

Joseph Beck and Brian Perdue
Power Sources Technology Group
Sandia National Laboratories
PO Box 5800
Albuquerque, NM 87185-0613
Contact Author: jbeck@sandia.gov

Abstract: *Thermal battery electrolyte-binder powder processing was investigated with design-for-manufacturing considerations with attempt to improve separator pellet production. Low separator pellet yields increase manufacturing costs and waste valuable or expensive battery materials. Alternative powder blending and sizing processes are reviewed and their impact on powder flow and compaction characteristics discussed. Reprocessing scrapped separator pellets was demonstrated to be a viable process to reclaim scrapped materials through mechanical and electrochemical test results.*

Keywords: Thermal battery; molten salt battery; electrolyte-binder; powder; pellet; reprocessing; LiCl/KCl; MgO; design for manufacturing

Introduction

A molten salt thermal battery is a reserve power source containing a stack assembly comprised of electrochemical cells made of anode, separator, and cathode pellets along with heat pellets for a heat source. The purpose of the separator pellet is to isolate the anode and cathode and provide ion transport during battery function. Thermal battery pellets are fabricated by compacting powder materials under a static force. Automated pellet presses, where the powder flows from a hopper into the die cavity, are utilized by industry to achieve higher throughput but introduce challenges related to the flow and compaction properties of the specific powder.

Low pellet production yields increase manufacturing costs, create financial and schedule opportunity costs, and scrap highly valuable battery materials. This research investigates and characterizes LiCl/KCl/MgO electrolyte-binder powder with intent to improve the manufacturability of separator pellets. The motivation of this work was design-for-manufacturing thermal battery powders and pellets while maintaining performance characteristics. This work investigates optimizing final powder characteristics during powder processing for high yield pellet production and the effects of using scrapped material on pellet performance.

Experimental results

Powder Processing – Blending: Overview of the thermal battery powder and pellet production process is shown in Figure 1. Electrolyte-binder powder processing operations are blending, fusing, grinding, and sizing with the final product being pelletized and accepted/rejected based on inspection criteria. In order to contain the molten electrolyte during battery operation, the LiCl/KCl eutectic is mixed with MgO as a binder in ratios ranging from 65/35 to 60/40 weight percentages. Traditionally, powder constituents are mixed using blending equipment, such as a "V"-blender, with no additional materials added. This process is commonly known as dry blending. Good homogeneity is difficult to ensure in dry blending even when using multi-axis blenders, such as the Turbula blender, due to magnesium oxide's high angle of repose which impacts its flow characteristics. To overcome the challenges of homogeneity extended mix times were required for dry blending. Powder homogeneity is a critical parameter impacting flow characteristics and especially important in the use of automated pellet presses where the material is flowing to fill a die [1].

In response to dry blending challenges, Sandia developed a process that used Freon TF as a mixing medium together with a Waring-type blender [2]. In the early 1990s due to environmental awareness, the Department of Energy began restricting and eliminating several common halogenated organics including Freons. Guidotti led research to identify alternative blending media and concluded that liquid nitrogen was the best replacement [3]. However, the use of liquid nitrogen created other issues including maintaining temperatures along with local condensation of moisture in water sensitive materials. In the mid-2000s, Sandia again pioneered the use of electrolyte-binder blending agents this time led by Moya. Vertrel XF, a hydrofluorocarbon, was selected as suitable material due to its similar physical properties of Freon TF. In all instances the media was added during the blending step to enhance mixing, which was then forced evaporated out before fusing. This process is referred to as wet blending.

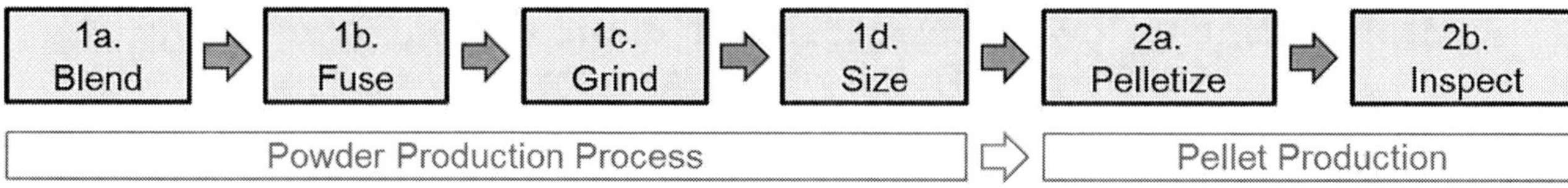

Figure 1: Thermal battery electrolyte-binder powder and pellet production process

The use of Vertrel XF decreased mixing time required for a homogenous blend compared to dry blending by almost two orders of magnitude, by acting as a fluidization aid decreasing inter-particle friction. While reducing mixing time is beneficial, an additional process step is required for wet blending to drive off the Vertrel XF prior to fusing. The implementation of wet blending was long accepted to improve pellet integrity. Experimental results from pressing dry and wet blended powders on automated pressing equipment exhibited no significant improvement in powder flow properties, as quantified by weight standard deviations, or pellet integrity. SEM/EDX was used to probe powder sample homogeneity and to ensure the Vertrel XF has been completely removed. Results indicate that both samples were equally homogeneous and the Vertrel XF had been completely removed.

Powder Processing – Sizing: After blending, the powder is fused at high temperatures to melt the electrolyte. The material is then ground using a relatively high energy mill through a 0.033" screen, before granulating and sieving through a #60 US Standard mesh (0.010"). The granulating and sieving operations are referred to collectively as the sizing operation. Granulating, widely adopted by the pharmaceutical industry, is the process of forming larger, multiparticle granules. Resulting granules typically have increased average particle size and are more isodiametric, both of which improve flow and compaction properties in an automated press [1]. Powder samples of both dry and wet blended powders were analyzed post-grinding, post-granulating, and post-sieving for particle size distribution. Samples were run in triplicate dry (not suspended in liquid medium) and measured using laser scattering.

The particle size distribution results for the wet blend are shown in Figure 2. As expected, the dry blended powder exhibited the same trends as the wet blended powder because powder homogeneity has no effect on grinding and sizing. After each sizing operation, the mean size and standard deviation decreased. Granulation of the electrolyte-binder resulted in high percentage of particles distributed around the mesh size. This was a result of both granulating the smaller particles and decreasing the size of the largest particles. The granulation equipment input enough energy to reduce the largest particles of the very soft electrolyte-binder. The material was then reduced in size again during the low-energy sieving operation but also the standard deviation decreased as well. The final powder exhibits a single peak whereas the post-grinding and post-granulating samples may exhibit a slight bimodal distribution or at least a wider particle size range. Further work is continuing on characterizing the impact on the final powder characteristics by the granulation step.

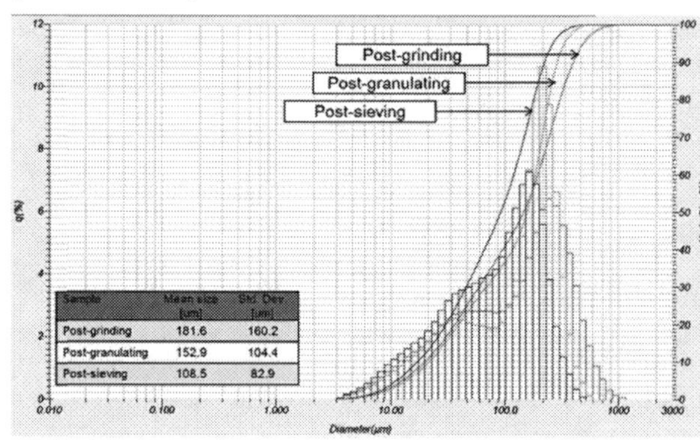

Figure 2: Particle size distribution of grinding and sizing

Pellet Reprocessing: Scrapped and rejected materials during the battery production process represent a significant portion of material losses. "Rejected" separator pellets were reprocessed using two different methods shown in Figure 3: fusing pellets before grinding (2b to 1b, "reprocess 1b") or just grinding the pellets back into electrolyte-binder powder (2b to 1c, "reprocess 1c"). The reprocessing was completed three times on the same materials in attempt to exaggerate any effects the reprocessing would have with all pellets fabricated on manual pellet presses. Mechanical and electrochemical performance impacts were investigated by comparing the mechanical and electrochemical properties of the 3X reprocessed pellets to control pellets, virgin pellets with no reprocessing, as the baseline.

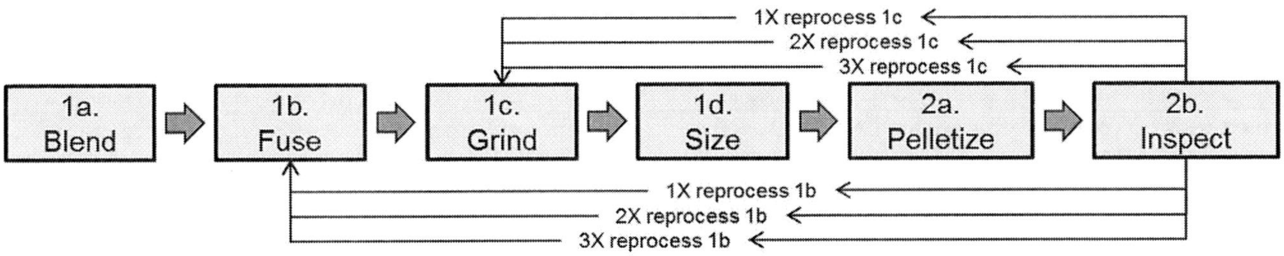

Figure 3: Separator pellet reprocessing processes

Firstly, acceptable pellets were fabricated using the reprocessed materials demonstrating that this process may be viable to reclaim scrapped materials. As the materials continued to be reprocessed, the pellet press operators qualitatively noted the powder was finer resulting in increased pellet defects of bad edges and soft spots. The reprocessed 1c powder without fusing exhibited a change in compaction properties requiring the forming force of the press to be reduced by almost 10% between the 1X and 2X reprocessing where it remained for the 3X pellets. The powder that was reprocessed 1b with fusing did not require any changes to the forming force, dwell time, or stripping force through the 3X pellets. Due to the pellets being pressed on manual presses where each charge is individually weighed and filled by hand, no data exists on its flow or compaction characteristics in automated pellet press.

Reprocessed materials were tested using Differential Scanning Calorimetry to identify bulk material property changes. Table 1 compiles the mean value of three replicates and one standard deviation for the various test results with the exception of surface area being a single measurement. Heat capacity at the lower temperature range when the eutectic is still in solid phase showed a minor decrease with reprocessing 1c but was only statistically significant using Student's t-test ($p<0.05$) at the reprocessed 2X and 3X pellets compared to the control. No data was statistically significant for the heat capacity at the higher temperature range when the electrolyte is molten. No change in melting point is estimated which is intuitive because no materials were added or removed from the eutectic salt formulation as part of either reprocessing. Finally, no change in the heat of fusion is estimated for any of the reprocessed pellets. BET surface area decreases with additional reprocessing. This is attributed to the additional grinding operations in both 1b and 1c reprocesses reducing the electrolyte particle size resulting in finer salts and a change in porosity.

Table 1: 3X reprocessed material properties

Material	Cp avg 150-250 °C [J/g°C]	Cp avg 400-500 °C [J/g°C]	Melting Point Onset [°C]	Heat of Fusion [J/g]	BET Surface Area [m²/g]
Control	1.21 ± 0.06	1.42 ± 0.07	343.6 ± 0.6	127.8 ± 1.0	5.3
1X reprocess 1b	1.14 ± 0.08	1.31 ± 0.09	343.1 ± 0.5	127.9 ± 0.2	2.4
2X reprocess 1b	1.07 ± 0.04	1.39 ± 0.05	343.3 ± 0.6	130.8 ± 2.5	2.0
3X reprocess 1b	1.09 ± 0.07	1.52 ± 0.06	343.2 ± 0.2	130.3 ± 0.6	2.2
1X reprocess 1c	1.04 ± 0.10	1.43 ± 0.12	343.4 ± 1.0	126.2 ± 1.7	4.2
2X reprocess 1c	1.11 ± 0.02	1.36 ± 0.07	344.0 ± 0.6	125.5 ± 0.8	4.6
3X reprocess 1c	1.08 ± 0.02	1.42 ± 0.02	342.4 ± 0.7	124.9 ± 0.5	2.6

To determine the effects of pellet reprocessing, electrochemical impedance spectroscopy was performed. Control, 3X reprocessed 1b, and 3X reprocessed 1c pellets were tested under a load force equating to 7.5 psi at 375, 400, 475, 500 and 550C with impedance spectra taken at each temperature in triplicate. To evaluate the performance of the pellets, slopes of the impedance spectra were calculated utilizing the last 10 data points comprising the most linear portion of the spectra. Results from these tests can be found in Figure 4. Control pellets were run to establish a baseline which contained no reprocessed materials. These pellets had spectra taken while the heating up to 550C as well as cooling down to 375C. It was found that when the temperature reached 475C the impedance spectrum remained constant indicating that the pellet had reached equilibrium and no longer changed when cooling. The test procedure was then altered to only measure on heating allowing for faster data collection. The performance of all pellets were compared at 550C which is in the normal operating temperature range of the cell chemistry. The control pellets exhibited an average slope of -0.565 with a coefficient of variance (CV) of 3.6. A small CV demonstrates how little variance there is between pellets which is to be expected for the control pellets. The 3X reprocessed 1b pellets with fusing exhibited an average slope of -0.541 with a CV of 5.4. The reprocessed pellets performed very similar to the control pellets suggesting that recycling material has little to no measurable effect on pellet performance even when made from three-times reprocessed materials with fusing. The 3X reprocessed 1c pellets showed a slope of -0.641 and a CV of 10.9. This suggests that reprocessing without fusing has an adverse effect on performance and variability likely due to non-uniform wetting. Thus, reprocessing scrapped pellets is a viable option in salvaging valuable material. Mechanical slump data collected from these experiments show that on average the reprocessed samples exhibit less slump than the controls. This is consistent with reprocessed pellets containing being grinded additional times reducing the electrolyte particle size resulting in lower porosity than virgin material.

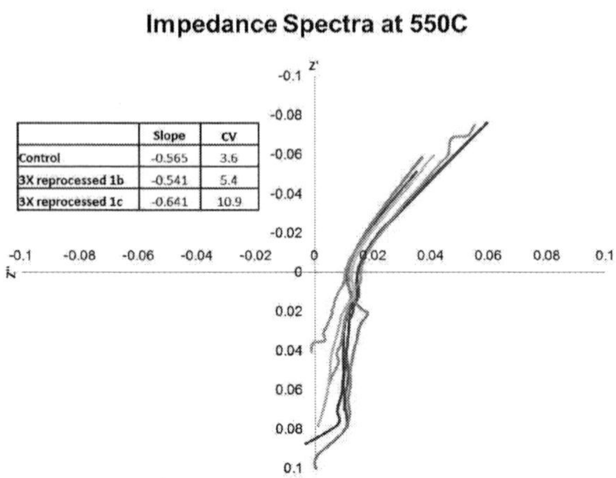

Figure 4: Reprocessed materials impedance spectra at 550C

Conclusion

The electrolyte-binder powder processing for thermal batteries was investigated and characterized in relation to separator pellet manufacturing and performance. Original hypotheses related to powder processing operations and their direct impact on pellet production did not hold fully true. Nonetheless, alternative powder blending and sizing processes are presented that each introduce both benefits and drawbacks. The use of a blending aid to improve mixing when using MgO significantly reduces the required mix time to achieve homogeneity but introduces additional processing steps. Granulation of the powder, while widely used in pharmaceutical industry to improve flow properties, may have influenced the final particle size distribution of the powder but experimental results did not show significant benefit on automated pellet press. Electrolyte-binder powder processing may be robust in that the process parameters evaluated as part of this research showed no significant impact on pellet production metrics evaluated.

While designing a powder process to result in improved pellet manufacturing was not immediately successful, reprocessing of scrapped separator pellets is a promising approach to reduce material waste. Separator pellets were reprocessed three times to exaggerate any effect using two different reprocessing methods. It was first demonstrated that reprocessed materials, both with and without fusing, can be fabricated into acceptable pellets requiring only minor adjustment in pellet press parameters attributed to a change in mechanical property of the reprocessed powders. 2X and 3X reprocessed pellets without fusing measured statistically significant changes in heat capacity over a temperature range when the electrolyte is still solid while all pellets behaved similarly in the molten phase. It is estimated that there is no change to melting point or heat of fusion for pellets using either reprocessing method. No change to the thermal properties of the reprocessed materials is important from the battery design perspective because it would not require a change to the heat balance if reprocessed materials were incorporated.

BET surface area showed a decreasing trend with reprocessing which is attributed to additional grinding reducing the electrolyte particle size and lowering the porosity. A reduction in porosity is supported by lower slump values for reprocessed pellets measured during impedance testing. At 550C and compared to control pellets, 3X reprocessed pellets with fusing exhibited similar impedance and coefficient of variance demonstrating that materials could likely be recycled. Reprocessed pellets that were not fused exhibited both higher impedance and coefficient of variance. Additional cell discharge data using reprocessed separators and cathodes is planned. It is recommended that reprocessed materials be fused to ensure good electrolyte wetting and then be mixed back in with virgin material at a defined maximum weight percentage.

Acknowledgements

Sandia National Laboratories is a multi-program laboratory managed and operated by Sandia Corporation, a wholly owned subsidiary of Lockheed Martin Corporation, for the U.S. Department of Energy's National Nuclear Security Administration under contract DEAC04-94AL85000. Approved for unlimited release, SAND2016-3756 C.

References

1. J. Prescott and R. Barnum, "On Powder Flowability," *Pharmaceutical Technology* (October 2000)
2. D. Nissen, "Processing Effects on Powders for Thermal Batteries," *SAND80-8024* (May 1980)
3. R. Guidotti, F. Reinhardt, and A. Andazola, "Blending Study of MgO-Based Separator Materials for Thermal Batteries," *SAND2002-1458* (June 2002)

Lithium-ion/Supercapacitor Hybrid Systems for Use in Man-Portable Applications

Yakira J. Howarth, Terrill B. Atwater, Kevin Chu
US Army-RDECOM-CERDEC
Aberdeen Proving Ground, MD 21005

Abstract: *Supercapacitors and supercapacitor hybrid systems are being sought as battery replacements in several military applications because of their lighter weight, better cyclability, and higher power density. They are additionally able to operate over a wider temperature range with minimal self-discharge at high temperature storage. The ability to build power sources that can demonstrate high power output and high energy in a single electrochemical system opens the doors to such applications as engine starters, radio power adapters, and microgrid sychronization, among others. Historically, capacitors have been used for peak-shaving in capacitor-battery hybrid systems for C4ISR equipment, but as a result of the advancements in supercapacitors, a new look is being taken to view their applications in the military. In this paper, we will present data on the effect of temperature and rate on performance and cycle life of new supercapacitor hybrid technologies. The goal of this effort is to analyze the systems' capabilities to meet the requirements of different applications, taking into consideration the military environment spectrum. Specifically, we will examine two proprietary configurations of lithium-ion/supercapacitor hybrid systems, and how they perform in man-portable applications.*

Keywords
Supercapacitors; Lithium-ion capacitors; High-rate electrochemical systems; Hybrid capacitors; Man-portable

Introduction
Advancements in supercapacitor technology have prompted the U.S. Army to explore systems that would benefit from the use of supercapacitors and supercapacitor hybrids in place of batteries. Specifically, the hybridization of lithium-ion batteries with supercapacitors creates a system that can operate in the same voltage range as batteries while still maintaining similar characteristics to supercapacitors. These hybrid systems combine the supercapacitor's ability to charge and discharge at high currents with the lithium-ion battery's ability to operate at a higher voltage range. They additionally maintain the supercapacitor's strength of running at a wide rate and temperature range for tens to hundreds of thousands of cycles with little detriment to the cell[1,2].

Hybridizing lithium-ion technology with supercapacitors presents trade-offs to the power system that need to be optimized for specific applications. The lithium-ion electrochemistry introduces a higher energy density to the system but reduces the high current capabilities of the supercapacitor element[1,3]. Depending on the method used for hybridization, the lithium-ion element may additionally decrease the cycle life and low temperature performance of the system[5,6]. This paper will analyze two proprietary configurations of lithium-ion/supercapacitor hybrid cells that utilize different hybridization methods, thus exhibiting unique strengths and weaknesses. The performance of these cells will be examined for use in man portable devices to determine which configuration can be optimized for this specific application.

Background
Lithium-ion/supercapacitor hybrid systems are uniquely suited to meet the power and energy needs of military man-portable devices as they utilize both battery and double layer capacitor-type electrodes[1,7]. The lithium-ion electrode contributes to the cell's energy density through faradaic redox reactions within the bulk electrode, while the supercapacitor electrode provides higher power density through buildup of electrostatic charge at its surface[6,8,9]. This combination gives the hybridized power system the ability to operate in place of batteries but at more extreme temperatures and for much greater lengths of time. While lithium-ion batteries have been the main power source for these systems in the past because of their high energy density, they have many limitations when it comes to power, cycle life, and operation under extreme temperatures. Traditional supercapacitors can address these limitations, making them an attractive hybridization element. Man-portable devices, such as radios, can have sizable load variations during operation as a result of how they are used. Such applications have relatively high "peak-to-average" power requirements, as a radio will require high "pulses" of power during transmission, but only low and steady power when in standby mode[3,10,11]. Furthermore, man portable devices can benefit greatly from these hybridized power systems due to the power source's quick recharge ability and high cycle-life, thus limiting the need for battery recharge or replacement[11,12]. Lithium-ion/supercapacitor hybrids can

function for over 100,000 cycles and therefore can outlast the lifetime of a device without any maintenance requirements. These power systems additionally have good performance at high and low temperatures, and can handle both the extreme climates in austere deployment environments as well as the heat generated during radio transmission[7].

Experimental

Two configurations of lithium-ion/supercapacitor hybrid prismatic pouch cells were tested for their performance at varying rates, temperatures, and application specific scenarios. Initially, five cells of Configuration A and three cells of Configuration B were tested for rate capability, followed by four cells of each tested for temperature performance. The two configurations were compared to each other in order to find which was optimal for application in man portable devices. Configuration A cells had an average volume of 12 cm^3 and weighed an average of 20.7 grams, and Configuration B cells had an average volume of 10 cm^3 and weighed an average of 20.8 grams. For each test, the cells were run on an ARBIN MSTAT4 Battery Cycler System, and TPS Tenney TJR temperature chambers were used for the temperature performance tests. Before beginning the tests, all cells were charged and discharged at a constant current of 0.8 A between 3.8 V and 2.2 V twenty times each to establish baseline performance.

For rate testing, the five cells of Configuration A and three cells of Configuration B were charged and discharged between 3.8 V and 2.2 V at 1 A for 20 cycles, followed by 2.0 A for 20 cycles, followed by a 0.8 A baseline test. The Configuration A cells were then tested at 4.0 A for 125 cycles, while the Configuration B cells were tested at 3.0 A because of their decreased performance when current was increased from 1.0 A to 2.0 A. Following another 20 cycles at baseline conditions, the Configuration A cells were run at 8.0 A for 20 cycles, while the Configuration B cells were run at 0.8 A for 500 cycles. The A cells were then also cycled at 0.8A for 500 cycles to conclude the rate capability testing. To test temperature performance, four of the original five Configuration A cells were used, while all three of the original Configuration B cells were used with an additional cell of the same configuration. All eight cells were run at 40°C, 10°C, 0°C, 50°C, -10°C, and -5°C for 20 cycles each before being cycled at baseline conditions at room temperature and run again at 55°C.

The two configurations of cells were additionally tested according to the discharge profile of a man portable device. To simulate a radio's load profile, the cells were alternatingly pulsed for 18 seconds at 0.55A and for 2 seconds at 2.9 A until they reached their discharged state at 2.2 V.

Results

In order to compare the performance of cells from Configuration A to Configuration B, plots were constructed showing charge and discharge capacity as a function of cycle number. Average cell weight with respect to each configuration was considered similar enough to gain an accurate comparison by charting capacity rather than specific capacity. These plots were analyzed for capacity output, cell matching, and capacity retention stability throughout each 20 cycle span. They were additionally examined to see the losses or gains in capacity due to rate and temperature deviations from the baseline.

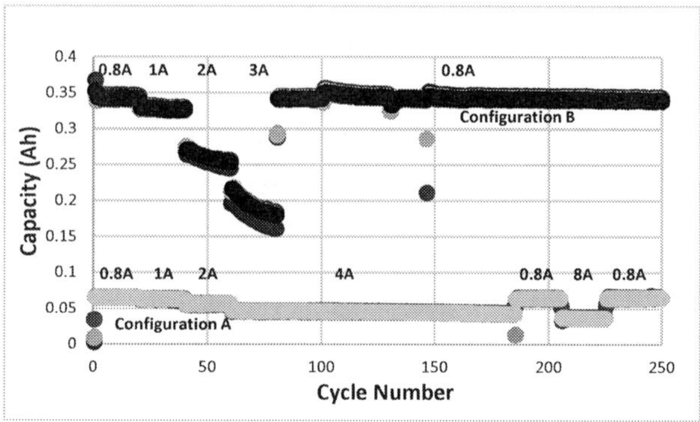

Figure 1: Configuration A and B Rate Comparison

Figure 1 shows the capacity yielded from each cell configuration at varying rates. It can be seen that the capacity output of Configuration B is much higher than that of Configuration A, with the 0.8 A baseline yielding around 5 times more capacity from the B cells. However, an increase in rate caused a much larger performance drop for the Configuration B cells than for the A cells. From the baseline cycling rate of 0.8 A, the B cells showed a 5% drop at 1.0 A, a 25% drop at 2.0 A, and a 45% drop at 3.0 A, while the A cells only showed a 3.5% drop at 1.0 A, a 14% drop at 2.0 A, a 29% drop at 4.0 A, and a 44% drop at 8.0 A. Configuration B cells were not cycled at 4.0 A or 8.0 A because of the trend they had shown when increasing the rate up to 3.0 A. Furthermore, the matching and overall consistent performance of the B cells was greatly diminished at the 2.0 A and 3.0 A rates, while the A cells never experienced a loss in matching or stability all the way up to 8.0 A. It is important to note that after both cell configurations experienced large capacity drops they recovered completely when cycled back at the baseline conditions.

Figure 2 shows the performance of the two cell configurations being cycled at varying temperatures. For 20 cycles each, four cells from both configurations were run at a 0.8 A rate at 23°C, 40°C, 10°C, 0°C, 50°C, -10°C, -5°C, 55°C, and 23°C. In addition to good performance at room temperature (23°C), the Configuration A cells also performed fairly consistently at 40°C and 10°C. At -10°C, the cells showed about a 57%

loss in capacity as well as a loss of consistent performance and matching between the cells. Although a slight gain in capacity was observed at 50°C and 55°C, capacity drops over the 20 cycles, as well as a loss of capacity matching, can be observed.

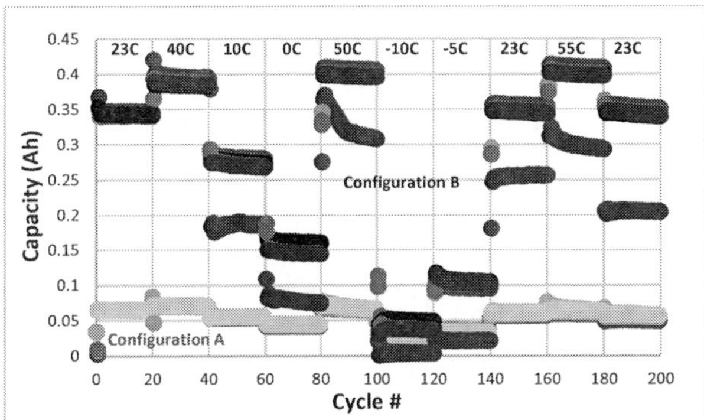

Figure 2: Configuration A and B Temp. Comparison

Figure 2 shows the performance of the two cell configurations being cycled at varying temperatures. For 20 cycles each, four cells from both configurations were run at a 0.8 A rate at 23°C, 40°C, 10°C, 0°C, 50°C, -10°C, -5°C, 55°C, and 23°C. In addition to good performance at room temperature (23°C), the Configuration A cells also performed fairly consistently at 40°C and 10°C. At -10°C, the cells showed about a 57% loss in capacity as well as a loss of consistent performance and matching between the cells. Although a slight gain in capacity was observed at 50°C and 55°C, capacity drops over the 20 cycles, as well as a loss of capacity matching, can be observed.

The Configuration B cells showed much more capacity variance from the baseline temperature of 23°C than the A cells when cycled in the same temperature range. Figure 2 shows a capacity loss of 89% at -10°C compared to Configuration A's 57% loss. However, even with this large capacity drop, three of the four B cells still performed at a higher capacity overall than the A cells. The B cells additionally showed much worse cell matching than the A cells at almost every temperature, with 10°C cycling apparently triggering the mismatch.

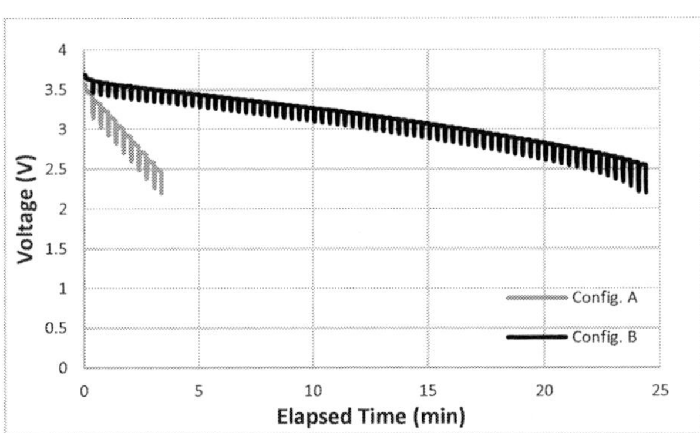

Figure 3: Configuration A and B Radio Profile

After being fully charged to 3.8 V, the cells were discharged according to a simulated radio profile by alternating between 0.55 A and 2.9 A for 18 seconds and 2 seconds, respectively. **Figure 3** shows that both Configuration A and B cells were able to handle a single discharge cycle according to this load, with the A cells completely discharging in about 4 minutes and the B cells discharging in about 24 minutes.

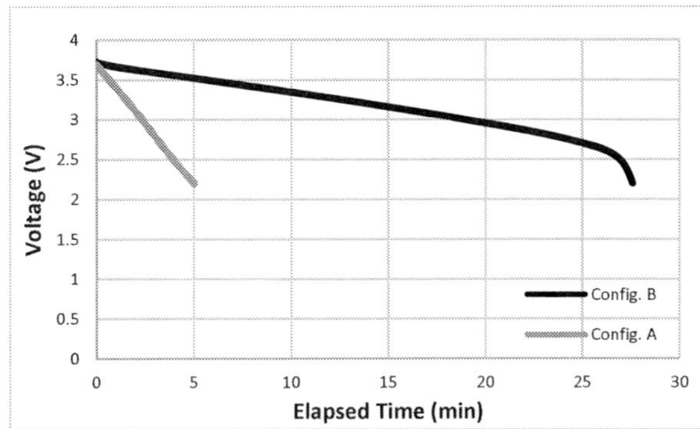

Figure 4: Configuration A and B Discharge Curve

When plotted for a single discharge cycle at 0.8 A, Figure 4 shows each configuration's voltage over elapsed time. Configuration A discharges from 3.8 V to 2.2 V in approximately 5 minutes, while Configuration B takes about 27. In addition to reinforcing the results from Figure 3, it is also important to note the shape of the discharge curves. Configuration A displays the linear relationship of voltage to state-of-charge normally exhibited by a supercapacitor, while Configuration B's curve appears more like a typical battery discharge curve.

Discussion

Hybridized lithium-ion/supercapacitor cells were tested in two configurations to assess their utility in man-portable devices. While both cells were approximately the same size and weight, the method of hybridization differed to an extent that rate and temperature capabilities were distinct. When compared at a baseline cycle test of 0.8 A and 23°C, Configuration B cells consistently yielded much higher capacity outputs than Configuration A cells, with an average difference of 438%. Higher rates greatly diminished the B cells' matching and overall consistency at 2.0 A and 3.0 A currents to such an extent that they were unable to be cycled at the 4 A and 8 A rates at which the A cells were successfully able to perform. A similar trend held true when compared at temperatures differing from the 23°C baseline, with the B cells unable to maintain cell matching and stability at temperatures below 10°C. When cycled according to a simulated radio profile, both configurations performed without noticeable losses throughout a single discharge, with the B cells lasting around 20 minutes longer than the A cells. It can additionally be observed from the radio profile test that although the Configuration B cells showed instability when cycled above 2.0 A during rate testing, being intermittently pulsed at 2.9 A did not have the same negative effects on the cell. Future testing would extend the duration of the radio profile simulation to observe the effects on the cells over the device's lifespan. Since the overall results show that the Configuration A cells closely resemble traditional supercapacitors while the Configuration B cells behave much more like a battery, the most fitting power source for man-portable applications may likely be a combination of the two.

Conclusion

The U.S. Army is investigating lithium-ion/supercapacitor hybrid systems for use in military applications because of their ability to sink sporadic and high-rate pulses of power without degradation, their wide operating temperature range, and their extremely long cycle life. The combination of the high operating voltage from the energy dense lithium-ion component with the high rate capability from the power dense supercapacitor component makes these power systems a promising replacement for lithium-ion batteries in man portable applications. However, these hybrid systems are not "one size fits all", and the balance of energy density and power density within the cells needs to be optimized for each specific application. The two cell configurations evaluated here provided distinct strengths and weaknesses that make them suitable for use in different applications. Configuration A demonstrated great stability and cell matching at rates as high as 8A and temperatures ranging from -10 to 55°C. While Configuration B cells yielded capacity outputs 5 times greater than those of the A cells, their stability and matching were greatly diminished as they were cycled at currents and temperatures that varied from the baseline. Based on the results of rate and temperature performance testing, the Configuration A cells demonstrated much better suitability for devices used in extreme temperature environments, while the Configuration B cells are the stronger choice for devices when longer runtime is needed. A power solution combining the strengths of each configuration is the likely path forward for man-portable applications.

Acknowledgements

The authors wish to thank Jeffrey Read for his assistance with this document and helpful discussion on cell testing. We would also like to acknowledge our colleagues who edited this paper.

References

1. Ronsmans J. and B. Lalande, "Combining energy with power: Lithium-ion capacitors," *2015 International Conference on Electrical Systems for Aircraft, Railway, Ship Propulsion and Road Vehicles (ESARS).* IEEE, pp. 1-4, 2015.
2. Lambert, S. M., Pickert, V., Holden, J., He, X., & Li, W. "Comparison of supercapacitor and lithium-ion capacitor technologies for power electronics applications," *5th IET International Conference*, IET, pp. 1-5, 2010.
3. Sikha, G. and B.N. Popov. "Performance optimization of a battery–capacitor hybrid system," *Journal of Power Sources*, vol. 134.1, pp. 130-138, 2004.
4. Cericola, D., et al. "Simulation of a supercapacitor/Li-ion battery hybrid for pulsed applications," *Journal of Power Sources*, vol. 195.9, pp. 2731-2736, 2010.
5. Simon, P. and Y. Gogotsi. "Materials for electrochemical capacitors," *Nature materials*, vol. 7.11, pp. 845-854, 2008.
6. Vangari, M, T. Pryor, and L. Jiang. "Supercapacitors: review of materials and fabrication methods," *Journal of Energy Engineering*, vol. 139.2, pp. 72-79, 2012.
7. Atwater, T. B., P.J. Cygan, and F.C. Leung. "Man portable power needs of the 21st century: I. Applications for the dismounted soldier. II. Enhanced capabilities through the use of hybrid power sources," *Journal of Power Sources*, vol. 91.1, pp. 27-36, 2000.
8. Chu, A. and P. Braatz. "Comparison of commercial supercapacitors and high-power lithium-ion batteries for power-assist applications in hybrid electric vehicles: I. Initial characterization," *Journal of power sources*, vol. 112.1, pp. 236-246, 2002.
9. Jiang, Jian, et al. "Recent advances in metal oxide-based electrode architecture design for electrochemical energy storage," *Advanced materials*, vol. 24.38, pp. 5166-5180, 2012.
10. Kuperman, A. and I. Aharon. "Battery–ultracapacitor hybrids for pulsed current loads: A review," *Renewable and Sustainable Energy Reviews*, vol. 15.2, pp. 981-992, 2011.
11. Halpin, M.S, R.M. Nelms, and J,E. Schatz. "Characterization of double-layer capacitor application issues for commercial and military applications," *IECON 97. 23rd International Conference on.* Vol. 3. IEEE, 1997.
12. Du Pasquier, A. et al. "A comparative study of Li-ion battery, supercapacitor and nonaqueous asymmetric hybrid devices for automotive applications," *Journal of Power Sources*, vol. 115.1, pp. 171-178, 2003.

Lithium Ion Capacitor-Battery Hybrid Power System for Portable Military Applications

Patricia H. Smith*[a], Raymond B. Sepe, Jr.[b], Kyle G. Waterman[b], and L. Jeff Myron[c]

[a]Naval Surface Warfare Center, Carderock Division, 9500 MacArthur Blvd., West Bethesda, MD 20817 [b]Electro Standards Laboratories, 36 Western Industrial Dr., Cranston, RI 02921 [c]JSR Micro, 1280 North Mathilda Ave, Sunnyvale, CA 94089

Abstract: *Portable military devices frequently require load profiles that fluctuate between a short high-power pulse (ranging from milliseconds to a minute) and a significantly longer, more modest power baseline draw. A hybrid combination of batteries and lithium ion capacitors (LICs) offers the promise of improved performance by shrinking the volume of batteries required and reducing the frequency of their replacement. High-power, short-duration pulses could be supplied by the LIC, while the batteries provide the low-power, long-duration demands of the load. This paper reviews the evaluation of LIC-battery hybrids that include lithium primary, lithium ion or alkaline batteries under a wide range of power and temperatures.*

Keywords: Lithium ion capacitor; hybrid

Introduction

Advanced electronic devices, such as the Single-Channel Ground and Airborne Radio System (SINCGARS) and various Satellite Communications (SATCOM) devices, are vital for the Marines to successfully complete their missions. The military presently relies on lithium and lithium ion batteries to meet the peak-power and energy requirements for this equipment. Unfortunately, current limitations in battery lifetime often lead to numerous batteries being required to complete a mission, thus creating a logistics problem that reduces the capability of the fighter force. Longer lasting batteries would be of great value to the Marine Corps and Army.

Hybrid power systems can be superior to batteries when the load profile is a series of intermittent high-power pulses superimposed over a steady, low-power baseline. Under these conditions, batteries are primarily limited by internal resistance that lowers cell voltage and results in premature cell failure. Combining a battery with a capacitor allows the capacitor to support high-power transients, thus lowering the battery discharge current and increasing battery efficiency. Hybrid systems should therefore be beneficial to communication systems such as SINCARS or SATCOM.

Until recently, the full potential of a hybrid-battery architecture could not be realized because of the low energy density of electrochemical double layer capacitors (EDLCs, 3-5 Wh/Kg). The development of Asymmetric EDLCs, where one of the capacitive carbon-electrodes is replaced with a faradaic battery-electrode [1], now makes this hybrid-battery feasible because the cell capacitance is considerably greater than that of its symmetric counterpart. One type of Asymmetric EDLC is the lithium ion capacitor (LIC) that utilizes a graphite or hard carbon for the negative electrode. The use of a lithium ion (Li^+) insertion carbon effectively pins the electrode voltage at a high negative potential, while the voltage of the positive electrode rises and falls. The net result is an increase in cell operating voltage, thereby providing higher energy according to the equation, $E = (1/2)CV^2$, where C and V are the capacitance and operating voltage of the cell, respectively. Energy densities as high as 14 Wh/Kg have been reported in commercial LIC cells. The energy is available over a wide range of power, and a cycle life of over 2 million cycles has been reported.[2] Such properties make the LIC a very attractive energy source for incorporation into hybrid-battery systems.

In this study, we investigated the potential benefit of a LIC-hybrid architecture for portable Marine Corps devices. Our goal was to identify under what conditions a hybrid system would be beneficial for SINCGARS and SATCOM-like devices.

Experimental

Primary lithium D-cells, alkaline D-cells, BA-5X90 and BB-2590 batteries were obtained from various commercial suppliers. The 1,000 F and 500 F LIC were supplied by JSR Micro.

An intelligent hybrid power management board (PMB) was developed and incorporated to regulate the current drawn from the battery and LIC when responding to the electric load. A basic diagram illustrating how the PMB functions is provided in Figure 1. The board employed an ultra-low power microprocessor and a bi-directional DC/DC converter. The microprocessor-based controller is activated upon detecting a power surge on the battery. Once activated, the controller ensures that the battery operates within a pre-determined current limit. During high-power transient conditions, the batteries supplies only a portion of the power with the LIC supplying additional power as needed. The PMB was also capable of monitoring temperature and adjusting current flow when battery temperatures exceeded the manufactures' recommended value. Thus the PMB ensures that the battery operates under highly efficient and safe conditions.

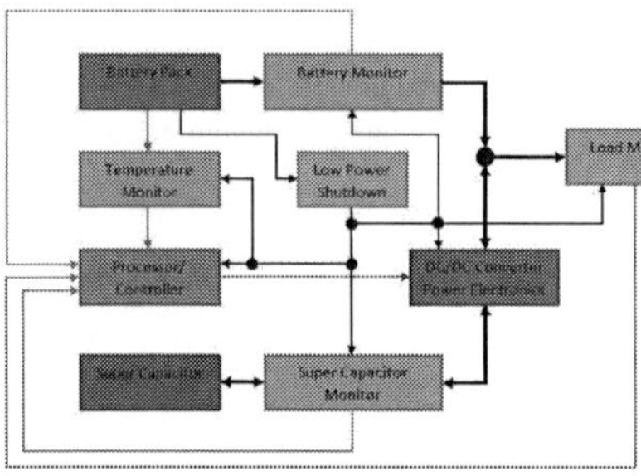

Figure 1. Block diagram of hybrid power management board.

The LIC (1,000 F) and PMB were packaged in a rugged container referred to as the "Power Augmentor" (Figure 2). The Power Augmentor prototype (12.5 cm x 11.0 cm x 3.8 cm, 404 g) had an ITT Cannon P/N CA 110821-6 mating connector for easy assembly to the BA-5X90 and BB-2590 batteries. The detachable housing was designed to facilitate easy conversion of a battery into a hybrid system when high power pulses were required, and easy removal for lower power demands.

Batteries and hybrid systems were evaluated using either a MACCOR Series 4000 Automated Test System or a BK Precision 8500 DC Electronic Loader. Tests were conducted using the following regimes:

Procedure 1: 100 W for 1 minute, followed by 12 W for 9 minutes, repeat until the battery/hybrid voltage drops to either 10V (primary) or 11 V (rechargeables).

Procedure 2: 20 W for 1 minute, followed by 6 W for 9 minutes, repeat until the battery/hybrid voltage drops to either 10 V (primary) or 11 V (rechargeables).

Test procedures were designed to provide harsh conditions that would clearly demonstrate the effect of high-rate pulse load applications on battery/hybrid service life and do not necessarily represent typical device usage.

Figure 2. Photograph of the Power Augmentor that includes a 1,000 F lithium ion capacitor and a power management board.

Results and Discussion

Figure 3 illustrates how the adding a LIC (in a hybrid setup) reduces the burden of the battery thus enabling it to operate under more favorable conditions. Here a five D-cell Li/SO_2 battery was hybridized with a 1,000 F capacitor. As shown, both the LIC and the battery contributed to 100 W pulse load while the battery provided the sole power during the 12 W load in addition to charging the capacitor.

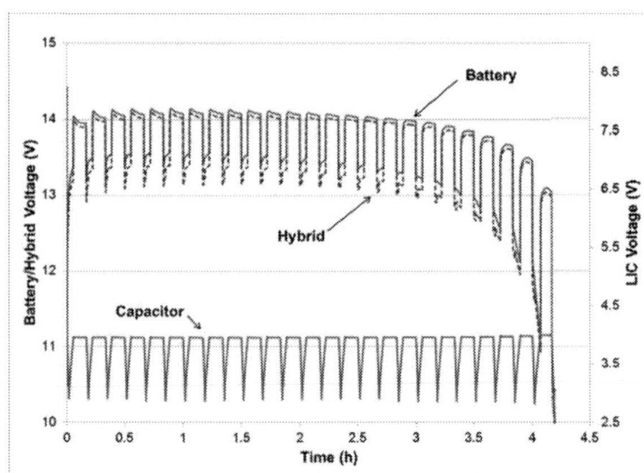

Figure 3. Voltage profiles of a five D-cell Li/SO_2 – 1,000 F LIC hybrid that was discharged for 1 minute at 100 W, 9 minutes at 12 W at RT.

The Power Augmentor allows BA-5X90 primary military batteries (5s2p) to be used for applications requiring power levels exceeding the battery's electrical fuse. This includes the BA-5790 (Li/CF_xMnO_2), the BA-5390 (Li/MnO_2) and the BA-5590 (Li/SO_2). As shown in Figure 4, significant capacity improvement was achieved when the Power Augmentor was connected to one Li/SO_2 BA-5590 battery (5s2p) discharged according to Procedure 1. The PMB was programmed so that the battery current never exceeded 2.5 A. As a consequence (and as seen in Figure 3), the LIC provided the majority of power during the 100 W one-minute pulse thereby allowing the battery to operate below the 3 A electrical fuse limit. Forty seven cycles were obtained compared to 0 cycles for the non-hybridized battery that failed immediately upon testing.

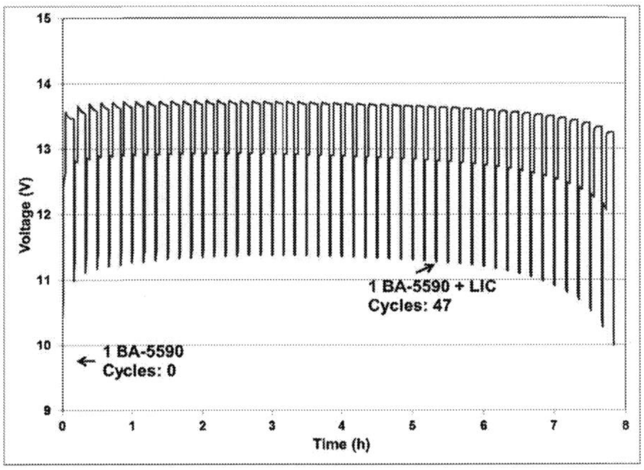

Figure 4. Discharge profiles of one BA-5590 Li/SO_2 battery (red) and one BA-5590 battery connected to the Power Augmentor (blue) that were cycled at 100 W for 1 minute, 12 W for 9 minutes and room temperature.

Additionally, one BA-5790 was able to deliver approximately the same number of cycles as two, BA-5590s when attached to the Power Augmentor and cycled using Procedure 1. This could result in a significant reduction in the number of batteries that the soldier must carry onto the battlefield.

The Power Augmentor was also shown to improve the performance of rechargeable BB-2590 batteries [3] when cycled at low temperatures, though they have a much higher current (20 A) and power limit (300 W) than the primary BA-5X90 batteries. As shown in Figure 5, the Power Augmentor extended the BB-2590 operational life by 23% when evaluated using Procedure 1 at -20°C. For certain missions however, this modest improvement in performance would not be offset by the additional weight and volume of the Power Augmentor.

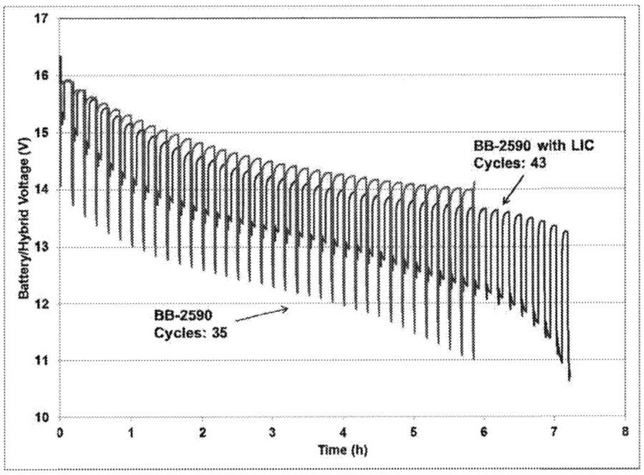

Figure 5. Observed performance enhancement of BB-2590 battery when hybridized to the Power Augmentor and cycled at 100 W for 1 minute, 12 W for 9 minutes and -20°C.

Additionally, the Power Augmentor may one day allow the military to use low-cost alkaline batteries for certain high-power applications. A ten D-cell alkaline battery hybridized to a 500 F LIC operated for approximately 9 hours (54 cycles) when discharged according to Procedure 2 (20 W for 1 minute, 6 W for 12 minutes, Figure 6). In comparison, the un-hybridized alkaline battery discharged for only 2.9 hours (17 cycles).

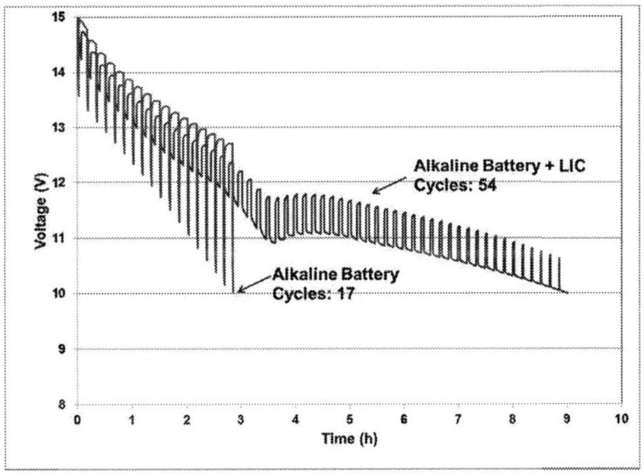

Figure 6. Voltage profiles of a ten D-cell alkaline battery hybridized to a 500 F LIC, discharged at 20 watts for 1 minute, followed by 6 watts for 9 minutes and room temperature.

Conclusions

We have demonstrated that high energy density lithium ion capacitors allow the soldier to achieve higher power and, for certain electrochemistries, longer operational life from existing military batteries. This was accomplished by hybridizing batteries with a lithium ion capacitor and interfacing the two energy storage devices with an intelligent power management board. Higher performance energy storage devices would reduce the number of batteries a soldier must carry onto the battlefield.

Acknowledgements

This work was financially support by the Office of Naval Research (Expeditionary Maneuver Warfare and Combating Terrorism Department) and is gratefully acknowledged.

References

1. Pell, W., and B. Conway, "Peculiarities and Requirements of Asymmetric Capacitor Devices Based on Combination of Capacitor and Battery-Type Electrodes", J. Power Sources, vol. 136, pp 334-335., 2004.
2. Ronsmans J.,and B. Lalande, "Combining Energy with Power: Lithium-Ion Capacitors", IEEE, 978-1-4799-7400-9/15/2015.
3. BB-2590 Spec sheet. SAFT, Doc N° 54092-0515-2, June 2015.

Development of High Power Supercapacitors for Hybrid Energy Storage Systems for Soldiers

Saemin Choi, Joseph Gallegos, Ryan Franck, Mahrokh Soltani, Leslie Alexander
Inmatech
schoi@inmatech-inc.com

Abstract

Development of High Power Supercapacitors for Hybrid Energy Storage Systems for Soldiers (Submitted to Capacitors session) Saemin Choi*, Joseph Gallegos, Ryan Franck, Mahrokh Soltani, and Leslie Alexander Inmatech, Inc. 1600 Huron Parkway, Ann Arbor, MI 48109 (734) 717-8247 / schoi@inmatech-inc.com Rechargeable Li-ion batteries such as BB-2590 are critical energy storage devices used for military applications. While these devices can have energy densities exceeding 150 Wh/kg, this energy is difficult to fully access in pulsed and high power applications due to the relatively slow kinetics associated with their redox processes1. As the demands for power and energy increase in the battlefield soldiers to access to new power and energy sources rapidly. Energy efficiency and recharge rates are critical for maintaining and sustaining equipment and communications. Supercapacitors are a class of electrochemical energy-storage device that could complement batteries in hybrid energy storage systems for applications in military and transportation, and load-leveling or uninterruptible power supply1-3. In terms of their specific energy and specific power, supercapacitors partially fill the gap between conventional capacitors and batteries. Accordingly, these devices can improve the performance of electronic power sources in applications where multiple cycles and high-power performance are required. Noticeably, supercapacitors can be included in a hybrid configuration to man¬age short, high power pulses, thereby minimizing stresses on the primary energy-storage device. Despite their proven performance benefits, supercapacitors have not found widespread commercial use, largely due to the need for higher energy densities and lower cost. Commercial off-the shelf (COTS) supercapacitors employing high area carbon electrodes and non-aqueous electrolytes can reach energy densities of 3-6 Wh/kg with power densities of 1000 W/kg. These devices have been highly optimized, and only incremental gains in energy density are expected in the future. Inmatech is commercializing next generation supercapacitor devices that incorporate low cost, high performance materials. We have demonstrated the technical feasibility of using proprietary nanostructured vanadium nitride (VN) based electrodes and an asymmetric cell architecture with non-flammable aqueous electrolytes (KOH) to manufacture commercially-attractive, high energy density (> 20 Wh/L) supercapacitors (Funded by NSF IIP 1113564, 1142998 and 1230387). These devices use aqueous electrolytes which are safe (nonflammable), inexpensive and have much higher ion conductivities at low temperatures than organic electrolytes used in COTS devices. We will report on the current status of our materials scale-up and high power cell development in cylindrical formats (e.g. 18650s) for military applications.

References

1. Miller, J.R. and Burke, A.F., Electrochemical capacitors: challenges and opportunities for real-world applications. Electrochem. Soc. Interface, 2008. 17(1): p. 53-57.
2. Song, Z., and Hoffman, H. and Li, J. and Han, X. and Zhang, X. and Ouyang, M. A system comparison of different semi-active hybrid energy storage system topologies for electric vehicles. J. Power Sources. 2015.
3. Simon, P. and Gogotsi, Y., Materials for electrochemical capacitors. Nat. Mater., 2008. 7(11): p. 845.

Metadielectric Materials

Matthew R Robinson, Paul Furuta, Ian Kelly-Morgan, Pavel Lazarev*, Hoang Ly, and Daniel Membreno

Capacitor Sciences, Inc.
Menlo Park, CA, USA 94025
***pavel.lazarez@capacitorsciences.com**

Abstract: We demonstrate progress towards the development of a Metadielectric material that enables a leap in the energy storage density of dielectric capacitors by extending the boundary of the tradeoff between bulk permittivity and resistivity. We demonstrate engineering the resistivity of solvent cast films to 10^{16} Ω•cm. We disclose material design principles aimed at achieving a 2 μm solvent-cast film with 10^{18} Ω•cm resistivity, 1000 V/μm dielectric strength, and 6 x 10^{-6} F/m permittivity. Metadielectric films meeting these specifications would enable capacitors with energy and power density of 250W•h/kg and 10^6 W/kg, respectively.

Keywords: film capacitor; hyperpolarizability; ferroelectric polymer; permittivity; resistivity; dielectric strength; energy storage.

Introduction: Energy storage devices having both high energy density and high power density would enable the development of machines and devices of the future including low cost grid energy storage. Conventional electrochemical batteries have power density, energy density, depth of discharge, charge and discharge rate, and lifetime limitations. Conventional capacitors have an energy density limitation. Metadielectric materials offer high energy density, high power density and long lifetime.

Table 1. Energy Density (E.D.), Power Density (P.D.), Self Discharge Time, and Lifetime expressed as number of charge/discharge cycles, for the major classes of energy storage devices [1,2].The projected properties of a film capacitor with a Metadielectric are shown in the last row.

Device	E.D. (Wh/kg)	P.D. (W/kg)	Self Discharge	Cycles
Battery	100 - 250	<10^3	months	10^3 - 10^4
Dielectric Capacitor	0.2	10^6	days	10^{10}
Supercap	10^0 - 10^1	10^0 - 10^1	weeks	10^5 - 10^6
Metadielectric	250	10^6	weeks - months	10^{10}

Permittivity vs. Resistivity Tradeoff: Materials with permittivity up to 10^{-5} F/m [3] have been demonstrated. However, the resulting resistivity has been impractically low (resulting in a high rate of self discharge) for a dielectric in a capacitor. High-permittivity (up to 10^{-6} F/m) polymer-matrix composites have been demonstrated with fillers such as metals, high k ceramics, carbon based materials, and conducting polymers and oligiomers [4]. Unfortunately, abundant data is consistent with a tradeoff between permittivity and resistivity in composite materials effectively bounding capacitor performance below the leap needed for energy storage applications [5]. This lack of successful use of the composite effect to increase the permittivity/resistivity boundary may lie with the interfacial structure of the composites. The predominate polarizability mechanism for composites exhibiting the highest permittivities is interfacial (Maxwell-Wagner) interactions [5]. But the penalty comes from the Lorentz/Mossotti field which alters the molecular orbitals, increasing conductivity and making bonds susceptible to breakage by standard Boltzmann processes and/or hole capture [6]. Broken molecular bonds leave percolation sites and result in lower dielectric strength.

Metadielectric: The Perfect Composite: Achieving high bulk permittivity without significant loss of resistivity requires a highly ordered material comprising densely packed highly polarizable units electrically isolated from one another by an envelope capable of withstanding the Lorentz/Mossotti field imposed from the nearby induced dipoles [7,8]. The natural choice for the envelope is a saturated hydrocarbon or fluorocarbon akin to polypropylene, polyethylene, or PTFE. In theory, highly crystalline polyethylene could achieve > 10,000 V/μm by virtue of the bond strength (3.6 eV) and size (0.15 nm). In reality, defects allow charge carrier breakthrough at much lower fields. Biaxially oriented (stretched) polypropylene (BOPP) exhibits 5x10^{16} Ω•cm resistivity and 600 V/μm dielectric strength [9], limited by defects. Laboratory measurements of vacuum deposited polypropylene films are reported as high as 1500 V/μm [10].

Metadielectric films are composed of units comprising a highly polarizable "core" covalently bonded to alkyl or fluoroalkyl chains - essentially fragments of polypropylene or PTFE. The units are engineered to self assemble into a highly ordered material whereby the "cores" are densely packed and enveloped by the ensemble of alkyl chains attached to the "core(s)" of the ensemble. Fig. 1 schematically illustrates the structure of a Metadielectric film and the self assembly process to create it. The alkyl groups in the Metadielectric materials can be more highly ordered than in BOPP. Furthermore, we employ fluoroalkyl groups known for more order and higher bulk resistivity than hydrocarbon alkyl groups [11]. Higher order means less random interfaces limiting the interfacial polarization to the covalent bond between the "core" and alkyl group. Hence this work targets composite electrical properties of 1000 V/μm dielectric strength and 10^{18} Ω•cm resistivity.

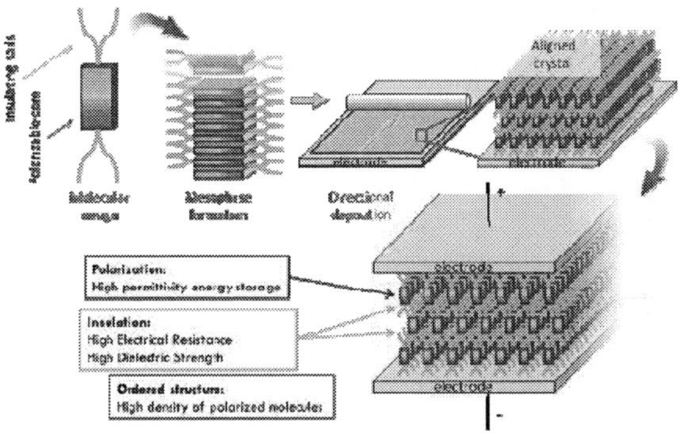

Figure 1. Metadielectric Material: Fabrication of capacitor comprising 1 – 2 μm Metadielectric film between charge collecting electrodes. The Metadielectric comprises a dense array of units each with a highly polarizable core all enveloped by the ensemble of insulating alkyl substituents.

Two classes of Metadielectric materials are introduced here: i) Conjugated π-stacking molecules, and ii) Ionic liquid crystalline side-chain polymers.

Conjugated π-stacking Molecules: In another paper we demonstrate π-conjugated molecules exhibiting hyperpolarizability [12] giving rise to permittivity as high as 10^{-6} F/m at fields > 500 V/μm. Fig. 2 depicts such a molecule without donor/acceptor substituents.

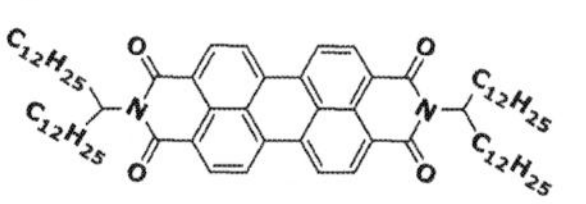

PDA Bis-Alk-PDI

Figure 2. An example of a conjugated π-stacking molecule comprising a flat π-conjugated polarizable core, with (**right**) and without (**left**) insulating alkyl substituents.

This class of Metadielectric material exploits the π–π stacking forces of the flat conjugated polarizable molecular unit to form a lyotropic liquid crystal (LLC) mesophase [13]. The LLC has long range order in the stacking direction. The ensemble of externally facing alkyl substituents envelopes a polarizable supramolecular stack. The coating and drying process used to generate the dielectric film is designed to preserve the order achieved in the LLC state.

Ionic Liquid Crystalline Side-chain Polymer, the second class of Metadielectric materials discussed here, comprise a mixture of an anionic copolymer and a cationic copolymer (Fig. 3). The ions are present as side-chains covalently attached to the copolymer backbone. Each ionic copolymer comprises electrically resistive alkyl or fluoroalkyl side chains (for resistivity).

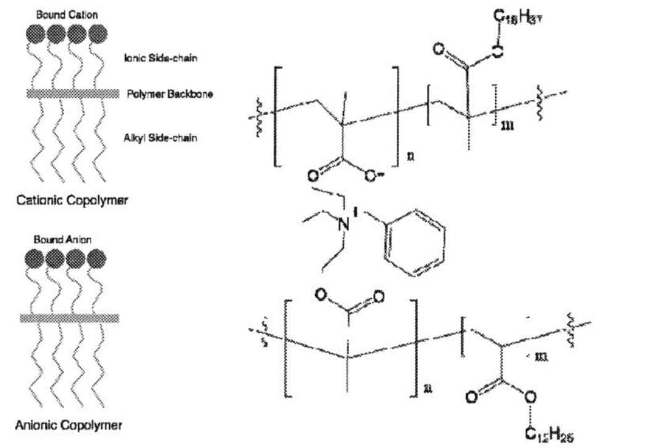

Figure 3. Schematic (**left**) and chemical formulae (**right**) of a cationic copolymer (**top**) and anionic copolymer (**bottom**), when mixed form an *Ionic Liquid Crystalline Side-chain Polymer Metadielectric material.* Each copolymer contains an electrically insulating alkyl side chain ($C_{18}H_{37}$ and $C_{12}H_{25}$) and a covalently bound ionic side chain.

Copolymers and polymer blends comprising monomers with significantly different polarity and solubility parameters are well known to result in solution cast films with high degree of order, e.g. lamella or micelles [14]. Metadielectric material properties emerge as the polarizable "cores" are formed as the cation/anion pair in the inside of a micelle or lamellar structures. The ion pair "cores" are electrically isolated by the enveloping alkyl side-chains that form the outside of the micelle or lamellar structure (Fig. 4). When a polymer contains ionic species, ionic polarization occurs below a few hundred Hz [15].

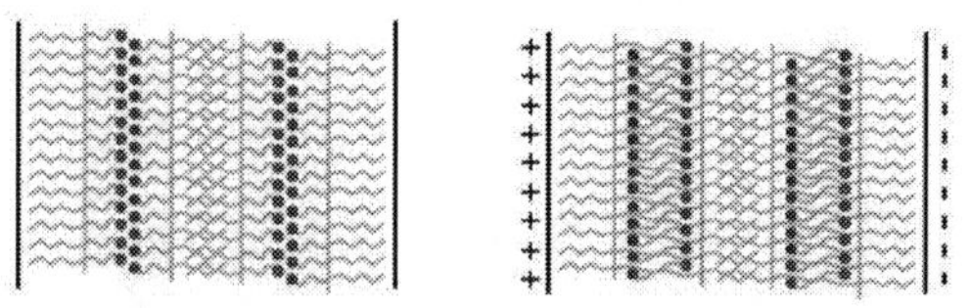

Figure 4. Schematic of ionic liquid crystalline side-chain polymer adopting a lamella structure, without (**left**) and with (**right**) an external electric field.

Nonpolar polymers free of ions are linear dielectrics, exhibiting a relative dielectric constant independent of electric field, $\varepsilon = D / E$. BOPP falls into this category. The stored (and released) energy density is thus $U = \int E \, dD = \frac{1}{2} \varepsilon E^2$.

Experimental:

Pellet

Sample Preparation of Pellet: Samples are pressed into a 13 mm x 1.3 mm pellet by grinding 0.2 g of powder and pressing it at 7 Tons in a standard KBr dye set. Silver epoxy electrodes are applied to both circular faces.

Sample Preparation of Thin Film Capacitors: Coating solutions are formulated by dissolving 0.2 g of powder into 1 mL of solvent and filtering the solution through a 0.45 μm PTFE filter. Patterned metalized glass substrates (9" x 5") are cleaned by exposing to UV-Ozone with 100%

oxygen process gas for 5 minutes. Coating and drying are all done in a laminar flow clean hood to prevent particle incorporation. Thin films are deposited on the substrates by dispensing 0.3 – 0.5 mL of coating solution and drawing a #2 ½ - #6 wire wound rod lengthwise along the glass at 1.5 in./s. The solution is allowed to dry.

Top aluminum electrodes (15 Ω/□) are thermally evaporated at 10^{-7} Torr at 0.1 – 0.2 nm/s through a mask defining 9 cm^2 capacitors per substrate. The high sheet resistance of the top electrode is designed to cause areas with current leaking defects to ablate and isolate themselves away from the circuit leaving the non-defective areas intact and connected ("clearing") [16]. Fig. 5 depicts the final test structure.

Figure 5. Top: Partial view of untested capacitors defined as |glass (1.1mm x 9" x 5") | Patterned ITO (0.2 μm x 9" x 4") | Metadielectric (1 μm x 9" x 5") | Al (2 nm x 4.5 cm x 2 cm) connected to circuit with pogo pins and silver epoxy; **Bottom:** Progression of one capacitor as voltage is increased. Defects clear electrode until it isolates at 600V.

DC Testing (Dielectric Strength & Field Dependent Resistivity & Permittivity): Capacitors are connected to a circuit with pogo pins inside a Faraday Cage. The pins are wired to a Keithley 2657A source meter where the testing protocol follows the DIN 62391-1 IEC. The DC resistivity as a function of soak voltage, "Soak Resistivity", is calculated from the current measured at the end of a 30 second voltage hold, or "soak. Capacitance at each voltage is recorded until the breakdown field is reached. The breakdown voltage is declared when less than half of the initial capacitance remains at the same low field. The thickness of the dielectric under each capacitor is measured using a stylus profilometer. The thickness and remaining device area are used to calculate the electric field, the permittivity, and resistivity.

Electrochemical Impedance Spectroscopy: For a deeper characterization of the material, Electrochemical Impedance Spectroscopy was performed by a Biologic SP-200 in a faraday cage. AC measurements were performed with 2 electrodes, 0.5 V_{rms}, and 0, 5 and 9 V/μm DC bias. The sample was measured at room temperature then heated to 30 and 50°C using a circulator and Lytron Al plate.

Results & Discussion: Resistivity engineering for the conjugated π-stacking class of Metamaterial was first demonstrated. The DC resistivity for perylene-3,4,9,10-tetracarboxylic dianhydride (PDA), a polarizable "core" without an insulating alkyl tail is 10^{11} Ω cm at 9 V/μm DC bias (Fig. 6). N,N-Bis(1-dodecyltridecyl)perylene-3,4,9,10-tetracarboxylic diimide (Bis-ALK-PDI) is 100x more resistive (10^{13} Ω cm at 9 V/μm DC bias). The solvent cast films (Fig. 1) of Bis-ALK-PDI show 10 – 1000x higher resistivity (up to 10^{15} Ω cm at 20 V/μm) than the pressed pellet, *increasing* with applied field as structure is pressed into place. The demonstrated resistance is higher than the best solution cast films of PMMA [17] and comparable with metalized BOPP [16]. This is consistent with a supramolecular stacking of "cores" to form an insulating envelope.

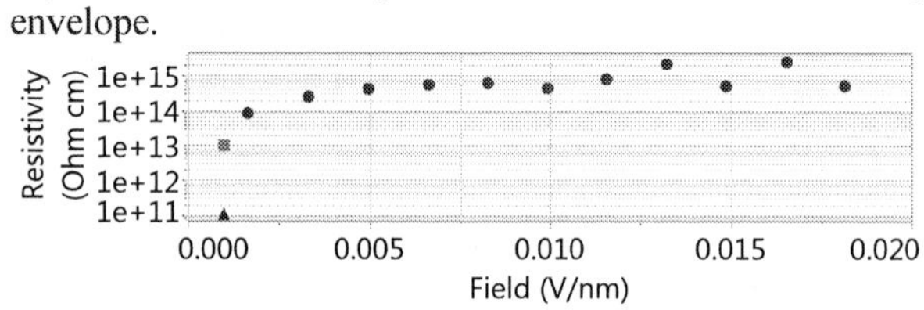

Figure 6. Resistivity at 9 V/μm of pellets of (▲) PDA - no alkyl substituent and (■) Bis-ALK-PDI – two branched 12 carbon alkyl substituents overlaid with the electric field dependency of (●) a 2 μm solvent cast film of Bis-ALK-PDI.

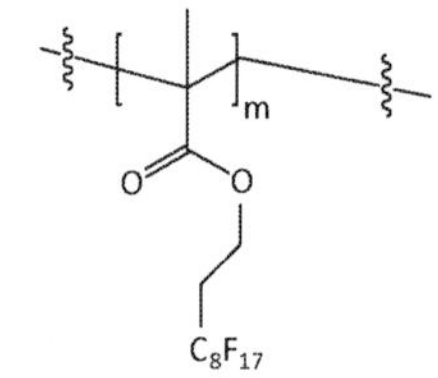

Resistivity engineering of ionic liquid crystalline side-chain polymer Metadielectric was also pursued. The insulating properties of the alkyl side groups are first discussed. Similar to Bis-ALK-PDI, we demonstrate increasing the resistivity of a solvent cast film compared to the bulk pellet. Before working with the mixture of anonic and cationic copolymers, the fluorinated acrylic shown to the right was investigated in order to understand the effect of fluoralkyl groups. The DC resistivity for the fluorinated fluoroacrylic is 10^{14} Ω cm at 9 V/μm DC bias (Fig. 7).

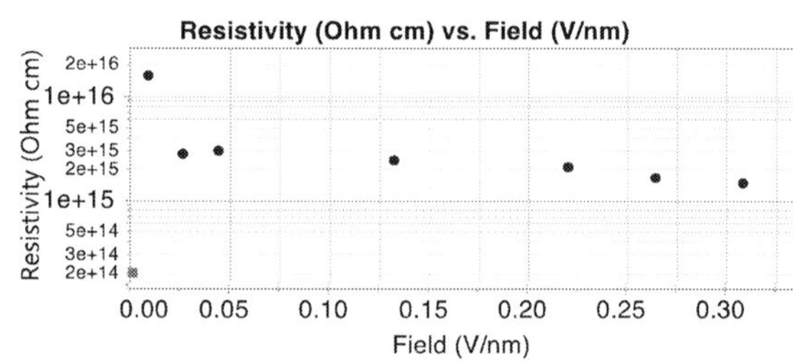

Figure 7. Resistivity of pellets (■) and a 1 μm solvent cast film (●) of a side chain fluorinated acrylic polymer.

The solvent cast films (Fig. 1) of the fluoro acrylic polymer is 10x to 100x higher resistivity (10^{15} – 10^{16} Ω cm) than the pellet. This demonstrates that order is induced by the side chain alkyl group. The breakdown field of the solvent cast films is > 500 V/μm, determined when 50% of the capacitive area remains after the electrode clears high current spots.

The sudden drop in resistivity at a low field (0.025 V/nm) shown in Figure 7 is troubling; resistivity of commercial fluorpolymer melt cast and extruded film is 10^{17} to 10^{18} Ω cm. Cyclic voltammetry was employed to detect impurities (free ions, monomers, water, etc.) which will undergo electrochemistry if present. Referring to Figure 8, peak current is proportional to concentration of species in the system and peak voltage is suggestive to the type of species.

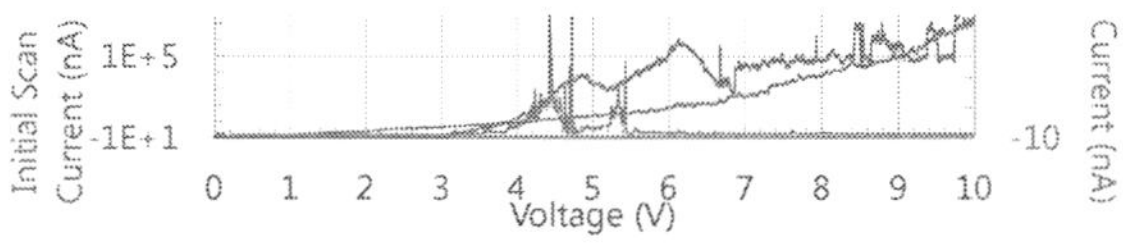

Figure 8. Cyclic voltammetry (200 mV/s) of a thin film device (Fig. 5) using the fluoropolymer acrylic as dielectric.

Oxidation (negative peaks between 4 and 6 volts) is occurring in the fluoro acrylic system likely from an impurity considering the substantial drop in peak height after cycling. Chemical synthesis and laboratory practices will be investigated and this testing will demonstrate the effectiveness of the improvements.

Continuing with the advanced analysis, electrochemical impedance spectroscopy was employed. The Nyquist plots were vertical lines with 20 ohms of equivalent series resistance ESR, which is consistent with the resistance of the ITO and the aluminum top electrode. There was no evidence of mobile ions or a diffusion process occurring at room temperature.

Conclusion: We have communicated design criteria for two classes of Metadielectric materials. Both require highly ordered molecular arrangement of polarizable "cores" covalently bonded to resistive alkyl groups as an ensemble envelope the "core". We have demonstrated the ability to make films from each of these classes with resistivity up to 10^{16} Ω·cm and 500 V/μm dielectric strength. Our next step for the π-conjugated Metadielectrics is to build in high permittivity by adding the theoretically determined donar/acceptor functional groups. Our next step for the ionic liquid crystal side chain polymers Metamaterials is better purification and annealing in order to increase the dielectric strength – to the point where the ion pairs separate. These dielectric metamaterials have the promise of creating inexpensive high power and high energy density energy storage devices with a virtually unlimited lifetime. When made into capacitive cells, energy could be safely stored at significantly less cost than that of grid energy. This would enable a suite of economically viable applications including Electric Vehicles, residential, commercial, industrial and utility energy storage.

References:

1. B. Dunn, H. Kamath, and J.-M. Tarascon, "Electrical Energy Storage for the Grid: A Battery of Choices", *Science* Vol. 334, pp. 928-935, 2011.
2. K. Yao, S. Chen, M. Rahimabady, M. S. Mirshekarloo, S. Yu, F. E. H. Tay, T. Sritharan, and L. Lu, "Nonlinear dielectric thin films for high power electric storage with energy density comparable with electrochemical supercapacitors", *Transactions on Ultrasonics, Ferroelectrics, and Frequency Control*, Vol. 58(9), pp. 1968-1974, 2011.
3. K. J. Hamam, M. A.-A. Mohammad, G. Mezei, R. Guda, and C. Burns, "High Dielectric Constant Response of Modified Copper Phthalocyanine", *Journal of Molecular Liquids*, Vol. 199 pp. 324-329, 2014.
4. C.-H. Ho, C.-D. Liu, C.-H. Hsieh, K.-H. Hsieh, and S.-N. Lee, "High dielectric constant polyananline/poly(acrylic acid) composites prepared by in situ polymerization", *Synthetic Metals*, Vol. 158, pp. 630-637, 2008.
5. Z.-M. Dang, J.-K. Yuan, J.-W. Zha, T. Zhou, S.-T. Li, and G.-H. Hu, "Fundamentals, processes and applications of high-permittivity polymer-matrix composites", *Progress in Materials Science*, Vol. 57, pp. 660-723, 2012.
6. J. McPherson, J.-Y. Kim, A. Shanware, and H. Mogul, "Thermochemical Description of Dielectric Breakdown in High Dielectric Constant Materials", *Applied Physics Letters*, Vol. 82(13), 2003.
7. A. Alu, "First-Principle Homogenization Theory for Periodic Metamaterials", *Phys. Rev. B*, Vol. 84(7), p. 075153, 2011.
8. R. Landauer, "Electrical Conductivity in Inhomogeneous Media, *AIP Conference Proceedings* Vol. 40(2), 1978.
9. Shin-Etsu Polypropylene Capacitor Films Technical Data Sheet, Jan. 2014, Shin-Etsu Film Co., Ltd. http://www.shinetsu-film.co.jp/e/products/pdf/ppfilm_r_e.pdf
10. T. Ogawa, S. Ochaia, T. Takagi, K. Kojima, M. Ieda, and T. Mizutani, "Electrical properties of ultra thin polypropylene film", *Properties and Applications of Dielectric Materials*, 1994. Proceedings of the 4th International Conference, Vol.1, Brisbane, Qld., 3-8 Jul 1994, pp. 211 – 214.
11. M. Friedman, and G. Walsh, "High Performance Films: Review of New Materials and Trends", *Polymer Engineering and Science*, Vol. 42(8), pp.1756-1788, 2002.
12. L. Mourokh, and P. Lazarev, "Organic molecules with high second-order permittivity: Energy storage applications", *Proceedings of the 47th Power Sources Conference*, 2016.
13. J. Lydon, "Chromonic Review", *J. Mater. Chem.*, Vol. 20, pp.10071-10099, 2010.
14. S. P. Samant, C. A. Grabowski, K. Kisslinger, K. G. Yager, G. Yuan, S. K. Satija, M. F. Durstock, D. Raghavan, and A. Karim, "Directed Self-Assembly of Block Copolymers for High Breakdown Strength Polymer Film Capacitors", *ACS Appl. Mater. Interfaces*, Vol. 8(12), 2016.
15. (a) L. Zhu, and Q. Wang, "Novel Ferroelectric Polymers for High Energy Density and Low Loss Dielectrics", *Macromolecules*, Vol. 45, pp. 2937-2954, 2012. (b) L. Yang, X. Li, E. Allahyarov, P. L. Taylor, Q. M. Zhang, and L. Zhu, "Novel polymer ferroelectric behavior via crystal isomorphism and the nanoconfinment effect", *Polymer*, Vol. 54, pp. 1709–1728, 2013. doi:10.1016/j.polymer.2013.01.035
16. http://www.vishay.com/docs/26033/gentechinfofilm.pdf
17. T. Tippo, C. Thanachayanont, P. Muthitamongkol, C. Junin, M. Hietschold, A. Thanachayanont, "The effects of solvents on the properties of ultra-thin poly (methyl methacrylate) films prepared by spin coating", *Thin Solid Films*, Vol. 546, pp. 180-184, 2013.

V_6O_{13}/C as High Capacity Cathode for Lithium Ion Batteries

Bijoy Das and Maximilian Fichtner
Helmholtz Institute Ulm for Electrochemical Storage (HIU)
bijoy.das@kit.edu

Abstract

Vanadium oxides, VOx (x = 2.5-2.0) are widely studied as prospective cathode materials for Lithium ion batteries (LIBs) due to their high specific capacity, multiple oxidation states of vanadium and low cost.1,2 Although V6O13 is least studied, the electrochemical performance is promising when cycled as cathode against Li- metal.2 It consists of an alternative single and double vanadium oxide layers with V5+ and V4+ ions. Such geometrical configuration of V6O13 provides ample sites for Li-ion intercalation. It can take up to 8 moles of Li theoretically where all the vanadium is being reduced to V3+, as a result a high specific capacity and specific energy of 417 mA h g-1 and 900 Wh kg-1 can be achieved. These values are higher than the conventional LiCoO2 (140 mA h g-1 and 540 Wh kg-1), LiFePO4 (170 mA h g-1 and 500 Wh kg-1) and LiMn2O4 (148 mA h g-1 and 500 Wh kg-1), respectively. Additionally, the metallic nature of V6O13 at room temperature is another advantage for better electrochemical performance. The high specific capacity and metallic nature make V6O13 as promising cathode for LIBs. In this work, we prepared V6O13 by simple sol-gel approach. A carbon coating was prepared by calcination of vanadium oxide-glucose complex at 400 oC for 6 h in N2-atm. The V_6O_{13}/C nanocomposite was characterized by XRD, SEM and XPS techniques. Li- cycling behavior was carried out by galvanostatic cycling and cyclic voltammetry (CV). V6O13/C showed a first cycle discharge capacity of 460 mA h g-1, when cycled at 100 mA g-1. A reversible capacity of 260 mA h g-1 was noticed at the end of 60 cycles, with capacity fading of 3.33 mA h g-1 per cycle. It also showed very good rate performance when cycled at different current rates. Cyclicvoltammetry (CV) and electrochemical impedance spectroscopy (EIS) were carried out to support the reaction mechanism. Ex-situ XPS measurement on discharged/charged electrodes was carried out to further support the reaction mechanism.

Development of High Energy Cathode Phosphates via High Throughput Methods

Bin Li, Jen-Hsien Yang and Dee Strand
Wildcat Discovery Technologies
bli@wildcatdiscovery.com

Abstract

Substantial improvement in the energy density of commercial batteries is required to meet the future needs for electric vehicles, plug-in electric vehicles, clean energy storage, consumer electronics, and medical devices. Li-ion batteries offer many attractive advantages over other rechargeable chemistries, including a much higher energy density, lighter weight, longer cycle life, superior capacity retention, broader ambient-temperature endurance, and higher current tolerance. Wildcat is using this high throughput system to develop new electrode and electrolyte materials for a variety of battery types (primary, secondary, aqueous, non-aqueous). In this talk, I will discuss the discovery of a new high energy density cathode doped-$LiCoPO_4$, ~700 Wh/kg. Compared to $LiFePO_4$, the significant energy density improvement obtained from higher voltage, about 4.7V, will be directly transferred into cell level. This promising cathode material has been scaled up to 1Kg per batch synthesis and tested in large format cells.

Advance Si Anode for High Energy Lithium Ion Cells

Pu Zhang, Peter Aurora, Sequoyah King, and Michael Wixom
Navitas Advanced Solutions Group
4880 Venture Drive, Suite 100, Ann Arbor, MI 48108
pzhang@navitassys.com

Abstract: *High energy lithium batteries are attractive power sources for vehicle propulsion, portable power units, and other battlefield applications. A low cost high performance Si anode material has been developed to enable high energy lithium cells at 600 Wh/L. The material also shows enhanced safety and abuse tolerance. The material is prepared using mass production process, the electrodes are coated in pilot scale, and prismatic pouch cells are built. A cycle life of 500 has been demonstrated for the Si anode. The high energy cells will be applied for portable power BB2590 and UAV battery packs.*

Keywords: lithium ion; silicon anode; porous Si; high energy; safety; BB2590; UAV

Introduction

There is a motivation to increase lithium ion cell energy density for mobile and stationary applications. Lithium-ion batteries have high energy density and long cycle life. They are flexible in design and one of the most promising energy storage devices. The specific energy and energy density of lithium ion cells today are typically 200 Wh/kg and 500 Wh/L respectively. However, the ever-growing need for higher capacity and higher power, especially for increasing number of emerging new applications, has further prompted widespread research efforts towards developing electrodes and other materials for higher energy, longer life, and lower cost.

Silicon-based materials have emerged as the anode of the future for lithium ion batteries, due to the high theoretical capacity of Si (4200 mAh/g, much higher than traditional graphite anode at 372 mAh/g). However, the enormous volume change of Si upon repeated lithium insertion and extraction leads to severe particle segregation and loss of particle–particle electronic contacts. Therefore pure silicon anodes suffer large capacity fading due to pulverization during cycling, which have prevented them from being commercially used.

Silicon-based alloy and composite materials are emerging as promising high capacity anodes for next generation lithium ion battery (NGLB). The benefit that metal alloy anodes offer in the NGLB can be realized through novel electrode designs that extend battery life cycle and improve abuse tolerance. Additionally, significant efforts have been made to improve the cycling reversibility of Si-based anodes by improving the micro-structural stability and connect-ability.

A novel nanostructured silicon composite anode developed by Navitas begins with a proprietary low-cost microporous silicon (µpSi) precursor. The silicon precursor is produced using a commercially scalable process that generates an innovative architecture through the creation of a controlled amount of metal oxide layer surrounding the silicon composite structure. Since the oxide is electrochemically inert, the high reversibility of the anode is not sacrificed. In addition, the oxide layer structure introduces an intrinsic safety of the anode. A µpSi composite is formed by protecting the µpSi core with a Si-metal alloy shell and a graphite buffer matrix.

In this paper, we will demonstrate >500 cycles and a safety advantage of the µpSi composite anode. With pilot scale electrode fabrication and large format cell assembly capability in house, we will deliver a prismatic cell of 600 Wh/L, through a novel chemistry design including a Si composite anode, a high energy cathode, and an advanced electrolyte. The safe, low cost, high energy cell will be applied to BB2590 battery and UAV power sources.

Experimental

Synthesis of Microporous Si (µpSi) Precursor

The µpSi production involves a two-step reduction process involving the usage of inexpensive commodity grade silicon oxide to produce Si/metal oxide solid state mixture. Following the reduction process is an etching process, which removes metal oxide and creates a desired porosity. A desired amount of metal oxide is retained in the microporous Si precursor for mechanical and safety advantage.

Synthesis of µpSi Core-Shell Material

The *µpSi* (with oxide) precursor is then milled with selected metal powder, which will form Si_xM_y alloy on the surface. A "Si core / alloy shell" structure is obtained as a result. The core-shell material is further milled with a carbon material (such as graphite). The latter forms another buffer layer around the core-shell composite.

Characterization

Physical properties: tap and true densities are measured with a tap density meter and a He pycnometer. BET surface area is measured with Micromeritics ASAP2020.

Morphology: The composite phase / structure is identified by using XRD, SEM, and EDAX.

Electrode Fabrication

The anode is a µpSi composite and the cathode is a high nickel content lithium metal oxide. Both the electrodes are fabricated by mixing the slurry containing active material, conductive additive, and binder in a mixer. The prepared slurry is coated on to Cu foil (anode) or Al foil (cathode). The coated electrode is then calendered to a desired thickness (porosity).

In lab scale, electrode slurry is mixed in a Flacktec Speed Mixer and electrode is hand-cast with doctor blades. In pilot scale, the slurry is mixed in a Ross high shear double-planetary mixer in the scale of 2 Gallons. Electrodes are coated using a Toyo 150 WI slot-die coater.

Cell Assembly
Si anode half cells are built in the form of CR2025, with lithium as counter electrode. Si anode formulation is "92% active / 1.5% carbon black / 6.5% Li-PAA" and the anode porosity is 35%.

Li ion pouch cells are assembled in a dry-room at <2% moisture. It includes Si anode (with the same formulation as in the half cells) and NCM 523 cathode. The cathode formulation is "93% active / 3% carbon black / 4% PVDF" and the cathode porosity is 30%. The N/P = 1.1.

Cell Test
The performance is evaluated based on cell capacity, rate capability, and cycle life on Maccor cyclers. The anode half-cell operates between 1.0 - 0.01V and the Li ion cell is cycled between 4.2 - 3.2V at +0.5C/-0.5C and at room temperature.

Safety Evaluation
Safety (abuse tolerance) of the anode is performed by differential scanning calorimetry (DSC) where the anode is at fully lithiated state (100% SOC). Onset temperature and heat flow are measured for exothermic peaks associated with SEI decomposition and electrolyte reactions. The DSC test is carried out under N_2 at 30 - 400 °C with a heating rate of 5 °C/min on a TA DSC Q200 instrument.

Results and Discussion

Anode Material Development
Navitas µpSi production starts with a two-step reduction process by using commodity grade SiO_2 precursor and a metal powder. The 1st step is a milling operation where the SiO_2 is partially reduced by the metal. The 2nd step is a thermal reduction treatment to fully reduce remaining oxide resulting in a nano-structured Si/metal oxide composite.

After the two-step reduction, the metal oxide is removed by acid etching (i.e., 3rd step) which creates micro porous Si network. Our investigation has shown a potential benefit of leaving small amounts of metal oxide dispersed on or in the silicon porous structure during the etching. The retained metal oxide can enhance the Si anode electrochemical properties as well as safety but the amount needs to be well controlled without sacrificing the anode capacity and rate capability [1-3]. Residual metal oxide also serves to reinforce the structural integrity of the electrodes by accommodating the substantial lithiation / delithiation strain and improving the cycling performance [4].

Navitas' previous work has shown that silicon-metal alloy can stabilize Si by limiting the formation high Li-content Li_xSi alloy, and that the alloy can be formed through mechanical milling process [5, 6].

With controlled milling process (i.e., 4th step), a "µpSi core - Si alloy shell" structure is obtained. The metal alloy can limit surface Si volume change and keep the large volume change within the Si core where the change is accommodated by the internal porous structure.

The "core-shell" material is further wrapped by a buffer layer (5th step). This last step grinds up the buffer materials (e.g., graphite) to encapsulate the core-shell material without breaking its structure. In the final composite (i.e., core-shell-buffer), the graphite serves three functions: (1) an active material itself, (2) a conductive network, and (3) a buffering matrix to accommodate volume change as a 2nd protective layer on the alloy shell.

The whole process (5 steps total) is shown in Figure 1. The µpSi structure is shown in Figure 2. The final core-shell-buffer composite structure is shown in Figure 3.

Table 1 compiles physical and electrochemical properties of the Si composite anode powder. In particular the tap density values are critical when making electrodes for high energy applications. Desired tap density (>0.8 g/cm^3) will ensure the electrode slurry to be mixed at high enough solid content and electrode to be calendered to low enough porosity. The specific capacity is high enough to accomplish high energy electrodes with loading of up to 4 mAh/cm^2.

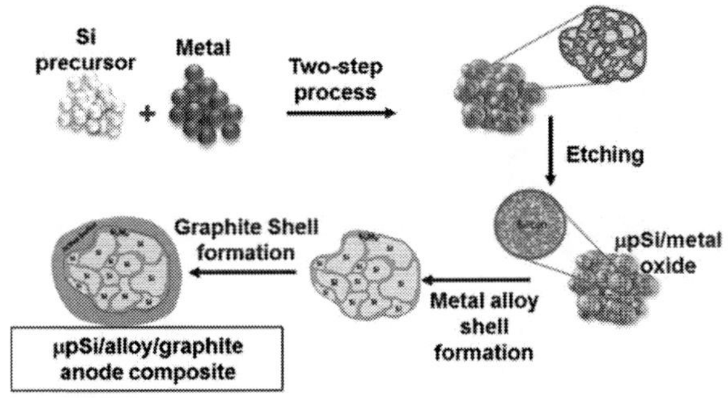

Figure 1. Si composite with novel architecture: micro porous Si core (with metal oxide ceramic reinforcing additive) protected by Si-metal alloy shell and additional layer of buffering matrix.

Electrochemical Performance Test
The Si composite anode is first tested in half coin cell format. The anode has reversible capacity of >600 mAh/g. More than 500 cycles have demonstrated at +1C/-1C cycling (Figure 4). This confirms the stability of the µpSi composite during accelerated cycling.

The anode material is then evaluated in a Li ion cell, coupled with a NCM 523 cathode. At a loading of 3 mAh/cm^2, the cell shows >90% capacity retention at 2C rate (Figure 5). Cycle life is under test (~200 at 88%

capacity retention) and it projects to be >500 at 4.2 – 3.2V and at +0.5C/-0.5C rate.

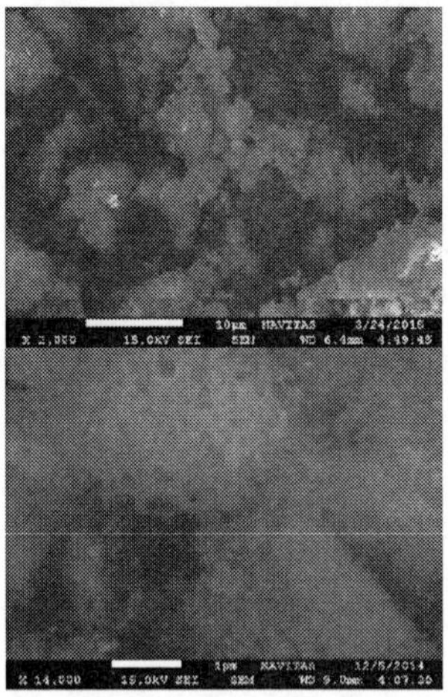

Figure 2. SEM micrographs of porous silicon: (left) Si and metal oxide mixture after the 2-step-reduction; (right) micro-porous Si after metal oxide removal.

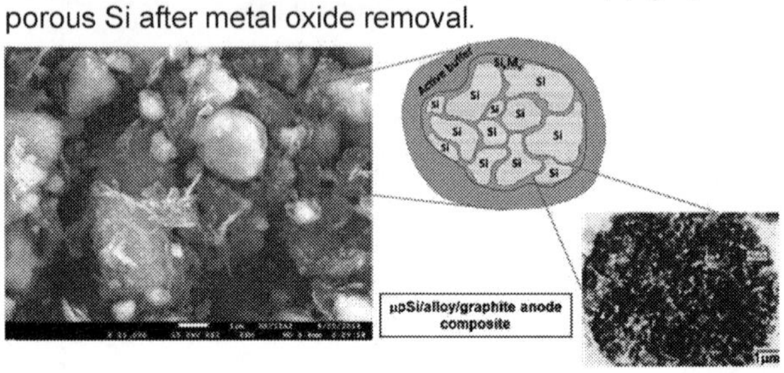

Figure 3. SEM micrographs of μpSi / Si-alloy / graphite composite. The inner core is composed of porous Si particle surrounded with a protective metal alloy shell, which enhances mechanical stability and suppresses stresses during cycling. The outer shell is a conductive/active graphite buffer matrix.

Table 1. Anode powder properties

Property	Target
Primary particle size (nm)	50 - 200
Secondary particle size (μm)	1 - 10
BET surface area (m^2/g)	< 20
Tap density (g/cm^3)	0.8 – 1.2
Specific capacity (mAh/g)	600 - 1000

Safety Test (DSC)

Differential scanning calorimetry (DSC) curves fully lithiated anodes are shown Figure 7. The two tested anodes are the new-developed μpSi composite (green solid line) and a mixed Si/graphite baseline (red dotted line). Both anodes show a breakdown in the SEI layer starting around 120°C but the μpSi composite shows higher onset temperature and lower rate of heat release, suggesting that the composite structure enhances safety and abuse tolerance. Additionally, the experiments on graphite anodes at similar conditions run by Sandia National Lab [7] showed >2x higher heat release than the Si/Graphite baseline. These results further confirm that the improved thermal properties are attributable to the novel architecture of the composite material.

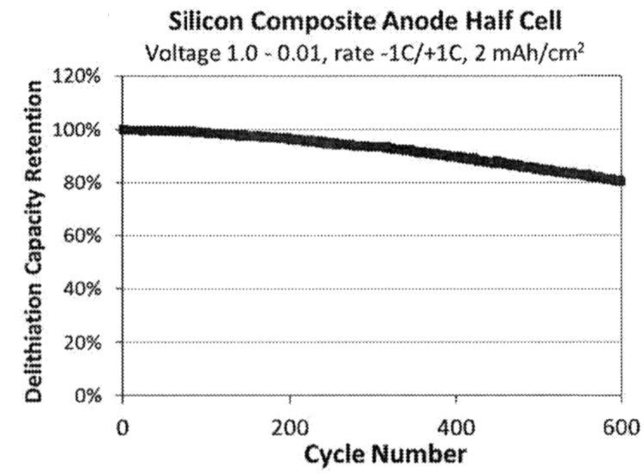

Figure 4. Half cell containing the Si composite anode material has attained > 500 cycles at +1C/-1C. The cut-off voltage is 1.0 V – 0.01V.

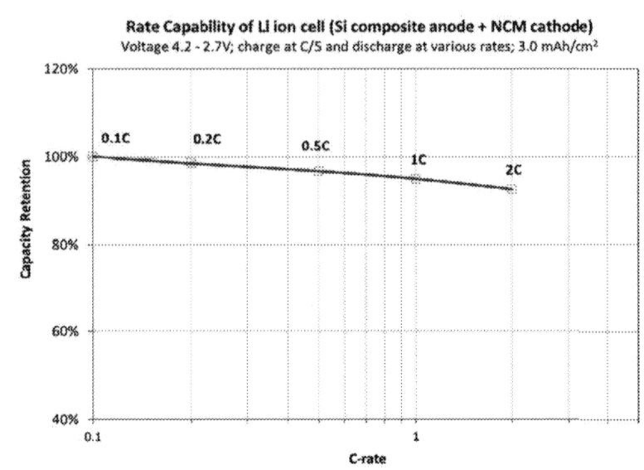

Figure 5. Rate capability of a Li ion cell with Si composite anode and NCM 523 cathode (loading at 3 mAh/cm^2). The cell is charged to 4.2V at C/5 and discharge to 2.7V at various rates. It shows >90% capacity retention at 2C.

Prismatic Pouch Li ion Cell Development

Navitas has developed various sized prismatic can or pouch cells. Table 2 summarizes the performance characteristics of the high energy cells, ranging from 2 Ah to 14 Ah. Figure 8 shows an example of a 2 Ah pouch cell.

High Energy Chemistry for BB2590 and UAV Applications

Navitas' High Energy Chemistry (HEC) cell technology has been applied in rechargeable BB 2590 batteries, which is the most common military battery, and other military systems including long endurance unmanned aerial vehicles (UAV).

BB2590 based on Navitas' 5.5Ah cells has shown 40% greater specific energy than COTS batteries. In the UAV application, a Navitas 6Ah prototype cell delivers 280 Wh/kg and 525 Wh/L. The flight time in AeroVironment Raven under Standard Profile (~0.3C avg., 1.1C peak) is 57% longer than the SOA (Figure 9).

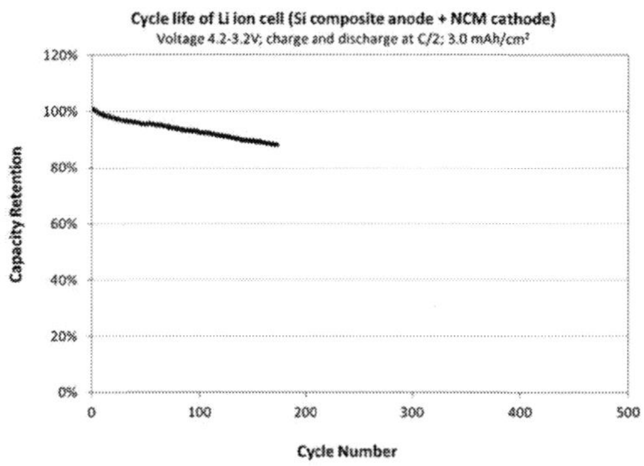

Figure 6. Cycle life of a Li ion cell with Si composite anode and NCM 523 cathode (loading at 3 mAh/cm^2). The cell is charged to 4.2V at C/2 (tapering to C/10) and discharge to 3.2V at C/2. The projected cycle life is >500.

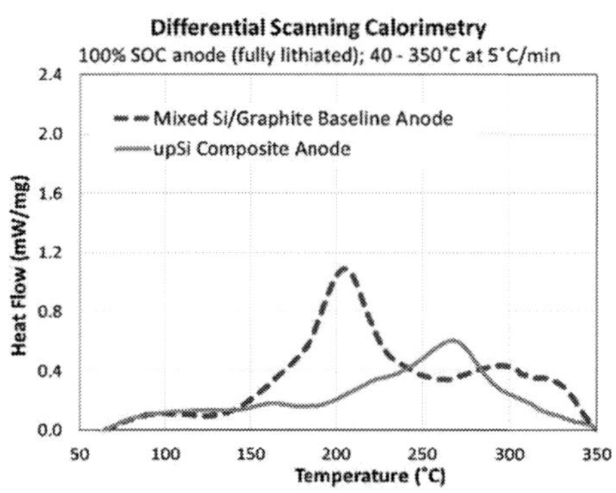

Figure 7. Differential scanning calorimetry (DSC) plots for µpSi composite anode and mixed Si/graphite baseline anode. The anodes are fully lithiated (100% SOC) before the test. The composite anode shows higher onset temperature and lower rate of heat release, suggesting that the composite structure enhances safety and abuse tolerance.

Table 2. Navitas high energy pouch cells (2 Ah - 14 Ah)

Operating Voltage	3.6 V
Max Voltage	4.3 V
Min Cut-off Voltage	3.0 V
Specific Energy	250-300 Wh/kg
Energy Density	520-730 Wh/L
Max continuous current	1C
Cycle life	>300 to 80% retention

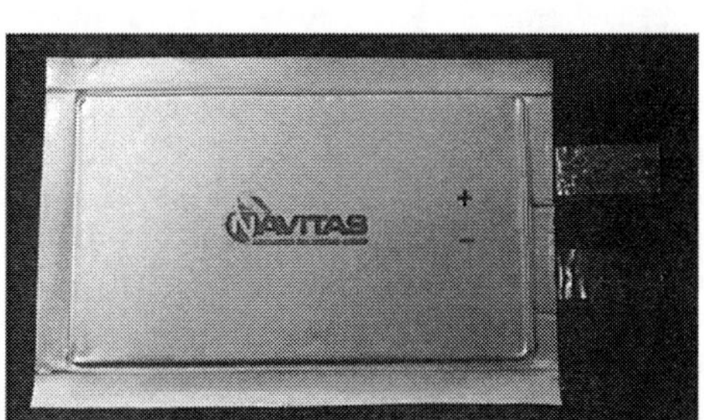

Figure 8. Navitas prototype 2 Ah prismatic pouch cell.

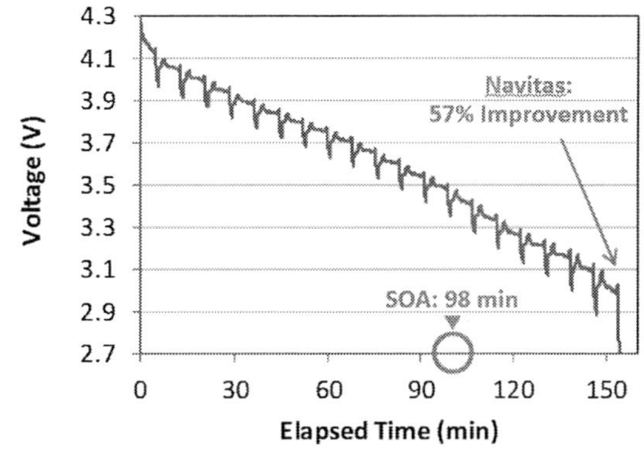

Figure 9. Navitas 6Ah UAV Cell Prototype Raven Flight Profile under standard load (0.3C avg., 1.1C peak)

Conclusion

A low cost, safe, and long cycle life Si composite anode has been developed in Navitas. A cycle life of >500 was demonstrated and safety advantage was confirmed by DSC. Large format prismatic Li ion cells have been fabricated based on the high energy chemistry enabling 300 Wh/kg and 600 Wh/L. Navitas BB2590 battery based on the high energy cells possesses >40% higher specific energy than COTS battery. Navitas UAV prototype cell delivers >50% more flight time.

Acknowledgement

This work was supported by Navitas IR&D, DOE SBIR, DOE VTO WIDE funding, and DARPA-LOTS programs.

Reference

1. He, Y., *et al.*, "Alumina-Coated Patterned Amorphous Silicon as the Anode for a Lithium-Ion Battery with High Coulombic Efficiency" *Adv. Mater.*, 23, 4938–4941, 2011
2. Hwang, G., *et al.*, "A high-performance nanoporous Si/Al_2O_3 foam lithium-ion battery anode fabricated by selective chemical etching of the Al–Si alloy and subsequent thermal oxidation", *Chem. Commun.*,51, 4429-4432, 2015
3. Li, J. *el al.*, "Atomic Layered Coating Enabling Ultrafast Surface Kinetics at Silicon Electrodes in Lithium Ion Batteries" J. Phys. Chem. Lett., 4, 3387–3391, 2013
4. Li, Y. *et al.*, "Tuning electrochemical performance of Si-based anodes for lithium-ion batteries by employing atomic layer deposition alumina coating" *J. Mater. Chem. A*, 2, 11417–11425, 2014
5. Zhang, P., *et al.*, "Silicon Based Composite Material", *US Patent*, 8679679, 2014
6. Dong H., et al., "Structural and electrochemical characterization of Fe–Si/C composite anodes for Li-ion batteries synthesized by mechanical alloying", *Electrochim. Acta,* 49, 5217–5222, 2004
7. Doughty D. and Roth P., "A General Discussion of Li ion Battery Safety", *Electrochem. Soc. Interface*, 37-44, 2012

High Energy Li-ion Pouch Cells with Silicon-Carbon Composite Anodes

Owen Crowther, Anson Yang, Aadil Benmayza, Hyun Joo Bang, Mario Destephen
R&D
EaglePicher Technologies
Joplin, Missouri, 64801
Owen.Crowther@EaglePicher.com

Abstract: *EaglePicher Technologies is currently developing high energy Li-ion pouch cells for the Title III LIMA program to be manufactured at the new Lithium Ion Center of Excellence production facility that will be online in 2017. The negative electrode of these pouch cells is a silicon-carbon composite material that demonstrates a higher specific capacity than the conventional graphite anode. However, silicon containing anodes historically suffer from poor capacity retention because of the large volume change of silicon during cycling, as well as parasitic reactions related to the solid electrolyte interphase. This presentation highlights EPT's approaches to extend the cycle life of these pouch cells. The rate, cycling, and safety performance of high energy Li-ion pouches will be given.*

Keywords: Lithium ion pouch cell; high energy; silicon anode

Introduction

The Department of Defense requires rechargeable batteries for several applications such as portable power, electric vehicles, aircraft, etc. However, most commercial Li-ion cells do not meet military performance requirements and are manufactured in foreign countries such as Japan, Korea, and China [1]. EaglePicher Technologies (EPT) received the sole phase II award for the Lithium-Battery for Military Applications (LIMA) project under the Defense Production Act Title III program in 2014. The program goal assures the affordable production of critical items deemed essential for national defense, alleviating concerns regarding market volatility and uncertainty within the current international market for Li-Ion. As a leading specialty battery manufacturer with a legacy of supplying U.S. military power needs, EaglePicher is poised to assist the defense industrial base by providing a timely, reliable supply of Li-Ion materials and products [2].

EPT is currently constructing a100,000-plus square foot production facility to support the Title III LIMA program. The facility will initially produce 1.75 and 10 Ah high energy Li-ion pouch cells, as well as a high power 26650. The pouch cells will contain a state-of-the-art silicon-carbon (SiC) composite anode to improve the cell's specific energy. This paper details the development of these two pouch cells with the Silicon containing anode.

Silicon anode background

Commercial-off-the-shelf (COTS) Li-ion batteries contain a graphite anode and transitional metal oxide cathode separated by an organic carbonate electrolyte. Typical COTS cells currently deliver between 200-250 Wh kg^{-1} for >300 cycles. Several applications, including portable power for the Soldier, require higher specific energies. One method for improving the specific energy is to use higher capacity alloy anode, such as silicon (Si). Table one shows capacity and deintercalation (discharge) potential of several potential anodes.

Table 1. Comparison of potential Li-ion anodes materials.

material	specific capacity / mAh g^{-1}	deintercalation potential / V
graphite	372	0.1
titanate	155	1.55
Si ($Li_{15}Si_4$)	3587	0.4
Sn ($Li_{4.4}Sn$)	993	0.5
SiO	1600	

Table 1 shows Si demonstrates nearly 10 times the capacity of the conventional graphite anode. However, several problems have delayed Si incorporation into COTS cells. The first is Si expands 280% during full lithiation [3]. This causes the Si to become electrically isolated either from the conductive carbon filler or current collector. The second problem is the large volume change can cause cracks in the solid electrolyte interphase (SEI), resulting in parasitic reactions at the anode. A third issue is the deintercalation potential is higher than graphite, causing full cells to reach the cutoff voltage prematurely.

EaglePicher employs several approaches to overcome these problems. The EPT anode consists of a silicon and graphite composite. The graphite acts a buffer to the volume change and provides an electronically conductive network. Electrode formulation (binder type and amount) and processing was optimized to improve the adhesion, minimizing electrode expansion. Finally, electrolyte additives were used to form a robust, flexible SEI that reduces parasitic reactions. The use of the Si-carbon composite also lowers the average deintercalation potential, since the carbon is electrochemically active.

Several types and morphologies of commercially available silicon materials were evaluated, as well as different types of carbon for the composite. Each material demonstrates different specific capacity, deintercalation potential, irreversible capacity loss (IRCL), and capacity retention when cycling. Figure 1 shows the 1st cycle deintercalation for several the screened anodes.

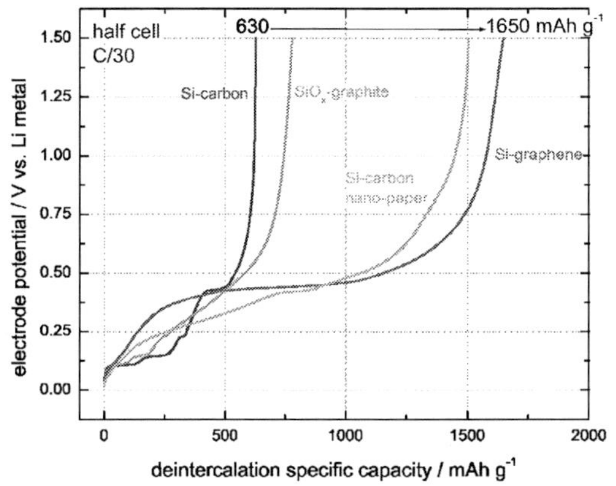

Figure 1. 1st deintercalation of various Si containing anodes.

Table 2 summarizes the results found in figure 1. The specific capacity of the screened anodes ranged from 630 to 1650 mAh g^{-1}. EPT selected the SiC composite, despite having the lowest specific capacity due to its low IRCL and relatively lower deintercalation potential. The SiC composite also demonstrates good rate capability and capacity retention during cycling.

Table 2. Comparison of screened Si containing anodes.

anode	specific capacity / mAh g^{-1}	IRCL / %
SiC	630	8
SiO_x-graphite	780	17
Si-CNP	1504	14
Si-graphene	1650	24

1.75Ah Li-ion pouch (SLC-202)

EPT SLC-202 cell is 1.75Ah designed to fit the conformal wearable battery (SLB-101). The first EPT deliverables for this application used a pouch cell that contained a standard graphite anode. SLC-202 is the same size as the original cell but is lighter due to the incorporation of the SiC composite anode. Table 3 is the preliminary specifications for the prototype cell.

Table 3. Preliminary SLC-202 specifications.

Name	SLC-202
Nominal capacity @ C/5	>1.75 Ah
Nominal specific energy @ C/5	230 Wh kg^{-1}
Current cycle life (80% retention)	>150
Target cycle life (80% retention)	≥224
Size	50 x 56 x 6.5 mm
Weight	~29 g
Anode	SiC composite
Cathode	High Ni metal oxide
Electrolyte	Organic carbonates
Separator	Shutdown
Cell type	Prismatic
Cell packaging	Polymer laminated Al film

The room temperature discharge curves for the cell are shown below in figure 2. The cell typically delivers 1.8 Ah at a C/5 rate. The cell also demonstrates good rate capability; retaining 94% of the nominal capacity at a 1C rate.

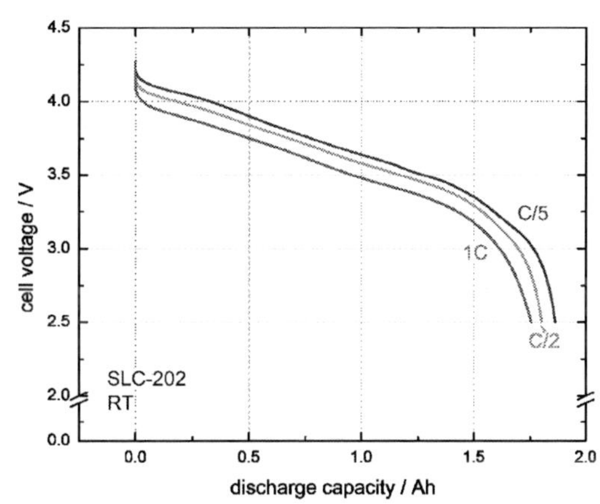

Figure 2. SLC-202 discharge curves.

Figure 3 shows the performance of the SLC-202 cell for various temperatures. The cells deliver high capacity from −20 to 40°C. The cell delivers 1.5 Ah capacity at −20°C, nearly 80% of the nominal room temperature capacity.

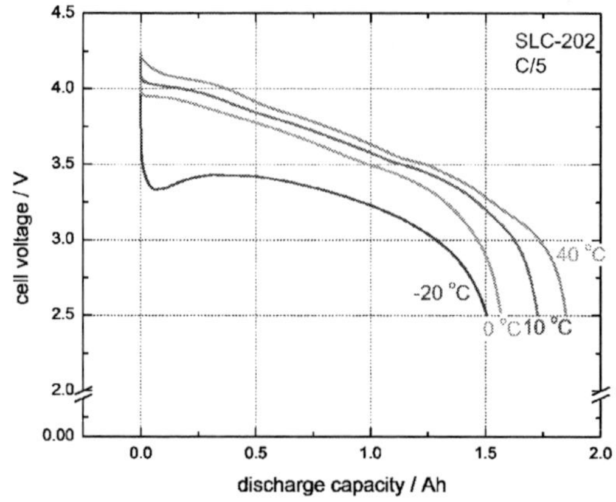

Figure 3. SLC-202 discharge curves at different temperatures.

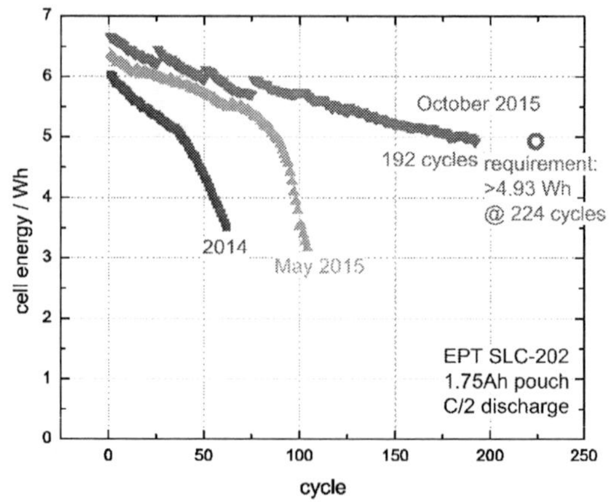

Figure 5. SLC-202 cycle life.

Figure 4 shows the nail penetration results for and SLC-202 cell at 50% state-of-charge. The cells temperature quickly spikes to ~40 °C then cools to RT within one hour. The cell voltage reaches 0V within 2 hours. No smoking or flames were observed throughout the 24 hour test.

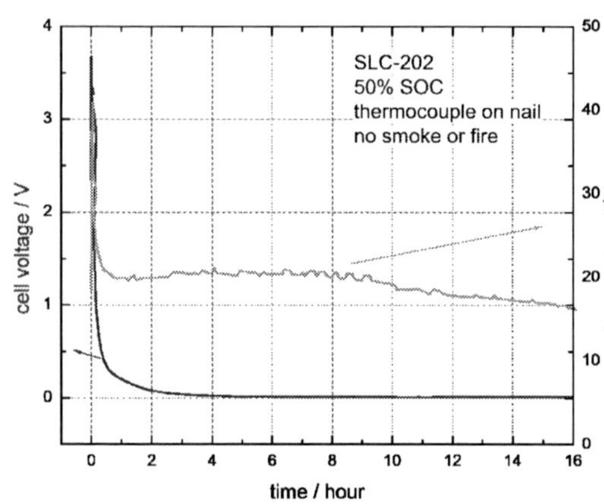

Figure 4. Nail penetration test for SLC-202 cell at 50% SOC.

Figure 5 shows the cycle life improvement of for the SLC-202 cell over the course of its development. The best performing cells deliver nearly 85% of the required cycle life for the SLB-101 conformal wearable applications. EPT will obtain the 224 cycle target through continued optimization of SiC anode formula and processing conditions, as well as through the optimization of the electrolyte composition.

10 Ah Li-ion pouch (SLC-203)

EPT is also developing a 10Ah pouch that meets the Title III requirement of delivering 250 Wh kg^{-1} at a 1C rate. The 10 Ah pouch fits into the BB-2590 packaging in a 8S or 4S2P configuration. Table 4 shows the preliminary specifications of the pouch.

Table 4. Preliminary SLC-203 specifications.

Name	SLC-202
Nominal capacity @ C/5	>10 Ah
Nominal specific energy @ C/5	>300 Wh kg^{-1}
Specific energy @ 1C	>250 Wh kg^{-1}
Target cycle life (80% retention)	≥100
Size	103 x 101 x 6.5 mm
Weight	~130g
Anode	SiC composite
Cathode	High Ni metal oxide
Electrolyte	Organic carbonates
Separator	Shutdown
Cell type	Prismatic
Cell packaging	Polymer laminated Al film

Figure 6 shows the current performance of the SLC-203 cell. The cell delivers 300 Wh kg^{-1} at C/20 rate and 240 Wh kg^{-1} at 1C rate. Current effort is focused on improving the rate capability of the cathode in the final cell. This will raise the average discharge voltage so the cell will deliver the target 250 Wh kg^{-1} at the 1C rate.

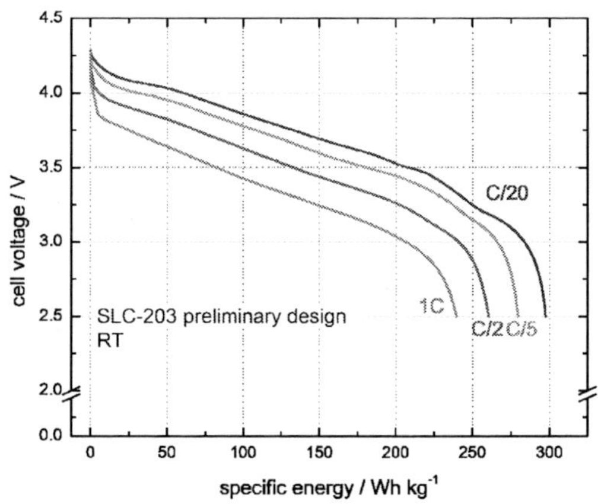

Figure 6. SLC-203 pathfinder cell performance.

Conclusions

EPT is developing 1.75 and 10Ah Li-ion high energy pouch cells for the Title III LIMA program. Both cells contain a silicon-carbon anode that lowers the cells wight, thus improving the specific energy. The SLC-202 cell is being designed to meet the SLB-101 conformal battery requirements. The SLC-203 cell will deliver 250 Wh kg^{-1} at the 1C rate. Both cells will be available for production volumes in 2017.

Acknowledgements

"This material is released to the public domain in accordance with ITAR 22 CFR 120.11"

References

1. Silberglitt, R., J. T. Bartis and K. Brady. "Soldier-Portable Battery Supply: Foreign Dependence and Policy Options". Santa Monica, CA: RAND Corporation, 2014. http://www.rand.org/pubs/research_reports/RR500.html. Also available in print form.
2. http://www.eaglepicher.com/news/eaglepicher-news
3. Obrovac. M. N., and V. L. Chevier, "Alloy Negative Electrodes for Li-Ion Batteries," *Chemical Reviews*, Vol. 114, no. 23, pp. 11444-11502, November 17, 2014.

Wide Temperature and Safer Li-Ion Cell Development

Ramanathan Thillaiyan, Wujun Fu, Mario Destephen and Owen Crowther
EaglePicher Technologies LLC, an OMG company
3220 Industrial Road
Joplin, MO 64801
Mario.Destephen@eaglepicher.com

Abstract: *EaglePicher Technologies (EPT) has developed reduced flammable electrolyte without sacrificing the performance at higher rates while maintaining a wide operating temperature range. We demonstrated the electrolyte fire-retardant properties in bulk electrolyte as well as in vapor pressure tests. We demonstrated a wide-temperature Li-Ion cell with reduced flammable capability with superior cell performance in the operational temperature range from -40°C to +85°C. Further, we designed a safer Li-Ion cell and demonstrated cell safety under overcharge abuse conditions.*

Keywords: Li-Ion; safety; reduced flammable; electrolyte; wide temperature Li-Ion cell development

Introduction

One of the greatest challenges of modern society is to stabilize a consistent energy supply that will meet our growing energy demands [1]. Developing high-performance power generation and storage devices would be benefited in many industries such as consumer electronics, hybrid electrical vehicles and defense applications [2]. Li-Ion battery (LIB) technology is the front runner that provides high energy density rechargeable batteries as compared to conventional Ni-Cd and Ni-metal hydrides [3]. Rechargeable LIB with liquid electrolytes was developed by Sony Corporation in 1991 [4]. Since then LIB are extensively used in various portable power applications. However, its safety is key obstacle for high rate and high capacity applications. Several incidents such as fire and explosion of LIB have been reported [5].

Non-flammable electrolyte development [6] and overcharge protection additives [7] have been studied extensively by many research groups for LIB safety improvements. EPT has been focused on the development of reduced flammable electrolyte using fire-retardant additives in liquid organic electrolytes to improve the safety of the LIB. There are two mechanisms proposed to explain the flame retardation: (1) physical char-forming process, which buildup an isolating layer between the condensed and gas phases to stop combustion process [8] and (2) chemical radical-scavenging process, which terminates radical chain reactions responsible for the combustion reaction in the gas phases [9]. Numerous organic phosphate fire-retardant compounds have been investigated as electrolyte additives to reduce the flammability of the liquid electrolyte used in LIB [10].

Besides the safety concern of LIB, increasing its operation temperature range is critical especially for military and aircraft applications. The optimization of the electrolyte formulation to achieve extreme cold temperature performance while maintaining the cell safety is a complex issue in current LIB technology. The performance and stability of LIB at temperature extremes has been a challenge using conventional organic solvent based electrolytes. Several studies suggest that Ionic Liquid (IL) based electrolyte can improve the safety and high temperature cell performance but it adversely affects the low temperature cell performance. Therefore, the development of reduced flammable electrolyte which will allow LIB to operate temperature extremes is very important for various industries [11].

EPT has developed a unique electrolyte formulation with fire-retardant for wide temperature Li-Ion battery applications. We demonstrated the reduced-flammability of our proprietary electrolyte formulation. We studied the reduced flammable electrolyte performance in Li-Ion full cell and demonstrated good rate capability including a wide temperature operating range. The wide temperature range was tested from -40°C to +85 °C and cycled at 60°C, 71°C and 85°C. This paper will describe the development of reduced flammable electrolyte, its wide temperature performance and safer cell design.

Experimental

EPT reduced flammable electrolyte formulation (RF electrolyte) was developed with various flame retardant additive in the mixture of carbonate solvents. $LiNi_xCo_yMn_zO_2$ (NCM) cathode and graphite anode were prepared using standard industrial processes by mixing the active material mixed with carbon, poy(vinylidene fluoride) (PVDF) and N-methyl-2-pyrrolidinone (NMP). The resultant slurry was coated on the current collector.

Flammability of the RF electrolyte and baseline electrolyte was tested using open flash point test in bulk electrolyte and vapor pressure test. Thermal properties of the different electrolyte formulation were studied using Differential Scanning Calorimeter (DSC). The electrolyte performance was studied in a stacked pouch cell with a calculated capacity ~14 Ah and a hard case prismatic cell with a capacity of 30 Ah. Electrochemical tests were monitored with an Arbin battery cycler for rate and cycle life for the EPT-RF electrolyte, and the results were compared with baseline cell with same cell design. Advanced Li-ion pouch cell design was developed to improve the safety.

Results and Discussion

The bulk electrolyte flame test was carried out by taking 2 mL of electrolyte in a watch glass and igniting using a torch. Baseline electrolyte caught fire instantaneously. Several concentrations of the flame retardant additive were added into mixture of carbonate solvents and the test was repeated in the same manner as baseline electrolyte bulk fire retardant test. We identified the optimum amount of additive required for non-flammable electrolyte. Baseline and EPT proprietary electrolyte formulation fire-retardant result are shown in Figure 1. The pictures in Figure 1 were saved from the video in "save frame" mode using video editing software. Figure 1a shows the constant flame with baseline electrolyte upon ignition. The absence of fire after several attempts in Figure 1b and 1c shows the non-flammability of EPT RF electrolyte.

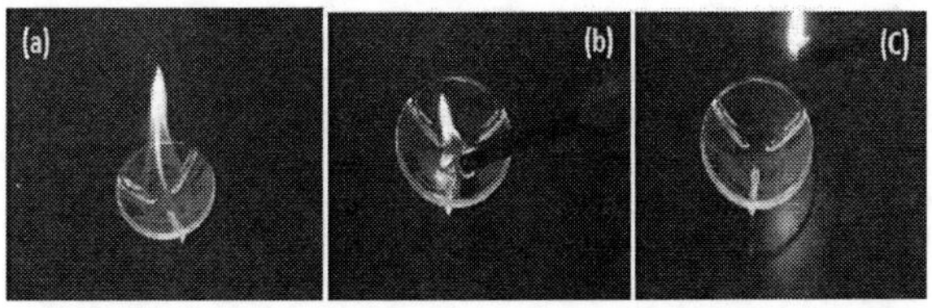

Figure 1. Bulk fire retardant test (a) baseline electrolyte catches fire instantaneously upon ignition and burnt continuously more than 2min; (b) and (c) EPT- RF electrolyte did not catch fire even after several attempts. The above photograph was saved as a picture frame mode from the video.

The bulk fire retardant test is a quick test, and was carried out in order to screen the optimum concentration of fire retardant additive to reduce the flammability of the electrolyte made at EPT. Furthermore, these electrolytes were tested for vapor pressure fire retardant which is shown in Figure 2. This test was carried out by heating electrolyte placed in a small aluminum pan using heating mantel. A gas torch was kept at a known fixed distance from the surface of the electrolyte in an aluminum pan in the heating mantel. The gas torch provides a continuous flame across the aluminum pan. The electrolyte temperature was increased through the heating mantel. The temperature corresponding to the first appearance of fire was determined for each electrolyte.

We found that baseline electrolyte caught fire at 44°C, whereas EPT-RF formulation only caught fire at 81°C. The test was repeated several times and found that ignition temperature for EPT- RF electrolyte is about 40°C higher than the baseline electrolyte formation.

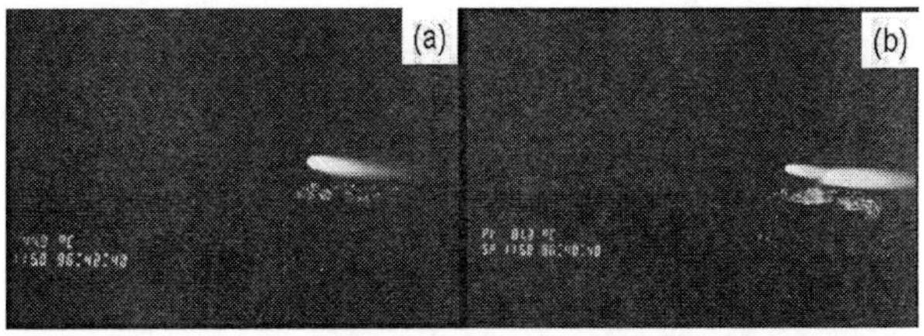

Figure 2. Vapor pressure flame retardant test (a) baseline electrolyte caught fire at 44°C; (b) EPT-RF electrolyte caught fire at 81°C at same heating rate. The gas torch flame was kept at the same distance above the electrolyte surface for both baseline and EPT-RF formulation.

The NCM/graphite pouch cells (calculated capacity 14Ah, is shown in Figure 3) were activated with baseline and EPT RF electrolytes respectively. Three cells for each formulation were tested. After formation cycles, these two sets of cells went through rate evaluation at different temperatures and thermal cycling tests. Figure 4 reveals that the rate capability of the baseline and EPT- RF formulation cells are similar at various discharge rates. There is no performance loss even at higher rate (4C), which is a significant achievement because the industry state of the art and the researcher usually observed performance loss with RF additive.

Figure 3. Photograph of EPT pouch full cell used for testing electrolyte formulations

It can be seen in Figure 5 that the EPT-RF electrolyte performance is very similar to the baseline electrolyte cells from temperature -40 °C to 50 °C. The cells were discharged at C/20 rate at sub-zero temperatures and at 1C discharge rate for higher temperatures. The cell capacity at -40°C is only ~38% of its room temperature capacity. However, this particular electrolyte was not developed to improve the low-temperature performance; it was developed to focus on the evaluation of reduced flammable additive in electrolyte at temperature extremes. This performance demonstrated that the flame retardant additive did not affect the cell performance over a wide temperature range, whereas the literature has demonstrated that fire retardant additives affect the cell performance. At very low temperatures the electrolytes are frozen, which reduces Li ion diffusion into the electrode. This loss of performance at sub-zero temperature is similar to many literature results [12].

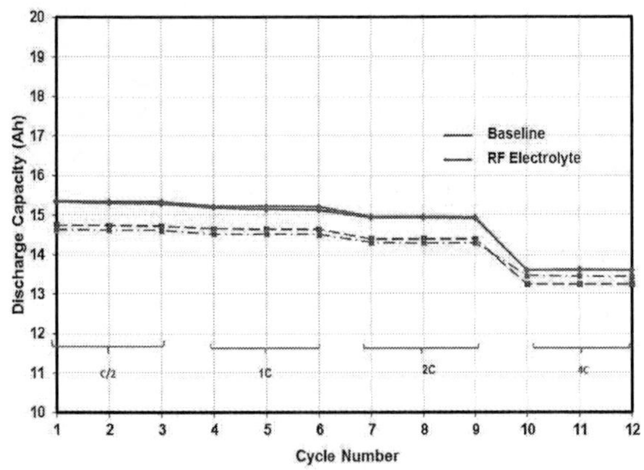

Figure 4. Comparison of rate capability of NCM/graphite full cell with baseline electrolyte and EPT-RF electrolyte.

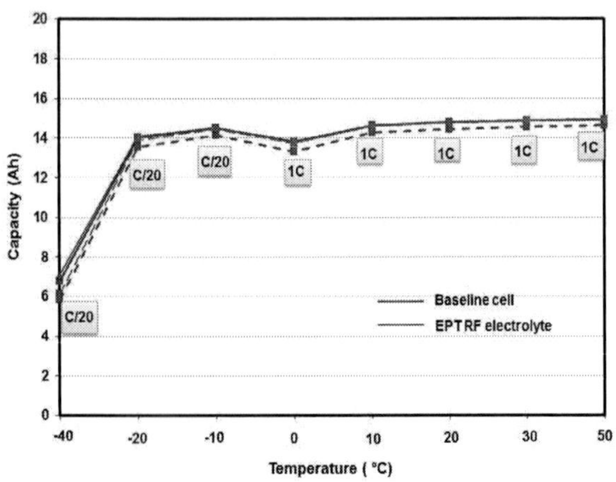

Figure 5. Temperature ramp tests of cells with baseline and EPT-RF electrolyte performance.

The reduced flammable electrolyte formulations were further optimized to improve the low temperature performance and high temperature stability. The cell performance is shown in Figure 6. Li-Ion cells using two different EPT formulations with reduced flammable electrolyte demonstrated superior performance over the baseline cell at the test temperature ranging from -40 °C and +50 °C.

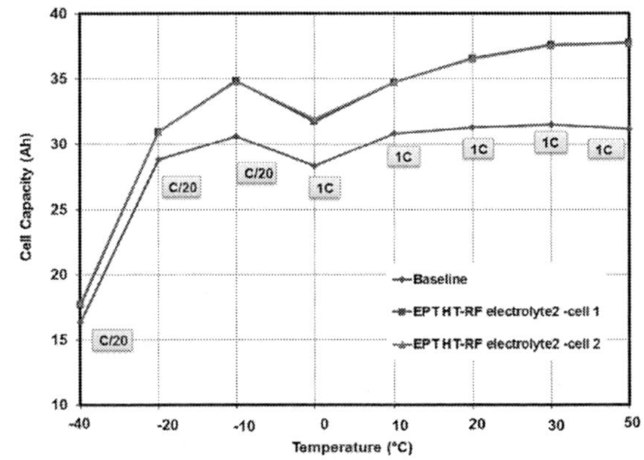

Figure 6. Wide temperature Li-Ion cell performances with reduced flammable electrolyte.

After the temperature characterization at 50°C, the cells were set to 60°C and cycle life tested for 100 cycles, and then the temperature was increased to 71°C for few cycles and again dropped to 60 °C for 25 cycles and then set to 85°C for few cycles. The high temperature cycle life stability of EPT Li-Ion cell performance is shown in Figure 7. The results in Figure 6 and Figure 7 demonstrated the EPT Li-Ion cell performance in a wide temperature range from -40°C to +85°C.

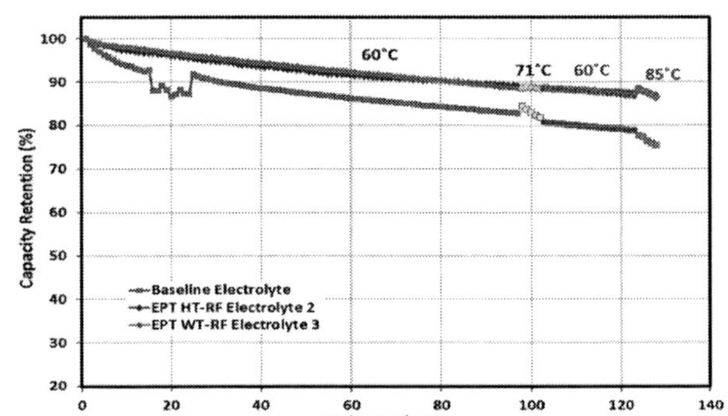

Figure 7 EPT Li-Ion Cell performances at higher temperature and compared with the baseline Li-Ion

A safer Li-Ion cell design was developed and the design was verified by an overcharge test carried out at 2C rate without any voltage control. Prior to the overcharge test, the cell was charge to 100% SOC.

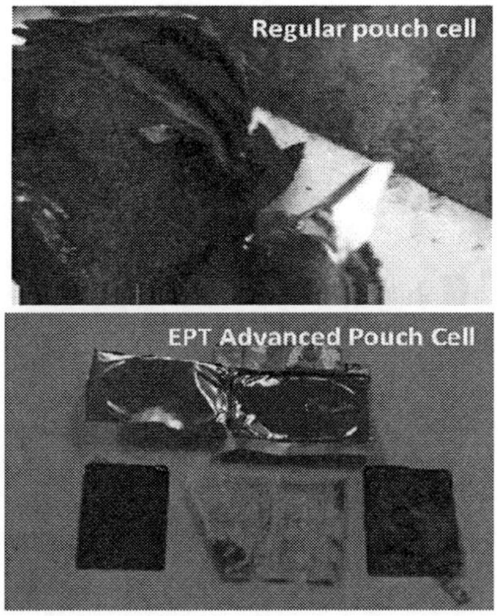

Figure 8. Photograph of overcharged test regular pouch cell after thermal runaway and EPT advanced pouch cell design which did not go through thermal runaway.

The regular pouch cell went to thermal runaway during the overcharge test within 20 min of overcharging at 2C rate. However, EPT advanced pouch cell design did not show any evidence of thermal runaway. The voltage profile in Table 1 summarized the series of safety tests that was carried out using 4Ah with NCM/graphite pouch cell. The DPA of the EPT advanced pouch cell in Figure 8 show that there is no evidence of fire inside the cell as we see a clean internal pouch materials and unburned separator. Figure 8 and Table 1 confirm that the EPT Li-Ion cell design is safer.

Conclusion

EPT Li-Ion cell demonstrated superior performance over wide temperature range from -40°C to +85°C. EPT pouch cell design was safer than the regular Li-Ion cell under overcharge abused test. EPT proprietary electrolyte formulations performance in NCM/graphite full cell demonstrates that there is no performance loss by adding fire retardant additive. The literature demonstrates that the fire retardant additive usually has a negative impact on the rate capability of LIB. We successfully developed reduced flammable electrolyte with good rate capability and wide temperature range for Li-Ion battery applications. EPT has designed an advanced pouch cell and demonstrated that the cell did not go to the thermal runaway and improves the overall safety of the Li-Ion battery.

Acknowledgement

"This material is released to the public domain in accordance with ITAR 22 CFR 120.11"

Table 1 Summary of safety test performance with 4Ah pouch cell

Test	Conditions	Observation	Result
Nail Penetration	Cell Tested at 100% SOC – 24hrs monitoring of the cell with nail inside the cell	No swelling, smoke, fire or flame.	Passed
External Short- Circuit	Cell tested at 100% SOC with 1.5mΩ external resistor	No smoke, fire or flame.	Passed
Heat-to-Vent	Cell tested at 100% SOC with heating rate of 5°C/min until it vents or voltage reached 0V	Cell swollen and vent with smoke, fire or flame.	Passed
Crush Test	Cell tested at 100% SOC with 17kN force	No physical damage	Passed
Over Charge Test	Cell over charged at 1C and 2C rate starting with 100% SOC. Single cell and 3 cells in module	Cell vented no smoke, fire or flame.	Passed

Reference

1. Marom R, Amalraj,S. F., Leifer N, Jacob D and Aurbach D., *J Materials Chemistry*, 21, (2011), 9938

2. Stura E., Nicolini C., *Anal. Chim. Acta*, 568, (2006), 57-64.

3. Li X., Kang F., Shen W., *Carbon*, 44, (2006), 1334-1336.

4. Tarascon J. M and Armand M., Nature, 414, (2001), 359-367.

5. Abu-Lebdeh Y and Davidson Isobel., *J Electrochem. Society*, 156, (2009), A60-65.

6. Levan S.L., Winandy J. E., *Fire Materials*, 24, (2000), 277.

7. Wang X., Yasukawa E., Kasuya S., *J Electrochem. Society*, 148, (2001), A1058.

8. Granzow A., *Chem Res.*, 11, (1978), 177.

9. Xu K., Zhang S.S., Allen J.L, Jow R.T, *J Electrochem. Society*, 149, (2002), A1079.

10.Feng J. K.,M Cao Y.L., Ai X. P. and Yang H. X., *Electrochimca Acta*, 53, (2008) 8265-8268.

11.Zhao J., Buldum A. and Lu J. P., *Phys. Rev. Lett.* 85, (2000), 1706.

12.Zhang S.S, *J Power Sources*, 162, (2006), 1379-1394.

Accelerated Aging of Li(Si)/FeS2 Thermal Batteries

Daniel Wesolowski, Ashley Allen, Chad Staiger, Andrea Ambrosini,
Nancy Missert, Henry Peebles and Travis Anderson
Sandia National Laboratories
dewesol@sandia.gov

Abstract

Modern Li(Si) thermal batteries have proven to be suitable for multi-decade missions, but longer shelf life is always desired. This work supplements analysis of real-time aged batteries with an accelerated aging study designed to elicit detectable responses with analytical tools. Simulated thermal batteries containing all the components except an explosive ignition system were fabricated. These components included Fe/KClO4 heat pellets, Li13Si4 anodes, KCl/LiCi eutectic electrolyte, and FeS2 cathode material in standard thermal battery formulations. A four-cell battery stack was wrapped and capped with aluminosilicate fiber insulation. The batteries were then aged up to 2 years at 75, 130, or 180°C. Moisture was also used as an accelerating factor. Moisture was controlled by first drying insulation according to standard practice then equilibrating with water at 25°C. A full suite of characterization was performed on the simulated thermal batteries, including evolved gas sampling, IR spectroscopy, combined thermal analysis (TG/DSC) on active materials, calorific output on heat pellets, cell capacity and impedance, and microanalysis (SEM/EDS). Cell capacity was reduced by as much as 10% in dry samples, but no less than 15% in moist samples and as much as 60%. Statistically significant correlations to temperature were found for heat pellet calorific output and carbon dioxide content. Large amounts of hydrogen accumulated quickly in sealed batteries and dissipated slowly, possibly through diffusion through the steel case walls. The reduction in calorific output with aging appears independent of moisture content. The correlation is strong and supported by calorific output measurements in real-time aged batteries, but the magnitude of this change is small (~1% over 30 years). Microanalysis and spectroscopy were used to define a probable reaction pathway for capacity fade through shelf-life aging. Thermodynamic calculations were used to support the proposed pathway. Cathode degradation was observed using FTIR, XRD and microanalysis. Degradation is hypothesized to be driven by the free energy drop associated with lithium reaction in the anode. A mobile sulfur species, most likely H2S, facilitates the reaction in the presence of moisture. A completely dry aging pathway exists with a larger change in free energy, but the lack of degradation observed in the absence of moisture shows that it is kinetically limited.

Lifetime Extension of Munitions Thermal Reserve Batteries

Frank C. Krieger and Michael S. Ding
U.S. Army Research Laboratory, 2800 Powder Mill Road, Adelphi MD 20783
frank.c.krieger.civ@mail.mil

Abstract: *Mathematical heat transfer analyses based on previously reported ARL developed FORTRAN programs and Sandia SIERRA TABS finite element models using measured thermal battery heat transfer parameters are used to characterize long life thermal batteries. Special emphasis is placed on systems that require nominal electrical outputs of 40–50 W at 20–50 V potentials and with operational lifetimes ranging from 300 to 900 seconds (15–36 kJ). Initial pyrotechnic heating of the thermal insulation packages and control of the insulation package thermal conductivity values can have significant effects on thermal battery lifetimes.*

Keywords: thermal battery life extension; heat transfer analysis; FORTRAN; SIERRA TABS; finite element modeling; transient heat transfer; statistical methods; gas control

Introduction

Batteries are modeled from previously measured thermal battery operating parameters using ARL developed FORTRAN programs and SIERRA TABS finite element modeling. Special attention was placed on 20–50 V batteries operating at 40–50 W that might be used in guidance applications. Previously reported attempts to control hydrogen and other gases in operating thermal batteries (1–5) are updated and discussed. The thermal conductivity values used in the models shown were reported by a commercial thermal insulation vendor for their insulation in an atmosphere of 50/50 H_2/air at 1 atmosphere of pressure. A program to simplify and accelerate the rate of data collection and analysis of gases from operating thermal batteries is in progress at ARL.

Significant amounts of heat are lost rapidly during the initial (10–60 s) transient heat transfer state immediately after pyrotechnic initiation (1, 4) when the thermal cell stack is rapidly heated from ambient temperature and a steady state temperature distribution is being closely approached in the thermal insulation package (Tables 1–9). Thermal insulation packages can be independently heated pyrotechnically or even temporarily overheated to prolong battery lifetimes. Later, during battery operation, the effective heat delivered from the cooling thermal insulation that prolongs battery life is much smaller, mostly because of the smaller temperature changes during cooling.

Battery construction methods can change markedly with or without significant changes in battery size. Multiple batteries are needed in some munitions applications for electrical or mechanical compatibility reasons. Energy and power density values for the 40–50 W thermal batteries modeled here are compared with experimental operating thermal battery volumes in Table 10.

In addition to the obviously significant heat transfer effects on thermal battery performance, other factors such as thermal cell stack force (lidding pressure), thermal cell stack pellet chemical compositions, chemical processing methods, and battery construction methods significantly affect thermal cell stack electrical outputs and reliabilities and can produce large changes in battery electrical output for specific applications. Thermal conductivity, heat capacity, density, physical state, and chemical compositional properties of the materials can all change significantly during battery operation. Pyrotechnic amounts, types, and locations within thermal insulation packages are typically chosen to avoid electrical short circuits, unfavorable chemical interactions such as decomposition of tape adhesives, or damage to other battery components. With such a large number of operating parameters and construction options possible, direct laboratory confirmation of individual experimental variations can become counterproductive because of time, personnel, and materials constraints. Statistical methods can then become helpful or essential as preliminary guides to thermal battery development experimentation (6) and will be applied during future ARL thermal battery investigations.

Thermal Battery Model Parameters

All of the batteries in this presentation use the LiBr-LiCl-LiF eutectic electrolyte (E) with the MgO binder (B). The batteries use 82/18 weight percent Fe/$KClO_4$ pyrotechnic heat pellets that deliver 340 cal/g of heat pellet. The anode pellet is 44/56 weight percent Li/Si alloy. The separator pellet (E/B) is 55/45 weight percent LiBr-LiCl-LiF eutectic electrolyte/MgO binder and the cathode pellet is 78/2/20 weight percent FeS_2/Fe/(E/B). Stainless steel (SS) electrodes are used to protect both the anode and cathode pellets from the initial pyrotechnic flash temperatures during activation.

This electrochemical system can supply current densities as high as 4 A/cm^2 of thermal cell area with single cell voltages as high as 1.4 V. At the 50 W current drain, and for all current densities of ~1 A/cm^2 or less, each thermal cell will initially supply nominally 1.8 V and will decline to nominally 1.35 V near the end of the electrical lifetime. All of the batteries analyzed in this paper are based on powder formulations that supply 14.0 A–min/g of FeS_2 and 20.0 A–min/g of 44/56 weight percent Li/Si alloy anode. Overall accuracy of the calculated cooling times in the absence of dedicated data from an experimental development program is estimated to be on the order of ±15%.

Thermal Battery Construction Detail for 32–24 V 50 W 1500 A–s Thermal Battery

The unit thermal cell shown in Table 1 is used in a thermal battery that is capable of supplying nominally 50 W at 32 V to 24 V at current densities of 1 A/cm^2 or less with a total capacity of 1500 coulomb (A–s). The battery uses 18 unit thermal cells with a calculated thermal lifetime of 615.9 s. The thermal cells all have 1.8 in. outer diameters and 0.25 in. inner diameters. The inner dimensions of the entire battery case are 2.195 in. diameter by 2.276 in. tall (total volume 141.1 cm^3). The individual component volumes, the volumetric heat content, and the total heat required for each component for the entire battery during activation (from 65 to 675 °C) are shown in Table 2. Table 2 shows the relatively large amounts of heat that are required to heat the thermal insulation. Values for those same parameters during a typical (much smaller) cooling interval of 593.5 to 540.7 °C are shown in Table 3. The volumetric thermal insulation heat contents shown in Table 3 are adjusted values applied by the FORTRAN thermal models used to closely approximate the effective heat lost from the thermal insulation package during the cooling interval.

Table 1. Unit Thermal Cell for 32–24 V 50 W 1500 A–s Thermal Battery

Component (Weight Percent)	Thick (inch)	Mass (g)	Density (g/cm^3)
SS Electrode	0.0030	0.9643	7.86
Heat Pellet	0.0307	4.389	3.5
SS Electrode	0.0030	0.9643	7.86
Li/Si Anode	0.0306	1.250	1.0
Separator	0.0100	1.046	2.557
FeS_2 Cathode	0.0155	2.289	3.618
Total	0.0928	10.903	

Table 2. Activation Heat Required for 32–24 V 50 W 1500 A–s Thermal Battery

Heat Required for Activation (65 to 675 °C)			
Component	Volume (cm^3)	Heat Required (cal/cm^3)	Total Heat (cal)
SS Electrodes	4.663	695.6	3244
Heat Pellets	29.37	347.5	10206
Anodes	22.50	338.8	7623
Separators + Cathodes	18.75	434.6	8149
Center Hole	1.481		
End Insulation	27.00	88.90	2400
Side Insulation	37.39	88.90	3324
Total	141.1		34946

Table 3. Heat Delivered During a Selected Cooling Interval for 32–24 V 50 W 1500 A–s Thermal Battery

Heat Lost During Cooling (593.5 to 540.7 °C)			
Component	Volume (cm^3)	Heat Delivered (cal/cm^3)	Total Heat (cal)
SS Electrodes	4.663	70.59	329.2
Heat Pellets	29.37	33.32	978.6
Anodes	22.50	29.65	667.1
Separators + Cathodes	18.75	35.30	661.9
Center Hole	1.481		
End Insulation	27.00	1.837	49.60
Side Insulation	37.39	1.837	68.69
Total	141.1		2755

Thermal Battery Construction Detail for 32–24 V 50 W 750 A–s Thermal Battery

The unit thermal cell shown in Table 4 is used in a thermal battery that is capable of supplying nominally 50 W at 32 V to 24 V with a total capacity of 750 coulomb (A–s). The battery shown in Tables 4–6 uses 18 thermal cells with a

Table 4. Unit Thermal Cell for 32–24 V 50 W 750 A–s Thermal Battery

Component (Weight Percent)	Thick (inch)	Mass (g)	Density (g/cm^3)
SS Electrode	0.0030	0.4180	7.86
Heat Pellet	0.0337	2.089	3.5
SS Electrode	0.003	0.4180	7.86
Li/Si Anode	0.0353	0.6250	1.0
Separator	0.0100	0.4533	2.557
FeS_2 Cathode	0.0178	1.145	3.618
Total	0.1028	5.1483	

Table 5. Activation Heat Required for 32–24 V 50 W 750 A–s Thermal Battery

Heat Required for Activation (65 to 675 °C)			
Component	Volume (cm^3)	Heat Required (cal/cm^3)	Total Heat (cal)
SS Electrodes	2.055	695.6	1429
Heat Pellets	13.83	347.5	4806
Anodes	11.25	338.8	3812
Separators + Cathodes	8.886	431.6	3835
Center Hole	1.634		
End Insulation	7.769	88.90	690.7
Side Insulation	21.18	88.90	1883
Total	66.60		16456

Table 6. Heat Delivered During a Selected Cooling Interval for 32–24 V 50 W 750 A–s Thermal Battery

Heat Lost During Cooling (593.3 to 540.5 °C)			
Component	Volume (cm^3)	Heat Delivered (cal/cm^3)	Total Heat (cal)
SS Electrodes	2.055	70.49	144.9
Heat Pellets	13.83	33.27	460.1
Anodes	11.25	29.61	333.1
Separators + Cathodes	8.886	35.16	312.4
Center Hole	1.634		
End Insulation	7.769	1.834	14.25
Side Insulation	21.18	1.834	38.84
Total	66.60		1303.6

calculated thermal lifetime of 318.0 s. The thermal cells all have 1.20 in. outer diameters and 0.25 in. inner diameters. The inner dimensions of the entire battery case are 1.50 in. diameter by 2.30 in. tall (total volume 66.60 cm^3). Tables 5 and 6 show the total heat required for battery activation and delivered for a selected cooling interval as before.

Thermal Battery Construction Detail for 50–38 V 40 W 900 A–s Thermal Battery

The unit thermal cell shown in Table 7 is used in a thermal battery that is capable of supplying nominally 40 W at 50 to 38 V with a total capacity of 900 coulomb (A–s). The battery uses 28 thermal cells with a calculated thermal lifetime of 959.9 s. The thermal cells all have 1.2 in. outer diameters and 0.25 in. inner diameters. The inner dimensions of the battery case are 2.25 in. diameter by 5.40 in. tall (total volume 351.8 cm^3). Tables 8 and 9 show the total heat required for battery activation and delivered for a selected cooling interval as before.

Table 7. Unit Thermal Cell for 50–38 V 40 W 900 A–s Thermal Battery

Component (Weight Percent)	Thick (inch)	Mass (g)	Density (g/cm^3)
SS Electrode	0.0030	0.4180	7.86
Heat Pellet	0.0381	2.364	3.5
SS Electrode	0.0030	0.4180	7.86
Li/Si Anode	0.0423	0.7500	1.0
Separator (E/B)	0.0100	0.4533	2.557
FeS_2 Cathode	0.0214	1.374	3.618
Total	0.1178	5.777	

The heat required to heat the thermal insulation during battery activation (Table 8) is 42.0% of the total heat required for the entire battery and can significantly shorten battery life in the absence of appropriate heat transfer engineering. The thermal lifetime for this battery could increase to 1017.8 s with a reduction in electrochemical-heat source cell stack (EHS) length of 1.505 in. while using the same internal case dimensions (or alternately, the internal volume could be reduced to 314.1 cm^3 for a thermal life of 938.2 s) if all of the insulation heat were supplied pyrotechnically from within the thermal insulation package rather than from the cooling EHS stack.

Table 8. Activation Heat Required for 50–38 V 40 W 900 A–s Thermal Battery

Heat Required for Activation (65 to 675 °C)			
Component	Volume (cm^3)	Heat Required (cal/cm^3)	Total Heat (cal)
SS Electrodes	3.086	695.6	2147
Heat Pellets	46.53	347.5	16169
Anodes	21.00	338.8	7115
Separators + Cathodes	15.59	428.0	6673
Center Hole	3.912		
End Insulation	35.00	88.90	3111
Side Insulation	226.7	88.90	20154
Total	351.8		55369

Table 9. Heat Delivered During a Selected Cooling Interval for 50–38 V 40 W 900 A–s Thermal Battery

Heat Lost During Cooling (592.7 to 540.1 °C)			
Component	Volume (cm^3)	Heat Delivered (cal/cm^3)	Total Heat (cal)
SS Electrodes	3.086	70.21	216.7
Heat Pellets	46.53	33.14	1542
Anodes	21.00	29.50	619.5
Separators + Cathodes	15.59	34.91	544.2
Center Hole	3.912		
End Insulation	35.00	1.828	63.98
Side Insulation	226.7	1.828	414.4
Total	351.8		3400.8

Thermal Battery Lifetime Extension Methods

The most obvious methods for extending thermal battery lifetimes remain the control of hydrogen gas and the proper transient heating of thermal insulation packages immediately following battery initiation as has been discussed previously (1 – 5). Hydrogen gas control has been confirmed in laboratory experiments using pyrotechnically heated thermal battery materials but has not yet been shown to be effective in operating thermal batteries. The effectiveness of heating the thermal insulation independently is clearly illustrated by optimization analyses of the 40 W 900 A–s battery of Tables 7–9. This effect becomes increasingly significant for thermal batteries like the Low Cost Competent Munition battery (LCCM) with small EHS stacks where large thermal insulation packages are required to achieve long thermal lifetimes (4).

Implementation of hydrogen gas removal from operating thermal batteries remains difficult because of the possibility of chemical reactions of the gas removal agents with the thermal insulation packages and with the EHS stack materials, especially considering the wide operating temperature ranges and the rapidly changing chemically active and chemically complex operating thermal battery environments. Appropriate thermal battery electrochemical powders have been prepared and test fixtures to simplify and speed the experimental investigation of hydrogen removal methods at ARL are being developed. Control of additional operating parameters as the importance of their effects for specific applications becomes identified through the use of thermal modeling and statistical parametric studies will also be used to help predict and extend thermal battery lifetimes.

Energy and Power Density Comparisons

Energy and power densities were calculated for the batteries modeled here at 40–50 W electrical loads and those results are compared with operating LCCM and Man Portable Non-line of Sight (MANLOS) thermal battery values (5) in Table 10. The energy and power density values for the modeled batteries in Table 10 include 304 SS cases with 0.030 in.

thick walls and 0.125 in. thick headers. The increase in power and energy densities from independent heating of the thermal insulation package for the thermally optimized 900 A–s battery shown in Table 10 is substantial but not dramatic. Decreases in thermal lifetimes from required heating of the thermal insulation packages can become quite large even for thermally optimized batteries that use good heat transfer engineering if the EHS stacks are significantly smaller than the thermal insulation packages.

The MANLOS thermal battery shown below was an exceptionally high energy and power (100 A) thermal battery developed at ARL to power a small aerial vehicle and the MANLOS values shown in Table 10 are for the EHS only. Thermal battery energy and power density values can vary greatly depending on whether high power or long life is emphasized. For most munitions thermal battery applications, when the case and thermal insulation package is included in the calculations, it would be difficult to exceed the values shown below for the MANLOS cell stack, and the MANLOS EHS numbers shown below can be used as approximate upper limits to thermal battery electrical output capabilities.

Table 10. Thermal Battery Energy and Power Densities

Battery	Wh/l	Wh/kg	W/l	W/kg
LCCM	20.4	8.23	649	262
MANLOS (EHS Only)	248	79	12470	3700
1500 A–s	53.8	21.9	314	128
750 A–s	57.4	22.3	650	252
900 A–s	28.0	16.7	105	62.5
900 A–s*	30.5	21.4	117	82.1
*Independently Heated Thermal Insulation				

Summary and Conclusions

Some examples of munitions thermal batteries operating at 40–50 W electrical loads were modeled using previously measured operating parameters with both ARL developed FORTRAN programs (1, 4) and SIERRA TABS finite element models (6, 7). Special attention was paid to 20–50 V 40–50 W thermal batteries with lifetimes of 300–900 s that might be used in guidance applications. Thermal insulation package thermal conductivity changes and independent pyrotechnic heating of the thermal insulation packages are two of the most obvious, readily altered, and commonly used methods of extending thermal battery lifetimes. Thermal conductivity values are typically optimized in industry by selecting known low thermal conductivity thermal insulators and by optimizing the resulting battery lifetimes with proven materials selection, chemical processing, and battery construction methods.

Test methods and fixtures being developed at ARL are expected to simplify and accelerate the evaluation of hydrogen gas control in operating thermal batteries. Much information, including measured cell stack exothermic and endothermic effects, is available from detailed analyses of operating thermal battery EHS stack temperatures. Mathematical models clearly show that proper selection and control of experimental operating parameters could extend many presently fielded munitions thermal battery operating lifetimes and thereby increase the corresponding volumetric energy densities by factors of four or more.

The high temperature chemically complex operating environment of thermal batteries is not well defined and many possibilities are best initially investigated statistically.
Statistical methods are being developed at ARL to evaluate the effects of thermal battery parametric interactions.

Acknowledgements

The authors would like to thank Ed Piekos, Chris Apblett, and Scott Roberts of the Sandia National Laboratories for their knowledgeable assistance and support on thermal battery technology and finite element models. Jeffrey Swank of ARL provided useful suggestions during his technical review of this paper.

References

1. Krieger, F., and M. Ding, "Experimental and Mathematical Confirmation of Munitions Thermal Battery Heat Transfer Using FORTRAN and SIERRA Finite Element Thermal Models," Proc. 46th Power Sources Conference, p. 403, (June 2014).
2. Krieger, F., and M. Ding, "Gas Analysis and Control Methods for Thermal Batteries," ARL-TR-6665, U.S. Army Research Laboratory, Adelphi MD, (SEP 2014).
3. Krieger, F., and M. Ding, "Thermal Battery Operating Gas Atmosphere Control and Heat Transfer Optimization," ARL-TR-6156, U.S. Army Research Laboratory, Adelphi MD, (SEP 2012).
4. Krieger, F., and M. Ding, "Heat Transfer in the LCCM Thermal Reserve Battery," ARL-TR-4843, U.S. Army Research Laboratory, Adelphi MD, (SEP 2009).
5. Krieger, F., and M. Ding, "Internal Heat Balance, Operating Gas Atmosphere, and Thermal Cell Heat Generation Optimization Methods for Thermal Batteries," Proc. 43rd Power Sources Conference, p. 381, (June 2008).
6. Piekos, E., A. Grillet, N. Streeter, and S. Showalter, "Assessing the Sensitivity of Thermal Battery Performance to Material Thermal Properties via Simulation," Proc. 46th Power Sources Conference, p. 399, (July 2014).
7. Roberts, S., Long, K., Clausen, J., Martinez, M., Piekos, E. and Grillet, A., Towards a Coupled Multiphysics Model of Molten Salt Battery Mechanics, Proc. 46th Power Sources Conference, p. 411, (July 2014).

Uncertainty Quantification, Verification, and Validation of a Thermal Simulation Tool for Molten Salt Batteries

Bradley L. Trembacki[1], Shaun R. Harris[1,2], Edward S. Piekos[1], and Scott A. Roberts[1]

[1]Sandia National Laboratories
P.O. Box 5800
Albuquerque, NM 87185-0840

[2]Utah State University
Mechanical and Aerospace Engineering Department
Logan, UT 84322

Abstract: *Thermal management is critical to the design of molten salt batteries, and the use of computational models to aid in this process has become widespread. An understanding of the relationship between uncertain inputs and probabilistic outputs allows for more realistic simulation results and model validation when compared to traditional deterministic simulation. This understanding also allows design engineers to make informed decisions when specifying material property and manufacturing tolerances. Thermal simulations of molten salt batteries using Sandia's Thermally Activated Battery Simulator (TABS v3) are employed to propagate uncertainty in input variables such as material properties, material response, initial conditions, and geometry through the model. The probability ranges of output responses such as rise time, maximum temperature, and lifetime are calculated, and the uncertain inputs that most significantly affect the output metrics are determined. Model validation results are presented by comparing the uncertainty quantification simulation results to temperature data from an instrumented model battery, and solution verification is discussed with a focus on computational grid spacing.*

Keywords: molten salt battery; thermal simulation; uncertainty; verification and validation; sensitivity

Introduction

Typical molten salt batteries are composed of a stack of electrochemical cells enclosed in a case, with each cell in the stack consisting chiefly of individual pellets of anode, separator, cathode, and pyrotechnic material. Additional materials such as insulation and current collectors are often included as well. The ignition of the pyrotechnic material introduces a large amount of heat energy into the system, causing the solid electrolyte within the porous separator to melt. The melted electrolyte flows into the porous electrodes and completes the electrochemical circuit, allowing the battery to deliver electric power.

Computational models of molten salt battery performance have traditionally focused on thermal transport, neglecting electrochemical or mechanical phenomena. By predicting the spatial temperature profile in each material, maximum temperatures reached in each material can be evaluated, and an approximation of battery rise time and lifetime can be made. We define several interpretations of these important performance metrics in more detail in the Quantities of Interest section below.

Specific heat and thermal conductivity are input parameters for each material in the domain. In addition, heat pellet pyrotechnic parameters like heat release and burn speed are provided as simulation inputs. The combination of material properties and number of materials in the domain results in a large number of input parameters that, combined with initial and boundary conditions, determine the overall behavior of a thermal simulation. Many of these properties are temperature dependent, making accurate characterization of each property for each material a significant challenge. Each value also has an associated uncertainty range, typically based on experimental or manufacturing variability. An understanding of the relationship between uncertain inputs and output quantities of interest allows design engineers to focus on input properties that most significantly affect battery performance. Incorporating uncertainty also allows for more realistic simulation results and model validation. In this paper, we investigate many thermal simulation input parameters and present their effects on battery performance. In addition, simulation results considering uncertainty propagation are compared to results from an instrumented validation battery.

Methodology

Throughout this paper, all results are obtained from thermal transport simulations of molten salt batteries using input configurations generated by Sandia's Thermally Activated Battery Simulator (TABS v3). The thermal model utilized by TABS has been developed within the Sierra mechanics framework [1], specifically in Sierra/Aria [2], and is based on the finite element method. All simulations are performed on a two-dimensional axisymmetric representation of a cylindrical battery.

Thermal Model: For thermal transport throughout the battery domain, the governing equation is the standard heat equation,

$$\rho c_p \frac{\partial T}{\partial t} = \nabla \cdot \kappa \nabla T + S_E, \tag{1}$$

where ρ is the density, c_p is the specific heat, T is temperature, t is time, κ is the thermal conductivity, and S_E is a volumetric energy source. The major energy source is from the burning of the pyrotechnic heat pellets, the location of which is tracked using a level-set method [3]. As materials change phase, latent heat also contributes to the S_E term.

Sensitivity Calculation: Each simulation input parameter has a nominal value obtained from Sandia battery designers or literature and an accompanying uncertainty range based on experimental or manufacturing variability [4, 5]. In many cases, an uncertainty range has not been studied for a given material or property, so a wide range is used here to represent a worst case scenario. Table 1 summarizes a typical list of battery input parameters and their uncertainty ranges used throughout this paper. For temperature dependent properties, the entire temperature range is scaled similarly.

Table 1. Input parameter relative uncertainty ranges used throughout this paper. HP=Heat Pellet.

Parameter	Lower Bound	Upper Bound
HP c_p	60%	140%
Separator c_p	60%	140%
Cathode c_p	60%	140%
Anode c_p	60%	140%
HP κ	10%	190%
Separator κ	10%	190%
Cathode κ	10%	190%
Anode κ	10%	190%
Insulation κ	10%	500%
HP Density (ρ)	97%	103%
HP Mass	99.5%	100.5%
HP Burn Speed	80%	100%
HP Heat Output	99%	101%
Ambient Temp	99.6%	100.4%
Emissivity (ϵ)	0	1

Using these input uncertainty ranges and assuming a uniform distribution on each parameter, a Latin Hypercube sampling of the parameters is used to perform 500 unique thermal simulations. This process was automated by using the open source DAKOTA toolkit [6], which provides an extensible interface between analysis codes and systems analysis methods. For each simulation, several quantities of interest (QOIs) are computed, which are detailed in the next section. This combination of various input parameters and their corresponding output QOIs is used to construct a surrogate model for a subsequent polynomial chaos response sampling, again using the DAKOTA toolkit. The result is a collection of uncertainty ranges and global sensitivity metrics of each output QOI with respect to each input parameter.

Quantities of Interest

As previously mentioned, the most important performance metrics of a molten salt battery are rise time and lifetime. Rise time represents the amount of time between initiating the heat pellet burn and achieving useful electric power. Similarly, lifetime represents the amount of time between heat pellet initiation and the point at which the battery ceases providing useful power. Since the simulations employed here model thermal transport only, a translation between useful electric power and temperature must be made for these metrics. The battery provides no power while the electrolyte within the separator region is solidified, thus the foundation for this translation will be that an activated battery corresponds to a separator region above the electrolyte melt temperature. While this assumption neglects some physical processes and/or non-uniform material composition, it serves as an acceptable approximation for our application. The amount of separator that needs to be above melt temperature in order for a battery to function remains unclear, so we use three definitions for an activated battery as our rise time and lifetime QOIs.

The two extremes for rise time are represented by *Rise Time Min* and *Rise Time Max*. The minimum time corresponds to an interpretation where the battery is activated if any point in a separator has melted, or $max(T) > T_{melting}$. Alternatively, the maximum time corresponds to the entire separator region being melted, or $min(T) > T_{melting}$. A third metric, *Rise Time Mid*, falls between the extremes by considering the battery active if the separator has reached melt temperature at at least one radial location, indicating that each cell in the stack now has a transport pathway between anode and cathode.

Three lifetime variations are similarly but inversely defined, where *Lifetime Min* and *Lifetime Max* represent the minimum and maximum extremes $min(T) < T_{melting}$ and $max(T) < T_{melting}$, respectively. *Lifetime Mid* corresponds to the point where the separator contains at least one frozen point at each radial location, meaning at least one cell in the stack has no transport pathway.

The last two QOIs are maximum temperature reached in the anode and cathode. While rise time and lifetime are mainly performance metrics, maximum temperatures are of interest due to safety. High temperatures in battery materials can lead to unacceptable consequences such as material degradation and thermal runaway [7].

These eight QOIs are all calculated by evaluating the spatial/temporal temperature results provided by the thermal simulations. For each QOI, the value is linearly interpolated between numerical time steps to offset inaccuracy due to the discrete nature of the simulation.

Results and Discussion

In this section, we provide results obtained from analysis of thermal simulations, beginning with uncertainty results for the QOIs, presented in Table 2. The standard deviations (σ) are quite large for some parameters, with the highest value being 130% of the mean for the long life battery *Rise Time Max*. The maximum temperatures reached show a significantly lower σ value than the other metrics, indicating that they are less sensitive to the specified variability in input parameters.

Table 2. Normalized QOI standard deviation ($\pm\sigma$) for both a short and long life battery design.

QOI	Short Life	Long Life
Lifetime Max	44%	32%
Lifetime Mid	62%	30%
Lifetime Min	76%	54%
Cathode max(T)	12%	10%
Anode max(T)	12%	9%
Rise Time Max	35%	130%
Rise Time Mid	47%	53%
Rise Time Min	59%	64%

Sensitivity Index: Here we present sensitivity index summaries for two battery designs, one designed to exhibit a short lifetime and the other a long lifetime. As described above, these sensitivity index values are calculated through variance-based decomposition using a polynomial chaos sampling of simulated QOI results and are useful when assessing which input variables are most influential in the resulting QOI uncertainty. Specifically, for each QOI, each sensitivity index corresponds to the fraction of the uncertainty that results due to each input variable alone and is often referred to as the main effect sensitivity index. Any effects that result from an interaction with another input variable are not included in the main index [6].

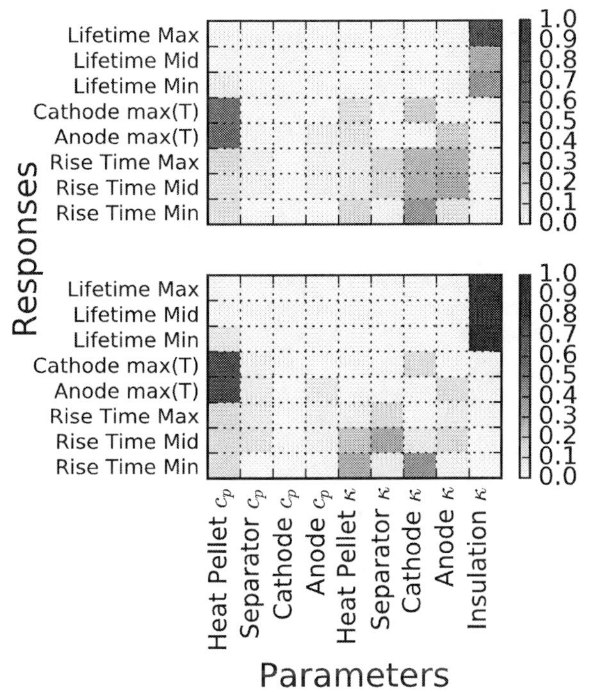

Figure 1. Sensitivity Index maps for both a short lifetime battery (top) and a long lifetime battery (bottom). The legend ranges from 0.0-1.0, representing the fraction of the uncertainty in each response that can be attributed to the uncertainty in each input parameter. Material property parameters plotted are specific heat (c_p) and thermal conductivity (κ) for each major battery material.

The sensitivity index results are summarized in Figure 1 where a few observations are immediately apparent. For both battery designs, all three lifetime calculations show high index values for the thermal conductivity of the insulation layer, which represents a heavy dependence. Between 80-90% of the variability in the lifetime predictions in the long life battery are due to the insulation conductivity alone. This is not surprising as the insulation dictates how quickly heat can leave the battery and the uncertainty range on the insulation conductivity is quite large. Interestingly, for both batteries *Lifetime Mid* shows a lower sensitivity than the minimum and maximum lifetime calculations, which indicates that the more complicated calculation is more significantly affected by a combination of parameters rather than solely conductive heat loss through the insulation material.

Maximum temperatures reached in the electrodes are predominantly sensitive to the heat pellet specific heat, where it alone accounts for 54% of the short life and 70% of the long life maximum temperature variability. For a given total heat release, a higher heat pellet c_p limits the maximum temperature reached by the heat pellet, and therefore limits the temperature reached by the electrodes as heat spreads. We see that the maximum temperature reached is also sensitive to a given electrode material's thermal conductivity, again dictating how quickly a buildup of heat can dissipate.

In contrast with the other responses, rise time calculations do not show a strong dependence on a single input parameter but instead depend on a collection of thermal conductivity parameters. The different rise time interpretations show significantly different sensitivities, which is highlighted by the long life battery cathode κ indices.

It should be noted that all responses showed negligible sensitivity to ambient temperature as well as heat pellet burn speed, heat output, and density, so they are not included in Figure 1. This is likely due to the relatively small uncertainty ranges associated with these parameters when compared to the large ranges used for the other material properties. As uncertainties of high-index parameters are narrowed, the sensitivity indices will change and other parameters may show themselves to be important. In a scenario with comparable relative uncertainty ranges in parameters, we would expect heat pellet pyrotechnic properties (burn speed, heat output, etc.) to be the dominant parameter for the rise time responses.

Despite the large uncertainty range on emissivity, it was also omitted from the plot due to a negligible sensitivity index, indicating that the effect of radiation variability is overshadowed by the other mechanisms in these simulations. Observations like these highlight the power and usefulness of this type of sensitivity study. Although there may be very limited information on a material property like emissivity, we can now be confident that resources would be better utilized characterizing other materials and/or properties that will have a more significant impact on simulation results.

Verification and Validation: Three replications of a molten salt battery design were manufactured and instrumented with 15 internal thermocouples to provide model validation data. We used this design when studying the long lifetime battery sensitivities presented in Figure 1. Comparisons between the temperature readings at the thermocouple locations and our thermal simulation results at similar locations in the computational domain were made, with one such comparison being presented here in Figure 2. The nominal simulation results do deviate from the validation data, but when accounting for the uncertainties in input parameters presented previously, the validation data falls within the 95% confidence interval provided by the previously described uncertainty quantification study. Improving nominal accuracy and narrowing the temperature variability bands are top candidates for continuing work and are currently being pursued.

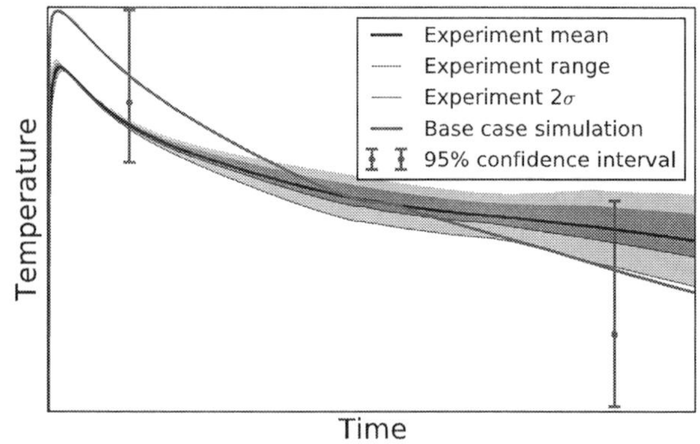

Figure 2. Comparison of experimental (3 replicates) and simulated separator temperature in an instrumented molten salt battery with both nominal and uncertainty propagation simulation results shown.

In an effort to assess solution verification, we focus here on physical space discretization (mesh refinement) error as the heat equation implementation in Sierra/Aria has been thoroughly verified [8]. Error results for the maximum temperature QOIs are presented in Figure 3, where error is relative to a Richardson extrapolation value for each QOI. We observe that the two temperature metrics show second order convergence as expected in a uniform mesh refinement study and note that even on the coarsest mesh, relative errors are less than 0.2%. Using this plot, it is possible to determine the mesh resolution required to provide an acceptable relative spatial discretization error (0.1%, 0.01%, etc.), avoiding waste of computational resources while maintaining desired accuracy. The rise time and lifetime QOIs are not plotted as they were not clearly convergent, making it difficult to confidently assess spatial discretization error. We are in the process of determining the cause of the unexpected convergence behavior with a focus on further mesh refinement as well as other error sources, such as temporal discretization or nonlinear solution tolerance.

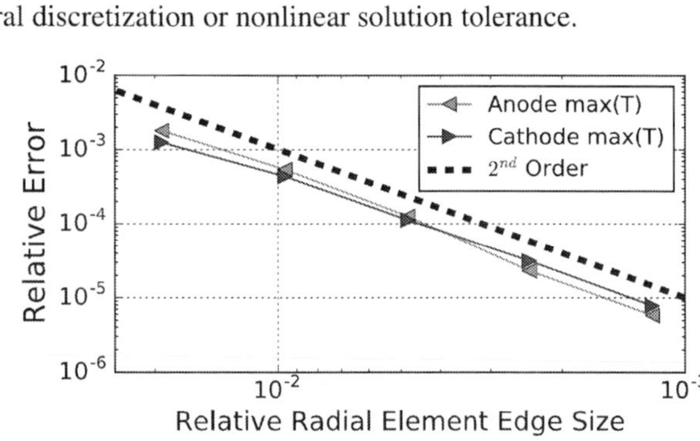

Figure 3. Plot of error relative to second order Richardson extrapolation values versus the uniform mesh refinement, where relative edge size is defined as the ratio of radial computational element edge length to the battery radius.

Conclusions

Accounting for uncertainty in input parameters and assessing how that uncertainty affects output quantities of interest can provide useful information for battery design engineers and motivate experiments to reduce uncertainty. We presented results of studies that use the DAKOTA toolkit for exploring the uncertainty space and discussed the importance of sensitivity index values. Finally, we demonstrated that efforts have been made to both verify and validate the models and techniques used.

Acknowledgments

The authors wish to thank Adam Hetzler, Richard Hills, Kenneth Hu, and the battery engineers and scientists of the Power Sources Group at Sandia for their continued insight. The authors gratefully acknowledge funding form the Advanced Simulation and Computing Verification and Validation Program Element. Sandia National Laboratories is a multi-program laboratory managed and operated by Sandia Corporation, a wholly owned subsidiary of Lockheed Martin Corporation, for the U.S. Department of Energy's National Nuclear Security Administration under contract DE-AC04-94AL85000.

References

[1] Stewart, J. R. and H. Edwards. "A framework approach for developing parallel adaptive multiphysics applications." *Finite Elements in Analysis and Design*, vol. 40, no. 12, pp. 1599 – 1617, 2004.

[2] Notz, P. K., S. R. Subia, M. M. Hopkins, H. K. Moffat, and D. R. Noble. "Aria 1.5: User Manual." Tech. rep., SAND2007-2734, Sandia National Laboratories, April 2007.

[3] Piekos, E. S., A. M. Grillet, D. T. Ingersoll, N. D. Streeter, and D. R. Noble. "Modeling of Thermal Battery Initiation Using Level Sets." In *Proceedings of the 45th Power Sources Conference*, pp. 595–598, 2012.

[4] Guidotti, R. A. and M. Moss. "Thermal conductivity of thermal-battery insulations." Tech. rep., SAND95-1649, Sandia National Laboratories, August 1995.

[5] Guidotti, R. A., J. Odinek, and F. W. Reinhardt. "Characterization of Fe/KClO4 heat powders and pellets." *Journal of Energetic Materials*, vol. 24, no. 4, pp. 271–305, 2006.

[6] Adams, B. M., M. Ebeida, M. Eldred, J. Jakeman, L. Swiler, W. Bohnhoff, K. Dalbey, J. Eddy, K. Hu, and D. Vigil. "Dakota, a multilevel parallel object-oriented framework for design optimization, parameter estimation, uncertainty quantification, and sensitivity analysis: Version 5.4 users manual." Tech. rep., SAND2010-2183, Sandia National Laboratories, December 2009, Updated November 2013.

[7] Guidotti, R. A. and P. Masset. "Thermally activated (thermal) battery technology: Part I: An overview." *Journal of Power Sources*, vol. 161, no. 2, pp. 1443–1449, 2006.

[8] Copps, K. D. and B. C. Carnes. "Sierra Verification Module: Encore User Guide - Version 4.28." Tech. rep., SAND2013-3344, Sandia National Laboratories, June 2013.

Multi-Physics, Multi-Plateau Reaction Model for LiSi/FeS$_2$ Batteries

Tyler G. Voskuilen, John C. Hewson, Harry K. Moffat, and Scott A. Roberts
Sandia National Laboratories
P.O. Box 5800, MS-0836, Albuquerque, NM 87185-0836

Abstract: *Prior modeling of LiSi/FeS$_2$ molten salt batteries used a multi-plateau approach for the anode reactions but used a reaction-extent model for the cathode. This required an assumption as to which reaction mechanism/interface is currently reacting and prevented multiple simultaneous reactions during high current discharge.*

We present an update to the previously presented multi-plateau model [1–3] for the cathode reactions with calibration against experimental data over a wide range of discharge currents using a 1D isothermal model. We then couple this new model with electrolyte phase-change and transport for single-cell simulations. Using this model, we present results from 2D axisymmetric single-cell coupled thermal-electrochemical simulations of start-up and freeze-out at varying load resistances.

Keywords: thermal battery; primary lithium cell; molten salt electrolyte; iron disulfide; computational modeling

Introduction

Predictive modeling of thermal batteries requires coupling between several key physical phenomena. A robust electrochemical model for the active components along with electrical transport is required to predict start-up times and operational performance, but this alone is not sufficient. The electrochemistry must be coupled with thermal transport, phase change, and porous flow in order to capture the relevant transport processes. The development of predictive models in order to guide battery design and enable efficient design optimization is a primary goal of this and our previous work [1–5]. In this work, we present a more robust multi-plateau electrochemical model for the FeS$_2$ cathode and compare isothermal 1D results with this model against experimental constant-current discharge data over a range of currents. Next, we couple this model with our 2D axisymmetric single cell model and show how thermal sources, such as Joule heating and phase change latent heat, influence the lifetime electrical performance. We also examine the effect that a partially saturated cell has on electrical startup performance.

Model

The electrochemical model described in previous work by Hewson et al. [1–3] used a concentric sphere multi-plateau model for the anode reactions and a reaction-extent model derived from Bernardi and Newman [6] for the cathode reactions. This reaction extent model, however, had a number of drawbacks. First, under high currents it did not allow multiple reactions to proceed simultaneously. Second, it suffered from numerical issues at the plateau transitions that could result in non-monotonic oscillating cell voltages even at constant current. Therefore, the first aspect of this work was to implement a robust multi-plateau model for the cathode reactions. The second aspect of this work is the integration of this new model into the multi-physics simulation capability described in [4] with necessary additional physics to allow simulation of battery start-up and freeze-out.

Multi-plateau model: In this work we present a graph-based model for phase change in the electrodes with an arbitrary number of volume phases and interconnecting reacting surfaces. The full cathode reaction pathway described by Hewson et al. [1] is

$$FeS_2 \leftrightarrow Li_3Fe_2S_4 \leftrightarrow Li_{2+x}Fe_{1-x}S_2 + Fe_{1-x}S \leftrightarrow Li_2FeS_2 \leftrightarrow Li_2S + Fe.$$

Experimental and thermodynamic analysis shows that the Li_2FeS_2 plateau is small relative to the overall cathode capacity so it can be safely neglected. The non-stoichiometric plateau involving $Li_{2+x}Fe_{1-x}S_2$ and $Fe_{1-x}S$ is another source of numerical instability, since the equilibrium chemistry between the different species in that system is numerically much stiffer than the other reactions. Fortunately, at the temperatures of interest for thermal battery operation that equilibrium strongly favors the formation of $Li_{7/3}Fe_{2/3}S_2$ and FeS. This leads to a reduced reaction set of

$$FeS_2 \leftrightarrow Li_3Fe_2S_4 \leftrightarrow Li_{7/3}Fe_{2/3}S_2 + FeS \leftrightarrow Li_2S + Fe.$$

To represent these reactions generally, and allow for inclusion of self-discharge reactions and other side reactions, we construct a graph representation of the mechanism whose vertices consist of volume phases and surfaces, an example of which is shown in Figure 1. This assumes that solid-phase diffusion to the reacting surface is not the rate-limiting step. The graph can be constructed completely from the reaction definitions at each surface, however the orientation (which phase is the inner phase) must also be specified for surface area calculations.

The three reactions for the reduced mechanism above are applied on three surface vertices, and with an appropriately selected electrode particle morphology model the surface area of each surface vertex can be constructed using its connectivity and the volume of its interior volume vertices. For the results shown in this work, we use a spherical morphology although a platelet morphology could be used with the same technique. This graph-based approach makes it easy to extend our implementation to alternate chemistries (e.g. CoS$_2$) or to add different self-discharge pathways.

The production and consumption rates for the individual phases in this system can also be discontinuous in time. If the reaction is not limited by its surface area going to zero, as is the case for reactions in the outer phases with a spherical mor-

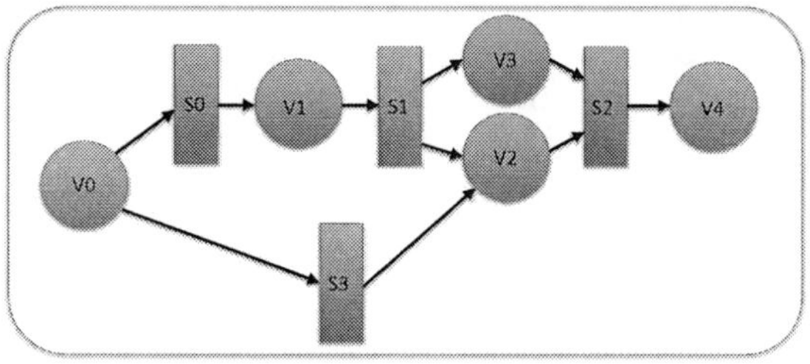

Figure 1. Example reaction graph for a three-plateau system including a self-discharge reaction pathway (S3) and non-stoichiometric phases (V2 and V3).

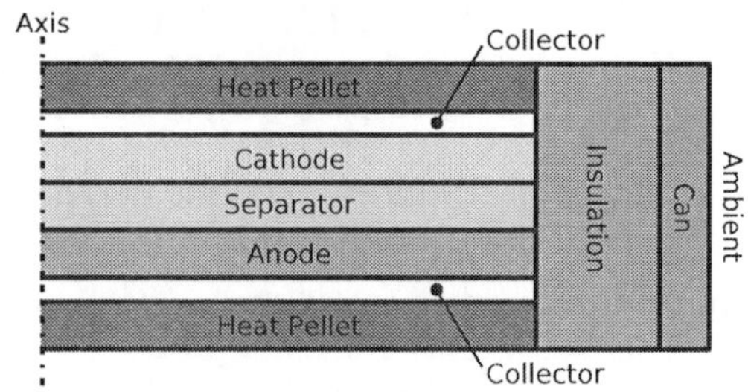

Figure 2. The 2D axisymmetric simulation domain for the multi-physics simulations (not to scale).

phology and with all reactions in a platelet morphology, then the rate will not have a continuous time derivative as the phase appears or disappears. This can cause numerical instabilities with the stiff ODE solvers used to solve the reaction mechanism, so we introduce rate smoothers at these discontinuities using hyperbolic tangent functions.

The most significant unknowns in this model are the reaction rates and the electrical conductivity in the cathode. Fortunately, these quantities influence the voltage profile under constant current differently at different currents, which gives us a way of using a data set with a range of currents to calibrate these parameters. In the prior work, a purely numerical optimization approach was used with the reaction extent model to determine appropriate reaction parameters [3]. Since we are using an updated model, we need to re-evaluate these parameters with the new model. Unfortunately, many of the optimization parameters only influence a small portion of the resulting voltage profile which leads to difficulty in obtaining a global minimum. For this work, we use the following observations from the simulation results (e.g. Figure 3) with the new multi-plateau model to calibrate these parameters against experimental data:

- Low current
  - Curvature of the voltage profile near the phase transitions is influenced by the reaction rate.
  - Location of the phase transitions is more apparent.
- High current
  - The initial voltage is highly dependent on the first cathode reaction rate.
  - The slope of the voltage profile during the first plateau is highly dependent on the cathode electrical conductivity.

We use these observations to adjust the unknown rate parameters one plateau at a time to minimize the error between simulation and experiment over discharge currents that vary by a factor of 40.

Multi-physics model: The basic components of the multi-physics thermal battery model we use have been described in our prior publications [4, 5, 7]. These include thermal transport, porous flow, and species transport in the electrolyte. These equations are applied on the axisymmetric domain shown in Figure 2, where thermal transport is solved on all regions, porous flow and species transport are solved in the anode, cathode, and separator, and electrical transport is solved in the anode, cathode, separator, and collectors. The level set burn front approach described in our prior publications is used to model the burn front movement in the two heat pellets. This burn front moves at a prescribed velocity, so we can use this velocity and the cell radius to calculate a non-dimensional time to compare the electrochemical startup against. For the electrical transport equations, we apply a constant 0.5 Ω resistive load boundary condition at the outer edge of the collectors.

The key additions to this model in the present work are the inclusion of the new electrochemical models, a modified form of the porous flow equation that is compatible with our melting and capillary flow models, and the addition of Joule heating and reaction heating.

In the porous flow system outlined previously, we use the van Genuchten model [8] to provide closure between saturation and pressure, providing two additional governing equations for the liquid and gas phases. This results in a different initial liquid pressure in each section of the cell (cathode, anode, and separator) that produces a large pressure gradient at their interface. In addition, we treat the solid electrolyte as a liquid with an artificially high viscosity and evaluate the liquid velocity using Darcy's law,

$$\boldsymbol{v} = -\frac{\boldsymbol{\kappa}}{\mu}\left(\boldsymbol{\nabla}P - \rho\boldsymbol{g}\right). \tag{1}$$

As a result of this combination, the large pressure gradient between the cell components results in a non-negligible velocity, even when the electrolyte is solid and μ is large. To compensate for this, we modify the Darcy flow equation to include the capillary pressure, P_c, as

$$\boldsymbol{v} = -\frac{\boldsymbol{\kappa}}{\mu}\left(\boldsymbol{\nabla}P + C\boldsymbol{\nabla}P_c - \rho\boldsymbol{g}\right), \tag{2}$$

where C is a smoothly transitioning scalar at the melt temperature (T_m) with a transition width of ΔT,

$$C = \frac{1}{2}\left(\tanh\left(\frac{T_m - T}{\Delta T}\right) + 1\right). \quad (3)$$

Since the capillary pressure gradient is opposite the liquid pressure gradient prior to melting and $C = 1$ below the melt temperature, these terms cancel below the melt temperature and there is no artificial flow of the solid electrolyte.

An additional change is that we calculate the effective density and specific heat using the porosity and saturation to combine the solid, liquid, and gas properties. This is different from the prior work, which neglected the gas when determining effective thermal properties. The effect of this is a higher thermal diffusivity during the heat-up period, which has a significant effect on the battery's electrochemical startup delay.

Results and Discussion

In this section, we demonstrate simulations of two separate physics models. First we show the results of the one-dimensional electrochemical model using the new multi-plateau model compared with data over a range of discharge currents. Second, we include this model in the 2D axisymmetric model of battery startup and show how different phenomena influence startup behavior.

One-dimensional electrochemical model: The results from the calibrated model are shown in Figure 3 at three currents, although the total data set used for the calibration included more intermediate currents between the high and low data sets shown here. There are a few interesting features to notice in this comparison. First, for the medium current case our model captures the change in slope that occurs at about 40% discharged but still includes a plateau from the third cathode reaction, which is not observed experimentally. This could be indicative of a transport limitation, such as changing electrical conductivity, which our model does not capture. Second, the phase transitions happen more sharply in the low current simulation than in the corresponding experiment. This could be due to a number of factors, including non-uniform particle sizes and the greater importance at low reaction rates of the non-stoichiometric phase we neglected in our initial simplifications of the FeS_2 mechanism or the omission of solid state diffusion limits as the reaction proceeds to secondary plateaus.

Two-dimensional multi-physics model: For comparisons of startup behavior we use the non-dimensional time, τ, which is the ratio of the physical time to the time it takes for the heat pellet to burn across the radius of the cell,

$$\tau = \frac{t v_b}{r_{\text{cell}}}. \quad (4)$$

The thermal diffusivity of the partially saturated materials is higher than the fully saturated materials in these simulations because the thermal conductivity is not treated as a function of the saturation but the thermal mass is. While this assumption may require further examination, its effect here is that the partially saturated system starts up at $\tau \approx 1.1$ while the fully saturated system starts at $\tau \approx 1.75$ (Figure 4).

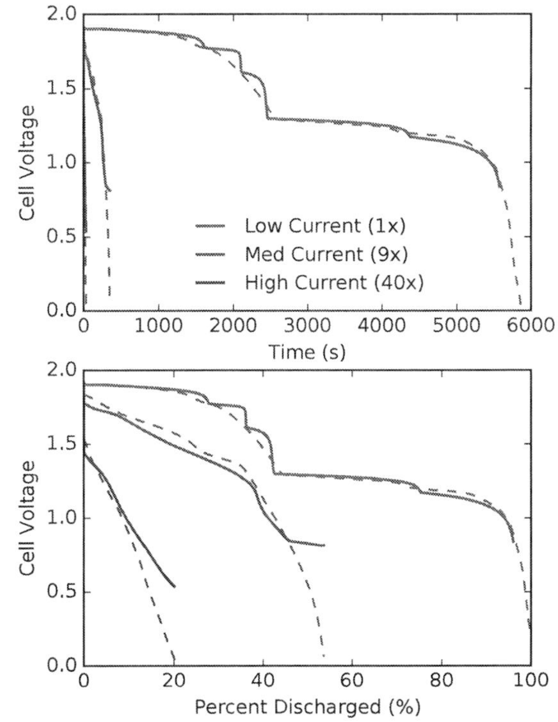

Figure 3. Comparison between the 1D isothermal model (solid lines) and experiments (dashed lines) at low (i), medium ($9i$) and high ($40i$) currents vs. time (top) and percent discharged (bottom).

Changing time scales, the behavior of the cell during the solidification phase change is strongly influenced by insulation properties and internal heat sources. Inclusion of sources such as Joule heating, while small compared to the heat pellet release, can be influential when analyzing the full life of the cell. For example, in Figure 5, the effects of different heat sources and sinks on the percentage of the battery capacity that can be discharged with a constant 0.5 Ω load are apparent. Omitting Joule heating results in a 9 % reduction in operating time (defined here as the time to fall to 1 V), while omitting the melting latent heat of the electrolyte increased the operating time by 15 % and changed the voltage response considerably. Obviously, using a higher discharge current or different thermal insulation will change the amount discharged, but the key here is the relative importance of the thermal source terms.

Summary

In this work we have shown a new graph-based multi-plateau electrochemical reaction model that is robust over the range of currents tested and does not exhibit the oscillatory behavior seen in the previous models. We have shown that this model can reasonably match the experimental voltage profiles over a

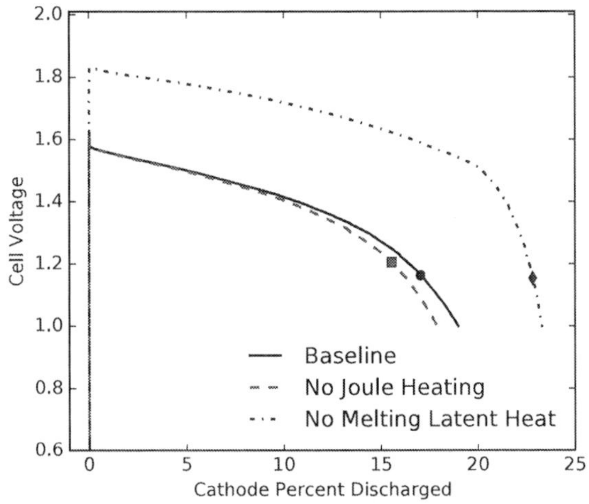

Figure 5. Comparison between freezeout behavior for a saturated cell with different thermal source/sink terms removed (markers indicate when the cell is 50 % re-solidified).

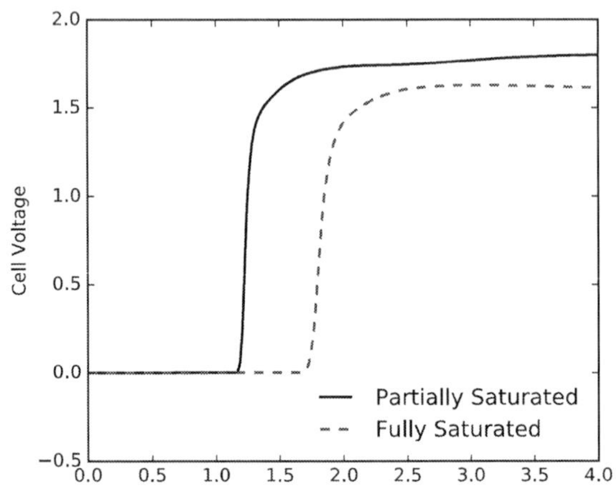

Figure 4. Comparison in startup behavior with fully saturated and partially saturated components.

wide range of currents. We have also demonstrated the utility of this model in a fully coupled simulation that successfully captures the effects of both small and large thermal sources and transport limitations on the electrochemical response.

Acknowledgments

The authors gratefully acknowledge funding from the Joint Department of Defense/Department of Energy Munitions Technology Development Program and from the Department of Energy Advanced Simulation and Computing Physics and Engineering Models program. Sandia National Laboratories is a multi-program laboratory managed and operated by Sandia Corporation, a wholly owned subsidiary of Lockheed Martin Corporation, for the U.S. Department of Energy's National Nuclear Security Administration under contract DE-AC04-94AL85000.

References

[1] Hewson, J., H. Moffat, C. Leuth, and D. Ingersoll. "Predicting Electrochemical Phenomena in Lithium Molten Salt Thermal Batteries." Proceedings of the 44th Power Sources Conference, 2010.

[2] Hewson, J., H. Moffat, C. Leuth, and D. Ingersoll. "Predicting Electrochemical Phenomena in Lithium Molten Salt Thermal Batteries." Proceedings of the 45th Power Sources Conference, 2012.

[3] Hewson, J., H. Moffat, and V. Brunini. "Model Parameterization for Electrochemical Predictions of LiSi/FeS2 Batteries." Proceedings of the 46th Power Sources Conference, 2014.

[4] Roberts, S. A., K. N. Long, J. R. Clausen, M. R. Martinez, E. S. Piekos, and A. M. Grillet. "Towards a Coupled Multiphysics Model of Molten Salt Battery Mechanics." Proceedings of the 46th Power Sources Conference, 2014.

[5] Roberts, S. A., K. N. Long, J. S. Rath, L. A. Mondy, and A. M. Grillet. "Modeling Separator Deformation and Electrolyte Flow in Thermally-Activated Batteries." Proceedings of the 45th Power Sources Conference, 2012.

[6] Bernardi, D. and J. Newman. "Mathematical Modeling of Lithium(alloy), Iron Disulfide Cells." *Journal of the Electrochemical Society: Electrochemical Science and Technology*, pp. 1309–1318, 1987.

[7] Piekos, E. S., A. M. Grillet, D. Ingersoll, N. D. Streeter, and D. R. Noble. "Modeling of thermal battery initiation using level sets." Proceedings of the 45th Power Sources Conference, 2012.

[8] van Genuchten, M. T. "A closed-form equation for predicting the hydraulic conductivity of unsaturated soils." *Soil Science Society of America Journal*, vol. 44, pp. 892–898, 1980.

Enhanced Nanostructuring Approach for Thermal Battery Cathode Materials

Ryan R. Carpenter
Powder Prototyping Technology Branch
U.S. Army Armament Research, Development and Engineering Center
Picatinny Arsenal, NJ, USA, 07806
E-mail: ryan.r.carpenter6.civ@mail.mil

Giuseppe L. Di Benedetto
Advanced Materials Technology Branch
U.S. Army Armament Research, Development and Engineering Center
Picatinny Arsenal, NJ, USA, 07806
E-mail: giuseppe.l.dibenedetto.civ@mail.mil

Abstract: *Understanding the potential and capabilities of nanoscale cathode materials can benefit the U.S. Army and the Armament Research, Development and Engineering Center (ARDEC) immensely. There is a growing concern over the power and energy needs of future munitions and military technologies. It is widely viewed that the current power and energy capabilities cannot meet the needs of future smart munitions, and improvements will need to be made at the materials level in order to make advancements. The use of Nanomaterials offers the potential to produce thermal batteries with performance improvements, such as higher voltages and increased current densities. In this study, nanoscale disulfide powders (iron, cobalt, and nickel) were synthesized using a fully scalable method, and characterized utilizing SEM, XRD, XRF, BET, EDS, and other techniques. High energy ball mills, which provide extremely high amounts of kinetic energy into the particles, were used to impart nanostructure into the* FeS_2*,* CoS_2*, and* NiS_2 *powders. All processing was carried out under an inert atmosphere to minimize oxygen pickup. The mechanical alloying process has multiple variables which were modified in order to create powders with tunable properties, and most importantly, to determine properties which are optimal for the disulfide cathode materials performance. Several processing variables were modified, such as rotational speed, milling time, and milling media type, in order to change the material properties. The nanoscale disulfide cathode powders were extensively characterized using the in-house U.S. Army ARDEC characterization facilities. This study successfully used powder processing technology to produce kilogram quantities of nanostructured disulfide powders for use as cathode materials in thermal battery systems, and this process can be applied to other potential cathode candidate materials.*

Keywords: nanomaterials; thermal battery; molten salt battery; cathode; nanostructure; disulfides; milling.

Introduction

Thermal batteries remain a key primary power source for critical military applications, such as precision munitions and missiles. Competitive technologies have yet to achieve the performance and reliability of thermal batteries for these applications. As the requirements for guided precision munitions increase, the thermal battery will need to supply a significantly higher level of power to the components of munitions while occupying less volume. Due to limited commercial usage of thermal batteries, industry investment in new designs, performance, and affordability is limited. It is therefore necessary to push the technology forward and investigate inexpensive material-based improvements.

An example of a material-based improvement is the investigation into the use of Nanoparticles in the thermal battery electrode pellets. Previous researchers have completed preliminary work on Nanostructured Iron Disulfide (FeS_2) for thermal battery designs. Nano-sized particles have been prepared by chemical hydrothermal synthesis at high temperature and pressures [1, 2] and by high energy ball milling particle size reduction [3], and have been reported to have enhanced properties when used in thermal batteries [4]. This enhancement is believed to come from the very small particle size (less than 100 nanometers average particle size) which results in an extremely large surface area per volume of active cathode material. Our previous study focused on consistently producing kilogram quantities of Nanostructured FeS_2, and evaluating performance in single cell tests [5]. The success of that study encouraged the utilization of these methods for other common thermal battery cathode materials, such as Cobalt Disulfide (CoS_2) and Nickel Disulfide (NiS_2).

This study aims to use a fully scalable high energy milling method to consistently produce kilogram quantities of Nanostructured FeS_2, CoS_2, and NiS_2 powders for cathode use in thermal batteries.

Experimental

Synthesis & Characterization of NiS_2 *and* CoS_2 *nanopowders:* Dry high energy mechanical attrition was used to synthesize nanoscale CoS_2 and NiS_2 powders from their original micron sized range. The starting materials were Cobalt Disulfide -200 mesh and Nickel Disulfide -80 mesh. All powders were handled, processed, and stored in an inert Argon environment with less than 10ppm O_2 atmosphere to prevent contamination, however atmospheric handling was done minimally for dependent characterization techniques. Chrome steel milling media was used and the powders were processed via horizontal high energy attritors under Argon to achieve particle size reduction. No processing control agents (PCA) were necessary during processing. A series of experiments were performed to observe the NiS_2 and CoS_2 powder properties as a function of processing times of 1h, 2h, 4h, 6h, and 10h. Microscopic inspection of powder size and morphology was performed via Scanning Electron Microscopy (SEM) using a Zeiss Supra V40 @ 10kV with In-Lens detector. The Barret-Emmet-Teller (B.E.T.) method for surface area analysis and particle size derivation was done using a Quantachrome Nova 4000e. Both X-Ray Diffraction (XRD) and X-Ray Fluorescence (XRF) were performed utilizing a Rigaku Ultima and ZSX Primus II equipment for phase identification and compositional analysis.

Results and Discussion

Scanning Electron Microscopy: SEM was used for a visual inspection of the Nickel and Cobalt Disulfides for morphology changes and size reduction. A comparison of the as received versus 10h processed powder can be seen in Figure 1. A 30kx magnified view of each material can also be seen in Figure 2. Particle size reduction can be observed as a function of increased processing time, but particle agglomeration is more apparent as compared to FeS_2 powders which were processed in a similar fashion making it more difficult to discern the actual particle size range. Sub 200nm particles are present for both materials.

Figure 1. Scanning Electron Microscope (SEM) images. Upper Left: As Received NiS_2 7kx. Upper Right: 10h Processed NiS_2 7kx. Bottom Left: As Received CoS_2. Lower Right: 10h Processed CoS_2 7kx.

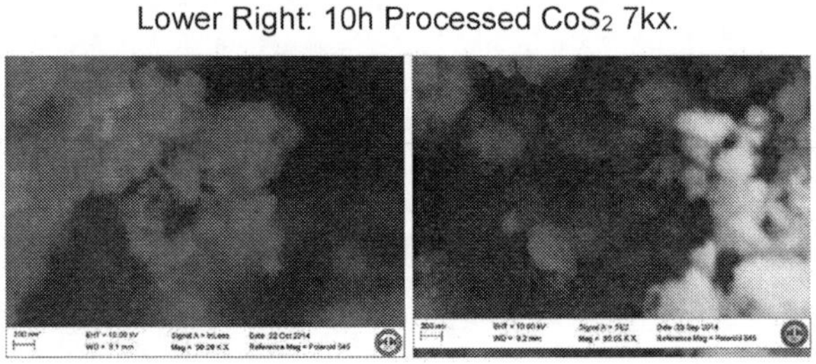

Figure 2. 30kx magnification of CoS_2 Powder (Left) and NiS_2 Powder (Right)

X-Ray Analysis: X-Ray Diffraction (Cu-Kα source) patterns are shown in Figure 3 for Cobalt Disulfide and in Figure 4 for Nickel Disulfide. The patterns match that of known references for those materials, and major peak broadening can be observed in both as well. CoS_2 did not show any outside contamination patterns, but NiS_2 did, showing possible moisture pickup due to characterization sample preparation in a non-inert environment. Both of these powders showed a much higher affinity for moisture pickup then that of FeS_2, which will be revisited when discussing the surface area analysis results. Figure 6 is a graphical representation of the reduction of measured crystallite size as a function of the processing time. Via the Scherrer equation, the lowest estimated average crystallite size for CoS_2 was 12nm and for NiS_2 was 62nm. The estimates for the CoS_2 material are lower than expected. X-Ray Fluorescence was used to determine the amount of elemental iron pickup as a function of processing time due to the use of steel milling media. Amounts for Fe pickup for NiS_2 ranged from .18% to .27% and for CoS_2 from .13% to .29% for increasing processing times.

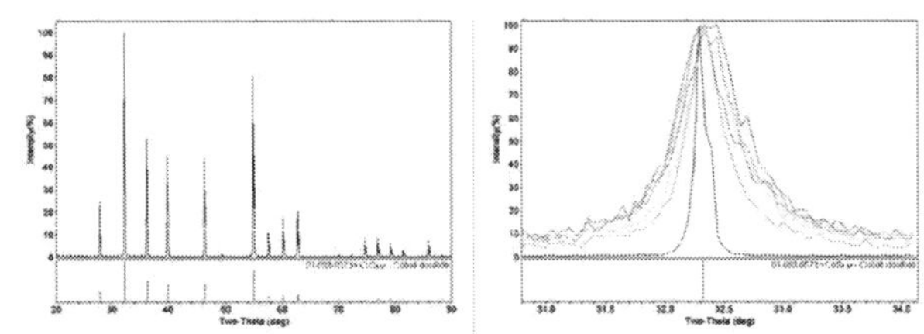

Figure 3. X-Ray Diffraction (XRD) Spectrum of As Received and Processed CoS_2 Powders

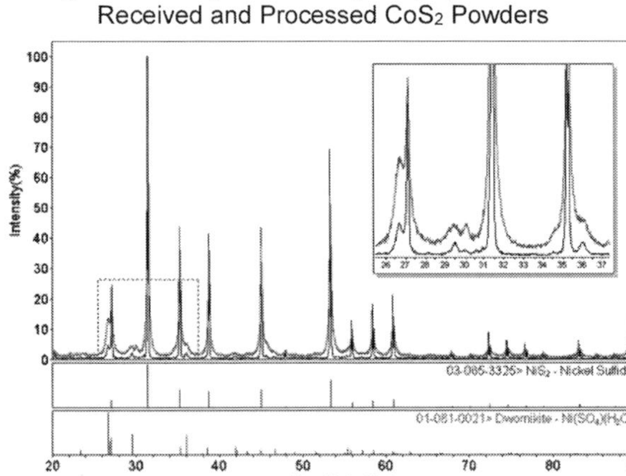

Figure 4. X-Ray Diffraction (XRD) of As Received and 10hr Processed NiS_2 powders.

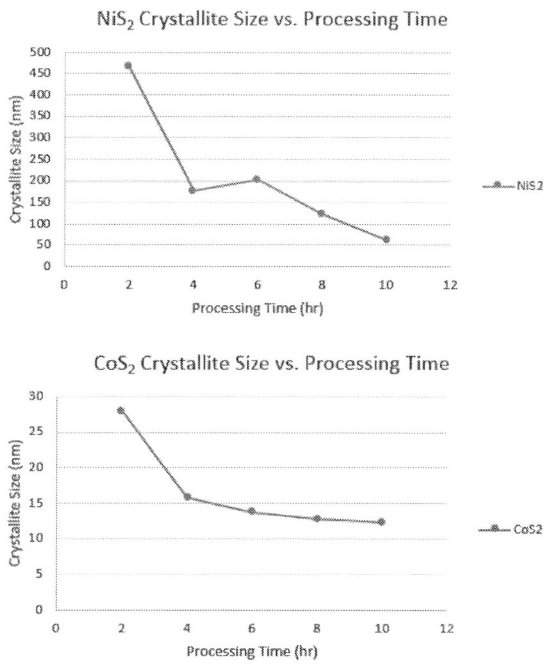

Figure 5. X-Ray Diffraction (XRD) Crystallite Size measured as a function of processing time.

Barret-Emmet-Teller Analysis: B.E.T. was used in conjunction with data acquired from SEM and XRD analysis to estimate particle size. Figure 7 shows the measured surface area in m^2/g as a function of processing time, as well as the estimated derived particle size as a function of time. A reduction in particle size is readily observed, but a trend in increasing processing time correlating to a smaller particle size is not as clear as what was seen with XRD data. A comparison of XRD and BET data is shown in Table 1. The data aligns well for NiS_2 but for CoS_2 the XRD estimate is much lower than that of the BET results which may be due to powder exposure to atmosphere. Nickel Disulfide has a lower measured surface area which trended towards reduction as a function of processing time, however, Cobalt Disulfide surface area peaked at 2hrs and then decreased. The lowest estimated particle size for CoS_2 was at 2hrs with 78nm and for NiS_2 at 8hrs with 123 nm. It was also noted that a study was done where the powder sampling jar was opened to load the samples, resealed, and then measured again after 24 hours. Powder was also left exposed in air for 1h to observe how moisture pickup could affect the measured surface area. These data points, presented in Figure 7, show that even 1 hour of powder exposure to atmosphere can decrease the measured surface area by around 360%. The exposed powder also had a visible macro texture of looking 'wet' and agglomerated.

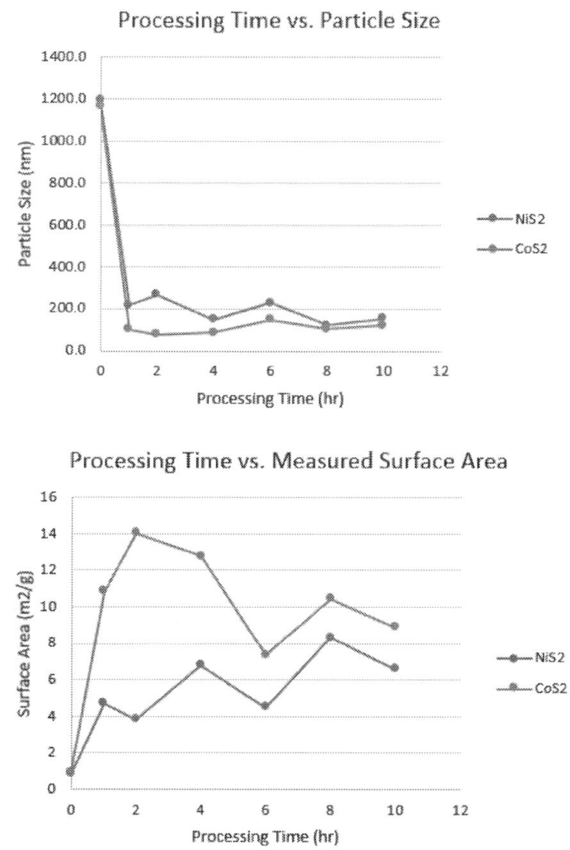

Figure 6. Measured Surface Area and Derived Particle Size as a function of Processing Time.

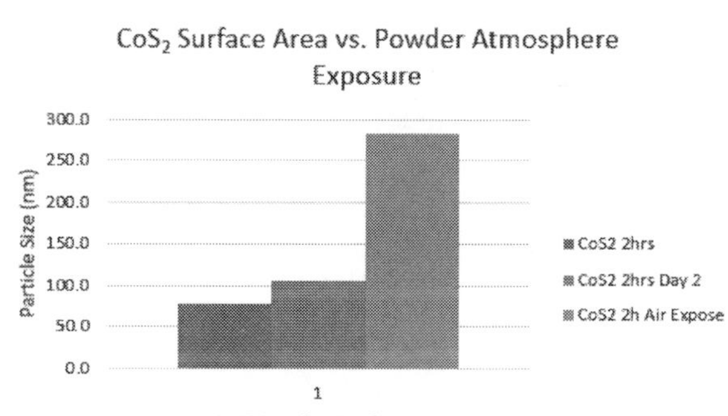

Figure 7. Derived Particle Size from Surface Area Measurements as a function of oxygen exposure.

CoS2	2h	4h	6h	8h	10h
B.E.T.	78 nm	86 nm	150 nm	105 nm	124 nm
XRD	28 nm	16 nm	14 nm	13 nm	12 nm

NiS2	2h	4h	6h	8h	10h
B.E.T.	266 nm	150 nm	227 nm	123 nm	154 nm
XRD	466 nm	176 nm	202 nm	123 nm	62 nm

Table 1. Comparison of B.E.T. and XRD Data for NiS_2 and CoS_2.

Conclusion

Nanoscale CoS_2 and NiS_2 particles were synthesized via a horizontal high energy attrition process and reduced to the nanoscale as comparted to the micron sized starting materials. For Nickel Disulfide, the particle size tended to decrease as a function of milling time up to 10h, but for Cobalt Disulfide, the material tended to reach its smallest size at 2h processing time and then increase after. Cobalt Disulfide also tended to have smaller particles sizes as compared to Nickel Disulfide, but both were still larger than previous work done with Iron Disulfide which reached 62nm. The lowest estimated particle size for CoS_2 was 78nm and for NiS_2 was 123nm. The powders' tendency for moisture pickup and agglomeration is an issue which appeared while characterizing the materials, and was a clear separation of properties from previously performed experiments on FeS_2. Future work will focus on testing these materials in single cell configurations to observe the single cell discharge performance as a function of processing time and materials properties.

Acknowledgements

This work was partially funded through the Life Cycle Pilot Process (LCPP) of Project Director for Joint Services (PD JS), and the In-House Laboratory Independent Research (ILIR) program of U.S. Army ARDEC.

References

1. Guidotti, R. A., F. W. Reinhardt, J. Dai, and D. E. Reisner, "Preparation and Characterization of Synthetic Pyrite for Thermal-Battery Cathodes," *Proceedings of 40th Power Sources Conference*, p. 339, 2002.
2. Guidotti, R. A., P. J. Nigrey, F. W. Reinhardt, and J. G. Odinek, "Evaluation of Nanoparticulate Metal Disulfides in Thermal Batteries," *Proceedings of 40th Power Sources Conference*, p. 250, 2002.
3. Au, M., "Nanostructured Thermal Batteries with High Power Density," *Journal of Power Sources*, vol. 115, pp. 360-366, 2003.
4. Au, M., Y. Lei, and T. Yadav, "Thermal Batteries Made with Nanostructured Material," *NASA Tech Briefs*, vol. 23, no. 4, pp. 28-29, April 1999.
5. Di Benedetto, G. L., R. Carpenter, D. Swanson, and B. Wightman, "Enhanced Nanostructuring of Iron Disulfide for Thermal Battery Cathode Materials," *Proceedings of 46th Power Sources Conference*, pp. 469-472, 2014.
6. Swift, G. A., "Cathode Materials for Use in Thermal Batteries," *Proceedings of 44th Power Sources Conference*, p. 581, 2010.
7. Masset, P. J., and R. A. Guidotti, "Thermal activated (thermal) battery technology Part IIIa: FeS2 cathode material." *Journal of Power Sources*, vol. 177, pp. 595-609, 2008.
8. Masset, P. J., and R. A. Guidotti, "Thermal activated (thermal) battery technology Part IIIb: Sulfur and oxide-based cathode materials." *Journal of Power Sources*, vol. 178, pp. 456-466, 2008.

Comparison of Natural and Synthetic Cathode Materials for Thermal Batteries

Geoffrey A. Swift
EaglePicher Technologies, LLC
Joplin, MO 64801

Abstract
Thermal battery technology has long relied on iron disulfide (FeS_2) as the primary active cathode material. Efforts to improve performance have included replacement of natural FeS_2 with synthetic FeS_2 or other synthetic sulfides, including nanosize powders. Several such materials were compared to natural FeS_2. Data are presented showing the performance of natural FeS_2 versus various synthetic cathode active materials.

Keywords: Thermal Batteries; Cathode

Introduction
Thermal batteries operate in hostile environments. This is due both to their use as power sources in various weapons systems, and from their very nature. Unlike most batteries, which operate at ambient or intermediate temperatures, thermal batteries require high temperature to operate. Thermal battery electrolytes are typically composed of two or more halide salts and an inert binder material. Thermal battery electrolytes are formulated to remain non-conductive when solid. This allows long-term storage of the batteries, since self-discharge is greatly inhibited by the solid electrolyte. High temperature (>300°C, typically) is required to melt the electrolyte, which is also usually incorporated into the anode and cathode to enhance performance. The battery is activated via a pyrotechnic ignition which inputs sufficient heat to melt the electrolyte, but without exceeding the temperature at which the anode and cathode materials melt, deflagrate, or decompose. With the electrolyte molten, the battery may be discharged.[1-2]

Thermal batteries often use pyrite-based cathodes. The low cost and easy availability of FeS_2 have kept it the primary thermal battery cathode material for decades. Despite its attractiveness for manufacturing, FeS_2 does possess some limitations. These include a high-impedance phase that forms during discharge and a firm upper operating temperature limit of 600°C, at which FeS_2 decomposes. The semiconductor nature of FeS_2 makes it the single largest source of impedance under pulsing in thermal batteries. Various means to overcome these disadvantages include using synthetic and/or nanosize pyrite, in hopes that eliminating naturally-occurring impurities will improve performance, and using alternate active materials to replace FeS_2 entirely. Nanosize FeS_2 has also been speculated to improve performance simply on the basis of the smaller particle size avoiding an interfacial layer of reaction product formed during discharge. This layer might prevent the complete reaction of the cathode active material, and thus "waste" active material in the battery. The origin of the nanosize material might be either a natural material or a synthetic material, the latter of which hypothetically benefitting from both the smaller particle size and the lack of impurities.[3]

Preparing synthetic pyrite incurs a significant cost premium to using natural material. Any impurities in the precursor will propagate into the final material. Thus, high-purity, and thus high-cost, starting materials must be used. Second, the precursor must be processed into a stoichiometric iron disulfide composition. Should the Fe:S ratio vary from the prescribed 1:2, the performance of the cathode in a thermal battery will be impacted. Thus, careful monitoring of the process and the resulting product must be performed to ensure quality control. All of these facts conspire to make synthetic pyrite orders of magnitude more expensive than simple natural pyrite.[3]

Synthetic pyrite can be produced in nanosize powders, provided the precursors and manufacturing method are properly selected. However, it is possible to mill natural pyrite into nanosize powders, with the caveat that any impurities present in the natural material will remain in the milled material. This at least partially defeats the purpose in eliminating those impurities to improve performance.[3]

Other disulfide materials have been demonstrated to perform adequately in thermal batteries. CoS_2 is one such example, offering the advantage of higher operating temperature over FeS_2 since it does not decompose at 600°C. CoS_2 also does not form high-impedance intermediate phases during discharge. CoS_2 also has a single stable voltage plateau, compared to multiple plateaus of decreasing voltage for FeS_2. Because CoS_2 does not occur in sufficiently large natural quantities, the material must be manufactured in order to produce thermal batteries with CoS_2 cathodes. This manufacturing is subject to the same conditions noted above for manufacturing FeS_2, with the same potential pitfalls. CoS_2 is also known to be a hazardous material, requiring handling precautions not necessary for FeS_2.[4]

The present investigation sought to compare naturally-occurring FeS_2 used by EaglePicher Technologies to manufacture thermal batteries with several alternative, synthetic materials. These include synthetic FeS_2; nanosize, synthetic FeS_2, and synthetic CoS_2. Comparison is based on single cell tests and battery discharge tests. Note that handling issues precluded building batteries with all the experimental materials.

Experimental Procedure

Experimental cathode materials were mixed with KCl-LiCl-MgO electrolyte to produce a flooded cathode. The amount incorporated was the same in the control (*i.e.*, EPT's standard, natural FeS_2) cathode materials. Powders were roll-mixed to ensure homogeneous blends. Mixed powders were used to produce pellets for single cell testing. Pellets were pressed at 45 tons force on a unidirectional, double-action, manual die. LiSi anode pellets and separator pellets were drawn from the same lot (for each comparison between experimental and control cathodes, not necessarily the same lots throughout the suite of experiments). All pellets of a given type were pressed under the same conditions to the same mass. Thickness measurements indicated that cathode pellet density varied insignificantly. Anode and cathode relative masses were selected to make the cells anode-limited. Some experimental cathodes showed high OCV. Cathode powders were then re-mixed to include a lithiation agent to reduce the OCV. Both experimental and control cathode were lithiated with the same material in the same amount. Single cell tests were repeated with the lithiated cathodes.

Single cells were discharged at 500°C in an inert-atmosphere glove box. The same discharge profile was used for all tests: 1A base load, with 5A pulses applied every 60s. The first 10s of discharge was open circuit, to determine OCV. Discharge was allowed to continue for 10min. Single cell data were compared in terms of OCV, voltage after 10min discharge, and impedance under applied pulses.

The synthetic FeS_2 and CoS_2 cathode powders were unable to be pressed on auto-feeding presses. Neither of these were used to construct thermal batteries as a result. The nanosize FeS_2 was used to build thermal batteries. In this case, the EPT and nanosize FeS_2 cathodes were hand-pressed in the same manner as the single cell cathode pellets. Anode, separator, and heat pellets were pressed on auto-feeding presses to the requirements of the battery being constructed. The thermal batteries were 72-cell stacks, discharged at room temperature (no hot or cold storage). Batteries were discharged under a 3A base load, with pulses of 10-20A during the 2min battery life. Performance was compared based on voltage and impedance under pulsing.

Results and Discussion

Synthetic FeS_2

Figure 1 shows single cell discharges for natural and synthetic FeS_2 cathodes. Both cathodes produced an OCV > 2V. The voltage profiles are nearly identical. Impedance under pulsing was higher for the synthetic FeS_2. The higher impedance and OCV were likely caused by surface oxidation; the synthetic material was finer (but not nanosize) than the natural FeS_2, Both cathodes were lithiated. Figure 2 shows the single cell discharge of the lithiated cathodes. Both lithiated cathodes exhibited reduced OCV. The natural FeS_2 displays greater impedance than the non-lithiated material, while the synthetic material's impedance is similar to its non-lithiated version. Overall, the two cathode materials performed comparably, with the natural material being superior without lithiation; lithiation reduces the performance of the natural FeS_2 to near-parity with the synthetic FeS_2.

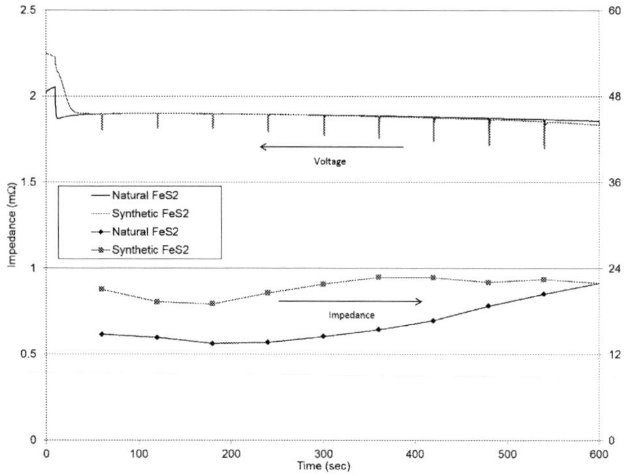

Figure 1. Single cell voltage traces and impedance under pulsing using synthetic and natural FeS_2-based cathodes.

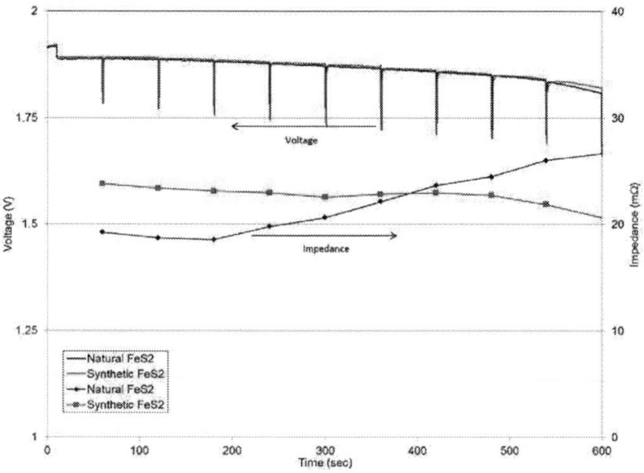

Figure 2. Voltage traces and impedance under pulsing for single cells using lithiated synthetic and natural FeS_2-based cathodes.

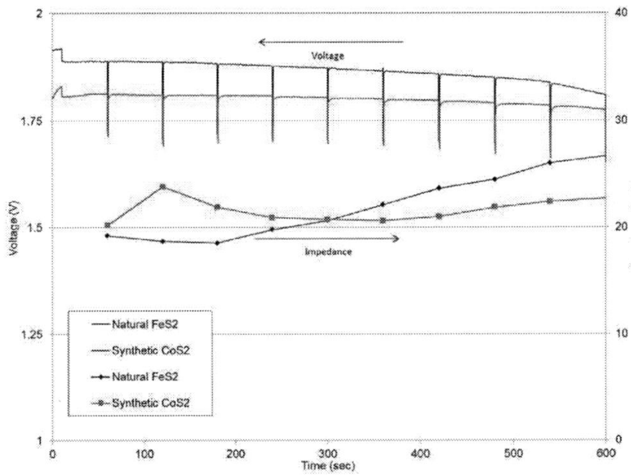

Figure 3. Voltage traces and impedance under pulsing for single cells using lithiated natural FeS_2- and synthetic CoS_2-based cathodes.

Synthetic CoS_2

Figure 3 shows the single cell discharges for natural FeS_2 and synthetic CoS_2 cathodes. The CoS_2 showed elevated OCV, likely for the same reason as synthetic FeS_2. Since CoS_2 has a lower voltage under load than FeS_2 against lithium, this OCV is actually relatively greater than that of the synthetic FeS_2. Of interest is the fairly constant, low impedance of the CoS_2 cathode throughout the discharge. This is expected from CoS_2. However, in the initial discharge, the natural FeS_2 has a superior impedance, which increased as the intermediate discharge phase was produced. Both materials were lithiated to compare performance. Figure 4 shows the single cell discharges for the lithiated natural FeS_2 and synthetic CoS_2. Lithiation clearly eliminated the high OCV issue for both materials.

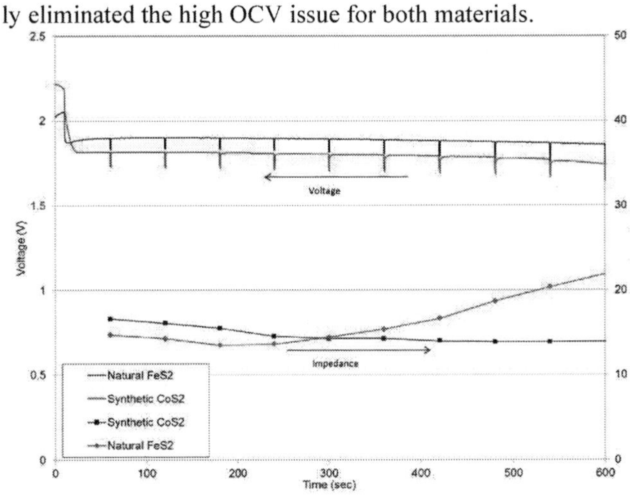

Figure 4. Voltage traces and impedance under pulsing for single cells using lithiated natural FeS_2- and synthetic CoS_2-based cathodes.

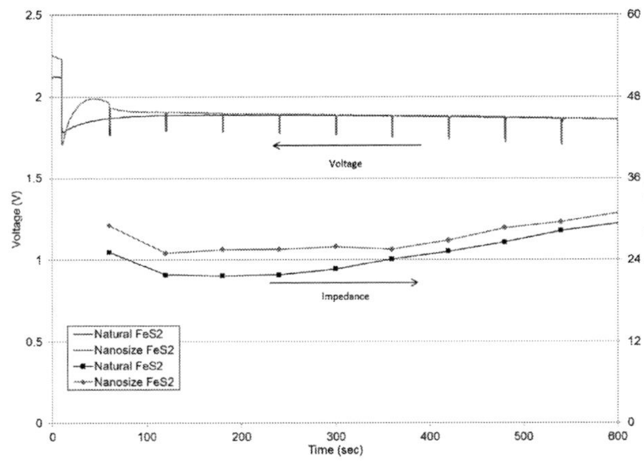

Figure 5. Single cell voltage traces and impedance under pulsing using natural and nanosizeFeS_2-based cathodes.

While the natural FeS_2 showed an increase in impedance, the synthetic CoS_2 cell nearly doubled in impedance. This indicates that a trade-off must be made. In the case of a battery with a firm upper voltage limit, using lithiated CoS_2 may result in a failure if the increased impedance causes a violation of a low voltage limit during pulsing.

Nano-size FeS_2

Figure 5 shows the single cell discharges for natural nanosize FeS_2 cathodes. The higher OCV of the nanosize FeS_2 was expected, due to its proportionally higher surface area favoring oxidation. However, while with the synthetic FeS_2 of Figure 1 the higher voltage was eliminated after applying the base current, for the nanosize FeS_2, higher voltage remained even after the first pulse was applied. This indicates that the surface oxide layer is relatively greater in concentration than for the synthetic material. Both materials were lithiated to eliminate the high OCV issue. The nanosize FeS_2 was not amenable to pressing on the auto-feeing presses. Instead, pellets were hand-pressed and a battery was built.

Figure 6 shows the battery discharges for the lithiated natural and nanosize FeS_2 cathodes. Even using lithiated cathodes, the nanosize FeS_2 exhibited a high OCV upon activation. The nanosize FeS_2 had a per-cell voltage of 2.19V, while the natural FeS_2 per-cell voltage was 1.97. The inability to mitigate the oxidation layer with lithiation indicates a problematic degree of surface oxidation. Because of the high specific surface area of nanosize powders, it is unknown whether this issue can be overcome such that standard powder pressing in air could be feasible. However, the impedance of the nanosize FeS_2 is lower than the natural FeS_2 after the first pulse application. At the end of discharge, the natural FeS_2 impedance is 10% greater than the nanosize FeS_2.

Conclusions

Various alternative cathode materials were compared to EaglePicher's standard, natural FeS_2 active material. In the case of synthetic FeS_2, higher impedance under pulsing and difficulty in handling do not justify the significant increase in costs for the synthetic material. While synthetic CoS_2 showed low impedance under pulsing, the performance was not sufficiently improved to justify the increased material cost, handling difficulty, and hazardous nature of the material to replace natural FeS_2. Nanosize FeS_2 possesses a much higher relative amount of surface oxidation. This presents serious difficulties meeting maximum voltage requirements. Combined with the additional cost burden, nanosize FeS_2 also fails to merit replacement of natural FeS_2, despite the low impedance under pulsing in a battery test, which is attributed to the smaller particle size. Despite the technological advances in material preparation, advanced, synthetic materials fail to justify the extreme cost associated with procurement. Natural FeS_2 remains the optimum manufacturing material for EaglePicher.

Acknowledgments

Thanks are offered to Trudy Harris for sample preparation and data collection. This material is released to the public domain in accordance with ITAR 22 CFR 120.11.

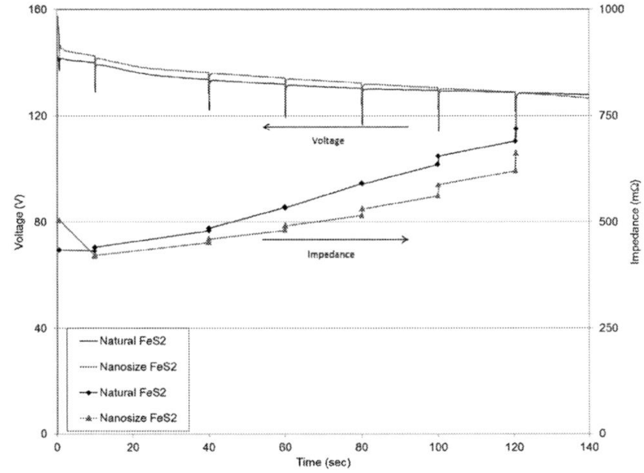

Figure 6. Voltage traces and impedance under pulsing for thermal batteries built using natural and nanosize FeS_2-based cathodes. Batteries were stored and fired at room temperature.

References

1. V. Klasons and C.M. Lamb, "Thermal Batteries," in *Handbook of Batteries*, 3rd ed., eds. D. Linden and T.B. Reddy, pp. 21.1-21.22, McGraw Hill, New York, NY, 2002
2. P. Masset, R.A. Guidotti, "Thermal Activated (Thermal) Battery Technology Part II: Molten Salt Electrolytes", *J. Power Sources*, **164**, pp. 397-414 (2008)
3. P. Masset, R.A. Guidotti, "Thermal Activated ("Thermal") Battery Technology: Part IIIa: FeS_2 Cathode Material", *J. Power Sources*, **177**, pp. 595–609 (2008)
4. P. Masset, R.A. Guidotti, "Thermal activated ("Thermal") Battery Technology Part IIIb: Sulfur and Oxide-Based Cathode Materials", *J. Power Sources*, **178**, pp. 456–466 (2008)

A High Power Thermal Battery based on High Voltage Cathode and Stable Electrolyte

Pyoungho Choi[1], Ivy Mills[1], Sameer Singhal[1], and Mohan Sanghadasa[2]

[1]CFD Research Corporation, 701 McMillian Way, Huntsville, AL 35806
[2]AMRDEC, US Army RDECOM, Redstone Arsenal, AL 35898

Abstract: *We have investigated several high voltage (OCV>3V) cathodes that provide higher energy and power densities than the current industry standard FeS_2 cathode. An electrolyte compatible with the high voltage cathodes was developed based on electrochemical stability, ionic conductivity, melting temperature, and cell performance. Mixed oxide V_2O_5-CuO with LiF-LiCl-Li_2SO_4 (30-48-22, mol%) electrolyte has shown operating cell voltage of 2.25V and 23% increase in capacity over the FeS_2 cathode.*

Keywords: high voltage cathode; metal oxides; molten salt electrolyte; high power applications

Introduction

Thermal batteries are used in many military applications with a potential immediate or sudden demand for electric power [1]. They are essential for providing power for radar and electronic guidance and are able to operate in the high spin and setback environment of artillery shells, and high shock experienced in an earth-penetrator weapon. They remain in weapon systems for 25 years or more over a wide range of storage (-55°C to 75°C) without degradation and should be hermetically sealed as the moisture and air degrade the battery significantly.

Thermal batteries run at temperatures between 350-550°C with molten salt electrolyte. They are inactive at room temperature as the molten salt electrolyte is in solid state bearing a low ionic conductivity minimizing self discharge and degradation processes. This low conductivity phase of the electrolyte promotes the capability for this type of battery to have a very long shelf life with practically no capacity fade and then can be activated within less than a second. For battery activation, internal pyrotechnics are ignited that generate thermal energy to raise the battery internal temperature to melting temperature of the electrolyte causing a large increase in its ionic conductivity thus allowing the battery to operate. The battery is active as long as the electrolyte is above its melting point (typically above 350°C) and generates power as long as enough active mass is available for the charge transfer reaction.

The most advanced common configurations feature lithium-silicon alloy powder as anode material, FeS_2 as cathode material, and eutectic electrolyte such as LiCl-KCl or halide electrolyte mixture of LiF-LiCl-LiBr [2]. The configurations operate at voltage less than 2V and the capacity is limited. The principal avenue for increasing thermal battery specific energy is to identify and develop new chemistry and electrode materials, which provide higher specific capacity at higher operating voltage (>2.0V). The combination of higher specific capacity and higher operating voltage translates directly to higher specific energy at the battery level.

We have investigated metal oxide composites $M'_aM''_bO_c$ that generate high cell voltage (OCV>3.0V) when coupled with lithium alloy anode. The lithium alloy anode is oxidized during the discharge process as

$$M_xLi \rightarrow M_x + Li^+ + e^- \qquad [1]$$

where M_x is a metal alloyed with lithium such as Sn or Si. Lithium ion Li^+ diffuses through the molten salt electrolyte and reaches the cathode where it combines with the electron at the interface by the following reaction

$$M'_aM''_bO_c + Li^+ + e^- \rightarrow LiM'_aM''_bO_c \qquad [2]$$

where M′ and M″ are V, Cr, Mn, Fe, Co, Ni, and Cu, as they can generate high discharge capacity. More specifically, electrochemical characteristics of CuO, Fe_2O_3, and V_2O_5 and their mixed oxides such as CuV_2O_6 and $Fe_2V_4O_{13}$ have been evaluated.

The current state of the art electrolytes such as LiF-LiCl-LiBr are effective for low voltage (<2.0V) cells employing FeS_2 or CoS_2, but not suitable for high voltage (>3.0V) cells as they decompose at the high voltage [3]. LiF-LiCl-Li_2SO_4 electrolyte has been evaluated for the high voltage cathode. The composition of the tertiary salt was optimized based on ionic conductivity, melting temperature, and cell performance.

Experimental

Thermal cells were assembled by piling up pellets of cathode, electrolyte and anode in order.

Cathode: The cathode was composed of oxide and separator MgO. Some cathodes were ball milled and heat-treated [4].

Electrolyte: LiF-LiCl-LiBr and CFDRC's proprietary LiF-LiCl-Li_2SO_4 electrolytes were prepared by fusing the constitutive salts and followed by ball milling.

Anode: LiSi was used as the anode. Molten salt electrolyte was mixed with the anode and ball milled [5].

DSC Measurement: 3 mg of the sample was heated at 10°C/min to 500°C to determine the melting point of electrolyte with various compositions.

Result and Discussions

Figure 1 shows discharge curves of V_2O_5-CuO with various treatments in LiF-LiCl-Li_2SO_4 electrolyte. Measured OCV of V_2O_5-CuO was 3.2V and stable. The initial overpotential was high (0.9V) and the cells show three plateau to 1V discharge. The average voltages of the cathodes to the time for the first plateau of FeS_2 cathode, i.e., 17 minutes, was 2.19V, 2.22V, 2.25V, and 2.11V for the cathode with ball milled, heat-treated at 500°C, 600°C, and 700°C, respectively. Compared to the average voltage of 1.83V in the conventional FeS_2 cathode, the V_2O_5-CuO heat treated at 600°C in LiF-LiCl-Li_2SO_4 (30-48-22) gives 23% increase in specific energy.

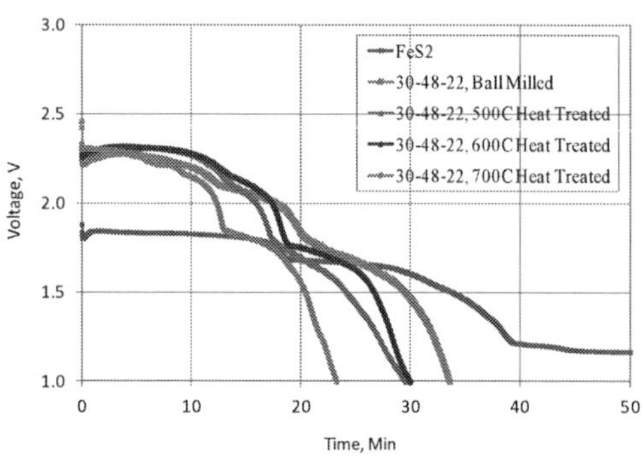

Figure 1. Discharge curves of V_2O_5-CuO cathode in LiF-LiCl-Li_2SO_4 electrolyte; compositions of the electrolyte are given in the box.

Figure 2 shows a DSC curve of the electrolyte LiF-LiCl-Li_2SO_4 (30-48-22). It shows eutectic point of 436°C for the composition. A number of compositions of the tertiary salts have been investigated for mixed oxide cathodes. Figure 3 shows a tertiary plot showing some of eutectic points of the electrolytes prepared by fusing three lithium salts; LiF, LiCl and Li_2SO_4. The melting points of binary mixture of LiF-LiCl (30-70), LiCl-Li_2SO_4 (60-40), and LiF-Li_2SO_4 (40-60) are 495°C, 485°C, and 530°C, respectively. Tertiary mixtures of LiF-LiCl-Li_2SO_4 generate salts with low melting points; 460°C, 433°C, and 445°C for the compositions of 35-48-17, 30-48-22, and 30-40-30, respectively.

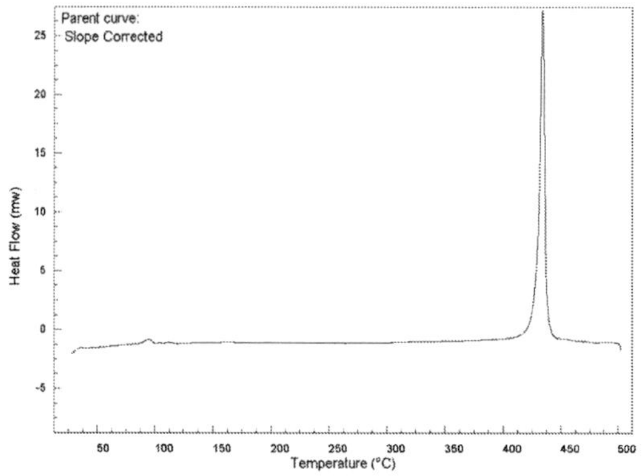

Figure 2. DSC curve of the electrolyte LiF-LiCl-Li_2SO_4 (30-48-22).

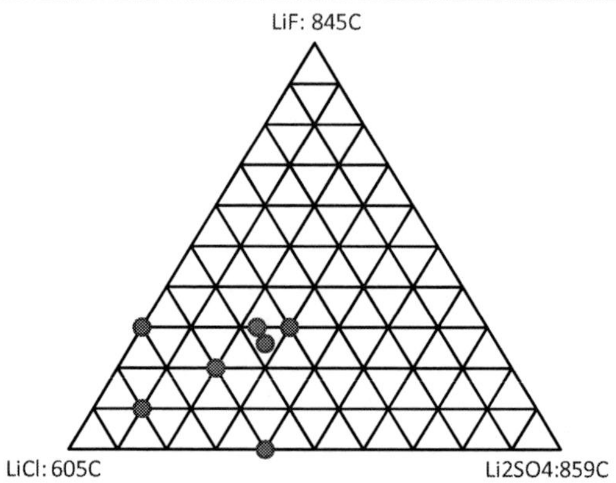

Figure 3. Phase diagram showing some of eutectic points below 500°C.

Conclusions

Vanadium-copper metal oxides have shown potential for use as cathode in high voltage thermal batteries. The cathode heat-treated at 600°C generates OCV of 3.2V and higher operating voltage (2.25V) than the FeS_2 (1.83V) resulting 23% higher capacity than FeS_2. A tertiary electrolyte composed of LiF, LiCl, and Li_2SO_4 was developed for the high voltage cell; LiF-LiCl-Li_2SO_4 (30-48-22) electrolyte has shown a melting point of 433°C and was successfully employed in the metal oxide cells. Further research of electrolyte materials and their compositions is being carried out to couple them with various high voltage metal oxide cathodes.

Acknowledgements

*This work was funded by the U.S. Army SBIR program (W31P4Q-16-C-0012) and U.S. Army AMRDEC Missile Science & Technology Program.

*Distribution Statement A. Approved for public release.

References

1. R. A. Guidotti and P. Masset, "Thermally activated ("thermal") battery technology: Part I: An overview." *Journal of Power Sources,* 161, 1443-1449 (2006).

2. P. Masset and R. A. Guidotti, "Thermal activated (thermal) battery technology: Part II. Molten salt electrolytes." *Journal of Power Sources,* 164, 397-414 (2007).

3. P. Masset and R. A. Guidotti, "Thermal activated ("thermal") battery technology: Part IIIa: FeS_2 cathode material." *Journal of Power Sources,* 177, 595-609 (2008).

4. P. Masset and R. A. Guidotti, "Thermal activated ("thermal") battery technology: Part IIIb. Sulfur and oxide-based cathode materials." *Journal of Power Sources,* 178, 456-666 (2008).

5. R. A. Guidotti and P. Masset, "Thermally activated ("thermal") battery technology: Part IV. Anode" *Journal of Power Sources*, 183, 388-398 (2008).

Li-Sulfur Chemistry: Challenges and Opportunities

Surya Moganty

Nohms Technologies, Inc.

surya@nohms.com

Abstract

Despite the excellent specific capacity (1672 mAh/g) and energy density (2567 Wh/kg), sulfur has several challenges that prevent the material from achieving commercial status. The primary setback with sulfur is its insulating property. The second detrimental problem is the dissolution of intermediate charge/discharge lithium polysulfide (Li2Sx) products in the electrolyte that leads to decreased utilization of sulfur, triggering parasitic side reactions with Li metal anode, poor cycle life. Hence, the design of electrolytes with lower solubilizing power for Li2Sx is perhaps the most straightforward and valid approach to suppress Li2Sx deduced redox shuttle. A liquid electrolyte designed for this purpose should act as a poor solvent for all of the Li2Sx species of the sulfur cathode, while enabling good Li-ion conduction by the originally doped Li salts. Given that the active species exhibit a wide range of hydrophilic−hydrophobic character: sulfur (hydrophobic, soluble in nonpolar solvents), lithium sulfide (soluble in highly polar solvents) and polysulfide species (intermediate solubility depending on the chain length). At NOHMs Technologies Inc, we have been developing functional ionic liquids as electrolyte additives in conjunction with novel cathode architectures to improve the Li-S battery performance. NOHMs has already demonstrated Li-S pouch cells that has exhibited full-cell specific energy density above 300 Wh/kg and excellent abuse tolerance during standard nail penetration tests. Figure 1 depicts the NOHMs Li-S cell level performance. This presentation will focus on the ongoing R&D work at NOHMs in maturing the Li-S battery chemistry.

The Benefit of $LiNO_3$ to the Cathode of Lithium-Sulfur Battery

Sheng S. Zhang
Electrochemistry Branch, RDRL-SED-C, Sensors and Electron Devices Directorate
U.S. Army Research Laboratory, Adelphi, MD 20783-1138
E-mail: shengshui.zhang.civ@mail.mil or shengshui@gmail.com

Abstract: *The effect of lithium nitrate ($LiNO_3$) on the Li anode in lithium-sulfur battery has been well studied, knowing that $LiNO_3$ incorporates the formation of a robust surface layer to protect the Li anode from reacting with the dissolved polysulfide. However, the benefit of $LiNO_3$ to the sulfur cathode has been little known, instead reporting that its reduction below 1.7 V vs. Li/Li^+ adversely affects the battery's cyclability. In this work, we reinvestigated the role of $LiNO_3$ with focus on the sulfur cathode, finding that $LiNO_3$ is capable of catalyzing the conversion of highly soluble polysulfide to slightly soluble elemental sulfur, and that the combination of a soluble nitrate in the electrolyte and an insoluble nitrate in the sulfur cathode leads to synergetic improvement. Additionally, the mechanism of $LiNO_3$ catalyzing the conversion of polysulfide to sulfur will be discussed.*

Keywords: Li-S battery; $LiNO_3$; nitrate; polysulfide; redox shuttle.

Introduction

Lithium nitrate ($LiNO_3$) has been widely used as the electrolyte additive or co-salt in the electrolyte of lithium-sulfur (Li-S) batteries. The known functions are that $LiNO_3$ effectively suppresses the redox shuttle of dissolved lithium polysulfide (PS, Li_2S_n) and reduces the battery's self-discharge rate [1, 2]. Understanding of these improvements has been mainly limited to the Li anode, knowing that $LiNO_3$ reacts with metallic Li to form a robust surface layer that consequently protects the Li anode from reacting with the dissolved PS. Few papers have reported that the robust surface layer on the Li anode is not the only cause for the suppression of redox shuttle in the Li-S batteries, showing that a Li anode pre-cycled in a $LiNO_3$-containing electrolyte does not suppress the redox shuttle [3]. On the other hand, we previously reported that $LiNO_3$ was subject to irreversible reduction on the sulfur cathode when the Li-S battery was discharged to lower than 1.7 V, and that the resultant reduction significantly reduced the cyclability of Li-S batteries [4, 5]. Therefore, further investigation is needed in order to better understand the role of $LiNO_3$ in the Li-S batteries. In this work, we studied the effect of $LiNO_3$ with focus on the sulfur cathode. We hereby demonstrate that $LiNO_3$ is capable of catalyzing the conversion of highly soluble PS to slightly soluble elemental sulfur (S_8) near the end of charging process (namely above 2.5 V vs. Li/Li^+), and discuss the mechanism for $LiNO_3$ catalyzing the conversion of polysulfide to sulfur.

Experimental

Two sulfur cathodes with an averaged sulfur loading of 2 mg cm^{-2} were prepared and punched into 1.27 cm^2 circular disks: one consisting of 77% S, 10% Super-P carbon, 10% Ketjenblack EC-300JD carbon black and 3% poly(acryl-onitrile-methyl methacrylate) binder and the other consisting of 65% S, 5% $Mg(NO_3)_2 \cdot 6H_2O$, 10% Super-P carbon, 10% Ketjenblack EC-300JD carbon black, and 10% poly(ethylene oxide) binder. Two solutions with a 0.5 mol kg^{-1} LiTFSI and a 0.25 mol Kg^{-1} LiTFSI-0.25 mol Kg^{-1} $LiNO_3$, respectively, dissolved in a 1:1 (wt.) mixed solvent of dimethyl ether (DME) and 1,3-dioxolane (DOL) were used as the electrolyte, and hereafter referred as to a "$LiNO_3$-free electrolyte" and a "$LiNO_3$-containing electrolyte", respectively.

A three-electrode cell with a platinum (Pt) wire as the working electrode and two Li foils as the reference and counter electrodes was used to evaluate the electrochemical property of liquid electrolyte. For cycling test, BR2335-type Li-S coin cell was assembled and filled with 30 μL electrolyte. The resultant cell was cycled on a Maccor Series 4000 cycler. Note that in this work, excess amount of liquid electrolyte was used for highlighting the effect of $LiNO_3$ although excess electrolyte increases the loss of sulfur active material.

Results and discussion

General benefit of $LiNO_3$ to Li-S battery

As indicated by Fig. 1a and Fig. 1b, the general benefit of $LiNO_3$ to the Li-S batteries is to suppress the redox shuttle of the dissolved PS. The cell with a $LiNO_3$-free electrolyte fails to pass the threshold at ~2.5 V (Fig. 1a), whereas that with a $LiNO_3$-containing electrolyte reaches the charge cutoff voltage (2.8 V) regardless of the discharge cutoff voltage. This difference clearly reveals the ability of $LiNO_3$ in suppressing the redox shuttle of the soluble PS formed during discharge. In order to observe the effect of $LiNO_3$ on the Li anode and sulfur cathode separately, a Li-S cell was first cycled in a $LiNO_3$-containing electrolyte for five times to enable the formation of a matured surface layer on two electrodes, and then was disassembled at the fully charge state (2.8 V). The harvested Li anode and sulfur cathode were carefully washed using a 1:1 DME/DOL mixed solvent to remove Li

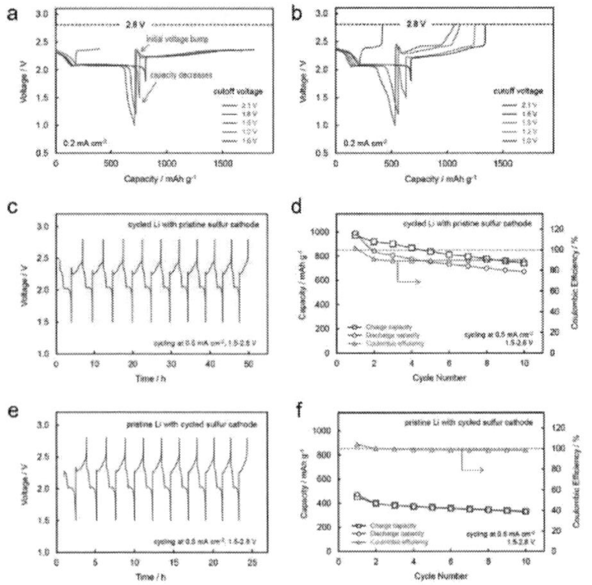

Figure 1. Voltage profile for two Li-S cells with a $LiNO_3$-free electrolyte (a) and a $LiNO_3$-containing electrolyte (b), respectively; Voltage profile and cycling performance for Li-S cells assembled with a pre-cycled Li anode (c and d) and a pre-cycled sulfur cathode (e and f), respectively.

salt and soluble PS, followed by re-assembling into two Li-S cells with a pristine sulfur cathode and a fresh Li anode, respectively. For the cell reassembled with the cycled Li, all charging reproducibly reached 2.8 V (Fig. 1c), however, the Coulbomic efficiencies (CEs) were somewhat low, being at a level of ~90% (Fig. 1d). These results suggest that the surface layer formed with $LiNO_3$ on the cycled Li anode could suppress the redox shuttle, but the redox shuttle still existed to some context. On contrary, the cell assembled with the cycled sulfur cathode could not only charge to 2.8 V (Fig. 2e), but also reach the CEs higher than 99% (Fig. 2f). By comparing the CEs in Fig. 2d and Fig. 2f, we conclude that the surface layer formed on the sulfur cathode with the incorporation of $LiNO_3$ plays a more important role than that on the Li anode in suppressing the redox shuttle of dissolved PS. It should be pointed out that the much lower capacities of sulfur in Fig. 2f than those in Fig. 2b are because all soluble PS species in the cell of Fig. 2f had been removed in the processes of cell disassembly and solvent washing.

Catalytic effect of $LiNO_3$ on sulfur formation

In order to avoid the interference of the Li anode, insoluble $Mg(NO_3)_2 6H_2O$ was directly used as the sulfur cathode additive without removing of crystal water. Fig. 2a shows the voltage profile of a Li-S cell with a sulfur cathode containing a 5 wt.% $Mg(NO_3)_2 6H_2O$ and a $LiNO_3$-free electrolyte. It is indicated that the cell can be normally discharged and charged without significant redox shuttle, being similar to those using the $LiNO_3$-containg electrolyte

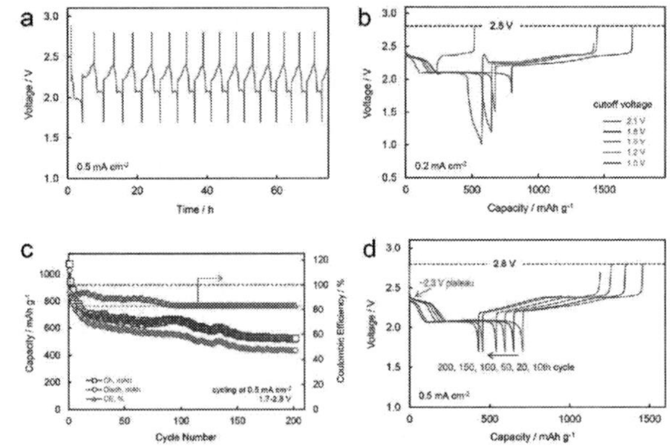

Figure 2. Catalytic effect of NO_3^- anions on the conversion of highly soluble Li_2S_n to slightly soluble S_8 in a Li-S cell with a $Mg(NO_3)_2 6H_2O$-containing sulfur cathode. (a) Voltage profile, (b) the effect of discharge cutoff voltage, (c) cycling performance, (d) voltage profile for selected cycle numbers.

as observed in Fig. 1b. In the same manner as the $LiNO_3$-containing electrolyte, the discharge cutoff voltage greatly affects the suppression of redox shuttle as indicated by Fig. 2b, in which the first discharging was intentionally terminated at 2.1 V so as to obtain a highly concentrated PS solution. We are interested to find that the voltage in the subsequent charging reached 2.8 V. This observation reveals that $Mg(NO_3)_2 6H_2O$, more exactly the NO_3^- anions, is able to catalyze the conversion of highly soluble PS to slightly soluble elemental sulfur (S_8), as described by eqn. 1

$$S_n^{2-} - 2e \rightarrow \frac{n}{8} S_8 \qquad (1)$$

Once the discharge cutoff voltage was lowered to 1.0 V, $Mg(NO_3)_2 6H_2O$ was irreversibly reduced so that it failed to suppress the redox shuttle and the charging voltage constantly stayed at ~2.5 V until the capacity limit.

Fig. 2c exhibits a typical cycling performance of the Li-S cells with a $Mg(NO_3)_2 6H_2O$-containing sulfur cathode and a $LiNO_3$-free electrolyte. Although the cell was successfully charged to 2.8 V, the CEs being in a range of 90~95% were relatively low compared with the cell using a $LiNO_3$-containing electrolyte, and the suppression of redox shuttle only lasted for about 70 cycles, after which the charging had to be terminated by the capacity limit, leading to a constant CE of 83%. This is not surprising because beside catalyzing the conversion of highly soluble Li_2S_n to slightly soluble S_8, $Mg(NO_3)_2 6H_2O$ is unable to prevent the dissolution of PS. Thus, the redox shuttle of the dissolved PS still takes place between the Li anode and sulfur cathode. Fig. 2d compares the voltage profile for several selected cycles of a Li-S cell using a $Mg(NO_3)_2 6H_2O$-containing sulfur cathode. At 10th, 20th and 50th cycles, the cell could be charged to 2.8 V, and accordingly there was a distinct discharge plateau at ~2.3 V with respect to the reduction of slightly soluble S_8 to highly soluble Li_2S_8

[6, 7]. At the 150th and 200th cycles, the charging failed to reach 2.8 V, instead constantly stayed at 2.4 V until the capacity limit. As a result, the discharging had a much shorter voltage plateau at ~2.3 V. This is because the NO_3^- anions in the sulfur cathode are progressively reduced during the repeated cycling, which led to an accumulated loss in the concentration of the NO_3^- anions. Based on the above observations, it can be concluded that the insoluble $Mg(NO_3)_2 6H_2O$ is able to catalyze the conversion of highly soluble Li_2S_n to slightly soluble S_8, which to some degree suppresses the redox shuttle of the dissolved PS.

Synergetic effect of $LiNO_3$ and $Mg(NO_3)_2 6H_2O$

Synergetic improvement of the soluble $LiNO_3$ in electrolyte and the insoluble $Mg(NO_3)_2 6H_2O$ in cathode can be observed from Fig. 3a, which shows that their combination results in the optimum capacity retention. When $LiNO_3$ and $Mg(NO_3)_2$ $6H_2O$ were applied independently as shown by Cell-1 and Cell-2 in Fig. 3a, the capacity only stabilized for about 100 cycles, after which the capacity fading rate accelerated. This is because the soluble $LiNO_3$ in the electrolyte was rapidly consumed (reduced) mainly on the Li anode while the insoluble $Mg(NO_3)_2 6H_2O$ in the cathode was unable to protect the Li anode. On contrary, when $LiNO_3$ and $Mg(NO_3)_2 6H_2O$ were used together (Cell-3 in Fig. 3a), the capacity constantly stabilized at ~570 mAh g^{-1} with CEs close to the unity until the end of cycling test (200 cycles). It should be noted that there was a rapid capacity loss during the initial 20 cycles, in particular Cell-3 suffered a loss from 1055 mAh g^{-1} in the 1st discharge to 612 mA g^{-1} in the 20th discharge. Such a loss in the capacity, which is generally attributed to the redistribution of the sulfur species from the cathode to throughout the entire cell as a result of the PS dissolution, is common for the liquid electrolyte Li-S batteries and can be reduced by optimizing the electrolyte/sulfur ratio or cell design [7]. Additionally, the excellence of the $LiNO_3$-$Mg(NO_3)_2 6H_2O$ combination can be observed from the voltage profile of the Li-S cell (Fig. 3b). It is shown that in all five selected cycles (namely at 10th, 20th, 50th, 150th and 200th cycles), there are a pair of distinct upper voltage plateaus corresponding to the reversible conversion between the highly soluble Li_2S_8 and slightly soluble S_8 (i.e., eqn. 1): one at ~2.36 V in discharging and the other at ~2.42 V in charging.

Catalysis mechanism of NO_3^- anions

Cyclic voltammetry was used to understand the catalytic effect of $LiNO_3$ on the conversion of the highly soluble Li_2S_n to slightly soluble S_8 (i.e., eqn. 1). Fig. 4 compares the cyclic voltammograms of a Pt electrode in a $LiNO_3$-free and a $LiNO_3$-containing electrolyte, respectively. In the $LiNO_3$-free electrolyte, the anodic (oxidation) current dramatically increases at 3.45 V vs. Li/Li^+ and quickly reaches a peak at 3.61 V due to the suppressed oxidation of electrolyte solvents (DME and DOL). This is typically attributed to the formation of a

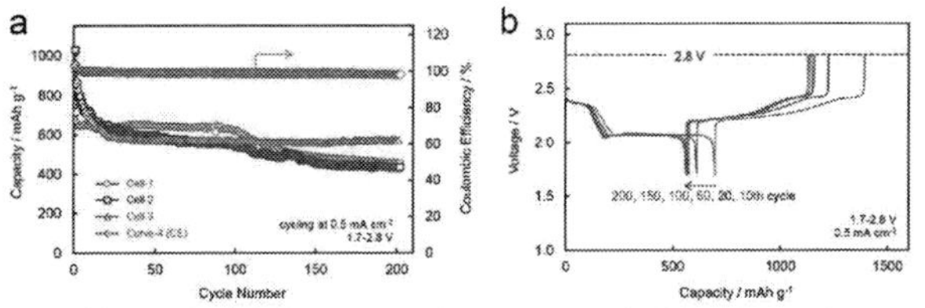

Figure 3. (a) Synergetic improvement of $LiNO_3$ and $Mg(NO_3)_2 6H_2O$ on Li-S cells, in which Cell-1 used a regular sulfur cathode and a $LiNO_3$-containing electrolyte, Cell-2 used a $Mg(NO_3)_2 6H_2O$-containing sulfur cathode and a $LiNO_3$-free electrolyte, Cell-3 combined a $Mg(NO_3)_2 6H_2O$-containing sulfur cathode and a $LiNO_3$-containing electrolyte, and Curve-4 shows the coulombic efficiency of Cell-3, and (b) selected voltage profile of Cell-3.

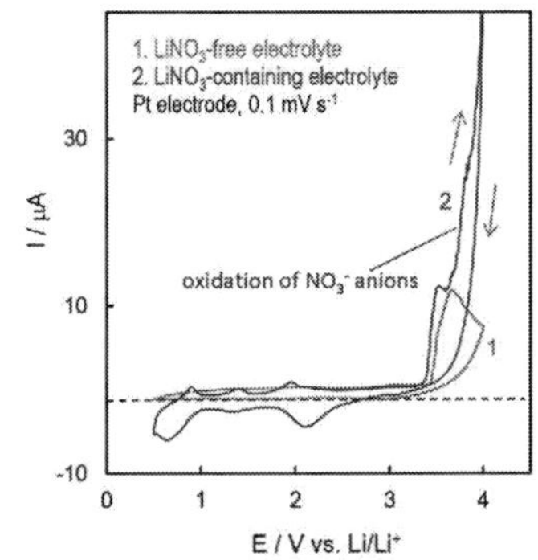

Figure 4. Cyclic voltammogram of Pt electrode in (1) $LiNO_3$-free electrolyte and (2) $LiNO_3$-containing electrolyte. Note that the arrows indicate the direction of potential scanning.

protective surface layer on the Pt electrode as a result of the dense accumulation of the insoluble solvent oxidation products. In the $LiNO_3$-containing electrolyte, the similar solvent oxidation is observed, however it is immediately followed by a dramatic oxidation of the NO_3^- anions, which does not stop until the potential end and can be described by eqn. 2 [8]:

$$NO_3^- - e \rightarrow NO_2 + ½O_2 \quad (2)$$

Scanning-back of the potential toward the low potential direction results in a broad reduction current peak at 2.14 V, followed by a reduction current plateau between 1.82 V and 1.05 V and a large reduction current peak at 0.67 V. In detail, the current peak at 2.14 V starts from 2.73 V, which is attributed to the reduction of oxygen produced according to eqn. 2 during the positive potential scanning. Whereas the subsequent current plateau and large peak at the potentials lower than 1.82 V are attributed to a series of rather complicated reductions, which involve not only the reduction of the NO_3^- to NO_2^- anions but also the reduction of peroxide and superoxide species resided by the incomplete reduction of oxygen. Based on the previous finding that the oxygen evolution reaction (OER) in non-aqueous electrolyte Li-air batteries suffers from very high polarization [9, 10], we speculate that the real potential for the oxidation of NO_3^- anions to oxygen (namely eqn. 2 that involves an OER) would be much lower than that observed in Fig. 4. On the other hand, it was reported that the NO_3 radicals widely exist in the nature with short life [11, 12], and are often formed as the reaction intermediate in electrochemical synthesis [13]. It is very likely that in a PS environment, the NO_3 radicals are formed near the redox potential of the polysulfide anions (S_n^{2-}) and reduced instantly by the S_n^{2-} anions. Therefore, we propose that the NO_3^- anions catalyze the conversion of Li_2S_n to S_8 through a NO_3 radical intermediate as described by eqn. 3 and eqn. 4, which lead to an overall reaction of eqn. 1:

$$2NO_3^- - 2e \rightarrow 2NO_3 \quad (3)$$

$$2NO_3 + S_n^{2-} \rightarrow 2NO_3^- + \frac{n}{8}S_8 \quad (4)$$

By taking the previous conclusions [1, 4] into account, the role of $LiNO_3$ in the Li-S batteries can be extended to such bi-functions that on the Li anode the NO_3^- anions enable the formation of a robust surface layer to protect the Li anode from reacting with the dissolved PS, and on the cathode the NO_3^- anions catalyze the conversion of highly soluble Li_2S_n to slightly soluble S_8. The combination of a soluble nitrate in the electrolyte and an insoluble nitrate in the cathode leads to synergetic improvement on the cycling performance of the Li-S batteries.

Conclusions

In summary, we found that the NO_3^- anions are capable of catalyzing the conversion of highly soluble Li_2S_n to slightly soluble S_8 in addition to the previous finding that $LiNO_3$ suppresses the redox shuttle of the dissolved PS. The suppressing efficiency of the redox shuttle is limited when $LiNO_3$ and $Mg(NO_3)_2 6H_2O$ are used individually as the soluble $LiNO_3$ in the electrolyte is rapidly reduced mainly on the Li anode whilst the insoluble $Mg(NO_3)_2 6H_2O$ in the sulfur cathode is unable to protect the Li anode. The combination of a soluble nitrate in the electrolyte and an insoluble nitrate in the cathode leads to synergetic improvement on the cycling performance of the Li-S batteries. It is proposed that the catalysis of the NO_3^- anions on the conversion of elemental sulfur involves a NO_3 radical intermediate, which instantly oxidizes the highly soluble Li_2S_n to slightly soluble S_8.

Acknowledgements

The author wishes to thank Drs. J. Read and C. Lundgren for their critical reading of the manuscript and valuable comments.

References

1 Zhang, S. S., and Read, J. A., "A New Direction for The Performance Improvement of Rechargeable Lithium/sulfur Batteries", *J. Power Sources,* 200, 77–82, 2012.

2 Lacey, M. J., Yalamanchili, A., Maibach, J., Tengstedt, C., Edstroem, K., and Brandell, D., "The Li-S Battery: An Investigation of Redox Shuttle and Self-discharge Behaviour with $LiNO_3$-containing Electrolytes", *RSC Adv.,* 6, 3632–3641, 2016.

3 Xu, R., Li, J. C. M., Lu, J., Amine, K., and Belharouak, I., "Demonstration of Highly Efficient Lithium-sulfur Batteries", *J. Mater. Chem. A,* 3, 4170–4179, 2015.

4 Zhang, S. S., "Role of $LiNO_3$ in Rechargeable Lithium/sulfur Battery", *Electrochim. Acta,* 70, 344–348, 2012.

5 Zhang, S. S., "Effect of Discharge Cutoff Voltage on Reversibility of Lithium/sulfur Batteries with $LiNO_3$-contained Electrolyte", *J. Electrochem. Soc.,* 159, A920–A923, 2012.

6 Zhang, S. S., and Tran, D. T., "A Proof-of-concept Lithium/sulfur Liquid Battery with Exceptionally High Capacity Density", *J. Power Sources,* 211, 169–172, 2012.

7 Zhang, S. S., "Improved Cyclability of Liquid Electrolyte Lithium/sulfur Batteries by Optimizing Electrolyte/sulfur Ratio", *Energies,* 5, 5190–5197, 2012.

8 Broder, T. L., Silvester, D. S., Aldous, L., Hardacre, C., Crossley, A., and Compton, R. G., "The Electrochemical Oxidation and Reduction of Nitrate Ions in The Room Temperature Ionic Liquid [C_2mim][NTf_2]; The Latter Behaves as A 'Melt' Rather Than An Organic 'Solvent'", *New J. Chem.,* 31, 966–972, 2007.

9 Lu, Y. C., Gasteiger, H. A., Parent, M. C., Chiloyan, V., and Shao-Horn, Y., "The Influence of Catalysts on Discharge and Charge Voltages of Rechargeable Li-Oxygen Batteries", *Electrochem. Solid-State Lett.,* 13, A69–A72, 2010.

10 Imanishi, N., and Yamamoto, O., "Rechargeable Lithium-Air Batteries: Characteristics and Prospects", *Mater. Today,* 17, 24-30, 2014.

11 Wayne, R. P., Barnes, I., Biggs, P., Burrows, J. P., Canosa-Mas, C. E., Hjorth, J., Le Bras, G., Moortgat, G. K., and Perner, D., "The Nitrate Radical: Physics, Chemistry, and The Atmosphere", *Atmos. Environ., Part A,* 25A, 1–203, 1991.

12 Geyer, A., Alicke, B., Konrad, S., Schmitz, T., Stutz, J., and Platt, U., "Chemistry and Oxidation Capacity of The Nitrate Radical in The Continental Boundary Layer Near Berlin", *J. Geophys. Res.,* 106, 8013–8025, 2001.

13 Tomat, R., and Rigo, A., "Electrochemical Oxidation of Aliphatic Hydrocarbons Promoted by Inorganic Radicals. II. Nitrogen Oxide (NO_3) Radicals", *J. Appl. Electrochem.,* 16, 8–14, 1986.

Advanced Lithium-Sulfur Batteries with Hybrid Electrolyte and Bi-functional Cathode

Jitendra Kumar, Priyanka Bhattacharya
University of Dayton

Stanley Rodrigues
AFRL, Dayton

Amarendra Rai, Rabi Bhattacharya
UES, Inc Services, Dayton

Guru Subramanyam
University of Dayton

jkumar1@udayton.edu

Abstract

Rechargeable lithium-sulfur (Li-S) battery is a promising technology with potential to provide high specific energy, high energy density (>450 Wh/kg, 1000-1500 Wh/L) and cycle life (> 100 cycles at C/5 rate). Li-S batteries with high specific energy (~500 Wh/kg) have been demonstrated and are close to commercialization. However, critical factors limiting the safety, durability and hence commercialization of Li-S batteries include Li dendrite formation at the Li anode, Li dendrite propagation through currently used polypropylene (PE) separator, low thermal stability of liquid electrolyte used and the lithium polysulfide (LiPS) shuttling from cathode to anode through PE separator. To overcome the afore-mentioned issues associated with the Li-S battery, our research includes modifications of all the three components of the battery viz. cathode, electrolyte/separator and anode. Cathode modification involves the use of highly branched (dendrimers) binders to encapsulate high sulfur loading and reduced LiPS shuttling. Specifically, a novel binder namely polyamidoamine (PAMAM) dendrimers with appropriate surface chemistries is being developed to enhance sulfur loading (>2 mg/cm2) and their encapsulation1. The modified electrolyte/separator2 comprises of a dendrite and LiPS proof super ion conducting ceramic electrolyte (lithium aluminum germanium phosphate, LAGP) coated polymer separator in conjunction with liquid electrolyte to obtain high room temperature ionic conductivity (~10-3 S/cm), low interfacial resistance, high liquid electrolyte uptake, low Li plating/deplating voltage polarization. For Li anode, an artificial SEI (ASEI) membrane has been developed3 to reduce dendrite growth and to enhance cycle life by stabilizing lithium-electrolyte interface. The latest data on combined effect of all the three modified cell components will be presented. Reference: 1. P. Bhattacharya, et. al., "Polyamidoamine dendrimer-based binders for high-loading lithium–sulfur battery cathodes", Nano Energy 19, 176 (2016) 2. J. Kumar, P. Kichambare, A.K. Rai, R. Bhattacharya, S. Rodrigues, G. Subramanyam, "A high performance ceramic-polymer separator for lithium batteries", J. Power Sources 301, 194 (2016) 3. J. Kumar, G. Subramanyam, F. Ouchen, J.G. Grote, "Method to Enhance Cycle Life and Usable Energy Density of Lithium Batteries based on Lithium Metal Anode," US Patent, 62107566 (01.26.15).

High Energy Density Li/S Prototype Development

Wujun Fu, Ramanthan Thillaiyan, Uma Viswanathan, Mario Destephen

EaglePicher Technologies
3220 Industrial Road
Joplin, MO 64801
Wujun.Fu@eaglepicher.com

Abstract: *Li/S battery is an alternative power source for advanced electronic devices for several defense applications due to its attractive high energy density and light weight. However, the poor cycle life and low system efficiency have plagued this system and prevented it commercial realization. To address those challenges, EaglePicher Technologies (EPT) has been developing various technologies including high loading cathode, proprietary electrolyte and separator to address the complex challenging involved in the Li/S chemistry. The typical high-energy prototype Li/S cells including our advanced technical approaches have been built and evaluated. The performance including rate capability, intermittence shelf life, storage life and safety evaluations have been demonstrated. The test results suggest a substantial opportunity for the development of Li/S battery for various industrial and defense applications including medical, portable power, unmanned aircraft and surveillance usage.*

Keywords: lithium; sulfur; Li/S battery; alternative power source; energy storage; high energy; prototype.

Introduction

The increasing consumption of fossil fuels and the resulting atmosphere pollute is one of the most critical concerns recently. The development of the renewable electrical energy production system helping to reduce the consumption of fossil fuel has attracted great attentions. Among the various candidates, lithium ion batteries (LIBs), representing the state-of-the-art energy storage technology, appeared to be the most promising because of their high energy and stable cycle life.[1-2] However, due to the limitation in energy density of LIBs (~ 200 Wh/kg) and expensive transition metals cathode materials, an alternative advanced rechargeable battery system, with an increased energy density, reduced cost and enhanced safety is essential.

Li/S system, a widely studied chemistry for decades, has the potential to meet such requirements because of its high capacity, earth abundance, inexpensive and environmentally benign attributes of the sulfur cathode material. Theoretically, sulfur can deliver a high specific capacity 1672 mAh/g and a specific energy density of 2500 Wh/kg assuming of complete reaction of Li with S to form Li_2S.[3-4] It was predicted that the Li/S cells will have two to three times higher gravimetric energy density than that of the current Li-ion batteries, with values of 400-600 Wh/kg. However, despite considerable advantages of Li/S batteries, the practical application of this system still remains as a huge challenge because of some major issues involved in this chemistry. The first one is the insulator nature of the elemental sulfur ($5x10^{-30}$ S cm^{-1} at 25°C) and its end discharge products Li_2S, leading to the poor electrochemical contact and low utilization of active material. Accordingly, a large amount of the conductive carbon has been added to address the above issue.[5] However, high fractions of non-active materials inevitably sacrifice the energy density of the Li/S cell since those light porous carbons do not contribute to the capacity but lower the cell gravimetric and volumetric energy density as well. The second challenge is more detrimental. The long-chain polysulfides generated during discharge, which are highly soluble in most organic electrolyte solutions, can easily migrate from the sulfur cathode to the Li anode. The reduced polysulfides can also diffuse back to the sulfur cathode during cycling to form a shuttle reaction, leading to the poor coulombic efficiency, fast capacity degrading and severe self-discharge of Li/S batteries.[6] To overcome this hurdle, various approaches have been proposed and demonstrated. For example, lithium nitrate ($LiNO_3$) has been employed as the electrolyte additive to form a stable passivation film on the surface of lithium anode therefore to inhibit the polysulfide shuttle reaction. Other challenges, such as huge cathode volume expansion, cathode and Li anode mismatch and electrolyte depletion during the cycling, which only can be realized in testing conditions close to practical applications, have not been well investigated.

Although the significant progress has been made to understand the reaction and kinetic mechanism of Li/S chemistry, the technical readiness level of this system is still in its early stage. One of the major reasons is the aforementioned complexity of Li/S system, and the other, which may not be well recognized, is the knowledge transfer from fundamental research into real systems. The numbers of related publications are accumulating rapidly in recent years and some of them showed that the sulfur utilization close to the theoretical capacity and stable cycling up to 500 cycles, however, most of the results were obtained based on the low active material loadings and testing in the coin cells, where the electrolyte and anode are significantly excessive. Herein, EPT are reporting a holistic technical approach spanning from the high loading C/S cathode development, electrolyte modification and utilization of novel separator to overcome the interlinked issues within Li/S chemistry. In order to progress at a relevant scale, all tests were performed and evaluated in the stack-bag pouch Li/S prototype cell with high sulfur loadings. We demonstrated an improved Li/S technology with increased capacity and energy density, prolonged storage life as well as the promoted safety performance.

Experimental

The C/S composite was prepared by mixing sulfur and conductive carbon at suitable ratio and followed by a heat treatment. The slurry was prepared by mixing C/S composite and the binder poly(vinylidene fluoride) (PVDF) using N-methyl-2-pyrrolidinone (NMP) as the solvent. Then the resulting slurry was then casted onto aluminum foil to achieve an electrode loading of around 16 mg/cm^2.

The baseline, additive-free electrolyte is composed of 1M lithium bis(trifluoromethane sulfone)imide (LiTFSI) in equal volumes of dioxolane and diglyme. EPT proprietary electrolyte was prepared by dissolving LiTFSI in organic solvents with addition of various additives in argon filled glove box. EPT proprietary separator was prepared via a conventional solution casting method.

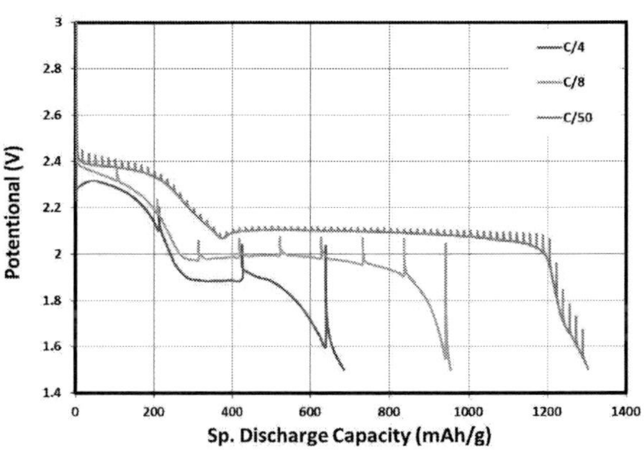

Figure 1. Discharge of high loading C/S cathode with baseline electrolyte at different C-rates.

The Li/S pouch cells were assembled by using lithium anode, C/S cathode, celgard 2325/EPT proprietary separator and the baseline/EPT modified electrolyte. The Li/S cells were evaluated by using Arbin battery test system between 2.7 V and 1.5 V (vs. Li+/Li). The intermittent discharge test was performed at the following procedures: the cells were discharged from OCV to 2.1V firstly, then stored at ambient conditions for 3 days, and followed by continuing to discharge to 1.5 V. The shelf life performance was evaluated at room temperature (RT) and 45 °C. The storage time was from one week to one month.

Results and discussion

Due to the insulating nature of sulfur, conductive materials must be added for the sulfur cathode preparation. C/S composite is most widely used cathode for Li/S system. To achieve high energy density, high sulfur fraction in the C/S composite and reasonable cathode lading is essential. However, most of the previously published results focusing on the cathode are based on the electrode with less than 2 mg/cm^2 of sulfur loading, significantly below the value of the commercialized LIB. For fundamental research, the low loading cathode may provide a convenient platform to validate new concept. However, there are huge uncertainties between lab-made low loading cathodes and those used for industrial scale. Firstly, the sulfur utilization is tightly linked to the electrode loading and it is meaningless to compare two cathodes with significant loading difference. Secondly, the approaches adopted in low loading cathode may not be applicable when the loading hugely increased. Thirdly, the stripping of lithium anode is more pronounced when using a high loading cathode while it can be well hidden when coupled with a low loading cathode.

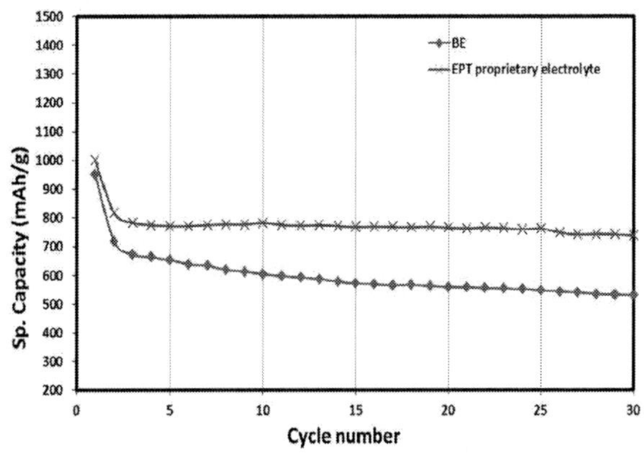

Figure 2. Cycling performance of EPT Li/S prototype pouch cells containing baseline electrolyte and EPT proprietary electrolyte.

In order to achieve the high energy density of Li/S system, EPT have designed high loadings of nanostructured C/S cathode using commercially available, low cost carbon material. By applying the traditional slurry coating process, we obtained a homogeneous coating on the current collector without apparent crackings. The loading of the obtained cathode was around 16 mg/cm^2, which is significantly higher than any values reported in literatures. As shown in Figure 1, the first discharge capacity of EPT high loading cathode can reach 1301 mAh/g at C/50, which is around 78% of the theoretical capacity. At C/8 discharge rate, the cell capacity dropped slightly below 1000 mAh/g. Higher sulfur ladings usually lead to lower sulfur utilization at the same C-rates, however, the performance of our high loading cathode is still better or comparable to other reported values.

The most popular electrolyte system for Li/S batteries is cyclic or linear ethers containing LITFSI salt. To modify physicochemical properties of the electrolyte, various additives have been included in EPT proprietary electrolyte formulation. The major functions of those additives are to adjust the viscosity of electrolyte, limit the polysulfide shuttle and avoid the deposition of insoluble Li_2S/Li_2S_2 on the lithium anode surface to improve the cell efficiency and extend the cycle life. As shown in Figure 2, The Li/S cell with EPT electrolyte showed the better utilization of active materials and cycle life than the cell with baseline electrolyte. After 30 cycles, the capacity retention of Li/S cell with EPT electrolyte displayed 38% capacity higher than that of the cell with baseline electrolyte. We disassembled the Li/S pouch cells after the cycling test. It was observed that lithium anode in the cell with baseline electrolyte turned greyish and mesh-like, indicating a dramatical stripping; while the lithium anode in the cell using EPT modified electrolyte still keep integrity and shiny, showing that the lithium anode is much more stable in our proprietary electrolyte during cycling.

By consolidation of high loading C/S cathode, EPT modified electrolyte and EPT proprietary polymer separator into a pouch cell, EPT Li/S cell not only showed the improved cycle performance but also promoted intermittence discharge and shelf life. As shown in Figure 3, after three days of holding, the capacity loss between continuous and intermittent discharge of EPT Li/S prototype cell was 7.91%. Even after three weeks of rest, the capacity loss is just slighter increased (8.78%), showing the good capacity holding of EPT Li/S pouch cell.

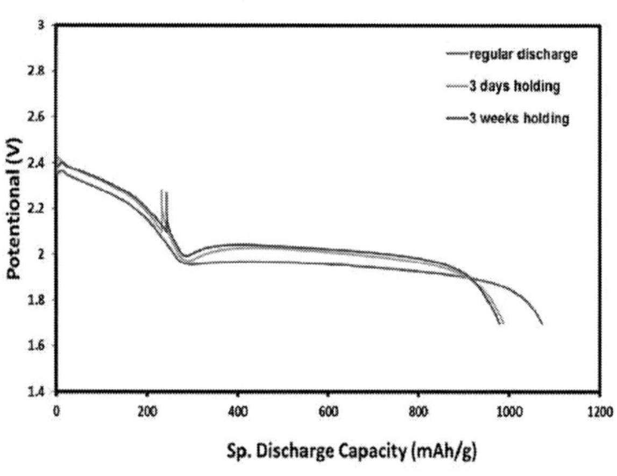

Figure 3. Intermittence discharge performance of EPT Li/S prototype pouch cell.

The shelf life performance is another major challenge involved in Li/S chemistry. Due to the self-discharge and shuttling, it is difficult to maintain the capacity, especially at higher temperatures. Table 1 showed the shelf life performance of the EPT Li/S prototype pouch cells. At room temperature, the capacity of the cell remained at 1072.90 mAh/g, which is ~3.17% lower compared to its original discharge capacity after one month storage. When stored at 45 °C for 1 week, although the voltage of the cell dropped, the capacity lost was only 0.93%. The promoted shelf life performance could be attributed to the better stability towards the self-discharge because of the using EPT proprietary electrolyte and improved cell design.

Table 1. Summary of the shelf life performance of EPT Li/S prototype cells.

Test Condition	Capacity (mAh/g)	Capacity Lost (%)
RT, regular discharge	1108.06	-
RT, 1 week storage	1090.85	1.56
RT, 1 month storage	1072.90	3.17
45°C, regular discharge	1074.22	-
45°C, 1 week storage	1064.22	0.93

Safety testing including nail penetration, overcharge, external short-circuit and forced discharge were carried out in EPT Li/S prototype pouch cells. One of the safety evaluations, short-circuit test, was showed in Figure 4. The test was based on the UN safety testing method by using 1.5mΩ as resistance. During the short, the current went up to 21 Amp and the cell temperature sharply increased to around 65°C; however, the Li/S prototype cell did not show any physical damage, and no fire or smoke was observed.

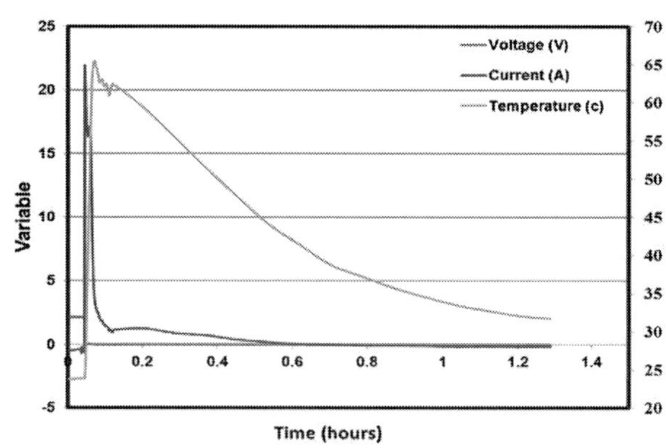

Figure 4. External short circuit test for Li/S prototype pouch cell.

All safety test conditions and results are summarized in Table 2. The Li/S prototype cells passed all the safety tests including nail penetration, overcharge/discharge as well as external short-circuit. The initial evaluation on Li/S prototype cell suggests this technology is very promising in terms of safety.

Table 2. Summary of safety test performance of EPT Li/S prototype cells.

Test	Conditions	Observation	Result
Nail Penetration	-Fresh cell at 100% SOC -After 5 cycles at 100% SOC -After 25 cycles at 100% SOC	No swelling, smoke, fire or flame	Passed Passed Passed
Over Charge at 1C rate	Cell cycled 5 times and tested overcharge started at 100% SOC.	Cell Swelled, no smoke, fire or flame Electrolyte leaked	Passed
External Short-Circuit	Cell cycled 5 times and tested at 100% SOC Resistance slightly lower than the cell internal resistance	Cell slightly swelled no physical damage	Passed
Forced Discharge	Cell cycled 5 times and tested at 100% SOC Discharge rate at C/8	No Physical damage	Passed

Conclusion

Targeting for commercial applications of Li/S batteries, EPT are systematically developing the Li/S technology to overcome the intrinsic challenges within Li/S chemistry. EPT Li/S prototype pouch cell, including high loading C/S cathode, EPT modified electrolyte and novel polymer separator, showed the good active materials utilization, better cyclability, improved intermittence and shelf life performance. In addition, EPT Li/S prototype cell demonstrated the inherent safety as well. The overall improvement represents a meaningful progress towards industrial practicality for Li/S system.

Acknowledgements

This material is released to the public domain in accordance with ITAR 22 CFR 120.11.

References

1. Armand, M., Tarascon, J. M. "Building Better Batteries," *Nature*, vol 451, pp. 652-657, 2008.
2. YOO, H. D., Markevich, E., Salitra, G., Sharon, D. Aurbach, D. "On the challenge of developing advanced technologies for electrochemical energy storage," *Materials Today*, vol 17, pp. 110-121, 2014.
3. Evers, S., Nazar, L. F. "New Approaches for High Energy Density Lithium-Sulfur Battery Cathodes," *Accounts of Chemical Research*, vol 46, pp. 1135-1143, 2013.
4. Bruce, P. G., Freunberger, S. A. Hardwick, L. J., Tarascon, J. M. " $Li\text{-}O_2$ and Li-S batteries with higher energy storage," *Natural Materials*, vol 11, pp. 19-29, 2012.
5. Liang, C., Dudney, N. J., Howe, J. Y. "Hierarchically Structured Sulfur/Carbon nanocomposite material for High-Energy Lithium Battery," *Chemistry of Materials*, vol 21, pp. 4724-4730, 2009.
6. Mikhaylik, Y. V., Akridge, J. R. "Polysulfide shuttle study in the Li/S battery system," *Journal of Electrochemical Society*, vol 151, pp. A1969-1976, 2004.

Electrochemical Performance of $Li_xMn_{2-y}Fe_yO_{4-z}Cl_z$ Synthesized Through In-Situ Glycine Nitrate Combustion

Ashley L. Ruth, Paula C. Latorre, and Terrill B. Atwater
U.S. Army Communications Electronics Research Development and Engineering Center
Power Division – Command Power and Integration
Aberdeen Proving Ground, MD, USA, 21005

Abstract: *Lithium manganese oxide spinel is an attractive material for lithium-ion battery cathodes due to its 3D network of lithium pathways within the structure. However, this material suffers from limited cyclability as a result of structural decomposition through extended lithium insertion and deinsertion cycling. This is due to the energy barriers for removing lithium from the octahedral sites as well as the formation of Mn^{3+} ions via the Jahn-Teller effect. The use of the glycine nitrate combustion synthesis produces small particles at reduced time and temperature during the calcining step of the synthesis process, which affords a uniform introduction of a Fe B-site modifier of AB_2O_4. This work incorporates chlorine to form more polarized Metal-Cl bonds to assist with liquid to solid transfer of Li^+ during the initial Fe-doping synthesis; this allows total production time to be achieved in less than 8 hours, preventing extended calcining times and at elevated temperatures which cause defect association leading to phase separation. These electrochemical cells cycle between 4.5 V and 3.5 V at 1.0 mA cm^{-2} (10 mA g_{active}^{-1}) and achieve over 250 cycles, maintaining 98% of original discharge at 71 mAh g^{-1}. Additionally, when cycled to a deeper potential at 2.25 V the electrochemical cell delivered a capacity of 142 mAh g^{-1} and is completely reversible without negatively impacting further cycling. This performance allows for access to energy at extended cycling and across potential regimes.*

Keywords: Li-ion battery; Lithium manganese oxide spinel; spinel cathode; Fe-doping; secondary lithium battery

Introduction

High voltage lithium manganese oxide spinels have been utilized in cathode materials for lithium-ion batteries due to their affordability and low toxicity while maintaining reasonable capacity [1-3]. However, this spinel suffers from capacity fading as a result of structural degradation either through the Jahn-Teller distortion, alternative phase formation via non-stoichiometry, or loss of crystallinity [4-6]. In an effort to combat these concerns, cycle life improvements have been achieved through stabilization of the spinel structure via transition metal doping on the B-site of the AB_2O_4 lattice [7-15]. The transition metal iron is a suitable dopant because of its low toxicity, but primarily due to affordability. Iron also has a high voltage redox couple of Fe^{3+} and Fe^{4+} at ~ 5.1 V allowing for high voltage applications [16-19]. Taniguchi and Bakenov demonstrate an increased capacity retention of $LiMn_{2-x}Fe_xO_4$ versus the undoped $LiMn_2O_4$ spinel over 100 cycles using a flame pyrolysis synthesis method [20]. While B-site doping has improved cyclability, adding anion dopants could enhance cycle life in $Li_xMn_{2-y}Fe_yO_4$ (LMFO). Our group as well as other researchers have added chlorine and more commonly fluorine and demonstrated performance enhancements [9, 13-14, 21-24]. However, many studies tend to coat the halide onto the surface of the spinel rather than incorporating it homogenously into the lattice. Liu et al. prepared a homogenous $LiMn_2O_{4-z}Cl_z$ material via a citrate gel method that demonstrated promising results [24]. Unfortunately only 10 charge/discharge cycles were reported. With regard to fluorine addition, Son and Kim as well as Amatucci et al. show an improvement in capacity with fluorine doping, however the discharge capacity rapidly declines resulting in short cycle life [14, 23].

This work intends to study the impact of adding the less common chlorine anion dopant on the cyclability of the B-site doped $Li_xMn_{2-y}Fe_yO_4$ material. By taking advantage of submicron ceramic synthesis, namely the glycine nitrate combustion process (GNP), we propose the capability for *in-situ* B-site doping and anion doping to synthesize the $Li_xMn_{2-y}Fe_yO_{4-z}Cl_z$ material.

Experimental

A glycine nitrate combustion method was used to synthesize iron doped chlorinated lithium manganese oxide spinel (LMFO-Cl). Stoichiometric amounts of $Li(NO_3)$ and $Mn(NO_3)_2{\cdot}4H_2O$ (Alfa Aesar) with $FeCl_3$ were mixed to incorporate both the iron and chlorine content then dissolved in DI H_2O. NH_2CH_2COOH (glycine, Alfa Aesar) was dissolved into the aqueous solution as a chelating agent in a 1:1 metal-ion to glycine ratio. The solution was heated to 80°C until the water fully evaporated and a gel was formed. The gel was heated further to 250°C when auto ignition occurs and formed a black ash. The ash was collected and ground in a mortar and pestle and fired at 600°C for two hours to achieve the desired phase.

Phase purity was determined using x-ray diffraction (XRD, Bruker D8 Advance, Cu-kα. chlorine content was determined from x-ray fluorescence spectroscopy (XRF,

Bruker S2 Ranger) after firing for phase formation. Experimental button cells were assembled using a lithium anode separated from the cathode by a 0.01 cm nonwoven glass separator. $Li_xMn_{2-y}Fe_yO_{4-z}Cl_z$ cathode was fabricated by mixing together the active material, carbon, and polytetrafluoroethylene (PTFE) in an 85:10:5 by weight ratio, respectively. The cathode mixture was rolled to 0.04 cm and dried in a vacuum oven. A 0.075 cm thick lithium foil was cut using a 12.7 mm hole punch. The cathode was cut into 1.0 cm^2 discs of approximately 0.13 g. The electrolyte used was 1 molar $LiPF_6$ in a proportional mixture of diethyl carbonate, dimethyl carbonate, and ethylene carbonate.

Cells were cycled with an ARBIN MSTAT4 battery cycler system controlled by MITS Pro software. The cells were charged and discharged from 4.5 V to 3.5 V, 4.5 V to 2.25 V, or 4.75 V to 3.5 V. The charge/discharge rates were maintained at 1.0 mA cm^{-2} or 2.0 mA cm^{-2}. A rest period of 15 minutes between charge and discharge cycles was used to allow for cells to achieve equilibrium on all experiments.

Results and Discussion

In order to confirm correct phase formation, XRD was performed on the $Li_xMn_{2-y}Fe_yO_{4-z}Cl_z$ cathode material after calcination. Figure 1 shows the resultant diffraction spectrum as compared with the JCPDS file for $LiMn_2O_4$ spinel (PDF 01-070-3120). While a slight shift is expected due to the iron dopant, no additional peaks are detected, indicating relative phase purity with no secondary phases that may not participate electrochemically.

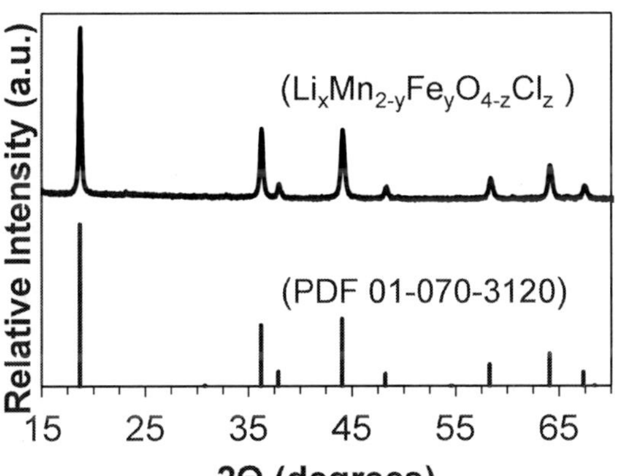

Figure 1. X-ray diffraction results for $Li_xMn_{2-y}Fe_yO_{4-z}Cl_z$ cathode material as compared with JCPDS file (PDF 01-070-3120) for $LiMn_2O_4$ spinel.

The energetic nature of the ignition synthesis method or the calcination process could have resulted in loss of the chlorine dopant. In order to address this concern, the $Li_xMn_{2-y}Fe_yO_{4-z}Cl_z$ cathode material was observed using XRF to confirm the maintenance of chlorine after the calcination to the correct phase is complete. Figure 2 shows the elemental components of the calcined material. Si, P, and S are expected background due to the polymer sample holder. The Pd peaks are the signature of the Pd x-ray source. As expected, there is very high (off the chart) intensity for the Mn and Fe peaks. Due to overlap, the Fe is confirmed by the Kb1 emission 7.06 keV. Most importantly, the Cl peak is clearly discernable, showing the presence of chlorine in the $Li_xMn_{2-y}Fe_yO_{4-z}Cl_z$ material after calcination.

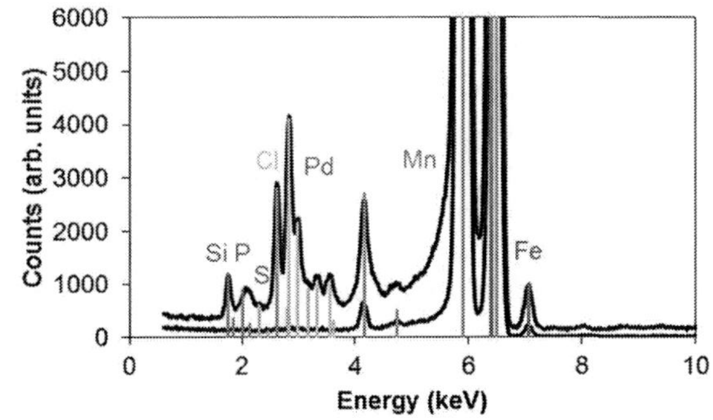

Figure 2. X-ray fluorescence results for the $Li_xMn_{2-y}Fe_yO_{4-z}Cl_z$ cathode material.

Electrochemical measurements were performed on the $Li_xMn_{2-y}Fe_yO_{4-z}Cl_z$ cathode material opposite a Li metal anode and results are shown in Figures 3-5 for y = 0.195 and z = 0.028. In Figure 3, the coulombic efficiency and charge and discharge capacities are shown up to 250 cycles. Beyond 250 cycles the periodic shorting indicated by overcharge data points worsens. However, the discharge capacity at cycle 250 is still greater than 98% of the original discharge capacity, demonstrating a very long cycle life.

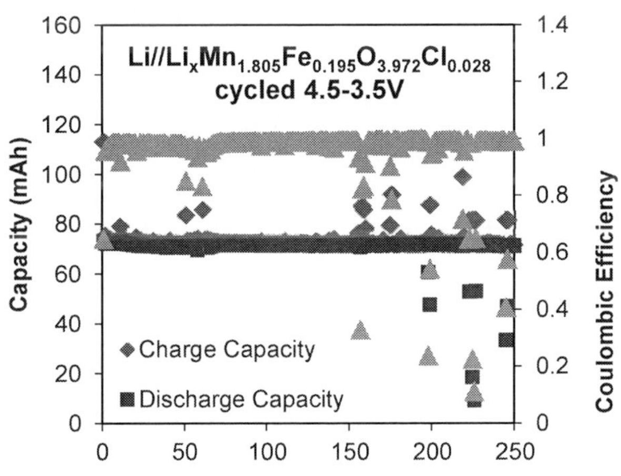

Figure 3. Specific capacity (bottom) and coulombic efficiency (top) during 250 charge/discharge cycles of a $Li_xMn_{2-y}Fe_yO_{4-z}Cl_z$ experimental button cell where $y = 0.195$ and $z = 0.028$.

The periodic shorting shown in Figure 3 is not a desirable characteristic for cells in operation, but these shorts are a result of the laboratory scale cell fabrication. The separator is a nonwoven glass separator that acts as a wick rather than a true separator that could prevent shorting through dendritic growth. So the lithium can easily form whiskers and subsequent cycling can grow them long enough to short. Once the short is alleviated, the cell returns to normal cycling behavior.

A differential capacity curve was generated from the charge/discharge data at several cycles to observe the changes over time. The resultant data is shown in Figure 4. The electrochemical peaks begin to shift in voltage and exhibit peak broadening. This shift could be due either electrolyte degradation or a breakdown of the spinel structure of the cathode. However, because the capacity remains intact through cycling, it is unlikely that the cathode is suffering from structural degradation. $LiPF_6$ electrolytes are known to degrade at high voltages (greater than 4.5V) and is a well-known culprit for poor extended performance in high voltage lithium-ion battery cathodes [25-26]. Therefore, the spinel chemistry is demonstrated to be robust enough for extended cycling should a suitable electrolyte be used.

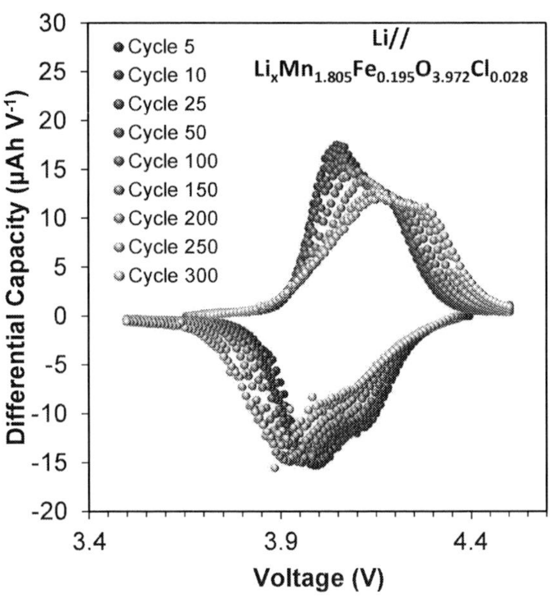

Figure 4. Differential capacity curves for cycles 5, 10, 25, 50, 100, 150, 200, 150, and 300 of a $Li_xMn_{2-y}Fe_yO_{4-z}Cl_z$ experimental cell for $y = 0.195$ and $z = 0.028$.

Beyond 250 cycles, an attempt to discharge the experimental cell below 3.5 V to 2.25 V was made in order to determine if there is any vulnerability of the cell at this deep discharge. This was performed at cycle 286 and is shown in Figure 5. Cycles 299 and 300 cycled from 4.5 V to 3.5 V and are also shown in Figure 5. These cycles are comparable to the deeper discharge of cycle 286 in the 4.5 V to 3.5 V regime, as expected. However, the fact that cycles 299 and 300 exist is a testament to the ability of this chemistry to withstand significant lithium insertion and still continue to cycle in the normal operating regime at 98% of original discharge capacity at 71 mAh/g. During the deep discharge to 2.25 V at cycle 286, a discharge capacity of 142 mAh/g is achieved. This is twice that of the upper voltage regime, as expected from the chemistry of inserting an additional lithium into the spinel cathode lattice.

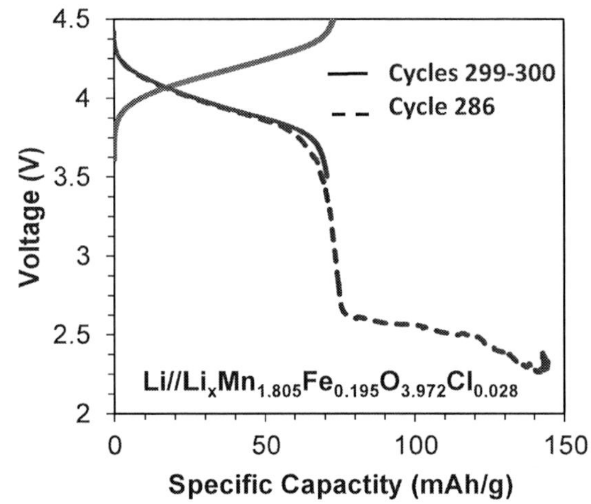

Figure 5. Charge (red) /discharge (blue) curves for cycles 286, 299, and 300 of an $Li_xMn_{2-y}Fe_yO_{4-z}Cl_z$ experimental cell for $y = 0.195$ and $z = 0.028$. A solid line indicates 4.5 V to 3.5 V cycling, and dashed lines indicates a full deep discharge to 2.25 V at 2.0 mA/cm^2.

Conclusions

A high voltage capable $Li_xMn_{2-y}Fe_yO_{4-z}Cl_z$ spinel cathode material was synthesized using very fast processing times taking advantage of the high energy precursor formation from the glycine nitrate combustion reaction. This allowed for a very short 2 hour calcination at just 600 °C to form the correct phase while retaining the chlorine addition. Testing this $Li_xMn_{2-y}Fe_yO_{4-z}Cl_z$ cathode material in an electrochemical cell opposite a lithium metal anode resulted in excellent cycle life up to 250 cycles and beyond with greater than 98% of the original discharge capacity. Future work would include incorporating a more robust separator as well as a high voltage electrolyte that will not degrade at advanced cycling at high voltages. More research is needed for selecting the appropriate high voltage electrolyte for this system. Should an adequate electrolyte be used in addition to a separator that can prevent dendritic shorts, an even greater cycle life of this $Li_xMn_{2-y}Fe_yO_{4-z}Cl_z$ cathode chemistry may be realized.

References

[1] H. Xia, Y.S. Meng, M.O. Lai, L. Lu, Journal of The Electrochemical Society, 157 (2010) A348-A354.
[2] B. Ebin, S. Gürmen, C. Arslan, G. Lindbergh, Electrochimica Acta, 76 (2012) 368-374.
[3] D. Liu, W. Zhu, J. Trottier, C. Gagnon, F. Barray, A. Guerfi, A. Mauger, H. Groult, C.M. Julien, J.B. Goodenough, K. Zaghib, RSC Advances, 4 (2014) 154-167.
[4] H. Xia, Z. Luo, J. Xie, Progress in Natural Science: Materials International, 22 (2012) 572-584.
[5] H. Huang, C.A. Vincent, P.G. Bruce, Journal of The Electrochemical Society, 146 (1999) 3649-3654.
[6] Y. Xia, M. Yoshio, Journal of The Electrochemical Society, 143 (1996) 825-833.
[7] N.M. Hagh, G.G. Amatucci, Journal of Power Sources, 256 (2014) 457-469.
[8] S. Jayapal, R. Mariappan, S. Sundar, S. Piraman, Journal of Electroanalytical Chemistry, 720 (2014) 58-63.
[9] X. He, J. Li, Y. Cai, Y. Wang, J. Ying, C. Jiang, C. Wan, Journal of Power Sources, 150 (2005) 216-222.
[10] J. Morales, L. Sánchez, J. Tirado, Journal of Solid State Electrochemistry, 2 (1998) 420-426.
[11] J. Amarilla, J. Martin de Vidales, R. Rojas, Solid State Ionics, 127 (2000) 73-81.
[12] H.J. Bang, V. Donepudi, J. Prakash, Electrochimica Acta, 48 (2002) 443-451.
[13] G. Amatucci, A. Du Pasquier, A. Blyr, T. Zheng, J.-M. Tarascon, Electrochimica Acta, 45 (1999) 255-271.
[14] G. Amatucci, N. Pereira, T. Zheng, I. Plitz, J. Tarascon, Journal of Power Sources, 81 (1999) 39-43.
[15] C. Wu, F. Wu, L. Chen, X. Huang, Solid State Ionics, 152 (2002) 335-339.
[16] A. Eftekhari, Journal of Power Sources, 124 (2003) 182-190.
[17] M. Pico, I. Álvarez-Serrano, M. López, M. Veiga, Dalton Transactions, 43 (2014) 14787-14797.
[18] H. Kawai, M. Nagata, M. Tabuchi, H. Tukamoto, A.R. West, Chemistry of materials, 10 (1998) 3266-3268.
[19] L. Herna, J. Morales, L. Sanchez, E. Rodriguez Castello, and M.A.G. Arandab, *Journal of Materials Chemistry*, 12 (2002) 734–741.
[20] I. Taniguchi, Z. Bakenov, Powder technology, 159 (2005) 55-62.
[21] T. Atwater, P. Tavares, SAE International Journal of Materials and Manufacturing, 6 (2013) 85-89.
[22] T.B. Atwater, P.C. Tavares, in, US Patent 8,900,756, 2014.
[23] J. Son, H. Kim, Journal of Power Sources, 147 (2005) 220-226.
[24] W.-R. Liu, S.-H. Wu, H.-S. Sheu, Journal of Power Sources, 146 (2005) 232-236.
[25] L. Yang, B. Ravdel, B.L. Lucht, Electrochemical and Solid-State Letters, 13 (2010) A95-A97.
[26] L. Hu, Z. Zhang, K. Amine, Journal of Power Sources, 236 (2013) 175-180.

Wireless Power Transfer in Military Applications

Edward Dawidowicz, Thomas Podlesak, Hon Tsang, Katherine Duncan
CERDEC

Abstract - *Wireless power transfer (WPT) is a diverse multidisciplinary field with a continuously growing number of applications supported by evolving technologies enabling its progress. There is great potential for WPT in military applications. These applications span from safe and efficient recharging in a vehicle of wearable devices to remotely supplying power to platforms miles away from the source. Such applications require diverse technologies and are subject to safety constraints focused on minimizing human tissue exposure to electrical, magnetic and electromagnetic fields, while maximizing efficiency of energy transfer.*

Keywords – Magnetic resonance, electric resonance, transfer efficiency, lasers, photovoltaic, microwave, rectenna, WPT.

Introduction

References to the history of wireless power transfer (WPT) customary begin with the works of N. Tesla [1, 2], who at the turn of twentieth century pioneered applications wireless electrical energy transmission across free space. By the end of the 1960s W. Brown [3] demonstrated WPT using a 2.45GHz microwave system to hover a "helicopter", 8 m above the source at 26% energy transfer efficiency. Industrial application require WPT capability to aid safety requirement and employ loosely coupled resonant inductive coils to transfer significant amount of power [4]. Recently the progress on resonant inductive power transfer has been stimulated by the work at MIT [5], coupled with a growing interest for small devices to be recharged wirelessly. The advances in near and far field WPT have many applications [6]. More recently, with lasers becoming more efficient and capable of delivering sufficient power, a helicopter was kept hovering for hours using laser-based WPT [7].

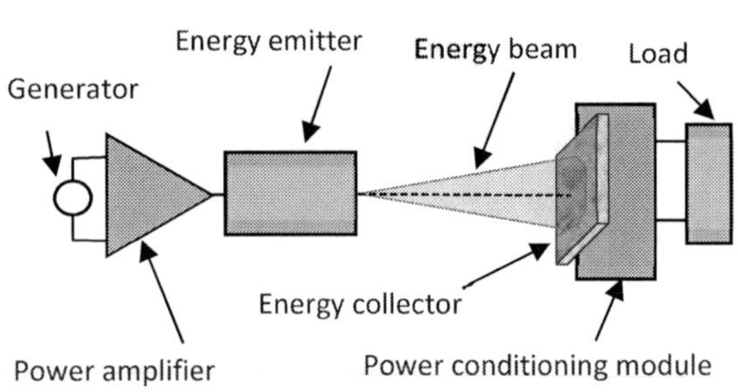

Figure 1. *Generalized WPT system*

While a traditional metallic wire is not ideal but is the most efficient medium to transport electrical energy between a source and a load, this efficiency comes at a price. The initial expense involves the cost of materials and labor required to set up the connections, and then the cost is compounded throughout the life of the system, to maintain damaged wires and clean dirty, corroded contacts. While WPT methods employ diverse physics phenomena they all share a common architecture as shown in Figure 1. The signal is amplified and transmitted across a medium to be captured by a collector. The collector transforms the received power to electricity. To maximize efficiency, the WPT network should match the impedance from the source to the load.

Methods and Applications

Before discussing application a short overview of particular methods of WPT is essential as a reference to this discussion. Notwithstanding conceptual similarities, WPT systems are rich in diversification and are subject to many disciplines. Here we mostly examine WPT based on electromagnetic phenomena, from near field to far field and from microwaves to infrared.

Resonant Magnetic and Resonant Electric Coupling

Electromagnetic induction, discovered in August of 1831 by Michael Faraday, is the foundation of both electrical machines and magnetically coupled WPT devices. Since air is a poor conductor of magnetic flux the transmitting and receiving coils should be in close proximity and well aligned.

Introducing resonance significantly improves magnetic coupling and allows for sufficient power to be efficiently transmitted. In 2007 the MIT group claimed transferring 60 W at 40% efficiency over the distance of 2 meters [8] for strongly coupled magnetic resonance. The size of the coils matters. The range can be extended further by employing resonant repeaters [9], however this is a subject of restricted geometry [10] since resonant repeaters are placed coaxially in the extended space, negating the advantage of gained distance in many applications. Use of metamaterial in place of resonating repeaters has been documented [11].

Strongly coupled magnetic resonance for midrange WPT has been recently revisited [12, 13] with application of both two and four coil systems. Whether two or four coil system is used the equivalent circuit is similar to one in Fig. 2(a).
Electric or capacitive power transfer allows the use of light conductive foils instead of more massive induction

coils, which would seem to save weight over their magnetically coupled counterparts Fig. 2 (b) [14, 15, 16]. While electric resonant circuit requires inductors their weight however is less than the transmitting and receiving coils in magnetic resonant device.

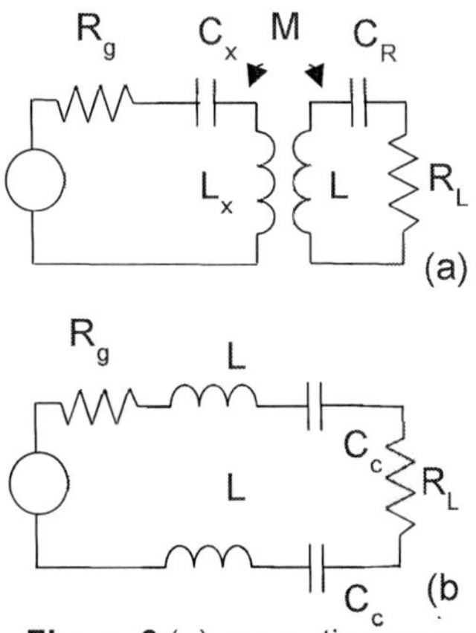

Figure 2 (a) magnetic resonant (b) electric resonant

In Vehicle en route charging

While en route, an individual needs to recharge a cell phone, computer or other personal devices. Today we simply plug in these devices into a cigarette lighter socket, often quickly realizing that the number of devices exceeds the number of sockets in a vehicle. It is possible to split the power sockets and to end up with an extension for every device requiring charging. When several people travel in the same vehicle, tangling of wires may even become a safety issue in a hastened or emergency egress.

For this application the use of a near field mid-range resonant power transfer of both magnetic and electric coupling is reasonable. The magnetic resonant technology appears safer and may have a lesser effect on the human body, compared to its electric counterpart. However, more studies are required, for each device, specifically with emphasis on power density and frequency considering exposure time and susceptibility of the human body organs to such exposure.

WPT Supply to Headgear

Lighter in weight, the electrical resonance WPT systems seems to be appropriate to deliver power to a vest and from a vest to a helmet. Wires, connecting vest to the helmet, can catch on external objects and cause injury to the user or break, rendering mission critical equipment mounted on the helmet inoperable.

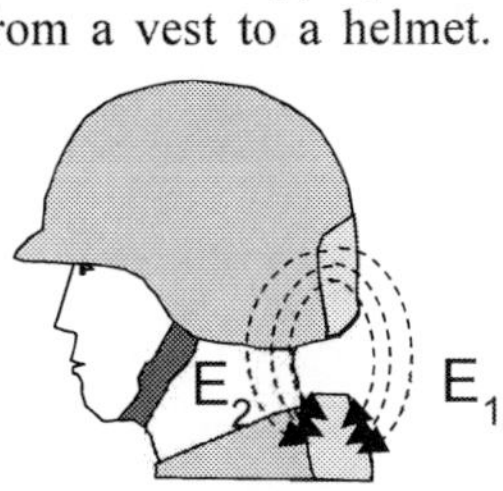

Figure 3 Insufficient electrical insulation can cause heating of

The electronics and power pack add a prohibitive weight to a helmet. Continuous supply of power from the main battery held by a vest could significantly reduce the power pack. The challenge would be in designing a receiver of lesser weight than the reduction attained on the power pack. Even at the breakeven point, where saved weight on the power pack is equal to the weight of the receiver, there is no need to burden a warfighter with carrying additional batteries for the mission duration. Light foils for capacitive coupling would appear to be more effective than more massive inductor coils. This application of capacitive WPT does encounter a couple of barriers.

In Fig. 3 the electric field has about equal path in length to take between coupling plates. The field E_2 is greater than E_1 since permittivity of biological tissue ε_{bt} is larger than that of air- ε_{air} [17]. The ε_{bt} is a complex quantity subject to frequency of the time varying electrical field. Such coupling is beneficial for power transfer, however may cause dangerous tissue exposure to electric field. Another issue emerges during parallel misalignment, shown in Fig. 4 where one of the load plates becomes effectively positioned between source plates, which will significantly disrupt power transfer to the load when a head is turned. To mitigate power interruption to the load, a small battery can keep the load energized during the power transfer disruption.

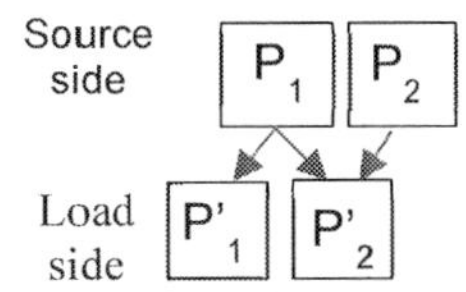

Figure 4 Drop in WPT caused by parallel misalignment

Microwave

Microwave is an attractive method for transferring energy across space using far-field radiation. The theory is well

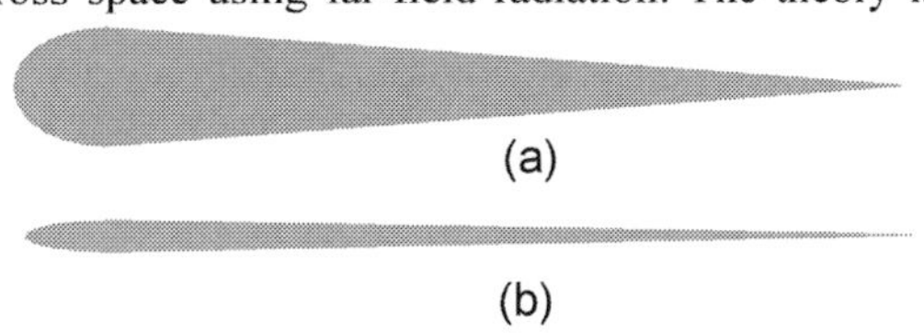

Figure 5 Effect of frequency on the beam of the same aperture (a) low frequency beam (b) high frequency beam

understood and technology is cost effective allowing the energy beaming across vast spaces to be possible, provided that the transmitted energy is not absorbed by the medium at the particular frequencies. Significant absorption of about 20dB of electromagnetic radiation by oxygen occurs in a narrow bandwidth around 60GHz [18], while water attenuates the same signal by only 2dB. Higher frequencies allow for lesser divergence and are desirable to minimize the size of both the receiving and transmitting antennas.

Antenna gain is proportional to the effective area of the aperture A_{eff} and inversely proportional to the square of the emitted wavelength λ:

Gain $G = 4\pi A_{eff}/\lambda^2$ (1)

The directivity of an antenna D is related to gain G by radiation efficiency of the antenna e_r:

$G = e_r D$ (2)

Finally by employing equation (1) the power density W at the receiver of total radiated P_{rad} through a solid angle $\Delta\Omega$ at a distance R is:

$$W = P_{rad} D / \Delta\Omega R^2 \quad (3)$$

Consider an example where a 500W of power delivered to the load over 500m by using dish antenna of: aperture efficiency $e_{ae} = 0.5$, antenna efficiency $e_r = 0.9$, gain 35dB, amplifier efficiency $\eta_{at} = 0.75$, transmitting efficiency $\eta_{rad} = 0.8$ at frequency f = 4GHz (λ=75mm). Total efficiency of conversion from electricity to radiated power is therefore 54%. The receiving antenna converts incoming power at an efficiency of $\eta_r = 0.8$ and an efficiency of power transfer to the load of $\eta_L = 0.85$ [19].

Using the above equations, the input power required was shown to be:

$$Pg = P_{rad}/\eta_{at}\eta_{rad} = 657\text{kW} / (0.75 \times 0.8) = 1095 \text{ kW}$$

The overall efficiency of this system at 500 m is:

$$\eta_{500} = 100\% \, (P_L/P_g) = 0.045\%$$

However, at 100m the efficiency significantly improves:

$$\eta_{100} = 1.1\%$$

The strong influence of the transmission distance on the efficiency of power transfer is evident. The efficiency can be increased by increasing the gain as shown in equation (1). From (1) the gain can be increased by increasing the size of the antenna, decreasing the wavelength or increasing the frequency. However in mobile applications the practical size of an antenna is severely limited suggesting that increase in frequency is an appropriate solution.

Laser

Referring again to equation (1) the gain of a transmitting antenna is inversely proportional to the square of the wavelength. Higher frequencies suggest higher gains and therefore higher power densities delivered to the target.

Using equation (3) we have:

$$W_t = P_{rad} \, A_{eff} / (e_r \, R^2 \lambda^2). \quad (4)$$

From equation (4) lasers, operating on even shorter wavelength, will deliver a greater power density at a larger distance [20]. There is no shortage of the variations of available lasers [21-23]; however, only those that are efficient in conversion of electric energy to light and systems capable of producing beams of low divergence are of particular interest to WPT applications. While the power conversion electrical-to-optical, or wall-plug efficiency, have been claimed to exceed 30% and propagations loses of about 10% over 1.5 km [24], is remarkable yielding a performance of 27% still has sufficient room for improvement.

The wall-plug efficiency is only a part of the overall transfer performance, and capture of light energy poses an even greater challenge. There are potentially several ways to capture energy emitted by a laser system: infrared rectenna, thermal photovoltaic (TPV), visible spectrum PV, pyroelectric devices, thermo-electric generators (TEGs).

Development of infrared rectennas has proven challenging in near infrared range [25] and so far their efficiency is in the range of a fraction of a percent. However the seeming simplicity of their construction makes them a particularly engaging area for further research. There are several other technologies. The thermal phovoltaic (TPV) [26] array in conjunction with TEG within allowable temperature gradient could potentially provide a reasonable efficiency in capturing and converting light into electrical energy; however, TEG plates could be too heavy to be used on small UAVs. The need of higher efficiency technology to convert photons to electricity is apparent for such applications and matching the wavelength of the transmitted light to the bandgap of TPV seems to be a viable solution. .

UAV and Sensor Grid Recharging

When it comes to WPT across large distances the microwaves and lasers systems are well suited to recharge UAVs in flight and replenish the energy storage of remotely located sensors. Such capability will extend the flight endurance of surveillance UAVs and prevent the exposing of personnel to hostile environments by allowing a UAV to recharge remotely position grid sensors. While laser are more efficient at longer distances microwave applications are viable players in 100-500m range.

The laser power densities required to recharge an airborne UAV, regardless of the wavelength, are in excess of permissible safety limits. Interlock safety devices must be in place to ensure that if anything comes close to the energy beam will trigger a safety interlock device capable to quickly interrupt the power beam. The beam also should not overshoot the target thereby exposing manned or unmanned airborne platforms to dangerous laser's emissions.

Conclusion

The WPT devices for military is analogous to commercial applications as they share similar human factors in safety, efficiency and utility. In military applications additional factors, include increased reliability, minimization of electromagnetic radiation emissions, electromagnetic interference, and effects of prolonged exposure of magnetic and electric fields is thoroughly considered.

While most consumer applications of magnetic or electric resonance WPT systems are content with stationary well aligned inductor coils and capacitor plates the military applications call for continually changing alignments between transmitting and receiving components while committed to maintain high efficiency in energy transfer which in turn add levels of complexity in design and operation.

Implementation of both microwave and lasers WPT methods offer new capabilities to allow remote recharging of stationary sensors including robotic and autonomous devices as far as several kilometers away. Such capability automates recharging process, prevents employing costly human labor, and exposing valuable personnel to existing threats.

References

1. N. Tesla "System of transmission of electrical energy", US Patent 645,576, Mar. 20 1900.
2. N. Tesla, "The Transmission of Electric Energy without Wires (The Thirteenth Anniversary Number of the Electrical World and Engineer). New York: McGraw-Hill, Mar. 5, 1904.
3. Brown W.C., Experiments Involving a Microwave Beam to Power and Position a Helicopter", *IEEE Transactions on Aerospace and Electronic Systems :AES-5*, 5, Sept. 1969
4. Chwei-Sen Wang, Grant A. Covic, Oskar H. Stielau, "Power Transfer Capability and Bifurcation Phenomena of Loosely Coupled Inductive Power Transfer Systems", *IEEE Transactions on Industrial Electronics, 51*, 1, Feb. 2004
5. A Karalis, JD Joannopoulos, M Soljačić , "Efficient wireless non-radiative mid-range energy transfer", *Annals of Physics*, 2008 – Elsevier
6. Garnica, J. ; Chinga, R.A. ; Jenshan Lin, "Wireless Power Transmission: From Far Field to Near Field", *Proceedings of the IEEE , 101* , 2013
7. Lin Edwards, "Lasers keep mini helicopter hovering for Hours", 9 September 2010, PhysOrg.com, http://phys.org/news203231075.html
8. André Kurs, *et al.,* "Wireless Power Transfer via Strongly Coupled Magnetic Resonances", *Science, 317*, 83 (2007).
9. K. E. Koh, et. al.,., "Multi-receiver and repeater wireless power transfer via magnetic resonance coupling impedance matching and power division utilizing impedance inverter," *The 15th Int. Conf. on Electrical Machines and Systems (ICEMS2012),* 2012
10. Bin Luo, Shichuang Wu, and Nanrun Zhou, "Flexible Design Method for Multi-Repeater Wireless Power Transfer System Based on Coupled Resonator Bandpass Filter Model" , , *IEEE Transactions on Circuits and Systems I: Regular Papers, 61* , 11
11. Wang, B.; Nishino, T.; Teo, K.H. Wireless Power Transmission Efficiency Enhancement with Metamaterials", *Proceedings of the IEEE International Conference on Wireless Information Technology and Systems (ICWITS),* Honolulu, HI, USA, 28 August 2010–3 September 2010; pp. 1–4.
12. Xuezhe Wei, Zhenshi Wang, and Haifeng Dai, "A Critical Review of Wireless Power Transfer via Strongly Coupled Magnetic Resonances", *Energies 2014, 7*,7, pp. 4316-4341;
13. S. Y. R. Hui, W. X. Zhong and C. K. Lee "A critical review of recent progress in mid-range wireless power transfer", *IEEE Trans. Power Electronics, 29,* 9, Sept. 2014.
14. Fnato, H. ; Chiku, Y. ; Harakawa, K., "Wireless power distribution with capacitive coupling excited by switched mode active negative capacitor" , *2010 International Conference on Electrical Machines and Systems (ICEMS) 2010* , pp. 117 - 122
15. M. Kline, I. Izyumin, B. Boser, and S. Sanders, "Capacitive power transfer for contactless charging", *Proc. of 2011 IEEE Applied Power Electronics Conference and Exposition (APEC)*, pp. 1398-1404, Mar. 2011
16. Jingook Kim ; Bien, F., "Electric field coupling technique of wireless power transfer for electric vehicles" , *2013 IEEE TENCON Spring Conference*
17. Mark J Schroeder, Anupama Sadasiva, Robert M Nelson "An Analysis on the Role of Water Content and State on Effective Permittivity Using Mixing Formulas", *Journal of Biomechanics, Biomedical and Biophysical Engineering, 2,* 1, 2008
18. FEDERAL COMMUNICATIONS COMMISSION OFFICE OF ENGINEERING AND TECHNOLOGY Bulletin Number 70 July, 1997
19. E. Dawidowicz, T. Podlesak, F. Leung, "Wireless Power Transfer Using Microwave and Infrared Radiation", *46th Power Sources Conference*, 2014
20. L. Summerer, O. Purcell, "Concepts for wireless energy transmission via laser", http://www.esa.int/gsp/ACT/doc/POW/ACT-RPR-NRG-2009-SPS-ICSOS-concepts-for-laser-WPT.pdf
21. Milonni P. W., Eberly J H., *Laser Physics*, John Wiley & Sons, 2010
22. Gary B. Hughes et al., "DE-STAR: Phased-Array Laser Technology for Planetary Defense and Other Scientific Purposes", *Nanophotonics and Macrophotonics for Space Environments VII Proceedings*: San Diego, CA, August 25, 2013.
23. M. A. Vorontsov, et al. "Adaptive array of phase-locked fiber collimators: analysis and experimental demonstration." *IEEE Journal of Selected Topics in Quantum Electronics, 15*, 2 (2009): 269-280.
24. P. Sprangle et al., "High-Power Fiber Lasers for Directed-Energy Applications", 2008 NRL REVIEW.
25. M. Dagenais, et al., "Solar Spectrum Rectification Using Nano-Antennas and Tunneling Diodes", Optoelectronic Integrated Circuits XII. Edited by Eldada, Louay A.; Lee, El-Hang. *Proceedings of the SPIE*, 7605, pp. 76050E-76050E-12 (2010).
26. N. G. Dhere, "Polycrystalline-Thin-Film Thermo photovoltaic Cells", American Institute of Physics, 1996.

Warfighter Wireless Recharging System

Kieran Peleaux and Charles Greene
Powercast Corporation
Pittsburgh, PA, USA

Abstract: *The system designed offers an alternative approach to powering and recharging electronic devices carried by soldiers which eliminates the need for traditional wired charging interfaces. Through the principles of magnetic coupling and mutual inductance, the system transfers power wirelessly from a transmitter embedded within the seatback of a military vehicle to a rechargeable battery carried on the soldier's person. The final developed system demonstrated 67% efficient wireless power transfer of 60 Watts over a distance of six inches, verifying the promising potential of a transparent solution for effortlessly charging the batteries in soldiers' tactical vests.*

Keywords: Wireless Power; Wireless Recharging; Inductive Coupling; Warfighter Recharging.

Introduction

In modern military environments, technology plays an invaluable role in everything from communications to weapon systems. Central to the functionality of these technologies is the requirement of power sources for charging and powering the electronics behind them. Oftentimes optimizing the availability of such power sources presents a significant challenge, which becomes even more difficult when dealing with portable electronics [1]. With a device that must be recharged, battery life must be carefully weighed against portability, and the charging procedure needs to be as hassle-free and unobtrusive as possible [2]. In seeking a system that can recharge on the fly—without a superfluous charging procedure—wireless power transfer emerges as an ideal solution.

Such a system requires careful consideration on numerous fronts. In examining current wireless power transfer technologies, those utilized for powering medical devices stand out for their high efficiency and tolerance over distance, alignment and load characteristics [3]. Other popular, short-range wireless power solutions, such as inductive magnetic coupling or magnetic resonance, sacrifice efficiency over distance or require highly resonant coils in a narrow frequency band [4]. Additionally, electromagnetic interference (EMI) requirements strictly limit the amount of electromagnetic emissions that a device can radiate, especially in a military environment with other potentially sensitive electronics [5].

This paper details a wireless power transfer system that addresses these considerations by examining existing technologies and their weaknesses and presenting a novel approach for charging the battery in a soldier's vest from a transmitter embedded in the seatback of a military vehicle. The system is capable of high efficiency over variation in distance, coil alignment and loads, and employs a custom spread spectrum magnetic coupling technology to comply with regulatory EMI requirements and minimize RF signature.

Overview

The Warfighter Wireless Recharging System is an adaptation of an existing patented spread spectrum magnetic coupling technology that was developed for efficiently transferring energy to a high-power medical implant. The developed system consists of two main components, the Vehicle Seat Transmitter and the Tactical Vest Receiver.

The Vehicle Seat Transmitter consists of a Primary Controller Printed Circuit Board Assembly (PCBA) and a transmitting coil integrated into the vehicle seatback. The Primary Controller drives the coil with an AC signal to create a magnetic field around the coil. A custom-fabricated ferrite sheet acts as low-loss shielding to prevent interference from conductive materials in the vehicle seat. Based on feedback communicated from the Tactical Vest Receiver via a high-speed wireless radio link, the Primary Controller manages the drive signal to the coil and regulates the power delivered to the Tactical Vest Receiver.

The Tactical Vest Receiver consists of a receiving coil—mounted in the back of the tactical vest—and a Secondary Battery Charger PCBA that contains receiver and battery recharging circuitry. The receiver circuitry rectifies and converts the signal received from the coil to DC power and the battery recharging circuitry manages the charging of a Li-Ion battery pack housed in the vest.

Regulation is accomplished by feedback from the system receiver to the transmitter, which communicates data via a high-speed wireless radio link. The system is powered by 28VDC from the vehicle. Figure 1 shows a block diagram of the described system.

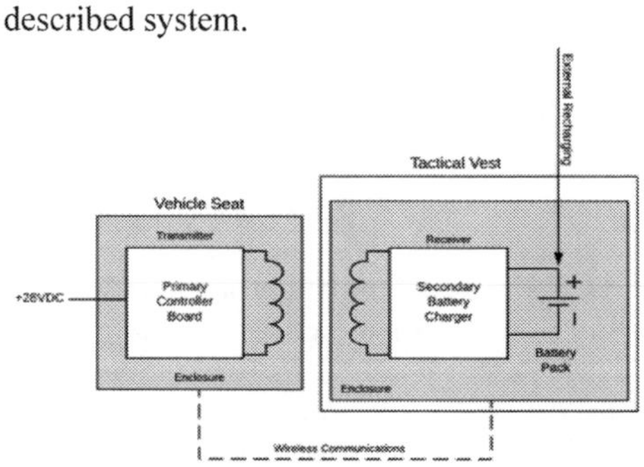

Figure 1. Block Diagram of Transparent Warfighter Recharging System

Theory of Operation

Spread Spectrum Magnetic Coupling: The designed system operates on the principal of magnetic coupling between two inductive coils. In such a system a transmitting coil is driven with an AC current to create a varying magnetic field in the vicinity of the driven coil. A receiving coil placed in this vicinity will have a voltage induced across it, provided that it intersects the flux created by the driven coil. This characteristic is described by Faraday's Law. The magnitude of the voltage induced across the receiving coil depends on the percentage of the transmitting coil's flux intersected by the receiving coil. The ratio of the partial flux enclosed by the receiving coil to the current in the transmitting coil is the mutual inductance between the two coils. The magnetic field of a conductor loop and the flux linkage between two coils are shown graphically in Figure 2.

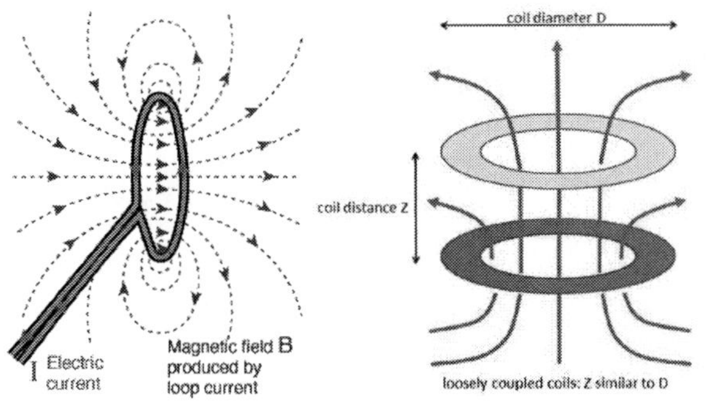

(A) (B)

Figure 2. (A) Magnetic Field of Conductor Loop (B) Flux Linkage Between Two Coils [6]

Narrow-band magnetic inductive power transmission can generate significant electromagnetic interference (EMI). This can result in failure to meet regulatory requirements laid out by the FCC and a large RF signature for the device. The designed system mitigates the problems associated with EMI by utilizing spread spectrum frequency modulation for power transmission. The spread spectrum modulation used is frequency hopping spread spectrum (FHSS). In FHSS modulation, power is transmitted via a primary coil at frequencies varying—or spread—within a specified range under according to a spread spectrum algorithm.

Use of frequency hopping spread spectrum modulation spreads the fundamental and harmonic energy across a number of frequency band channels on a wider electromagnetic spectrum, resulting in decreased narrowband interference and lower average power per channel.

The specifics of the coils developed for this system were primarily dictated by the size of the Tactical Vest and by the need for highly efficient power transfer. In testing the transfer efficiency of various coil diameters, a 9-inch diameter coil was found to yield the highest transfer efficiency at a distance of 6 inches. Additionally, the 9-inch coil was found to fit on a large range of body types—from the 95th percentile male down to the 5th percentile female—making it the optimal size for all aspects of the system. The material of the coil was also carefully selected to optimize power transfer efficiency. Litz wire was used to minimize coil resistance and dramatically increase transfer efficiency.

Primary Controller Board: The Primary Controller Board takes in +28V from the vehicle as its primary power supply. A DC/DC converter is required to optimize the coil supply voltage for maximum transfer efficiency. The coil supply voltage is then transformed to produce the spread spectrum AC drive signal that is sent to the attached Primary Coil. This was accomplished with an H-bridge containing low on-resistance MOSFETs and an H-bridge driver. The spread spectrum clock signal needed by the H-bridge driver is produced by an embedded software algorithm executed by a microprocessor.

The Primary Controller Board also contains a Control Loop Receiver which receives data commands from the Secondary Battery Charger. These data commands are based on power signals received from the Primary Coil. The commands are used by the Primary Control Board to vary the on-time of power transmission pulses, and therefore the amount of energy transferred to the Secondary Battery Charger. This method provides the most efficient transfer of energy because the wireless power transfer is optimized for maximum efficiency at peak power transfer. This functionality is controlled by a microprocessor and embedded software that responds to the data communication commands. The Primary Controller Board was designed to detect the presence of a Secondary Battery Charger and negotiate energy transfer. Without the presence of a Secondary Battery Charger, the Primary Control Board remains in a low power sleep state with periodic pings to check for a Secondary Battery Charger's presence. A block diagram of the Primary Controller Board can be seen in Figure 3.

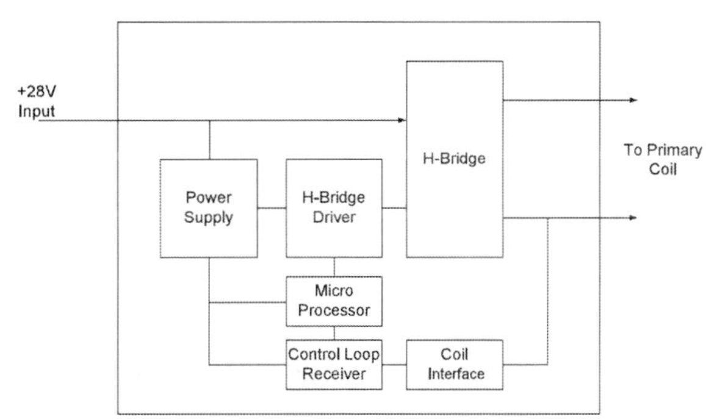

Figure 3. Block Diagram of Primary Controller Board

Secondary Battery Charging Board: The Secondary Battery Charging Board transforms the signal captured by the Secondary Coil into DC voltage, which then charges the battery within the soldier's tactical vest. First, the received signal is rectified with a highly efficient bridge rectifier constructed of Schottky diodes. A bank of capacitors filters the resulting signal and stores its energy. For the next stage, commercially available battery recharging chips were explored, but these chips tend to have lower efficiencies that dramatically reduce the overall system efficiency. Therefore, a custom battery recharging circuit was designed to help maximize the end-to-end efficiency of the system. The Secondary Battery Charger also includes a Control Loop Transmitter for sending control signals to the Primary Controller Board using a separate frequency from the wireless power transfer. The data, generated by a microprocessor, monitors the conditions of the battery charging and makes control decisions using an embedded software algorithm. This data includes commands to increase, decrease, stop, start or maintain the current charging status.

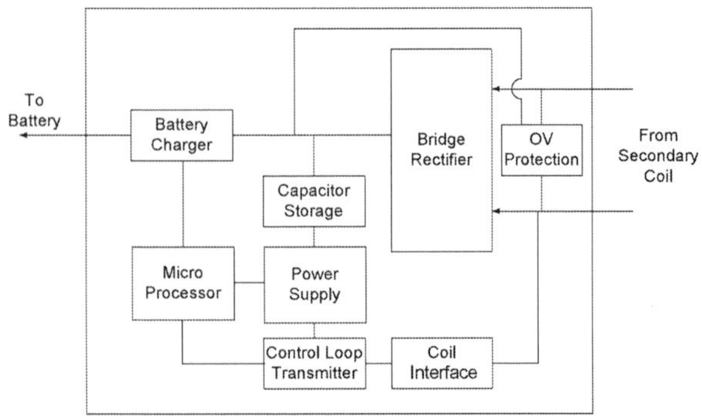

Figure 4. Block Diagram of Secondary Battery Charging Board

The Secondary Battery Charger also includes a fail-safe overvoltage protection circuit to ensure the battery is never damaged due to overcharging. The fail-safe circuit detunes the Secondary Coil in an event where the voltage reaches a predetermined unsafe threshold. The fail-safe circuit then retunes the Secondary Coil when the voltage has discharged back to a safe level. A block diagram of the Secondary Battery Charger can be seen in the Figure 4.

Experimental Results

The prototype system was tested for different performance metrics, mainly targeting the end-to-end efficiency over variable coil separation and offset, and the effectiveness of frequency hopping on EMI. The tests were performed by using a 28VDC power supply to both power the Primary Controller Board and to measure the amount of input current being sourced by the supply. The output of the Secondary Battery Charging Board rectifier was then attached to an electronic load, which was programmed to draw the maximum amount of current that the transmitter could provide without exceeding 60W.

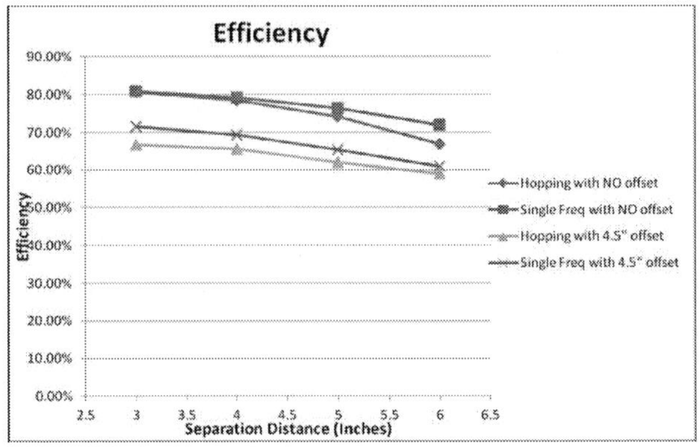

Figure 5. Efficiency vs. Separation Distance Between Seatback and Vest

Figures 5 and 6 show the overall system efficiency and power transferred respectively, where both performance metrics were taken over four different test setups. First, the measurements were taken by driving the Primary Controller Board with the frequency-hopping signal and optimally aligning the two coils. Then, the same measurements were taking with the same coil alignment, but with the transmitter being driven by a single fixed frequency. These two tests were then repeated with coils offset laterally by one radius. The results of these tests are summarized in Table 1.

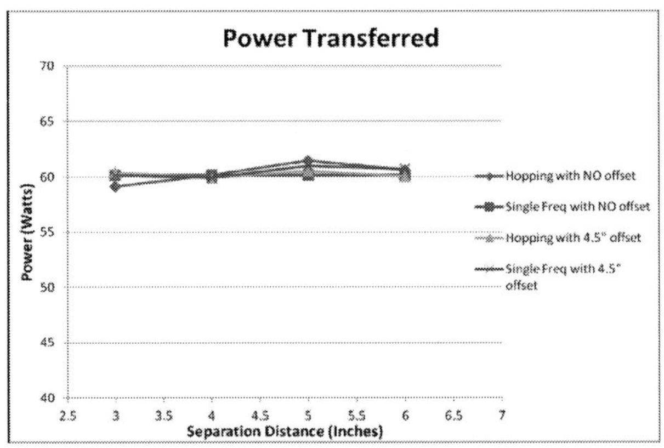

Figure 6. Power Transferred vs. Separation Distance Between Seatback and Vest

Next, the system was tested with a lithium ion rechargeable battery pack serving as the electrical load. The coils were aligned optimally and separated by a distance of 6 inches. Figure 7 shows several different characteristics of the charge cycle over time. While Table 1 references a measured efficiency of 67%, the recharging circuit necessary for charging the lithium ion battery is not 100% efficient, hence the peak efficiency of approximately 63% shown in Figure 7.

Test Scenario	Efficiency at 3 inches	Efficiency at 6 inches
FHSS without offset	80.64%	67.00%
Single frequency without offset	80.96%	72.03%
FHSS with 4.5" offset	66.78%	59.01%
Single frequency with 4.5" offset	71.62%	61.03%

Table 1. Warfighter Wireless Recharging System Prototype Assessment

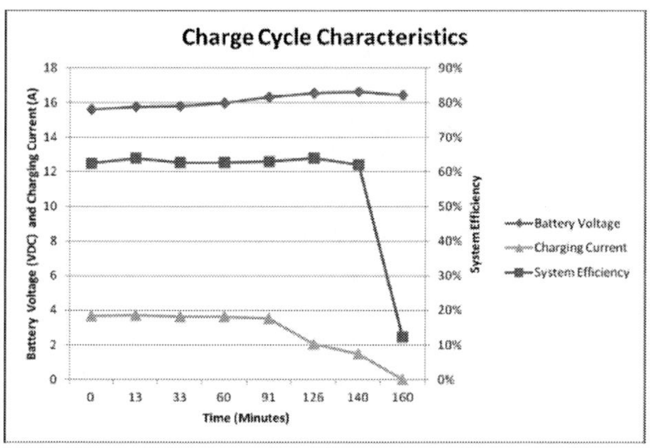

Figure 7. Battery Charge Cycle Characteristics

Conclusion

The data taken from testing the Warfighter Wireless Recharging System demonstrates that a 28VDC powered system utilizing resonant inductive coils can wirelessly transfer 60 Watts over 6 inches with high efficiency. The system is capable of recharging a lithium ion battery, offering a unique, unencumbered solution for power concerns in remote military settings. With such a system integrated into existing vehicle seatbacks, a soldier is not only able to maintain power to portable devices more consistently, but he or she can do so with little to no extra effort.

The design has also proven to be robust with respect to variance in coil offset, distance and load characteristics. The use of custom spread spectrum drive signals to the transmitter enables the system to have a lower RF signature and to comply with FCC and other regulatory constraints with minimal impact on efficiency. This contributes to the overall goal of making the system as unobtrusive as possible, where it can be integrated into existing systems without requiring significant modifications or adjustments.

While there are other improvements that could be targeted in future systems, this initial Warfighter Wireless Recharging System clearly illustrates the feasibility of the concept and its potential to reduce the size, weight, volume and quantity of batteries a soldier must carry. Such improvements not only reduce the strain and demand on a soldier, but also offer significant environmental benefits by reducing the amount of battery waste generated by military operations.

Acknowledgments

Powercast would like to acknowledge and thank the US Army CERDEC for support on this effort.

References

1. Z. C. Nxumalo, P. Tarwireyi and M. O. Adigun, "Lithium-based batteries in tactical military applications: A review," Computer, Communications, and Control Technology (I4CT), 2015 International Conference on, Kuching, 2015, pp. 575-579.
2. R. P. Hamlen, H. A. Christopher and S. Gilman, "US Army battery needs-present and future," Battery Conference on Applications and Advances, 1995., Proceedings of the Tenth Annual, Long Beach, CA, 1995, pp. 123-127.
3. Y. Wu, A. P. Hu, D. Budgett, S. C. Malpas and T. Dissanayake, "Efficient Power-Transfer Capability Analysis of the TET System Using the Equivalent Small Parameter Method," in IEEE Transactions on Biomedical Circuits and Systems, vol. 5, no. 3, pp. 272-282, June 2011.
4. Z. Bin and H. Xiao-hong, "Modeling and analysis of wireless power transmission system via strongly coupled magnetic resonances," Mechatronics and Control (ICMC), 2014 International Conference on, Jinzhou, 2014, pp. 70-75.
5. S. Mazzola, "MIL-STD-461: The basic military EMC specification and it's evolution over the years," Systems, Applications and Technology Conference, 2009. LISAT '09. IEEE Long Island, Farmingdale, NY, 2009, pp. 1-5.
6. "Wireless Power Consortium", Wirelesspowerconsortium.com, 2016. [Online]. Available: https://www.wirelesspowerconsortium.com.

Autonomously Adaptable Wireless Power Charging System

Craig DeLuccia and Eric Ehrbar

Busek Co. Inc.
Natick, Massachusetts, USA 01760

Abstract: The Busek Wireless Power System (WPS) enables automated, cordless charging of Soldier devices, increasing Soldier speed and safety on vehicle exit and entry, reducing Soldier cognitive load, and eliminating replacement of fouled connections in harsh environments. Automated wireless power recharging reduces the already ,,.overburdened Soldier's need to carry spare power sources, extending operational readiness, and response times

Keywords: wireless power; alternative power source; cordless; magnetic resonance; electromagnetics; Nett Warrior; rechargeable batteries; power hubs

Introduction:

The WPS operates from a vehicle bus power supply (28V nominal) where a vehicle mounted power supply controller provides conditioning, system control, and interfacing to a low profile power transmitter pad designed to be installed on vehicle. The supply controller and transmitter pad autonomously transfer regulated power to a Soldier-worn receiver pad. The Soldier-worn receiver is thin, lightweight, and flexible, and contains all Soldier-side electronics along with magnetic and electric field shielding. Communications between the receiver and transmitter relays data between the devices. In this manner, the system continually monitors and adjusts the vehicle-side electronics to maintain peak power transfer at maximum efficiency in dynamic environments. The Soldier worn receiver is connected to a Soldier worn ISPDS-C compliant power hub via a physical connection. The intended use of the system is to supply Soldiers wireless power from a power source such as a vehicle, generator, solar panel, etc. to power Soldier worn electronics while recharging a central battery. Presumably, Soldiers could utilize the system while on-base, allowing for charging of their entire kit without disconnecting components or harnessed devices from their ISPDS-C. The system is able to provide power through air, water, fabrics, wood, fiberglass, glass, and other materials such as cement block (not sheet metals such as aluminum or steel), potentially opening up new operational uses providing power through sealed enclosures or through other materials if desirable.

The WPS system consists of three (3) major components:

1) Lightweight Soldier-worn power receiver pad with integrated electronics, carried on Soldier (e.g. Improved Outer Tactical Vest), (#1, Figure 1 & **Error! Reference source not found.**).
2) Vehicle mounted power transmitter pad, mounted on vehicle (#2, Figure 1).
3) Vehicle mounted power supply controller, connected to transmitter pad and vehicle power source. Vehicle/platform power can include power sources such as solar panels, generators, etc. (#3, Figure 1).

Figure 1. Wireless Power System Major Components

Figure 2. Soldier receiver pad on tactical vest

System Specifications

A summary of the current system features and specifications of the Engineering Model (EM) prototype is shown below:

- WPS Features
  - Range 0-4"
  - Power output - up to 60W at 19 volts DC.
  - Efficiency ≥75%
  - Automatic Power Tuning - maximizes transfer efficiency, adjusts power according to distance and alignment between Power Supply and Receive Pads.
- Solider Power Receiver Pad Prototype
  - Weight 14.5 oz (0.9 lb)
  - Pad & Dimensions 8" x 10" (includes electronic controls)
  - Advanced Combat Uniform fabric pouch (50% nylon, 50% cotton) with MOLLE webbing or Velcro attachments.

- Vehicle Power Transmitter Pad Prototype
  - Weight 25.4 oz (1.6 lb)
  - Size 6.25" x 7.5"
  - Advanced Combat Uniform fabric pouch (50% nylon, 50% cotton) with MOLLE webbing or Velcro attachments.
- Vehicle Power Supply Controller Prototype
  - Weight 136 oz (8.5 lb)
  - Size 17.1" x 5.1" x 25.5" *(Supply Controller packaging to be reduced in future design iteration)*

Summary of Test Data and Results

A photograph of the final EM system prototype is shown below in Figure 3Figure 3. The system operates from a single supply (nominal 28V). The vehicle side electronics contain all of power conditioning and system control required to operate the wireless power system autonomously. The system consists of a Vehicle Transmitter Pad and a Soldier-worn Receiver Pad. Both pads contain electric and magnetic shielding capabilities. All soldier worn WPS electronics have been integrated into the Receiver Pad package. The Receiver Pad has been optimized to provide a thin, lightweight, and flexible unit while maintaining functionality and safety. Pad-to-pad communication capabilities relay data from the receiver pad to the vehicle power supply controller. In this manner, the system constantly monitors and adjusts the vehicle power transmitter to maintain peak power transfer at maximum efficiency.

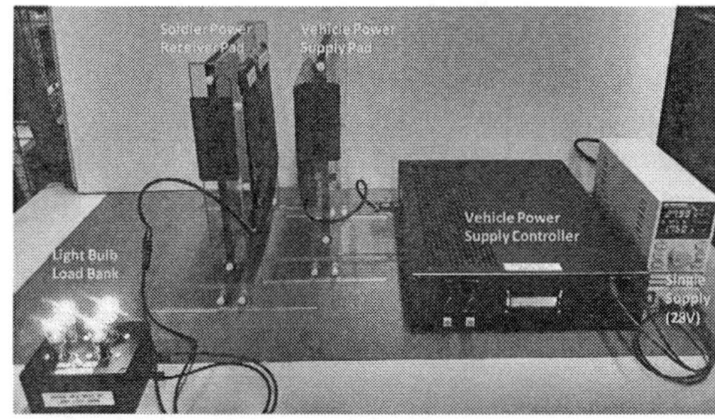

Figure 3. Complete EM Prototype Wireless Power System (shown with lab power supply and 60W light bulb load bank)

The final EM prototype unit was verification tested. The test setup was configured as shown in Figure 3. The performance was measured using three key metrics: distance, power, and efficiency. The results of these tests are shown graphically in Figure 4 and in tabular form in Table 1. The WPS was tested at three different power levels, 30W, 45W, and 60W using light bulbs as a "dummy" load. The system was tested at each power level from a distance of 0 inches (transmitter & receiver touching) up to 3.5 inches.

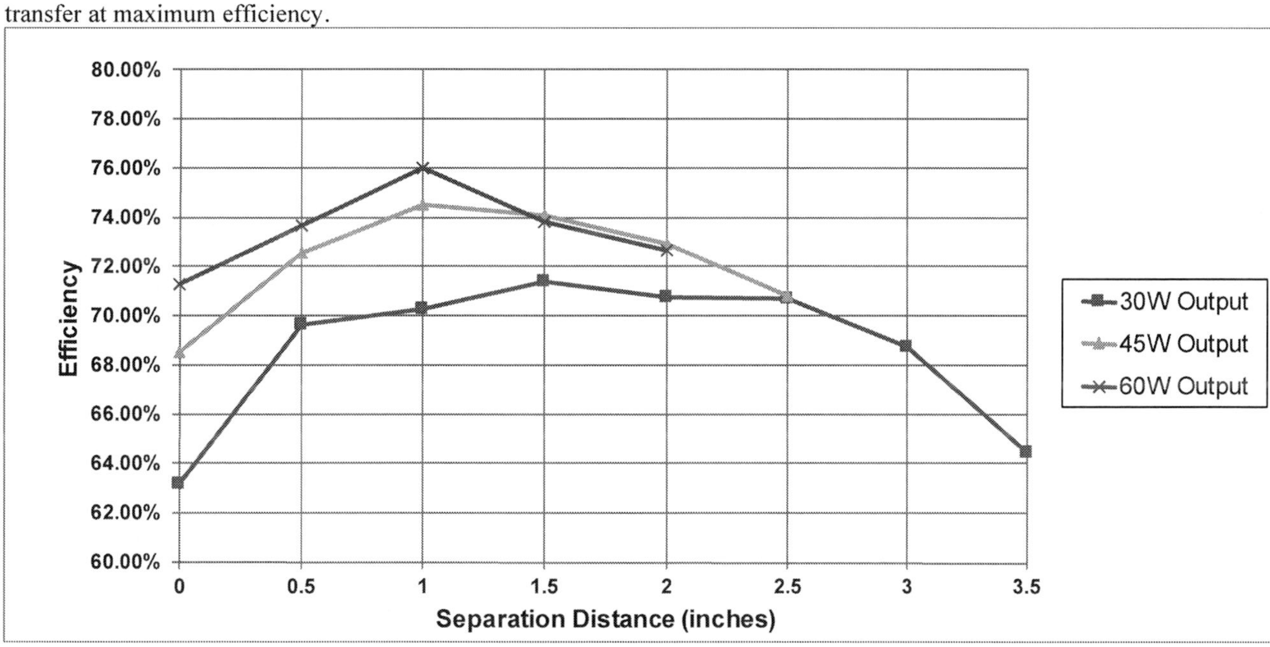

Figure 4. WPS Efficiency Plots at Various Power Levels and Distances

Table 1. Tabular View of WPS Efficiency, Distance, and Power Level

Separation Distance (inches)	Efficiency		
	30W	45W	60W
0	63.15%	68.50%	71.27%
0.5	69.65%	72.55%	73.69%
1	70.27%	74.51%	75.97%
1.5	71.38%	74.09%	73.83%
2	70.72%	72.92%	72.63%
2.5	70.70%	70.79%	
3	68.73%		
3.5	64.44%		

Overall the WPS has demonstrated the ability to provide up to 60W of power at a distance of up to 2.0 inches. Reduced power can be transmitted at greater distances as shown above. The peak efficiency of the system is ~76% while transmitting 60W or more at approximately 1.0 inches. Even across the wide power and distance ranges the system maintains roughly >65% efficiency. The system can be optimized for peak performance at given ranges and power levels.

Future Work

With the core WPS technology established and demonstrated at the prototype level, Busek's next steps include functional testing with ISPDS-C hubs, batteries, and peripheral devices as well as integration into specific platforms (e.g. ground vehicles and aircraft) in addition to advanced safety features and functionality.

Conclusions

Over the course of the Phase II effort, Busek made great strides in advancing its wireless power system prototype. The end result is an efficient, compact, lightweight system capable of autonomously tuning and maintaining up to 60W power transfer at a distance of up to 2.0 inches, with power transmissions at reduced power over greater distances up to 4.0 inches. The test results show a peak efficiency (>75%) while transmitting 60W at 1 inch.

In addition to the rigorous hardware development, an initial safety assessment was performed to examine and identifies any safety hazards, both to humans as well as environmental concerns (vehicle instruments). The results of this initial assessment indicate that when the WPS is used properly, the system is safe.

Acknowledgements

Busek Co. Inc. would like to thank the US Army PM Soldier Warrior for funding this effort under contract W91CRB-14-C-0049. In particular, we would like to thank Mr. Dave Schimmel, and Mr. Jose Lopez-Merced.

Alternative Energy-Platforms

Elvis Bertrand Nougoum Ngombissi

e-mail:ngombissi@yahoo.com.

Engineering Department. E-Soft Corporation Co.Ltd,

Yaounde 1, Centre, Cameroon, 00237

Abstract: *Until recently, the offshore wind energy potential in Cameroon was ignored because vast onshore wind resources have the potential to fulfill the electrical energy needs for the entire country. However, the challenge of transmitting the electricity to the large load centers may limit wind grid penetration for land-based turbines. Offshore wind turbines can generate power much closer to higher value coastal load centers. Reduced transmission constraints, steadier and more energetic winds, and recent Africa success, have made offshore wind energy more attractive for Cameroon However, Cameroon. Waters are generally deeper than those on the Africa coast, and will require new technology. This paper presents an overview of Cameroon. Coastal resources, explores promising deepwater wind technology, and predicts long-term cost-of-energy (COE) trends. COE estimates are based on generic 5-MW wind turbines in a hypothetical 100- MW wind power plant. With sufficient R&D technology improvements and volume production, analysis shows that costs could reach $0.051/kWh for deployment of deepwater offshore wind turbines by 2035, and $0.041/kWh by 2012 for shallow water in class 4 winds. Offshore wind systems can diversify the Cameroon electric energy supply and provide a new market for wind energy in the west region that is complementary to onshore development. Background The worldwide installed capacity of grid-connected wind power has now exceeded 40 GW, corresponding to an investment of approximately $20 billion.*

Keywords: wind Energy, Wind grid, offshore wind, wind technology.

Introduction

Wind energy installations in Cameroon have not grown during the past decade from about 1800MW to 6.000MW at the end of 2015 .Development has mainly focused on class 4 (low wind sites with an annual average wind speed of 15mph) in remote areas of the West, and on a few ridgelines East. The Ministry of Energy is conducting the Low Wind speed Technology project, which targets development of cost-effective Wind turbines for class 4 sites that can produce electricity onshore for $0.03/Kwh and offshore $0.05kwh by the end of

2035. This will open up 20 times more land in Cameroon for wind energy development, and since many of these sites tend to be closer to urban load centers, the problem of transmission line will be greatly simplified.

Offshore Resource

This resource estimation methodology has been validated for onshore application against actual anemometer data for several Cameroon geographic regions. Although these models are new and have not been fully validated in all climatological situations, they are more accurate than the earlier boundary layer prediction methods used in conjunction with measured data. This table includes the effects of wind shear referenced to a 60-m elevation.

Table 1: Reference Table for Wind Speed Classes at Offshore Sites (Ranges are given in m/s)

Ws m/s 40M	Class
3.4-4.2	Class1
4.2-5	Class2
5.-5.4	Class3
5.4-6	Class 4

Although the modeling is not validated for offshore conditions, and modeling of the entire Cameroon coastline has not been completed .Table 2 provides a summary of the estimated offshore resources by region and water depth.

In the analysis it was assumed that the offshore zone from shoreline to 5nm is100% excluded to reduce view shed issues and to avoid ecosystem near shore, where environmental concerns are likely to be primary concerns.

Water depth

Offshore wind development has been limited to waters shallower than 30 m in the Littoral and Atlantic Seas.

Current Offshore turbine Technology

Operating experience has shown that there is much to be learned about deployment of offshore wind turbines in terms of achieving the same reliability and low COE as their land-based counterparts.

Future Deep Wind Turbine Technology

When Offshore wind installation arrive in Cameroon, more severe ocean condition and greater water depth will challenge designers. At some depth, the development of floating platforms for wind turbines will be necessary to deploy wind turbines in even deeper waters. This progression is illustrated in Figure 2

Table 2: Cameroon offshore wind energy resources by region for shallow and deep water

Offshore Resources Estimates Resources in MW						
	4-20 Nautical Miles			20-40 Nautical Miles		
Region	Shallow<30m	Deep	% Exclusion	Shallow<30m	Deep	% Exclusion
West	6,600	33,600	55%	2,500	99,200	22%
Littoral	22,400	7,500	55%	20,145	120,00	22%
East	2,650	42,00	55%	0	198,30	22%
North	7,10	31,075	55%	0	85,90	22%
East	6,20	32,045	55%	1	100,20	22%
Totals	43,95	146.22	55%	23,643	600,50	22%

Figure 1: Progression of Expected Wind turbine Evolution to Deeper Water

This deepwater technology will require extensive development effort because of the added difficulty of dynamic floating platforms and other design conditions at the more exposed sites further from shore. The proven offshore floating platforms used by the oil and gas industry have characteristics similar to those being considered for floating wind turbine platforms, but their differences will allow the necessary cost reductions:

- Oil platforms 'safety margins are higher to provide permanent residences for personnel
- Oil platforms must provide additional safety for spill prevention.
- wind platforms need only be deployed in water as 600ft.

Estimated Cost of Energy

The approach that was taking for this cost study was to assume a nominal 300-Mw wind plant composed of 60 machines, each with a 5-mw rating. The cost of the machines, including marinazation and industry data,was scaled from WindPACT studies[1,2,3,4].Two platforms concepts were used, as described by Rob and Enestson[5].one was a concept developed by ARSEL;the other under a European study[6].First the cost estimates for shallow water technology, taken from a number of African Offshore project papers, are provided in table 3.

Table 3: Shallow water estimates for offshore wind class 4 winds

Shallow water wind COE estimates –class4-<30m depth ,15m from shore				
	Year of installation			
	2012	2015	2020	2035
Turbine Size	3	3	3	3
Wind farm Size	100 MW	100 MW	100 MW	100 MW
Rotor diameter	128	128	128 M	128 M
HUB HIGH	80	80	80 M	80 M
Assumed water depth	<30-m	<30-m	<30-m	<30-m
Electrical infrastructure	€100 ,20	€99.80	€114.45	€113.25
Icc /rating (€/kw)	€1,092	€709	€608	€600
Capacity factor (%)	0.39	0.40	0.42	0.42
Availability (%)	0.93	0.93	0.94	0.94
Shallow water COE (€/kw)	€0,046	€0.039	€0.034	€0.031

Deepwater cost of Energy-results

For deepwater systems, costs were calculated for 600ft water depth, although studies show that significant resources can be developed in much shallower water with correspondingly lower costs. The deeper water turbine and tower are assumed to be the same for shallow and deep water, with an initial minimization cost premium of 11% higher than the land-based value.The major differences between deep and shallow water were due to the higher cost of floating platforms and the additional electrical cabling in deeper water. In additional, baseline O&M costs for deeper turbines were assumed to be higher ($.018kwh) than shallow water turbines due to the added platform hardware and nominally greater distances to shore .most other assumptions remain the same. Electrical infrastructure costs were based on an unpublished ARSEL report. These costs were higher for the deep-water cases because of greater distances offshore and riser designs necessary to reach from the bottom to the floating platforms. In both cases 34.5 kV service was used for distribution among the wind plant and 138 kV was used for interconnection from the plant to shore. Redundancy was incorporated in the distribution system to allow for full power transmission with a single fault within the system.

Musial et al. [7] estimated platform costs for two 5-MW floating platform configurations, one designed by ARSEL (Figure 3) and a Dutch Tri-Floater concept (Figure 4) designed under a European Union-funded study on floating platforms [6]. ARSEL's design was less detailed than the Dutch Tri-Floater, but ARSEL used the Dutch study to attain similar levels of conservatism and estimates for miscellaneous hardware. These assumptions are described by Enestson and Hub [5].

This study focuses on the ARSEL TLP concept. Enestson et Hub, estimate that low volume TLP production costs would be \$2.88 to \$6.50 million. The midrange cost of \$4.69 million was chosen as the mean baseline deepwater platform cost, with the upper and lower costs estimates taken as conservative and optimistic values to define a range of reasonable baseline platform costs. These costs are shown in Table 4.

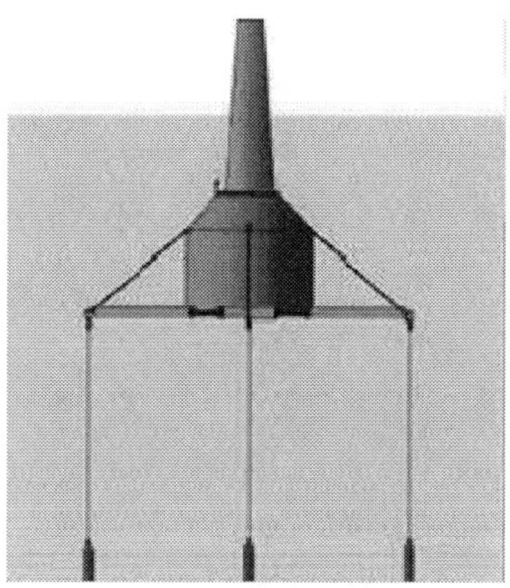

Figure 2a: ARSEL TLP concept

Figure 2b: Dutch trifloater concept

With the assumptions stated earlier, and if research, design, and production begin in the near future, results shown in Table 4 indicate that class 4 baseline deepwater COE estimates for wind energy will range from \$0.095/kWh to \$0.071/kWh. The mean baseline for class 6 winds is \$0.083/kWh. By 2020, mean costs drop below \$0.045 for the ARSEL TLP. These costs put deepwater offshore wind energy solidly in competition with onshore electrical energy generating sources, but they are not possible without research to initiate the technology..

Given the breadth of ongoing research and innovation opportunities, there could be significant changes in the supply chain as the offshore wind industry grows and matures. For example, firms specializing in monopile foundation production may need to diversify into pipe production for jacket structures, and subsequently floating assemblies, should they desire to continue to serve the offshore wind sector. However, the technology ranking exercise demonstrates that progress in the industry will take time; many innovations see a notable increase into their potential impact as one moves five, ten, or even more than ten years into the future.

Deepwater Research and development strategy

In the arena of floating wind energy platforms, a pathway composed of a comprehensive **R&D** program, commercial demonstration, and subsequent mass production can probably reduce costs by 50% or more .significant research is needed in the areas of anchoring, platform/turbine interactions, and understanding wind and wave loading on structure. To successfully achieve cost-competitive deepwater technology, key collaboration must take place between three critical groups:

1. The oil and gas /marine industry
2. The present shallow water offshore wind energy industry
3. A targetad deepwater wind energy research community.

Summary

Offshore wind energy development is an unexplored Cameroon domestic power resource that is estimated to be economically developable using megawatt-scale wind turbines in large offshore wind farms within a decade. New wind technology can be developed that could make floating wind turbines economical, at energy costs as low as \$0.051/kWh in class 4 winds by 2020, given sufficient volume production .Though current technologies can be deployed today in shallow water, improvements in wind turbines designed and installation methods are essential to minimize the COE and make Offshore wind electricity competitive with conventional technology.

Acknowledgments

I would like to recognize Pr. Onana Noah Roger Patrick, Sodea,Marcus, AkonoAristide, Dr Degoudé Didier (I.R.A.D) for their contributions to the content of this paper. In additional, the Ministry of mines water and Energy of Cameroon for its support of this project.

References

1. Central Africa Wind association Accessed july19, 2014.

2. SIL, B SeaWind Africa Association accessed September 2014 N/r125471250

3. Web site for ENEO CAMEROON www.eneocameroon.cm

4. www.arsel-cm-org web site for Arsel,accessed april 2014

5. Rob, H, Enestson W, Hub T feasibility of floating platforms systems for wind Turbines, Arsel /pjt/054178 4 December 2014.

6. Studie narr haalbaarheid van en randvoorwaarden voor drijvende offshore windturbines. ECN, MARIN, Lagerwey the Windmaster, TNO, TUD, MSC, Dec. 2002

7. Musial W.D, Butterfield, C. P and Boone, A, Feasibility of floting plaforms systems for wind turbines. NREL/CP-500-34847, November, 2003.

Update: Solvent Free, Additive Manufacturing Process for Lithium Electrodes

Michael D. Eskra and Paula K. Ralston
Eskra Technical Products, Inc.
Saukville, WI 53080

Abstract: *Under a DLA BATTNET Short Term Project (STP) Eskra Technical Products, Inc. (ETP) developed a dry, additive manufacturing process for lithium electrodes, successfully eliminating the use of solvents and/or liquids. The ETP process involves the use of powder coating subsequent layers of active material and PVDF binder and thermal processing. This novel additive manufacturing system can be used with all common active materials for both anodes and cathodes, as well as differing particle sizes for the production of Li-ion electrodes. The ETP dry process totally eliminates the use of solvents and/or liquids enabling a reduction in processing steps required such as slurry preparation, wet-coating, drying, and solvent reclaiming. Product line changeovers are simplified, enabling fast change over from anode to cathode pairs using a web based process. This simplification also allows more cost effective small run production. Significant cost savings are possible along with reduction in organic contamination. Development is also underway for using this same process with a novel ceramic separator.*

The ETP additive manufacturing process and equipment has been reported on throughout its development. The final stages of development and the state of readiness for pre-production equipment will be covered here.

Keywords: lithium ion; additive manufacturing; dry process; battery.

Introduction

Under a DLA BATTNET Short Term Project (STP), Eskra Technical Products, Inc. (ETP) developed a dry, additive manufacturing process for lithium electrodes. The ETP process involves the use of a charged, fluidized bed and powder coating subsequent layers of active material, premixed with a PVDF binder and thermally processed.

Proof-of-Concept

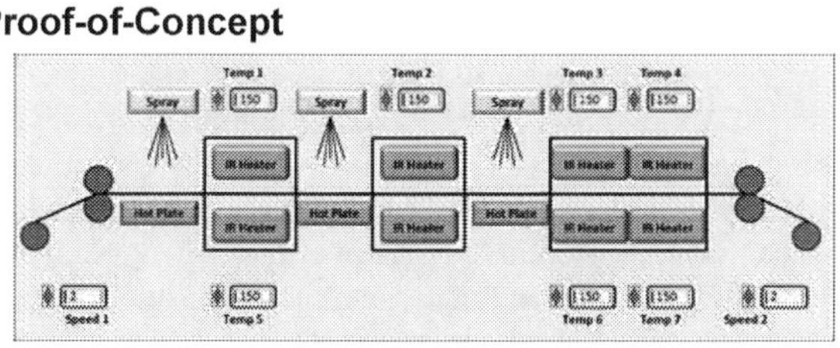

Figure 1. Concept of Dry Process Manufacturing Line

A proof-of-concept line was built with results showing this novel manufacturing method to be successful. ETP's process successfully eliminates the use of all solvents and/or liquids, allows for quick change over between active materials and offers a significant cost savings when compared to standard electrode manufacturing processes. The same binder and active materials as conventional lithium ion batteries are used in the process, leaving no issues with non-compatible components being added to limit cell life or hinder performance

Figure 2. ETP's Proof-of-Concept Line

This proof-of-concept line produced both cathodes and anodes for lithium ion batteries. Performance of test cells were near, or at the level of commercially made electrodes.

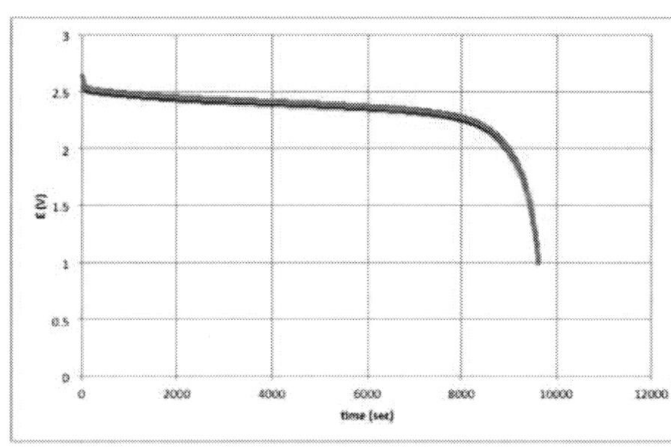

Figure 3. LTO Anode-Limited Cells With an Initiall Specific Capacity of 0.485 mAh/cm^2

Prototype

With the success of the proof-of-concept line, ETP received follow-on funding through DLA BATTNET and moved forward with the building of a prototype line.

Figure 4. ETP Prototype Line

This prototype line allowed ETP to get closer to the goals of a fully capable electrode fabrication line, spraying two sided at 10 feet per minute. ETP understands that its manufacturing line must be competitive and offer the same capabilities as the solvent based systems in which it competes, but at lower costs and similar to better electrical performance. At the beginning of the second phase development effort ETP and MEGTEC developed an additional scope of requirements which were intended to help guide the development towards ultimate commercialization. Higher speeds, better uniformity of active material density and thickness controls were part of these goals. The ability to apply active material to the current collector at one nominal particle thickness along with the use of no solvents were industry wants, as well as ultra-thin coatings of 1-2 micron. One of the issues of trying to coat at a micron thickness is how to measure the coating thickness on a continual basis.

Some of the inherent issues with developing a new process to manufacture electrodes is in a dry state is control of the active material in air, or dusting of the active materials. Transport of the active materials, and of course uniformity of the dispersion and adhesion of the active materials to the current collectors are also issues. During the early phase of the development effort, many active material combinations were used to verify that the active materials would not be the limiting factor in the use of the process. Initially the concept was to use multiple layers of active materials which used a higher polymer layer at the electrode interface and significantly lower polymer content in subsequent layers as the electrode was manufactured. This has several benefits, the first of which is that you can increase the active material adhesion with the foils, different active materials characteristics can be layered or added to benefit the electrical performance of the resulting electrode, and much lower binder and perhaps even a third type characteristic of the active material can be put into the electrode. In later trials a ceramic separator was added to the surface of the electrode.

The ability to layer differing active materials or even different ceramic separator materials can improve the electrical performance of the resulting electrochemical couple. Most recently, ETP has also expanded the use of the process line to non-lithium ion chemistries including lithium primary, lead acid and nickel metal hydride.

The Process Line Development

The evolution of the process development was to move from hobby tools and techniques to commercial off the shelf (COTS) to custom made equipment on an as needed basis. During the first effort we migrated to use powder coating equipment for hobby car enthusiasts. Under Phase II we reviewed alternative methods to apply the various active materials and evolved to use the Wagner Powder Coating System. Issues with uniformity of powder delivery to the gun were the most significant hurdle in the project. Unlike a solvent based slurry system where pumps are used to deliver a pre-measured slurry, the dry process faced many issues.

One of the first concerns, was active materials segregation in transport and fluidization. It is a well know issue with hoppers of mixed dry materials that fines will either float or gather along the edges of a cone feeder. We found that the commercial fluidization hoppers commonly used in the powder coating industry could be used and surprisingly did not cause the fines to separate. Instead they could be set so that the uniformity of the active material was enhanced with the fluidization. However, the pressure and volume of the air to fluidize correctly, required constant attention to ensure the proper amount of "action" and to prevent air pockets to be delivered to the spray gun. As an alternative method a screw feeder was developed and later acquired to feed the active materials at a more uniform rate. It was found that different active material compositions could require different feed screws and speeds. In addition some active materials were much more prone to bridging and rat holing. Fluidization of the hopper slightly above the feed screw seemed to alleviate this issue. Higher feed screw speeds and a cascade hopper reduced pulsing of active materials to the spray gun.

Spray uniformity across the surface of the electrode is a matter of spray tip design. Typical commercial powder coating tips are not well developed for precision powder dispersion. Over spray and cloud spraying is typical in a powder coating facility. However, when spraying expensive and hazardous materials, the wild spray patterns of these nozzles cannot be tolerated.

Typically powder coat spraying is performed with one of two types of spray guns, Tribo or Corona. We found that the Corona guns performed the best overall for all the active materials types. We did find though that the combination of the longer style gun gave us some challenges when trying to pattern coat or any time to get a crisp clean start stop, due to active material falling instead of being sprayed on the foil. To eliminate this, the top were turned 90 degrees and a shorter nozzle was used. This allowed the powder in the air stream to be shut off and active material to fall inside the gun.

Another issue was to develop a methodology with which to insulate and prevent active material build up where it was not needed, prevent unwanted powder escape from the spray zones, maintain spray operations while maintaining environmental health and safety for the employees operating the machine and anyone else in the area. Typically the powder coating method is to charge the particles being sprayed in the 15K to 100K volt range. Compared to the target area where you want the material to be sprayed. This high attraction provides minimum overspray but quickly points out if machine grounding is not adequate. Electrical hazards from such a high voltage can be mitigated and appear to stay mitigated once solved.

B&W MEGTEC Systems, Inc. was responsible for the unwind, rewind, web tracking and the calendar roller. Due to the industry want of micron control, and belief it could be achieved through this process MEGTEC also put design effort into developing a method to calendar with micron control. Conventional Calendar systems (Nip Rollers) typically are not accurate enough to control to better than 5 microns. Usually there is more play in the bearings and the roll surface than what we wanted to control too. The tool was assembled and worked well for most of the development. Unfortunately the hardening of the calendar rolls was not uniform and they needed to be sent back to the manufacturer for repair.

Figure 5. Calender Rolls

MEGTEC Systems assembled the final version of the machine and began spraying some of the active materials, such as titanate, manganese oxides and graphite in their facility. Titanate was chosen throughout the program for Start-up experiments for several reasons. Titanate is difficult to process due to caking, bridging, hydrophilic nature and its environmental issues compared with other materials (easy cleanup). After several weeks running Titanate, and mutual belief that the process was in control, MEGTEC moved to graphite and manganese oxide. The machine is scheduled to be moved to ETP in mid-May where the other active materials will be sprayed and additional cells built.

Figure 6. Web-Tracking

Figure 7. Pre-Commercial Machine

The end result of the project was that a new process was further developed resulting in a pre-commercial prototype machine which can handle 8 inch wide foil up to 40 feet per minute while spraying two sided electrodes. Masking of the current collector and uniform spray can be accomplished. Waste powder is minimized and can be recycled back into the respective spray zone. The technology transition was begun with MEGTEC being the likely provider to the industry.

Cell performance is comparable or slightly better than solvent cast systems. The new machine provides a more consistent electrical performance compared to the proof of concept machine.

The revised cost study shows that significant cost savings can be had both in the initial investment and ongoing operations.

The authors would like to thank B&W MEGTEC Systems, Inc. and our sponsor, Matt Hutchens of DLA, BATTNET.

Additive Manufacturing Technique for Dry Sprayed Ceramic Separators for Lithium Ion

Michael D. Eskra and Paula K. Ralston
Eskra Technical Products, Inc.
Saukville, WI 53080

Abstract: *Eskra Technical Products, Inc., using its previously developed, dry, additive manufacturing technique, has begun developing a dry, sprayed on, ceramic separator for lithium ion batteries. This will significantly lower cost and improve safety. Separators are a significant cost element in battery construction. By using ETP's additive manufacturing technique and directly spraying the separator on the electrode, ETP will eliminate bottle necks in production due to the need to acquire and store specific separator materials to meet size and performance criteria. Additionally, lowering the overall polymeric component of the separator will help in preventing thermal runaway and possibly propagation from cell to cell. The net result of using a sprayed separator of Al_2O_3 and MgO will show improved life, better power and energy, while lowering separator cost by 80%. Also, because the separator will be sprayed directly on to, and physically attached to, the electrode, shorts, due to misalignment will be eliminated and cell and battery assembly will be further simplified, furthering cost savings. The ETP low cost, additive manufacturing separator process will allow thinner separators while improving separator performance and safety. The separator development is a follow on to our dry lithium ion electrode process.*

Keywords: lithium ion; additive manufacturing; dry process; battery Ceramic separator

Introduction

Under a DLA BATTNET Short Term Project (STP), Eskra Technical Products, Inc. (ETP) developed a dry, additive manufacturing process for lithium electrodes. The ETP process involves the use of a charged, fluidized bed and powder coating subsequent layers of active material, premixed with a PVDF binder and thermally processed.

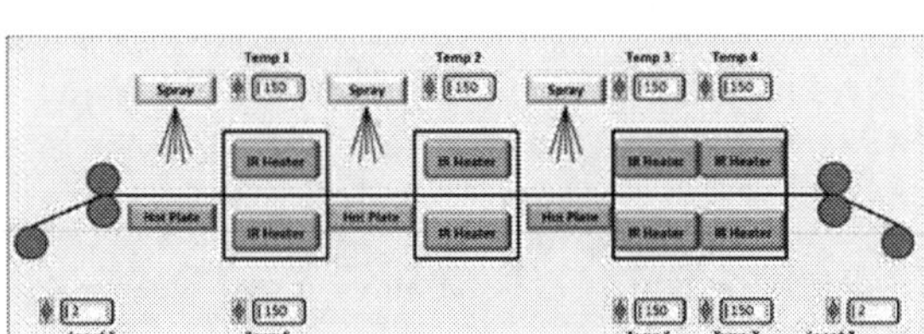

Figure 1. Concept of Dry Process Manufacturing Line

A proof-of-concept line was built with results showing this novel manufacturing method to be successful. ETP's process successfully eliminates the use of all solvents and/or liquids, allows for quick change over between active materials and offers a significant cost savings when compared to standard electrode manufacturing processes. The same binder and active materials as conventional lithium ion batteries are used in the process, leaving no issues with non-compatible components being added to limit cell life or hinder performance. Under a Phase I DLA SBIR and Phase I Option, ETP expanded the use of the dry process to address manufacturability of a ceramic separator.

The separator of a lithium ion battery provides a significant performance and cost advantage. Typically, battery separators are a free standing polyolefin film, which can be difficult to handle, keep in stock and many times can create a handling issue. Battery cell winders have a difficult time transitioning from one type of separator to another sometimes turning a 15 minute changeover to days and creating a large volume of scrap. In some cases, such as when making very small cells, the separator placement and subsequent alignment are major cost drivers.

In addition, the robustness of the separator is the deciding factor in determining whether an internal short will occur, if it will be thermal runaway or a catastrophic failure. Ceramic separators containing 20 to 40% polymer are commercially available. The polymer is used to maintain flexibility and strength. These are typically more expensive than non-ceramic separators but do improve safety.

Proof-of-Concept

To improve manufacturing flexibility, ETP worked to develop a direct spray ceramic separator using its solvent free dry process. This process can either be an additional stage on an existing electrode process line or can be added to a winder, prior to the final nip. The process provides a direct spray separator to the surface of the electrode, attaching the separator as part of the electrode. A slight over spray of the separator is possible providing either a totally enclosed electrode, if two sided sprayed or a conventional separator overlap in a single or double sprayed separator.

The advantages of such a process are reduced cost due to lower processing cost, reduced inventory of separators, easier handling, reduced scrap and it appears, improved safety and performance.

There are several articles about putting different ceramics alongside the graphitic anode or cathode improving electrical performance. While this is possible in a solvent extracted conventional ceramic separator it is much easier in a direct sprayed ceramic separator.

The overall process is nearly identical to the ETP dry electrode process. The electrode surface is heated slightly to soften polymer of the electrode soft and the ceramic polymer composition is sprayed onto it. In our early experiments we lightly calendared the resulting composite structure. By varying the composition of the individual ceramic, temperature, polymer and spraying distance, different porosities and tortuosity's can be obtained within a given thickness. It is also likely that the separator can me made thinner.

Ideally ETP was looking to improve safety as well as improve manufacturability. The first attempt of spraying a separator was done on a marginal scrap electrode by spraying a 10% PVDF MgO layer onto a NMC cathode. The separator was approximately 25um thick and was 35 cm^2 in area. We deliberately used a small cell to test whether we could make a safe cell and not short or cause a fire. The results are shown below in Figure 1.

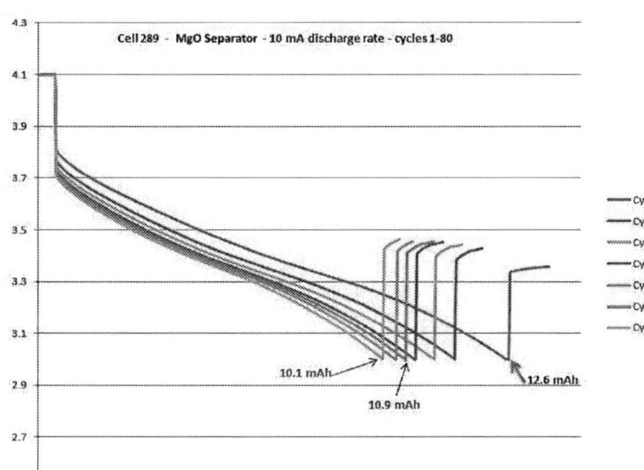

Figure 1. Dry Process Separator Results

This cell, while not overly exciting electrically, was exciting in that the sprayed separator appeared to work, and eased assembly.

The Phase I Option ended and since then ETP wanted to understand if the characteristics of the sprayed separator could possibly lead to a safer lithium ion battery. To do this we began a study to determine if a lower polymer based separator could be beneficial in preventing thermal runaway events. To this end we began an internal effort to model what we see in the reaction of this separator when it gets hot.

A mathematical model was used to help understand the potential role a ceramic-based separator could play in a lithium-ion cell. Of particular interest was the mitigating role it could play in reducing thermal runaway, in thermal abuse conditions, especially the occurance of an internal or external electronic short.

The cell modeled was spirally-wound and cylindrical-shaped (18650). The cell sandwich was composed of porous positive and negative electrodes, with metal current collectors on the back of each electrode region, and a separator between them. The electrodes consisted of active material, conductive carbon, and polymer binder (PVDF), as well as the electrolyte in the electrode pores. The separator consisted of ceramic powder and the same binder used in the electrodes (PVDF). Its pores also contained electrolyte. Electrode capacities were calculated from the thickness, active material mass fraction, porosity, and the height and length of the electrode (calculated from cell thickness and volume considerations for the cell interior). The overall cell capacity (A•hr) was the lesser of the two electrode capacities (i.e. that of the positive).

The cell modeled an electronic (internal) short between the electrodes at a given location, close to the center of the cell wrap (i.e. approximately half-way between the outer and inner edges of the cell wrap. The heat transfer in a cell is inherently a three-dimensional problem, and ideally would be modeled accordingly. The simple needs of this study were to provide an approximate idea of the rate of cell heat-up, temperature increase and the rates of various side reactions. As such a one-dimensional model was used, with variations being in the radial dimension (i.e. there were no variations in the axial or angular dimensions). In addition, temperatures were assumed to be constant within each cell sandwich. The thermal conductivity in the radial dimension of the cell sandwich was calculated assuming thermal resistors in series (current collectors, electrode and separator regions), with the thermal resistances of the electrodes and separator calculated in turn assuming thermal resistors in parallel. Heat capacities and specific gravities for each cell were obtained from the mass fractions and properties of the cell components. Heat was removed from the cell via convection at the outer edge of the cell.

The heat source terms for the energy balance were the sum of heats from reactions and the electronic short. The electronic short heat dissipation rate was calculated from the total cell energy, short time, and the fraction of the cell energy released during the short time. This energy fraction was a variable in the calculations. Values were always < 1% of the total cell energy (higher values resulted in huge temperature rise, as would take place in real cells). The specification of the energy fraction released during a short is easily related to a short resistance. The heat rate (W/cm^3) from the short was varied linearly from a maximum close to the middle of the cell wrap, and zero at the edges of the wrap. This profile was used for numerical stability reasons, with these preliminary calculations. The time length of the model solution was typically 1000 seconds, with the short taking place at the first part of the time period. The model was used to study the effect of heat-up rates on cell temperatures and composition, at different values of ceramic content in a MgO-PVDF separator. Three values of ceramic mass fraction were used: a high (0.85), a medium value (0.50), and a low value (0.01), such as when ceramic powder is sparingly incorporated into a predominantly polymer separator.

Results

The model was run for a variety of different conditions. Shown in this section are a few of the results. Figure 1 shows the temperature and heat evolution as a result of the various reactions, at ten seconds, just as the ohmic heating from the short ceases. The fractional cell energy that is dissipated during the short was 0.003, and the ceramic content in the separator was 0.85 (i.e. 15% PVDF binder). The peak in the profiles occurs at around 0.48 cm. This is due to the heating profile that was assumed; it would differ with a change in that profile. This peak nearly disappears after a few tens of seconds, as the temperature profile flattens. It is noted that the only two of the reactions are significant, the SEI layer decomposition and negative active material-electrolyte reaction. The temperature that is reached does indeed cause degradation in the electrolyte, negative electrode active material and SEI layer on the negative. The homogeneous electrolyte decomposition, positive active material-electrolyte and negative active material-binder interactions are insignificant. Furthermore thermal runaway does not occur. At higher values of short heating runaway does take place, and the positive-electrolyte and electrolyte decomposition reactions are important. However, binder decomposition does not contribute significantly to heat evolution, unless the cell is already so hot that it has been destroyed. The heating rates are very small compared to the short heating rates (up to 40 W/cm^3, depending on conditions). Finally it should be noted that heat is not evolved in the core of the cell (radius < 0.15 cm) or at the outer edge (i.e. the battery case).

Figures 2, 3 and 4 show profiles of temperature, heat from the SEI decomposition reaction (the most important), and the fraction of original SEI layer material still present at different times, respectively. As mentioned earlier, the temperature decreases after the short heating ceases, indicating runaway has not taken place. The profiles of temperature are substantially flat as well, after a few tens of seconds. Temperature is decreased due to the convective heat removal at the case of the surface, despite the heat being evolved due to decomposition reactions (which is insufficient to sustain runaway). The reaction rate of SEI decomposition decreases almost solely due to the temperature change. Nearly a third of the SEI material is decomposed after 1000 seconds.

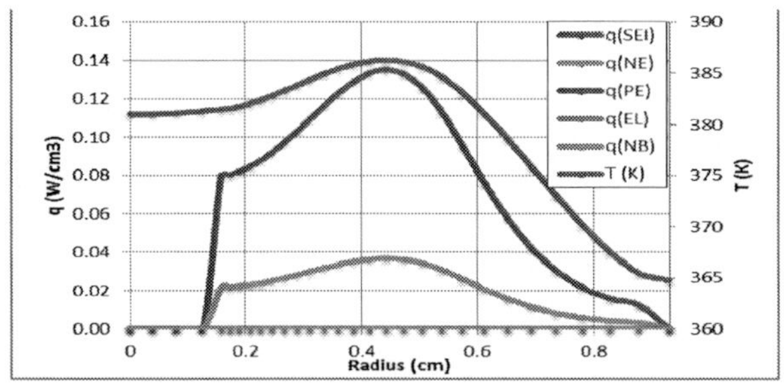

Figure 1. Temperature and Heat Evolution from Various Reactions as Function of Radial Position

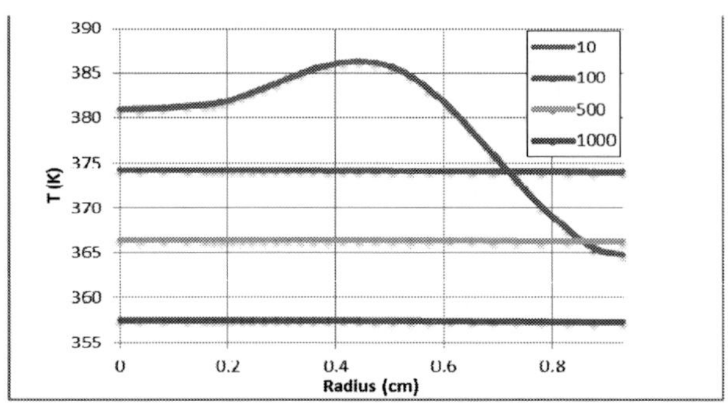

Figure 2. Temperature Profiles at Different TImes (Short Energy Fraction = 0.003; Short Time = 10 Seconds).

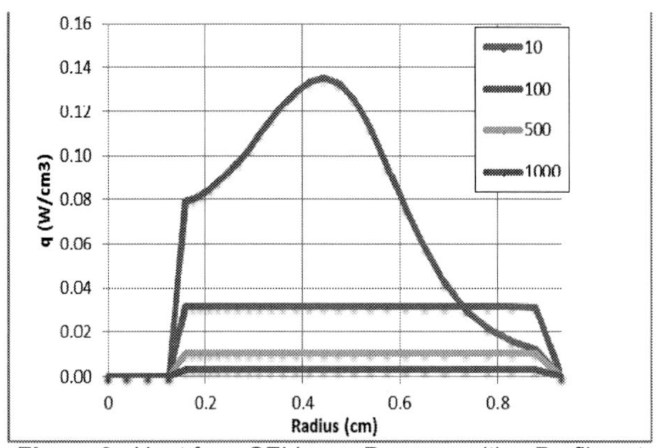

Figure 3. Heat from SEI Layer Decomposition Profiles at Different TImes (Short Energy Fraction = 0.003; Short Time = 10 Seconds).

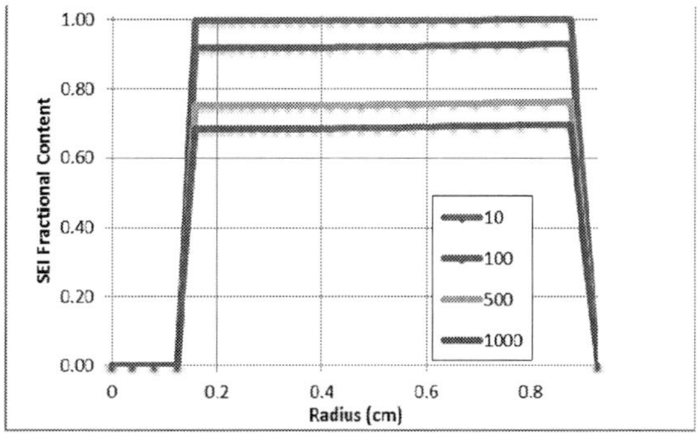

Figure 4. SEI Fractional Content Profiles at Different Times

Results for a short time of 1.0 second and an energy fraction of 0.002 are shown in Figures 5, 6 and 7. As can be seen, the temperature profiles settle down to a nearly flat radial profile within a few seconds; however these conditions lead to thermal runaway. The temperatures gradually increase until just over forty seconds have elapsed. At this point temperatures rapidly escalate at a given position (just under 0.5 cm), and then the SEI decomposition reaction greatly accelerates. The SEI content is quickly exhausted at this particular point. The predicted temperatures are high enough to melt the aluminum current collector used at the positive electrode. The heat evolution from SEI decomposition reaction goes to zero, as the reactant (SEI material) is gone; however the thermal damage has been done by this time.

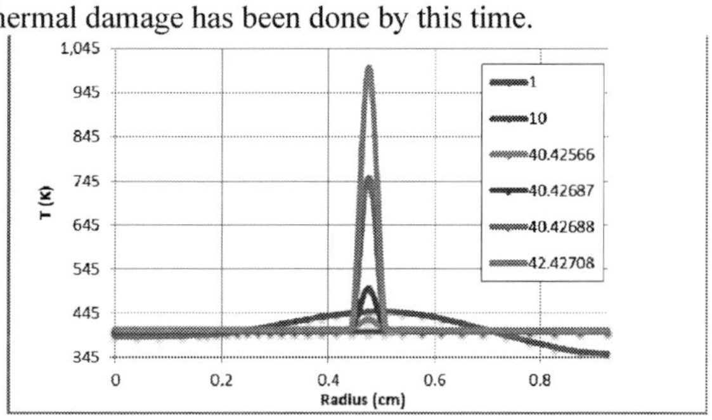

Figure 5. Temperature Profiles at Different Times

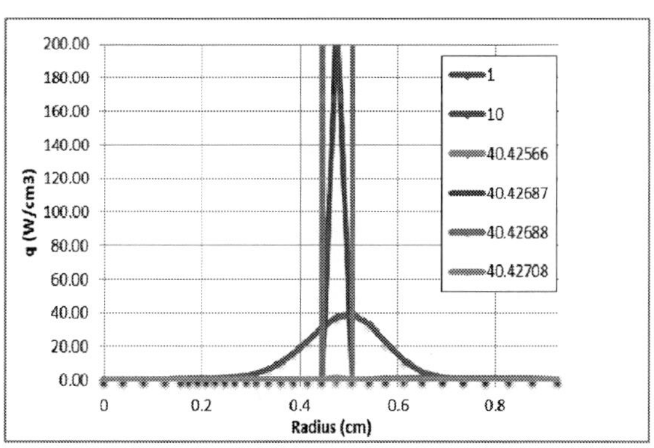

Figure 6. Heat From SEI Layer Decomposition Profiles

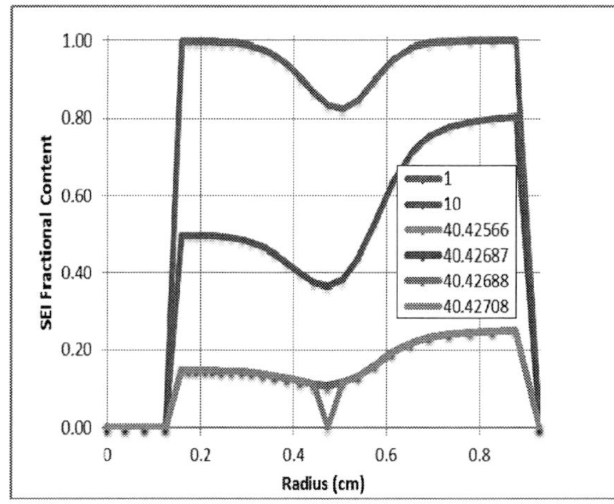

Figure 7. SEI Fractional Content Profiles at Different Times (Short Energy Fraction = 0.002; Short Time = 1 Second).

It should be noted that the temperatures shown are sufficient to soften and perhaps melt a polyolefin separator, such as is used in commercial Li-ion cells. This would lead to an electronic short as the separator moves in the region of the short, possibly causing catastrophic cell failure. In the case of a ceramic-PVDF separator though, this will not happen, due to the higher melting point of PVDF and the presence of (insulating) ceramic powders. It should be noted that the binder content (not shown) was essentially unaffected during this simulation. In more aggressive short conditions (not shown) the temperature approaches or surpasses the melting point of PVDF, where the PVDF can migrate throughout the cell (including into the pores of the separator ceramic and/or electrode materials. It is likely though that the presence of the ceramic powder would prevent a catastrophic internal short. This could extend the temperature range where Li-ion cells could operate without causing thermal runaway.

ETP would like to thank Traci Myers of DLA Land and Maritime.

Development of Safe Rechargeable Li-S Battery Chemistries

Tony Thampan, Clifford Cook, Lauren Marzocca, Ronald Thompson, David Shoemaker, and Terrill Atwater
U.S. Army RDECOM, CERDEC
Aberdeen Proving Ground, MD

Abstract: *Communications-Electronics Research, Development and Engineering Center (CERDEC) is developing wearable power sources for dismounted Soldier applications in the U.S. military. As part of this development, a novel 1.5 Ah lithium Sulfur (Li-S) pouch cell prototype has been characterized. This work presents the results, including promising performance during abusive overcharging and over-discharging conditions. Furthermore, thermal simulation of Li-S cells in a wearable configuration showed the potential of high power density without thermal runway.*

Keywords: wearable; safety; lithium sulfur; overcharge, over-discharge; thermal simulation

Introduction

Power and energy are critical to assure communications and situational awareness capabilities for Soldiers. To effectively deploy these capabilities on the Soldier and to avoid increased risks of musculoskeletal injuries [1, 2], higher density power and energy sources are required. As a potential solution, the authors, together with industry partners, are investigating lithium-sulfur (Li-S) batteries. Li-S batteries have a very high theoretical specific capacity (1675 mAh/g S) resulting in a cell discharge capacity almost twice that of Li-ion (> 900 mAh/g S vs. 400 mAh/g) at high discharge rates [3].

However, there are significant technical challenges to overcome due to the complex multi-step discharge process by which S is reduced to Li_2S through various lithium polysulfide intermediates, as shown in Figure 1.

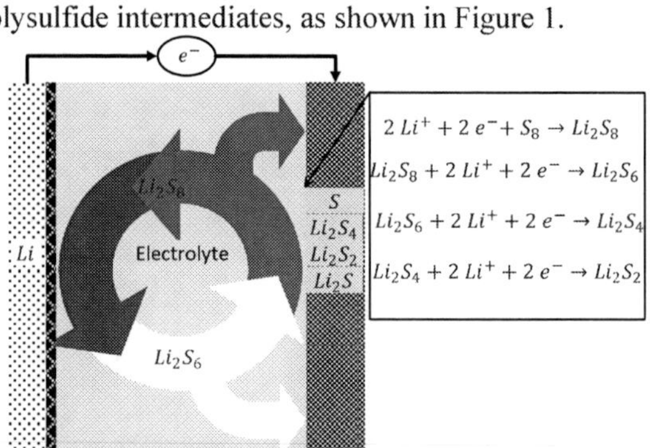

Figure 1: Li-S multistep discharge process. Higher order sulfides $\boldsymbol{Li_2S_8}$, $\boldsymbol{Li_2S_6}$ are highly soluble in conventional electrolytes leading to redox shuttle and loss of active material [12].

These highly reactive polysulfides dissolve into the electrolyte and are known to react with the conventional ester and carbonate electrolytes and salts [4]. However, electrolyte solvents such as ethylene glycol-dimethyl ether, 1,3-dioxolane [5] and room temperature ionic liquids, with $LiSO_3CF_3$ or $LiN(SO_2CF_3)_2$ salts have shown promising results with Li-S systems. Furthermore, the use of $LiNO_3$ as a protective barrier on the lithium anode to avoid polysulfide passivation has also been shown to increase cycle life [6].

This work investigates the development a high performance, safe Li-S system. It includes a discussion of battery safety failure and experimental results, including safety tests for a prototype 1.5 Ah Li-S pouch cell and thermal modeling of a battery pack comprised of Li-S cells.

Battery Safety

Conventional Li-ion battery safety incidents are related to the flammable electrolytes utilized. The electrolytes are based on alkyl carbonates [7] with lithium salts such as $LiPF_6$, $LiBF_4$, $LiB(C_2O_4)_2$, and $LiBF_2C_2O_4$ [8]. In the event of self-heating from a cell short event and subsequent exothermic reactions with active electrode materials, the cell goes into thermal runway [9]. The large temperature rise leads to electrolyte decomposition and gas production. This rapid over-pressurization leads to the venting of the volatile and highly flammable electrolyte, generating an explosive mixture near the cell. Ignition of this mixture leads to damage and rupture of adjacent cells, resulting in cascading battery failure [7] and catastrophic damage.

In the case of Li-S systems, it has been reported [10] that, as a result of the reactive nature of the polysulfides, self-heating of fully charged Li-S systems can occur as low as 50 °C. For comparison, a 1.35 Ah $LiCoO_2$ 18650 format cell shows a onset of thermal run way at 104 °C [11].

To develop a high performance Li-S system with acceptable safety, it is necessary to evaluate potential failure mechanisms associated with the electrolyte/electrode materials, including cell evaluation as discussed below.

Experimental

CERDEC, together with industrial partners, has developed prototype Li-S cells. The specifications of a Li-S cell acquired from a partner are shown in Table 1.

Table 1. Li-S cell specifications

OCV	3.0 V
Voltage Discharge Cut-off	1.7 V.
Voltage Charge Cut-off	2.7 V
Cell Length	5.4 cm
Cell Width	4.0 cm
Cell Thickness	0.8 cm
Cell Volume	17 cm^3
Cell Mass	19.5 g
Cell Packaging Materials	Aluminum w/ polymer layer

Cell samples were tested utilizing an ARBIN 5A PBT electronic load for capacity, forced overcharge, and forced discharge. A thermocouple was placed on each cell to monitor cell temperature during test. All tests were performed at room temperature (20 °C).

Capacity Tests –The test procedure began with a 30-minute open circuit rest period followed by a 180 mA charge to the charge voltage (2.7 V), 30 minutes at open circuit, and a 180 mA discharge to the voltage cut-off (1.7 V), followed by a final 30-minute rest. This cycle was repeated until the discharge capacity decreased to 80% of the original discharge capacity.

Forced Over-Discharge Test – A cell that had already undergone a capacity cycle test was subjected to an abuse test to examine safety when the cell is discharged beyond specifications. This test procedure began with a 160 mA discharge to 0.5 V followed by a 160 mA charge to 2.7 V and a 160 mA discharge to 1.7 V. The cell was then recharged to 2.7 V at 160 mA, and the cycle began again with the discharge to 0.5 V at 160 mA.

Forced Overcharge Test – A cell that had already undergone a capacity cycle test was subjected to an abuse test to examine safety when the cell is overcharged. The cell was charged at 160 mA to 10 V. The voltage was maintained at 10 V for three hours and the test was ended.

Results and Discussion

Capacity Tests – Figure 2 shows the results of the capacity test with the cell voltage response to the charge and discharge current. For the second cycle, the total discharge capacity is 1.49 Ah and the total energy is 3.2 Wh. The cell was cycled more than 50 times without an unacceptable loss in performance, i.e., > 20% loss compared with the beginning of the test. As observed by others, the discharge voltage curve shows three regions – an upper plateau, a sloping region, and a lower plateau, indicative of the different products present during the discharge [12].

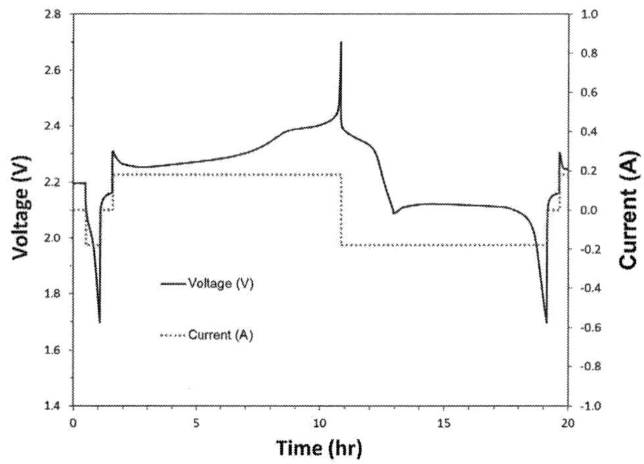

Figure 2: Li-S cell charged at 180 mA to 2.7 V, followed by 180 mA discharge to 1.7 V.

Forced Over-Discharge Test – Figure 3 shows the performance of the cell with a discharge to 0.5 V. When the cell was discharged to 1.7 V, the resulting energy was 0.52 Wh, while when discharged to 0.5 V, the energy was 0.70 Wh, possibly due to increased sulfur utilization. As the cell had already seen capacity fading due to the capacity tests, the starting cell capacity was lower the capacity test results (i.e 3.2 Wh). Subsequent cycles were lower in energy, indicating loss of active material. However, no temperature rise or cell swelling was observed.

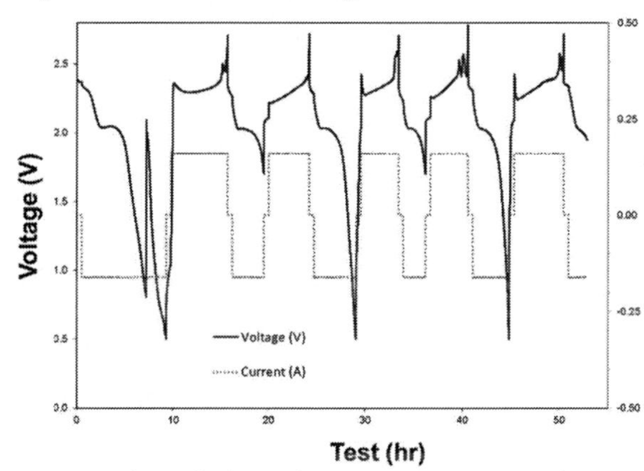

Figure 3: Li-S cell charged at 160 mA to 2.7 V and discharged at 160 mA to 1.7 V, followed by a charge to 2.7 V and discharged to 0.5 V.

Forced Overcharge Test – Figure 4 shows the cell undergoing a forced overcharge. During the test, the cell demonstrated a temperature increase almost 10 °C higher than ambient, although no catastrophic failure occurred. Cell pack swelling was also observed, and post-test results showed a 27% expansion in the thickness.

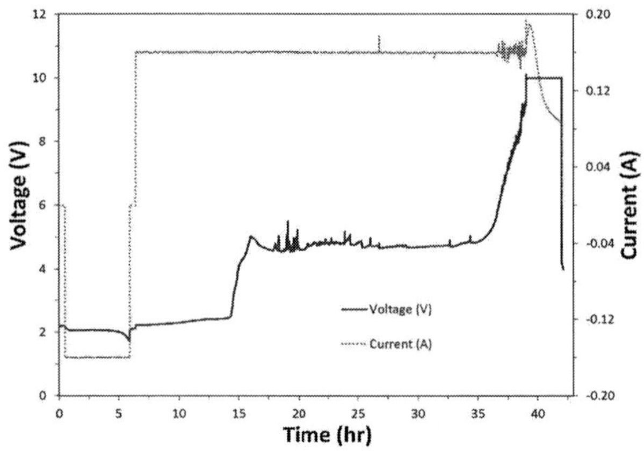

Figure 4: Li-S cell discharged at 160 mA to 1.7 V and then charged at 160 mA to 10 V. The cell was maintained at 10 V for 3 hours.

The increased temperature and swelling are potentially due to the exothermic breakdown of the electrolyte, resulting in gas production.

Thermal Modeling of a Wearable Li-S Battery

To appropriately consider the development of safe, wearable Li-S batteries, a system energy balance is useful. This will be useful to predict thermal characteristics, including the maximum temperature of the battery to avoid thermal runway during operation.

The existing Conformal Wearable Battery (CWB), which is comprised of Li-ion prismatic cells, is shown in Figure 5. This 22 cm x 20 cm x 1.8 cm battery has been well accepted in the Army because of its form and fit, and it serves as a basis for the design of the Li-S battery.

Figure 5: CWB that is 22 cm x 20 cm and 1.8 cm.

The temperature ( ) profile in the battery can be modeled using the heat equation:

$$Q_T = C_p \frac{dT}{dt} - \nabla \cdot (k \nabla T) - h(T_{ext} - T) \qquad (1)$$

This parabolic partial differential equation can be simplified, since the thickness (z) dimension is small enough that the Biot number is ~0.1, resulting in lumped parameter analysis and reducing its solution to two dimensions.

Utilizing the first law of thermodynamics, the overall heat generation rate ( ) in the cell can be represented as [13]

$$Q_T = I(E - E_{OCV}) + IT\left(\frac{\partial E}{\partial T}\right)_P - \sum_i \Delta H_i r_i + C_p \frac{dT}{dt} \qquad (2)$$
$$- \int \sum_j \left(\bar{H}_j - \bar{H}_j^{avg}\right) \frac{\partial c_j}{\partial t} dv \,,$$

where the first term on the right is the irreversible heating due to cell impedance to current, the second term is the reversible entropic heat, the third term is the heat of reactions, the fourth term is the heat capacity, and the final term is the heat of mixing.

Unlike Li-ion systems, the contribution of the heat of reaction is significant for a Li-S system [10] and cannot be ignored. Furthermore, it not clear if the heat of mixing can be ignored at high discharge rates. It is therefore difficult to calculate the heat generated without experimental measurements. However, experimental results using coin cells [10] are available in literature and can be utilized to model the temperature profile in a Li-S battery.

Utilizing the MATLAB PDE toolbox, it is possible to solve Eq. 1 for different pouch cells placed in the form factor of the CWB. Figure 6 shows an example of simulation results for a 1.5 Ah cell in a CWB being discharged at 1 C. The maximum temperature can be observed from the simulation.

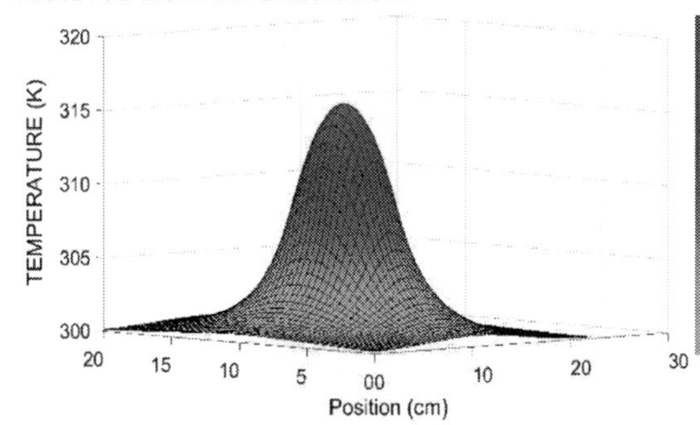

Figure 6: Solution for a 1.5 Ah Li-S cell in a CWB at 1 C discharge, showing the maximum temperature (315 K).

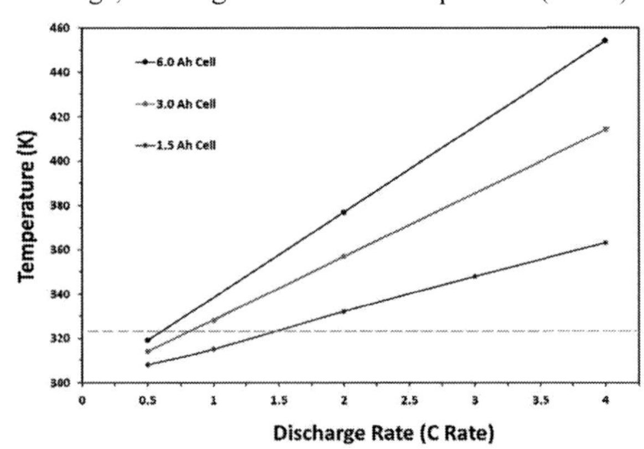

Figure 7: Simulated maximum temperature profile at different discharge rates with different cell capacities. Temperature safety limit at 350 K is also indicated.

In a similar manner, the temperature profiles of 1.5 Ah, 3.0 Ah, and 6.0 Ah cells at various discharge rates were calculated and are shown in Figure 7. Additionally, an estimate of the self-heating temperature onset of 50 °C based on literature [10] for Li-S cells is also shown in Figure 7. Operation of cells at temperature beyond this may lead to self-heating and potentially thermal runaway in the absence of effective cooling. From Figure 7, it can be seen that the 1.5 Ah cells can be operated up to a 1.5 C-rate discharge in a CWB configuration, while the larger cells of 3 Ah and 6 Ah have maximum C-rates of 0.8 C and 0.6 C, respectively.

Conclusion

Li-S technology offers a promising pathway to develop high energy density batteries. However, their full potential remains to be developed. This work has shown that prototype Li-S cells have acceptable safety performance in overcharge and over-discharge abuse tests. Furthermore, based on thermal modeling, it appears that Li-S technology can safely offer a high power density in a wearable configuration.

Nomenclature

Q_T	Heat generation rate (W)
C_p	Heat capacity (0.837 J g^{-1} K^{-1})
k	Thermal conductivity (4x10^{-4} W m^{-1} K^{-1})
T	Temperature (K)
T_{ext}	Ambient temperature (300 K)
h	Ambient heat transfer coefficient (5x10^{-4} W m^{-2} K^{-1})
I	Current (A)
E	Battery voltage (V)
E_{OCV}	Open circuit voltage (V)
ΔH_i	Heat of reaction (J/mol)
r_i	Rate of chemical reaction *i*, (mol/s)
$\bar{H}_j$	Partial molar enthalpy of species *j*, (J/mol)
$\bar{H}_j^{avg}$	Partial molar enthalpy of species *j* evaluated at the overall volume average concentration (J/mol)
c_j	Concentration of species *j* (mol/m^3)
v	Differential volume element (m^3)

References

1. E. J. Zambraski, M. K. Yancosek, *J. Strength Cond. Res.* 26/ 2, (2012) S101–S106
2. E. Beidel, *National Defense Magazine*, April (2011)
3. M-K. Song, Y. Zhang, E. J. Cairns, *Nano Lett.* 13 (12), (2013) 5891-5899
4. J. Gao, M.A. Lowe, Y. Kiya, H.D. Abruna, *J. of Physical Chem.* C 115 (2011) 25132
5. S.S. Zhang, *Electrochimica Acta* 97 (2013) 226 – 230
6. S.S. Zhang, *Electrochimica Acta* 70 (2012) 344-348
7. E.P. Roth and C. J. Orendorff, *The Electrochemical Chemical Society Interface* Summer 2012, 45-49
8. S.S. Zhang, *J. Power Sources* 231 (2013) 153-162
9. S. Abada, G. Marlair, A. Lecocq, M. Petit, V. Sauvant-Moynot, F. Huet, *J. Power Sources* 306 (2016) 178-192
10. J. Seo, S Sankarasubramanian, C-S Kim, P. Hovington, J Prakash, K Zaghib, *J. Power Sources* 289 (2015) 1-7
11. S. Al. Hallaj, H. Maleki, J.S. Hong, J.R. Selman, *J. Power Sources* 83 (1999) 1-8
12. Y-Sheng Su, Y. Fu, T. Cochell, A. Manthiram, *Nature Communications* **4**, 2985: 1-8 (2013)
13. K.E. Thomas, J. Newman, J Electrochem. Soc. 150 (2003)

Hyperlinked References

1 E. J. Zambraski, M. K. Yancosek, *J. Strength Cond. Res.* 26/ 2, (2012) S101–S106

2 E. Beidel, *National Defense Magazine*, April (2011)

3 M-K. Song, Y. Zhang, E. J. Cairns, *Nano Lett.* 13 (12), (2013) 5891-5899

4 J. Gao, M.A. Lowe, Y. Kiya, H.D. Abruna, *J. of Physical Chem.* C 115 (2011) 25132

5 S.S. Zhang, *Electrochimica Acta* 97 (2013) 226 – 230

6 S.S. Zhang, *Electrochimica Acta* 70 (2012) 344-348

7 E.P. Roth and C. J. Orendorff, *The Electrochemical Chemical Society Interface* Summer 2012, 45-49

8 S.S. Zhang, *J. Power Sources* 231 (2013) 153-162

9 S. Abada, G. Marlair, A. Lecocq, M. Petit, V. Sauvant-Moynot, F. Huet, *J. Power Sources* 306 (2016) 178-192

10 J. Seo, S Sankarasubramanian, C-S Kim, P. Hovington, J Prakash, K Zaghib, *J. Power Sources* 289 (2015) 1-7

11 S. Al. Hallaj, H. Maleki, J.S. Hong, J.R. Selman, *J. Power Sources* 83 (1999) 1-8

12 Y-Sheng Su, Y. Fu, T. Cochell, A. Manthiram, *Nature Communications* **4**, 2985: 1-8 (2013)

13 K.E. Thomas, J. Newman, *J Electrochem. Soc.* 150 (2003)

Custom High Energy Batteries for Small Unmanned Air System Applications

Stephen Cordova, Steven C. Arzberger and Weibing Xing

stephenc@adatech.com, stevena@adatech.com, weibingx@adatech.com

ADA Technologies, Inc.

8100 Shaffer Parkway, Suite 130

Littleton, CO 80127

Abstract: The United States military has identified a need for increased range, payload and endurance for Group 1 Unmanned Air Systems (UAS) to carry out critical intelligence, surveillance and reconnaissance (ISR) missions down range. The existing commercial battery options provide only brief mission durations. Higher specific energy batteries are critical to longer flight times. ADA Technologies, Inc. (ADA) is working to mature a high-energy/high-power lithium ion (Li-ion) battery technology for integration into UAS platforms for a series of qualification and operational test and evaluation activities. A recent and successful Group 1 UAS flight demonstration employing an ADA large-format, Li-ion battery pack prototype has piqued the interest of the UAS community. This battery prototype is part of a custom energy storage product offering as part of our 'agile battery manufacturing' capability.

Keywords: Lithium ion (Li-ion); battery; unmanned air systems; unmanned air vehicle; remotely piloted air vehicle; agile battery manufacturing; Group 1 UAS.

Introduction

Group 1 UAS platforms are typically hand-launched, portable systems (*i.e.*, 0-20 lbs.) employed at the small unit level or for base security.[1] They are capable of providing "over the hill" or "around the corner" type ISR and target acquisition. Payloads are modular including, for example, electro-optical (EO), infrared (IR) and synthetic aperture radar (SAR) imaging. They have small logistics footprint.

Their advantages include their low mass, man-portable format and ability to provide timely and accurate situational awareness for small groups in forward operating environments. This is because they offer a minor logistical footprint, without much burden on a unit's supply infrastructure.

This UAS class has traditionally been limited to missions that can be accomplished by an operator within his line-of-sight (LOS) at low altitudes, generally less than 1200 feet above ground level (AGL), and within a limited local endurance. They tend to have poor performance in high wind environments in excess of 15 knots and are limited to missions of 40 minutes or less. For example a typical cruise/loiter ISR mission would only allow roughly a 2-mile range from the base station with a 30 minute loiter over the ISR area of interest.

Identification & Significance of the Problem or Opportunity

The U.S. does not expect a near-peer symmetric military competitor in the foreseeable future.[1] Our military does anticipate operations in a global environment of increasing instability and uncertainty. Operations will be necessary in urban settings or uncertain, inaccessible lawless areas with an absence of local security or effective local government. This includes regions containing competing factions locked in internal conflict. Opponents are anticipated to develop strategies that are adaptive and assymetric, with forces that are trained to exploit U.S. vulnerabilities and patterns while countering or mitigating U.S. strengths. The ability to equip our special operation forces with beyond line of sight (BLOS) ISR capabilities represents a mission critical advancement. Thus, the ability to offer Group 1 UAS platforms with significantly increased endurance is viewed as a critical need of the U.S. military.

In recent years, the U.S. military has been highly reliant on a limited number of Group 1 UAS original equipment manufacturers. Closed UAS system designs and sluggish improvements in piece-part technologies, including energy storage systems and mission duration capability, have opened an opportunity for competitive solutions.

The existing commercial batteries are either too large or heavy, and do not possess adequate specific energy to meet the BLOS ISR needs of the U.S. special operation forces. While technologies exist that would undoubtedly lead to enabling batteries for Group 1 UAS platforms, the current market volume demand for military-specified batteries is too small for domestic battery manufacturers to address. As a result, UAS manufacturers have had to rely on a small number of commercial batteries that exist to serve the remote control airplane, hobby community. These batteries are not qualified to military-specifications and thus, may pose safety and/or tampering concerns. There is a critical need for a cost-effective, reliable and consistent supply of custom, high energy and military-specified batteries that can address the rapidly changing needs of the U.S. special operation forces.

ADA High Energy/High Power Li-ion Battery

ADA Technologies, Inc. (ADA) has designed, developed and fabricated a custom high energy/high power Li-ion battery prototype for UAS platforms (**Figure 1**).

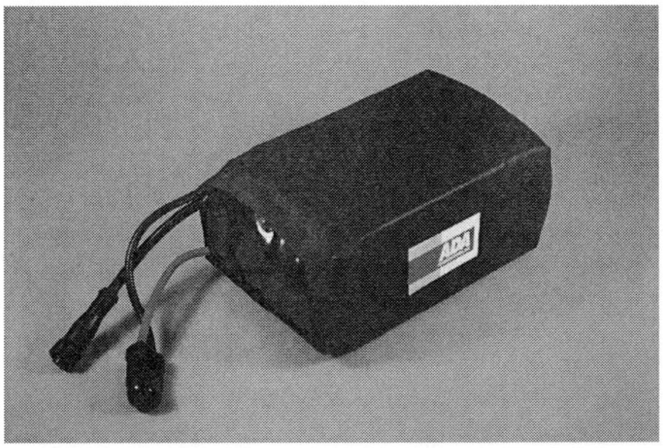

Figure 1. ADA high energy/high power Li-ion battery.

Table 1 summarizes and compares the performance of the ADA Li-ion battery with a relevant commercial UAS lithium polymer (LiPo) battery. The ADA battery offers more than a 25% increase in energy resulting in a substantial increase in endurance. It also offers a significant improvement in power of nearly 2x. It is important to note that the enhanced endurance performance permits operation in high-wind environments of 20 knots or greater. This translates into substantial improvements in mission capabilities.

Table 1. Performance comparison of ADA Li-ion battery to a commercial UAS battery

Performance Goal	Commercial (UAS) LiPo Battery	ADA Li-ion Battery
Cell design	Standard footprint	Energy-optimized footprint
Energy	< 200 Wh/kg	> 250 Wh/kg
Power	Up to 9A discharge	Up to 15A discharge
Custom Chemistry	No	Yes
Mission Endurance	1-2 hours	3+ hours

The higher energy offered by the ADA Li-ion battery provides a 100% increase in operating range for typical BLOS ISR missions (**Figure 2**) with greater air vehicle mission endurance planned in future product spirals.

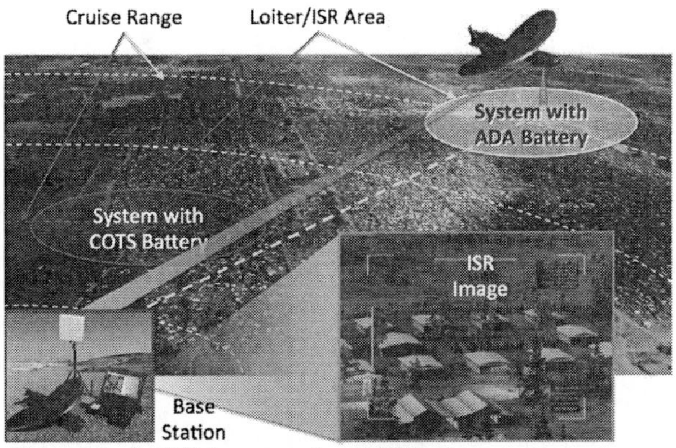

Figure 2. A 20% increase in sUAS battery energy gives a 100% increase in operating range.

ADA 'Agile Manufacturing' Capability

Battery fabrication was achieved using an ADA agile battery design, manufacturing and delivery to ensure custom battery solutions for the UAS community to best meet their evolving operational needs. An agile manufacturing ability is a prominent aspect of the ADA strategic vision to become a domestic, high throughput manufacturer and supplier of critical, custom energy storage products.

At ADA, we define agile manufacturing as the ability to: (1) efficiently transition between different products in a *responsive* manner, and (2) rapidly fabricate different products using *tool-less* infrastructure. Our goal is to serve the under-represented battery customer, by rapidly responding to customer needs without extensive up-front tooling and setup costs. In this manner, we have planned a sustainable business based on the manufacturing production of a moderate total volume (see **Figure 3**) of a diverse set of energy storage products.

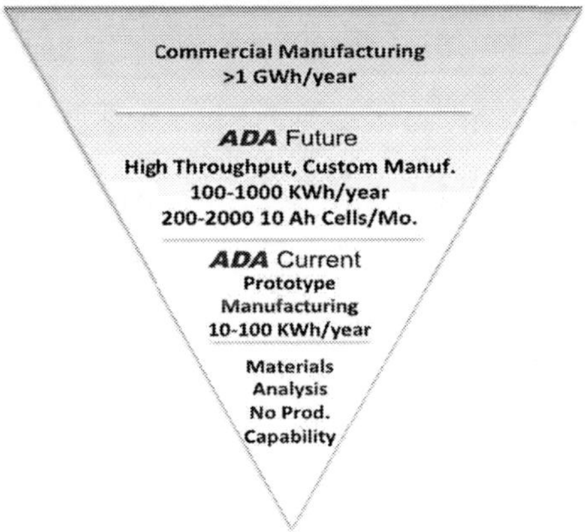

Figure 3. ADA current and future battery product manufacturing goals.

This effort showcased two unique aspects of the ADA agile battery manufacturing capability: (1) the use of commercial electrode active materials to provide increased mission energy and power needs, and (2) the development of a custom battery design configuration/footprint by leveraging an ADA custom electrode cutting system.

Figure 4 presents an image of the ADA manual electrode laser cutter unit. This unit has been used to demonstrate laser processing of virtually any size or shape electrode (for example, **Figure 5**), producing outstanding electrode cut quality (**Figure 6**) at rates of up to 1.4 m/s. It offers tremendous flexibility at the research and development, and manufacturing stages of technology development and product fabrication, respectively. ADA is currently working to expand the capabilities of this unit to offer semi-continuous, roll-to-roll processing of electrodes for planar prismatic and cylindrical cells at similar cut quality and rates as high as 5 m/s. Our laser cutting infrastructure offers tremendous advantages when compared to common planar electrode processing via matched die sets.

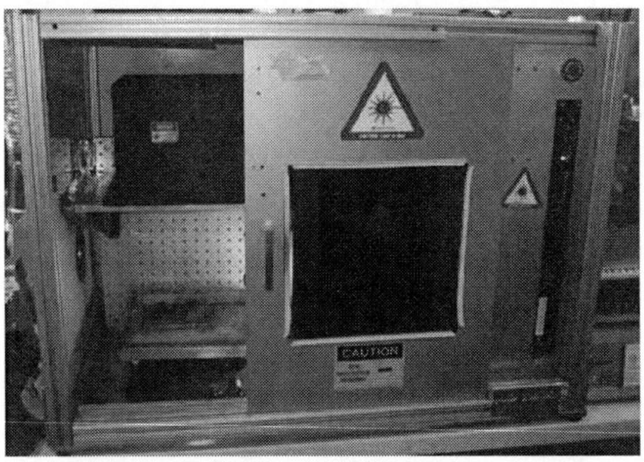

Figure 4. ADA custom electrode cutting system.

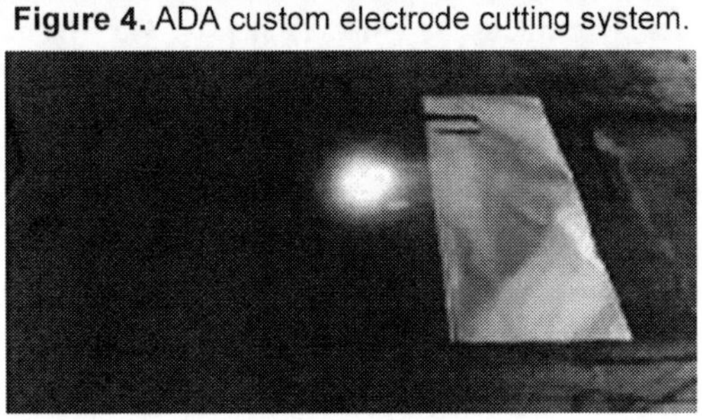

Figure 5. Still screenshot of Li-ion electrode being processed using the ADA laser cutting unit.

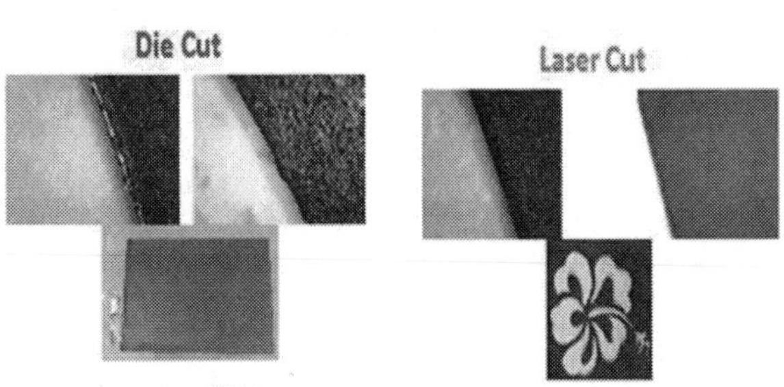

Figure 6. Comparison of die cut and laser cut electrodes.

The use of commercial active materials represents the willingness of ADA to work with our customers to produce a custom battery prototype without the incorporation of ADA active materials. In this manner, ADA can rapidly demonstrate meaningful battery products without having to also establish all elements of a new material supply chain.

The custom electrode footprint allowed ADA to make use of all available volume in the UAS power bay, and reduce parasitic mass by reducing the magnitude of the common elements (*e.g.*, packaging materials) through a reduction in the number of cells. These elements were critical in achieving the highest possible battery specific energy.

A significant aspect of the ADA efforts to automate the processing of battery electrodes is the establishment of critical sub-systems. While a number of sub-systems will be fabricated and integrated into the automated laser electrode cutting system, we highlight the design and development of a robotic, pick-in-place processing unit, necessary for rapid unit throughput. We do so because of its applicability to also streamline electrode and separator stacking and assembly processes, and thus improve our fabrication efficiency and planar prismatic cell quality.

These activities are part of a broader technology and capability portfolio that includes applied research and development activities for a wide range of energy storage technologies. This includes efforts ranging from the large-format, Li-ion batteries (to address UAS community needs) to high-power Li-ion batteries; high performance electrode active materials (*e.g.*, high voltage LNMO and LCO products) and novel electrodes; high specific energy supercapacitors; hybrid electric energy storage systems based on enabling management electronics; solid state batteries; and unprecedented performance lithium-based chemical reserve batteries.

Acknowledgements

The authors wish to acknowledge the contributions and support of Larry Toomey of Army Tank Automotive Research, Development and Engineering Center (TARDEC, contract W56HZV-12-C-0005) and Stanley Rodrigues of Air Force Research Laboratory, Aerospace Directorate (AFRL-RQ, contract FA8650-11-C-2143) in the development of key material constituents and processes involved in the UAS Li-ion battery prototype activities at ADA. We also wish to acknowledge the contributions and support of Mather "Matt" Hutchens and Traci Myers of the Defense Logistics Agency (DLA) for their continued support and funding (contract HQ0147-15-C-800) in the development of the ADA automated laser electrode cutting unit.

References

1. U.S. Army Unmanned Air Systems Roadmap 2010-2035;http://www.rucker.army.mil/usaace/uas/US%20 Army%20UAS%20RoadMap%202010%202035.pdf

Power Sources Conference
Palisades Convention Management
411 Lafayette Street, Suite 201
New York, NY 10003

ISBN 978-1-5108-5235-8

BioNLP Shared Task 2013

Sofia, Bulgaria
9 August 2013

ISBN: 978-1-62748-981-2